ENCYCLOPEDIA OF WORLD BIOGRAPHY

SUPPLEMENT

34

ENCYCLOPEDIA OF WORLD BIOGRAPHY

SUPPLEMENT

A
Z

34

GALE
CENGAGE Learning

Farmington Hills, Mich • San Francisco • New York • Waterville, Maine
Meriden, Conn • Mason, Ohio • Chicago

GALE
CENGAGE Learning®

Encyclopedia of World Biography Supplement, Volume 34

Project Editor: James Craddock

Editorial: Tracie Moy, Jeffrey Muhr

Image Research and Acquisition: Lynn Vagg

Rights Acquisition and Management:
Mollika Basu, Jermaine Bobbitt, Jackie Jones

Imaging and Multimedia: Sheila Spencer

Manufacturing: Rita Wimberley

Gale
27500 Drake Rd.
Farmington Hills, MI, 48331-3535

ISBN-13: 978-1-57302-442-6
ISSN 1099-7326

This title is also available as an e-book.
ISBN-13: 978-1-5730-2443-3
Contact your Gale sales representative for ordering information.

Printed in Mexico
1 2 3 4 5 6 19 18 17 16 15 14

CONTENTS

INTRODUCTION

The study of biography has always held an important, if not explicitly stated, place in school curricula. The absence in schools of a class specifically devoted to studying the lives of the giants of human history belies the focus most courses have always had on people. From ancient times to the present, the world has been shaped by the decisions, philosophies, inventions, discoveries, artistic creations, medical breakthroughs, and written works of its myriad personalities. Librarians, teachers, and students alike recognize that our lives are immensely enriched when we learn about those individuals who have made their mark on the world we live in today.

Encyclopedia of World Biography Supplement, Volume 34, provides biographical information on 175 individuals not covered in the 17-volume second edition of *Encyclopedia of World Biography (EWB)* and its supplements, Volumes 18 through 33. Like other volumes in the *EWB* series, this supplement represents a unique, comprehensive source for biographical information on those people who, for their contributions to human culture and society, have reputations that stand the test of time. Each original article ends with a bibliographic section. There is also an index to names and subjects, which cumulates all persons appearing as main entries in the *EWB* second edition, the Volume 18 through 33 supplements, and this supplement—more than 8,000 people!

Articles. Arranged alphabetically following the letter-by-letter convention (spaces and hyphens have been ignored), articles begin with the full name of the person profiled in large, bold type. Next is a boldfaced, descriptive paragraph that includes birth and death years in parentheses. It provides a capsule identification and a statement of the person's significance. The essay that follows is approximately 2,000 words in length and offers a substantial treatment of the person's life. Some of the essays proceed chronologically while others confine biographical data to a paragraph or two and move on to a consideration and evaluation of the subject's work. Where very few biographical facts are known, the article is necessarily devoted to an analysis of the subject's contribution.

Following the essay is a bibliographic section arranged by source type. Citations include books, periodicals, and online Internet addresses for Web pages, where current information can be found.

Portraits accompany many of the articles and provide either an authentic likeness, contemporaneous with the subject, or a later representation of artistic merit. For artists, occasionally self-portraits have been included. Of the ancient figures, there are depictions from coins, engravings, and sculptures; of the moderns, there are many portrait photographs.

Index. The *EWB Supplement* index is a useful key to the encyclopedia. Persons, places, battles, treaties, institutions, buildings, inventions, books, works of art, ideas, philosophies, styles, movements—all are indexed for quick reference just as in a general encyclopedia. The index entry for a person includes a brief identification with birth and death dates *and* is cumulative so that any person for whom an article was written who appears in the second edition of *EWB* (volumes 1-16) and its supplements (volumes 18-33) can be located. The subject terms within the index, however, apply only to volume 34. Every index reference includes the title of the article to which the reader is being directed as well as the volume and page numbers.

Because *EWB Supplement,* Volume 34, is an encyclopedia of biography, its index differs in important ways from the indexes to other encyclopedias. Basically, this is an index of people, and that fact has several interesting consequences. First, the information to which the index refers the reader on a particular topic is always about people associated with that topic. Thus the entry "Quantum theory (physics)" lists articles on people associated with quantum theory. Each article may discuss a person's contribution to quantum theory, but no single article or group of articles is intended to provide a comprehensive treatment of quantum theory as such. Second, the index is rich in classified entries. All persons who are subjects of articles in the encyclopedia, for example, are listed in one or more classifications in the index—abolitionists, astronomers, engineers, philosophers, zoologists, etc.

The index, together with the biographical articles, make *EWB Supplement* an enduring and valuable source for biographical information. As school course work changes to reflect advances in technology and further revelations about the universe, the life stories of the people who have risen above the ordinary and earned a place in the annals of human history will continue to fascinate students of all ages.

We Welcome Your Suggestions. Mail your comments and suggestions for enhancing and improving the *Encyclopedia of World Biography Supplement* to:

The Editors
Encyclopedia of World Biography Supplement
Gale, a Cengage Learning company
27500 Drake Road
Farmington Hills, MI 48331-3535
Phone: (800) 347-4253

ADVISORY BOARD

OBITUARIES

The following people, appearing in volumes 1-33 of the *Encyclopedia of World Biography,* have died since the publication of the 33rd supplement. Each entry lists the volume where the full biography can be found.

ANDREOTTI, GIULIO (born 1919), Italian politician and leader of Italy's Christian Democratic Party, died in Rome, Italy on May 6, 2013 (1).

BENN, TONY (born 1925), British Labour Party politician, died in London, England on March 14, 2014 (2).

BLACK, SHIRLEY TEMPLE (born 1928), American actress and public servant, died in Woodside, CA on February 10, 2014 (2).

BROTHERS, JOYCE (born 1927), American psychologist, died in New York City, NY on May 13, 2013 (3).

CHYTILOVÁ, VERA (born 1929), Czech filmmaker, died in Prague, Czech Republic on March 12, 2014 (24).

DAVIS, COLIN REX (born 1927), British conductor, died on April 14, 2013 (22).

GARCIA MARQUEZ, GABRIEL (born 1928), Colombian author, died in Mexico City, Mexico on April 17, 2014 (6).

GIAP, VO NGUYEN (born 1912), Vietnamese Communist general and statesman, died in Hanoi, Vietnam on October 4, 2013 (6).

GREELEY, ANDREW M. (born 1928), American Catholic priest, sociologist, and author, died in Chicago, IL on May 30, 2013 (6).

JANCSO, MIKLOS (born 1921), Hungarian filmmaker, died on January 31, 2014 (25).

JHABVALA, RUTH PRAWER (born 1927), British screenwriter and novelist, died of complications from a pulmonary disorder in New York, NY on April 3, 2013 (18).

JOHNSON, VIRGINIA E. (born 1925), American psychologist and sex therapist, died in St. Louis, MO on July 24, 2013 (8).

KALASHNIKOV, MIKHAIL (born 1919), Russian inventor, died after a long illness in Izhevsk, Russia on December 23, 2013 (28).

KUMIN, MAXINE WINOKUR (born 1925), American poet and author, died in Warner, NH on February 6, 2014 (26).

LEONARD, ELMORE (born 1925), American writer, died of complications from a stroke in Bloomfield Village, MI on August 20, 2013 (32).

LESSING, DORIS (born 1919), South African expatriate writer, died in London, England on November 17, 2013 (9).

MANDELA, NELSON (born 1918), South African leader, died in Qunu, East Cape, South Africa on December 15, 2013 (10).

PATRICK, RUTH (born 1907), American limnologist, died in Lafayette Hill, PA on September 23, 2013 (12).

RESNAIS, ALAIN (born 1922), French filmmaker, died in Paris, France on March 1, 2014 (23).

ROHRER, HEINRICH (born 1933), Swiss physicist, died in Wollerau, Switzerland on May 16, 2013 (25).

SANGER, FREDERICK (born 1918), English biochemist, died in Cambridge, England on November 19, 2013 (13).

SEEGER, PETE (born 1919), American folksinger and activist, died in Manhattan, NY on January 27, 2014 (14).

SHARON, ARIEL (born 1928), Israeli politician and defense minister, died of renal failure in Ramat Gan, Israel on January 11, 2014 (14).

SHAW, RUN RUN (born 1907), Chinese cinema executive, died in Hong Kong on January 7, 2014 (30).

SIEBERT, MURIEL (born 1932), American businesswoman, died of complications from cancer in New York City, NY on August 24, 2013 (18).

TALLCHIEF, MARIA (born 1925), Native American ballerina, died on April 11, 2013 (15).

THOMAS, HELEN (born 1920), American journalist, died in Washington, DC on July 20, 2013 (19).

TOYODA, EIJI (born 1913), Japanese automotive manufacturing executive, died of heart failure on September 17, 2013 (15).

VIDELA, JORGE RAFAEL (born 1925), military President of Argentina (1976-1981), died in Buenos Aires, Argentina on May 17, 2013 (15).

WILLIAMS, ESTHER (born 1921), American swimmer and actress, died on June 6, 2013 (30).

WILSON, KENNETH GEDDES (born 1936), American scientist, died in Saco, ME on June 15, 2013 (23).

A

Stella Adler

The American educator, director, and actress Stella Adler (1901–1992) shaped both the style of American theater and many of its individual practitioners. She was one of the key exponents of the ideas of Russian theater innovator Konstantin Stanislavsky in the United States, but she put her own stamp on those ideas with her outsized personality and energy.

Adler was a member of the innovative 1930s theater ensemble known as the Group, and she appeared in many plays and several films herself. She was also active and influential as a stage and cinematic director. But her greatest influence was as a teacher, at several of the top drama schools in the U.S. and at her own Stella Adler Theater Studio (later renamed several times), which continues to operate. Her students there included some of the most famous names in American acting: Robert DeNiro, Anthony Quinn, Warren Beatty, Harvey Keitel, *Star Trek: Voyager* lead Kate Mulgrew, and perhaps most famously of all, Marlon Brando, whom Adler mentored in the days leading up to his rise to superstardom and who demonstrated in dramatic fashion the power of her ideas.

Grew Up in Yiddish Theatrical World

Stella Adler was born in Manhattan, New York, on February 10, 1901. Her parents, Russian Jewish immigrants Jacob Pavlovitch Adler and Sara Levitzky Adler, were major figures in New York's Yiddish-language theatrical scene, operating their own Independent Yiddish Art Company and appearing in serious dramas such as Yiddish translations of Shakespeare. Most or all of her eight siblings or half-siblings became actors, and Stella's own career began when she was a small child. Her earliest memory was of seeing her father transforming himself before a play with costumes and makeup.

Adler's education was spotty, for she was usually appearing in a play in New York or elsewhere in the U.S., or even abroad. But she attended classes at New York University as a teen and tried to learn about the background behind classics of the stage. By her late teens she was taking lead roles in Yiddish-language plays as far afield as London, England. Adler married Horace Elashieff in 1922. and around that time she began to appear in Broadway plays, taking the name Lola Adler for a part in a show called *The World We Live In (The Insect Comedy).* The couple had a daughter, Ellen, but Adler's marriage ended in divorce soon after.

The most important part of Adler's education began when troupes from the Moscow Art Theatre and other Russian theatrical innovators arrived in the U.S. in the early and middle 1920s and began to give acting classes. Adler took classes at the American Laboratory Theatre with Russian instructors from 1925 to 1927, soaking up the so-called Method Acting techniques pioneered by Stanislavsky. She and several of her classmates began to dream of an American counterpart to the Moscow Art Theatre, and her friends Harold Clurman and Lee Strasberg became cofounders of the Group Theatre in 1931. Adler appeared in several of the Group's earliest productions and went on to star in some of its most famous productions, including Clifford Odets's *Awake and Sing!* (1935).

Studied with Stanislavsky

The atmosphere within the Group was volatile as Adler became romantically involved with Clurman, whom she

Ron Galella/Ron Galella Collection/Getty Images

married in 1943 and divorced in 1960. She later attested to Clurman's influence on her own thinking, but she rebelled against what she considered the subsidiary position of women within the ensemble, and against Strasberg's interpretation of Stanislavsky's ideas: Strasberg insisted that actors had to draw on their own experiences in creating a character, while Adler argued in favor of a greater role for the actor's own imagination. On a trip to Paris in 1934, Adler took acting lessons from Stanislavsky and learned that the aging Russian master had come to adopt much of her own outlook.

Returning to the U.S., Adler tried her luck both in Hollywood films and on the New York stage. For the movies, she took the less Jewish-sounding name Ardler and appeared in several films, including *Love on Toast* (1937) and *Shadow of the Thin Man* (1941). She also served as associate producer for several musicals released by the MGM studio, including *For Me and My Gal* (1942); she was one of the first women to hold that position. Adler directed the international stage tour of Odets's play *Golden Boy* in 1938 and 1939.

As early as 1939, Adler sought to apply ideas as a teacher, giving classes at the New School for Social Research in New York. Her classes grew in renown, and she emerged as something of a rival to Strasberg, whose Actors Studio taught his own version of Stanislavsky's method. Some actors, such as Ellen Burstyn, however, studied with both teachers, drawing from each. In 1949, Adler opened her own Stella Adler Acting Studio in New York. Later renamed the Stella Adler Conservatory of Acting and then the Stella Adler Studio of Acting, the school expanded, opening a branch in Los Angeles in 1986. Adler's school developed into an institution of fundamental importance in American dramatic arts, training many of the leading film and theater actors of the second half of the 20th century.

Mentored Brando

None of those Adler students was more celebrated in his own time than Marlon Brando, who studied with Adler in the mid-1940s and went on to make sensational lead appearances in both the stage (1947) and film (1951) versions of the Tennessee Williams play *A Streetcar Named Desire.* According to Budd Schulberg, writing in *Vanity Fair,* Adler "virtually adopted" Brando, taking him in at the apartment on the Upper East Side of Manhattan that she shared with Clurman and had decorated in a flamboyant Italian Renaissance style. Brando dated Adler's daughter, Ellen, for many years, and Adler encouraged them to marry, but Brando resisted the match. In Schulberg's words, Adler "sensed the quivering mass of sensitivities within [Brando] and taught him how to relate them to the expanding horizons of her own interpretation of the Stanislavsky method, which she had studied with the master in Paris. She provided the base on which Brando would build his art."

In addition to all her educational activities, Adler maintained her own theatrical career for a time, directing a 1956 production of the Kurt Weill musical *Johnny Johnson.* She appeared in the 1961 stage comedy *Oh Dad, Poor Dad, Mama's Hung You in the Closet and I'm Feelin' So Sad,* but retired after her performance received bad reviews. In 1960, Adler's long, tempestuous marriage to Clurman ended in divorce. She married novelist Mitchell Wilson; that marriage lasted until Wilson's death in 1973.

Adler was by all accounts a dynamic teacher with a gift for imparting her ideas and energy to her students. "You can't be boring. Life is boring. The weather is boring. Actors must not be boring," she would say (according to Peter B. Flint of *The New York Times*). "Never go on stage without your motor running." Yet Adler's art was also grounded in a thorough knowledge of dramatic literature. Her schools incorporated play analysis as an integrated part of the curriculum, and her lectures on various playwrights were collected after her death into a pair of volumes, *Stella Adler on Ibsen, Strindberg, and Chekhov* (1999) and *Stella Adler on America's Master Playwrights* (2012). Adler expressed her ideas on acting in a book of her own, *The Technique of Acting,* in 1988.

Adler lived in Los Angeles in her later years and died there of heart failure in 1992. Her *New York Times* obituary quoted writer Foster Hirsch, who called her "theatrical royalty who [instilled] in her students a sense of the nobility of acting. She dares her students to act, to lift their bodies and their voices, to be larger than themselves, to love language and ideas." Adler was honored with a star on the Hollywood Walk of Fame in 2006.

Books

Adler. Stella, *The Technique of Acting,* Bantam, 1988.
Clurman, Harold, *The Fervent Years,* Da Capo, 1983.
Encyclopedia Judaica, Keter, 2007.

Periodicals

Austin American-Statesman, February 16, 2006.
Back Stage, April 8, 2010.
Globe & Mail (Toronto, Ontario, Canada), August 7, 2006.
International Herald Tribune, September 6, 2012.
New Republic, February 1, 1993.
New York Times, December 22, 1992.
Vanity Fair, March 2005.

Online

"Stella Adler," *Jewish Women: A Comprehensive Historical Encyclopedia,* http://jwa.org/encyclopedia/article/adler-stella (September 1, 2013).
"Stella Adler," *Stella Adler Studio of Acting,* http://www.stellaadler.com/about/history/ (September 1, 2013).□

Qing Ai

Chinese writer Jiang Haicheng (1910–1996), better known by his pen name Ai Qing, was a prolific writer whose largest output was free-verse poetry. His works greatly influenced the development of what is called "xinshi," known in the western world as "new poetry." He was also a political activist and a member of China's Communist Party.

Ai Qing was one of China's major poets and a remarkably prolific writer. During his career, which lasted for more than sixty years, he produced more than twenty lengthy lyrical and narrative poems, more than 1,000 short poems, and about 200 essays. His works typically were sympathetic depictions (in simple, naturalistic language) of the difficult lives of his country's poor people. Considered a "radical activist," he became a fervent communist, and his works extolled the communist philosophy. He joined the Communist Party in 1941. Because of his attitudes and activities, however, he endured exile and imprisonment.

Ai Qing was born as Jiang Haicheng on March 27, 1910, in Zhejiang, a coastal province in China. He was the son of a wealthy landowner, but was brought up by a Chinese peasant woman. Reportedly, this was a situation that resulted from difficult circumstances: His mother suffered painful and extended labor in giving birth, and he was sent away to be reared by the surrogate. Supposedly, this impoverished Chinese woman felt compelled to drown her own child to raise this wealthy family's son. Nevertheless, the five years that Qing spent with the woman significantly influenced his later poetic works. She loved Qing as if he were her own child. The experience instilled in him passionate empathy for his nation's poor people. Indeed, his early work *Dayanhe* (translated as *My Nurse* and composed in 1933) received high praise and pointed to his eventual embrace of Maoism, a political philosophy—based on Marxist and Lenin principles—fostered by revolutionary Chinese leader Mao Zedong (1893–1976).

As his works well indicate, Qing enjoyed a strong educational background. Early in life, he was advised to learn Western languages, and after his primary education, his youthful interest in art gained him admittance to the National Hangzhou West Lake Art Academy. There, the institution's principal Lin Fengmian (1900–1991), an acclaimed painter, encouraged Qing. With ambitions bolstered by his mentor, Qing travelled to France to study painting, from 1928 to 1932. But his interests were diverted from paint to the pen, as he developed a great appreciation of Western literature. In particular, his exposure to modernist poetry guided his mode of artistic expression. His major influences were Belgian poet Emile Verhaeren (1855–1916) and the Russian poet Vladimir Mayakovsky (1893–1930).

Imprisoned for Three Years

Qing returned to China in 1932. As writing was not his only passion—he was equally passionate about politics—this influenced much of his writing. It also proved problematic, as his attitudes and activities led to imprisonment. After coming back to China, he became a member of the League of Leftist Writers. Also, he helped establish the Shanghai-based Spring Earth Painters. He expressed opposition to the reigning Nationalist regime, and for this he was incarcerated in July 1932. Imprisonment proved a turning point in his life, as he began focusing his artistic efforts on poetry, since he was not able to paint while jailed. But what he had learned from painting—insights about color, light and image capture—enhanced his writing skills. During his three-year imprisonment, he translated Verhaeren's works into Chinese and he wrote poetry, now using his pen name. He also produced his first collection of poems, *Dayanhe,* in which he communicated his compassion for the common people of his home nation. It also recalled with great fondness the very kind woman who raised him. It would be published in 1936.

Qing was released from prison in October 1935. Two years later, during the War of Resistance, a Japanese-Chinese conflict, he wrote *Xue luo zai Zhongguo de tudi shang* (*Snow is falling on the land of Chinardquo*). With this work he strove to accurately and forcefully depict the true suffering of the poorest portion of the Chinese population.

Joined the Communist Party

During the Sino-Japanese conflicts, which lasted from 1931 to 1945 and was initiated in part by the swelling tide of China's patriotism, Qing went to Yan'an, the center of Communist control in China. There, he officially became a member of the Communist Party in 1941. He made this decision because the Communists were looking to protect the rights of China's peasant population. The poet joined Mao Zedong (often spelled in the Western world as Mao Tse-tung) in his mountain cave headquarters in Yan'an. The two men discussed philosophy, politics, and literature. Mao Zedong, who became known as Chairman Mao, is regarded as the guiding force of the People's Republic of China. During his governance of the nation, he was the Chairman of the Communist Party until his death in 1976. Qing went with Mao's troops into Beijing in 1949 when the Communists gained power.

During the 1940s, Qing produced several poetic volumes, such as *Kuangye* (*Wilderness,* 1940); *Xiang taiyang,* (*Toward the Sun,* also 1940); and *Beifang* (*North,* 1942). Each volume demonstrated his social consciousness in free-form verse.

When Qing returned to Beijing in 1949, he was greatly inspired by Mao Zedong—as well as Russian leader Joseph Stalin— and produced poems in praise of the Communist philosophy. By that year, he was considered part of China's revolutionary nucleus. During this period, he produced compilations of his poetry. Utilizing language that was at once both basic and moving, his works conveyed a love of China's land, its soldiers and, most especially, its people.

His efforts led to him gaining important cultural positions in his country. For instance, he became the leading editor of a national poetry journal (*Shi kan*). As a representative of his nation, he traveled to Europe and South America. Ironically, he fell out of favor, as he expressed criticism of China's Communist regime. During an anti-rightist campaign in 1958, he was deemed a "rightist", and he was forced into a period of exile in the Manchuria province and then in the Xinjiang province. An influential literary journal deemed his works as "counter-revolutionary," even though Qing remained a fervent Maoist.

His troubles continued through the "Cultural Revolution" of 1966–1969, and its aftermath. It was not until 1979 that he was considered "rehabilitated" and allowed to again publish his writings. That led to a collection of poems, *Guilai de ge* (*Songs of Returning*), which was published in 1980. That same year, Qing returned to France. In 1985, French President François Mitterrand awarded him the Commandeur de l'Ordre des arts et des letters.

Died in Beijing

Ai Qing died in Beijing, China on October 10, 1996, at the age of 86 years old. By that time, he was considered China's best known poet, and his works were included in the standard literary educational curriculum in his country, which displeased some younger poets: They disliked his establishment stance and his criticism of the works of the new generation of writers.

Married twice, he was survived by five sons and three daughters. One son, Ai Weiwei (born 1957), became a noted artist and, like his father, an activist. He was also an architect. Another son, Ai Xuan (born 1947), also became an artist.

Today Qing's works are part of standard college courses on modern Chinese literature. Opinions tended to vary about his body of work. The general Chinese population embraced his poetic expression. Reportedly, a Chinese factory worker sent him a letter that said (according to *The Independent,* "I don't read much. But I like your poems. I understand what you say in them. I am always moved by your works." But the emerging generation of young poets criticized him and his output. They perceived him as old-fashioned and even a puppet of the reigning political power. Further, they condemned him for blocking the way for other poetic styles and, in turn, the recognition of the new breed of younger poets. Still, throughout his career, he demonstrated a knack for describing nature, in language that was at once simple and powerful. More importantly, he portrayed the basic nature of human concerns. "The wind,", he wrote in his poem of the same title as recorded in *The Independent,* "like a grief-stricken old woman, closely following behind, stretching out her ice claws, tugs at the travelers clothes." Humanity and nature were closely entwined, in his world view.

Where criticism might be justified is in his more political works. This passage, from *On Top of the Wave,* demonstrates the difference: "All policies must be carried out / All unjust cases must be righted/Even those who are dead/ Must be rehabilitated." It reads as very didactic.

But as Lee Ruru wrote in a 1996 obituary for *The Independent,* a British newspaper, "Regardless of how one views Ai Qing's political stance and the political aspects of his later writing, his powers of description, depth of feeling and artistic passion mark him out as a poet of considerable presence. His works were indelibly marked by the period of turmoil in which he lived, worked, loved, hated and survived, and as such are powerful expressions of the human spirit and hold a special place in modern Chinese poetry."

Before his death, his poetry was published as *Ai Qing quanji* (*The Complete Works of Ai Qing,* 1991). His major works are considered *Kuangye* (*Wilderness,* 1940); *Xiang taiyang* (*Toward the Sun,* 1940); *Beifang* (*North,* 1942), and *Guilai de ge* (*Song of Returning,* 1980). His poetry has been translated into both French and English.

Books

Encyclopedia of Modern China, Charles Scribner's Sons, 2009.

Periodicals

Chicago Tribune, May 6, 1996.

The New York Times, May 6, 1996.

Online

"Ai Qing," *Britannica.com,* http://www.britannica.com/EBchecked/topic/10366/Ai-Qing (December 10, 2013)

"Obituary: Ai Qing," *The Independent,* http://www.independent.co.uk/news/people/obituary-ai-qing-1348347.html (December 10, 2013).□

Otl Aicher

German graphic designer Otl Aicher (1922–1991) is widely credited with creating the first official Olympic mascot, a modernist little dachshund dubbed "Waldi" for the 1972 Summer Games in Munich. As design director for the event, Aicher

was responsible for the look of the Munich Olympics, and the result was a cheerful, contemporary palette of signage and pictograms that later became commonplace symbols in public spaces around the world.

Otto "Otl" Aicher was born on May 13, 1922, in Ulm, a cathedral city on the Danube River in the southern German state of Baden-Württemberg. His father Anton had a plumbing and heating business in the city, and Aicher and his sister Hedwig, called "Hedl," were raised in the Roman Catholic faith. When Aicher was ten years old, the right-wing Nazi Party led by Adolf Hitler came to power in Germany. Three years later, Hitler and senior Nazi leaders used the 1936 Summer Olympic Games in Berlin as an international showcase for their political ideology—a breach of the spirit of the Games, which were created to foster peace and cooperation between nations.

Forced into Uniform

As a rebellious teenager, Aicher found the right-wing authoritarian Nazi regime loathsome. He first came to the attention of local authorities for refusing to join Ulm's branch of the Hitler Youth organization. Among his like-minded peers were the Scholl siblings, whose father had spent most of the 1920s as mayor of a nearby town called Forchtenberg. Aicher was close friends with Werner Scholl, the second son, and with Sophie, the third Scholl daughter. Hans, the elder brother, was enrolled at Ludwig-Maximilians-Universität in Munich, where Sophie eventually joined him.

Aicher's refusal to join the Hitler Youth group hindered his chance at a university education. He was prevented from taking the *abitur,* or school-leaving examination for college-bound students, and in 1941 was drafted into the Wehrmacht, or German Army, during the second year of World War II. At the time, Nazi Germany was fighting a land, sea, and air war against Britain, had overrun and occupied a large swath of Europe, and recently launched an attack on its eastern flank to invade the Soviet Union. Aicher was sent to the dreaded Eastern Front, where casualties were high on both sides, and was wounded in the long mission to capture Russia's valuable oilfields in the Caucasus mountains.

Aicher became a lance corporal, but his stint as a soldier reaffirmed his loathing of German authoritarianism and belief that the German national character was both easily corrupted by political ideology and deeply, heartlessly corrupted by the Nazi war machine. When he was assigned radio-operator duties, he was able to clandestinely listen to broadcasts from English-language news services out of British-occupied Iran and Lebanon, and realized the war against the Allies would be even longer and more ruthless than the German public had been led to believe. He dreamed of defecting over to the British side, but was fortunate to contract a case of jaundice and was placed on medical leave in the fall of 1942.

Friends Executed by Regime

Aicher made a journey that took weeks, via trains and stops at field hospitals in German-occupied Ukraine, Czechoslovakia, and finally Austria. Sophie Scholl, with whom he had been corresponding, came to visit him while he was recuperating in an Austrian convent during the winter of 1942–43. Her brother Werner had also been drafted into the Wehrmacht, but in Munich she and Hans had become the core founders of an underground resistance network called the "Weisse Rose" (White Rose). The two Scholl siblings and their fellow activists printed and distributed anonymous leaflets urging Germans to resist, but were discovered and beheaded by guillotine at a Munich jail in February of 1943.

Aicher was questioned by the Gestapo, or German secret police, but the Scholls had been cautious about their network and he did not realize the extent of their activities until their shocking deaths. The entire Scholl family was arrested except for Werner, who was permitted to return to the Eastern Front and was presumed to have been killed in action in 1943 or 1944. Aicher finally managed to desert the Wehrmacht and fled to a hideout in the Black Forest where the newly freed Scholls had been staying. In 1985, four decades after Nazi Germany's defeat in World War II, he completed a memoir he titled *Innenseiten des Kriegs* (*Inside the War*), in which he gave a detailed account of these years and his ties to the Scholls.

Co-Founded "Neu" Bauhaus

After the war ended, Aicher went to Munich and enrolled in its famed art school, the Akademie der Bildenden Künste (Academy of Fine Arts). He found the rigors of a prescribed course in sculpture unappealing, and eventually dropped out to take freelance book-design work. In 1948, he opened his own graphic design studio in Ulm and four years later he married the eldest Scholl daughter, Inge, who took the name Inge Aicher-Scholl. It was Inge who wrote a book about her siblings' actions during the war, a story that resonated with many Germans of their generation who knew that to resist the Nazis was to court death. The Geschwister Scholl Foundation (Scholl Siblings' Foundation) was established to commemorate their bravery, and scores of sites around Munich are named for them and other slain White Rose resistance members.

In 1953, Aicher and his wife, along with Swiss architect Max Bill, opened the new Hochschule für Gestaltung Ulm (Ulm School of Design). Bill had been trained under the original Bauhaus artists' and architects' collective in Dessau in the 1920s. A catchword for design with an utter absence of extraneous flourishes, Bauhaus ("house of construction" in German) set new standards for Modernist twentieth-century architecture and the decorative arts, but its school was forced to close almost immediately after Hitler came to power in 1933.

Realizing how lucky he was to have survived the war, Aicher made it his personal mission to resurrect a new-era Bauhaus for a new Germany. Known in Germany by its acronym HfG, the Ulm School of Design soon became a leading font of creativity and attracted international attention. Its students and teachers took commission work for companies like Braun, a Frankfurt-based manufacturer of electronics, to develop streamlined consumer goods that were soon winning awards at prestigious industrial-design competitions. The school also lured a stellar roster of visiting professors, including original Bauhaus pioneer Mies van der Rohe. The *New York Times* wrote about HfG and journalist George O'Brien visited the compact, modernist campus overlooking the Danube in 1964. "We want to produce ideas in students, not products," Aicher told O'Brien about the school.

Chosen for Olympics Project

The Ulm School of Design was riven by internal battles between its founding members, and it also experienced financial difficulties. Aicher was serving as rector when the *New York Times* interviewed him, but stepped down later that year. The school was finally forced to close in 1968, a much-lamented end of an era for industrial-design enthusiasts and a new generation of graphic artists. By that point Aicher was living in Munich, the capital of the German state of Bavaria, and had won an important but time-consuming commission as design director for the 1972 Munich Olympics.

Munich had been chosen in 1966 over Madrid, Montreal, and Detroit, Michigan, as the site of the 20th Olympiad's 1972 Summer Games. They would be the first Olympics held on German soil since the blighted 1936 Berlin Games, which had been widely derided as the "Nazi" Olympics. As chief graphic artist for the upcoming event, Aicher laid out an ambitious presentation to the decision-makers who sat on the organizing committee of the Munich Olympics, and won them over with his visionary pitch. "Will the world believe us if we say that Germany is different today to what it was then?" he was said to have argued, according to Kay Schiller and Christopher Young's book *The 1972 Munich Olympics and the Making of Modern Germany*. "Trust cannot be gained through words, but instead only through visual proof and the winning of sympathy," he continued. "It is not about explaining that this Germany is different, but about *showing* it."

Aicher worked with several other leading creative authorities on Olympia-Park, the site carved out of a pile of World War II-era rubble that had been moved north of the city. For the Munich Games' modernist sports venues, guest facilities, and athletes' housing he designed a series of pictograms whose meaning could be quickly understood by visitors from around the world. "Through these breathtakingly stark images, sometimes no more than three geometric blocks on a white background, Aicher effortlessly evoked the human body in flight: sprinting to the finish line; rowing a boat across the water; plunging a basketball into the hoop," wrote Benjamin Secher in the *Daily Telegraph* 35 years later. The original 21 sport pictograms were joined by other examples of what Aicher called *Zeichensprache,* or a language of symbols, not words.

Created "Waldi"

Aicher's graphic designs for the 1972 Munich Games included its official "Strahlenkranz" logo, a circular radiant spiral, and all of its signage, posters, and even clothing uniforms for its host personnel and security employees. He chose a palette of green and blue primary tones, with silver, orange, and white used as counterbalance. The idea of an official Olympic mascot came from Munich Olympic Committee chairperson Willi Daume, who thought the adorable dachshund would make an ideal stuffed toy. The breed was particularly popular with Germans and Aicher devised a striped version that incorporated the 1972 Games' signature palette colors. He also supervised the design of "Waldi" Olympic souvenirs, which proved enormously popular.

Sadly, Aicher's imaginative, almost universally praised graphic-design achievements for the 1972 Summer Games were overshadowed by events happening in real time in Munich that were broadcast around the world. Members of a Palestinian guerrilla group breached lax security at "Oly-Dorf" (Olympic Village) and took several Israeli athletes and their coaches hostage. It was the first act of violence ever to disrupt an Olympiad, and the German security forces' rescue operation was badly bungled. The death of Jewish athletes on German soil, less than 30 years after Hitler's genocidal plan to exterminate all of Europe's Jews, was especially galling, and the relaxed atmosphere that the Munich Organizing Committee had sought to create became the target of criticism.

Aicher was devastated by the massacre in Munich. He retreated to a small village called Leutkirch in Baden-Württemberg and returned to product design and typography. For many years, he was a consultant to Bulthaup, a maker of modular kitchen-cabinet systems. The informational pictograms he created for the Olympics were adopted by the U.S. Department of Transportation and can be found in almost every public space in the developed world, showing exits, restrooms, and access points for the disabled.

Aicher had five children with Inge Aicher-Scholl. One daughter, Pia, died in a car accident in 1975. Aicher himself was struck by a motorcycle while backing up his riding lawnmower onto the road and died of his injuries on September 1, 1991. One of his final commissions was done for British architect Norman Foster, who revered Aicher and other HfG figures. In 1988, Foster won an architectural competition to build the rapid-transit system in Bilbao, Spain, which took ten years to complete. Aicher designed the lettering, signage, and ticketing materials, all of which feature a vivid orange-red against a white background.

Books

Rathgeb, Markus, *Otl Aicher,* Phaidon Press, 2007.

Schiller, Kay, and Christopher Young, *The 1972 Munich Olympics and the Making of Modern Germany,* University of California Press, 2010.

Periodicals

Creative Review, March 1, 2007.

Daily Telegraph (London, England), February 17, 2007.

Guardian (London, England), September 11, 1991.

New York Times, February 4, 1964.□

Alexandra, Empress, consort of Nicholas II, Czar of Russia

German-born Princess Alix of Hesse became Alexandra Feodorova (1872–1918), the last tsarina of imperial Russia. Her 1894 marriage to Tsar Nicholas II sowed distrust and political unrest in their Empire that reached a fevered pitch during World War I and, ultimately resulted in a finale that shocked the world: in July of 1918, the ex-tsar, his wife, and their five children were taken into a basement chamber and assassinated by Bolshevik revolutionaries.

Princess Alix of Hesse was the granddaughter of England's Queen Victoria and was born on June 6, 1872, at her family's royal palace in Darmstadt, Germany. She was christened Viktoria Alix Helena Luise Beatrice of Hesse and by Rhein but called Alix by her family. Her father was Grand Duke Louis IV of Hessen, who had married one of the five daughters produced by Queen Victoria and her consort, the former Prince Albert of Saxe-Coburg and Gotha. Alix herself was one of six children, which included three older sisters and her toddler brother, Prince Friedrich. Little Frittie, as he was called, suffered from hemophilia, a genetic disorder of the blood that was often deadly until the modern age. Just before Alix's first birthday, Frittie died of a brain hemorrhage after a fall from a window.

© Heritage Image Partnership, Ltd/Alamy

Endured Family Tragedies

Five years later, Alix's mother died during a diphtheria outbreak that also claimed Alix's younger sister, Marie. The string of tragedies cast a pall on the Hessian princess's childhood and, as she grew into her teens, Alix was shy, socially awkward, and deeply religious. She first met Nicholas, heir to the Russian throne, at the St. Petersburg wedding of her sister Elisabeth to Grand Duke Sergei Alexandrovich, who was the son of the late Tsar Alexander II, assassinated three years earlier. That tsar was succeeded by Alexander III, the father of Nicholas. All were descendants of the House of Romanov, a family of stupendous wealth that had ruled Russia as autocrats since the 1600s.

The 16-year-old Nicholas was impressed by 12-year-old Alix, a pretty but quiet girl, and their courtship began in earnest five years later in 1889 when the 17-year-old Alix came to visit her sister Elisabeth. Because of complex intermarriage practices among European royalty, Alix and Nicholas were actually second cousins, sharing a great-grandmother, Princess Wilhelmina of Baden. Nicholas's mother, the Empress Maria Feodorovna, was born a princess of Denmark. Both the Empress Maria and Queen Victoria tried to discourage the match, as did Nicholas's father. As a future ruler of Russia it was thought that Nicholas should unite with another royal dynasty, possibly French, as a wiser political strategy.

Nicholas and Alix discussed marriage but she initially balked at converting from her Lutheran faith to the Russian Orthodox church, as the law demanded for a future tsarina. In an odd twist of events, their marriage was hastened when the 49-year-old tsar fell ill at his Livadia palace in Crimea in the fall of 1894, and Alix was one of several royal family members who traveled there to pay their respects. She finally accepted Nicholas's proposal, and the tsar gave his blessing for their union before he died on October 20, 1894.

Became Empress of Russia

To provide a sense of the pomp and pageantry of the House of Romanov, the late tsar was laid to rest after a 17-day-long funeral. When that concluded, a more subdued wedding could take place; in the interim Alix had converted to the Russian Orthodox faith. On November 26, 1894, she and Nicholas were wed at the Grand Church of the Winter Palace in St. Petersburg. The bride wore jewels that belonged to one of the House of Romanov's most famous women, Empress Catherine the Great, and among the 8,000 guests were two future kings of England, Edward VII and George V, the latter the grandfather of Queen Elizabeth II.

Alix became Empress Alexandra on May 26, 1896, at her husband's coronation as Tsar Nicholas II. Again, protocol dictated a long and tiring affair, preceded by days of fasting and prayer for the couple, with the coronation ceremony itself lasting an exhausting five hours. Her husband sat on the famous Diamond Throne, and Alexandra was seated next to him on a spectacular throne of ivory brought to Russia in 1472 by a Byzantine princess who married Ivan the Great, the Grand Prince of Muscovy.

Worried Over Son's Health

Alexandra was already a mother by then. She had given birth to the first of four daughters, Grand Duchess Olga Nikolaevna, in November of 1895. After the coronation she and her husband made a limited tour of the European imperial capitals, ending with an enjoyable visit to her beloved grandmother Queen Victoria at Balmoral, the royal retreat in Scotland. Three more daughters for Nicholas and Alexandra followed, each of whom took the patronym of their father, Nikolaevna, after their given names: Tatiana was born in June of 1897, Maria arrived in June of 1899, and Anastasia in June of 1901. The Empress suffered miscarriages in 1896 and 1902, and finally in August of 1904 she gave birth to a long-awaited male heir, Alexis Nikolaevich, the new tsarevich.

In the first weeks of their son's life the couple realized Alexis was a "bleeder," and that Alexandra was an asymptomatic carrier of the hemophiliac gene. Hemophilia was a terrifying, incurable condition characterized by the blood's inability to produce its own clotting agent. A minor cut could lead to heavy blood loss and death within a matter of hours if left untreated. Alexandra's uncle Prince Leopold, son of Queen Victoria, lived as an invalid for much of his life and died at the age of 30. Alexandra also knew that her sister Irene had passed it on to two of her three sons, one of whom died in 1904 at the age of four. Irene was married to the brother of Germany's emperor Kaiser Wilhelm II, and the disease was kept a closely guarded secret by family members; common wisdom at the time was to advise against marriage at all for sisters or nieces of hemophiliacs—advice both Alexandra and Irene ignored, as did other female descendants of Queen Victoria. Women carried the gene but were rarely afflicted with the condition.

Nicholas and Alexandra spent the next 14 years living in a state of constant anxiety and fear over their son's health. Some princes elsewhere were clad in padded suits to prevent potentially fatal internal bleeding, but the tsar and Alexandra assigned a pair of imperial Russian navy sailors to guard over their son and prevent injury on a round-the-clock basis. The royal couple also managed to keep the tsarevich's condition a closely guarded secret for many years.

Influenced by Rasputin

Empress Alexandra was an unpopular tsarina, both at court and among the superstitious Russian rabble. Her shyness was interpreted as Teutonic frostiness, and she suffered from various physical ailments that kept her confined to her palace rooms at the opulent Tsarskoye Selo, or Tsar's Village, near St. Petersburg. Given to long periods of prayer and reflection, she fell easily under the sway of a curious interloper who had conned enough nobles to gain entrance to the imperial court. This was Grigori Rasputin, an itinerant monk and Russian Orthodox mystic who claimed to have faith-healing powers. Of peasant origins, Rasputin was utterly filthy in his personal grooming habits, sexually rapacious, and a talented grifter who had already seduced some well-born women in St. Petersburg. Nicholas and Alexandra first met the "Mad Monk" in late 1905. Rasputin claimed he could devote his powers to the tsarevich Alexis and keep him in good health. The couple grew increasingly reliant on him, despite warnings from many others about the loathsome Rasputin's motives.

If Russians privately called Alexandra *Niemka,* a derogatory term for a German woman, her husband was an unpopular tsar who hopelessly blundered through the 23-year duration of his reign. In retrospect, his rule was characterized by indecisiveness and inaction, alternating with imprudent decisions and an inability to delegate to ministers and military leaders when the moment called for a more experienced approach. He led Russia into a disastrous war with Japan in 1904–05 that brought the country to the brink of revolution and set in motion a series of events that spiraled out of even his authoritarian control. Intently adherent to what he considered his divine right to rule, the tsar resisted all efforts at reform until his hand was forced by civil unrest. A succession of Imperial Dumas, or parliaments, met from 1906 to the start of World War I, each marked by either chaos and opposition to the tsar, or ineffectiveness because they consisted of handpicked allies of the status quo. The Empress's reliance on Rasputin was one of the livelier subjects the Duma debated. Her marriage to Nicholas was an extraordinarily solid union, and their letters and correspondence show that she encouraged Nicholas to act independently and supported his vision for Russia.

World War I marked the final chapter of Alexandra's life as Tsarina of Russia. Nicholas led his troops in battle, against all advice, and delegated authority to Alexandra to act on his behalf when he was away at the front. Rasputin was still lurking about, but finally in December of 1916 a clique of high-ranking nobles carried out an assassination. Rasputin was said to have survived a poisoned meal, was shot by pistol, made an attempt to escape from his host's palace, and was finally shot several more times before the conspirators dumped his body in the icy River Neva. Alexandra, who spoke to Rasputin by telephone daily, was distraught and fearful for her own safety when she learned the news.

Taken into Custody

Within weeks Russia's heavy losses in the war sparked political unrest in St. Petersburg, where soldiers, malnourished workers, and other disaffected elements took to the streets. A Provisional Government was formed in February of 1917, at first led by a Council of Ministers of the newly created Russian Republic. Nicholas was forced to abdicate while he was en route back to St. Petersburg.

Meanwhile, guards moved in place as Alexandra, her daughters, and Alexis were put under house arrest at Tsarskoye Selo, where Nicholas joined them. In August of 1917, they were moved to a governor's mansion in Tobolsk, a city in Siberia. By then a vicious civil war had erupted between the hard-line Communist Bolsheviks—who had seized control in October of 1917 by ousting the Provisional Government—and the White Guards, who called for the restoration of Romanov power. In 1918, the eventual outcome between the Whites, who enjoyed foreign aid and arms, and the Red Army factions remained unclear. In April of 1918, Alexandra and her family were moved yet again, this time to Ipatiev House in Yekaterinburg. The ex-tsar begged to be allowed to emigrate to Britain, or at least let his wife and children leave, but Alexandra refused to part from her husband, and the Bolsheviks knew they had a tremendous advantage in keeping the family hostage, and a potentially lucrative source of ransom payment, too.

As a unit of Whites neared Yekaterinburg on July 16, 1918, the 46-year-old mother of five and former Empress was woken by her son's physician after midnight, on July 17. With Nicholas and the children, Alexandra was taken to a basement room where, they were told, a photograph proving their safety was to be taken to send abroad. Instead the Bolshevik commander read a short statement condemning them to death and eleven soldiers marched forward and opened fire. Having instructed her daughters to sew jewels into their corsets, the former Grand Duchesses, who ranged in age from 22-year-old Olga to 17-year-old Anastasia, appeared to be bulletproof, as their fortified undergarments deflected the bullets. Soldiers panicked and fired round after round. Thirteen-year-old Alexis died while holding the family dog, a King Charles spaniel named Jimmy. Their bodies were dismembered and buried in a location that remained a secret for decades. In 1991, the graves were conclusively located, DNA tests were run, and Alexandra and her family's remains were reinterred at Sts. Peter and Paul Cathedral in St. Petersburg in 1998.

Books

Massie, Robert K., *Nicholas and Alexandra: The Tragic, Compelling Story of the Last Tsar and his Family,* Head of Zeus Ltd., 2013.

Rounding, Virginia, *Alix and Nicky: The Passion of the Last Tsar and Tsarina,* Macmillan, 2012.

Periodicals

Times (London, England), July 22, 1918.□

Raúl Anguiano

One of the most industrious artists to emerge during Mexico's post-Revolutionary modernist period, Raul Anguiano (1915–2006) enjoyed a long and productive career that took his artwork around the globe. Anguiano tackled a number of styles and themes in his artwork but is most remembered for his immense murals, his images concerning political and social structures, and his ability to capture the inner and outer beauty of Mexico's indigenous people, particularly its females.

While Anguiano respected all artists, he believed the painter was exceptional. In 1999, Anguiano told the *Orange County Register's* Daniel Chang that painters were superior to other artists: "The painter is a more complete artist than the musician or writer. A composer lacking manual ability can still write music. An author can be blind and still write. But a painter must work with his brain, eyes, heart and the hand. Only a surgeon comes close to the painter."

Began Sketching as Child

Raúl Anguiano (pronounced ahn-gee-AH-no) was born February 26, 1915, in Guadalajara, Mexico. He was the eldest of ten children born to Abigail Valadez and José Anguiano. His family's livelihood involved manufacturing shoes. Early on, Anguiano's mother recognized his passion for drawing and provided him with endless sketchbooks. As a youngster, Anguiano favored figure work over landscapes. At the age of five, he impressed his elders with sketches of Mexican President Álvaro Obregón and famed bullfighter Rodolfo Gaona.

Growing up, Anguiano practiced his skills by trying to copy portraits of famed movie stars and photographs of the Mexican Revolution. Early on, he emulated the style of Cubist artists, rendering abstract, geometric images in his sketches. At 12, Anguiano began art classes, forgoing regular school to attend the Museum of Guadalajara's Free School of Painting. While attending the school, Anguiano expanded his interests. He began drawing live models and objects from his surroundings. In addition, he copied famed masterpieces by looking at prints, completing an in-depth study of Michelangelo. As the youngest student in his class, Anguiano earned the nickname "Rafaelito" or "small Raphael." Along the way, he met drawing instructor Jose Vizcarra, who was so impressed with Anguiano's potential that he tutored him for free.

Eager to forge his own course, the teenaged Anguiano joined an artists and intellectuals collective known as the Bandera de Provincias. The group published a magazine and organized exhibitions and lectures. Inspired by members of the collective, Anguiano read Machiavelli's famed political tract *The Prince,* as well as Franz Roh's *Magical Realism,* an essay on visual arts. Anguiano also studied poets and philosophers, thus broadening his intellectual ideas about the world. During this time, Anguiano began to adopt a more radical ideology with an interest in social affairs, economic issues, and workers' unions. In 1928, Anguiano exhibited his first artwork in a group show. By 17, he was teaching in Guadalajara's schools to help support his family.

Studied Muralism in Mexico City

In 1934, Anguiano moved to Mexico City and hooked up with other painters to improve and explore his craft. At this time, Anguiano befriended several revolutionaries, including Jesús Guerrero Galván and Máximo Pacheco. Anguiano assisted other artists as they painted murals, in this way honing his own fresco technique and learning to use scaffolding. At one point, Anguiano joined a troupe of young painters who dubbed themselves the "Group of 18." Galván and Pacheco were part of this group. Working together the group members painted murals, yet since they each had their own style, the images in the murals lacked uniformity and cohesion. One series of panels created by the Group of 18 stood out, noted MacKinley Helm in *Mexican Painters.* This one was painted on the outside walls of a polytechnic institute and emblazoned with the words, "Let us dynamite the schools and cut off the ears of the teachers."

After settling in Mexico City and taking an interest in murals, it was not long before Anguiano crossed paths with Diego Rivera, the prominent Mexican muralist and husband to portrait artist Frida Kahlo. Anguiano told Vivian Letran of the *Los Angeles Times* that when he first met Rivera at the National Palace of Mexico, Rivera was up on a platform painting. "He climbed down from the scaffold to introduce himself to me. He regarded my work. I know this because after he painted another mural at the National Palace, a journalist asked him who could continue the tradition of Mexican mural painting, and he said only three artists: Pablo Higgins, Frida Kahlo and Raúl Anguiano."

In 1935, Anguiano celebrated his first exhibition in Mexico's capital city with a show at the country's most noted cultural center, the Palacio de Bellas Artes (Palace of Fine Arts). It was a joint show, with Pacheco's work on display, too. At the time, Anguiano was the youngest painter to date to display his work there. For this exhibition, Anguiano focused his artwork on industrial topics. There were factories, depictions of the workers' movement, and other images meant to illustrate Anguiano's views on how capitalism affected the working class.

During the 1930s, Anguiano taught at the National Autonomous University of Mexico and at the Las Esmeralda School of Painting and Sculpture. He also served as a supervisor of drawing teachers in the Mexico City public schools. In 1936, Anguiano enjoyed his first mural commission, painting *Revolución* and *Contrarevolución* in Morelia, a city located in central Mexico. He would go on to paint some 50 murals during his lifetime.

Explored Painting, Graphic Arts

Around 1936, Anguiano began experimenting with surrealism by adding slightly offbeat, dream-like features to his paintings and drawings. During this period, Anguiano took his inspiration from the world around him, exploring a parallel reality to the political and proletarian topics he had been focused on. Anguiano visited run-down neighborhoods, cabarets and circuses, capturing the prostitutes, circus freaks, clowns, and acrobats he came across. Some critics consider these pieces to be among Anguiano's best artistic creations. Noted pieces from this period included *Marihuanos* (1938); *La Mujer Rosa y el Cirquero Gris* (The Pink Woman and the Grey Circus Performer) (1941), which showed a Picasso-like influence; and *La Llorona* (The Wailing Woman), a sober pencil drawing from 1942 depicting the devil, a child, and a mother-like human. The latter piece was acquired by the Museum of Modern Art in New York.

In the mid-1930s, Anguiano joined the League of Writers and Revolutionary Artists, a collective of artists and intellectuals who used their art as a vehicle to combat war, fascism, and the oppression of the working class. After the group fell apart, Anguiano joined the artists' print collective known as the Taller de Gráfica Popular, or People's Graphic Workshop in 1937. The group used graphic arts—particularly woodcuts and lithography—to advance the revolutionary cause and communicate its message through posters. After joining, Anguiano explored lithography.

Anguiano's first international trip took place in 1938, when the Ministry of Public Education dispatched him and Xavier Guerrero to Havana to show off the work of several Mexican painters. In 1940, Anguiano traveled to New York City and received a scholarship to attend the Art Students League. When he was not painting or attending class, Anguiano visited the city's galleries and found inspiration in the works of Paul Cézanne, El Greco, Diego Velazquez, Rembrandt, and Vincent Van Gogh. The influences were clear in Anguiano's Expressionist pieces that followed, particularly his portraits.

Inspired by Indigenous People

In 1949, Anguiano took a journey into Mexico's jungles that changed the focus of his artwork for the rest of his life. That year, the National Institute of Fine Arts tapped Anguiano to join an expedition of anthropologists and archaeologists visiting the ancient Mayan archaeological site of Bonampak. Located in eastern Chiapas, the site included a temple filled with frescos. American archaeologist Charles Frey had examined the ruins and discovered the ancient frescoes. The Mexican government did not believe Frey when he divulged their existence, so Frey contacted muralists Rivera and David Alfaro Siqueiros for help in financing an expedition to document the artwork. "They asked me to go," Anguiano told the *Los Angeles Times'* Letran. "I was intelligent, I was young and I was eager to go."

The experience had a lasting impact on Anguiano. The jungle surrounding Bonampak was home to the Lacandones—an isolated, indigenous Mexican tribe little known to the rest of the world. The Lacandon people, their culture, and their lifestyle captivated Anguiano. When he was not sketching the ruins and ancient frescoes, Anguiano stayed busy painting portraits of the Lacandon people and their huts, the exotic vegetation, and the wild game they cooked for dinner. Anguiano produced more than 70 pieces of artwork inspired by the Lacandon landscapes and people. Noted works from this collection include *Lacandons Roasting Sarahuato Monkeys* (1950), a painting showing Lacandon women sitting around a fire, making their dinner, and *La Espina* (The Thorn), a piece from 1952 depicting a pious Mayan woman sitting on the ground, picking at a splinter in her foot with a knife. *The Thorn* was one of Anguiano's better-known images and sold at auction for $156,000 in 2004. Another memorable piece was 1953's *Nacimiento en la Selva* (Birth in the Jungle) in which Anguiano drew Mayan women through the lens of realism. The trip so impacted Anguiano that he wrote a book about the experience entitled, *Aventura en Bonampak,* published in 1959.

During the 1950s and '60s, Anguiano exhibited his work in Paris; San Francisco; Moscow and Leningrad, Russia; Havana, Cuba; Santiago, Chile; and Rome. In the 1970s, he focused on several book-illustrating projects and in the 1980s, turned his attention back to lithographs, displaying a series of them at the Chicago International Art Exposition and also in Paris. In 1988, Anguiano taught mural-making and painting at the Art Academy of Latvia. In 1995, Anguiano donated a 1963 painting called *La Crucifixíon* to the Vatican.

Returned to Mural-Making

In the last decade of his life, Anguiano rendered more murals than ever. In 1999, Anguiano painted a mural called *Mexican Greatness* at the Consulate-General of Mexico in Los Angeles. That same year, he started a "multicultural" mural at the Bowers Museum of Cultural Art in Santa Ana, California. The mural was so well-received he was asked to paint a second. Titled *The Mayas: Magic, Science and the History of the Maya,* the latter mural was commissioned as part of a permanent Mayan culture exhibit at the museum and incorporated images from his trip to Bonampak alongside objects from the museum's collection. In 2001, Anguiano painted a mural depicting the creation story at the Monterrey Institute of Technology and Higher Education in Mexico City.

Over the course of his life, Anguiano painted more than 50 murals, leaving his work behind in his native Mexico at the National Museum of Anthropology and History, the Ministry of Public Education, and the Ministry of Environment and National Resources, all in Mexico City. Anguiano completed his final U.S. mural in 2002 at the performing arts center of East Los Angeles College. This enormous mural—68 feet long by 13 feet high—traced the history of Mexican art from the Mayans through the 20th century. It featured portraits of prominent artists who shaped the Mexican mural tradition, such as José Clemente Orozco, Rivera, and Siqueiros.

By the 1990s, Anguiano was splitting his time between his home in Mexico City and his home in Huntington Beach, California. Working until the end, Anguiano finished his last painting—a sunset—on December 14, 2005. He was in California when he fell ill toward the end of 2005 and was flown in a presidential jet back to his homeland. Admitted to the hospital for heart failure, Anguiano died in Mexico City on January 13, 2006. He was 90. Anguiano left behind his son, daughter, and wife, Brigita (Liepins) Anguiano, a former art student whom he married around 1970. In a 1996 interview with Wendy Lee of the Long Beach *Press-Telegram,* Brigita Anguiano discussed her husband's ability to capture the beauty and dignity of his fellow compatriots, even in the midst of their suffering. "His love is for the human," Brigita Anguiano said. "To him, there isn't a person ugly in the world. There is no class distinction in his heart or mind. He just loves the people."

Books

Helm, MacKinley, *Mexican Painters,* Dover Publications, 1968.

Periodicals

Independent (London), February 8, 2006.

Los Angeles Times, January 12, 1999; July 26, 2000; January 16, 2006.

Orange County Register, December 25, 1999.

Press-Telegram (Long Beach, CA), January 13, 1996.

Online

"Biography," Raúl Anguiano Official Website, http://www.raulanguiano.com/Ingles/biografia.html (November 23, 2013).□

Mordecai Anielewicz

Mordecai Anielewicz (c. 1919–1943) was a Polish resistance fighter and one of the key leaders of the Warsaw Ghetto Uprising of 1943. This was the only open, armed rebellion against Nazi German occupation anywhere in Europe during World War II, and it was significantly outmatched by the German war machine. Known in the resistance network by his *nom de guerre* "Aniolek," or Little Angel, Anielewicz was just 24 years old when he perished in a bunker at 18 Miła Street after nearly three weeks of fighting.

Mordecai Anielewicz was born around 1919 in Wyszków, Poland, a railroad town north of Warsaw. His parents settled in a part of Warsaw known as Riverside, along the Vistula River. Riverside was a rough part of town, situated in a flood zone, and was the site of grain depots, gambling dens, and poorhouses. The family lived on Solec Street and Anielewicz grew up close to his younger brother Pinchas, a teenage wrestling champion. Near the Poniatowski Bridge was an open-air flea market where their mother sold fish, and their father Abraham had a small corner store. His parents invested in their sons' education, sending Anielewicz to Laor, the top Jewish private school in Warsaw.

Joined Zionist Organization

Anielewicz came of age during a revival of deep-rooted anti-Semitism in Europe. Poles, Czechs, Ukrainians, and other Eastern Europeans had lived for generations under repressive imperial regimes that instigated and took advantage of tensions between the two religious groups. On one side was imperial Russia, which had fought for Poland and its surrounding territories for centuries; on Poland's western flank was the gateway to the rest of Europe, where religious tolerance had been imposed in some progressive nations by decree. The upheaval of World War I, and with it the end of the Russian, Austro-Hungarian, and German empires, destabilized all of Europe. In the new modern era, newspapers inflamed anti-Semitism by blaming Jewish-owned banking institutions for the ongoing economic hardship of the 1920s. In Germany and elsewhere, right-wing political parties gained popular support.

In response, a homeland movement that originated in the nineteenth century began to gain wider support. This was known as Zionism, and its goal was a permanent, independent Jewish state. For politically moderate and culturally assimilated Jews the idea of a separate country, in effect a permanent exile, was unthinkable. Others, like Anielewicz, envisioned it as a place of progress and freedom. In his teens Anielewicz joined the Zionist youth group Betar, which provided self-defense training and advocated for resettlement in the British Mandate for Palestine. Anielewicz came to consider the Betarim too conservative for his emerging political views, and went over to a more leftist Zionist youth group, Hashomer Hatzair, or the Young Guards. After finishing his education at Laor, he went to work as an organizer for Hashomer Hatzair, traveling to cities and towns in southwest Poland to recruit and train new branches.

On September 1, 1939, Nazi Germany invaded Poland, an act that marked the start of World War II. Anielewicz's family and friends knew what would happen if Poland fell to Germany: a strict military government would impose the same humiliating, discriminatory laws against Jews as elsewhere in German-occupied lands as part of German leader Adolf Hitler's plan for a new *Reich,* or empire. Barred from the professions, stripped of their bank accounts, businesses, and even homes, Jews were ordered by law to wear a yellow Star of David on their clothes, and in some places were being deported to work camps in remote parts of Eastern Europe.

Sought Aid in Vilnius

Many Polish Jews seized the opportunity to flee Poland forever, heading toward Palestine or unoccupied parts of southern Europe. Anielewicz stayed, believing the Polish Army could stave off a total collapse to Nazi assault. But the Polish leadership capitulated after a month of fighting, and a Soviet-German non-aggression pact prompted the Soviet Union to seize coveted parts of eastern Poland and the Baltic regions. Anielewicz went to Vilnius in Lithuania for a time. This Baltic urban center was, like Warsaw, home to a sizable Jewish population. Anielewicz attempted to convince leaders of Zionist groups there that the time was right for an organized, armed resistance. That idea was anathema to many, and an occupation by Soviet Russia—the world's first Communist state, and brought into being by some of the most prominent Jewish Marxists of the era—was considered preferable to rule by German overlords.

In the first year of the war, Anielewicz tried to open up a safe route to Palestine south from Vilnius, through Belarus, Ukraine, and Romania, to the Black Sea. His plan was foiled by Soviet authorities, and he spent some time in a Soviet detention center for political operatives. His exploits, which exposed others in the Young Guards, led to his formal ouster from Hashomer Hatzair. He went to Warsaw in late 1941, traveling incognito and carrying a prized, extremely forbidden firearm.

By that point Nazi commanders in Poland had ordered cities with large Jewish populations to restrict them to ghettoes, a tactic dating back to anti-Semitic practices of the Middle Ages. Warsaw, along with Vilnius, Łódż, and Kraków, had its urban footprint remapped as Jewish residents were forced into an 840-acre district. The Nazis' feared national police corps of SS soldiers, or *Schutzstaffel,* carried out orders from Berlin. High brick walls were erected, and access to the rest of Warsaw was controlled by soldiers at a few military-checkpoint intersections. Overpopulated thanks to a flood of newly homeless Jews from towns outside Warsaw, the Ghetto quickly became a place of misery, disease, and starvation. Internal control was handed over to a few elders on a newly created *Judenrat,* or Jewish Council, who set up a Jewish police force and attempted to alleviate the most abject poverty cases through relief charities. The war meant shortages of food, heating fuel, and other basics for all of Europe, but the Jews' rations were even more diminished.

Urged Combat, Not Cooperation

Warsaw's Jews toiled in factories for the German war effort, even making uniforms for the German Army. Resistance organizations inside the Ghetto established communication networks and smuggled goods in and even Jewish children out; in some cases ingenious basement tunnels were used to connect the two zones. Anielewicz took part in these activities and allied with another young rebel, a Vilnius-born organizer named Yitzhak Zuckerman, who looked "Aryan" and thus could move easily between sectors without attracting much attention.

The main group of resisters in Warsaw came to call themselves *Żydowska Organizacja Bojowa* or the Jewish Fighting Organization and referred to by its Polish-language acronym ŻOB. It had been founded by a Communist named Pinkus Kartin, who had combat experience from the Spanish Civil War of the 1930s. For much of 1941, the ŻOB was divided over whether to help Jews or aid the Soviet effort against the Germans; they managed to negotiate for weapons and ammunition, secreted into the Ghetto by deft smugglers' networks, but by the spring of 1942, hints came from the outside of a newly built "labor" camp at Treblinka, near Warsaw.

In July of 1942, German officials in Warsaw began the *Grossaktion,* or mass liquidation of the Warsaw Ghetto. About a third of Warsaw's Jewish population of around 400,000 were taken to a train depot known as Umschlagplatz, or Collection Point. The round-ups were conducted in terrifying, utterly random seizures designed to instill terror in the already-despairing populace, and went on daily for eight weeks. About 250,000 were deported for "resettlement in the East," as the Judenrat leaders were told. Instead the freight-train cars deposited the Jews at Treblinka, where they were sorted according to work abilities; those too elderly, too young, or too malnourished were sent directly to gas chambers.

The acquiescent leader of Warsaw's Judenrat was a former Polish senator named Adam Czerniaków. When the mass deportations began in July of 1942, Czerniaków was aghast by his own complicity and committed suicide by cyanide capsule. This event in itself roiled the resistance network, and finally the younger generation of resisters like Anielewicz and Zuckerman took over in late 1942.

Allied with *Armia Krajowa*

Anielewicz had been in southwest Poland on organizing and recruitment missions when the Grossaktion began. He had by then taken over the leadership of ŻOB from Pinkus Kartin, who had been arrested by the Germans in the spring of 1942 and died in custody. Anielewicz and other ŻOB commanders begged their contacts inside the Polish government-in-exile in London, and the Home Army—the official Polish resistance network inside Poland—for weapons and supplies. ŻOB erected a secret bunker and command post at 18 Miła Street, and practiced making pipe bombs and other incendiary devices.

On January 18, 1943, when deportation round-ups began again, the ŻOB made its first bold move by picking off a few German soldiers in the escort march. Anielewicz led the action, which included blockading Zamenhoff and Niska streets, and the sight of dead Germans in uniform was galvanizing to Warsaw's suffering Jews, who began to rally around the idea of an uprising. Four days later, the Germans ordered a halt to the deportations, which was a victory of immense symbolism for Anielewicz and others in the ŻOB. Of course, the Germans were merely reshuffling their Warsaw command team and removing officers deemed responsible for the debacle. On April 17, 1943, a new SS commander, General Jürgen Stroop, arrived in Warsaw. Deportations from Umschlagplatz began again two days later, and this date also marked the official start of the Warsaw Ghetto Uprising. It was also the start of one of the Jewish calendar's most important holidays, Pesach, or Passover, which commemorates the Jews' escape from slavery in Egypt under Moses as described in the Old Testament's Book of Exodus.

Fought for 19 Days

Some 2,000 German troops surrounded the Warsaw Ghetto overnight to begin another round of deportations. This time, Anielewicz and the others were prepared: he led teams of rooftop snipers and assigned the planting of homemade bombs. They threw Molotov cocktail bombs and traversed rooftops in aerial assaults. The roughly 600 ŻOB fighters were hopelessly outnumbered and outgunned by their enemy, but the rebel leaders did have the advantage of familiarity with the Ghetto's buildings, its secret tunnels, and other hiding places. Again, Anielewicz and the ŻOB viewed the Ghetto itself as a strategic advantage, since the Germans had constructed so few exit points; that meant that ŻOB cells could carry out an attack that would trap the maximum number of Germans in a single spot. Zuckerman was hiding out in Aryan Warsaw when the Uprising started on April 19, 1943, and worked to send more arms and ammunition to the fighters.

Hitler and Berlin's Reichsministers were enraged about the Warsaw Ghetto Uprising. Stroop decided to burn the ghetto down, and set about systematically blasting out buildings and blocks. Anielewicz was holed up at the fairly well constructed bunker at 18 Miła Street on May 8, 19 long days since the start of the Uprising. Surrounded by German forces, he chose suicide for himself and his girlfriend, Mira Fuchrer, rather than surrender or be shot by German bullets. About 80 other ŻOB fighters were also in the bunker and chose to die. They were discovered by Marek Edelman, another key leader, and Zivia Lubetkin, the highest ranking female in the ŻOB command. Edelman and Lubetkin managed to escape through tunnels, as did some other fighters. In all, just 34 Jewish rebels survived the Uprising, which came to a conclusion on May 16, 1943. It remained the only concerted Jewish-led effort against Nazi oppression during the Holocaust, and the only time civilians in a German-occupied place had openly taken up arms against their occupiers.

Books

Brzezinski, Matthew, *Isaac's Army: The Jewish Resistance in Occupied Poland,* Random House, 2012.

Periodicals

New York Times, November 4, 2001.

World War II, January–February 2013.□

Estelle Axton

As the cofounder of what became the soul music label Stax Records in Memphis, Tennessee, American music executive Estelle Axton (1918–2004) exerted a strong influence over the course of popular music worldwide.

Estelle Axton remains one of the few women to have held a top executive position at a major American music label. As a white woman working among a predominantly African American group of artists in the Deep South in the 1960s, she might have been out of place in other ways as well, but by all accounts Stax, at least in its earlier years, was a largely integrated organization. Axton's own outlook contributed to Stax's progressive attitude, and she helped shape the label's musical direction in many ways. Axton was held in great affection by many musicians at Stax: "She was like a mother to us all," singer Isaac Hayes was quoted as saying in the *Times* of London after her death.

Charlie Gillett Collection/redferns/Getty Images

Sang in Gospel Quartet

Estelle Axton was born Estelle Stewart in the small southwest Tennessee town of Middleton on September 11, 1918, and grew up there on a farm. Musical from the beginning, she played the organ as a girl and sang in a family gospel-music quartet. At 16, she moved to Memphis to attend Memphis State University, studying to become a schoolteacher. She returned to Middleton, became a first grade teacher, and then met Everett Axton. The pair married in 1941 and returned to Memphis. Estelle Axton stayed home to take care of the couple's two boys but, as they grew older, joined the workforce as a teller at Union Planters National Bank in Memphis in 1950.

She was still at the bank when her brother, Jim Stewart, appealed for financial help with his fledgling recording activities in 1958. The previous year, Stewart had made a few country recordings on a reel-to-reel tape recorder borrowed from his barber and tried to distribute them locally, hoping to replicate the success of the local rockabilly label Sun. With his sister's help he intended to buy a top-of-the-line Ampex 350 tape recorder and professionalize the sound of his releases. Estelle Axton suggested to her husband that they take out a second mortgage on the couple's house, and Everett, although he was earning only $18 a week at the time, agreed. With a contribution of $2,500, Estelle financed the tape recorder and bought out Stewart's partners, becoming a full partner in the new Satellite Records label that the pair set up in a warehouse in nearby Brunswick, Tennessee.

At first the label recorded mostly country artists, but after gaining some national distribution from the Mercury label with a release by an African American rhythm and blues group, the Veltones, Axton and Stewart began to experiment with that genre. In 1960, they moved Satellite to a disused movie theater they rented for $150 a month on East McLemore Street on Memphis's south side, in a neighborhood whose proportion of African American residents was increasing. Renovating the theater into a recording studio themselves to make money, they also converted its candy counter into a record store. At first Axton, who enjoyed dancing to music in the latest styles, sold records from the shop to her friends at the bank, but later she began to work there herself and became a sort of gatekeeper, spotting talent among the young local performers who came through the doors.

Remortgaged House

Even these measures did not put the young label in the black, however, and once again Axton came to the rescue, taking out a third mortgage on her house and investing another $4,000. Fortunately, Satellite scored a pair of hits in 1960 with releases by the 17-year-old rhythm and blues singer Carla Thomas, the daughter of a disc jockey, Rufus Thomas, on the pioneering black-oriented radio station WDIA. The first of these, "Cause I Love You," led to a $5,000 distribution deal with the large Atlantic label; Atlantic in turn released Carla Thomas's "Gee Whiz" nationally, and it reached the pop top ten.

A 1961 Satellite release, "Last Night," by the interracial group the Mar-Keys, featuring Axton's son Packy on saxophone, also became a national hit; it was recorded at Axton's insistence, and Stewart bet $100 that it would fail. At this point the label, fearing litigation from a California label also named Satellite, changed its name to Stax. The name was formed from the first two letters of Stewart's and Axton's last names.

As musicians began to gravitate toward the Stax studio, it was often Axton who they first encountered in the front record store. Mar-Keys guitarist Steve Cropper worked for Axton in the record store for a time, and he joined forces with another Axton discovery, keyboard player Booker T. Jones, to form the nucleus of Booker T. and the MGs, a band that recorded the major instrumental hit "Green Onions" on its own and also served as Stax's house band in the early years. Cropper was white and Jones was African American, and the integrated MGs were a rarity in an environment where audiences remained largely divided by race. But Axton, according to Garth Cartwright of the London *Guardian,* insisted that "[w]e didn't see color, we just saw talent." Hayes was quoted as saying by Cartwright that "You didn't feel any back-off from her, no differentiation that you were black and she was white."

Led Music Analysis Sessions

The Stax studio itself was Jim Stewart's domain, but Axton's input on Stax's musical direction was substantial. During the label's first years, the street-level record store served as an informal musical laboratory in which Axton and Stax's stable of writers, who included the young Isaac Hayes, would evaluate hits on other labels in search of ideas for Stax artists. "When a record would hit on another label, we would discuss what made this record sell, we analyzed it," Axton was quoted as saying by Pierre Perrone in the London *Independent.* "That's why we had so many good writers. They knew what would sell." Axton championed the release of Eddie Floyd's "Knock on Wood," in the face of Stewart's initial resistance, and the song became one of Stax's biggest hits in 1966.

Vocalist Otis Redding was another Axton record-store associate who went on to major stardom. His death in a plane crash in late 1967 was one of a series of tragedies that marked the end of Stax's first successful phase; the assassination in Memphis of the Rev. Martin Luther King Jr. in 1968 also strained relationships among Stax's musicians. In the late 1960s, Axton handled many of Stax's business affairs. She helped organize the company's sale to the film studio Gulf & Western in 1968 and during that process sold her own stake in the company, signing an agreement not to compete with Stax for five years. Stax reorganized and reverted to Stewart's ownership, scoring major hits by Hayes and the gospel-flavored group the Staple Singers in the early 1970s, but Axton's time with the company was over.

For several years in the early 1970s, Axton was active in the real estate business in Memphis, but she returned to music in partnership with her son Packy to establish the Fretone label in 1973, continuing to run the label after her son's early death the following year. She outlasted Stax in that capacity; Stax went bankrupt in 1975, forced into final foreclosure by Axton's former employer, Union Planters Bank. The following year Fretone scored a hit with the novelty recording "Disco Duck" by Memphis disc jockey Rick Dees.

In her later years she remained involved in Memphis music, helping to establish several industry groups that remain active. The Stax studios were demolished in 1989, but Axton lived to see a museum erected on the site, incorporating many of the features of the original building's design and telling the story she had done so much to create. Axton died in Memphis on February 25, 2004. She was survived by a daughter, Doris Axton Fredrick. Three years later, she was posthumously honored with a Trustees Award at the 2007 Grammy awards ceremonies.

Books

Bowman, Rob, *Soulsville U.S.A.: The Story of Stax Records,* Schirmer, 2003.

Periodicals

Daily Telegraph (London, England), March 4, 2004.

Guardian (London, England), February 28, 2004.

Independent (London, England), March 13, 2004.

New York Times, February 27, 2004.

Times (London, England), March 8, 2004.

Online

"Estelle Axton,"*Allmusic,* http://www.allmusic.com (September 3, 2013).

"Jim Stewart and Estelle Axton's Stax Records," *The History of Rock 'n' Roll,* http://www.history-of-rock.com/stax_records.htm (September 3, 2013).

"Jim Stewart & Estelle Axton," *Memphis Music Hall of Fame,* http://memphismusichalloffame.com/inductee/jimstewartestelleaxton (September 3, 2013).□

B

Hobey Baker

American amateur athlete Hobey Baker (1892–1918) has been honored since 1981 with his name on the award given to the best college hockey player in the United States, the Hobey Baker Award. A gifted hockey and football player for Princeton in the early 1900s, Baker was also known for being a well-rounded gentleman. Baker lost his life as a pilot shortly after the end of World War I.

Born Hobart Amory Hare Baker on January 15, 1892, in Wissahickon, Pennsylvania, he was the son of Alfred Thornton Baker and his wife Augusta Pemberton. He was named for an uncle, Hobart Amory Hare, who was the president of Jefferson Medical Hospital. Baker's family was wealthy and privileged, and his parents were members of Philadelphia society. A graduate of Princeton University, Baker's father was an upholstery manufacturer. Baker was raised primarily in Bala Cynwyd, a well-to-do suburb of Philadelphia.

Because of their parents' affluence, Baker and his elder brother Thornton enjoyed special advantages throughout their childhood. This included an elite education, beginning in 1903, at Concord, New Hampshire's Saint Paul's School. Baker's brother was a solid athlete but after completing his schooling there, joined his father's firm. Baker took a different path.

Demonstrated Athletic Skills

During his years at Saint Paul's, Baker was able to become skilled in every sport offered there, including gymnastics, golf, baseball, swimming, running, football, and hockey. Baker favored the latter two sports, spending hours learning to play better and becoming a leader who emphasized fair play in the process. By the time he was a senior at his school, his hockey team was beating the best college teams.

After graduating from Saint Paul's, Baker entered Princeton University in 1910. There, he continued to stand out as a student, an athlete, and an ideal gentleman. Baker was a B student, member of the fashionable Ivy Club, and gave up his vacations to do social work at the YMCA. Baker was widely considered a selfless athlete, one who stood only 5′9″ and 160 pounds.

Became Star at Princeton

Because the school only allowed students to play two varsity sports, Baker focused on and shined in both football and hockey at Princeton. In this era, Ivy League college football was the center of national attention. At the time, the football was itself larger and rounder, there was no forward pass, and recent rule changes intended to limit injuries favored the defense. A versatile and well-respected college football player, Baker played as a punter, kicker, quarterback, halfback, and punt-returner for the Tigers.

In addition to demonstrating considerable skill on the freshman team, Baker played on Princeton's varsity team for three years and was an All-America selection. In 1912, he set a Princeton record for scoring with 92 points, which lasted until 1974. During Baker's three years on Princeton's varsity team, the Tigers posted a record of 20-3-4 and were the top ranked team in the United States in 1911. He also memorably played all 73 minutes of the lauded January 1914 Harvard-Princeton overtime game. Over the course of his football career at Princeton, he returned more than 900 punts and averaged more than 300 yards per game in punt returns.

©PF-(bygone1)/Alamy

Though Baker was a great college football player, his skills in hockey were even greater and the Tigers won two national hockey titles in 1912 and 1914. At this time, hockey was played with seven players per side, and the positions were slightly different than today. Baker was a rover and was able to control the game from any point on the ice. During his years at Princeton, the Tigers had a record of 27-7 when he was playing.

Not only did he play well, he embraced good sportsmanship and was only penalized one time. After every game, Baker also thanked the opposition for playing a good game. When his hockey playing days ended with Princeton, he was voted the best hockey player in his senior class. At the end of his Princeton playing days, Baker had accumulated more than 120 goals and 100 assists, thus averaging about three goals and assists per game.

Played Elite Amateur Hockey

By the time Baker graduated from Princeton in 1914, he was known as the "Prince of Princeton." Baker then joined the Wall Street-based J.P. Morgan Bank, and later was employed by his father's company. Though he disliked working for the bank, Baker took the job at J.P. Morgan so he could stay in New York City and in contact with fellow Princeton alums. He also garnered attention for dating and being briefly engaged to a prominent socialite, Jeanne Marie "Mimi" Scott. The world of work and society proved not nearly as satisfying as his college athletic pursuits and competition had been, and he found one outlet in New York playing hockey.

Baker had turned down offers to play hockey professionally in New York and Canada after college, primarily because it did not pay much, the players were not his intellectual and social equals, and he believed that one should play sport strictly for the love of the game. However, Baker did play for the talented amateur hockey team at New York's St. Nick's Arena, the St. Nicholas Skating Club. The team attracted some of the best players from Ivy League schools like Yale, Harvard, and Princeton, and was backed by such rich men as Cornelius Vanderbilt, J.P. Morgan, and John Jacob Astor. Yet Baker played better than most American players on any level and attracted much attention, in part because amateur teams of the time played professional teams in their off season. Baker dominated in many of these games, showing that he could skate with the best. And when the St. Nicholas Skating Club played in Madison Square Garden, crowds would show up to watch Baker fly down the ice. Baker would play for the team from about 1915 to 1917, with his last game most likely occurring in Pittsburgh on March 24, 1917.

Seeking other new challenges, the restless Baker also did some automobile racing with race car driver Eddie Rickenbacker, learned to play polo, and, in 1916, participated in volunteer flight training at Mineola, Long Island, New York, with General Leonard Wood's Civilian Aviation Corps. In addition, Baker became a lieutenant in the U.S. Army in May 1917. By this time, the United States had entered World War I, and Baker went to France in August 1917. There he joined the Lafayette Escadrille, a group of pilots who served in the French Air Service.

Used Piloting Skills in World War I

Becoming a distinguished pilot and marksman after receiving more training in France, Baker began flying for the Allies by early 1918. He was based in Toul and used his skills to shoot down three enemy planes from his plane. During the war, Baker flew a Spad, a light plane driven by a single propeller, with distinction, winning honors from both France and the United States, and served as a squadron leader for the Lafayette Escadrille.

After becoming a captain in August 1918, Baker was disappointed when the war ended with an armistice on November 11, 1918. Before returning to the United States, he wanted to take one last flight in a Spad. On December 21, 1918, he decided to test pilot a plane determined to be faulty that had been repaired. Though he was advised by friends not to fly the plane, he insisted on taking it for a test run. The decision proved fatal.

Within a quarter of a mile, the Spad stalled, the engine quit, and Baker tried to land it on an airstrip intact instead of crash land it as he could have done. He failed however, and the plane nosedived into the ground. Baker died in an ambulance in Toul, France, shortly after the accident. His body was returned to the United States and was buried in Bala Cynwyd.

Though Baker's name lives on through various memorials, many authors note that Baker and his ideals represented the era in which he lived, but transcended them as well. Jeffrey Hart wrote of Baker in the *Weekly Standard,* "For Baker, the epitome of the gentleman ideal and an athletic perfectionist, the game itself was the point. How the game was played was what mattered: sportsmanship, modesty, good manners. Even when he had been hammered bloody on the hockey rink or the gridiron, and if the opposing team had played fairly, he always went to their locker room and congratulated them on a game well played. If fouled, he sometimes wept, not because he had been hurt but because the game itself had been betrayed."

After his death, Baker was honored, if not idealized, in many ways. Author F. Scott Fitzgerald, who also attended Princeton in this era, greatly admired Baker and his legacy at Princeton. In Fitzgerald's 1920 novel *This Side of Paradise,* the author based the character of the football captain Allenby on Baker. Other fiction writers also used Baker and his legacy in various ways, including John Tunis, Mark Goodman (in his 1985 novel *Hurrah for the Next Man Who Dies*), and Geoffrey Wolff. For many authors, Baker's death reflected the decline in American optimism and idealism after World War I.

Memorialized After Death

Baker was also immortalized in other ways, many related to sports. In 1923, Princeton dedicated the Hobey Baker Rink. In 1945, when the Hockey Hall of Fame elected its charter class, he was the first American player to be inducted. The other original inductees included Art Ross, Georges Vezina, and Lord Frederick Stanley. In 1973, the United States Hockey Hall of Fame also made him a charter member. Four years later, the College Football Hall of Fame inducted Baker, making him the only athlete to be elected to both the Hockey Hall of Fame and the College Football Hall of Fame. Since 1981, U.S. college hockey has given its best player the Hobey Baker Award, due to the efforts of Chuck Bard and the Decathlon Athletic Club who established the honor. Many of the winners of the honor have gone on to distinguished careers in the NHL, including Paul Kariya, Ryan Miller, and Chris Drury.

Many hockey players appreciated how Baker's character was positively reflected in the award. Tom Kurvers, who won the Hobey Baker Award in 1984 while playing for the University of Minnesota-Duluth and later served as the assistant general manager for the National Hockey League's Tampa Bay Lightning, told Joe Smith of the *Tampa Bay Times,* "He died before his time—he was a legend. The name Hobey Baker probably, outside of a few people who studied it, doesn't mean a whole lot. But if you take a quick look at what he stood for, who he was and how he died, it makes you stop and think about it. They found a guy who really measures up."

Books

Scribner Encyclopedia of American Lives, Thematic Series: The 1960s, edited by William L. O'Neill and Kenneth T. Jackson. New York: Charles Scriber's Sons, 2002.

Periodicals

Daily News (New York), April 16, 2003.
Philadelphia Inquirer, November 11, 2010.
Pittsburgh Post-Gazette, April 13, 2013.
Pittsburgh Tribune Review, December 27, 2010.
Record (Bergen County, NJ), May 16, 2005.
Tampa Bay Times, April 5, 2012.
Weekly Standard, April 28, 2008.□

Françoise Barré-Sinoussi

French scientist Françoise Barré-Sinoussi (born 1947) is credited with playing a significant role in the discovery of HIV (human immunodeficiency virus). She was a co-recipient of the 2008 Nobel Prize in Medicine as a result. Barré-Sinoussi continued to focus on the study of the virology of HIV after winning the award.

Barré-Sinoussi was born on July 30, 1947, in Paris, France, the daughter of Roger and Jeanine Sinoussi. Raised in modest circumstances, Barré-Sinoussi was interested in plants and animals from an early age. When Barré-Sinoussi started going to school, her interest in biology and related biological sciences soon emerged.

Had Early Interest in Science

By the time Barré-Sinoussi entered university for her undergraduate degree, she had determined that she wanted to pursue medicine or science. She ultimately chose science because she liked discovering things and seeing valuable work emerge from the lab. She was also interested in cancer research after a young cousin died of leukemia.

Though it was not typical for students to work in labs—especially while rarely attending class—Barré-Sinoussi began conducting research in the role of retroviruses, which are slow-acting viruses that insert themselves into host cell genomes and replicate indefinitely if not stopped, in cancer while working in the laboratory of Jean-Claude Chermann. She landed in the lab two years into her studies by agreeing to volunteer in his lab on a part-time basis. There, she found her calling. In this period, she was able to pass her classes by using the notes of friends after spending full days in the lab instead of going to class.

After completing her undergraduate degree, Barré-Sinoussi continued her education at the University of Sciences in Paris. She earned her master's degree in biochemistry from the school in 1971. Barré-Sinoussi then entered the Pasteur Institute where she was granted her doctorate in 1975.

Faced Discrimination

In this time period, Barré-Sinoussi found her career path was often difficult because she was a woman. Even one of

Jacques DeMarthon/AFP/Getty Images

the heads of the Pasteur Institute dismissed her desire for a job there after completing her doctorate because of her sex. She told Andrew Jack of the *Financial Times,* "It was a lot more difficult at the time. Certain people—men, of course—discouraged me, saying it was not a good career for women. That pushed me even more to persevere. But I was from the generation of 1968. It was a period of activism and women were demanding their rights. I was not out demonstrating on the streets, but I shared a lot of those ideas."

With Ph.D. in hand, Barré-Sinoussi went to the United States to complete a post-doctoral fellowship granted by the National Science Foundation. Working at the National Institutes of Health, she conducted research on mouse retroviruses and their genetic restrictions. The experience proved important in her later research because it showed her the value of establishing partnerships with researchers around the world. She also was exposed to strict measures related to biosecurity in her lab, which were implemented to limit the risk of infection in researchers. She remained in the United States until the end of the 1970s, but adopted these measures in her own labs when she went back to Paris.

Returning to France and the Pasteur Institute with a large grant funding her research, Barré-Sinoussi began teaching as well. By the 1980s, Barré-Sinoussi was focusing on AIDS research with colleague Luc Montagnier. In 1981, the U.S. Centers for Disease Control and Prevention (CDC) recognized AIDS (acquired immune deficiency syndrome) after describing the mysterious illness in five young homosexual men, but the cause was unknown. In December 1982, a doctor named Willy Rozenbaum came to the lab helmed by Luc Montagnier hoping to find help for his many young gay male patients who were quickly dying and had these symptoms. (Rozenbaum later became the president of France's National AIDS council.)

Helped Discover HIV Virus

One of Rozenbaum's patients provided a lymph node biopsy, and the team first noted the distinct HIV virus on February 4, 1983. Barré-Sinoussi herself was the first scientist to isolate the HIV virus, which was originally called the lymphadenopathy-associated virus. Barré-Sinoussi and Montagnier eventually discovered that HIV was the virus responsible for AIDS. The team also developed the first diagnostic test to confirm the presence of the virus.

Barré-Sinoussi was listed as the first author of the publication which outlined the discovery of HIV, which was then labeled as a type of retrovirus. The paper was published in the prestigious journal *Science* in May 1983. Barré-Sinoussi presented her team's findings shortly thereafter. Because of their breakthrough, many advances were eventually made related to AIDS and its diagnosis, treatment, and prevention. Barré-Sinoussi and Montagnier's team continued to conduct research on HIV/AIDS, and by 1985, had decoded the HIV genome.

During this era, Barré-Sinoussi conducted research with a sense of urgency. From the first, she connected with community groups as she saw many young patients dying from this disease in a horrible fashion. Such relationships compelled her to use real patients instead of animal research. She also focused on HIV/AIDS prevention, including vaccines and ways to prevent HIV positive mothers from infecting their babies.

Emerging Controversy Over Credit for Discovery

Yet there was controversy as Barré-Sinoussi and Montagnier had an American rival, virologist Robert C. Gallo. In March 1983, Gallo publicly announced that he had isolated the virus that caused AIDS. Over time, it came to light that what he found—what he called HTL-V—had nothing to do with AIDS. Despite this setback, Gallo continued to produce significant work on HIV/AIDS. An employee of the National Cancer Institute, he received a patent on an HIV-related test. Gallo also claimed to have discovered the link between HIV and AIDS at the same time as the French scientists.

Because of the disagreement over the matter, French president François Mitterrand and the United States president Ronald Reagan had to intervene. In 1987, Barré-Sinoussi, Montagnier, and Gallo were named co-discoverers of the virus. They also split the royalties from the HIV blood test that was created as a result of their work. Most of the money from the royalties was deposited into a fund for AIDS research.

Despite such distractions, Barré-Sinoussi conducted related research through the Pasteur Institute in Africa. She also had a short-lived but illuminating study in Vietnam. There Barré-Sinoussi examined a small group of intravenous drug-users who had been exposed to HIV but had an innate immunity. In 1992, she became the head of the Virology of Retroviruses Unit at the institute, a position she held through at least 2013.

Won Nobel Prize

In 2008, Barré-Sinoussi received the Nobel Prize in Physiology or Medicine along with her colleague Montagnier and a German researcher named Harald zur Hausen. They were all given the honor for playing significant roles in discovering viruses. While Barré-Sinoussi and Montagnier identified HIV, zur Hausen discovered the first type of HPV (human papilloma virus), which can cause cervical cancer in women. Barré-Sinoussi was honored in particular as the first scientist to isolate the HIV virus. The Nobel Committee also cited how their discovery helped in AIDS treatment and prevention, while decreasing its spread.

After the winners of the award were announced, there was immediate controversy. Montagnier was better known than Barré-Sinoussi, and there were questions about the role she played in its discovery because her role had been publicly obscured. A bigger storm emerged concerning the snubbing of Gallo and his claim to be the first to link HIV to AIDS. However, the Nobel Committee noted that the award was given for the identification of HIV in particular, not his contribution. The controversy served to conceal, if not undermine, Barré-Sinoussi's key contribution to the identification of HIV.

Remaining the head of the Virology of Retroviruses Unit at the Pasteur Institute, Barré-Sinoussi continued to conduct research into the virology of HIV after winning the award. She also traveled around the world to help health professionals better understand HIV. In addition, she served as a consultant to the World Health Organization and the Joint United Nations Programme on HIV/AIDS. She also published regularly, with more than 250 original publications by 2011.

Continued HIV/AIDS Research

By 2012, Barré-Sinoussi was also serving as the president of the International AIDS Society, among other leadership positions. This organization included the leading researchers working on the disease, and focused on facilitating the search for a cure that was safe and affordable. In 2012, Barré-Sinoussi and the society announced a plan to find a cure for HIV. Though HIV/AIDS research had funding problems, there was a need to improve research infrastructure, and the lack of wide HIV research in animals. Despite the best efforts of scientists, there were only drugs that made HIV manageable and it still resulted in 1.7 million deaths per year. Between the 1980s and 2013, more than 35 million people have died of AIDS.

There was hope, however. Barré-Sinoussi supported and followed the Visconti study in which 14 French HIV-positive patients were given anti-viral drugs within ten weeks of infection. They then stopped taking the drugs for at least seven years, but showed no recurrence of HIV. Such studies demonstrated that a cure was possible, and Barré-Sinoussi firmly believed at least a functional cure would eventually emerge as well as a vaccine. When this would occur was unclear. She did not believe that a total elimination of the virus would ever be possible.

Barré-Sinoussi explained to the *Bulletin of the World Health Organization,* "if we can treat people early, then we can bring them hope. Prolonging life might provide time to develop new strategies for the future. I'm not sure that we will succeed in eradicating the disease but I am convinced that we'll be able to treat all HIV carriers so that they no longer have detectable levels of the virus and cannot transmit it to others."

Emphasized Humanitarian Causes

Barré-Sinoussi also focused on related humanitarian causes, including increasing access to treatment for those with HIV living in impoverished countries in sub-Saharan Africa and Southeast Asia. She participated in at least 250 international conferences on HIV/AIDS. In May 2013, Barré-Sinoussi chaired a conference at the Pasteur Institute to mark the 30th anniversary of the announcement in *Science.* Montagnier and Gallo took part as guests of honor. The emphasis, however, was not on the past but on discussing the work of young researchers and the future of HIV/AIDS research.

For her work, Barré-Sinoussi received numerous honors in addition to the Nobel Prize, such as the 2011 Porter Prize from the University of Pittsburgh Graduate School of Public Health. This particular honor was given to recognize her achievements related to HIV/AIDS research that helped promote health and disease prevention. Explaining the power of the Nobel Prize, Barré-Sinoussi told Jen Christiensen of the *CNN Wire,* "This is a good thing of the Nobel Prize—it is easier for me to get an appointment with the first lady or the president of the country. It gives me an opportunity to try to be the voice for others. This is something that for me seems to be my responsibility, my duty."

Books

Encyclopedia of Women in Today's World, Volume 1, edited by Mary Zeiss Stange, Carol K. Oyster, and Jane E. Sloan. Thousand Oaks, CA: SAGE Reference, 2011.

World of Microbiology and Immunology, Volume 2, edited by Brenda Wilmoth Lerner and K. Lee Lerner. Detroit: Gale, 2003.

Periodicals

Bulletin of the World Health Organization, January 2009.

CNN Wire, June 4, 2013.

Deutsche Presse-Agenteur, October 6, 2008.

Financial Times, May 18, 2013.

Independent (London), March 8, 2002.

International Herald Tribune, October 7, 2008.

Nature, July 19, 2012.

Targeted News Service, May 29, 2011.□

Thomas Bartholin

Danish scientist and professor Thomas Bartholin (1616–1680) was the first to discover the pancreatic ducts and parotid glands, which proved key in understanding how human and animal digestive systems work. Bartholin also was the first Western scientist to describe a case of spontaneous human combustion.

© Chronicle/Alamy

Born on October 20, 1616, in Copenhagen, Denmark, he was the second son of Caspar and Anna (Fincke) Bartholin. Caspar Bartholin was a professor of anatomy, religion, and eloquentaia at the University of Copenhagen, and wrote the famous 1611 book of human anatomy, *Institutiones anatomicae.* Anna Bartholin's father, Thomas Fincke, was also a professor at the university. In addition to Thomas Bartholin, the Bartholins had four more sons, and several of Bartholin's brothers became famous in their own right. Among them was Erasmus Bartholin, a younger brother who dabbled in medicine but is primarily known for his studies in pure mathematics, astronomy, and physics, especially concerning the Icelandic spar.

Had Early Interest in Medicine

In 1634, Bartholin entered the University of Copenhagen. He spent three years at the school before moving to another city in Denmark, Leiden, where he studied at its university from 1637 to 1640. There, though he had interest in the humanities, he also decided that he wanted to study and practice medicine. While living in Leiden, Bartholin also began writing the first revised edition of his father's *Institutiones anatomicae,* with the assistance of Sylvius (real name: Franciscus de le Boë) and Johannes de Wale. (Caspar Bartholin had died when his son was 13 years old.) This version, which included information about the recent discoveries of physicians Gaspare Aselli and William Harvey, would be published in 1641, and Bartholin would produce more revised versions of this text over the years.

Also in 1641, Bartholin described the first known case of spontaneous human combustion—that is, when a person self-ignites—in Western culture when he described a case of a woman in Paris who burned to death in her sleep. The straw mat she was resting on was relatively untouched. He also described the death of Polonus Vorstius who burst into flames in 1470 after drinking wine at his home in Milan. It would be more than a century before this and other stories of spontaneous human combustion became commonly known. Jonas Dupont related this and other examples in his 1763 work *De Incendiis Corporis Humani Spontaneis.*

Studied in Padua

Ill health, primarily in the form of pulmonary tuberculosis, prompted Bartholin to travel around France, moving from Paris to Orlénes, and Montpellier, before reaching Padua, in present-day northern Italy, beginning in 1640 through about 1643. While living in Padua, he continued his medical education. In Paris, for example, Bartholin studied with Johan Rhode and Johann Vesling. Bartholin began his second revision of *Institutiones anatomicae,* written with the help of Vesling. It was published in 1645.

Though Bartholin was cured of his ailment in Padua, he soon developed another, chronic renal stones, which would plague him while his studies continued. Bartholin spent much of the mid-1640s in various Italian cities, visiting Rome, Naples, Sicily, and Malta in 1643 and 1644 alone. He also had job offers, including a philosophy professorship at a university in Messina, which he declined, and wrote an unpublished thesis about the teeth of the fossil shark. Also conducting research, he discovered the pancreatic duct in 1644. By 1645, Bartholin had returned to Padua where he wrote and published a treatise *De unicornu.* It was similar to the one he declined to publish on fossil shark's teeth, which were believed to have medicinal value.

Became Chair of Anatomy

Around this time, Bartholin moved to Basel, Switzerland. Attending a medical school there, he was granted his degree in medicine. Returning to Copenhagen in October 1646, Bartholin became a faculty member at the University of Copenhagen, first teaching mathematics. In about 1649, Bartholin was selected as the anatomy chair at the

University of Copenhagen. When he became the head of anatomy at the university, he updated methods of teaching and research. Greatly influenced by his time in Padua, human dissection occurred more often. Until this point, such dissections were infrequent and only with the permission of the king.

As anatomy chair, Bartholin could extensively and frequently study anatomy. Because of this experience, his third edition of *Institutiones anatomicae* included greatly improved knowledge of human anatomy. It also featured better illustrations created by Vesling and Iulius Casserius.

Bartholin also conducted important research of his own. He learned that French scientist Jean Pecquet had located both the thoracic duct and cisterna chyli (parts of the lymphatic system) in dogs. Bartholin then decided to try to find similar glands on humans, using cadavers. In 1652, in his treatise *De lacteis thoracis in homine brustique nupperime observatis,* Bartholin reported finding the thoracic duct in humans. However, he did not find the cisterna chyli, at least consistently, and stated in his publication that it was not always present in humans. (It was later shown that humans have this as well.)

Made Discoveries of the Lymphatic System

More noteworthy was Bartholin's discovery related to the lymphatic system. By this time, human lymphatics were already known as anatomical structures but their purpose was a source of controversy. Initially, he believed that lymphatics gave chyle—a milky fluid of lymph and free fatty acids produced by the small intestine—to the liver to make blood. After further studies conducted with the help of assistant Michael Lyser, however, he concluded on February 28, 1652, that the human lymphatic system was separate from other systems and had previously not been fully identified. Bartholin published his discovery in 1653 in his treatise, *Vasa lymphatica nuper hafniae in animalibus inventa et hepatis exsequiae* (*The Lymphatic Vessels and the Secretion of the Liver*). It included color plates, introducing the concept to the anatomical publications.

The date of this discovery was important as there were some who claimed Bartholin did not make it before another scientist, Olof Rudbeck. Rudbeck stated that he found the lymphatics in April 1652, and that Bartholin only included the date in his second edition of the treatise's publication in an attempt to best Rudbeck. Rudbeck insisted that Bartholin did not make his discovery until 1653. Despite the drawn-out drama, scientists now generally agree that Bartholin made the discovery first. Bartholin went as far as to confirm the existence of the lymphatic system in humans in his 1654 treatise, *Vasa lymphatica in homine nuper inventa.*

Though Bartholin continued to conduct research, his on-going problems with renal stones compelled him to step down as anatomy chair in 1656. In 1661, he was elected a professor honorarius, and after this point, had no formal academic duties for the University of Copenhagen. Two years later, Bartholin bought an estate, Hagerstedgaard, located about 45 miles away from Copenhagen, where he focused on not only medical studies but also literary, historical, antiquarian, and other work. Still, he was recognized as the most distinguished physician in Denmark.

Discovered the Parotid Glands

Bartholin made many breakthroughs between the mid-1650s and about 1670. In 1659, for example, he discovered the parotid glands, which are the major salivary glands in humans. A few years later, in 1656, he described what came to be known as Patau syndrome or Bartholin-Patau syndrome. Also known as trisomy 13, it is a congenital disorder which includes the presence of up to three extra copies of the thirteenth chromosome. These extra chromosomes cause many physical and mental abnormalities, such as heart defects, incomplete brain development, and unusual facial features.

During this period, Bartholin also published numerous treatises. The four volumes of *Historarium anatomicarum rariorum cemuria,* published between 1654 and 1661, considered issues related to human and comparative anatomy. He wrote the first Danish pharmacopeia, or guide to identifying and making drugs, with *Dispensatorium hafniense* (1658). Another noteworthy work was *De pulmonus substantia et motu* (1663). It provided the second European publication of Marcello Malpighi's breakthrough work on the lungs, *De pulmonibus* (1661), which provided proof of the existence of the capillaries. Capillaries link arteries and veins, providing a system of circulation of the blood.

After the move to his estate, Bartholin was prolific, publishing *De medicinia danorum domestica* (1666) and *Carmina varii argumenti* (1669). In 1670, there was a devastating fire at Hagestedgaard, which destroyed many unpublished works by Bartholin. He described the event and its effects later that year in his treatise *De bibliothecae incendio.*

Became Royal Physician

Though the fire resulted in the loss of much work, Bartholin remained an important scientist and physician in Denmark. Indeed after the fire, the king of Denmark, Christian V, named Bartholin as his personal physician. In 1671, Bartholin added another post as the librarian at the University of Copenhagen. Because Christian V thought highly of Bartholin, Bartholin was able to get a 1672 royal decree which outlined the way medicine in Denmark would be organized for the next century. The following year, Bartholin both founded the first examination in midwifing in Copenhagen and launched *Acta medica et philosophica hafniensa,* the first Danish scientific journal.

In declining health beginning in the mid-1670s, Bartholin sold his estate in 1680 and went back to Copenhagen. Bartholin died there on December 4, 1680. Married in 1649 to Else Christofferdatter, his survivors included his children. One, also named Caspar Bartholin, in keeping with family tradition, became involved in medical research. He was known for the discovery of the Bartholin's gland and Bartholin's duct on the female genitalia.

Books

Complete Dictionary of Scientific Biography, Volume 1. Detroit: Charles Scribner's Sons, 2008.

Encyclopedia of Death & the Human Experience, Volume 2, edited by Clifton D. Bryant and Dennis L. Peck. Thousand Oaks, CA: SAGE Publications, 2009.

Gale Encyclopedia of Medicine, Volume 4. 3rd edition. Detroit: Gale, 2006.

Science and Its Times. Volume 3: 1450 to 1699, edited by Neil Schlager and Josh Lauer. Detroit: Gale, 2001.

Periodicals

Cambridge Evening News, August 21, 2012.

New Scientist, August 18, 2012.

Online

"Bartholin, Thomas," *Galileo Project,* http://galileo.rice.edu/Catalog/NewFiles/bartolin_tho.html (September 10, 2013).□

Nina Bawden

British author Nina Bawden (1925–2012) was a prolific and critically acclaimed novelist who penned more than 40 works for adults and children during her nearly 50-year career.

© Presselect/Alamy

Nina Bawden wrote critically acclaimed fiction works for both children and adults. Perhaps best known for the Phoenix Award-winning children's novel *Carrie's War,* which drew on Bawden's own experiences in World War II-era England, the author enjoyed a literary career spanning some 50 years. Along with her respected children's stories, Bawden wrote adult works that realistically explored the world of the British middle class such as the Booker Prize-nominated novels *The Birds on the Trees* and *Circles of Deceit.* In later life, she struggled with physical and psychological damage after a train she was riding derailed, killing her husband and seriously injuring Bawden. She was made a Commander of the British Empire in 1995.

Grew Up in Wartime England

Born Nina Mary Mabey on January 19, 1925, in Ilford, Essex, near London, England, Bawden was the daughter of merchant navy engineer Charles Mabey and his second wife, Judy. Because her father's work kept him mostly at sea away from his family, Bawden grew up largely under the care and influence of her mother. "Someone once pointed out to me that my children's books were full of absent fathers though as far as I remember I didn't consciously miss mine," she wrote in her memoirs, *In My Own Time: Almost an Autobiography.* "His absence was accepted and explicable; not the social embarrassment it might have been if my mother had been unmarried or divorced."

From an early age, Bawden enjoyed creating stories, and she thrilled to take classes in reading and writing literature in school. But what had been to that point a rather ordinary childhood was interrupted by the onset of World War II. With other students at her grammar school, Bawden was evacuated to safer locales in the countryside. She stayed with foster families in Suffolk and Wales, and her experiences and observations during this period later informed the storyline of her most famous children's book, *Carrie's War.* Published in 1973, the novel recounted the fictional story of a young English girl evacuated to a town in South Wales during World War II. Although the author asserted that the novel was not directly autobiographical, she acknowledged that some of the day-to-day realities of Carrie and her peers—carrying photographs of their mothers, for example, and feelings of fear and separation—stemmed from her own recollections of the situation.

Bawden's stay in Wales during World War II also influenced her lifelong political and social beliefs. After she saw a speech by the Welsh-born British Labour Party politician Aneurin Bevan, Bawden—angered by what she saw as the injustices perpetuated against the workers who lived in the South Wales valley she was then inhabiting—quickly became politicized. She remained a supporter of socialism throughout her life.

Although the young Bawden had not necessarily set her sights on a university education, she successfully won a place at Britain's prestigious Oxford University in 1943, impressing her interviewer with a passion for correcting injustice and a certain youthful naiveté. At Oxford's Somerville College, she studied philosophy, politics, and economics. By the time Bawden completed her degree, World War II was drawing to a close and she had become engaged to an older ex-serviceman, Harry Bawden. The couple married in the fall of 1945 and moved to London.

The youthful Bawden found work in post-war London as the assistant to the director of the Town and Country Planning Association, but soon left to seek a job in journalism. Pregnancy interfered with her plans, however, and she gave birth to two sons, Nicholas and Robert, over the next few years. In the early 1950s, she had a chance encounter with Austen Kark, a married man and journalist, on a bus. Both Bawden and Kark divorced their respective spouses and married, remaining wed until Kark's death in 2002.

Published Respected Novels

Unable to pursue a full-time job while raising two small children, Bawden began writing novels while her two sons slept. Her first novel for adults, *Who Calls the Tune,* was published in 1953; her first children's novel, *The Secret Passage,* followed a decade later. Throughout her literary career Bawden published more than 40 novels for both adult and juvenile readers. Often, she traded back and forth among the genres, publishing about one book each year from the mid-1950s through the late 1990s. Although the author acknowledged the differences in style and tone required to write for two different audiences, she believed that the two forms had intimate connections that meant even her best-known stories for children could easily have been retold as slightly refocused tales for adults. A profile in the *St. James Guide to Young Adult Writers* quoted Bawden as explaining, "To my mind, [the stories] are all part of a coded autobiography; the jottings that make up a life. One leads to the other and because of the difference between the child and the adult point of view, themes often overlap."

Bawden reached what was arguably the zenith of her abilities as a children's novelist in the mid-1970s with the publication of *Carrie's War* and, two years later, *The Peppermint Pig.* The titular protagonist of *Carrie's War* looks back on her time as an evacuee in the 1940s upon a visit to the Welsh town where she stayed, all the while dealing with lifelong feelings of guilt over a terrible crime that she may not have actually committed. Densely plotted and realistically characterized, the novel became a best-seller that inspired television adaptations and theatrical interpretations; it won the Phoenix Prize in 1993, an award given for works of enduring literary value that failed to win a major prize at the time of their publication.

Like *Carrie's War,* Bawden's *The Peppermint Pig* wove threads of personal struggle into a realistic story of a young English girl who travels with her mother and siblings to live with family in the British countryside. The protagonist adopts the titular "Peppermint Pig," a runt named Johnny, and by raising him as a pet enjoys some escape from the stresses of her enforced move from the city and the somewhat mysterious absence of her father. Amidst this turmoil, the family pet pig cannot survive the harsh realities of the adult world. A critic for the *New York Times Book Review* declared the novel to be "webbed with a delicate network of inter-personal complications," and its publication spurred a British literary panel to grant Bawden the Guardian Children's Fiction Prize in 1976.

Despite these professional successes, Bawden's life was not without challenges. One of her children by her first husband, Nicholas, suffered from a series of psychological problems caused by the mental illness schizophrenia and exacerbated by drug use. He was arrested and imprisoned for a time, including a period in a secure mental health ward. In 1982, he disappeared from a clinic where he was receiving treatment; several anguished months later, Bawden learned from authorities that his body had been found drowned in London's Thames River. Her son's suicide depressed Bawden and made her extremely disheartened about the ability of British society to support the mentally ill.

Among Bawden's most respected works of adult fiction was the 1987 novel *Circles of Deceit.* In this novel, the characters perpetuate a series of lies and misrepresentations that affect their professional and personal lives as the characters consistently mistreat one another. "Ms. Bawden makes comic use of these characters' foibles," assessed Laurel Graeber in the *New York Times,* "but there is considerable sadness beneath her evocative scenes and lively dialogue." Again the author drew on her own life to shape her narrative. One character, the mentally ill son of the narrator, disappears mysteriously, as did Bawden's own mentally ill son; unlike the author's real child, however, the fictional character returns by the end of the novel. *Circles of Deceit* was shortlisted for the prestigious Booker Prize.

Train Derailment Troubled Later Years

In May of 2002, Bawden and her husband boarded a high-speed train at travel from their home in London to Cambridge for a friend's birthday party. Shortly after departing London and traveling at a speed of nearly 100 miles per hours, the train derailed near the Potters Bar railroad station. The train's final car left the tracks altogether, crashing into a bridge and landing on the station platform. More than 70 people were injured; seven, including Bawden's husband Austen Kark, were killed. The author herself experienced a broken collarbone; she blacked out during the incident and learned of the crash and her husband's death only after awakening in the hospital.

As Bawden recovered from her injuries, she became infuriated that the accident had occurred. The cause of the derailment was eventually determined to be linked to a set of poorly maintained rail points, the mechanism that shifts a train's wheels from one track to another. But the private company hired to maintain that stretch of railroad track argued that that mechanism was not in their contract, and even that the crash had been caused by a deliberate act of sabotage. "To begin with I felt only pain and emptiness. It dawned on me only slowly that Austen, who was a notably conscientious man, had died because other men had not done their jobs properly," she stated in an article printed in the *Times* about six months after the accident. "And instead of accepting responsibility, the railway industry had responded with weasel words of condolence and the pretence, picked up by the press, that handsome compensation would be paid to the bereaved families... In fact, although there can be no real compensation for this kind of permanent loss, no payments have been made to anyone,'' Bawden continued.

Struggling with deep grief and post-traumatic stress, Bawden became one of the loudest voices demanding a full investigation of the event, decrying poor government oversight of the railways, and blaming the private company for negligence. "Quietly but effectively, she recalled the horror of her recent experience, contrasting it with the respect she felt for railway workers whom she had known as a child. It was an impressive contribution to the public controversy,'' assessed Janet Watts in the *Guardian*. Bawden published her only literary work after the crash, *Dear Austen,* in 2005. An emotionally wrenching memoir addressed to her deceased husband, *Dear Austen* recounted the train derailment and its aftermath.

Although her written output declined after the derailment, Bawden's past writings continued to earn her plaudits in the twenty-first century. She received the Golden PEN Award for a Lifetime's Distinguished Service to Literature from the English PEN organization in 2004. Six years later, *The Birds on the Trees* was shortlisted for the Lost Man Booker Award, a one-time prize for which books published in 1970 were eligible because shifts in the Booker Prize's qualification criteria had prevented them from being considered at the time of their publication four decades previously.

Bawden died at her home in London on August 22, 2012. She was 87 years old. Writing for the *New York Times,* Margalit Fox suggested that the author's literary legacy lay in "her finely drawn characters and her keen, sympathetic understanding of those characters' inner lives.'' In the *Guardian,* Watts praised the author as having "a strong power of survival at her core. Her courage and resourcefulness were helped by the art that transformed everything she experienced.''

Books

Bawden, Nina, *In My Own Time: Almost an Autobiography,* Clarion, 1994.

St. James Guide to Young Adult Writers, Gale, 1999.

Periodicals

Guardian, August 22, 2012.

New York Times, November 16, 1975; November 29, 1987; August 22, 2012.□

Cristina Belgiojoso

DEA/De Agostini/Getty Images

Italian aristocrat and writer Cristina Trivulzio Belgiojoso (1808–1871) led a bold and adventurous life as a writer, political activist, and intrepid traveler. Known for her support of the Italian independence and unification movement of the mid-19th century, Belgiojoso possessed a sizable fortune and wrote prodigiously about her progressive beliefs and travels through Europe and the Middle East.

Cristina Trivulzio Belgiojoso was born into a distinguished family of aristocrats based in Lombardy and its main city, Milan. Her paternal Trivulzio line included several renowned cardinals, diplomats, and book collectors. One of them was Gian Giacomo the Great, who made an uncommon and quite arduous pilgrimage to the Holy Land in the 1470s and was favored with a prestigious appointment as a Marshal of France by King Louis XII. Later generations of Trivulzios became important book collectors, amassing one of the largest collections of rare manuscripts in private hands in Europe. Belgiojoso's paternal grandfather, like others in the family preceding him, maintained strong ties to France and served under Napoleon Bonaparte in the years before her birth in Milan on June 28, 1808.

Married at 16

Belgiojoso's father Gerolamo opposed Austrian control over Lombardy, the northern Italian principality that had close ties to the French and Swiss. Milan had emerged as a distinctly different Italian city from its counterparts further south in Florence and Rome, settling into an uneasy relationship with the port of Venice, another outlier. Like Venice, Milan had prospered in the Middle Ages because of its proximity to routes that enabled trade between Europe and the East. Gerolamo Trivulzio's troubles with Austrian authorities would shape his only daughter's mission to liberate Lombardy and the other rivalry-ridden Italian kingdoms from foreign control and unite under a single flag.

Belgiojoso's mother was Vittoria Gherardini, who came from another fairly prominent family in northern Italy. Widowed in 1812 when Gerolamo died, Vittoria remarried a marquis named Alessandro Visconti d'Aragona, with whom she would have four more children. Belgiojoso was close to her half-brother and three half-sisters, but she was a headstrong teenager and eager to move forward with her life by age 16. With a substantial fortune left to her as Gerolamo's only heir, she was considered one of the most eligible young women in Italy but made a poor decision in choosing her husband, 24-year-old Prince Emilio Barbiano di Belgiojoso. The prince came from an aristocratic family, too, and shared her progressive political views, but he spent money recklessly, had affairs, and allegedly infected her with syphilis. They were wed in Milan in September of 1824 but separated after four years. Belgiojoso never formally divorced Prince Emilio, but they remained on friendly terms until his death many years later.

Penniless in Paris

Belgiojoso became involved in the nascent Italian independence movement. In Milan and Lombardy there was ardent opposition to Austrian rule, and others involved included Belgiojoso's stepfather, who was arrested for his political activities at one point. There was also a strong push to unify Italy, and it was these dual goals with which Belgiojoso involved herself for the next twenty-odd years. The Austrian overlords used spies and other underhanded tactics to quash dissent, and Belgiojoso was eventually forced to flee Lombardy. She went to Genoa, then on to the French cities of Marseille and Lyon. Her political activities aroused the suspicions of Austrian agents working abroad, and at one point she was commanded to move back to Lombardy. She refused, and in April of 1831 Austrian authorities issued an edict compelling her to either return to Lombardy or forfeit her assets, which included a still-sizable endowment from her father as well as real estate. Moving to Paris instead, she survived on funds sent by her family and her estranged husband for a time. "Never had I touched money and I could not imagine what a five-franc piece represented," she wrote about suddenly finding herself a destitute woman of noble stock, according to *Great Women Travel Writers: From 1750 to the Present.* "I could paint, sing, play the piano, but did not know how to hem a handkerchief, cook a boiled egg, or even order a meal."

Belgiojoso began writing about Italy's independence movement to support herself. Her essays appeared in *Revue des Deux Mondes* and attracted favorable attention from other Italian progressives and European intellectuals, who agreed that Italy would remain impoverished and a weak, ineffectual power despite its impressive legacy of political and cultural achievements dating back two millennia. Belgiojoso joined other figures in the Italian independence movement, among them Giuseppe Mazzini, Vincenzo Gioberti, Niccolò Tommaseo, and Camillo Benso Cavour. Some were living in exile, like her, and she also came to know prominent French and German influencers like Alexis de Tocqueville, Honoré de Balzac, Victor Hugo, Heinrich Heine, and Franz Liszt. One especially crucial friend of Belgiojoso's in Paris was Gilbert du Motier, better known as the Marquis de Lafayette. He had fought against the British in the American Revolutionary War and was among her supporters who interceded with Austrian officials to let Belgiojoso regain control of her sequestered assets.

Became Single Parent

Belgiojoso was a renowned beauty, and the salons she held at her Paris apartment were attended by noted cultural figures of her day. Intelligent and engaging, she was reportedly pursued by a few high-profile men, and in 1838 had a child, a daughter she named Maria Cristina. Technically, Belgiojoso was still married to Prince Emilio, though he was not thought to have been the girl's father. One source of parentage was possibly the historian François Mignet, who wrote extensively on the French Revolution and was the founding editor of *Le National,* a newspaper for which Belgiojoso wrote. Mignet's writings influenced the later work of German political philosopher Karl Marx.

In 1839, Belgiojoso visited England and Ireland with some of her half-siblings. On the trip she hired an English nursemaid named Mary Ann Parker to help care for her infant daughter, and brought Parker back to the Continent. Parker would remain in Belgiojoso's employ for many years. In 1840, the Trivulzio heiress was finally allowed to reenter Italy, after ten years of exile, and settled into a villa she had inherited in Locate, a village south of Milan. There she established an experimental community with a kindergarten, hospital, and even a large heated room at her villa where villagers were welcome to take shelter during frigid Lombardy winters. Wary about the Roman Catholic-instilled values that seemed to stall social progress in Italy, Belgiojoso expressed her ideas in a 1842 tract, *Essai Sur la Formation du Dogme Catholique* (Essay on the Formation of Catholic Dogma), which predictably landed on an official list of publications the Church prohibited its members from reading.

Finally in 1848, a series of minor revolutions began to sweep across Europe, most of them centered on calls for economic reform, political enfranchisement, and nationalist sovereignty. When an uprising began in Milan to oust the Austrians, Belgiojoso was in Naples and raised money to form a regiment. The force of about 160 men sailed from the southern Italian port city to Lombardy, the intrepid Belgiojoso also on board. In Milan she took part in the formation of a new regime under Carlo Alberto, the King of Sardinia. The Lombardian-Sardinian alliance was short-lived, however, and the Milan insurrection was quashed when Carlo was defeated at the Battle of Novara. For her involvement Belgiojoso was fined with a tax of around 800,000 *lira,* an enormous sum at the time, by the reinstalled Austrian government. To escape this punitive measure she fled to France once again.

Nursed Victims of War

Mazzini, considered the founding father of a unified Italy, had had some success further south in Rome in the tumultuous events of 1848. In early 1849 he and two others founded the Republicca Romana, or Roman Republic. It was a short-lived state, however, unrecognized by its European neighbors, and France came to the aid of the Papal States out of which the Roman Republic had been created. There was heavy bombardment from French forces and many wounded and dying patriots loyal to Mazzini's cause. When Mazzini asked for Belgiojoso help, she readily accepted and made her way to Rome. There she took over as hospital director and cared for hundreds of maimed men, many of them with fatal injuries. In a letter to her friend Caroline Jaubert, she wrote of the long days and nights tending to the wounded. "When, overcome by fatigue, I was looking for that condition where you can forget everything which is called sleep, could I sleep when I knew that when I would have waken up, I would not have found all those who had wished me a quiet night with a weak voice?" Belgiojoso wrote Jaubert, according to *Cristina Trivulzio di Belgiojoso: An Italian Princess in the 19th C. Turkish Countryside.* "Could I predict how many hands shook mine for the last time, how many sheets turned upside down on the pillow would have announced, in the morning visit, a new martyr?"

The above-mentioned volume was part of a long-overdue academic examination of Belgiojoso's intriguing and adventure-filled life. Edited by Antonio Fabris, it was a collection of papers presented at a 2009 symposium at Ca' Foscari University of Venice. When Mazzini's Roman Republic forces were defeated after just three months of independence, Belgiojoso was forced to flee once again, leaving via boat at the ancient port of Civitavecchia near Rome. She stopped first at Malta, the Mediterranean isle, where she was fascinated by the sight of Muslims en route to the Arabian peninsula to make their *hajj,* or pilgrimage to Mecca. Recalling her own Trivulzio ancestor's journey to the Christian and Jewish holy lands several centuries before, Belgiojoso decided to head east, too.

Bought Rundown Farm in Turkey

Belgiojoso's visit to Jerusalem was delayed by a productive delay in Anatolia, Turkey, in the early 1850s. She was able to buy a run-down parcel of land and once again, attempted to establish a prosperous and egalitarian community. This was at Çakmakoĝlu in Karabuk province, but the place name is sometimes spelled Ciaq-Maq-Oglou in a Gallicized version, for Belgiojoso's letters to Jaubert were eventually published in a Paris newspaper and also ran in the New York *Tribune.* The Ciaq-Maq-Oglou community cultivated wheat and tended cattle and other livestock; many of its inhabitants were Italian exiles like Belgiojoso herself. In 1852 she continued on her journey through the Middle East, stopping in Syria and Lebanon before reaching Jerusalem. This was a long and arduous trek on horseback, and Belgiojoso relied on the guides she had hired to lead and guard her, especially when they were forced to sleep in tents. In some rural areas the sight of a European, let alone a woman traveler, was so strange a sight that people would just run up to her and touch her, she wrote.

Belgiojoso wrote about gender inequality in the Middle East in an 1866 tract, *Of Women's Condition and of Their Future,* in which she argued that women must be educated just as solidly as men, otherwise they become complicit in oppressive systems. By then she was living back in a united and free Italy, which came into being in 1861. Her daughter had married an Italian aristocrat, the Marchese Ludovico Trotti Bentivoglio, and had two daughters, Cristinetta and Antonietta. Belgiojoso spent her final years near family in Lombardy's Lake Como, where she bought a villa. Among her staffers was a Turk named Bodoz, a former slave whose freedom she had purchased back in the early 1850s. Belgiojoso died there on July 5, 1871, at age 63. She remains a fairly well known figure in Italy for her role in the independence movement, and there is a wealth of biographical information about her. Only some of it is in English or English translation, though American expatriate author Henry James modeled the title character of his 1886 novel, *The Princess Cassamassina,* on Belgiojoso's devotion to the Italian independence movement.

Books

Fortunati, Sandro, "The Life of Cristina Trivulzio di Belgiojoso," in *Cristina Trivulzio di Belgiojoso: An Italian Princess in the 19th C. Turkish Countryside,* edited by Antonio Fabris, Fillippi Editore Venezia, 2010.

Great Women Travel Writers: From 1750 to the Present, edited by Alba Amoia and Bettina Knapp, Continuum, 2005.□

Chadli Bendjedid

Chadli Bendjedid (1929–2012) served as the third president of an independent Algeria. A top-ranking military officer during the North African nation's long war with France from 1954 to 1961, Bendjedid held high-ranking posts before taking office in 1979. During his 12-year tenure he conceded to demands to restore democratic, multiparty elections to the Algerian political process, but in the end he was removed by military coup to prevent an Islamic fundamentalist majority government, and Algeria descended into a decade of civil war.

Some Western media sources transposed Bendjedid's first and last names when he first came to power, referring to him as Colonel Bendjedid Chadli. He was born on April 14, 1929, in Bouteldja, a village in the northeastern part of what was then French Algeria. At the time, Algeria was an overseas territory of France, which

AP Photo/File

had ruled this part of the Maghreb, as Arabic-speaking, Berber-populated North Africa is called, since the 1840s. As a young man he joined the French armed forces and was sent to fight France's war in Indochina, which at the time was also an overseas colony France was desperate to retain. The military experience radicalized young men like Bendjedid, who resented having to serve as soldiers under French officers. A growing independence movement was emerging in Algiers, the cosmopolitan main port city on the Mediterranean, and elsewhere in French Algeria.

Fought Against French Colonial Forces

After his overseas deployment, Bendjedid returned to Algeria and discovered the Front de Libération Nationale, or National Liberation Front, which later became independent Algeria's ruling party and known by its French acronym, FLN. The FLN's armed wing, the Armée de Libération Nationale (ALN), had launched a war at home against French rule in November of 1954, just months after the French were finally ousted from Indochina.

Bendjedid was one of thousands of Algerians who deserted the French colonial forces to join the ALN, rather than fire against their own people. The ALN carried out a stealth guerrilla war against French targets in Algeria, and French military authorities reacted with particularly lethal force. The seven-year-long war divided France and attracted international attention for years; the Algerians' fight for independence was considered a just cause and there was a belief among liberals and moderates in Europe that France should divest itself of its foreign territories conquered by force in previous eras, no matter how great the investment in infrastructure had been since then.

Spent Years as Trusted Policy-Maker

Like other ALN fighters, Bendjedid was arrested by French military police, but managed to escape into exile in Tunisia, a haven for the independence fighters. By 1960 Bendjedid was placed in charge of the ALN's 13th Battalion, a unit that played a key role in helping to push the war to a conclusion. He became one of a cadre of trusted advisors to Colonel Houari Boumédiènne, the ALN chief of staff. When France finally capitulated in 1961, Abderrahman Farès became the transitional president. In September of 1962, Algerians voted overwhelmingly in favor of self-rule, and a respected FLN figure named Ahmed Ben Bella became the first president of a fully independent Algeria.

Bendjedid remained in the military. He was promoted to the rank of major in the newly legitimatized ALN, which had become the national army of Algeria, and given charge of a vital eastern section of Constantine. In 1964, he was put in charge of the military units in a major port of Oran in the western part of Algeria. He also took part in an independent Algeria's first foreign mission to Communist China; the Soviet Union also welcomed the Socialist FLN leaders into their international circle.

Internal rivalries soured the excitement of Algerian independence in its first years. Ben Bella was ousted in a bloodless coup on June 16, 1965, by Boumédiènne, the country's defense minister. Bendjedid was made a regional commander on the Council of the Revolution and promoted to the rank of colonel in 1969. Various experiments in a Maghreb version of socialism were notable failures, including an agricultural collectivization program in the early 1970s that was widely resented. Algeria lost the ability to feed its people, and an authoritarian, socialist party controlled the limited jobs in the civil service, which included the lucrative natural gas and oil industries.

Became Compromise Candidate

Algeria's birthrate began to soar in the 1970s, and the school and social-service systems were unable to maintain order. Even in major cities like Algiers and Oman, running water came on only during certain times of day, and there were brownouts and power outages. Pledging an end to military rule, Boumédiènne dissolved his Council of the Revolution in 1976 and named himself president in 1976. Bendjedid retained a high rank and took over as minister of defense when Boumédiènne suddenly lapsed into a coma after contracting a rare blood disorder in November of 1978. Boumédiènne died on December 27, 1978, causing a power vacuum, and there was a secretive battle for control of the FLN's future at its party congress in January of 1979. One faction wanted closer ties with the West, including aid dollars and investment, and these moderates were allied with Abdelaziz Bouteflika, who had served as

Algeria's longtime minister of foreign affairs. A more conservative faction aligned with an emerging new Islamist fundamentalist movement in the Middle East and were determined to maintain the one-party socialist program.

Bendjedid was chosen as a compromise candidate between those two factions. He was not known for having a particularly pro-West or pro-Moscow stance, had served his nation since its fight for independence, and was viewed as a pragmatist and valuable asset in courting foreign investment, which had been wary of planting roots in a relatively untested socialist regime that still received military aid from the Soviet Union. Another Maghreb country, Libya, had an authoritarian leader but was raking in petrodollars; the kingdom of Morocco, on Algeria's western border, was still ruled as a monarchy but had become an elite tourism destination for the new jet set in the 1960s. In an election held on February 7 in which his was the only name on the ballot, Bendjedid won with 94 percent of the vote and was sworn into office on February 9, 1979.

Islamic fundamentalists in Algeria were a problem for the regime and elsewhere in the Mahgreb and Middle East. In oil-rich Iran, students allied with conservative Muslim clerics and overthrew the police state of the longtime Shah, Mohammed Reza Pahlavi, a longtime ally of the West. On April 1, 1979, Iran became the modern world's first Islamic republic. When the ailing Shah traveled to the United States for medical treatment, Iranian protesters stormed the U.S. Embassy in Tehran and took hostages. The siege began in the first week of November in 1979, just as Algeria was hosting an international celebration to commemorate the 25th anniversary of the start of its fight for independence. The Americans remained under guard for the next 443 days.

Bendjedid made some bold moves to prevent unrest in Algeria. He loosened many of the authoritarian restrictions in place since the 1965 coup, such as the requirements for exit visas for travel abroad, and also cut back on state surveillance. He ordered the release of Ben Bella after 14 years of house arrest and permitted the former president to move to Switzerland. Bendjedid also worked to establish firm and trustworthy relations with the leading organization of Arab political dissent in the Middle East, the Palestinian Liberation Organization (PLO). Its chair, Yasser Arafat, flew to Algiers to visit Bendjedid during his first month in office, and Bendjedid later welcomed to Algiers PLO delegates who adopted the Palestinian Declaration of Independence in 1988, an historic event in the Arab-Israeli conflict.

Won Respect for Diplomatic Role

Bendjedid's most significant role in international relations was letting his key ministers and diplomats broker the release of the American hostages in Iran in January of 1981. They worked with officials at the U.S. State Department and representatives of the new regime in Iran under Ayatollah Ruhollah Khomeini for months, and finally Bendjedid sent two Boeing planes and pilots to wait for clearance. "The Americans were taken to Algiers not only as part of the arrangement," reported Bernard Gwertzman in the *New York Times,* "but to demonstrate the United States Government's gratitude for the Algerian efforts, State Department officials said."

Bendjedid sought to mend ties with France, too. In November of 1983, he became the first Algerian head of state to visit France, at the invitation of French president François Mitterrand. Two years later he was the first president of Algeria to visit the United States in April of 1985, where he discussed the Palestinian cause with President Ronald W. Reagan.

Despite successes on the diplomatic front, Bendjedid faced turmoil at home. World oil prices had plummeted in the early 1980s, and with that came a decline in revenue for Algeria's state-run oil and gas company, Sonatrach. After another election in which Bendjedid was the sole candidate in 1984, he pledged economic reforms aimed at raising the standard of living. Under the revised National Charter of 1985, Algerians were allowed to operate some limited forms of free-enterprise businesses, but the cost of food remained high and there were riots in the city of Constantine in late 1986.

More tumult followed in October of 1988, after another election in which Bendjedid ran unopposed but had ordered the military and security forces to round up and detain Islamic radicals. In the weeks that followed, Bendjedid was forced to declare a state of emergency and appear in a special television broadcast to plead for calm. He promised immediate political reforms, and in November of 1988, agreed to multiparty elections.

Ousted in Early 1992

A new party called the Front Islamique du Salut, or Islamic Salvation Front (FIS) was formed and quickly gained support. In the first free and open elections in Algeria in June of 1990, the FIS won heavily in municipal and provincial contests. Elections for the Algeria National Assembly were slated to take place a year later, but in March of 1991, Bendjedid's government announced changes to electoral districts and voting rules that would give the FLN a significant advantage. This provoked a new round of protests, and Bendjedid declared another state of emergency in June of 1991 and postponed the June 27 elections for six months.

In the first round of balloting in December 1991, FIS candidates won a significant majority, and hardliners in Bendjedid's administration moved against him. Before the second round of balloting was to take place on January 16, Bendjedid stepped down from his post as FLN chair, then was forced out as president by a military coup on January 12. He followed all of his predecessors to leave office, transitioning immediately into a period of house arrest. He was succeeded by Mohammed Boudiaf, a founder of the FLN, who was assassinated five months later. "In 2002 Bendjedid gave an interview in which he explained that he had wanted to accept the result of the 1991 elections and work with the FIS," reported Mohamed Ben-Madani in the *Guardian.* "He believed that the constitution gave him the power to prevent the FIS taking over all government institutions, but he failed to persuade the army chiefs."

Algeria dissolved into civil war after the Boudiaf assassination. The FIS was outlawed, and the country became a haven for radical Islamic mujahideen fighters from

Afghanistan and the Iran-Iraq war. Finally, in 1999, civilian rule was restored and the terms of Bendjedid's house arrest were revoked by his long-ago ALN comrade in arms, Abdelaziz Bouteflika, who became president. Bouteflika, too, overstayed his term in office as Algeria's standard of living remained abysmal. In the Arab Spring of 2011, Algeria became the second nation to remove a longtime authoritarian leader by force when Bouteflika was ousted.

Bendjedid lived the remaining years of his life in Oman. He was married and was father to four sons. Diagnosed with cancer, he went to Paris for treatment, but died at a military hospital in Algiers on October 6, 2012, at the age of 83. His memoirs were published posthumously.

Periodicals

Guardian (London, England), November 16, 2012.
New York Times, February 1, 1979; January 21, 1981.
Sunday Times (London, England), October 16, 1988.
Times (London, England), February 6, 1981; January 13, 1992; October 8, 2012.□

Maeve Binchy

The Irish writer Maeve Binchy (1940–2012) was, in the words of the London *Independent,* "the queen of Irish popular fiction." Translated into more than 30 languages, her 16 novels have sold an estimated 40 million copies worldwide.

© Liam White/Alamy

The London *Guardian* commented that Binchy "inspires great devotion in her fans and a complete lack of critical interest," and it was true that Binchy's audience lay more among ordinary fiction readers than among the literary set. Binchy once said that she wrote exactly as she spoke, and thus she could not say that any other writer had influenced her at all. Many observers have noted, and many readers prized, the plainspokenness of Binchy's writing, its familiar feel. Man Booker Prize winner Anne Engright was quoted in the *Independent* as saying that "Reading Maeve was like being with a good friend—wise, generous, funny, and full-hearted, she was the best of good company on the page and off it." Binchy's novels of small-town Ireland had a universal appeal, selling widely in countries beyond the British Isles.

Inspired by Philosophy Assignment

Maeve Binchy was born in Dalkey, Ireland, near Dublin, on May 28, 1940. Her father was a lawyer and her mother a nurse. "Even though I was fat and hopeless at games, which are very unacceptable things for a schoolgirl," Binchy wrote on her website, "I was happy and confident. This was simply because I had a mother and father at home who thought I was wonderful." Still, Binchy was more than six feet tall and overweight, and she was self-conscious as a young woman. She attended University College in Dublin, majoring in English, French, and history, and continuing to live at home. While reading a philosophy assignment on a park bench one evening, she came across the idea that one should be true to oneself and not worry about the perceptions of others. She would later refer to that moment as a revelation.

After graduating, Binchy got a job teaching at a girls' school in Dublin. But she was restless, and after a few years, when she was 24, she went to Israel and got a job on a kibbutz, or collective farm. Her stint in Israel had several long-lasting effects. First, it led to the loss of what had been an intense Catholic faith. She visited the site of the biblical Last Supper, imagining it as the sumptuous scene that has been shown in religious iconography but finding only a small cave. An Israeli guard (quoted by her biographer, Piers Dudgeon, in the London *Sunday Telegraph*) asked her, "What were you expecting, lady, a Renaissance table set for 13?" Binchy's disillusionment was instantaneous: "One minute I believed that lot, angels with wings and a special Irish God, and the next I didn't believe a word of it."

Binchy broke the news of that shift to her family only later, but on other matters she was more forthcoming: she wrote detailed letters home about her life in Israel, and her father was so enthusiastic about them that he sent them to the *Irish Independent* newspaper, which serialized them and cut her a check for 16 pounds, equal to the salary she would receive for a week and a half of teaching.

Binchy's writing career was launched, and she began contributing columns to the *Irish Times* in Dublin and then, although she had no editorial experience, became the paper's women's editor in 1968.

Had Radio Career

By that time, Binchy was living at home, caring for her aging father after her mother died of cancer at age 57. She continued to develop professionally, doing radio broadcasts for the Irish RTE network and for the British Broadcasting Company (BBC). Personally, though, she was unfulfilled: beginning in Israel, she had a series of unsatisfying relationships with men. Divesting herself of religion had led her to sexual freedom, but not to a formula for a long-lasting, committed relationship.

That changed when Binchy met BBC broadcaster Gordon Snell through her BBC job. After carrying on a long-distance relationship for a year, Binchy moved to London, submitting to the *Irish Times* a down-to-earth description of the wedding of Princess Anne to Mark Phillips (as quoted by Conor O'Clery in the London *Guardian*): "The bride looked as edgy as if it were the Badminton Horse Trials and she was waiting for the bell to gallop off." Binchy and Snell married in 1977. The marriage survived the revelation of Binchy's infertility and lasted until her death. Surrounded by Snell's friends, Binchy knew no one in London, and her husband encouraged her to try her hand at writing fiction as a new project.

Binchy flourished as a writer, soon completing her first novel, *Light a Penny Candle* (1982). The book followed the lifelong friendship of two girls, one Irish, one English, that began in Ireland in the years after World War II, and it announced two of Binchy's favorite themes, female friendship, and changes in the Irish cultural landscape in the modern world. Binchy delivered the manuscript in stages to agent Chris Green, whom she dubbed the Stormtrooper; Green confidently visited publishers, telling them that he represented the next big female fiction writer. As it happened, he was right. Binchy was given an advance of 50,000 pounds from the book's eventual publisher, Arrow Books, and she and Snell moved back to Binchy's hometown of Dalkey. They bought a house there and converted a second-floor room into a writing studio where they would work together daily from early morning until lunchtime.

Light a Penny Candle was the first of Binchy's 16 novels, which were almost uniformly successful and set several more sales records. A survey of Irish best-sellers in 1998 put books by Binchy in first, third, and fourth places. *Evening Class* stayed in the London *Times* hardback fiction best-seller list for 17 weeks in a row. Her sixth novel, *Tara Road*, appeared in 1998 and concerned two women, one in Ireland and one in the United States, who exchange houses. The book was the first in history to have more than one million hardback copies printed in advance. It remains one of the best-selling novels in the history of the British Isles, having received a major sales boost in the U.S. after its selection for the book club of popular television host Oprah Winfrey. Binchy's character-driven stories were ideally suited to cinematic adaptation, and *Tara Road* was made into a film starring Andie McDowell and Stephen

Rea. Binchy's *Circle of Friends* (1990) was filmed with Minnie Driver and Chris O'Donnell in lead roles.

Announced Retirement

After the publication of *Scarlet Feather* in 2000, Binchy announced her retirement due to longstanding health problems. She had already written a nonfiction book, *Aches and Pains* (1999), about the travails of her medical treatments. Binchy recovered, however, and fed the ongoing demand for her writing with six more novels, including the posthumously published *A Week in Winter*. Her 2006 novel *A Time to Dance* focused on life in old age. Binchy also published six more collections of short stories, three novellas, a stage play, and radio dramas for RTE, even after she became famous as a novelist.

Binchy was hardly a critical favorite. One writer quoted in the *Telegraph* opined: "It cannot be said that her prose style is a pleasure to read. It is a little too short on punctuation, and a little too much like being gossiped at by a loquacious neighbor." Some readers took Binchy to task for ignoring one of the defining features of Irish life in the 1970s and 1980s, the so-called "Troubles" between Catholics and Protestants in Northern Ireland, but Binchy replied that those problems had little impact in the middle-class world she knew. Nor did Binchy follow the vogue for explicit sex scenes in contemporary fiction. "I am not going to do it—not because I'm a Holy Joe, far from it, Not because I'm very moral, far from that," she explained in a *Daily Mail* interview quoted by Margalit Fox in the *New York Times*. "But because I'm afraid I'll get it wrong. You see, I've never been at an orgy and I wouldn't know where legs should be and arms should be."

In her later years, Binchy's writing made her one of the wealthiest women in the British Isles. "I used to think if I was very rich I'd be Mother Teresa and give it all away, but of course, when you get it you don't," she observed with typical straightforwardness in the *Telegraph*. Nevertheless, she rarely turned down direct appeals for help, and she gave generously to charitable causes. Binchy died in Dublin on July 30, 2012.

Books

Dudgeon, Piers, *Maeve Binchy: The Biography*, Robson, 2013.

Periodicals

Belfast Telegraph (Belfast, Northern Ireland), August 10, 2013.

Daily Mail (London, England), November 8, 2012; August 16, 2013.

Daily Telegraph (London, England), August 1, 2012.

Guardian (London, England), August 1, 2012.

Independent (London, England), August 1, 2012.

Irish Examiner, August 1, 2012.

New York Times, August 1, 2012.

Sunday Telegraph (London, England), August 4, 2013.

Sunday Times (London, England), August 4, 2013.

Online

"About Maeve," *Maeve Binchy Official Website,* http://www.
maevebinchy.com/ (September 14, 2013).
"Maeve Binchy," *Guardian Books,* http://www.theguardian.
com/books/2008/jun/10/maevebinchy (September 14,
2013).□

Otis Blackwell

**The African American songwriter Otis Blackwell
(c. 1932–2002) fundamentally shaped the rock and
roll music genre in its early years, contributing
compositions that became hits and classics for Elvis
Presley, Jerry Lee Lewis, and many other artists.**

Michael Ochs Archives/Getty Images

B lackwell's style as a songwriter drew on the energy
of rock and roll's rhythm and blues antecedents, but
he was among the first writers to harness that energy
to pop song structures and wit. When Presley topped
Billboard magazine's pop, country, and rhythm and blues
charts simultaneously with Blackwell's "Don't Be Cruel" in
the fall of 1956, rock and roll jumped from niche music to
American musical mainstream, and Blackwell's songs,
which also included the Jerry Lee Lewis hit "Great Balls
of Fire" the following year, played an important role in that
transformation. The exact nature of Blackwell's creative
relationship with Presley, whom he never met, has been
debated. He wrote some 1,000 songs, and recordings of
them, by a great variety of artists, have reportedly sold
nearly 200 million copies.

Influenced by Music of Westerns

Otis Blackwell was born in Brooklyn, New York, on February 16, 1932 (or, according to some sources, 1931). Considering the familiarity of his major creations, biographical
writings on his early years are sparse. He enjoyed the rhythm
and blues songs his father listened to on the radio but also
acknowledged an influence from the cowboy music he
heard in western films as a child and named cowboy balla-
deer Tex Ritter as his favorite singer. "Like the blues, it told a
story," he said of cowboy music (as reported in *New York
Times*). "But it didn't have the same restrictive construction.
A cowboy song could do anything." Blackwell learned to
play the piano when he was young, and soon he was
accompanying a music-loving uncle to open-
performance nights at small bars where he would play and
sing for pocket change.

Blackwell's uncle introduced him to a small-time
agent named Willie Saunders, who launched the 16-year-
old Blackwell's career as a blues singer in small clubs. He
was nowhere near the point where he could make a living,
and he worked on the side as a theater janitor and then as a
clothes presser. But he experienced a breakthrough in 1952
with a win at one of the amateur-night contests at Harlem's
famed Apollo Theater, a venue closely watched by music
executives at the time. He was signed to the Jay-Dee label

operated by entrepreneur Joe Davis, who encouraged him
to focus on writing songs and signed him to a $25-a-week
publishing contract. From the beginning the move was a
smart one. Blackwell recorded a song called "Daddy
Rollin' Stone" for Jay-Dee; it was only a minor hit for
Blackwell himself, but Jamaican vocalist Derek Martin
scored big with it.

With several more singles on the RCA and Groove
labels, Blackwell made his name better known in the music
industry for songs that were on the verge of what would
soon be known as rock and roll. Blackwell and Eddie
Cooley cowrote the blues ballad "Fever," which became
a steamy blues hit for the Detroit blues singer Little Willie
John in 1956 and later (with sanitized but uncredited lyrics
by Lee herself) for pop star Peggy Lee in 1958. Blackwell
began making demo recordings of his songs, accompanying himself on piano and a drum fashioned from a card-
board box. In late 1955 he compiled six of these and turned
them over to a song promoter from the music publisher Hill
and Range for a fee of $150, reportedly because he needed
the money for Christmas presents.

One of these was "Don't Be Cruel." Hill and Range
pitched it to Elvis Presley, newly signed to RCA, who
identified at it as the perfect vehicle for the next, still rock
and roll-oriented, but more pop-flavored style of his
career.

Song Recorded by Elvis Presley

What happened next remains controversial in several respects. Presley's Dutch-Jewish-born manager, Colonel Tom Parker, insisted that if Presley were to record "Don't Be Cruel," Blackwell would have to agree to have Presley listed as co-author of the song. Blackwell, well aware that many African American songwriters had sold songs outright, earning no royalties whatsoever, accepted the deal. Presley recorded the song in 28 takes at RCA's New York studios on July 2, 1956, and it was released nine days later as the B side of the "Hound Dog" single to nearly instant and massive demand.

Presley associate Freddy Bienstock pointed out (as quoted by Spencer Leigh in the London *Independent*) that Presley's perfectionistic tendencies often involved changes to Blackwell's originals: "Elvis would show dissatisfaction with some lines and he would make alterations, so [the publishing deal] wasn't just what is known as a 'cut-in.'" Others familiar with the industry at the time have told an opposite story; agent Joe Yeager, also quoted by Leigh, asserted that "I've heard many of the original demos by Otis Blackwell and I know that Elvis would record them note for note and also inflection for inflection from the way Otis sang them." The disappearance of Blackwell's demos over time has made the authorship question difficult to resolve.

Whatever the truth of these questions, Blackwell profited handsomely from his association with Presley, whom he never tried to contact personally. "We had a great thing going, and I just wanted to leave it alone," he said in an interview quoted by the *Times* of London. Several more Presley records appeared listing the two as co-writers, and Blackwell continued as a major supplier of hits to Presley through the early 1960s. Blackwell-penned Presley hits included "All Shook Up" (which Blackwell wrote after a challenge from an executive who shook a soft-drink bottle and challenged him to write a song on that theme), "Return to Sender" (with Winfield Scott), "Paralyzed," and "One Broken Heart for Sale."

Equally important was the demand that arose for Blackwell's songs from other artists in the wake of his successes with Presley. "Great Balls of Fire," which Blackwell heavily modified from an initial idea by songwriter Jack Hammer, was pitched to Jerry Lee Lewis, who, as a former Assembly of God minister, was disturbed by the song's blatant sexualization of a biblical image ("cloven tongues like as of fire," in the Book of Acts). But Blackwell persuaded Lewis to record the song for a soundtrack of a low-budget musical, *Jamboree,* for which he served as music director. The song topped the charts in 1957, and Lewis soon scored another major hit with Blackwell's "Breathless" and later recorded other Blackwell tunes including "Let's Talk About Us" and "It Won't Happen with Me."

Produced Mahalia Jackson Recordings

Other artists, too, recorded Blackwell's songs. Later rockabilly artists followed Presley and Lewis in seeking out his material; Gene Vincent recorded "It's No Lie," and Carl Perkins released "Hollywood City." The British pop singer Cliff Richard hit top chart levels in the United Kingdom with Blackwell's "Nine Times Out of Ten." By the early 1960s Blackwell was plying his trade at New York's Brill Building, the center of the city's music publishing community. He did production work for gospel singer Mahalia Jackson, who recorded Blackwell's "For My Good Fortune" in 1958.

The rise of the Beatles and the Rolling Stones, groups who wrote their own material, dented the success of Blackwell and the other Brill Building songwriters as the business model in which publishers pitched songwriters' songs to vocalists was partly eclipsed. Blackwell still scored occasional successes; in Britain, The Who released a version of "Daddy Rollin' Stone" as the B side to the single "Anyway, Anyhow, Anywhere." But Blackwell's career suffered further as a result of alcohol abuse, and his free-spending ways led to difficulties with tax authorities.

Blackwell attempted a comeback as a vocalist in 1976 with the release of a new album, *These Are My Songs,* and after Elvis Presley's death the following year he penned a song, "The King's Not Dead," for members of Presley's fan club. Still enamored with country music, Blackwell moved to Nashville in 1990 with plans to establish a new music label in partnership with Tom Parker. In 1991, however, Blackwell suffered a stroke that left him unable to communicate without using a computer.

In 1991, Blackwell was inducted into the Songwriters Hall of Fame, and a group of rock stars that included Chrissie Hynde and Debbie Harry recorded a Blackwell tribute album, *Brace Yourself,* in 1994. But during his later years Blackwell lived mostly in obscurity. He died in Nashville on May 6, 2002. The *New York Times* noted in its obituary that "[h]is songs joined the sentimentality of pop, the twang of country music and the propulsive rhythm of the blues, and his lyrics, even at their hottest, could be playful." Otis Blackwell was inducted into the Rock and Roll Hall of Fame in 2010.

Books

Contemporary Musicians, Vol. 57, Gale, 2006.

Periodicals

Daily Telegraph (London, England), May 9, 2002.
Independent (London, England), May 9, 2002.
Investor's Business Daily, May 20, 2002.
Jet, May 27, 2002.
Music Week, September 21, 2012.
New York Times, May 9, 2002.
Times (London, England), May 9, 2002.

Online

"Otis Blackwell, 1931–2002," *Spectropop,* http://www.spectropop.com/remembers/OBobit.htm (September 8, 2013).
"Otis Blackwell, 1931–2002," *Stereophile,* http://www.stereophile.com/news/11337/ (September 8, 2013).
"Otis Blackwell: Biography," *Songwriters Hall of Fame,* http://www.songwritershalloffame.org/exhibits/bio/C152 (September 8, 2013).
"Otis Blackwell Biography," *Rock and Roll Hall of Fame,* http://rockhall.com/inductees/otis-blackwell/bio/ (September 8, 2013). □

George Blake

George Blake (born 1922) is one of the most infamous names in the annals of Cold War espionage. A high-ranking station chief with Britain's Secret Intelligence Service (SIS), Blake was actually a double agent who covertly provided reams of information to the Soviet Union for several years. The disgraced former MI6 agent made headlines again in 1966 when he escaped from prison and defected to the Soviet Union.

AP Photo/Boris Yurchenko, File

George Blake's ties to Britain came through his father, Albert Behar, who had been born in Egypt into a family of Sephardim origin; these were the Jews expelled from the Iberian peninsula in 1492, who then dispersed to other parts of Europe and the Middle East. Blake's father was of mixed Turkish-Lebanese origins and served with the French Foreign Legion, then fought for the British side during World War I and was decorated for valor. His family allegedly spurned him when he married Blake's mother, a non-Jewish Dutch woman named Catherine Beijderwellen. So great was Albert's patriotism for England, it was said, that he named his first-born son in honor of the reigning monarch, King George V. The future spy was born George Behar on November 11, 1922, in Rotterdam, Netherlands. Albert and Catherine had two more children, both daughters, and lived in modest prosperity in Rotterdam and then The Hague. Blake was raised in his mother's Dutch Reformed faith and as a youngster dreamed of becoming a minister in the church.

Joined Dutch Resistance

Albert Behar died in 1936, when his son was 13, and Catherine accepted her Egyptian sister-in-law's offer to take him for a time. Blake was enrolled in a British school in Cairo and grew close to his cousins, who included Henri Curiel, a member of Egypt's nascent Communist Party. Curiel would go on to a noted if slightly infamous career as a figure in Algeria's war for independence and supporter of Palestinian rights. He was assassinated in Paris in 1978, in a case that remains unsolved.

In early 1939, Blake returned to Rotterdam and lived with his maternal grandmother while finishing his education. War between England and Germany broke out later that year, which imperiled the rest of Western Europe. Blake was 18 years old when Nazi troops marched into the Low Countries—Belgium, Luxembourg, and the Netherlands—in the spring of 1940, and also conquered France. He joined the underground Dutch Resistance, working as a courier, but eventually made his way to France, then over the Pyrénées into Spain, traveling some of the way with false papers and in the guise of a Roman Catholic monk. In early 1943, he was able to join his mother and sisters, who had been safely evacuated to England and were living near London. The family began using a new surname, Blake, and it was George Blake who enlisted in Britain's Royal Navy in October of 1943. Because he was fluent in Dutch, he was recommended for assignment as a translator with the Secret Intelligence Service's (SIS) MI6, or Military Intelligence Section 6 branch. MI6 handled foreign intelligence-gathering operations and Blake stayed with it when the war ended in 1945. He worked as a translator of German documents after having picked up the language quickly, and even interrogated captured Nazi submarine commanders in British-occupied Hamburg.

Imprisoned in North Korea

Blake remained with MI6 but also joined the British Foreign Office, the diplomatic corps, as his "cover," or public identity. He requested to enter an accelerated language course at Cambridge University to become fluent in Russian, and after completing was assigned to the Foreign Office's Far East division. Posted to Seoul, the South Korean capital, as vice consul at the British Embassy, he was charged with setting up a network of pro-British informants, but war on the Korean peninsula loomed. In June of 1950, Communist China came to the aid of their North Korean allies and armed conflict erupted. On the other side were anti-Communist Koreans who were supplied with major U.S. military support that came from nearby Japan, which was home to a massive U.S. military base set up after American forces occupied Japan after World War II.

Both Blake and the British envoy in Seoul, Sir Vyvyan Holt, were taken prisoner by Communist Korean forces shortly after the Korean War began. Along with some remaining foreign missionaries they were marched northward and interned inside Communist-held territory; their whereabouts were not known until early 1953, when Britain successfully brokered a release arrangement with officials in Pyongyang, the capital of what would become Communist North Korea. Blake, Holt, and the other detainees returned to Britain in April of 1953 in a widely reported news story that hailed them as heroes for surviving their ordeal.

Blake later revealed that it had been his time in captivity that had turned him into a double agent, along with the crash course in Communist philosophy he passed at Cambridge. He said that on the march northward he had witnessed scores of civilian casualties inflicted by U.S.-provided aircraft, and saw firsthand the effects of Cold War tensions on blameless women, children, and the elderly. In prison he read Karl Marx's *Das Kapital,* and was stirred by its message, which he likened to a religious awakening.

Stationed in West Berlin

Back in London Blake went to work at the Foreign Office headquarters at Whitehall, where several other U.K. cabinet ministries are also located, and in late 1954, married a woman named Gillian Allen, whose father was a Russian-affairs consultant at the Foreign Office. In early 1955, Blake was assigned to the MI6 station in West Berlin and the couple moved to the pretty Charlottenburg section of the city. Berlin was divided along the same lines as Germany itself had been in the immediate aftermath of World War II, with four zones controlled by the each of the four Allied victors—the U.S., British, French, and Soviets. Yet the Soviets distrusted their wartime allies, and moved to secure the loyalties of Eastern European nations like Poland, Czechoslovakia, and Hungary in the decade after the war ended. Even Germany was divided, with freewheeling West Berlin stranded in the middle of an increasingly militarized Communist state called the German Democratic Republic (DDR), also known as East Germany.

Blake's task as an MI6 officer in West Berlin was to recruit Soviet spies willing to work as double agents. In reality, he told his handlers from the KGB—the Soviet spy agency for domestic and foreign intelligence-gathering—what other MI6 agents were doing in Eastern Europe. It is not known how many of those agents were taken into custody, sentenced to death, or disappeared into the Soviet prison-camp system known as the *gulag,* but he may have divulged as many as 400 names. Blake also revealed to Russian and East German sources that the agents of the American espionage corps, the Central Intelligence Agency (CIA), had worked with MI6 to construct a secret tunnel beneath the two Berlins that let them tap into special telephone lines that carried communications to Moscow.

Blake stayed in Berlin until 1959, when the Foreign Office decided to transfer him to the Middle East. Once again, given his facility for languages, he was sent for Arabic training at the Middle East Center for Arabic Studies near Beirut, Lebanon. He and Gillian and their two young sons lived in Shemlan, Lebanon, after 1960, and he continued to make contact with his KGB handlers in Beirut.

Confessed to Espionage

Blake's downfall came when a high-ranking Polish military counterintelligence expert named Michael Goleniewski was "turned" by the CIA and began reporting on networks in Europe. CIA officials shared this information with their SIS counterparts, and these details led first to the exposure of a British man named Harry Houghton, a British Navy employee who had been passing scientific research about submarine technology and weapons to Polish spies in Britain. Goleniewski also said someone in MI6 used to give him information, and that leak was soon traced to Blake and his time in West Berlin. Blake was recalled from Lebanon in early April of 1961, and obeyed the order. He underwent three days of interrogation in London and initially denied the charges of violating Britain's Official Secrets Act.

Blake's case went to trial in May of 1961 at the Old Bailey, the Central Criminal Court building in London. Most of it was conducted in a closed session due to potentially compromising security issues presented as evidence of espionage in Blake's confession, and Lord Chief Justice Lord Parker of Waddingham handed down an unusually punitive sentence: under the terms of the Official Secrets Act, a defendant's maximum sentence was 14 years, but it was decided that Blake could be held responsible for three different breaches and found guilty of each. Lord Parker set the prison term at three 14-year terms, or 42 years.

Escape Prompted Prison Reform

Blake began serving his term at Her Majesty's (HM) Prison Wormwood Scrubs in London, a shabby Victorian-era building in London. As one of the prison's more well-known inmates, Blake made friends and allies. One was a petty thief and raconteur from Ireland named Sean Bourke, who had been incarcerated after mailing an explosive device to a law-enforcement official. When Bourke was released he began working on a plan to help Blake escape; Blake had also recruited two fairly well-known anti-nuclear activists, Michael Randle and Pat Pottle, also detained at Wormwood Scrubs and sympathetic to his plight. On October 22, 1966, as pre-arranged, Blake used a saw to cut through iron bars of a second-story window during the prison's weekly movie night. Bourke had provided him with a walkie-talkie radio and fashioned a ladder made of rope and knitting needles to toss over the wall at a predesignated spot marked by a flower pot. Blake actually fell while climbing the prison's high perimeter wall and was knocked unconscious, forcing Bourke to carry him to the getaway vehicle.

Blake was moved around various safe houses in London to elude a massive police dragnet, but made it safely to Berlin by hiding inside a wooden box transported in a cargo van. His whereabouts were finally confirmed when Bourke turned up in Moscow a few years later, and the Soviet daily *Izvestia* published an article on Blake, hailing him as a Soviet hero, in February of 1970. He was by then divorced from his first wife and had remarried a Russian woman, with whom he had a son. His 1990 memoir, published in Britain as *No Other Choice,* was subject to a court case in which British authorities blocked proceeds from its sale. An attempt was made to extradite Bourke from Ireland to Britain, but Ireland's Supreme Court refused the request.

In the Soviet Union Blake was given the rank of retired colonel in the KGB and a pension. In 2007, on the occasion of Blake's 85th birthday, Russian president Vladimir Putin—himself once a KGB agent in East Berlin, but long after Blake's transgressions—awarded Blake the Order of Friendship in 2007.

Books

West, Rebecca, *The New Meaning of Treason,* Viking Press, 1964, Open Road Media, 2010.

Periodicals

Independent (London, England), November 7, 2012.

New York Times, September 22, 1967; February 15, 1970; November 12, 2012.

Times (London, England), May 4, 1961.□

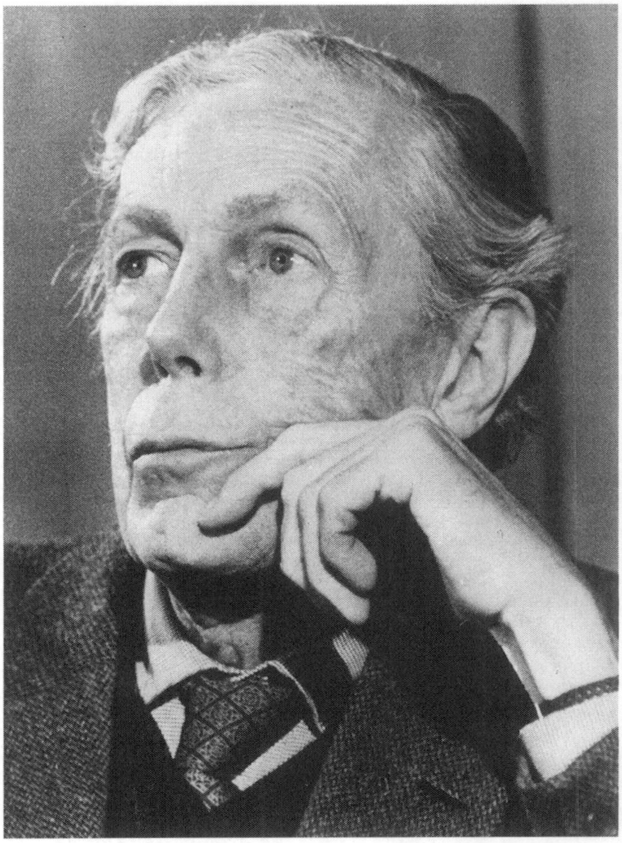

© Keystone Pictures USA/Alamy

Anthony Blunt

Anthony Blunt (1907–1983) lived much of his adult life in subterfuge as a secret member of the infamous "Cambridge Five" espionage ring. Named for the elite British university where the Communist Party sympathizers first met in the 1930s, the ring worked clandestinely to provide the Soviet Union with classified information for almost a quarter-century. Blunt functioned as a recruiter and had less access to vital information than his colleagues, and went on to become one of the foremost art historians in Britain during his lifetime.

Like other members of the Cambridge Five, Anthony Frederick Blunt came from a modest but privileged background with firm ties to the establishment. His paternal grandfather was serving as the Bishop of Hull when Blunt was born on September 26, 1907, while his father, Rev. Arthur Stanley Vaughan Blunt, was a vicar in the Anglican Church, too. Blunt was the youngest of three sons in his family and his mother, Hilda Master Blunt, was distantly related to Elizabeth Bowes-Lyon, who in 1923 married the third in line to the English throne, Prince Albert, the Duke of York. Thirteen years later the Princess Elizabeth became queen when her brother-in-law, King Edward VIII, abdicated and Albert succeeded him as King George VI.

Entered Cambridge

Blunt was born in Bournemouth, Hampshire, but spent a large part of his childhood in Paris, where his father served as chaplain at the British Embassy chapel. The young Blunt was a bright, talented student who spoke excellent French by the time he arrived at Marlborough College, a prestigious private school that was single-sex during his tenure; one of its later alumni would also go on to a royal title as Her Royal Highness, the Duchess of Cambridge, who married King George VI's great-grandson, Prince William of Wales.

In 1926, Blunt entered Trinity College of Cambridge University after winning a scholarship to study mathematics. He later switched to modern languages and earned his degree in 1930. Working as a French tutor while pursuing graduate studies in art history at Cambridge, he was active in the Cambridge Apostles, a secret debate society with limited membership. Most of his future spy-colleagues were also part of this elite, Marxist-tilted club during the early 1930s. The Apostles—like other young intellectuals in Britain in this era—were aghast by right-wing fascist movements that were taking hold in Britain and elsewhere. In Germany in 1933, the National Socialist (Nazi) Party came to power under Adolf Hitler and began enacting punitive laws against Jews and Communists. Hitler's plan for a new fascist Reich, or German Empire, began with his annexation of Austria in 1938. Later that same year German troops invaded neighboring Czechoslovakia. Blunt and other progressive young Britons were shamed by their government's policy of appeasement to Hitler and Nazi Germany.

Friends of Blunt's from the weekly Apostles' meetings included Donald Maclean, son of a prominent Liberal Party politician, and Victor Rothschild of the European banking dynasty. The circle also included Harold Adrian Russell (Kim) Philby and Guy Burgess. Maclean, Philby, and Burgess were a few years younger than Blunt and still undergraduates when they were recruited to spy for the Soviet Union around 1934. Their common link was an Austrian graduate student named Arnold Deutsch, who was an undercover agent for the Soviet Union, the world's first Communist nation. Deutsch had contacts with the Soviet secret police/intelligence-collecting service known by its Russian-language acronym, NKVD. The NKVD recruited Communist sympathizers abroad in part to build up a network of "sleeper" cells should a potential Communist revolution overtake one of Western Europe's economically beleaguered democracies.

"Biggest Mistake of My Life"

Arnold Deutsch was believed to have first secured Philby's cooperation. Philby, in turn, recruited Maclean, and Maclean suggested Blunt's name. Blunt later revealed in an unpublished memoir that Guy Burgess was a major influence on his entry into the Cambridge spy ring, describing the younger man as "an extraordinarily persuasive person," according to the *Guardian* newspaper. Blunt added that in the mid-1930s "the atmosphere in Cambridge was so intense, the enthusiasm for any anti-fascist activity was so great, that I made the biggest mistake of my life" by agreeing to participate in the spy ring, he wrote with regret.

On the public front, Blunt was emerging as one of Britain's most gifted art-history experts. In 1939, he joined the Courtauld Institute of Art as deputy director then entered the British Army after the outbreak of World War II in September of 1939. In 1940, after he was part of a massive emergency evacuation of British troops from western France at Dunkirk, Blunt was recruited to work for MI5 of Britain's Secret Intelligence Service (SIS). MI5 (Military Intelligence Section 5) dealt with domestic intelligence-gathering, while MI6 was in charge of foreign intelligence-data collection. In a remarkably fortuitous decision, he was made the personal assistant of a high-ranking MI5 figure named Guy Liddell, who headed the MI5 counter-espionage division. Blunt's duties at MI5 seemed to involve finding and planting low-level household help for foreign diplomats stationed in wartime London. His own quarters were a flat in central London at 5 Bentinck Street, which he rented from Rothschild; Burgess lived there as well but the two were never romantically involved. The Bentinck address was said to have been the site of wartime parties fabled for their debauchery. Blunt led a quiet personal life, however, in contrast to Burgess's almost openly gay lifestyle.

One of Blunt's recruits, and the so-called "Fifth Man" exposed as a member of the Cambridge spy ring, was John Cairncross, a Cambridge student who went on to work at Bletchley Park during the war in a top-secret assignment. The Bletchley manor house was home to a team of brilliant code-breakers who worked to decipher encrypted messages used by the German military. Through Cairncross, Blunt likely passed on these codes to his Soviet handlers in London.

Posted to Royal Household

Blunt rose to the rank of British Army major, and left both the army and MI5 in 1945 with the end of World War II. That same year he was given a royal-household appointment of enormous prestige as Surveyor of the King's Pictures. This made him the chief art historian and curator for the vast trove of art and other objects held in trust by the House of Windsor. He spent years cataloguing the collection and readying it for a new home, the Queen's Gallery, which opened to the public at Buckingham Palace in 1962. This was the tenth year in the reign of Queen Elizabeth II, who succeeded her father King George VI. Blunt remained on friendly terms with Bowes-Lyon, who used the title Queen Mother. Senior palace officials were reportedly aware of Blunt's possible ties to the Cambridge spy ring, but the job of Surveyor of the Queen's Pictures did not give him much access to sensitive policy matters.

In his field Blunt was an expert on Italian and French Baroque art and a leading authority on seventeenth-century French painter Nicolas Poussin. He wrote several scholarly works, held a professorship at University College of London, and from 1947 to 1974 was director of the Courtauld Institute of Art, one of Europe's most respected schools for advanced study of the history of art. The directorship came with a palatial apartment in the Courtauld Gallery's top floor, whose windows overlooked Portman Square. Blunt was knighted in 1956 for his service to the royal family as a Knight Commander of the Royal Victorian Order (KCVO).

The SIS suspected Blunt of spying for the Soviet Union during the war because of leaks from the Bletchley Park operation, but there was not enough evidence to confirm this. He came under heightened suspicion in the spring of 1951, when Guy Burgess and Donald Maclean vanished one night in May after taking a midnight ferry to France. Both had attained high-ranking positions inside the British Foreign Office in the 1940s and had served at the British Embassy in Washington, as had Kim Philby. Burgess and Maclean turned up in 1956 in Moscow, admitting they had defected to the Soviet Union. The revelations renewed a furor against the two and they were reviled in the media as traitors to Britain.

Confessed in 1964

The "Cambridge Five" first came into use in the early 1960s when a high-ranking Soviet agent of the KGB—the successor agency to the NKVD intelligence services—defected to the West and provided a wealth of detailed information. Anatoliy Golitsyn claimed there had been a ring of five well-placed Britons working for the Soviets since the mid-1930s and asserted Burgess and Maclean were among them. The third person was Philby, who also fled to Soviet protection in early 1963. Once again, Blunt denied any involvement in the ring, though he admitted he had harbored Communist sympathies, which was not a prosecutable offense.

Another incident in 1963 finally confirmed Blunt as the so-called "Fourth Man" in the Cambridge spy ring. Back in the 1930s, one of the Cambridge students he recruited for the spy network was an American, Michael Whitney Straight, who came from a prominent art-collecting clan that established the Whitney Museum of American Art. Improbably, Straight went back to the United States after leaving Cambridge, worked as a speechwriter for U.S. president Franklin D. Roosevelt, and ran the *New Republic* magazine. He was offered a post in the administration of U.S. President John F. Kennedy in 1963, and knew that more rigorous background checks were now in place because of Cold War tensions. Straight confessed his Cambridge-ring connections to a Kennedy advisor, who then passed on the information to MI5. On April 23, 1964, an SIS official confronted Blunt at his Portland Square home and offered him immunity from prosecution in exchange for full cooperation, which he accepted. The revelation of "the Fourth Man" was kept secret, however, and Blunt retained his post as Surveyor of the Queen's Pictures. He retired in 1972, and from the Courtauld directorship in 1974.

Outed in 1979

Irate former colleagues of Blunt's at MI5, who resented the fact that he had betrayed his country to the Soviets but suffered no reprisals nor even a public shaming, were believed to have leaked details to veteran journalist Andrew Boyle, whose 1979 book *The Climate of Treason* featured a thinly disguised gay man connected to Burgess, Maclean, and Philby. Ten days after the publication of Boyle's book, British Prime Minister Margaret Thatcher confirmed in a session of the House of Commons that Blunt was in fact the fourth figure in the Cambridge spy ring. The news that the esteemed former art advisor to Queen Elizabeth II had committed acts of espionage on behalf of the Soviet Union during World War II made headlines across Britain, and Blunt was forced into hiding. His longtime partner was stunned by the revelation and attempted to commit suicide a few months later, and Blunt admitted that he, too, had considered acting to end his life. Stripped of his knighthood, he resigned from his private clubs to spare any further embarrassment, gave a mostly measured interview to a BBC television journalist, and tried to write his memoirs. The content was hampered by Blunt's desire not to expose others at Cambridge or in the SIS.

Blunt died of a heart attack at his home in London on March 26, 1983. The unfinished autobiographical manuscript was given to the British Library in 1984 by a trusted associate of Blunt's, with the stipulation that access to it be granted 25 years from thence, in 2009. John Cairncross, the Fifth Man in the Cambridge spy ring, was exposed in 1991 and admitted blame several months later. He, too, was granted immunity from prosecution.

Books

Hamrick, S.J., *Deceiving the Deceivers: Kim Philby, Donald Maclean, and Guy Burgess,* Yale University Press, 2004.

Kitson, Michael, "Blunt, Anthony Frederick (1907–1983)," in *Oxford Dictionary of National Biography,* 2004, revised by Miranda Carter, Oxford University Press, 2013.

Periodicals

Guardian (London, England), July 22, 2009.

Times (London, England), March 28, 1983.□

Robert Bly

The American poet, translator, and editor Robert Bly (born 1926) has been an influential figure in late 20th-century American poetry, publishing over 20 collections of original poems known for their visionary images of the natural world, as well as translating luminary European and South American poets who had been previously unknown to American readers. Among mainstream circles, Bly is known for organizing and leading the myth-oriented men's movement, which seeks to help men discover their masculinity through ritualized gatherings.

On December 23, 1926, Robert Bly was born on a farm in the rural area of Lac qui Parle, Minnesota, to Jacob T. Bly and Alice Aws Bly. Bly's ancestors had immigrated from Norway to the United States in the mid-19th century, and his father Jacob had been born in Illinois before settling among fellow Norwegian immigrant farmers in Minnesota. It was in this sparsely inhabited region of farms and lakes that Robert Bly and his older brother, James, were raised and educated. In some years, the Bly brothers were the only students in their school. Bly's interest in poetry emerged in high school, under the instruction of an attractive teacher for whom he wrote poetry. After graduating, he enlisted in the Navy in 1944, near the end of World War II, but he proved less than enthusiastic about military life. He was instead motivated to write poetry, thanks to the encouragement of a Navy friend, Eisy Eisenstein, who was the first person Bly had known to write original poems. According to Bly, in an interview appearing on his website, "We conspired to flunk out of the radar program on the grounds that we were poets who couldn't be bothered with science. We didn't succeed." Bly served for two years in the Navy, but was never sent overseas.

Transferred to Harvard

After the Navy, Bly attended St. Olaf College in Minnesota, a school popular among Midwestern Scandinavians. He studied there for one year and then transferred to Harvard University in 1947. There, he landed among a cohort of

© ZUMA Press, Inc./Alamy

students who would turn out to be some of the most distinguished writers of their generation: John Ashbery, Donald Hall, Kenneth Koch, Frank O'Hara, George Plimpton, Adrienne Rich, and Bob Crichton. Bly served as the literary editor of the *Harvard Advocate,* where he and his peers published their work alongside pieces from well-known writers.

Upon graduation from Harvard in 1950, Bly retreated from this brilliant and lively literary circle whose members would spend nights arguing over which poems and stories to publish in the *Harvard Advocate.* "I think I had spent up my available capital for extroversion in college, and I had to be by myself. I intended to take one year, but ended up taking four," Bly said (as quoted on his website). He holed up in a cabin in northern Minnesota, surviving on illegally hunted partridge. In this isolated and austere life, Bly nourished himself with dreams of writing like the exalted English poet John Milton.

After one year, he moved to New York, where he lived and wrote in a series of tiny rented rooms and sublets. He wrote for 12 hours a day, six days a week. On the seventh day, he worked odd jobs such as file clerk, typist, and painter. The only profit he turned from his writing came from two poems he published in the first issue of the *Paris Review.* His poetry during this period was formal and concerned with classical subjects; he specialized in composing ten-line iambic poems that incorporated events from Greek and Roman history. So single-minded was Bly in his solitary devotion to his craft that he might go a month without speaking to another living person.

Inspired by Landscape

After his four years of solitude, Bly attended the University of Iowa Writers' Workshop. In 1955, he married a former Harvard acquaintance, the writer Carolyn McLean. They moved back to Bly's native Minnesota and lived on a farm a half-mile from the one where Bly had grown up. Bly did not farm, but passed his days sitting alone in fields or driving the roads, composing poems about the surrounding pastoral landscapes. These poems were later collected in his first book, *Silence in the Snowy Fields* (1962). In "Hunting Pheasants in a Cornfield," Bly writes, "The mind has shed leaves alone for years. / It stands apart with small creatures near its roots. / I am happy in this ancient place."

In 1956, Bly received a Fulbright Fellowship, allowing him to travel to his ancestral home of Norway and translate Norwegian poetry into English. In the library in Oslo, Bly had a pivotal encounter. He happened upon a couple of lines of poetry by the Chilean poet Pablo Neruda: "Young girls with their hands on their hearts, / Dreaming of pirates." Neruda's poems brimmed with fresh, surreal images that were absent from American and English poetry. Bly was also drawn to the poetry of Juan Ramón Jiménez, George Trakl, Cesar Vallejo, and Gunnar Ekeloef. These poets were internationally known and beloved, yet Bly, with his first-rate Harvard education, had never heard of them, since they had not been translated into English. Bly decided to commit himself to this task of translation, convinced that other readers would feel as moved and invigorated as he had felt.

Once back home in Minnesota, Bly and his friend William Duffy started a literary magazine named *The Fifties.* It was dedicated to publishing translations of important European, South American, and Scandinavian poets, and challenging the dominant lyrical aesthetic in America, English metrical verse and formal poems, which Bly now considered to be boring and old-fashioned. Bly and Duffy published angry response letters written by poets whose work Duffy had cruelly rejected in letters that read, for example (as recorded on his website), "Dear Mr. Smith: These poems remind me of false teeth. Yours sincerely, William Duffy." Despite such antics, *The Fifties* was important for its thoughtful translations of foreign poets, and for publishing the work of up-and-coming American poets like Gary Snyder and David Ignatow. *The Fifties* eventually became *The Sixties* and then *The Seventies,* with the title changing to match the decade.

Wrote Antiwar Poetry

In 1964, Bly began writing poetry protesting the Vietnam War. The poem "Driving through Minnesota During the Hanoi Bombings" juxtaposes the lush and tranquil Minnesota countryside of "lakes just turning green" with the horrific and sudden violence taking place in Vietnam, where moments of terror "become crystals, / Particles / The grass cannot dissolve." This poem and others were collected in his book *The Light around the Body* (1967), winner of the 1968 National Book Award. At the ceremony, Bly publicly denounced the American literary culture for celebrating and rewarding itself while people were dying in Vietnam, and handed over the $1,000 prize to a representative from an antiwar group. Bly also founded, along with fellow poet David Ray, the organization American Writers against the Vietnam War, and participated in countless antiwar readings.

During the 1970s, Bly wrote continuously, publishing eleven books of poetry, essays, and translations. His poems in his collections *Sleepers Joining Hands* (1973) and *This Tree Will Be Here for a Thousand Years* (1979) continued to draw upon antiwar and rural themes and images, and they also incorporated elements of mythology, storytelling, Jungian psychology, and pre-Christian religion. Bly also continued to absorb the work of foreign poets, including the 15th-century Indian mystic poet Kabir and the 13th-century Sufi mystic poet Rumi, both of whose ecstatic poetry influenced Bly's collection of prose poems, *This Body is Made of Camphor and Gopherwood* (1977).

The solitude and silence of Bly's twenties gave way to numerous readings and public appearances during his thirties and forties, as he worked to provide for his wife Carol and their four children, Mary, Bridget, Noah, and Micah. In 1979, he and Carol divorced, and the next year Bly married Ruth Ray, a Jungian therapist whom Bly had known since 1972.

Bly's increasing interest in mythology, and a need to supplement his income, led him to develop seminars for adult men and women whose purpose was to share and discuss fairy tales, myths, and stories. These seminars were part of a larger cultural discussion that used psychology and fairy tales to explore individual growth and development. According to Bly (as quoted on his website), "I wasn't the first to have discovered that many of the classic fairy tales lay out stages of initiation into adulthood which we've entirely forgotten, that our ancestors apparently knew a lot about."

Focused on Male Rituals in Seminars

During the seminars, Bly noticed that men were less willing than women to open up and share their feelings and experiences. Bly believed that this repression among contemporary men was due to a lack of older male role models and initiation rituals. Bly gradually began to focus his attention on masculine development, and with the help of the American psychologist James Hillman and Michael Meade, he created seminars exclusively for men with the goal of helping them discover healthy and productive masculine traits. In outdoor seminars and workshops that began in the early 1980s, Bly, Hillman, and Meade shared stories, recited poetry, and led the attendees in rites and rituals. Bly also wrote the book *Iron John: A Book About Men* (1990), which critically explored the story of Iron John, an archetypal character originating from a Brothers Grimm tale, to discover lessons useful to contemporary male growth. The book drew criticism for being anti-feminist and a hodgepodge of myths and stories, but it was also well received by many men, and spent several weeks at the top of the *New York Times* best-seller list. It is now regarded as a pioneering work in the men's movement.

Other notable Bly books from the 1990s include *The Sibling Society* (1997), a work of social criticism arguing that a lack of respected and influential elders has created a society of Americans who refuse to grow up, and *Morning Poems* (1997), a collection of poems written in bed in the morning, a practice Bly adopted from William Stafford, who wrote a new poem every morning for forty years. Bly found the process of writing these poems liberating: "The first detail that arrives is treated as if it were the end of a thread. When one follows that thread, whatever comes along is welcomed into the poem. It could be a three-legged dog or an old stick or a character out of *Madame Bovary.* Whatever it is, I'll welcome it into the poem. You can always take it out later. One has no idea where the poem is going. That's what I like," he was quoted as saying on his website. This free association of images was likely influenced by the unending stream of visionary surprises he encountered in the work of poets he chose to translate.

These poets came from practically every corner of the globe, and include Neruda, Jiménez, Trakl, Vallejo, Ekeloef, Tomas Tranströmer, Rainer Maria Rilke, Antonio Machado, Francis Ponge, Issa Kobayashi, and Basho. In recent decades, Bly has translated ghazals, a centuries-old Middle Eastern form of love poetry, written by the Persian poet Hafez and the Urdu-language poet Ghalib. Bly's time spent with this form led him to compose original ghazals, collected in *My Sentence Was a Thousand Years of Joy* (2005). His translations of 22 poets were collected in the book *The Winged Energy of Delight: Selected Translations* (2004). In a *Bloomsbury Review* article quoted on the Poetry Foundation's website, Ray Gonzalez acknowledged the debt English language poetry owes Robert Bly, writing that Bly "has opened the doors of experience, insight, and language, lifting them toward a universal understanding of what poetry means in the lives of people throughout the world." In 2008, Bly was named the first poet laureate of Minnesota, where he continues to live.

Books

Bryson, J. Scott, and Roger Thompson, eds., *Twentieth-Century American Nature Poets* (*Dictionary of Literary Biography, Vol. 342*), Gale, 2008.

Davis, William Virgil, *Robert Bly: The Poet and His Critics,* Camden House, 1995.

Galens, David M., ed., *Poetry Criticism,* Vol. 39, Gale, 2002.

Roberson, William H., *Robert Bly: A Primary and Secondary Bibliography,* Scarecrow, 1986.

Periodicals

Star Tribune (Minneapolis, MN), December 2, 2001; September 27, 2009.

Online

"Robert Bly," *Poetry Foundation,* http://www.poetryfoundation.org/bio/robert-bly (September 25, 2013).

"A Short Biography of Robert Bly," "An Interview with Robert Bly," *Robert Bly Official Website,* http://www.robertbly.com/ (September 25, 2013).□

Ruth Brown

The African American rhythm and blues vocalist Ruth Brown (1928–2006) was a major figure in the rise of blues-based popular vocal genres after World War II, becoming one of the first successes in the stable of the key Atlantic label. Later in life, Brown experienced a strong career revival and emerged as a spokesperson for the rights of African American musicians who had not been adequately compensated for their contributions during the era of rhythm and blues and early rock and roll.

Atlantic, indeed, was known (according to Brown's biography on the Rock and Roll Hall of Fame website) as "The House that Ruth Built," and she had various other honorary sobriquets, including 'The Queen of Rhythm and Blues' and, as pop singer Frankie Laine dubbed her, 'Miss Rhythm.' During the early 1950s Brown was a consistent presence on rhythm-and-blues charts, and she even, exceptionally for an African American artist in the genre, made inroads into the pop realm with her biggest hit, "(Mama) He Treats Your Daughter Mean." Her career slowed down with the rise of the rock and soul genres in the 1960s, but she bounced back, showing talent as an actress and continuing to record and perform rhythm and blues in the classic style. Brown was inducted into the Rock and Roll Hall of Fame in 1993.

J. Vespa/Wireimage/Getty Images

Picked Crops on Farm

Brown was born Ruth Alston Weston in Portsmouth, Virginia, on January 12, 1928. Her father, Leonard Weston, was a dock worker. She grew up hearing music at a local African Methodist Episcopal church where her father was the choir director, making her debut at age four when her father lifted her up so she could sit on top of the church's piano. There were sharecroppers in the family, and Brown's summer vacation was to pick crops on a family farm in North Carolina with her six siblings. "That made me the strong woman I am," she was quoted as saying by Jon Pareles of *The New York Times*.

As a teenager, Brown became seriously interested in music and began taking any chance she could to perform. She landed gigs at Navy U.S.O. clubs, sneaking out of the house to make them by telling her family she was going to choir practice. She ran away from home at 17, joining the band of trumpeter Jimmy Brown and then marrying him. The marriage was never really legal, for the musician was already married. But Ruth Brown had established the beginnings of a reputation and kept using that name. She joined the big band of Lucky Millinder in Detroit in 1946 but was fired after the band returned to Washington. reportedly because she had served a round of drinks to the band's members without Millinder's consent.

At loose ends in 1947, Brown made friends with singer Blanche Calloway (sister of bandleader Cab Calloway), who landed her a gig at Washington's Crystal Caverns nightclub and began to manage her career. Brown got a break when the popular Voice of America jazz broadcaster Willis Conover, who had been active in the desegregation of Washington's nightclub scene, heard her set at the Crystal Caverns and recommended them to his friends Ahmet Ertegun and Herb Abramson, partners in the new Atlantic label in New York that was specializing in a new music that was tougher, sexier, and more vocally oriented than jazz. Soon it would have the name rhythm and blues.

Atlantic offered her the chance to record a session, and Brown accepted enthusiastically and headed for New York to record. On the way she was involved in an auto crash that left her in the hospital for almost a year. Ertegun stuck with his new find, visiting Brown in the hospital and on one occasion bringing a recording contract. His faith was justified: a 1949 session yielded the moderate hit "So Long," and soon Brown was generating rhythm and blues chart-toppers like the upbeat "Teardrops from My Eyes" (1950) and "5–10–15 Hours" (1952).

Developed Distinctive Style

At first, Brown recorded mostly ballads and torch songs in a smooth style, but with "Teardrops from My Eyes" she developed a personal sound, a vocal crack upwards that Abramson called a tear. In the early 1950s, Brown became the best-selling African American female performer in the country. Even though she suffered the indignity of seeing some of her songs covered by white performers, who turned them into the national hits denied her in the still-segregated music world, she put the young Atlantic label permanently on the map, and her combination of distinctive vocals backed by a sharp rhythm and blues ensemble set the pattern for followers such as LaVern Baker and Etta James. Even the high-powered rock and roller Little Richard pointed to Brown as a major influence.

Brown's trademark vocal tear was prominently featured in her biggest hit, "(Mama) He Treats Your Daughter Mean," recorded in 1953. Brown conceded in later years that she had resisted recording the song. "For some reason, I just wasn't impressed with it," she was quoted as saying by the London *Independent.* She thought the song "felt kind of crude. It was one of those times where Ahmet "insisted that this tune was for me." Ertegun's judgment was vindicated when "Mama" not only topped rhythm and blues charts, but even cracked the pop top 25.

In the late 1950s, despite the rise of rock and roll and the more directly gospel-influenced style of Ray Charles, Brown continued to score hits. In 1954 she topped rhythm and blues charts again with "Oh What a Dream" and "Mambo Baby," and she adapted well to rock and roll with the top-30 hits "Lucky Lips" (1957) and "This Little Girl's Gone Rockin" (1958). Brown was romantically linked to Clyde McPhatter, lead vocalist of the Drifters; she had a son (named Ronald Jackson, after the man whom Brown initially named as the father) by him, and the two released a hit duet, "Love Has Joined Us Together," in 1955. That year, Brown married saxophonist Earl Swanson; the couple had a son, Earl Jr., but the marriage would later end in divorce.

Deprived of Royalties

In the 1960s, Brown left Atlantic, recorded two albums for the Philips label, and contributed vocals to several jazz albums with only minimal success. Finally she stopped performing and settled in suburban New York City with her husband Bill Blunt, who abused her. "I could pick a good song but I sure couldn't pick a man," Brown was quoted as saying by Perrone. After she and Blunt divorced, Brown was forced to look for work; she took various jobs including maid, cook, and teacher's assistant. Her financial situation was complicated by the fact that she received no royalties during this period from Atlantic, which claimed that she owed the label reimbursement for expenses.

Brown returned to show business in the mid-1970s at the invitation of comedian Redd Foxx, who recruited her to play gospel singer Mahalia Jackson in a musical about the civil rights movment. That led to more acting work, including guest appearances on the *Little House on the Prairie* television series. Brown appeared in the 1988 film *Hairspray* as disc jockey Motormouth Mabel; initially she did not warm to the role, but, as she was quoted as saying by Perrone, director John Waters persuaded her that "'[t]hat's not Ruth Brown out there, that's Motormouth Mabel.' That role was very possibly one of the luckiest things that ever happened to me because I really got a whole new audience of young people."

Brown resumed her recording career, releasing a critically acclaimed series of albums on the Fantasy and Bullseye Blues labels in the late 1980s and 1990s. Her 1989 release *Blues on Broadway* won a Grammy award. She was also active as a radio host on the National Public Radio programs *Harlem Hit Parade* and *BluesStage.* In 1989, Brown appeared in the Broadway revue *Black and Blue,* winning a Tony award for her performance.

Brown also hired a lawyer and succeeded in recovering a portion of the royalties she had earned over the years from the Atlantic label. That experience inspired her to form the Rhythm and Blues Foundation in 1988; Ertegun contributed a reported $2 million in seed money. The foundation aimed to aid rhythm and blues musicians from the 1940s through the 1970s, many of whom had suffered worse treatment at the hands of the music industry than Brown did. Brown was inducted into the Rock and Roll Hall of Fame in 1993, and three years later she released an autobiography, *Miss Rhythm.* She suffered a stroke in 2000 but returned to nightclub performances in which she sat in a chair, quoting blues singer B.B. King to the effect that she had earned the right to sit down. Brown died in Henderson, Nevada, on November 17, 2006; blues singer Bonnie Raitt, quoted by Pareles, called her "one of the original divas."

Books

Brown, Ruth, with Andrew Yule, *Miss Rhythm: The Autobiography of Ruth Brown, Rhythm and Blues Legend,* Dutton, 1995.

Contemporary Black Biography, Vol. 90, Gale, 2011.

Periodicals

Back Stage, July 30, 2004.

Independent (London, England), November 20, 2006.

Jet, December 11, 2006.

New York Times, November 18, 2006.

Online

"Interview: Miss Ruth Brown: Better Late, Than Never," *BroadwayWorld.com,* http://www.broadwayworld.com/article/Interview-Miss-Ruth-Brown-Better-Late-Than-Never-20060829 (September 5, 2013).

"Ruth Brown," *Allmusic,* http://www.allmusic.com (September 5, 2013).

"Ruth Brown Biography," *Rock and Roll Hall of Fame,* http://rockhall.com/inductees/ruth-brown/ (September 5, 2013).□

Charles Buller

Charles Buller (1806–1848) was one of the leading radical political figures of his era. A Whig Party factionalist and staunch advocate for parliamentary reform, he held numerous civil-service and judicial posts granted to him by well-connected friends, and moved in London social circles that included the writer-philosopher John Stuart Mill, novelist William Makepeace Thackeray, and literary giant Thomas Carlyle.

Charles Buller was born on August 6, 1806, in Kolkata, the bustling port city of British India known formerly as Calcutta. His father was also named Charles and held positions with the Bengal Civil Service and British East India Company. On his father's side the future reformer had roots in Cornwall, where the Bullers had been prominent landowners with roots in the western corner of the British Isles dating back to the 1550s. The family holdings in Cornwall included large estates of Shillingham, Morval, and the Isle of Thanet. Buller's mother was Barbara Isabella Kirkpatrick, who preferred to use her middle name. Her father was General William Kirkpatrick, who had a long and distinguished record of military service in Persia and India with the British colonial army; Buller's maternal grandfather had even been sent by the Governor-General of India to mediate a dispute in Nepal, and thereby became one of the first Britons to enter one remote section of the Himalayan mountain kingdom.

Tutored by Carlyle

Buller spent his early years in Calcutta as the eldest of three sons. He permanently injured a leg in a childhood accident, but that failed to dampen what was consistently deemed a lively personality. He was sent to the prestigious Harrow School in 1819, but neglected his studies for amateur boxing matches that eventually forced him out. His parents had temporarily settled in Scotland after leaving Calcutta, and a plan was formed to have Buller and his younger brother Arthur enter the University of Edinburgh, but some tutoring was deemed necessary. A famous orator and cleric, Edward Irving, suggested to the Buller parents that they might hire a promising young teacher named Thomas Carlyle to tutor the teens. Carlyle would later go on to immense acclaim as one of the leading essayist on British politics, culture, and religion during the Victorian era; he also wrote extensively on the French Revolution and its impact on the rest of Europe and promoted the works of German philosophers in Britain. This was one of the first jobs that Carlyle ever held, and he wrote extensively about the Buller family and their habits, as it placed him directly in contact with members of a class much more elite than his own background. In his posthumously published *Reminiscences,* Carlyle wrote that "Charles, by his qualities, his ingenious curiosities, his brilliancy of faculty and character, was actually an entertainment to me rather than a labour."

Buller entered the University of Edinburgh twice, but eventually transferred to Trinity College at Cambridge University, where he was elected president of the Cambridge Union, its famous debating society. He earned his degree in 1828 and then studied for a career in law. His entry into politics was effortless: the Buller family held one of the so-called "rotten boroughs" who sent barely elected representatives to the House of Commons, the lower house of parliament. The seat for West Looe in Cornwall had been controlled by several members of the Buller family and dated back nearly 300 years; these electoral districts were known as "rotten" in the words of an earlier reformer because they contained very small rural populations within their boundaries, most of whom were related to the local landowner, and the privilege of voting was only open to men who possessed a certain financial benchmark anyway. At the time that Buller entered parliament, there were serious calls for electoral reform. The question of eliminating the "rotten boroughs" and adding newer boroughs to reflect growing urban populations in cities like Manchester and Liverpool dominated much of the political discourse of the day.

Buller set out to reform the system from within. His father resigned his seat for West Looe and passed it to him in February of 1830, and Buller became one of the supporters of a controversial Reform Act of 1832. During these two years Britain teetered on the brink of internal political collapse, and the House of Commons was a fractious, battling morass of reformers and status-quo adherents. The peers who sat in the House of Lords—the upper chamber of Britain's parliament—were by nature opposed to most of the reform measures proposed by the Whigs, a liberal party, and the life peers acted against any proposals to increase voter enfranchisement. Buller actually voted in favor of eliminating his own seat from West Looe. The House of Lords attempted to block the bill, and with that riots broke out in Bristol, Derby, Nottingham, and several other cities.

Returned as M.P.

Buller argued the case for change both on the Commons floor and in pamphlet form. In his 1831 treatise *On the Necessity of a Radical Reform,* Buller cited unrest and recalcitrance by the Old Guard in pre-Revolutionary France in the 1780s, and what a crushing blow that nation suffered when public sentiment was inflamed enough to engage in physical protest and force the abdication of the French sovereign. "The insolence of the aristocracy and their hirelings can no longer represent the reformers as a stupid and needy rabble, ignorant of the consequences of a revolution, or uninterested in the maintenance of order," he wrote in his pamphlet. "They are, on the contrary, the very class in which the moral power of the country is lodged, which every theory of free government acknowledges to be the fittest depository of political power, which has the most undeniable claim to a share in representation, and the most irresistible power of enforcing its claims."

The political turbulence in Britain continued, and as a remedy parliament was dissolved, new elections were held, and the Reform Act reintroduced. When it finally passed, Buller stood for election as a Member of Parliament (M.P.) from Liskeard, also in Cornwall, and held that seat from 1832 until his unexpected death 16 years later. He also attained the professional qualification of a barrister when he was called to the bar of Lincoln's Inn in June of 1831. A friend of several prominent figures dating back to his Cambridge days, he was a contributing writer for the *Edinburgh Review* and the *Westminster Review,* and maintained a lifelong friendship with Carlyle, his former tutor. John Stuart Mill, the philosopher, was Buller's sponsor for entrance into the London Debating Society, another prominent group. One of Buller's closest friends in parliament was Lord Durham, born John George Lambton into a landed family with a vast coal-mining fortune. Lambton was already a member of the House of Commons and had married into another politically influential family when he was created the first Earl of Durham in 1828. Durham emerged as a significant player in Whig Party politics and was known as "Radical Jack" for his leftist ideals; it was Durham who drafted much of the Reform Act of 1832.

Sorted Out Troubles in Canada

Buller's friend Durham served as Britain's ambassador to Russia in the mid-1830s and was appointed Governor General of one of the Crown's most important colonies, the Province of Canada, in 1838. In the previous year rebellions had erupted in Lower Canada (present-day Quebec) and Upper Canada, which later became the province of Ontario. Durham was dispatched by the prime minister to deal with the insurrection, and persuaded Buller to join him as chief secretary. Buller was thought to have authored some parts of Lord Durham's famous document, *Report on the Affairs of British North America,* published in early 1839. It urged a more representative form of government to forestall outright rebellion and secession, as Britain's colonies in New England and the Atlantic Seaboard region had done in the 1770s. The *Report* argued, moreover, for the union of Upper and Lower Canada as a preventative measure to end sectarian violence between English Protestant colonists and Francophone Catholics in Quebec, who were holdovers from the French colonial era.

Another prominent friend of Buller's was Edward Gibbon Wakefield, who advocated the establishment of "model" colonies in South Australia and New Zealand. Buller was a founding member of the New Zealand Company, created to establish a more equitable version of an English-speaking society in the Antipodes. For several years in the late 1830s Buller involved himself in contentious negotiations between the Company and officials of the British Colonial Office, who were fiercely resistant to Wakefield's schemes. Originally founded as a penal colony, Australia was emerging as a potentially lucrative player in the global economy, and Buller, Wakefield, Durham, and others believed that settlement to Australia, New Zealand, and Canada, too, should be encouraged as a way to relieve growing social tensions in an overcrowded England. A ski resort in the Australian state of Victoria, Mount Buller, is named in Buller's honor, as is Buller River and Buller Gorge, both in New Zealand.

Appointed to Reform Poor Laws

Buller's other government posts include a stint as head of the Public Records Commission in 1836 and secretary of the Board of Control, which supervised British interests in India. Another close friend was Lord Russell, a Whig Party leader and fellow advocate for reform. When Russell became prime minister in 1846, he named Buller to the high bench as a Judge Advocate General, and a year later put him in charge of a newly established Poor Law Board. Laws regarding public-welfare stipends and workhouses were a sharply contested topic in England of the 1840s; the writer Charles Dickens secured his place in English literature by writing about the widening gap between rich and poor in Victorian England. Buller attempted to draft new laws regarding workhouses and almshouses, which had become egregiously punitive and were exposed by new crusading journalists as little better than prison factories or farms for the most destitute in England.

Buller never married, but his mother Isabella informally adopted a little girl thought to have been the result of his relationship with a woman named Teresa Reviss. The daughter, also named Teresa but called Tizzy, was discussed in diaries and correspondence of Jane Welsh Carlyle, wife of Thomas Carlyle, and was said to have partly inspired the venal, social-climbing Becky Sharp in *Vanity Fair,* the 1848 novel by William Makepeace Thackeray—another friend of both Buller brothers.

Buller died on November 29, 1848, in London at the age of 42 from a bacterial infection. Carlyle, who had previously deemed Buller "the genialest radical I have ever met" (as recorded in the *Dictionary of National Biography*), wrote an obituary that ran in the *Examiner* newspaper a few days later, according to William Howie Wylie's *Thomas Carlyle, The Man and His Books.* "This man was true to his friends, true to his convictions," the usually obtuse Carlyle commented, "and true without effort, as the magnet is to the north."

Books

Buller, Charles, *On the Necessity of a Radical Reform* (pamphlet), James Ridgway, 1831.

"Buller, Charles, (1806–1848)," *Dictionary of National Biography,* Leslie Stephen, editor, Volume 7, Macmillan, 1886.

Carlyle, Thomas, *Reminiscences,* edited by James Anthony Froude, Charles Scribner's Sons, 1881.

Wylie, William Howie, *Thomas Carlyle, The Man and His Books,* Marshall Japp, 1881.□

Guy Burgess

Former British intelligence officer Guy Burgess (1911–1963) remains one of the most infamous names in the history of espionage. Through his career with the British Foreign Office, the Cambridge University graduate was able to pass highly sensitive material over to agents of the Soviet intelligence services during the most tension-filled years of the Cold War. Burgess was not alone in his treachery: he and two other members of the "Cambridge Five" spy ring defected to the Soviet Union.

Guy Francis de Moncy Burgess was born at home at 2 Albermarle Villas on April 16, 1911, in Devonport, a section of Plymouth. His father Malcolm was a high-ranking Royal Navy officer who died in 1924, the year Burgess turned 13. Burgess had a younger brother named Nigel and their mother Evelyn later remarried

Express/Hulton Archive/Getty Images

another distinguished military officer, John Bassett. As a youth Burgess attended Eton, the prestigious private school, and then entered the Royal Navy College at Dartmouth. Imperfect eyesight was given as the reason for his return to Eton, where he completed his schooling and went on to Trinity College of Cambridge University. At Cambridge he studied history, was granted a teaching fellowship, and became a member of a secret debate society known as the Apostles.

Recruited as Soviet Agent

In the early 1930s Burgess was among the privileged Cambridge and Oxford youth who were uneasy with the Britain in which they were coming of age. Rife with pernicious class divisions, seemingly hidebound to a preposterously old-fashioned monarchy, and plagued by high unemployment due to the Great Depression, Britain was to many idealistic, well-educated young adults like Burgess merely an anachronistic empire ready to be toppled. Some among these dissenters gravitated toward right-wing politics, looking with favor upon the sudden turns of fortune in both Germany and Italy, where Fascist regimes had taken over. Adherents of leftist politics on the other side saw the momentous changes that had taken place in Russia since its 1917 Bolshevik Revolution overthrew the repressive Romanov dynasty and installed the world's first Communist regime.

Marxism appealed to Burgess and others in the Cambridge Apostles group. One was Harold Adrian Russell (Kim) Philby, another Cambridge history major, whose faith in Communism as a better way brought him into contact with a relief organization seeking to help victims of Nazi Germany, which was taking a punitive line against both declared and suspected Communists. Some of these "charities" and aid societies were secretly funded by the Soviet Union, whose foreign-intelligence services were recruiting allies in Europe and elsewhere with the goal of spreading the revolutionary message. In the spring of 1934, through his connection to Philby, Burgess met Soviet agent Arnold Deutsch, an Austrian graduate student in London. Deutsch was a key figure in assembling the Cambridge Five, of whom Philby and Burgess were the first recruits. Burgess was said to have suggested two other potential ring members, Anthony Blunt and Donald Maclean. Blunt was slightly older and a member of the Apostles; Maclean was the son of a prominent Liberal Party politician.

Burgess had planned to join the Communist Party of Great Britain, but was advised by his Soviet handlers to avoid political activities and instead seek a role inside the British establishment. He found a job as an aide to a Conservative Party (Tory) member of parliament, then joined the British Broadcasting Corporation (BBC) Radio service as a radio producer in 1936. In December of 1938, with war against Germany looming, Burgess was recruited to work for a propaganda unit of Britain's Secret Intelligence Service (SIS). He joined Section D of MI6—with "MI" the acronym for Military Intelligence Section 6, which handles foreign intelligence operations—and continued to pass along information to his handlers in London. The fact that there were almost no security checks for those recruited into British intelligence services later caused consternation and rebukes against the affinity networks, where elites inside an "old boy" network culled from Eton, Cambridge, and other top schools were considered above reproach in matters of patriotism.

Recruited for Foreign Office

Burgess rejoined the BBC in 1941 after an alcohol-related incident raised some concerns about his SIS suitability, and went on to produce radio panel programs and news roundups like *The Week in Westminster.* In wartime London he lived a barely closeted life as a gay man, and the flat he shared with Anthony Blunt at 5 Bentinck Street was the scene of raucous wartime parties. The property was owned by Victor Rothschild, scion of the venerable banking family and a member of MI5, the domestic-intelligence branch of SIS.

In June of 1944, Burgess left the BBC to take a new post with the news department of the British Foreign Office. The Foreign Office—equivalent to the U.S. Department of State—conducted diplomatic relations with other nations, and this was an especially delicate moment in the modern history of Britain. The nation had gone to war against Nazi aggression in 1939, endured heavy aerial bombardment in the first years of World War II, then allied with the United States and Soviet Union in 1941 to roust the Nazi menace in Europe. Burgess joined the Foreign Office as the Allies were approaching the sixth and final year of world war.

Remarkably, Burgess continued to work for the Soviet intelligence services undetected, and his job at the Foreign Office made him privy to even more confidential correspondence and dispatches. World War II ended in 1945, and a year later he became secretary to Hector McNeil, a Minister of State and United Nations economic-recovery specialist for Europe. This post gave Burgess even more access to classified documents, which he removed from McNeil's desk at night. They were passed on to his Soviet contact, and who then photographed them and gave them back; Burgess would simply return the documents the following morning.

Dispatched to Washington

Burgess also worked for the Information Research Department (IRD) of the Foreign Office, which sought to discredit Soviet-propaganda campaigns. His job took him across Europe, but he continued to drink heavily and engage in reckless personal behavior. In November of 1948 he was assigned to the Far Eastern section of the British Foreign Office, and worked to convince British diplomats to recognize a newly Communist China. In June of 1950 he was informed that he was being transferred to the British Embassy in Washington, D.C. Another member of the Cambridge spy ring, Donald Maclean, had gone on to even more impressive service at the Foreign Office and rose to become first secretary at the Embassy in Washington in the mid-1940s. When Burgess moved to Washington the first secretary was yet another Cambridge spy-ring member, Kim Philby, who later claimed to have stopped spying for the Soviet Union after the war.

A complex set of fortuitous circumstances and determined code-breaking work had permitted American intelligence operatives to decipher encrypted cables sent from the British Embassy in Washington to Moscow during World War II. It was this effort that led U.S. officials to warn their British counterparts that there was a double agent—a British official agent who was colluding with the enemy—at their Washington embassy. Burgess lived with Philby in Washington and allegedly the two conspired to have Burgess recalled to London, where he could make contact with Maclean and warn him that he was suspected of being that "mole" inside the British Embassy. Burgess managed to get himself pulled over by District of Columbia police cruisers for driving under the influence of alcohol three times in a single day; he claimed diplomatic immunity and Britain's ambassador to the United States, Oliver Franks, ordered him to return to England.

Burgess was also under cautious surveillance by MI5 and MI6 personnel for an incident that had occurred in the autumn of 1949, when he visited Gibraltar and Morocco for a vacation. He drank heavily and identified covert agents of British intelligence services. Maclean was also showing signs of mental strain and had suffered a brief nervous breakdown while stationed in Egypt in 1950. Blunt, now a prominent art historian with a royal appointment as Surveyor of the King's Pictures, met Burgess upon his return from America in May of 1951, and let him stay at his flat for a time.

Vanished for Half-Decade

Burgess made contact with Maclean and they met at a private gentlemen's club in Pall Mall. Maclean was suspected of providing information to the Soviet intelligence services about the Allies' plans to build a weapon of mass destruction, the atomic bomb, which was used to end the war with Japan in 1945. Maclean was to be questioned jointly by MI5 and U.S. intelligence officials on May 28, 1951. On the night of May 25, Burgess drove to Maclean's home in Tatsfield, Kent, which was in a remote area that made physical surveillance too obvious, though it was thought to have been bugged with hidden microphones. It was a Friday night and Maclean's birthday, and his American-born wife greeted Burgess by a different name—Roger Styles, from an Agatha Christie mystery novel. Burgess had already purchased two tickets for them aboard the ferry from Southampton to St. Malo, France, which did not require passport documentation. They left in an Austin sedan Burgess had rented and just barely made the ship's 11:45 p.m. departure time.

The next morning, Burgess and Maclean made their way by train to Paris and then on to Switzerland, where Soviet handlers gave them false identity papers. From Zurich they flew to Prague, the capital of Communist-allied Czechoslovakia, where they were met by Soviet handlers as they debarked from the plane, then promptly vanished from public view for the next five years. The news of two missing diplomats broke on June 7, and British and international authorities announced a massive search operation. The case made international headlines for several months, and they were believed to have defected to the Soviet Union. Soviet authorities denied this until February of 1956, when Burgess and Maclean appeared at a hastily convened press conference at a Moscow hotel. Reporters from TASS, the Soviet news agency, and *Pravda,* the Russian Communist Party daily, were joined by a London *Sunday Times* correspondent and a Reuters journalist, both of whom were astonished to see the two infamous Britons in apparently good health and speaking with no signs of duress. In an official joint statement, Burgess and Maclean asserted they had moved to the Soviet Union of their own free will and strongly denied they had ever been involved in any espionage activities on behalf of the Soviet Union.

Tale Continues to Enthrall

The story of the Cambridge Five remains one of the most fruitful sources of examination by historians, journalists, novelists, and screenwriters. Even decades later some parts of the story remain murky. Philby, who also claimed to have ended his espionage activities years before, would later defect to the Soviet Union in the early 1960s to escape prosecution. Anthony Blunt, the "fourth man" in the ring, was identified through his connections to Burgess and Maclean and confessed in 1964, but was promised immunity from prosecution and allowed to remain as Surveyor of the Queen's Pictures until 1979.

Cold War historians and espionage analysts have theorized that Burgess had only agreed to accompany Maclean on the trip out of a sense of duty and had been promised he would be allowed to return to England. Unlike Maclean, Burgess never renounced his British citizenship and occasionally expressed a desire to visit England to see his aging mother. Accounts that surfaced after the fall of the Soviet Union revealed that Burgess desperately missed his hedonistic life in London, finding Moscow drab and the puritanical Soviet police state devoid of any underground gay culture. He continued to drink heavily and died on August 30, 1963, at the age of 52 at Botin Hospital in Moscow. The cause of death was heart disease. Burgess had requested that his ashes be buried on English soil, in the family plot in Hampshire, and permission was granted.

Blunt and Maclean died in 1983, the former in England and the latter in Moscow. Philby wrote his memoirs from Moscow in 1968 and claimed that the defection of Burgess had stunned their circle. Philby died in Moscow in 1988. The "fifth man" was John Cairncross, who was exposed in 1991, after the fall of the Soviet Union.

Books

Hamrick, S.J., *Deceiving the Deceivers: Kim Philby, Donald Maclean, and Guy Burgess,* Yale University Press, 2004.

Kerr, Sheila, "Burgess, Guy Francis de Moncy (1911–1963)," in *Oxford Dictionary of National Biography,* 2004.

Periodicals

New York Times, February 12, 1956; April 24, 1962.

Times (London, England), February 13, 1956; September 2, 1963.□

C

John Cale

Welsh musician and composer John Cale (born 1942) is best known for co-founding the rock group the Velvet Underground with singer/songrwriter/ guitarist Lou Reed. After leaving the group, he continued making music and produced albums for many other artists. He was inducted into the Rock and Roll Hall of Fame (as a member of the Velvet Underground) in 1996. The recognition underscored the influence his musicianship had on many subgenres of rock and roll music.

John Cale's name is inextricably linked with the late musician Lou Reed (1942–2013). In the mid-1960s, they founded the Velvet Underground, an innovative rock band that influenced many later musical artists–and art is a key word, for the gulf between what most contemporary performers purveyed and what the Velvet Underground offered was immeasurable. Reed's lyrics were deemed brutal but honest, and Cale's musicianship helped bring those lyrics to life on vinyl, during the age of the twelve-inch, long-playing record album. Typically, during the 1960s, an album from a popular group contained one or two inclusions of hit singles and was filled out with fluff, or filler material comprised of poor versions of other bands' songs; but an album from the Velvet Underground, song for song, demonstrated ambition and excellence.

Cale's entrance into rock and roll was interesting: He was a classically trained musician, but he achieved his greatest success with the minimalistic rock and roll musical structure that afforded him expression as well as reputation. Working with Reed, Cale helped produce works marked by their dissonance: basic conventions of the rock and roll format mixed with ear-blunting noise. The result was groundbreaking, even if the contemporary audience—who were, after all, mostly teenagers—failed to grasp the complexities. But rock critics and music historians certainly did.

While rock and roll provided Cale with notoriety, he also worked in genres such as drone and classical music. His path into the commercial arena, which began with the Velvet Underground, subsequently led to more than thirty solo albums as well as a body of work that included collaboration with a diverse list of artists and bands such as LaMonte Young, John Cage, Hector Zazou, Cranes, Nick Drake, Brian Eno, Patti Smith, Iggy and the Stooges, Jonathan Richman and the Modern Lovers, Squeeze, The Replacements, and Siouxsie and the Banshees, among many others who appreciated how Cale's classical training-cum-rock and roll experience could enhance their own output. Even so, Cale was not keen on accepting the mantle as a pioneer of progressive music. Always, his main interest was classical music; rock and roll merely gave him a setting in which to express musically his ideas—and to earn some money. That does not mean he was a "sell out," however; he was a survivor and, above all, an innovator.

Earned Musical Scholarship

John Cale was born March 9, 1942, in Garnant, Wales, in the United Kingdom. His father, Will Cale, was a Welsh coal miner and his mother, Margaret Davies, was a teacher. Their son proved to be a musical prodigy. Even before he was a teenager, Cale performed a self-written musical composition on a British Broadcasting Corporation (BBC) radio show. He studied in Britain under famed composer Humphrey Searle (1915–1982). This led to a scholarship, granted in 1963, to study music in the United States, within

© Presselect/Alamy

programs developed by renowned American composers Aaron Copland and Leonard Bernstein.

The scholarship took him to the Tanglewood Music Center in Lenox, Massachusetts. But he was not allowed to play his own compositions; his educators considered his pieces too violent. One piece involved the destruction of a table with an axe. Later in his career, Cale would be able to indulge in such inclinations.

As his talents ripened, Cale's musical interests drifted toward the avant-garde, and he took part in a 19-hour piano recital—Erik Satie's "Vexations"—with equally innovative musician John Cage (1912–1992).

From there, Cale attached himself to LaMonte Young (born 1935), an avant-garde musician who became known as the first important composer of minimalism, an experimental musical form which on the surface seemed repetitive but, with a careful listening, proved to be quite complex. Cale then became part of Young's music ensemble named the Theatre of Eternal Music. Experience with the minimalist ensemble, and its drone music experimentation, would greatly influence Cale's next professional connection—with the Velvet Underground.

Connected with Lou Reed

This came about through Cale's friendship with Lou Reed, who would become a legendary New York singer/songwriter. In the early 1960s, Reed was churning out pop tunes for Pickwick Records, a minor record label that specialized in novelty songs. As is the case with any young and financially-challenged college student residing in unfamiliar territory, Cale needed money. So he acquired work at Pickwick and eventually joined Reed in a band called the Primitives, in which the eclectic Cale played bass. Early efforts were trivial, but Reed filled Cale with a headful of ideas about the potential of popular music. Reed also pointed out to Cale how his diverse talents could be integrated into a rock band format. Cale was a keyboardist, bass player, and viola player. At the time, a typical rock band structure was simplistic: lead guitar, rhythm guitar, bass guitar, and drums. Cale and Reed helped break those traditional boundaries by bringing other instruments into the mix, broadening sonic possibilities. Cale provided musical backing to Reed's lyrics and seemingly emotionless vocals, and the two men became friends and roommates.

Reed and Cale then connected with Reed's former college classmate Sterling Morrison, who became a guitarist in Reed's envisioned band. They added Maureen Tucker—a percussionist with somewhat eccentric ideas about how to provide a backbeat—to be their drummer. Thus, the Velvet Underground was born in 1965. The group took its title from a lurid paperback book of the same name about modern sexual mores, written by Michael Leigh, that was published in 1963. With their leather jackets, dark clothing, and dark glasses, the group members' look embodied the sexual subculture that Leigh wrote about. Also, it was unusual at the time for a rock band to have a female drummer. Further, the group's musical and lyrical slant was New York City street smart, and Cale's classical approach added a unique dimension to the overall sound.

As with many rock groups aspiring to fame in that period, the Velvet Underground struggled. This discouraged Cale. He suggested that his bandmates test their talents in his home territory, the British Isles, where they might find better success. Group members were sold on the idea, and the band prepared to leave for England. However, their path was diverted: One of their New York City appearances excited pop artist Andy Warhol (1928–1987). He had witnessed a performance at the Cafe Bizarre in Greenwich Village. He was delightfully startled by the band's look and Reed's lyrics, and Cale's musical audacity was equally attractive. Warhol then made the group his "house band" at his studio, called the "Factory."

Warhol integrated the Velvet Underground into his "Exploding Plastic Inevitable," a series of multi-media events that combined music with film. The group proved perfect for Warhol's artistic vision. Jon Dolan wrote in *Rolling Stone* magazine, "Reed's matter-of-fact descriptions of New York's bohemian demimonde, rife with allusions to drugs and S&M, pushed beyond even the Rolling Stones' darkest moments, while the heavy doses of distortion and noise for its own sake revolutionized rock guitar."

Reed provided the words, Cale provided the music—all of that distortion and noise—for this new form of rock expression. The distinctive sound that Cale helped create was discordant and dissonant and, in true rock and roll fashion, attractively minimalistic. Dolan described the results of the partnership: "Reed fused street-level urgency with elements of European avant-garde music, marrying beauty and noise." Cale made the beautiful noise.

Warhol acted as the band's manager and producer, placing the Velvets on stage and in film. He even secured the group a recording contract with MGM's subsidiary Verve record label. Warhol had his own ideas about the band's direction, and he forced the group to take into their ranks an attractive and talented singer and actress, Nico. She has been described as a "chanteuse," a female nightclub singer typically accompanied by a pianist. The group initially objected, then relented. This resulted in one of the most stunning debut albums in rock history, *The Velvet Underground & Nico,* released in 1967. Warhol supplied the album cover artwork with one of his most famous images: a very yellow banana. Still, the album did not sell well.

Encountered Little Commercial Success

During its brief existence, the Velvet Underground would deliver four albums, all critical successes. But at the time of their releases, each album sold poorly and only made a disappointing and fleeting appearance on industry record charts. For instance, *Billboard* magazine, a trade industry publication that on a weekly basis charts the top 200 best-selling albums, only placed the 1967 debut album at number 171. Following that weak incursion, the album listing disappeared. The band's second album, *White Light/White Heat,* in 1968, only flirted with chart recognition, experiencing a week at the 199 position.

One of the sales problems could have been that the Velvet Underground was far ahead of its time. Its songs addressed issues not typically mentioned in the rock and roll song format: drug addiction ("Heroin," "I'm Waiting for the Man" and "White Light/White Heat") and alternative sexual lifestyles ("Venus in Furs" and "Sister Ray"). Compositions were at once avant-garde and basic rock and roll. After the aforementioned albums, the Velvet Underground, despite being a creative and influential band, only released two more albums, *The Velvet Underground* (1969) and *Loaded* (1970).

Left The Velvet Underground

But Cale was only around for the first two albums. By the time that *White Light/White Heat* was being recorded, Cale and Reed had artistic disagreements. Arguments were ferocious enough to end both a friendship and a professional collaboration.

Cale left the band in 1968. Whether he was fired or merely decided to move on remains a matter of debate. He was replaced by Reed's friend Doug Yule (born 1947).

Cale had no problem finding work in the post-Velvet phase of his career. During the early 1970s, he served in the A&R (artist and repertoire) function for the Warner Brothers and Elektra record labels, a position that required him to scout talent and help develop recording artists' careers.

Recorded Solo Albums

Meanwhile, Cale made solo albums. His major works in the 1970s included *Vintage Violence* (1970), *The Academy in Peril* (1972), *Paris 1919* (1973), and *Fear* (1974). Such works demonstrated an eclectic mix of styles: pop (with the appropriate lush orchestration), hard rock (with its aggressive minimalism), and punk rock (even more minimalistic). From this period, *Paris 1919* is widely considered to be his finest achievement. For *Rolling Stone* magazine, reviewer Stephen Holden described it as "the most ambitious album ever released under the name 'pop.'" But like the Velvet Underground's ambitious works, the record sold poorly.

To promote his work, Cale toured during the decade. Performances combined music with theater, sometimes with controversial results. In one performance—like the guitar smashing Peter Townshend, founder of The Who—Cale destroyed a musical instrument onstage, a piano. During an April 24, 1977 performance in Croydon, England, Cale decapitated a dead chicken with a meat cleaver, to the horror of his band members. His drummer at the time, Joe Stefko, who had threatened to quit if Cale went through with his plan, immediately walked off the stage and left the band.

Bass player Mike Visceglia also stormed off of the stage in mid-performance. In his 1999 autobiography *What's Welsh for Zen,* Cale described the circumstances, which were not pretty. It occurred during the performance of a classic rock and roll song. "I had the chicken killed backstage and put on a wooden platter with a handle," wrote Cale. "I told the roadie: 'When I get into the second verse of Heartbreak Hotel, slide it out to me on the platter.' I already had the meat cleaver stashed on stage. So I thought, try a little voodoo! I am singing, 'We could be so lonely,' swinging the chicken around by its feet, nobody in the audience knowing it was dead, 'we could be so'—Twhok! I decapitated it and threw the body into the slam dancers at the front of the stage, and I threw the head past them. It landed in somebody's Pimm's. Everyone looked totally disgusted. The bass player was about to vomit and all the musicians moved away from me. Even the slam dancers stopped in mid-slam. It was the most effective show-stopper I ever came up with." Despite this braggadocio, Cale would later apologize for his disturbing onstage act. But the autobiographical anecdote provides insight into the late 1970s performance environment.

Became a Sought-After Music Producer

During this period, Cale also established himself as a record producer. He engaged in the conventional, working on albums by Barbra Streisand and pop group Paul Revere and the Raiders for Columbia; and he plied his talents to the unconventional, as in early albums by Iggy Pop and the Stooges, Patti Smith, and Jonathan Richman and the Modern Lovers, among others.

In the 1980s, he continued writing songs and producing music, and he contributed to film soundtracks such as director Jonathan Demme's *Something Wild,* a musical collaboration that included famed performance artist and musician Laurie Anderson, who later married Lou Reed, and David Byrne, who founded the Talking Heads rock band.

Reconnected with Reed

In the late 1970s, Cale and Reed re-established their friendship, but it would be about ten years before they would again work together. In 1988, they collaborated on the *Songs for Drella* album, a musical tribute to Warhol. This led to thoughts about a new Velvet Underground effort. In 1993, and twenty-five years after their glory days, founding members of the Velvet Underground decided to reunite. The result was a brief European tour and a subsequent live album. Hopes were that there would be an American tour and that another studio album would emerge, but old conflicts again reared their ugly heads. Hopes were scuttled as, once again, Cale and Reed indicated that it was impossible for them to work together. But the new Velvet Underground fans could find solace in a major reissue: the 1995 compilation titled *Peel Slowly & See*, a boxed set that included five CDs: the group's first four albums and unreleased tracks.

Cale's post-Velvet Underground career proved he did not need to be attached to Reed to be successful. In the 1990s and into the 2000s, he continued demonstrating productivity as a solo performer, a composer, and a producer. Even if his relationship with Reed provoked conflict, Cale proved he could collaborate with numerous artists and musical ensembles. Further, the passage of time appeared to be no roadblock to interest in Cale's career. An overview of his output, *Conflict & Catalysis: Production & Arrangements 1966–2006*, was well received. The title of this music compilation underscores the ongoing interest in his work.

Also, readers were provided an overview of Cale's life with his autobiography *What's Welsh for Zen*, which was supplemented by a 2003 biography *Sedition and Alchemy: A Biography of John Cale*, written by Tim Mitchell. Details of Cale's life were revealed. In 1968, he wed fashion designer Betsey Johnson, but the marriage lasted less than a year. In 1971, he married Cynthia Wells, a member of the all-female rock band the GTOs (Girls Together Only). They divorced in 1975. In 1981, Cale married Risé Irushalmi. They had one child, Eden Myfanwy Cale (born 1985), but the third time was not a charm; the couple divorced in 1997. Cale also endured substance addiction throughout his life. The trigger stemmed from childhood, when he suffered bronchial problems and a doctor prescribed opiates. Cale came to depend upon prescribed drugs to function, and when he landed in New York City, he found that any illicit drug was readily available. Ultimately, the birth of his daughter compelled him to free himself from dependence.

In 1996, Cale was inducted into the Rock and Roll Hall of Fame (as a member of the Velvet Underground). In 2010, he was award an OBE (Officer of the Order of the British Empire) in recognition for his services to music and art. The honors were appropriate as Cale, with his participation in Velvet Underground and with his solo efforts, influenced seminal punk, new wave, and progressive bands such as the New York Dolls, the Sex Pistols, Television, Patti Smith, the Talking Heads, Roxy Music, U2, and REM. In turn, all of those artists helped chart the future course of rock and roll.

Books

Cale, John (with Victor Bockris), *What's Welsh for Zen*, Bloomsbury, 1999.

Contemporary Musicians, Gale, 2005.

Mitchell, Tim, *Sedition and Alchemy: A Biography of John Cale*, Peter Owen Publishers, 2003.

Stokes, Geoffrey, Ken Tucker and Ed Ward, *Rock of Ages: The Rolling Stone History of Rock & Roll*, Rolling Stone Press/Summit Books, 1986.

The Rolling Stone Encyclopedia of Rock & Roll, Simon & Schuster, 2001.

Periodicals

Associated Press, October, 28 2013.

Rolling Stone, May 10, 1973; October 27, 2013; November 21, 2013.

Online

"John Cale," *AllMusic.com*, http://www.allmusic.com/artist/john-cale-mn0000224638/biography (November 24, 2013)

"John Cale Biography," *BBC*, http://www.bbc.co.uk/wales/music/sites/john-cale/pages/biography.shtml (November 24, 2013)

"John Cale Biography," *IMDb*, http://www.imdb.com/name/nm0129816/bio?ref_=nm_ov_bio_sm (November 24, 2013)

"Lou Reed," *Rolling Stone*, www.rollingstone.com/music/artists/lou-reed/biography (October 31, 2013).

"The Velvet Underground Biography," *Rock and Roll Hall of Fame*, https://www.rockhall.com/inductees/the-velvet-underground/bio/(November 24, 2013)□

Orlando Cepeda

The Latin American baseball player Orlando Cepeda (born 1937) was one of the stars in the game in the 1960s, a consistently productive slugger who played through pain over a long career in which he routinely notched batting averages of over .300 and hit 25 or more home runs.

A Puerto Rican of African descent, Cepeda was among both the earliest Latino players and the earliest African Americans to play in the major leagues. Beginning his major league career with the San Francisco Giants in 1958, he was one of the first minority players to command a strong fan base. "You have to remember that Orlando was the most popular player when the [Giants] franchise moved from New York," Giants owner Peter A. Magowan told George Vecsey of the *New York Times*. "Orlando played the game with flamboyance. He was an all-around player. He got our fans interested in the team." Cepeda was one of the first of a wave of players of Latin background who reshaped the game of baseball in the 1960s. Cepeda's life after he left the field was troubled, but over time he has become a respected

© Everett Collection, Inc./Alamy

baseball elder statesman. Cepeda was inducted into the Baseball Hall of Fame in 1999.

Father Was Caribbean Baseball Star

Orlando Manuel Cepeda was born in Ponce, Puerto Rico, on September 17, 1937. His father, Pedro Cepeda, known as Perucho, was a famed slugger who was known across the Caribbean as "El Toro," or The Bull. The elder Cepeda was recruited to play in the U.S. Negro Leagues but feared the degree of racism he would encounter there. Instead he played in leagues in the Dominican Republic and moved closer to home to play for a team in Guyama, Puerto Rico, after his son was born. The young Orlando was quickly dubbed Peruchín and "El Torito," The Baby Bull.

Learning the game directly from his father, Cepeda vacillated between a desire to emulate him and a spirit of independence. After hearing his father play in a Puerto Rico–Cuba all-star game on the radio in 1944, he was hooked. He probably overdid his baseball exercises as a child and thus contributed to the leg problems he would experience as an adult player, but he also set his sights on basketball for a time, returning to baseball at age 13 after injuring his knee. In 1952, Cepeda underwent knee surgery that left him bedridden for two months. He gained weight, reaching the big slugger's build that he would have as a major leaguer.

It was two years before Cepeda could return to the field, but he soon won places on amateur teams. The family moved to the economically distressed San Juan neighborhood of Santurce after Pedro Cepeda fell on hard times and began to accumulate gambling debts. Orlando Cepeda got a job as a batboy with a local team, the Santurce Crabbers, and began to rub elbows with other up-and-coming Puerto Rican players and with visiting major-leaguers. At his father's urging he prevailed upon a member of the Crabbers' coaching staff to send him to Florida for a tryout with the New York Giants. Cepeda was signed in 1955, and sent to a Giants farm team, the Salem Rebels in Salem, Virginia. Just before he was due to take the field in American organized baseball for the first time, his father died. Cepeda returned home for the funeral but quickly realized that his baseball salary was now the family's sole means of support. He pressed on, although at this point he spoke very little English.

Rose Quickly Through Minor Leagues

Cepeda was depressed by the institutions of segregration in the American South, but once he moved later in 1955 to another team in Kokomo, Indiana, he began to show what he could do, hitting 21 home runs with a .393 batting average in his first season. In 1956, Cepeda moved to the St. Cloud Rox in Minnesota and won the Northern League Triple Crown with 26 home runs, 112 runs batted in (RBIs), and a .355 batting average. The Giants moved him to the Minneapolis Millers of the AAA-level American Association, one step below the major leagues, in 1957, and he did nearly as well, hitting 25 home runs with a batting average of .307. When the Giants moved to San Francisco, Cepeda was ready to join them.

The 20-year-old Cepeda quickly became a star in San Francisco: in his first game he hit a home run and led the Giants to a victory over the Los Angeles Dodgers and pitching ace Don Drysdale. Giants manager Bill Rigney remarked (according to *JockBio.com*) that Cepeda was "three years away" from the Hall of Fame. Cepeda took National League Rookie of the Year honors in 1958 and remained remarkably consistent over his first seven seasons in San Francisco, hitting at least 24 home runs and batting close to .300 each year. In 1961, he hit a career-high 46 home runs but suffered the first of a series of knee injuries that aggravated childhood trauma to the joint and plagued him with increasing severity for the rest of his career. Cepeda adapted to playing in the outfield after he faced competition from another sensational young first baseman, Willie McCovey.

With Cepeda and outfielder Willie Mays providing a nearly unstoppable hitting juggernaut, the Giants defeated the Los Angeles Dodgers in a three-game playoff to reach the World Series in 1962, losing to the New York Yankees in seven games. Cepeda reinjured his knee in 1965, playing only 33 games that year, and he was dissatisfied with the Giants' management's support for his recovery. Early in the 1966 season he was traded to the St. Louis Cardinals and quickly returned to form with a .303 batting average and 17 home runs. The following year he achieved the distinction of playing for a world championship team as the Cardinals topped the Boston Red Sox in a thrilling seven-game series even though Cepeda's bat went cold. Cepeda was named the National League's Most Valuable Player.

First Player Signed as Designated Hitter

After the Cardinals lost the 1968 World Series to the Detroit Tigers, squandering a three-games-to-one lead, Cepeda and several other players were traded. Cepeda ended up with the Atlanta Braves, where he joined slugger Henry "Hank" Aaron to lead the team to the National League West divisional title. Cepeda turned in very strong performances with the 1970 Braves, hitting 34 home runs, but he injured his left knee and was sidelined for much of the 1971 and 1972 seasons. Traded to the Oakland Athletics and then released, he was signed to the Boston Red Sox as a designated hitter—then a recent baseball innovation. Cepeda was the first designated hitter signed in baseball history, and the position was tailor-made for Cepeda, who hit 20 home runs for the Red Sox in 1973. That made him the first player in history to hit 20 home runs for four separate teams. After one more season with the Kansas City Royals, Cepeda retired with 379 career home runs and a .297 lifetime batting average.

Cepeda floundered after leaving the baseball diamond. In December of 1975 he was arrested at San Juan International Airport in Puerto Rico after he claimed two boxes that authorities alleged contained 170 pounds of marijuana. He was sentenced to five years in prison. Released after ten months during which his work assignments included cleaning toilets and washing underwear, he found his reputation in shreds in culturally conservative Puerto Rico. He tried to find work in the Los Angeles area but was ejected from Dodger Stadium due to the drug conviction. Cepeda's second marriage dissolved, and he lost custody of his two younger children to his ex-wife, Nydia.

The Nichiren Shoshu sect of Buddhism, to which he was converted partly by singer Tina Turner and jazz musician Herbie Hancock, helped Cepeda in his recovery from this low point. "With Buddhism, I opened up my mind and cleaned it out," Cepeda explained to Bernie Miklasz of the Toronto *Globe & Mail*. "There is a Buddhist phrase—'Change the poison into medicine.' That's what I've tried to do. I took the bad and made it into good." Cepeda embarked on a new career as a lecturer. "I don't lecture by books. I use my life," he told Miklasz. He also worked for the organization Athletes Against AIDS and the I Have a Dream Foundation.

Cepeda was still interested in returning to baseball, however, and in the mid-1980s he began working for the Giants as a community ambassador. The great honor of his life was his induction into the Baseball Hall of Fame in 1999, after years of rejections caused primarily by his drug conviction. Puerto Ricans forgave him as well: a large crowd chanted "Viva Puerto Rico" as he gave his induction speech. In addition to his work for the Giants and his speaking career, he has founded the Cepeda Baseball Clubs, a youth organization where, according to the group's website, "[w]e strive to help our players build that bridge between life and sports."

Books

Cepeda, Orlando, with Herb Fagen, *Baby Bull: From Hardball to Hard Time and Back,* Taylor, 1998.

Contemporary Black Biography, Volume 98, Gale, 2012.

Periodicals

Fresno Bee, June 26, 2006.

Globe & Mail (Toronto, Ontario, Canada), September 8, 1993.

New York Times, February 9, 1989; July 7, 1993; December 12, 1993.

Online

"Cepeda Baseball," *Cepeda Bulls,* http://cepedabaseball.com/ (October 28, 2013).

"Orlando Cepeda: Baby Bull," *JockBio.com,* http://www.jockbio.com/Classic/O_Cepeda/O_Cepeda_bio.html (October 28, 2013).

"From Shame to Frame," *Sports Illustrated,* http://sportsillustrated.cnn.com/vault/article/magazine/MAG1016498/index.htm (October 28, 2013).

"Orlando Manuel Cepeda," *Latino Sports Legends,* http://www.latinosportslegends.com/cepeda.htm (October 28, 2013).□

Giorgio Chinaglia

One of Europe's most magnetic soccer stars of the 1970s, Giorgio Chinagalia (1947-2012) joined the legendary New York Cosmos in 1976 and, with his brazen on-field antics, helped popularize soccer in the United States. Regularly booed by crowds, Chinaglia spent eight years with the New York Cosmos. During that time, he scored 242 goals in 254 games, leading the league in scoring five years and retiring as the North American Soccer League's all-time leading scorer.

Giorgio Chinaglia (Kee-NAHL-yah) was born January 24, 1947, in Carrara, a small town 50 miles northeast of Florence, Italy, best known for its marble quarries. At the time of Chinaglia's birth, Italy suffered from an economic depression touched off by the end of World War II. Like many Italians at the time, Chinaglia's parents were poor. As an infant, Chinaglia lived at his grandmother's house—along with some 25 other relatives, most of them unemployed. He was still a baby when his father, Mario, moved to Wales, England, to work in the iron industry. Initially, his mother, Giovanna, stayed behind but soon joined her husband in England. Chinaglia and his sister remained in Carrara for several years, living under their grandmother's care. Around the time Chinaglia turned

Focus on Sport/Getty Images

nine, he and his sister were summoned to Cardiff, Wales, to join their parents. Chinaglia's father later ran a restaurant.

Began Professional Career in England

Chinaglia started playing soccer as a youngster. He was well-acquainted with the game by the time he moved to England and played on his school soccer team at St. Mary's Catholic School. By the time Chinaglia was 15, scouts showed up at his games. As a teen he signed with Swansea Town, a professional men's team that was part of England's Premier League. As a young apprentice, Chinaglia's duties included team chores like cutting the grass, sweeping the stands, scrubbing the showers, and cleaning the players' cleats. In exchange for his services, Chinaglia got to work out with the team a few days a week. In his four years with Swansea, Chinaglia made only six appearances with the first team, but was the top scorer on the reserve squad.

Chinaglia never hit it off with the Swansea coaches. He reportedly stayed out late playing cards and chasing girls and was regularly fined for showing up late to practice. There was also an incident in which Chinaglia was asked to help spruce up the team's stadium but instead of helping, the hotheaded teen threw a can of paint against the wall. When Chinaglia was 19, Swansea Town let him go. Chinaglia's father quickly arranged a tryout with Massese, an Italian soccer club in Massa, Italy. While Chinaglia—with his long Beatles-style haircut and tight-fitting pants—preferred the British youth culture to that of Italy, he accepted the offer when Massese offered him a Fiat sports car with his contract. Chinaglia joined Massese in June 1966. After the 1966-67 season, Chinaglia made the under-21 Italian team and got to play his first international game in a match against the under-21 Austrian team. Italy won the match 2-1 with Chinagalia putting in the winning goal.

Soon after the match, Chinaglia, an Italian citizen, had to report for mandatory military service. He was sent to Rome, but ended up in military jail after sneaking out one night and getting into a tussle with the officer who caught him. Before Chinaglia finished his military service, Massese traded him to Internapoli, an Italian club based in Naples. He joined them for games during the 1967-68 season, playing on extended weekend passes and furloughs.

Became Standout in Italy

In the summer of 1969, Chinaglia began playing for Lazio, a team based in Rome. Lazio struggled to make an impact and in 1971 hired Tommaso Maestrelli as its new manager. Maestrelli and Chinaglia hit it off well, with Maestrelli adopting an offense that positioned Chinaglia as the first attacking player of the offense. Under Maestrelli's system, Chinaglia never ran back to play defense. Every time Lazio's defenders won the ball from the other team, they passed it to Chinaglia, who hung out 40 yards in front of the other team's goal. During the 1973-74 season, Chinaglia scored 24 goals, leading Lazio to its first championship in Italy's premier Serie A league and winning the Capocannoniere, or top-scorer award.

Ever confident—and often called conceited by the press—Chinaglia was known to taunt members of the opposing team by muttering his own name as he dribbled past opponents. He celebrated his goals in style, flinging his arms into the air and running around the field screaming at the top of his lungs. There was also an incident in 1973 when he taunted fans of the opposing team. It happened during the Coppa Italia cup when Chinaglia's Lazio team was locked in battle with cross-town rival Romanisti. According to Graham Henry of the *South Wales Echo,* Chinaglia scored a goal in the 68th minute to break the tie, then sprinted up into the stands to face the Romanisti fans and shouted, "Look at me. I am Giorgio Chinaglia. I beat you!"

In Lazio, Chinaglia was a local hero. The press followed his every move. Chinaglia liked to joke that when he did something, it ended up on the front page of the paper, whereas the pope was relegated to page 3. During his career with Lazio—from 1969 to 1976—Chinaglia scored 98 goals in 209 appearances. In 2000, when Lazio celebrated its 100th anniversary, Chinaglia was honored as the team's greatest all-time player.

Chinaglia's success as a striker for Lazio led him to be selected for Italy's national team. His international career included many highs and lows. In 1973, Chinaglia was chosen to play for Italy in a friendly match against England held at London's famed Wembley Stadium. As the minutes dwindled in regulation play, the game remained tied at zero. On the attack, Chinaglia beat England's defender Bobby Moore and sent a cross to Fabio Capello, who put in the winning goal. It was a momentous occasion, as Italy had never beat England in all of their matches at Wembley.

In 1974, Chinaglia represented Italy in the World Cup, which was held in West Germany. Substituted during mid-match in a game against Haiti, Chinaglia threw a fit. He insulted the coach with an obscene gesture, then stormed down the tunnel and into the dressing room, where he smashed several bottles of mineral water against the wall. Chinaglia was never chosen to represent Italy again and his international career ended brusquely with 14 appearances and 11 goals.

By 1975, Chinaglia's wife and children were living in New Jersey, with Chinaglia commuting to Rome to play for Lazio. Chinaglia met his wife, Connie Eruzione, around 1970. The daughter of a U.S. Army sergeant, Eruzione was an American citizen. Her family was living in Italy when she met Chinaglia. They married on July 9, 1970. During the summer of 1973, Chinaglia's team had toured the United States. Chinaglia liked the United States and his wife yearned to return home, so they bought a home in Englewood, New Jersey.

Signed with New York Cosmos

In 1976, the 6-foot-1 Chinagalia signed with the New York Cosmos, which enabled him to relocate to New Jersey to be with his family. The fans from Lazio, however, did not want to see him go. On the day of Chinaglia's departure, police informed him that thousands of fans had descended on the airport and were threatening to block his flight. To escape Rome, Chinaglia chartered a private plane to Genoa, then boarded a flight to Paris and, finally, a plane to New York.

When Chinaglia joined the Cosmos, the team was building a collection of aging stars to increase attendance. The team's lead attraction was Brazilian superstar Pele. During his time with the Cosmos, Chinaglia played alongside a star-studded roster that included Germany's Franz Beckenbauer, Dutchman Johan Neeskens and Belgian forward François Van der Elst. While many international soccer stars were migrating to the United States to play in the North American Soccer League, many of them were at the end of their careers. Not yet 30, Chinaglia was still in his prime. The Cosmos' celebrity lineup attracted crowds of 70,000 at Giants Stadium in New Jersey.

Chinaglia played with the Cosmos from 1976 to 1983. During that time, he led the league in scoring five years. Chinaglia scored 193 goals in 213 official matches, was named the league's most valuable player in 1981 and helped the Cosmos win the league championship in 1977, 1978, 1980, and 1982. One of Chinaglia's most remarkable matches occurred in 1980 when he scored a record-setting seven goals during a playoff game against the Tulsa Roughnecks. In that one game alone, Chingalia broke several playoff records, including most goals in a half (5), shortest time between two goals (4 minutes, 48 seconds), and most points in a playoff game (15—two for each goal and one for an assist).

Known as Polemic Player

Despite Chinaglia's formidable foot and uncanny ability to maneuver around defenders, his peers were quick to downplay his success. "He's a great scorer, but he's on a great team." Dallas midfielder Zequinha told author Diane Ackerman in a profile for the *New York Times.* "Put him in Memphis and then see what happens." Some critics attributed Chinaglia's goal-scoring success to his teammates, who were able to deliver the ball to him frequently as he stayed forward in scoring position, rarely retreating to help on defense. *Sports Illustrated's* Clive Gammon noted that Chinaglia had earned a reputation as "Garbage-goal George, finishing off the efforts of players with greater skill and less egotism."

True to form, Chinaglia's hotheadedness caused trouble with teammates, particularly Pelé. Chinaglia once told reporters that Pelé was not playing on all cylinders and another time complained that the Brazilian star had shown up for spring training out of shape. According to Douglas Martin of the *New York Times,* there was also a heated locker-room quarrel between the two. During the argument, Chinaglia criticized Pelé for not passing the ball to him enough and Pelé responded that it was foolish to pass the ball to a teammate who shot from unfeasible angles. Chinaglia responded by jumping from his seat and yelling, "I am Chinaglia! If I shoot from a place, it's because Chinaglia can score from there!"

Needless to say, Latin American soccer fans were not fond of Chinaglia. Chinaglia also infuriated European fans by suggesting that the Cosmos sign some younger American players instead of the aging Beckenbauer. Because of his criticism and his arrogance, Chinaglia was booed with regularity—even in his home stadium. According to the London *Times,* Beckenbauer summed up his teammate this way: "Giorgio is a brilliant player, but he has no career as a diplomat." Chinaglia also raised eyebrows by showing up at postgame press conferences wearing silk robes.

After retiring from the Cosmos in 1983, Chinaglia stayed in the United States, though he served as president of the Lazio club from 1983 to 1985. Chinaglia, who had become a U.S. citizen in 1979, owned a 22-room Mediterranean-style mansion in New Jersey. He later worked as a broadcaster for ESPN and Sirius XM. In 2000, Chinaglia was inducted into the U.S. National Soccer Hall of Fame. He died at his home in Naples, Florida, on April 1, 2012, shortly after undergoing surgery for a heart attack. Chinaglia's body was returned to Italy, where he was buried next to his former Lazio coach, Maestrelli. Well after his departure from the country, Chinaglia remained an icon in Italy and even entered the national lexicon. In Italian, "chinagliata" means uniquely unpredictable.

Books

Chinaglia, Giorgio (with Basil Kane), *Chinaglia!* Simon and Schuster, 1980.

Periodicals

New York Times, May 31, 1981; April 3, 2012.

South Wales Echo (Cardiff, Wales, England), April 3, 2012.

Times (London), April 4, 2012.
Western Mail (Cardiff, Wales, England), April 3, 2012.

Online

"Ciao, Giorgio," ESPN, http://espn.go.com/sports/soccer/story/_/id/7765419/david-hirshey-says-goodbye-giorgio-chinaglia (November 1, 2013).
"What A Night for Giorgio!," *SI Vault,* http://sportsillustrated.cnn.com/vault/article/magazine/MAG1123766/1/index.htm (November 2, 2013).□

Colley Cibber

English actor, playwright, poet, and theater manager Colley Cibber (1671–1757) is best known for his encompassing autobiography that depicted stage life in his era and for his revised version of William Shakespeare's *Richard III,* which became a template for future productions. However, important contemporaries considered him foolish, despite his literary prolificacy and his comedic talents. When he became England's Poet Laureate in 1730, the appointment generated passionate disapproval.

Hulton Archive/Getty Images

Colley Cibber enjoyed success—and endured denunciation—as an actor, playwright, poet, and theater manager. Personal accomplishments were somewhat overshadowed by his revised version of William Shakespeare's play *Richard III,* which his contemporaries considered a "bowderlization"—that is, a taking of liberty to remove important parts of a work to serve the general tastes of the public. Indeed, Cibber was not above pandering to the crowd.

Cibber's contemporaries, such as Alexander Pope (1688–1744), a poet and influential literary critic, considered his revisions to be hubris—or an arrogant, overbearing display of pride of one's own talents. In fairness to the often maligned Cibber, his edited version of *Richard III* became the *de reguere* for the play's subsequent productions. Centuries after Cibber's perceived blasphemy, famed actor Sir Laurence Olivier was guided in part by Cibber's editing when he produced a highly regarded 1955 film version of the Shakespearean play. Cibber's interpretation is how modern audiences came to view Richard III: twisted in mind and body, totally villainous, but above all a humorous bad guy who delighted in his own devious schemes.

Cibber, indeed, liked humor. In his own plays, he often willingly took on the part of a fool. Contemporaries felt this suited him well. But he was not quite the dolt that they made him out to be. He actually did display talent. His entertaining autobiography, *Apology for the Life of Mr. Colley Cibber, Comedian, and the Late Patentee of the Theatre-Royal With an Historical View of the Stage During His Own Time,* published in 1740, was considered—and is still considered—an insightful, humorous, and compellingly readable account of the theater. Not only did it depict a past theatrical era, it was a seminal work; even up to the twenty-first century, it represented a tradition of actor memoirs that recounted personal observances and anecdotal accounts of "treading the boards." English actor Peter O'Toole's enormously successful three-part autobiography *Loitering with Intent*—started in 1995—could be considered part of this tradition. But Cibber's autobiography also provided a textbook study of the art of acting as it then existed.

Also, Cibber advanced the direction of staged plays in his time. With at least one of his works—*Love's Last Shift; or The Fool in Fashion*—Cibber fashioned a stage genre: sentimental comedy. This type of entertainment would endure on the English stage for nearly a hundred years. Eventually, the style fell out of favor. It was no fault of Cibber's, though: he merely catered to current audience tastes. And the genre never truly died; consider episodes of 1970s sitcoms such as *Three's Company,* which included misunderstandings that led to ribald dialogue.

Cibber was a high-profile actor in his time, though often criticized for his portrayals. In twentieth century theater parlance, he would be considered "hammy." But he was still a governing force in the 18th century theatrical landscape. He not only acted, but as a theatrical manager, he selected plays, and he even wrote plays that, at the time, were considered a degree better than the existing average. His contemporary playwrights may have produced better works, and contemporary actors may have offered far better performances, but it was hard to match Cibber when it came to success in all areas of the theater. Further, his longevity far exceeded anyone else in his time: His career lasted longer than fifty seasons on the London stage. Still, Cibber's career coat was stained through politics, which he had little control over, and devious machinations, in which he too willingly engaged.

Born in London

Colley Cibber was born in London, England, on November 6, 1671. He was the oldest child of Caius Gabriel Cibber, a renowned Danish sculptor. His mother was the well-heeled heiress Jane Colley (who was Cibber's father's second wife). Early on, during his formal education, Cibber demonstrated a talent for writing that endeared him to his teachers. But this early recognition alienated him from his schoolmates—the first of many personality-based conflicts that would follow Cibber throughout his life.

For instance, even parental connections could not secure him a most advantageous educational placement. Cibber was educated at the King's School at Grantham in Lincolnshire. Education for the precocious Cibber began in 1682, but when he was 16 years old, he did not qualify for Winchestor College, an educational institution founded by his maternal ancestor, William of Wykeham (1324–1404). Rejection—one can imagine that it was injury added to insult—was apparently based on his father's failure to provide the institution with a promised statue of William of Wykeham. So, Cibber remained at Grantham. While the young scholar appeared unready to make a mark in letters of public service, he achieved early notice by writing odes about the death of Charles II and the coronation of James II.

Cibber's rejection from Winchestor College greatly disappointed his father, who hoped that his son would become a cleric. However, Cibber reportedly found the rejection a welcomed diversion, as he had entertained hopes of a theatrical career. He was now free to pursue his chosen path. But his aim was temporarily diverted when war broke out within England. The underlying cause of the conflict was the abdication of James II, which led to a claim to the title by William of Orange. This, in turn, led to the so-called "Glorious Revolution" of 1688. Cibber and his father sided with William, fighting under the Devonshire flag. But the seemingly under-achieving Cibber proved unable to earn an army commission. When his nation's fighting ended, he continued serving Devonshire for a short time in London, where he inserted himself into the theatrical circles, establishing a friendship with John Downes, a prominent theater figure.

Joined Theatre Company

Cibber's ambitions and early connections gained him entrance into an arena in which he hoped to thrive, even if his efforts only offered him the merest compensation. In February 1690, Cibber joined the United Company at the Theatre Royal, on an unpaid probation status. His first roles were small: He played a servant in Thomas Southerne's play *Sir Anthony Love.* For the next several years, he played in similar small roles. Essentially these roles were what the profession later termed as "spear carriers." But he experienced his big break in 1694, when he took the place of aging actor Edward Kynaston (1640–1712) in *The Double Dealer,* a comedy written by William Congreve (1670–1729). Cibber's performance garnered some positive reviews.

An ensuing rift within the United Company—popular actor Thomas Betterton and other important leading actors left for Lincoln's Inn Fields—allowed Cibber to seize new opportunities via acting and writing. With the Theatre Royal, he would write prologues, and his performance as "Fondlewife" in Congreve's *The Old Bachelor* garnered him more positive reviews. He then began writing plays that provided him with larger roles. These included *Love's Last Shift* (1696) and *The Relapse* (1697). In these works, he played "Sir Novetly Fashion" and "Lord Foppington," respectively, and the roles helped develop his reputation as a stage comedian. Character titles, particularly *Fondlewife,* left little to the imagination, as was par for the course in this period of theatrical history. In his autobiography, Cibber indicated that the only way for him to gain important stage roles was to write his own plays. In this way, he established a career not only as an actor and but as a playwright.

Soon, Cibber also became an influential figure beyond just the stage boards. In 1700, he began serving as an advisor to Christopher Rich (1657–1714) in the management of the Drury Lane Theatre in London. Rich, a former lawyer, gained a share in the management of the Theatre Royal. By 1704, Cibber—who had just written another well-received comedy *The Careless Husband*—gained a five-year contract for acting and management. Four years later, Cibber benefited from the uniting of the Drury Lane and Haymarket companies: He became one of three managers of the Drury Lane Theatre. A year later, Cibber and other actors secretly plotted to subvert Rich's power by moving to the Haymarket and shutting down the Drury Lane Theater. That shutdown lasted until 1712. It was just one of Cibber' power plays.

Appointed Poet Laureate

Cibber staged his next major play in 1717, *The Non-Juror.* The work was controversial, as it exploited the strong feelings generated by the 1715 Jacobite uprising fostered by supporters of James II and the Stuart royal line. The play portrayed Whig principles in a positive light. This gained Cibber the approval of the Hanoverian monarchy, a faction that would appoint him England's Poet Laurate in 1730. The appointment was certainly nothing less than a political reward, as Cibber demonstrated little talent when it came to writing poetry, a fact that relegated him to merely a subject of scholarly research, and not a figure of importance when it came to that literary art form.

At the time, his appointment as Poet Laureate was considered a scandal. Among the literati, far better poets plied their feathered pens. Also, Cibber made important enemies. These included Pope, whose *Essay on Criticism* remained a subject of study in twentieth century college literary courses; Henry Fielding (1707–1754), who produced the early English novels *Joseph Andrews* and *The*

History of Tom Jones, A Foundling, now considered seminal classics; and Samuel Johnson (1709–1784), the highly esteemed biographer, essayist, literary critic, and lexicographer. Johnson's *The History of Rasselas, the Prince of Abisinnia* is considered the equal of Jonathan Swift's *Gulliver's Travels* and Miguel de Cervantes's *The Ingenious Gentleman Don Quixote of La Mancha* as far as humor and insight into the human condition. Cibber's works came nowhere near that level, as his main purpose was merely to entertain. This Shakespeare did well, and Cibber did too, but his works could be considered the modern equivalent of a television sitcom episode: popular and laugh inducing, but not a literary hallmark.

During his career, Cibber would either write original plays or revise already existing texts. Revisions included editing tragic plays. But his specialty was comedy and he enjoyed placing himself in the role of ridiculous, foppish characters. The comedies he wrote were considered his major works, while his revisions were often considered a defilement of classic works. His revision of Shakespeare's works were deemed as sacrilege. To place his efforts in historical context, however, during Cibber's time, Shakespearean plays had yet to be afforded the reverence now granted. As such, Cibber's revision of *Richard III* became an accepted norm. Indeed, the basic template he provided existed for about 150 years.

As for his own work, no one could seriously regard him as Shakespeare's equal, but Cibber was as prolific as "The Bard." He churned out at least 26 original or revised works. His last play, *Papal Tyranny in the Reign of King John* was considered a "bastardization" of Shakespeare's *King John.*

Along with the aforementioned plays, Cibber's major works included *Love Makes a Man* (1700), *She Wou'd and She Wou'd Not* (1702), *The Double Gallant* (1707), *Three Hours After Marriage,* and *The Provok'd Husband* (1728). As the titles indicate, these works involved comedic misunderstandings and the resulting romantic mishaps. Among his works, *The Careless Husband* even gained the grudging praise of the highly critical Pope.

But Cibber's crowning achievement was perhaps his autobiography, which proved popular with both critics and the reading public alike. The *apology* phrase in the title did not indicate regret for past actions; rather, in the parlance of the times, it meant a defense of actions taken. The work was certainly self aggrandizing, but it was also full of gossip and insights into theater history and the art of acting. It included humorous—if apocryphal—anecdotes and a tendency toward endearing self promotion. Indeed, it was a vain piece of writing, and it was filled with inaccuracies, but the work remains of interest as a resource for theater historical research and a groundbreaker for a literary genre, the actor autobiography. Even the hard-to-please Johnson reluctantly endorsed the work.

Omitted Family from Autobiography

Interestingly, the autobiography completely ignores Cibber's wife and family, which underscores his self-absorbed personality: He has been described as "tactless, rude, and supremely self-confident." For the record, Cibber married Katherine Shire on May 6, 1693. Apparently, their love for each other was as lusty as an early English novel, for the couple would have 12 children, born between 1694 and 1713. Sadly, though, six died in infancy. Late in his life, his much beloved daughter Catherine took care of the failing Cibber, who suffered health problems following his wife's death in 1734. Catherine inherited most of the Cibber estate.

Cibber died in 1757, and his death generated little notice, which this vainglorious man no doubt would have considered the ultimate insult. However, for more than 50 years after his passing, Cibber's plays continued to be staged. Today, his life—as depicted by biographer Helene Koon—and his observations, which he recorded in his autobiography, provide valuable insight about the development of the western art of theater.

Books

Adams, W. Davenport, *A Dictionary of the Drama,* J.B. Lippincott Company, 1904.

Cibber, Colley, *Apology for the Life of Mr. Colley Cibber, Comedian, and the Late Patentee of the Theatre-Royal With an Historical View of the Stage During His Own Time,* Dover, 2003.

International Dictionary of Theatre, (Volume 2), Gale, 1993.

Koon, Helene, *Colley Cibber: A Biography,* University Press of Kentucky, 1986.

Online

"Colley Cibber," *Encyclopedia Britannica,* http://www.britannica.com/EBchecked/topic/117512/Colley-Cibber (November 22, 2013).

"Colley Cibber," *IMDb,* http://www.imdb.com/name/nm1410377/bio?ref_=nm_ov_bio_sm (November 22, 2013).

"Colley Cibber," *NNDB,* http://www.nndb.com/people/203/000101897/ (November 22, 2013).

"Colley Cibber," *TheatreHistory.com,* http://www.theatrehistory.com/british/cibber001.html (November 22, 2013).

"Colley Cibber," *The Twickenham Museum,* http://www.twickenham-museum.org.uk/detail.asp?ContentID=229 (November 22, 2013).□

Liviu Ciulei

Romania's Liviu Ciulei (1923–2011) was one of the pioneering figures in twentieth century drama as a director and set designer. The former head of a Bucharest theater company, Ciulei came to the United States in the 1970s after having made his name as a daring reinterpreter of Shakespearean classics. *New York Times* theater critic Richard Eder hailed him as "one of the great contemporary theater directors" after Ciulei made his New York directing debut. "Ciulei brings a sense of the civilization of the Western world to our theater, and that is a precious and not at all a common thing," Eder asserted.

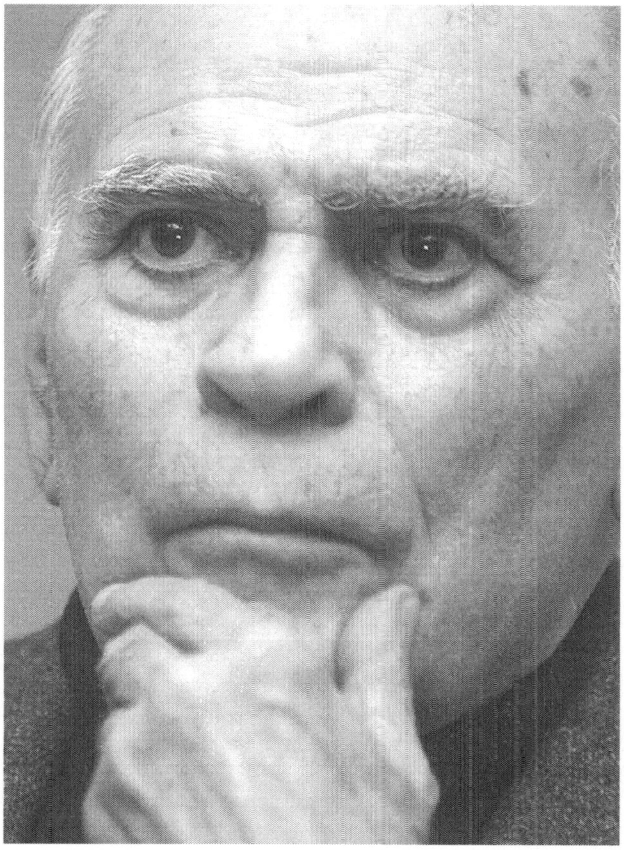

RAVZAN CHIRITA/AFP/Getty Images

Liviu Ioan Ciulei was born on July 7, 1923, in Bucharest, the Romanian capital. His father was an architect and owner of a building company, and Ciulei originally trained as an architect. He favored the performing arts, however, and entered Bucharest's Royal Conservatory of Music and Theater. Romania's monarchy was not to last much longer by that point: during World War II the Central European nation became a fascist dictatorship allied with Nazi Germany, then switched sides in 1944. Troops from the Soviet Union remained on Romanian soil in the war's aftermath, and the country became a socialist republic in 1947.

Began Career as Actor

Ciulei began his career as an actor with his 1946 stage debut at the Odeon Theater in Bucharest, one of the city's leading venues. He played Puck in a production of Shakespeare's *A Midsummer Night's Dream*. For the next decade he appeared with the Teatrul Municipal, a new theater company in Bucharest headed by Lucia Sturdza Bulandra, an actor and its first artistic director. After a decade on the stage—and working on sets and costumes at the company, too—he made his directorial debut with a 1957 staging of a Romanian-language version of N. Richard Nash's Broadway hit *The Rainmaker,* an import that enjoyed surprising international success.

Romania had a long and proud tradition of producing and nurturing particularly gifted theater professionals who went on to wider renown. Eugène Ionesco began his career there and though his later works were written in French, Ionesco's plays are considered part of the country's modernist literary legacy. Before Ionesco there was Costache Caragiale, a playwright who served as director of the first National Theater in the 1850s. Ciulei belonged to a generation who started to adapt classic plays into modern settings. At the Teatrul Municipal, Ciulei first made his mark with a daring adaptation of Shakespeare's *As You Like It* in 1961, a production in which he also appeared—in the role of melancholy Jacques—and designed the sets. In 1963 he was named the new artistic director of the Teatrul Bulandra, the newly renamed Teatrul Municipal, following Bulandra's death. He also ventured into filmmaking with *The Waves of the Danube* in 1959.

Romania remained a socialist republic, and like other national theaters in Eastern Europe during the Cold War era, the plays of Shakespeare were deemed mostly safe to stage, as were works from approved left-leaning writers. The dramas of Russian playwright Maxim Gorky were frequently staged, or Bertolt Brecht's droll musical the *Threepenny Opera,* which satirized the fatuous bourgeoisie and their institutions of power. Ciulei's star rose inside Romania and then he began to gain notice in the West. His career trajectory almost mirrored that of Romania's Communist Party leader Nicolae Ceauşescu. Taking over the party apparatus in 1965, Ceauşescu worked to modernize the country while pursing more cordial diplomatic relations with the West as he rebuffed the Soviet Union's attempts at imposition.

Feted at Cannes

Ciulei's third feature film, *Forest of the Hanged,* was a sensation when it premiered at the Cannes Film Festival in France in the spring of 1965. Based on a 1922 Romanian novel whose original title was *Padurea Spânzuratilor, Forest of the Hanged* revealed the psychological torment experienced by a soldier who is forced to take part in a firing squad and kill a comrade for desertion during World War I. Ciulei won the Best Director honors at Cannes, and the film was also nominated for the prestigious Palme d'Or.

The Ceauşescu regime initially welcomed such publicity and courted drama critics from the West to visit Bucharest and see the sharply modernist versions of classics that stage directors like Ciulei were making. *Times* of London writer Henry Popkin was among those who hailed Romania's current theater scene as among the most exciting in Europe, as did *New York Times* writer Irving Wardler. In 1971 Ciulei made his foreign directorial debut on the stage of a glittery annual cultural event in Scotland, the Edinburgh Festival. He staged *Leonce and Lena* there in August, and his updating of the satire from Georg Büchner won enthusiastic acclaim. The London *Times* theater critic Michael Billington remarked that the Teatrul Bulandra's reputation preceded it in Edinburgh, and enthused over the staging of the Büchner work, which dated back to 1836. "Ciulei's palimpsest of a production is held together partly by its own organic vitality and partly by a towering central performance by" the Romanian lead, Ion Caramitru, whom Billington compared to a young Ian McKellen. "I only hope we shall have a chance to see this splendid company again."

Forced into Exile

The drama critic's hopes were short-lived. In 1972, after a staging of the famous Russian satire *The Inspector General*—a Nikolai Gogol play set in tsarist Russia—that veered too close to truth in Ceauşescu's increasingly authoritarian state, Ciulei was removed from his post at the Bulandra. He was forced to leave the country to work, and was fortunate in that he was permitted to do so. Zelda Fichandler, at the time the artistic director at the Arena Stage in Washington, D.C., invited him to stage *Leonce and Lena* there in 1974. Another influential supporter for Ciulei was Alan Schneider, an esteemed stage director in New York who was skilled at producing darkly modern new works. Schneider had won the Tony Award for Best Director of a Drama a few years before for Edward Albee's classic *Who's Afraid of Virginia Woolf?* Schneider helped Ciulei find steady work in the United States, beginning with a 1977 production of Frank Wedekind's *Spring Awakening* with senior-level students of the Juilliard School. It went on to a wider stage in the summer of 1978 when Joseph Papp's respected Public Theater mounted a production with Ciulei as director.

Ciulei has one legitimate Broadway credit, for a 1978 staging of *The Inspector General* at the Circle in the Square playhouse. He worked again at the Arena Stage that year, too, putting together a new version of *Hamlet* that moved the action from medieval Denmark to late-imperialist Germany. "His work with actors is extraordinary," declared Eder, the *New York Times* critic. "He draws performances from them that make the most of their abilities and sometimes, it seems, more than that."

Ciulei even ventured into opera, creating the sets for a little-seen but infamously racy tale of infidelity and murder, *Lady Macbeth of Mtsensk,* a work by Russian composer Dmitri Shostakovitch dating back to 1934. Ciulei also directed this production, which enjoyed a resurgence at the 1980 Spoleto Festival in Italy, and came to the United States three years later at the Lyric Opera in Chicago, again under Ciulei's direction, and then was staged in New York at the Juilliard American Opera Center in 1984. By then Ciulei had taken a position at the respected Tyrone Guthrie Theater in Minneapolis, Minnesota, considered one of the top regional theater companies in the United States.

Brought Daring Sensibility to Classics

Ciulei's half-decade at the Guthrie was an exuberant period of creativity for the Romanian émigré. His first major production there was a reworking of *The Tempest* in 1981, the Shakespeare saga about an exiled ruler and his desire for revenge. In Ciulei's staging, Prospero's island is a parcel of land surrounded by a moat of blood in which artifacts representing Western culture bobble by. "The symbolism is straightforward," contended a new *New York Times* theater critic, Frank Rich. "Man's noble attempts to create a beautiful and humane civilization have always, finally, been drowned in the blood of wars." Rich went on to describe the actors as "first-rate," but remarked that "it is most of all Mr. Ciulei who fills this 'Tempest' with the stuff of dreams—and then, with equal force, cracks Shakespeare's fantasy open to show us the bottomless melancholy that lies within."

Utilized Architectural Training

Ciulei often put his training as an architect to use in creating sets and renovating playhouses. He redesigned the Guthrie stage, which permitted more flexibility in its productions, and during Ciulei's tenure the Minneapolis venue won the Regional Theater Tony Award in 1982, given to an outstanding company outside of Broadway's purview. His tenure at the Guthrie came to a close in 1985, after which he worked in New York City for the New York Shakespeare Festival presented by the Public Theater. He staged a controversial production of *Hamlet* with a young Kevin Kline in the lead role, and *A Midsummer Night's Dream* that featured music from contemporary composer Philip Glass. He also taught stagecraft and drama directing to students at Columbia University and New York University.

Returned to Romania

In late 1989 Nicolae Ceauşescu's detested regime came to a swift and justifiably brutal end, and Ciulei was eventually invited to return to his post at the Teatrul Bulandra, whose stage he redesigned. He worked almost into his eighties, with his last U.S. directing credit at the Lucille Lortel Theater in 2002 in its staging of *Andorra,* the Max Frisch play. Twice married and divorced, Ciulei divided his final years between Bucharest and Munich, Germany, where he died on October 24, 2011, at the age of 88. His son Thomas, by his marriage to film critic Helga Reiter-Ciulei, became a filmmaker and producer in Romania. Another protégé of Ciulei's was Andrei Serban, whom he had mentored in the 1960s at the Bulandra and who also went into exile in the United States during the Ceauşescu regime. "Ciulei gave us the courage to free our imaginations and seek to satisfy a spiritually starved audience, taking refuge from the gray life under communism," wrote Serban in an obituary tribute that ran in *American Theater.*

Ciulei's career in film might have eclipsed his theater work had the timing been more fortuitous. His 1965 saga *Forest of the Hanged* was his final film, and at Cannes it was bested for the festival's top Palme d'Or honor by a frothy mod-London farce called *The Knack... And How to Get It* by Richard Lester, who made the musical comedies featuring the Beatles. Ciulei claimed the final scene of *Forest of the Hanged* was the favorite concocted moment of his entire career, he once said, according to his *New York Times* obituary. "We see a young peasant woman preparing the last meal for the man she loves who is sentenced to death by hanging—a man, a woman, bread, salt and wine, love, life and death."

Periodicals

American Theater, January 2012.
New York Times, June 12, 1971; July 23, 1978; April 7, 1979; August 20, 1980; July 4, 1981; March 30, 1986; October 6, 1991; October 27, 2011.
Star-Tribune (Minneapolis, MN), October 26, 2011.
Times (London, England), June 21, 1966; July 19, 1969; September 1, 1971.□

Jimmy Cliff

Michael Ochs Archies/Getty Images

Jamaican singer Jimmy Cliff (born 1948) was the first artist to popularize the reggae genre internationally, and the 1972 film *The Harder They Come,* in which he starred and for which he composed some of the music, remains an icon of the rough-and-tumble environment in which reggae emerged.

"My role has always been as the shepherd of reggae music," Cliff was quoted as saying by the Rock and Roll Hall of Fame, which inducted him in 2010 and made him the first native Jamaican artist so honored. "When they wanted to bring reggae to America, they sent Jimmy Cliff. When they wanted to bring reggae to England, they sent Jimmy Cliff. When they wanted to bring reggae to Africa, they sent Jimmy Cliff." During a long apprenticeship in London, Cliff was groomed for international stardom by producer and recording executive Chris Blackwell, one of the pioneers of world music. In the 1970s, Cliff's music was eclipsed somewhat by that of the simultaneously more political and more mystical Bob Marley, and Marley's early death turned him into a legend. But Cliff continued to record, scoring several more reggae hits and experimenting with other genres over a long career that has also included acting.

Grew Up in Poverty

Jimmy Cliff was born James Chambers in Jamaica on April 1, 1948. His birthplace has sometimes been given as St. Catherine, near Kingston, but he stated in a version of his website biography that he had been told he was born in Adelphi Land in western Jamaica's Somerton district, in the highlands east of Montego Bay. The eighth of nine children, he was raised by his father and grandmother in a strict Pentecostal home with three bedrooms. The family was poor. "Everybody comes into this planet in some kind of way—it has something to do with how we are," Cliff told Nick Hasted of the London *Independent.* "I was born in a hurricane."

Cliff once recalled being told that he had come out of the womb singing, and he made his debut performing in church at age six. In his early years, he had to defy his family's religious restrictions. "I was supposed to be singing the songs of the church, but I was singing things like calypso songs," he recalled to Nick McGrath of the London *Guardian.* "There was a song called Water the Garden and it wasn't about watering the garden—it was about sex, so I couldn't let dad hear it. But if one of my bigger brothers heard me, he'd say, 'OK, I'm going to tell on you,' . . . and then they said: 'You go and do my chores today.'"

When he was 12, he went to Kingston, by himself, with the plan of attending technical school and escaping a life of farm labor. He was already hoping to become a performer, though, and soon after settling in an East Kingston boarding house he began entering talent shows and trying to persuade producers to record him. He had little success until he sang a song for Chinese-Jamaican record store and restaurant operator Leslie Kong praising Kong's establishment, Beverley's. Kong agreed to record Cliff, who took that stage name in reference to his high aspirations and to his highland home. Forming the Beverley label, Kong (also the first to record Bob Marley) released Cliff's "Hurricane Hattie," which became a hit in 1962.

Several more Cliff singles, including "King of Kings," "Miss Jamaica," and "Pride and Passion," became classics of Jamaica's ska music scene, which also had a strong following in Britain. Cliff performed at the 1964 New York World's Fair as a representative of Jamaica, moved to Paris for a time, and then, at Blackwell's urging, settled in Britain for several years. With an eye toward attracting a wider audience for Jamaican music, he wrote songs that included progressive rock elements. Cliff released his debut album, the highly regarded *Hard Road to Travel,* on Island in 1968.

That LP spawned the major Brazilian hit "Waterfall," and Cliff headed for South America to tour with Brazilian songwriter Gilberto Gil.

Influenced Simon's Move to Reggae

Cliff followed that album with *Wonderful World, Beautiful People,* which was titled *Jimmy Cliff* in the United Kingdom. The album's title track, which was a reworking of the Cat Stevens hit "Wild World," reached the British top 10 and the American top 25, and the protest song "Viet Nam" was praised by American folk-rock songwriter Bob Dylan, among others. Another single "Many Rivers to Cross," became a reggae standard. American pop star Paul Simon was inspired by Cliff to take a sharp turn in the direction of reggae; he headed for Kingston to record his single "Mother and Child Reunion" with Kong and members of Cliff's band. Cliff was thrown off balance by Kong's sudden death in 1971 but bounced back with the album *Another Cycle* later that year.

Before he died, Kong suggested that Cliff contribute songs to an upcoming film, *The Harder They Come,* written and directed by Jamaican filmmaker Perry Henzell. After hearing Cliff's songs, Henzell asked Cliff to star in the film as well. It was easy to see why—the film's story concerned a young man, Ivan, who comes from the Jamaican countryside to Kingston with hopes of becoming a singer and then becomes ensnared in the activities of the capital's organized crime gangs, and it closely paralleled Cliff's own life. The film was only moderately successful but became an underground hit and a staple of college film societies for many years to come.

The Harder They Come was released as an album on Island's Mango imprint in 1973, and included the irresistible title track as well as several other Cliff compositions, some of which had appeared on previous releases. Like the film, it built slowly. By March of 1975 the album had entered *Billboard* magazine's album sales chart in the United States, and it generated another Cliff classic, "You Can Get It If You Really Want," which had already been a hit for fellow Jamaican Desmond Dekker. Cliff seemed poised for international success.

Recorded Protest Song

Two months later, Marley and his band the Wailers released *Natty Dread,* the first of their albums to appear in the U.S., and the attention of reggae fans shifted toward Marley. There were several reasons for this, Marley's gift for capturing the essential themes of reggae in simple terms primary among them. Cliff tried several new directions in the middle and late 1970s, a period during which he converted to Islam for a time. Leaving Island, he recorded for the Reprise label and experimented with spiritual ideas on the album *Follow My Mind* and political ones on *Give Thanx* (1978), which contained the protest anthem "Stand Up and Fight Back."

Cliff returned to a rootsier reggae style with the 1981 album *Give the People What They Want* and with *Special* in 1983. The latter was the first of a series of albums he recorded for the Columbia label. He gradually became more involved with Rastafarianism, telling Richard Ouzounian of the *Toronto Star* that "If you look at the major monotheistic religions of the world, you will see that there is much violence in their history. But Rasta is not a religion. It is a spiritual movement that came reborn to keep the peace in the world, to appeal to the conscience of the world." For the albums *The Power and the Glory* (1983) and *Cliff Hanger* (1985) Cliff collaborated with the R&B group Kool and the Gang. The latter album earned a Grammy award for Best Reggae Album.

Continuing to benefit from his work in films, Cliff appeared opposite comedian Robin Williams in *Club Paradise* in 1985, and in the 1990 thriller *Marked for Death.* The soundtrack for the 1993 film *Cool Runnings,* about an unlikely Jamaican team of bobsledders, yielded another Cliff hit, a remake of the ska classic "I Can See Clearly Now." "Acting has always been my first love," Cliff told Ouzounian. "When you see me perform my music, that's me. But when I'm acting, I'm becoming someone other than myself and oh, I love that." Cliff continued to record through the 1990s and 2000s, mostly for small Jamaican labels.

Cliff received two major honors in his later years: the Jamaican Order of Merit (one of Jamaica's highest civilian honors) in 2003, and induction into the Rock and Roll Hall of Fame in 2010. In 2012, with his career entering its sixth decade, Cliff released the *Rebirth* album on the major Universal label; the album was produced by the much younger American punk musician Tim Armstrong. As of 2013, Cliff was planning a return to acting in the form of a sequel to *The Harder They Come.*

Books

Contemporary Black Biography, Volume 92, Gale, 2011.

Periodicals

Electronic Musician, September 2012.

Guardian (London, England), July 20, 2012.

Independent (London, England), September 5, 2003; July 28, 2012.

Toronto Star, February 22, 2009.

Sunday Herald (Glasgow, Scotland), April 22, 2001.

Online

"Bio," Jimmy Cliff Official Website, http://www.jimmycliff.com/home (September 7, 2013).

"Biography: Jimmy Cliff," *Reggaeville,* http://www.reggaeville.com/nc/artist-details/artist/jimmy-cliff/ac/biography.html (September 7, 2013).

"Jimmy Cliff," "Leslie Kong," *AllMusic,* http://www.allmusic.com (September 7, 2013).

"Jimmy Cliff Biography," *Rock and Roll Hall of Fame,* http://rockhall.com/inductees/jimmy-cliff/bio/y (September 7, 2013).

"Leslie Kong's Reggae Pioneer,"l *Jamaica Observer,* http://www.jamaicaobserver.com/Entertainment/Leslie-Kong-s-reggae-pioneer_11989294 (September 7, 2013).□

Sam Cooke

The African American vocalist Sam Cooke (1931–1964) was a pioneer in bringing African American vocal styles into the American popular musical mainstream.

Beginning his career in African American gospel music, Cooke transferred vocal techniques from that field to secular popular songs, many of them of his own composition. For that reason, he is considered one of the founders of soul music, in which such sacred-secular mixtures are common. But equally important were Cooke's pop instincts. Other African American vocalists, such as Nat "King" Cole, had achieved wide popularity among white audiences, but few had done so with material rooted directly in the African American tradition. Suave and photogenic, Cooke showed with a series of hits like 1962's "Bring It on Home to Me" that it was possible to appeal to audiences across the board with songs based on models from the African American musical tradition. Cooke established his own record label, publishing company, and management company, taking control of his own career in a way that few other African American artists of his time succeeded in doing.

Gilles Petard/redferns/Getty Images

Raised in Religious Household

Cooke was born Sam Cook on January 22, 1931, in Clarksdale, Mississippi; he added the "e" to the end of his name as an adult performer. His father was a minister in the Holiness church, and during Cooke's childhood movies and watching sports were forbidden in the household; church services or preparation for them took up most of the weekend anyhow. The Rev. Charles Cook Sr. moved to Chicago in 1933, worked in a metal plant, and became a minister at a Holiness church in suburban Chicago Heights. Once established, he sent for his family. Cooke grew up in the South Side Chicago neighborhood of Bronzeville. He excelled as a student at the city's Wendell Phillips High School but also had an obstreperous side, sometimes tearing down fence slats in neighbors' backyards and then selling them back to their unfortunate owners as firewood.

Music was in Cooke's blood from the start, and he, along with two brothers and two sisters, formed a gospel quintet called The Singing Children that graduated beyond local church appearances to paying gigs. When he was 15, Cook joined a gospel quartet called the Highway QC's and began to make waves with his soaring lead vocals. The group's career was interrupted when Cooke was sentenced to 90 days in the Cook County Jail for the crime of giving a salacious book to one of his girlfriends at school. When he returned to the group, however, they resumed their ascent, performing at New Bethel Baptist Church in Detroit and its pastor, the Rev. C.L. Franklin, and his daughter Aretha.

The Highway QC's were modeled closely on the leading black gospel quartet of the day, the Soul Stirrers, and when that group's lead vocalist slot fell open in 1951, Cooke was asked to accept it. Joining the group, Cooke took home a salary of $50 a week. They encountered overt racism while touring in the segregated South. Signed to the Specialty label by its white, Jewish owner Art Rupe, the group recorded numerous gospel singles in Los Angeles in the early 1950s, including "Peace in the Valley" and "Jesus Paid the Debt." For some devotees of Cooke's singing, these recordings represented his finest hours as an artist. On tour, too, Cooke was successful, proving an especially strong draw among young women who otherwise had little interest in gospel music. In the words of Gene Santoro, writing in *The Nation,* "Like Aretha Franklin, whom he knew well and with whom he performed as both a young gospeler and a pop artist, Sam Cooke was one of the clearest embodiments of the tension between the sacred and the secular that continues to define the American political and cultural landscapes."

Released Secular Single Under Pseudonym

In his gospel recordings, Cooke developed a set of unusual vocal techniques, including a yodel-like jump around high notes that came into sharp relief when backed by the Soul Stirrers' harmony singing. Specialty producer Robert "Bumps" Blackwell realized that Cooke's vocal style was tailor-made for pop and rock music, and Cooke himself had reached similar conclusions. Under the name Dale Cook he released a single, "Lovable," that he had written himself, claiming that Dale Cook was his brother when fans instantly identified his singing. The problem was that gospel fans refused to accept artists who crossed over to secular music, and the Soul Stirrers were booed during appearances with Cooke at the helm.

Undaunted, Cooke signed with a small label called Keen and released the single "You Send Me" in the fall of 1957. A gentle piece of romantic pop distinguished by Cooke's effortless upper register, the song topped both rhythm and blues and pop charts and made Cooke an instant star among both black and white audiences. The Specialty label pressed Cooke and Blackwell for a share of the profits, claiming that the song had been written while Cook was under contract to that label, but Cooke avoided a lawsuit by crediting the song to an actual brother, L.C. Cook.

Such problems, along with the long history of exploitation of African American artists, convinced Cooke that he had to take financial control of his own career. In 1958 he entered into a partnership with gospel singer J.W. Alexander in the KAGS music publishing firm, using it as the publisher for his own compositions and ensuring that he would receive royalties from them. Cooke, Alexander, and S. Roy Crain joined to create the SAR record label in 1959. Cooke was active with the label not only as a recording artist but also as a producer and artist-and-repertoire talent spotter, helping to launch the careers of Bobby Womack, Billy Preston, and other artists. Motown Records founder Berry Gordy is often cited as a pioneer among African American music executives, but Cooke anticipated many of his innovations by several years.

Although Cooke's career was continuing to develop—in 1959, he toured with vocalist Jackie Wilson and drew huge crowds that in at least one case broke down Southern regulations that required blacks and whites in concert audiences to be divided from each other—his personal life was difficult. In 1958, his marriage to Dolores Mohawk ended in divorce, and several other women filed paternity suits against him; Mohawk killed herself by driving into a tree. Cooke himself was almost killed in an auto accident. In 1959, Cooke married childhood sweetheart Barbara Campbell, with whom he had already had a daughter, Linda. This marriage, too, was troubled.

Signed to RCA

In 1960, Cooke was signed to RCA, becoming only the second African American (after Harry Belafonte) signed to the venerable label; his manager, Allen Klein, later negotiated a deal whereby RCA would distribute SAR product—a common arrangement in the later history of urban music, but rare or unprecedented at the time. RCA's added promotional muscle, together with Cooke's increasingly timely commercial instincts and smooth pop productions showcasing Cooke's vocals brought the singer a string of hits that have remained popular evergreens: "Chain Gang" (1960), "Cupid" (1961), "Twistin' the Night Away," and "Havin' a Party," and "Bring It on Home to Me" (1962), and "Another Saturday Night" and "Little Red Rooster" (1963). "Bring It on Home to Me" was especially notable for its strong gospel tinge, and it significantly influenced the development of the soul genre.

Still, Cooke seemed surrounded by personal demons. In the summer of 1962 the music world was swept by a rumor that he was suffering from leukemia and near death. That was untrue, but the following summer Cooke's infant son, Vincent, drowned in his swimming pool. Cooke's singles in the first part of 1964 were only moderately successful as the taste of American teenagers shifted toward the music of the Beatles and other so-called British Invasion bands. Cooke made plans to combat the trend with a new, harder-edged sound that drew more strongly on African American traditions, and he recorded a protest song, "A Change Is Gonna Come," that may have been inspired by the thematically similar Peter, Paul & Mary hit "Blowin' in the Wind."

On December 11, 1964, Cooke met Elisa Boyer at a Los Angeles restaurant, Martoni's. The pair drove to the Hacienda Motel in south central Los Angeles, where, according to Boyer, Cooke began attacking her. While Cooke was in the bathroom, Boyer fled with the singer's clothes. An enraged Cooke, wearing only a coat and one shoe, demanded to know whether Boyer was in the office of manager Bertha Franklin. Cooke and Franklin struggled, and she shot him with a pistol, killing him soon after he managed the words "Lady, you shot me." The shooting was ultimately ruled a justifiable homicide, but the exact nature of Cooke's death has remained a subject of speculation and conspiracy theorizing. In 1986 Cooke was part of the inaugural group of inductees to the Rock and Roll Hall of Fame, and he received numerous other posthumous awards, including a Grammy Lifetime Achievement Award in 1999. In 2013, director Carl Franklin announced plans for a film about Cooke's life.

Books

Contemporary Black Biography, Vol. 17, Gale, 1998.

Guralnick, Peter, *Dream Boogie: The Triumph of Sam Cooke,* Little, Brown, 2005.

Wolff, Daniel, *You Send Me: The Life & Times of Sam Cooke,* Morrow, 1995.

Periodicals

Nation, March 13, 1995.

Village Voice, August 5, 2003.

Online

"Sam Cooke," *History of Rock,* http://www.history-of-rock.com/cooke.htm (November 14, 2013).

"Sam Cooke: About," *ABKCO Music & Records,* http://www.abkco.com/index.php/artists/artist/16/Sam-Cooke (November 14, 2013).

"Sam Cooke Biography," *Rock and Roll Hall of Fame,* http://rockhall.com/inductees/sam-cooke/bio/ (November 14, 2013).

"Sam Cooke Biography," *Rolling Stone,* http://www.rollingstone.com/music/artists/sam-cooke/biography (November 14, 2013).☐

Norman Corwin

Norman Corwin (1910–2011) produced some of the finest hours of radio broadcasting for the CBS network in the 1930s and '40s. Hailed by his contemporaries as the "poet laureate" of the medium, Corwin was the author or adapter of plays, poems, and special broadcasts designed to boost public morale during World War II. "Corwin's programs, which CBS aired without sponsors, are considered classics of the era when radio was the primary news and entertainment venue for Americans," wrote Dennis McLellan in the *Los Angeles Times* about Corwin's pioneering career.

CBS Photo Archive/Getty Images

Norman Lewis Corwin came from a Boston family of Anglo-Jewish background. Born on May 3, 1910, he was the son of Rose Corwin and Samuel Corwin, a printer and engraver. Corwin, his older brother Emil, and his father all lived remarkably long lives: Corwin died in October of 2011 at age 101, several months after Emil's passing at age 107; their 110-year-old father lived until 1987. Like his brother, Corwin's career did not slow with age—he taught at the University of Southern California until he died, and Emil retired from the U.S. Food and Drug Administration at the age of 96.

Began as Newspaper Reporter

Corwin's future in radio was foreshadowed by a gift for mimicry he showed at an early age as he repeated Emil's homework in memorizing and reciting poems. After finishing at Winthrop High School in East Boston, Corwin decided to try to find a job as a newspaper journalist. He was hired by the *Greenfield Daily Recorder* in north-central Massachusetts, and later moved on to the *Springfield Republican*. It was the late 1920s, and the number of households who owned radio sets in the United States was skyrocketing, and newspapers teamed with local radio stations to secure their listeners' and readers' loyalties. Westinghouse Electric, a corporate giant with divisions that manufactured radios and operated broadcast stations, approached the newspaper *Springfield Republican* with an idea to launch a nightly news broadcast on its Springfield station, WBZ. Corwin had a decent baritone and was invited to take the job. He wrote his own copy and signed off with the words, "This is Norman Corwin of the *Springfield Republican*."

WBZ was one of the oldest radio stations in the United States and was a dominant player in the New England market during these years. At a time when station managers attempted a something-for-everyone programming approach, Corwin was given the go-ahead to start his own poetry show on WBZ. He was fortunate that the Springfield station owned by Westinghouse also had a simultaneous broadcast from a Boston studio, which gave his *Rhymes and Cadences* a wider audience. In 1935, he moved to New York City to take a job in the publicity department of the 20th Century-Fox film studio. Part of his job was handling major stars like Shirley Temple and Tyrone Power, but he missed the broadcast booth and took an idea for a new poetry show to WQXR, another venerable broadcaster from radio's golden era. His 15-minute *Poetic License* was again a surprising success in the New York City market and led to a job offer with the Columbia Broadcasting Service, or CBS, radio network in 1938. *Norman Corwin's Words Without Music* debuted on December 4, 1938, on the New York City flagship station later known as WCBS and became a Sunday-afternoon staple.

Wrote Enduring Christmas Play

Words Without Music was an example of Corwin's gift for producing top-quality content with broad appeal. He wrote and directed poetic dramatizations, read by trained actors, that proved surprisingly popular. In a 1939 *New York Times* article about his program's success, Corwin revealed that the network received a steady stream of listener mail about the program—some from reluctant listeners who disliked radio in general but liked the program, or disliked poetry but enjoyed hearing it recited over the airwaves. "I think there is little doubt that this program has been helpful in dispelling the idea that poetry is a 'sissy' idea," Corwin told the *New York Times*. "It proves my theory that when poetry is made entertaining and has overtures of enjoyment, the public is eager to embrace it."

One of Corwin's greatest successes from this era was "The Plot to Overthrow Christmas," which he wrote himself and directed on Christmas Day of 1938; it proved a popular annual event on the CBS radio network, and helped turn Corwin into a household name. "Soon he had virtual carte blanche at the network," wrote *New York Times* journalist William Grimes. "As part of his series 'The Pursuit of Happiness,' he presented Paul Robeson singing Earl Robinson's cantata 'Ballad for Americans,' the first performance of Maxwell Anderson and Kurt Weill's 'Ballad of Magna Carta,' and an adaptation of Stephen Vincent Benet's poetry performed by Charles Laughton and Elsa Lanchester."

Set Radio Ratings Record

Corwin recruited well-known Hollywood figures for one of a handful of epic radio programs indelibly associated with his career at CBS. *We Hold These Truths* was an hour-long radio drama arranged to honor the 150th anniversary of the U.S. Bill of Rights on December 15, 1941. These are the first ten amendments to the U.S. Constitution and were designed to secure more firmly the rights of citizens and preserve the balance between state and federal powers. They include the First Amendment—freedom of speech—and the Fourth Amendment, which prohibits unreasonable search and seizure. Corwin structured the broadcast as a walk back through American history starring film star Jimmy Stewart as a time-traveling reporter. Others who appeared on the broadcast, which aired just eight days after the United States entered World War II after the bombing of a U.S. naval installation at Pearl Harbor, Hawaii, included Orson Welles, Lionel Barrymore, Rudy Vallee, Edward G. Robinson, and Walter Huston.

The *New York Times* offered Corwin a chance to promote the *We Hold These Truths* broadcast in his own words. In an article dated December 14, 1941, he said he carried out a fair amount of research for the project, but at times struggled to convey his message. He asked experts about what some parts of the Bill of Rights could mean to an ordinary citizen—those displaced in recent years by the Great Depression and the Dust Bowl, for example. "None of us could give a cheerful answer," Corwin wrote in the newspaper. "But two days later the Supreme Court answered by deciding that no State could bar the entry of a migratory worker simply because he was jobless and propertyless. It ruled that a hungry man has the right to wander over the face of his country looking for work."

We Hold These Truths was unusual in the fact that it was broadcast live over all four major national radio networks—a strategic cooperative decision by network executives, who were already signed on to broadcast a live radio address to the nation by President Franklin D. Roosevelt from the White House that immediately followed—and it pulled in an estimated 63 million listeners, or about half the U.S. population in 1941. *We Hold These Truths* remains a ratings record-holder for a work of drama in radio. Newspaper writers and commentators across the nation hailed Corwin's achievement. In retrospect, opined Walter Goodman in the *New York Times,* Corwin's "was the strongest radio voice in behalf of the World War II Allies, specializing in hard-boiled-sounding, soft-at-the-center sentiments about the little guy." Goodman also noted that "by network standards, the Corwin plays were innovative and, in their use of verse, daring."

Created Special Broadcast to Commemorate Victory

Corwin worked tirelessly to promote a message of freedom and moral decency for the American and Allied powers' war effort. He directed and wrote radio programs like the 1942 series *An American in England* about the privations suffered by British civilians on their home front, and a 1943 dramatic series called *Passport for Adams* that starred future television star Robert Young as a war correspondent. When joint Allied forces finally defeated Nazi Germany in early May of 1945, Corwin was asked to prepare another special broadcast of a dramatic poem, which he titled *On a Note of Triumph.* It aired on May 8, 1945, the day when Germany capitulated and again, Corwin's special broadcast pulled in enormous numbers, again nearing the 60-million mark. Voiced by a well-known radio actor and director named Martin Gabel, Corwin's epic verse "is considered by many to be one of radio's greatest works," wrote McLellan in the *Los Angeles Times.* "So they've given up," begins Gabel, who then goes on to reference the "Übermensch" of German philosophy, which posited that a superior race of humans would prevail against lesser beings. "They're finally done in, and the rat is dead in an alley back of the Wilhelmstrasse. Take a bow, G.I. Take a bow, little guy. The superman of tomorrow lies at the feet of you common men of this afternoon."

Corwin's work at CBS added immense prestige to the radio network's emerging reputation in the 1940s. Corwin himself was honored with the first ever One World Award a few months after the war's terrible end with the dropping of atomic weapons on two Japanese cities in August of 1945. "Corwin made good use of the prize, setting out on a four-month journey in June 1946 accompanied by a CBS recording engineer," wrote Carmel Dagan in *Daily Variety.* "His 100 hours of recorded interviews with world leaders and ordinary citizens were molded by CBS into a 13-part documentary that aired in 1947."

Taught at USC

Corwin transitioned to Hollywood in the late 1940s after losing out on some tough contractual battles with CBS over copyright issues. He married actor Katherine Locke and they settled in Los Angeles, where Corwin wrote screenplays for film and television. Among his best-known works from this period was an adaptation of a novel about the life of Dutch painter Vincent Van Gogh that starred Kirk Douglas. Corwin was nominated for an Academy Award for Best Adapted Screenplay for *Lust for Life,* but lost to the writers of *Around the World in Eighty Days.* In the 1960s and '70s, he compiled television-movie writing credits and eventually took a post as writer-in-residence at the Annenberg School for Communication and Journalism at the University of Southern California. A 39-minute film, *A Note of Triumph: The Golden Age of Norman Corwin,* won the 2006 Academy Award for Best Documentary Short.

Corwin's journal of his *One World* trip was published in 2009 as *Norman Corwin's One World Flight: The Lost Journal of Radio's Greatest Writer.* Emmy-winning television writer Norman Lear penned the foreword and wrote of the pride he took in having had the opportunity to work with the man behind *We Hold These Truths,* which Lear first heard as a teenager in 1941. Corwin's writing, Lear asserted, showed "a deep connection to people of all races and nations; in words that reveal an artist of social conscience who takes endless inspiration from the genius of the American founders."

Corwin became a widower in 1995. He died on October 18, 2011, at the age of 101 at his Los Angeles home, and is survived by his and Locke's two children, Diane and Anthony.

Books

Corwin, Norman, *Norman Corwin's One World Flight: The Lost Journal of Radio's Greatest Writer,* edited by Michael C. Keith and Mary Ann Watson, foreword by Norman Lear, Continuum Books, 2009.

Periodicals

Daily Variety, October 20, 2011.

Los Angeles Times, October 19, 2011.

New York Times, March 26, 1939; December 14, 1941; December 21, 1941, June 13, 1996; October 19, 2011.

Radio World, January 12, 2011.□

Demetrius Cydones

The Byzantine theologian and statesman Demetrius Cydones (c. 1324–1397) was an influential thinker and political figure during the last century of the Byzantine Empire. He served three terms as the empire's *Mesazon,* or prime minister.

Today, the combination of theologian and political leader seems an unusual one. But to a resident of Constantinople (now Istanbul), the empire's capital, in Cydones's time, it would not have been unusual at all. Byzantines of that day were concerned with the doctrinal differences that had, over a thousand years of clashes, driven them away from the Western church in Rome. But they were equally worried about the military threat from the Islamic Ottoman Empire, which would defeat the Byzantines militarily in 1453, and put an end to a thousand-year-old state rooted in ancient Rome—and in the early traditions of Christianity, for members of the Eastern Orthodox faith practiced in Byzantium considered (and still consider) their church the direct descendant of the religion preached by Jesus Christ. It was Cydones who brought together religion, history, and culture in an attempt to persuade the leaders of what is now Turkey that their future lay with the West.

Educated in Classics

Much of what is known about Cydones comes from his own writings, including an unusually large number of well-preserved letters. Not much is known, therefore, about the first years of his life. He was born around 1324 in Thessalonica (now Thessaloniki, Greece), the second most important city in the empire, and he received an excellent education by the standards of the day. The curriculum was rooted in the classics of ancient Greece, which as a Greek speaker he could read in the original language. He also benefited from studies with the Orthodox religious elders in Thessalonica, and he was interested in mathematics and astronomy.

In 1341, when his father died, Cydones ended his formal education and took responsibility for his family. In 1347, he entered the service of the Byzantine emperor John VI Kantakuzenos, who had met Cydones during his student years and been impressed by his erudition. Kantakuzenos was himself a vigorous anti-Islamic polemicist who believed generally that the main threat to Byzantium came not from Rome but from the Ottoman Turks. He brought Cydones to the capital of Constantinople, and Cydones was annoyed at having to rely on interpreters when Latin-speaking dignitaries and even early tourists visited from Rome. So he undertook on his own the difficult task of learning Latin, seeking instruction from a local Dominican monk.

Cydones became fascinated by the classics of Latin-language theology he read as his skills deepened, and, encouraged by his superiors at the imperial palace, he began translating them into Greek. He became a major source of knowledge of the Latin classics in the Byzantine Empire. translating works by St. Thomas Aquinas, St. Augustine, and Boethius, as well as more contemporary works bearing on the issues that had helped to split the Eastern and Western churches in the first place. One of those issues was the question of the so-called Filioque, of whether the Holy Spirit proceeded from God alone or "filioque," "and from the Son (Jesus)."

Resigned Government Post

While still quite a young man, Cydones became John VI Kantakuzenos's Mesazon, an influential position that required him to negotiate with foreign powers and to formulate the empire's position on theological matters. The requirements of these tasks were the stimulus for the large body of writing Cydones produced over the course of his career. In 1354, Cydones resigned his position to undertake a period of study in Rome. His timing was good: Kantakuzenos was overthrown by John V Palaiologos. But the reason for his departure seemed to be a disagreement with Kantakuzenos over the doctrine of Palamism, which emphasized, among other things, the importance of monastic inner prayer and religious inner life in the Orthodox tradition.

Palamism, of which Cydones's younger brother Prochorus Cydones was a staunch opponent, was one of the issues Cydones addressed in his religious writings. Others included the *filioque,* the contributions of the Western church fathers, the authority of the Western pope, and the sources of religious authority generally. The doctrinal questions active in the Eastern Orthodox church and in its relationship to Roman Catholicism are complex ones, but in general Cydones emphasized the importance of divine revelation and its manifestations in the temporal world. At first Cydones remained a follower of the Orthodox faith, but by 1365, he had converted to Catholicism.

That did not impede his career, for as the Ottoman Turks grew stronger, Byzantines increasingly turned their gaze to the West. Several conclaves had already tried, unsuccessfully, to reunite the Christian church's Eastern and Western branches, and Cydones was among the voices advocating stronger ties with Rome. He remained in close touch with John V Palaiologos, and in 1369 he returned to Constantinople at John's command to become Mesazon once again, this time with the added portfolio of imperial adviser. Cydones accompanied John to Rome on a diplomatic trip in 1369, at which closer ties between Byzantium and Rome were agreed upon. On this trip he formally professed his faith as a Catholic.

Cydones's positions were by no means universally accepted in Constantinople, and his writings and those of his brother remained topics of strong debate. Yet the steady military advances of crack Turkish troops under their leader Osman I in the first decades of what became known as the Ottoman Empire were matters of deep concern, and Cydones seems to have been considered an expert in the field. His writings on political and cultural matters as well as on religion were voluminous. The extent of their diffusion in the Byzantine world is unclear, but their sheer volume suggests that he had a wide audience.

Evaluated Turkish Threat

In the words of Judith R. Ryder in her book *The Career and Writings of Demetrius Cydones,* Cydones "presents the Turks as the antithesis of civilization and of freedom." He essentially considered the Turks barbarians, but he also respected them as a military force and wrote unsentimental evaluations of their power and of potential Byzantine strategies for combating it. He also wrote extensively about other societies that found themselves in conflict with the Turks: Bulgarians, Serbs, and Hungarians in Eastern Europe, and Mongol tribes to the north. And he asserted that the Papal States of Rome had extensive experience in fighting the Ottomans made them natural allies.

Beyond these weighty matters of church and state, Cydones was an energetic letter-writer who might discuss a wide range of topics. He described his own serious illnesses and gave the modern reader an idea of common health conditions in the times before modern medicine: at one point he spent an entire year bedridden, and he described feeling as though he were nailed to his bed. Cydones complained about the difficulties in mail delivery in a time when letters had to traverse thousands of miles and might be diverted by pirates or bandits at any time. Cydones loved the outdoors, liked to walk around Constantinople and take in the views from its hills, and envied a friend who had a country home where he could hunt and fish.

Cydones lived an unusually long life for his time and place. In 1383, he retired. He made a trip to Venice, where he apparently came in contact with some of the thinkers exploring the ideas that led to the European Renaissance. In 1391, at the age of nearly 70, he was recalled to the court by John V Palaiologus's son, the emperor Manuel II Palaiologus. His influence was weakened by this point, possibly due to his Catholic faith, and he spent his last years in exile on the island of Crete, then under Venetian rule. He died there in 1397 or 1398. His life has been the subject of scholarly treatments but awaits a general biography befitting his importance in the history of the Near East.

Books

Dendrinos, Charalambos, et al., eds., *Porphyrogenita: Essays on the History and Literature of Byzantium and the Latin East in Honour of Julian Chrysostomides,* Ashgame, 2003.

Harris, Jonathan, Catherine Holmes, and Eugenia Russell, eds., *Byzantines, Latins, and Turks in the Eastern Mediterranean World After 1150,* Oxford, 2013.

Likoudis, James, *Ending the Byzantine Greek Schism: The 14th Century Apologia of Demetrios Kydones for Unity with Rome,* Catholics United for the Faith, 1983.

Ryder, Judith R., *The Career and Writings of Demetrius Kydones: A Study of Fourteenth-Century Byzantine Politics, Religion, and Society,* Brill, 2010.□

Carl Czerny

The Austrian composer, piano teacher, and pianist Carl Czerny (1791–1857) is known by name to most serious students of the piano, for the piano exercises he devised in the middle of the 19th century are still in use, more than 150 years later.

Czerny was at the very least an influential figure in 19th-century classical music. He was a student of Beethoven, the teacher of such noted virtuosos as Franz Liszt, and one of the first musical researchers to try to prepare accurate performing editions of older music. Many composers of the period admired both his music and his piano technique, although a few believed that as a composer he was, as Robert Everett-Green characterized this view in *Globe & Mail,* "an uninspired hack." Czerny was an astonishingly prolific composer; at a time when many composers tended to produce only modest numbers of works in large forms, he completed nearly 900 published works plus an assortment that remained unpublished. Some of his music has been rediscovered and promoted in the 21st century, but his pedagogical (teaching) materials remain his best-known works.

Began Playing at Three

An only child, Carl Czerny (roughly pronounced CHAIR-nee) was born in Vienna, Austria, on February 21, 1791. The family was of Czech ethnic background, and Czerny's native tongue was Czech. His father was a well-trained

Imagno/Hulton Fine Art Collection/getty Images

musician and piano repairman, but in highly competitive Vienna he was able only to eke out a living. Czerny immediately showed musical talent, taking up the piano when he was only three, and his parents rested their hopes on him, keeping him away from other children and bringing him up in an atmosphere of intense musical training. The youngster obliged, and by seven he was writing compositions of his own. Czerny made his public debut in 1800, at age nine, performing a Mozart concerto for piano and orchestra, and around that time he began to study the comparatively more difficult music of Beethoven. Czerny lived with his parents until their deaths, and he never married.

When Czerny was ten, his violin teacher, one Wenzel Krumpholz, introduced him to Beethoven. After Czerny played Beethoven's difficult "Pathétique" piano sonata, among other works, Beethoven agreed to take him on as a pupil, giving him several lessons a week. Those lessons lasted for several years, ending in 1802 because of time constraints on Beethoven's part and financial ones on that of the Czerny family. However, Beethoven remained close to his young student, writing an enthusiastic blurb for a projected Czerny concert tour in 1805, and later hiring him as a piano teacher for his nephew, Karl. Czerny's own writings remain valuable sources of information on Beethoven's career and on the effects of his encroaching deafness.

As a teenager, Czerny dreamed of a career as a touring pianist, but for a variety of reasons, including the desire to be close to his family during the instability generated by the Napoleonic Wars, he eventually discarded this goal. He felt that he lacked star quality, writing in an autobiographical sketch (quoted in the *New Grove Dictionary of Music and Musicians*) that "my playing lacked the type of brilliant, calculated charlatanry that is usually part of a traveling virtuoso's essential equipment." Despite the fact that he could reputedly play all of Beethoven's music from memory, Czerny decided to remain in Vienna and focus on teaching piano and, increasingly, on composition.

Taught Liszt

As a teacher, Czerny was one of the most influential of his time. His most famous student was Franz Liszt, later a major composer and arguably the biggest piano star of the 19th century; Liszt began studying with Czerny when he was nine. Another top virtuoso who began as Czerny's student was Sigismund Thalberg (1812–1871). A number of second-line touring pianists also studied with Czerny, but equally important were the hundreds or thousands of ordinary Viennese pianists who came through the doors of his studio despite the increasingly high prices he commanded: he recalled that he often gave 12 lessons per day, lasting from 8 a.m. to 8 p.m., and attended to his own voluminous composing after that.

To supply the needs of those students, Czerny wrote a large number of study pieces designed to strengthen every aspect of a pianist's technical arsenal. Some of these, most of all the very difficult *Die Schule der Geläufigkeit* (The School of Velocity, 1834), Op. 299, are still in use among piano teachers and students today. He also wrote a good deal of music intended specifically for piano students. Czerny divided his music into four categories: technical exercises, simple works for students, concert pieces intended for pianistic display, and serious music.

He was most attached to the last of these, and he worried that he had diluted his talent by writing too much light music. Nevertheless, Czerny's output of serious music was substantial. He composed seven symphonies, 11 piano sonatas, 28 sonatinas, numerous shorter piano works, six piano concertos, operas, and more than 300 sacred works, many of them large pieces with orchestral accompaniment. Czerny always had new works in progress along a kind of assembly line, a series of desks in his studio, each of which held a partly finished composition. He would walk from one desk to another, adding new material, and then move on to the next desk so that he would not waste time waiting for the ink to dry.

Criticized by Schumann

This method did not endear itself to hard-core Romantics, who cultivated an image and ethos of spontaneity. Their leader around the middle of the century, composer Robert Schumann, who was also an influential music critic, delivered the withering judgment (as quoted by Everett-Green) that "a greater bankruptcy of imagination ... could hardly exist" than that displayed in Czerny's music, and he opined that Czerny ought to be forced to stop composing. But opinions differed: Beethoven remained supportive of his former pupil, and Johannes Brahms praised Czerny's piano studies and contended in general that he had fallen into undeserved obscurity. Fryderyk Chopin often visited Czerny and corresponded with him, and Liszt invited Czerny to contribute to his *Hexameron,* a collection of variations by different composers on the tune from an opera aria by Vincenzo Bellini.

For many decades, Czerny's technical studies and piano etudes (exercise-like pieces) were the only works for which he was known. In the early 21st century, however, his work has experienced a modest revival. Among his champions was the Austrian-Canadian pianist Anton Kuerti, who organized a series of seven concerts devoted to Czerny's music in Toronto in 2002. Britain's Nimbus label issued a complete cycle of Czerny's piano sonatas beginning in 2010, and many other Czerny works appeared in new recordings.

Opinions remain divided on the value of Czerny's more ambitious pieces; *New York Times* critic Anne Midgette reviewed a 2004 performance of Czerny's variations on the *Deutschlandlied* (the future German national anthem) by writing that "Czerny was better at showcasing brilliance than at thinking of anything particularly original to do with it." But as of the 2010s his reputation seemed to be on the rise. Another interesting and little-examined facet of Czerny's career was his work as an editor: he was one of the first to prepare careful editions of music by earlier composers such as J.S. Bach and Domenico Scarlatti, whose compositions had come down from the 18th century in irregular ways.

Czerny stopped teaching in 1836 but remained active as a composer and writer until the end of his life, producing major theoretical-musical works such as the *Schule der praktischen Tonsetzkunst,* Op. 600 (School of Practical Compositional Art), and the *Nouvelle école de la main gauche,* Op. 861 (New School of the Left Hand). He lived alone after his parents' death, reportedly sharing space with as many as a dozen cats. Czerny died in Vienna on July 15, 1857.

Books

Slonimsky, Nicolas, ed. emeritus, *Baker's Biographical Dictionary of Musicians,* Schirmer, 2001.

Sadie, Stanley, ed., *The New Grove Dictionary of Music and Musicians,* 2nd ed., Macmillan, 2001.

Periodicals

Globe & Mail (Toronto, Canada), June 13, 2002, August 22, 2002.

New York Times, November 20, 2004.

Online

"Carl Czerny," *AllMusic,* http://www.allmusic.com (September 4, 2013).□

D

Alexander Dalrymple

Scottish geographer Alexander Dalrymple (1737–1808) served as the first hydrographer of the British Admiralty. A former executive with the British East India Company, he spent years collecting seafarers' data on oceans, coastlines, and islands. Dalrymple was adamant about the possibility of a vast, as-yet undiscovered land mass somewhere in the Southern Hemisphere that could yield untapped natural resources and possibly even wealth comparable to the kingdoms of India or China, he believed. Explorer Captain James Cook used Dalrymple's maps on his historic 1772–75 expedition, but found only frigid waters and penguin-bedecked ice floes.

Alexander Dalrymple came from an elite, politically engaged family. Born on July 24, 1737, he was the son of James Dalrymple, whose father had been created a baronet in 1700 for his support of the Act of Union between England and Scotland. His father, known as Lord Hailes, served as Auditor of the Exchequer of Scotland. Dalrymple's maternal ancestors were similarly distinguished: his mother, Lady Christian Hamilton, was the daughter of Thomas Hamilton, 6th Earl of Haddington, who created one of Scotland's most impressive gardens at their Tyninghame estate.

Loved Explorers' Tales

Dalrymple's childhood was spent at Newhailes, his family seat in Musselburgh just outside of Edinburgh. He had four older brothers and several younger siblings; by some accounts his mother bore as many as 16 children, though not all survived to adulthood. Dalrymple's eldest brother was David, who attended Eton College and studied law in the Netherlands before inheriting his father's baronetcy and becoming a respected judge. The other Dalrymple brothers included James, a poet, and John, who served as Lord Provost of Edinburgh.

A large part of Dalrymple's education took place at home by private tutors, and he did not show much academic promise. He turned 13 the year his father died in 1750, and that placed his brother David in charge of the family affairs. The new Lord Hailes attempted to improve his younger brother's grasp of Latin and Greek—prerequisites for almost any academic path at the time—but Dalrymple's lack of formal education showed in his poor study skills. He did love adventure tales, however, and he longed to see Asia. A few books had mentioned the 1738–39 South Atlantic exploratory voyage of Jean-Baptiste Charles Bouvet de Lozier, a French sea captain who had discovered an island about 1,500 miles southwest of Cape Town, South Africa. Lozier named the bay Cape Circoncision because it was sighted on January 1, 1739, which is the Feast of the Circumcision in the Christian liturgical calendar. Some explorers surmised that Bouvet Island, as it was called, marked the entry point to a major undiscovered continent.

Dalrymple's family connections helped secure a job with the British East India Company, the vast corporation that managed trade routes between Britain and a large swath of Asia. It controlled ports along the Indian Ocean, operated warehouses stocked with textiles, spices, and other valuable commodities, and operated the fleet of ships that traversed the routes from British ports like Manchester and Liverpool to Mumbai and Calcutta. Dalrymple's brother brought him to London, where he undertook a crash course in merchant recordkeeping. He was hired as a writer, or copyist, by the British East India Company on November 1, 1752, and assigned to its port office in Madras, India. After four months at sea, Dalrymple arrived in Madras in May of 1753 to begin work. His penmanship was abysmal, however, and he was demoted to a warehouse job. Again, family connections helped him secure a better post, this one with George Pigot, the British governor of Madras. He also impressed Robert Orme, another leading colonial official.

Ventured to Pacific Rim

Dalrymple proved to be a gifted researcher, planner, and manager. He convinced his superiors to let him embark upon a mission to set up a trade zone in a remote part of South Asia, one where the Dutch and Spanish had already stationed a few barely staffed forts and outposts. Dalrymple seized upon Balambangan Island, located between the Philippine and Indonesian archipelagoes, to be the next free-trade zone under British control. The Philippines had been a Spanish stronghold for 200 years by that point, and the Dutch controlled large chunks of Borneo, Malaysia, and other parts of Indonesia. Dalrymple believed a trading port at Balambangan could extend the British presence into the Pacific Rim and prove a boon in the East India Company's trade with China. He sailed to the Sulu Sea islands several times, beginning in 1759, and negotiated terms with the Sultan of Sulu. The British East India Company, however, found itself caught up in a dynastic drama overthe next decade involving the sultan's heirs, complicated by a brief war against the Spanish in Manila, the largest Philippine port. Balambangan failed to thrive after it was finally set up as a full-fledged port in 1773, and its main product, shipped to Chinese ports, was opium.

Dalrymple had actually quit his job by then after he and his superiors failed to agree upon a new salary contract. Already keenly interested in hydrography, or the mapping of oceans, coastlines, and islands, he had begun collecting charts and data from others who had sailed this region. He published *An Account of the Discoveries Made in the South Pacifick Ocean, Previous to 1764* in 1767. He posited that the western coast of New Zealand was actually part of a major land mass, one that had been rumored to exist since Roman times and had been dubbed Terra Australis (Latin for "South Land"). Sailors and explorers were wary of venturing too far south, for even when they were close to land these seas were known for fierce, shipwrecking storms. The passages around the tips of Africa and South America—respectively, the Cape of Good Hope and Cape Horn—were frightening confluences of storm activity, unknown rocky shoals, and sudden losses in standard navigational abilities. The Dutch had mapped part of Australia in the 1600s, along its north and west coasts near to its Indonesian colonies, but the exact dimensions of the continent were as yet unknown in Dalrymple's day. The Dutch had planted a flag at one port on the Australian continent near to its Javanese holdings and named it New Holland.

Obsessed with *Terra Australis*

Dalrymple was intrigued by new accounts given by British explore Samuel Wallis, whose *H.M.S. Dolphin* had finished its circumnavigation of the globe in 1768. Wallis was the first European of record to set foot on Tahiti, which he named King George III's Island in honor of the reigning British monarch. Wallis found an elaborate Polynesian society who hinted at other areas full of promise eastward in the Pacific. *Dolphin* crew had also reported that at Tahitian sunsets they thought they sighted mountain peaks in the far distance to the south, lending credence to the possibility of a major continent. This was likely an optical illusion, because Tahiti and other South Seas islands in the Pacific Ocean are among the sparsest populated parts of the planet. In fact, large areas of the Pacific were simply labeled *nondum cognita* (not yet known) on maps of the time.

Dalrymple assumed there was a wealth of riches yet to be discovered on a southern land mass, either the as-yet-to be mapped Australian continent or a second site. He maintained "that trade with a continent of this size can replace trade with those two million ungrateful wretches in the American colonies," he wrote, according to Alan Gurney's book *Below the Convergence: Voyages Toward Antarctica, 1699–1839.* "For without a doubt there must live in this great southern continent at least fifty million inhabitants, and 'the scraps from this table would be sufficient to maintain the power, dominion, and sovereignty of Britain by employing all its manufacturers and ships.'"

Bypassed by Captain Cook

In 1768, Britain's esteemed Royal Society announced plans to observe the transit of Venus, an event predicted by British astronomer Edmond Halley 50 years earlier. The planetary phenomenon would occur on June 3, 1769, and not again for another hundred years, and the transit would give astronomers a more precise measurement of the distance of the Earth from the sun. The Royal Society drew up plans to follow Halley's instructions and set up three measurement sites around the globe, and one of them was to be in the South Seas near Tahiti. The Royal Society plan recommended Dalrymple to be put in charge of the South Sea mission, but the British Admiralty Office refused, on grounds he had no experience captaining ships or major expeditions. A relatively unknown young officer named James Cook was chosen instead.

Cook went on to achieve immense fame for this journey, setting foot in Hawaii and going much further south on the Australian continent than any previous European of record. Cook also circumnavigated all of New Zealand, showing that it was its own separate land mass. Cook made a second voyage, from 1772 to 1775, trying to locate a land mass in the South Atlantic that Dalrymple and others believed was actually the fabled Terra Australis. He used Dalrymple's *Chart of the Ocean between South America and Africa* which Dalrymple had drawn up in 1769, but it was based on older, faulty sources some 200 years old by then. All Cook found in early 1775, where Dalrymple's map showed a land mass would be, were major ocean swells—a sign that no land was near. The air had turned frigid, too, and the crew on Cook's *H.M.S. Resolution* spotted icebergs, penguins, and enormous cliffs of what appeared to be ice.

Dalrymple was still convinced that the Bouvet Island and another parcel, South Georgia Island, were the entry ports to another continent. Bouvet Island's closest inhabitable land mass was present-day South Africa, a distance of some 1,600 miles. South Georgia Island had been chanced upon by a British explorer of French origin, Antoine de la Roche, in 1675 after having been blown off course while rounding Cape Horn. South Georgia's closest land mass was the tip of South America, some 1,100 miles away, and it seemed mostly uninhabitable.

Dalrymple publicly disputed Cook's findings. In 1775, the same year that Cook returned from his second historic trek, Dalrymple published another tome, which he titled *Collection of Voyages, Chiefly in the Southern Atlantick Ocean.* "Here he suggested colonizing the island discovered by de la Roche and the *Leon,*" wrote Gurney. "Food could be grown for the East India ships by West Indian slaves, an industry set up to exploit the whales and seals (an idea ahead of its time), and, finally, the island could be used as a base for exploration of the southern continent of which Cape Circumcision was but a small indication."

The First Hydrographer

Dalrymple's most lasting contribution to geography came through his work at the Admiralty Office in London. He was one of the main proponents of establishing an official Hydrographic Office, which was done in 1795, and he was its first director. He wrote a pamphlet distributed to all ships' captains on how to maintain a proper ship's log, and he is thought to have suggested to Francis Beaufort, an Irish hydrographer who later succeeded Dalrymple at the Admiralty, a method of measuring wind speed by observation, since there were no scientific tools to measure velocity at the time. The famous Beaufort Scale of Wind Force can be traced back to an unpublished manuscript Dalrymple authored in the late 1780s titled *Practical Navigation,* which featured a method of describing wind velocity based on the work of a civil engineer named John Smeaton, who had studied windmills.

Dalrymple was often described as a difficult personality, obstinate in his ideas and reliably ready to engage in debate. He was dismissed from his post as Hydrographer of the Admiralty on May 28, 1808, after refusing to hand over some charts taken during the capture of a French ship in the Napoleonic Wars. He died 23 days later on June 19, 1808, at his home in London, unmarried and without children.

Books

Fry, Howard T., *Alexander Dalrymple (1737–1808) and the Expansion of British Trade,* Frank Cass & Company, 1970.

Gurney Alan, *Below the Convergence: Voyages Toward Antarctica, 1699–1839,* W.W. Norton, 1997.

Periodicals

Geographical, November 1998.□

Walter Damrosch

The German-born American conductor Walter Damrosch (1862–1950) was responsible in many ways for spreading the popularity of classical music in the United States.

Damrosch's career began in the 1880s and lasted until the 1940s. During that time he presented the American premieres of numerous European symphonic works and laid down patterns that classical music in America would follow well into the future. These included financial patronage from captains of industry, an emphasis on training in Europe, and the use of mass media in popularizing the classics. Although Damrosch's own tastes were conservative, rooted firmly in the traditions of German 19th-century music in which he was raised, he recognized the talent of the purely American George Gershwin and conducted the premieres of two of Gershwin's most important works. Damrosch was also a composer of moderate repute. Compared with immigrant contemporaries such as Arturo Toscanini he is not generally regarded as a top conductor of his time. The legacy of his engaging presentation of classical music to ordinary listeners, however, is immense.

Raised Among Famous Musicians

Walter Damrosch was born in Breslau in the kingdom of Prussia (now Wroclaw, Poland, but at the time predominantly German), on January 30, 1862. His father, Leopold Damrosch, was a symphony conductor. The Damrosch home was a frequent stopping-place for the top musicians in German-speaking Europe, including composers Richard Wagner, and Franz Liszt, pianists Anton Rubinstein and Clara Schumann, and conductor Hans von Bülow, and Damrosch grew up in an intensely musical environment. He saw Wagner conduct his own operas at the composer's combined theater and shrine in Bayreuth in 1882. The family moved to New York when Damrosch was nine so that Leopold Damrosch could accept a position as conductor of a German chorus there. Walter Damrosch continued his studies of music with immigrant German teachers, and Europe would continue to play a role in his musical life. But he would begin his autobiography *My Musical Life,* with the words "I am an American musician."

Largely trained by his father, Damrosch at first labored very much in his shadow. Playing percussion in an opera orchestra under his father's baton, he once missed a crucial cymbal crash. But he built experience on his own in a variety of small gigs, from organist at Brooklyn's Plymouth Church to conductor of a 300-voice New Jersey choir called the Newark Harmonic Society. He toured the South as accompanist to a visiting virtuoso. When his father successfully persuaded the new Metropolitan Opera in New York to add German opera to its schedule, Damrosch assisted him with performances of operas by Richard Wagner. He was unexpectedly thrown into the spotlight by his father's sudden illness in the winter of 1884–1885, taking to the podium to lead performances of two Wagner operas.

AP Photo/Charles Kenneth Lucas

After his father's death, Damrosch was offered the conductorship of New York's Symphony Society and Oratorio Society. His hope was to conduct German opera at the Metropolitan Opera, but that organization offered him only an assistant conductor position; his brother Frank became chorus master. Taking the setback well, Damrosch agreed to go to Germany to recruit new talent for the Metropolitan's German-language productions. He returned in 1887 for further study with von Bülow in the interpretation of the works of Beethoven.

Damrosch saw in America's growing industrial might a source of funding for classical music that could replace the traditional aristocratic patronage it had enjoyed in Europe. On the boat to Europe to study with von Bülow he met steel magnate Andrew Carnegie and convinced him to fund a handsome new concert hall on Seventh Avenue, designed to serve New York's growing orchestral music scene. By 1891, when the venue had been named Carnegie Hall and was ready to open (with then unheard-of air conditioning achieved with fans blowing air through a huge ice chamber), it was Damrosch who inaugurated the work by conducting the American premiere of Pyotr Tchaikovsky's Symphony No. 4 in F minor—and persuaded the Russian composer to come to New York for the premiere. Damrosch and Carnegie remained good friends, ensuring that a steady flow of conducting opportunities would come Damrosch's way.

Founded Opera Company

Damrosch remained as conductor of the Oratorio Society of New York (an oratorio is a dramatic choral work) until 1898, and of the New York Symphony until it merged with the New York Philharmonic Orchestra in the 1920s. But at this point in his career, with his youthful experiences at Bayreuth still in his ears, he still dreamed of being a major opera conductor. Once again, Damrosch's artistic aims dovetailed with his fundraising talents, and he succeeded in founding the Damrosch Opera Company in New York in 1894. The troupe mounted productions of German opera in New York and as far away as Denver, attracting prominent singers such as Nellie Melba for lead roles.

In 1896, Damrosch tried his hand as a composer himself, penning an opera in Wagnerian style with a libretto based on Nathaniel Hawthorne's novel *The Scarlet Letter.* When the Damrosch Opera Company disbanded in 1899, it was less because of financial problems than because Damrosch himself seemed to have gotten German opera out of his system. He expressed disillusionment with Wagner's overarching dramatic theories and for the first decades of the 20th century devoted himself mostly to symphonic conducting. He gave the American premieres of major works by Gustav Mahler and Edward Elgar in addition to those of Tchaikovsky's fourth and sixth symphonies. During World War I, he organized an orchestra in France that played in hospitals for wounded members of Allied military forces, and in 1924 his New York Symphony became one of the first American orchestras to tour major European cities.

Damrosch's repertoire as a conductor was squarely in the symphonic mainstream, and unlike Toscanini, who recorded music by Stravinsky and Shostakovich, Damrosch had little sympathy for modern trends in European music. In this he was in tune with American audiences, which did not warm to modernist styles until much later, if at all. Damrosch was an able advocate of the mainstream classics and stressed the importance of bringing classical music to parts of the U.S. where it was little heard. He jumped at the chance to use the new medium of radio, hosting "University of the Air" broadcasts for NBC radio in 1927 in which he offered listeners a verbal guide to the music they would hear. From 1928 Damrosch was the well-loved host of the NBC Music Appreciation Hour broadcasts for children and families, whose estimated audience reached seven million in the 1930s. That program ran until 1942.

Championed Gershwin's Music

Along with such projects aiming at musical uplift, Damrosch championed the jazz-classical fusions of George Gershwin, becoming one of the few conductors of the time to program Gershwin's music in the classical concert hall. Damrosch commissioned Gershwin's Piano Concerto in F (1926) and conducted the premiere of his enduring favorite *An American in Paris* in 1928. An *American Mercury* article in 1935 chastised Damrosch for "musical vulgarity," and it was likely the music of Gershwin the writer had in mind.

Damrosch continued to compose music, and he completed two more operas, *Cyrano* (1913) and *The Man*

Without a Country (1937). Both had their premieres at the Metropolitan Opera, making Damrosch one of just three American composers to have enjoyed multiple premieres there. He also penned some widely performed songs, including a setting of Rudyard Kipling's poem "Danny Deever." Damrosch's music is not often played today. Damrosch was honored in later life by such bodies as the American Academy of Arts and Letters, whose gold medal he received in 1938. But he was perhaps most proud of his work for the Musicians Emergency Fund, for which he served as president from 1933 to 1943, and for which he raised money tirelessly through benefit performances.

In 1890, Damrosch married Margaret Blaine, daughter of Secretary of State James G. Blaine, in a ceremony attended by the cream of American political society. The couple raised four daughters, Alice, Margaret, Leopoldine, and Anita. Damrosch died in New York on December 22, 1950. Damrosch Park at New York's Lincoln Center performing arts complex honors him as well as other members of his musically high-achieving family.

Books

Damrosch, Walter, *My Musical Life,* Scribner's, 1926.

Sadie, Stanley, ed., *The New Grove Dictionary of Music and Musicians,* 2nd ed., Schirmer, 2001.

Slonimsky, Nicolas, ed. emeritus, *Baker's Biographical Dictionary of Musicians,* centennial ed., Schirmer, 2001.

Periodicals

American Mercury, March 1935.

New York Times, December 23, 1950.

Online

"Walter Damrosch," *New York Philharmonic Orchestra,* http://nyphil.org/about-us/ArtistDetail?artistname=walter-damrosch (September 7, 2013).

"Walter Damrosch, 1862–1950 (Biography)," *Library of Congress,* http://lcweb2.loc.gov/diglib/ihas/loc.natlib.ihas.200035728/default.html (September 7, 2013).□

Jack Daniel

American distiller Jack Daniel (1849–1911) founded the Tennessee distillery that bears his name. His sour-mash whiskey blend evolved from a do-it-yourself rural operation in the rough years following the end of the U.S. Civil War to one of America's most successful signature exports in the global marketplace.

Dates vary on the arrival of Jasper Newton Daniel, allegedly born in September of 1849 or 1850, near Lynchburg, Tennessee. Daniel's biographer Peter Krass cites it as January of 1849 instead in his book, *Blood & Whiskey: The Life and Times of Jack Daniel.* Little Jasper may have been born prematurely as the tenth child of an Irish immigrant named Lucinda Cook, who married Calaway Daniel in 1822, and possibly died shortly after this birth.

Ran Away from Home

The Daniels were of Scotch-Irish origin, a particularly problematic ethnic group both in Ireland and Britain's North American colonies before the American Revolutionary War. Back in the 1600s some land-poor Scots had been invited to settle Ireland to help populate the isle after its definitive conquest by the English crown. Their descendants were later the target of discrimination and outright expulsion, however. Daniel's paternal grandfather Joseph, nicknamed "Job," was among those who left Ireland in the mid-18th century and settled in what later became North Carolina.

Like many other Scotch-Irish immigrants who loathed British imperialism, Daniel's grandfather eagerly took up arms against the British in the war for American independence. He married and had several children, and the family was among the first wave of permanent settlers in Franklin County, Tennessee, arriving around 1809 with their family, which included at least five sons. Some of those Daniel boys fought in War of 1812, and Jack's father Calaway was a teenager when he took over the farm his father had cleared and built.

Calaway and Lucinda had moved to Lincoln County, near Lynchburg, around 1835. They were known to follow a breakaway sect known as Primitive Baptism. Jack's father grew corn and raised sheep and cattle, and his farm prospered in the years before the Civil War. In June of 1851, he remarried and had more children with a woman named Matilda Vanzant. Little "Jackie Boy," as Daniel was known to his family, was mistreated by his new stepmother and claimed to have first run away from home at the age of ten. He may have been returned unwillingly, and it is known he attended at least one year of school. The Krass biography claims Daniel was 14 years old when he was taken in by a local Lutheran evangelical preacher named Dan Call. This would have been around 1863, and in January of 1864, Daniel's father Calaway died. There was little left of his once-prosperous farm, for Union Army troops had sacked and burned much on their march through Tennessee.

Learned Whiskey-Making from Ex-Slave

Dan Call also had Scotch-Irish roots. More significantly, before the war he had enjoyed a prosperous side business as a distiller. This was a long tradition that had come with them from Ireland but one with roots in Scotland, where Scots quaffed a single-malt beverage known as *uisgebeatha* or water of life. The shortened form, *uisge,* was pronounced "wees-gay," and later evolved into the word "whiskey." The Scots made theirs from fermented malt barley, and toasted the grain by burning peat, the decomposing plant matter from area bogs. The peat-barley combination gave Scotch whiskey its distinctive flavor. When the Scotch-Irish settled in Ireland, the peat-toasting process fell away. They later developed a similar process for using grains other than barley, including corn, which grew plentifully in Tennessee, Kentucky, and other southern states. This type of whiskey, whose variants include bourbon, was aged in barrels whose staves had been charred, which mellowed the flavor.

Dan Call and his wife Mary Jane were kind to Daniel, who was a penniless orphan with few prospects, and whose older brothers were either serving in the Confederate Army or had moved west to Texas. Even hard work seemed out of the question, because Daniel was still runty and suffered from bouts of ill health. With the end of the Civil War, Tennessee's economy was wrecked and Daniel convinced Call to let him operate the still. Call paired him with an older man who lived on the Call farm, Nearis Green, a former slave. Uncle Nearis, as he was known, was a skilled distiller and taught Daniel the process. The Call lands also included part of Louse Creek, which was a particularly fine source of fresh water with a low iron content, and this yielded an ideal whiskey. In the years before the Civil War, local distillers like Call had developed what became known as the Lincoln County Process, which used charcoal filtering to give the final product an even smoother finish. The term "Lincoln County Process" remained even after 1871, when parts of Lincoln and neighboring counties were combined into Moore County, with Lynchburg as the county seat.

There was tremendous demand for alcohol in the traumatized years after the Civil War. Daniel found a ready market for the jugs of Tennessee sourmash whiskey in Lynchburg and nearby towns, which he visited in his mule-drawn wagon loaded with earthenware jugs. Other distillers in the county began operating stills again, sensing the quick profit to be made as the economic troubles of the Reconstruction Era continued. Customers in Tennessee were divided in their allegiances to sourmash whiskey, which uses a starter batch of the previous fermenter to begin the chemical process, and sweetmash, which used only new yeast.

Company Registered in 1875

Daniel was able to start his own large-scale distillery enterprise when he came into an inheritance from his late father, whose once-profitable farm had been sold after his death in 1864. The children were each to receive a share of the proceeds, but the terms of the will had been challenged in court by one of Daniel's brothers and the case dragged on for a decade. Finally, in 1874 Daniel came into an inheritance of $1,000, which let him launch his own company and buy a 140-acre farm with a ten-room house and various outbuildings. Land-claim deeds and court records hunted down by Krass reveal that the founding date of Jack Daniel's company was November 27, 1875, when it was registered as Daniel & Call, showing that he was still a business partner of Dan Call.

Federal officials recognized that an excise tax on whiskey would be a profitable source of revenue. Government revenue agents were among the most loathed figures in the South, for they represented "Yankee" northern authority. Agents of the Internal Revenue Service who were responsible for collecting the excise tax on spirits were especially hated in Tennessee, and their attempts to dictate the details of production at Daniel's distillery and other large operations aroused immense resentment. Daniel took part in a major protest action against the interference in the late 1870s, showing solidarity with his Tennessee competitors after a decree was made to combine tax-collection districts.

Daniel's business also faced a threat from local temperance, or anti-alcohol activists, who argued that alcohol consumption rates were the root of many social ills. His longtime partner and father figure, Dan Call, finally bowed to increasing pressure from his Lutheran church elders and sold his share of the business back to Daniel in the early 1880s. The dissolution of the partnership meant that Daniel would have to change the brand name, and he feared he might lose loyal customers. He rebranded it first as "Jack Daniel Whiskey, Lynchburg, Tennessee." That evolved to "Jack Daniel's Old Time Distillery Whiskey," and finally he named it "Old No. 7," the origins of which remain part of company lore.

Chose Famous Square Bottle

Daniel's biographer Krass dismissed several near-folklore status tales about the origins of "No. 7" and explained that the branding was actually a sly bit of marketing. Previously, his and Call's company had been registered as distillery No. 7 in Tennessee's Fourth District for tax-collection purposes. When the Fourth and Fifth Districts were combined in 1876, their distillery became "No. 16" in the new district. "By adopting what appeared to be a bland, even boring label name, Jack was actually indulging in civil disobedience," Krass wrote. "He was effectively rebelling against the federal government by reminding everyone of the despised consolidation of the two districts." Moreover, the old jugs had long carried "No. 7" as their official government stamp, and resurrecting it as part of the label reminded old-timers of their favorite Lynchburg sourmash whiskey.

Daniel never married and had no children. Once his distillery began to prosper, he adopted the uniform of the successful southern gentleman farmer, with a knee-length suitcoat, necktie and vest, topped by a wide-brimmed hat. He kept the sartorial signature long into the 20th century as his Lynchburg distillery grew and expanded into regional markets. A major event came in 1884, when he purchased a distillery just outside of Lynchburg, which was close to another equally important freshwater source, Cave Spring. This site was known as "the Hollow" in local lore, revered as the site where the first distiller in the county, a man named Alfred Neaton, chanced upon the charcoal-filtering process back in the 1820s. The company transitioned from barrels and jugs to sealed glass bottles in the 1890s, and then began using a distinctive square bottle, which fortuitously would not roll across a moving vehicle.

Daniel's sister Finnetta, called Nettie, had married a man from another longtime Lincoln County family, the Motlows. Their son, Lemuel, began working at the distillery in 1880, when he was just ten years old, as a wood-chopper and hog-tender. Daniel brought him into the distillery itself in 1887, and also brought in other nephews as his business expanded. "Captain Jack," as the founder was known around Lynchburg, was one of the area's wealthiest men and was a beloved local patriarch.

Deeded Company to Nephews

Daniel's passing became part of the legend of his company's brand: one day in late 1906, he went to the office and tried to open the safe, which worked by a predetermined combination of numbers. Unable to get the sequence to unlock the door, he kicked the iron box, stubbed his toe, and the wound became infected. Already suffering from poor health, his condition weakened, and he handed over the daily operations to Lemuel. He also signed a deed that gave Motlow and another nephew, Richard Daniel, control of the company, but Richard soon accepted a cash payout from his cousin. Daniel went to Hot Springs, Arkansas, in an attempt to restore his health. Moore County went "dry" in 1909, a sign of a growing temperance movement across America, meaning that whiskey, wine, beer, and or other intoxicating beverages could not be manufactured nor sold within its confines. The state of Tennessee followed with its own edict in 1910, and Lemuel supervised the company's relocation to St. Louis, Missouri.

Daniel's original leg wound continued to deteriorate to the point where his left leg became infected with gangrene, and he underwent surgery to amputate it in the summer of 1911. He died several weeks later, on October 9, 1911, at the age of 62. His funeral was held at the original Primitive Baptist church congregation to which his parents had belonged. His distillery survived the dire period of Prohibition, when the sale of all alcoholic beverages was banned by constitutional amendment, but was the first distillery allowed to begin operation once Prohibition was repealed in 1933. Motlow's sons eventually sold the company to Brown-Forman Distillers in 1956, which turned it into one of the world's most recognized liquor brands.

Books

Krass, Peter, *Blood & Whiskey: The Life and Times of Jack Daniel,* Wiley, 2004.

Periodicals

American History, June 2010.
Brandweek, November 15, 2004.
Popular Mechanics, September 1998.□

Bobby Darin

American singer and actor Bobby Darin (1936–1973) gained fame as a teen idol in the late 1950s. The singer of "Mack the Knife," "Dream Lover," and other early rock and roll classics, Darin effortlessly segued into a film career and married blonde screen icon Sandra Dee in what appeared to be a fairy-tale cinematic romance of two young stars at the peak of fame. A move to more serious films and folk music failed to keep Darin's fans interested, and he died at an unexpectedly young age of 37 after open-heart surgery.

RB/Redferns/Getty Images

Bobby Darin's birth name was Walden Robert Cassotto, and his childhood was blighted by the Cassottos' financial hardships and his own serious health concerns. Born at Bellevue Hospital in New York City on May 14, 1936, he was ostensibly the long-awaited second child of Vivian "Polly" Walden Cassotto, who was in her late forties. Polly's husband, however, had recently disappeared from their neighborhood, and both were morphine addicts. They already had a 16-year-old daughter, Nina, and as an adult Darin was traumatized to learn that Nina was actually his mother. Polly and Nina conspired to hide the unplanned pregnancy from family and neighbors. and then pretend the newborn was a surprise "midlife" fertility event for Polly.

Polly Walden Cassotto, the woman Darin believed to be his mother, came from a well-to-do Rhode Island family and had grown up in Chicago. Somewhat of a free spirit, she had once been a vaudeville singer and was said to have married but not divorced two other men before she wed Savierio Cassotto in New York City around 1912. He was the son of Italian immigrants and a cabinetmaker by trade, but worked as an aide to an organized-crime boss named Frank Costello. Known on the streets as "Big Sam Curly," Cassotto was eventually overcome by his opiate and gambling addictions, and his recklessness prompted the Costello group to disown him. He went to prison for theft in 1934, and died of pneumonia. Nothing is known about

Darin's biological father, except for the fact that he was a college student whom Nina had briefly dated.

Polly, Nina, and little Bobby lived in a series of rundown apartment buildings, first at 125th Street and Second Avenue in Harlem, then in the South Bronx, and later in a Lower East Side public-housing project called Baruch Place. The family received municipal welfare benefits for a time but their circumstances improved when Nina began working full-time and married a hardworking man named Charlie Maffia. Darin was a sickly child from an early age, often confined to bed with weakness and fevers, and finally at age eight doctors pinpointed the condition as rheumatic fever. Polly and Nina were told the boy would probably die before he reached adulthood from the aftereffects of the fever, which had weakened his heart. The family managed to keep this secret from him for several more years.

Dreamed of Broadway Career

Darin was smaller and less robust than his playmates, but remained energetic, active, and musically gifted. From an early age he showed a talent for memorizing songs and an obvious love of performing for an audience of any size. By middle school he was a talented mimic of top radio stars of the day, and later in his teens demonstrated prowess on the drums, piano, and even the xylophone. Though he dreamed of a career in the performing arts, he obediently followed a more professional academic path to the Bronx High School of Science, a highly competitive magnet school. He spent summers working with friends as a busboy at a resort in the Catskills, occasionally taking summer-school classes at a nearby high school in the morning hours to make up for his poor grades at Bronx Science. He started his first band with friends at the resort, and dazzled guests with his dance moves, too. In the era of acrobatic stage virtuosos like Gene Kelly and Donald O'Connor, Darin dreamed of a career as a Broadway hoofer, but eventually learned about his heart condition and the lifelong physical limitations he faced.

Darin turned to songwriting as a creative outlet and path to stardom. After graduating from Bronx Science in 1953, he enrolled at Hunter College as a drama and speech major. He eventually dropped out to play in a nightclub combo, and that led to an introduction to another Bronx native, Don Kirshner. Kirshner already had some music-business connections, but they struggled to land a publishing deal; their first successes were radio advertising jingles for local businesses. They eventually won over executives at Decca Records, who signed them, and Darin was offered a recording deal, too. He changed his name from "Bobby Cassotto" to "Bobby Darin" for his 1956 debut single, "Rock Island Line," a cover of a blues classic; on its B-side was "Timber," a song Darin co-wrote with Kirshner and another writer.

Warned Away from Francis

Darin and Kirshner eventually went over to Atco, a subsidiary of Atlantic Records, and had some success writing for others, but Darin's solo career as an Elvis Presley-type failed to gain much notice. During this period Darin also had an ill-fated romance with singer Connie Francis, who rose to fame in 1958 with her number one single "Who's Sorry Now?" Of Italian heritage and a New Jersey native, Francis had much in common with Darin, but her controlling father allegedly threatened Darin at gunpoint. Francis had a hobbled career for years and later revealed that she never got over the loss of Darin from her life.

Darin finally had his first hit record with "Splish Splash," which he had co-written on a lark as a dare from DJ Murray "Murray the K" Kaufman. It was released in May of 1958 and peaked at number three on the U.S. pop charts; it took several more singles before Darin became a star with "Dream Lover" in early 1959, which peaked at number two in the United States but went to number one in Britain. "Mack the Knife," released in August of 1959, cemented Darin's name in the early history of rock and roll. The snappy song was actually based on a much earlier work from German composer Kurt Weill's *Threepenny Opera* of 1928, and was a gloomy dirge about a criminal named Mackie "the Knife" Messer. Others had sung an English-language version, including popular big-band leader Louis Armstrong in 1956, but it was Darin's that became one of the best-selling records of 1959 and earned him the Grammy award for Record of the Year in early 1960 after nine weeks at the number one spot.

A bonafide star not yet 25, Darin was offered film roles, television series, and an array of lucrative performing gigs. He opted for a choice film debut in *Come September,* a 1961 romantic comedy whose main stars were Rock Hudson and Gina Lollobrigida. Hudson was cast as a wealthy American bachelor tycoon who turns up at his Italian vacation home to find that his caretaker has turned it into a youth hostel on the sly; Darin played one of the young vacationers and sang the title song, which he also wrote. In the film his character, Tony, romances a young blonde played by Sandra Dee, and the pair fell in love instantly—a boon to the publicity departments at Universal Studios, at Darin's label, and on Dee's management team. The couple announced their engagement in November of 1960 and were wed on December 2, 1960. They welcomed their first and only child, son Dodd Mitchell Darin, just after their first anniversary.

Struggled with Fame

After this point, Darin's film and music career never regained its initial momentum, and the giddy whirlwind romance with Dee also spiraled into a downward trajectory of a typical unhappy Hollywood marriage. His attempts to take control over his creative life resulted in a series of curious forays. To distance himself from the teenybopper rock singers with whom he had been classed, he wrote and recorded country-and-western tunes, then signed with Capitol Records, whose executives positioned him as their new crooner act to replace its top star, Frank Sinatra, who had parted ways with the label. Trussed up in a tuxedo and bow tie, Darin began singing engagements at the Copacabana nightclub in New York City, eventually adding Las Vegas dates.

Darin's acting career also took a curious turn when he co-starred with Sidney Poitier in the 1962 drama *Pressure*

Point. Darin's character is an obviously deranged young man detained on sedition charges during World War II; he hurls racial insults at Poitier's character, a psychiatrist sent to evaluate him. The tagline of the film's promotional material announced "Some Men and Some Motion Pictures Just Won't Conform"—an apt summary for the film, which confused newly racially sensitized audiences at the peak of the civil-rights movement in America.

Darin was nominated for an Academy Award for Best Supporting Actor in 1964 film for *Captain Newman, M.D.* in which he played a sufferer of post-traumatic stress disorder. He and Dee made two lightweight romantic comedies together: *If a Man Answers* released in 1962, and *That Funny Feeling* in 1965. But Darin and Dee's marriage did not survive the decade, and they divorced in 1967. Musically, he continued to defy expectations, recording jazzy standards then moving into folk music. The folk scene failed to take his work seriously, recalling his teen-idol status and nightclub act, which tied him culturally to a slightly older demographic.

Emotionally Gutted by Events of 1968

Darin later explained his decisions as weighted by historical events and a rapidly changing American culture. "Years ago I had the choice between ethnic and plastic, and I chose plastic," he told one interviewer, according to David Hajdu in *The Atlantic.* "And twelve or thirteen years later, it dawned on me that I'd chosen the wrong one." Active in Democratic Party politics, he was one of the major stars who took part in a gala 46th birthday event/fundraiser for President John F. Kennedy in 1963 just months before Kennedy was assassinated. In the 1968 presidential race, Darin campaigned for U.S. senator Robert F. Kennedy Jr., brother of the slain president, and was at the Ambassador Hotel in downtown Los Angeles celebrating Bobby Kennedy's victory in the California primary on Tuesday, June 4, 1968. The presumptive Democratic Party candidate gave a speech then went through the hotel kitchen, where he was shot by a lone assailant and died 26 hours later.

Darin was traumatized by the second Kennedy assassination, the end of his marriage, and his inability to regain his footing on the charts. He had been so ardently committed to liberal causes that he considered entering politics, but finally his sister Nina revealed the secret of his parentage, fearful that his attempt to run for office would finally expose the family's secret. Shocked, Darin went into seclusion, giving away most of his possessions and moving into a small trailer at Big Sur, a scenic but remote part of northern California.

Darin reemerged with his own record label, Direction Records, that promoted folk and protest-music artists, and signed a deal with the NBC network for a comeback series that premiered in the summer of 1972 under the title *The Bobby Darin Amusement Company.* It became the *The Bobby Darin Show* when NBC renewed it for a weekly run in 1973, but Darin's health issues had finally started to take a visible toll on him. He underwent heart surgery in 1971 to install artificial valves damaged from his childhood rheumatic fever. Dental surgery in 1973 resulted in a rare infection that turned to sepsis and weakened his heart once again, and his team of physicians at Cedars-Sinai Medical Center in Los Angeles opted to repair the valves with another open-heart procedure. After five hours in surgery Darin died in post-operative care, never having regained consciousness. He was 37 years old.

Books

Evanier, David, *Roman Candle: The Life of Bobby Darin,* Rodale, 2004.

Starr, Michael Seth, *Bobby Darin: A Life,* Rowman & Littlefield, 2004.

Periodicals

The Atlantic, January–February 2005.

Los Angeles Times, January 17, 1990.

New York Times, December 21, 1973; November 21, 2004.□

Danielle Darrieux

Danielle Darrieux (born 1917) is one of French cinema's most beloved icons. A performer whose career began in the 1930s with romantic comedies and musicals, Darrieux had worked steadily for nearly eight decades. Her list of screen credits, which run from 1931 to 2010, make hers one of the longest careers in the history of film.

Danielle Yvonne Marie Antoinette Darrieux was born on May 1, 1917, in Bordeaux, France, as the musically gifted daughter of an ophthalmologist who served with the French forces in World War I. After the war's end later in 1917 the family, which included two more children, moved to Paris. Darrieux's father died when she was seven and her part-Algerian mother, who had some professional experience as a singer and music teacher, struggled to provide for them.

Debuted at 14

Darrieux trained on the cello at an early age and began the *concours,* or selection process for entrance, at the Paris Conservatory. She did not do well, she admitted in a *Times* of London interview with writer Ronald Hayman, and when an offer to appear in a film turned up, she convinced her mother to let her accept it. She was 14 years old when *Le Bal,* a French comedy made by Wilhelm Thiele, was released in theaters in September of 1931. Thiele was an Austrian by birth but made films for both French and German-language audiences. "I thought it was a joke," Darrieux later told Hayman about her role as Antoinette. "I didn't realize what I was doing. It was just like a game. It took me four years to realize what it was and to like being an actress."

Darrieux was the unlikeliest of actors, she revealed, because she was paralyzed by a natural reticence and

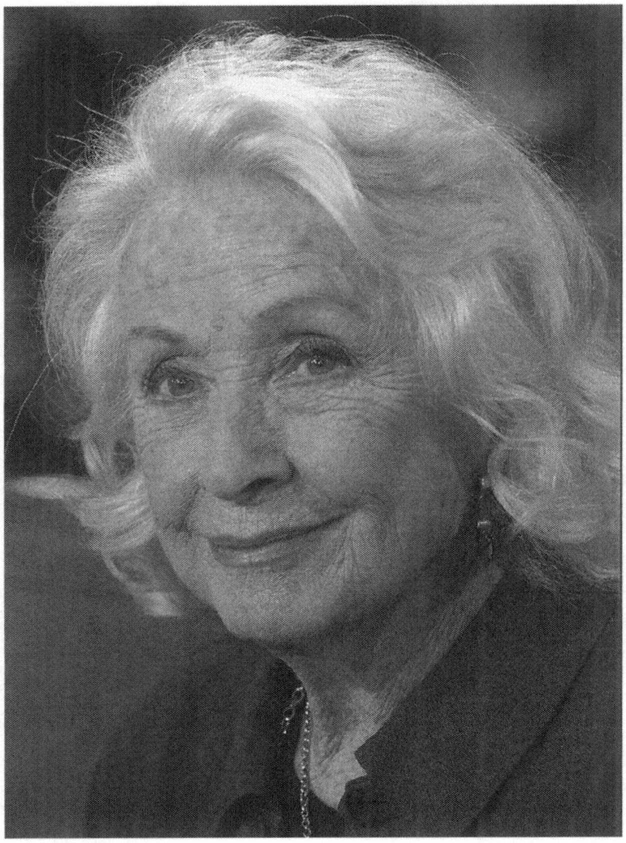

rederic Souloy/Gamma-Rapho/Getty Images

typical teenage self-consciousness. Recalling how ill at ease she always felt when she had to speak before unfamiliar faces, she said that the heavy-duty spackle used during film's black-and-white era gave her courage. "It was exactly like a mask," she told Hayman in the London *Times.* "I felt, 'Oh, it's marvellous because when I blush nobody can see.'"

Darrieux went on to appear in a flurry of French movies while still in her teens. These include *Coquecigrole,* a lead role for her in 1931 and only her second film, and the comedies *Château de Rêeve* (Dream Castle), and the musical *Mon coeur t'appelle* (My Heart Is Calling You). Between 1932 and the end of 1934 she had appeared in eleven films, a few shot on location elsewhere in Europe. In 1935 she wed Henri Decoin, a screenwriter and director, in between five other cinema releases that year. He directed her in several projects that decade and helped turn Darrieux into one of France's most appealing film stars of the day—and one of its highest-paid females of her era.

Moved to Hollywood

Darrieux's breakout role came as the doomed Baroness Marie Vetséra in the 1936 epic *Mayerling.* Paired with French cinema's newest leading male star, Charles Boyer, Darrieux was cast as the lover of the Austrian crown prince, Archduke Rudolf, who was found shot to death in 1889 an apparent double-suicide pact with Vetséra in the hunting lodge of the film's title. A familiar tale to Europeans of the era, the doomed Rudolf/Marie love story was characterized as a struggle between the feudal and the progressive in Central Europe and the heir's death inadvertently led to a shifted royal succession and events that sparked the outbreak of world war in 1914. Anatole Litvak directed the film and it made international stars of both him and Darrieux. In 1937 *Mayerling* won the New York Film Critics Circle Award for Best Foreign Film of the previous year. Darrieux's hairstyle in the film, a modernized version of a nineteenth-century updo, was widely copied by young women in America and ignited a minor debate over the merits of a no-fuss bob cut and the return to more complicated retro styles.

Darrieux was lured to Hollywood by the prospect of a lucrative studio contract. Universal signed her in January of 1937, despite the fact she barely spoke English, and she embarked upon a crash course to learn it. Her first American film was *The Rage of Paris,* which co-starred her with Douglas Fairbanks Jr. A classic screwball comedy in which she played a Parisian transplant to New York on the hunt for a rich husband, the movie premiered July 2, 1938, to excellent reviews, but did not cement Darrieux's career as a star of the American screen. The process of making it was long and difficult, and Darrieux balked at the amount of publicity she was expected to do for it. Contract negotiations over her next project broke down, and she and Decoin returned to France for a jubilant welcome.

Throughout the 1930s, Darrieux continued to make musicals, costume dramas, and romantic comedies. Most of them were shown in U.S. cinemas, including *Mademoiselle ma mère* and *Katia.* Her career skidded to a halt, however, when France was invaded by neighboring Nazi Germany in the spring of 1940. Paris was placed under a military-government administration, and the creative professions faced an onslaught of new regulatory oversight. There was even an office set up to ensure French films were in line with Nazi political ideology. Both Darrieux and Decoin's careers stalled when the Occupation began, and their marriage would soon come to a highly publicized end.

Criticized for Contacts with Nazis

Darrieux's life changed dramatically when she met famed raconteur Porfirio Rubirosa at a party in Paris during the first year of the Occupation. A rakish diplomat from the Dominican Republic with a reputation as an ardent and indefatigable womanizer, Rubirosa charmed Darrieux and she left Decoin. Rubirosa had less success with Nazi officials, who arrested him and transferred him to an internment camp in Germany. Bad Nauheim was less a prison camp than a form of luxury house-arrest for high-profile detainees, and Darrieux, her divorce from Decoin final, managed to secure permission to visit Rubirosa after traveling to Berlin for the German opening of the last film she had made under Decoin's direction, *Premier Rendez-vous* (Her First Affair). She met with Germany's Reichsminister for Propaganda, Joseph Goebbels, and secured permission to visit her fiancé at Bad Nauheim, which caused a stir.

Rubirosa was released and the couple were wed in September of 1942. They lived in France and then Switzerland for the remainder of the war.

When World War II ended in 1945 Darrieux was roundly criticized for having collaborated with the enemy. The French Resistance shamed her for traveling to Germany and for a pair of films she reportedly made under pressure in 1942 for a company run by a German producer in France. These were *Caprices* and *Le Fausse maîtresse* (Twisted Mistress), which had limited release in Europe. She had trouble resuming her film career in France after the war, but she and Rubirosa traveled to Italy for the filming of *Ruy Blas,* a major costume drama with a screenplay written by Jean Cocteau from a story by Victor Hugo. While there, Rubirosa met American heiress Doris Duke and parted ways with Darrieux, who married a third time in 1948. Her third husband was screenwriter George Mitsikidès, and their union lasted until his death in 1991.

The prestige of *Ruy Blas,* in which Darrieux played a Spanish queen, did much to restore Darrieux's reputation. The 1948 production featured a handsome French lead, Jean Marais, with Cocteau's lavish sets and costumes. "As usual in her pictures, Danielle Darrieux is beautiful and intense as the queen who is made the victim of an innocent love and elaborate intrigue," wrote Bosley Crowther in his *New York Times* review. The onetime French box-office leader even returned briefly to Hollywood when MGM persuaded her to star in a musical titled *Rich, Young, and Pretty* in 1951. A year later Darrieux was cast opposite James Mason in an espionage thriller set in Istanbul during World War II, *5 Fingers.* Based on the true story of a German agent who worked as a valet for British consul, the film was directed by noted Hollywood tastemaker Joseph L. Mankiewicz and earned terrific reviews.

Emerged as Art-House Favorite

Darrieux's career in European cinema was bolstered by her alliance with Max Ophüls, a German Jew who had trained in the theater and then fled to Hollywood when the Nazis came to power in the 1930s. Ophüls put Darrieux in three of his movies, starting with *Le Ronde* (The Round) in 1950, followed by *Le Plaisir* (Pleasure) in 1952 and *The Earrings of Madame de...* a year later. These were films with serious literary credentials but usually racy content. *Le Ronde* was nominated in two Academy Award categories and won the British Academy of Film and Television Award (BAFTA) for best film. In 1955, Darrieux appeared in the lead in *Lady Chatterley's Lover,* another risqué tale and adapted from the D.H. Lawrence novel of the same name. The film version was the target of influential Roman Catholic censors at the Vatican and its showing was even banned by the New York state legislature.

One of Darrieux's last English-language films was *The Greengage Summer* in 1961. Later that decade she appeared with upstart Catherine Deneuve in Jacques Demy's 1967 musical *Les Demoiselles de Rochefort* (The Young Girls of Rochefort). In 1970 she made her Broadway debut when she replaced Katherine Hepburn in *Coco,* a musical version of the life of French fashion legend Coco Chanel—a figure who was still alive at the time, and whom Darrieux of course knew. "I've invited her to come to my opening," Darrieux reported to *New York Times* writer Thomas Quinn Curtiss. "She didn't say yes and she didn't say no. She just smiled enigmatically."

Darrieux confessed to experiencing major stage fright, though she had some stage experience in Paris before coming to Broadway. "When the curtain goes up you feel you are doomed. Nothing will stop the progress of the play once it starts," she explained to Curtiss in the *New York Times* interview. Despite lackluster reviews, Darrieux gamely attempted another musical, this one in London in 1972. *Ambassador* was a musical version of the Henry James novel *The Ambassadors* and closed after a short run.

Darrieux spent the rest of the decade in semi-retirement, living with Mitsikidès in Paris and at their second home on an island off the coast of Brittany. She appeared in the occasional French-television miniseries in the 1980s and '90s, but a younger generation of filmmakers began to cast her in their well-received art-house projects. She appeared with Deneuve again in André Téchiné's *La lieu du crime* (Scene of the Crime) in 1986, and a third time in a 2001 film from François Ozon, *8 Femmes* (8 Women), that featured an all-star roster of French cinematic legends. In 2007 she contributed a voice to *Persepolis,* the acclaimed animated film based on Iranian-born writer Marjane Satrapi's graphic novel of the same name about a young woman in Iran in the 1970s and '80s. That marked Darrieux's 137th screen credit and 76 years since her debut in *Le Bal.*

Books

Riding, Alan, *And the Show Went On: Cultural Life in Nazi-occupied Paris,* Random House, 2010.

Periodicals

New York Times, March 2, 1952; October 4, 1948; July 16, 1970.

Times (London, England), October 16, 1971.□

Al Davis

American Al Davis (1929–2011) is perhaps best remembered as the colorful, controversial long-time managing partner and owner of the Oakland Raiders of the National Football League (NFL). Davis had a long history with professional football and the NFL, working not only as a scout, head coach, and general manager, but also briefly as the commissioner of the American Football League in 1966.

Born Allen Davis on July 4, 1929, in Brockton, Massachusetts, he was the son of Louis Davis, a successful businessman. Davis was primarily raised in Brooklyn, New York, and during his youth, he worked selling hot dogs at Ebbets Field. He graduated from Erasmus Hall High School, then entered Wittenberg College. Davis

later transferred to and received his undergraduate degree in English from Syracuse University. There, he played junior varsity football.

Began Coaching Career

After graduating from Syracuse, Davis coached football at Adelphi University, then for the U.S. Army at Fort Belvoir in Virginia. Davis began his career in professional football at the age of 24 with the Baltimore Colts, a National Football League (NFL) team. He then was an assistant football coach at the Citadel military school in South Carolina. After leaving the Citadel, he spent two years on the coaching staff at the University of Southern California. At the time, recruiting violations meant that the Trojans were on probation for two years. Davis left Los Angeles when Don Clark, the head football coach, retired and was replaced by John McKay, instead of Davis.

An upset Davis joined the American Football League (AFL), a newly formed professional league intended to challenge the established NFL. He worked for the Los Angeles Chargers beginning in 1960. Davis remained in the team's employ after they moved to San Diego in 1961 until January 1963, when he was hired by the lowly Oakland Raiders as the team's head coach and general manager. Davis was 33 years old at the time, and the youngest person in the history of professional football to hold this position.

Over the next three seasons, the Raiders went 23-16-3. In 1963, Davis was named the AFL's coach of the year after the Raiders, a 1-13 team in 1962 improved to a record of 10-4. In April 1966, Davis was appointed the AFL commissioner. Though Davis only served for six weeks, he essentially brokered an agreement for a merger between the AFL and NFL. After his task was done, he stepped down to return to the Raiders.

Became Part-Owner of the Raiders

Davis had bought a ten percent stake in the team, and served as one of the team's three partners, along with Wayne Valley and Ed McGah. Upon his return, Davis served as Oakland's managing general partner and head of football operations. It was Davis who chose the Raiders colors—black and silver—which were selected to intimidate. He also chose their pirate-inspired insignia, which was a shield with an image of a pirate and crossed sabers. In 1968, he made history when the Raiders became the first NFL or AFL team to draft an African American quarterback, Eldridge Dickey, in the first round.

It took several years for the merger between the AFL and the NFL to be completed. In that period, the Raiders won the AFL championship in 1967. In 1970, the merger was complete. Davis was disappointed, however, when he was not named commissioner of the merged league. Pete Rozelle was given the honor.

Focusing on his team, the Raiders became one of the new NFL's dominant teams, a trend that would continue until the 1980s. In addition to winning numerous division championships and regularly making the playoffs, the Raiders also won three Super Bowls, in 1977, 1981, and 1984. Though he hired a string of bright young coaches, Davis essentially remained deeply involved in coaching decisions, one who would call plays and make substitutions from the sidelines. Overall, he emphasized a forceful style of play, which emphasized long passing on offense and brutal physicality on defense. Davis wanted his teams to be feared, not respected.

Gained Control of the Team

Davis had a significant role in the Raiders' success. In 1972, a revised partnership agreement was signed which gave him almost absolute control over the team. From this position, he was often given credit for making risky choices that led to success for the Raiders. He supported giving players second chances. Davis also took chances on misfit players who potentially had game-changing speed but also might have lacked a football background or had a checkered past.

There was a reason for Davis's choices as the head of the Raiders. According to Phil Elderkin of the *Christian Science Monitor,* Davis once said, "I always wanted to take an organization and make it the best in sports. I admired the New York Yankees for their power and intimidation. I admired the Brooklyn Dodgers under Branch Rickey for their speed and player development. I felt there was no reason the two approaches couldn't be combined into one powerful organziation."

Moved Team to Los Angeles

Davis was also controversial, and made decisions that angered his team's fan base. In 1980, he tried to move the Raiders from Oakland to Los Angeles but was stopped by a court injunction. Davis then filed an antitrust lawsuit against the NFL. A federal district court ruled in his favor in June 1982 and he won millions from other owners in the process. Davis moved the team to Los Angeles in time for the beginning of the 1982 NFL season. In Los Angeles, the team played at the Los Angeles Coliseum. The following year, Davis made modern-era NFL history when he hired the first African American head coach, Art Shell. Steve Cockran of the *San Jose Mercury News* quoted Davis as saying "The Raiders have never been interested in a man's color, only his ability."

The Raiders would remain in Los Angeles until 1995. Davis returned the team to Oakland only after the Raiders tried and failed to build a new stadium at Hollywood Park in Inglewood. After returning to Oakland, Davis sued the NFL, claiming the league had sabotaged his stadium-building efforts. The legal matter dragged on for years. Though the NFL won a decision in 2001, a new trial was ordered after accusations were made that one juror was biased against Davis and another committed misconduct. An appeals court ultimately overturned the decision, and the case was thrown out by the California Supreme Court in 2007.

This was not the only lawsuit against the NFL brought by Davis in this time period. In the mid-1990s, after the move back to Oakland, Davis sued the NFL for $1.2 billion on behalf of the Raiders to retain exclusive rights to the Los Angeles market despite the fact that the Raiders were located in Oakland. The Raiders lost this suit. At the same time, Davis sued the city of Oakland for not having the sold-out games that were promised if he brought the team back from Los Angeles.

Experienced Less Success

During the 1990s and first decade of the 21st century, the Davis-led Raiders did not have the same success as they had in the 1970s and 1980s. Yet Davis remained respected, if not admired, as a maverick, innovator, and influential team owner who built the Raiders into an international franchise. His sense of style also brought him attention as he frequently wore sunglasses and warm-up suits in his team's colors. In 1992, Davis was honored with election to the National Football Hall of Fame. Five years later, he again made NFL history when he hired Amy Trask as the first woman chief executive officer (CEO) for an NFL franchise. Trask was also the first woman CEO in any of the four major sports in the United States.

The last best year for the Raiders under Davis's leadership was 2002, when Oakland won the AFC championship and made it to the Super Bowl. The Raiders lost to the Tampa Bay Buccaneers in the final game, however. In 2005, Davis acquired majority interest in the Raiders after buying the shares of the McGah family. Two years later, Davis turned around and sold a minority stake in the team for $150 million. Still a respected leader in the NFL even in his seventies, Davis helped broker the labor deal between the owners and the players union in 2006.

Yet the Raiders had one of their worst stretches as a franchise after 2002, posting some of the NFL's worst records and going through five coaches in one six-year period. Though Davis was always present at practice, training camp, and in the locker room, he made fewer and fewer public appearances except for when coaches were hired and fired. When introducing a new coach, he would often spend more time criticizing the fired coach than lauding his new coach.

Focused on Football Until Death

Throughout his years with the Raiders, Davis not only believed in protecting the sanctity of football and building the sport, but also remaining loyal to those who had played and worked for him and had been loyal in return. Davis regularly paid medical bills for former players, and gave them jobs when they needed a break. When Kansas City Chiefs player Derrick Thomas died, Davis paid for his funeral. Former Raiders coach John Madden told Steve Cockran of the *San Jose Mercury News,* "He gave his whole life to football. Not only to the Raiders but to the NFL. He did a lot of things for people and for players and for coaches. The good that he does is really going to come up some day."

In declining health at the end of his life, Davis was less publicly involved with the Raiders in his last few years and attended fewer league functions. Behind the scenes, he remained involved with Oakland by preparing for the draft, negotiating contracts, and discussing strategies with the coaches. In the months before his death, however, Davis did not attend any training camp practices and missed one of the team's games. When he missed that Raiders game in Buffalo in September 2011, it was only the third game he had not attended in his 49 seasons with the franchise.

Davis died of congestive heart failure, cardiomyopathy, and ventricular fibrillation at the Oakland Airport Hilton in Oakland, California, on October 8, 2011. He was 82 years old. According to *ESPN NFL,* the Raiders released a statement saying "The Oakland Raiders are deeply saddened by the passing of Al Davis. Al Davis was unique, a maverick, a giant among giants, a true legend among legends, the brightest star among stars, a hero, a mentor, a friend."

After his death, Davis's widow, Carol, became the Raiders' majority owner. His son, Mark, became the head of operations. Davis's legacy, however, would not be forgotten. Upon Davis's death, the owner of long-time rival Denver Broncos, Pat Bowlen, told Jeff Legwold of the *Denver Post,* "During my 28 years with the Broncos, I came to know Al Davis as one of the most influential and innovative people in the history of the National Football League. His competitive spirit and intensity grew our rivalry with the Raiders into one of the fiercest in all of sports. I respected Al for what he meant to the NFL. He was a visionary who defined the Raiders and had an enormous responsibility for the prosperity of this league."

Periodicals

Christian Science Monitor, October 11, 2011.
Contra Costa Times (CA), October 28, 2011.
Denver Post, October 9, 2011.
New York Times, October 8, 2011; October 10, 2011.
San Jose Mercury News, October 8, 2011.

Online

"Raiders Owner Al Davis Dead at 82," *ESPN NFL,* http://espn.go.com/nfl/story/_/id/7074380/oakland-raiders-owner-al-davis-dies-82 (December 11, 2013).□

Emily Davison

The death of British suffragette Emily Wilding Davison shocked the world in 1913. The 39-year-old former teacher and activist with Britain's Women's Social and Political Union (WSPU) had been arrested on several previous occasions for committing acts of public disorder designed to call attention to the issue of women's suffrage. On June 4, 1913, she stepped out onto the racecourse at the elite Epsom Derby in Surrey, England, and attempted to grab the bridle of Anmer, a bay colt belonging to King George V. Badly mangled within a matter of seconds, she never regained consciousness and died of her injuries four days later.

Hulton Archive/Getty Images

Emily Wilding Davison was born on October 11, 1872, in Blackheath, a neighborhood in southeast London. Her parents were originally from Northumberland, in the north of England, and she grew up with two sisters and a brother, plus two half-siblings from her father's first marriage. She was educated at the single-sex Kensington School in London and entered the University of London's Royal Holloway College, another women's institution, until her family could no longer afford the tuition payments following the death of her father. For a few years she worked as a schoolteacher in order to save the funds to complete her education. At the time, women were permitted to take full courses at Oxford University, where she attended its St. Hugh's College, but the school did not grant women official degrees.

Joined WSPU

British women had been campaigning publicly for the right to vote since the 1820s. The Reform Act of 1832 had expanded voting privileges to a wider range of men—previously, only males who owned property of a certain monetary value could cast ballots in local and general elections—but further expansion to include women property owners and taxpayers was bitterly opposed by conservative elements in Britain. Another Reform Act of 1867 enacted by Parliament expanded the right to vote to thousands of men of humbler origins living in cities, which renewed the push for women's suffrage. In what some women activists considered the ultimate irony, since 1837 Britain had actually been ruled by a woman, Queen Victoria, whose 63-year-long reign until her death in 1901 was one of the longest in the history of the crown.

In 1906, the 34-year-old Davison joined the Women's Social and Political Union (WSPU). The three-year-old organization was founded by Emmeline Pankhurst, who formed it after an older suffragist group had rejected her demands calling for a more radical course of action. The WSPU's slogan was "Deeds Not Words," and by the time Davison joined it was gaining a reputation for civil disobedience and militant protest actions that crossed the line into criminal hooliganism. After well-attended demonstrations outside the Houses of Parliament proved ineffective, some WSPU activists took to smashing shop windows and vandalizing property. Two women managed to send themselves via Royal Mail to No. 10 Downing Street, the official residence of British prime minister Herbert Henry Asquith, leader of the Liberal Party. Some in Asquith's party supported women's suffrage, but he was staunchly opposed. Women, traditionalists argued, were incapable of complex reasoning required to evaluate a political matter, and they seemed to be ruled by emotions, too—a denigration bolstered by the WSPU activists, who were considered dangerously irate.

Force-Fed in Prison

Davison had been living and working in Northhamptonshire as a governess, a post she left in 1908 to move to London. Soon after that she became one of the scores of WSPU activists arrested, tried, and convicted on public disturbance charges. In jail the suffragists went on hunger strikes, refusing to eat, in order to call attention to their plight and the injustice of being incarcerated for demanding the right to participate in the political life of their homeland. In 1909 alone, Davison was arrested five times. In the first event she served a sentence of one month on the charge of obstruction. In July of 1909, a judge sentenced her to two months on another obstruction charge, but she went on a hunger strike and was given early release. Twice more in 1909 she was charged and convicted on stone-throwing charges. She was detained at two sites, His Majesty's Prison for women in Holloway, London, and at another H.M.'s Prison with women inmates, Strangelands, in Manchester.

The British government was in a quandary about the WSPU's actions. Hunger strikes were a particularly effective form of political protest in detention, but the Asquith government was loath to have any women detainees die in custody, fearing it would only inflame the cause. Government authorities approved force-feeding measures to break the hunger strikers at Holloway prison. This was a particularly heinous and gruesome procedure, requiring physical restraint and subjecting the women to extreme psychological discomfort through the use of wooden or steel mouth gags and rubber tubing inserted by force into the esophagus; the victims often vomited from the ordeal, and it would then have to be restarted. The barbaric procedure was widely condemned and helped sway public opinion toward the women's voting-rights campaign.

Davison managed to elude prison until the infamous Black Friday of November 18, 1910, when Asquith ended a debate in parliament on a bill that would have granted the vote to a limited number of women who owned property. The WSPU's 300-strong protest outside parliament was rebuffed by London police, and some women were victims of police brutality and even sexual assault. Davison was charged with breaking a window in the House of Commons and sentenced to one month in prison. She declared another hunger strike, but was force-fed and so traumatized by it that she managed to barricade herself in her cell with two plank beds. To remedy this stalemate, prison authorities inserted a water-hose through her cell window and flooded the room with cold water until she relented.

Seemed Willing to Become Martyr

Davison launched an arson campaign later in 1911, apparently without the approval of WSPU leadership. Her targets were the red Royal Mail pillar boxes, into which she threw paraffin-soaked rags and a lit match. In January of 1912, she was apprehended and sent once again to Holloway prison. This time, she received a six-month sentence and again embarked upon a hunger strike. When she was being taken to another force-feeding procedure she managed to elude guards and leapt from a balcony on the upper floors, but was saved by a preventive net; she jumped again from that and tumbled down a staircase. "When I attempted to commit suicide in Holloway prison on June 22 I did it deliberately and with all my power because I felt that by nothing but sacrifice of human life would the nation be brought to realise the horrible torture our women face," she wrote in a letter to the *Sunday Times*.

Davison was jailed a total of nine times. The matter of WSPU hunger-strikers was resolved in April of 1913 by the passage of a new Prisoners Act of 1913 called the Temporary Discharge for Ill Health but widely referred to as the Cat and Mouse Act. It permitted detainees the right to go on hunger strike, up to the point their health was compromised, and prison doctors then signed off on a temporary release; when the women's health was restored they were required to report to prison again to serve out the remainder of their sentence. Again, the measure provoked widespread outrage and did little to serve the opposition's arguments.

On June 4, 1913, Davison left her flat in Lambeth, London, and went to Victoria Station, where she bought a round-trip ticket to the town of Epsom in nearby Surrey. The Epsom Downs racecourse hosted one of British thoroughbred racing's most exciting events, the Epsom Derby, which was usually attended by the king or queen, who reliably had a proverbial horse in the race. In this case the monarch was King George V, grandson of the late Queen Victoria and grandfather of another long-reigning monarch, Queen Elizabeth II. The king's horse was a three-year-old bay colt named Anmer. Huge crowds turned out at Epsom every year, eager to see the excitement of the race and the pageantry of the upper classes, who arrived in grand carriages wearing the newest spring fashions to wager large sums on the outcome of the race.

Captured by News Cameras

Davison obtained a race card and made some notations about the entrants. The king's jockey was a man named Herbert Jones, who raced in a pre-Derby event at 1:30 p.m. The main Derby Stakes race started at 3 p.m. It was a mile-and-a-half-long course with an exciting bend called the Tattenham Corner. Davison had two WSPU banners concealed on her. These were well-known flags of the movement, with the signature colors of purple, green, and white, embroidered with the lily-flower symbol and the slogan "Deeds Not Words." One was pinned inside her dress and the other was rolled up inside the sleeve of her jacket. She jostled for a position near the simple wooden barriers separating spectators from the course after the frontrunner thoroughbreds stormed past. After two more horses came by, she dipped under the barrier and walked out to the track. Jones, riding Anmer, had little time to react as Davison raised both arms above her head and tried to grab Anmer's bridle. Instead she and the horse collided with a brute force as captured by three newsreel cameras set up for the race. "The horse struck the woman with its chest, knocking her down among the flying hoofs," reported the *Daily Mirror* newspaper, according to the *New Statesman.*

"Blood rushed from her mouth and nose. Anmer turned a complete somersault and fell upon his jockey."

Anmer rose and cantered off, but Jones's foot was still stuck in a stirrup and he was dragged a few yards. Both he and Davison were unconscious. Spectators rushed through the barriers and a mounted police guard cordoned off the area. Someone shielded Davison's badly injured head in a newspaper. Jones regained consciousness and refused medical treatment. Davison was taken by car to Epsom Cottage Hospital, where doctors performed surgery to relive cranial pressure, but she never regained consciousness and died of her injuries four days later on June 8, 1913.

Davison's shocking death was deemed a suicide mission, though an official inquiry ruled it a death by misadventure, and historians surmise she was likely attempting to attach the WSPU colors to Anmer's bridle for a subversive photo finish. Britons flocked to the cinema the next day to watch the newsreel footage of the trampling, and hate mail decrying the suffragettes' militancy flooded the newspapers. Davison's funeral procession on June 14, 1913, was a major demonstration of WSPU support. Some 6,000 people watched the cortege as it proceeded to St. George's Church in Bloomsbury, London, to the King's Cross train station, from which her casket was transported to a family burial plot in Morpeth, Northumberland. Her grave marker bears the epitaph "Deeds Not Words."

The women's suffrage movement advanced little after that, then was disrupted by the outbreak of World War I. In 1918 a new law granted limited women's suffrage, followed by universal suffrage a decade later. In 2013, the Epsom Derby marked the hundredth anniversary of the tragedy with a special historical display about Davison, her life, and the women's suffrage movement.

Periodicals

Guardian (London, England), May 30, 2013.
Independent (London, England), May 25, 2013.
New Statesman, June 6, 2005; May 24, 2013.
Sunday Times (London, England), February 9, 1986.
Times (London, England), June 5, 1913; June 11, 1913.□

Lisa Della Casa

Swiss opera singer Lisa Della Casa (1919–2012) was one of the leading interpreters of the operatic works of Richard Strauss during the mid-20th century.

© INTERFOTO/Alamy

Swiss opera singer Lisa Della Casa was one of the leading European operatic sopranos of the 20th century. Particularly known for her interpretations of the works of the German Romantic composer Richard Strauss and Austrian Classical composer Wolfgang Amadeus Mozart, Della Casa graced the stages of opera houses both in Europe and in the United States, where she spent 15 years performing with the prestigious Metropolitan Opera company in New York. Her talent, beauty, and charm made her popular with audiences and with her peers, and her early retirement in the 1970s was met with widespread disappointment. Della Casa spent the last 40 years of her life in retirement in Europe.

Born on February 2, 1919, in Bergdorf, near Bern, Switzerland, Della Casa was the daughter of an Italian-Swiss father, Francesco Della Casa, and a German-born mother, Margarete Mueller. Her family was a middle-class one, with her father—himself a frustrated singer barred from pursuing his dream by his parents—working as an ophthalmologist and her mother running a restaurant. Della Casa's parents shared a love of music and encouraged their daughter to study voice from a young age. As an adult, Della Casa recalled that she had first developed an ambition to sing on stage at the age of eight upon hearing a performance of the Strauss opera *Salome* sung by soprano Else Schulz. When she was 15, the aspiring performer entered the Zurich Conservatory in Zurich, Switzerland, to study with Margarete Haeser. "She instructed me in a mixture of bel canto and the Viennese school," Della Casa later recalled in an interview with Lanfranco Rasponi in *The Last Great Divas,* "and if I was able later to sing both repertoires, it is all due to her."

Began Career in Switzerland

The singer first appeared on stage in 1941 in the role of Butterfly in a German-language staging of Italian opera

Madama Butterfly at the small Solothurn-Biel theater in Switzerland. Two years later, Della Casa made her debut with the Zurich Opera House in a minor role as the First Genie in the opera *Die Zauberflöte* (*Magic Flute*)—a step down from the role she had been originally engaged to perform, Pamina. She soon made another professional move forward in Zurich, however, in the role of Annina in the Strauss opera *Der Rosenkavalier.* Although the role was written for a slightly lower mezzo soprano register, the turmoil of World War II limited the availability of opera singers and the company took a chance on Della Casa, believing that her dark-haired good looks would make her appealing as an on-stage Italian.

Della Casa's performance was a success, and more roles with the Zurich company followed on its heels. She sang the role of the Queen of the Night in Mozart's *Magic Flute* soon after, and even performed in blackface as Clara in the American opera *Porgy and Bess.* Della Casa later explained the nature of these early roles to Elizabeth Forbes of *Opera News.* "You arrive as a young singer and do what you are asked, in opera, operetta, everything," Della Casa said. "I was always ready to jump in if the star was sick or was not good enough."

A few years later, with the war ended, the respected Romanian soprano Maria Cebotari came to Zurich to sing the title role in Strauss's *Arabella,* with Della Casa singing the supporting character of Zdenka. Although the young soprano was initially disappointed to appear as Zdenka after expecting to sing the lead role of Arabella herself, the pairing proved a fateful one for her career. Della Casa's performance impressed both the composer Strauss himself, who legendarily predicted that she would one day progress not only to play the starring role but to be its defining interpreter, and the soprano Cebotari, who recommended her to the organizers of the Salzburg Festival in neighboring Austria. The young singer was hired to perform Zdenka in Salzburg and received strong critical notices there. As a result of her successes in Salzburg, she received a contract from the Vienna Opera House, appearing there within the year as Gilda in Verdi's *Rigoletto* and Nedda in the Italian opera *Pagliacci.* Over the next few years, she divided her time among singing in Vienna; Salzburg; Zurich; and Munich, Germany, all places that she would return to repeatedly over the next few decades.

In 1949, Della Casa wed her second husband, Yugoslavian journalist and violin player Dragan Debeljevic. An earlier, unhappy marriage had lasted just a short time before ending in divorce. Debeljevic dedicated much of his time to supporting his wife's artistic endeavors, and she acknowledged that his critical feedback was invaluable to her. The couple's only child, daughter Vesna, was born in March of 1951.

Famed for Interpretations

Beginning in the late 1940s, Della Casa became increasingly known for her interpretations of the works of Strauss. "I soon realized I had the right feeling for the music of Strauss," she told Forbes. "He always wrote the expression and the movement into his music. One could hear what one had to do—it was so simple, so right. But I also found you have to start to sing Strauss very early. If you cannot manage all the difficult passages, that's not important, but if you start too late, you have much greater difficulty coming into the feeling of the music." Over the course of her career, Della Casa appeared as many of Strauss's operatic heroines, including Salome, Ariadne, Chrysothemis, and Marschallin. Through these performances she developed working relationships with some of the leading music talents of the time, including stage directors Rudolf Hartmann and Herbert Graf and conductors Wilhelm Furtwängler and Georg Solti.

In 1950, she first sang the part of Arabella in Zurich, inaugurating what became one of her best-known and respected roles. Della Casa's command of the character was established through further performances at London's Covent Garden Opera House and New York's Metropolitan Opera, where she also sang the role in English. Writing favorably of Della Casa's premiere of the role at the Metropolitan in 1957, *New York Times* reviewer Howard Taubman declared that "a great deal of the credit for the spell woven by *Arabella* at its best belongs to Lisa Della Casa... The Swiss soprano was altogether credible and appealing.... There was a youth in her movements and a beauty in her appearance.... And her singing was unfailingly lovely—accurate, well-focused and sensitively phrased."

Indeed, the critical response to Della Casa's performances during her long tenure at the Metropolitan were typically strong ones. Writing in the *New York Times* about a Metropolitan staging of *Die Meistersinger* in 1956, Taubman called Della Casa's performance of Eva "musically the most satisfying performance.... She sang with sensitivity and feeling, and she made an appealing-looking heroine." Della Casa, however, was less enthused about her years with the Metropolitan Opera. She recalled that she bookended her fifteen-year tenure with the company with performances in the role of Countess Almaviva in Mozart's *Marriage of Figaro,* telling Rasponi that in this repetition "lay the trouble, for in those all years at the Met I was assigned only eleven roles.... It was the same fare over and over again," she complained. Della Casa wished to sing French and Italian roles, but Metropolitan General Manager Rudolf Bing preferred her to perform in the German-language roles that were her specialty. She occasionally appeared in these Italian or French roles in other companies, however, singing Elvira—a part she rather disliked—in *Don Giovanni* at Salzburg in 1954 and Mimi in *La Bohème* in her 1958 San Francisco Opera House debut.

The singer was also known for her interpretations of German lieder, or art songs; during her career Della Casa performed songs by composers including Strauss, Schubert, and Brahms, among others. Writing about a 1957 recording of these types of works, Martin Bernheimer of *Opera News* noted that Della Casa's approach to German songs "tended to concentrate on familiar challenges. But...she enriched them with limpid tone and understated pathos. She savored the power of an insinuating legato and, only when imperative, a soaring climax. She knew the secrets of intimate communication,'' he concluded, applauding her ability to express emotion dynamically but without melodrama.

Retired Early

Beginning in the late 1960s, Della Casa chose to perform less often, dedicating more time to her family. Her only daughter, Vesna, suffered a life-threatening aneurysm in 1970, leading the opera singer to appear even less frequently. Her daughter's continuing ill health preyed on the singer's psyche, and she began to feel that the demands of her family life and her frustrations with the contemporary group of stage directors and conductors made singing an unwanted chore. ''In my contracts I always demanded a full rehearsal, and in the last years no one turned up,'' she complained to Rasponi.

In 1973, Della Casa made her last stage appearance at the Vienna Opera House in *Arabella* and then announced her retirement from performance to the great shock of the music world. She cancelled years' worth of scheduled engagements before making her final performance. On stage, she put extra feeling into her rendition of the operatic line ''Dann fahr ich fort von euch auf Nimmerwiedersehn,'' (''Then I shall leave you, never to see you again,'') which she delivered not to another performer on stage but directly to the audience. As she recalled to Rasponi, it ''was my way of saying goodbye. But of course no one realized that I was bidding goodbye to my loyal public as well.''

Despite hopes to the contrary, the singer spent her retirement years entirely off stage, splitting her time between her family's castle near Lake Constance, Switzerland, and a Spanish villa along the Mediterranean coast. Speaking to Rasponi, Della Casa noted that her retirement was complete. ''Since that night [of her final performance] I have not sung a single note again, not even for my pleasure,'' she admitted. Yet recordings of her music continued to enjoy critical respect and listener enthusiasm, and the singer was remembered fondly as one of the great operatic singers of the German repertory of her era.

Della Casa died on December 10, 2012, in Muensterlingen, Switzerland. She was 93 years old. The Vienna Opera House announced her death soon after, and music critics around the world paid tribute to her memory. Writing for the *Guardian,* Alan Blyth hailed the singer's ''sure sense of style, and her firm characterization, but above all her lovely, even tone.'' F. Paul Driscoll declared that ''Della Casa achieved such small miracles of subtlety that it was impossible to tell the difference between the artist at work and the character she was playing'' in his *Opera News* obituary even as Jonathan Kandell of the *New York Times* recalled her ''outstanding voice, stunning beauty and exceptional stage presence.'' All of these accolades contradicted Della Casa's own expectation for her legacy as she explained it to Rasponi. ''The imprint we [singers] leave is like the snow you see falling.... Tomorrow it will be gone, and there will be nothing. Yes, a few people will remember, but only for a very short time.''

Books

Rasponi, Lanfranco, *The Last Prima Donnas,* Knopf, 1982.

Periodicals

Guardian (London, England), December 11, 2012.

New York Times, January 12, 1956; January 8, 1957; December 12, 2012.

Opera News, March 4, 1995; November 2004; March 2013.□

Cathérine Deneuve

Cathérine Deneuve (born 1943) is one of French cinema's most venerated actors. Cast in a wide range of roles since the 1960s by some of Europe's most acclaimed filmmakers, Deneuve has made a chilly, regal blond beauty her on-screen trademark in more than 100 films over five decades. She once conceded that her career was merely the result of a happy confluence of circumstances in the 1960s, when directors like Roman Polanski and François Truffaut discovered her. "I have never really known what it is to struggle," she told Joan Goodman in a 1981 interview for the *Times* of London. "When everybody thinks I'm so strong and independent, they forget how much luck I have had."

Cathérine Fabienne Dorléac did experience one piece of misfortune, that of being born under the Nazi occupation of France during World War II. The second of four daughters born to mother Renee Deneuve, a former child star whose family name Deneuve later adopted, she was born on October 22, 1943. Her father was Maurice Dorléac, who also worked as an actor and later headed the sound-dubbing department at Paramount Pictures' Paris office. Deneuve's older sister Françoise Dorléac was considered an especially promising new talent in French cinema, and Dorléac's rise was a swift one. Deneuve made her film debut at age 13 in a 1957 movie *Les Collégiennes* (The Twilight Girls), but her career was cemented by 1960's *Les Portes claquent* (The Door Slams), for which Françoise had suggested to the director that her own sibling should be cast as her on-screen sister.

Married Fashion Photographer

In 1961 Deneuve met filmmaker Roger Vadim, who had made a star out of his first wife, Brigitte Bardot, in the 1950s. Deneuve and Vadim became romantically involved during the making of *Le Vice et la vertu* (Vice and Virtue), released in 1963 just as Deneuve had a son by Vadim, named Christian. Though the couple never married, she was 20 years old, and it was a time when becoming a single mother by choice was still frowned upon, and Deneuve risked derailing her career. Instead she sailed forward, impervious to moralists' barbs, and eventually married London high-fashion photographer David Bailey after splitting up with Vadim, who then took up with

©MARKA/Alamy

American film star Jane Fonda. The Deneuve-Bailey nuptials took place in 1965 in London, where Rolling Stones singer Mick Jagger served as best man, and dissolved after Deneuve became romantically involved with Italian screen star Marcello Mastroianni, with whom she had another child, Chiara Mastroianni, in 1972.

A year after the birth of her son, Deneuve became a star in France with the release of an unusual musical film, *Les Parapluies de Cherbourg* (The Umbrellas of Cherbourg), by filmmaker Jacques Demy. Every line of dialogue is sung, and the vividly lensed work and tale of thwarted love resulted in a Palme d'Or award at the Cannes Film Festival; since then it has achieved minor cult status as a curiously sentimental work made at a time of dark shifts toward modernity and realism in postwar European cinema.

Deneuve became a sensation outside of France with her first English-language film, 1965's *Repulsion.* She played a Francophone Belgian manicurist living in London with her more carefree sister. Deneuve's Carol is a stunning beauty, but unnerved by the near-constant attention she receives from men as she moves through her day. It was also Polanski's feature-length debut in English, and the minimal dialogue made Carol's descent into madness when her sister leaves her alone for a vacation all the more chilling; the character's emotional turmoil eventually drives her to murder. As a psychological thriller, *Repulsion* is considered one of Polanski's groundbreaking works and also vaulted Deneuve into international stardom.

Caused Sensation as Séverine

Deneuve worked steadily for nearly all of her career, making at least one and sometimes as many as four films in a single year. She made another sunny romance with Demy in 1967's *Les Demoiselles de Rochefort* (The Young Girls of Rochefort), which co-starred her sister and also featured American movie-musical icon Gene Kelly. It was released in France in March of 1967, and followed six months later by what would become Deneuve's most famous film, *Belle de jour* (Beauty of the Day). It premiered at the 1967 Venice Film Festival and won the Golden Lion award for best film. The first color film directed by Surrealist master Luis Buñuel, *Belle du Jour* elevated Deneuve to the status of cinematic icon. Séverine, her character, is a placid Paris housewife who consistently rejects her physician-husband's attempts at affection. Her dreams, however, are full of shocking images in which she is violated and humiliated, and she eventually learns about a discreet "madame" who runs a high-priced prostitution service out of a posh apartment. Séverine becomes one of the sex workers, but in the end her secret life unravels when she becomes involved with a troubled young man—instead of the similarly secretive, bourgeois married men who are the brothel's usual customers.

Belle du Jour is one of the most famous films of the era, as much for its racy themes as for Deneuve's costumes, designed specifically for the film by Yves Saint Laurent. Three decades later *New York Times* fashion writer Amy M. Spindler wrote about the impact of the film, asserting that "Buñuel's erotic parable profoundly influenced fashion photography when it was released. Helmut Newton's images of Saint Laurent in the years that followed were full of the same suggestiveness that Buñuel imparted to the clothes: bisexuality, violence and bodies for sale."

Deneuve's name would become indelibly associated with *Belle du Jour,* but she later confessed that she had been reluctant to take the role, knowing how tough a taskmaster Buñuel could be; the film even featured one dream-sequence in which Séverine is tied up and pelted with what appears to be mud. "I was very resistant to it initially," Deneuve told journalist Gaby Wood in the London *Observer* years later. "I thought he wanted to do something cruder, more naked. It wasn't a lack of confidence in him that made me resistant, but my own prudishness and anxiety."

Lost Sister in Tragic Accident

Deneuve's rise to stardom after less than a decade of work was marred by tragedy: in June of 1967, her sister Françoise was killed in a horrific car accident in which she lost control of the car, which hit a post, flipped over, and burst into flames. Dorléac perished as she struggled to free herself. The haunting loss gave Deneuve's public image a frisson of tragedy, and made her a particularly prickly interviewee for journalists, who asked her about it for decades. "It's like a wound that you always have," she told Kevin Maher in the *Times* of London 44 years after her

25-year-old sister's death. "It's a wound that hurts, but can also help you appreciate the people around you more, and the value of everything and everyone you have."

There was a brief period in the early 1970s when Deneuve's career slowed down, around the time of the birth of Chiara, her daughter with Mastroianni. She returned full-force in another prostitution-themed drama, *Zig zig,* and made a rare appearance in a Hollywood project called *Hustle* that paired her with Burt Reynolds, both of which were released in 1975. For a few years, none of the movies in which Deneuve appeared received the same level of critical accolades as *Repulsion* or *Belle du Jour,* but she became a familiar face to television viewers through her television commercials for Chanel fragrances for an eight-year span in the 1970s.

Deneuve made a surprising mid-career comeback in 1980 when veteran director François Truffaut cast her as one of the leads in *Le Dernier Métro* (The Last Metro), a 1980 drama set in Paris during World War II. Her co-star was a younger French actor, Gérard Depardieu, and the movie was an enormous box-office success in France and on the art-house circuit elsewhere. *New York Times* film critic Vincent Canby hailed the film, asserting that "Deneuve is elegant without being frosty, grand without being great lady-ish. It's a star performance of a star role."

Paired with David Bowie

Deneuve still made the occasional forays into English-language films. In the 1983 cult favorite *The Hunger,* she co-starred with rocker David Bowie in a racy, stylish tale about dissolute vampires who prey upon New York City's nightclub scene for new victims. She and Susan Sarandon had an especially torrid scene that turned Deneuve into an object of sapphic fascination, and a few years later an attempt to title a lesbian-oriented magazine *Deneuve* came to an abrupt rebranding when the French star filed a lawsuit against its publishers, and it was forced to rename itself *Curve.* "It was something commercial," Deneuve explained to *Guardian* writer Howard Feinstein about her successful lawsuit. "They tried to use the fact that I had played lesbian roles in films, but it has nothing to do with my life. I wouldn't have let any magazine use my name."

Deneuve literally became a national icon in France in 1985 when her visage was chosen as the new model for "Marianne," a national emblem that appears on coins, stamps, and other official items issued by the French Republic. She continued to make several films a year, mostly in French, and with a newer generation of directors like François Ozon, Leos Carax, and Lars von Trier. She passed her 100 film mark in 2008 with *Je veux voir* (I Want to See), followed by *La Fille du RER* (The Girl on the Train) a year later. Another burst of publicity followed her starring role in 2010's *Potiche* (Trophy Wife), about a wife in small-town France in the early 1970s who finds herself involved in leftist politics; the film was said to have been inspired by the real-life rise of Ségolène Royal, a prominent Socialist Party figure in France and former government minister who became the country's first female candidate for president in 2007.

Won Two Césars

Deneuve has worked on occasion with her son and daughter, each of whom followed their famous parents into film careers. She and Christian Vadim appeared in 1999's *Le Temps retrouvé* (Time Regained) and with Chiara Mastroianni, Deneuve starred in *Les Voleurs* (Thieves), a 1996 drama. Only twice has Deneuve won a César Award, the French equivalent of the Academy Awards. The first was in 1981 for *Le Dernier Métro,* and the second was twelve years later for *Indochine,* a period piece set during the French occupation of Vietnam; Deneuve was nominated for an Academy Award for *Indochine,* too, but lost to Emma Thompson for *Howard's End.*

As her 70th birthday approached, Deneuve remained an enigmatic beauty, celebrated as much for her acting abilities as for her seemingly effortless transition into an older femme fatale. Of the icy Gallic blonde hauteur which filmgoers and critics claim she embodies, Deneuve has said that she eventually learned to use that to her advantage. "In the beginning, it hurt me very much to be perceived as so cold, but then I realised it was quite helpful to be perceived as a person who does not feel familiar with people," she explained to Feinstein, the *Guardian* journalist. "It was better to have an approach that is in my real character: to be warm with people I feel close to, and not to be warm with everybody else."

Periodicals

Guardian (London, England), March 13, 1998.
Independent on Sunday (London, England), April 18, 2004.
New York Times, August 18, 1968; October 12, 1980.
New York Times Magazine, January 9, 2000.
Observer (London, England), January 2, 2000.
Times (London, England), June 13, 1981; June 18, 2011.□

George Devol Jr.

American inventor George Devol (1912–2011) was granted more than 40 patents over the course of his lifetime. Devol developed innovations in many areas—including radars and microwave technology—but was best remembered as the brains behind Unimate, the first programmable, electronically controlled industrial robot. In 1961, Unimate entered its first U.S. factory and went on to revolutionize the modern manufacturing industry all across the globe.

George Charles Devol Jr., was born February 20, 1912, in Louisville, Kentucky. Devol's (pronounced de-VAHL) father was a manager on the Louisville and Nashville Railroad and the family was well-off financially. Devol developed an early interest in electrical and mechanical items—particularly those with a practical application. He also read a lot of fantasy comic books and science-fiction stories. As a teenager, Devol began daydreaming ways to synthesize these two passions. He attended Riordon Prep School in Highland, New York, reading everything he could find about mechanical devices. Devol was interested in finding new applications for vacuum tubes, which were, at the time, regularly used for radios. Besides bookwork, Devol got some hands-on experience at Riordan when he was allowed to help design some buildings and operate the school's electric light plant.

Developed Practical Products

Devol skipped college, choosing practical experience instead. He worked for several electronics companies and in 1932 founded his own business, United Cinephone Corp., with the idea that he would develop new recording technology for movies. The silent film era was coming to a close as studios turned their attention to "talkies." Devol understood that studios needed a better way to record dialogue directly on the film in a synchronized manner. Devol worked on this idea, but after realizing the fierce competition he faced with RCA and Western Electric, he abandoned the project.

Devol, however, had plenty of other ideas floating around in his head. He kept Cinephone alive by inventing several practical products, most of them relying on vacuum tubes, sensors, and photoelectric switches. While still in his 20s, Devol invented a mechanized door that used photoelectric switches to automatically open and close. Devol licensed the product to lock manufacturer Yale & Towne, which manufactured and marketed the invention as the "Phantom Doorman." These doors were predecessors to the automated doors still used at grocery stores in the 21st century. Devol also dreamed up innovations with color printing presses and packaging machines. He invented a primitive bar code system that was used at a railway shipping agency to sort packages. In the late 1930s, Devol developed a photoelectric entrance-counter. This device—dubbed "electric eyes"—was installed at the 1939 New York World's Fair to count fairgoers in lieu of the traditional turnstile.

During World War II, Devol worked in the special projects department at Sperry Gyroscope developing counter-radar devices and microwave test equipment. He invented the "Speedy Weeny," a coin-operated vending machine that offered electron-cooked hot dogs. The heating mechanism on the "Speedy Weeny" was a predecessor to the modern microwave. In 1947, this machine dispensed dogs to commuters at New York's Grand Central Station. During the 1940s, Devol also developed a magnetic recording system, which he hoped could be used for business data applications, though it never panned out. Devol also designed a laundry press that used a radio frequency field to open and close automatically as a worker came near.

Brought Robot to Life

In 1954, Devol applied for a patent for a "programmed article-transfer" device. According to the *Atlantic's* Rebecca J. Rosen, Devol's patent application began: "The present invention relates to the automatic operation of machinery, particularly the handling apparatus, and to automatic control apparatus suited for such machinery." The invention Devol described and diagrammed in the three-page patent application could perform repetitive tasks with absolute precision. In 1961, Devol received patent number 2,988,237 for universal automation.

Just as it took Devol years to receive a patent for his invention, it took years before he could persuade someone to make it. No one was eager to back his idea. "It was years of talking with presidents of companies and hearing no in every language of the world," Devol told the *Miami Herald's* Emilia Askari. A big break came in 1956, however, when Devol met Columbia University engineering grad Joseph Engelberger at a cocktail party. What began as a discussion of author Isaac Asimov's fictitious robots turned into a business venture. During the course of their conversation, Devol announced that he had already invented a mechanical arm for universal automation. According to the *New York Review's* Roger Drape, Devol spoke to Engelberger with excitement, and "waved his hands a lot and said, 'You know, we ought to realize that 50 percent of the people in factories are really putting and taking.'"

As Devol went on to describe his creation, Engelberger realized the invention he was describing was a robot. The idea excited Engelberger, who coined the term "Unimate" as an abbreviation for *uni*versal auto*mation*. The two set up a new company, Unimation Inc., in Danbury, Connecticut, in 1956. At the time the company was founded, the Unimate was just an idea. Unimation was founded to develop and manufacture the actual product. Devol supplied the ideas and staff engineers, who, working under Devol's direction, figured out how to bring the ideas to life. Engelberger marketed it. In other words, Devol was the inventor of the technology and Engelberger, the entrepreneur behind selling it.

The Unimate was so far ahead of its time in terms of available technology that the engineers at Unimation had to create every part, as there were no "shelf-existing" parts already in existence. Engineers had to design a solid-state memory system since the Unimate was to move and store step-by-step digital commands. The first Unimate, which weighed some 4,000 pounds, was controlled by a program stored on a magnetic drum. It moved through hydraulic actuators. The machine was accurate within 1/10,000th of an inch.

Found Market Entry Slow

Devol's robot was ahead of its time and Unimation struggled through its first decade trying to drum up customers. In 1961, the first Unimate—with serial number 001—entered the assembly lines at General Motors in Ewing Township, New Jersey. The robot's job was to remove sizzling-hot car parts that had just been formed in the die-casting machine, then dunk them into a coolant and move them onto an assembly line. The Unimate went online without much fanfare because GM figured there would be resistance from the labor force. Instead, workers mostly thought of the robot as a curiosity and harbored little animosity, figuring it would fail.

As Unimation refined the robot, the company began to show how the robot could move humans away from a factory's more dangerous and tedious jobs. Through the 1960s, Unimation continued to develop its product and came up with robots that could weld, handle spray paint, apply adhesives and conduct other hazardous jobs. During a trade show in Chicago in 1961, the Unimate showed off its dexterity by picking up letters and spelling out simple phrases. Despite the potential, only about 30 Unimates had been sold by 1964.

In 1966, Engelberger took a series 1900 Unimate to appear as a guest on *The Tonight Show with Johnny Carson.* The hydraulic robot wowed American viewers who had never seen a machine like it. Using a remote console plugged directly into the robot, Engelberger "programmed" the robot right in front of the studio audience. The robot was programmed to do several tasks, which included directing the *Tonight Show* orchestra, pouring a beer into a mug and putting a golf ball into a cup. The robot performed as planned, but the beer can had to be partially frozen because the Unimate's "hand"—which was really a set of pincers—lacked the discretion to keep a light grip on the can and kept squeezing it so hard the contents sprayed all over the place.

Ford and Chrysler eventually joined GM in installing the robot, but in general, U.S. manufacturers were slow to warm to the Unimate. According to Drape of the *New York Review,* after Ford Motor Company's Del Harder read the specifications for the Unimate in the 1950s, the manufacturing chief announced, "We could use two thousand of them tomorrow." Yet Ford did not order any robots at the time. Unimate's first robots cost upwards of $25,000 apiece. Factory workers at the time made about $6 an hour. When corporate accountants looked at the figures, they did not see any initial savings. Robot makers argued that purchasing robots was a sound investment because robots could work around the clock, did not need a pension, a vacation, or a bathroom break, and could increase output, thus over the long run, they made sense. Businesses, however, tended to prefer investments that broke even quicker, and this made the Unimate a tough sell.

The Unimate entered the European industrial market in 1967 when one of the machines was installed in Sweden at Svenska Metallverken (Swedish Metal Works). Engineers in Japan jumped on the idea as well. In 1967, when the Japanese government invited Engelberger to discuss the Unimate he found an audience of more than 700 engineers and executives eager to hear about the invention. They grilled him for hours after his lecture, wanting to know more. In 1968, Kawasaki Heavy Industries licensed the Unimate and in 1969 produced the first industrial robot in Japan, called the Kawasaki-Unimate 2000. Kawasaki's robots allowed Japan to become a leader in the modern manufacturing industry. By 1983, Kawasaki had shipped some 2,400 Kawasaki-Unimate robots.

Unimation turned its first profit in 1975 and was acquired by Westinghouse in the early 1980s. After divesting himself of obligations to Unimation, Devol moved to Fort Lauderdale, Florida, and ran a tech consulting firm. He continued to work on robotic improvements for the rest of his life and was particularly interested in visual and touch sensors. Devol applied for his last patent at the age of 98. According to the *Miami Herald's* Askari, Devol said he worked out all of his ideas in his head, never relying on a drafting board or workshop mockups. "I never had any of that stuff. I just write things down and give them to my lawyer," he told Askari. In addition, Devol was known for boiling his inventions down to their essential elements. According to the *New York Times'* Jeremy Pearce, Devol once said, "We should take refuge in the fact that very crude systems can accomplish an awful lot. Elegant capabilities are nice, but often unnecessary."

Changed The Course of History

In 2005, *Popular Mechanics* named Unimate to its list of the top scientific and technological advances of the last half of the twentieth century. The Unimate took its place on the list right alongside the jet airplane, the television remote, the birth control pill, and the microwave oven. The Smithsonian National Museum of American History acquired an early model for its collection, as did the Henry Ford Museum in Dearborn, Michigan. The Unimate was also featured in a 2012 volume by Eric Chaline titled, *Fifty Machines That Changed the Course of History.*

After manufacturers warmed to the idea of the robot, the invention went on to improve safety and consistency in the manufacturing industry. To acknowledge his work in this area, Devol was inducted into the National Inventors Hall of Fame in 2011. According to the *New York Times'* Pearce, the citation read, "George Devol's patent for the first digitally operated programmable robotic arm represents the foundation of the modern robotics industry." In 2011, there were more than 1 million industrial robots in use around the world.

In his later years, Devol and his wife, Evelyn Jahelka, retired to Connecticut. The couple, who married in the late 1930s, had two sons and two daughters. Evelyn died in 2003. Devol died at his home in Wilton, Connecticut, on August 11, 2011. He was 99. After Devol's death, daughter Christine Wardlow remembered her father as a visionary. "My father was so ahead of his time he had to do a lot of things in rudimentary ways," she told Brian Koonz of the Danbury, Connecticut *News-Times.* "To me, that just makes what he accomplished even more amazing. He had all these incredible ideas, and he found ways to make them work."

Books

Chaline, Eric, *Fifty Machines that Changed the Course of History,* Firefly Books, 2012.

Periodicals

Miami Herald, March 19, 1984.

News-Times (Danbury, CT), August 20, 2011.

New York Review, October 24, 1985.

New York Times, March 21, 1982; August 15, 2011.

Online

"'Father of Robotics' Who Helped to Revolutionise Carmaking," *Financial Times*, http://www.ft.com/intl/cms/s/0/b16e00b8-c9b7-11e0-b88b-00144feabdc0.html (September 16, 2013).

"Unimate: The Story of George Devol and the First Robotic Arm," *Atlantic*, http://www.theatlantic.com/technology/archive/2011/08/unimate-the-story-of-george-devol-and-the-first-robotic-arm/243716/ (September 15, 2013).□

Hazel Dickens

The American singer and songwriter Hazel Dickens (1935–2011) was a pioneering figure among women in the bluegrass music genre, and she left a long trail of influence in country and folk music as well. As a songwriter, Dickens broached topics rarely raised by Appalachian women before her: the difficult and dangerous lives of coal miners, the treatment of women, and the rights of working people.

Dickens was never a chart-topping artist; she recorded sporadically for small folk- and bluegrass-oriented labels, and for much of her career she performed mostly at small gatherings of traditional-music enthusiasts. Yet superstars as major as the country duo the Judds have cited her as an influence. She directly inspired many members of the generation of female bluegrass singers that began to challenge men for dominance in the 1980s. Dickens's songs became anthems of the labor movement, especially in her native Appalachian coal country, and she had a strong following in feminist circles. Her duet recordings with folksinger Alice Gerrard helped bridge the gap between traditional music's native practitioners from the southern United States and revivalists from the urban Northeast. Many of her compositions, including "Black Lung" and "It's Hard to Tell the Singer from the Song," have endured as country and bluegrass classics.

Left School After Seventh Grade

According to biographer Bill C. Malone, Hazel Jane Dickens was born June 1, 1935, in Montcalm, West Virginia, in the heart of the state's coal country. But a report in the *Old-Time Herald,* citing public records, asserted that Dickens was ten years older than that, and pictures of her taken in the early 1950s do not appear to show a teenage girl. Her father, H.N. Dickens, was a coal and lumber truck driver and part-time Primitive Baptist preacher; several of her brothers were miners. The family was enthusiastic about music, listening to broadcasts of the Grand Ole Opry country variety show from Nashville and the Carter Family singing family group on clear-channel radio stations. Dickens left school after seventh grade. In search of a better life, Dickens's family moved in stages to Baltimore, Maryland, in the 1950s. Painfully shy, Dickens would later describe herself as unsocialized.

Chris Felver/Getty Images

Working in a can factory and keeping mostly to the family's predominantly Appalachian neighborhood, Dickens nevertheless began to meet individuals who would bring out the musical talent that had until then had displayed itself only at family gatherings. The most important was Mike Seeger, a banjoist and the child of a family of folk music researchers who had refused Korean War service as a conscientious objector and was performing community service in a tuberculosis sanatorium where one of Dickens's brothers was a patient. Seeger became fascinated by the mountain talent of the Dickens family group and suggested that they all perform together, At first, Dickens was quoted as saying by *Smithsonian Folkways Magazine,* they were suspicious, considering Seeger a "city guy" who might "want to make fun of us or laugh at us or something." But soon the new group was playing for change and traveling to early bluegrass events at venues like Maryland's New River Ranch.

It was probably through someone in Seeger's circle that Dickens met Alice Gerrard (then Alice Foster), a classically trained singer who had attended the experimental Antioch College in Ohio. The backgrounds of the pair were vastly different, but their vocal blend was perfect: with Gerrard's alto balancing Dickens's raw mountain soprano, they had a combination that could compete with male bluegrass vocal pairs featuring a mid-range lead and a high harmony vocalist. There had been women singers in the old-time country tradition Dickens had grown up with, but very few women had sung bluegrass prior to the release of the Dickens and Gerrard duo album *Who's That Knocking* in 1965. That album featured a mixture of traditional bluegrass players with northeastern newcomers like mandolinist David Grisman.

Formed Strange Creek Singers

In 1967, Dickens and Gerrard joined with Seeger and others to form the Strange Creek Singers, which released a single eponymously titled album in 1970. Then, as a duo, they released *Won't You Come and Sing for Me* in 1973. After that release Gerrard, to Dickens's disappointment, departed to pursue solo projects. As it happened, Gerrard would not release another solo album until 1994, and it was Dickens who went on to a prestigious solo career. The early Dickens-Gerrard albums appeared on the academically oriented Folkways label, but after Dickens was signed to the leading folk and bluegrass label Rounder, several more collections of Dickens-Gerrard material appeared on that label, including *Hazel & Alice* (1973).

Dickens married youth counselor Joel Cohen in 1965, but the couple divorced three years later. For a time she worked as the manager of a store called Old Mexico Imports, but eventually she gave up that job in order to focus on music full-time. Beginning in the late 1960s she wrote the songs that made her into a revered figure in country music: "Black Lung," "Mannington Mine Disaster," and "Working Girl Blues," in which Dickens intoned the plaint "When the Lord made the working girl, He made the blues."

That song combined two of Dickens's characteristic themes: feminism and the lives of the working class, especially coal miners. Although raised a Primitive Baptist, Dickens largely abandoned religion as an adult. She was quoted by Bill C. Malone in *Working Girl Blues* as saying, "If I have a religion, that's it: to take what I have, and be able to share it with somebody that needs it. If there's any religion in my life, it's for the working class. And I want to be that way as long as I have a breath." Dickens gained a strong following among young feminist women while still appealing to traditional bluegrass fans; she was perhaps the only artist to do so.

Dickens released three albums on Rounder: *Hard Hitting Songs for Hard Hit People* (1981), *By the Sweat of My Brow* (1984), and *It's Hard to Tell the Singer from the Song* (1986), as well as the compilation *A Few Old Memories* (1987). Although many of her songs dealt with political or gender-related matters, she also wrote love songs and the perhaps autobiographical "It's Hard to Tell the Singer from the Song." "Don't Put Her Down, You Helped Put Her There" was a country song with a feminist outlook. Dickens had a small but memorable role in the 1987 John Sayles film *Matewan,* set amidst labor strife in the West Virginia coal fields, and she performed in several other films.

Influenced Judds

Dickens's 1980s albums remain in print, and both those and her albums with Gerrard have influenced various female singers in the fields of bluegrass, country, and women's music. Naomi Judd of the Judds told Richard Harrington of the *Washington Post* that the duo had been inspired by the 1973 *Hazel & Alice* album, which Judd found in a used record store. "Their whole sound was so unpolished, so authentic, they were unabashedly just who they were—it was really like looking in the mirror of truth," she told Harrington. "We felt like we knew them, and when we listened to the songs, it crystallized the possibility that two women could sing together." Country singer Emmylou Harris's arrangement of the Carter Family's "Hello Stranger" was drawn directly on that of Dickens and Gerrard.

Although she suffered from some health problems, Dickens continued to perform a choice selection of concert dates in her later years. The Smithsonian Festival of American Folklife organized a major Dickens concert and tribute, "Hazel Dickens: A Life's Work," in 1996. By that time she was beginning to see young rock fans who knew little of traditional music at her concerts. Dickens received an honorary doctoral degree from Shepherd College in West Virginia, after which she asked to be referred to as Dr. Dickens. The National Endowment for the Arts bestowed upon her a fellowship and $10,000 stipend, one of the highest arts awards in the U.S., in 2001.

Dickens issued *Working Girl Blues,* a group of commentaries on her own songs paired with a biography by Malone, in 2008. She died from complications from pneumonia in Washington, D.C., on April 22, 2011. Reflecting on her pioneer status as a woman in the male-dominated field of bluegrass, she said, "I had one thing that most of the good old boys didn't have. I had a mind. I had every song that you could think of in my head, and they didn't. People were always asking me for the words of songs, and I could sing them authentically, just the way they were supposed to be sung," according to *The Independent.*

Books

Dickens, Hazel, and Bill C. Malone, *Working Girl Blues,* University of Illinois, 2008.

Periodicals

Guardian (London, England), May 17, 2011.

Independent (London, England), June 3, 2011.

New York Times, April 23, 2011.

Sing Out!, Summer 2011.

Washington Post, July 6, 1996.

Online

"Final Notes, Hazel Dickens," *Old-Time Herald* http://www.oldtimeherald.org/here+there/final-notes/hazel-dickens.htm (November 12, 2013).

"Hazel Dickens," *AllMusic,* http://www.allmusic.com (November 12, 2013).

"Remembering Hazel Dickens," *Smithsonian Folkways Magazine,* http://www.folkways.si.edu/magazine/2011_spring/archive_spotlight-hazel.aspx (November 12, 2013).□

Carl Djerassi

Austrian-born chemist Carl Djerassi (born 1923) achieved a revolutionary milestone in reproductive science in 1951 when he created norethindrone, a synthetic form of the hormone progesterone, with colleagues at a small research company in Mexico City. Djerassi is often hailed as the "father" of the birth-control pill, or oral contraceptive for women, that became widely available in the early 1960s.

Carl Djerassi was born on October 29, 1923, in Vienna, Austria. Both of his parents were physicians and from Jewish families. His father Samuel was originally from Bulgaria and in Vienna ran a successful private practice that treated suffers of sexually transmitted diseases. When Djerassi was four his mother Alice took him to live with her mother in Vienna, though she did not reveal that she had divorced Samuel. All four were imperiled by the increasingly bolder moves of neighboring Nazi Germany after 1933, especially the restrictive laws against Jews. When Germany annexed Austria in the 1938 Anschluss, Djerassi's parents quietly remarried in order to help them obtain exit visas. They moved first to Sofia, Bulgaria, when Djerassi was 16, and then he and his mother were able to emigrate to the United States with the help of Jewish refugee organizations.

© jeremy sutton-hibbert/Alamy

Hired at CIBA

Djerassi first lived in New Jersey, where he enrolled at Newark Junior College. Already a promising student with a clear aptitude for science, Djerassi won a scholarship to Kenyon College in Ohio and earned an undergraduate degree in chemistry in 1943. He recalled living in fear and uncertainty in his first years in the United States, which coincided with World War II. "When I came to America I had a phobia, like most Jewish refugees," he told Deborah Ross in an interview for the London *Independent*. "'Are you Jewish?' someone would ask, and I'd worry they had an anti-Semitic agenda.... In Vienna, the Nazis put up a poster showing a smiling kid with a hooked nose. 'Kill The Jews,' the poster said."

By 1945, Djerassi had earned his Ph.D. in chemistry from the University of Wisconsin in Madison and was working at the New Jersey laboratory of the Swiss pharmaceutical giant CIBA. Under the supervision of another Austrian-émigré scientist, Charles Huttrer, Djerassi received his first patent for one of the first-generation antihistamines to be approved for use, a compound called pyribenzamine. During this decade he also became a naturalized U.S. citizen and married a woman named Virginia Jeremiah, though the couple divorced in 1950.

In 1949, Djerassi was offered a job at a small pharmaceutical company in Mexico City called Syntex. Lured with the promise that he would be able to head his own research group, he accepted the offer and began working on steroid chemistry projects in the Syntex lab. Djerassi initially worked on synthesized cortisone, an injectable form of a steroid hormone that effectively alleviated arthritis pain.

Used Obscure Mexican Tuber

Syntex had been set up in Mexico because an American chemist, Russell Marker, had discovered that a chemical from a certain type of Central American yam, the barbasco, contained a chemical that mimicked the effect of the hormone progesterone. Progesterone is a steroid hormone produced by the body, and its levels in the blood rise and fall according to the reproductive cycle in women of childbearing age. Scientists knew that injections of progesterone could help infertile women conceive, but the injections were painful and costly to manufacture.

Syntex possessed a stupendous supply of the inedible barbasco tuber thanks to Marker's efforts, and tasked Djerassi with concocting a synthetic form of progesterone that could be ingested and pass through digestive system unmolested by enzymes. Transversing the digestive system was the key element in the process—stomach acids and liver enzymes tended to nullify or interfere with a chemical ingested in pill or syrup form, preventing the synthetic hormone from entering the bloodstream and producing the desired effect in the body's endocrine system. This was the key to inhibiting ovulation in the female reproductive cycle, an idea that had been bandied about by a few

European researchers in the 1920s and described in science literature of the era as temporary induced infertility. "Women don't get pregnant during pregnancy, that's nature's contraceptive, and that was our lead," Djerassi explained to *Guardian* writer Dina Rabinovitch years later.

Working with two other Syntex colleagues, Djerassi created the first stable version of norethindrone in the laboratory on October 15, 1951. His senior colleague, George Rosenkranz, had suggested certain tweaks to create an ingestible form, and it was a young Mexican scientist named Luis Miramontes who conducted the final steps in the first successful synthesis of the hormone. Djerassi's name appeared first on the patent filed for it, and he signed the rights over to Syntex for the amount of $1. He was given stock shares in Syntex, however, and that decision proved an enormously lucrative one in the decades to come. His work with Rosenkrantz, Miramontes, and others at Syntex continued on and their published papers regularly appeared in the *Journal of the American Chemical Society.*

Dubbed "Father" of "The Pill"

It was two other pioneers, the biologist Gregory Pincus and an infertility specialist named John Rock, who worked to create the first combined oral contraceptive pill, which was first tested on animals. The first round of human clinical trials were done in Puerto Rico in the mid-1950s—because artificially restricting reproduction was a felony charge in some U.S. states—and the U.S. Food and Drug Administration approved the first version of the oral-contraceptive pill, Enovid, for use in treating menstrual disorders in 1957. A new formulation was approved in 1960 for contraceptive use, and the breakthrough was heralded around the world as a milestone in human reproductive science. "The Pill," as various forms of the combined synthetic progesterone-estrogen contraceptive became known, unshackled women from the fear of an unplanned pregnancy and helped usher in an era of dramatic social upheaval across much of the developed world. American pharmaceutical giant G. D. Searle controlled the market in the first years, but other companies came up with equally effective lower-dose pills, which still relied on Djerassi's breakthrough process for creating norethindrone.

Just how revolutionary Djerassi's discovery was can be tracked by its legal status in the United States alone: only in 1965 did a U.S. Supreme Court decision remove restrictions on its use for married women, and it took another seven more years before some states' laws against dispensing oral contraceptives to unmarried women were finally eliminated by the High Court. By the late 1980s, one study estimated that 80 percent of all U.S. women born after 1945 had taken oral contraceptives at some point during their childbearing years.

Dreamed of Lab-Based Procreation

In 1952, Djerassi moved to Detroit, Michigan, where he became an associate professor of chemistry at Wayne State University. Seven years later Stanford University offered him a post, and he spent the remainder of his teaching career there until semi-retiring in 2002 as professor emeritus. Over the years, Djerassi made many more discoveries in organic chemistry, and one of them contributed to a long-awaited treatment for male infertility in the early 1990s known as intracytoplasmic sperm injection (ICSI). In a 1994 interview with London *Sunday Times* journalist Margarette Driscoll, Djerassi forecasted a future in which scientific advances would fully separate human reproduction from sexual relations. He theorized that young adults of ideal childbearing age could freeze and "bank" their respective gamete-containing cells for use a later date. Women would have a cache of eggs extracted from their ovaries, and men could freeze a supply of sperm and then undergo a vasectomy. He explained to Driscoll that the U.S. armed forces would be the ideal place to begin such a trial experiment because of its large population of young males and already-established medical record-keeping experience. "I realise it is an unusual and controversial proposal," he said in the *Sunday Times* article. "But I have long felt that if women must bear the reproductive burden, men should bear the contraceptive burden. This way we can use the technology we already have. The chance of a new male contraceptive by the year 2000 is zero."

Djerassi's own family life had some storied twists: he divorced his first wife in 1950 to wed Norma Lundholm, who was expecting a child by him. His daughter Pamela was born that same year, followed by a son with Lundholm, Dale, a few years later. During his tenure at Stanford he spent part of the year on a 600-acre ranch he acquired in the Santa Cruz Mountains. The California estate was dubbed "SMIP," an acronym for "Syntex Made It Possible." In 1976 he and Lundholm divorced, and two years later his daughter Pamela—a 28-year-old artist who suffered from clinical depression—committed suicide in a wooded parcel near the ranch. Djerassi was deeply affected by the loss and established an artist-residency program at the ranch in her honor. "I believe suicide should not be kept quiet—one shouldn't be ashamed of talking or writing about it, it does a dishonour to the person who killed herself," he told the *Observer*'s Gaby Wood. "Suicide is a message to the survivors—it's very different from any other form of death—and one should have at least the respect to read it."

Became Writer and Art Collector

Djerassi also embarked upon a second career as a writer of novels and plays. His books include the science fiction-themed thrillers *Cantor's Dilemma, Marx, Deceased,* and *Menachem's Seed.* He also produced a 1990 memoir, *Steroids Made It Possible,* followed two years later by *The Pill, Pygmy Chimps, and Degas' Horse: The Autobiography of Carl Djerassi.* His literary spark, he admitted, began as a way to win back the renowned scholar who would become his third wife, Diane Middlebrook. A poet who became a professor of English at Stanford, Middlebrook married Djerassi in 1985, but died of cancer in 2007. In the interim years she produced a pair of acclaimed biographies of a two well-known American poets who committed suicide, Sylvia Plath and Anne Sexton.

In 1998, Djerassi's one-act play *An Immaculate Misconception* premiered at the Edinburgh Fringe in Scotland.

That work and subsequent dramas were staged in New York City and earned critical plaudits. In 2001, he produced another volume of autobiography, *This Man's Pill: Reflections on the 50th Birthday of the Pill.* In 2003, on the occasion of his eightieth birthday, Austrian officials honored him with a postage stamp that bore his image and the words: "Born 1923, Expelled 1938, Reconciled 2003."

The "Degas' Horse" referenced in the title of Djerassi's second volume of his memoirs refers to a third career as an avid art collector. Focusing on the works of early twentieth-century masters like Pablo Picasso and Alberto Giacometti, Djerassi eventually amassed one of the largest collections of the works of Swiss artist Paul Klee in private hands. In what can only be described as one of the more fabled twists in Djerassi's already storied life, he was once the father-in-law of Isabel Maxwell, the daughter of British media mogul Robert Maxwell, who died near the Canary Islands after falling off his yacht in 1991. Isabel Maxwell had married Dale Djerassi and the two made documentary films together before divorcing.

Books

Djerassi, Carl, *This Man's Pill: Reflections on the 50th Birthday of the Pill,* Oxford University Press, 2001.

Periodicals

Guardian (London, England), August 5, 1998.
Independent (London, England), October 15, 2001.
Observer (London, England), April 15, 2007.
Sunday Times (London, England), July 17, 1994.□

Daily Mail/Rex/Alamy

Basil D'Oliveira

Classified as "colored" under South Africa's apartheid system, cricket master Basil D'Oliveira (1931–2011) was unable to play professionally in his own country because government-enforced racial segregation kept him from South Africa's elite white teams. In the 1960s, D'Oliveira immigrated to England and earned appointment to England's national team but the South African government refused to let D'Oliveira play during an international tour scheduled for South African soil. The 1968 incident, dubbed the "D'Oliveira Affair," opened eyes to the inequality of apartheid and led to South Africa's exclusion from international sporting events for the next two decades.

Basil Lewis D'Oliveira was born October 4, 1931, in Cape Town, South Africa, to Lewis and Maria D'Oliveira. He grew up at the bottom of "Signal Hill," a historic hill used as a signaling post for ships coming into harbor. The area was originally settled by freed slaves brought in during Dutch colonization. D'Oliveira was of Indian-Portuguese descent. Under South Africa's apartheid system, the government classified the D'Oliveiras as "colored." In *Basil D'Oliveira—Cricket and Conspiracy: The Untold Story,* author Peter Oborne included D'Oliveira's analysis of race classification. "A Cape-coloured is somebody who is not Indian, not African, but a combination of either Indian and white or African and white. Out of this mixing a new race was born. In South Africa, if you are mixed you are coloured and that's the end of it."

D'Oliveira attended a Roman Catholic school. As a child, he played cricket on the sloped, pitted streets of his neighborhood. Sometimes, he and his friends played on the streets nearer to Cape Town's center because the neighborhoods were more level there, but since this was a "white-only" area, they risked being arrested. At 15, D'Oliveira quit school and helped support his family by working at a printing firm.

Joined South African Cricket Club

As a teen D'Oliveira joined St. Augustine's Cricket Club. D'Oliveira's father was the club captain. Lewis D'Oliveira did not like his son's approach to the game. Whenever Basil D'Oliveira batted, he tried for "sixes." In cricket, if a batter hits the ball in the air over the boundary, six runs are awarded. Four runs are awarded if the ball bounces on the ground before going over the boundary. D'Oliveira's father believed it was too risky to hit the ball in the air because the fielding team might catch it and get the batter out. In cricket, the batter gets to keep going until being put out. Lewis D'Oliveira thought it safer to knock the ball across the ground, but his son would not comply. Lewis D'Oliveira went so far as to offer his son a new bat if he could score a century—100 runs in one innings—without a six (in cricket, an innings is a team's turn at bat, and it is always plural). D'Oliveira never even attempted to win the bat.

South Africans began to take notice of D'Oliveira during the 1948-49 season when he displayed his remarkable bat skills as a member of the Western Province select team. During a game against Griqualand West, D'Oliveira shot a ball over the offside boundary for six points. The opposing captain immediately positioned a player at the offside boundary, so D'Oliveira smacked the next one up the middle and across the boundary for six more points. The captain responded by moving a player into that position. D'Oliveira sent his next six whizzing right between the two fielders.

During the 1950-51 season, D'Oliveira's father resigned as captain. Members decided that the younger D'Oliveira should take over and he proved to be a humble, inspiring leader. "Even if you were just mediocre, he made you feel you were something special," player Peter Manuel told Oborne. "I broke my leg and Basil was the one guy who came to see me in [the] hospital. He was so interested in us. He would never think of looking after himself." D'Oliveira required his players to endurance-train by running Signal Hill and he frequently invited teammates to his home to socialize and discuss the game.

Relocated to England to Play

As his skills progressed, D'Oliveira aspired to play Test matches on an international level. Test matches—competitions between national teams that last several days—represent the highest form of cricket. At the time, South Africa's Test-match teams always comprised white players. By the late 1950s, D'Oliveira realized he had risen as high as he could in South African cricket circles. He knew he would never be chosen to represent South Africa at the international level. Desperate to test his skills against the game's greatest players, D'Oliveira wrote letters to BBC cricket commentator John Arlott. Through his connections, Arlott secured a spot for D'Oliveira to play professionally for the Middleton Cricket Club in northwestern England.

D'Oliveira traveled to England in the spring of 1960 to join the team. It was the first time he experienced life outside the apartheid system and he struggled to adjust to the changes. First off, D'Oliveira nearly missed his train after landing at Heathrow because he walked around the airport in a daze, looking for a "non-white" exit. In South Africa, separate public facilities for whites and non-whites were the norm. In England, D'Oliveira got to ride in the same train car as his white teammates and sit with white people in pubs. He suffered severe culture shock, always looking for colored entrances to public places and walking a few yards behind white teammates on the street.

D'Oliveira also struggled to adjust his cricket-playing. In South Africa, apartheid prevented him from playing on well-manicured fields with actual turf. These were reserved for white teams. Instead, D'Oliveira came of age playing on crude, hard-baked, rocky fields. D'Oliveira soon found that the ball reacted differently on the puffy turf as the thick, green grass slowed it down. This affected his batting and fielding. In his first five innings of batting, D'Oliveira scored just 25 runs. He was used to averaging more than 40 runs in each innings he batted. He felt like a failure and like he had let down everyone in his community who had raised the funds to send him to England.

D'Oliveira began studying other players and received coaching from teammate Eric Price, who helped him adapt his Cape Town skills for the English pitch. D'Oliveira persevered and ended the season at the top of the Central Lancashire League batting averages, scoring 930 runs for the season with an average of 48.95. As a bowler, he took 71 wickets, for an average of 11.72. To "take a wicket" means to eliminate the batter. A bowler's average is computed by taking the runs conceded and dividing it by the wickets taken. At the end of the season, according to Oborne, the *Wisden Cricketers' Almanac* declared, "Middleton had every reason to be satisfied with their gamble in signing the non-European, Basil D'Oliveira, from South Africa."

After the season ended, D'Oliveira returned home to his wife, Naomi, and celebrated the birth of a son, Damian. Middleton renewed his contract and in early 1961, the D'Oliveiras left South Africa by boat and headed to England. They would never live in South Africa again. D'Oliveira spent four seasons with Middleton. During that time, he scored 3,663 runs, averaging 48.20. He also took 238 wickets, for an average of 14.87.

In 1964, D'Oliveira joined the Worcestershire County Cricket Club. County cricket in England represented the highest level of professional play in the country. That same year, he became an English citizen. In 1965, D'Oliveira appeared in his first county championship match and scored a century, helping his team take the title. In 1966, D'Oliveira was chosen to play for England. Already in his mid-thirties, D'Oliveira lied about his age to the selection committee, fearing they would not select an aging player past his prime. D'Oliveira believed his best days were behind him. "In terms of eyesight, coordination, instinct and fitness, I was at my peak when playing with non-whites in the Fifties," D'Oliveira wrote in his 1980 autobiography *Time To Declare,* according to the *Daily Telegraph.* The next year, playing India, D'Oliveira scored his first century in a Test match.

Stirred Race Storm

In 1968-69, the English national team was scheduled to tour South Africa. No colored man had ever played a Test match there. D'Oliveira was determined to make the team, whereas many apartheid supporters made it clear they did not want him to play. In the run-up to the tour, South African Prime Minister John Vorster told the English selection committee that the tour would be canceled if D'Oliveira made the team. In hopes of preventing an embarrassing ordeal for the South African government, one wealthy South African tobacco businessman offered D'Oliveira a lucrative deal to become the cricket coach and organizer for the "colored" cricketers of the South African Sports Foundation. The deal was, in effect, a bribe because the catch was that D'Oliveira had to make himself unavailable for the English side.

Just before the English side was selected, D'Oliveira played brilliantly in a Test match against Australia. He scored 158 runs in one innings, yet was left off the roster for the South African tour even though he had the top Test average of the season. "When Basil left the field after that innings, I think he and everyone else had thought that he had booked his place on the boat to South Africa," former teammate Norman Gifford recalled in a CNN interview. "We were all shocked by the decision, we couldn't believe it."

Disappointment seized D'Oliveira. "I was like a zombie," D'Oliveira told Ian Hawkey of the *Sunday Times.* "The stomach had been kicked out of me. I remember thinking, 'You just can't beat the white South Africans.'" Most Britons were outraged—a national poll found that two-thirds of Britons thought it wrong that D'Oliveira had been left off the squad. Before the tour commenced, British cricketer Tom Cartwright dropped out after an injury and England chose D'Oliveira to replace him. But D'Oliveira's dream of playing Test cricket in his homeland was not to be. The South African government responded by saying that a team containing D'Oliveira would be unable to play. Vorster contended that the team was chosen for political reasons in a quiet protest of apartheid. In the end, England called off the tour.

Left a Legacy

After the incident, South Africa was barred from international Test cricket. No country wanted to play there or host the South African team after the D'Oliveira Affair. For the next two decades, South African cricket lived through a period of international isolation. Other sports steered clear of South Africa as well. South Africa resumed international cricket in 1991, after apartheid broke down.

Speaking to CNN, Oborne discussed the impact of the D'Oliveira Affair. "I think the importance of Basil D'Oliveira was that he educated ordinary people who until then had instinctively sympathized with white South Africa about the sheer horror and nastiness of the racist regime. Basil was such a decent, unassuming and honest man that it seemed outrageous that he should not be allowed to play in his own country."

After the incident, D'Oliveira continued to play for England. In 1972, D'Oliveira competed in his final Test match. His international career included 2,484 runs and five centuries for an average of 40.06. He took 47 wickets for an average of 39.55. D'Oliveira continued to play at Worcestershire until 1980, then became the coach, leading the team to the title in 1988 and 1989 and retiring in 1990. During that period, his son Damian played on the team.

Another highlight in D'Oliveira's life came in 1996 when South African President Nelson Mandela invited D'Oliveira to lunch as he wrapped up a coaching trip there. According to Oborne, Mandela parted ways with D'Oliveira by telling him, "Thanks for coming, Basil. You must go home now. You've done your bit." In his later years, D'Oliveira suffered from Parkinson's disease. He died in England on November 19, 2011, leaving behind his wife and two sons.

Books

Oborne, Peter, *Basil D'Oliveira—Cricket and Conspiracy: The Untold Story,* Time Warner Books, 2004.

Periodicals

Daily Telegraph (London), November 21, 2011.

Sunday Times (London), November 14, 1999; November 20, 2011.

Online

"Basil D'Oliveira—The Early Years," Basil D'Oliveira Official Website, http://basildoliveira.com/about/biographies/basil-doliveira/ (November 1, 2013).

"Basil D'Oliveira: The Man Who Took On South Africa's Apartheid Regime," *CNN,* http://edition.cnn.com/2013/03/08/sport/cricket-basil-doliveira-apartheid-south-africa/index.html (November 1, 2013).□

E

Bernie Ecclestone

The British entrepreneur Bernie Ecclestone (born 1930) has become, in the words of the London *Daily Telegraph*'s Peter Dron, "the uncrowned head of Formula One" auto racing.

Beginning his career in extremely modest circumstances, Ecclestone built Formula One racing into the most popular sport aired regularly on television; Formula One, which had its roots in Europe but now extends its reach worldwide, is broadcast in about 150 countries, and its ratings are exceeded only by those of the quadrennial Olympics and soccer World Cup. Ecclestone rose to the top of his industry partly by outmaneuvering his contemporaries and partly by sensing the importance of television and other forms of marketing auxiliary to the sport of racing itself. A controversial figure, he has at times been embroiled in legal and political problems, but he has become a fascinating figure to business and sports journalists who see in him a remarkable example of the self-made man phenomenon. Though he has suffered setbacks in his old age, Ecclestone remains one of the wealthiest men in the United Kingdom.

Grew Up in Poverty

Bernard Charles Ecclestone (the name was, he told Dron, "a bit upmarket for me") was born in the tiny crossroads settlement of St. Peter South Elmham, near Bungay in England's Suffolk region, on October 28, 1930. His father operated a trawler that fished for herring and mackerel, and was shaken by a storm that threw his boat onto a beach. The family home had no indoor plumbing or running water, and Bernard was blind in one eye from birth. Ecclestone's parents rarely spoke to each other, and they never took vacations or celebrated holidays or Ecclestone's birthday. Ecclestone went to school on a horse-drawn milk wagon, and he learned the value of frugality early on.

The family moved to Dartford, in the Kent region, in 1938, where an aunt gave Ecclestone his first birthday party, and then to Bexley on the edge of the London metropolitan area. As a schoolboy Ecclestone delivered newspapers each morning, invested his earnings in baked goods, and resold them at a profit to his classmates. "I started racing pushbikes there, then I raced motorbikes when I was 14 or 15," he told Adam Sweeting of the London *Guardian*. "I've been racing something all my bloody life. None of this happened until we'd moved from Suffolk." He earned a degree in chemical engineering at Woolwich Polytechnic school, finishing his classes when he was 16 and taking a job in a gasworks laboratory. Bored, he soon quit and opened a small motorcycle parts store. Ecclestone's timing was good, for motorcycle parts were in short supply after World War II, and when he joined forces with a partner to form the Compton & Ecclestone motorcycle dealership, it became one of the largest in Britain.

Ecclestone enjoyed racing motorcycles and later cars himself, but he retired permanently from racing after a 1949 incident in which his car was thrown into the track's parking lot after a collision. Unwilling to face the possiblity of a life spent as a quadriplegic, he stayed away from racing for several years, managing a weekend auto auction and dabbling in real estate. Later in the 1950s, he purchased a Formula One team called Connaught and managed the career of driver Stuart Lewis-Evans, who was killed in an accident on a track in Casablanca, Morocco. Ecclestone attended his driver as he lay in a hospital bed covered with burns.

© Presselect/Alamy

He left the racing scene for another decade in the 1960s, building a highly successful chain of auto dealerships whose showrooms were marked by his own fastidious sense of cleanliness and neatness. Once he ripped a phone out of the wall after employees persistently placed the receiver on the hook in what he considered the wrong direction. He was not averse, however, to rolling back the odometers of used cars. In the late 1960s Ecclestone managed the career of Austrian Formula One driver Jochen Rindt; he, too, was killed in a 1970 crash, and Ecclestone quit racing once again. He could not stay away, however, and purchased the Brabham team later in 1970.

Founded Race Car Makers' Group

Ecclestone would remain as Brabham's owner until 1987, by which time he had taken major steps toward dominance over Formula One racing as a whole. When Ecclestone came on the scene, the sport was dominated by owners with a mechanical mindset, not those alert to its large-scale marketing potential. "F1 teams have not always been the sharpest commercial entities," team owner Martin Whitmarsh told Adam Cooper of *Racer,* "and world motorsport governing bodies have not been the sharpest commercial entities! Bernie is one of the sharpest commercial entities, so that's why he got to where he is." His first step came in 1974, when he founded the F1 Constructors Association of team owners (FOCA) and began to challenge the authority of the sport's governing body, the France-based Fédération Internationale de l'Automobile (FIA), demanding that team owners have more ability to control their own financial dealings.

As Ecclestone began to assert control over the FOCA (he became its chief executive in 1978), he simultaneously sharply increased the revenues earned by Formula One as a whole; he essentially made other team owners so wealthy that they were hardly inclined to worry about the vastly larger money-making machine he was setting up for himself. In 1978, he established the Formula One Products and Administration group (FOPA), giving himself control over promotions associated with Formula One races (where he was already successful—Brabham won world championships in 1981 and 1983). In FOPA's first year, he centralized the negotiation of television contracts in FOPA's offices. That was probably his single most important move; annual television revenues, which had been about $1 million per team when Ecclestone began his rise, reached an estimated $500 million in 2001. Through a complicated series of legal arrangements, more than 50 percent of that went to Ecclestone himself.

As auxiliary sources of profit began to accumulate along with television revenues, Ecclestone, aided by his financial advisor Max Moseley, who he installed as FIA president in 1993, insinuated himself into the revenue stream, and his personal wealth began to grow sharply. The FOCA's cartel-like control over racing as well as Ecclestone's own many-tentacled hold on the business began to attract the attention of government regulators, who among other things attempted to extend a ban on television tobacco advertising to Formula One broadcasts. Ecclestone made large contributions to British Prime Minister Tony Blair's Labor Party shortly before the ban was lifted, and Ecclestone found himself at the center of a scandal. Although the government claimed that it was only worried about losing business to Middle Eastern countries where there was no ban, the party was forced to return Ecclestone's contributions.

Sold Home for Record Price

By 2003, the London *Sunday Times* ranked Ecclestone as the third-wealthiest individual in Britain; by 2008, after an unsuccessful attempt to introduce Formula One racing into the United States, his ranking had dropped to 24th, but his fortune was still estimated at 2.4 billion pounds. Ecclestone owned several posh London mansions; he sold one in 2004 to steel entrepreneur Lakshmi Mittal for 57.1 million pounds, at the time the highest price ever paid for a house. Observers wondered whether the septuagenarian Ecclestone might slow down or groom a successor, but in the mid-2000s decade he supervised the transfer of many of his interests to capital investment firms in dizzyingly complex deals that filled his coffers anew.

As his wealth accumulated, the unassuming Ecclestone began to attract gossip press attention commensurate with his jet-setting status. Much of it centered on his Croatian-born second wife, Slavica, a former model who, at six feet, two inches, towered over the five-foot-four executive. Ecclestone courted and married her in 1984 in spite of the fact that she spoke only Croatian and Italian and he spoke only English. Before ending in 2008, the marriage produced two daughters, Petra and Tamara; Petra's marriage to businessman James Stunt, at a medieval Italian castle, cost 12 million pounds (about $19 million) and was attended by Paris Hilton and serenaded by rock singer Eric Clapton (who donated his services) and tenor Andrea Bocelli.

By the early 2010s, Ecclestone seemed to be running into personal, business, and legal problems. He was mugged twice outside his London home, losing a $40,000 watch on one occasion. After his divorce, he told Rachel Sylvester and Alice Thomson of the London *Times* that "I'm not a good cook but I can prepare cold things like salads," and mused that "apart from the fact that Hitler got taken away and persuaded to do things that I have no idea whether he wanted to do or not, he was in the way that he could command a lot of people able to get things done." Most seriously, he was indicted in Germany on charges of having bribed German financier Gerhard Gribkowsky to undervalue shares of assets that were being transferred to a Munich bank. As of the fall of 2013, Ecclestone was facing trial and a possible prison term in Germany, something that would force him to relinquish his long and transformative leadership of Formula One.

Books

Bowers, Tom, *No Angel: The Secret Life of Bernie Ecclestone,* Faber & Faber, 2012.

Watkins, Susan, *Bernie: The Biography of Bernie Ecclestone,* Haynes, 2011.

Periodicals

Auto Racing Digest, January 2001.

Cape Times (South Africa), January 19, 2012.

Guardian (London, England), March 29, 1999; December 10, 2004; March 4, 2011; October 25, 2012; May 15, 2013.

Investor's Business Daily, May 21, 2008.

Observer (London, England), November 13, 2011.

Racer, September 2012.

Telegraph (London, England), March 8, 2003; October 28, 2010.

Times (London, England), July 4, 2009.

Online

"Bernie Ecclestone, the Man Behind Formula One," *BBC,* http://news.bbc.co.uk/2/hi/uk_news/29426.stm (September 10, 2013).

"Formula 1 Boss Indicted on Bribery Charge," *BBC,* http://www.bbc.co.uk/news/(September 10, 2013).

"Poor Suffolk Boy to Formula One Billionaire," *Eastern Daily Press* (Norwich, United Kingdom), http://www.edp24.co.uk/lifestyle/ (September 10, 2013).□

Marek Edelman

Polish resistance fighter Marek Edelman (1919–2009) played a vital role in the events of the Warsaw Ghetto Uprising of 1943. One of just a handful of Jewish guerrilla-warfare combatants who survived both the Nazi occupation of Poland during World War II and the Holocaust, Edelman became a respected cardiologist after the war and was active in Poland's struggle toward democracy as the Cold War neared to a close in the 1980s.

Marek Edelman was born in Warsaw, Poland, on September 19, 1919. His father Natan Feliks Edelman came from an area near Minsk, in present-day Belarus, and had been active in the Socialist Revolutionary Party, the Russian leftist group that worked to overthrow Tsar Nicholas II and bring about revolution in the neighboring superpower in 1917. Natan died in 1924, and ten years after that Edelman was orphaned when his mother Cecylia, who worked as a hospital secretary in Warsaw, passed away. Her work colleagues looked after the teenaged Edelman and helped him complete his education.

Joined the *Bund*

Edelman grew up in a city with an impressive Jewish population of about 350,000, or one third of Warsaw's residents. Like Vilnius, the capital of Lithuania, Warsaw was a center of religious and academic importance for Eastern European Jews, plus an important buffer site between the poorer *shtetl* Jews in Russian lands and the wealthier, more assimilated Jews of Germany, France, and the rest of Western Europe. The Zionist movement worked to establish a permanent Jewish homeland in the British Mandate for Palestine, but Edelman was staunchly opposed to the Zionist cause. He considered himself both a Jew and a Pole, was proud of his Polish roots, and uninterested in living in a self-imposed exile in an all-Jewish homeland. As a youngster he joined the *Sotsyalistishe Kinder Farband,* as the Socialist Children's Union was known in the Yiddish language. The group was part of the powerful Jewish *Bund,* or Union. More formally known as the Jewish Anti Zionist Socialist Bund in Poland, the Polish Bund had its origins in an older organization that had included Russian and Lithuanian Jews at its founding in Vilnius in 1897. Bundists were internationalists, believing that Jews had a right to citizenship and freedom to practice their religion in their land of origin.

Edelman was an admittedly indifferent student and aimless about his career plans on the outbreak of World War II in September of 1939. The Bund was his primary interest, and he became active in its young-adult section, *Tsukunft* (Future). When Nazi German forces invaded Poland on September 1, 1939, Edelman followed other leftists toward the eastern borders, where it was hoped they could count on support from the Soviet Union's socialist

Janek Skarzynski/AFP/Getty Images

regime. But the Soviets and Germany's Foreign Minister, Joachim von Ribbentrop, had signed a non-aggression pact just before the invasion. Large sections of western Poland fell quickly to Nazi military power, and Warsaw held out for a few more weeks. The end came on October 6, when Poland ceased to exist as a nation.

Edelman recalled one incident early in the Warsaw occupation, when two German soldiers had placed an elderly Jewish man on top of a barrel. With enormous shears they were cutting off his long beard and the crowd, some of them Jews, were laughing at the spectacle. "Objectively, it was really funny," Edelman told Matthew Brzezinski in the book *Isaac's Army: The Jewish Resistance in Occupied Poland.* "A little man on . . . a barrel with his beard growing shorter by the moment. Just like a movie gag. After all, nothing really horrible was happening to that Jew. Only now that it was possible to put him on a barrel with impunity." Edelman vowed at that moment never to let himself fall into German custody.

Ghetto Officially Sealed

Over the next several months of 1939–40, Jewish homes and businesses were confiscated and all of Warsaw's Jews were relocated into an old quarter that became known as the Warsaw Ghetto. It was literally walled off from the rest of the city by brick and sealed on November 16, 1940, with military checkpoints and gates at otherwise normal-looking urban intersections. As other Jews from elsewhere in occupied Poland were forced into the already over-crowded Warsaw Ghetto, food and fuel shortages made living conditions grim; emaciated Jews literally died on the street, either from hypothermia or starvation.

Edelman was fortunate to have a job as an orderly at a Warsaw Ghetto hospital, the Berson and Bauman Children's Hospital. At night, in defiance of a 9 p.m. curfew, he worked with other young Bund members on illegal pamphlets they printed by a hand-cranked mimeograph machine. The fliers and other materials urged Jews and Poles to work together to undermine the Nazi occupation. Even the location of the machine was top secret, and paper and ink to use it had to be purchased on the black market, which was flourishing in occupied Warsaw.

Edelman remained active in Tsukunft, which he had relaunched as an underground group inside the Ghetto. His hospital job and pamphleteering work gave him a familiarity with the zigzag streets, alleys, and secret passageways of the city. There were even basement access points and sewer tunnels that allowed resistance activists to make contact with sympathizers on the other side of the Ghetto wall, which was called Aryan Warsaw. From there they sent couriers to other Polish cities to make contact with Jewish and Polish-nationalist resistance cells elsewhere.

Witnessed Misery of Death Transports

The Warsaw Ghetto was supervised by a Nazi-sanctioned *Judenrat,* or Jewish Council. These were the elders in charge of job assignments, charity relief efforts, and other municipal details. They were largely hostile to any idea of underground resistance, fearing it would endanger the lives of all Jews in the Ghetto. On July 22, 1942, however, mass deportations began from Warsaw after the Germans proclaimed a new "resettlement" program. Warsaw's Jews were told to report to Umschagplatz, or Collection Square, a train depot. From there they would be sent to new work camps, where fresh air and produce were plentiful, they were told. In reality, these were recently constructed concentration camps on Polish soil, where the healthiest workers toiled in prison-labor workshops; those too old, too young, or too sickly were dispatched to concrete bunkers, told to strip for showers, and instead gassed to death with hundreds of others. Resistance activists in Warsaw had already learned about these camps and what had happened to Jews recently deported from other cities in Poland.

For more than a month, Edelman watched as German military authorities fulfilled daily quotas and rounded up Warsaw's Jews. In this first wave, about 265,000 men, women, and children were packed onto freight cars, which were then boarded shut to prevent escape. Edelman was stationed at Umschagplatz in his role as a messenger for the hospital. He brandished a sheaf of papers that could save lives, and searched for persons to match his names. These were special permits from the hospital that claimed the person was too ill to travel, but in many instances they contained names of resistance fighters considered vital to the future fight.

The underground Jewish resistance in Warsaw had failed to coalesce until the terror of the July deportations began. During that first week, Adam Czerniaków, head of the Judenrat, committed suicide once he realized what his long-argued policy of non-resistance meant for Jews. The formation of a solid resistance movement had been hampered by ideological differences among groups, too: some were ardent Zionists and leftists, like Yitzhak Zuckerman, Zivia Lubetkin, and Mordechai Anielewicz, while a few others had a strongly anti-Communist ideology. Finally, these differences were put aside as the ghetto's population dwindled to just 60,000 Jews. Shortly after the deportations began and Czerniaków committed suicide, Edelman and three aforementioned fighters, plus others, formed the *Żydowska Organizacja Bojowa,* or Jewish Fighting Organization, known by its Polish-language acronym of ŻOB. Edelman was not initially on its five-member high command, but was a deputy commander who advanced up the chain as its ranks were decimated by the guerrilla warfare that followed.

Tour Guide for Shocked Visitor

One of ŻOB's first actions was an assassination attempt on Jósef Szeryński, a widely reviled figure in the Warsaw Ghetto, in October of 1942. Szeryński served as commander the Jewish Ghetto Police, a loathed cadre of turncoats who carried out German orders against their fellow Jews with a particular zeal and violence. Another hopeful moment that autumn was the arrival of Jan Karski, a Polish resistance figure who had masterfully escaped capture several times and went undercover on important missions. Karski worked for Poland's government-in-exile in London and was tasked with reporting on Nazi war crimes with the help of contacts in the Armia Krajowa (AK), or Polish Home Army, the nationalist Polish resistance movement. It was Edelman who smuggled Karski into the Ghetto and took him on a tour that left the latter traumatized by what he saw. Karski was the first credible source to alert other nations to German chancellor Adolf Hitler's crimes against Jews, and Karski personally debriefed U.S. President Franklin D. Roosevelt.

When a new round of deportations began on January 18, 1943, ŻOB was ready to fight back. A few Germans were shot, and this temporarily halted the deportations. The act of aggression energized the movement, and more fighters were trained. Deportations began anew on April 19, 1943, and this time Edelman's and other ŻOB units were armed with slightly more firepower, including grenades and homemade Molotov cocktails. The fighting continued for three weeks, but the 500 or so members of the ŻOB and another group, the *Żydowski Związek Wojskowy,* or Jewish Military Union, were largely decimated. The Slavic-looking Zuckerman was trapped on the other side of the city, and served as an information and arms conduit. Edelman worked with Zuckerman's future wife, Lubetkin, who was one of the members of the high command. Finally, as they ran out of ammunition and the Germans began to use aerial bombs and chemical weapons to root out the remaining Warsaw Ghetto holdouts, Edelman and other leaders agreed on a plan to evacuate themselves via sewer tunnel and hide in Aryan Warsaw.

Discovered Tragic Miła Site

On May 8, 1943, Edelman had not received an expected message from Anielewicz at the ŻOB command post at 18 Miła Street, regarding coordination of their planned exodus. He and Lubetkin, along with a third ŻOB member, waited until dark then sneaked through alleys and passageways. At what was supposed to be a concealed entrance at the bunker they found signs of a disturbance, and called out the password. There was no reply, and Edelman realized that Anielewicz and several dozen other ŻOB fighters had committed suicide once the Germans had encircled their hideout. Edelman, Lubetkin, and the others regrouped and literally went underground as the Germans set fire to the Warsaw Ghetto. After a 20-hour trek through the sewer system, they emerged at Frosta Street on the other side. "In broad daylight with almost no cover, the trapdoor opened and one after another, with the stunned crowd looking on, armed Jews appeared from the depths of a black hole," Edelman wrote in his 1946 memoir, *The Ghetto Fights,* according his obituary in the London *Independent.*

Edelman lived to a remarkable age of 90, making him one of the oldest survivors of the Jewish resistance movement in Poland and even one of the rare Polish Jews who survived the Holocaust without leaving Polish soil or ever being captured. He took part in a second uprising, this one led by Polish nationalists, in August of 1944, that also proved disastrous. After the war, he married Alina Margolis, who had worked as a nurse inside the Warsaw Ghetto then became a pediatrician; Edelman also trained as a physician and became a renowned cardiologist in Poland. He was active in the Solidarity movement of the early 1980s and died in Warsaw on October 2, 2009. Of his actions in April and May of 1943, he famously claimed it was not really an uprising, because he and the others knew they no chance of success. "It was a defensive action," he asserted, according to his *New York Times* obituary. "We fought simply not to allow the Germans alone to pick the time and place of our deaths."

Books

Brzezinski, Matthew, *Isaac's Army: The Jewish Resistance in Occupied Poland,* Random House, 2012.

Periodicals

Guardian (London, England), November 17, 1990.
Independent (London, England), October 7, 2009.
New York Times, October 3, 2009; April 18, 2013.□

Richard Lovell Edgeworth

Anglo-Irish polymath Richard Lovell Edgeworth (1744–1817) applied his talents to a broad range of fields. An inventor, writer, and member of the

© Oldtime/Alamy

Irish House of Commons, Edgeworth built clocks, wind-powered vehicles, and even a primitive form of the telegraph. His ideas on the proper secular education of children were widely read in Britain during his lifetime, and in translation in other parts of Europe.

Born on May 31, 1744, Richard Lovell Edgeworth was the third of four children born to his father, also named Richard Edgeworth, and Rachel Jane Lovell Edgeworth. His immediate family included one older and one younger sister, Mary and Margaret, and a brother named Thomas who preceded Edgeworth's birth but died in childhood, which meant that young Richard would inherit his father's estate. At the time of his birth, the Edgeworths were living in the fashionable resort of Bath, England, but the family were part of the Anglo-Irish landed gentry and owned vast tracts in County Longford, Ireland. Edgeworth's middle name, Lovell, came from his mother's side, who was descended from an infamously punitive judge who once fined the novelist and pamphleteer Daniel Defoe for his writings and ordered him to be pilloried, or whipped, in public.

Edgeworth was keenly interested in the sciences as a child, especially mechanical gadgets, the laws of physics, and astronomy. At age seven he visited Dublin, Ireland, where he first saw an orrery, a mechanical model of the solar system that showed the Earth and other planets as well as demonstrating their paths of orbit around the sun. At age eight he was sent away to a boarding school for boys in Warwick, run by a Dr. Lydiat, where he spent a tormented year, and then completed more school terms at institutions in Drogheda—a city in Ireland—and then at Longford, close to the family seat at Pakenham Hall Castle, owned by wealthier relations known as the Earls of Longford.

Eloped to Gretna Green

Edgeworth spent six months at Trinity College of Dublin before enrolling at Corpus Christi College of Oxford University in October of 1761. Pursuing his interest in astronomy and horology—the science of measuring time by means of watches, clocks, sundials, and other devices—Edgeworth built his own camera obscura, a projection device that was the precursor to the modern camera. His Oxford education was cut short by romance, however: his father had asked a family friend named Paul Elers to look after him, and Edgeworth fell in love with a daughter of the household, Anna Maria Elers. Escaping a restrictive English law that prevented anyone under the age of 21 from marrying if one of their parents objected, the pair ran off to a town just across the border of Scotland, Gretna Green, to be wed there in 1763. When Anna Maria became pregnant with their first child, the couple were remarried at a church at Black Bourton, near Oxford, on February 21, 1764. Their son Richard was born three months later.

The young family moved to Edgeworthstown, in County Longford, Ireland, in 1765. Edgeworth built his own orrery while there and studied law. They eventually left Ireland and settled in the village of Hare Hatch in Berkshire, where Edgeworth continued with his inveterate tinkering and gadget-devising. He constructed a type of land cart propelled by sail, for example, and an umbrella to keep rain from spoiling haystacks in the countryside. In London in 1766, he sought to aid some acquaintances who were placing bets on a derby in Newmarket, a city in Suffolk that was the center of British thoroughbred racing. He promised some that he would be able to deliver the news of the winning horse several hours before the first courier arrived on horseback in London. Edgeworth successfully demonstrated a rudimentary system of transmitting information through signaling poles, based in part on the semaphore flag communication method used by sailors aboard Royal Navy ships.

From his mother, who had read the works of progressive philosopher John Locke, Edgeworth came of age with a deep interest in the ideas of the Age of Enlightenment. He was a particularly devout follower of the French philosopher Jean-Jacques Rousseau, who wrote extensively on how best to educate a child and future model citizen. One of Rousseau's most influential works was *Émile, ou De l'éducation,* published in 1763, and Edgeworth used it as a guide to homeschool his own son and daughter Maria, who was born in 1768. His marriage to Elers produced two more daughters, Emmeline and Anna, and the family spent some years in Lichfield, a city in Staffordshire that had become a hub of British scientific and literary achievement in a period known as the Midlands Age of Enlightenment.

Earned Medals and a Patent

In Lichfield, Edgeworth befriended the physician, poet, and botanist Erasmus Darwin, grandfather of Charles Darwin, and many other prominent figures. With the elder Darwin, Edgeworth became one of the founding members of the Lunar Society of Birmingham. Other members included James Watt and Matthew Boulton, who perfected the steam engine that launched the Industrial Revolution in the mid-eighteenth century. Edgeworth's various inventions were awarded medals from the Society of Arts in 1767 and 1769. His most lasting patent was registered as a "portable railway or artificial road to move along with any carriage to which it is attached," as its 1770 patent title reads. This was a precursor to the caterpillar track, or a continuous-tread type of wheel used by tractors, tanks and other vehicles. Also used in tractor construction, the caterpillar track permitted heavy equipment to move more efficiently across hilly or damp terrain.

Among the other figures in Lichfield during Edgeworth's time there was the poet Anna Seward. Seward was serving as guardian to a teenager named Honora Sneyd. Edgeworth became so smitten with Sneyd that he decided to leave England, traveling to France with his friend Thomas Day in 1771. Anna Maria eventually joined him in Lyon, where Edgeworth was attempting to perfect a land reclamation device for the Rhône River. When she became pregnant again, she went back to England with Day as her travel companion. She died in childbirth in March of 1773, and Edgeworth returned, too. He learned that Sneyd was not yet married, and the pair were wed in July of 1773. They had two children together: Honora the younger, born in 1774, and a son named Lovell, who arrived the following year. His new wife was keenly interested in progressive education theories, and they took the family to County Longford, where Edgeworth had inherited property in Edgeworthstown after the death of his father in 1769. They kept detailed records of the children's lessons and intellectual progress, and that *Register,* as it was known, provided the basis for several books by both Edgeworth and his eldest daughter Maria.

Devised Cross-Ireland Defense Network

Edgeworth was widowed again at age 35 when Honora died of tuberculosis in April of 1780. On her deathbed she urged him to marry her younger sister, Elizabeth Sneyd, who agreed to the match. This was not illegal, but was considered highly irregular, and so the pair moved to what was then the outskirts of London and were wed at St. Andrew's parish church in Holborn on December 25, 1780. This marriage produced six more children, all of whom lived to adulthood: Elizabeth, Henry, Charlotte, Charles, a second Honora, and William. Edgeworth's eldest daughter Maria, by then approaching her teens, took an active role in educating her younger siblings at Edgeworthstown, where they settled once again in 1782. The family's Georgian-era manor home, Edgeworthstown House, became the focus of Edgeworth's inventive mind, too, with a system of central heating he devised after undertaking extensive renovations; it also boasted a primitive form of running water via a pump-action apparatus.

Edgeworth had inherited an estate on which Irish tenant farmers eked out a living. Many of them would later be hard hit by Ireland's Potato Famine of the 1840s. During his lifetime he worked to improve agricultural practices and drew up new contractual agreements designed to help both tenant and landlord turn more of a profit. He brought Maria along when he made the rounds on estate business and taught her how to manage it effectively. In the 1790s parts of Ireland were in political turmoil over Anglo-Irish domination and the rights of its Roman Catholic population, who were often at odds with Protestant minority rule. Twice in that decade there was a threat of an invasion by France, and Edgeworth sought government patronage for his idea of a "tellograph" system. His proposal, submitted to the Royal Irish Academy in 1797, was titled *An Essay on the Art of Conveying Secret and Swift Intelligence.* A few years later, a young Anglo-Irish naval officer and hydrographer named Francis Beaufort visited County Longford and helped Edgeworth set up a system of towers that stretched from the west coast of Ireland, in Galway, to Dublin on the other side of the Emerald Isle. The Irish landscape and weather proved a poor choice of location, with fog and consistently inclement weather hindering visibility between the 30 stations.

Edgeworth was widowed a third time when Elizabeth Sneyd Edgeworth died in November of 1797. On May 31, 1798—his 54th birthday—Edgeworth married Beaufort's sister Frances, called Fanny. Already the father of 12, Edgeworth began a fourth family with Beaufort that added six more young minds to educate: Frances, Harriet, Sophia, Lucy, Francis, and Michael. His brother-in-law, who became Sir Francis Beaufort and chief hydrographer of the British Admiralty, was partially inspired by Edgeworth's tellograph line of 1803 when he drew up the Beaufort Scale of Wind Force. The tellograph system had failed because the optical-signaling codes that Edgeworth had devised to transmit data were incredibly complicated to master. Beaufort's Scale of Wind Force, by contrast, assigned numbers to easily observable wind conditions at sea. After Edgeworth's death, an American inventor named Samuel Morse created a code that replaced the letters of the alphabet with dots and dashes. Transmitted via electrical current, the Morse Code could be easily tapped out by finger over devices that relied on electrical current, and it launched the era of modern global telecommunication.

Inspired Other Inventors

Another prescient work from Edgeworth was *An Essay on the Construction of Roads and Carriages,* which he wrote in 1813. In an era just before rail transport and steam-powered locomotives enabled more efficient long-distance travel, land routes in the British Isles were in need of constant repair and maintenance. Edgeworth wrote of a method of pulverizing hard stone into gravel and mixing it with a binding agent. A Scottish engineer named John

Loudon MacAdam later improved upon this a few years after Edgeworth's death, and the tar-based surface was known for decades to come in the British Isles as "macadam"; the word "tarmac" is also derived from the Scottish inventor's recipe.

Edgeworth's ideas for a continuous track vehicle, known as the caterpillar tread, also inspired other inventors, and the first wartime machines using this were successfully deployed in Britain's battle against the Russian Empire in the Crimean War of 1853–56. One of his more enduring but minor achievements was a prefabricated spire for the church in Edgeworthstown. Made of iron bars and covered with slate, it was erected in July of 1811 and remained a County Longford landmark until 1935. Edgeworth died at Edgeworthstown House on June 13, 1817, two weeks after his 73rd birthday. His daughter Maria became a well-known novelist and writer of educational tracts. Though he is credited as the co-author of a widely reprinted title called *Professional Education,* which first appeared in 1808, Maria was assumed to have written the bulk of it. She also completed his two-volume set of memoirs, published posthumously in 1821.

Books

Colvin, Christina Edgeworth, "Edgeworth, Richard Lovell (1744–1817)," *Oxford Dictionary of National Biography,* Oxford University Press, 2004.

Edgeworth, Richard Lovell, and Maria Edgeworth, *Memoirs of Richard Lovell Edgeworth, Esq.,* R. Hunter, 1821.□

Martinie/Roger Viollet/Getty Images

Paul Éluard

The French poet Paul Éluard (1895–1952) was one of the founders of the Surrealist movement. Considered one of France's greatest writers of the modern era, he lived through and addressed in his writing many of the tumultuous events of 20th-century European life.

Some of Éluard's poems were political; others were experimental. Yet what has made his poetry compelling for students and general readers in France, and often for those reading it in translation, has been its personal qualities. Éluard fell deeply in love several times over the course of his life, and many of his love poems, addressed directly to one of his three wives, are classic expressions of romantic and sexual impulses. For Éluard, the personal and the political were linked: he saw love as a source of creativity and liberation that provided sustenance even in the face of the despair he and others felt as they lived through the carnage of two world wars.

Spent Early Life in Poverty

Paul Éluard was born Paul-Eugèene Emile Grindel on December 14, 1895, in the working-class Paris suburb of Saint-Denis. He was called Eugè or Gégè by his family. His father, Clément, was a poorly paid accountant, and his mother, Jeanne, took on dressmaking jobs to help with the always stretched family budget. Around 1899, the family moved to another suburb, Aulnay-sous-Bois, which suffered less from industrial pollution, and in about 1908, they moved to Paris. Éluard attended school there and showed a gift for language; he learned English quickly, and, as his family's fortunes improved, he was able to spend two months in England to master the language.

In 1912, however, Éluard contracted a lung infection that was probably tuberculosis. Confined in a sanatorium in Switzerland for more than a year to recover and regain his strength, he found himself with time to read and think, and he was given books of recent French poetry by the likes of Arthur Rimbaud and Guillaume Apollinaire. Soon Éluard had issued a small book optimistically titled *Premiè Poèmes* (First Poems). He began using the pen name Paul Éluard, formed from part of his given first hame and the surname of his maternal grandmother.

The mature themes of Éluard's poetry had their roots in both personal and political developments. At the sanatorium, he fell in love with a beautiful young Russian woman named Helena Diakonova, known as Gala. Éluard's mother forbade him to see her after his release, but the pair married in 1917 in Paris and had a daughter, Cécile. By that time Éluard's view of human nature had been darkened by his experiences in World War I. Joining the French army after the beginning of the war in 1914, he was sent to the front as a medic and at one point was the victim of a chemical weapons attack. That exacerbated the lung damage that Éluard had already suffered, and for the rest of his life he would struggle with fragile health.

Met Surrealist Writers

Éluard continued to write poetry prolifically, both in the midst of his war experiences and after the war, when he returned to Paris and his family. He issued several more books, including *Poèmes pour la paix* (Poems for Peace, 1919), and an editor introduced him to a group of young writers and artists who would go on to create some of the most innovative work in interwar France. These included the poets André Breton and Louis Aragon, and later the German artist Max Ernst. At first Éluard identified himself with the nihilistic Dada movement, which rejected what they saw as the bourgeois values that had led to the carnage of World War I. Later, when Dada ran its course, Éluard began to experiment with Surrealism, a movement that reached into art, literature, and even music.

The atmosphere among these young arists was sexually as well as creatively experimental, and Éluard's wife entered into liaisons with Ernst and later the Spanish artist Salvador Dali. Ernst even moved in with the young couple. Éluard's father, who by this time had become a successful real estate developer and was supporting his son financially, pressured Éluard to put a stop to this situation, but Éluard responded by dropping out of it completely, disappearing from Paris and leading family and friends to think he was dead. He resurfaced in the Far East, having visited India, New Zealand, the Malay peninsula, and what is now Indonesia. Gala traveled to Singapore to get him, and by the fall of 1924, Éluard was back in Paris.

Over the next several years, Éluard wrote some of his best-known poetry. The book *Capitale de la douleur* (Capital of Pain, 1926) reflected both the violence he had experienced and his belief in the redemptive power of love. The poem "Paris pendant la guerre" (Paris During the War) contained these lines: "Les oiseaux qui secouent leurs plumes meurtrières, / Les terribles ciels jaunes, les nuages tout nus, / Ont, en toute saison, fêté cette statue. / Elle est belle, statue vivante de l'amour." (The birds which shake their deadly feathers, / The terrible yellow skies, the clouds in their nakedness / Have in all seasons celebrated this statue. / It is beautiful, a living statue of love. [The English translations of Éluard's poems are taken from an article by Kenneth W. Meadwell in the *Dictionary of Literary Biography*]).

In 1926 Éluard joined the French Communist Party. He became disillusioned with Communism as Stalinist repression closed in on the Soviet Union and was expelled from the party, along with Breton, in 1933. Éluard's marriage to Gala finally dissolved in the late 1920s, and in 1930 he met the actress and circus performer Maria Benz, nicknamed Nusch. The pair married in 1934, and this new romance brought about a fresh burst of creativity from Éluard even though she had an affair with artist Pablo Picasso. Éluard joined with the photographer Man Ray to create a book, *Facile* (Easy, 1935), consisting of poems directed to Nusch as well as photgraphs of her; the book was dubbed a *Photopoème* or Photopoem.

Participated in French Resistance

In the late 1930s Éluard once again affiliated himself with Communism. He would remain a steadfast Communist for the rest of his life despite mounting evidence of Stalin's atrocities. During World War II Éluard participated in the resistance to Nazi rule in France, writing, printing, and distributing anti-German flyers. He published new poetry under pen names and frequently moved from place to place to avoid detection by the Germans. Éluard's poem "Liberté" published in the 1942 book *Poèsie et Vé* (Poetry and Truth), was broadcast on pirate anti-Nazi radio stations and became a classic of French poetry that is still taught in French schools.

The poem was typical of Éluard's style, which was concise and muscular, retaining surrealist elements. Of the titular Liberty, he wrote, "On my school exercise books / On my desk and the trees / On the sand on the show / I write your name." Crisis seemed to stimulate the poet's creativity once again, and he issued no fewer than 25 books of poetry in occupied Paris during the war. An extraordinarily productive writer despite periods of ill health, Éluard published at least 110 books of poetry during his lifetime, with several more appearing posthumously.

Éluard's second wife died suddenly in 1946, and his grief over her death was abundantly reflected in his poetry. In 1949, at a meeting of the World Peace Council in Mexico, he met single mother Dominique Laure, and the two married in 1951 after touring the Communist East Bloc; Dominique began to perceive flaws in the Communist social model, but Éluard remained devoted to the cause. After suffering a heart attack in September of 1952, Éluard died at his home in Paris on November 18. Reportedly "Dominique" was his last word. Many of Éluard's poems have been translated into English, some of them by the bilingual *Waiting for Godot* author Samuel Beckett.

Books

Leroux, Jean-François, ed., *Modern French Poets* (*Dictionary of Literary Biography,* Vol. 258), Gale, 2002.

Nugent, Robert, *Paul Éluard,* Twayne, 1974.

Online

"Biography of Paul Éluard," *PoemHunter.com,* http://www.poemhunter.com/paul-Éluard/biography/ (November 12, 2013).

"Paul Éluard (1895–1952)," *Books and Writers,* http://www.kirjasto.sci.fi/Éluard.htm (November 12, 2013).

"Paul Éluard," *Poetry Foundation,* http://www.poetryfoundation.org/bio/paul-Éluard (November 12, 2013).□

F

Horst Faas

German-born photographer Horst Faas (1933–2012) played a key role in bringing the emotionally searing images of the Vietnam War to the world's doorstep in the 1960s and '70s. The photojournalist spent several years as an Associated Press photographer and then the agency's bureau chief for South Asia. He won two Pulitzer Prizes for his work, and became a revered figure to a generation of photojournalists, many of whom he had personally trained.

Horst Faas was born on April 28, 1933, in Berlin, Germany, just three months after the Nazi Party and its leader, Adolf Hitler, came to power. He was the first of three sons of parents Adalbert and Gerda, and the family moved several times to escape the perils of World War II. They lived in Kattowicz, a city in present-day Poland, but in early 1945 fled advancing Russian forces and returned to Berlin, which was in the process of being bombed into ruins. As an adolescent Faas was not particularly bothered by the ominous rumble and searing noise of the Allies' aerial raids on the city, nor was he shaken by the earth-shattering booms of German anti-aircraft guns designed to shoot down the enemy planes. Finally, with the city in utter ruins, the family fled Berlin once again and eventually made their way to Munich. In the immediate aftermath of the war, Germany was divided into military zones under occupation, and the Bavarian city was inside the American zone. As a teen, Faas was musically talented and became a jazz drummer for a band formed by U.S. service members.

Sent to Cover African Wars

Faas eventually became a darkroom assistant, helping to develop rolls of film via a special chemical process. He eventually began taking photographs himself and moved to London to work for the Keystone Press Agency in 1953, a well-known supplier of photojournalism for newspapers and magazines of the era. The Associated Press news agency (AP) hired him in 1956, and sent him on his first combat assignment in 1960, to the Democratic Republic of Congo in Central Africa, which at the time was experiencing violent civil strife in its transition to self-rule. Faas saw even grimmer scenes when the AP sent him to Algeria, then in its final year of a eight-year battle for independence from France. Faas proved so adept at handling himself in battlefield conditions that in 1962, his AP bosses tapped him for a post in former French Indochina, which had also emerged as an independent nation called Vietnam. There remained internal divisions, however, and the United States had sent personnel—both armed units and undercover operatives—to keep the nation from tilting toward Communism. Vietnamese Communists had played a key role in the fight for independence in the early 1950s, but an anti-Communist Vietnamese, anchored in the south of the country around Saigon, were ruling an over an increasingly authoritarian state and proved unwilling to share power.

The fight in Vietnam escalated into a full-scale conflict in 1965 with the arrival of U.S. combat forces. On one side were the Communists in North Vietnam, based in Hanoi, and a government in Saigon that managed to hold off a takeover for the next ten years partly with the help of enormous military aid from the United States; the North Vietnamese, meanwhile, were supported by two Communist behemoths, the Soviet Union and China. The fighting took place in the jungles and Central Highlands of middle

© ZUMA Press, Inc./Alamy

Vietnam, drew in nearby Laos and Cambodia, and its casualty toll included thousands of impoverished civilians.

Faas won his first major honor, the Robert Capa Gold Medal from the Overseas Press Club, in 1964 for his coverage of the war in Vietnam. In 1965, he won the prestigious Pulitzer Prize, one of journalism's top honors, for his image of a Vietnamese man holding the lifeless body of a young child and looking up at the South Vietnamese army rangers, crowded into the back an armored truck. Faas had taken the shot on March 19, 1964, just after South Vietnamese forces came through the area, near the border with Cambodia, searching for Viet Cong, the name given to North Vietnamese sympathizers and guerrilla combatants.

Nearly Lost Legs, and Life

Just how close Faas put himself to the action is visible in another image he took that went out over the AP wires and was widely reprinted: he appears to be standing in waist-high water in a line of women and children under deep jungle cover. The photograph was taken on January 1, 1966, and the civilians were being escorted by the U.S. 173rd Airborne Brigade to safety as the Airborne fought off a Viet Cong attack. The fear on the women's faces is visible as they cower against the riverbank foliage.

Faas always carried $50 in U.S. currency on him in the event he was wounded and needed help; as a civilian journalist he had to win the trust of soldiers who agreed to take him along on their missions, sometimes via helicopter, and his luck finally ran out on December 6, 1967, when he was hit during a grenade attack in Bu Dop in South Vietnam's Central Highlands. He nearly bled to death but his legs were saved by U.S. Army medics. Waving off any idea of reassignment, Faas settled into a desk job as the AP's Chief of Photography for South Asia once he could get around on crutches. He had already been training local amateur photographers to work for the AP; some of them were just teenagers but spoke Vietnamese and English, knew the city well, and sped to and from hot spots via motorbike.

Ran Controversial Images

From his office in Saigon, Faas sent out photographers during the Tet Offensive of January-February 1968. Both sides had agreed to a ceasefire for the two-day South Asian lunar holiday known as Tet, but the North Vietnamese launched a surprise attack, aided by Viet Cong working inside South Vietnam. Even Saigon was shelled, and one of Faas's AP staffers named Eddie Adams went out with a patrol headed by the Saigon chief of police on February 1, 1968. One section of the city had been taken by the Viet Cong but reverted within hours to South Vietnamese control. Adams was with an NBC cameraman as the police chief's force found a man wearing a plaid shirt and grabbed him. The man's hands were bound behind his back and he was brought to Lt. Colonel Nguyen Ngoc Loan, who raised a pistol to the young man's head and fired the weapon; the first milliseconds of the actual blast is visible.

"The Saigon Execution," as Adams's photograph became known, was an appalling image in which a man dressed in civilian clothing is shot in broad daylight in the middle of a deserted but otherwise normal urban street. Adams later said he did not expect the police chief to shoot the man, as it was not uncommon to hold a gun to the head of prisoners. Adams rushed the film roll back to Faas's AP office, where it was developed and Faas quickly scanned the contact sheet. "I saw what I had never seen before on the lightbox of my Saigon editing desk: The perfect news-picture—the perfectly framed and exposed 'frozen moment' of an event which I felt instantly would become representative of the brutality of the Vietnam War," Faas wrote years later in an account of the photograph for *Digital Journalist* magazine. "The photo of the execution at the hands of Vietnam's police chief, Lt. Colonel Nguyen Ngoc Loan, at noon on Feb. 1, 1968 has reached beyond the history of the Indochina War—it stands today for the brutality of our last century."

The photo won Eddie Adams the 1969 Pulitzer Prize and became one of the most iconic images of the war. There was one more emblematic photograph of the Vietnam War that also passed across Faas's desk and went out over the wires, a 1972 image of children fleeing an aerial napalm attack. A deadly chemical agent that burned the skin and damaged the respiratory system, the weapon was especially effective against the enemy but also caused massive civilian casualties. On June 8, 1972, one of Faas's AP photographers was at a village called Trang Bang when the South Vietnamese launched a napalm bomb. A nine-year-old girl is among the children photographer Huynh Cong "Nick" Ut captured fleeing from the smoking village. Her clothes have been burned off in the attack and her face is contorted in agony. The photo won Ut a Pulitzer Prize in 1973, though Faas later said his AP bosses had been skittish about running it because of the nudity. Faas convinced them it was newsworthy and it appeared on the front page of hundreds of American newspapers the next day, becoming the first image millions of people saw around the world as the morning edition of their newspaper appeared on their doorstep.

Shot Iconic Munich Olympics Image

Protests against U.S. involvement in Vietnam dated back to the first troop deployments, but the scale of rancor and disgust among the public was bolstered by inescapable images taken by Faas and other photojournalists, many of whom did not survive the job. Troop withdrawals were already underway by the time Nick Ut took that shot at Trang Bang, and U.S. forces pulled out altogether as North Vietnamese advanced on Saigon in April of 1975.

Faas won a second Pulitzer Prize, shared with French photographer Michel Laurent, for images of civilian unrest and ethnic conflict in Bangladesh in December of 1971. Remarkably, Faas managed to capture yet another memorable image back in peaceful West Germany, which was excited about hosting the 1972 Summer Olympic Games. In a land where armed conflict had ceased 27 years earlier at the end of World War II, Faas captured the shocking image of a hooded Palestinian guerilla peering out over a balcony of the newly built Olympic Village; behind the ski mask-wearing Palestinian is a door to a room where Israeli athletes were being held hostage by members of the Black September terrorist group. The athletes and several Palestinians died in a shootout during a botched rescue attempt at a nearby airfield, and Faas's image remains the most iconic of the 1972 Munich Olympics, and virtually the only one captured of any of the Black September operatives—whose surviving members were rooted out and assassinated by agents of Mossad, the Israeli intelligence agency.

Faas had an eye for more hopeful images, too: one of them was U.S. President Richard M. Nixon shaking hands with Egyptian President Anwar Sadat in June of 1974 on Nixon's visit to Egypt. The Pyramids at Giza serve as a dramatic backdrop. Two years later, Faas settled in London and became the AP's senior photo editor for Europe. Remarkably, he had been married for more than a decade by then, to Ursula Gerienne, with whom he had a daughter. He retired from the AP in 2004, a year after co-authoring his account of a search to find the remains of four other photojournalists who had died in a 1971 helicopter crash during the South Vietnamese Army's invasion of Laos. *Lost over Laos: a True Story of Tragedy, Mystery, and Friendship* was written with Richard Pyle and detailed the trip back to the mountainside where the accident had occurred.

Faas returned to Vietnam again in 2005 for a reunion of war correspondents, where he suffered a spinal hemorrhage. He was confined to a wheelchair for the remainder of his life, and died on May 10, 2012, at age 79, in Munich. Despite the pair of Pulitzer Prizes and the awards his protégés also earned over the years, Faas disavowed any personal political crusade in his job with the AP. "I tried to be in the newspapers every day, to beat the opposition with better photos," he told a BBC interviewer a few years before his death, according to his *Times* of London obituary. "I didn't try to do anything grandiose. The photos were used and published and asked for because Vietnam was on the front pages year after year."

Periodicals

Independent (London, England), May 12, 2012.
New York Times, May 12, 2012.
Times (London, England), May 12, 2012.

Online

Faas, Horst, "The Saigon Execution," *Digital Journalist,* October 2004, http://digitaljournalist.org/issue0410/faas.html (February 10, 2014).□

Marino Faliero

Marino Faliero (1285–1355) served a brief but scandalously concluded term as the 55th Doge of Venice. Beheaded in 1355 after he was linked to a plot to oust the aristocracy from power, the veteran diplomat and formerly esteemed military commander has the ignominious designation of being the only Venetian doge ever executed for treason.

The title Doge of Venice dates back to 700 CE. One of Faliero's forebears was Vitale Faliero, who ruled as the 32nd Doge of Venice from 1084 to 1095. The Faliero family was thought to be from Fano, an ancient town in the Marches region on Italy's Adriatic Sea coast. As Doge, Vitale Faliero had the honor of presiding over a newly consecrated St. Mark's Basilica, one of Venice's most breathtaking landmarks even a millennium later. Vitale was married to a woman named Cornelia Bembo, and their son Ordelafo Faliero was elected Doge a few years later, in 1102. An experienced military commander, Ordelafo led armies against Hungarian incursions to the north and in the Balkans, and he was also commander in chief of a fleet that sailed to present-day Israel and Syria and made some territorial advances.

Descended from Prominent Family

It would be another 230 years before a Faliero returned to the Doge's throne in Venice. Marino Faliero's name is alternately spelled in Venetian-dialect form as "Marin Falier." He was born in 1285, and spent his ablest years at sea and at war. He was known to have taken part in one of the battles at Zara, also known as Zadar, a Croatian coastal jewel and long a thorn in Venice's mission to control Adriatic Sea commerce. Faliero was eventually appointed commander of the Venetian fleet in the Black Sea, a vital strategic post. The Republic of Genoa, another maritime power, also had a foothold there, and in Faliero's lifetime Venice would resume a long-running rivalry with its northern Italian enemy for control of important trade routes.

Faliero's first wife was a woman named Tommasina Contarini, scion of another elite Venetian family. After her death, he remarried a woman whose given name has been spelled Aloica, Aluica, Aluycia, or Alucia; her surname was Gradenigo, and she, too, was from an esteemed Venetian clan. Later accounts of Faliero's tenure attempt to portray Gradenigo as much younger than her husband and a less-than-faithful spouse, but the future Dogaressa was probably in her late 40s and likely as primly behaved as her husband, whom the historical record has sometimes mischaracterized as reckless and with a temperament unsuited for leadership.

Faliero was nearly 70 years old when he became Doge and had previously held a number of noteworthy political posts. A member of the Republic of Venice's Council of Ten ruling body, he had also served as *podestà* or provincial governor in Chioggi and Treviso, a pair of northern Italian parcels that were part of the Republic of Venice. Faliero was formally ennobled as the Count of Valdemarino in the Marches of Treviso, and in 1353, he went to Vienna, the seat of the Holy Roman Empire, to be knighted by the Holy Roman Emperor Charles IV.

Passed Through Molo Pillars

A trusted diplomat, Faliero had been sent to the papal court at Avignon, France, to request Pope Innocent IV's intercession in the Venetian Republic's war with Milan and Genoa, which had erupted once again. He was still in the south of France when he received word that he had been elected the next Doge following the death of Andrea Dandolo on September 7, 1354. In the era when communication was only as fast as its human messenger could travel, Faliero learned of his appointment several days after the September 11 election and immediately made plans to sail home. It was early October when his vessel finally reached the Venice lagoon, and the city was covered by a heavy fog. A tender from the main ship carrying him missed the main pier, and Faliero came ashore a short distance from the primary Doge's Palace dock, landing at a stone quay called the Molo instead. Some superstitious Venetians avoided walking between the pair of landmark columns at the site, where public executions were sometimes held, and his return to Venice at Molo was later deemed an inauspicious moment.

Faliero's inauguration ceremony took place not far from this spot, too, near the magnificent Doge's Palace, the seat of government of the Republic of Venice. His first weeks in office were troubled by news of Venice's resounding loss in the Battle of Portolungo against the Genoese. Portolungo was a Venetian stronghold at Modon in the southern Greek Peloponnesian peninsula, later called Methoni. In early November of 1354, the Venetian commander at Portolungo made several tactical errors and was forced to surrender. The Venetians lost 30 galley ships and at least 5,000 men, who were either killed or taken prisoner by the detested Genoese. When news of the terrible loss reached Venice, there was major unrest and infectious fear that Venice's long and fabled tradition of rule by nobility—a system with several internal checks and balances to guard against tyranny and corruption—had at long last come to an end. The nobles were blamed for leading Venice once again into war with Genoa, and with inflicting such a calamitous loss of men and resources on the Republic.

Venice had a rising middle class of merchants and artisans, of humble origin but financially prosperous, and many had become contemptuous of the old-guard elite. Faliero found himself caught between these opposing forces. One of his first decisive acts as Doge was to install commoners as chiefs of some new galley ships he commissioned, and this smaller fleet scored a few successes against Genoese targets in the months that followed. The *popolo* of Venice, as the commoners were classed, were exultant over these victories, and some among Venice's noble families began to resent Faliero for his actions.

Blamed on Scurrilous Graffiti

The events leading up to Faliero's conviction for treason allegedly began during Carnival week, the pre-Lenten celebrations that take place just before the 40-day period of fasting and penance on the Christian liturgical calendar preceding Easter. At a banquet at the Doge's Palace, a young nobleman named Michele Steno took advantage of the ribald Carnival atmosphere and behaved inappropriately to one of Gradenigo's attendants. The Dogaressa was insulted, brought the matter to her husband, and Steno was ejected by security guards. Legend holds that Steno scribbled a slur against the Dogaressa and left it on the Doge's throne in the official council chamber. His honor insulted, Faliero had Steno brought up on charges, but the magistrates who dealt with such matters gave the young man a light, barely punitive sentence, on the grounds that it was Carnival week and Steno had no prior record of serious troublemaking.

There were other names linked to the alleged plot to remove the old nobility from power that ended with Faliero's beheading. The chain began with a man named Bertucci Isarello, a commoner and a ship captain. Isarello became embroiled in a dispute with a noble named Giovanno Dandolo, paymaster of the Venetian navy. Dandolo had assigned a commoner to one of Isarello's ships. Isarello rejected the appointment of the other man to his galley, an argument ensued, and Dandolo was said to have slapped Isarello. Enraged, Isarello left the navy office and roamed the docks and wharves, gathering men to carry out a retributive assault on Dandolo. When word of this reached Faliero, he summoned Isarello for a formal reprimand and ordered him to disband his men, so that Dandolo could leave the building.

Isarello complied, and Faliero reportedly summoned him back for a private meeting later that night. Another ringleader was Filippo Calendario, a wealthy stonemason involved in renovations of the Doge's Palace. Both were commoners but quite wealthy, and Calendario even owned his own ship. At the stealth meeting that night, both offered to recruit 20 men for a force, each of whom would recruit another 40. The supposed coup would involve 800 men, sworn to secrecy, who would massacre the nobles in one vicious and bloody reprisal.

Level of Involvement Remains Mystery

Faliero's plot was also alleged to involve the Arsenalotti, or guards of the Arsenale, the Venetian naval yard. Some Arsenalotti also served as a personal security detail for the Doge. The coup was to take place on April 15, 1355, when the city would be roused by false rumors that the Genoese were about to attack and invade the famously untouchable Venetian Republic. With this, Faliero was supposed to summon the Great Council for a meeting, and at a prearranged signal the coup participants, some of them Arsenalotti guards, would move to secure the palace exits, then use their weapons to kill as many nobles as they could. Faliero was to appear on the Doge's Palace balcony after the bloodshed and plead for calm, and humbly request the *popolo* affirm him as the Prince of Venice, not just the Duke.

The plot to overthrow Venice's elites was foiled by lack of secrecy. Reportedly a furrier from Bergamo came to Venice on April 14 and warned one of his customers not to leave the house the next day. The customer was a nobleman named Nicolò Lioni, who interrogated the furrier further and was able to glean some names attached to the plot. Lioni went to Faliero to warn him, but Faliero dismissed the rumors as idle gossip. Lioni then shared his concerns with the Council of Ten, who had already heard rumors of a potential Arsenalotti uprising. Meeting in secret, the Council of Ten summoned an emergency summit and on the morning of April 15 made sure that 7,000 loyal men were mustered to the Piazzetta, the smaller plaza adjacent to St. Mark's next to the Doge's Palace. Another hundred cavalry officers were stationed elsewhere in the city to quash any revolt. The Council voted to enact emergency powers, ordered the arrests of Isarello and Calendario, and they in turn implicated Faliero on April 16.

Isarello and Calendario were tried by a special *zonta,* a tribunal assembled at times of extreme peril to the Republic. Both confessed their guilt and were sentenced to death by hanging, which took place from the loggia of the Doge's Palace. Another nine conspirators were also hanged, then finally Faliero also admitted his guilt and was condemned to die. Historians still puzzle over his confession, for he seemed the least likely of rebels—a man of seventy, who already ruled Venice, and who had no sons to inherit his title. In any case, in a terrifying sequence of events he was taken from his residence chambers to the grand staircase at the palace, formally stripped of the insignia of his office, including the distinctive *corno,* or Doge's hat, and beheaded by long sword. His body and head tumbled separately down the staircase, and then the doors were opened for public viewing.

Inspired Various Artistic Works

The Florentine scholar Petrarch visited Venice a month after Faliero's death and was the first to report on events, though his account was based on hearsay. When the Republic of Venice finally fell to Napoleon's forces in 1797, its archives were opened to historians. Accounts of Faliero's grim end fascinated early nineteenth-century Europeans. Lord Byron wrote a play about him in verse in 1821, and Gaetano Donizetti used the tale as the basis of his 1835 opera also titled *Marino Faliero.* French master Eugne Delacroix completed *The Execution of Marino Faliero* in 1827, which hangs in the Wallace Collection in London. In Venice, Faliero is commemorated only by a black veil over the historical frieze of doges' portrait in the Great Hall of the Doge's Palace. The black cloth bears the Latin inscription *Hic est locus Marini Faletro decapitati pro criminibus*—"This is the space reserved for Marino Faliero, beheaded for his crimes."

Books

Lane, Frederic Chapin, *Venice, A Maritime Republic,* Johns Hopkins University Press, 1973.

Madden, Thomas F., *Venice: Islands of Honor and Profit: A New History,* Viking/Penguin, 2012.□

Lizhi Fang

The Chinese scientist Fang Lizhi (1936–2012) was a leading political dissident in China. A thorn in the side of China's totalitarian government for many years, he helped to inspire the pro-democracy activism of the 1980s and was forced into exile after the brutal Tiananmen Square crackdown of 1989.

Fang (his family name in the Chinese naming system) was also one of China's pioneering scientists, and he spent much of his career alternating between officially approved celebrity and condemnation from Chinese officialdom. He did not consider his political activism something separate from his scientific work; instead, his activism sprang from his commitment to scientific truth. "Scientists must express their feelings about all aspects of society, especially when unreasonable, wrong, or evil things emerge," he said in a Chinese interview quoted by the *Times* of London. Indeed, a major stimulus to his activism early in his career was the government's attempt to make science conform to strict Marxist principles in the 1950s and 1960s. For his resistance to that trend, Fang was sent to the countryside to do manual labor during China's repressive Cultural Revolution period.

Built Radio from Scratch

Fang Lizhi was born on February 12, 1936. His birthplace has been variously reported as Beijing and Hangzhou, China, and his father's occupation as postal clerk and railroad accountant. His family was middle-class, but their lives were disrupted by the Japanese occupation of China during World War II. The presence of American troops and the surplus electronic parts they brought with them after the

Forrest Anderson/Time & Life Pictures/Getty Images

war stimulated the first stirrings of Fang's scientific interests: he saved his lunch money to buy the components of a radio, which he assembled himself. Around the same time, he saw police beat a group of students. Fascinated by the radio and the principles behind it, he began to read Western physics texts, such as the writings of Danish physicist Niels Bohr, on his own.

That was enough to get Fang into Beijing University, one of the most prestigious in China, at age 16. Majoring in nuclear and theoretical physics, he graduated at 20 and was put to work building a nuclear reactor that in 1996, he proudly noted, was still in operation. Following a Russian design, Fang and his co-workers lacked computers and calculators; they did the necessary calcluations on an abacus. Fang enthusiastically joined the Communist Party, but in 1957, he had his first brush with authority. After he and other scientists were invited by Chinese leader Mao Zedong to give their opinions freely on the country's development (a ploy that may have been intended to trick critics into giving themselves away), "I made trouble for the first time. Even though I believed very deeply in Marx, Lenin, and Stalin, I could not go along with what the Party was saying in physics," Fang recalled to Arthur Fisher of *Popular Science.*

One issue that troubled Fang was that official Chinese textbooks condemned the ideas of Bohr's Copenhagen School, ideas that Fang's own reading had convinced him were correct. Calling for freedom of inquiry in Chinese science, he was expelled from the Communist Party in 1957. Nevertheless, Fang remained a promising young scientist, and the government could not afford to do without his expertise completely. He was permitted to organize a new physics department at the University of Science and Technology in Beijing and to publish papers in the field of theoretical physics, albeit without his name attached to them at first. In the late 1950s and early 1960s, Fang was part of a team that built China's first lasers. He married fellow physicist Li Shuxian in 1961, and the couple had two sons.

Held in Cow Shed

During the first half of the 1960s, Fang published a number of scientific papers and was a member of a productive physics institute at the Chinese Academy of Sciences. But beginning in 1966, the Cultural Revolution disrupted his life once again, and this time the situation was much more serious than in 1957. The Cultural Revolution was an attempt by Mao and a radical faction that included his wife, Jiang Qing, to return Chinese Communism to its pure Marxist roots. Reading materials other than official Communist texts were forbidden. Like many other Chinese intellectuals, Fang was sent to the countryside. He was held for a year in solitary confinement in a cow shed and then forced to do agricultural work. "In the field, I pulled a donkey cart loaded with sick people suffering from heat," he told Fisher. "Then, I was the donkey." Fang, however, was able to physically carry a single book as he entered internal exile: *Classical Theory of Fields,* by Lev Landau. As he worked, he reflected on the deeper physics concepts it contained.

The Cultural Revolution waned after it resulted in disastrous famines, and in 1969 Fang was permitted to return to active teaching and writing. He still faced criticism: after he wrote that the universe was finite, he was censured by the Communist Party because one of the early theoreticians of Communism, Friedrich Engels, who had no training as a physicist, had once remarked in a letter that the universe was surely infinite. After Mao's death in 1976 the environment for academics and intellectuals was liberalized, and Fang's Communist Party membership was restored. That gave him the opportunity to join the first wave of Chinese scholars who were allowed to communicate with their Western colleagues and even attend academic conferences in the West. Fang himself spent six months at Cambridge University in England in 1979, meeting famed physicist Stephen Hawking there. In 1986, he did research at the Institute for Advanced Study at Princeton University in the United States.

Fang soon emerged as a leader in attempts to free Chinese education from political influences, and students looked to him as a promoter of the ideal of free expression in general. In 1984, Fang was made a vice president of the University of Science and Technology, and he used his new position to strengthen the independence of the school's faculty. He called for wholesale reform of China's educational system according to principles of intellectual freedom, and at first official government press organs praised his reform efforts. Soon the official tide turned against him, but by then he was a hero among young Chinese students, who copied out his speeches by hand and passed them along.

Once again, Fang landed in trouble with Chinese officialdom, which made repeated but futile requests that he tone down his position. "Although human rights are fundamental privileges that people have from birth ... we Chinese consider these rights dangerous," he was quoted as saying in the *Times*. "We Chinese lump freedom, equality and brotherhood together with capitalism and criticize them all in the same terms." In January of 1987, Fang was stripped of his Communist Party membership once more and demoted from his university vice-presidency to a research post at an observatory. Defiant, Fang wrote a letter to Chinese leader Deng Xiaoping urging the release of political prisoners.

Took Refuge at Embassy

Despite official disfavor, Fang's name still carried great weight among China's restive students, who denounced his demotion and continued to agitate for reform. A Party newspaper article summarizing Fang's supposed intellectual crimes instead resulted in an outpouring of support. Things came to a head in 1989 with the outbreak of massive student protests in Beijing's Tiananmen Square. The Chinese army crushed the protests on June 4, 1989, with numerous civilian deaths, and Fang, although he had earlier specifically warned students against illegal street demonstrations, realized that he would be blamed for the Tiananmen Square protests. In an autobiography posthumously published in China, Fang denied responsibility for organizing the protests, but at the time he correctly guessed that he was in danger, and he and his wife sought refuge at the U.S. Embassy in Beijing. They were admitted as guests of President George H.W. Bush.

Chinese authorities soon issued a warrant for his arrest, but the embassy refused to release him. Fang would spend more than a year within the embassy walls. "I am an astrophysicist yet I cannot see the sky," he was reported to have said by the London *Independent*. Finally, after a series of negotiations involving former U.S. president Richard Nixon and secretary of state Henry Kissinger, the U.S. agreed to several commercial concessions and Fang was allowed to board a U.S. military transport plane leaving China in June of 1990. His departure was announced with the pretext that he was going to receive medical treatment abroad. After spending six months in Britain, Fang and his wife arrived in the U.S.

In fact Fang's health was strong enough that he would live for more than two decades. In 1992, he accepted a position in the physics department at the University of Arizona in Tucson. In his later years he served as co-chair of the organization Human Rights in China and continued to speak out against repressive laws in his home country. Fang was a frequent contributor to such publications as the *New York Review of Books* toward the end of his life. He died in Tucson on April 6, 2012. Chinese dissident Wang Dan was quoted in the *New York Times* as saying that "Fang Lizhi has inspired the '89 generation and has awakened the people's yearning for human rights and democracy."

Books

Scientists: Their Lives and Works, Gale, 2006.

Periodicals

Daily Telegraph (London, England), April 9, 2012.
Economist, April 14, 2012.
Guardian (London, England), April 11, 2012.
Independent (London, England), April 10, 2012.
New York Times, April 8, 2012.
Popular Science, August 1996.
Science, April 28, 1989.
Times (London, England), April 10, 2012.

Online

"Fang Lizhi uses posthumous autobiography to deny any role in Tiananmen protests," *South China Morning Post* (Hong Kong), http://www.scmp.com/news/china/ (October 15, 2013).□

Leo Fender

The American musical instrument manufacturer Leo Fender (1909–1991) was the creator of the Fender Telecaster and Fender Stratocaster electric guitars, two instruments that revolutionized the sound of popular music.

Fender guitars were icons of the era of rock and roll music. Singer-guitarist Buddy Holly was pictured on the cover of his *Chirping Crickets* album holding a Fender Stratocaster, and numerous other top instrumentalists in the rock, soul, and rhythm and blues genres played Fender guitars or the Fender Precision bass. The latter instrument was radically innovative, but in general Fender was the sort of inventor who refined, perfected, and streamlined the innovations of others. Fender did not invent the solid-body electric guitar, for example, but he created a version of it that was simple, stylish, and powerful. The results changed the face of music and created an ongoing business juggernaut; the Telecaster and Stratocaster remained in common use decades after they were invented, and in the 21st century the Fender Musical Instruments Corporation remained by far the largest guitar manufacturer in the United States.

Born in Barn

Clarence Leonidas Fender, known as Leo, was born on August 10, 1909, in Anaheim, California. The area was then rural; his parents, Clarence "Monty" and Harriet Fender were farmers; and his birth took place in a barn on the family ranch. Fender attended nearby Fullerton Union High School and then went on to Fullerton Junior

College, majoring in accounting and intending to follow that career. After graduating in 1930, Fender got a job with Anaheim's Consolidated Ice and Cold Storage, and later with a tire company. Fender had no formal training in electronics (and never played the guitar), but he was an enthusiastic amateur experimenter with radios, amplification, and other electrical devices.

A 1939 layoff spurred Fender to form a small radio repair shop, Fender Radio Service, in Fullerton, California. Taking on a partner, a street performer named Clayton "Doc" Kauffman, he soon expanded into musical instrument repairs. With numerous country and Western swing musicians gravitating to the Los Angeles area to take advantage of its rapid growth and large population of wartime military service members, Fender soon prospered, and also received a strong informal education as to what musicians liked and did not like about their instruments. Fender, blind in one eye because of a childhood accident, was exempt from military service himself, and he and Kauffman began to experiment in their workshop with electric guitars, ampifiers, and country steel guitars.

Kauffman departed in 1946, and Fender changed the name of the company to the Fender Electric Instrument Company and went into business making electric guitars. He began work on what became the Telecaster around 1947 after a salesman, Charlie Hayes, suggsested that there was a strong market for an inexpensive electric guitar among ordinary players. At the time, many electric guitars were essentially amplified acoustic guitars, but Fender created something new, putting together features of several guitars he had seen.

Adopted Solid-Body Design

From the horizontal country steel guitar he took the idea of purely electronic pickups, with no body to amplify the sound. A Rickenbacker Vibrola guitar owned by Kauffman featured a Bakelite body and a detachable neck that appealed to Fender, who was thinking in terms of cheap, modular design. And he eventually adopted the idea of a solid body, which was already the subject of experimentation by guitarist-inventor Les Paul and other researchers. Fender first called his new guitar the Esquire, then the Broadcaster. After that name was found to have infringed a trademark by the guitar maker Gretsch, Fender changed the name in 1950 to the Telecaster. The instrument was an immediate hit; guitarists could not wait to adopt it and accepted prototype models. One record featuring an in-house version, Arthur Smith's "Guitar Boogie," became a country hit in 1947.

The Telecaster's sound was perfectly suited to the new barroom environments in which country, blues, and proto-rock and roll increasingly found themselves in the 1950s. Fender aimed at a sound with clear, strong highs and lows, explaining (as quoted by Richard Savage in *Guitar Player*) that "[w]hen you make lemonade, you want to taste the tangy lemon flavor and the sweet sugar." Fender's next invention was even more innovative sonically. The Fender Precision bass, which hit the market in 1951, did not resemble any previous bass guitar. Its lower end did not rest on the ground, but rather was held like a guitar, giving bassists greatly increased flexibility on stage. The instrument was fretted, delivering the tonal precision its name promised.

Ultimately even more popular than the Telecaster (although it by no means supplanted the earlier instrument, as Fender had intended) was the Fender Stratocaster, which appeared in 1953. The instrument introduced numerous small improvements to Fender's earlier designs. It had an unprecedented three pickups (other electric guitars had two), with plastic covers to eliminate feedback, and an unusual tremolo unit that became the stock-in-trade of later rock guitarists such as Jeff Beck, later augmented by a cutting-edge vibrato arm.

Many aspects of the Stratocaster's design were copied by later makers, but its most influential aspect was its appearance, which the *Times* of London called the "flashy epitome of 1950s American style." Its contoured exterior, with double indentations at the top of the body, was initially designed for player comfort but became instantly and enduringly fashionable. Fender's guitars were never boutique items but were inexpensive because they could be mass produced. Guitar maker John Carruthers was quoted as saying in the Toronto *Globe & Mail* that Fender was "the Henry Ford of electric guitars. He basically turned it into an assembly-line situation." Fender, in fact, adopted the idea of a solid-body guitar only after he realized that it lent itself to mass production. "Leo was single-minded about his work and totally dedicated to the old-school notion of perfection," museum curator Richard Smith told Nancy Gondo of *Investor's Business Daily.* His professional rival, Les Paul, was quoted as saying by the Rock and Roll Hall of Fame that "Fender could look at something and immediately discern the simplest method of doing whatever had to be done."

Instruments Adopted by Rock Guitarists

The musical ramifications of Fender's guitars were immense. Fender's own favorite music was country, and his guitars have had a long history within that genre. But their greatest impact has come in the genres that developed in the 1950s and 1960s, partly as a result of Fender's instruments themselves. James Burton, longtime guitarist for Elvis Presley among other rock vocalists, played a Fender Telecaster beginning in 1952, as did Memphis soul stalwart Steve Cropper. The Stratocaster, with its tone-bending capabilities, was a favored instruments of classic rock musicians including Jimi Hendrix, Keith Richards (of the Rolling Stones), Eric Clapton, and Stevie Ray Vaughan. The instrumental capabilities built into the Stratocaster were in some cases not exploited until many years after the instrument's invention, and the instrument itself changed very little over several decades.

Fender went on to create other instruments, such as the Jazzmaster (1958), Jaguar (1961), and Starcaster (1975) guitars, and the Jazz Bass (1960), Bass VI (1962), and Telecaster Bass (1968). Suffering years-long aftereffects from a bout with strep throat, he became convinced that he was going to die, and sold Fender Electric Instruments to the CBS broadcasting firm for $13 million. Shortly after that he recovered completely, forming his own CLF Research Company and working for CBS as a consultant until 1970. Later he became a partner in the Music Man firm, created by some of his own former employees, and in 1980 he formed his own firm, G & L Musical Products. In later years, Fender suffered from Parkinson's disease, but he continued to work on new instrument designs.

Fender lived for his entire life in the Anaheim-Fullerton area. He married Esther Klosky in 1934; the marriage lasted until her death in 1979, and the following year he married Phyllis Dalton. He had no children. Fender died in Fullerton on March 21, 1991. The following year he was inducted into the Rock and Roll Hall of Fame. A Leo Fender Gallery is the only permanent exhibition of the Fullerton Museum Center. "What's distinctive," Steve Cropper told Neville Marten of the London *Guardian,* "is that you can recognize a Fender when you hear it played and you can tell who's playing when they're playing a Fender."

Books

Contemporary Musicians, Vol. 10, Gale, 1993.

Smith, Richard R., *Fender: The Sound Heard 'Round the World,* Garfish, 2000.

Periodicals

Globe & Mail (Toronto, Ontario, Canada), March 23, 1991.

Guardian (London, England), March 23, 1991.

Guitar Player, August 1996; November 2005.

Investor's Business Daily, January 11, 2010.

Music Trades, April 2009.

New York Times, March 23, 1991.

Times (London, England), March 25, 1991.

Online

"History," Fender Musical Instruments Corporation Official Website, http://www.fender.com/history (September 5, 2013).

"Leo Fender," *AllMusic,* http://www.allmusic.com (September 5, 2013).

"Leo Fender Biography," *Rock and Roll Hall of Fame,* http://rockhall.com/inductees/leo-fender/bio/ (September 5, 2013).□

Enzo Ferrari

Italian automaker Enzo Ferrari (1898–1988) created the high-performance sport roadsters that bear his family name. The famously expensive—and lethally fast—status symbols turned out by his factory near Modena were merely a way to finance Ferrari's real passion, which was his equally celebrated Ferrari racing team.

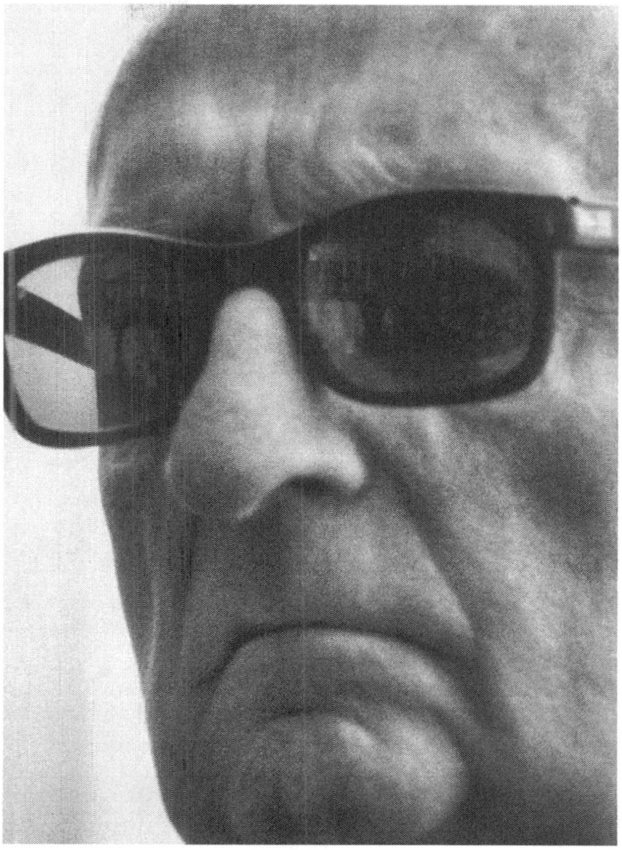

© Martyn Goddard/Alamy

Enzo Anselmo Ferrari's birth date is sometimes given as February 20, 1898, but he insisted that he had actually arrived in the world two days earlier, on February 18, and a snowstorm that hit the Maddalena Pass region near Modena delayed his father from getting into town to register the birth. Italy's automotive industry was in its infancy, too, and the early carmakers used racing and rally events to demonstrate superiority over competitors in the emerging industry. Ferrari's father Alfredo, who ran a metalworking shop, took him to see his first car race when he was ten years old. This was the 1908 Circuito di Bologna, a rally-type event in Bologna, the nearest big city, and Ferrari became obsessed with motor sports, the internal-combustion engine, and the new land-speed records that drivers were setting.

Rose to Fame as a Racer

Ferrari's late teens were disrupted by death and war. First, his father died of bronchitis in 1916, in the middle of World War I, and then Ferrari's older brother, also named Alfredo, succumbed during an influenza outbreak when serving in the Italian army. Ferrari was called up for military service, too, and assigned to a mountain artillery and put to work shoeing mules for the troops because of his experience at his father's smithworks. By the time the war ended in 1918, he was in poor health himself, and returned to Modena with few financial resources or job prospects. His father's workshop had gone out of business, and there were scores of newly discharged veterans across Italy also seeking employment. He went all the way to Turin, where Italy's most successful carmaker was headquartered, but his application for a job at Fiat (Fabbrica Italiana Automobili Torino) was passed over.

In the years just after World War I, Ferrari became a largely self-taught mechanic and engine tinkerer. He worked for a firm that turned military-type vehicles into passenger cars, and the experience helped him secure a job at CMN, or *Costruzioni Meccaniche Nazionali,* the forerunner of the company that made Vespa scooters. He entered his first race as a driver for CMN on October 5, 1919, in an ascent contest from Parma to Berceto. He placed fourth, and went to the island of Sicily for what was then one of Italy's oldest motor-sports events, the Targa Florio. He placed ninth in that, but came in second place in the 1920 contest.

Ferrari drove his second Targa Florio endurance race for the Alfa Romeo team. Another early-era Italian automaker and competitor to Fiat, Alfa Romeo prided itself on its racing prowess, and the company's team was attracting talented drivers. Ferrari raced for Alfa Romeo, developed its race cars, and managed the team in the decade to come. In 1924, he won the first-ever Coppa Acerbo in Pescara, which became one of Italy's most challenging courses. In 1929, he set up Scuderia Ferrari, his own "stable" of drivers, and the team raced cars on behalf of Alfa Romeo.

Lost First-Born Son

In 1932, Ferrari retired from the racetrack after the birth of his son, whom he named Alfredo in honor of his father and brother but called Dino. Ferrari's wife, Laura Dominica Garello, was a former dancer whom he had wed in 1923, but he conducted numerous extramarital affairs, one of which resulted in the birth of another son, Piero, in 1945. Dino was born with the Duchenne form of muscular dystrophy and showed promise as a race-car driver and automotive engineer before his death in 1956, at the age of 24. Ferrari was devastated by this tragedy, which recalled the early losses of his father and brother. Already famously temperamental as a boss and a reluctant public figure, Ferrari became even more reclusive and eccentric.

Ferrari spent much of the 1930s building race cars and training drivers, some of those years with Alfa Romeo. His goal was to establish his own automotive nameplate, but the process was stalled by multiple issues. There was interference from Italy's Fascist government, led by Benito Mussolini; financial problems at Alfa Romeo, which had scarcer financial resources to commit to race events during the Great Depression; a non-compete clause he was compelled to sign when he left Alfa Romeo, which barred him from racing or designing cars for four years; and then the onset of World War II. The company he created as a stopgap source of income during this non-compete interim was an parts supplier called Auto-Avio Costruzioni, and its facilities were forced to convert to war production. The factory was hit by Allied bombs, but relocated.

Ferrari was finally able to set up Ferrari S.p.A. in 1947, in the town of Maranello, a few miles outside of Modena. The "S.p.A." designation is the acronym for *Società per azioni,* or joint stock company. Its logo was a fabled one: a black horse with its front legs raised, called *Il Cavallino Rampante,* the Prancing Horse. The quasi-medieval insignia had been used by one of Italy's first aviator-heroes, Francesco Baracca, who rose to fame in World War I as the country's most successful aerial attackers. Baracca's plane carried a plate bearing the image when it was shot down in combat in 1918. The plate was removed from the wreckage and given to his family, and Baracca's mother in turn bestowed it on Ferrari after he began winning his first auto races in the early 1920s. It was a storied emblem that only added to the allure—and, some said, the doomed glamour—of the Ferrari brand name.

Delivered Excellent Race Results

The first car to come out of Ferrari's automobile factory was the Ferrari 125S. His Scuderia Ferrari team now had a permanent source of race cars—whicháwere expensive to build and rarely lasted past a few seasons—and they began racking up significant wins. When the top tier of motor sports was created in 1950 with the Formula One (F1) circuit, a Ferrari piloted by José Froilán Gonzalez, an Argentinean driver, won the 1951 British Grand Prix, snatching the cup from Ferrari's previous employer, the Alfa Romeo team.

Ferrari did not attend the British Grand Prix at the Silverstone race track, nor the French Grand Prix, the fabled Monaco one, or the notoriously deadly Nüburgring Nordschleife track, the site of the German Grand Prix. He even stopped attending the Italian Grand Prix after the death of his son in 1956, though he always kept tabs on his drivers on race day via a bank of television sets in his headquarters. Ferrari's cars and drivers were associated with several spectacular crashes, though aficionados agreed they were certainly built to handle high speeds. Deaths of fellow drivers had been an ever-present danger since the earliest days of automotive racing: Ugo Sivocci, the friend who helped him get a job at CMN, then went with him to Alfa Romeo in 1920, was killed on the Alfa Romeo track. Another friend was Antonio Ascari, who died at the Montlhéry, racetrack near Paris in 1925. Ascari's son Alberto joined Scuderia Ferrari and became the team's first Italian winner of the British Grand Prix, a great coup in the intensely competitive F1 races that carried an undercurrent of nationalist pride. The younger Ascari repeated his Silverstone victory in 1953, then was killed in 1955 in a Ferrari car during test laps at Monza, where the Italian Grand Prix was held.

Another highly publicized tragedy occurred at the 1957 Mille Miglia, or Thousand-Mile Race. This was an endurance contest that spanned a figure-eight swath of the Italian peninsula and was enormously popular, but crowd-control features were almost nonexistent. A Spanish aristocrat named Alfonso de Portago crashed his Ferrari in an accident that resulted in his death plus that of nine spectators, five of them children. The Mille Miglia incident aroused great public sentiment and even resulted in criminal charges against Ferrari's company and the tire manufacturer. The 1957 Mille Miglia was the final one, and de Portago's fatal wreck was one of several that helped lend an air of doom to the Ferrari brand.

Brokered Deal with Fiat

Ferrari's drivers and their cars racked up victory after victory on the F1 circuit, and even the seven hundred or so production cars his factory turned out every year for wealthy buyers were elevated to cult-status luxury-brand purchases. The V12 engine parts were hand-tooled, the sleek exteriors polished to a high-gloss and signature blood-red, and the cars easily reached speeds of 180 miles per hour. Built only with the manual transmission option, they barely fit two people and Ferrari liked to emphasize that his cars were meant to be piloted, not driven. He left much of the details of the business to others, preferring to concentrate only on improvements to engines and the chassis of the race cars. In 1969, he sold a 50 percent stake in the company to Fiat in a deal that let him keep control of his racing team. The high-profile stable of Ferrari drivers, who included Niki Lauda and Gilles Villeneuve, continued to win F1 titles and season championships. Villeneuve was another Ferrari casualty, killed in qualifying laps during the 1982 Belgian Grand Prix.

In 1978, Ferrari's wife Laura died, and her death enabled him to file the necessary documents to legitimize his second son, Piero, who was born in 1945 to Ferrari's mistress, Lina Lardi. Piero worked for the company for many years and eventually became a vice president at the company. Ferrari was one of Italy's most famous figures, but was a solitary, enigmatic figure who only occasionally engaged with the press, avoided elevators, and wore dark glasses even indoors. *Il Commendatore,* as he was known in Modena, was likewise both revered and feared by his seemingly fearless F1 team drivers and company managers alike. His day started in his Ferrari 131 with a visit to the cemetery to brood over the graves of his parents, brother, and son. In his later years he rarely left Maranello, save for a pre-race day visit to the Monza track for the Italian Grand Prix, and he reportedly traveled out of the country only once, to neighboring Switzerland. He died at the age of 90 on August 14, 1988, in Maranello.

Ferrari left behind a 1962 autobiography, whose original Italian-language title was translated as "My Terrible Joys," and a racing team that continued its long and fabled winning streak. Its lead driver was Germany's Michael Schumacher, who in the 1990s became the highest-paid F1 competitor in history, but the aura of almost operatically tragic death that seemed to stay with the Prancing Horse badge endured: in 2013, Schumacher was badly injured in a skiing accident in the French Alps, and the medical team attending the now-retired driver—statistically, the most adept in the history of F1 racing—remained unsure that Schumacher would ever regain consciousness.

Periodicals

Guardian (London, England), September 11, 1998; November 17, 2001.

New York Times, June 8, 1958; March 11, 2012.

New Yorker, January 15, 1966.

Times (London, England), October 4, 1977: September 5, 1986; August 16, 1988.□

Pretty Boy Floyd

American outlaw Charles "Pretty Boy" Floyd (1904–1934) captured enormous public interest in the early 1930s as one of the most brazen bank robbers of the Great Depression. The armed and clever Oklahoman managed to elude law-enforcement authorities for nearly four years, achieving the designation "Public Enemy No. 1" by J. Edgar Hoover's Federal Bureau of Investigation (FBI).

Charles Arthur Floyd came from a respectable Baptist family in Adairsville, Georgia, where he was born on February 3, 1904. The Floyd family's roots in this part of northwest Georgia dated back to the 1830s, and "Charley," as he was called, was the fourth of Walter and Mamie Floyd's eight children and second-eldest son. The Floyds moved to Sequoyah County, Oklahoma, in 1911, settling into a community that already had a significant population of former Georgia farmers. They lived near the notorious Cookson Hills, which had served for decades as a hideout for bandits and others on the run in Oklahoma's freewheeling early years prior to statehood. The Cookson range connected this part of Oklahoma to the Ozark Mountains in nearby Missouri and Arkansas.

Quit School at 12

Walter Floyd eventually opened a small general store in Akins, also in Sequoyah County, but his wife and children put in long hours on the family farm, where they raised produce, kept hogs, and bred foxhounds. Floyd left school after finishing his sixth-grade year to find full-time work. He found it as a seasonal harvest laborer on farms in both Oklahoma and across its northern border with Kansas. When he was not working, he frequented pool halls in Sallisaw, the county seat, and picked up the nickname "Choc" for his preference for Choctaw beer, a potent brew made by the local Native American communities. Floyd occasionally tried to find steady work, but conditions in the area's mining and smelting camps were brutal, with workers forced to live in filthy barracks for scant wages. Oklahoma and Texas were experiencing oil booms and Floyd tried out another grimy, dangerous job as an oil field roustabout, which he also hated. It was thought he probably earned a living making bootleg runs between communities in the Oklahoma-Arkansas-Missouri area.

On June 28, 1924, Floyd married 16-year-old Ruby Hardgraves, who had grown up on a farm in nearby Bixby, Oklahoma. Part Cherokee, she was tall, lithe, and by most contemporary accounts devastatingly attractive. She was also a few months pregnant when they wed in Sallisaw, and a son they named Charles Dempsey Floyd was born in December of 1924. The middle name came from boxing legend Jack Dempsey, and Floyd and Ruby called their son "Jackie" to distinguish him from his father Charley.

© Pictorial Press Ltd/Alamy

Floyd's official criminal record dates back to a robbery of the Akins post office on May 16, 1922, that netted him and a friend named J. Harold Franks a paltry sum of $3.50 in coins. Any mail-related crimes were automatically federal crimes, and eleven months later Floyd and Franks were arrested for the break-in. Floyd was acquitted in March of 1924, at a trial conducted by the U.S. federal court for the Eastern District of Oklahoma when two key witnesses failed to appear. The close call may have spurred Floyd to marry and attempt to farm a plot of land in Sequoyah County, but the long hours and lack of profit again proved unappealing.

Payroll Heist Made Headlines

Returning to seasonal harvest labor in 1925, Floyd worked on a crew with a man named in sources as either Fred or John Hilderbrand or Hildebrand, who was from St. Louis, Missouri. Hilderbrand confided that he had almost effortlessly robbed a small electrical-manufacturing company in St. Louis simply by barging into the office with a pistol and demanding the cash on hand. Floyd teamed with Hilderbrand for a string of robberies at five Kroger grocery stores and an unknown number of gas stations in the St. Louis area in August of 1925. A month later, after recruiting a third man to carry out their plan, they intercepted an armored truck on its way to the Kroger offices in St. Louis and netted the entire payroll amount for the week, about $13,000. Famously, the paymaster of the Kroger offices told police that "the fellow who carried the gun was a mere boy—a pretty boy with apple cheeks" according to Jeffery S. King's *The Life and Death of Pretty Boy Floyd.*

Floyd, Hilderbrand, and the third man were able to flee, but back in Sallisaw Floyd was arrested almost immediately upon his arrival because he was driving a new Studebaker car. Local law-enforcement authorities detained him and found in the car cash wrappers bearing the logo of the Tower Grove Bank of St. Louis, which tied him to the payroll heist. The sheriff in Oklahoma contacted police in St. Louis, who came to Sallisaw to question Floyd and Hilderbrand, who denied involvement in the Kroger payroll robbery. The third man, Joseph Hlavaty, was a less experienced criminal and quickly caved under police questioning. At his trial in November of 1925, Floyd pled guilty for highway robbery and was sentenced to five years in the infamous Missouri State Penitentiary.

Located in Jefferson City, the Missouri Pen had the designation of being the first U.S. prison west of the Mississippi River. It was decades old by the time Floyd arrived and dangerously overcrowded. Its workshops were also a profitable source of revenue and Floyd worked as a plumber's helper during some of his 39 months inside. With time off for good behavior, he was released on March 7, 1929, shortly after the divorce petition that Ruby had filed was granted by an Oklahoma court.

Joined Larceny Gang

Floyd had learned much in prison, staying away from troublemakers, the obvious mentally ill criminals, and the luckless types. He listened to chatter from seasoned big-city racketeers and came to learn that there were crime "families" in most major U.S. cities, and those families had ties to one another. There were also certain places where cops, judges, and even elected officials profited by bribes and kickbacks paid to them by bootleggers, brothel-keepers, and illegal-gambling entrepreneurs. Kansas City, Missouri, was one particularly lawless place, and Floyd headed there when he left prison.

After a brief attempt at finding honest work, Floyd was recruited as a junior member of the Bradley gang, an older, experienced group of robbers run by Jim Bradley. They went to Akron, Ohio, and set up operations there. Their first hit was the Farmers and Merchants' Bank in Sylvania, Ohio, just outside of Toledo, on February 5, 1930. Floyd was arrested on another charge, tied to the robbery, and in November of 1930, was sentenced to a minimum of 12 years in the Ohio State Penitentiary. En route to the Columbus prison, Floyd managed to escape by kicking out a window in a train bathroom and jumping from the moving carriage. He was never again taken into police custody.

Floyd headed for Toledo and teamed with a new, ruthless accomplice named Willis Miller, known as "Bill the Killer." In early 1931, they began robbing a string of banks in Oklahoma, sometimes with a third man, George Birdwell, and sometimes they even hit a target twice. In April of 1931, while in Bowling Green, Ohio, Floyd was involved in a police shootout in which Patrolman Ralph Castner was fatally wounded.

Dubbed "Sagebrush Robin Hood"

In 1932, Floyd robbed at least three banks in Oklahoma. Newspaper stories about the state's most notorious bandit elevated him to folk-hero status, especially when rumors circulated that during the robberies he deliberately searched out the banks' mortgage deeds and either tore them up or set fire to them. These were the worst years of the Great Depression and the start of the catastrophic Dust Bowl environmental and financial disaster that swept through Oklahoma and other Great Plains states, and bank foreclosure rates were high. The absence of clear title records meant that financially strapped farm owners were able to keep their home and property.

Floyd's misdeeds made him Oklahoma's favorite local outlaw. The state's acting governor, Robert Burns, announced a $1,000 reward for information leading to the capture of Floyd, to which Floyd allegedly responded by letter, dated January 20, 1932, urging Burns to withdraw the offer "or suffer the consequences," the unsigned letter warned, according to King in *The Life and Death of Pretty Boy Floyd.* "I have robbed no one but the monied men." During this period he reunited with his ex-wife and now-six-year-old son Jackie, living under assumed names in Fort Smith, Arkansas. They later moved to Tulsa, Oklahoma, and on April 7, 1932, an attempt was made by a retired sheriff and special investigator named Erv Kelley to apprehend Floyd and Birdwell at a farm hideout, but Floyd shot from a .45 caliber gun and Birdwell used a machine gun to fire a 21-bullet round, a bullet from which hit Floyd in the foot. Floyd and Birdwell hid out in the impenetrable Cookson Hills, and also used the Ozarks as a retreat from a manhunt that received daily newspaper coverage.

Tied to Kansas City Massacre

On June 17, 1933, a bank robber named Frank Nash was being escorted by armed guard into Union Station in Kansas City. In the parking plaza, a gang of Nash allies were lying in wait to ambush the guards and free Nash. In what became known as the Kansas City Massacre, four law-enforcement officials were killed. Witnesses to the scene claimed that Floyd was among the Nash accomplices, but he vehemently disputed his involvement in the bloody public shootout. Criminologists believe it many have been a case of mistaken identity, but J. Edgar Hoover, director of the Federal Bureau of Investigation (FBI), used the massacre to call for a war on what he described as roaming bands of thugs and cop-killers. Hoover secured additional funding for staffing his regional offices to hunt down those he termed public enemies. Also on Hoover's hit list was John Dillinger, another enormously successful bank robber, and the Barker Gang, led by "Ma" Barker, whose sons had kidnapped a bank president and kept him for three weeks until the $200,000 ransom was paid.

Dillinger was slain in a famous shootout in front of a Chicago movie theater on July 23, 1934, which elevated Floyd to the status of the FBI's official "Public Enemy No. 1." Once again, he returned to Ohio, and was on the run with an accomplice named Adam Richetti. They robbed a bank in Tiltonsville, Ohio, on October 20, 1934, but their car broke down and police were tipped off when a farmer spotted two men camping whom he first mistook for hobos, but was perplexed by the fact that they wore relatively nice suits. Richetti was apprehended but Floyd managed to flee after firing at the officers. He roamed through farmlands until he reached East Liverpool, Ohio, where he offered to pay a local couple to drive him to Youngstown. His plan was to buy a bus ticket and disappear into the hills of Appalachia. A husband and wife agreed to drive him part of the way, but Floyd was spotted in their car and it was quickly ringed by law-enforcement authorities. Floyd took off running but was shot at by the local police captain, a former World War I sharpshooter. The sequence of events that occurred after Floyd was cornered behind a farmer's corn crib vary, but one of the FBI's most famous agents, Melvin Purvis, took credit for killing Floyd on October 22, 1934.

Floyd's funeral in Akins, Oklahoma, was the final chapter in his Depression-era saga. It quickly evolved into a mob scene, with some 20,000 onlookers descending upon the small town to see the end of "Pretty Boy" Floyd, a nickname he was said to have hated. It remains the most well-attended funeral in Oklahoma state history.

Books

King, Jeffery S., *The Life and Death of Pretty Boy Floyd,* Kent Library State University Press, 1999.

Wallis, Michael, *Pretty Boy: The Life and Times of Charles Arthur Floyd,* W. W. Norton & Company, 2011.

Periodicals

American History, August 2009.

New York Times, June 17, 1933; October 12, 1934.□

Joan Fontaine

Anglo-American actress Joan Fontaine (1917–2013) spent her Hollywood career fighting her illustrious sister—Olivia de Havilland—for awards, acting jobs, and men. When Fontaine won the Academy Award for best actress in 1942 (for her role in Hitchcock's *Suspicion*) she won it over her sister. Fueled by rivalry and resentment, the sisters' long-standing feud led to decades of animosity that often played out in the press.

Fontaine came to filmmaking during Hollywood's "Golden Age" and appeared in nearly 50 movies. In summing up Fontaine's career, the London *Observer* called Fontaine "a delicately feminine adornment in movies for nearly 30 years and a fine actress." The paper went on to commend Fontaine for giving "at least half-a-dozen outstanding performances." The *Observer* noted that Fontaine's "most distinctive work

© AF archive/Alamy

was as good women experiencing troubled relationships with older men—as the second Mrs. de Winter in Hitchcock's *Rebecca* (1940), the heiress who marries the duplicitous Cary Grant in *Suspicion* (1941) . . . and the eponymous heroine of *Jane Eyre* (1944)."

Locked in Sibling Rivalry

Joan de Beauvoir de Havilland was born in Tokyo on October 22, 1917. Her sister, Olivia, was 15 months older. Their parents—Walter and Lilian de Havilland—were British transplants. Walter de Havilland grew up in Guernsey, an English Channel island off the coast of France. He studied theology at Cambridge University. After graduating, he felt restless. As Fontaine related the story in her autobiography *No Bed of Roses,* her father simply placed his hand on the globe opposite the United Kingdom and found it had landed on Hokkaido, Japan's second largest island. He moved there and taught English and French, then became a patent attorney and settled in Tokyo. Lilian (Ruse) de Havilland was born in Reading, Berkshire, England. She studied piano and voice. She also studied acting at London's Royal Academy of Dramatic Art and toured with British composer Ralph Vaughan Williams. Lilian Ruse left England to join her brother in Japan, where he taught at Waseda University. Walter de Havilland taught there as well.

Lilian Ruse and Walter de Havilland married in 1914 and welcomed their daughters in 1916 and 1917. Writing in the *St. Louis Post-Dispatch,* Angela Fox Dunn said that Fontaine maintained that the sibling rivalry started at birth. "I was the usurper, and she the berater," Fontaine said. "My sister was born a lion, and I a tiger, and in the laws of the jungle, they were never friends."

In 1919, Lilian de Havilland took her daughters to the United States after learning her husband had an affair. They settled in San Jose, where Lilian met George Milan Fontaine, a widower and part-owner/manager of the Hale Brothers department store. He later became an investment counselor and married Lilian in 1925. The family settled in Saratoga. According to Fontaine's autobiography, life in the Fontaine household was anything but fun. For punishments, the girls were subjected to public humiliations in the schoolyard at the hands of their authoritarian stepfather. In her book, Fontaine described an evening she was led outside by her stepfather. "There under the oak trees, in the fallen leaves, he had dug a shallow grave. 'This is where I shall put you if you don't stop biting your nails,' he warned."

Started Acting as Teen

Lilian Fontaine and her husband sought to raise the girls to be proper, cultivated English ladies. The girls took ballet, received walking lessons and had to practice their diction by reading Shakespeare. If they slurred a sentence or mispronounced a word, they were hit on the knuckles with a ruler, Fontaine said in her autobiography. They were also smacked with brooms. The sisters found solace in acting. Fontaine enjoyed her first lead in an eighth-grade production of *Flyin' High.* The girls attended Saratoga Grammar School and Los Gatos High School, appearing in one production together—*Hansel and Gretel.* Olivia de Havilland earned the lead role of the witch, while little sister Joan was cast in the angel chorus.

After a blow-up in the household, Olivia de Havilland moved out and Fontaine soon followed. Fontaine left home at 15 and moved in with the editor of the Los Gatos newspaper, earning her room and board as the family nanny. She soon reconnected with her father and returned to Tokyo, attending an American school in the nearby suburb of Kami-Meguro. After a rift with her father, Fontaine returned to her mother's home in the United States in 1934. Her sister had already begun her acting career.

At this time, Fontaine began taking drawing lessons from family friends and artists George Dennison and Frank Ingerson. The artists were friends with stage and screen star May Robson, who was looking to cast an English ingénue for a production called *Kind Lady.* They suggested Fontaine audition. Just 17, she won the part and soon made her stage debut. The mystery drama opened in Santa Barbara with Ralph Forbes and Robson in the lead roles. Fontaine was billed as Joan Burfield because her mother refused to let her use the de Havilland name so as not to impinge on sister Olivia's career. Soon enough, Fontaine took on her stepfather's name to distinguish herself from her sister.

After Fontaine's *Kind Lady* tour ended, she found herself back under her mother's roof with her sister running the household as the breadwinner. Fontaine was required to run personal errands for her sister, like chauffeuring her to jobs and delivering her lunch. One day, as Fontaine waited for her sister at Warner Bros., producer-director Mervyn LeRoy offered her a contract. Fontaine's mother, however, forbade her to accept the offer because her sister already had a contract with Warner Bros. as a leading lady.

Joined R.K.O. as Screen Actress

Fontaine eventually landed a contract at R.K.O. Radio Pictures and made her feature-film debut in *No More Ladies* (1935). She started in supporting roles, then moved to playing leading ladies in the studio's B-grade films. In 1937, Fontaine appeared in *Quality Street* with Katharine Hepburn and *A Damsel in Distress* with Fred Astaire. In 1939, she acted in *Gunga Din* with Cary Grant and *The Women* with Joan Crawford and Norma Shearer. The latter film was directed by George Cukor. In her autobiography, Fontaine said Cukor gave her the best acting advice of anyone in her career. During filming one day, Fontaine inquired about how to personate her character. "George simply said, 'Forget all that. *Think* and *feel* and the rest will take care of itself.'"

In 1939, Fontaine married British actor Brian Aherne. At the time, de Havilland was involved with eccentric billionaire Howard Hughes. Prior to her wedding with Aherne, Fontaine said Hughes proposed to her. Hughes urged Fontaine not to marry Aherne and slipped her his personal number, should she want to rendezvous. As Fontaine tells the story in her autobiography, she warned her sister that Hughes was not to be trusted. "No one two-timed my sister, whatever our domestic quarrels might be." Naturally, the situation increased the sisters' animosity.

Fontaine's marriage to Aherne lasted only a handful of years. During that time, Fontaine learned to fly a plane because Aherne owned an aircraft. During the marriage, Fontaine appeared in *Rebecca* (1940), *Suspicion* (1941), *This Above All* (1942), *The Constant Nymph* and *Jane Eyre* (both 1943), and *Frenchman's Creek* (1944). Fontaine's breakout role came with Alfred Hitchcock's *Rebecca,* a role that took numerous screen tests to win and a role she won over her sister. Incidentally, around this same time, de Havilland landed the role of Melanie in *Gone with the Wind,* beating out Fontaine.

In 1940's *Rebecca,* Fontaine starred opposite Laurence Olivier in this psychological thriller about a new bride overwhelmed by the memory of her husband's previous wife. As filming began, Fontaine felt extremely insecure, knowing Olivier had wanted his wife, Vivien Leigh, in the lead role. Fontaine realized her performance in this film would make or break her career. Hitchcock fed her doubt by telling her that the rest of the cast questioned her ability to carry the role. This burdened Fontaine with an enormous amount of insecurity, which she inadvertently transferred onto her screen character—just as Hitchcock hoped. With this mental manipulation, Hitchcock coaxed an outstanding performance out of Fontaine and she earned her first Academy Award nomination, though she did not win.

Earned Academy Award

In 1941, Fontaine appeared in *Suspicion,* another Hitchcock thriller, this one about an heiress named Lina (Fontaine) who marries a charming bachelor (Cary Grant). As their marriage drags on, Lina suspects her husband may be trying to kill her for her money. The role earned Fontaine another Academy Award nomination for best actress. Other nominees that year included Bette Davis, Greer Garson, Barbara Stanwyck, and her very own sister, de Havilland, for *Hold Back the Dawn.* This time, Fontaine won.

At 23, Fontaine was the youngest actress to date to win in the category. She was also the only actor to win an Academy Award in a Hitchcock film. The jubilation of winning, however, was short-lived. In her autobiography, Fontaine described the moment as bittersweet. "I felt Olivia would spring across the table and grab me by the hair. I felt age four, being confronted by my older sister." In 1943, Fontaine earned another Academy Award nomination for best actress, this time for playing Tessa in *The Constant Nymph.* Writing in the *Saturday Evening Post,* Fontaine said this was one of her favorite roles. "Tessa was interesting and fun to play because she took me completely out of my own personality. She was a musician, which I am not; had a weak heart, which I certainly have not; and was fifteen years old—I was twenty-three."

Married Film Producer

In 1946, Fontaine married film producer William Dozier. After giving birth to Deborah Leslie Dozier in 1948, the couple separated and divorced. In 1951, Fontaine traveled to South America to attend some film festivals and adopted a Peruvian girl named Martita Pareja. They were later estranged. In 1952, Fontaine married Collier Young, another film producer. They divorced in 1961 and Fontaine married *Sports Illustrated* writer Alfred Wright Jr., in 1964, divorcing in 1969.

During the 1950s, Fontaine appeared in a number of mediocre films that did little to advance her career. In her autobiography, Fontaine wrote that she signed on for several films without even looking at the scripts because she needed money to support her daughters. Films of this era included *Darling, How Could You!* (1951), *Something to Live For* (1952), *Flight to Tangier* (1953), and *Casanova's Big Night* with Bob Hope (1954). In 1957, Fontaine starred in the controversial *Island in the Sun,* which explored interracial romance—a taboo topic at the time. Fontaine's love interest in the film was Harry Belafonte, the son of Caribbean immigrants. Fontaine received hate mail for kissing Belafonte in the film. One bright spot during the 1950s included Fontaine's return to Broadway in 1954 when she took over for Barbara Kerr in *Tea and Sympathy,* which also starred Anthony Perkins. Reviews were positive.

The feud between Fontaine and de Havilland escalated in 1975 after their mother died. In her autobiography, Fontaine criticized her sister for not notifying her of their mother's death in a timely manner and for setting the memorial service for a date Fontaine could not make. Chances for a reconciliation came to an end after Fontaine published her tell-all autobiography (*No Bed of Roses*) in 1978. In the book, Fontaine was critical of her parents, her sister, and her former husbands. She said her sister pulled her hair and once fractured her collarbone. According to Michael Thornton of the *Mail Online,* Fontaine's ex-husband, Dozier, referred to the book as *No Word of Truth.* In 1979, during an Academy Award winners' reunion in honor of the 50th anniversary of the awards, the sisters refused to acknowledge each other and had to be seated at opposite ends of the stage.

Fontaine continued acting throughout the 1970s and '80s. In her later year she spent more time on stage than on the big screen. In 1980, Fontaine appeared on the daytime serial *Ryan's Hope* and earned an Emmy nomination for outstanding cameo appearance. She continued to live alone into her 90s at her home in Carmel, California. Fontaine told the *Daily Breeze's* Jerry Roberts that she preferred living alone, which perhaps contributed to all of her estrangements. "I'm pretty unhappy with someone else around all the time. I'm my best company. The other morning I had gone and got *The New York Times* and bought a new book. I got home to find the telephones out of order. I built a fire in the fireplace and sat down to read. When I looked up, it was six o'clock. It was heaven. It's what happiness is."

Fontaine died December 15, 2013, at her home in Carmel. She was 96. According to *CBS News,* within 24 hours of Fontaine's death, de Havilland—in a rare about-face—publicly acknowledged her sister, saying she was "shocked and saddened" by the news. For decades, de Havilland had refused to discuss her sister. Their rivalry was so intense that Fontaine once told *People* she figured de Havilland would be angry if she died first. "Olivia has always said I was first at everything—I got married first, got an Academy Award first, had a child first. If I die, she'll be furious, because again I'll have got there first!"

Books

Fontaine, Joan, *No Bed of Roses,* William Morrow and Co., 1978.

Periodicals

Daily Breeze (Torrance, CA), October 1, 1985.

Independent (London), May 15, 2008.

Observer (London), September 6, 2009.

Saturday Evening Post, May 10, 1947.

St. Louis Post-Dispatch, December 23, 1992.

Online

"And the Oscar for Sibling Rivalry Goes to . . .," *Mail Online,* http://www.dailymail.co.uk/femail/article-1311426/Olivia-Havilland-Joan-Fontaine-Their-decade-feud.html (November 12, 2013).

"Joan Fontaine, Oscar-Winning Best Actress, Dies at 96," *People,* http://www.people.com/people/article/0,,20766598,00.html (December 16, 2013).

"Olivia de Havilland 'Shocked and Saddened' by Sister Joan Fontaine's Death," *CBS News,* http://www.cbsnews.com/news/olivia-de-havilland-shocked-and-saddened-by-sister-joan-fontaines-death/ (December 16, 2013).□

Jimmie Foxx

American Major League Baseball player Jimmie Foxx (1907–1967) played for the Philadelphia Athletics, Boston Red Sox, Chicago Cubs, and Philadelphia Phillies. Called the "right-handed Babe Ruth," he was one of the best power hitters of the late 1920s, as well as the 1930s and 1940s. He recorded 534 career home runs and posted a .325 career batting average. He was inducted into the Major League Baseball Hall of Fame in 1951.

Jimmie Foxx was known as "the Beast," a sportswriter-given nickname that belied his friendly personality. But at the plate, Foxx was monstrous. He played his best years in Philadelphia in the late 1920s and early 1930s for Connie Mack's Athletics, and in Boston in the late 1930s and early 1940s. In some peoples' minds he was a better power hitter than his more famous contemporary Babe Ruth. In his sundown years, Foxx played for the Chicago Cubs (1942–1944) and the Philadelphia Phillies (1945), a shadow of his former self. But during his peak years, he hit 30 or more home runs in 12 consecutive seasons, and drove in more than 100 runs in 13 consecutive seasons.

Foxx was formidable, boasting Herculean deltoids and biceps that accentuated his farm-grown, five-foot, eleven-inch, 195-pound body. Reportedly, he had to cut the sleeves of his baseball uniforms, not to show off but to accommodate his arm size. Those arms propelled 534 home runs out of stadiums during a 20-year career (1925–1945). He was the second player in baseball history to hit more than 500 career home runs (after Babe Ruth), and his offensive production garnered him the sport's Most Valuable Player award three times. When his career ended in 1945, he boasted a .325 lifetime batting average. But he was not a one-dimensional player counted on only to put balls out of the stadium; he was a talented fielder and could—like Ruth—even pitch.

Foxx was an integral part of the Philadelphia Athletics (or A's) during a three-year glory span of 1929–1931, in which the Athletics won three American League pennants and two world championships. When those teams were broken up and the players sold off by Connie Mack, Foxx was a star with the Boston Red Sox in the late 1930s and early 1940s. At Boston's Fenway Park, the friendly Foxx mentored rising star Ted Williams, another Hall-of-Fame

AP

player. Williams would forever remain friends with the Foxx family. But for opposing players, Foxx was a horrific force of nature that grew like a sturdy cornstalk from the Maryland farmlands.

Excelled at Many Sports

James Emory Foxx was born in Sudlersville, Maryland, on October 22, 1907, to farming parents of Irish heritage: Dell and Mattie Foxx. His father played baseball for state county teams and instilled in his son a love for the sport. Meanwhile, Foxx's farming chores helped build his menacing physique. He also excelled in basketball, soccer, and track-and-field competition. Raised in a peaceful, pastoral setting, Foxx developed a pleasant and affable personality that made him a well-liked individual in his professional career. He was also low-keyed. Whereas Babe Ruth tended to be flamboyant, Foxx was unassuming.

As for baseball, Foxx was an all-round player: He could hit, play behind the plate, play the outfield and infield, and he could even pitch. His versatility would make it hard for Philadelphia Athletics manager Connie Mack to place this hard-hitting youngster into a single role. But Mack would settle him in at first base. Years later, baseball analyst Bill James, who developed the statistical science of Sabermetrics, used his numerical evaluations to demonstrate that Foxx was arguably one of the best first basemen ever—maybe even better than another mythic player: Lou Gehrig.

Recruited by "Home Run" Baker

In 1924, Hall-of-Famer Frank "Home Run" Baker (who, despite his nickname, hit only hit 96 home runs in his entire career), recruited the sixteen-year-old Foxx to join his team in the Eastern Shore League. Foxx made the most of his debut: He slugged a home run in his first game with the Easton, Maryland-based team.

Foxx performed so well that Baker informed Connie Mack (Cornelius McGillicuddy)—owner and manager of the Philadelphia A's—of his young prospect. In July of that year, Foxx dropped out of high school and signed on with Mack's Athletics. He played his first Major League game in 1925. He was only seventeen years old.

Mack knew he had acquired a valuable resource; the only question that remained was where to position this farm boy powerhouse. Foxx had played catcher for his Sudlersville high school team, but the Athletics already had an all-star catcher, Mickey Cochrane (1903-1962; inducted into the Hall of Fame in 1947). So, for two years, the multi-talented Foxx was relegated to being a utility player: He did back-up catching duties, played in the outfield, and anywhere else needed. By 1927, Foxx played in sixty-one games, mostly at first base. The next year, he played third base, first base, and catcher for the Athletics, a team that was striving to catch up to its American League rival, the New York Yankees. Eventually, the Mack team would crush its much despised enemy, with Foxx's help.

By 1929, Connie Mack's Athletics were the predominant force in baseball, which has led to ongoing arguments about who was the better team, the 1927 New York Yankees of Ruth and Gehrig or the 1929-1932 Philadelphia Athletics. The Yankees, in 1927, with its "Murderer's Row," had a combined .307 batting average, and its hitters drove in 951 runs. But the Athletics of 1929 had more depth: a better pitching staff and better defensive abilities. Also, as William Nack reported in his August 19, 1996 article for *Sports Illustrated* "Lost in History," the A's had the edge over the Yankees when it came to catching. The Yankees platooned two journeymen catchers, Pat Collins and Johnny Grabowski. In contrast, the A's started Cochrane, a lifetime .320 hitter.

In 1929, the A's superior pitching roster included the sullen, combative Robert "Lefty" Grove who won 20 games matched against six losses, and George Earnshaw (24-8) and Rube Walberg (18-11). As for offensive production, the team had six hitters that batted above .300, including Cochrane (.331), and outfielders Al Simmons (.365), Bing Miller (.331), Mule Haas (.313) and, of course, infielder Foxx (.354). In 1929, Mack's Athletics—which included four future Hall-of-Famers (Foxx, Simmons, Grove, and Cochrane)—won the American League pennant with a robust 18-game lead over the flailing New York Yankees.

About which team was better, Joe Reilly, a longtime scout for many decades with the Brooklyn Dodgers and Philadelphia Phillies told *The Kennett Paper* in a 1989 interview, "It is like arguing about who was better, Joe

Louis or Jack Dempsey. You could argue about it forever. [But] I don't care what anyone says. Jimmie Foxx could hit the ball harder than anyone I ever saw."

Integral to Philadelphia's Success

During the 1929 season, Foxx, now the regular first-baseman, batted .354 which included 183 hits (which included 23 doubles, nine triples, and 33 home runs). But numbers written on paper do not even begin to suggest his power. Some of Foxx's home runs are what legends are made of. During his career, he was the first player to hit the ball over the roof of Comiskey Park in Chicago (home of the American League White Sox). He also sky-rocketed a home run over the center field wall in Fenway Park in Boston. From Philadelphia's Shibe Park (later renamed Connie Mack Stadium) he drove a home run over the wall that sailed past neighboring streets and landed on a rooftop. Perhaps his most famous home run came in Yankee Stadium. Described Nack: "[Foxx] hit a home run with such force that it shattered a wooden seat three rows from the top of the upper deck."

In its July 29, 1929 issue, *Time* magazine placed Foxx on its cover. In that year's World Series, the Athletics beat the Chicago Cubs four games to one. Foxx recorded a post-season .350 batting average and hit two home runs in the first two games.

Maintained Consistent Production

The next year (1930), Foxx helped the Athletics to another pennant. He boasted a .335 season batting average, which included power production of 37 home runs and 13 triples. Against the National League's St. Louis Cardinals, his team won a second-straight world championship. In 1931, the Athletics posted a 107-win season. Again, the team met the Cardinals in the World Series; but the St. Louis "redbirds" won the seven-game matchup four games to three. That year, Foxx hit 30 home runs and drove in 120 runs.

During this era, Foxx was impressive. In 1932, he was voted the American League Most Valuable Player, as he hit 58 home runs and posted a .364 batting average. His home run numbers that year generated some controversy. If not for certain factors, Foxx should have well exceeded Ruth's record of 60 home runs (which stood until 1961). Some of Foxx's home runs were eliminated by rained out games. Other potential home runs were stopped by new netting placed in ballparks. By 1932, the protective screening for spectators had been placed in St. Louis, Cleveland, and Detroit, which reduced the number of home runs players could hit into the stands. Such protective screening was not in place in 1927, the year that Ruth hit his record 60 home runs. Foxx's teammate Bing Miller said that Foxx should have had at least 65 homers in 1932 (as recorded on baseball-reference.com). "[But] rainouts robbed him of two and the right field screen at Sportsman's Park in St. Louis robbed him of at least five more."

In a 1988 interview with *The Kennett Paper*, Foxx relative Charles Wallace—who played high school and semi-pro baseball and earned a tryout with the National League Braves— revealed, "[Connie Mack] told my uncle, Dell Foxx, that Jimmie could have hit 75 home runs that year [1932]." The protective screening erected in League Park in Cleveland, then the home of the American League Cleveland Indians, proved especially problematic for Foxx, who hammered three line drives off of the screen in left field that surely would have fallen in the stands. If not for such circumstances, Ruth's single-season record would have been erased and Roger Maris' home run chase with Mickey Mantle would never have made sports page headlines.

Won Triple Crown

Ensuing years would not be kind to the Athletics. The team did not make it to the World Series in 1933. However, Foxx had one of his best years. He won his league's "Triple Crown" when he batted .356, hit 48 home runs, and drove in 163 runs. He also won the Most Valuable Player award and played in the sport's first All Star game. In 1935, the Athletics finished in last place in the American League with a meager 58 wins. By this time, Mack was having financial difficulties, brought on by the Great Depression. He was compelled to sell some of his biggest stars that he felt he could no longer afford (Simmons, among others, were already gone). But Mack held on to Foxx. Mack sincerely liked Foxx. But in 1936, a contract dispute ended the Foxx-Mack-Athletics relationship.

Sold to The Red Sox

That year, Foxx was sold to the Boston Red Sox for $150,000. Foxx would play for the American League rival from 1936 to 1942. These years would prove to be some of Foxx's most offensively productive years, but the period would also witness his decline.

In his first year with the Red Sox, he batted .338, slugged 41 home runs, and drove in 143 runs. His production fell a bit in 1937, as his average dipped to .285, but still hit 36 home runs. He responded the next year with a league-leading .349 batting average, and he hit 50 home runs and recorded 175 runs batted in. The numbers earned him another MVP award. In 1939, Foxx batted .360. Surprisingly, this was not enough to earn him the American League batting crown, but his 35 home runs were the league's top. It would be the last year that he would win a home run title. In 1940, his average fell to .297 and he hit 36 home runs. This would be the 12th consecutive season that he hit more than 30 home runs.

By 1941, Foxx's numbers significantly diminished: While he batted .300, he only hit 19 home runs. The following years would witness him suffering problems related to illness, injury, and personal issues such as alcohol abuse. During the 1942 season, Foxx suffered a broken rib during batting practice, and the Red Sox management placed Foxx on waivers. This seemed a heartless move, but by this time Foxx had gained a reputation as a heavy drinker, a habit that led to the deterioration of his health and seasonal statistics. The legendary player was sold to the National League's Chicago Cubs for a mere $10,000 price tag.

Returned Home to Philadelphia

For health reasons, Foxx decided to sit out the entire 1943 baseball season. When he returned to the sport in 1944, he only played in 15 games, for the Cubs, mostly as a pinch hitter. In 1945, he ended his career in Philadelphia, not with the Athletics but with the then-woeful Phillies in the National League. For that team, he filled in as a utility player at first and third base and performed pinch hitting chores, playing in only 89 games. But he demonstrated some of his old competitive spark when he was handed the ball as a pitcher. He pitched 22.2 innings and recorded a highly respectable 1.59 earned run average, even if his won-loss record was just 1–0. "In one game, he pitched seven no-hit, no-run innings," Wallace told *The Kennett Paper*. On the offensive side for the 1945 Phillies, Foxx went to bat 224 times, hit seven home runs, and batted .268. After the season, he announced his retirement.

Managed in the Minor Leagues

Retirement did not mean that Foxx was completely divorced from the sport, however. He spent a period in the late 1940s managing minor league teams—and in that capacity, he could still demonstrate some of the old spark, sometimes assuming the role of player/manager. In an interview with *The Kennett Paper*, Howard Lynn, who umpired in the minor leagues, recalled, "I was working in the Florida International League in 1948 and was introduced to Al Lang [a state politician who brought spring training baseball to the St. Petersburg area]. He said, 'Have you met our manager?' It was Jimmie Foxx. When I told Foxx I was from Kennett Square, he said 'Herb Pennock's home town! He told me to get on you.'"

Lynn had many times watched Foxx play in Shibe Park in Philadelphia, but his most vivid memory of "The Beast" occurred in a game that Lynn umpired in Florida. "[Jimmie's minor league] team was getting beat, and he didn't like that. So, Jimmie decided he'd go in and pinch hit. There were a couple of men on base, and he thought he'd tie the game up. Jimmie still had those big shoulders. He was a big man. Well, the pitcher threw him a real nice curveball, and I called it a strike. Jimmie got out of the [batter's box] pointed at me and shouted right in my ear. 'That damn pitch was outside! And you know it was outside!' I didn't say a thing."

Lynn continued: "He got back in the box, digging them cleats into the dirt, his shoulders so broad. And I thought, 'uh-oh, look out.' Then the next pitch—I've never seen a ball hit that hard. It cleared the left field fence. It cleared the parking lot. It then cleared the street, then it landed on the porch of a rowhouse. He was mad, you see, so he really tagged the ball. He circled the bases and when he crossed home plate, he said to me, 'You can tell Herb Pennock about that!' There was no one who hit one farther than that."

But the seemingly combative attitude that Lynn suggested was merely Jimmie Foxx having fun with the game he loved so much. As sportswriter Al Hirshberg revealed, "[Foxx's] personality was one of the gentlest in the game. Foxx hated no one and no one hated him. From the day he first went into the major leagues, he was pleasant to everyone, never impatient with the fans or admirers, always accessible to anybody who appreciated him."

That is but one reason why Foxx's later years take on a sense of tragedy: How could such an amiable and talented man fall upon such hard times. Foxx found it difficult to hold down a job. After toiling in the minor leagues, his times got harder, and this baseball legend even took on menial blue collar work to make ends meet. The root of his financial difficulty, it seemed, was his unquenchable thirst for alcohol.

Managed a Female Professional Baseball Team

Still, people were ready to give him another chance. After his minor league managing and coaching roles did not work out, he was asked to helm the all-female Fort Wayne Daisies team of the All-American Girls Professional Baseball League. He held this field manager position for only one year (1952), even though he led the team to the league playoffs. The problem was not necessarily alcohol fondness (his female players loved the gentlemanly Foxx); rather it was more because Foxx didn't like the league lifestyle, which included long, uncomfortable bus rides—it was like being back in the minor leagues. Still, from this experience, Foxx's likable presence earned him a much later honor: The Tom Hanks character in the 1992 film *A League of Their Own* (named "Jimmy Dugan"), was based on Foxx. The movie, which depicted the war-time female baseball leagues, placed a very sympathetic light upon the manager.

There were other jobs in baseball–Foxx served as head coach for the University of Miami baseball team (1956–57). But times were hard. Several factors—a painful and costly divorce, failed business ventures, including a golf course, and the inability to hold down a steady baseball job—left Foxx bankrupt.

Despite all of his problems, Foxx remained a likeable and powerful figure, as baseball beat writer and columnist Bill Conlin recalled. While Conlin, an award-winning journalist, was trying to establish his writing career, he took a part-time job at a tavern in Coral Gables, Florida, a place that Foxx frequented. This was in the late 1940s. Conlin relates that Foxx (then working in the minor leagues) was 47 years old, but possessed a face that was "sallow and jowly" and looked ten years older. Still, Foxx's arms "belonged to a man who was 'blacksmith strong,'" wrote Conlin. He adds: "I never shook his hand, but I could imagine the grip of a man my father said could hit a baseball farther than Babe Ruth. He made a baseball look like a golf ball, my father said. 'Ruth hit them high and far, Foxx hit them higher and farther.'"

By this time, Foxx had to forsake his favored Scotch whiskey for glasses of beer. Conlin described the daily bar room regimen: "The ritual was always the same. [Foxx] would lay a $5 bill on the table and hand me a $1 tip in advance. At exactly 7 p.m., he would catch my eye and nod toward the door. I would pick up the phone behind the bar and order him a cab." What Conlin described is a sorrowful shadow. Foxx, as Conlin related, was the most underpaid player in his era–someone who was even forced to swallow a pay cut after one of his greatest years. Today,

Foxx would garner a multi-million dollar contract, instead of that meager $12,000 salary in 1933.

The suffering ended on July 21, 1967, in Miami, Florida, when Foxx—broke and almost forgotten—choked on a piece of food that led to fatal asphyxiation. But someone like Foxx cannot remain forgotten for long. For years, drivers passing through the major road artery through Sudlersville, Maryland would be greeted with this sign: "Home of Jimmie Foxx." In 1987, a better cement monument was erected to celebrate his 80th birthday. Finally, in October 1997, Foxx's hometown built a bronze life-sized statue to honor its favorite son.

Books

Kashatus, William, *Baseball's White Elephants: Connie Mack & The Philadelphia Athletics,* Chester County Historical Society, 1999.

Nemec, David, et al, *Players of Cooperstown: Baseball's Hall of Fame,* Publications International LTD, 1994.

Reichler, Joseph (editor), *The Baseball Encyclopedia,* MacMillan, 1988 edition.

Smith, Ron, *The Sporting News Selects Baseball's Greatest Players: A Celebration of the 20th Century's Best,* The Sporting News Publishing Co., 1998.

Periodicals

Sports Illustrated, August 19, 1996.

The Kennett Paper, April 7, 1988; June 12, 1988; August 17, 1989

Online

"Foxx, James Emory (Jimmie)" *Pennsylvania Center for the Book,* http://pabook.libraries.psu.edu/palitmap/bios/Foxx__James.html (October 31, 2013.

"Jimmie Foxx," *BaseballReference.com,* http://www.baseball-reference.com/players/f/foxxji01.shtml (October 31, 2013.

"Jimmie Foxx," *SABR: Society for American Baseball Research,* http://sabr.org/bioproj/person/e34a045d (October 31, 2013.□

Martine Franck

Belgian photographer Martine Franck (1938–2012) was an inveterate chronicler of the world around her. Franck began her career in photojournalism as a freelancer for *Life* and other top publications, and had a long association with Magnum Photos, the prestigious agency founded by her husband, Henri Cartier-Bresson.

GINIES/SIPA/1110050958

Martine Franck came from a well-to-do family in Antwerp, Belgium, where she was born on April 2, 1938. Her father Louis was a merchant banker with ties to London financial institutions, and the family moved there shortly after Franck's birth. Both her father and her mother, born Evelyn Aéby, were avid art collectors in their later years and instilled in their daughter and her older brother, Eric, a love of painting, sculpture, and other visual arts. When World War II erupted between Britain and Nazi Germany in 1939, Franck's father remained in England and joined the British military intelligence corps; Evelyn Franck and her two young children moved to the United States. They lived for a time in the Oyster Bay area of Long Island and later in Arizona. When she was sent off to boarding school at age six, Franck looked forward to a daily postcard in the mail from her mother, which was often a reproduction of a well-known work of art.

Traveled Through Asia

Franck's formative years were spent in postwar England. She attended the single-sex Heathfield School in Ascot from 1947 to 1954, where she decided upon a career in art history. "I had a wonderful teacher who really galvanized me," she told *Wall Street Journal* writer Tobias Grey, and her interest was further spiked by trips to London museums and galleries, "which was the big excitement of the year for me," she added. *Times* of London society pages for 1956 recorded that Franck participated in that spring's debutante season, including a dance hosted by her mother at Buck's Club in London. By her own admission, Franck was introverted and disliked the social whirl required of young women of her standing. "I never really dared to go up to people and talk to them," she explained to Grey in the *Wall Street Journal* interview. "I started by taking wedding photographs. Then, when I went to parties, I would take my camera with me, just to give myself a sense of composure, or a necessity to be there."

Franck spent a year at the University of Madrid before moving to Paris to earn her art history degree at the École du Louvre, the institute attached to the landmark museum of the same name. She finished her studies in 1963, completing a thesis on Modernist sculptor Henri Gaudier-Brzeska, then embarked upon an extended trek through Asia, some of it in the company of her friend Ariane Mnouchkine, a Parisian drama student who was the daughter of a fairly well-known Russian-émigré film producer named Alexandre Mnouchkine. The younger Mnouchkine would soon launch an avant-garde theater company in Paris, Théâtre du Soleil, that drew heavily from classical Asian drama traditions. Franck served as the official photographer for the highly regarded Théâtre du Soleil from its founding in 1964 until her death.

Franck had borrowed her cousin's Leica camera for her trip to Asia, and ventured through Cambodia, India, Afghanistan, and Turkey. When she came back to Paris, she was hired as a photographic assistant at the prestigious Time-Life bureau. She worked under two established photojournalists, an American named Eliot Elisofon and Gjon Mili, of Albanian birth; both were important contributors to *Life* magazine during its peak years as a weekly chronicle of images and stories from around the world.

Married Cartier-Bresson

By 1966, Franck had started picking up freelance jobs, shooting images for *Life,* Paris *Vogue,* the Style section of the *New York Times,* and on assignment for *Fortune* and *Sports Illustrated.* Around this same time she met legendary French photographer Henri Cartier-Bresson, who was 30 years her senior. Cartier-Bresson came from a similarly wealthy background and had led a roaming, unconventional life before establishing his career in the 1930s as a pioneer of street photography. As a ruse to see Franck after their initial introduction, he asked to take a look at her contact sheets, the resulting cache of images from a roll of film once they had undergone the darkroom-development process. "He always judged a photographer by looking at their contact sheets upside down to see the composition of a photo," Franck said of her future husband in the interview with Grey in the *Wall Street Journal.*

Franck and Cartier-Bresson were married in 1970 and a child, their daughter Mélanie, was born in the spring of 1972. Still forging her own professional career, Franck was skittish about being tagged as the wife of the famed Cartier-Bresson. She was offered a show at the Institute of Contemporary Arts in London in 1971, but promptly cancelled it when the gallery sent out opening-night invitations that boasted Cartier-Bresson would be present at the gala. Before she became a mother she worked for a Paris photo agency called Vu, then co-founded an agency called Viva in 1972 that operated for the rest of the decade before closing.

Work Lauded by Curators, Collectors

Franck and Cartier-Bresson lived in Paris and spent time in the South of France. By this point he had moved away from photography as a visual medium and took up drawing and painting. The couple socialized with an impressive roster of living legends of 20th century art, and Franck began to experiment with portraits and documentary photography. One of her most famous images is of three figures grouped around a modernist swimming pool in Provence on a summer day in 1976. This is titled *Le Brusc* and was later used as the cover photograph for a retrospective volume of her work, *I Grandi Fotografi,* published in 2003. "The delicate horizontal and criss-crossing lines of the hammock in the foreground are echoed in their shadows on the square-tiled terrace floor, while the sweeping curve of the terrace stands out against a dark slope," wrote Louise Baring in the *Sunday Telegraph.* "The three figures in the photograph all seem absorbed in their own world." Franck told Baring that she recalled "running to get the image while changing the film in the camera and quickly closing down the lens as the sunlight on the tiles was so intense," she said in the *Sunday Telegraph* interview. "A second later and the composition would have broken up."

Like her husband and scores of other professional photographers and artists of the medium, Franck used a German-made Leica 35-millimeter camera. She also preferred black-and-white film. "Colour is actually very distracting for photographers," she explained in an article for the London *Guardian* in 2007. "In some ways, shooting in black and white enables you to concentrate more on the composition.... Shape, tone and texture are accentuated in monochrome, and if you don't act quickly, shadows will move, shapes will change, and the composition will break up."

Back in the late 1940s Cartier-Bresson had co-founded Magnum Photos, a photographers' cooperative agency established with Robert Capa and several other prominent photojournalists. The group met annually to admit new members, and the process was an intellectually and emotionally bruising one. Franck joined in 1980 as a nominee photographer, and in 1983, became one of the few women ever admitted to full member status at Magnum.

Returned to Asia in 1990s

Franck's portraits of important cultural figures cemented her artistic reputation. She photographed French painter Marc Chagall in 1980, the Irish poet Seamus Heaney in the mid-1990s, and took a rare joint assignment with her husband in Switzerland at the estate of the famously reclusive painter Balthus. A portrait of her husband, looking into a mirror as she takes the photograph, is another oft-reproduced image of Franck's. "We've always shown each other everything," she told London *Times* journalist Candida Crewe about her professional relationship with her husband. "He's been critical and inspirational, and taught me to say no—not to accept all the work that's offered. And he doesn't allow anyone to do anything with his work. I've also learnt from him to be discreet and respectful, but I think that was in my nature, too."

Some of Franck's other subjects were from the opposite end of the spectrum of publicity: she visited nursing homes and remote communities to depict aging and poverty. A collection of her images of elderly French citizens was published in a 1980 tome, *Le Temps de Vieillir* (A Time to Grow Old), with text by Robert Doisneau and Dr. L. Kaprio. For many years Franck also worked with an international volunteer organization called Petits Frères des Pauvres, or Little Brothers of the Poor, which provides support to senior citizens. Franck later worked on a series of portraits of French men and women who were born before 1900 as part of the cultural events surrounding the 1999–2000 millennium year.

A roamer since her earliest years, Franck became fascinated with a remote and storied place off the northern coast of Ireland, Tory Island, and made frequent visits to photograph its Gaelic-speaking community. In the early 1990s, she became interested in Tibetan Buddhism, and particularly its belief that its most venerated spiritual guides, known as lamas, are reincarnated upon the end of their natural lives. Their successors are infants or toddlers, and these youngsters are raised in monasteries in Tibet and Nepal by monks. Another of Franck's most well-known images is a photograph of a child monk and his much-older tutor in their traditional robes at a monastery in Nepal. A pigeon has landed on the older monk's head, and he tilts it toward the little boy, who laughs in delight. As Franck recalled in an interview with *Guardian* writer Leo Benedictus, she had been in the room for an hour, listening to the youngster recite mantras with his teacher. "I never imagined for a second that the bird would perch on the monk's head," she said. "That's the wonder of photography—you try and capture the surprises."

"A Tough Profession for Women"

Franck attained a career milestone in 1998 with her first solo show, a retrospective in Paris at the Maison Européenne de la Photographie (MEP). A year later, she joined with some of the other women photographers of Magnum, including Eve Arnold and Inge Morath, to stage an exhibition with an accompanying book, both titled *Magna Brava.* "It's difficult for women to get in," she reflected in the *Times* of London interview with Crewe. "There should be more, but it is a tough profession for women. In a way, I was very privileged. I had help when my daughter was small which meant I could go away, but even so I never went for long."

Franck's husband died in August of 2004 at the age of 95. She and her daughter became directors of the Fondation Henri Cartier-Bresson, an exhibition space in Paris and repository of his archives. In 2010, Franck was diagnosed with leukemia, and died on August 16, 2012, in Paris, at the age of 74.

Periodicals

Guardian (London, England), November 29, 2006; October 27, 2007.

Sunday Telegraph (London, England), April 8, 2007.

Times (London, England), November 18, 2000; August 28, 2012.

Wall Street Journal, October 21, 2011.□

Itamar Franco

As president of Brazil for a brief period in the early 1990s, Itamar Franco (1930-2011) implemented an economic plan which essentially saved the Brazilian economy. He was also a member of the Brazilian national senate, the Constituent National Assembly, and a state governor.

Itamar Augusto Cautiero Franco was born prematurely on June 28, 1930, on a boat that was traveling in the Atlantic Ocean between Salvador, located in the Brazilian state of Bahia, and Rio de Janeiro. Franco's unusual name was inspired by his birth, as he was born on a ship called *Ita* and *mar* is the Portuguese word for sea. His father, César died shortly before his birth, and he was raised in poverty by his single mother, Itália, the daughter of Italian immigrants. His mother worked as a seamstress, and with her son's help, sold lunchboxes to local factory workers in the city they adopted as their home, Juiz de Fora, located in the Minas Gerais state of Brazil. His late father's family was originally from this area.

Participated in Student and Local Politics

To improve the lives of herself and her son, Franco's mother encouraged him to pursue as much education as possible. He attended a traditional college in Juiz de Fora then studied civil and electronic engineering at a local university's school of engineering. While a university student, he became active in student politics. He graduated in 1955. This interest in politics eventually translated into involvement in local politics within a few years of earning his degree, starting a construction company, and serving as his city's director of water and sewers.

After being elected a local councilor and vice mayor, Franco won the office of mayor of Juiz de Fora in 1967. He served for four years during this stint, then was mayor again from 1973 to 1974. As mayor, Franco was a member of the Brazilian Democratic Movement (MDB) party. He was known for being quite ethical, open, and honest, an exception in Brazilian politics.

In 1974, Franco moved into federal politics when was elected to the Brazilian Senate. He was re-elected to his senate seat in 1982. During this period, Franco switched party allegiances, becoming a member of the Liberal Party. At the time Brazil was under military rule, as it had been since 1964, and Franco successfully pushed for democratic elections for the presidency. By this time, Franco had developed a reputation for being difficult and temperamental, but this was countered by the respect he earned for his transparent decency.

Military rule ended in Brazil in the mid-1980s, and Franco was a member of the National Constituent Assembly in 1987 and 1988. This body was charged with creating a new democratic constitution for Brazil. As a member of the assembly, Franco voted for severing relationships with countries that practiced racial discrimination (the measure was specifically targeting South Africa and its apartheid

AP Photo/Eraldo Peres

policies), making abortion legal, and limiting the work week to 40 hours. Franco voted against reintroducing the death penalty.

Became Vice President, Then President

Franco's political career reached new heights in 1989, when he joined the small National Reconstruction Party (PRN) and was elected Brazil's vice president. Playboy Fernando Collor de Mello was elected president, but his government soon faced difficulties including allegations of corruption and embezzlement. In December 1992, Franco became president when Collor left office to avoid an impeachment trial because of corruption charges.

Unlike Collor, Franco had no tolerance for corruption. Indeed, Franco was characterized as a man of dignity who kept his interest in gaining power in check. As Hugh O'Shaughnessy wrote in the *Ottawa Citizen* shortly after Franco took office, "After years of the arrogance of President Fernando Collor de Mello, Brazilians are revelling in the down-to-earth unpretentiousness of their new leader." O'Shaughnessy added, "While Collor was loud and flashy, an arrogant man with the tall good looks of a matinee idol, Itamar is quiet and sober, an unprepossessing man with the simple touch."

When he took office, Franco faced immediate challenges, including many lingering effects from the era of military rule followed by the corrupt years of Collor. For years, the military had run the country to benefit themselves, industrialists, landowners, and other elite groups with power and money, while millions of Brazilians suffered from poverty and hunger. Immediately, Franco spoke out in support of the poor and average Brazilians, and stood against profiteering of drug companies. He also refused to sell off the many nationalized major industries quickly, fearing that Brazil would get a bad deal.

More importantly, Franco faced a major economic crisis as Brazil dealt with an extended phase of hyperinflation. Annual inflation was anywhere from 1000 to 2500 percent, and caused prices to rise by as much as 5000 percent annually, limited investment in the country, and forced more Brazilians to live in poverty. Because of hyperinflation, new denominations of the country's currency lost their value as soon as they were printed. Brazil was also in a recession for more than a year before he took office. One reason for the economic situation was that rich and middle class Brazilians were determined not to pay taxes, and there was no state apparatus to force them to do so.

Franco made several failed attempts to fix the inflation situation through the efforts and ideas of three different finance ministers. These endeavors included expanding foreign trade, aggressively cleaning up his government, and liberalizing the economy of Brazil. In addition to stabilizing relations with the international finance community as much as possible, Franco supported the expansion of liberalization policies to expose Brazil's long-protected state-run industries to international competition. The state industry sector was highly debt ridden, laden with privileges and high salaries, and the sector was a drain on national finances. Most of the companies were inefficient as well, adding to the economic chaos.

Implemented Real Plan

In 1993, Franco took a bold chance and asked Fernando Henrique Cardoso to be his new finance minister. A sociologist, Cardoso came up with a plan that Franco endorsed and introduced on July 1, 1994, in an attempt to check an inflation rate which had reached at least 50 percent per month. Cardoso's Real Plan (Plano Real) raised interest rates, ensured that the new version of Brazil's currency, the *real,* which was pegged to the U.S. dollar, and controlled government spending. Salaries and other prices were converted to into what were called Real Value Units (URVs) which were also then linked to the dollar. Because the plan attracted foreign capital and calmed interest rates down, it was ultimately the most successful anti-inflation program introduced in Brazil, with interest rates rapidly decreasing within months.

Because of Franco's actions in implementing the Real Program, Brazil's economy ultimately improved—inflation dropped to only four percent in two years—and boomed by the first decades of the twenty-first century. Later in 1994, Franco lost the presidential election to Cardoso, who had been praised as Brazil's miracle worker for the plan. Cardoso ultimately served as Brazil's president from 1995 to 2002.

While Franco was in office and trying to handle the economic crisis, he unintentionally launched a personal political crisis. During the Rio Carnival in February 1994, Franco was watching the parade from the presidential box when he allowed a 28-year-old dancer and *Playboy* cover girl, Lilian Ramos, into his box after they blew kisses to each other. A cameraman recorded the meeting, which included more kissing and gyrating. Most notoriously Ramos revealed she was wearing nothing under a t-shirt after she raised her hands to participate in the Mexican Wave.

Unaware that cameras had taken pictures of the whole incident, Franco called her the next day, lavished praise on her, and invited her to dinner, again while the exchange was recorded by cameras on Ramos's end. When he learned that it had been recorded, Franco cancelled the date and spent the next four days in hiding. It soon came to light that Franco wrote erotic short stories—as well as other types of fiction and nonfiction—in his spare time as well. Though the Roman Catholic Church demanded Franco resign while others called for his impeachment, only 18 percent of the Brazilian public supported such a move. Franco survived the scandal, though he left office in January 1995.

Left Positive Legacy

Overall, Franco's legacy for his brief, just over two-year term as president was generally positive. Though Cardoso gained most of the credit for the Real Plan, Franco was lauded for leading Brazil out of the crisis and quelling ever-increasing amounts of social unrest. He alson helped restore stability to the still fragile political system in Brazil. By doing so, democracy in Brazil gained traction at a time when the military was becoming restless after losing power after decades of rule. At the same time, critics and the public mocked the modest, unassuming Franco who was often awkward in public. Franco was even labeled the Forrest Gump of Brazilian politics.

Served as State Governor

Franco took on new challenges in 1998, when he was overwhelmingly elected governor of Minas Gerais over a candidate supported by Cardoso. A year after taking office, he declared a 90-day moratorium on his state's debt to the federal government. Franco stated that the debt, some US $11 billion, could not be paid because Minas Gerais was insolvent. Because of Franco's decision, there were national and international fears that Brazil as a whole would default on debt payments. As a result, investors withdrew billions of dollars from Brazil, creating a temporary national crisis. This decision negatively impacted his image and his country because of the financial chaos that ensued. Despite this mishap, Franco remained governor until 2003.

After leaving the office of governor of Minas Gerais, Franco supported the presidential campaign of Luiz Inacio Lula da Silva, a member of the left-leaning Workers Party, in 2002. In the early 2000s, he also held other political posts, including serving as Brazil's ambassador to Portugal. During his time as ambassador, Franco was given credit for improving relations between Brazil and its mother country. He served as the ambassador to the Organization of American States, located in Washington, D.C., as well. Later breaking with Lula da Silva, Franco returned to national politics in 2010 when he was again elected a senator as a member of the left-wing Popular Socialist Party. He continued to serve until he fell ill in early 2011.

At the end of his life, Franco was hospitalized at the Albert Einstein hospital in São Paulo for several months after being diagnosed with leukemia and pneumonia. On July 2, 2011, Franco suffered a stroke there and died. Franco was survived by two daughters, Georgiana and Fabriana, from his ten-year marriage to Ana Elia Suerus, whom he divorced in 1978.

Upon his death, Brazilian president Dilma Rousseff declared a seven-day period of mourning. Another former president, Lula da Silva told Tom Phillips of the London *Guardian,* "Itamar helped the country take positive political, economic and social paths. Da Silva added that Franco had made "a fundamental contribution to the collective construction of a democratic, more equal country without poverty."

Periodicals

Associated Press, July 2, 2011.
Daily Telegraph (London), July 6, 2011.
Financial Post (Toronto, Canada), February 20, 1993.
Guardian (London), July 5, 2011.
Independent Extra, July 8, 2011.
Journal of Commerce, January 7, 1993.
Ottawa Citizen, February 21, 1993.
Times (London), July 14, 2011.□

Ford Frick

American sportswriter Ford Frick (1894-1978) moved from the press box to baseball's front office, serving 14 years as the commissioner of Major League Baseball and 17 as president of the National League. During this time, Frick oversaw the expansion of the league to the West, the racial integration of professional baseball, and the creation of the National Baseball Hall of Fame and Museum.

Ford Christopher Frick was born December 19, 1894, on the family farm in Noble County, Indiana. He was the only son of five children born to Jacob and Emma (Prickett) Frick. There was always work to be done on the farm. The family grew corn, wheat, potatoes, hay, and alfalfa. Nonetheless, Frick found free time to play baseball, a favorite pastime in his rural community. "You could go out in the cow pasture, after the hay was cut, and take four or five bricks for bases and a slab of stone for home plate," Frick recalled in Jerome Holtzman's book *The Commissioners.* "We made our own baseballs and the guy who

Transcendental Graphics/Getty Images

had the best baseball was captain of the team—until that ball was lost. If you had a bat you made the team."

Frick's first baseball hero was a pitcher named Albert John Inks, who went by the nickname "Big Bert." Inks, who played for the Brooklyn Bridegrooms in the 1890s, hailed from nearby Ligonier, Indiana. Frick had a chance to shake his hand and it made a lasting impression. In 1907, Frick's infatuation with the game increased after the Chicago Cubs came to town to play an exhibition game against the local Kendallville Blues at the Noble County Fairgrounds.

With no dugouts, the players changed outside the park and walked in. As the team paraded by Frick and his boyhood friends, Frick caught the eye of Cubs catcher Johnny Kling, who asked him if he would like to attend the game. Kling gave Frick his shoes to carry and suggested the boy walk in with him to see if the gateman would let him through. It worked and Frick spent the game sitting on the ground near the players' bench. The experience had a lasting impact. As Frick noted in his memoir—*Games, Asterisks, and People*—"One thing sure. That day in 1907 convinced me that baseball was the greatest game in the world, and he its greatest player."

Entered Newspaper Business

As a teenager, Frick expressed a desire to go into the newspaper business. Everyone told him he needed to learn to type, so he spent a summer taking a typing and stenography course at a business college in Fort Wayne, Indiana. During that summer, he landed a job at the *Fort Wayne Journal Gazette*. In 1912, Frick enrolled at DePauw University in Greencastle, Indiana. He played collegiate baseball and also ran on DePauw's track team. To pay for his schooling, Frick waited tables at a student boarding house and worked as a correspondent for the dailies in Indianapolis and Terre Haute. Occasionally, Frick received a special assignment from the *Chicago Tribune* to cover noteworthy sporting events in the area.

In 1915, Frick graduated from DePauw and headed west, settling in Colorado. He got a job teaching English at the high school in Walsenburg and business English at Colorado College in Colorado Springs. Frick also joined the Cubanolas, a semi-professional baseball club from Walsenburg, Colorado. He played first base but struggled immensely against left-handed pitchers, having faced few of them in Indiana. In most accounts of his playing career, Frick often said he was mediocre at best. Frick married a local gal, Eleanor Cowing, on September 15, 1916. After the birth of a son, Frick decided he needed a job that paid better than teaching, so he went back into the newspaper business, landing a job at the *Colorado Springs Gazette* in 1917. During World War I, he worked for the Veterans Bureau in Denver.

In 1919, Frick returned to the paper in Colorado Springs. He wrote editorials, covered sports stories and the crime beat, and also conducted "hotel" interviews of noted personalities when celebrities passed through the resort town. Frick interviewed actress Ethel Barrymore, entertainer Al Jolson, and New York Governor Al Smith. Frick's big break came in 1921 when a flood devastated the region and he was the only reporter with access to the area. Frick persuaded a pilot to fly him over the destruction so he could take pictures to accompany his story. Frick's flood coverage drew nationwide attention and impressed Hearst newspaper editor Arthur Brisbane. Brisbane offered Frick a job at the *New York American* with a focus on sportswriting.

Covered New York Sports Teams

Frick arrived in New York in 1922 and worked at the *American* until 1923 when the Hearst conglomerate bought the *New York Evening Journal* and Brisbane transferred him to the new paper. Working in New York, Frick covered sports exclusively. Baseball was big business in the city, with a large majority of the sports section devoted to the city's three teams—the Giants, Yankees, and Dodgers. There were no televisions yet and radio was in its infancy, so fans relied on the newspaper for in-depth coverage. The *Journal* frequently carried three baseball stories a day—one for each team. Frick often covered the Yankees and in this capacity got to know Babe Ruth. Frick served as Ruth's ghostwriter for *Babe Ruth's Own Book of Baseball,* which was published in 1928. In addition to covering sports stories for the paper, Frick wrote a regular column called "Ford Frick's Comments," a blend of news and commentary.

Around 1930, Frick entered the radio business doing sports broadcasting and hosting a nightly 15-minute radio sports show summarizing the day. He also kept his newspaper column. Initially, New York's Major League Baseball teams banned live broadcasts from their stadiums. Head office executives feared that fans would stop buying tickets if they could hear the game for free. In 1933, as the crosstown rivalry between the Giants and Dodgers heated up, Western Union hired Frick to "broadcast" the games. Because he was not allowed to broadcast from inside the stadium, Frick followed the ticker tape report from the stadium pitch-by-pitch and recreated the action on the air as if he was watching it live.

Elected National League President

Frick's sportscasting and sportswriting brought him national recognition and also led to a friendship with Giants manager John McGraw. In 1934, McGraw persuaded the National League to hire Frick to oversee its newly created Service Bureau, which was in charge of publicity for the National League. Nine months later, Frick was elected president of the National League, serving from 1934 to 1951.

As NL president, Frick took over during tough financial times, as the Great Depression challenged the financial security of several teams in the league. Frick's innovations helped save the Brooklyn, Philadelphia, and Boston franchises from bankruptcy. Ford was also instrumental in establishing the National Baseball Hall of Fame and Museum in Cooperstown, N.Y. Plans for the Hall of Fame originated in the mid-1930s after philanthropist Stephen Clark contacted Frick asking if a major league all-star team could play a celebratory game in Cooperstown to commemorate the life of Union Army officer Abner Doubleday.

A native of Cooperstown, Doubleday at one time was thought to be the inventor of the game. As Frick and Clark talked, they decided to do something longer lasting and came up with the idea for the Hall of Fame. Clark put up funding and Frick persuaded Major League Baseball to join in. That was a tough sell since the presiding baseball commissioner, Kenesaw Mountain Landis, never warmed to the idea. But Frick persuaded enough people and the doors opened in 1939. In his book on baseball's commissioners, Holtzman noted that Frick considered the founding of the Hall of Fame his most noteworthy achievement. "That's my baby, the thing I'm proudest of," Frick told Holtzman.

Baseball integration also took place under Frick's watch. While Frick did not lead the push toward integration, once the Dodgers called up Jackie Robinson to the majors at the start of the 1947 season, Frick backed integration wholeheartedly. When Frick heard there was a boycott brewing among some St. Louis Cardinals players, he threatened to suspend anyone who refused to take the field with Robinson. As the story goes, Cardinals owner Sam Breadon approached Frick with the news that some of his players were threatening to derail racial integration.

Frick recalled the event in his memoir and said he told Breadon to deliver this message to the players: "Tell them this is America and baseball is America's game. Tell them that if they go on strike, for racial reasons, or refuse to play a scheduled game they will be barred from baseball even though it means the disruption of a club or a whole league." Frick went on to say that he did not know specifically how Breadon delivered the message, but a few days later Breadon said the issue had been resolved. *New York Herald Tribune* writer Stanley Woodward broke the story and printed Frick's words on the matter. Because Woodward printed Frick's message, his stance was available for all players and managers to read. After that, no one else threatened a boycott.

Served as Baseball Commissioner

In 1951, Frick was chosen by club owners to become the third commissioner of Major League Baseball. During his tenure as commissioner, Frick testified 17 times before Congressional committees concerning anti-trust laws. Because of a court ruling, baseball was (and remains) exempt from federal anti-trust laws, which were put in place to prevent anti-competitive behavior in the marketplace. Some players had challenged the reserve clause—which essentially makes a player the "property" of the team—as a violation of anti-trust interstate commerce laws. Frick defended the reserve clause and Congress never acted on the matter.

As commissioner, Frick was best remembered as the "asterisk" guy. The asterisk controversy started during the summer of 1961 as Roger Maris' bat got hot and he approached Babe Ruth's single-season home run record of 60. During a press conference, a reporter inquired about the record. Ruth hit his 60 homers during a 154-game schedule, while Maris was playing a 162-game schedule. According to Allen Barra of the *New York Times,* Frick responded by saying, "If a player does not hit more than 60 until after his club has played 154 games, there would have to be some distinctive mark in the record books to show that Babe Ruth's record was set under a 154-game schedule." A *New York Daily News* sportswriter applied the term "asterisk" to Frick's remark. Frick never used the word and tried to downplay the idea, saying he was just stating an opinion about the matter—not making a definitive ruling.

Nonetheless, the idea of the asterisk took off and Frick was vilified by Maris fans for "footnoting" his accomplishment, but applauded by old-timers who revered Ruth. Maris ended up hitting 59 homers in 154 games but closed out the season with 61. According to *USA Today's* Hal Bodley, Maris once complained to the paper, "that was the only record Ford Frick put an asterisk on and tried to diminish. I never understood why." The truth, however, was that there never was an asterisk. Major League Baseball did not keep an "official" record book in 1961. Baseball historian Dan Gutman told the *New York Times'* Barra that the myth persisted because "the majority of the fans believed that Maris should have had the asterisk, and so he did."

Besides taking criticism from Maris fans, Frick was regularly lambasted by the press who called him a do-little commissioner and accused him of being too tolerant of the status quo. The press also accused him of bias toward the league's owners. In addition, the press said Frick skirted away from making tough decisions. It was true that Frick often said controversial matters were not for the commissioner to decide. "I got panned very frequently for saying, 'This was a league matter,'" Frick told Holtzman. "The owners try to throw a lot of their disputes in the commissioner's lap that were never meant for the commissioner to decide. You can't remain on a judicial level, protecting honesty and integrity and holding the confidence of the fans, if you're going to be required to roll in the dirt down at a lower level. Being criticized is part of the job. But in your heart there is a scar."

Frick retired in 1965 and was elected to the National Baseball Hall of Fame in 1970. He died April 8, 1978, at a hospital in Bronxville, New York. Annually, the National Baseball Hall of Fame offers the Ford C. Frick Award to a sportscaster for meritorious contributions to baseball.

Books

Frick, Ford C., *Games, Asterisks, and People: Memoirs of a Lucky Fan,* Crown Publishers, 1973.

Holtzman, Jerome, *The Commissioners,* Total Sports, 1998.

Holtzman, Jerome, *No Cheering in the Press Box,* Holt McDougal, 1974.

Periodicals

Chicago Tribune, April 10, 1978; December 26, 1985.

Lowell Sun (MA), September 21, 1951.

USA Today, August 11, 1998.

Online

"An Asterisk Is Very Real, Even When It's Not," *New York Times* http://www.nytimes.com/2007/05/27/weekinreview/27barra.html?_r=0 (December 11, 2013).□

G

William M. Gaines

The American magazine publisher William M. Gaines (1922–1992), who founded *Mad* magazine as well as several controversial and widely read comic book series in the 1950s, exerted a strong influence on American satire and on irreverent, liberatarian attitudes more generally.

At its peak in the early 1970s, *Mad*'s circulation reached about 2.4 million copies a month and extended well beyond the United States. The magazine's gap-toothed boy mascot Alfred E. Neuman and his "what, me worry?" trademark phrase were nearly universally known among American youth. Gaines was only rarely a writer, but he was in many ways the magazine's guiding light, building *Mad* into a long-lasting institution at the same time as other satirical efforts appeared briefly and then quickly flamed out. In the 1950s, Gaines became known for his challenges to censorship of comic books, and his horror comic book series *Tales from the Crypt* enjoyed a long life in print, film, and television media. Gaines's corpulent frame and Santa Claus–like beard were common topics of ridicule in the pages of *Mad,* which, true to its original spirit, did not shrink from poking fun at its founder.

Served in Army

Gaines was born into comic-book publishing. His father, Max C. Gaines (born Maxwell Ginzburg), was an early major publisher of mass-circulation comic books in the U.S.; his company All-American Publications introduced such characters as Wonder Woman. Gaines grew up seeing copies of his father's publication *Famous Funnies* on sale for a dime apiece at newsstands around New York and beyond. He attended Brooklyn Polytechnic Institute (now the Polytechnic Institute of New York University), where he became known as a better prankster than student. He left school in 1942 to join the U.S. Army, serving until 1946. The following year he completed a Bachelor of Science degree at New York University.

In that same year, Max Gaines died in a boating accident, and William Gaines, known as Bill, set aside his plans to become a chemistry teacher and assumed control of his father's new company, Educational Comics. The firm had published such inoffensive volumes as a picture book based on the Bible, but Gaines quickly took it in a new direction, renaming it Entertaining Comics (EC Comics for short, a name under which it became widely known) and launching new horror comics, including *Shock Suspenstories* and, in 1950, *Vault of Horror* and *Crypt of Terror.* The latter series was renamed *Tales from the Crypt* after three issues, and its lurid, gory drawings began to attract the attention of congressional investigators as EC's products became more and more popular. By 1952 a host of Gaines imitators had pushed horror comics to a 25 percent U.S. market share.

In 1954, Gaines was called to testify before the U.S. Senate subcommittee on juvenile delinquency. Senator Estes Kefauver brandished a copy of Gaines's *Crime Suspense #22,* with a cover showing a man carrying an ax and holding a severed human head. Kefauver demanded to know whether Gaines thought the cover was in good taste, and Gaines's reply has been widely quoted (for example in his *Times* of London obituary); "I think it would be bad taste if he were holding the head a little higher so the neck would show with the blood dripping from it." The result was official pressure on the comics

Ron Galella/WireImage/Getty Images

industry to police itself; a Comics Code Authority was formed, and it had the effect of slowing or eliminating major parts of EC's output.

By that time, however, Gaines was already nurturing a new product. *Mad,* formed in 1952 after cartoonist Harvey Kurtzman approached Gaines with an idea for something he could draw during a bout with jaundice, featured detailed comic cover artwork and a variety of parodies that took aim at complacent 1950s mainstream culture. By 1954 *Mad* was gaining popularity, and Kurtzman was urging Gaines to transform it from a comic book to a full-fledged magazine.

Changed Format to Retain Writer

It has been reported that Gaines agreed to the conversion, executed in 1955, to avoid the strictures of the Comics Code, and it did indeed have that effect. But Gaines told *Comics Art* in 1991 that the conversion occurred because Kurtzman, by then *Mad*'s editor, had received a job offer from a competing publication. "At the time I didn't think I wanted to because I didn't know anything about publishing magazines. I was a comics publisher. But, remembering this interest, when he got this offer, I countered his offer by saying I would allow him to change Mad into a magazine, which proved to be a very lucky step for me. But that's why it was changed. It was not changed to avoid the Code. Now, as a result of this, it did avoid the Code, but that's not why I did it."

Kurtzman ended up leaving *Mad* soon after that anyway, but by then the magazine had a growing staff of talented cartoonists that could produce a varied issue of consistently high quality. Each issue of *Mad* would feature a madcap parody of a familiar serious film or television drama of the day, but that was augmented by contributions from a diverse set of artists. Beginning in 1960, Cuban-born artist Antonio Prohías poked fun at Cold War espionage with his *Spy vs. Spy* cartoons, while artist Don Martin contributed strips with a pure slapstick quality. In the magazine's first years, noted Barry Fantoni in the London *Guardian,* "aspiring modern comic illustrators were challenged by the dexterity of the artists and the sharpness of the writing, always given equal credit at the top of the page." Gaines told *Comic Art* that his own politics were "part-liberal, part-conservative. It depends on which part you're talking about. In foreign policy I'm a conservative. In domestic policy, in things having to do with sex, abortion, pornography, and what have you, I'm completely liberal."

The anarchic atmosphere at the magazine's New York headquarters, encouraged and often directly created by Gaines himself, contributed to its creative successes. He filled the office water coolers with wine and, to celebrate the magazine's passing the one-million circulation mark, took the entire staff on a vacation to Haiti, where there was only one subscriber to the magazine. Gaines and his staff tracked the subscriber down and presented him with a subscription-renewal card.

Refused to Run Advertising

In 1961 Gaines sold *Mad* but stayed on as financial director and was for many years still the de facto publisher. *Mad* was one of the few magazines that carried no advertising, a policy that was also largely Gaines's own doing; he believed that to run ads would compromise the magazine's satirical integrity. Gaines also mostly declined to commercialize the Alfred E. Neuman mascot, although he did appear on some T-shirts and a *Mad*-themed board game.

Well before 2 Live Crew and other hip-hop artists tested the legal boundaries of fair use of prior materials, Gaines emerged as a vigorous defender of the rights of humorists to parody existing work. A series of humorous poems designed to be sung to the tunes of Irving Berlin songs drew a lawsuit from that prolific popular song composer, but a judge ruled in Gaines's favor, noting (according to Gaines's second wife, Ann, quoted by *Comic Art*): "We doubt that even so eminent a composer as Irving Berlin should be permitted to claim a property interest in iambic pentameter."

Gaines remained active at *Mad* for the rest of his life, displaying a tight control over expenses that seemed outwardly at odds with his anarchic nature, and that kept the magazine afloat as its circulation declined from its 1970s peak. (It is still being published.) He died quietly at his New York home on June 3, 1992. Gaines married twice and had three children, Wendy Bucci, Cathy Missud, and Chris Gaines, whom he raised to believe in Santa Claus but not in God. In 2007 Iron Mountain Media acquired the rights to make a film based on Gaines's life.

Books

Jacobs, Frank, *The Mad World of William M. Gaines,* Lyle Stuart, 1972.
Newsmakers, Gale, 1993.

Periodicals

Globe & Mail (Toronto, Ontario, Canada), June 4, 1992.
Guardian (London, England), June 6, 1992.
Hollywood Reporter, June 6, 2007.
National Review, July 6, 1992.
Times (London, England), June 6, 1992.

Online

"The Long, Gory Life of EC Comics," *Reason,* http://reason.com/archives/2005/06/01/the-long-gory-life-of-ec-comic (September 5, 2013).
"William M. Gaines Interview II," *Comic Art & Graffix Gallery,* http://www.comic-art.com/intervws/gaines11.ht (September 5, 2013).□

Carleton Gajdusek

The American medical researcher and physician Carleton Gajdusek (1923–2008) was first to identify the mysterious infectious agent that later became known as the prion and has been linked to bovine spongiform encephalopathy, also known as mad cow disease.

Keystone/Hulton Archive/Getty Images

Gajdusek received the 1976 Nobel Prize in medicine for his work, the foundations of which were laid under extremely difficult research conditions among the remote Fore people of highland Papua New Guinea. Carrying out backwoods autopsies on Fore individuals who had died of a little-understood disease called kuru, he began to suspect that the malady was unlike anything else he had encountered in his training as a physician. Drawing on information across disciplinary lines, Gajdusek learned more about the infection, its mode of transmission, and the course of the infection it caused. Kuru was, he believed, caused by cannibalism among the Fore, and when scientists identified the cause of mad cow disease in the 1990s, they were building ultimately on Gajdusek's long record of research. Unfortunately, Gajdusek's reputation was marred in his later years by a 1997 conviction for child molestation, an activity that may have begun during his years doing research in the Pacific Islands.

Collected Insects on Family Outings

Daniel Carleton Gajdusek (pronounced GUY-dah-shek) was born in Yonkers, New York, on September 9, 1923, and grew up in an extended family that included grandparents and an aunt. He had one younger brother, Robert, who became as interested in the arts as he was in science. Gajdusek was of Slovak background on his father's side, Hungarian on his mother's. Both his parents had university educations, and both children were raised with a positive attitude toward learning and observation. Gajdusek trapped insects on outings with his aunt, a trained entomologist, and while other students were content to keep insects in jars, he would experiment on them with different substances and bring specimens to school in jars labeled "Poison: potassium cyanide."

A local scientist, however, encouraged the young man's talents: William Youden, a researcher at Yonkers' Boyce Thompson Institute, let him play with chemical solutions and a slide rule. By the time he was in middle school, Gajdusek was using his after-school time to attend science lectures at New York's Museum of Natural History. He worked on insecticide compounds at the Boyce Thompson Institute as a teen and then enrolled at the University of Rochester, majoring in science. Gajdusek graduated in 1943, at age 19, and went on to Harvard Medical School. His interests were not completely academic, however; beginning in his teens he was an avid outdoorsman.

Earning his M.D. degree from Harvard in 1946, Gajdusek moved on to a lab at Boston Children's Hospital and then to a postdoctoral research post at the California Institute of Technology, where one of his teachers was double Nobel Prize winner Linus Pauling. Gajdusek was drafted into the United States Army in 1951, serving as a research virologist at

Walter Reed Army Medical Center in Washington, D.C. In 1952 and 1953 he worked at the Pasteur Institute in Tehran, Iran, when that country still had friendly relations with the U.S. Although he had gone to Iran feeling that his best years were behind him, it was there that he found his calling: working on third-world epidemics of such diseases as rabies and plague, "I learned of the excitement and challenge offered by urgent opportunistic investigations of epidemiological problems in exotic and isolated populations," he wrote in his Nobel Prize autobiography.

Heard About Rare Disease

Gajdusek began to travel widely, to the Hindu Kush region of Afghanistan and Pakistan, to South American rain forests, and to southeast Asia and Australia. In the latter country he undertook further studies in virology and immunology and immediately began to apply what he had learned in studies in the field among Australian aboriginal populations and in Papua New Guinea, then under Australian control. In 1957, in the Papuan capital of Port Moresby, he heard about a disease called kuru that had afflicted the Fore, a group in eastern Papua New Guinea. He set off for the area to investigate.

What he saw was horrible: Fore people lost control of their bodies and minds, screamed, stumbled, laughed uncontrollably, and for the most part finally died. The death rate was 100 percent. Gajdusek established a makeshift hospital and tried various treatments on the Fore, none of which worked. Using a carving knife he conducted autopsies on the Fore dead, trading axes and salt for permission to do so. He sent brain samples to Australia and the U.S. in search of answers. None were immediately forthcoming, but Gajdusek did notice one thing: the Fore, unlike other tribes in the area, had a tradition of cannibalism of the dead: they told him that they cooked and ate the brains of deceased relatives, as a sign of respect. (Some researchers have questioned whether cannibalism actually occurred.) Another strange aspect of the disease was that it seemed to take years to develop.

Leaving Papua New Guinea for a job at the National Institutes of Health in Washington, Gajdusek inoculated a group of chimpanzees with extracts taken from the brains of deceased Fore. Another piece of the puzzle came together when he heard from American and British scientists who had read his papers about the Fore brains and noticed that they looked similar to those of sheep stricken by a disease called scrapie, which, like kuru, was little understood: the brains of the affected sheep developed a strange sponge-like texture, and, as with kuru sufferers, all eventually died.

Two years after he returned to the U.S., the chimpanzees Gajdusek had inoculated fell ill, and subsequent investigations showed that they had contracted a disease similar to kuru. Gajdusek had his answer: kuru was caused by a hitherto-unknown kind of infectious agent that affected the brains of its victims. He called it a slow-moving virus and, in the 1960s and early 1970s, published about 150 papers describing his work. For these, he, along with Baruch S. Blumberg, was awarded the 1976 Nobel Prize in Physiology or Medicine.

Further work by later researchers showed how prescient Gajdusek had been. In 1982, Stanley Prusiner suggested that Gajdusek's slow-moving virus was in fact not a virus at all or even a living thing, but rather a deformed self-replicating protein that he called a prion. Prusiner too later received the Nobel Prize, and prions have since been implicated in mad cow disease (called variant Creutzfeld-Jakob disease in its human form). Some researchers have suggested that prions may even be involved in the development of common degenerative ailments such as Alzheimer's disease.

Adopted Children from South Pacific

Meanwhile, Gajdusek had begun to adopt boys, and a few girls, from the south Pacific. The adoptions began on the island of Yap, now part of the Federated States of Micronesia, in the early 1960s and continued, also including some youngsters from Papua New Guinea. Local families supported the adoptions, for Gajdusek, who had provided medical care in the area, was a well-loved figure. Gajdusek moved back into his family home in Yonkers, where he cared for the young people and financed their high school and college educations. Several of them returned to their home countries and were appointed to high-ranking positions in health care and government.

Gajdusek's world fell into disarray after an unknown party noticed passages in his journals from his years in Papua New Guinea and Yap that indicated he had slept the night with multiple local young men. U.S. Senate investigators turned evidence over to the Federal Bureau of Investigation (FBI), which arrested Gajdusek in April of 1996. After being sought out by the FBI, one of his adoptees charged that Gajdusek had sexually abused him during the four years he lived in Gajdusek's house; others backed Gajdusek, and some cultural observers pointed out that sexual play between younger people and adults was common in the societies from which the boys came. Most damning when Gajdusek went on trial in 1997 was a telephone call, placed by the complainant and recorded by the FBI, in which Gajdusek characterized himself as a pedophile, said of the phone line (according to Justin Gillis of the *Washington Post*), "I hope it's not being tapped," admitted that the two had engaged in mutual masturbation, and asked the young man to lie to investigators.

Gajdusek remained unrepentant, contending that he was acting according to different cultural norms than those of American society. But on the advice of his attorney, he accepted a plea deal that saw him released after serving one year in prison. He left the U.S. and spent most of his time in Amsterdam and in Tromsø, Norway, continuing to work and follow scientific literature. He chose the latter city, which is above the Arctic Circle and completely dark in winter, because he felt that the darkness allowed him to concentrate on his work. Gajdusek was found dead in a hotel room in Tromsø on December 12, 2008. In 2013, there appeared a novel based on Gajdusek's story, *The People in the Trees,* by Hanya Yanagihara.

Books

Klitzman, Robert, *A Personal Account of Kuru, Cannibals, and Mad Cow Disease,* Plenum, 1998.
World of Health, Gale, 2007.

Periodicals

Age (Melbourne, Australia), May 10, 1996.
Globe & Mail (Toronto, Ontario, Canada), January 12, 1991.
Guardian (London, England), February 25, 2009.
Independent (London, England), August 5, 1996.
International Herald Tribune, October 3, 2013.
Los Angeles Times, December 18, 2008.
New York Times, April 6, 1996; February 19, 1997; April 30, 1997; Deecember 15, 2008.
Oceania, November 2007.
Science, June 20, 1986.
Washington Post, April 6, 1996; April 27, 1996; April 30, 1997.

Online

"D. Carleton Gajdusek—Biographical," *NobelPrize.org,* http://www.nobelprize.org/nobel_prizes/medicine/laureates/1976/gajdusek-bio.html (October 3, 2013).□

Harold Garfinkel

The American educator Harold Garfinkel (1917–2011) created an entirely new field within American academic sociology. He called this new field ethnomethodology, which he defined as the study of common-sense knowledge.

Garfinkel's writings, in comparison with those of other academic figures, were somewhat sparse, and his major contribution lay in a single book, *Studies in Ethnomethodology* (1967), which consisted of a series of essays. Yet Garfinkel's influence loomed large, even in fields beyond sociology. "You wouldn't get any argument if you said [*Studies in Ethnomethodology*] was among the ten most important books in sociology in the 20th century," Garfinkel's colleague John Heritage told Bruce Weber of the *New York Times.* Within the field of sociology itself, Garfinkel's impact was fundamental. When he began his work, most sociologists believed that they were studying the rules that governed human society. Garfinkel "dropped a bomb on that idea, by saying rules need to be specified and interpreted in light of real-world situations," Heritage told Weber.

Inspired by Graduate Student Instructors

Harold Garfinkel was born in Newark, New Jersey, on October 29, 1917. Garfinkel's father was a small businessman in the housewares field, and Garfinkel set out to follow him into a similar line of work, taking business and accounting courses at the University of Newark (now Rutgers University, Newark). Some of his professors at the school were graduate students from Columbia University in New York, and conversations with them kindled Garfinkel's interest in sociology. After graduating from Newark with a bachelor's degree in economics in 1939, he headed for the University of North Carolina, earning a master's degree in sociology there in 1941. While he was there, he wrote a short story, "Color Trouble," about an African American woman who refused to move to the back of a bus as it crossed into the Southern states; the story was published in *Opportunity* magazine and named to a list of best short stories of 1941.

From 1942 to 1946, Garfinkel served in the United States Army Air Force in a noncombatant role. He then moved on to the PhD program at Harvard, where he studied under sociologist Talcott Parsons. Parsons was a major figure in American sociology who was largely responsible for putting the field on a more theoretical footing; his students would study the German and French roots of sociological thought as well as later developments in pure philosophy that followed from them. Parsons himself had a notoriously difficult-to-understand writing style, and Garfinkel would follow in his footsteps. Garfinkel earned his PhD from Harvard in 1952 and did postgraduate work and teaching at Ohio State and Princeton universities and the University of Chicago. Even during this period he was developing the ideas that would later bear the name of ethnomethodology.

Hired at the University of California at Los Angeles (UCLA) in 1954, Garfinkel developed a reputation as a brilliant, if eccentric, teacher and lecturer. His style was theatrical: he would often outline an idea partially and then let it hang in silence as students digested his words. "Often," noted Michael Lynch in the London *Guardian,* "he would break the silence with enigmatic pronouncements and anecdotes that left his students with problems to work out." Garfinkel taught at UCLA for the rest of his career, becoming a professor emeritus in the late 1980s, and his students have continued to exert a strong influence on American sociology.

Based Ideas on Jury Deliberations

In his early years at UCLA, Garfinkel continued to think about social rules and norms, and to test his own conceptions of them against established sociological ideas. One key step occurred as Garfinkel was doing research for a project on jury deliberations and the interpersonal relationships involved in them. He realized that even in this intensely rule-driven setting, the concept of people acting according to established rules and norms often did not apply. Instead, he noticed, jurors tried to convince each other of what they considered common-sense insights, telling each other, for example, that "anyone can see" that a certain assertion was true. Garfinkel coined the term ethnomethodology to describe his new outlook in the late 1950s.

Garfinkel defined ethnomethodology as the study of common-sense knowledge. How, he asked, did ordinary individuals make sense of the social structures in which they lived? Garfinkel rejected the idea that they simply learned to apply social norms. Instead, he believed, such understanding developed as a result of negotiations between individuals in society. Prior to Garfinkel, sociologists had believed that everyday interactions were inherently almost random, and certainly not susceptible to detailed sociological study. Garfinkel set out to change that.

He devised a set of research techniques that collectively became known as breaching experiments, in which he and his students created situations in which ordinary social interactions were somehow violated. Then they would observe the steps the subjects involved would take to make sense of their unexpected new reality. In one experiment, a tic-tac-toe player placed by Garfinkel made marks on the lines of the board instead of within the squares. In another, Garfinkel's researchers pretended that they were guests in their own homes and recorded the reactions of family members. The depth of Garfinkel's influence is attested to by the fact that such experiments have come to be known as garfinkeling.

Never a prolific writer, Garfinkel summarized many of his ideas in a single book, *Studies in Ethnomethodology* (1967). That and other writings introduced key concepts of ethnomethodology, including reflexivity, accounts, and indexicality. Garfinkel defined reflexivity as the process in which social groups create their own reality through their thoughts and actions. It refers to the fact that society evolves through group interactions rather than through the imposition of external rules. Accounts are the explanations of social situations that individuals give to each other. By indexicality Garfinkel meant the meaning of social relationships in the context of a specific setting.

Wrote in Difficult, Abstract Style

The abstractness of these terms was typical of the difficulty of Garfinkel's ideas. Reviewing Garfinkel's book *Toward a Sociological Theory of Information,* M. Oromaner wrote in *Choice: Current Reviews for Academic Libraries* that the book was "likely to pose some difficulty to readers, which will likely restrict it to specialists in the development of Garfinkel's contributions." His prose style has largely limited the audience for his writings to professional sociologists, although as a teacher he was charismatic and accessible.

Despite the difficulty of Garfinkel's ideas, their influence in 20th-century thought in the social sciences has been significant. Partly this was due to the way Garfinkel reached across disciplines and created ideas that were relevant to multiple disciplines in addition to sociology. His ideas were read and used by scholars in the fields of philosophy, linguistics, cognitive science, and artificial intelligence. Garfinkel's view of social interaction as essentially being built from the bottom up, from the negotiations of ordinary individuals, dovetailed well with the efforts of scholars in other fields to distance themselves from the view that social institutions and power structures are essentially imposed from above by the powerful. Garfinkel's writings were addressed by prominent European intellectuals such as Pierre Bourdieu and Jürgen Habermas, although they did not entirely concur with his ideas.

Garfinkel remained active after his retirement from UCLA, continuing to contribute articles to scholarly journals and to collect them into books under his own name as well as collections edited by others. Two of those books were *Seeing Sociologically: The Routine Grounds of Social Action* (2006) and *Toward a Sociological Theory of Information* (2008), which brought together many of Garfinkel's early writings. Garfinkel married Arlene Steinbach in 1945, and the couple raised a daughter, Leah Hertz, and a son, Mark Garfinkel. He died of congestive heart failure at home, in Pacific Palisades, California, on April 21, 2011.

Books

Heritage, John, *Garfinkel and Ethnomethodology,* Polity, 1991.
World of Sociology, Gale, 2001.

Periodicals

Choice: Current Reviews for Academic Libraries, July 2009.
Guardian (London, England), July 14, 2011.
Los Angeles Times, May 4, 2011.
New York Times, May 9, 2011.□

Edmund Berry Godfrey

The death of English magistrate Edmund Berry Godfrey (1621–1678) remains one of Britain's oldest unsolved crimes. A justice of the peace officer for a district in London, Godfrey was found dead in a ditch near Primrose Hill on an October night in 1678, at a time when enmity between Protestants and Roman Catholics in England was intensifying. His death is tied to the so-called "Popish Plot" that supposedly involved a plan to reunite the Anglican church with the Church in Rome.

Born on December 23, 1621, Edmund Berry Godfrey came from a prosperous family in Kent. His father was Thomas Godfrey, who owned a parcel of land called Hodiford Farm and served in the troubled Short Parliament of 1640, whose three-week tenure was one of the events leading up to the English Civil War and the beheading of King Charles I in 1649. Among the charges against the king were plotting with Britain's enemies, particularly the staunchly Roman Catholic kingdoms of Spain and France, to remain on the English throne despite widespread domestic opposition to his policies.

Antipathy between Protestant sects and those who had remained faithful to the Roman Catholic church had raged for nearly a century in Britain before Godfrey's birth, beginning with King Henry VIII's break with Rome in the 1530s. Henry forced his subjects to swear an oath of allegiance to him as head of the English church, and this marginalized the remaining Roman Catholic population, whose spiritual obedience was to the pope in Rome, not the English monarch. Later in the sixteenth century there were bitter battles over the throne among Henry's heirs. King Charles's grandmother was Mary Stuart, a staunch Roman Catholic also known as Mary, Queen of Scots, who plotted against Henry's daughter, Queen Elizabeth I, and was executed in 1587.

Entered Oxford

Such was the atmosphere and enmity between the two religious camps, a split that had also sparked wars across the European continent during Godfrey's youth. As the son of an elite, landowning family, Godfrey was raised in the Anglican faith, but in his adulthood he had Roman Catholic friends and was not biased or hostile to the "Papists," as English Protestants derisively called them. Godfrey attended an elite boys' academy in London, Westminster School, and from there went on to Christ Church College of Oxford University. Historians know that his plans for a career in law were cut short by his increasing difficulties with his hearing as a young man, which forced him to drop out of his studies at Gray's Inn.

Godfrey came from a large family. He was a product of his father's second marriage to a woman named Sarah Isles Godfrey, and the seventh son out of a total of 18 children. He first went into business with a man named James Harrison, probably the husband of one of his sisters, as a woodmonger and coal merchant in London. Their business was at Greene's Lane, a now-vanished street beneath the Charing Cross train station, but later Godfrey set up his own wharfside enterprise at Hartshorn Lane, which later became Northumberland Avenue. Hartshorn Lane ran directly to the Thames and was located in the City of Westminster, one of several London districts that had limited local governance.

Became Influential Merchant

Godfrey was often described as a curious figure, prone to occasional bouts of melancholy. Unmarried, he lived in an adjacent house on Hartshorn Lane with a maid named Elizabeth Curtis and Henry More, his business secretary. Two of his brothers, Michael and Benjamin, also lived in London and were successful merchants. Godfrey rose to become Master of the Woodmongers' Company and was appointed a justice of the peace for the City of Westminster in 1658. This was a position of some prestige and power, and even during the Interregnum period following the beheading of Charles I the local magistrates wielded police and prosecutorial power in their districts, and had the authority to order arrests and hear cases.

The Stuart throne was restored in 1661 with the ascension of Charles II, son of the beheaded king and his French Catholic wife, Henrietta Maria. Charles II chose a foreign bride, too, in the form of Catherine of Braganza, a Portuguese princess. She, too, was Roman Catholic and her term as queen consort was nearly as disastrous as her mother-in-law's had been. Powerful forces allied against the king and attempted to drum up opposition by focusing on Queen Catherine and her "foreign" ways. Godfrey would be inadvertently drawn into this drama and his death would become a rallying cry to rid England of its Roman Catholic population, whose patriotism to their sovereign was deemed insufficient.

Did Not Flee Great Plague

London endured two major catastrophes in the 1660s. The first was the Great Plague of 1665, an outbreak of bubonic plague that struck down about 15 percent of the London population. At the time, public health remedies amounted to little more than ordering the home of a plague victim to be quarantined, with a seal over the door and a guard posted to keep the occupants inside. Commerce came to a halt and bodies piled up by the thousands. Godfrey was commended for remaining at his post as justice of the peace in the City of Westminster district. In one incident, a graverobber had dug up a mass grave and removed the winding sheets to resell. The man was chased to a house, but Godfrey's constables, fearful of falling ill from contact, refused to enter the address. Godfrey entered it himself and took the graverobber into custody.

A year later, disaster stuck London again with the Great Fire of 1666. It began at a bakery on Pudding Lane in the City of London district, and destroyed large sections of the oldest part of the city, which dated back to the Roman Empire's conquest of Britain 16 centuries before. This time, casualties were fewer, but the conflagration was blamed on foreigners and vengeful Roman Catholics. Again, Godfrey was lauded for his heroic efforts, though he suffered financial losses to his businesses. He was knighted by Charles II later in 1666.

Though the Restoration era of Charles II was a solid attempt at mending the political divide—especially regarding questions of religious freedom and the powers of the throne versus parliament—opposition to Charles and his Catholic queen consort continued. One example was the Green Ribbon Club, a loose-knit group that met regularly at the Swan Tavern coffeehouse in London. During Godfrey's time, some of the Green Ribbon adherents—taking their name from the green ribbons once worn by the radical Levellers of the English Civil War era—worked to undermine Charles's moderate approach to Roman Catholicism in the Kingdom of Great Britain and Ireland. The more fanatical opponents spread rumors that the king was plotting to seek the aid of his wife's family connections and reunite the English Church with the one in Rome.

Drawn into "Popish" Conspiracies

A troublemaker named Titus Oates was tied to the Popish Plot, as this series of events became known. Oates made several increasingly alarming claims. He said that while visiting a college in France run by one of the Roman Catholic Church's most tightly organized religious orders, the Society of Jesus, or Jesuits, he heard rumors of various schemes, including one that involved the death by poison of Charles. This would spark an uprising of Roman Catholics in England and Ireland, which would then be aided by armies from France and Spain.

Oates divulged this information in August of 1678, then gave testimony to Godfrey in his capacity as a justice of the peace twice in September, each time with another witness, Israel Tonge, in sworn affadavits. Charles ordered an investigation, which discovered little merit to the claims, save for the fact that an English Catholic named Edward Colman, who served as secretary to Charles's sister-in-law the Duchess of York, had corresponded with a Jesuit priest with ties to the French court. Colman was arrested, tried, convicted, and put to death on December 3, 1678.

Godfrey, who knew Colman, was already dead by then. On October 12, 1678, he left his house in Hartshorn Lane and was observed walking north to Oxford Street. Rumors of his disappearance began almost immediately that same day when he failed to turn up at a scheduled lunch engagement. London was captivated by the drama of the missing magistrate, and five days later his body was found in a muddy ditch near Primrose Hill in north London, impaled on his own sword. Curiously, there was an absence of blood around the wound, and Godfrey's shoes were unmuddied—leading to the assumption that he had been killed elsewhere and his body dumped there. Nor was it deemed a robbery, for he still had a sum of money on him and some jewelry. A coroner's inquest found marks around his neck and evidence that he had been strangled and his neck broken.

Funeral Became Protest March

Godfrey's mysterious death was immediately tied to the Popish Plot because of his handling of the affadavits. His body was laid out for public viewing and his funeral was a massive event, delayed until October 31. "Those who saw the corpse apparently went away distressed and 'inflamed,'" wrote Alan Marshall in a *History Today* essay. "Gilbert Burnet, who himself made a visit, was to later note that this unofficial lying-instate, possibly organised by Michael Godfrey, had the desired effect of sharpening 'men's spirits', leading to fears that the already confused and enraged London mob would precipitate a massacre of the Catholics in the city." A prominent London vicar and future Bishop of Winchester, William Lloyd, delivered an inflammatory sermon at the funeral that warned about the dangers of religious tolerance in so divided a kingdom.

A man named William Bedloe claimed to have seen Godfrey's body at Somerset House, the palace in London sometimes used by Charles's wife, Catherine, and her Roman Catholic courtiers. Bedloe claimed another man named Miles Prance was also there. Arrested on December 21, Prance was a Roman Catholic silversmith who had done work at Somerset House, and he testified that three Roman Catholics with ties to the queen were the murderers: Robert Green, Henry Berry, and Lawrence Hill. The trio was arrested, but Prance recanted his testimony before the trial, then reversed his recantation. Green, Berry, and Hill were found guilty of Godfrey's murder and hanged at Primrose Hill in February of 1679. For years this parklike part of London was called Greenberry Hill in reference to their deaths.

Godfrey's death incited enmity toward Roman Catholics in England. An annual demonstration every November 17—the date of Queen Elizabeth I's accession—was held in which Godfrey's murder was reenacted and effigies of the pope were burned. Scores of publications and even mementos with his image appeared for those who firmly believed in the treachery of English Catholics. The Popish Plot came to encircle five Roman Catholic lords, who were jailed in the Tower of London and targeted by impeachment proceedings; one was beheaded after a guilty verdict on the treason charge. One of the most enduring consequences of the hysteria surrounding Godfrey's death was the Second Test Act, enacted at the end of 1678. It barred Roman Catholics from holding a seat in the House of Lords or the House of Commons, and remained in effect until 1829.

Books

Long, James, and Ben Long, *The Plot against Pepys,* Faber & Faber, 2012.

Stroud, Angus, *Stuart England,* Routledge, 2002.

Periodicals

History Today, March 1997.□

Beate Gordon

Austrian-born Beate Sirota Gordon (1923–2012) spent decades promoting Asian culture, especially the performing arts, in the United States. After a childhood spent in Japan, Gordon became a naturalized U.S. citizen and was one of the first civilians permitted to reenter Japan in the aftermath of World War II. Much later in life, Gordon was revealed to have authored two important articles of Japan's 1947 Constitution: the first secured important legal rights for Japanese women—an historic first—and the second addressed civil rights matters, prohibiting discriminatory laws and practices.

Born on October 25, 1923, in Vienna, Austria, Beate Sirota was raised in a household in which classical music exerted a strong influence. Her mother, Augustine Horenstein Sirota, was the sister of conductor Jascha Horenstein, who gained fame with the Berlin and Vienna Philharmonic orchestras in the 1920s. The Horensteins were of Ukrainian Jewish heritage, as was the family of Gordon's father Leo Sirota, a highly regarded pianist who also emerged as a rising talent in German-speaking Europe after World War I. In 1929, after her father made a successful concert tour of Japan, he was invited to become head of piano faculty at the Imperial Academy of Music in Tokyo. Gordon, an only child, settled with her parents in the Nogizaka district of Tokyo and quickly picked up Japanese as her second language, adding it to the German she spoke at home.

Entered College at 16

Gordon was installed at a private school in Tokyo for the children of German diplomats and business executives. At age 12, however, her parents reacted to the school's increasingly politicized curriculum—a shift tied to the rise of Adolf Hitler's anti-Semitic Nazi Party in Germany in 1933—and enrolled her instead at the American School of Tokyo. As a teenager, she was surprised at the differences between young women from foreign families like her own, who could plan to go on to college or train for a profession, and her Japanese friends from middle-class households, who learned flower-arranging and other traditional arts in preparation for an early marriage arranged by their families. The Imperial

Kyodo/Newscom

Academy where her father taught, for example, did not even permit women to enroll.

Gordon left Japan at a fortuitous time, thanks in part to an accelerated completion of her high-school graduation requirements and admission to Mills College, a prestigious women's school in Oakland, California. She was 16 years old when she parted from her parents in Tokyo in 1939, and settled in the San Francisco Bay Area, but there was tremendous unease on both sides of the Pacific Ocean: Japan's fiercely imperialist and increasingly militarized regime had allied with Nazi Germany, which was at war against England and on the verge of forcibly occupying most of Europe. Gordon was devastated by Japan's surprise attack on the U.S. naval installation at Pearl Harbor, Hawaii, on December 7, 1941. Within hours, the United States joined the Allied Powers' fight against the Axis coalition of Germany, Japan, and Italy.

Fretted Over Parents for Years

Because of World War II, Gordon was unable to contact her parents or receive word about their whereabouts for nearly four years. Her fluency in Japanese, however, was of use to the United States Office of War Information, and Mills College administrators granted her a special leave from her classes while she worked in San Francisco at a U.S. military facility monitoring radio broadcasts from Tokyo. She also worked for the War Office's Foreign Broadcast Information Service, writing and delivering special radio broadcasts transmitted to Japan in which the United States exhorted clandestine listeners in Japan to overthrow the imperial regime that had led them into a disastrous world war.

In 1943, Gordon earned her undergraduate degree and continued to work for the Office of War Information, and she also was employed at *Time* magazine. In January of 1945, she became a naturalized U.S. citizen, and in May of that year the Allied forces declared victory in Europe against a defeated Nazi Germany. The war against Japan in the Pacific Rim dragged on, however, and U.S. troops were readying for a major land-sea invasion of the Japanese island nation. In August of 1945, the United States launched a surprise attack of their own, dropping two newly developed atomic weapons on the cities of Hiroshima and Nagasaki, which resulted in a conflagration and devastation on a catastrophic scale in both cities. Fearful of a third attack that would target Tokyo, Japanese officials agreed to an unconditional surrender, and U.S. troops moved quickly to de-arm and occupy a defeated Japanese nation.

One of the most famous U.S. military leaders of the war, General of the Army Douglas MacArthur, was appointed Supreme Commander for the Allied Powers (SCAP) in Occupied Japan. Gordon applied for and was approved for a slot as translator on his Political Affairs staff. That allowed her to travel to Japan, and on December 24, 1945, she was the first American civilian woman allowed to enter Japan after the end of World War II. She flew to Atsugi Airport, near the port city of Yokohama, and made her way to Tokyo. Her first attempt to locate her parents—a visit to their last known address—revealed just a single pillar, charred from a fire that engulfed the quarter during the nine-month bombardment of the city by U.S. aerial forces. She finally found them, alive but emaciated, at their summer home in Karuizawa, a nearby summer resort.

Became Trusted Translator

MacArthur's mission was to dismantle the Japanese military, oversee a large influx of foreign aid to help the Japanese economy rebuild, and establish a democratic form of government. He and other senior officers worked to recruit Japanese political figures whose wartime service was not tarnished and could be therefore be permitted to participate in a transition government. The future role of Japan's revered leader, Emperor Hirohito, was the subject of much debate. MacArthur appointed a former cabinet official from the 1930s, Joji Matsumoto, as a minister without portfolio in charge of drafting a new post-war constitution to replace Japan's 1889 Meiji Constitution. Matsumoto presented to MacArthur a first and then a second draft, both of which MacArthur deemed unsatisfactory. The famously autocratic American commander then summoned two trusted, high-ranking aides at his General Headquarters (GHQ) and ordered them to write an entirely new document.

Both Brigadier General Courtney Whitney and Lieutenant Colonel Milo Rowell were law-school graduates and legal affairs specialists. They, in turn, chose a group of 24 at MacArthur's GHQ, and Gordon was the sole woman included. It was Whitney who "called us in and said, 'Ladies and gentlemen, you are now a constitutional assembly and you will now write a new draft of the Japanese Constitution, and it has to be done in seven days,'" Gordon told *New York Times* journalist James Brooke years later. "We were stunned." They were also sworn to secrecy. The final draft, after long negotiations with Japanese officials, was presented to the public as having been based on a "template" provided by MacArthur's GHQ/SCAP. Only years later was it revealed that Gordon and others had actually written the Articles of Japan's Constitution of 1947.

Fluent in English, Japanese, German, French, and even Russian, Gordon's multilingual skills served her well. Assigned to the subcommittee for civil rights, she took a Jeep and drove to libraries she remembered from her long-ago decade in pre-war Tokyo. Some were still standing, and some had books with copies of the constitutions of other nations, which she read to give herself a crash course on the governance of democratic societies. She drafted Article 14, which guaranteed equality under the law regardless of sex, race, creed, or social status. It also outlawed a feudal-era peerage, barring titles of nobility and political or economic privileges associated with them.

"Miss Sirota's Heart Is Set"

Gordon remembered the sharply curtailed lives of her teenaged friends in Japan of the 1930s, who were expected to fulfill roles as wives and mothers and had almost no legal or political rights under the Meiji Constitution. With this in mind she drafted Article 24, which prohibited forced marriage and introduced basic civil rights for women in Japan. "With regard to choice of spouse, property rights, inheritance, choice of domicile, divorce and other matters pertaining to marriage and the family," Article 24 states, according to the Web site of the Prime Minister of Japan, "laws shall be enacted from the standpoint of individual dignity and the essential equality of the sexes."

MacArthur delivered the draft constitution to senior Japanese officials on February 13, 1946, and Gordon was present at the Steering Committee as MacArthur's translator as negotiations ensued. There was opposition, she recalled, even from some of her American colleagues. One of them was Lieutenant Colonel Charles L. Kades, who huffed, "My God, you have given Japanese women more rights than in the American Constitution," Gordon recalled him saying, according to the 2005 *New York Times* article by Brooke. "I said, 'Colonel Kades, that's not very difficult to do, because women are not in the American Constitution.'" In the end, it was Kades who pressed her case when the Japanese politicians balked, telling them that "'Miss Sirota's heart is set on this,'" reported the *Economist,* though he did not mention that she herself had written it. "But during the previous 14 hours of debates, the young American woman had won the gratitude of the Japanese leaders for backing them in previous disagreements with the Americans," wrote Brooke in the *New York Times,* and in the end both Articles 14 and 24 were left in the document.

The outline of the Constitution of Japan was publicly revealed on March 6, 1946. On April 10, 1946, Japanese women went to the polls for the first time in the nation's history to cast their votes. They chose representatives for a new Diet, or National Assembly, which approved the Constitution of Japan in October of that year. Emperor Hirohito signed it into law on November 3, 1946, and it went into effect six months from that date, on May 3, 1947. For both critics and champions of the Constitution of Japan, the document's most notable paragraph is Article 9, in which Japan formally renounced war.

Promoted Asian Arts

Gordon went back to United States with her parents in 1947, and a year later married one of her GHQ/SCAP colleagues, Lieutenant Joseph Gordon. They had two children and in 1954 Gordon became director of student programs for the Japan Society of New York. In this role she welcomed Japanese students studying at U.S. colleges and universities. One of them was performance artist/musician Yoko Ono, who later married ex-Beatle John Lennon and became a longtime friend of Gordon and her family. In 1958, the Japan Society invited Gordon to become its director of performing arts, and she worked to bring Japanese drama and dance to the United States. In 1970, she took the same post with the Asia Society, and remained there for the next two decades. This job allowed her to travel extensively throughout many parts of Asia, seeking out authentic folk traditions, and it was through Gordon's persistence and persuasion that American audiences were exposed to new sights and sounds, such as Vietnamese puppet shows and gamelan music from Bali.

In the 1970s, Gordon and others who had been involved in the drafting of the Constitution of Japan began to reveal their roles in its development. She became a revered figure among women's-rights advocates in Japan and her life story was chronicled in documentary films and even a play. She delivered her version of events in a 1997 memoir, *The Only Woman in the Room.* Her husband of 64 years died in August of 2012 at age 93, and Gordon succumbed to pancreatic cancer four months later at age 89 on December 30, 2012, in New York City. "The women of Japan," she told *Japan Times* contributor Roger Pulvers, "have done extremely well. They have gone to court; many have been elected not only to the Diet but to local legislatures; they are really peace-loving and ready to fight for peace."

Periodicals

Economist, January 12, 2013.

Independent (London, England), January 18, 2013.

Japan Times (Tokyo, Japan), January 13, 2013.

New York Times, May 28, 2005; January 2, 2013.

Times (London, England), January 14, 2013.

Online

"The Constitution of Japan," Prime Minister of Japan Web site, http://www.kantei.go.jp/foreign/constitution_and_government_of_japan/constitution_e.html (February 3, 2014). □

Danny Greene

American mobster Danny Greene (1933–1977) engaged in a years-long battle against fellow northeast Ohio racketeers in the 1970s that the national media dubbed the Cleveland Mob Wars. A fiercely proud Irish-American, ex-labor union official, and federal informant, Greene sought to wrest control of Cleveland's lucrative gambling and illegal-drugs operations from Italian American syndicates. Nonfiction accounts of his life, which ended by a car bomb, became the basis for the 2011 film *Kill the Irishman.* Greene's death ultimately brought down several members of New York's Five Families.

© Bettmann/Corbis

Danny Greene had a rough early life marked by loss and neglect. Born at a Cleveland Roman Catholic hospital to a recently married pair of 20-year olds on November 14, 1933, Daniel John Patrick Greene never knew his mother, who died just days after his birth from a heart condition. Greene's father sank into depression and alcoholism, and for a time lived with his recently widowed father, a printing-press operator, in Cleveland's Collinwood neighborhood. Neither were able to adequately care for him, and the infant was handed over to a local orphanage. When Greene was six, his father remarried and retrieved him from the home, but his new stepmother disliked him and he ran away several times. He eventually wound up back with his grandfather, who worked the night shift at a newspaper plant. As a result, Greene often turned up unwashed and hungry at St. Jerome's, his parochial school.

Rose to Dockworkers' Union Boss

Greene struggled to stay on the right side of the law as a youth. He loved the structure of school and was a solid athlete, but struggled to pass his grades. The nuns showed charity by feeding him and helping guide him toward St. Ignatius High School, where he played sports but was ultimately expelled for fighting. Collinwood was home to many ethnic groups, but there was a longstanding animosity between Irish American and Italian American youths, and Greene loathed the latter group and continued to engage in turf battles and fisticuffs. After he was kicked out of St. Ignatius, Greene took advantage of a chance to leave town by enlisting in the U.S. Marine Corps in 1951. Stationed at Camp Lejeune, North Carolina, he rose to the rank of corporal, trained new recruits on the artillery range, and was honorably discharged in 1953.

After returning to Cleveland, Greene took a job as a dockworker at Cleveland's busy port on Lake Erie, into which the Cuyahoga River emptied. Massive amounts of copper, iron ore, and other resources were extracted from mines in the northern Great Lakes region and loaded onto freighters that set sail for ports serving industrial and manufacturing hubs like Detroit, Pittsburgh, and beyond. From Cleveland some vessels went south to Akron, the center of U.S. rubber production for decades. Greene entered the field in the mid-1950s, when local and federal officials sought to end the notorious union corruption as depicted in *On the Waterfront,* the title of 1954 drama that starred Marlon Brando and won the Academy Award for Best Film.

Greene married and began a family while rising through the ranks of the International Longshoremen's Association (ILA), one of the oldest labor unions in the United States. In Cleveland, as elsewhere, the dock businesses had illicit ties to both the union leadership and organized crime. Ambitious and shrewd, Greene emerged as the local boss of the Cleveland port when he won the presidency of the ILA local in the early 1960s. He made several enemies along the way, and a series of newspaper stories in the Cleveland *Plain Dealer* exposing the dockworkers' union practices resulted in his ouster in 1964. Charged with embezzling union funds, Greene beat that conviction and narrowly escaped prison on a second charge of falsifying union records.

Formed the Celtic Club

It was reportedly around this time that Greene entered into an arrangement with the local Federal Bureau of Investigation (FBI) office to become an informant. The FBI had long sought to end the control of organized-crime syndicates across the United States, and a network of informers was part of the strategy to collect evidence on mob bosses who controlled municipal union and construction contracts but also profited handsomely from gambling rackets, prostitution, and illegal drugs. Though nearly every ethnic group in American history had their own organized-crime racket, it was the ruthless and well-organized southern Italians in the New York City area who gained enormous power and influence during the Prohibition era. Referred to as La Cosa Nostra (Our Thing) or more informally as the Mafia, the five major crime families in New York City had ties to organized crime rackets all the way from the Tri-State area to Ohio, the West Coast, and even Las Vegas.

Greene was famous for branding himself as Cleveland's most patriotic Gaelic son. When he moved into the ILA office, he had it repainted green and ordered green carpeting. He wore green suits, drove a green car, and handed out promotional pens with green ink. Long resentful of the hold that Italian American cabals had on lucrative gaming and union rackets, Greene read books on Irish history and trumpeted his Celtic origins. Though he often declared his enmity toward Italian Americans, he entered into partnerships with a few of them as a way to gain entrance into Cleveland's rackets, which had been in the hands of the associates of the Licavoli family for decades. He also worked for Alex "Shondor" Burns, a Hungarian Jewish mobster who had long ties to the Licavoli family and its associates.

In the early 1970s, Greene tried to gain control of the garbage-collection routes and waste-disposal business, another union-and-mob profit center. He engaged in a long battle with Mike "Big Mike" Frato, and at one point sent his longtime confidante, Arthur Sneperger, to wire the bomb on Frato's car. Greene apparently detonated it too early and Sneperger was killed. Years later, records show that Greene had learned that Sneperger had just given an account to the Cleveland Police Department, and probably planned to kill his friend. Rumors of his personal ruthlessness made Greene a feared figure in Cleveland.

By this point Greene had separated from his wife and children and was living back in the Collinwood area. A health fanatic, he liked to jog near the Lake Erie waterfront at a park known as White City Beach. One day in November of 1971 Greene was shot at from a distance, and he ducked, pulled out his own weapon, and fired back, though he could not see his assailant. He later told reporters it had been a lucky shot to have hit Frato in the head, killing him instantly.

Took Out Birns

Greene was popular in working-class, transitional Collinwood. He handed out free frozen turkeys to the poor on Thanksgiving and paid tuition and medical bills for those in need. When a motorcycle gang took up residence on one street and the noise level went up considerably, Greene turned up at their property holding a lit stick of dynamite as a threat. His official business was Emerald Industrial Relations, a labor "consulting" firm. Its aim was to cut legitimate deals with general contractors building skyscrapers and other projects in Cleveland, which was attempting to revitalize its downtown and waterfront. If a company balked at hiring Emerald as workforce consultants, the job site would suddenly be plagued by workers calling in sick and a delay in material deliveries.

Cleveland's Mob Wars began with a dispute between Greene and Shondor Birns. Greene wanted to open his own "cheat spot," a gambling den and unlicensed bar. He asked Birns for a loan, and Birns arranged it through New York associates. Birns also wanted a protégé of his named Billy Cox in on the cheat-spot revenues. Greene did not trust Cox, an instinct that proved correct when Cox was sent as a courier to pick up the $75,000 loan and instead used it to make a major cocaine purchase, which he planned to dilute and resell for enormous profit. The inexperienced Cox was targeted by police and dumped the drugs, and Birns was left indebted to the Gambinos, one of New York's powerful Five Families. Birns pressured Greene for repayment of the money anyway, which was an affront to Greene, as he claimed he was not liable for a loan he had never received in the first place.

On March 29, 1975, Birns was leaving a burlesque bar at 2515 Detroit Avenue in Cleveland when a massive bomb blew his body into pieces. Six weeks later, an explosion rocked the Collinwood apartment building that Greene had bought; he and his girlfriend ran into the kitchen, where they slid down into the rubble alongside the refrigerator as the floor collapsed. This second, high-profile attempt on Greene's life made him a local legend, and he proclaimed himself the target of the Cleveland mob. He erected a trailer on the property and sat outside, shirtless and sunbathing, under an enormous Irish flag, proclaiming to the local news media who came to interview him that anyone who wanted to kill him knew where to find him.

Cleveland Dubbed "Bomb City"

By 1976, James Licavoli, known to most by the alias "Jack White," was the acting capo, or boss, of the Cleveland branch of La Cosa Nostra. One of Licavoli's foes was another Italian mobster named John Nardi, and Nardi allied with Greene to decapitate the senior leadership of the Cleveland mob. Car bombs like the one used to kill Birns were the weapon of choice, and Greene regularly switched vehicles with his underlings and almost never entered a car without checking under the hood first. More than 30 homemade explosive devices went off in the Cleveland metropolitan area in a single year, prompting an influx of U.S. Bureau of Alcohol, Tobacco, and Firearms (ATF) agents to work with federal and local law-enforcement officials to quell the turf war. Nardi was killed by a car bomb on May 17, 1977.

Licavoli and his plan to "kill the Irishman" involved a West Coast operator named Jimmy "the Weasel" Fratianno. They paid Fratianno to recruit a hitman from Erie, Pennsylvania, named Raymond Ferritto. He and a Licavoli associate from Youngstown, Ohio, named Ronald Carabbia planned the hit on Greene after a phone tap revealed he had a dentist appointment on October 6, 1977. They hollowed out the door panel of a maroon Chevy Nova, drove it to the medical building parking lot, and waited for Greene, who was late and parked, as was his habit, between two other cars.

By luck, one of the adjacent cars left shortly afterward, and the Nova was moved next to the 1976 Lincoln Continental Greene was driving that day. Greene had a filling replaced and went out to his car. An eyewitness at a traffic intersection recalled letting Ferritto's blue Plymouth sedan pass and noticed a man was sitting in its back seat intently looking at something in his hand while glancing toward the parking lot just before the explosion. The bomb that detonated blew Greene to pieces and seared one piece of his jewelry, a distinctive Celtic cross, into the asphalt.

The witness identified Ferritto as the driver, and police were able to link his license plates to the exploded Nova. Ferritto "sung," in mob parlance—giving up names of other associates, and Carabbia went to prison for the Greene hit. Fratianno also rolled, entering the federal witness protection program after cutting deals with prosecutors to reveal other mob secrets. Licavoli was convicted on federal anti-racketeering statutes in 1982. The Cleveland FBI investigation had a domino effect: the information obtained led to wiretap authorizations and increased surveillance on mob figures. In 1980, the feds taped a conversation between Licavoli's successor as Cleveland boss, Angelo Lonardo, and another figure. "Big Ange," as he was known, was indicted and then gave testimony that helped bring down New York's Genovese family. In the end, Genovese associates fingered other Mafia associates in exchange for leniency, and the power of New York's Five Families—the Gambino, Genovese, Colombo, Lucchese, and Bonanno families—was sharply curtailed.

Books

Porrello, Rick, *To Kill the Irishman: The War That Crippled the Mafia,* Next Hat Press, 1998.

Periodicals

Cleveland Magazine, August 1978.
New York Times, October 2, 1977; February 22, 1983.□

Richard Grenville

English adventurer Richard Grenville (1542–1591) was one of the ruthless "Sea Dogs" of the Elizabethan Age. A wealthy landowner with political influence, he crossed the Atlantic Ocean on several voyages and was part of the first attempt to establish a permanent British settlement in North America on Roanoke Island. Of all his storied exploits, Grenville is perhaps best known for dying in battle against the mighty Spanish Armada as his single vessel attempted to fend off more than 50 enemy ships.

© North Wind Picture Archives/Alamy

Richard Grenville was born in June of 1542 in the final years of the reign of King Henry VIII, the controversial, oft-married Tudor ruler. The Grenvilles were a family of landed gentry whose title dated back to the 1200s, and their service to the Crown reached even further back into English history as allies of William the Conqueror, the leader of the Norman Conquest of Britain in 1066. Their estates were in Devonshire and Cornwall, both in the southwestern section of England. Grenville was born in Bideford, a seaside town in Devon, and was named for his grandfather, Richard Grenville, who for years had served as the Marshal of Calais, the last remaining English fort on French soil.

Killed Another in Gang Fight

As the first-born son, Grenville was to inherit the family title and lands. His father Roger Grenville was an enthusiastic participant in Henry VIII's growing Royal Navy and captained the fleet's flagship, an enormous Tudor-era warship called the *Mary Rose.* When England was attacked by France near the Isle of Wight in July of 1545, the *Mary Rose* engaged with the enemy but made a swift tack that caused water to flood into the open gunports on one side. The heavily armed vessel capsized and sank in the Portsmouth harbor in one of England's deadliest naval disasters. Roger Grenville was among the *Mary Rose* casualties.

Grenville's mother Thomasine eventually remarried an Arundell, scion of another well-born family from the counties and shires of Devon and Cornwall. The Arundells also had connections at court, and through the second marriage

Grenville became a distant cousin of Walter Raleigh, one of the Elizabethan Age's most legendary figures and a man whose exploits occasionally crossed the line into criminal behavior. Grenville was of a similar temperament: he was sent to London at age 17 to study law at one of the four Inns of Court, which train and certify barristers to practice law in England, but at age 20 was involved in a street brawl between two groups of youth on the Strand, a main thoroughfare of the capital. The November of 1562 fracas ended when Grenville's sword delivered a fatal slice to a man named Robert Bannister, who died of his wounds. Grenville was arrested and jailed, but was fortunate to win a pardon by Queen Elizabeth I. Several months later, he returned to Bideford to assume his title and lands, which passed to him on his twenty-first birthday.

In 1565, Grenville married Mary St. Leger, daughter of a prominent family with venerable roots dating back to the Norman Conquest era. A year later, Grenville and his half-brother, Alexander Arundell, are recorded as having fought as mercenary soldiers in Hungary against an Ottoman Empire invasion of Central Europe that was successfully repelled. Following that, Grenville went to Ireland, to County Cork on the south coastline, with Warham St. Leger, a relative by marriage.

Fought in Ireland

Grenville arrived in Ireland as the newly appointed Sheriff for Cork and quickly became embroiled in a local dispute known as the Desmond Rebellion. This was the first of two uprisings against Queen Elizabeth's rule and named for its ringleader, James Fitzmaurice Fitzgerald, heir to the Anglo-Irish Earldom of Desmond. The conflict was over land rights and local rule, but had a religious element, too, as Anglo-Irish nobles chose to maintain their allegiance to the Roman Catholic Church and resisted the imposition of Protestantism. Grenville was a staunch Protestant and fierce opponent of anything Papist, as those who maintained their allegiance to Rome were called. Henry VIII's break with the Church in Rome had been momentous, but it was the actions of each of his daughters that inspired religious violence. Mary I restored Catholicism, but her successor Elizabeth outlawed the faith and priests who celebrated Mass in private homes were subject to the most debasing form of capital punishment, to be drawn and quartered.

Back in London, Grenville was involved in various intrigues at Elizabeth's court, which had a surfeit of well-born and politically connected men competing to win the unmarried queen's favor. He sat for Cornwall in the House of Commons and in 1576 was appointed High Sheriff of this corner of England, a peninsula with vital strategic importance to English shipping and defense. As sheriff he arrested a Roman Catholic priest named Cuthbert Mayne, who had secretly converted and was suspected of involvement in a plot against the throne. Grenville led the house-to-house search for the fugitive Mayne and handed him over to authorities. The priest was sentenced to death later in 1577, becoming one of the English martyrs of the Roman Catholic pantheon of saints.

Grenville returned to Ireland to tamp down the Second Desmond Rebellion of 1579–83. For his role he was awarded one of the Plantations of the Province grants, which gave him the right to bring over English and Scottish families to settle lands in the southern part of Ireland that had been cleared of Gaelic inhabitants. He acquired an estate called Kinalmeaky and recruited settlers, but like many of the Plantations the colony failed and Elizabeth was finally forced to halt the program after reports of widespread human-rights abuses, including the killing of civilians.

Involved in Scheme for Virginia Colony

Walter Raleigh was among the other beneficiaries of confiscated Irish lands, and he and Grenville colluded to make their mark even further west. Raleigh had sent an exploratory mission to North America in 1584 that landed in present-day North Carolina. Indigenous peoples lived inland, and Raleigh believed the area was ripe for settlement and rich in major resources. There was also a push to gain a toehold in North America, for the Spanish and French had already established missions and trading posts elsewhere. Granted a charter from Elizabeth, Raleigh placed Grenville in command of five ships bound for Roanoke Island to establish a military colony. The flotilla left Plymouth, England, in April of 1585, but the ships were separated by an Atlantic storm. Grenville's ship, the *Tiger,* was blown off course and sailed for Puerto Rico, where he and the other captains had agreed to meet if separated. One vessel turned up after a few more weeks, and Grenville led it and his own to the Outer Banks of North Carolina, where two of the other five ships already were, in late June of 1585.

The expedition had already suffered costly setbacks, and Grenville decided to return to England for more supplies. An army officer named Ralph Lane was placed in charge of 107 men on Roanoke Island, but there were problems with the Croatan and Algonquian communities and it was a difficult winter. Grenville's planned return in the spring of 1586 was delayed, and the remaining colonists were discovered by another famous "Sea Dog," Francis Drake, who offered them passage back to England. When Grenville finally returned to Roanoke, he found it deserted and left behind a party of 15 men to stake England's claim.

Raleigh had recruited another boatload of settlers, who arrived to find Roanoke deserted of Grenville's men in July of 1587. That party also established themselves on Roanoke Island, but were left stranded for years when England went to war with Spain and transatlantic shipping was disrupted. The whereabouts of Grenville's party plus the 1587 Roanoke colonists remains one of history's most intriguing puzzles—some may have been killed by Native Americans, while others apparently fled inland or were taken captive, then intermarried with Native Americans and began families.

Return to Roanoke Delayed

In 1588, Grenville outfitted another Roanoke expedition, this one with seven ships, but when the queen received news that a Spanish invasion of England was imminent, all ships were ordered to remain at port. Grenville had already been placed in charge of defending Devon and Cornwall, and he sent some of the ships originally destined for Roanoke to instead defend Plymouth, a major port.

The Anglo-Spanish War preoccupied the last few years of Grenville's life. Grenville's friend Francis Drake was in charge of repelling the Spanish Armada, an enormous fleet of warships sent to invade the island and overthrow the Tudor queen. In mid-1588, the Spanish made a tactical error by opting against an attack on Plymouth, and instead the Armada were either harried by English fire ships, blockaded by England's Dutch allies, or blown off course by storms. A year later, Drake and other commanders attempted to set up a naval base in the Azores Islands, about 850 miles off the coast of Portugal. In 1591 Grenville arrived there with a massive galleon called, fittingly enough, the *H.M.S. Revenge.* The ship had seen much service already and was one of the most fearsome moving weapons in the English arsenal. Already an experienced privateer, Grenville was dispatched to the outpost of Flores, one of the remoter Azorean isles, to intercept the Spanish treasure ships, which brought gold, silver, and other riches from Spain's tightly guarded posts in Central and South America.

Like his father, Grenville took command of a well known ship and disaster occurred: on August 30, 1591, Spanish ships were sighted from Flores, one of the westernmost Azores Islands. But it was a much larger detachment than expected, and Grenville's superior, Thomas Howard, ordered a withdrawal. Livid, Grenville stayed with the *Revenge* and ordered his men to do as much damage as possible to the 53 Spanish ships that surrounded them. The Battle of Flores was a legendary 12 hour fight in which Grenville was gravely wounded. He ordered his men to blow up the ship with the last of its gunpowder rather than surrender to the enemy, but they disobeyed.

Grenville died of his wounds in early September of 1591, age 49, while in Spanish custody and fuming about the defeat to the very end. After he passed, the Spanish ships and their English sailors were hit by a fierce Atlantic storm on their way to the larger Azores Island of Terceira, and *Revenge* was one of the ships that sank. Grenville's actions in the Battle of Flores were immortalized by Alfred Lord Tennyson in his 1878 poem *The Revenge: A Ballad of the Fleet.* In it Tennyson repeats the lore of superstitious sailors, who maintained that Grenville's burial at sea caused the storm that wrecked the rest of the Spanish fleet in the Azores.

Grenville had four sons and his later descendants went on to positions of enormous influence, including the prime minister's office. Grenville's legacy remains the port of Bideford, which he developed from a small fishing village into a major harbor and dockworks capable of handling large cargo ships. Eventually Bideford became the center of tobacco importation from the Virginia Colony, which finally prospered when the settlement at Jamestown was established. He also built Buckland Abbey at Yelverton, Devon, as his family home. This was the site of a long-abandoned Cistercian abbey that dated back to the 1200s, but had lain in ruins for several decades by the time Grenville inherited it. He spent lavishly on its renovation, and it became a splendid example of Tudor decorative arts, especially its plaster-fresco work done by Devonshire artisans. Grenville later sold Buckland Abbey to Francis Drake, and it eventually passed to the United Kingdom's National Trust, which operates it as a tourist site.

Books

Rowse, A.L., *Sir Richard Grenville of the Revenge,* Faber & Faber, 1937, reprint, 2013.

Periodicals

Financial Times (London, England), June 28, 2003.

North Devon Gazette (Bideford, Devon, England), June 20, 2012.

Western Morning News (Cornwall, England), December 13, 2012.□

H

Marvin Hamlisch

The American composer, conductor, and pianist Marvin Hamlisch (1944–2012) was a prolific creator of film scores, popular songs, and musical events showcasing his frequent collaborator, vocalist Barbra Streisand.

Hamlisch was one of just two people in musical history (the other was Broadway composer Richard Rodgers) to have won a Pulitzer Prize and Academy, Emmy, Grammy, and Tony awards. The range of honors Hamlisch received indicated his versatility; though his main field of activity was the Hollywood film score, of which he wrote more than 30, he was also the composer of *A Chorus Line* (one of just three musicals in history to win the Pulitzer Prize) and of several evergreen popular song hits, including "The Way We Were." Hamlisch virtually reintroduced ragtime music to the public with his score for the 1973 film *The Sting,* and his film scores were notable for their musical variety and their intelligent, original matching of music to subject matter. Though more active as an orchestral pops conductor in his later years, Hamlisch remained creative and fresh over his long career. "He would pick up on conversations and words and ultimately use them in his music," recalled Pasadena Symphony executive Paul Jan Zdunek. "He was always absorbing everything around him."

Father Fled Nazism

Marvin Frederick Hamlisch was born in New York on June 2, 1944. His father, Max, was a Jewish accordionist who had fled Austria after its union with Nazi Germany; in New York, he led his own band and encouraged Marvin's budding musical talent. After Marvin, at the age of five, proved able not only to play on the piano songs he had heard on the radio but to transpose them into different keys, his parents dreamed of turning him into a classical piano virtuoso. At seven, he became the youngest student in the history of the prestigious Juilliard School of Music in New York. Hamlisch did well there but suffered from extreme stage fright. "Before every recital, I would violently throw up, lose weight, the veins on my hands would stand out," he said in an interview quoted by Rob Hoerburger in *The New York Times.* More than classical music, he enjoyed show tunes, which he played enthusiastically on his own time.

Hamlisch would remain at Juilliard for more than a decade, completing various programs and finally graduating in 1964. By that time he had already gotten his first big music-business break: singer Liza Minnelli, who was dating a friend of Hamlisch's, asked him to write some songs that she could record and package as a gift for her mother, actress Judy Garland. Hamlisch, with some help on lyrics from Howard Liebling, complied. Garland loved the songs, and the result was an invitation for Hamlisch to her 1960 holiday party. There he met the pioneering pop producer Quincy Jones, who connected Hamlisch's material with singer Lesley Gore. She had a top-15 hit with Hamlisch's "Sunshine, Lollipops, and Rainbows" in 1962.

Soon after that, Hamlisch made another valuable connection when he served as a rehearsal pianist for the 1964 musical *Funny Girl,* which starred Streisand. Their collaboration would last into the next century. During rehearsals, Hamlisch got another break: he was asked to perform at a party hosted by producer Sam Spiegel, who wanted to recruit a new composer for his challenging upcoming drama *The Swimmer* (1968). Hamlisch quickly

© Everett Collection Inc/Alamy

sketched out a theme and soon had his first film scoring assignment. In the words of Turner Classic Movies, "The haunting themes he created did much to enhance this character study about a wealthy advertising man ... confronting his disturbing past."

Wrote Streisand Hit

Foot firmly in the film-industry door, Hamlisch proceeded to show his impressive emotional range as a composer. He scored a pair of madcap early comedies by director-star Woody Allen, *Take the Money and Run* (1969) and *Bananas* (1971), as well as the drama *Kotch* (1971), which brought him his first Academy Award nomination for Best Original Song. Perhaps the highlight of Hamlisch's film career was his score for *The Way We Were,* which reunited him with Streisand. Both Hamlisch's title song and the soundtrack as a whole were major winners at the Academy and Grammy awards ceremonies in early 1974.

The year 1973 was an extremely productive one for Hamlisch, who in addition to *The Way We Were,* earned major awards for a second, and completely different, film score: his soundtrack for *The Sting,* a period caper tale starring Paul Newman and Robert Redford, sold more than three million copies. To match the film's early 20th century setting, Hamlisch turned to ragtime, a syncopated piano-based ancestor of jazz that until then had been mostly the province of jazz buffs and academics. With the score propelled by the catchy Scott Joplin piano rag "The Entertainer," ragtime experienced a major revival.

A still greater Hamlisch triumph, the stage musical *A Chorus Line* (with lyrics by Edward Kelban), followed in 1975: the show won nine Tony awards, including Best Musical and Best Score, and subsequent versions scored four Emmy awards, two Grammy awards, and three Academy Awards. The stage version even won the 1975 Pulitzer Prize for Drama, a rare feat for a musical. These accomplishments loomed even larger considering the fact that the show's format was entirely new: in place of the usual romantic leads and supporting cast of the classic musical, it featured ensemble numbers by members of a stage chorus line. Twenty years after its premiere, *A Chorus Line* was still running on Broadway.

Based Musical on Own Relationship

Hamlisch never quite matched the heights of popularity he achieved during the 1973–1975 period, but he remained one of the leading film-music composers in the industry and wrote several more major pop hits. Hamlisch's score for the James Bond film *The Spy Who Loved Me* (1977), co-written with his then-girlfriend Carole Bayer Sager, contained the song "Nobody Does It Better," which became a number-two hit for the vocalist Carly Simon. Although the Hamlisch–Bayer Sager relationship dissolved, the pair remained both friends and collaborators, even co-writing a stage musical, *They're Playing Our Song* (1979), that chronicled the ups and downs of their own relationship. That show ran for more than 1,000 performances on Broadway and was also successful in Britain.

In the 1980s and 1990s, Hamlisch's name continued to be associated with scores for a great variety of successful films, including the dramas *Ordinary People* (1980) and *Sophie's Choice* (1982), the comedy *Three Men and a Baby* (1987), and the romantic comedy *The Mirror Has Two Faces* (1996). The latter film reunited Hamlisch with Streisand and earned him another Academy Award nomination. Hamlisch won an Emmy award for arranging and conducting the music for the *Barbra Streisand—Timeless* television special in 2001. He also wrote scores for television dramas, including the 1985 production of the Tennessee Williams play *A Streetcar Named Desire.*

Hamlisch's popularity even extended to the R&B genre: his "Break It To Me Gently" became a number-one hit for vocalist Aretha Franklin in 1977. In later years, Hamlisch seemed to return to his childhood roots in classical music. He conducted and performed as a pianist with major symphony orchestras, including the New York Philharmonic, the Cleveland Orchestra, and England's Royal Philharmonic, most often in crossover-oriented pops programs that featured orchestral arrangements of his scores and show tunes. In 1993 Hamlisch composed a full-scale symphonic piece, *Anatomy of Peace.*

Hamlisch composed the score for the Steven Soderbergh caper film *The Informant!* in 2009 and continued to tour as a conductor almost until his death on June 6, 2012, which came quite suddenly. At the time of his death he was at work on a stage musical adaptation of the film *The Nutty*

Professor and the score for a new film about pop pianist Liberace. Hamlisch was survived by his wife, television news anchor Terre Blair, to whom he left most of his estate—even if she had left him, which she did not. "I'm devastated,' Streisand told Carmel Dagan of *Variety.* "When I think of him now, it was his brilliantly quick mind, his generosity, and delicious sense of humor that made him a delight to be around."

Books

Contemporary Musicians, Volume 1, Gale, 1989.

Hamlisch, Marvin, *Marvin Makes Music,* Dial, 2012.

Hamlisch, Marvin, with Gerald C. Gardner, *The Way I Was,* Scribner, 1992.

Periodicals

Billboard, August 18, 2012.

Daily Telegraph (London, England), August 9, 2012.

Guardian (London, England), August 9, 2012.

Investor's Business Daily, October 4, 2012.

New York Times, August 8, 2012.

Times (London, England), August 8, 2012.

Variety, August 8, 2012.

Online

"Biography," Marvin Hamlisch Official Website, http://marvinhamlisch.us/ (October 15, 2013).

"InDepth InterView: Marvin Hamlisch," *BroadwayWorld.com,* http://www.broadwayworld.com/article/InDepth-InterView-Marvin-Hamlisch-20100722 (October 15, 2013).

"Marvin Hamlisch," *Turner Classic Movies,* http://www.tcm.com/tcmdb/person/80172l108273/Marvin-Hamlisch/ (October 15, 2013).

"Marvin Hamlisch Biography," *Film Reference,* http://www.filmreference.com/film/14/Marvin-Hamlisch.html (October 15, 2013).

"Marvin Hamlisch Willed Oscars to Wife Even if She Divorced Him," *DNA Info,* http://www.dnainfo.com/new-york/20121004/new-york-city/(October 15, 2013).□

Lang Hancock

Lang Hancock (1909–1992) was one of Australia's most colorful and outspoken self-made millionaires. The former sheep rancher and asbestos miner laid claim to discovering the world's largest iron ore deposit, and the profits from his stake made him a millionaire several times over. His vision of the remote, underpopulated state of Western Australia as a potentially lucrative site of mineral wealth proved true, and the region's natural-resources boom that began in the 1960s continued decades after Hancock's death in 1992.

Langley George Hancock was born on June 10, 1909, in Perth, the capital of Western Australia. His ancestors had come to Australia from Coldridge, England, in 1830, to start a timber business. One of the their descendants was John Hancock, Langley Hancock's grandfather, who moved the family to Pilbara, a forbidding, mountainous part of Western Australia previously deemed unfit for European settlement. It was prone to floods and droughts, but the Hancocks eventually built a successful sheep ranching business in its more fertile region. Hancock was raised in the rough-and-tumble world of sheep shearers and resisted being sent away to a private boys' school, Hale, in Perth at age eight. At the time, the journey from the family sheep station in Ashburton to Perth took days by land, but was even more treacherous by sea.

Discovered Blue Asbestos

Eager to return to the family business, Hancock opted against university studies and instead joined his father's business. The Pilbara in central Western Australia was also home to the Hamersley Range, and Hancock initially found success with deposits of blue asbestos he discovered in the Wittenoom Gorge in the early 1930s. The gorge was a parcel of land his father had bought from a man named Wittenoom several years earlier. Asbestos was a soft mineral whose fibers were famously fireproof, and it had been mined around the world for centuries for use in consumer goods, manufacturing, and construction sectors. The fibers, however, were highly carcinogenic and caused certain types of lung diseases; the cancer affected not only those who mined and handled it, but even those who lived with someone who worked in the industry.

Teaming with Peter Wright, a friend from the Hale School in Perth, Hancock became a prospector and staked his first mining claim on the trove in Wittenoom Gorge. Representatives of a British company expressed an interest in the blue asbestos—which state mining officials had told Hancock was worthless—and Hancock and Wright's company, Hanwright, began exporting it. In the 1940s they sold a 51 percent stake to CSR, a major Australian company whose initials reflected its older origins as the Colonial Sugar Refining Company. After World War II, Hancock began searching Hamersley and other ranges for potential mineral wealth.

Hancock's first marriage, to Susette Maley in 1935, produced no children, and reportedly ended because she disliked the isolation of living at a remote sheep station at Mulga Downs, which he had inherited from his family. In 1947 he married Hope Margaret Nicholas, and the couple was fairly surprised to become parents late in life when their daughter Georgina was born in 1954; Hancock was almost 45 and his wife in her late 30s. Hancock had been certain the baby would be a boy, and planned to name it after his father George; instead the Hancocks named her Georgina and Hancock brought her into family business at an early age.

Sat on Claim for Years

Hancock had been flying his plane on November 22, 1952, with his wife alongside him. They were making a late-spring trip from an asbestos mine he owned in Nunyerry to Perth when bad weather, he claimed, forced him to fly in and out of the Hamersley Range. He saw long rust-colored walls in the mountain gorges, and the rust was a sign that iron ore was present and had been oxidized by moisture. "I noticed the walls," he told Pamela G. Hollie in a 1982 *New York Times* article. "They were made of iron ore, but I figured it had to be poor grade. At the time, they said Australia didn't have any grade iron ore"—that is, of a grade or quality high enough to be a traded commodity on world markets. In fact, Australia's reserves of decent iron ore were so small that export was forbidden, for the cache was considered vital to its national defense and manufacturing sectors. Hancock realized the long-held assumption that Australia had no such grade-high trove was disastrously wrong, he told Hollie. "I followed the iron ore in the walls for 70 miles."

Hancock kept his discovery of this deep ore vein a secret for nearly a decade as he lobbied government officials to overturn a ban on mining-claim stakes in Western Australia, and then to remove the ban on iron-ore export. Convinced Western Australia contained vast deposits of mineral wealth, he set up a prospecting company, and began to seek out foreign investment. Hancock was never able to own a mine on his own, for the start-up costs were astronomical, but he convinced executives of a massive London-based mining company, Rio Tinto, to develop his discovery. He named it Hope Downs after his wife, and his royalty rights on every single bucket of iron ore that came out of it gave him a 2.5 percent fee on the sale price. In the early 1960s, with Japan the biggest customer of Hope Downs's ore deposits, Hancock became one of Australia's richest men with about $12 million in income annually just from Hope Downs alone.

Profiled in Television Documentaries

Hancock's name appeared regularly on the business pages of the *New York Times* and the *Times* of London. He was often described as a genuine Outback-style cowboy from the other side of the world, who visited bankers in New York and London on his own private Learjet. The British Broadcasting Company (BBC) found him so intriguing they sent a film crew to Pilbara to make a 1966 documentary film titled *Man of Iron,* about his discovery of the Hope Downs mine and the formation of his company, Hancock Prospecting. In 1969, the Australian Broadcasting Company (ABC) featured Hancock in another documentary, *Dig a Million, Make a Million.* Hancock's teenage daughter, who went by the shortened form of her name, Gina, was often filmed by his side, and Hancock once boasted to a journalist, "She's a lot tougher than me," according to 2013 profile of his daughter that ran in the *New Yorker.*

Like her father, Gina bypassed university. She married and became a mother, but her career at Hancock Prospecting remained her primary focus. Her father once brought her along to a meeting with British Conservative Party leader Margaret Thatcher, which was said to have profoundly influenced her. Hancock himself shared some of the future British prime minister's famously draconian beliefs about free enterprise and the stranglehold of trade unions and regulatory laws. He became friendly with one of Australia's most conservative figures, Joh Bjelke-Petersen, the longtime premier (or governor) of the state of Queensland, and was on good terms with other influential figures in Australian industry and commerce.

In the 1970s, Hancock became a staunch opponent of a new Labor Party government that swept to power in 1972 elections. He even wrote a short book titled *Wake Up, Australia!* that set forth his vision for the country to become a major player in the Pacific Rim economy. One of his pet causes was secession for Western Australia, a long-dormant idea that dated back to the 1930s when resentment from Australia's eastern seaboard elites was at a peak. Hancock financed a political party to promote the idea of a sovereign nation called Westralia, which would have lower taxes, fewer regulations, and dismiss Aboriginal land claims, which were a major political issue in Australia at the time.

Chastised for Television Interview

Hancock was among those who opposed any form of land claims, reparations, or affirmative action policies to remedy the injustices shown to the country's Aboriginal inhabitants, who had lived off the land and traded with neighbors for centuries before European settlement. Hancock was particularly vehement about Australia's mixed-race populace, the result of intermarriage or affairs between Aboriginals and those of European origin. Criticizing unemployment and welfare-benefit recipients on a Brisbane-produced news program called *Today Tonight* in October of 1981, Hancock suggested that mixed-race welfare recipients be forced to pick up their benefits checks at a central location, where officials could poison drinking water and make the population sterile. "I'm not talking about the full-bloods. I'm not talking about the people who are assimilated already. They are happy enough. But what I'm talking about is the ones that are in real trouble and can never get out of trouble. I'm just terminating that, not terminating them," he said in the television interview, according to Adele Ferguson in *Gina Rinehart: The Untold Story of the Richest Woman in the World.*

Hancock's remarks prompted public outrage. Moreover, personal troubles closer to home were already mounting: his wife Hope was suffering from cancer, and now-divorced Gina had become involved with a shady American lawyer whom Hancock saw as an interloper. She married the man, Frank Rinehart, in Las Vegas in January of 1983, two months before her mother died. The couple spent time in the United States, but Gina arranged for a housekeeper to help her newly widowed father at his Perth home. A Filipino woman named Rose Lacson answered the newspaper ad, and soon began an affair with Hancock, who removed her from his payroll and installed her in a luxury apartment. Gina was outraged, and attempted to have Lacson deported back to the Philippines.

Opened Deep Vein of Resentment

Hancock, meanwhile, was outraged at the costly hotel bills and luxury vacation jaunts that Frank Rinehart was enjoying on his dime. From 1984 onward, the Hancock-Rinehart saga emerged as one of Australia's longest-running real-life family feuds. Gina was ousted from her executive role at Hancock Prospecting, but reconciled with her father after Frank Rinehart died in 1990. Hancock died on March 27, 1992, in one of the guest cottages of a palatial Swan River estate in Perth he had built for Rose, which they called Prix d'Amour. He was 82 and the coroner's report listed the cause of death as natural causes exacerbated by arteriosclerotic heart disease. Following that, Gina Rinehart mounted a long and expensive legal battle against her widowed stepmother, and even managed to have an official inquest opened against her in the late 1990s, accusing her of Hancock's murder.

Hancock's daughter Gina is Australia's richest woman, and one of the richest women in the world. An active steward of Hancock Prospecting and related ventures, she spent much of the 1990s expanding its mineral leases and holdings. Gina's late father had set up a trust for her four children which she controlled as sole director, but the terms of the trust mandated that her four children would each become fully vested directors with control over the income from that fortune when the youngest of the four, Ginia Rinehart, turned 25. A few days before her youngest daughter's 25th birthday in 2011, Gina forced the three elder children into signing a document that gave her sole control over the fortune until 2068. The drama played out over the next few years in almost daily revelations in the Australian media about Gina and the ongoing feud with three of her adult children, who filed suit against their mother for violating the terms of the trust Hancock had established for them.

Unlike her father, Gina Rinehart is famously media-averse, but did permit *New Yorker* writer William Finnegan to tour the construction site of her company's new iron-ore mine at Roy Hill, part of the trove Hancock had discovered back in 1952. It was still producing tons of ore for the export market daily, just as Hancock had predicted. "The deep stuff is best," a company geologist named Greg Almond told Finnegan, showing him hematite, an ore named because of its resemblance to blood. "Most of it was laid down about three billion years ago, when this iron formation was sea bottom. It was bacteria, producing oxygen as a waste product. Some of the oldest rocks you can still see on the earth's surface are here in the Pilbara."

Books

Ferguson, Adele, *Gina Rinehart: The Untold Story of the Richest Woman in the World,* Macmillan Australia, 2012.

Periodicals

Guardian (London, England), April 1, 1992.

New York Times, January 27, 1974; September 4, 1975; December 12, 1982; March 12, 2012.

New Yorker, March 25, 2013.

Times (London, England), July 7, 1972.□

Elliot Handler

American toy manufacturer Elliot Handler (1916–2011) co-founded and served as a creative force behind the toy company Mattel.

American toy manufacturer Elliot Handler co-founded one of the world's largest and most successful toy companies, Mattel. Along with his wife, Ruth, Handler helped develop some of the 20th century's seminal toys, including plastic Barbie dolls and Hot Wheels cars. Handler's background was in art, and his primary contributions to the Mattel line were creative ones in product design and development; his wife acted as the company's main business leader, although Handler served as a co-chair of Mattel. The Handlers lost control of Mattel in 1975, and Handler spent his retirement years living quietly in Los Angeles until his death at the age of 95.

Co-Founded Mattel

Born Isadore Elliot Handler on April 9, 1916, in Chicago, Illinois, Handler was the son of Jewish immigrants who had come to the United States from Matziv, Ukraine. When Handler was a boy, his father Samuel contracted tuberculosis, a lung disease, and moved the family to Denver, Colorado, where a Jewish organization operated a tuberculosis sanatorium. Colorado's clean air and atmosphere were then considered the best treatment available for tuberculosis sufferers, and the family remained in Denver after Samuel Handler's sanatorium stay. From a young age, the future toy maker was an enthusiastic artist who drew cartoons, which he tried unsuccessfully to sell to newspapers as a teen. At the same time, he worked at a local lighting design company and attended the Denver Art Institute as a scholarship student.

As a teenager, Handler met and became instantly infatuated with Ruth Mosco, the daughter of Jewish immigrant parents from Poland. "I was attracted to everything about her," Handler recalled of the couple's first meeting to Jerry Oppenheimer in *Toy Monster: The Big, Bad World of Mattel.* "Everything worked. We just hit it off and kept going together." The Mosco family was less enthused about their daughter's suitor; they had become successful business owners, and the Handler family's working-class social status did not live up to their dreams of marrying Ruth into money and prestige. Handler followed Ruth to Los Angeles, where she had moved in 1936 and taken a job as a secretary at Paramount Pictures. Handler found work in that city at a lighting company and enrolled part-time in industrial design courses at the Art Center College of Design. The couple resumed their relationship, and the Handlers married in Denver on June 26, 1938.

Handler put his design training to use by making objects out of a then-new material, Plexiglas, using tools that the couple bought on installment at Sears. At first, Handler worked in a garage; later, the Handlers rented a workspace, and from here the artist crafted Plexiglas and Lucite trays, bookends, and other small goods. Ruth Handler proved an

Jean-Paul Aussenard/WireImage/Getty Images

able salesperson and before long, Handler had a small but growing operation producing Plexiglas and Lucite home goods and costume jewelry. Handler joined with a partner, Zachary Zemby, who handled marketing and other business affairs for the newly-christened company, Elzac. Finances remained tight, however, especially when Ruth gave birth to the couple's first child, Barbara, in 1941.

His business relationship with Zemby and other new investors became strained over the next few years, and Handler became unhappy with his involvement in the business. Not long after Ruth bore the second Handler child, Kenneth, in the spring of 1944, Handler and another Elzac associate, Harold "Matt" Matson, left the company to strike out on their own. Handler designed picture frames, Matson produced them, and Ruth sold them. The three named the new enterprise "Mattel"—a portmanteau of "Matt" and "Elliot." Ruth Handler, although not included in the company's name, was a significant part of its operation. Robin Gerber quoted the assertive woman in *Barbie and Ruth: The Story of the World's Most Famous Doll and the Women Who Created Her* as recalling, "Yes, it was Elliot's designs. Yes, it was Elliot's name. Yes, he was very much a part of it.... But I actually started Mattel."

Launched Successful Toys

Soon, Handler and Matson began using pieces of leftover wood and plastic from their picture frame production to craft dollhouse furniture. Handler was drafted for domestic military duty as World War II drew to a close, and he divided his time between Mattel and military service near Los Angeles. Sales of the company's doll furniture took off, with Ruth Handler developing a nationwide network of sales representatives. Mattel turned a respectable profit of $30,000—more than $350,000 when adjusted for inflation—in 1945, its first complete year in business. A few years later, the company scored a major hit with its 1947 introduction of the "Uke-a-Doodle," a cheap plastic ukulele that sold more than 10 million units. Not long after, Matson sold his share of the company to members of the Mosco family.

Over the next few years, Mattel produced and marketed a series of popular children's musical toys, including a Handler-designed toy piano that sold some 300,000 units after appearing at the New York Toy Fair. The company had mispriced the hit toy, however, and went deeply in debt as its costs ate up Mattel's profits. An innovative cheap music box mechanism that allowed all types of toys to play music with a simple hand crank saved Mattel, and the company's business exploded in the mid-1950s after it became the sole sponsor of the television program *Mickey Mouse Club,* using the show to advertise products such as the Burp Gun and "Mouseguitar." Over the next several years, Mattel produced a string of successful toys, including the Chatty Cathy doll, the See and Say, and a group of Handler-envisioned dolls known as the Kiddles.

Mattel's best-known product, the Barbie doll, was born after a family trip to Europe in 1956. The Handlers had been considering ways to enter the market for toy dolls, and Ruth Handler knew she had found the perfect model when she saw a German doll created for an adult audience. With long legs and a curvaceous figure, the doll represented an idealized womanhood that Elliot Handler and most of Mattel's other male employees believed would never appeal to American mothers. Ruth Handler prevailed, however, and her husband traveled to Japan for a time to oversee production of Barbie, a doll named for the Handler's daughter. It became a massive success and was soon joined by a male counterpart, Ken, named for the Handlers' son.

During the late 1960s, Handler envisioned another of Mattel's signature toys: Hot Wheels. "Elliot was kind of a frustrated automotive designer," commented Fred Adickes, a Mattel employee who helped develop Hot Wheels, to Oppenheimer. "He did a couple of toy cars years before, but they were a failure." Hoping to create a toy car that was more functional and more realistic than the competing Matchbox models, Mattel designed a die-cast body with innovative plastic wheels that could roll quickly across hard surfaces. The first Hot Wheels cars, based on contemporary popular U.S. automobile models, received orders in excess of 50 million upon their debut at the New York Toy Fair. Hot Wheels cars, race tracks, and other accessories were among the most popular toys of the 1968 and 1969 holiday seasons. By the time of Handler's death, the Hot Wheels product line had produced some 10,000 different models.

Despite this immense success and its accompanying pressures, Handler remained enthusiastic about his creative work as a toy designer. "We do kind of wonder sometimes whatever happened to that little toy factory of ours, but it's still a lot of fun," Handler told C. Robert Jennings in a 1968 *New York Times* profile. "When you see your displays used in toy fairs all over the world and thousands of people producing for you, it's a little overwhelming." The Handlers were also known for their casual management style in which they encouraged employees to call them by their first names well before such a practice was common, and for their support of a diverse workplace when segregation and discriminatory hiring practices were still the norm. "We hired black and brown people; it did not matter to us," Gerber quoted Handler as explaining. "Our families weren't racist. One of my first managers was a black guy, a very capable mechanic. We were very liberal."

Retired Amid Scandal

As the 1970s began, Mattel seemed unstoppable. But a major scandal managed to bring the company—and the Handlers—temporarily screeching to a halt. The corporation had reported record profits year after year, but a warehouse fire and labor strike meant that profits for 1970 seemed likely to be weak. Worried, the Handlers and other Mattel executives sought ways to bolster the company's profits on paper in order to keep investors and stock analysts happy. Their solution was to encourage Mattel salespeople to make large sales for products to be delivered at a later date in the future. Although this tactic was ethical, a second one was not; salespeople were also allowed to permit customers to cancel orders without removing the billings from Mattel's books. This artificially inflated profits but still failed to protect overall corporate earnings. In 1972, Mattel lost more than $30 million; projections for 1973 were also poor.

The value of Mattel stock crashed. Investigations and analysis placed the blame for the fiasco mostly on Handler and his wife. In October of 1975, Mattel's board of directors forced both Handlers to resign from their positions at the company that they had founded some three decades previously. To make matters worse, Ruth Handler was indicted for fraud and other charges related to the income falsification; Handler was spared from legal charges because his work dealt mostly with creative rather than financial management. Ruth Handler was eventually ordered to pay a fine and perform community service.

After these events, Handler spent his later years largely out of the public eye. He was inducted into the Toy Industry Hall of Fame in 1989 alongside Ruth Handler, with the two sharing the distinction of being the first two living inductees to that body. The Handlers' son Ken died in 1994 from a brain tumor, and Ruth Handler followed in 2002. Handler spent much of his time pursuing a rediscovered love of painting. His works were typically painted in a realistic style enlivened by bold, primary colors. In time, Mattel healed its relationship with its founders, and after Ruth Handler died in 2002 commissioned a sculpture for its corporate headquarters that shows both Handlers with a Barbie doll.

Handler died from heart failure on July 21, 2011, at his home in Los Angeles's Century City neighborhood. His passage made international news as those who had grown up with some of his company's offerings remembered its co-founder fondly. "They were something—my mother was ahead of her time, that's for sure, and [my father] was such a great designer. He had such a great flair for creativity," Handler's daughter Barbara recalled of her parents in an obituary of Handler written by Andrea Chang of the *Los Angeles Times*. Handler's brother, Sid, told Charles Duhigg in a *New York Times* obituary that Handler "was a quiet, kind man. I think that's why he liked toys so much. They make people happy."

Books

Gerber, Robin, *Barbie and Ruth: The Story of the World's Most Famous Doll and the Woman Who Created Her,* HarperCollins, 2009.

Oppenheimer, Jerry, *Toy Monster: The Big, Bad World of Mattel,* Wiley, 2009.

Periodicals

Los Angeles Times, July 23, 2011.

New York Times, May 19, 1968; July 22, 2011.

Online

"Elliot Handler," Mattel Official Website, http://corporate.mattel.com/about-us/elliot-handler/ (December 7, 2013).□

Ray Harryhausen

Ray Harryhausen (1920–2013) is regarded as the master of stop-motion animation, a process that combines moveable miniature models with live actors and manufactured settings to create a fantastical confrontation between man and monster in a fantasy environment. Harryhausen enjoyed a 50-year career that reaped recognition and awards and influenced a younger generation of filmmakers. In 1992, he received a special Academy Award for his body of work.

On the cover of his legendary magazine *Famous Monsters of Filmland,* editor Forrest J. Ackerman (1916–2008) emblazoned issue No. 20 (November, 1962) with a garishly large headline: "Read About the Man Who Saw King Kong 90 Times." This was well before the era of cable TV and DVD, so it was quite a feat. The man was Ray Harryhausen, and, as Ackerman's article related, his obsession with *King Kong* led to a career as a master film animator. Harryhausen developed techniques that went beyond previous special effects methodology. He created film creatures that destroyed major cities and that did battle with mythic heroes such as Jason, Perseus, and

ZUMA Press, Inc./Alamy

Sinbad, all the while making everything look as realistic as possible.

For fans of fantastic films, wrote Danny Peary in his book *Cult Movies,* "there [was] no greater treat than the not-frequent-enough release of a new spectacle featuring the special effects of Ray Harryhausen. It is Harryhausen—not the actors, not the director—who is the 'star' of the pictures with which he is involved: he is the attraction." Peary's comment on the frequency of Harryhausen's films is key, for Harryhausen revolutionized the existing art of stop-motion animation—a painstaking process that involves minute movements photographed one film frame at a time. When projected on a screen, the process creates realistic fluidity of action. As such, his films would often take several years to finish. Months could be spent filming just one scene. Harryhausen attached his art to science-fiction movies and films based on tales from mythology. For fantasy film aficionados, he became a legend, and his movies—such as *The 7th Voyage of Sinbad* (1958) and *Jason and the Argonauts (1963)*—are considered cult movie classics.

Harryhausen practiced his methodology in the pre-CGI (computer generated imagery) era, so his accomplishments are astonishing. His models, animated with a ball-and-socket jointed technique, were combined with live action, and his creatures could be frightful menaces (such as the dragon in *The 7th Voyage of Sinbad* or the army of sword-wielding skeletons in *Jason and the Argonauts*), or imbued with personality and even sympathy, such as the "Ymir" in *20 Million Miles to Earth.*

Encouraged By Parents

Born on June 29, 1920, in Los Angeles, California, Raymond Frederick Harryhausen had an early interest in dinosaurs and the fantastic tales from Greek, Roman, and Arabian mythology. His parents, Frederick W. and Martha Harryhausen, encouraged his interests and curiosity. "They never tried to discourage me in any way from my obsession," the late film technician is quoted on his official website. He added that they nurtured his passion by exposing him to plays and films. Growing up, Harryhausen loved to frequent museums, puppet shows, amusement parks and movie theaters. Indeed, inside a dark "spookhouse," he was not fearful; rather, his analytic mind tried to figure out how the shocks were created.

Inspired by Two Films

Two films most provoked his imagination and drove his ambition. The seeds of Harryhausen's career were planted when his parents took the five-year-old boy to see *The Lost World* (1925), a silent-film adaptation of the Sir Arthur Conan Doyle novel. The film featured stop-motion special effects by animation pioneer Willis O'Brien (1886–1962), who would later create "King Kong." Harryhausen was intrigued by the sight of his favorite creatures—giants and dinosaurs—coming to life.

The pivotal moment in his life, however, came eight years later, in 1933, when his aunt and mother took him to Grauman's Chinese Theater on Hollywood Boulevard in California to see O'Brien's next major production: *King Kong,* released by RKO and produced by David O. Selznick. But the movie was essentially the vision of the filmmaking team of Merian C. Cooper and Ernest B. Schoedsack, who were adventurers as well as filmmakers. Selznick merely gave the go-ahead and provided the money.

In his autobiographic overview of his techniques and films, *Film Fantasy Scrapbook,* Harryhausen wrote, "All of this excitement over a film that some might call 'trivial entertainment' could suggest that I may be a fanatic about the subject, but I have found over the years that 'extravagant enthusiasm' can be half of the battle of turning mere desire into actuality."

Engaged in Early Experiments

Harryhausen wanted to know how figures such as the film's *tyrannosaurus rex* came alive on the screen. He did his own early experiments with marionettes, but he realized this method was totally inadequate, even ridiculous. Undaunted, his continuing interest led him to read articles about the stop-motion animation that filmmakers like O'Brien deployed. His obsessive research revealed to him the secret. As quoted on his website, Harryhausen said: "As I continued to study and learn how the effects for Kong were achieved, I realized [stop motion animation] was something I really wanted to try for myself and perhaps even be part of, so I began to construct my own miniature dioramas and crude models, which eventually led me to take the step in making larger moveable figures."

In his late teens, Harryhausen began taking night courses in motion picture photography at the University of Southern California in Los Angeles. There, he learned about the intricacies of special effects, matte shots, and multiple exposures, all of which would come into play in his later film career. He supplemented this by taking art classes such as sculpture and drawing, which would aid him in designing the models of his fantastic creatures. His designs were influenced by the murals painted by Charles R. Knight (1874–1953). These were showcased in the Los Angeles County Museum of Art and depicted the early interpretation of what prehistoric animals looked like. In 1938, the 18-year-old Harryhausen submitted a diorama—which included his modeled stegosaurus, based on Knight's paintings—into the Junior Museum Hobby Show at the County Museum. He won first prize.

During this period, Harryhausen became friends with writer Ray Bradbury (1920–2012) and Ackerman. The relationships would influence and promote Harryhausen's career. Harryhausen's early animation attempts were crude: He utilized wooden armatures, which proved lacking in realism. He had to improvise. Also, the 16mm Victor camera he deployed did not offer a one-frame-at-a-time capability, which is critical to creating the lifelike movements that stop-motion animation engenders. During his early efforts, his studio was his parents' backyard and garage. Ever supportive, Harryhausen's father even parked his car on the driveway and not in the garage, to give free reign to his son's creativity.

Later, Harryhausen bought a Kodak Cine II camera with a one-frame shaft that enabled him to film much smoother animation sequences. Still, he was in the amateur ranks. In 1938, bolstered by his Junior Museum Hobby Show award and his new tools, Harryhausen began a project called *Evolution of the World,* which would include short episodes about the dinosaur age. He populated his vision with his favorite creatures—a tyrannosaurus rex, triceratops, brontosaurus and pterodactyl—all sculpted by his own hands. He also began experimenting with mattes, a process that integrated animated forms and live action figures with false but realistically painted backgrounds to form a cohesive scene. His vision included a sequence where a brontosaurus arose from the water and stomped about on dry land.

For sure, it was a personal development, but Harryhausen became discouraged when he went to a movie theater and saw Walt Disney's 1940 film *Fantasia.* The film's "Rite of Spring" sequence depicted what Harryhausen had envisioned and beat him to the punch. Further, Harryhausen knew that he obviously could not compete with the Disney studio's highly talented and experienced staff of technicians and the organization's money. He realized his own creations were comparatively crude.

Encouraged by Willis O'Brien

During this period, the disappointed but undaunted Harryhausen met O'Brien. At the time, O'Brien was working on a war picture at Metro-Goldwyn-Mayer (MGM). Harryhausen called and told him about his interests. The affable but somewhat eccentric O'Brien invited him to visit the studio. Harryhausen showed his hero some of his dinosaur models. O'Brien was critical but encouraging; he told Harryhausen to study anatomy, which would make his models more realistic. Harryhausen realized that O'Brien was right. He enrolled in night classes at local universities, taking classes in art and anatomy at Los Angeles City College, where he acquired the insight that drawings were the first step in the animation process. Ever ambitious, Harryhausen then signed up for classes in film technique at the University of Southern California, where he studied art direction, editing, and photography. At the same time, and inspired by O'Brien's accomplishments, he strove to imbue his animated models with character. His formal education was supplemented by informal education: Harryhausen went to zoos, so that he could observe animal movements up close.

Moved into the Professional Ranks

With new skills and knowledge, Harryhausen sought work as a professional film animator. He answered a newspaper advertisement for a film technician position and met Hungarian film producer George Pal (1908–1980), who would later produce fantasy and sci-fi film classics such as *The War of the Worlds* (1953), *The Time Machine* (1960), *Atlantis, the Lost Continent* (1961), and *The Wonderful World of the Brothers Grimm* (1962). Pal hired him, and Harryhausen worked on a series of short films called *Puppetoons.* He worked on 13 of these shorts, but he felt that Pal's techniques were limiting. He had greater ambitions.

Harryhausen's career—but not his education—was interrupted by World War II. In 1942, he enlisted in the Army and was assigned to the Army Signal Corps (Special Service Division), where he worked with famed film director Frank Capra (1897–1991), who had won an Academy Award for Best Director in 1934 for *It Happened One Night* and later directed *It's a Wonderful Life* (1946). Capra was impressed by Harryhausen's 1941 short technical film *How to Bridge a Gorge,* and he realized that animation could be used effectively in training films. During this period, Harryhausen made another animated short, *Guadacanal.*

Even before his military service, Harryhausen received national recognition. In 1946, *Popular Mechanics* magazine reported: "Harryhausen's ability to create naturalistic, smoothly moving miniatures is the secret of his success. It is this skill in making animals of the past, or monsters of fantasy, look and move as if alive that has turned his hobby into a successful job with Hollywood motion picture companies."

In 1946, after his military service, Harryhausen decided to make his own short films, a series called *Mother Goose Stories,* which included animated tales about

Humpty Dumpty, Little Miss Muffet, and Old Mother Hubbard, among others. The films were distributed to schools. He deployed the ball-and-socket technique that he designed with his father. The ball-and-socket technique, as *Famous Monsters of Filmland* magazine reported, "is the basis of each Harryhausen [creation], be it prehistoric or futuristic. Sponge rubber is modeled over the metal frame, directly on the frame, without the use of a mold or a cast. The method [was] Harryhausen's secret."

Worked with O'Brien

Three years later, in 1949, Harryhausen experienced a dream come true: O'Brien asked him to work on another "big ape" film project. The working title was *Mr. Joseph Young of Africa.* The film was eventually released as *Mighty Joe Young,* a much beloved film classic—albeit not on the level of *King Kong.* Harryhausen animated about 90 percent of the scenes. His work helped O'Brien win the Best Special Effects award at the 1950 Academy Awards. Harryhausen then worked with O'Brien on at least two projects that never came to fruition: *Valley of the Mist,* which would feature animated dinosaurs, and *War of the Worlds.* George Pal would later produce the H.G. Wells novel without Harryhausen's help.

Harryhausen then decided it was time to strike out on his own. His early independent efforts included short Fairy Tale-based films: *The Story of Little Red Riding Hood* (1950), *The Story of Hansel and Gretel* (1950), and *The Story of King Midas* (1953).

Moved into Feature Films

In 1951, Harryhausen was offered a chance to work on his first feature film without O'Brien. The film was based on a short story, *The Foghorn,* by his friend Ray Bradbury, about a prehistoric creature that hears a call from a modern man-made siren and arises from the sea. The film was released in 1952 as *The Beast from 20,000 Fathoms.* The film featured only one monster, a vicious quadruped called a "Rhedosaurus" that, like King Kong, rampaged through New York City. However, this creation had none of the charm or personality of the 50-foot ape; rather, it was simply a creature of destruction.

At first, studio head Jack Dietz at Mutual Films wanted to use a live lizard that would be visually enlarged onscreen to look enormous—a cost-saving technique previously used in *One Million B.C.* (1940)—but Dietz was impressed by Harryhausen's proposal and portfolio. He decided to go with stop-motion animation. Audiences were enthralled. Harryhausen's feature film career was launched.

Developed Dynamation

For the film, Harryhausen developed a technique that would later become known as "Dynamation." This innovative process split the live action so that a small miniature model could be inserted into the frame, making it appear that it was present on the set and much larger than the actors it interacted with. The split-screen technique was an advancement over the glass methods that O'Brien had used in *King Kong* and *Mighty Joe Young.* Harryhausen knew that this new technique would be less time consuming and less expensive. Also, it allowed an animator greater freedom in creating a screened scene–in turn creating a more enthralling image.

As *Famous Monsters of Filmland* reported in 1963, Charles H. Schneer, who became Harryhausen' business partner and collaborator, described Dynamation as "a photographic process which combines a live background [sometimes in color] with a 3-dimensional animated figure in combination with flesh and bone actors."

The description sounds fancy, but it was an artistic development born of practical consideration: Harryhausen appreciated that he was given the opportunity to ply his animation methodology in a feature film, but he realized there was a limiting film budget. After many hours of experimentation, he knew that the split-screen technique not only worked but was more time-efficient and, more importantly, more dynamic: hence the name Dynamation. However, the name would not be trademarked until later in the decade with *The 7th Voyage of Sinbad* (1958), and it would continue to evolve through the years.

Began Collaboration with Charles H. Schneer

It would be film producer Charles H. Schneer who would come up with the Dynamation name. Schneer watched *The Beast from 20,000 Fathoms* and envisioned another oversized beast-on-the-rampage scenario: one that would involve an enormous octopus that would attack San Francisco and enwrap its tentacles around the Golden Gate bridge. While Harryhausen was reluctant to do another "monster" film, he was intrigued by the plot elements that could be achieved by stop-motion animation.

The result was *It Came From Beneath the Sea* (1955). Again, budget and time considerations came into play, so Harryhausen had to fashion a six-tentacled monstrosity, while making it appear that the invading giant octopus had eight arms. This he did by keeping the creature always partially submerged in water. Audiences were not counting how many tentacles this resulting "sixtopus" possessed. Again, the film was a monster-amok saga that took place in a major American city–a recurrent theme that was quickly becoming old hat.

Meanwhile, Harryhausen had a chance to work one more time with O'Brien, on a film called *Animal World* (1956). The subject matter was evolution, and the student and his mentor provided a short segment about dinosaurs. The film is largely forgotten—remembered by only those who appreciate the talents of Harryhausen and O'Brien. Their segment lasts a mere eight minutes, but it is the reason the film lingers in some minds.

The Harryhausen-Schneer collaboration continued, however. Interested in UFO reports that were pervading the news during the late 1940s and early 1950s, Schneer wanted to produce a film about "flying saucers." Apparently tired of beasts-on-the-loose scenarios, Harryhausen accepted the assignment and animated extraterrestrial, plate-shaped vehicles that destroyed American iconographic architectural structures such as the Washington Monument and the Capitol building. Interestingly, the film was populated with alien pilots (robotic anthropomorphs), but Harryhausen did not animate these invaders; they were actors in rubber suits due to budget restrictions.

Harryhausen's next film, *20 Million Miles to Earth* (1957), returned to the monster-on-loose scenario, this time with a creature from Venus running wild in Rome and eventually being shot down from the Coliseum. However, the so-called "Ymir" was a somewhat sympathetic creation. Rather than being an invader, it was a creature snatched from its home planet by astronauts while it was still in a gelatinous egg.

The film included one of Harryhausen's greatest scenes: the creature hatching itself from its soft egg. At first, the entity looked absolutely cute, but it soon grows into an anthropomorphic reptilian beast with broad shoulders, large biceps, a dragon-like head and a brontosaurus tail. Even so, when soldiers tried to bait it with food, the other-worldly creature eats with the urgency of a hungry dog or cat, further evoking sympathy.

Moved into Color Production

20 Million Miles to Earth would be the last film that Harryhausen would shoot in black-and-white cinematography. Schneer wanted the next movie to be shot in color, but Harryhausen insisted on the grey shades. He helped explain his reasoning in an interview with *Castle of Frankenstein* magazine in 1973: "[An animator] can do much more in black and white. I think there are certain subjects I would still prefer to do to in black and white. But most [film] distributors want color and will often refuse to play a black and white picture."

One problem that Harryhausen pointed out was the maintenance of proper balances with the Dynamation process. Nevertheless, Schneer insisted on the move toward color, and Harryhausen's next effort was a very colorful—and very successful—rendering of Arabian Nights tales titled *The 7th Voyage of Sinbad,* released in 1958. Harryhausen also moved toward the inclusion of multiple—and thrilling—monstrosities that included a giant, single-horned cyclopean beast, a two-headed bird, and a dragon. The film climaxed with Sinbad engaged in a swordfight with a nasty, grinning skeleton, animated by Harryhausen.

The move to color created headaches for Harryhausen, but Schneer knew he found a sustainable partnership: He would insure his animator's hands for a million dollars. Also, with the film, Schneer trademarked the name Dynamation. Success led the partners into a four-year contract with Columbia Pictures. Despite color versus black-and-white disagreements, Harryhausen and Schneer remained friends and enjoyed a longstanding business partnership. Their next film was *The Three Worlds of Gulliver* (1960), a superficial adaptation of the Jonathan Swift classic *Gulliver's Travels.* Despite some interesting special effects, the film is largely forgotten.

Harryhausen' next effort was another multi-monster film called *Mysterious Island* (1961), very loosely based on the Jules Verne novel. But with this outing, Harryhausen's creations took a back seat to the rousing, Civil-War era adventure tale that involved Union soldiers escaping from a Confederate prison camp in a hot-air balloon, only to be caught up in a storm and swept cross-country to an uncharted Pacific island where they fight for survival. Viewers were more interested in the characters' efforts. Still, it contained a memorable scene involving a giant crab. Other beasties included giant wasps, a huge chicken, and a giant undersea mollusk.

Animated his Masterpiece

If *Mysterious Island* disappointed, Harryhausen responded with his best film: *Jason and the Argonauts.* Originally titled *Jason and the Golden Fleece,* the film depicted the mythic Jason's quest for a treasure that hung from a tree at the "at the end of the world." As good as *The 7th Voyage of Sinbad* was, *Jason and the Argonauts* was even better. It is Harryhausen at his peak, wrote Peary: "It is a truly glorious fantasty-adventure film." Harryhausen not only animated but designed the models.

The film's unforgettable episodes include the awakening of the "Titan" Talos. Also, Harryhausen has star Todd Armstrong (Jason) do battle with a seven-headed hydra and an army of skeletons. "Sometimes in the skeleton scene, I only averaged 15 frames a day," Harryhausen revealed to *Castle of Frankenstein* magazine in 1973. The skeleton battle scene comprises four minutes and thirty-seven seconds of screen time, but it took four and a half months to film. To make the scene come alive, Harryhausen reportedly needed to manipulate an estimated 184,800 animated movements.

Another film highlight is when Jason sails his ship through the strait of clashing rocks, where huge boulders tumble from high cliffs that border both sides of the water passageway. Assisted by Olympian gods, Jason and his sailors are saved from catastrophe when the sea god Triton, a merman with his large fish tail flapping, is summoned, arises from the waters, and holds back the tumbling rocks. This scene was done without animation. An actor (William Gungeon) portrayed Triton. Harryhausen explained why for *Castle of Frankenstein* magazine: "I have always believed that there is no point in animating anything you can photograph successfully in the normal course of photography."

His comments point to one of the strengths of the Dynamation process: It was not just about animation. Painted landscapes and live actors could be perfectly blended to create an image that is seamless and realistic. When the Argonaut ship sails through the strait, viewers are treated to an amazing scene where the sailors look up beneath Triton's (the live actor's) outstretched arm.

Unfortunately, the film failed at the box office, and critics were unimpressed. As Peary reported, Leo Mishkin of New York's *Morning Telegraph* wrote, "[The film] is strictly hot weather entertainment, suitable for keeping the children off the streets, perhaps, but hardly to be taken seriously by anybody beyond the age of puberty."

Years later, others begged to differ. Peary is but one writer who considers the film a genuine classic. Also, in 1992, the Academy of Motion Pictures Arts and Sciences acknowledged Harryhausen's accomplishments with its Gordon E. Sawyer Award for "technological contributions [which] have brought credit to the [film] industry." Actor Tom Hanks made the presentation and commented about the pinnacle of cinematic success: "Some people say 'Casablanca' or 'Citizen Kane.' I say 'Jason and the Argonauts' is the greatest film ever made."

True, Hank's comment may have been a bit over-enthusiastic, but it suggests the love that film aficionados have for such a well-made movie, whose birth was back-boned by a true artist. But in the mid-1960s, Harryhausen's film were dismissed as drive-in theater fodder or showcased at Saturday matinee showings that catered to kids, mostly boys. This was unfortunate, for Harryhausen would next launch his most technologically complex and visually intriguing film.

While working on *Jason,* Harryhausen was developing a project that would become *First Men in the Moon,* which helped him realize another dream: to adapt an H.G Wells novel. If Harryhausen thought color was problematic, he had to deal with another technological development. This would be a film shot in widescreen—the Panavision process—and it caused him even more headaches. But Harryhausen rose to the occasion. The film was released in 1964, and it included visions of lunar landscapes that could rival anything Stanley Kubrick later developed for *2001: A Space Odyssey.* Thanks to the Dynamation process, it allowed viewers to experience the silence of the vacuum of outer space, the desolation of the moon, and the exoticism of an unfamiliar landscape.

Also, the film included one of Harryhausen's most intricate creations: the so-called "moon calf," which was essentially an enormous caterpillar with numerous appendages. It was a stunning model brought to life, but what remains most memorable about the movie are those lunar landscapes, and the silence of dark space that Dynamation produced. Harryhausen took audiences where no man had ventured before, well in advance of the *Star Trek* television series or Kubrick's *2001: A Space Odyssey.* Again, the film did little business outside of Saturday matinees: unfortunate for a film that demonstrated such technical innovation and creativity. This was not a film for kids; this was a motion picture designed to prod the imagination of an adult.

The remainder of the decade was even less kind to Harryhausen. His next project, released in 1966, when he was freelancing and was called upon by Hammer Pictures, was *One Million Years B.C.* It is now remembered more for the promotional poster depicting Raquel Welch wearing a fur bikini—even though the dinosaur-populated film featured one of Harryhausen's best creations, the giant turtle. Critics' complaints were justified. The film's concept was ludicrous and foolishly anachronistic: dinosaurs did not co-exist with cavemen and well-endowed starlets.

His next film was *The Valley of Gwangi,* released in 1969, and it was as equally ridiculous. This minor effort depicted cowboys lassoing and capturing an Allosaurus that somehow survived in Mexico. Based upon ideas first generated by O'Brien, it was the Kong story all over again: adventurers capture a big beast and take it for display to the big city, where it breaks loose. Despite some stunning animation, the film suggested a boredom on Harryhausen's part. Harryhausen and Schneer decided to return to what they did best: exotic mythology. Next, they came up with one of their best collaborative achievements.

Revitalized Career

By 1973, many people had forgotten about Harryhausen and his splendid creations of the 1950s and 1960s. But he revitalized his presence in fine form with *The Golden Voyage of Sinbad.* The film, as *Castle of Frankenstein* magazine reported, represented "a radical improvement of Harryhausen's animation." Indeed, Dynamation evolved into Dynarama, a step forward that made it virtually impossible to detect any travelling matte work. The work was so seamless that it appeared the filmmakers were working on location, instead of with some painted landscapes.

The film entailed a four-year planning schedule. Special effects alone required a year of production. It was another multi-monster film for Harryhausen, and the movie climaxed with a splendid battle between a one-eyed centaur armed with a club and a ferociously feline gryphon that ripped flesh with stiletto-sharp claws.

Unfortunately, Harryhausen's next effort—*Sindbad and the Eye of the the Tiger* (1977)—was a major disappointment. It essentially rehashed the same plot as the previous Sinbad story. Instead of a warlock, Sinbad battled a witch, and once again the hero hoped to restore a kin dom's leader's good looks. Further, the creatures Harryhausen created demonstrated a paucity of imagination.

While the third Sinbad film disappointed, Harryhausen closed his feature-film career on a high note with *Clash of the Titans* (1981). At last, he was given a large budget from a major studio (MGM), and his cast included major actors including Sir Laurence Olivier, Burgess Meredith, and Maggie Smith. But Harryhausen fans could have cared less about who starred in the picture. They wanted spectacle. This Harryhausen provided.

The film included what is considered the scariest scene Harryhausen ever envisioned: the visit to the gorgon Medusa's castle. Bradbury described it as the "best thing that Ray ever photographed." If the young Harryhausen sought to determine how *haunted house* shocks are created, he went a step beyond.

Further, the climax included one of Harryhauen's best-ever creations: the four armed, fish-tailed Kraken, an enormous monster summoned from the depths of the sea. It seems appropriate that the creature's head resembled the "Ymir", as this film and this creation summarized all that everyone had ever loved about the Harryhausen creature portfolio.

Reluctantly Retired

This final film was well received, but Harryhausen did not mean for it to be his career end. He still had plans. He hoped to do at least two more Sinbad movies. It became clearly evident, though, that new technology was making his type of artistry obsolete. Hollywood became disinterested in the time-consuming skills and talents that Harryhausen could provide.

Thankfully, Harryhausen was not forgotten. Along with the 1992 Oscar award, he received the 2010 BAFTA award (the British Academy of Film and Television Arts) which recognized his cinematic contributions. In 2011, the Visual Effects Society bestowed upon him a Lifetime Achievement Award. Without Harryhausen, "there never would have been a *Star Wars* or *Jurassic Park,*" said director Steven Speilberg, as quoted in a *Los Angeles Times* obituary. Harryhausen's films inspired "awe," said Geoge Lucas, producer of *Star Wars.* Fortunately, Harryhausen received these awards while still alive. Harryhausen passed away in London, England on May 7, 2013, at the age of 92. He was survived by his wife Diana (Livingstone) who he married in 1962. He was also survived by his daughter, Vanessa.

Books

Harryhausen, Ray, *Fantasy Film Scrapbook,* Barnes and Co., 1972.

Peary, Danny, *Cult Movies,* Delta Publishing Company, 1981.

Periodicals

Castle of Frankenstein, volume 5, number 4 (summer), 1973; volume 6, number 1, 1974.

Famous Monsters of Filmland, November, 1962; June, 1963.

Filmfax, Jan/March 2005.

Los Angeles Times, May 7, 2013.

The New York Times, May 7, 2013.

USA Today, May 7, 2013.

Online

"Biography," The Official Ray Harryhausen Website, http://www.rayharryhausen.com/index.php (October 31, 2013.

"Monsters, Inc.-An Interview with Ray Harryhausen," *Bright Lights Film Journal,* http://brightlightsfilm.com/58/58harryhauseniv.php#.UgtyQVLD9Mw(October 31, 2013).

"Ray Harryhausen," *TCM,* http://www.tcm.com/tcmdb/person/82065%7C127790/Ray-Harryhausen/biography.html (October 31, 2013).□

Elizabeth Lee Hazen

American scientist Elizabeth Lee Hazen (1885-1975) is the co-discoverer, with Rachel Fuller Brown, of the antifungal antibiotic nystatin.

Born August 24, 1885, in Rich, Mississippi, Elizabeth Lee Hazen was the daughter of William Edgar Hazen and his wife, Maggie Harper. Her father was a cotton farmer, and the couple had three children. Hazen suffered much early tragedy, with her parents both dying before she was four years old. In the same period, sadly, her younger brother also died.

Hazen and her elder sister, Annis, joined the family of a paternal uncle, Robert Henry Hazen and his wife Laura Crawford, in nearby Lula, Mississippi. Though he was not educated, he wanted his daughters and nieces to attend college. After attending public schools in Coahoma County, Hazen went to the Mississippi Industrial Institute and College at Columbus (now the Mississippi University for Women). While an undergraduate, she became interested in science and earned her B.S. in 1910. She also earned a certificate in dressmaking.

Worked in Army Labs During World War II

From 1910 to 1916, Hazen worked as a high school teacher in Jackson, Mississippi. During the summers, Hazen would further her education at the University of Tennessee and the University of Virginia. Eventually, she decided to pursue graduate studies. Moving to New York City, Hazen studied biology at Columbia University. She received her M.S. in biology in 1917, then volunteered to work in the laboratories of the U.S. Army. At this time, the United States had entered World War I, and many scientists supported the war effort. Hazen worked for the U.S. Army's diagnostic laboratories at Camp Sheridan in Alabama from 1918 to 1919.

When the war ended, Hazen further delayed continuing her graduate work by working in a hospital laboratory in Fairmont, West Virginia. From 1919 to 1923, she was the assistant director of the Clinical and Bacteriology Laboratory of Cook Hospital there. In 1923, Hazen finally went back to Columbia and began working on her Ph.D. in microbiology. Four years later, she earned the degree, and was one of the few women medical scientists with a Ph.D. She was also one of the first women doctoral candidates at Columbia.

She was soon recognized as an expert in diagnosing and treating viral and bacterial infections. In 1928, she was named resident bacteriologist at Presbyterian Hospital. From 1927 to 1931, Hazen was also employed as an instructor at the Columbia College of Physicians and Surgeons.

Joined New York State Lab

Beginning in 1931, Hazen focused on research, initially joining the New York State Department of Health as the head of the bacterial diagnosis lab in the Division of Laboratories and Research in New York City. For at least a decade, she concentrated on infectious diseases. Hazen also specialized in identifying disease-causing fungi, and was widely recognized as an expert in a field which had been underinvestigated. In addition, she had developed a reputation as a gifted scientific investigator.

During this period, Hazen was able to discern what caused an outbreak of anthrax, linking it to a Westchester County-based brush factory. Anthrax is a disease that is primarily linked to cows and horses, not humans. Hazen figured out that the outbreak was caused by animal bristles used in the production of the brushes.

Hazen also located the cause of the first American case of a type of food poisoning called Clostridium botulinum. It is found in foods that have not been properly preserved, and in this particular case, came from canned fish imported from Germany and Labrador that had spoiled. In addition, she discovered unknown sources of tularemia, also known as rabbit fever, in New York. This infection is commonly found in wild rodents, but can be passed to humans through insect bites or the handling of the flesh of infected animals.

Focused on Antifungal Research

During and after World War II, Hazen's research shifted further to focus on fungal, or mycotic, infections in humans. Influenced by the recent discovery of penicillin, an antibacterial antibiotic, Hazen focused nearly exclusively on mycology, or fungi-focused, research. She worked with an organic chemist named Rachel Fuller Brown, who was also employed in the division of laboratories at the New York State Department of Health, but based in Albany.

One reason for the importance of this research was penicillin itself. A side effect of penicillin was that it encouraged the growth of fungus in the mouth and stomach, and could lead to fatal infections. This side effect needed to be addressed so that penicillin could be used widely, instead of just on bacterial diseases, as was the case in this time period. Hazen's research focus was influenced by the discovery, in 1944, by Selman A. Waksman that antibiotics were produced by certain bacteria, called actinomycetes, that live in the soil.

Also in this era, fungal infections were common and rapidly spreading among school children in New York City. These infections included moniliasis, also known as thrush, a condition found in the mouth that could make swallowing painful. There were antifungals available, but they were not safe for human consumption. Though Hazen had her own health problems, she focused much time and energy on her vital research.

Hazen began examining cultures of fungi from local laboratories, other researchers, and various collections to further educate herself about mycotic sources and diseases. She also worked with Rhoda Benham, who was an authority on pathogenic fungi, and took additional coursework at Columbia. Originally, Hazen formed her own collection of systemic fungi to develop standard methods of examination for disease-conducting fungi. This collection of culture ultimately provided Hazen with comparative data she used in her research.

Together, Hazen and Fuller began looking for an antifungal actinomycete in nature. Hazen collected and analyzed soil samples with streptomycetes with strong anti-fungal activigeis from around the United States. The pair were looking for microbes that might be effective antifugnals for humans. Brown tested Hazen's samples, and extracted any active agents from the microbes. Brown sent the results to Hazen, who continued the analysis. Hazen tested the antifungal agents on the fungi.

Discovered Nystatin

In 1948, Hazen and Fuller had a breakthrough when they discovered what they called fungicidin, an antifungal antibiotic, in the dirt from a farm near Warrenton, Virginia, owned by a friend of Hazen. It proved to be the first highly active fungal agent that was safe and effective in humans. Hazen and Fuller renamed it fungicidin nystatin in 1950, to honor their employer, New York State laboratories. Its discovery was announced by the National Academy of Science that year as well.

Since its commercial introduction in 1954, Nystatin has been taken to treat infections caused by a fungus, primarily yeast infections like candida and Asprgillus of the skin, intestines, vagina, and mucous membranes. Athletes' foot, for example, is one fungal condition that nystatin can treat. It is also used to fight mold in food for humans and animals, and, in 1966, even used to restore murals and manuscripts from mold and water damage after the Arno River flooded Florence, Italy. Nystatin worked in this scenario because it did not effect pigments found in paints. In addition, nystatin is used to prevent Dutch elm disease in trees and to kill molds on produce.

It took several years to settle patent rights and begin commercial production of the drug. The process by which Hazen and Brown produced nystatin was far too expensive for commercial production. Also, the state entity for which the pair worked had no patent policy. The New York State Department of Health suggested Hazen and Brown approach the Research Corporation, a nonprofit that focused on patenting and licensing inventions for research and educational institutions. Because of the Research Corporation's policy, Hazen and Brown had to give all rights to nystatin to the nonprofit, which in turn would use any financial profits philanthropically. Both Hazen and Fuller decided that their profits from the sale of nystatin would be given to support further scientific research.

Funneled Profits to Support Science

In the final agreement drawn up between the scientists and the Research Corporation, half of nystatin's royalties went to the nonprofit for its philanthropic work. The other half went to the Brown-Hazen Fund which supported research into biology and related sciences, especially by women and young researchers. The Brown-Hazen Fund administered such research grants beginning in 1951. Later, it was used to fund undergraduate education in biology as well as research and training in medical mycology.

During its first year on the market, nystatin was used across the United States and earned $135,000. The drug would earn a total of $13.4 million in royalties between 1955 and 1976, when the patent expired. The patent on nystatin had been held by the drug company E.R. Squibb and Sons throughout this time period.

Continuing to do research for another decade, Hazen and Fuller discovered an antibacterial agent called phalamycin in 1953, though it was too toxic for human use. Hazen also co-wrote a book, *Laboratory Identification of Pathogenic Fungi Simplified* in 1955. She became an associate professor at the Albany Medical College in 1958. Hazen and Fuller announced their discovery of the antifungal agent capacidin in 1959. Like phalamycin, it was also extremely toxic and unfit for use on humans. Hazen spent two years at the Albany, New York-based school, before retiring. In retirement, she returned to the mycology lab at Columbia as a full-time guest investigator. She continued to conduct research there until 1973.

Though Hazen and Fuller worked together on their discovery of nystatin and other projects, Hazen avoided the spotlight and allowed Brown to present their joint papers. The pair received many awards together over the years, including the Squibb Award in chemotherapy in 1955, the Sara Benham Award from the Mycological Society of America in 1968, and the first Chemical Pioneer Award from the American Institute of Chemists in 1975. The latter award was given to Hazen only after a change in bylaws, because she was a microbiologist, not a chemist. It also marked the first time that the award had been given to women.

Inducted into Inventors Hall of Fame

In failing health by 1973, Hazen then entered a retirement home in Seattle, Washington, where her sister already was living. Hazen died at Mount St. Vincent Hospital in Seattle on June 24, 1975. Posthumously, Hazen and Brown were inducted into the National Inventors Hall of Fame in 1994. They were the second and third women inducted. Describing their impact, the Massachusetts Institute of Technology's *Inventor of the Week* website stated, "Their generosity has provided a great deal of further medical research; their example has inspired many women to pursue a scientific career."

Books

American Inventors, Entrepreneurs, and Business Visionaries, Revised ed., Facts on File, 2011.

American Women of Science Since 1900, Volume 1., ABC-CLIO, 2011.

Dictionary of Women Worldwide: 25,000 Women Through the Ages, edited by Anne Commire and Deborah Klezmer, Yorkin Publications, 2007.

Encyclopedia of World Scientist, Revised ed., Facts on File, 2007.

UXL Biographies, Gale, 2003.

Women in World History: A Biographical Encyclopedia, edited by Anne Commire, Yorkin Publications, 2002.

World of Microbiology and Immunology, edited by Brenda Wilmoth Lerner and K. Lee Lerner, Gale, 2003.

Periodicals

Gazette (Montreal, Quebec, Canada), February 7, 1994.

Online

"Elizabeth Lee Hazen," *Inventor's Hall of Fame,* http://www.invent.org/hall_of_fame/75.html (September 11, 2013).

"Elizabeth Lee Hazen (1885-1975) and Rachel Fuller Brown (1898-1980)," *Inventor of the Week,* http://web.mit.edu/invent/iow/HazenBrown.html (September 11, 2013).

Levon Helm

The American musician Levon Helm (1940–2012) exerted a strong influence over the development of roots rock and later alternative country and Americana styles, both as a member of The Band and during his solo career.

Helm, a drummer and vocalist, has never been a household name, but he was present at the birth of rock and roll, and over a career lasting more than 50 years he was often, as his official website biography put it, "in the right place at the right time." His music-making intersected with, and contributed vitally to, the emergence of Bob Dylan's electric style, and when he and a group of Canadian musicians associated with Dylan took the name of The Band and released the album *Music from Big Pink* in 1968, they created something new—a form of rock music that was influenced by traditional country and other roots genres but did not seek to imitate them. The list of musicians shaped by Helm's music is long, running from Eric Clapton and the Eagles in the 1960s and 1970s through Emmylou Harris and Steve Earle in the 1980s, down to My Morning Jacket in the 2000s. Despite health problems and tragedies among his longtime bandmates, Helm lived and remained active long enough to become an elder statesman of Americana music.

Inspired by Bill Monroe

Levon Helm was born Mark Lavon Helm on May 26, 1940, in Elaine, Arkansas, in the Mississippi River delta. His father was a cotton farmer; his mother claimed to be descended from members of the Chickasaw Native American tribe. The area was musically rich, with both blues and country bands active in live appearances and on local radio, and the family enjoyed listening to such shows as King Biscuit Time on the Helena, Arkansas, station KFFA. Helm began to show a strong interest in music after hearing a concert by Bill Monroe and His Blue Grass Boys when he was six years old, and three years later his father gave him a guitar. Three years after that, Helm made a rudimentary string bass from a washtub and some wire, gave it to his sister, and began performing with her as Lavon and Linda at 4-H events and the like.

In high school, with the new rockabilly style rapidly gaining fans in nearby Memphis, Helm formed a new band of his own, the Jungle Bush Beaters. When he saw an Elvis Presley performance in 1955 that featured drummer D.J. Fontana, he decided to switch from guitar to drums. The first non-local musician to spot his talent was vocalist Conway Twitty, later a major country star but at that time active in the rockabilly field. When Helm was 17, Lavon and Linda opened for Twitty, and the singer invited Helm to sit in at some of his shows. Later that year, rockabilly singer Ronnie Hawkins was looking for musicians to join him in touring Canada, where rockabilly was just taking off. He heard about Helm from his guitarist, Jimmy Ray Paulman, and offered him a slot as his drummer and driver. Helm, after keeping a promise to his parents to finish high school, headed north to join Hawkins on tour.

Several of Helm's youthful Arkansas-born bandmates soon tired of the road and returned home to Arkansas, but Helm, encouraged by a pair of hit singles Hawkins and the band scored on the Roulette label, stayed on in Canada. As Hawkins, pleased by the lack of competition there, laid plans for further Canadian tours, Helm emerged as the de facto leader of his band, the Hawks. In the early 1960s, the pair recruited a group of ambitious teenage Canadian musicians: guitarist Robbie Robertson, vocalist Richard Manuel, keyboardist Garth Hudson, and bassist Rick Danko. By 1963, the Hawks were tiring of Hawkins' taskmaster ways and decided to strike out on their own. They used the names Levon and the Hawks (Helm's bandmates found "Lavon" difficult to pronounce) and the Canadian Squires at first.

Recommended to Dylan by Secretary

Pickings were lean at first, and the band recorded two singles that went nowhere. But they got a break when a Canadian secretary, Mary Martin, who worked for Bob Dylan's manager, Albert Grossman, recommended them as possible Dylan collaborators. At the time, Dylan was in the early stages of his then-controversial decision to begin perfomring with electric instruments, but the group that had backed his tumultuous first foray at the Newport Folk Festival, the Paul Butterfield Blues Band, had its own future commitments and was unavailable. Dylan turned to Helm and Robertson, who suddenly found themselves backing one of the best-known musicians in the United States at such major venues as the Hollywood Bowl and the Forest Hills Tennis Club in New York. Later in 1965, the rest of the Hawks joined Dylan. Sometimes Dylan called them the Crackers, but most often he simply referred to them as The Band, and that name stuck.

As the first Dylan tour developed, however, Helm was unhappy. Hardcore folk music fans, dismayed by Dylan's move in the direction of electric music, heckled and booed the singer and the band, and to Helm, for whom music was essentially a positive communal experience, the audience's reaction was disturbing. Helm finally left the band and returned to Arkansas, believing that his musical career was over, and with Dylan out of commission for much of 1966 after a motorcycle accident, it began to look as though he might be right.

As Dylan recovered in a pink house in West Saugerties, New York, near Woodstock, however, he was joined by Helm's bandmates and soon by Helm himself. At first the group recorded with Dylan, creating music in a new, sparse style marked by the use of American traditional instruments. These recordings, later issued as *The Basement Tapes,* created intense excitement among musicians looking for an alternative to the complex high-concept music of the Beatles that was in vogue at the time, and the stage was set for The Band's signing to the Capitol label and the release of their album debut, *Music from Big Pink,* in 1968, with artwork by Dylan on the cover; Big Pink was the pink house that had come to serve as the group's creative center, although the album itself was not recorded there.

That album and its successor, *The Band* (1969), were among the most influential releases of the rock era. British guitarist Eric Clapton made the decision to embark on a solo career after hearing *Music from Big Pink,* and even the Beatles moved in a noticeably rootsier direction at the end of the 1960s. A unique feature of The Band's music was that all the members took lead vocals at times, and Helm, in addition to propelling the music with his loose, organic drumming, contributed lead vocals to about a quarter of The Band's songs, including the much-covered "Ophelia" and "The Night They Drove Old Dixie Down." The Band released nine albums between 1968 and 1976, never achieving superstar status but placing all their releases in the upper reaches of pop album sales charts. Their most successful album was their third, *Stage Fright* (1970). The group was less oriented toward singles, but "Up on Cripple Creek," again with Helm on lead vocals, cracked the pop top 25. As The Band's sole American member, Helm added a note of authenticity to the group's down-home sound: "With their stories of medicine shows and moonshine, many of his songs recalled his Deep South upbringing," noted the *Telegraph.*

Avoided Hall of Fame Induction

The Band broke up in 1976 after a farewell concert, titled *The Last Waltz,* which was released as an album and also became the basis for a famous documentary film by director Martin Scorsese. The film marked the beginning of a longstanding disagreement between Robertson and Helm, who felt that his role in the group had been slighted. When The Band reunited for tours beginning in 1983, Robertson was not included, and Helm refused to attend the induction of the group into the Rock and Roll Hall of Fame in 1994. The deaths of Manuel, by suicide, in 1986 and of Danko in

1999 ended The Band's activities as a group after they recorded three albums in the 1980s and 1990s.

Helm's solo career began with the album *Levon Helm and the RCO All-Stars* in 1977, followed by *American Son* (1980) and two albums entitled *Levon Helm* in 1978 and 1982. He made several successful film appearances, most notably as the father of country singer Loretta Lynn in the biographical film *Coal Miner's Daughter* (1980). Helm was diagnosed with throat cancer in 1998, and treatments left him unable to sing. He continued to perform, however, on drums, mandolin, and harmonica.

In the 2000s, Helm's voice gradually returned and he inaugurated a series of live concerts and recordings called the *Midnight Ramble,* at his studio in Woodstock, New York, at the beginning of 2004. Helm performed at some of these shows, but mostly they were given over to appearances by a large collection of roots musicians of all ages, from veteran blues pianist Johnnie Johnson to country singer Emmylou Harris to rootsy alternative rockers My Morning Jacket to tejano accordionist Steve Jordan. The Midnight Ramble sessions produced three albums, plus the live *Ramble at the Ryman* road-show album recorded at the Ryman Auditorium in Nashville.

Helm also recorded two more solo albums, *Dirt Farmer* (2007) and *Electric Dirt* (2008). Both albums earned widespread acclaim. *Dirt Farmer* included songs Helm had learned from his parents, and won a Grammy award for Best Traditional Folk Album. *Electric Dirt* won a second Grammy, for Best Americana Album, by which time Helm was seen as the progenitor, not only of his musician daughter Amy (a member of the alternative country band Ollabelle), but of a great deal of music that had come to be called Americana. *Ramble at the Ryman* earned Helm a third Grammy, for Best Americana Album, early in 2012. By that time, though, his cancer had returned, and he died in New York on April 19, 2012.

Books

Contemporary Musicians, Volume 75, Gale, 2013.

Helm, Levon, with Stephen Davis, *This Wheel's on Fire,* Plexus, 1993.

Periodicals

Guardian (London, England), April 21, 2012.

International Herald Tribune, April 21, 2012.

New York, October 29, 2007.

Telegraph (London, England), April 21, 2012.

Times (London, England), April 21, 2012.

Toronto Star, April 20, 2012.

Variety, April 20, 2013.

Online

"Biography & Movies," Levon Helm Official Website, http://www.levonhelm.com/biography.htm (September 15, 2013).

"Levon Helm," *AllMusic,* http://www.allmusic.com (September 15, 2013).□

Henrietta Maria, Queen, consort of Charles I, King of England

Henrietta Maria of France (1609–1669) was one of the most unpopular queens in English history. The daughter of the King of France and wife of King Charles I, she was neither English nor Protestant, and her interfaith marriage occurred not long after decades of religious wars left a lasting imprint on the British Isles and Continental Europe, too. Her husband's reign ended disastrously, when his refusal to submit to Parliament spurred the English Civil War; in 1649 he was convicted of treason and publicly beheaded—a nadir in the history of England for which his foreign-born wife was widely, and unjustly, blamed.

Queen Henrietta Maria was named after her father, King Henry IV of France, the founder of the House of Bourbon dynasty. He ruled from 1589 to 1610 and also possessed the kingdom of Navarre, one of Spain's oldest royal titles. Henrietta's mother was Marie de' Medici, daughter of the Grand Duke of Tuscany. Born in the Palais du Louvre in Paris on November 25, 1609, the infant Princess of France was the last of the couple's five children. Six months later, her mother was crowned queen of France in one of a long list of incautious decisions made by her father. He was slain by an assassin's knife the next day, and Henrietta's mother ruled as regent for her eldest son, who became King Louis XIII of France.

Henrietta was raised in an atmosphere of sumptuous extravagance and meticulous protocol as a Princess of France. From an early age her future spouse was the subject of much discussion and negotiation. A union with England was almost unthinkable, but Charles Stuart—England's Duke of York and the second son of King James I of England and his wife Anne of Denmark—met the teenager during a brief thaw in relations between the two longtime enemies in 1623, and a match was summarily arranged.

Henrietta's new fiancé was the son of a Scottish king who had advanced to the English throne, and Charles became next in the line of succession after the sudden death of his brother, Henry Frederick, in 1612. England had been rocked by religious unrest since the 1530s, when King Henry VIII famously broke with the Church in Rome and established himself as head of the Church of England. The Protestant Reformation in Germany and other parts of Western Europe had destabilized the entire continent and complicated England's foreign relations with ardently Roman Catholic kingdoms in Europe, especially Spain and France.

© Image Asset Management Ltd./Alamy

Married King of England

Henrietta's future father-in-law, King James I, died on March 27, 1625. Six weeks later, her and Charles's first marriage ceremony took place in Paris, France, with a relative, the Duc de Chevreuse, standing for the English monarch. This permitted Henrietta to sail for England with full privileges accorded a queen. A second ceremony took place, with Charles, on June 13, 1625, at St. Augustine's Church in Canterbury. Theirs was an interfaith marriage by agreement on both sides, but there was major opposition in England to a foreign-born, Roman Catholic queen, and because Henrietta was not a member of the Church of England she could not be crowned at Charles's coronation; instead she took the title Queen Consort.

The first years of Henrietta and Charles's marriage were turbulent. She had brought with her an enormous retinue of French courtiers, including a dozen Roman Catholic priests, and their presence at Charles's court was problematic. Henrietta's foreign ways and devout Roman Catholicism stirred rumors of yet another plot to cut ties with the Church of England and reunite with the Church of Rome. Charles bowed to some internal pressure and dismissed members of Henrietta's entourage in June of 1626.

As king, Charles battled Parliament over finances and executive powers. The Parliaments of 1625 and 1626 voiced major opposition to him, and a 1628 Parliament proved even more unwilling to compromise. After that, Charles governed without any parliament for eleven years, which incited widespread dissatisfaction inside many strata of English society. In the 1630s, Charles dealt harshly with a religious sect known as the Puritans, and their persecution prompted many of them to settle new colonies in North America. Persons accused of making libelous statements against Henrietta also faced harsh punitive measures. Henrietta was criticized for spending lavishly, including an ornate chapel she had built at Somerset House, and for taking part in masques, or plays at court, in which she appeared onstage in disguise. So scandalous was this last action to religious conservatives that all performances of drama would be banned when the Puritans, under Oliver Cromwell, eventually seized power.

Mettle Battle-Tested

Henrietta and Charles had several children. The first was a stillborn son, Charles James, in March of 1629. Eleven months later she gave birth to a crown prince, also named Charles. In late 1631, the couple's first daughter, Mary, was born, followed almost two years later by a son who would also eventually rule England as James II. In December 1635, a second daughter, Elizabeth, was born, but she died at age 14. In early March 1637, Henrietta gave birth to daughter Anne, and in 1640, a third son, Henry—the future Duke of Gloucester—arrived.

During these years England was divided between the Royalists, who supported Charles and his autocratic rule, and the Parliamentarians, who campaigned for a more democratic form of government. When Charles raised taxes without parliamentary approval, and issued edicts that were considered favorable to English Catholics, he roused further ire. Another issue was Ireland: Charles had sent the Earl of Strafford to deal with a rebellion, and Strafford was widely loathed for his actions there, but the king remained supportive. Charles finally summoned Parliament again in 1640 in order to pass new tax laws, but instead the so-called Long Parliament presented to him a list of grievances. This was known as the Grand Remonstrance of 1641. Charles then attempted to have some of his most vociferous critics in Parliament arrested, and later tried to dissolve Parliament. That led to the start of the First English Civil War.

When the war erupted, Henrietta made her way to the Netherlands to plead for financial aid for the Royalist cause from the Prince of Orange. Reports of her attempts to sell off jewelry and tin mines in Cornwall to raise funds came back to England and incited additional furor against the Catholic queen. There was even an attempt to block Henrietta from returning to England in early 1643, and her ship—loaded with arms and soldiers—evaded a naval blockade set up by vessels controlled by Parliamentarians.

Fled to France

Henrietta and Charles spent the winter of 1643–44 at their new royal court established at Oxford, living at a house at Merton College under heavy guard. In early 1644, pregnant once again, Henrietta traveled southward, part of the way with Charles; they parted at Abingdon, never to see one another again. Henrietta made her way to Exeter, where she gave birth to the Princess Henriette-Anne. She was forced to leave the child with one of her ladies-in-waiting and sailed again for France in July. Once again, the ship carrying her was fired upon by the Parliamentarian navy. She retreated to the safety of her French family, but even her presence in Paris was fraught with peril, as civil unrest percolated through France, too.

A turning point in the war came at the Battle of Naseby in June of 1645, when Charles's Royalist forces were routed in their attempt to reach allies in Scotland. He was forced to flee for his life, and left behind a cache of personal correspondence between him and Henrietta; this was published in booklet form under the title *The King's Cabinet Opened,* and it proved ruinous to the Royalist cause, showing that the royal couple had indeed been seeking foreign aid from England's Catholic enemies. Henrietta remained in France, where her son Prince Charles joined her. She and her husband continued to correspond, using a cipher key to encrypt their letters. Both seemed to believe either time or a foreign power would come to their aid. Charles rejected one proposed peace settlement in late 1647, and a renewal of hostilities began with Scottish support in the Second English Civil War in early 1648.

News from England took agonizing weeks to reach Henrietta in Saint-Germain-en-Laye, her castle hideout near Paris. She learned days or even weeks after the fact that her husband had made his way to the Isle of Wight on the southern coast of England, where he had tried to sail for France in late November of 1648. Instead Charles was betrayed by a local lord and taken into custody by the Parliamentarians. Parliament voted to try him on charges of treason, and he was convicted and sentenced to death on January 27, 1649. England's king was beheaded three days later in front of enormous crowds at the Palace of Whitehall in London, with a heavy cordon of hundreds of guards protecting the scaffold to prevent a riot. There were even iron wedges and ropes built onto the platform, in case Charles resisted, but he did not.

Henrietta did not learn that the death sentence had been carried out until ten days later, on February 9. She was devastated and already in poor physical health. "I have been the artificer of my misfortunes," she later wrote to her son, according to *Letters of Queen Henrietta Maria, Including Her Private Correspondence with Charles the First.* "I ought never to have left the king my lord and husband, and our most loving father, since if I could not have prevented an end so disproportionate to the so great worth of such a king, at least I should have had the consolation of accompanying him to prison and the horrors of death."

Returned for Restoration

Charles's barbarous death finally galvanized opposition to the Parliamentarians and spurred a Third English Civil War that lasted until 1651. Along with Louis XVI of France, who died during the French Revolution, and Russia's Tsar Nicholas II, Charles is one of just three reigning European monarchs to be put to death as a political gesture. In 1653 the leader of the Parliamentarians, Oliver Cromwell, took the title Lord Protector and assumed powers equal to that of the monarchy. After Cromwell's death, Prince Charles, Henrietta's first son, was invited to return to the throne in what became known as the Restoration. He ruled as King Charles II. She returned with him and lived at Somerset House. In 1665, she moved back to Paris, where she died on September 10, 1669, two months short of her sixtieth birthday. James, her second son, succeeded Charles in 1685 upon the latter's death, but King James II was the last Roman Catholic ever to wear the British crown. In 1688, an act of parliament deemed that from henceforward no Roman Catholic could succeed to the throne.

Charles and Henrietta's youngest daughter, Henriette-Anne, married the brother of France's King Louis XIV. That couple's daughter, Anne Marie d'Orléans, married the Duke of Burgundy and gave birth to a future King Louis XV of France. Other descendants married into royal lines across Europe, including the Habsburgs. The House of Hanover, which succeeded the House of Stuart in 1714, was descended from the sister of Charles I, Elizabeth Stuart, who was married to a German prince, Frederick V. The German connection was broken off from that house and its heirs still held the British throne as the renamed House of Windsor. The reigning monarch, Queen Elizabeth II, is a direct descendant of Henrietta's sister-in-law Elizabeth Stuart.

Books

Ashley, Maurice, "The Stuarts," in *The Lives of the Kings & Queens of England,* edited by Antonia Fraser, Weidenfeld & Nicolson, 1975; revised edition, University of California Press, 2000.

Letters of Queen Henrietta Maria, Including Her Private Correspondence with Charles the First, edited by Mary Anne Everett Green, Richard Bentley, 1857.

Whitaker, Katie, *A Royal Passion: The Turbulent Marriage of King Charles I of England and Henrietta Maria of France,* W. W. Norton, 2010.□

Bert Hinkler

Australian pilot Bert Hinkler (1892–1933) has been called one of the forgotten heroes of aviation history. The first person to complete a solo flight from England to Australia in 1928, Hinkler set five new records on that 12,000-mile trek alone, including the first nonstop flight from London to Rome. Three years later, the daring Australian became the first person to fly across the southern Atlantic Ocean, piloting his De Havilland-built Puss Moth from Brazil to Senegal in just 22 hours.

Herbert John Louis Hinkler was born on December 8, 1892, in the town of Bundaberg, Queensland, Australia. This was the coastal, tropical part of Queensland, and the region produced timber and sugarcane. Hinkler's father was originally from Germany and worked as a laborer to support his family. The future aviator's mother, Frances Bonney Hinkler, was from a family with roots in Brisbane, the nearest major city to Bundaberg.

Built Glider

Hinkler was raised with four younger siblings in a simple cottage at 69 Gavin Street in North Bundaberg. He attended local public schools until age 14, at which point he joined the workforce to help support his family. Obsessed by stories of planes and pilots at an early age, Hinkler was about to turn eleven years old in 1903 when Americans Orville and Wilbur Wright made their historic flight on the beaches of Kitty Hawk, North Carolina. In his teen years, Hinkler amassed a small library of newspaper clippings and issues of magazines devoted to advances in aviation science. With parts taken from the scrap heap of the foundry where he worked, he built a wood glider using calico fabric and a flour paste to hold it together. A pair of bicycle wheels served as the undercarriage, and Hinkler convinced friends to help him try to get it aloft at the local beach. When that worked, Hinkler literally strapped himself in onto a board and repeated the takeoff, trying to use a rudimentary steering device he had added to it. A combination of luck and good winds helped him safely return to the sand, and Hinkler and his glider were photographed for a Brisbane newspaper story.

After completing a correspondence course in aviation science in 1911, Hinkler tried to find steady work with some of Australia's first pilots and visiting stunt flyers, but decided to move to England to pursue his career. He worked as a furnace stoker aboard a tramp steamer, the cheapest way to reach Europe. The trip took weeks and the conditions aboard such vessels were grim; the accommodations were grubby and the route included perilous waters around the southern tip of Africa at the Cape of Good Hope. He arrived in England in early 1914, and found a job with Sopwith Aviation, one of the new plane-manufacturing firms. When World War I erupted later in 1914, Hinkler enlisted in the forerunner of the Royal Air Force, the Royal Naval Air Service. Finally, his quest for flight was fulfilled, and Hinkler flew as both a pilot and a gunner in what became the first aerial-combat war in human history. He and his fellow pilots flew daring missions over the English Channel to fire at German targets in Belgium and France, and also engaged in gun battles against Germany's equally new and formidable air force.

Made First Notable European Treks

After the war's end in 1918, Hinkler was hired by A.V. Roe and Company, another British aircraft manufacturer, and became the firm's chief test pilot. Hinkler was a particularly gifted master of its tiny Avro 534 model, also known as the Avro Baby. It was in one of these 35-horsepower, single-seater open-air biplanes that he made the first-ever nonstop solo flight from London to Turin, Italy. It took him nine hours and 35 minutes, and for it he was awarded the prestigious Britannia Medal of the Royal Aero Club for the most meritorious aviation achievement of 1920.

Hinkler's dream was to make the first solo flight to Australia, an enormous distance that would take him over the Alps, the deserts of the Middle East, and the Indian Ocean; it would also require multiple refueling stops. Ongoing conflicts on the ground made this unfeasible in the early 1920s, so he disassembled an Avro Baby and sailed back to Australia with it to visit family and demonstrate his flying skills. He made several notable jaunts up and down the Australian coastline, and back in England continued to make news for his flights in new Avro planes. He won the Royal Aero Club's Grosvenor Cup race in 1924 for light aircraft, and traveled to the United States a year later as a reserve pilot for the Schneider Trophy seaplane contest, held in the Baltimore/Chesapeake Bay area that year. On December 22, 1926, he made British aviation history again by completing the first mountaintop landing in Britain at Helvellyn, a peak in England's Lake District.

In 1926, Hinkler began flying a new experimental aircraft made by Avro, the Avian. He worked with designers and engineers to fine-tune it for longer-distance flights. In August of 1927, he made the first nonstop flight from England to Latvia, touching down near the capital city of Riga in just ten and a half hours. Three months later, he and another pilot, Robert H. McIntosh, attempted to make the first nonstop flight from England to India. They flew in a Dutch-made Fokker monoplane, but were forced to land in Poland due to mechanical issues.

Catapulted to Fame

Hinkler secured his place in aviation history with his historic flight from England to Australia, which began on February 7, 1928. He flew his Avro Avian, taking off from Croydon Airfield near London and 900 miles later landed it safely in Rome, setting a new record time for a nonstop flight from England to the Italian capital. He stopped in Malta while flying over the Mediterranean Sea, then landed in Tobruk, Libya, for another round of refueling. He was welcomed by Royal Air Force (RAF) personnel in Ramla in British-controlled Palestine, then ventured east to another British-held air station in Basra, Iraq, on February 12. From there he continued to Karachi, Pakistan—again, another thriving British colonial outpost—and further south to Kolkata, India, which he reached on February 16. After that came Rangoon, the main city in British Burma, and he landed in Singapore on February 19. From Bandung in the Dutch West Indies he flew to another part of the Indonesian archipelago, the island of Sumbawa, where he spent a sleepless, mosquito-plagued night in Bima. The final leg of his journey was a 970-mile flight to Darwin, the capital city of Australia's Northern Territory. This was the most perilous stretch, taking him across more than 400 miles of open sea. Enormous crowds waited for hours for his arrival in Darwin on February 22, 1928.

Hinkler's feat was the longest solo flight ever made by an aviator to that date, and he had also set a remarkable average speed of 92 miles per hour for the 15-day flight, of which he had spent a total of 134 hours in flight, or nearly six consecutive days. There had been previous flights from England to Australia, but they were not solo flights, and the fastest time on record was 28 days, almost as long as the standard sea route. Hinkler received a hero's welcome on his tour of Australia, and news of his feat made headlines around the world.

Hinkler was often compared to Charles Lindbergh, the American aviator who made the first nonstop, solo Atlantic Ocean crossing between New York City and Paris in 1927. Lindbergh was given a ticker-tape parade when he returned to America and named *Time* magazine's Person of the Year. Hinkler had a more difficult time turning his feat into a source of steady income, however, and even Avro struggled to stay solvent. In the spring of 1929, the *New York Times* announced that Hinkler would be joining the American company that made Avro planes for the U.S. market, Whittelsey Manufacturing in Bridgeport, Connecticut. Distance flights over open sea roused his interest in seaplanes, but his plan to design and build them was stalled by the onset of the Great Depression, which began with the Wall Street Crash in October of 1929. He was also dejected when another Australian aviator, Charles Kingsford Smith, beat Hinkler's solo England-to-Australia record in October of 1930, shortening it by five days.

Flew Through Atlantic Storm

One of Avro's main competitors was another British firm, De Havilland. In the spring of 1931, Hinkler turned up in Toronto, Canada, and bought an enclosed-cockpit plane, a De Havilland Puss Moth, that had a Canadian registration number. He flew on to Buffalo, New York, then to Pawtucket, Rhode Island. Later that year, after several test flights at the North Beach, Long Island airfield—which later became New York's LaGuardia Airport—he set out for the Caribbean island of Jamaica, but failed to alert any journalists or raise any publicity prior to his mission. The *New York Times* reported on October 28, 1931, that Hinkler made a perfect landing in Kingston, Jamaica, and brandished a copy of the same newspaper dated October 27 as proof of his feat. Hinkler had flown over 1,800 miles nonstop in 18 hours, nearly all of them over the Atlantic Ocean and Caribbean waters.

Several days later Hinkler turned up in British Guiana, on the northeastern coast of South America. He took the Puss Moth on to Brazil, where authorities detained him for flying without a permit. British Embassy officials interceded on his behalf and he was released after four days. On November 26, 1931, he took off from the Brazilian port city of Natal and headed for West Africa. Twenty-two hours later he landed in St. Louis, the capital city of French West Africa. Once again, Hinkler had set a new record for solo overseas flight and also won the distinction of becoming the first lone pilot to cross the southern Atlantic Ocean. "I ran into every kind of weather and wind imaginable," he told reporters, according to a *New York Times* account. He added that his adventure included "the worst electrical storm I have ever seen. It was accompanied by high winds and I battled it for six full hours. I was completely blinded."

Hinkler's feat brought him a second Britannia Trophy from the Royal Aero Club, and he spent much of 1932 planning a reprise of his England-to-Australia solo flight to beat the latest record time. Shortly after 3 a.m. on January 7, 1933, Hinkler took off from a runway at the Harmondsworth Aerodrome, near what later became London's Heathrow Airport. His flight diary records that he passed over the English Channel, the Swiss Alps, and the city of Florence, Italy. Nothing more was heard from him, and several days later his pilot friends organized a search mission for his plane, which was assumed to have crashed in dangerous Alpine territory. But Hinkler had made it safely into the Italian peninsula and crashed in a remote, mountainous part of Tuscany, the Pratomagno range of the Apennines, at the Passo Delia Vacche. The plane and Hinkler's body were not discovered until late April. Hinkler's watch had stopped at 5:10 a.m. The De Havilland had apparently burst into flames upon impact but Hinkler had managed to free himself before dying of severe head injuries.

The final curious footnote to Hinkler's extraordinary life is his place of burial, in the Protestant cemetery in Florence after Italy's Fascist government, led by Benito Mussolini, gave him a full military funeral. There was apparently some conflict over the legitimate next-of-kin; his heirs included his aged mother in Bundaberg and two women who claimed to have been his wife, a British woman named Hannah "Nance" Jervis, whom he never married but lived with in Southampton, England, for most of the 1920s, and a woman named Katherine Rome whom he had secretly wed in Connecticut in 1932.

Books

Dymock, D., *Hustling Hinkler: The Short Tumultuous Life of a Trailblazing Australian Aviator,* Hachette Books, 2013.

Kieza, Grantlee, *Bert Hinkler: The Most Daring Man in the World,* HarperCollins Australia, 2012.

Periodicals

Daily Telegraph (Sydney, Australia), May 9, 1998.

New York Times, February 23, 1928; May 6, 1931; October 28, 1931; December 4, 1931; April 29, 1933.

Times (London, England), August 31, 1927; February November 28, 1931.□

Eric J. Hobsbawm

The British historian and educator Eric Hobsbawm (1917–2012) was a primary exponent of Marxist ideas in the writing of history in the 20th century. Until the collapse of Communism, he remained a member of Britain's Communist Party, and he outraged many observers with his stout defenses of the excesses committed by the Soviet Union.

Yet, even as Communism in general fell out of favor, Hobsbawm remained a widely respected figure. As a writer, he was clear and compelling. "Eric J. Hobsbawm was a brilliant historian in the great English tradition of narrative history," New York University history professor Tony Judt was quoted as saying by William

© LondonPhotos -Homer Sykes/Alamy

Grimes of the *New York Times.* "On everything he touched he wrote much better, had usually read much more, and had a broader and subtler understanding than his more fashionable emulators." Indeed, Hobsbawm's works were widely read not just in Britain, with its strong tradition of leftist, labor-oriented thought, but in the comparatively centrist United States. His books, which covered such diverse topics as banditry and the rise of industrial capitalism, have been staples of college and university curricula, and his wide interests included jazz, about which he wrote numerous critical essays under a pen name in a kind of parallel career.

Name Altered by Clerical Error

Eric John Ernest Hobsbawm was born in Alexandria, Egypt, on June 9, 1917. His father, Leopold Hobsbaum, was a carpenter of Polish Jewish background who had moved to Egypt to take a job in a shipping office; there he met and married an Austrian woman, Nelly Gruen. A clerical error resulted in the new spelling of Hobsbawm's last name. He was raised mostly in Vienna, where he witnessed major street violence between left-wing and right-wing forces after a bank failure, and later in Weimar Republic–era Berlin, where he joined a socialist student group at the age of 14 and published a newsletter called *School Struggle.* Both of his parents died around this time, and he was cared for by an uncle whose work sent him to England in 1933—a fortunate development considering Adolf Hitler's rise to power that year.

In Britain Hobsbawm flourished as a student at London's Marylebone Grammar School and then at King's College, Cambridge, where he earned top grades as a history major. His early education in Austria had given him a broad background in European history and culture, and his Cambridge classmates, according to Martin Kettle and Dorothy Wedderburn of the London *Guardian,* were fond of asking, "Is there anything Hobsbawm doesn't know?" Hobsbawm joined the Communist Party in 1936. Cambridge was a hotbed of sympathy for the Soviet Union's Communist government at the time, and the Soviets succeeded in recruiting a ring of spies from among the university's upper-class intellectual elite. Hobsbawm, who was already an open Communist, had no covert potential, however, and was ignored. Hobsbawm earned a master's degree from Cambridge in 1942 and a doctorate in 1951, writing his dissertation on the development of the moderate socialist Fabian Society.

In the meantime, Hobsbawm volunteered in 1939 to serve in the British army. He hoped to become part of Britain's intelligence services during World War II, but his superiors, mistrustful of his leftist affiliations, kept him away from any real responsibility, and he was put to work with a group of largely working-class recruits building a defensive fortification of dubious value. Hobsbawm was unhappy, but he got along well with his comrades-in-arms. "That experience converted me to the British working class. They were not very clever, except for the Scots and Welsh, but they were very, very good people," he was quoted as saying by Kettle and Wedderburn.

Taught at Small College

In 1943, Hobsbawm married Muriel Seaman, whom he described (according to the *Guardian*) as "a very attractive LSE [London School of Economics] communist girl." That marriage ended in divorce in 1951, and Hobsbawm became involved in short-term relationships with a variety of other women, all of them Communists. By one of them, a married woman, he had a son, Joshua, who became a writer and teacher. His second marriage, to Marlene Schwarz, produced two more children, Julia and Andrew. Hobsbawm joined the faculty at the small Birkbeck College (now part of the University of London). Although he amassed an impressive publication record in the late 1950s and 1960s, he was barred from professional advancement because of his political outlook; he became a professor of history at Birkbeck in 1970, but was turned down for more prestigious posts at Oxford and Cambridge.

In the 1950s, Hobsbawm wrote jazz columns for the *New Statesman* and *Nation* magazines, using the pen name Francis Newton. The name referred to American jazz trumpeter Frankie Newton, a fellow Communist. His jazz writings were collected into a book, *The Jazz Scene,* in 1959. That same year, Hobsbawm issued the first of his famous historical studies: *Primitive Rebels* was an account of secret societies in rural Europe, groups that few historians had even noticed before. Hobsbawm continued to be interested in early European outlaw types, such as Robin Hood, and he synthesized many of his ideas in another influential book, *Bandits* (1969).

Hobsbawm's best-known writings are his grand overviews of the period of industrialization in Britain and beyond. In these, his political outlook is evident in his focus on the lives of working people, but the books are erudite and highly readable histories fully accessible to those who do not share that outlook. These books include *Industry and Empire* (1968), and a tetralogy, *The Age of Revolution: 1789–1848* (1962), *The Age of Capital: 1848-1875* (1975), *The Age of Empire: 1875–1914* (1987), and *The Age of Extremes: The Short Twentieth Century, 1914–1991* (1994).

Retained Communist Affiliation

Although many of his fellow Communists in Britain deserted Communism after the Soviet Union invaded Hungary in 1956 and Czechoslovakia in 1968, Hobsbawm remained a party member. He finally let his membership lapse as Communism began to collapse in Eastern Europe in 1989, but continued to defend Communist ideals. He was slow to accept evidence of atrocities committed by the regime of Josef Stalin during the collectivization of the rural Soviet Union in the 1930s.

Hobsbawm shocked listeners of a British Broadcasting Company interview in 1994 by saying that the deaths of millions of ordinary Russians during that period would have been justifiable if Stalin's actions had led to the establishment of a genuine Communist state. Hobsbawm was criticized not only by conservatives but by liberals such as Judt, who was quoted by the *Guardian* as saying that Hobsbawm clung "to a pernicious illusion of the late Enlightenment: that if one can promise a benevolent outcome it would be worth the human cost. But one of the great lessons of the 20th century is that it's not true. For such a clear-headed writer, he appears blind to the sheer scale of the price paid."

Hobsbawm remained an influential teacher, offering courses at New York's New School for Social Research from 1984 to 1997 after retiring from Birkbeck. Despite his continuing affiliation with Communism, he supported Britain's increasingly centrist Labor Party and even helped orchestrate its newly moderate policies. Some saw Hobsbawm's thinking as self-contradictory, but part of his motivation was his fear of rising nationalism in Europe, expressed in his 1990 book *Nations and Nationalism Since 1780.* Hobsbawm saw social-democratic institutions as a bulwark against a resurgence of nationalism. Labor Party leader and British prime minister Tony Blair paved the way for Hobsbawm's induction into the Order of the Companions of Honor, one of Britain's highest awards.

Hobsbawm remained active into his tenth decade. His later books include *Uncommon People: Resistance, Rebellion, and Jazz* (1998), the autobiography *Interesting Times: A Twentieth-Century Life* (2002), *Globalisation, Democracy, and Terrorism* (2007), and, at age 94, *How to Change the World* (2011). He became president of the Hay Festival of Literature and the Arts at age 93. Hobsbawm died in London on October 1, 2012. A posthumous collection of lectures and essays, *Fractured Times,* appeared in 2013.

Books

Hobsbawm, Eric, *Interesting Times: A Twentieth-Century Life,* Allen Lane, 2002.

Periodicals

Financial Times, October 2, 2012.

Globe & Mail (Toronto, Ontario, Canada), October 6, 2012.

Guardian (London, England), October 2, 2012.

New York Times, October 2, 2012.

Observer (London, England), March 31, 2013.

Sunday Business Post (Ireland), April 21, 2013.

Online

"Profile: A Question of Faith," *Guardian* (London, England), http://www.theguardian.com/books/2002/sep/14/biography.history (October 3, 2013).□

Bohumil Hrabal

Bohumil Hrabal (1914–1997) is regarded is one of the best Czech writers, and his works have been translated into 27 languages. One of his best known novels, *Ostre sledované vlaky* (1965) (translated as Closely Watched Trains). The film adaptation, for which he wrote the screenplay, was a huge critical success and garnered him international fame. He was the subject of a two-volume biography, *Kdo jsem* (1989).

Bohumil Hrabal became one of the Czech Republic's most famous writers. He penned novels, novellas, short stories, poems, and film screenplays. His best known works, in addition to *Ostre sledované vlaky,* include *Tanecni hodiny pro starsi a pokrocile,* which was first published in 1964 and translated as "Dancing Lessons for the Advanced in Age," and *Obsluhoval jsem anglické ho krále* (I Served the King of England, 2006). His works typically portrayed people confronted by circumstances upon which they had no control. While his style was colloquial and seemingly rambling and wordy, he nevertheless communicated with powerful force the experience of his characters—people who populated a harsh, hard-hearted world indifferent to an individual's suffering.

Influenced by Uncle

Bohumil Hrabal was born on March 28, 1914 in Brno, Czechoslovakia. His mother, Marie Kiliá Nová, was not married, and Hrabal never met his biological father, nor did his father's name appear on his birth certificate. During his boyhood, Hrabal was mostly reared by his grandparents. His mother later married František Hrabal in 1916,

Ulf Andersen/Hulton Archive/Getty Images

and the family moved to Polná, where his stepfather worked as a brewery bookkeeper. In 1919, the stepfather took a job a manager of a brewery in Nymburk.

Hrabul enjoyed a positive relationship with his loving stepfather, but he did not take to schooling very well and performed poorly. In 1920, he entered a primary school in Nymburk. Five years later, he attended a Brno grammar school. He was an undistinguished student. He preferred a very informal education, rambling around town and observing people at their jobs and closely listening to how they spoke and what they liked to talk about. This predilection would later greatly influence his adult writings. Another major influence came via his uncle who came to visit his stepfather's family and stayed for an extended period. Hrabal grew very close to this uncle, and he enjoyed listening to the garrulous man's long-winded reminiscences. The way in which the much beloved uncle recounted his stories in rambling fashion formed the style that Hrabal would apply to much of his prose writings.

All the while, Hrabul found it difficult to concentrate on his formal studies. Still, he would advance into higher education. In June 1934, he entered a university and signed up for a year of private classes in Latin. He barely made graduation, but the passing grade he achieved in October 1935 enabled him to enter the Charles University in Prague, where he studied law. But he would not complete his course curriculum until March 1946, as the German Nazis—who occupied his country starting in 1939—closed down Czech universities. He eventually earned a law degree from the university, but he was never able practice his profession, due to the post-World War II political environment of Czechoslovakia.

Such circumstances led to Hrabal assuming various jobs. During the war, he worked in his country's railway system, first as a general laborer and then as a dispatcher. The experience led to one of his most famous works: *Ostre sledované vlaky* (Closely Watched Trains). From there, he worked at various odd jobs: an insurance agent (1946–1947), a traveling salesman (1947–1949), a manual laborer within a steel works plant (1949–1952), and as a paper packer in a recycling facility (1954–1959). The imposition of communism upon the Czech population in 1949 was a major factor in preventing him from working as a lawyer.

Became a Full-time Writer

All the while, he was writing—which was his true passion—while toiling at all of the other jobs. From 1959 to 1962, he worked as a stage hand in a theater. In 1956, he married Eliška Plevová. In 1965, the couple bought a cottage home in Kersko, in the Czech Republic.

Writng eventually became his main profession. His first published efforts involved poetry. He produced a collection in 1948, *Ztracená ulička*, which was banned when the communist regime took over his country. From there, he joined an underground literary society. He wrote short stories, poetry and literary criticism. Much of his early work went unpublished at first.

Along with his short stories, he wrote novels. His early short stories were published in collections: *Perlicka na dne* (A Pearl at the Bottom, 1963), *Pábitelé* (Palaverers, 1964), and *Automat svet* (The Death of Mr. Baltisberger, 1966). The stories have been described as free-association anecdotes without plot and filled with dark humor. Characters tended to be disreputable, social outcasts who were oddly charming. His works could be quite creative. For instance, the novel *Tanecni hodiny pro starší a pokrociilé* (Dancing Lessons for the Advanced in Age), published in 1964, fills more than 100 pages with one long sentence, as an elderly man recounts his life history.

Gained Fame with "Trains"

The novel that gained Hrabal international fame was *Ostre sledované vlaky* (Closely Watched Trains, 1964), a somewhat comedic work. Hrabal subsequently co-authored the screen adaptation with film director Jiri Menzel. The film, initially released in 1966, would receive the 1967 Best Foreign Film award from the Academy of Motion Picture Arts and Sciences. It was produced by the Barrandov Film Studio, and then released in 1968 in the United States as *Closely Watched Trains* and in Great Britain as *Closely Observed Trains.*

The film made Hrabal's name known in the United States. The novel, which was noted for its humor despite its dark subject matter, took place in Nazi-occupied Czechoslovakia. Its story focused on a young railroad employee eager to prove his manhood, particularly after an embarrassingly bad experience with a pretty young woman. The novel maintains a prevailing sense of impending doom.

Hrabal would write several more screenplays. He collaborated with another film director, Ivan Passer, on the film adaptation of his short story *Fádní odpoledne* (A Boring Afternoon, 1968). The award-winning short film was set in a Prague pub and depicted elderly patrons bemoaning the indifference of the younger generation.

His other best-known novel, *Obsluhoval jsem anglické ho krále* (I Served the King of England), was also made into a film, again directed by Menzel and released in 2006. Menzel and Hrabal became close friends.

Works Banned During Soviet Occupation

Hrabal's life was not unlike many of his characters, whose individual lives were caught up in larger situations. In 1968, he witnessed the invasion of Czechoslovakia by the Soviet Union and its Warsaw Pact allies. His autobiographical writings would describe his fear of the conquering empire's secret police. After the invasion, his published works were destroyed and his subsequent writings were banned. Subsequently, he would publish his writings in the Czech underground.

The censorship of his work would be eased in the mid-1970s. In 1975, during an interview for the Czech publication *Tvorba,* he offered some "self-critical" observations. This seemed a political apology and enabled some of his works to be published above ground. In 1976, he was considered "rehabilitated" by the communist government. But the situation infuriated many young Czechoslovakian dissidents, who considered him a "sell out" to the oppressors. They denounced him publicly and even burned some of his books.

Hrabal had convinced the Czech government of his loyalty and was able to openly publish a semifictional short story collection entitled *Postriziny* (The Haircutting, 1976). He based the stories on the lives of his ancestors. It was his first work available above ground in his country in more than a decade. Reportedly, it took only two hours for the first printing, which totaled twenty thousand copies, to be sold out.

Obsluhoval jsem anglické ho krále (I Served the King of England), widely considered to be the second of his best-known works, first saw Czech publication in 1982. It was followed by an English translation in 1989. This novel takes place in the years preceding World War II. The main character, Ditie, is a self-absorbed hotel waiter whose work provides him with exposure to many other characters as well as transformative experiences. The result is that he develops a greater comprehension of the human condition as well as of himself.

Another major work, *Tanecni hodiny pro starsi a pokrocile,* was first published in 1964. It was translated into English in 1995 and published as *Dancing Lessons for the Advanced in Age,* and it is Hrabal's famous one-sentence novel. The narrator is a cobbler (or shoemaker) who, like Hrabal's real life uncle, is a long-winded raconteur.

In an essay published in 2010 in the *New York Times Book Review,* Ed Park wrote that "'Dancing Lessons' unfurls as a single, sometimes maddening sentence that ends after 117 pages without a period, giving the impression that the opinionated, randy old cobbler will go on jawing ad infinitum. But the gambit works. His exuberant ramblings gain a propulsion that would be lost if the comma splices were curbed, the phrases divided into sentences. And there's something about that slab of wordage that carries the eye forward, promising an intensity simply unattainable by your regularly punctuated novel."

Fell to his Death

Hrabal died on February 3, 1997, in Prague in the Czech Republic when he fell from a fifth-floor hospital window. He had been admitted to the Bulovka Hospital in December 1996, as he had been suffering pain in his back and his joints. According to eyewitness accounts, he was trying to feed pigeons from a window sill. The table he was standing on tipped over and he fell. Reportedly, he died instantly. He was 82 years old. Before his death, he was the subject of a two-volume biography, *Kdo jsem,* published in 1989.

The body of work that Hrabal left behind is defined by visual style, eccentric expression, complex sentences, recurrent themes of politics and moral ambiguities, and they are peopled with characters who have been called "wise fools"—that is, individuals who appear outwardly stupid but who are capable of entertaining and expressing an occasional profound thought. These characters are crude and lewd, and seem only intent on finding base pleasure within the cruel environments they find themselves in. The works also perceive a dichotomy: the world that Hrabal depicts is at once filled with beauty and horrific cruelty. Above all, his complex works are accessible because they are filled with humor.

In a 1995 *Los Angeles Times* article, renowned novelist Horward Norman wrote, "Simply put, first-hand experience informs Hrabal's work with wonderful detail, deceptive folksiness, irascibility and charm. One of the grand patriarchs of the unprecedented cacophony of Czech film, writing and painting in the late 1960s, known as "Prague Spring," Bohumil Hrabal has invented some of the most memorable characters in world literature."

Like Park, Norman also uses *Dancing Lessons for the Advanced in Age* to underscore his points: "His novels enhance the soul, distill complicated human behavior to its basic—albeit at times repugnant, at times joyful—motivations, telescope in on village life and spin yarns that no one practicing naturalistic fiction (since Isaac Bashevis Singer) can spin with such unmitigated savvy."

Periodicals

Los Angeles Times, October 22, 1995.

New York Times, December 10, 2010.

Online

"Bohumil Hrabal,"*Contemporary Authors Online,* http://ic.galegroup.com/ic/bic1/ReferenceDetailsPage/ (December 13, 2013).

"Bohumil Hrabal," *Encyclopedia Britannica,* http://www.britannica.com/EBchecked/topic/273633/Bohumil-Hrabal (December 13, 2013).

"Bohumil Hrabal (1914–1997)," *Pegasos,* http://www.kirjasto.sci.fi/hrabal.htm (December 13, 2013).

"Bohumil Hrabal," *University of Glasgow,* http://www.arts.gla.ac.uk/Slavonic/Hrabal1.htm (December 13, 2013).

"Bohumil Hrabal—the Close Watcher of Trains," *In the Art Bin,* http://art-bin.com/art/ahrabaleng.html (December 13, 2013).

"Bohumil Hrabal," *The New York Review of Books,* http://www.nybooks.com/books/authors/bohumil-hrabal/ (December 13, 2013).

"Czech literary legend Bohumil Hrabal died 10 years ago," *Radio Prague,* http://www.radio.cz/en/section/ (December 13, 2013).□

James Hunt

James Hunt (1947–1993) remains a legendary figure in British motor sports. A long shot to win the 1976 Formula One (F1) world championship title, the handsome and reckless Hunt had a personal life best described as debauched and was known for his fearlessness on the track. The media attention his antics garnered boosted interest in Formula One racing in the 1970s, although Hunt has sometimes been described as the most inexperienced driver ever to make it to that elite level of auto racing.

© Presselect/Alamy

Born James Simon Wallis Hunt on August 29, 1947, the future motor-sport celebrity came from respectable, middle-class roots in suburban London. He was born in Surrey as the second child and first son in a family that would eventually number six children at their home in the village of Belmont. His father Wallis worked in the City, London's financial epicenter, and sent his sons off to his own alma mater, Wellington College, an elite private academy. There Hunt excelled in cricket, soccer, track and field, and racquet sports.

Started on Club Circuit

Hunt obtained a much-coveted driver's license just after his seventeenth birthday in 1964, and soon began compiling what would be a long list of traffic violations and smash-ups. He first crashed his parents' car, was banned from using their replacement vehicle, and managed to wreck a little Fiat 500, which they thought would be a safe choice for him because it had minimal horsepower. Hunt's racing career began on the club circuit in a souped-up Mini Cooper he had cobbled together himself, despite limited mechanic skills. In 1968, he signed with Formula Ford, a beginners' circuit for drivers using cars powered by Ford engines.

In 1969, Hunt moved up to Formula Three (F3) racing, where he spent three years racing single-seat, open-wheel cars consisting of little more than a chassis frame to support an amped-up engine, four tires, a roll bar, and a space for the driver. The F3 circuit is considered the farm league for auto racing hopefuls, giving them experience and a chance to attract the attention of Formula One (F1) teams and sponsors. The F1 season includes the prestigious international Grand Prix races, which begin in Southern Hemisphere countries like Argentina and South Africa early in the calendar year.

On the F3 circuit Hunt was known for smashing up costly cars on the track, and friends and foes dubbed him "Hunt the Shunt" after the British slang word for car crash. In 1972, he joined the March Engineering team, named for its race-car manufacturer whose name was taken from the first initials of its founders. The "M" in March stood for Max Mosley, who later became head of the governing body that oversees F1 racing. Hired as an F3 driver, Hunt crashed March cars and quickly clashed with Mosley and his other bosses. In 1973, he moved to a newly created team called Hesketh Racing. Founded by a maverick young aristocrat, Alexander Hesketh, the team also built their own cars but disdained corporate sponsorship and the obligatory decals on cars and drivers. Lord Hesketh, as he was known, wanted only a version of Britain's distinctive Union Jack flag design on his cars.

Debuted in Monte Carlo

Hunt's first race on the F1 circuit was one of the most fabled of all: Monaco's Grand Prix, in which he placed an impressive ninth. He came in sixth on July 1, 1973, in the French Grand Prix at the Ricard track in Le Castellet, and then took fourth place two weeks later in the British Grand Prix at Silverstone. At the end of July he won the third-place trophy in the Dutch Grand Prix at Zandvoort, and finished the 1973 season by almost beating a top Swede, Ronnie Peterson, in the U.S. Grand Prix at the course in Watkins Glen, New York. Hunt lost that last race by less than one second, which earned him the Royal Automobile Club (RAC)'s award for best British driver of the year.

Hunt drove again for Hesketh in the 1974 Grand Prix season, but dropped out of more races than he finished that year due to mechanical failures and crashes. He finished third in the Swedish, Austrian, and U.S. Grand Prix races and ended 1974 as F1's eighth-place competitor in the points tally, a match of his rookie season total. The 1975 season was Hunt's launching pad to stardom, and he racked up 33 points for a fourth-place season finish. On June 22, 1975, he won his first Grand Prix trophy at Zandvoort, the sandy-landscape Dutch event.

Hunt's personal life attracted almost as much media attention as his track mishaps and lap times. He lived as a British tax exile in the glitzy resort town of Marbella, Spain, where in 1974 he met a Zimbabwean-born model named Suzy Miller. The pair had a short and tempestuous courtship that ended with an ill-advised marriage in October of that same year—a union, some hoped, would put an end to Hunt's legendary drinking binges and womanizing. Lord Hesketh served as best man at the lavish London affair and reportedly underwrote the cost of the wedding, too. Having regretted his marriage proposal and too nervous about backing out as the date neared, Hunt turned up staggeringly drunk at Brompton Oratory church in Kensington, London, and at his wedding reception was said to have been mostly incoherent.

The Miller-Hunt liaison was doomed from the start and sputtered for 14 months, with Miller bored by the racing circuit and Hunt unable to control his impulsive, self-destructive behaviors. In December of 1975, the couple went to Gstaad, Switzerland, where Miller fortuitously met the actor Richard Burton. Just two months earlier, Burton had married Hollywood star Elizabeth Taylor for the second time, after their famously turbulent first ten-year marriage ended in 1974. Burton became enamored with Hunt's wife and abandoned Taylor shortly after the Gstaad holiday. This incident fueled an already frenzied tabloid interest in Hunt's personal life. Six months later, Burton paid Hunt's share of a divorce settlement to Suzy so that the two could marry in August of 1976, a sum reported to be $500,000.

The F1 Rebel

By that point Hunt was heading toward the finish of his only winning F1 season. In his first race of the 1976 season, the South African Grand Prix, he came in second to his chief rival, Austrian driver Niki Lauda. Lord Hesketh and Hesketh Racing had run into financial trouble, and by that season Hunt was racing for the McLaren International team. This was a well-funded winning outfit, with the Marlboro cigarette manufacturer Philip Morris as its chief sponsor. Hunt's contract included a clause that removed a dress-code stipulation for public events he was obligated to attend, and when not in his racing jumpsuit Hunt eschewed the jacket and tie for t-shirts and jeans, even showing up at black-tie events casually dressed. On May 2, 1976, he won the Spanish Grand Prix at the Jarama course, but his McLaren M23 car was disqualified after the race for being 1.8 centimeters too wide, and Lauda was declared the winner. Team McLaren filed a formal appeal and Hunt was reinstated as the winner by the Fédération Internationale de l'Automobile (FIA), F1's governing body.

On July 4, 1976, Hunt won the French Grand Prix and two weeks later entered into another heated bid with Lauda for the winner's trophy, this time on Hunt home turf at the British Grand Prix. His M23 collided with Lauda's Ferrari, the race had to be halted, then restarted, and there was a major debate over whether Hunt would be permitted to use a McLaren backup car. When FIA officials said no, patriotic Brit fans at the Brands Hatch racecourse bleacher stands jeered and threw beer cans onto the track. Hunt won, but this time Lauda and Team Ferrari filed their own legal challenge to the FIA that the race should not have been allowed a restart, and Hunt had to forfeit his win to Lauda.

The weeks of F1 drama reached a feverish pitch when the teams readied for the German Grand Prix at the infamous, crash-prone Nüburgring Nordschleife track, or North Loop. It wound 14.2 miles through the Eifel Mountains and was justly feared: between 1928 and 1976 a total of 51 drivers had been involved in fatal crashes during races or practice laps. The 1976 Grand Prix was actually going to be the final one at the Nordschleife, with German racing officials planning to build a less treacherous route elsewhere at the Nüburgring site. Lauda had unsuccessfully attempted to organize a drivers' boycott that year for safety reasons. The race went ahead as planned on August 1, 1976, despite wet road conditions, and Lauda almost became the 52nd fatality when he took a corner at 150 miles an hour and lost control. His Ferrari exploded into flames, caused two other wrecks, and Lauda was trapped inside the flaming wreck until other drivers pulled him out. He was badly burned and suffered extreme lung damage. When the race resumed, Hunt overtook South African driver Jody Scheckter and Germany's Jochen Mass for the winner's cup.

Raced Against Determined Lauda

Hunt went on to win the 1976 Dutch Grand Prix at the end of August and the rivalry with Lauda resumed when the still-injured Austrian driver returned to the racetrack on September 12, 1976, at the Italian Grand Prix in Monza. It was just six weeks after Lauda's near-fatal accident and underneath his helmet were bandages that were leaking blood. Hunt's McLaren M23 spun out on the eleventh lap and he walked away from the race. In North America, Hunt won the Canadian Grand Prix on October 3, and then the U.S. Grand Prix a week later. The last race of the season was the first-ever Japanese Grand Prix on a newly built track in the foothills of majestic Mount Fuji. Lauda was forced to drop out, and though American driver Mario

Andretti won the inaugural Japanese Grand Prix, Hunt ended the season with 69 points, taking the 1976 F1 world championship title by a single point from Lauda, the 1975 champion.

Hunt raced for another two and a half seasons, but came in fifth place for Team McLaren in the 1977 F1 final standings, though he won the British Grand Prix and the challenging second Fuji Speedway race that year. In the summer of 1978, his third-place win at the Ricard track in France was his best result. Weeks later, he dropped out of the Italian Grand Prix on September 10, 1978, when his longtime friend and rival, Ronnie Peterson, crashed his Lotus into a barrier; Hunt, along with two other drivers, pulled the Swede out of the flaming wreckage but Peterson died the next day.

Made Exit at Monaco, Too

Hunt started the 1979 F1 season on a new team, Wolf Racing, but disliked the WR7 and WR8 cars. He managed to finish the South African Grand Prix but dropped out of the Monaco Grand Prix after four laps when the car's transmission failed. He announced his retirement on June 8, 1979. "It was over," the *Sunday Times* quoted him as saying about the Monaco debacle. "I knew this was my last race, and I hated that car, anyway. I felt no sadness at all, just immense relief."

Hunt had an enjoyable second career as a commentator for British Broadcasting Corporation (BBC) motor sports events, where he freely disparaged drivers and team executives. He married a second time, in 1983, had two sons, and lived in a palatial home in Wimbledon. Divorced in 1989, he was living in financial penury when he died of a heart attack on June 15, 1993, at the age of 45. A legend in a field littered with outsized personalities, Hunt was the subject of a long-awaited film treatment of his life and career in 2013, *Rush,* which focused on his rivalry with Lauda for the 1976 F1 title.

Books

Rubython, Tom, *Rush to Glory: Formula 1 Racing's Greatest Rivalry,* Globe Pequot Press, 2013, originally published as *In the Name of Glory,* Myrtle Books, 2011.

Periodicals

Guardian (London, England), June 16, 1993.
Observer (London, England), October 22, 2006.
Sports Illustrated, September 27, 1976.
Sunday Times (London, England), June 20, 1993.
Times (London, England), June 16, 1993.□

Constantijn Huygens

The Dutch diplomat, composer, and poet Constantijn Huygens (1596–1687) is remembered outside of the Netherlands mostly as the father of the physicist Christiaan Huygens, the discoverer of Saturn's moon Titan and the inventor of the pendulum clock. His own career, however, was important in the long history of diplomatic and cultural interchange between the Netherlands and England in the 17th century.

Huygens was what is now known as a Renaissance man. Given a superb education as a young man, he spent much of his career as a diplomat and later as a member of the Council of Domaines of the House of Orange, the ruling family that essentially founded the modern Dutch state. But Huygens's leisure activities, which he thought of as strictly separate from his governmental and business affairs, were lively and varied. He was a poet whose own verse, unusually for the time, seemed to directly reflect his own experiences, and who translated the writings of English poet John Donne into Dutch. Huygens was an energetic composer who is thought to have written almost 1,000 works, most of which have been lost. Something of a patron of the arts and of philosophy, he aided and corresponded with some of the top thinkers and artists of the time, including the French philosopher René Descartes and the Dutch painter Rembrandt van Rijn. The fruits of Huygens's own efforts as a landscape architect, the estate he called Hofwijck, are still visible in the Netherlands today. In all, Huygens spent his long life at the center of the splendor that was the Dutch Golden Age, and he contributed to that splendor in many ways.

Born into Political Elite

Constantijn Huygens (pronounced close to HU-i-kens in Dutch, but anglicized to HI-gens, with a hard "g") was born on September 4, 1596, in The Hague, which was then part of the Republic of the Seven Northern Provinces—the direct ancestor of the Netherlands as a unified state. His father, like his son named Christiaan Huygens, had been a secretary to William of Orange, the leader of the rebellion that ended Spanish rule over the Netherlands. Huygens's first name, Constantijn, meant "Constant One" and was intended to honor the support of a town council that had remained faithful to the Dutch revolt. Huygens thus grew up in the top social circles of the emerging country. His father, according to Adelheid Rech (writing on the *Essential Vermeer* website), remarked that "we are born from respectable folk, are not washed to shore on a straw, or pissed down at the horse-fair." His mother, Susanna, came from a family of well-off Antwerp merchants.

Accordingly, Huygens received the best education that money could buy. His father personally instructed him in Latin grammar, and he studied logic, writing and speaking, mathematics, law, riding, fencing, dancing, ice skating, and foreign languages, for which Huygens showed a particular aptitude. By the time he was a teen he was conversant in Latin, ancient Greek, French, and Italian. Soon after that, as a law student at the University of Leiden, he began to study English. Huygens was able to sing back church melodies to his mother at the age of two, and he enthusiastically pursued music as a hobby in the midst of all his other studies.

After completing a Latin-language law dissertation at the university in 1617, Huygens began his career in the Dutch diplomatic service. At the time, England was a natural ally of the Netherlands against potentially hostile states farther south, and the Dutch ambassador to England suggested that Huygens be sent to London to deepen his understanding of diplomatic life. Arriving in London in 1618, Huygens immersed himself not only in state affairs but in England's rich cultural life. He studied the viola da gamba and became so expert on the instrument that he was knighted by King James VI on a later visit in honor of his talents. He took art lessons from a printmaker and read the works of major English poets including Sir Philip Sidney and John Donne, whose works he would later translate.

Accumulated Large Library

Back in The Hague, Huygens continued to combine business with pleasure. Becoming the private secretary to a nobleman named François Aerssen, he traveled to Italy (he was the only member of the delegation with knowledge of the Italian language) and heard the pioneering music of Claudio Monteverdi, the first major opera composer. In 1621, he traveled with Aerssen to England once more, this time meeting the renowned scientist Francis Bacon. Huygens accumulated a library of some 8,000 books, an enormous number for that time, and he began to write poetry of his own during this period. After his father's death in 1624, Huygens became secretary to Prince Frederick Henry of Orange, the stadtholder (or ruler) of The Hague in 1625, remaining in that position until 1647. He married Susanne van Baerle in 1627, and the couple had five children; the scientist Christiaan Huygens was the second.

Huygens once wrote a 2,000-line poem about a single day in his marriage to his wife, and he was badly shaken by Susanne's unexpected death in 1637. He moved his five children into the magnificent new house in the center of The Hague, next to what is now the Mauritshuis art museum, having planned it as the home for the entire family. During this time he wrote some of his best-known poetry, mostly memorializing Susanne. The growing importance of the court at The Hague, and Frederick Henry's determination to make the court a center for the arts, helped snap Huygens out of his depression, for he was ideally suited for the job.

In 1628, Huygens had already visited the studio of the young Rembrandt and had correctly identified his once-in-a-century talent. In his autobiography he provided a memorable description of Rembrandt's early painting *Judas Repentant, Returning the Pieces of Silver*, one that captures the artist's emotional insight: "The singular gesture of the despairing Judas—leaving aside the many fascinating figures in this one painting—that one furious Judas, howling, praying for mercy, but devoid of hope, all traces of hope erased from his countenance, his appearance frightening, his hair torn, his garment rent, his limbs twisted, his hands clenched bloodlessly tight, fallen prostrate on his knees on a blind impulse, his whole body contorted in wretched hideousness. Such I place against all the elegance that has been produced throughout the ages."

Designed Formal Garden

Huygens collected a large number of paintings himself and also served as an agent for Rembrandt, Jan Lievens, and other Dutch artists, arranging a commission for Rembrandt over the course of the 1630s to execute a series of five paintings illustrating the biblical Passion story for Frederick Henry's court. In 1639, he began work on a country estate that he called Hofwijck (meaning "garden place," as well as other more subtle concepts simultaneously), designing an elaborate formal garden to go with it. His designs drew on the ideas of the ancient Roman architect Vitruvius, as communicated partly through Leonardo da Vinci, and he chronicled the garden's entire development in a long poem. Hofwijck still exists today, with a superhighway slicing off one edge.

Taking a lively interest in musical matters, Huygens composed prolifically. Only one set of works that were published in 1647 in Paris, a group of vocal pieces in the style of Monteverdi, has survived, but Huygens himself said that he had written nearly 1,000 pieces. They were probably short instrumental dances suitable for use at court functions. In 1641, Huygens plunged into the controversy over whether organ music should be allowed to accompany the singing of psalms in the Dutch Reformed Church, publishing a short treatise arguing in the affirmative.

Frederick Henry died in 1647 and was succeeded by his son William II, who died after just three years. After that, The Hague entered an unstable time known as the First Stadtholderless Period, in which Huygens's Orangists and other groups jockeyed for control. On the foreign front too Huygens faced difficulties: the relationship between the Netherlands and Britain was fraught during the Commonwealth period (1649–1660) when the English monarchy was displaced. Relations with France, with which the Orange faction clashed militarily in 1660, were also problematic. Huygens put a great deal of energy into promoting the idea of a paved road between The Hague and the coastal city of Scheveningen; the road was finally built in 1665. Huygens's youngest son, Philips, died while on a diplomatic mission to Poland and Sweden in 1657.

Huygens lived an unusually long life for his time. On his 69th birthday he wrote a poem that read in part: "How many more Septembers, ... Lord, will you suffer me? What do I hope on earth, why not now leave?" The following year he traveled to England on a diplomatic mission once again. He lived out his life as an elder statesman, writing some long autobiographical poems as well as one on the death of his puppy, Geckie: "This is my puppy's grave: / No more than this be said, / I'd wish (and were it so, the world were none the worse) / My little dog alive, all this world's great ones dead." Huygens died in The Hague on March 28, 1687, at the age of 91. Despite his importance in early Dutch cultural life, a full-scale English biography of Huygens has not yet appeared.

Books

Alpers, Svetlana, *The Art of Describing: Dutch Art in the Seventeenth Century,* University of Chicago, 1984.

Colie, Rosalie L., *Some Thankfulnesse to Constantine: A Study of English Influence upon the Early Works of Constantijn Huygens,* Nijhoff, 1956.

Sadie, Stanley, ed., *The New Grove Dictionary of Music and Musicians,* 2nd ed., Macmillan, 2001.

Schoenberg, Thomas J., and Lawrence J. Trudeau, eds., *Literature Criticism from 1400 to 1800,* Vol. 114, Gale, 2005.

Online

"Constantijn Huygens: Lord of Zuilichem (1596–1687)," *Essential Vermeer,* http://www.essentialvermeer.com/history/huygens.html (November 14, 2013).□

Chrissie Hynde

The American singer and songwriter Chrissie Hynde (born 1951), the lead singer of the band the Pretenders, has been one of the best-known and most durable performers to emerge from the punk rock movement in Britain at the end of the 1970s.

Hynde wrote most of the Pretenders' material, and her strong, independent perspective certainly made her a pioneer among women in rock music. Yet Hynde rejected the feminist label, telling David Belcher of the Glasgow (Scotland) *Herald* that her music was "not a social statement. It's something that transcends gender. I just play guitar in a rock band. I have a female voice, because I'm female. But I haven't done anything for women. ... I've done it for myself." Hynde's songs were vigorous, honest explorations of love, hate, fear, and her personal reactions to the social trends of the day. Unlike with many singers rooted in the punk movement, the lyrics of Hynde's songs were of paramount importance, and she articulated them clearly and if necessary angrily. She never treated the punk style as an end in itself, drawing freely on styles from mainstream rock to pop to reggae when they suited what she wanted to express. While the careers of many punk musicians burned out after a few intense years, Hynde has continued to make new music at a deliberate pace over three decades.

Became Vegetarian

Christine Ellen Hynde was born in Akron, Ohio, on September 7, 1951. Her father, Melville Hynde, known as Bud, was a telephone company employee; her mother, Dolores, owned a beauty salon. Hynde grew up in a home that had been owned by her grandmother; it was later moved on rollers to a different part of the city to make way for a superhighway, something Hynde recalled sadly in her song "My City Was Gone." Attending Firestone High School in Akron, Hynde took little interest in the usual school social whirl, preferring to listen to rock music on a transistor radio and to go to nearby Cleveland to hear bands when she could. Hynde became a vegetarian when she was 17. "My whole life changed," she told the London *Independent.* "I spent a lot of time hanging out in the woods near my house and felt a connection to the birds and the trees."

After graduating from high school in 1969, Hynde enrolled at Kent State University near Akron, majoring in art. She was present when Ohio National Guard members killed four Kent State students during an antiwar demonstration in 1970. Hynde saved money by working as a waitress, and by 1973 she had saved about $1,000. With that money she fulfilled her dream of moving to London, England, leaving her nearly completed college degree unfinished. In London Hynde made a living by writing for the rock magazine *New Music Express* and working at a store called Sex that supplied many of the bondage-themed clothing styles of the nascent punk movement.

All the while she was trying to break into London's music scene, but for several years she had no luck. "Nobody I met had ever heard of Iggy Pop, but I kept at it until I finally met people who had," she recalled to Andrew Perry of the London *Daily Telegraph.* Hynde came close to slots in bands that soon became punk's first stars: she had a few rehearsals with a band called Masters of the Backside that evolved into the Damned, and she was acquainted with Mick Jones, who went on to form the Clash. Back in Ohio in 1975, she joined an R&B band called Jack Rabbitt whose members included future Devo frontman Mark Mothersbaugh. But attempts on both sides of the Atlantic to form her own band came to nothing. Hynde later summed up this difficult period in her career, telling *Rolling Stone,* "For every act of sodomy I was forced to perform, I'm getting paid £10,000 now."

Single Produced by Lowe

Hynde's breakthrough finally came in London in 1978 when she met bassist Pete Farndon. The pair recruited guitarist James Honeyman-Scott and drummer Jerry Mcleduff, soon replaced by Martin Chambers, and the group recorded a demonstration tape that included the Hynde originals "Precious" and "The Wait," plus a cover of a song called "Stop Your Sobbing" originally recorded by the proto-punk British band the Kinks. The latter song impressed British rock star Nick Lowe, who produced it as a single release. The band took the name the Pretenders after Hynde was moved by the experience of a white-supremacist motorcyclist in a bar who confessed to her that his favorite song, which he could never admit to his friends, was Sam Cooke's version of the 1950s Platters hit "The Great Pretender." "Stop Your Sobbing" reached the British top 30 and stirred interest among independent music fans in the United States.

The group's debut album, *The Pretenders,* was released early in 1980, with additional production work from Roxy Music producer Chris Thomas after Lowe mistakenly concluded that the band was not destined for stardom. *The Pretenders* made its debut at number one in Britain and reached the U.S. top ten. The album served notice of an entirely new punk-based style: its most successful single, "Brass in Pocket," a poetically inventive portrayal of female romantic initiative, fused Hynde's rough but flexible vocals with a chordal and rhythmic structure based in American Motown-label pop. Hynde herself disliked the song and had to be persuaded to release it as a single. The band's follow-up, *Pretenders II,* also reached the U.S. top ten; it contained a second Kinks cover, "I Go to Sleep."

The Pretenders underwent major personnel changes after Honeyman-Scott died of a drug overdose and Hynde fired Farndon due to substance abuse problems; soon Farndon was dead as well. Hynde recruited new musicians and recorded the album *Learning to Crawl* (1984); a tuneful single released in advance of the album, "Back on the Chain Gang," remains one of the Pretenders' best-known songs, and *Learning to Crawl,* both popularly successful and critically acclaimed, expanded the range of Hynde's songwriting. Hynde toned down her own drug and alcohol use in the wake of her bandmates' deaths.

Raised Two Children

Partly that was due to the fact that Hynde had become a mother to daughter Natalie after becoming involved in a relationship with Kinks' frontman Ray Davies. The relationship dissolved, but Hynde continued to cite Davies as a major songwriting influence. In 1984, she married vocalist Jim Kerr of the Scottish band Simple Minds and had another daughter, Yasmin. After that, Hynde's musical output slowed somewhat. "I never struggled with my decisions," she told the *Mercury* (Hobart, Tasmania, Australia). "Never. I had kids. I put them first. I was a single mother. That was that." Hynde and Kerr divorced in 1999. She married Colombian artist Lucho Brieva in 1997; that marriage, too, ended in divorce.

The Pretenders released their fourth album, *Get Close,* in 1986, after which Hynde took a hiatus and consciously avoided the trappings of the rock lifestyle. She released the moderately successful album *Packed!* in 1990, using session musicians. In the early 1990s Hynde formed a new version of the Pretenders, and in 1994 they released *Last of the Independents,* widely regarded as a strong comeback; the album spawned the pop ballad "I'll Stand by You," which reached the top 10 in Britain and the top 20 in the U.S.

Despite her more stable lifestyle, Hynde shed none of her rocker's image and retained what Perry called her "classic Exile on Main Street–era Keith Richards hairdo." The Pretenders did not tour heavily, but they opened for the Rolling Stones on a 2002 U.S. tour. The group released four more albums, the live acoustic *The Isle of View* (1995), *Viva el Amor* (1999), *Loose Screw* (2002), and the country-flavored *Break Up the Concrete* (2008). In 2010 she joined a band called JP and Chrissie and the Fairground Boys, which released an album, *Fidelity.* Carefully shielding her children from the glare of publicity, Hynde continued to live in London. "I definitely feel like I'm at home here now," she told Perry. "I feel displaced when I'm back in America, like a visitor. I feel like, if I don't get a cup of tea, I'm going to lose my mind."

In 2007, however, Hynde announced plans to open a vegetarian restaurant called VegeTerranean on Akron's north side, and she has also maintained a small apartment in Akron. The restaurant, which foundered in 2011 amidst the U.S. economic recession, fit in with Hynde's commitment to animal rights. She once said that McDonald's restaurants should be firebombed, and in 1994 she altered her will giving the organization People for the Ethical Treatment of Animals permission to use her image as they desired after her death. The Pretenders were inducted into the Rock and Roll Hall of Fame in 2005. As of late 2013 the band's website was defunct, although a Facebook page with messages apparently posted by Hynde remained active.

Books

Newsmakers, Gale, 1991.

Periodicals

Billboard, October 14, 1995.

Daily Telegraph (London, England), April 19, 2003.

Herald (Glasgow, Scotland), September 30, 1999.

Independent (London, England), June 6, 2009.

Mercury (Hobart, Tasmania, Australia), July 15, 1999.

Nation's Restaurant News, July 23, 2007.

Online

"Chrissie Hynde," *AllMusic,* http://www.allmusic.com (November 15, 2013).

"Chrissie Hynde Biography," *The Biography Channel* (UK), http://www.thebiographychannel.co.uk/biographies/chrissie-hynde.html (November 15, 2013).

"Homegrown Heroes: Chrissie Hynde," *Cleveland.com,* http://www.cleveland.com/homegrown/index.ssf?/homegrown/more/chrissie/vital.html (November 15, 2013).

"The Pretenders, 'The Pretenders,'" *Rolling Stone* (Women Who Rock: The 50 Greatest Albums of All Time), http://www.rollingstone.com/music/lists/women-who-rock-the-50-greatest-albums-of-all-time-20120622/the-pretenders-the-pretenders-20120621 (November 14, 2013). □

I

Pope Innocent VIII

Pope Innocent VIII (1432–1492) was the leader of the Roman Catholic Church from 1484 until his death.

History has not treated Innocent kindly, with even the generally sympathetic *New Catholic Encyclopedia* remarking that "[t]he moral and political disorders of the time called for a pontiff of character and ability. Innocent possessed neither." For observers critical of Catholicism's role in European history, he was a villain of his time. He lived lavishly while engaging in military adventurism that left the church in a precarious state, a situation he attempted to remedy by creating make-work church offices that he sold off to those who shared his noble background. What can be said in Innocent's defense is that he ascended to the papacy in a chaotic period, when corruption ruled ecclesiastical structures as much as it did secular ones, and power struggles were the norm both inside and outside the church. Innocent's actions were comparable to those of other popes of his time.

Fathered Illegitimate Children

Innocent was born Giovanni Battista Cibo in Genoa in 1432. His father, Aran Cibo, was a powerful aristocrat. The family name was also spelled Cybo or Zibo, with an accent mark sometimes used over the final "o" in all cases. As a young man he lived at the court of Naples, where he apparently had free rein with the area women; he had at least two or three illegitimate children, whom he acknowledged, and he may have had more. *The Catholic Encyclopedia* termed his youth "licentious." Apparently resolving to mend his ways, he decided to become a priest and studied in Rome and Padua before taking holy orders and entering the service of Cardinal Filippo Calandrini in Bologna.

Apparently having a gregarious nature, Cibo made friends easily across the often-competitive spectrum of churches and church bureaucracies in Italy's warring city-states. He became the Bishop of Savona in northwestern Italy in 1467, moving to the same post in Molfetta, in the southeastern part of the peninsula, in 1472. He was made a cardinal himself the following year. Around this time Cibo seems to have hitched his rising star to the career of Cardinal Giuliano della Rovere, who later became Pope Julius II.

For the next decade, Cibo served the church faithfully while deftly currying favor with members of its numerous competing factions. He served as the legate of Pope Sixtus IV (Sixtus' uncle) in Rome when the latter fled an outbreak of bubonic plague there. He served as governor of the city of Siena and represented the church at a meeting of cardinals with Holy Roman Emperor Friedrich III in Hungary in 1482. As Sixtus meddled in wars between northern Italy's increasingly powerful secular families in Venice, Florence, Milan, Ferrara, and other cities, Cibo, his eye apparently on the papacy, tried to maintain cordial relations with players on both sides.

Chosen as Pope

Soon Cibo got his chance. After the death of Sixtus IV, the Papal Conclave of 1484 quickly devolved into factionalism and even chaos as militias loyal to one candidate or another battled in the streets of Rome. Leading one faction was della Rovere, who had the support of Rome's powerful Colonna family and argued in favor of trying to extend the power of the papacy in the growing southern Italian city of

© INTERFOTO/Alamy

Naples. His rival, Cardinal Rodrigo Borja (later Pope Alexander VI), was backed by the Colonna family's nemeses the Orsinis. As has often happened in the history of the Cardinals' deliberations, they turned to a compromise candidate, which was Cibo. Della Rovere supported the compromise, believing that he could control Cibo, and Cibo became Pope Innocent VIII.

Largely at della Rovere's urging, Innocent plunged military forces loyal to the Papal States into conflict with Naples, where he sided with a group of barons attempting to enforce the payment of papal taxes by the Neapolitan king, Ferdinand I. He formed an alliance with the Medici family in Florence, marrying his illegitimate son Franceschetto off to a daughter of Lorenzo de' Medici and naming Lorenzo's son a cardinal even though he was just 13 at the time. He attempted to persuade the cardinals to launch a crusade against encroaching Islamic forces from the Ottoman empire, but, perhaps tired of military adventurism, they refused.

Innocent's personal lifestyle was luxurious. Richard P. McBrien noted in *Lives of the Popes* that "Innocent VIII's papal court was indistinguishable from that of any contemporary prince, and his cardinals (appointed mostly by Sixtus IV) lived in the grand style." In this Innocent was not alone; Bernhard Schimmelpfenning wrote in *The Papacy* that "[m]ost of the popes of this epoch fit the picture of an Italian Renaissance prince that was common at the time." The combination of domestic spending and military budgets drained the Vatican treasury.

Created, Sold Church Offices

The solution Innocent attempted ranks along with the sale of indulgences, or remission of sins, in the catalog of church abuses in the century prior to the Protestant Reformation and subsequent Catholic reaction. He (and other popes) sold off offices within the papal administration to noble investors who had cash to offer, often creating offices for just that purpose. The buyers were then free to reap profits associated with their newly purchased powers. Innocent may have been especially notorious in this regard; he created 52 new posts for officials called *pulumbatores,* who did nothing but affix lead seals to official documents. "The sale of office," noted Eamon Duffy in *Saints & Sinners: A History of the Popes,* "paralyzed reform, for it created a huge class of officials with a vested interest in preventing the streamlining of the papal administraiton or any attempt at removing financial abuses within the Curia."

For many, the worst action for which Innocent remains historically culpable was his papal Bull, or decree, of December 5, 1484, condemning witchcraft and urging its vigorous prosecution in Germany, where he believed its incidence was on the increase. A pair of inquisitors dispatched by Innocent may have condemned numerous Germans, mostly women, to death on slender evidence. Innocent also persecuted Count Giovanni Pico della Mirandola, one of the major early exponents of Renaissance humanism; he declared della Mirandola a heretic and forbade the public reading of della Mirandola's 900 theses, which he had posted publicly in Rome. The penalty was excommunication from the church.

Innocent's promotion of a crusade against the Islamic world was apparently not motivated by deep theological differences, for during the later part of his papacy, beset with problems at home, he readily entered into negotiations with the Turkish sultan Bayezid II. In return for Innocent's keeping Bayezid's brother and rival Jem, who had been detained after seeking help from a Western military-religious order, imprisoned at the Vatican, Bayezid would make a large annual payment and send to Rome a spear, the Holy Lance, said to have pierced the body of Jesus Christ during his crucifixion. As a result, noted Duffy, "four centuries of papal commitment to the pushing back of Islam was abandoned." Innocent did live to see the final reconquest, however, of Spain from Moorish forces in 1492.

Other charges against Innocent VIII have been leveled by historians, including that he profited from the slave trade between Naples and northern Africa and distributed slaves to favored cardinals. He apparently confessed his failings during his final illness, exhorting his cardinals to choose a successor who was better than he himself had been. One writer reported that as the Pope fell into a coma, his doctor (who according to the *Encyclopedia Judaica* was Jewish) ordered history's first attempted blood transfusion; the blood of three ten-year-old boys was administered to Innocent by mouth, the function of the venous system being little understood at the time. The three boys died, and Innocent died as well on July 25, 1492, in Rome.

Books

Duffy, Eamon, *Saints & Sinners: A History of the Popes,* Yale, 2006.

Encyclopedia Judaica, Gale, 2007.

McBrien, Richard F., *Lives of the Popes,* Harper, 1997.

New Catholic Encyclopedia, Gale, 2003.

Schimmelpfennig, Bernhard, *The Papacy,* Columbia, 1992.

Online

"Cibo, Giovanni Battista (1432–1492)," *The Cardinals of the Holy Roman Church* (Florida International University), http://www2.fiu.edu/~mirandas/bios1489.htm (December 1, 2013).□

Issa

The Japanese poet Kobayashi Issa (1763–1828) is, along with his predecessors Matsuo Basho and Yosa Buson, known as one of the three pillars of haiku, the classic three-line form of Japanese poetry.

Prized for their subtlety, haikus are known for descriptions of the natural world that aim at an impersonal, timeless quality. Issa, by contrast, inhabits his own poetry, much of which directly reflects the events of his life. In the words of biographer Makoto Ueda (as taken from *Dew on the Grass: The Life and Poetry of Kobayashi Issa*), "Issa always had an earthly perspective, with a mind that looked at nature from his highly personal point of view.... His poetry is lacking in the viewpoint that transcends time and space. Yet on the other hand it is filled with personal feelings, intense and livedly, that we can easily identify with." Isaa sometimes, like other haiku poets, depicted natural scenes, but he was just as likely to write about animals around him—cats, birds, insects—and his own interactions with them. While Basho and Buson might write about a wild duck in flight, Issa wrote: "a wild duck in my yard / when I arrive back home / glares at me." Issa's accessible and down-to-earth poetry is enjoyed by ordinary speakers of Japanese and is often taught to schoolchildren.

Grew Up on Farm

Issa was a pen name the poet took as he was establishing himself in his career, meaning "cup of tea" or, according to one translation, "a single bubble in steeping tea." His official name at birth was Kobayashi Nobuyki (with Kobayahsi, the last name, written first according to the Japanese sytems). The first son of a fairly prosperous farmer, Yagobei, he was born in the village of Kashiwabara about 150 miles northwest of present-day Tokyo, on June 15, 1763. As a child he was called Yataro. After Issa's mother died when he was three, he was raised by a grandmother and sent to the home of a local poet and wine dealer named Shimpo to study reading and writing. He later claimed to have begun writing poetry at age five, although this is now considered unlikely.

Issa's life took a turn for the worse after his father remarried in 1770. He clashed with his stepmother, Hatsu, who forced him to babysit his half-brother, Senroku, and frequently beat him; Issa recalled carrying the baby until he was soaked with its urine. Ueda has characterized this recollection as "not fair" to Issa's father and stepmother, pointing out that babysitting was an easier job than field labor and that corporal punishment was common in Japan at the time. Nevertheless, the tension in the family was such that Issa's father sent him to Tokyo, then called Edo, to study in 1777.

Little is known of the next years of Issa's life, perhaps because they were difficult ones. Of his first days in the city he later wrote (as quoted by Ueda): "Like a pitiful bird without its nest, I immediately faced the difficulty of finding a place to sleep. One night I would take shelter from dew under the eaves of one house; another night I would seek protection from frost in the shade of another house. One day I would wander into an unknown forest and call out at the top of my voice, but with no one except a lonely wind among the pines responding to me, I would make a bed out of tree leaves and go to sleep there." Issa may have worked for a clerk in a Buddhist temple. He apparently studied writing under the poet Norokuan Chikua, for after Chikua's death Issa assumed some of his teaching duties.

Wandered Across Japan

By 1790, Issa's poetry was being published in collections, and he also attracted a patron, the wealthy rice merchant Seibi Natsume. However, whether by necessity or by temperament, Issa would spend much of the next 25 years on the road, as a wandering poet and teacher. He shaved his head. In addition to writing poetry he kept meticulous journals that were almost works of poetry in themselves. In one, quoted by Ueda, he described himself this way: "I am a homeless lunatic, now roving in the west, now roaming in the east. I eat breakfast in Kazusa Province in the morning and take lodging in Musashi Province that night. I am like a white wave that has not shore to land, or foam that vanishes as soon as it forms. I therefore call myself Issa the monk."

Nevertheless, Issa began to gain a reputation as a poet, although he was long less popular in eastern Japan than in the west. He visited his hometown of Kashiwabara at one point but then departed once again because, Ueda speculated, he had teaching opportunities elsehwere. Issa compiled a listing of all the poets he could find in Japan, probably with the intention of offering his services as a teacher. In 1795, Issa published a collection of his own poetry, entitled *Tabishui.* In 1801, Yagobei died of typhoid fever. Issa recorded his final illness in a diary called *The Record of My Father's Last Days,* and after his cremation Issa collected his bones.

As the firstborn son, Issa should by tradition have inherited his father's substantial farm, and his father's will stated that the farm was to be his. However, Hatsu and Senroku challenged the will, and they succeeded in rallying some of the local villagers to their side, probably because it was they who had actually farmed the land and made improvements that saw the farm increase in value. A rancorous dispute over the land and family house unfolded over the next 13 years, with several local officials and religious leaders unsuccessfully trying their hand at mediation. Finally an agreement was signed between Issa and Senroku that divided not only the farm but also the farmhouse itself in half.

Children Died Young

Finally, at age 50, Issa had become a homeowner. He soon married, and his wife, Kiku, had a baby boy. The baby died in infancy, and in 1818, the couple had a daughter, Sato. She lived for about a year, long enough for Issa to become attached to her and to describe her activities and personality in great detail in his poetry and diaries; he expressed great sorrow at her death from smallpox. Two more sons were born in 1820 and 1822; both died soon afterward, followed, in 1823, by the death of Kiku herself. A second marriage, to the 38-year-old daughter of a local samurai warrior, lasted only a few weeks. In 1826, Issa was married yet again, to a farmer's daughter, Yawo.

Through the tumultuous events happening in his life, which included his own bout with malaria and a variety of other medical problems, Issa continued to write, and his reputation as a writer steadily grew. In 1819, he issued one of his most famous works, *Ora ga haru,* which has been translated as *The Year of My Life* or *The Spring of My Life.* The book was another in his series of diaries, written in elevated poetic language (a distinctively Japanese genre known as *haibun*); it recorded his sorrow over Sato's death. Issa also wrote haikus of a personal nature, touching on such subjects as disputes with his wife. Sato's death also inspired this haiku, quoted on the website of the Kobayashi Issa Museum and translated by Lewis Mackenzie: "The world of dew— / A world of dew it is indeed, / And yet, and yet . . ."

Issa wrote more than 20,000 haikus, as well as poems in other genres and prose works. Because of his background, but also because of the directness and honesty of his writing, he was sometimes called the peasant poet. Issa's haikus were populated by living things: people and animals. Often he employed humor, most often directed at himself. In 1807 or 1808, he wrote this haiku (as quoted by Ueda): "is it hard to crawl / on my wrinkled palm / first firefly of the year?" The website *PoemHunter.com* quoted this economical evening scene: "Blossoms at night / and the faces of people / moved by music."

The last year of the aging poet's life was marked by a fire in his family homestead. The house was destroyed, and Issa and his family moved into a storehouse that is still in existence. During the year 1827 Issa became temporarily mute, probably from a precursor to the stroke that would soon kill him. Yuwo became pregnant, but she would not give birth until after Issa's death on January 5, 1828. He continued writing poetry on his deathbed, almost until the end.

Books

Bickerton, Max, *Issa's Life and Poetry,* in *Transactions of the Asiatic Society of Japan,* Asiatic Society of Japan, 1932,

Ueda, Makoto, *Dew on the Grass: The Life and Poetry of Kobayashi Issa,* Brill, 2004.

Periodicals

Horn Book Magazine, March-April 2007.

Online

"Biography of Kobayashi Issa," *PoemHunter,com,* http://www.poemhunter.com/kobayashi-issa/biography (November 7, 2013).

"Kobayashi Issa," *Poetry Foundation,* http://www.poetryfoundation.org/bio/kobayashi-issa (November 7, 2013).

"Kobayashi Issa (1763–1827)," *Books and Writers,* http://www.kirjasto.sci.fi/koba.htm (November 7, 2013).

"The Life of Kobayashi Issa," *Kobayashi Issa Museum,* http://www.kobayashi-issa.jp/en/about-issa (November 7, 2013).

"Nobuyuki Kobayashi—ISSA," *HaikuOz: The Australian Haiku Society,* http://www.haikuoz.org/2007/04/nobuyuki_kobayashi_issa.html (November 7, 2013).□

Toyo Ito

The Japanese architect Toyo Ito (born 1941) has gained renown for original, entirely modern designs that, unlike much other contemporary architecture, maintain a human scale and reflect the needs and emotions of their users.

Ito has not been an adherent of any particular architectural style. Rather, his buildings differ greatly from one to another, and over his career he has continued to experiment relentlessly. Each building he has completed, he told Elaine Kurtenbach of the Associated Press (as quoted in the Kitchener, Ontario, *Record*), has made him "painfully aware of my own inadequacy, and it turns into energy to challenge the next project." Ito's career as a whole, wrote Nicolai Ourousoff of the *New York Times,* "can be read as a lifelong quest to find the precise balance between seemingly opposing values—individual and community, machine and nature, male and female, utopian fantasies and hard realities." Novel and unexpected in his designs, Ito was called by Thomas Daniell of *Artscape Japan,* "the definitive architect of the cyberspace era." Ito received the Pritzker Prize, the architecture profession's highest honor, in 2013.

Worked in Family Miso Factory

Toyo Ito was born in Seoul, Korea, which was then under Japanese occupation and called Keijo, on June 1, 1941. His family was Japanese, and he and his mother, along with two sisters, returned to Japan in 1943, and they were

© epa european pressphoto agency b.v./Alamy

followed by his father in 1945. Ito was raised in the town of Shimosuwa-machi in Japan's Nagano Prefecture. Ito's father enjoyed traditional Japanese painting and liked to draw up plans for friends' houses to assist his own father, who was a lumber dealer. After his father's death in 1953, Ito and the rest of his family all pitched in to work at a small plant that made miso (a fermented grain paste).

The business prospered, and Ito's mother asked a well-known modern architect, Yoshinobu Ashihara, to design the family's new house in Tokyo. As a young man, however, Ito had no interest in architecture. Attending Hibiya High School in Tokyo, he hoped to become a professional baseball player. Classes at the University of Tokyo ignited his interest in architecture, however, and his talents quickly bloomed: for his undergraduate final project he devised a redesign of Tokyo's Ueno Park, and the project won the school's top prize.

The project was indicative of Ito's lifelong concern for the human usability of spaces, but when he was being trained, in the 1960s, modernism was the rule in architecture, and Ito followed the example of such Japanese architects as Kenzo Tange and Kiyonori Kikutake, in whose studio he worked after graduating from the university in 1965. The massive ambitions—the dreams of remaking the world through architecture—of modernist projects depressed the young architect. It was very disappointing for the young generation," he recalled to Ourousoff. "It became very hard to have any outward hope about the future." Restless, Ito opened his own studio in Tokyo, calling it Urban Robot or Urbot. In 1979, he renamed it Toyo Ito & Associates.

Designed Home Associated with Mourning

Unlike the modernists, for whom a prize commission was a giant skyscraper that could become a canvas of concrete and steel, Ito began his independent career by building mostly small residences that seemed to reflect the specific feelings of their owners. One of the first Ito buildings to gain wide attention in the profession was the so-called White U house, which Ito designed in 1976 for a sister who had recently lost her husband to cancer. U-shaped, entirely white, and featuring a peaceful central courtyard that was largely isolated from the outside world, the house was intended as a therapeutic environment, and it was unlike any other structure of its time. Eventually, after Ito's family had moved out, the house was demolished in 1996; Ito attended the demolition and approved of it, for it signified that the family's period of mourning had ended.

In the 1980s and 1990s, Ito's career continued to develop steadily but slowly. He won an Architecture Institute of Japan award for a 1984 house dubbed the Silver Hut in Imabari, Japan, in 1986; the building, in which Ito himself lived for a time, experimented with unusual ways of admitting light into an airy space with an open floor plan. Already Ito was beginning to challenge what architects call the grid, the orderly system of walls and ceiliings with which architecture imposes order on a natural space. In 1986. Ito turned his attention to a larger structure with the acclaimed Tower of Winds in Yokohama; constructed from a complex set of reflecting materials, it is defined at night by lights whose intensity is controlled by computers that sense wind velocity and direction. *Archdaily* referred to the building as a "technological sculpture" that "creates an infinite relationship between technology, architecture, the city, and its inhabitants, emphasizing the profound impact of the city on the human race and the crucial role of technology and architecture."

In 1992, Ito received his first commission for a major public building—the Yatsushiro Municipal Museum. His design for the museum received the Mainich Art Award. Working in a small space in a city park that limited the extent of the building both vertically and horizontally, Ito achieved a design featuring vaults with deep overhangs. Hiroshi Watanabe of *Progressive Architecture* noted that the museum was "a summing up of ideas that have preoccupied Ito in the past, such as the lightness and transparency of materials of the Silver Hut, and the autonomous, geometrical object first seen in his 1986 Tower of Winds," but that the building also marked a new emphasis on stability in Ito's work.

The same combination of lightness and stability was evident in the Sendai Mediatheque (2001), a library in Sendai, Japan, that marked Ito's international breakthrough. The building at first glance looks like a glass box typical of the modernist style, but it is pierced by shafts (which hold elevators, stairs, and mechanical systems, which protrude above the top of the building like growing things. "The tubes are often compared to trees in a forest," Ito told Ourousoff.

"But they are also like objects in a Japanese garden, where space is created by movement around carefully arranged points, like ponds or stones." The Sendai Mediatheque won major prizes both in Japan and abroad, and led to the honoring of Ito with a Golden Lion award at the prestigious Venice Biennale in 2002. The building even survived the 2011 Japan earthquake; a viral YouTube video showed the structure swaying but not falling even as other buildings in the area collapsed.

Received Opera House Commission

As Ito's international renown grew, he began to receive important commissions from outside Japan. He designed the Taichung Metropolitan Opera house in Taiwan, which has been compared to a giant sponge; scheduled for completion in late 2013, the building, in Ourousoff's words, "comes closest to an ideal [Ito] has been chasing for decades: a building that seems to have been frozen in a state of metamorphosis." Still more visible to the general public was another Taiwanese Ito design: the main stadium for the 2009 World Games in Kaohsiung, Taiwan. At home, Ito earned plaudits for the Tama Art University Library and for a Tokyo store for the Italian shoe retailer Tod's. He also designed a set of flatware patterns for another Italian company, Alessi.

Despite his growing personal renown, Ito was committed to collective action in the wake of the 8.9-magnitude 2011 earthquake. He brought together three young architects and worked with them on a project called Home-for-All that provided space for earthquake survivors. "An architect is someone who can make such places for meager meals show a little more humanity, make them a little more beautiful, a little more comfortable," Ito was quoted as saying by Robin Pogrebin of the *New York Times.* Ito's work on behalf of earthquake victims was considered an important factor leading to his reception of the Pritzker Prize, architecture's counterpart to the Nobel Prizes, in 2013.

Ito was married; he and his wife, who died in 2010, raised one daughter, who became the editor of the Japanese edition of *Vogue* magazine. A Toyo Ito Museum of Architecture opened in Imbari in 2011, featuring a re-creation of Ito's Silver Hut. As of 2013, Ito's first major American commission, for a design for the new Berkeley Art Museum and Pacific Film Archive in California, was under construction.

Periodicals

Architectural Review, May 2008.
New York Times, July 12, 2009; March 18, 2013.
Progressive Architecture, October 1992.
Record (Kitchener, Ontario, Canada), March 30, 2013.

Online

"AD Classics: Tower of Winds," *Archdaily,* http://www.archdaily.com/344664/ (October 11, 2013).
"AD Classics: White U/Toyo Ito," *Archdaily,* http://www.archdaily.com/345857/ (October 11, 2013).
"Toyo Ito," *Appalachian State University,* http://www.appstate.edu/~fletcherag/Architect/Biography.html (October 11, 2013).
"Toyo Ito: Biography," *Pritzker Architecture Prize,* http://www.pritzkerprize.com/2013/biography (October 11, 2013).□

J

Joe Jackson

The British singer and songwriter Joe Jackson (born 1954) has been perhaps the most musically versatile figure to have emerged from the New Wave rock music scene of the late 1970s.

In the words of *Variety*'s Steve Chagolian, "Joe Jackson has always experienced a thorny relationship with convention, zigging left when fans and critics expect him to zag right." His own attitude has been almost anti-commercial: "You [can't] start trying to figure out what people are going to like. It's an ass-backwards way of trying to create anything," he told Chagolian. Yet Jackson experienced considerable commercial success during the first part of his career, with the punk-oriented yet tuneful single "Is She Really Going Out with Him?" and the Latin jazz–flavored album *Night and Day* especially. Since then, Jackson, a classically trained musician, has delved into swing, film scores, rock, jazz, and classical music, according to the direction of his interests at the time. No longer inhabiting upper chart reaches, Jackson has been a prolific creator of original music that has amassed a cadre of fans despite—or because of—his unpredictability.

Nickname Came from Television Puppet

Joe Jackson was born David Ian Jackson on August 11, 1954, in Burton Upon Trent, England. He acquired the nickname Joe early in his musical career when some bandmates decided that he resembled a television puppet named Joe and began calling him that. His father was a member of the British navy who became a plasterer; his mother worked at her family's pub in the city of Portsmouth. Jackson was raised mostly in that city and grew up in poverty, suffering from asthma and other health problems as a result. He hated sports in school and signed up for music classes to escape them. To his surprise he found that he both enjoyed and had an aptitude for such difficult subjects as music theory, and he quickly gained some piano skills. On an early version of his website (as quoted in *Contemporary Musicians*) he said that music saved him from being one of those sad [people] you see milling around the pub at closing time, looking for a fight."

From the beginning, Jackson vacillated between popular and classical music. His first ambition was to become a classical composer. Then, finding that most people around him enjoyed popular songs, he began to try to write those. By 16 he was landing gigs in pubs and as an accompanist to a bouzouki player at a Greek restaurant. He won a scholarship to attend the prestigious Royal Academy of Music in London, studying both classical music and jazz, and working with an experimental theater group. By the time he graduated in 1975, Jackson had become involved with an early punk band called first Edward Bear, then Edwin Bear, then finally Arms & Legs, which released several singles on the small MAM label.

With an eye on bigger things, Jackson worked at a Playboy Club and as musical director for a cabaret act to raise money. In 1977, he formed his own Joe Jackson Band, and the group recorded a demo tape that impressed David Kershenbaum, an executive and talent scout for the venerable American label A&M. The label's catalogue, with its eclectic mixture of popular styles, would prove a congenial home for Jackson, and after he was signed to A&M in the summer of 1978 his demo tape, entitled *Look Sharp,* was rerecorded and released in Britain in early 1979.

The single "Is She Really Going Out with Him?" had already been released with little impact, and the album was slow to build. But Jackson and his band toured heavily in the U.S., where the album was released in March, and the U.S. single version of "Is She Really Going Out with Him?" hit the top 40, gained substantial airplay on rock radio stations (which few songs from the New Wave sphere yet had by that point), and even earned Jackson a Grammy nomination for Best Rock Male Vocal Performance. Jackson's sophomore release, *I'm the Man,* made the top 20 in Britain and began to earn Jackson comparison with other British singer-songwriters who combined punk anger and New Wave pop sensitivity: namely, Elvis Costello and Graham Parker.

Exposed to Salsa in New York

Jackson's next album, *Beat Crazy,* featured Jamaican influences and was only moderately successful. Jackson, in poor health, left the road in order to rest at his family home, and while there he became fascinated with the jump blues music of the late 1940s. In 1981 he released the album *Jumpin' Jive,* which, in the words of *AllMusic*'s William Ruhlmann, "was not so much 35 years behind the times as 15 years ahead of them." Danceable jump blues and swing became very popular in the U.S. in the 1990s. After Jackson's marriage broke up he moved to New York, where he was exposed to another new influence: the piano-based salsa music that flourished in the city's Latin American neighborhoods. The result was the album *Night and Day,* released in the summer of 1982.

For several reasons, *Night and Day* became the high point of Jackson's career, commercially and perhaps artistically. For the first time the music allowed him to showcase his considerable skills as a pianist. And the music found a winning contrast between the bright sounds of salsa and Jackson's often doubt-riddled lyrics in such songs as "Steppin' Out:" "We . . . are young but getting old before our time. / We'll leave the TV and the radio behind. / Don't you wonder what we'll find, / Steppin' out tonight." That song and "Breaking Us in Two" both hit ths U.S. top 20; the album as a whole reached the top ten and earned a pair of Grammy nominations. He followed up *Night and Day* with *Body & Soul,* another album in the same vein, and he also worked on the soundtrack to the film *Mike's Murder* (1983).

Once more, Jackson dropped out of the music scene temporarily to recharge his creative impulses, and returned with a completely new direction: in 1987, he released the orchestral *Will Power,* on which he began to explore what he had learned during his training in classical music. After the commercially disappointing *Blaze of Glory,* Jackson left A&M and signed with Virgin. He released *Laughter and Love* (1991) and *Night Music* (1994), another album with classical elements.

Signed with Classical Label

In 1995, Jackson signed with the Sony Classical label and was able to give full attention to this side of his musical popularity. He recorded a classical song cycle, *Heaven & Hell,* with guest vocalists that included figures from both the pop (Suzanne Vega) and classical (Dawn Upshaw) worlds. Jackson's 1999 album *Symphony No. 1* was not quite the pure classical outing its title might suggest, for it included jazz and rock players rather than a symphony orchestra, and it won a Grammy award for best instrumental album—on the pop side. Jackson's 2000 release *Summer in the City: Live in New York* featured sparse arrangements for piano, bass, and drums of Jackson's earlier hits.

Jackson returned to pop music in the 2000s, issuing *Night & Day* in 2000 (Jackson himself considers it his most underrated work). The original Joe Jackson Band reunited for *Volume 4* in 2003, and the resulting tour was successful enough to spawn a live album, *Afterlife,* the following year. Jackson toured in the mid-2000s on a pop-classical tour with experimental Philadelphia soul singer Todd Rundgren and a string quartet called Ethel. In 2007, Jackson returned to the piano-bass-and-drums accompaniment format for the album *Rain,* which generated a three-year tour reaching as far as Israel and South Africa.

Jackson has issued an autobiography, *A Cure for Gravity.* As of this writing his most recent album is *The Duke,* a tribute to jazz bandleader Duke Ellington that draws on a typically diverse array of stylistic sources including samba, art-rock, and hip-hop. Jackson lives in Berlin and has announced plans for a new release in 2014.

Books

Contemporary Musicians, volume 64, Gale, 2008.

Jackson, Joe, *A Cure for Gravity,* Da Capo, 2000.

Periodicals

Billboard, July 7, 2012.

Birmingham Evening Mail (Birmingham, England), February 20, 2001.

Variety, June 25, 2012.

Online

"Bio," Joe Jackson Official Website, http://joejackson.com/info (November 14, 2013).

"Joe Jackson," *AllMusic,* http://www.allmusic.com (November 14, 2013).□

Wanda Jackson

The American vocalist Wanda Jackson (born 1937) was one of the first women to sing rock and roll music. Elvis Presley, among others, called her the Queen of Rockabilly.

Jackson broke into popular music as a teenager in the mid-1950s, touring with a pair of stars: the country singer Hank Thompson and the fast-rising rockabilly star Elvis Presley. It was Presley who suggested that she try to sing the then-new rockabilly music. For several years Jackson tried to straddle the divide between country and rockabilly, recording in both styles—occasionally within the same song. In several of her rockabilly songs, Jackson offered a level of sexual innuendo that had hitherto been unknown in mainstream, major-label music releases, and her bare-shouldered, tight-skirted sexy image was also very rare at the time. Rock singer Jack White, who produced one of Jackson's remarkable series of comeback albums, told Craig McLean of the London *Times* that "Wanda was the first female badass—the first rock 'n' roll queen."

Performed with Father

Wanda Lavonne Jackson was a native of the small town of Maud, Oklahoma, born on October 20, 1937. Her father was a barber and part-time musician, and jobs in Oklahoma at the height of the Dust Bowl years were scarce. When Wanda was four, the family joined other Oklahomans on a westward migration, settling in Bakersfield, California. There her parents took her to Western swing concerts, and she dreamed of being a singer from the start. As soon as she could fit her hand around the instrument's neck, she took up the guitar and played duets with her father, a fiddler. "Wanda wasn't like other children after the guitar came into her life," her mother was quoted as saying by Mike Walsh of *Mission Creep*. The Jacksons moved back to Oklahoma when Wanda was 12, over the objections of her father, who agreed on the condition that Wanda and her mother pitch in to contribute to the family finances.

Wanda held up her end of the bargain, winning a talent contest at her Oklahoma City high school and landing a 15-minute slot on radio station KLPR. Soon the show had expanded to 30 minutes, and Jackson was performing on vocals at dances with a local Western swing band, Merle Lindsey and the Oklahoma Night Riders. Her local fame as a radio and live-performance star brought her to the attention of Thompson, who heard her on the radio in Oklahoma City. He was Jackson's favorite singer at the time, and when he invited her to audition, she jumped at the chance.

Jackson, still in her mid-teens, continued to attend high school and toured with Thompson's Brazos Valley Boys on weekends, accompanied by her father. Thompson showed the young singer the ways of show business and tried to arrange for her signing to his label, Capitol. But the label demurred due to Jackson's age. Signed instead to

© ZUMA Press, Inc./Alamy

Decca, she released several singles; a duet with Thompson band member Billy Gray, "You Can't Have My Love," reached the number eight spot on country charts. That propelled Jackson to a spot on the Ozark Jubilee, a major country music touring package that also included Presley; Jackson joined the tour in 1955 after graduating from high school. "As it's turned out, I've been on tour ever since," Jackson remarked in an interview with Scott Jenkins of *Elvis Australia*.

Soon Presley and Jackson were dating, with Jackson's father accompanying them as a chaperone on dates. "Our dating amounted to what we could do on the road," Jackson recalled to Jenkins. "If we got in town early, we might take in a matinee movie. Then after shows we could go places with his band—and my dad, of course." The couple was apparently able to enjoy some privacy, however; Jackson told Marjorie Hernandez of the *Ventura County Star* that Presley was "a very good kisser." The couple was in a committed relationship for a time, and Presley gave Jackson a ring that she wore around her neck in concerts later in life. But they parted ways when Presley left the South for California to pursue his movie career.

Sang Rockabilly at Presley's Urging

More lasting was Presley's musical influence on the young singer. On tour, Jackson shared bills not only with Presley, but such high-energy stars as Johnny Cash, Carl Perkins, Jerry Lee Lewis, and Buddy Holly. It was Presley who urged

Jackson to add the new rockabilly style to her vocal repertoire. "I can't, I'm just a country singer," Jackson objected (as quoted in the *Guelph Mercury*). But she soon mastered the hiccups, yells, and belted vocals of rockabilly. When Jackson was finally signed to Capitol in 1956, she chose a song written by a friend, "I Gotta Know," that inventively combined rockabilly and country in its verse-chorus structure.

"I Gotta Know" was a moderate country hit, but it may have hampered her long-term prospects: Capitol was unsure whether to market Jackson as a country singer or as a rock and roller. Her singles for the rest of the 1950s had little success in the United States despite production work by influential Capitol executive Ken Nelson. But such Jackson tracks as "Hot Dog! That Made Him Mad" are prized by collectors today as fine examples of rockabilly with a strong female perspective. "Fujiyama Mama," with its double-entendre imagery ("When I start erupting, ain't nobody gonna make me stop"), may have proved too sexy for Bible Belt American audiences but reached top chart levels in Japan, where Jackson has maintained a strong following.

On records and in performance, Jackson was backed by a top-flight band that, alone among major rockabilly touring ensembles, included an African American musician, pianist Big Al Downing. Jackson finally cracked the pop top 40 in 1960 with the single "Let's Have a Party," which reached number 37. The song had previously been recorded by Presley, but several modern critics have opined that Jackson's hard-rocking version was superior. In 1960, Capitol collected Jackson's rockabilly singles into an LP album, *Rockin' with Wanda,* which has remained a consistent seller.

In 1961, Jackson returned to her first love, country music, and scored a pair of top 40 country hits with "Right or Wrong" and "In the Middle of a Heartache." Her protofeminist edge was dulled under the weight of countrypolitan string arrangements, but not eliminated; in one single she threatened a cheating partner with attack from her "Big Iron Skillet." Jackson was a major attraction on the growing Las Vegas Strip country scene, and in 1964 in Las Vegas she saw Presley for the last time—he had reserved an entire corridor of a hotel, except for the room where she and her husband were staying.

Recorded Gospel Music

Jackson's husband, Wendell Goodman, was a computer programmer whom she married in 1961. He gave up his career to manage Jackson's. The couple had two children and several grandchildren who have begun to show an interest in performing. In the early 1970s, Jackson embraced evangelical Christianity, a decision she credited with the preservation of her marriage. She recorded several gospel albums, which resulted in her departure from Capitol after the initial *Praise the Lord* (1972); her gospel releases appeared on the Christian-oriented Word and Myrrh labels. Jackson never completely renounced secular music, and she maintained a strong following in Europe. She also issued a Swedish-language autobiography.

Jackson began her rockabilly comeback with *Rock 'n' Roll Your Blues Away,* released in 1987 on the Varrick label. Her renewed rockabilly-oriented touring saw her venerated by younger female rockabilly singers such as Marti Brom, Rosie Flores, and Kim Lenz. Jackson saw many of her recordings collected into anthologies in her later years by both American and European labels, and she received such accolades as a National Endowment for the Arts fellowship in 2005 and a Smithsonian Institution documentary, *The Sweet Lady with the Nasty Voice,* devoted to her career in 2008. She remarked to *Smithsonian* that "I'm not sure that's right, because I'm not sure I'm a sweet lady at all." Jackson was inducted into the Rock and Roll Hall of Fame in 2009. In 2011, she toured as an opening act for British pop vocalist Adele.

Perhaps the most remarkable aspect of Jackson's late-life legacy, however, has been her continuing production of new music. After releasing the Presley tribute album *I Remember Elvis* in 2006, she planned to assemble a collection of duets with contemporary vocalists but was dissuaded from doing so by rock star Jack White (of the band the White Stripes), who offered to produce an album of covers of songs that were familiar to younger audiences but unexpected for Jackson, including Bob Dylan's "Thunder on the Mountain" and Amy Winehouse's "You Know That I'm No Good." White rewrote some of the lyrics of the latter song to make it acceptable for Jackson's Christian sensibilities. Jackson returned to the studio in 2013 for the new album *Unfinished Business,* her 31st studio album release, which was produced by rising Americana star Justin Townes Earle. She has continued to live with her husband in the Oklahoma City area.

Books

Contemporary Musicians, Volume 72, Gale, 2012.

Periodicals

Entertainment Weekly, January 21, 2011.
Guelph Mercury (Guelph, Ontario, Canada), January 10, 2013.
Herald (Glasgow, Scotland), January 23, 2009.
International Herald Tribune, January 22, 2011.
Toronto Star, July 4, 2013.
Smithsonian, November 2008.
Star Tribune (Minneapolis, MN), August 6, 2011.
Times (London, England), January 15, 2011.
Ventura County Star (Ventura, CA), June 9, 2012.

Online

"Biography," Wanda Jackson Official Website, http://www.wandajackson.com/pages/biography.html (October 15, 2013).
"Interview with Wanda Jackson," *Elvis Australia,* http://www.elvis.com.au/presley/interview_wanda_jackson.shtml#sthash.hCKAtZTZ.dpbs (October 15, 2013).
"Nitroglycerine!!!!! The Rock & Roll Eruption of Wanda Jackson," *Mission Creep,* http://www.missioncreep.com/mw/jackson.html (October 15, 2013).
"Wanda Jackson," *AllMusic,* http://www.allmusic.com/artist/wanda-jackson-mn0000814606/biography (October 15, 2013).
"Wanda Jackson Biography," *Oldies.com,* http://www.oldies.com/artist-biography/Wanda-Jackson.html (October 15, 2013).
"Wanda Jackson Biography," *Rock and Roll Hall of Fame,* http://rockhall.com/inductees/wanda-jackson (October 15, 2013).□

Nucky Johnson

American political boss Enoch "Nucky" Johnson (1883–1968) dominated Atlantic City for more than three decades and inspired the HBO drama *Boardwalk Empire.*

AP Photo

American political boss Enoch "Nucky" Johnson dominated Atlantic City and strongly influenced New Jersey Republican politics for some 30 years as the most powerful person in the seaside resort town. Johnson commanded a slate of illicit activities that helped make him immensely rich but that also attracted a federal investigation that ultimately sent him to prison for tax evasion in the 1940s. His colorful lifestyle and connections with high-profile mobsters who were involved in Prohibition-era bootlegging inspired the lead character of the HBO drama *Boardwalk Empire,* which debuted more than forty years after the real Atlantic City boss's death.

Became Political Boss of Atlantic City

The son of Smith Johnson and his wife Virginia, Enoch Lewis Johnson was born on January 20, 1883, in Smithville, New Jersey. His lifelong nickname, "Nucky," was a diminutive of his first name. Both parents were of Scots-Irish descent and came from families that had long lived in the state. Smith Johnson was a physically imposing man who was a close ally of Atlantic City's political boss, Louis "Commodore" Kuehnle. He was first elected sheriff in 1886, and the family divided their time between Atlantic City and nearby Mays Landing as young Johnson grew up, depending on whether the elder Johnson was acting as sheriff or undersheriff. Johnson graduated from May Landing High School and briefly attended the Trenton Model Preparatory School for Boys before returning to take on the job of undersheriff himself in 1905. The following year, he married his first wife, Mabel.

Johnson's political ascent continued rapidly. In 1909, at the age of 25, he was sworn in as sheriff, becoming the youngest person in New Jersey history to hold that office to date; his father served as undersheriff in that term. This position afforded Johnson a great deal of power within the county's Republican Party establishment at a time when Atlantic City was essentially a one-party community. But his tenure was short-lived. In 1910, New Jersey Governor Woodrow Wilson initiated an investigation into irregular voting practices by the Republican Party in Atlantic City. Although Johnson was acquitted of all charges, he lost his seat as sheriff. In truth, he had performed few of the duties associated with the office anyway. He soon became the secretary of the Republican County Committee, however, allowing him to closely manage party affairs, especially as a conviction for corruption had removed Kuehnle from the city's political scene.

Johnson's personal life fared worse. Mabel Johnson was diagnosed with tuberculosis and died weeks later in 1913. The death of his wife deeply affected the young man. "My father said that Nucky mourned Mabel for months," recalled an unnamed interviewee in Nelson Johnson's *Boardwalk Empire: The Birth, High Times, and Corruption of Atlantic City.* "Her death, like it was, broke his heart. After she was gone, he was a changed man." Local legend reputes that the death drove Johnson to cease being a teetotaler, and certainly it encouraged him to focus his energies on his career.

Later that year, he gained appointment as the county treasurer, an influential position that he would hold for the next 30 years. As treasurer, Johnson had the power to manage the county's money to line his own pockets and those of Republican supporters, and to funnel money to anointed Republican candidates for office. In 1916, Johnson's support helped Atlantic City native Walter Edge win election as New Jersey's governor. These efforts led Edge to appoint Johnson clerk of the New Jersey Supreme Court in return, giving him a foothold in state-level politics.

Dominated a "Boardwalk Empire"

By 1920, Johnson had established himself as the boss of Atlantic City. A behind-the-scenes kingmaker, he was arguably the most powerful figure in New Jersey state politics. He won the support of Atlantic City's African American population through financial support to the city's Northside neighborhood, and in return gained a loyal black voting bloc that helped him deliver elections time after time.

Purveyors of gambling holes, numbers games, brothels, and other illicit institutions paid him bribes in order to operate without the interference of the authorities. The ratification of the Eighteenth Amendment barring the production and sale of alcoholic beverages served only to increase Johnson's power.

Atlantic City's reputation as a haven for vice and its location on the coast made it a natural destination for illegally imported liquor. Local authorities simply declined to enforce Prohibition, and alcohol flowed freely from its restaurants, bars, and drugstores. Visitors flocked to the resort town to enjoy its unmitigated pleasures. "We have whiskey, wine, women, song and slot machines," Johnson explained in an oft-repeated quotation that appeared in Jon Blackwell's *Notorious New Jersey: 100 True Tales of Murders and Mobsters, Scandals and Scoundrels.* "I won't deny it and I won't apologize for it. If the majority of the people didn't want them, they wouldn't be profitable and they wouldn't exist. The fact that they do exist proves to me that the people want them."

For every drop of alcohol that passed through the city, Johnson got a small cut of the proceeds. Combined with his existing revenue streams, Prohibition made Johnson immensely wealthy; estimates of his annual untaxed income range as high as $500,000 in a time when a Model T cost just a few hundred dollars. He rented out the entire ninth floor of Atlantic City's Ritz Carlton and employed a valet, two chauffeurs, and three maids. A tall, imposing man with a deep voice and an engaging personality, Johnson spent lavishly on clothing, often appearing in the Ritz Carlton lobby in a full-length raccoon fur coat and never seen without a fresh red carnation in his lapel. Johnson frequently slept until late afternoon and then spent his evenings strolling the boardwalk, meeting with potential voters and business associates, and partying at local nightclubs with a rotating cast of young beauties at his side.

Johnson's involvement in graft and politics put him in contact with some of the era's most notorious gangsters, particularly New York City-based mob boss Charles "Lucky" Luciano. Atlantic City was itself a relative safe zone where high-level criminals could congregate and relax without fear of assassination. In May of 1929, Johnson orchestrated a convention of the bosses of competing crime rackets in Atlantic City. There, mob bosses including Luciano and Al Capone agreed to stop the infighting among rival families, with Capone pointing out that plenty of opportunities for bootlegging and other criminal activities existed for all of them to operate profitably. Historians consider this meeting of the "Seven Group" to be the true birth of organized crime syndicates in the United States.

Convicted of Tax Evasion

By the mid 1930s, the federal government had determined to unseat and prosecute Johnson. Federal investigators decided to pursue charges of tax evasion, the same charge which had sent mobster Capone to prison earlier that decade. According to Blackwell, Johnson "was an easy target, for he lived like a millionaire while drawing a county salary of $6,000." Over the course of five years, the Roosevelt administration and other federal agencies dedicated more than $200,000 in resources and countless hours put in by 18 federal agents to collect incriminating interviews from Johnson's associates and low-level criminals about the corrupt activities in Atlantic City. Using threats of jail time and other persuasive tactics, government investigators managed to gather enough evidence to indict more than 40 of Johnson's underlings by early 1939.

After one Johnson lieutenant, a minor gambling operative named Austin Clark, was convicted for tax evasion, Johnson became increasingly worried. He tried to rig juries and discourage witnesses from testifying to the FBI. A case involving 14 defendants that was tried in 1940 produced incriminating testimony against Johnson as the accused tried to win leniency in their own cases. His situation was further complicated when a new Atlantic City major, Thomas Taggart, began closing many of the illicit operations that provided Johnson with off-the-books revenue.

The following summer, Johnson's own case went to trial. Witnesses testified that Johnson had received large kickbacks on government contracts and extorted protection money from local illegal operations. Johnson defended himself by claiming that the funds had gone to support policies that benefited Atlantic City's poor residents. But his arguments proved fruitless. The court found Johnson guilty of tax evasion and sentenced him to ten years in a federal penitentiary and a fine of $20,000. In total, the grand jury determined that his income for the year 1935 was nearly $108,000—about $1.8 million in 2013 dollars.

Shortly before reporting to serve his prison sentence, Johnson remarried to his longtime girlfriend, a former showgirl named Florence "Flossie" Osbeck. The pair remained wed for the remainder of Johnson's life. The convicted political boss spent the next few years at Lewisburg Federal Penitentiary in Pennsylvania, receiving a release on parole in August of 1945. He swore a pauper's oath to avoid paying the fine levied in his sentence and returned to Atlantic City. Johnson avoided involvement in politics despite opportunities to run for city commission. Nelson Johnson explained in *Boardwalk Empire* that "he remembered the humiliation the Commodore had experienced when he tried to regain control of the Republican Party and refused to expose himself to another defeat." Instead, he worked as a salesman for an oil company and lived quietly in a house owned by members of his wife's family. Johnson died in a New Jersey nursing home on December 9, 1968, at the age of 85.

Inspired Fictional Character

Johnson's high-flying lifestyle and involvement with some of the century's most notorious criminals made him an intriguing figure to cultural historians and observers even well after his death. Historians wrote several studies of Johnson's influence on New Jersey politics and mentioned him in works on the growth of organized crime. Most notably, a 2002 study of the changing fortunes of Atlantic City from the 19th century through the era of legalized casino gambling inaugurated in the 1970s entitled *Boardwalk Empire: The Birth, High Times, and Corruption of Atlantic City* by the local historian Nelson Johnson—no relation to the former political boss—inspired the creation of a dramatic series also called *Boardwalk Empire* that debuted on cable network HBO in 2010.

The show's central character, the Steve Buscemi-protrayed Enoch "Nucky" Thompson, was a fictionalized version of the real Johnson. Like Johnson, Thompson was an Atlantic City political boss who profited from the city's host of illegal enterprises. The differences between the characters were numerous, however. The fictional Thompson actively engaged in bootlegging, organized crime, and murders while the real Johnson is not recorded to have ordered any killings or operated his own bootlegging operations. Other characters on the show drew on actual Atlantic City figures from Johnson's era, including Kuehnle, although with notable variations in personality and life history. "I've always loved the way people talked in the '20s, and the clothes, the cars," show co-creator Terence Winter explained of the decision to create the show in an interview with Charles McGrath of the *New York Times*. "It was such a transitional period. The world was changing so much. And in some ways it was a very modern time. This was almost a hundred years ago, but they had airplanes, telephones, people went to the movies all the time."

Books

Blackwell, Jon, *Notorious New Jersey: 100 True Tales of Murders and Mobsters, Scandals and Scoundrels,* Rivergate Books, 2007.

Johnson, Nelson, *Boardwalk Empire: The Birth, High Times, and Corruption of Atlantic City,* Plexus, 2002.

Periodicals

New York Times, December 10, 1968; September 3, 2010.

Online

"Boss Nucky Johnson," *Atlantic City Experience,* http://www.atlanticcityexperience.org (December 8, 2013).□

K

Franklin Kameny

American activist Franklin Kameny (1925–2011) challenged federal-government hiring rules that permitted employment discrimination based on sexual preference. The Harvard-trained astronomer and World War II veteran fought what was then a largely solo battle in the early 1960s to be reinstated to his job with the U.S. Army Map Service. He holds a place in U.S. civil rights history as the first openly gay person to petition the U.S. Supreme Court to hear a discrimination case based on sexual preference.

Franklin Edward Kameny was born on May 21, 1925, in New York City into a Jewish family and was one of four children. Fascinated by the nighttime sky as a child, he earned solid grades at Richmond Hill High School in Queens. He began a physics undergraduate degree course at Queens College, but his studies were interrupted by World War II. He served with a U.S. Army division that fought in Germany and the Netherlands, then returned to Queens College after the war's end in 1945 to complete his degree. In 1949, he earned a master's degree in astronomy from Harvard University, then attained a doctorate with a dissertation on a distant star, RV Tauri, and its properties in 1956.

Arrested on Spurious Morals Charge

Kameny's research had taken him out west to Arizona, and while in San Francisco he was targeted in an entrapment encounter at a bus station by an undercover police officer. Such stings were commonplace in public areas where local cops believed homosexuals met, and could prove terrifying and ruinous to one's career. Kameny did not contest the charge, and the court handed down a three-year probation sentence for an encounter that began when an officer groped him. San Francisco court officials told him the charge would be expunged after the three years had passed without another offense. In 1956, Georgetown University in Washington, D.C. hired him to teach astronomy, and he was soon recruited for work with U.S. Army Map Service as staff astronomer. This was a prestigious start to a career that would have likely propelled him directly into the civilian agency about to be assembled from various other scientific and military-related research efforts, the National Aeronautics and Space Administration (NASA).

Kameny was a civilian employee of the Army, which classified him as a federal worker subject to oversight by the U.S. Civil Service Commission. A few months after he started his Army job, Kameny had another encounter with local police, this time in Lafayette Park near the White House. Security clearance officers discovered the San Francisco misdemeanor charge and questioned him about the matter, but he would not divulge his sexual orientation. In late 1957, Kameny was fired from the Army Map Service, a terrible blow after spending nearly a decade pursuing advanced science degrees. Furthermore, his name was placed on a no-hire list for any future employment on the grounds that he presented a potential national security risk.

Kameny appealed his dismissal with the U.S. Civil Service Commission. The commissioners set policy guidelines according to various directives, including Executive Order 10450, signed by President Dwight D. Eisenhower in 1953. Replacing a previous "loyalty test" parameter, E.O. 10450 permitted the federal government to deny security clearances for employees deemed a risk to national security. Gay men and women were included under its terms, on

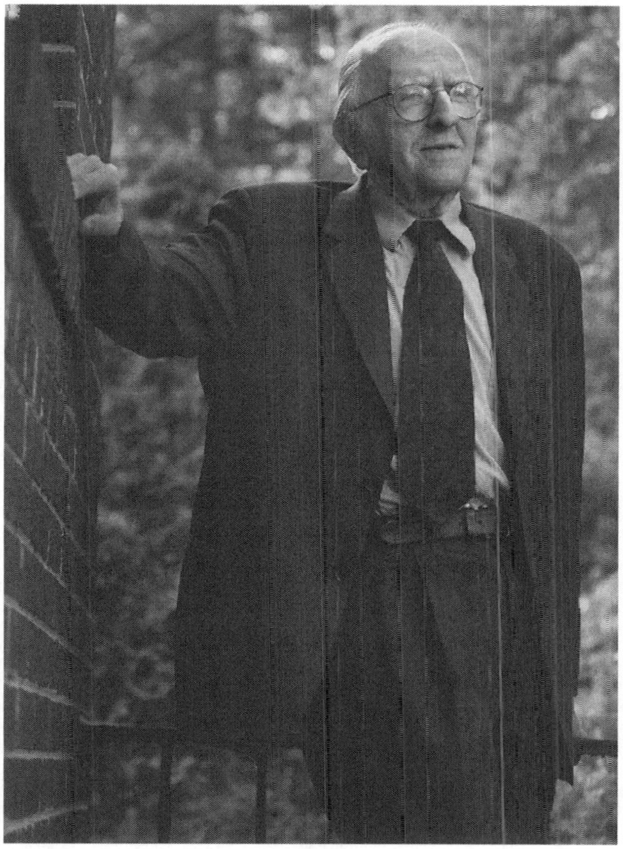

Jahi Chikwendiu/The Washington Post/Getty Images

the grounds of "sexual perversion." The Civil Service Commission rejected his appeal to be reinstated, and his arguments that he was not a security risk. At that, Kameny hired an attorney to take the case to court.

Took It to Supreme Court

As Kameny explained to writer Eric Marcus, author of *Making History: The Struggle for Gay and Lesbian Equal Rights, 1945-1990,* it was the "morals" charge that galled him into action. "The government put its disqualification of gays under the rubric of immoral conduct, which I objected to," he told Marcus, according to the *New York Times.* "Because under our system, morality is a matter of personal opinion and individual belief on which any American citizen may hold any view he wishes and upon which the government has no power or authority to have any view at all."

Kameny lost his first court case, with the court ruling that the dismissal had been justified, and he took it to the U.S. Court of Appeals, which also upheld the lower court's decision. His attorney abandoned the case when Kameny announced he would take it to the U.S. Supreme Court. Kameny—still unemployed and without income—was forced to become his own attorney, writing the legal brief required to petition the Supreme Court to hear a case. He drafted a 60-page brief, but the High Court passed and did not place it on its upcoming docket. Nevertheless, Kameny became the first openly gay American to appear in a discrimination-related case read for review by U.S. Supreme Court justices.

Kameny had applied the same zeal to legal studies as he had to his astronomy degree, and his 60-page legal brief asking the Supreme Court to hear his case used wording that became the template for subsequent legal challenges. "The government's regulations ... are a stench in the nostrils of decent people, an offense against morality, an abandonment of reason, an affront to human dignity, an improper restraint upon proper freedom and liberty, a disgrace to any civilized society, and a violation of all that this nation stands for," it read, according to Joyce Murdoch and Deb Price, authors of *Courting Justice: Gay Men And Lesbians V. The Supreme Court.* Murdoch and Price traced the paper trail of Kameny's petition, debated in closed chambers on March 17, 1961, and called the High Court's refusal to hear it—in legal terms, denying it *certiorari,* or judicial review, an accidental history-making error. "The greatest unintentional favor the Supreme Court has ever done gay Americans was infuriating Kameny by turning his case away unheard," they wrote. "The court's refusal to restore a 35-year-old astronomer to an obscure government post arguably did more to advance homosexual rights than any ruling it has ever handed down in favor of homosexual litigants," Murdoch and Price argued.

Protested at White House

Kameny became a hero to gay men and women in the early 1960s as his story quietly spread through professional circles. He and another area activist, Jack Nichols, founded the Mattachine Society of Washington, which staged some of the first public protests in support of gay rights in the United States. The D.C. Mattachine chapter was modeled on an earlier group founded in Los Angeles created to combat ongoing police harassment. In Washington, Kameny and about ten others quietly picketed in front of the White House in April of 1965. The conservatively dressed protesters held up signs urging the destigmatizing of homosexuality in America, arguing it amounted to relegating them to "second class citizenship." They also carried signs terming the Civil Service Commission rules "Un-American."

Kameny became a paralegal and worked to help other fired federal employees. He also worked with military personnel who had been dishonorably discharged on the grounds of sexual orientation. These efforts were almost the only avenues of legal recourse at a time when few attorneys were interested in taking on discrimination cases on behalf of gay men and women. The first small victory came in 1965, when a U.S. Court of Appeals bench agreed that rules barring applicants for federal employment on the basis of their sexual orientation failed to be concisely worded enough to demonstrate any risk to national security. It would take another ten years for the Civil Service Commission to finally eliminate the rule altogether.

The Stonewall Bar riots in New York City in late June of 1969 are usually considered a turning point in the history of gay rights in America, but Kameny, Nichols, and others had been working for nearly a decade by then to overturn discriminatory laws. Their efforts, plus the Stonewall rebellion, helped usher in a new era and many previously closeted gay men and women began to speak up. In Washington, Kameny launched a small monthly newsletter, called the *Gay Blade* that eventually became the *Washington Blade,* the oldest weekly newspaper in the United States serving the gay, lesbian, bisexual, and transgendered (GLBT) community. During this era he also popularized the term "gay" as an affirmative community identifier, promoting the effort with the slogan "Gay Is Good."

Led Action Against APA

One of Kameny's most notable successes he also described as the own high point of his career: in the early 1970s, he led a highly publicized effort to persuade the American Psychiatric Association (APA) to remove homosexuality from its list of personality disorders. His arguments with the APA were bolstered by his own résumé as the holder of a Ph.D. from Harvard University. He derided pervious studies on gay men and women as "junk" science, arguing that the data had been collected from men and women who had either sought or were forced to accept psychiatric treatment for their lifestyle choices or sexual desires. Therefore, the studies' published findings about the mental health of gay men and women was scientifically unsound, because they did not represent an accurate sampling of a population group. The APA finally assented at their 1973 convention, and homosexuality was removed from the seventh printing of the APA's influential reference tome, the *Diagnostic and Statistical Manual of Mental Disorders,* or DSM, in 1974.

In 1970, Kameny made history again as the first openly gay person to run for a seat in Congress, entering the race to represent the District of Columbia as a non-voting delegate in the U.S. House of Representatives. He placed fourth out of sixth. For many years he and other Mattachine Society activists, along with a newly created Gay and Lesbian Activists Alliance (GLAA) of Washington, also worked to overturn state sodomy laws, which remained in place in some states until as late as 2003. Dudley Clendinen and Adam Nagourney, in their 1999 book *Out for Good: The Struggle to Build a Gay Rights Movement in America,* described him as "perfectly equipped to do battle with the federal establishment by speech, testimony and memoranda. Almost single-handedly, he formed and popularized the ideological foundations of the gay rights movement in the 1960s: that homosexuals constituted 10 percent of the population, that they were not mentally ill, that they didn't need to be spoken for by medical experts, and that they had a right not to be discriminated against."

Kameny was witness to scores of other milestones in the civil rights movement for gay Americans, but perhaps the most heartfelt one was a 2009 formal apology for his 1957 firing from the U.S. Army Map Service and civil-service blacklisting of his name. The director of the U.S. Office of Personnel Management (OPM), the successor to the Civil Service Commission, delivered the apology, and in a suitable twist that same man, John Berry, was himself an openly gay federal employee. Kameny also attended the first same-sex unions held in the District of Columbia when those were legalized in 2010.

"All of Us . . . Are Indebted"

Kameny died in his sleep on October 11, 2011, age 86, at his longtime home in Washington. "Dr. Kameny stood up for this community when doing so was considered unthinkable and even shocking, and he continued to do so throughout his life," Chuck Wolfe told Lou Chibbaro Jr., a writer for the *Washington Blade.* Wolfe was director of the political action committee (PAC) the Gay & Lesbian Victory Fund, which raises money for campaigns to overturn discrimination based on sexual orientation. "He spoke with a clear voice and firm conviction about the humanity and dignity of people who were gay, long before it was safe for him to do so," Wolfe affirmed. "All of us who today endeavor to complete the work he began a half century ago are indebted to Dr. Kameny and his remarkable bravery and commitment."

Books

Clendinen, Dudley, and Adam Nagourney, *Out for Good: The Struggle to Build a Gay Rights Movement in America,* Simon & Schuster, 1999.

Murdoch, Joyce, and Deb Price, *Courting Justice: Gay Men And Lesbians V. The Supreme Court,* Basic Books, 2002.

Periodicals

Los Angeles Times, October 13, 2011.

New York Times, October 12, 2011.

Washington Blade, October 11, 2011.□

Stan Kenton

The American bandleader Stan Kenton (1911–1979) was among the most innovative figures in the world of jazz big bands, and his new ideas allowed him to keep working in the big band tradition even after it had fallen from popularity.

Kenton was a controversial figure whose audiences reached beyond core jazz fans in several different directions. His brass-heavy arrangements, often spiked well ahead of their time with Latin American rhythms, attracted young listeners, who attended the Kenton band's live shows in droves. Later in his career Kenton experimented with classical styles, attempting to bridge the gap between jazz and classical music. He constantly explored new ideas in orchestration, making use of a brand-new instrument, the mellophonium, on several of his albums. All these traits attracted criticism, but Kenton remained unperturbed and musically curious. "Never look back," he would tell his band members (according to J. Bonasia of *Investor's Business Daily*). "It's lost energy."

© Pictorial Press Ltd/Alamy

Family Moved to California

Stanley Newcomb Kenton was born December 15, 1911, in Wichita, Kansas. His birthdate was given as February 19, 1912, by his family, probably to conceal the fact that he was conceived before his parents were married, and earlier reference sources reproduced that date. Kenton's father, Thomas Floyd Kenton, was an unsuccessful roofer and mechanic, and the family wandered west, settling first in Huntington Park, California, and then in Bell, both suburbs of Los Angeles. Kenton had a few piano lessons from his mother and then rededicated himself to the instrument after hearing jazz for the first time in the early 1920s. He took lessons with a Los Angeles theater organist and showed a gift for absorbing contemporary European classical music as well as jazz.

As early as age 15, Kenton was organizing his own bands at Bell High School and writing arrangements for them. He took more lessons, this time in arranging, from Hollywood composer Tony Arreta. After graduating from high school Kenton worked in a speakeasy in San Diego, picked up work in Las Vegas, and played with a variety of jazz bands including a big band led by Los Angeles pianist Everett Hoagland. In the late 1930s, Kenton took time off from performing in order to study classical music theory. Armed with this knowledge he began to produce a body of original jazz compositions. In 1940, he organized a 13-piece band, which he first called the Stan Kenton Orchestra and then the Artistry in Rhythm Orchestra.

Perhaps surprisingly, in view of its complicated harmonies and dense textures, this band was a hit from the beginning. Kenton landed engagements at the Pavilion, the Rendezvous, and other large Los Angeles–area dance halls, and they were well attended by young jazz fans. Kenton's arrangements were high-energy, marked by staccato wind blasts that became a Kenton trademark very early on. "The teenagers of southern California discovered Kenton," noted biographer Michael Sparke in *Stan Kenton: This Is an Orchestra!* "They related to his music, and the crowd's enthusiasm was reflected in the band's spirit, and urged the men to greater heights." By 1942, the Kenton band was recording for the Decca label and touring nationally, landing a weeklong gig at the Roseland Ballroom in New York.

Signed to Capitol

The Artistry in Rhythm name came from the title of the Kenton orchestra's theme song, which became one of their most recognizable numbers. Its rich wall of brass sound was typical of the band's style. In 1943 Kenton signed with the Capitol label and released a series of 78 rpm singles that became major hits: "Eager Beaver," "The Peanut Vendor," "Tampico" (these two were among the first jazz recordings to explore Latin influences), and "Across the Valley from the Alamo." The last of these featured June Christy on vocals, and Kenton also recorded several tracks with vocalist Anita O'Day, cannily balancing his increasingly experimental instrumental style with vocal-based recordings.

During the 1940s, Kenton steadily increased the size of his band, reaching a temporary peak of 19 members. He called his music progressive jazz and tried to play not just for dancers but also, when he could, in concert settings. Young players such as trumpeter Kai Winding and saxophonist Art Pepper began to gravitate toward Kenton's band, attracted by the breakneck brass and wind lines devised by Kenton and arranger Pete Rugolo, whose contributions were sometimes difficult to distinguish in the music. Kenton's high-volume style, echoes of which can be heard in the work of contemporary trumpeter Maynard Ferguson, drew criticism at the time from more cerebral jazz critics: *Metronome* magazine writer Barry Ulanov, quoted by National Public Radio's *A Blog Supreme,* complained that "[t]here is a danger of an entire generation growing up with the idea that jazz and the atom bomb are essentially the same phenomenon."

Kenton calmly pointed to the legions of young fans who traveled considerable distances to hear his music, and those fans several times voted him to the top of jazz popularity polls even as the big bands declined after World War II. By 1948, the Kenton orchestra's five trumpets, five trombones, five saxophones, and four rhythm instruments had become a top attraction on the jazz circuit, turning out a crowd of 15,000 at the Hollywood Bowl in Los Angeles and selling out New York's Carnegie Hall, where 300 folding chairs had to be set up on stage to accommodate the crowd. Increasingly, though, Kenton was hungry for new innovations. He sometimes refused to play his hits, except for "Artistry in Rhythm," and in 1949, at the height of his commercial success, he took a one-year hiatus in order to work on new music.

Formed 39-Piece Group

When he reemerged, it was with something unlike anything else in the jazz scene before or since: a 39-piece group called the Innovations in Modern Music Orchestra. Over the two years of its existence the group's output ranged from swing to pieces, some of them by composer and arranger Bob Graettinger, that approached contemporary classical music. Kenton's thinking in combining the two forms was at least ten years ahead of the so-called Third Stream experiments of the 1960s that aimed at jazz-classical fusions. Although the music appealed neither to jazz purists nor to classical music devotees, the Innovations in Modern Music Orchestra attracted favorable critical notice and undertook two national tours. Boston Pops conductor Arthur Fiedler praised Kenton as a figure who bridged the gap between jazz and classical music. The sheer expense of keeping 39 musicians on the road eventually doomed the project, however.

In the early 1950s, Kenton reverted to his relatively more conventional 19-piece big band. He encountered controversy in 1956 after protesting a 1956 *Down Beat* magazine critics' poll that protested the exclusion of what he called (according to National Public Radio) "a new minority, white jazz musicians." Kenton's defenders, some of whom were African American, pointed out that he had employed a number of African American players, including soprano saxophonist Lucky Thompson, and helped them along in their careers. The Kenton orchestra continued to serve as an incubator of future jazz talent, with major players such as saxophonist Lee Konitz passing through the group at one time or another. In 1958, Kenton released two hit albums with a Latin tinge: *Cuban Fire* and *Viva Kenton!* (both 1958).

Kenton launched yet another innovative group in 1960: it featured a section of four mellophoniums, an instrument Kenton popularized but did not invent. The mellophonium was something like a partially unwould French horn. In 1961 Kenton's jazz rendition of pieces from the musical *West Side Story* earned him one of his two Grammy awards. Increasingly in the 1960s Kenton devoted himself to educational activities: his jazz camps at Indiana University, Michigan State University, and Redlands University in California, attracted teenage musicians. He continued to experiment with unusual large bands such as the Los Angeles Neophonic Orchestra, which he founded in 1965 and, again in advance of any similar move by other musicians, established his own label to record.

Kenton continued to perform in the 1970s but was sometimes sidelined by health problems. He died in Los Angeles on August 25, 1979. Kenton was married three times; all three marriages ended in divorce. He had two children. His son, Lance, was arrested in 1978 and charged with putting a rattlesnake in the mailbox of a lawyer; his daughter, Leslie, published a book in 2010 in which she alleged that Kenton, struggling with alcoholism, had molested her during her preteen and early teen years.

Books

Contemporary Musicians, volume 21, Gale, 1998.

Kenton, Leslie, *Love Affair: The Memoir of a Forbidden Father-Daughter Relationship,* St. Martin's, 2011.

Lee, William F., *Stan Kenton: Artistry in Rhythm,* Creative, 1994.

Sparke, Michael, *Stan Kenton: This Is an Orchestra!,* University of North Texas, 2011.

Periodicals

Investor's Business Daily, February 6, 2001.

New York Times, August 26, 1979.

Online

"Kenton Biographical Information," *Stan Kenton & His Orchestra: The Creative World of Stan Kenton,* http://www.stankenton.org (November 15, 2013).

"Stan Kenton," *AllMusic,* http://www.allmusic.com (November 15, 2013).

"Stan Kenton," *Kansaspedia,* http://www.kshs.org/kansapedia/stan-kenton/12124 (November 15, 2013).

"Stan Kenton at 100," *A Blog Supreme* (National Public Radio), http://www.npr.org/blogs/ablogsupreme/2012/02/17/147040413/stan-kenton-at-100-artistry-in-rhythm (November 15, 2013).□

Abdur Rahman Khan

Abdur Rahman Khan (1844–1901) was Emir of Afghanistan from 1880 until 1901, the year he died. During his reign, he became known as "The Iron Amir," as he stifled many rebellions in his country and centralized Afghanistan's government, often to the woe of those who opposed him.

Abdur Rahman Khan, the "The Iron Amir," of Afghanistan, assumed his nation's throne as a result of the second British invasion of his country. His name is spelled several different ways: Abd al-Rahman Khan Barakzai, Abd er-Rahman, Abdur Rahman Khan, and Abdor Raham Khan. His tenure was characterized by an unrelenting leadership policy that focused on the centralization of government and power. His reign lasted from 1880 to 1901, a period that witnessed four civil wars and numerous rebel uprisings, all of which he successfully quelled.

For many who met him, Abdur Rahman came across as a driven individual not afraid to take what he considered necessary action. His aim was to preserve his nation's freedom to self govern and, at the same time, maintain the integrity of his purpose. Physically, he has been described as a man of average height who demonstrated manners that were at once frank and courteous. This demeanor proved advantageous, as it lent him a well-heard voice at the international negotiating table.

One could say he was precocious in his early life. He was only thirteen years old when he received his first appointment in the government. He later displayed leadership abilities when he was assigned to command the army in the northern region, an area where his father served as governor, while still a young man. Twice during an ensuing five-year war of succession, he helped determine rule,

© North Wind Picture Archives/Alamy

winning the throne for his father and one of his uncles. But there was internal and external family strife: Another uncle, Sher Ali, proved the conquerering force and ruled from 1863 to 1866, and again from 1869 to 1879. Circumstances forced Abdur Rahman into exile. For eleven years he lived in the Asiatic colonies in Russia, but he would eventually return from exile and regain power.

Involved in Succession Dispute

Abdur Rahman Khan was born in 1844, the son of Afzul Khan. His grandfather was Dost Mahomed Khan, who ruled from 1826 to 1839 and from 1842 to 1863. His father, Afzul Khan, the oldest son of Dost Mahomed Khan, helped the Barakzai family establish a dynasty in Afghanistan. Dost Mohammad Khan died in 1863. Before his death, he nominated his third son, Sher Ali Khan, as his successor. This did not sit well. Afzal Khan was one of two older brothers, along with Azam Khan, that were passed over in the traditional line of succession. Subsequently, Afzal Khan led an insurrection in the northern portion of the country, where he had been governing when his father died. This began a fierce power struggle that involved all of Dost Mohammad's sons, a situation that lasted for nearly five years. During this period, Abdur Rahman distinguished himself in the nation's army for his daring nature, coupled with his ability to effectively command troops.

The *Encyclopedia Britannica* described the conflict as "in character, and in its striking vicissitudes [resembling] the English War of the Roses at the end of the [fifteenth century]." Abur Rahman displayed great leadership qualities that his father, Afzul Khan, lacked. Afzul Khan negotiated terms with Amir Sher Ali Khan. Still, Abdur Rahman Khan's nature and ability—as demonstrated in the northern province—provoked the existing amir's ire and suspicion. This led to Abur Rahman's flight into exile. Meanwhile, Sher Ali Khan imprisoned Afzul Khan, which led to a rebellion in the southern region of Afghanistan.

Sher Ali Khan held on to power after a fierce internal battle. Abdur Rahman's reappearance led to a mutiny among military ranks in the northern region. Eventually, Abdur Rahman and his uncle, Azim Khan occupied Kabul in March 1866. Sher Ali confronted the battalion in Kandahar in May, but his ranks were depleted by desertion. The resulting circumstances allowed Abdur Rahman to release his father, Afzul Khan, from prison and make a marked change the leadership of Afghanistan. After more conflicts—particularly in Kandahar in 1867—Afzul Khan died and Azim Khan assumed leadership. Abdur Rahman then served as governor in Afghanistan's northern province.

From there, Sher Ali made a return that was celebrated by a good portion of the population, but ongoing unsettled circumstances forced him to seek a safe refuge in what was then known as Persia, later known as Iran. Subsequently, Abdur Rahman also sought refuge. His haven was in Russia, and his flight took place in 1869, the same year that Azim Khan died.

Returned from Exile

Abdur Rahman remained in exile for eleven years, but Sher Ali's death in 1879 opened the door for a return. Bolstered by the Russians, Abdur Rahman sought once again to seize power in Afghanistan. In 1880, British-ruled India learned that he was in northern Afghanistan. That year, Britain was surprised by the will and the force of Afghan resistance. The governing nation sought an acceptable leader that would both satisfy the governing entity and resistance movements. The ongoing power struggle seemed, at least for the moment, revolved by British Governor-General Lord Lytton. Lytton indicated to Abdur Rahman that the British government was willing to withdraw troops and recognize Abdur Rahman as amir of Afghanistan, but with some territorial exceptions: Kandahar and several adjacent districts.

Agreement came after many negotiations, and finally, in 1880 Abdur Rahman was officially recognized as his nation's amir. This recognition came with a bolstering of arms, as well as financial support and further aid in the face of foreign aggression. Of course, Abdur Rahman had to align his foreign policy with that of Britain. In addition, in 1881, Britain eventually turned over Kandahar to the newly recognized amir.

But peace was nowhere near at hand, however. In 1881, after Britain ceded Kandahar to the new amir, a son of Sher Ali, Ayub Khan, led troops into the city and defeated Abdur Rahman's army. The situation was soon reversed, however, and Ayub Khan fled to Persia. With his seat seemingly solidified, Abdur Rahman then began

the task of consolidating his power over all of Afghanistan. Any insurrection was met with repressive, sometimes even cruel, authority.

Following the British invasion of Afghanistan, several power centers emerged, each controlled by family. Despite his blood ties, Abdur Rahman rejected the idea of shared power. He had already defeated one cousin in 1880. He defeated another family-based insurrection in 1885, which was a difficult year. While the recognized amir held conference with the British viceroy, Lord Dufferin, in India, a small-scale war broke out between Russian and Afghan troops, resulting from a dispute involving a border demarcation in the northwestern region. Specifically, the dispute centered in Panjdeh. Abdur Rahman demonstrated his leadership abilities. As the *Encyclopedia Britannica* described "Abdul Rahman's attitude at this critical juncture is a good example of his political sagacity. To one who had been a man of war from his youth up, who had won and lost many fights, the rout of a detachment and the forcible seizure of some debatable frontier lands was an untoward incident." In other words, Abdul Rhaman had accomplished what no previous Afghan leader could.

Indeed, he did not see the conflict as sufficient reason for applying for British assistance, even though it could be helpful. As the *Encyclopedia Britannica* explained, " [Britain] had guaranteed his territory's integrity, to vindicate his rights by hostilities which would certainly bring upon him a Russian invasion from the north, and would compel his British allies to throw an army into Afghanistan from the south-east."

The aim was to keep the strong neighboring countries—friend or enemy—from gaining incursion into the nation. He felt strongly that his people would most likely support that stance, and made plans for any possible separation from Russia if the situation changed. As Abdur Rahman was strongly focused on centralizing his policies within his nation, he realized that this meant a transformation of national systems. Immediately, this meant the army. For the militaristic leader, the army was the primary vehicle to carry out his policies. During his reign, he reorganized and increased military power. Indeed, most of the nation's money went toward this purpose.

His efforts did not stop there, though. Abdur Rahman bureaucratized judicial and administrative functions. Further, he invoked religion, making the law of Islam the prevailing spiritual principle of his country. Abdur Rahman's reign proved successful, and one of the reasons involved international relations: Britain and Russia had no wish to confront one another. Afghanistan was an important piece of the world puzzle: It became a buffer state between these two empires, one that had longstanding interests throughout the world (Britain) and one that was emerging as a new power player (Russia). Abdur Rahman took advantage of his nation's position between the two, exploiting the British-Russian rivalry.

Succeeded by his Son

Abdur Rahman died on October 1, 1901. He was 57 years old. He was succeeded by his son Habibullah Khan, who ruled until 1919. During his reign, Abdur Rahman preserved his power by defeating all rivals to his throne. He diminished the power of localized chieftains and quelled insurrections by rebellious tribes. His power became complete via military despotism. His army, the basis of his power, was strong; it was operated by high-ranking officials who simultaneously embraced and were held in check by his rigid will.

One of Abdur Rahman's major accomplishment was the imposition of a well-organized government on one of the Middle East's most unmanageable populations—his own nation. He followed the European example to increase his strength. At the same time, he strategically shunned modern innovations such as railways and telegraphs. There was a purpose in this seemingly negative tactic in that he felt this would keep European nations from gaining influence in his country.

The *Encyclopedia Britannica* commented, "Abdul Rahman left on those who met him in India the impression of a clear-headed man of action, with great self-reliance and hardihood, not without indications of the implacable severity that too often marked his administration."

Books

"Abdor Raham Khan," *Encyclopedia Britannica,* Encyclopedia Britannica Inc., 2010.

"Abd al-Rahman Khan (1844-1910)," *Encyclopedia of the Modern Middle East and North Africa,* Macmillan Reference USA, 2004.

Online

"Amir Abdur Rahman Kahn, *afghandland.com,* http://www.afghanland.com/history/abdulrahman.html (December 8, 2013).

"Khan, Amir Abdur Rahman (Amir Abdur Rehman Khan)," *S9.com,* http://www.s9.com/Biography/Khan-Amir-Abdur-Rahman (December 8, 2013).

"Abdur Rahman Khan, 'The Iron Amir,' 1880-1901," *countrystudies.us,* http://countrystudies.us/afghanistan/15.htm (December 3, 2013).□

Noor Inayat Khan

Noor Inayat Khan (1914–1944) was a British patriot of Indian birth and Muslim background who risked her life to work as a radio operator behind enemy lines in France during World War II. One of the famous Special Operations Executive (SOE) agents recruited for espionage and saboteur work in German-occupied France, Khan eluded a Nazi dragnet for several weeks but was captured, tortured, and finally shot by firing squad at the Dachau concentration camp.

Though her British colleagues knew her as "Nora Baker," Noor Inayat Khan's full name was Noor-un-Nisa Inayat Khan. She was born in Moscow, Russia, on January 1, 1914, to Ora Meena Ray Baker Khan, an American from Albuquerque, New Mexico. On her mother's side Khan was related to Mary Baker Eddy, the founder of

the Christian Science religious movement. Khan's father was Hazrat Inayat Khan, a noted musician and Sufi Muslim teacher. The couple, who had married in London, were visiting Russia as part of Hazrat's concert tour with his Royal Hindustani musicians. Khan's father actually was of royal birth, with a lineage that stretched to Tipu Sultan, the "Tiger of Mysore." The sultan received that moniker for his leadership of a rebellion against British encroachment on the Indian subcontinent, a fight to which he gave his life in battle in 1799. Tipu Sultan would be the last ruler of an independent Mysore, which became a British crown colony and part of the British Raj, or empire, until 1947.

Studied at the Sorbonne

The first few years of Khan's life were spent in London, but in 1920, after the end of World War I, her parents settled in France. One of her father's patrons gave them a house in Suresnes, outside Paris, where Khan grew up with three younger siblings. Her father died in 1927, when she was 13, and her mother struggled financially—and emotionally—after that. Khan cared for her siblings and finished her education at a lycée. She spent much of the 1930s pursuing two academic paths: she studied child psychology at the Sorbonne, and was enrolled in a composition course for harp and piano at the Paris Conservatory. She eventually found her niche as a writer of poetry and children's stories. Her work aired on Radio Paris and appeared in *Le Figaro*. In 1939, her first English-language book, *Twenty Jataka Tales* for children, was published in Britain.

Khan peers later revealed to biographers that as a young woman she was romantically involved with another music student, a Romanian Jew who was the son of a humble laundress, but her elitist Sufi Muslim uncles were vociferously opposed to the idea of marriage. The outbreak of World War II in September of 1939 put Khan, her fiancé, and her family at risk. A right-wing fascist dictatorship in Germany under Nazi Party leader Adolf Hitler was making bold territorial advances across Europe, while persecuting Jews and other non-ethnic Germans at home. In the spring of 1940, the Nazis invaded France, and Khan and her family fled first to Bordeaux, in northern France, then sailed as refugees to England. Their travel party consisted of their ailing mother Ora, Khan's brother Vilayat, and Khan's only sister, Khair. Her youngest brother, Hidayat, stayed in France and joined the underground movement known as the French Resistance.

Joined Women's RAF Auxiliary

Settling in Oxford, England, Khan and Vilayat set out to join the British war effort. On November 19, 1940, Khan officially became a member of the British Women's Auxiliary Air Force (WAAF). With several other recruits she was trained as a radio operator in Harrogate, and passed her first course in learning Morse code. After earning high marks in a more advanced course in Edinburgh, she was assigned to code work for the Royal Air Force (RAF) near Oxford, and then singled out for further training in Wiltshire on a new, more technically advanced type of radio. Her work and her trustworthiness attracted the attention of her superiors, and her name was passed along to British military intelligence bosses after she had applied for a more challenging WAAF commission.

In October of 1942, Khan was recruited for participation in the Special Operations Executive (SOE), a secret branch of the British military intelligence apparatus. A mystery writer named Selwyn Jepson recruited her, explaining the risks of the mission—which had only recently been approved by the British War Office—to send female SOE agents into Nazi-occupied France. SOE agents passed through several levels of vetting and clearance set up by British military intelligence officers. Their task was to infiltrate Nazi-occupied France, where they joined up with a fairly well-developed network of underground resistance against German occupation. SOE and French Resistance operatives proved fairly successful at disrupting German supply lines, sabotaging railways and machinery, and sent back useful information about positions and movements via clandestine radio sets. Women were particularly vital to the effort, because all able-bodied men were recruited for military service or war work; thus female civilians could move about more easily in Nazi-occupied lands and elude the suspicion of the Gestapo, the German secret police force.

Khan underwent an SOE training course and her final report described her as inept with handling firearms but in possession of near-flawless, unaccented French. Her course included a four-day exercise during which she traveled somewhere in England, made contact with another supposed agent, recited a plausible cover story and received a password, then carried out dead-letter drops. Her training exercises also included searching out apartments for rent and assessing the risk of detection for a wireless radio and its antenna. She became one of the first female SOE agents sent as radio operators into Nazi-occupied France.

Landed in Loire Valley

SOE agents were dropped into the French countryside during moonlit nights via special Lysander aircraft, which could fly low enough to elude German radar devices and land with the help of bicycle lights or torches held by waiting Resistance network members. Khan's infiltration took place on the night of June 16–17, 1943, when an RAF Lysander landed her in a farmer's field in the Loire Valley. Her code name was Madeleine and she carried false identity documents naming her as Jeanne-Marie Regnier. Her cover occupation was that of a private nursemaid for the children of a wealthy French family. One of the French Resistance contacts, Henri Déricourt, had arranged her assignment, and the arrival party gave her a bicycle and instructed her to pedal seven miles to the next village and board a train for Paris. Following further instructions, she met up with her contact there and went on to Grignon, where SOE agents were debriefed by Resistance operatives. She became part of a three-member cell that was part of a larger Resistance network code-named Prosper. She also received her radio set, which were often dropped by parachute in separate Lysander missions.

Khan headed back into Paris and sent her first transmission back to London. Even this first week in France was fraught with drama, as the Prosper network was suddenly exposed and the Gestapo discovered the Grignon offices. At one point she had to get rid of her radio, which was the size of a small suitcase, bicycle several miles, and move to a safer flat in Paris.

Unbeknownst to Khan or her superiors, Déricourt was actually a double agent and provided information to the Gestapo, too. She and two other SOE women had been sent to Paris, but they were discovered by Gestapo's twin organization, the Sicherheitsdienst (SD, or Security Service). Her London contacts ordered her home, but she declined, promising to keep quiet for a few weeks. For a time, she remained the only SOE agent transmitting between Paris and London. "General Sir Colin Gubbins, the head of SOE, said that she occupied 'the principal and most dangerous post in France,'" wrote London *Times* journalist Alan Hamilton. "She had remarkable luck; stopped by the Gestapo as she cycled with her radio, she persuaded them that it was a [film] projector." The SD also used a specially equipped vehicle that drove through the streets of Paris searching for covert wireless radio signals. Some of Khan's messages relayed information on the locations of downed Allied pilots in France that had managed to go into hiding; the replies helped rescue Lysander missions and saved several lives.

Hunted by Gestapo

In another incident Khan was less lucky: a message to meet two new Canadian SOE agents had been intercepted, and the Gestapo sent two impostor foreigners instead. Thus Khan inadvertently exposed herself and others in her network, who began to disappear. Because of this the Gestapo also now knew what the radio operator known as "Madeleine" or "Nurse" looked like and had some information on her whereabouts, though she moved frequently. Her chief in the Resistance network was a man named Henri Garry, who had a sister named Renée with whom Khan shared living quarters at one point. It was Renée Garry who gave the Gestapo crucial information that led to an attempt to arrest Khan on the street near her latest flat. The deft Khan sensed danger and managed to flee, but a French collaborator broke into her apartment, hid, and apprehended her several hours later. Khan fought the ambush physically, and the traitor had actually telephoned SD headquarters while pointing a gun at her, unable to take her into custody on his own.

Khan's date of arrest was October 13, 1943. She was taken to SD headquarters on the Avenue Foch—coincidentally, just around the corner from her flat—and her interrogation lasted a month. She was forced to continue her regularly scheduled radio transmissions to London, so that her London spymasters would not realize she was in custody. She attempted to escape the first night, and almost succeeded; after that she was kept under stricter guard but communicated with another detainee, a man named Léon Faye, via Morse code. They planned a more elaborate escape with another SOE agent in custody, John Renshaw Starr, and very nearly succeeded on November 25, 1943, with the aid of a stolen screwdriver, to remove the bars on their windows. They made it to the roof of 84 Avenue Foch and scrambled over into another building, but were discovered hiding in an apartment after an air raid alert mandated a prisoner count of SD cells.

Khan's Gestapo handlers treated her brutally after this, but when the Germans were finally ousted from Paris several months later, the head of Paris Gestapo station reported to his Allied captors that Khan had never given them any useful information. On November 27, she was transported to a prison camp in Pforzheim, Germany, which ensured that SOE agents would never be able to retrieve her. Her case vanished into the Germans' dreaded *Nacht und Nebel* (Night and Fog) program, in which authorities denied having any record of the detainee or information on their location. She was kept in virtual isolation and often in handcuffs and ankle shackles for the next ten months.

Anticipated Release, Not Execution

In September of 1944, Khan was informed that she would be moved to a farm outside Munich; Allied troops were advancing on several parts of Germany and such prisoner-transfers were not unexpected. In her train car she was surprised to find another SOE agent, Yolande Beekman, with whom she had trained, plus two more SOE women, Eliane Plewman and Madeleine Damerment. Instead the quartet were taken to the Dachau concentration camp, held overnight in separate cells, and taken out the next morning. Ordered to kneel, the women joined hands and were shot separately in the back of the head. Khan died on September 13, 1944. A witness to the scene later said Khan shouted the word "Liberté!" just before she was shot.

Khan's family and friends had no knowledge her SOE work. In 1949, she was posthumously awarded the George Cross from the British government, the highest honor for civilian service in wartime.

Books

Foot, M.R.D., *SOE in France: An Account of the Work of the British Special Operations Executive in France 1940–1944,* revised edition, Routledge, 2013.

Vargo, Marc E., *Women of the Resistance: Eight who Defied the Third Reich,* McFarland & Company, 2012.

Periodicals

Independent (London, England), January 4, 2011.

Times (London, England), May 13, 2006.□

Larry King

The American television and radio broadcaster Larry King (born 1933) has been perhaps history's most successful figure in the broadcast interview medium.

King has done somewhere between 30,000 and 50,000 interviews, including sessions with every United States president from Gerald Ford to Barack Obama. He has been called the Pope of Talk (and popes have been among the few famous figures to have eluded an

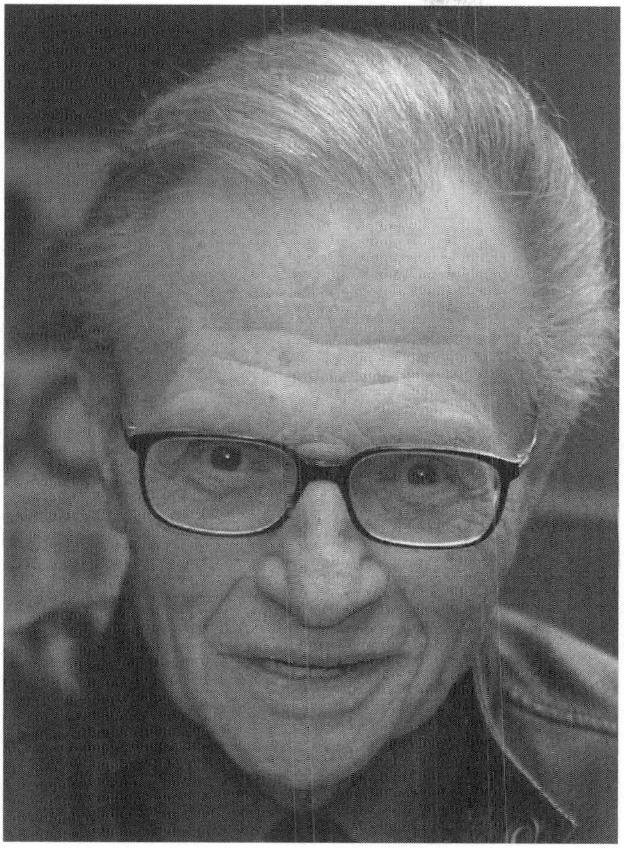

© ZUMA Press, Inc./Alamy

interview with him) and the Muhammad Ali of the broadcast interview. Unlike nearly every other figure in the heavily topical world of broadcast talk, King was well known internationally. In a world of opinionated and often polarizing talk show hosts, King was self-effacing. "I don't use the word 'I,'" he told Andrew Ryan of the Toronto *Globe & Mail.* "Never have." Instead he projected an everyman's curiosity and often drew revelations from guests who felt that he was genuinely listening to what they had to say.

Family Struggled After Father's Death

Larry King was born Lawrence Harvey Zeiger in Brooklyn, New York, on November 19, 1933. His parents were Orthodox Jews who had emigrated from Russia and still retained some of their old-world ways: King was called by a Yiddish nickname, Leibel, as a child and attended Hebrew instruction after school. King's own religious convictions were shattered by the death of his father at age 43; he later became agnostic. The family struggled financially as King's mother took in sewing, and King immediately went to work after graduating from high school—which he barely did. King's brother Martin was quoted in King's autobiography, *My Remarkable Journey,* as saying that King "couldn't stay focused. He was always talking to other kids. If there had been Ritalin back then, maybe he wouldn't have become Larry King."

King's favorite job was a stint in the mail room at radio station WOR, where he could nurture his dream of becoming a radio announcer. Ever since he held a crowd rapt as he delivered a speech at his bar mitzvah, he had been convinced that he had the voice of a radio star. He attended Brooklyn Dodgers games and provided his own commentary, speaking into a rolled-up newspaper. Asking an announcer for advice, he was told to try his luck in rapidly growing Florida, and when he turned 22 he did just that, applying at Miami radio station WAHR and agreeing to sweep floors until an on-air position became available.

King acquired his professional name when his supervisor complained that the name Larry Zeiger was too ethnic, and his eye fell on a newspaper advertisement for a liquor store named King's. He later changed his name to King but has said that he would prefer that Zeiger appear on his tombstone. King succeeded quickly in Miami despite an early snafu in which he asked a priest how many children he had, moving up to stations WKAT and then WIOD, where he hosted his own talk show at a restaurant (interviewing random customers and employees) and began to attract a devoted following with his friendly, approachable style. In 1960, King moved to television on a serious discussion show called *Miami Undercover* on station WLBW, and in 1964, he had a regular late-night show on television station WTVJ.

Suffered from Gambling Addiction

King seemed inexhaustible. He continued to work for WIOD, where he was part of the on-air team for the station's Miami Dolphins football broadcasts. He wrote columns for Miami newspapers and married former Playboy bunny Alene Akins in 1961. The marriage ended in 1963, began again in 1967, and ended in divorce once again. King began to spiral downward into problems caused by gambling, and in 1971 he hit bottom: he was arrested after Miami corporate raider Louis Wolfson alleged that King had been given $5,000 as a payoff intended for New Orleans district attorney Jim Garrison but had pocketed the money himself. King was never prosecuted because the statute of limitations had expired on his crimes, but he was fired from his radio jobs and spent four years making a living wherever he could, for a time serving as announcer for a team in the ill-fated World Football League.

In 1975, after convincing WIOD's managers that he had reformed, King was rehired. Three years later he was well enough known across Florida that he was given the chance at a national show—an overnight talk show, *The Larry King Show,* on the Mutual Broadcasting System where he would interview a guest, allow telephone callers to ask the guest questions, and then offer an "Open Phone America" segment. The radio show was an immediate hit, gaining affiliates in major markets and rising from 28 affiliates in 1978 to 118 five years later. It ran until 1994. In 1982, King began writing a weekly column for the newspaper *USA Today.*

By that time, King had become a television star. In 1985, he was hired for the five-year-old Cable News Network (CNN) by its president, Ted Turner, and the new *Larry King Live* show went on the air at 9 p.m. (Eastern time) on

June 3, 1985. King transferred the basic format of his radio show to television, with a combination of guests and calls from viewers. Even at a time when cable television penetration of American households was much lower than it is today, King's show became the number-one television talk show. By the early 1990s, King's shows were seen or heard in 130 countries internationally, eventually reaching 250. In 1989, he was already listed in the *Guinness Book of World Records* as having broadcast for more hours on national radio than any other talk show host.

Hosted Perot Annoucement

King interviewed most of the world's most famous people, focusing on politics and the arts more than on business or sports. In addition to presidents and their spouses, his guests included actor Marlon Brando, the Soviet Union's leader Mikhail Gorbachev, singers Madonna and Prince, and religious leader Billy Graham. It was on *Larry King Live* that Texas technology executive Ross Perot announced his run for the U.S. presidency. His personal favorite among his interviews was a session with singer Frank Sinatra.

"King's technique," wrote Jonathan Freedland of the London *Guardian,* "is to have no technique. He simply talks, like a regular guy. No elaborate, policy-concerned probes, just stuff from the gut." When interviewing authors he rarely read their books ahead of time—but this worked to his advantage, for he approached the guest with genuine curiosity. Unlike numerous other radio personalities, King was a listener rather than a talker, and he had a gift for making guests and ordinary callers feel that their perspectives were valuded. "I always knew that I never learned anything in my life while I was speaking," he once said (according to *Jewish Virtual Library*). Sometimes King was criticized for the softball questions he asked his interviewees, but the affection he commanded among the American public was wide, and crossed political boundaries.

In 1987, King, a heavy cigarette smoker, suffered a heart attack. He later quit smoking and established the Larry King Cardiac Foundation to provide heart surgery procedures for low-income individuals. Among the dozens of awards King has received was a star on the Walk of Fame in Hollywood, added in 1997. *Larry King Live* remained vital into the new century, and in 2010, he celebrated its 25th anniversary with a week of all-star interviews of figures ranging from Barack Obama to pop star Lady Gaga. He has written or edited 18 books; many of them are autobiographical, but one was a novel, *Moon over Manhattan* (2003). King's most recent autobiography is *My Remarkable Journey* (2009). He has made cameo appearances in more than 20 films and several television series.

King has been married eight times and has six children, Larry Jr., Chaia, Andy, Kelly, Chance, and Cannon. He married the last of his wives at this writing, country singer Shawn Southwick, as he was being wheeled into cardiac surgery in 1997; the couple accused each other of infidelity in 2010 and filed for divorce, but then reconciled. The final regular *Larry King Live* show aired on December 16, 2010, but he has remained busy, launching an online series, *Larry King Now,* in 2012. King received an Emmy award for lifetime achievement in 2011.

Books

Encyclopedia Judaica, Gale, 2007.
King, Larry, *My Remarkable Journey,* Weinstein, 2009.

Periodicals

Atlanta Journal-Constitution, February 15, 2000.
CNN Wire, May 27, 2013.
Globe & Mail (Toronto, Ontario, Canada), January 26, 2007.
Guardian (London, England), January 3, 1994.
Times (London, England), July 1, 2010.
Vanity Fair, September 2009.

Online

"Larry King," *Jewish Virtual Library,* http://www.jewishvirtuallibrary.org/jsource/biography/larryking.html (November 13, 2013).
"Larry King," *Wall Street Journal,* http://topics.wsj.com/person/K/larry-king/6171 (November 13, 2013).
"Larry King Biography," *Us Magazine,* http://www.usmagazine.com/celebrities/larry-king/biography (November 17, 2013).□

Néstor Kirchner

The Argentine politician Néstor Kirchner (1950–2010) served his country as president from 2003 to 2007. Leading Argentina out of difficult economic and poltical problems, he has been one of the country's most popular contemporary leaders.

Kirchner was not well known even in Argentina when he began his rise to power in the early 2000s. He came not from the capital, Buenos Aires, but from the country's remote and sparsely populated south, where he was a popular regional governor. Kirchner played an important role in bringing some of the perpetrators of violent repression in 1970s and 1980s Argentina to justice. Taking office in the midst of a severe economic crisis, Kirchner pursued a growth-oriented strategy that returned Argentina to political stability faster than even some of his supporters had expected. Tending toward the left in his political outlook, Kirchner nevertheless pursed a prudent fiscal path and avoided a heavily state-oriented economic direction. Kirchner was aware of the global nature of modern economic activity, but he favored, as quoted by Uki Goñi in *Time,* "a kind of globalization that works for everyone and not just for a few." Kirchner ceded the Argentine presidency to his wife, Cristína Fernández de Kirchner, in 2007, and the pair became South America's premier political power couple.

Met Wife at Law School

Néstor Carlos Kirchner was born in the small city of Río Gallegos, in southern Argentina's Santa Cruz province, on February 25, 1950. Kirchner's parents, like many other Argentines, were of immigrant stock. His father was a

© vario images GmbH & Co.KG/Alamy

postal worker of Swiss background, and his mother, born in Chile, came from a Croatian family. Kirchner attended schools in Río Gallegos and went on to law school at the University of La Plata in Buenos Aires. It was there that he met fellow student Cristina Fernández; the pair married in 1975, and raised two children.

At the university, Kirchner was a member of a progressive student group associated with the populist Argentine leader Juan Perón and his wife, Isabel Martínez de Perón, who succeeded her husband as president upon his death. Kirchner was in the crowd in 1973 when rightist Perón followers opened fire on left-wing students at Ezeiza Airport in Buenos Aires as Juan Perón returned from exile. Kirchner's views put him in grave danger following the right-wing military takeover in Argentina in 1976, after which numerous members of the progressive Peronist faction were arrested, and some disappeared during Argentina's so-called Dirty War. Kirchner kept a low profile during this period, returning to Santa Cruz province and opening a small law office there. He was arrested and imprisoned once for a period of several days, but in remote Santa Cruz, far from the centers of political intrigue, he fared better than many of his compatriots.

Argentina's military leadership was deposed following the loss of the 1983 Falkland Islands war with Great Britain, and Kirchner was able to think once again of a political career. In 1987, he was narrowly elected mayor of his hometown of Rio Gallegos under the banner of the Peronist Partido Justicialista or Justicialist Party. Retaining his post as mayor, he won election to the Santa Cruz provincial legislature in 1989, and in 1991, after the impeachment of the incumbent governor, Kirchner was elected governor of Santa Cruz. He remained in that post until he entered the race for the Argentine presidency in 2003.

As governor of Santa Cruz, Kirchner gained a moderately positive iamge as an efficient administrator with center-left political tendencies. He invested in infrastructure projects, schools, and hospitals, avoiding the fraud and intimidation of political opponents that still plagued much of Argentina's political system. Kirchner was aided by the fact that Santa Cruz was both relatively wealthy, with abundant revenues from oil and other natural resources, and sparsely populated, with a population of only about 200,00 at the time. Kirchner's administration doled out public jobs generously, with the result that almost half of the region's working population held jobs that depended on the government or collected direct social welfare payments.

Moved Provincial Funds out of Country

Some residents questioned Kirchner's decision to push through a change in the province's constitution to permit him to run for reelection an unlimited number of times, a change facilitated by a provincial legislature and courts packed with Kirchner allies. Kirchner nevertheless began to earn a reputation for honesty and clean government, especially after he invested $500 million in provincial oil royalties on the grounds that leaving the money in Argentina, whose financial system was marked by ruinous waves of inflation and repeated currency fluctuations, meant risking its loss. Despite coming under scrutiny around suspicions that his financial situation had benefited under less than auspicious means while he was in office, no proof of unlawfulness was found.

Part of Kirchner's motivation in holding on to the governorship was that he hoped to ascend into the realm of national politics as established leaders moved aside. In 2002 and 2003, as Argentina fell into economic crisis, he saw his chance. The country's debt to the International Monetary Fund was at ruinous levels, resulting in sharp devaluations of the Argentine currency, the peso, and middle-class Argentines were threatening to precipitate disastrous bank runs by withdrawing their savings. After Argentina spiraled through six new governments over 18 months, Kirchner jumped into the race for the Argentine presidency in the general election of April 27, 2003.

He was hardly a promising candidate. Almost unknown outside Santa Cruz province, he suffered from a lack of charisma that led pundits to dub him El Pingüino, or The Penguin, in reference to his origins in the nearly Antarctic region of Patagonia. Kirchner and his followers deftly turned the nickname on its head by adopting it proudly, with his followers calling themselves *pingüinos.* Running under the banner of a Justicialist Party offshoot called the Front for Victory, Kirchner promoted himself as an advocate of clean, progressive government. In the first round of voting, he finished in second place, narrowly behind former

Argentine president Carlos Menem. With polls showing him losing badly to Kirchner in a second-round runoff, Menem withdrew, and Kirchner ascended to the presidency even though he had won the support of only about 22 percent of Argentine voters.

Removed Military Officers' Immunity

Once in office, Kirchner pursued a canny mixture of progressive and nationalist policies, establishing himself as an ally of the flamboyant Venezuelan leader Hugo Chávez. During his first months in office, he surprised observers by attacking corruption in the government and stripping retired military officers of immunity from prosecution for their misdeeds during the Dirty War. Rejecting IMF demands for new austerity measures, he offered international holders of defaulted Argentine bonds a deal attractive enough to be seriously considered—payment of 33 cents on the dollar—and many accepted it. By 2005, Kirchner was able to pay off Argentina's debt to the IMF in full. Kirchner appealed to Argentine nationalists by reasserting the country's claim to ownership of the Falkland Islands, known in Argentina as the Islas Malvinas, and he cultivated working-class support with stable social-welfare payments and controls on utility bills. He encouraged business investment in emerging economic sectors such as biotechnology.

Kirchner's approval rating skyrocketed as Argentina's growth rate returned to a healthy 8 percent in the mid-2000s decade and unemployment and poverty rates, contrary to nearly all expectations, fell sharply. Again, he benefited to some extent from factors external to his own policies: prices for Argentine exports such as meat and soybeans increased during this period, benefiting the economy as a whole. By 2007, Kirchner was an extraordinarily popular figure. But he stepped aside rather than run for reelection that year, clearing the way for the landslide vote in favor of his wife, Cristina Fernáandez de Kirchner. Speculation has varied as to the causes for Kirchner's decision, which he has never fully explained; he may have been worried about encroaching health problems, or have wanted to lay the groundwork for longer-term control of the reins of power. Indeed, the Kirchners soon drew comparisons to the powerful duo of Bill and Hillary Clinton in American politics.

Kirchner ran for and won a seat in Argentina's chamber of deputies in 2009, and was involved in mediating several conflicts both within and outside Argentina. Allegations that he and his wife had enriched themselves substantially through local investments while in office failed to yield clear evidence of wrongdoing despite an increase in the couple's wealth from about $2.3 million in 2003 to more than $12 million in 2010. After inflation that may have been caused by his own policies led to sharp Peronist losses in Argentina's legislative elections in 2009, Kirchner began to make plans to run for the presidency once more in 2011. Those plans were cut short as Kirchner suffered a heart attack and died suddenly in El Calafate, in Santa Cruz province on October 27, 2010. Argentines genuinely mourned his death: in the words of the London *Independent,* "There were Princess Diana–like scenes at the presidential palace in Buenos Aires yesterday as hundreds of thousands ... gathered to greet his corpse from his home province of Santa Cruz, where he had died on Wednesday."

Periodicals

Daily Telegraph (October 28, 2010.
Economist, February 27, 2010.
Financial Times, October 28, 2010.
Guardian (London, England), October 29, 2010.
Independent (London, England), October 29, 2010.
Newsweek, November 8 2010.
Times (London, England), October 28, 2010.

Online

"Néstor Kirchner (1950–2010): Half of Argentina's Presidential Duo," *Time,* http://content.time.com/time/world/article/0,8599,2027848,00.html (October 3, 2013).□

Sergei Kirov

The mysterious death of Sergei Kirov (1886–1934) was a momentous, fear-inducing incident in the Soviet Union in 1934. A respected Communist Party boss and close friend of leader Josef Stalin, Kirov was shot in his Leningrad office building in a questionable security lapse. His assassination incited a period known as the Great Terror in the world's first socialist state, with Stalin using it as a pretext to launch a political witch-hunt that decimated the Communist Party ranks and sent thousands to early deaths either by firing squad or in Siberian labor camps.

Sergei Kirov was born Sergei Mironovich Kostrikov on March 27, 1886, in Urzhum, a town near Russia's Vyatka River. His parents struggled financially, though his father Miron had once had a civil-servant post with the imperial forestry department. The elder Kostrikov was a heavy drinker and prone to violence at home, and disappeared around 1890. Kirov's mother Yekaterina and his two sisters relied on her parents for help, but the boy's situation worsened when Yekaterina died of tuberculosis. He was eventually sent to a local orphanage.

Active in Russian Underground

School records show that young Kirov was a studious, serious child, with one of his teachers commenting that his chores at the orphanage prevented him from achieving higher marks. Locals in Urzhum knew his family and tried to help; funds were collected to send him to an industrial training institute in Kazan in 1901, when he was 15. Possessed with an effortless charm from an early age, Kirov was also gifted in appearance, with a robust physique and

© ITAR-TASS Photo Agency/Alamy

cinema-idol level looks. It was rumored that he had an affair with the young woman who ran the boarding house where he lived rent-free, which resulted in an unplanned pregnancy. Both the woman and her infant vanished from the Kazan area within a year.

After graduating with an engineering degree in 1904, Kirov sought a graduate degree in his field. Since he had attended a vocational college, however, he needed to complete the equivalent of a high school diploma for college-bound students. He moved to the Siberian city of Tomsk and worked as a draftsperson by day while taking night-school courses. He soon fell in with other young revolutionaries in the city, who were part of a growing leftist movement that would soon spring to action during Russia's ill-fated war with Japan of 1904–05. As a member of the underground Russian Social Democratic Labor Party (RSDLP), Kirov participated in demonstrations against Tsar Nicholas II and was taken into custody by the imperial-era secret police in a dragnet sweep of political agitators.

Kirov read and distributed the writings of RSDLP's enigmatic theorist, Vladimir I. Lenin. With other underground activists he learned how to use an unregistered printing press they concealed in a sub-basement. He was arrested several times in roundups for distributing leaflets, and after a third violation a 16-month sentence was handed down by the court in 1907 on charges of disseminating material that advocated the overthrow of the tsarist regime.

Named Astrakhan Party Chief

Unable to find work because of his criminal record, Kirov fled to the Caucasus region and took a new surname, Mironov. In the city of Vladikavkaz on the Terek River he began working at a relatively liberal, mainstream newspaper called *Terek.* Authorities in Tomsk finally discovered the printing press after a building collapse and jailed him once again. By then he was romantically involved with the woman whom he later married, Maria Lvovna Markus, who also worked at the newspaper and whose two brothers were fellow revolutionaries.

Kirov was fortunate to win an acquittal and was able to return to Vladikavkaz, where he married Markus using new identity documents. His new papers named him as Dmitry Zakharovich Kornev and he began using the pen name "Kirov" in 1912 when he resumed writing for *Terek.* His new identity document also featured a coveted exemption from military service, which aided him greatly when Russia entered World War I in 1914. Tsar Nicholas so badly bungled the war effort, and the privations at home were so dire, that the regime inevitably collapsed upon its own incompetence. A group of moderate Socialist Democrats removed the Tsar and formed a Provisional Government in March of 1917, and Kirov became active in the new era of democratic participation. His RSDLP credentials earned him a seat on the new Soviet of Workers' Deputies in Vladikavkaz and by October of 1917 he had allied with the hardliners in the RSDLP, who seized control of the Provisional Government in what became known as the October Revolution. This was the Bolshevik Revolution, taking its name from the more leftist faction in the RSDLP.

In the turbulent years of civil war that followed, as the Bolsheviks fought supporters of the tsar, moderate Mensheviks, foreign-funded armies, and other enemies on many sides, Kirov rose to a position of prestige and influence. Working out of the southern city of Astrakhan, he coordinated Red Army operations and traveled back and forth to Moscow to secure additional troops and arms. Soviet Communist lore attributes to him the final Bolshevik control of the south, which was vital to their victory in the Russian Civil War and the formation of the Union of Soviet Socialist Republics. Skilled in dealing with the non-Russian populations in the Caucasus, he negotiated the special "autonomous" republics that permitted resistant populations in Azerbaijan and Armenia to retain some semblance of local control.

Elected to Politburo

Kirov came to know both Vladimir Lenin and Josef Stalin during this period, as well as others who were known as "Old Bolsheviks" for their longtime commitment to the socialist cause. In March of 1921, Kirov was elected to the Central Committee of the Communist Party, and that same year he was installed as head of the Azerbaijani Communist Party, a post he held for the next five years. In the interim, Lenin's health began to decline and Stalin moved to take control of the party. To do so, Stalin—who was viewed as somewhat uncouth and even more ruthless an operator than his already-zealous Bolshevik comrades—eliminated his main political opponents through various deceptions and maneuverings. One was Leon Trotsky, whom Lenin had designated as his successor in a troika (trio) that included two other Old Bolsheviks, Grigory Zinoviev and Lev Kamenev, both of whom had played decisive roles in the 1917 October Revolution. Trotsky was expelled from the party and eventually forced into exile; Zinoviev was removed as head of the Leningrad Communist Party and Kirov installed in his place in 1926.

Despite the prestige attached to running the Communist Party in the former St. Petersburg, Kirov was uneasy about taking the job but accepted the post out of loyalty to Stalin. Many members of the Leningrad party organization were still loyal to Zinoviev and resented Kirov's rise. For the next seven years Kirov faithfully carried out Stalin's directives, and the two spoke daily by telephone. Kirov and Maria Lvovna even vacationed with Stalin and his wife in Sochi, the Black Sea resort.

Kirov had served as a delegate to the semi-regular party congresses and was elected to the Central Committee of Communist Party, or Politburo, in 1926. This was the upper echelon of Soviet leadership, and behind the scenes were various personal feuds and ideological alliances. When opposition to Stalin amplified, there were rumors that one faction wanted Kirov to replace Stalin. As the Leningrad party boss, Kirov was well-known even outside the Soviet Union, and had a strong following inside the secretive regime. "Kirov had a forthcoming and approachable demeanor that made people feel they could trust him," wrote Amy W. Knight in *Who Killed Kirov?: The Kremlin's Greatest Mystery*. "In contrast to Stalin, who rarely left the confines of the Kremlin and was uncomfortable with spontaneity, Kirov was a man of the people, who would leap out of his chauffeur-driven car to shake hands on the street. Whereas Stalin spoke Russian with a heavy Georgian accent, Kirov's words rang out in the clear, forceful tones of a native Russian, a real muzhik, a man of the soil."

Shot by Lone Assassin

Kirov's violent death has spurred numerous theories from historians of the Soviet era, and an investigation was even launched 20 years later by new Soviet premier Nikita Khrushchev, who laid the blame on Stalin in another series of revelations that rocked the Soviet nation. On Saturday, December 1, 1934, Kirov left his apartment on Leningrad's Kamenoostrovsky Prospekt and ordered his driver to take him to his office at the Smolny Institute, a grand building that had been an elite girls' school in the tsarist era and then became the Bolsheviks' headquarters during the October Revolution. A unit of the NKVD secret police was responsible for his personal security. This was the Russian-language acronym for the *Narodnii Komissariat Vnutrennikh Del,* or People's Commissariat of Internal Affairs. A man named Feodor Medved was in charge of the Leningrad NKVD, and Medved's boss in Moscow was the much-feared NKVD Commissar Genrikh Grigoryevich Yagoda. Stalin allegedly conspired with Yagoda to eliminate Kirov, with Yagoda recruiting an unhappy underling of Medved's to find a suitable assassin. They located a troubled former factory worker named Leonid Nikolaev, who had been elevated to an office job within the party organization, which he then botched. Expelled from the party ranks and newly impoverished, Nikolaev reportedly sought revenge.

Kirov always had a security detail with him, and there were various guard checkpoints inside the Smolny building, which also served as offices of the Leningrad municipal government. Nikolaev had been given his orders and a Nagant M1895 revolver to use, and had been stopped by guards back in October—then mysteriously released, and his weapon and bullets returned to him. Around 4:30 p.m. on December 1, Kirov entered the building with just one of his guards trailing on the stairs behind him; the party boss was expected at a meeting already in progress. Nikolaev came out of a bathroom and fired the gun, and meeting attendees ran out to find Kirov bleeding from a head wound and Nikolaev unconscious after collapsing beside the victim. Kirov was pronounced dead at the scene.

Prompted Infamous Show Trials

Nikolaev was revived and seemed justly terrified, giving contradictory answers. News of Kirov's death was announced over a state radio broadcast that same evening, and there were fears that foreign spies had infiltrated the country and were conducting high-level political assassinations. Kirov was laid to rest with full honors in a state funeral, and his ashes interred in a Kremlin mausoleum. His lone bodyguard died the day after the assassination while in police custody. Nikolaev was tried, found guilty, and sentenced to death by the end of December. Stalin appointed another trusted confidante, Nikolai Yezhov, to a special investigative task force that spiraled into a massive dragnet. Leningrad Party officials and then senior Politburo members were accused of various crimes, including treason and espionage. The most notorious of the Moscow Show Trials accused respected Bolshevik veterans of the crime, including Zinoviev and Kamenev, who were shot by firing squad.

In 1936, Stalin replaced Yagoda with Yezhov as NKVD Commissar and the dragnet came to include NKVD officials, top-ranking military personnel, rank-and-file Communist Party figures, Soviet citizens with foreign-sounding names, and then just ordinary Russians in what became known as Stalin's Great Terror. Even Yagoda and Yezhov were eventually accused of being enemies of the state and executed. "This killing has every right to be called the crime of the century," wrote Sovietologist Robert Conquest about the Kirov murder in his 1990 work *The Great Terror: A Reassessment.* "Over the next four years, hundreds of Soviet citizens, including the most prominent political leaders of the Revolution, were shot for direct responsibility for the assassination, and literally millions of others went to their deaths for complicity in one or another part of the vast conspiracy which allegedly lay behind it. Kirov's death, in fact, was the keystone of the entire edifice of terror and suffering by which Stalin secured his grip on the Soviet peoples."

Books

Conquest, Robert, *The Great Terror: A Reassessment,* Oxford University Press, 1990.

Getty, J. Arch, and Oleg V. Naumov, *Road to Terror: Stalin and the Self-Destruction of the Bolsheviks, 1932–1939,* Yale University Press, 2010.

Knight, Amy W., *Who Killed Kirov?: The Kremlin's Greatest Mystery,* Hill & Wang, 2000.

Periodicals

New York Times, December 2, 1934.□

Klemens Von Klemperer

German-born historian Klemens von Klemperer (1916–2012) wrote extensively on his homeland's most destructive and calamitous period, the rise and fall of the Nazi Party from 1933 to 1945. The longtime Smith College professor was not just a scholar of the Third Reich's plan to remap Europe for German settlement, but also a refugee from it, too. To honor the numerous childhood friends and family members who suffered or died during World War II, von Klemperer devoted his academic career to researching underground anti-Nazi activities and wrote what is considered the definitive study of the German *Widerstand,* or Resistance.

Klemens Wilhelm von Klemperer was a rare historian who was encouraged to write his own autobiography, and accepted the challenge. "I was not an extraordinary person, but I did live in extraordinary times," he once reflected, according to his *New York Times* obituary. As he recounted in *Voyage Through the 20th Century: A Historian's Recollections and Reflections,* he was born in the middle of World War I on November 2, 1916, as imperial Germany fought Britain, France, and other nations. He came from a prominent family of bankers and industrialists with ties to the political, economic, and cultural elite across Europe. His paternal grandfather, Gustav Klemperer, had started his career as a teenaged bank clerk in Dresden, Germany, and rose to become head of the main branch of the powerful Dresdner Bank. In 1910, his grandfather was honored by the Austrian government and ennobled with the title "von Klemenau" added to the name. Both Gustav and his wife were Jewish but had converted to Christianity many years before. Gustav served as honorary U.S. consul in Dresden and amassed an enormous, museum-worthy collection of priceless Meissen porcelain before his death in 1926 that was later seized by the Nazis.

Descended from Prominent Families

Von Klemperer's father Herbert was a successful industrialist and president of Berliner Maschinenbau-AG (Aktien-Gesellschaft), which produced trains, submarines, and torpedoes for the German military. Von Klemperer's mother was born Frieda Kuffner and came from a distinguished Austrian family that had made its fortune in beer brewing and sugar refining, then became patrons of the arts and sciences. They, too, had converted from Judaism, and as a child von Klemperer spent extended periods of time with his mother's relatives, who lived in a palatial villa near Vienna known as Palais Kuffner. Von Klemperer and his three siblings grew up in a lively part of central Berlin opposite the splendid Tiergarten park.

Even as a toddler, von Klemperer possessed a keen eye for detail: he recalled watching the events of the Communist Spartacist uprising in January of 1919 from the windows of his home. Though he was just two months past his second birthday, von Klemperer concisely remembered the shock of peeking out of a curtain and seeing a machine gun swivel its turret toward their window. The Spartacist rebellion was quashed, and the new post-imperial Weimar Republic, with elected representatives and a president, continued on. Germany's defeat in World War I had fractured the country, however, and in the 1920s, Germany struggled to pay onerous financial penalties, or reparations, imposed on it by the League of Nations, a forerunner of the United Nations. Hyperinflation and then the Great Depression pushed the country toward right-wing extremism, which led to an emergency-powers act in 1930, and then the appointment of a new chancellor, Nazi Party leader Adolf Hitler, by the Weimar Republic's elderly, addled 84-year-old president, Field Marshall Paul von Hindenburg, in January of 1933.

In German, this event is referred to as *Der Machtergreifung,* or seizure of power. Von Klemperer was 16 years old and a student at the Französiches Gymnasium of Berlin. The Nazis were rabidly anti-Semitic, casting the blame for the country's economic woes on Jewish bankers and industrialists—like von Klemperer's own paternal grandfather. When he completed his studies in 1934, his parents were eager to send him out of the country and away from danger. His brothers Alfred and Franz, and sister Lily, were also encouraged to emigrate. A place was arranged for von Klemperer at Balliol College at Oxford University, but he left after a few weeks to join his cousins in Vienna, the Austrian capital. Though he was born in Berlin, von Klemperer felt a keen sense of kinship with the Austrian side of his family.

Fled Nazi Germany

Von Klemperer was aware of the risks he took by going to Austria in late 1934, which was one of Hitler's first targets in his plan to create the new German Reich, or empire. Enrolled at the University of Vienna's history of law program, he witnessed the Anschluss, or Nazi annexation of Austria, in March of 1938. With his mountain-climbing friends from the city von Klemperer was drafted into a makeshift defense group, but Austria's beleaguered government quickly capitulated to the Nazi threat. Two close friends of his were forced into hiding for their political activities, and von Klemperer spent several weeks at a well-protected mini-castle where his widowed aunt, who had been married to the writer Hugo von Hofmannsthal, lived. He helped her close up the house, went to Berlin to obtain exit-travel documents for himself, and was shocked to find his grandparents' Palais Kuffner overrun with Nazi soldiers when he returned to Vienna. The paratroopers formally evicted the Kuffners, and as he packed some possessions von Klemperer managed to leave behind notes that read, "You can take our house, yet not our pride."

Both of von Klemperer's brothers were in New York City by then, and von Klemperer's father worked tirelessly to secure an entry visa for his third son. At one point, von Klemperer received a summons for a medical exam for induction into the *Wehrmacht,* or German Army, but an older police officer at the barracks, who had once worked at his father's factory, recognized him and told him to leave. He and his sister were finally able to sail for the United States, arriving on Thanksgiving Day of 1938. A year later, his parents safely emigrated to Britain, where they waited out the war that began officially on September 1, 1939.

Von Klemperer entered Harvard University as a refugee scholar, but his fluency in German and anti-Nazi political views propelled him into wartime service for U.S. military intelligence, and he served at the London headquarters of General Dwight D. Eisenhower's Allied Expeditionary Force. His espionage work was anything but glamorous, and consisted mostly of combing through the paystub books of German prisoners of war to glean data on troop movement and strength. Von Klemperer became a naturalized U.S. citizen in 1943 and was posted to Frankfurt once the war was over. The sight of his homeland, its cities flattened by bombs and its population traumatized, shocked him deeply, and he pursued a Ph.D. in history when he returned to Harvard in order to focus on what had happened to his wrecked country in the space of his own lifetime.

Studied the *Widerstand*

Von Klemperer taught at Smith College for 37 years and produced numerous works of scholarship on the history of modern Germany. His published works included *Germany's New Conservatism* in 1957 and *Mandate for Resistance: The Case of the German Opposition to Hitler* in 1969. He focused on a small cadre of high-ranking Nazi military officials who mounted a plot to remove Hitler from power via assassination. One of them was Adam von Trott zu Solz, and von Klemperer wrote about von Trott's correspondence with a British journalist who was friends with Britain's Prime Minister Winston Churchill in *A Noble Combat: The Letters of Shiela Grant Duff and Adam von Trott zu Solz 1932–1938.* This work appeared in 1988, followed four years later by von Klemperer's best-known book, *German Resistance Against Hitler: The Search for Allies Abroad 1938–1945.*

In *German Resistance Against Hitler* von Klemperer sought to counter the general assumption that most Germans obediently went along with Hitler and his right-wing extremism. There were pockets of opponents deep in the underground left, but also in the uppermost echelons of the party. One was a high-ranking Wehrmacht colonel and aristocrat, Count Klaus von Stauffenberg, who carried out the failed July 20 Plot to kill Hitler. On July 20, 1944, Colonel von Stauffenberg placed a briefcase containing explosives in a map room at Hitler's bunker in East Prussia, Wolfsschanze, during a senior-level meeting. As prearranged, von Stauffenberg was called out of the room and the blast rocked the map room, though the briefcase had been inadvertently moved out of a direct path to Hitler's body by one of the officers; instead it went off next to a leg of the enormous map table, and that helped diffuse the blast. Hitler was unharmed save for a perforated eardrum; three officers and a secretary died. Von Stauffenberg and his co-conspirators were rounded up, convicted of treason, and hanged.

Von Klemperer's 487-page opus traced all the attempts to kill Hitler, though the July 20 Plot was the most well known among them and eventually became the basis for a 2008 Hollywood film, *Valkyrie,* that starred actor Tom Cruise as von Stauffenberg. Some of the *Widerstand,* or resistance inside Germany, came from religious figures like the prominent Lutheran theologian Dietrich Bonhoeffer—also executed by the regime—or aristocrats like von Stauffenberg and another elite, a Count Helmuth von Moltke, a high-ranking legal-affairs official inside the Nazi government who, also, was exposed and sentenced to death. Von Klemperer sought to show how many other diplomats and even military officers risked their lives to make contact with the Allies, for they were ardent patriots and did not want to see Germany fall to foreign powers, as it became increasingly clear would happen as Hitler vowed to fight until the end. Some hoped to broker a peace treaty, but Allied decision-makers—Churchill and U.S. President Franklin D. Roosevelt among them—had already agreed that Germany's war crimes were so egregious that the enemy had to be forced to an unconditional surrender.

Rebuked President for Bitburg Visit

Von Klemperer continued his research into the twenty-first century with the publication of his 2001 book, *German Incertitudes: The Stones in the Cathedral.* His memoir, *Voyage Through the 20th Century,* appeared in 2009. He retired from Smith College in 1987. Two years earlier, he had been one of many figures who publicly criticized U.S. President Ronald Reagan for visiting a military cemetery in Bitburg, West Germany, with German Chancellor Helmut Kohl as part of 40th-anniversary events marking of the end of World War II in Europe. The burial grounds included some members of Hitler's detested Waffen-SS corps, and the controversy provoked a fresh round of effrontery that a U.S. president participated in a commemoration on soil in which Nazis had been laid to rest for their service in a genocidal regime. In response, Reagan gave a speech in which he noted that many ordinary Germans suffered, too, during the war, especially those who were drafted as teenagers. Von Klemperer chastised the president in a letter to the *New York Times* that ran on May 5, 1985. "Reagan betrayed an abysmal ignorance of history and an absence of memory" by that remark, von Klemperer asserted.

Von Klemperer died on December 23, 2012, at his home in Easthampton, Massachusetts, at age 96. He had a long marriage to another professor at Smith, Elizabeth Gallaher, and they had two children. He traveled frequently back to Germany for both work and pleasure, and he also spent years tracking down what happened to nearly everyone he remembered from his childhood idylls in Dresden and Vienna, his Berlin friends and classmates at the Französiches Gymnasium, and the other students at the University of Vienna who had expressed shock and dismay at the Anschluss. "My ultimate intention," he once said, according to his London *Times* obituary, "was to bear witness to the fact that, whatever the conflicts of interest and misunderstandings on either side, righteous Germans had existed."

Books

Von Klemperer, Klemens, *Voyage Through the 20th Century: A Historian's Recollections and Reflections,* Berghahn Books, 2009.

Periodicals

New York Times, May 5, 1985; July 21, 1990; January 7, 2013.
Times (London, England), February 19, 2013.□

Alice Kober

The American linguist and classical studies scholar Alice Kober (1906–1950) laid the groundwork for the deciphering, soon after her death, of the writing system known as Linear B, which recorded one of the earliest forms of the Greek language.

The 1,000 writing-covered clay tablets that first alerted the academic world to the existence of Linear B were originally discovered by the British archaeologist Arthur Evans (1851–1941) during excavations on the Greek island of Crete. The actual discovery that Linear B represented a form of ancient Greek and the understanding of what each of its individual characters signified came from an amateur linguist from Britain, Michael Ventris (1922–1956), who announced his findings on BBC radio in 1951. But the bulk of the work done in deciphering Linear B, in the words of *New York Times* writer Matti Friedman, "an unknown script that an unknown society used to write an unknown language," was done by Kober. She rejected erroneous hypotheses by Evans, who worked on Linear B until his death at age 90, and others including Ventris. Instead, she chose to approach the problem of Linear B systematically and scientifically, undertaking heroic labors that nearly solved one of the great mysteries of Greek antiquity.

Won College Scholarship Prize

Alice Elizabeth Kober was born in New York on December 23, 1906. Unlike many classical scholars, she was not born into money. Her parents, Franz and Katharina Kober, were Hungarian immigrants of modest means; Franz worked as an upholsterer and apartment-building superintendent. Not much is known of Alice's early life—or of her personal life in general (she never married or wrote of any romantic relationships). She was a standout high school student, placing third among 115 New York students in a scholarship contest in 1924, and winning a prize that helped her attend the then all-female Hunter College, which had a strong classics program.

At Hunter, Kober took a course in early Greek culture, and it was probably there that she first encountered the Linear B script. She impressed her teachers, including one who wrote (as quoted by Margalit Fox in *The Riddle of the Labyrinth*), "As an undergraduate she impressed me by her earnest application to her work, and even more by her independent judgment ... Coupled with this was a still more valuable trait, an intellectual honesty, which induced her readily to revise her own opinion when she became convinced of the correctness of the opposition." Kober graduated magna cum laude from Hunter in 1928 with a major in Latin and a minor in Greek, and announced that she would one day decipher Linear B. The problem had stumped Evans for a quarter-century, and Kober's assertion seemed an unlikely one.

Kober went on for a master's degree in classics at Columbia University in 1929 and a Ph.D. there in 1932, writing her dissertation (published as a book in 1932) about color terminology and working her way through by teaching Latin and Greek at Hunter College. In 1930, she was hired as an instructor at Brooklyn College. Her salary was low (about $30,000 in 2013 dollars), and her course load was heavy, leaving her little time for independent research. She remained at Brooklyn College for the rest of her life, occasionally trying without success to find a job at an institution that would allow her more time for research. In the 1930s, she went on several archaeological digs, one of them in Greece.

Although she published nothing on the subject for several years, Kober began working seriously on Linear B in the 1930s. At the time, Evans was the acknowledged reigning specialist in the field, and he was loath to share his materials with others. Evans had discovered the tablets, which were the oldest instances of writing in Europe, at his excavation of Knossos on Crete, an elaborate city that revealed the presence of a complex Bronze Age civilization that had apparently flourished between about 1600 and 1100 B.C.E. Some of the characters on the tablets were pictograms whose meanings were clear (such as an image of a horse), but others were purely linguistic in nature. Evans and others had correctly guessed from the number of different characters involved that the script was syllabic: each character represented not a sound (as in English), nor a whole word (as in Chinese), but a syllable (as in modern Korean and other languages). Further, Evans surmised that the tablets contained inventories of materials, and he successfully translated a single word, meaning "total."

Learned Multiple Ancient Languages

But there Evans hit a wall. He and others tried to solve the riddle of Linear B by guessing what language it represented. Some, including Ventris, believed that it recorded the Etruscan language, the ancient language of Italy that was displaced by Latin. Kober dismissed this method. "It is possible to prove, quite logically, that the Cretans spoke any language whatever known to have existed at that time—provided only that one disregards the fact that half a dozen other possibilities are equally likely," she said in a lecture quoted by Fox in the London *Telegraph Online.* Kober resolved to approach the whole problem more systematically. To prepare herself, she learned, to various degrees, written languages of great antiquity (and difficulty) that were organized in various ways; Sanskrit, Chinese, Akkadian (a language of ancient Mesopotamia), Persian, Hittite, Old Irish, Basque, and several others.

Working late at night in a house in Brooklyn's Flatbush neighborhood that she shared with her mother, Kober began to apply what was essentially an exhaustive version of the reasoning processes used by solvers of newspaper cryptogram puzzles. Instead of trying to make the Linear B characters fit existing languages, she started from scratch by making a giant inventory of all the characters—tabulating how frequently they occurred and whether they appeared at the beginning, the middle, or the end of a word. Without the aid of computers (which did not yet exist), she painstakingly tabulated the frequency with which characters appeared next to one another.

Money was scarce, and during World War II paper was at times expensive and difficult to obtain. Kober improvised by recycling and cutting up any heavy paper she could find: backs of greeting cards, exam book covers, and library checkout slips. In this way she accumulated about 180,000 index cards that she used to record her findings. She stored her cards in empty cigarette cartons. After the war she was able to travel to Britain to examine new materials and to copy out the Linear B characters they contained—but in the middle of winter, with wartime shortages still acute, she found herself having to make elaborate drawings of the characters by hand in unheated rooms that were barely above freezing—the common office photocopier was also years in the future.

Discovered Inflections in Linear B Language

In the middle and late 1940s, aided by a one-year Guggenheim fellowship in 1946, Kober's laborious efforts began to pay off. She realized that many groups of words had identical beginnings but different endings, and thus that Linear B represented an inflected language—a language in which word endings affect a word's grammatical function (English, which is lightly inflected, contains groups of words such as read, reader, reading). In 1945, Kober published a paper, "Evidence of Inflection in the 'Chariot' Tablets from Knossos," in the *American Journal of Archaeology.* She issued lists of groups of three words that seemed closely related, and Ventris, a British architect and enthusiastic amateur linguist who followed Kober's work closely in spite of the fact that the two did not get along personally, dubbed these groups Kober's triplets.

Clearly Kober was close to solving the problem of Linear B, while Ventris, who still believed that the script represented a form of Etruscan, was farther from the goal. In 1949, however, Kober began to suffer the effects of an illness (she never said what it was nor gave up hope that she might soon recover), and soon it was impossible for her to work. In January of 1950, Brooklyn College promoted her from assistant professor to associate professor. A few months later, on May 16, 1950, Kober died. Her father had died of stomach cancer, and in Fox's words "[i]t seems probable, given Kober's heavy smoking, that she had some form of cancer."

After Kober's death, Ventris began experimenting with her triplets, assigning actual sounds to them. With this method one word seemed to appear frequently: "Ko-no-so." Ventris realized that this might mean the city of Knossos itself—and with this insight the puzzle of Linear B fell into place. Quickly Ventris derived other place names on Crete from the script, and soon he had a large corpus of actual syllables to work with. He realized that he had been wrong all along: Linear B recorded not Etruscan but an early form of Greek now known as Mycenean. Ventris announced to wide acclaim in 1952 that he had deciphered Linear B, but the backbone of his discovery was provided by Kober's research. She was largely forgotten, however, until Fox's *The Riddle of the Labyrinth* appeared in 2013.

Books

Fox, Margalit, *The Riddle of the Labyrinth,* HarperCollins, 2013.

Periodicals

Guardian (London, England), August 3, 2013.

International Herald Tribune, June 17, 2013.

New York Times, May 12, 2013; May 31, 2013.

Telegraph Online, July 11, 2013.

Online

"How an American Linguist Helped Unlock the Secrets of Linear B," *Public Radio International,* http://pri.org/stories/2013-05-13/how-american-linguist-helped-unlock-secrets-linear-b (November 1, 2013).

"Professor Alice Kober: 1907–May 16, 1950," *Breaking Ground: Women in Old World Archaeology,* http://www.brown.edu/Research/Breaking_Ground/bios/Kober_Alice.pdf (November 1, 2013).□

Rem Koolhaas

Dutch architect and urbanist Rem Koolhaas (born 1944) was honored with the Pritzker Architecture Prize in 2000 after a 25-year career. Known for his daring ideas about space and form, Koolhaas has created just a handful of buildings, but all of them are visually stunning and marvels of structural engineering. One of his most iconic works is the China Central Television (CCTV) headquarters in Beijing, China, a 44-story tower which features an enormous open space in its center.

Remment Lucas Koolhaas was born to Selinde Pietertje Roosenburg Koolhaas, the daughter of a prominent Modernist architect, on November 17, 1944, in Rotterdam. The Dutch city had been a center of global commerce and the maritime industries since the Middle Ages, but had been flattened by a destructive aerial raid four years before Koolhaas was born, when neighboring Nazi Germany moved to occupy the Netherlands at the onset of World War II. During the first six months of his life, Koolhaas lived in a city whose residents endured a terrible famine known as the Hunger Winter, which lasted until Rotterdam was liberated by Allied forces on May 5, 1945.

Enthralled by Indonesian Adventure

Koolhaas was the first of three children born to Selinde and her spouse Anton Koolhaas, a left-leaning journalist who wrote in support of the Indonesian independence movement in the postwar years. The massive archipelago-colony known as the Dutch East Indies eventually won the right to self-rule and its mononymed leader, Sukarno, invited Koolhaas's father to run a cultural program in the capital of Jakarta. The Koolhaas family moved there from Amsterdam in 1952, and the future architect spent three impressionable late-childhood years there. "It made me at an early age aware of very many different peoples, many different ways of living, many different ways of being happy—probably also many different ways of being religious," he reflected in an interview with *Newsweek*'s Christopher Dickey. "Because I had seen Christianity, Islam, Buddhism when I was 8, and actually experienced them. So all of that I think was very crucial. We went to Indonesian schools and had to live more or less an Indonesian kind of life."

Koolhaas had been fascinated by Jakarta's once-grand colonial buildings and the surrounding ramshackle sprawl, and was disoriented by the family's return to a rebuilt Western Europe in the mid-1950s, where "everything had been fixed up and was straight and boring," he told Tim Adams, a journalist with the London *Observer*. "I craved the previous animation, the getting of things done."

Koolhaas failed to complete the requirements for his baccalaureate, which prevented him from continuing on the standard path to a university education. Instead, at age 18 he went to work for a tabloid newspaper, *Haagse Post*. In the early 1960s newspapers were still composed by a hot-metal process known as linotype, and Koolhaas was captivated by the technique. He recalled "standing at a table surrounded by steel plates, telling people where to put things," as he told Jay Merrick in an interview with another London paper, the *Independent*. "You had to be able to imagine everything upside down and in mirror images, and totally feel the consequences of a gesture here or there."

Studied in London

Koolhaas wrote for the *Haagse Post* and became involved with a loose-knit group of renegade Dutch filmmakers. He co-wrote some unproduced screenplays, and was asked by a friend to give a lecture on film to a group of architecture students in Delft. A pivotal shift happened that day, when he suddenly realized he would rather be sitting among them. In 1968, Koolhaas moved to London to begin studies at the Architectural Association School of Architecture (AASA). His thesis explored how the Berlin Wall—an enormous structure that divided the former German capital into a tightly controlled Communist sphere and a freewheeling West German exclave—had redefined the city in a little over a decade since it was first erected as a political barrier by the East Germans.

In the early 1970s, Koolhaas spent some formative years in the United States. He studied under a German architect, Oswald Mathias Ungers, at Cornell University in New York, and also lived in New York City as a visiting scholar at the Institute for Architecture and Urban Studies. During this time, he produced the first of several books on architectural theory and urban design that have become classic texts in both fields. *Delirious New York: A Retroactive Manifesto for Manhattan* appeared in 1978, and garnered Koolhaas a minor cult following for his ideas about urban congestion and the future of cities. "Change tends to fill people with this incredible fear," Koolhaas reflected in a 2012 interview with Nicolai Ouroussoff for *Smithsonian* magazine. "We are surrounded by crisis-mongers who see the city in terms of decline. I kind of automatically embrace the change. Then I try to find ways in which change can be mobilized to strengthen the original identity."

Founded OMA

In 1975, Koolhaas joined with one of his professors from London's Architectural Association School, Elia Zenghelis, and opened a small four-person practice in London. They called it OMA, the Office for Metropolitan Architecture. The other partners were Zenghelis's wife, Zoe, and Koolhaas's spouse, Madelon Vriesendorp. The firm entered many competitions for public and private projects, but failed to win any income-generating commissions for several years. Finally, in 1981, their proposal for the Netherlands Dance Theater in The Hague was approved. The space housed a modern-dance company and served as a performance venue, too, when it opened in 1987. It won critical accolades and secured Koolhaas's reputation as a visionary architect of a newly emerging generation.

In 1988, Koolhaas and OMA won a prestigious commission after submitting a masterplan for Euralille, a new business and transportation district to be built on the edge of Lille, France. Connected to Paris and to Brussels—the capital of the European Union—by new high-speed trains, the site would also be the gateway to a long-delayed Chunnel, the undersea tunnel connecting England and France. Koolhaas's Congrexpo convention center for Euralille won particular acclaim, with architectural critics often remarking upon how difficult it was to give such immense spaces any sense of exhilaration to visitors.

By this point OMA's original partnership structure had changed, and Koolhaas had offices in London and Rotterdam. As staff expanded and the number of competition entries grew, the firm struggled to remain financially solvent. Some notable projects fell through in the early 1990s, and Koolhaas was forced to downsize. Interest in his work was reignited by a show at New York's Museum of Modern Art in 1994 titled "O.M.A. at MOMA: Rem Koolhaas and the Place of Public Architecture," which featured drawings and three-dimensional models of his firm's work—much of which remained unbuilt. He also collected all of his writings and drawings of as-yet-unrealized ideas into another hefty tome, *S, M, L, XL,* that also became an instant classic.

Returned to Asia

In 1995, Koolhaas began teaching a seminar at Harvard University's Graduate School of Design. The course focused less on architecture than on urban studies, and he led a small group of students in conducting a special research project each term. The first of these investigated a site that Koolhaas believed would soon become the world's biggest urban metropolis by size: China's Pearl River Delta, which connected Hong Kong and Macau with Guangzhou and Shenzhen. He and another group of seminar students were co-authors of a summary of a subsequent project, *The Harvard Design School Guide to Shopping,* which posited that late twentieth-century consumerism was driving urban growth, even for art museums and other citadels of high culture. "The market economy thrives on spectacle and novelty," he explained to *Guardian* writer Jonathan Glancey. "Its buildings are ever more dramatic. It offers the promise of total freedom, but in architecture this quickly leads to the danger of grotesqueness. It is hard to do serious, disciplined buildings in such a condition." Koolhaas's theories led to an offer from Italian fashion designer Miuccia Prada, who commissioned him to design new state-of-the-art flagship stores for the Prada luxury label in New York City and Los Angeles.

In the spring of 2000 Koolhaas's name was announced as that year's recipient of the Pritzker Architecture Prize. Named for the philanthropic family associated with the Hyatt hotels empire, the Pritzker Prize was created to remedy the absence of a Nobel Prize category for architecture. Koolhaas joined a esteemed list of luminaries and Pritzker laureates, including I.M. Pei, Frank Gehry, and Oscar Niemeyer.

One of Koolhaas's first significant buildings in North America was the new Seattle Central Library, which opened in 2004. Made up of polygon forms clad in reflective glass, the eleven-story structure features book stacks that spiral through several floors and a light-filled tenth-floor reading room overlooking the city. The *New Yorker*'s architecture critic, Paul Goldberger, hailed it as "the most important new library to be built in a generation, and the most exhilarating.... The building manages the neat trick of seeming exotic but not bizarre."

Designed Tilted CCTV Towers

Koolhaas's prolonged interest in Asia and its cities drew him to China, which launched a massive building boom in advance of the 2008 Summer Olympics in Beijing. Working once again with OMA collaborators, Koolhaas created a dazzling new headquarters for China's state-run television network, China Central Television. The 44-floor CCTV Building in Beijing is essentially a rectangle with an enormous void in the center, plus a taller tower on one side. A marvel of architectural creativity and structural design, the iconic skyscraper can be seen for miles and quickly came to symbolize China's rapid modernization and entrance onto the global stage. "It introduced a level of daring that had not been shown in China," Koolhaas said of this work in an interview with *Wall Street Journal* reporter J.S. Marcus "I am very convinced that it had a positive effect on Chinese culture in general. It pushed the edge of possibility."

Koolhaas has often credited one longtime collaborator, Cecil Balmond of the British structural-engineering firm Ove Arup, for turning his ideas into reality. The two have worked together since the mid-1980s, and both travel extensively and often communicate via electronically transmitted sketches. Koolhaas coined the term "junk space" to refer to airports, hotels, and other anonymous places in which he is forced to spend time. He has homes in both London and Rotterdam, as well as offices in both Rotterdam and in Beijing. Separated from Vriesendorp, with whom he has two adult children, he lives in the Netherlands with Petra Blaisse, an interior designer. His firm continues to enter commission competitions, which can be a drain on an architecture practice's overhead and staffing costs and give scant guarantee of future revenue; only if the firm's design is chosen can it expect to collect fees related to the projected budget. "I've absolutely never thought about money or economic issues," Koolhaas asserted to Ouroussoff in the *Smithsonian.* "But as an architect I think this is a strength. It allows me to be irresponsible and to invest in my work."

Periodicals

Guardian (London, England), August 27, 2007.
Independent (London, England), February 18, 2004.
New Yorker, May 24, 2004.
Newsweek, July 30, 2012.
Observer (London, England), June 25, 2006.
Smithsonian, September 2012.
Wall Street Journal, April 24, 2009.□

Janusz Korczak

Polish author, educator, social worker, and physician Janusz Korczak (1878–1942) devoted much of his life to caring for and educating orphaned Jewish children. He achieved martyrdom when he vanished in a Treblinka death camp, apparently a victim of Germany's comprehensive elimination of European Jews.

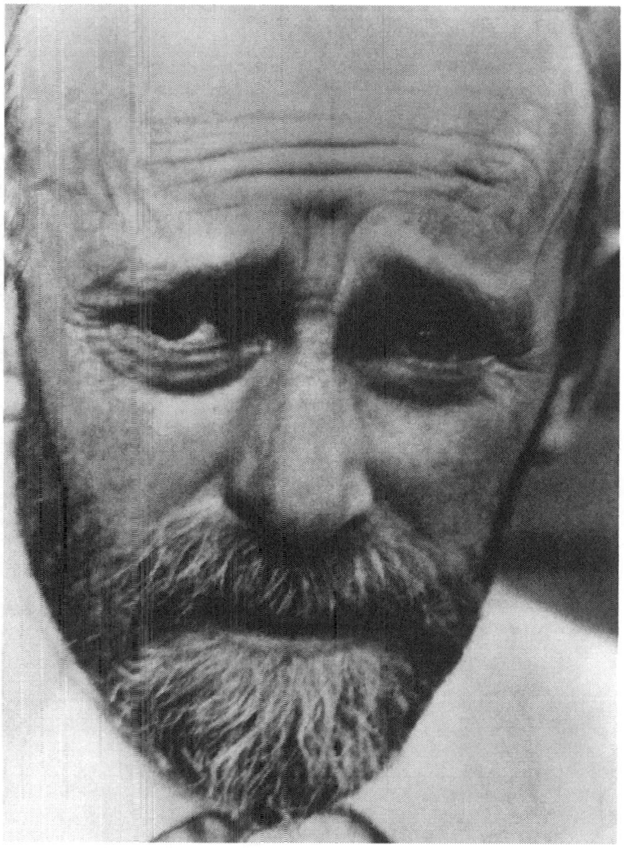

© INTERFOTO/Alamy

Born into a wealthy and assimilated Jewish family in Warsaw, Poland, Janusz Korczak had a compassionate interest in the welfare of underprivileged children. This came about through his childhood familiarity as well as his adult experience as a physician.

A versatile individual, Korczak was also a writer and educator. As a writer, he first expressed his concern for poor children in *Dzieci ulicy* (Children of the Street), which was published in 1901. The work described the terrible plight of homeless orphans who were forced to steal to survive. But it also expressed how these children managed to maintain moral values: Korczak communicated how they maintained a basic comprehension of what was right and what was wrong. In 1906, he produced a work—*Dziecko salonu* (A Child of the Salon)—that took a different, but equally powerful slant. It depicted a privileged middle-class male child whose life was governed by money. Though it came from a different direction as the previous work, the message was the same. Both works were controversial, as they criticized the reactionary elements of his country. Naturally, these gentle but inflammatory works provoked criticism from those elements.

In 1912, Korczak established a Jewish orphanage in Warsaw, and he would remain involved with this institution until his death. Korczak also was noted for his revolutionary educational ideas, which offered children a concept of self-government that, in turn, gave the young people the opportunity to publish a weekly newspaper supplement *Maly Przeglad* (Little Journal), which was included in a Zionist daily newspaper, *Nasz Przeglad,* from 1920 to 1939. He would also become involved in another orphanage, a non-Jewish institution located near Warsaw. Relentless in delivering his message, he also lectured at educational institutions and frequently spoke on radio about child and adult-related issues.

Janusz Korczak was born as Henryk Goldsmit in Warsaw, Poland, on July 22, 1878. He was an only child. Though his family was well off—his father was a successful lawyer—he played with children who were poor and lived in bad neighborhoods. Early on, he demonstrated a sensitivity and empathy toward people less fortunate.

His family was assimilated—that is, while his family was Jewish, his parents did not practice the religion. Rather, they considered themselves as liberated Jews and Polish patriots. At the time, Poland was occupied by Czarist Russia, a situation that fostered a militant Nationalism in the Polish population.

Studied to be a Physician

As his family was prosperous, Korczak benefited from the best education then offered. He wanted to be a physician, and his specialty—quite naturally—would be pediatrics. He wanted to devote his life to the welfare of children, even if this meant he would never marry and have a family, a personal sacrifice he decided upon.

From 1898 to 1904, he studied medicine at the University of Warsaw. His father died in 1896, and this meant that in addition to his educational activities, he needed to become his family's sole money earner. He supported his mother, sister, and grandmother. Some income came from his work as a writer for several of Poland's newspapers, as Korczak demonstrated literary talent. While practicing medicine, he began writing plays and essays. During this period, he assumed the pen name of Janusz Korczak, which came from the nineteenth-century novel *Janasz Korczak and the Pretty Swordsweeperlady,* written by Polish writer Jóef Ignacy Kraszewski.

After graduating, he became a pediatrician and worked at a children's hospital. During the Russo-Japanese War (1905–1906) he served as a military doctor. Following the war, he returned to his medical practice in Warsaw. Meanwhile, he wrote plays and essays (using his pen name), and these works were regularly published in Polish periodicals. His name and reputation expanded beyond the medical arena. But some people found him to be highly sensitive, didactic, and a bit morose.

Established an Orphanage

In 1906, Korszak organized a summer camp for youths who lived in Warsaw ghettos. Though this camp, "Summer Colony Michalowka," lasted but a month, it would prove to be a turning point in his life. He decided he wanted to establish an orphanage that would offer children both justice and respect. In 1911, he took a shameful Warsaw Jewish orphanage, and with the help of a Jewish organization, "Help for the Orphans," turned it into a respectable habitat called "Dom Sierot," which translates into "House of the Orphans." In this setting, Korszak applied his own progressive educational concepts combined with those of Swiss educational reformer Johann Heinrich Pestolazzi (1746–1827) and his student, Germany's Friedrich Fröbel (1782–1852). Essentially, Korszak created a microcosmic republic for children that included a small parliament, a court, and its own newspaper. One of Korszak's main strategies was to reveal to young people how they had the power to take control of their own lives.

Wrote During World War I

When World War I broke out in Europe, the 36-year-old Korszak was conscripted into the Russian army and assigned the position as the chief physician in a division hospital. As this division traveled throughout the Ukraine region, Korszak passed his time at night in his tent by continuing his writing activities. This eventually led to the publication of a book, published in German as *Wie man ein Kind lieben soll,* or "How to Love a Child." The work included his ideas about the need for proper feeding and sleep for infants, a parent's responsibility for a child, and the recognition and respect that each child requires. Though he could be at times pedantic, even tiresome, the writings offered readers examples of his humor. But while demonstrating wit, he never lost sight of his essential message, which was a fervent plea for the care of children. Also during this period, he wrote several essays that were compiled in a volume called *Der Fruhling and das Kind* ("Spring and the Child"). He based these writings on his experiences of witnessing how parents and children interacted in a war-torn environment.

During the war, after he was removed from his division, Korszak served as a pediatric physician in Kiev, Ukraine, where he met Polish nurse Maryna Rogowska-Falska, a woman whose membership in the Polish Socialist party led to her banishment to Siberia. Later freed, she worked in post-war Warsaw with Korszak in 1919 to establish a new orphanage, this one for Christian Polish children. It became known as *Nasz Dom,* or "Our House." During this difficult European period, Poland witnessed starvation and disease. A typhus epidemic killed Falska's husband and child. But the partners were careful for children's welfare, and children from both Dom Sierot and Nasz Dom orphanages were able to play together in peace in Poland's rural countryside.

Increased Literary Output

In the decades between World War I and World War II, Korszak produced major literary accomplishments. Along with *How to Love a Child* (which was also published as *Jak kochac dziecko*), he also wrote *Prawo dziecko do szacunka* (The Child's Right to Respect, 1929). Previously, he wrote two books for children: *Mośki, Jośki, Srule* (1910) and *Franki* (1911), works about Jewish children. Like a writer working in a garret, he penned many of his works in the small, sparsely furnished room he allowed for himself in the orphanage he established. There, he wrote *Sam na sam z Bogiem* (Alone with God, 1922), a book about prayer; *Kiedy znów bede maly* (When I am Small Again, 1922); *Król Macius Pierwszy* (Matthew the Young King, 1928); and *Kajtus czarodziej* (Kajtus the Magician, 1934). These works were translated into several languages and, understandably, they would prove popular in Israel.

Affected by Anti-Semitism

The decades that Korszak toiled as a physician, writer, and educator were a period of turmoil for Europe. By 1933, the world was reeling from the effects of the Great Depression, which indeed had global impact. By 1935, in Poland, democracy was being supplanted by fascism. Even so, the fascistic Germany threatened Polish independence. All these developments had a negative impact on Korszak's inherent optimism. What made all of this even worse was the rising level of anti-Jewish sentiment. Indeed, anti-Semitism was a major theme that ran through political rhetoric.

In 1934 and 1936, Korczak visited Palestine and embraced the Kibbutz movement, and he felt that all Jews should return to the homeland of Palestine. But he quickly divorced himself from this idea. The notion of a "Jewish Paradise" sounded unrealistic to him. Rather, he envisioned a world, unrestricted by national boundaries, where "universal brotherhood" prevailed, where class nor race was a factor.

But as he envisioned this utopia, the German war machine was becoming inexorable, threatening force. By September 1939, the Germans gained occupation of

Poland following a huge air and ground attack. A year later, the Germans had established the Warsaw Ghetto. Korczak's orphanage was consigned to the ghetto. Korczak was offered many chances from underground resistance to be surreptitiously removed to safety beyond the ghetto, but he chose to remain behind; he did not want to leave the children. He even went out into the streets where he begged for food and money for them. He also refused to wear the Jewish Star that German occupiers required. Meanwhile, Jews in Poland and Germany were being forced into the Warsaw Ghetto, which soon had a population of nearly 400,000 people who suffered from hunger, the region's harsh elements, and disease.

In August 1942, Korczak, orphanage staff, and nearly 200 children were deported to Treblinka, a Nazi extermination camp located near Warsaw. They were transported by train in horrendous conditions. Three written passages described the situation. One came from Korczak's own journal: "Today," he wrote on August 5, "I watered the flowers, the poor plants of the orphanage, a Jewish orphanage. The parched earth breathed in the water. A [German] sentry looked at me as I worked. Did he envy me in my peaceful task at this early morning hour, or was he moved by it perhaps? With his legs apart he stands there and watches. I water the flowers. My reflection on the window pane, a good sign. He has a rifle. Why does he stand there and watch me so peacefully? He gives no command. Perhaps he once led a normal life as a village school teacher, perhaps a lawyer, or a street sweeper in Leipzig or a waiter in Cologne. What will he do if I nod to him? Wave in a friendly fashion? Perhaps he has no idea that things are as they are. Perhaps he just arrived yesterday from somewhere else."

Another description came from a witness from the Warsaw Ghetto (as recorded on the *Center for Holocaust & Genocide Studies* webiste): "The scene I shall never forget. In contrast to the mass of humanity being driven like animals to slaughter, there appeared a group of children marching together in formation. They were the orphanage children walking four abreast in a line behind Korczak. His eyes were lifted to heaven. Even the military personnel stood still and saluted."

A third description came from a survivor who managed to escape from the railroad yard and who witnessed Korczak and the children being placed in windowless railroads cars typically used to transport cattle, not humans: "These children did not cry, these innocent little beings did not even weep. Like sick sparrows they snuggled up to their teacher, their caregiver, their father and their brother Janusz Korczak, that he might protect them with his weak, emaciated body."

Once transported to the Treblinka death camp, Korczak and his beloved children were never heard from again. In August 1942, Korczak died in one of the most brutal periods of world history. Korczak's legacy is that he helped reshape adult attitudes toward children. Children, he averred, have a right to be respected, and an adult must help them achieve their goals, not impose goals. This attitude is summed up from one of his most famous quotes: "There are no children—there are people."

Books

"Janus Korczak," *Encyclopedia Judaiaca,* Macmillan Reference USA, 2007.

Periodicals

Journal of Teacher Education, 56.2, 2005.

Online

"Biography," *The Janusz Korczak Association of Canada,* http://www.januszkorczak.ca/biography.html (December 1, 2013).

"Janus Korczak," *Jewish Virtual Library,* http://www.jewishvirtuallibrary.org/jsource/biography/Korczak.html (December 1, 2013).

"Janus Korczak's Biography," *Center for Holocaust & Genocide Studies,* http://chgs.umn.edu/museum/responses/hergeth/bio.html (December 1, 2013.

"New Janusz Korczak biography published," *Thenews.pl,* http://www.thenews.pl/1/11/Artykul/25272,New-Janusz-Korczak-biography-published (December 1, 2013).□

Karl Kraus

The Austrian writer Karl Kraus (1874–1936) was one of the foremost satirists of the 20th century.

Kraus's writings are difficult to translate from German into any other language, and he has remained best known in German-speaking countries. The critic Clive James observed, in an *Australian Literary Review* article reproduced on his website, that "[t]hough he had no computer on his desk, Kraus was essentially a blogger before the fact: his basic technique was to write a couple of hundred words about something silly in the newspaper." Like modern-day bloggers, he favored the literary feud as a mode of expression. Kraus was a fascinating and often self-contradictory figure; a Jew who was bitterly critical of artists; a conservative who longed for the stable days of the Austro-Hungarian monarchy but espoused such progressive causes as women's rights; a journalist who saw journalism as the source of a degradation of language that threatened society itself. Kraus wrote plays, including a giant opus that was hardly performable, but his own dramatic activities were restricted to his frequent public dramatic readings of plays and even an operetta. For most of his life, Kraus published his own magazine, devoted mainly to his own writings.

Dropped Out of Law School

Karl Kraus was born April 28, 1874, in Jicin, a Czech town then part of the Austro-Hungarian Empire. He was the youngest of nine children born to the prosperous Jewish paper manufacturer Jacob Kraus. The Kraus family moved to Vienna, Austria, when Kraus was three. Later Kraus would often complain about Vienna and even ascribed stress symptoms to the hubbub of its streets, but he lived there for the rest of his life. An unimpressive student, Kraus

© DIZ Muenchen GmbH, Sueddeutsche Zeitung Photo/Alamy

attended the college-preparatory type of Austrian high school called a gymnasium and then enrolled in law school at the University of Vienna. He showed up consistently only for literature and philosophy classes and left school after several years without graduating.

Exempt from military service because of a spine problem and supported by his family and later by an inheritance, Kraus essentially could do what he pleased. After a poor showing in an initial outing as an actor he switched to journalism, writing a review of a play by Gerhart Hauptmann in 1892. Kraus became a denizen of Vienna's coffee houses, spending time there with other rising writers like Hugo von Hofmannsthal and Arthur Schnitzler—and then turning on them in a satirical essay called *Demolierte Litteratur* (Literature Wrecked) in 1897. In 1899, he founded a journal of his own, called *Die Fackel* (The Torch). He was the editor and often sole contributor, and he accepted little advertising, believing that advertising could only corrupt his journalistic voice. Kraus continued to edit and produce *Die Fackel* until shortly before his death.

That year, Kraus was baptized as a Catholic. The move was not unusual for educated Viennese Jews, who faced discrimination of various kinds. Kraus was often harsh toward those who shared his Jewish background, denouncing them for having a ghetto mentality. In his essays he attacked two of the most prominent Jewish thinkers of the age: Theodor Herzl, the founder of the modern Zionist movement, and psychoanalysis pioneer Sigmund Freud. He quipped that psychoanalysis (he called its practitioners psychoanals) was the disease whose cure it purports to be and was in turn denounced by adherents of the new science. Kraus's religious affiliation with Catholicism was never a deep one, and he renounced Catholicism in turn in 1923.

Satirized Own Café Milieu

Kraus's essays in *Die Fackel* directed satirical ire at a wide range of modern phenomena. He poked sharp fun at political leaders, other publications (including very often the leading Viennese daily newspaper of the time, the *Neue freie Presse* or New Free Press), and artists and writers whom he disliked—which was most of them. He could, however, be very loyal to contemporaries he admired, including the Swedish playwright August Strindberg and the Austrian poet Peter Altenberg, for whom he organized a fundraiser when Altenberg faced large medical bills. Another target of Kraus's pen was Vienna's intellectual café society—of which he himself was a part.

Although he often seemed to long for an idealized past in which the classics of literature and art held cultural sway, Kraus held a number of progressive viewpoints. He was a staunch advocate of women's rights, although he once remarked (according to James) that "a liberated woman is a fish that has fought its way to shore." But perhaps Kraus's biggest personal annoyance was what he considered to be a decline in the elegance and precision of the German language, a phenomenon for which he held the new medium of the time, the mass-circulation daily newspaper, primariy responsible. He aimed particular criticism at the *feuilleton,* a sort of literary-political supplement containing topical criticism. In the words of *Toronto Star* writer Rick Salutin, "In a way, [Kraus] was the first critic of mainstream media: their lies and the damage wrought. . . . 'He deplored advertising's demeaning effects way back then, including gun makers to whom he suggested the slogan: Murder yourself."

Perhaps the most comprehensive catalog of Kraus's satirical concerns was his five-act play (plus prologue and epilogue) *Die letzten Tage der Menschheit* (The Last Days of Humankind), written between 1915 and 1919, during World War I. Broadly antiwar in theme, the play included 500 characters ranging from professors to prostitutes, deployed in a total of 209 scenes. The play required ten evenings to stage in full, and it was never presented in full during Kraus's lifetime, although he did read his own abridgement in a public performance in 1930. Complete performances were given in Basel, Switzerland, and Vienna in 1980, with an English version having its premiere in Edinburgh, Scotland, in 1983.

Drew Capacity Crowds to Readings

Kraus wrote several more plays in the 1920s, and although they did not seem to have the realities of theater in mind, these were performed in Vienna; they included the surreal *Traumstüuck* (Dream Play, 1923), the comic *Wolkenkuckucksheim* (Cloudcuckooland, 1923), and *Traumtheater* (Dream Theater, 1924). Most of all he liked to read dramas aloud himself in public. He gave 700 of these performances, in Vienna and elsewhere in Europe, titling them simply "A Reading by Karl Kraus" or later "Theater of Poetry." Newspapers ignored this aspect of Kraus's career, but he drew capacity crowds. Of the 700 performances, 123 were musical and were accompanied by a pianist; for these, Kraus liked to perform the comic operettas of French composer Jacques Offenbach. Although he could not read music, he sang all the parts himself. He also presented his own adaptations of Shakespeare's plays, working from established German translations.

Kraus never married, but he had a number of high-profile lovers. His relationship with the Baroness Sidonie Nádherný lasted from 1913 until his death. She inspired a good deal of Kraus's poetry, which was not humorous in tone, and he proposed marriage to her several times. She turned him down because of the difference in their social backgrounds, and she eventually married someone else—but their relationship continued, sometimes nurtured in overnight train compartments or in a car Kraus bought to satifsy her desire for travel.

With the rise of fascism in Germany, Kraus seemed to be depressed that his worst fears about contemporary culture were coming true. He wrote an essay called *Die dritte Walpurgisnacht* (The Third Witches' Sabbath) in 1933 that began with the words "I can't think of anything to say about Hitler" but went on to forecast the Nazi threat and was not published in full until 1962. Kraus supported the right-wing Austrian government of chancellor Engelbert Dollfuss, something for which he was criticized by liberal writers; Kraus saw Dollfuss as a bulwark against a German takeover of Austria. Kraus suffered a heart attack and died on June 12, 1936; the last issue of *Die Fackel* had appeared just four months earlier. Dollfuss had been asssassinated in a fascist coup attempt in 1934, but Kraus did not live to see Austria's annexation to Germany in 1938.

German occupiers destroyed all of Kraus's papers. The majority of the writings on his career have been in German, for his language, depending on wordplay and humor, is extremely difficult to translate, and his works are not well known among English-speaking readers. In 2013, however, a selection of Kraus's essays was presented in the book *The Kraus Project*. They were translated by the American novelist Jonathan Franzen, whose attitude of social critique had some affinities to Kraus's: "These men share similar obsessions, notably in regard to the soul-draining natures of mass media, high tech, consumer capitalism and hack writing," noted Dwight Garner of *The New York Times*.

Books

Elfe, Wolfgang, and James N. Hardin, eds., *Twentieth-Century German Dramatists* (*Dictionary of Literary Biography, Vol. 118*), Gale, 1992.

Encyclopedia Judaica, Gale, 2007.

Reitter, Paul, *The Anti-Journalist Karl Kraus and Jewish Self-Fashioning in Fin-de-Siècle Europe*, Chicago, 2008.

Timms, Edward, *Karl Kraus: Apocalyptic Satirist*, Yale, 1989.

Periodicals

New York Times, October 2, 2013.

Toronto Star, January 3, 2014.

Online

"Karl Kraus," *The Undergraduate Review* (State University of New York), http://www.theabsolute.net/minefield/kraus.html (January 9, 2014).

"Karl Kraus (1874–1936," *Books and Writers*, http://www.kirjasto.sci.fi/kkraus.htm (January 9, 2014).

"The Question of Karl Kraus," *CliveJames.com*, http://www.clivejames.com/karl-krau (January 9, 2014).□

Béla Kun

Hungarian revolutionary Béla Kun (1886–1938) led a short-lived experiment in Communism in the chaotic aftermath that followed World War I. A left-leaning journalist radicalized by his experience as a prisoner of war in Russia in 1917–18, Kun managed to marshal enough popular and military support to establish the Hungarian Soviet Republic, the world's second Communist state, in March of 1919, but it lasted just 133 days.

Kun was born Béla Kohn on February 20, 1886, in Transylvania, a mountain region in present-day Romania. His hometown was called Szilaágycseh at the time, but later resumed a Romanian-language place name, Lelei. There were many Hungarians living in Transylvania during this period, and the mixed ethnic population also included Germans who came during the Protestant Reformation of the 16th century and Jewish families like the Kohns. Kun changed his name as a young adult when he became more politically active and attuned to a growing Hungarian nationalist sentiment.

Taken Prisoner by Russians

During Kun's childhood, Transylvania was part of the enormous Austro-Hungarian Empire, which ruled from Vienna over a wide swath of southern and eastern Europe. Two larger cities near Szilaágycseh were Zalău, which was home to a Protestant academy Kun attended in his youth, and then the regional capital of Kolozsvár, also known as Cluj-Napoca. A talented writer and orator, the teenage Kun won a scholarship to the Hungarian-language Franz-Joseph University in Kolozsvár with an essay about the poet Sándor Petőfi, a Hungarian cultural hero. Kun abandoned his plans for a law degree around 1905, when he was 19, and went to work as an investigative journalist for a Kolozsvár newspaper. His first direct experience with political repression came in 1907 when he was jailed for authorship of a leaflet supporting a local labor strike. Most reports of Kun's early years reveal that he had frequent squabbles with others that sometimes escalated into duels, and that he lost his seat on Kolozsvár's social-welfare/workers'-compensation committee after he was accused of embezzling funds.

In the spring of 1913, Kun married a music teacher and fellow Hungarian, Iren Gal, after a two-year courtship

and apparently over the objections of her family. In the summer of 1914, Archduke Franz Ferdinand, heir to the Austro-Hungarian throne, was assassinated by a Serbian nationalist. The incident magnified long-simmering hostilities across Europe, from Britain to Russia, and tensions erupted into World War I within a matter of weeks. Kun was drafted into the Austro-Hungarian army to fight against England, France, and imperial Russia. One of the few tactical successes the Russians managed to achieve was the Brusilov Offensive, which lasted from June to September of 1916, and took place on Ukrainian soil. Kun fought in it and was taken prisoner by Russian troops.

Kun was one of several thousand Austro-Hungarian soldiers captured and transported far into the Russia empire. This population later found themselves at an historical crossroad at the end of the war as both empires disintegrated and Russia became the world's first Communist state. At his prisoner of war (POW) camp in Tomsk, Siberia, Kun was exposed to radical Communist teachings and witnessed firsthand the Russian Revolution's rapid transformation of the social order.

Agitated for Hungarian Revolution

Released from the POW camp at the end of the war, Kun went from Tomsk to Moscow, where in March of 1918, he became a founding member of the Hungarian Group of the Communist (Bolshevik) Party of Russia. He also spent time in the former St. Petersburg, the capital of imperial Russia and newly renamed Petrograd, and published a Hungarian-language newspaper called *Social Revolution* and a widely distributed pamphlet titled *What Do the Communists Want?* He came to know both Vladimir I. Lenin, the leader of the Bolshevik Revolution in Russia in 1917, and a couple of hardline leftists in the Russian Communist Party named Karl Radek and Grigory Zinoviev.

The new Soviet Russia knew it needed allies to survive as the world's first Communist state. With that in mind, its leadership sent money and other forms of aid to leftist parties in Europe, hoping that the chaos of the postwar months—still-armed returning war veterans, widespread food and fuel shortages, and a war-wrecked economy—would tilt these countries, too, toward revolution. Kun was deemed the best hope to lead a serious Hungarian revolution, and he returned in early November of 1918 with this goal. With him was a contingent of former POWs and other Hungarian Socialists. They made up the newly renamed Party of Communists of Hungary (*Kommunisták Magyarországi Pártja,* or KMP).

Kun went to Budapest, Hungary's largest city and cultural capital. By then the country was in the hands of a provisional government run by Mihály Károlyi, known as the "Red Count." An aristocrat with strong leftist leanings, Károlyi had led October demonstrations in Budapest that had forced from power the last emperor of Austria and King of Hungary, Charles I. To the KMP and other hardline Communists, Károlyi's elite family background was unsavory, and he was also a political moderate chosen by the Hungarian Social Democratic Party, a center-left party that had been the party of the liberals in the years before World War I.

The armistice bringing World War I to a close was signed on November 11, 1918, and it also dissolved the Austro-Hungarian Empire. Kun formally registered the KMP in Budapest on November 24, 1918. Károlyi's provisional government, meanwhile, struggled to maintain order during the tough winter months that followed. With the end of the Austro-Hungarian Empire, its former principalities—led by nationalist movements of various political stripes—had declared themselves sovereign and independent nations. Neighboring Czechoslovakia was one of them, and with that, Hungarians lost access to the vast coal mines of Czech lands. In Budapest and other cities there was mass unemployment,hyperinflation, and food shortages.

Joined with Social Democrats

Kun was active throughout the winter months, calling for strikes and civil action on the pages of the KMP newspaper, *Vörös újság* (Red News). Another major issue was the finalization of an independent Hungary's borders. There were disputes on all sides—Slovakians claimed a chunk, villages like Kun's birthplace of Szilaágycseh were caught between Hungarian sympathies and Romanian loyalties, and there was also contested territory in the south between Hungary and various Balkan populations. Hungarians desperately wanted to retain as much territory as possible, and it was this mind-set that enabled Kun's KMP to rise to power.

Kun had actually been jailed after one mass meeting in February of 1919 turned violent; he was arrested and beaten in police custody. The prospect of war loomed in March of 1919 when Károlyi's government balked at new delineated borders for Hungary. On March 19, 1919, an emissary from France sent the dispatch known as the Vix Note, named after French lieutenant-colonel Fernand Vix, who controlled the French and other Entente (Allied) troops stationed in this part of Europe in the months following the war before the Treaty of Versailles could be finalized. The Vix Note ordered Károlyi to recall Hungarian troops backward to the new border lines. There was major outrage in Hungary over this, and the Social Democrats realized their position was hopeless. They looked to Bolshevik Russia for help. From jail, Kun agreed to act as an emissary, but demanded that the two parties—the Social Democrats and his KMP—be merged. They did so the next day, becoming the Hungarian Socialist Party, which proclaimed the establishment of the Hungarian Soviet Republic on March 21, 1919.

Released from jail, Kun became the de facto leader of the new Communist regime, only the second one in the world and this one completed in a bloodless handover. Copying the Bolshevik model, Kun and other leaders formed an all-volunteer Hungarian Red Army, which launched wars against Romania and Czechoslovakia in April 1919. He and the Revolutionary Governing Council began a major overhaul of all aspects of Hungarian society. Private property was abolished, as were titles of nobility. Banks, major industries, and any business with more than 20 employees were nationalized. Agricultural collectivization in Hungary's still-fertile rural areas, however, provoked intense resistance, especially when government trucks began confiscating grain stores and livestock to feed urban residents. One of Kun's cohorts was Tibor Szamuely, the People's Commissar for Military Affairs. Szamuely, too, had spent time in Russia during the revolutionary period and deployed the same tactics by recruiting his own personal security detail, whom he then sent out to arrest, attack, and in some cases even murder civilians for what were judged to be counterrevolutionary crimes. This was known as the Red Terror, and though it was brief, it instilled great fear among a generation of Hungarians and long-simmering resentment against anything Bolshevik or even vaguely Russian.

Focused Meager Resources on Romania

The Russians did not come to Hungary's aid to help it secure its borders, though a Soviet Red Army detachment was sent but halted in Ukraine. On June 30, 1919, Kun complied with another directive from France, ordering the removal of troops from a part of Slovakia his Red Army had managed to take, and with that the Hungarian Socialists lost the support of their own military and much of the populace. There was enormous public resentment that France and other Western nations were punishing Hungary for its role in World War I, a conflict it had not instigated. In mid-July Kun ordered all resources be directed toward the Romanian front, but a better-equipped enemy defeated them and began a forward advance toward Budapest. Kun was forced to resign on August 1, 1919, fleeing first to Vienna. With that, Hungary's experiment in Bolshevik-style socialism came to an end after 133 days.

A new right-wing regime eventually prevailed in Hungary, even restoring the monarchy. Political power, however, rested in Admiral Miklós Horthy. Some participants in the 1919 Red Terror were tried and executed, and Horthy's government fought unsuccessfully with Austria for Kun's extradition. In the end, Kun was traded in a prisoner exchange in July of 1920, and placed on a train bound for Moscow. He worked with Zinoviev on the Comintern, or Communist International, and was sent to Germany in March of 1921 to help instigate a Communist revolution there. This ended in another ignominious defeat, as did his attempt to infiltrate the Austrian left in 1928, when he was arrested in Vienna with false identity papers. Hungarian authorities demanded once again that he be extradited, but Kun still had friends with high-ranking connections and he was spared a treason trial and certain execution when he was deported a second time back to Moscow.

Denounced Others

One recurring theme in Kun's life was his utter inability to retain friends and allies. He fought with Hungarians, with Russians, with Communists, and Lenin was said to have greatly distrusted him. Kun even made enemies among the expatriate Hungarian Communists in Moscow, and his grudge-settling betrayals of former friends to the Soviet secret police in the early 1930s came back to haunt him. In 1937, he was arrested and tried on charges of engaging in espionage and counterrevolutionary acts, sent to a prison camp, and executed after a quick trial. This occurred during the Great Terror, Soviet leader Josef Stalin's effort to purge all opposition within the Russian Communist Party, when many foreigners were rounded up and accused of spying, along with enormous sections of the Communist Party, the secret police, and even the military.

Stalin's successor Nikita Khrushchev admitted that serious human rights abuses had taken place in the 1930s and made efforts to correct the record. Kun was posthumously rehabilitated and his wife allowed to return to Hungary, where she died in 1974. Kun was also hailed by a newly resurgent Hungarian Communist Party that gained power in 1956, this time with the help of Soviet troops still stationed there more than a decade after the end of World War II.

Books

Mink, András. "Kun, Béla (1886–1938 or 1939)," in *Europe Since 1914: Encyclopedia of the Age of War and Reconstruction,* edited by John Merriman and Jay Winter, Charles Scribner's Sons, 2007.

Periodicals

New York Times, May 6, 1928.

Times (London, England), April 16, 1919; June 11, 1919.□

L

Jean de Labadie

French cleric Jean de Labadie (1610–1674) was among the high-profile defectors from the Roman Catholic Church during Europe's Protestant Reformation of the seventeenth century. In 1670, the former Jesuit priest founded his own Christian religious community, the Labadists. Their small, utopian-idealist communities flourished in the Netherlands, Germany, and even the Province of Maryland for a few decades after Labadie's death, but eventually passed into historical oblivion.

The Labadie surname is sometimes spelled "de la Badie." The future religious leader was one of seven children in a family headed by Jean-Charles Labadie, a French army officer who was granted a governorship of Guyenne for his service to King Henry IV, who died in 1610, the same year Labadie was born on February 13. The family lived in Bourg-en-Guyenne, near the larger city of Bordeaux, and Labadie's parents had once been part of a French Protestant population known as the Huguenots, who faced tremendous pressure from other French rulers to counter-reform, or return to the Roman Catholic faith.

Raised in Atmosphere of Dissent

Huguenots were followers of John Calvin, a French theologian who founded the Protestant Reformed Church of France in the 1530s. Like many other French Huguenots, Labadie's parents returned to their Roman Catholic customs and even sent their sons to a well-known school in Bordeaux, the Collège de La Madeleine, run by priests of the Society of Jesus, also known as the Jesuits. This brotherhood had a reputation for turning out excellent scholars and future leaders in their schools, and they played a major role in establishing the church's missions in the Americas.

Because of the Catholic/Huguenot divide, Labadie grew up in an atmosphere of vigorous religious debate and dissent. In Bordeaux and elsewhere in Europe, Protestant adherents railed against what they viewed were the excesses and corruption of the Church in Rome, while "papist" traditionalists acceded to the rule that their spiritual leader in Rome was the true representative of divine authority on earth. Firmly in the latter camp as a youngster, Labadie took readily to Roman Catholic religious instruction and the memorization of requisite Latin-language prayers. He entered the Jesuit order in 1625 as a novice, and in 1628, advanced to the level of subdiaconate. Yet as he came of age and read more religious-philosophy and theology texts in the course of his Jesuit education, he began to question some key tenets. Ordained a priest in 1635, he engaged in rancorous debates with his teachers and fellow students. He left the order to become a simple diocesan priest in 1639.

Experienced Religious Visions

Labadie had been a frail child and suffered from health problems as a young man. These may have prompted the onset of religious visions, or mystical events, in which he believed he was being singled out for a special divine purpose. He had been profoundly impacted by the writings of Augustine of Hippo, one of the so-called Fathers of the Church whose extensive writings had shaped Christian theology in its formative fourth and fifth centuries in the West. Labadie found some kindred minds inside the French Oratorians, a group of priests who believed the clergy could benefit from much-needed reforms to create a more worthy group of spiritual guides for the Roman Catholic faithful.

The beginnings of Labadie's break with Rome came during his tenure as a canon in Amiens, the great cathedral city. He was popular with his congregation and as a teacher of theology. Breaking with the French Oratorians, he allied with the Jansenists, named after Dutch theologian Cornelius Jansen, who died in 1638. Jansenist theology also hewed closely to the teachings of St. Augustine, but the Jansenists were especially loathed by the Jesuits, many of whom were in positions of ecclesiastic power in France. Labadie was initially protected from official reprimand thanks to the patronage of Cardinal Richelieu, a Roman Catholic bishop who was one of the key advisors to French King Louis XIII. Richelieu's successor, Cardinal Mazarin, took a stricter approach to potential dissenters within church ranks when he came to power in 1642 as chief minister to the King of France.

Abjuration Caused Sensation

Labadie was forced out of his post as canon priest in Amiens after he clashed with Mazarin. His religious visions had persisted, and he took shelter with a group of Cistercian nuns near Paris at the Port-Royal-des-Champs abbey, a Jansenist stronghold, where he spent long periods in solitary prayer and contemplation. While visiting another abbey, the Carrmelite Priory of Graville in Le Havre, he read Calvin's *Institutes of the Christian Religion,* an important and influential Protestant text.

Labadie had already began to lay out his own ideas in tracts published in the early 1640s. He wrote about spiritual sanctity, the sacraments, and interpretations of St. Augustine's texts. The books earned him further censure from Mazarin but were widely read, and he was banished to Toulouse in the south of France, where he stopped wearing his priest's robes and finally made a break with the Roman Catholic church on October 16, 1650, in nearby Montauban, France. Word of his formal abjuration, or rejection of Roman Catholicism, and conversion to the Protestant Reformed Church of France spread quickly, and the Jesuits denounced him publicly. Montauban had been an historic Huguenot stronghold in the past century and was a center of French Protestant theology. From 1652 to 1657, Labadie served as a pastor in the Montauban school of theology, but his zeal to reform continued, and he was eventually expelled from Montauban for his dissenting ideas, too. He continued to publish tracts in French, and was even threatened with sedition. From 1657 to 1659 he lived in Orange, also in the south of France.

Labadie's repudiation of Roman Catholicism, and his arguments that even the Reformed Church needed improvement, continued to establish him as a high-profile dissenter, and his name was known as far as England. The esteemed British poet and religious influencer John Milton wrote to him in the spring of 1659, inviting him to become pastor of the French-speaking Reformed Church congregation in London, but instead Labadie found his way to the Swiss city of Geneva, another epicenter of Protestantism. In the tolerant atmosphere of Geneva he began to gain a small following among a younger generation of religious seekers. Some had been inspired by his sermons, like Pierre Yvon, who had been a teenager in Montauban when Labadie preached there. Dutch Protestants were also drawn to Labadie's vision of a purer, more refined version of a Christian community. Among them was Johan Gottschalk van Schurman, who was pastor of a Reformed congregation in Basle, Switzerland. Van Schurman, who came from a wealthy, well-born German-Dutch family, urged Labadie to bring his ideas to the Netherlands.

Founded Own Church

In 1666, Labadie moved to the city of Middelburg, in the Dutch province of Zeeland, where he completed and published his best known work, *La Réformation de l'Église par le Pastorat* (The Reform of the Church Through the Pastorate). On his way there he stopped in Utrecht, where he met van Schurman's brilliant and equally renowned sister, Anna Maria van Schurman. The first woman ever permitted to attend the University of Utrecht, she was an accomplished scholar and polymath, wrote a widely reprinted text arguing in favor of the education of women, and was also an artist and sculpture. Van Schurman eventually gave away or sold all of her possessions to join Labadie's communal-living sect.

Labadie had quickly emerged as a leading figure in the Dutch Reformed church, though his teachings once again caused trouble with church hierarchy. He failed to follow the standard liturgy and refused to abide by a few fundamental beliefs and practices. Knowing the scripture and studying the Bible, he argued, were unnecessary, and a genuine believer needed no priestly or liturgical intercession to attain spiritual grace; long contemplative periods of prayer would bring the Holy Spirit, he maintained. He also rejected the practice of baptizing of infants—to cleanse them of the so-called Original Sin of Adam and Eve, as told in the Old Testament's Book of Genesis—and asserted that only conscientious adult minds should consent to this sacrament. Another major Labadist principle was the idea that the Second Coming of Christ was imminent, and those who had achieved spiritual grace and would participate in the Rapture were called Regenerates, or those who had been "born again."

In 1668, a Dutch Reformed Church synod suspended Labadie from its clergy, but he continued to gather with his followers and give lectures. A year later he was formally banished from Middelburg. With his followers he went to Amsterdam, where they acquired three adjoining houses and lived in what they called a "house church." About 60 Labadists formed this original group. Like Anna Maria van Schurman they sold or gave away their property and possessions, dressed in the plainest of clothing, and shared equally in the duties of running a self-sufficient community. The children were homeschooled and the Labadists even rejected the idea of Sunday as a day of rest and spiritual enrichment. They had their own printing press, which allowed them to disseminate Labadie's ideas to a wider audience.

Influenced William Penn in Germany

As the Labadist community continued to thrive in Amsterdam and gain new followers, Labadie was once again pressured to move on, with municipal authorities enacting various measures to halt their growth. In 1670 he accepted a generous offer from a friend of Anna Maria van Schurman's, Princess Elisabeth of Bohemia. A member of the powerful Wittelsbach dynasty, Elisabeth was the daughter of Frederick V, Elector Palatine and King of Bohemia, and on her mother's side she was the granddaughter of King James I of England. A staunch Protestant, Elisabeth had taken religious vows and was abbess of a religious community in Herford, Westphalia, in northern Germany. Her Herford Abbey became the Labadists' new home until 1672, when local unrest forced them once again to search for a new site. Labadie led his sect on a pilgrimage to Altona, near present-day Hamburg, Germany, that at the time was under Danish royal rule. He died there on his 64th birthday on February 13, 1674.

Other Labadist settlements were established shortly after Labadie's death. One was at Schloss Waltha in Wiuwert, which was part of the Dutch province of Friesland. The castle and its lands were donated to the Labadists by three of their followers, the van Aerssen van Sommelsdijck sisters. Their brother was governor of the Dutch colony of Surinam, located on the northeast tip of South America, and some Labadists went to build a settlement there, too. Their Providence Plantation was short-lived, decimated by tropical diseases and piracy. Another of Labadie's followers was the son of a prominent early New Yorker, Augustine Herman, one of the leading citizens of what was called New Amsterdam. His son Ephraim became a Labadist and helped secure a parcel of land in Cecil County, Maryland, in 1683, from his father's extensive holdings at what the elder Herman called Bohemia Manor. This was known as the Ephrata Labadist settlement at Bohemia Manor, and it holds a historical designation as the first successful communistic utopian group established in the Americas by those of European origins. The early Marylanders raised sheep, grew tobacco, and even prospered for a few years, but died out in the 1730s.

Books

Durnbaugh, Donald F., "Communitarian Societies in Colonial America," in *America's Communal Utopias,* edited by Donald E. Pitzer and Paul S. Boyer, University of North Carolina Press, 1997.

Frank, G., "Labadie, Jean de, Labadists," in *The New Schaff-Herzog Encyclopedia of Religious Knowledge,* edited by Samuel Macauley Jackson, Volume VI, *Innocents-Liudger,* Baker Book House, 1953.

Muller, H. J., "Labadie, Jean de," *New Catholic Encyclopedia,* 2nd edition, Gale, 2003.□

John Kinder Labatt

Irish-born brewer John Kinder Labatt (c. 1803–1866) founded the Canadian beer company that became one of North America's most popular beverage brands. His London, Ontario-based Labatt Brewing Company remained in the hands of Labatt descendants through Canada's short-lived experiment with Prohibition and, with the Molson Brewing Company, soldiered on into the 21st century as one of the most recognized Canadian beer labels in the world.

John Kinder Labatt's exact date of birth remains unknown, but he was likely born in 1803 and more definitely in Mountmellick, a sizable village in County Laoighis. This was in the middle of Ireland, in Leinster Province, and his family had been in the area for about a hundred years before that. The first "Labat" of note, as the family name was originally spelled, was a prominent lawyer in Bordeaux, France, named Etienne de Labat, born in 1625. The Labats were Huguenots, as French Protestants were called, and Etienne served for a time in Bordeaux's independent legislature.

Great-Grandfather Aided Stuart Restoration

A fiercely protective and extremely wealthy Atlantic coastal region renowned for its viticulture, Bordeaux had to be forcibly annexed into the Kingdom of France in the 1650s. Religious clashes between French Catholics and Huguenots were resolved with an Edict of Nantes, which guaranteed freedom of religion for French Protestants in Bordeaux and elsewhere. The famous edict went into effect before Etienne was born but was revoked in 1685 after continuing religious strife. Etienne's son André joined an army of Huguenots and other Protestants led by William of Orange, a Dutch prince and claimant to the English throne. William eventually prevailed and seized the British Isles and their thrones in 1689.

Soldiers like André Labat were among the Huguenots who were invited to settle in Ireland during the reign of William and his queen, Mary. André wound up in Mountmellick, a town that featured a fairly new and growing community of Quakers, also known as the Society of Friends, who came to Ireland from England. In 1707, André Labat married a woman named Christina Peppard, a union that produced two children, Marie and Andrew. Their son Labat married and had three sons, the second of whom was Valentine Knightley Chetwode Labat, father of John Kinder Labatt.

Left Laoighis for London

Labatt's mother was born Jane Harper and was the daughter of an Anglican vicar named Ephraim Harper; the grandfather's given name would be passed on through successive Labatt generations. Labatt was the first of seven children born to Jane and Valentine. Little else is known of the family save for the fact that one of Valentine's brothers, Dr. Samuel Labatt, was a well-known Dublin surgeon and expert on vaccination, an emerging medical field of the era.

Little is known of Labatt's early life, save for the fact that his mother was likely preoccupied with pregnancies and newborns until Valentine died in 1813. The family's Irish Huguenot background set them apart in County Laoighis, which was well settled by Anglo-Irish elites and prospered in the years before the Great Potato Famine struck in the 1840s. Labatt had left Mountmellick by then, setting out for England in 1830 at a relatively late age of 27. He was close to another Irish Huguenot family from Leinster, the Claris brothers, who were also in London. It is known that he found a job as a clerk for a timber merchant, and in August of 1833, he married a woman named Eliza Kell, whom he had met through the Claris family.

Eliza was just 17 years old when she wed Labatt, and while her background appeared to signify another solid match for a Labatt man, in reality her father Robert Kell was in serious financial trouble. A senior clerk at the Bank of England, Kell had made a bad investment and owed several others fairly large sums; in order to escape debtors' prison it was agreed that he would stay on in London and pay off his debts from his bank salary while Eliza, her new husband, and the rest of her family would emigrate to Canada, where the new bridegroom might make his fortune. This entourage included Eliza's mother, her younger brother, and younger sister.

Sailed for Canada

The ultimate success of Robert Kell's debt-repayment plan remains unknown, but shortly after the Kell-Labatt marriage in Twickenham, Middlesex County, the family set out for North America on a ship named the *William Osborne,* according to a family history traced by Labatt's descendants. The transatlantic crossing landed the party in New York City, from whence they sailed up the Hudson River to Albany, and then traveled via the recently opened Erie Canal into the Great Lakes region. They arrived in York, near Toronto, after a two-month journey.

Labatt and Eliza eventually relocated to the London, Ontario, area. This was an inland city but situated almost equidistantly from the shores of Lake Huron, Lake Erie, and Lake Ontario. At the time, the future Province of Ontario was called Upper Canada and belonged to Britain; nearby was another British colony, Lower Canada, which had been originally been settled by the French and had a large Francophone population.

Owned 400 Acres of Farmland

The couple, in addition to supporting Eliza's family, produced an astonishing 14 children, counting five sons and nine daughters. Before Labatt entered the beer-brewing business he appeared to have prospered as a farmer. He first acquired 200 acres south of London in 1834, deeded to him by the Canada Company, a charter company established by an Act of Parliament in Britain to encourage settlement of Upper Canada. Nine years later, he bought another 200 acres of land next to his farm. It is known that he made at least one trip back to England around 1846, probably to deal with some financial matters that his father-in-law was handling. He also apparently assessed the possibility of moving back permanently, but was appalled by the high cost of living in England.

Labatt had grown barley and sold the crop to brewers in Upper Canada. A beverage that had been perfected by the English a few centuries earlier, beer had become the alcoholic drink of choice in British Canada. The soil and climate of Ontario and Quebec were ideal for barley crops, and the hops plant that gave beer its distinctive tang also flourished in the brisk air. The Great Lakes region and St. Lawrence River basin, moreover, featured a plentiful supply of unpolluted freshwater, which was crucial to the brewing process.

The London in Ontario also featured a Thames River, like its English namesake, and which also snaked through the metropolis. Near one bend was the oldest brewery in the city, dating back to 1827. Its original owner was a brewer named John Balkwill, and what was called the Simcoe Street London Brewery was destroyed by a fire that engulfed much of London's city center—which had been built from the seemingly limitless supply of nearby timber—in April of 1845. The Balkwill family rebuilt the brewery but incurred heavy debts from construction costs, and sold it to Samuel Eccles, another London landowner. When Labatt learned that Eccles, a farmer-neighbor of his, had bought the property, he proposed a co-investment scheme. The pair went into business together in 1847, renaming the brewery "Labatt and Eccles." With six employees they began producing three brews, which were labeled simply XXX, XX, and X.

Established Line of Succession

Labatt bought out Eccles' share in the partnership a few years later, around the same time that a railroad line was built in London. This expanded the market for beer barrels from the London Brewery, as it was now called, and Labatt brought his sons into the business with him. One son was Ephraim, named after the great-grandfather Harper, and another was Robert, named after the bank clerk grandfather in England. A third son, John Jr., was born in 1838, and was shipped off to Wheeling, West Virginia, in 1859, to apprentice with an English brewer there named George Weatherall Smith, who taught the younger Labatt the process of making India pale ale, a popular beer that had proven exceptionally suitable to long-distance travel. When the U.S. Civil War ruined Smith's business in West Virginia, he headed north to Upper Canada and set up a brewing operation in Prescott, Ontario, near the border with New York State. That business was eventually purchased by Labatt's sons Robert and Ephraim and operated as Labatt's Prescott Brewery.

Labatt became one of the leading citizens in London, Ontario. He is listed as a donor to the building of Christ Church in 1844, an Anglican congregation, and was an also investor in the London and Port Stanley Railway a few years later. In the early 1850s, he became a member of the London municipal council, and held a seat on the London Board of Trade after 1863. His brewery became a monumental success, expanding along with the rest of Western Ontario, and Labatt was a savvy entrepreneur who occasionally joined forces with competitors like John Carling, who inherited a London brewing dynasty from his Yorkshire-born father.

Labatt died on October 26, 1866, in London, Ontario. His son Ephraim died a year later, and his widow Eliza outlived him by another 31 years. Labatt had arranged for his son John Jr. to take over the brewery, which became John Labatt Ltd. before his death in 1915. Labatt's designated successor was not a particularly successful investor in the other schemes through which he tried to expand the family fortune, but he did leave another large brood of children and his will specified that all nine of his children—including his daughters—take part in decisions that affected the business and its future legacy. That left Labatt's grandsons John Sackville Labatt and Hugh Francis Labatt, plus their seven sisters, responsible for carrying forward the family brand. One of those Labatt granddaughters was Frances Amelia Labatt, who married the son of an even more established Ontario family, the Cronyns. The Cronyn fortune was much tidier, coming from banking and railroad investments, and the couple's son Hume Cronyn became a well-known actor on the New York stage and in Hollywood films.

Grandson Kidnapped in 1934

The Labatt company, along with Molson, Carling, and O'Keefe, were among the handful of breweries to survive Canada's brief experiment with Prohibition. Labatt's heirs stayed in business by exporting to the U.S. market before Prohibition went into effect there, too, and were established enough to thrive in an illicit black market that transported beer brewed legally in Canada—which was permissible during Canadian Prohibition, whose laws criminalized only alcohol consumption, not its production—to border U.S. crossings during the years from 1920 to 1933, when the production and sale of alcoholic beverages in all U.S. states was illegal, but there were almost no laws to enforce consumption.

In August of 1934, Labatt's grandson John Sackville Labatt was kidnapped and held for ransom for several days in a case that made headlines as the first crime of this kind in Canadian history. John S. Labatt was one of Canada's richest men and had disappeared while traveling from the family's Sarnia-area summer home to downtown London. His luxury REO sedan was left parked in downtown London by his abductors with a ransom note on the windshield. The men later arrested in the abduction were a loosely organized gang of former bootleggers and rum-runners with ties to Windsor, Ontario, and Detroit, Michigan.

The Labatt Brewing Company became a publicly traded firm in 1945. The decision enriched a now-enormous clan of Labatt grandchildren and great-grandchildren, but in 1964, the company was acquired by the Joseph Schlitz Brewing Company of Milwaukee, which aroused intense public sentiment in Canada. The original London brew works continued to make and bottle the legacy brand, adding a lighter pilsner style in the early 1950s, Labatt Blue, to tie in with the company's sponsorship of a Canadian Football League team, the Winnipeg Blue Bombers. The company was purchased by Interbrew, a Belgian company, in 1995.

Books

Armstrong, Frederick H., "Labatt, John Kinder," in *Dictionary of Canadian Biography,* vol. 9, University of Toronto/Université Laval, 2003.

Goldenberg, Susan, *Snatched!: The Peculiar Kidnapping of Beer Tycoon John Labatt,* Dundurn, 2004.

Labatt, Arthur, *A Different Road: A Memoir,* BPS Books, 2012.□

Guy Lafleur

Canadian professional hockey player Guy Lafleur (born 1951) was one of the most popular and exciting players in the National Hockey League (NHL) in the 1970s. He was known as "le Démon Blond" (the "Blond Demon") while playing for the Montreal Canadiens. Though he later played for other teams, including the Quebec Nordiques, and owned a restaurant, among other activities, he remains deeply identified with the Canadiens and as a French-Canadian.

Born September 20, 1951, in Thurso, Quebec, Canada, Guy Damien Lafleur was the only son of the five children of Rejean and Pirrette Lafleur. His father worked as a welder in the McLaren pulp mill which dominated the small community of Thurso. When Lafleur was four years old, his father bought him ice skates and he soon began playing hockey. By the age of five, he was playing hockey at every opportunity in the rink his father built in the family's backyard.

Became Passionate about Hockey

By the time he was seven years old, Lafleur passionately focused on playing hockey outside of school. He even slept in his hockey equipment. Idolizing NHL player Jean Béliveau of the Montreal Canadiens, Lafleur also wore a number four jersey and wanted to play for the Canadiens or the Quebec Nordiques. Beginning at the age of eight, Lafleur's talent as a player began showing as he quickly moved through the levels of youth hockey.

At ten years of age, Lafleur played for Thurso in the Class C championship at the Quebec City International Pee Wee Tournament. It was at this game that scouts began noticing the gifted young player who was named most outstanding player after scoring 30 of his team's 48 goals. Three years later, in 1965, a major amateur team, the Quebec Junior A Aces (later known as the Remparts), invited Lafleur to join the team. Because Lafleur was only 14 years old, his father would not let him take the offer and move to Quebec City.

Became Outstanding Junior Hockey Player

A year later, the Remparts made the same offer and this time Lafleur's father allowed him to go. While finishing school and living away from home, Lafleur played center and right wing. He also demonstrated determinatoin and a penchant for working hard, being the first to arrive at the rink and the last to leave.

Lafleur's hard work paid off as he set a junior hockey record with 103 goals in the 1969-1970 season. In the next season, 1970-1971, he topped those numbers with 130 goals and 79 assists, making him the top junior player in the country. His Quebec Remparts won both their league title and a national championship, the Memorial Cup. Because of his success, the still teenaged Lafleur was treated like a hero in French Canada and drew thousands to his games.

© ZUMA Press, Inc./Alamy

Ready for the NHL, many scouts came to watch Lafleur as well, but Lafleur had been coveted by the Canadiens since at least 1968. Until 1970, Montreal's general manager, Sam Pollock, thought it would be easy to draft Lafleur because the NHL gave the Canadiens special considerations to draft the two top French-speaking prospects. This practice, however, ended the year before Lafleur entered the NHL amateur draft.

Drafted by the Montreal Canadiens

Through numerous trades and deals, primarily with the worst team in the league—the Oakland Seals—Montreal gained the first draft pick of the 1971 NHL draft and used it to select Lafleur. As soon as he was drafted, Lafleur was pressured to immediately live up to the legacy of Béliveau. Lafleur did not meet these expectations during his first three seasons, though his numbers were decent. As a rookie, Lafleur played in 73 games, with 29 goals and 35 assists. In his next season, 1972-1973, he had 55 points and won his first Stanley Cup.

It was during Lafleur's third season that his formidable skills started to show. Playing in one game against the Chicago Blackhawks, Lafleur deked (faked out) the entire Chicago squad and skated through them on the way to the goal. By the 1974-1975 season, Lafleur's confidence shone through and he began playing aggressive, dominant hockey. Though he had 56 points in 1973-74, Lafleur doubled that in 1974-1975 with 53 goals and 66 assists for 119 points. That year, Montreal won the first of four straight Stanley Cups.

Lafleur's numbers continued to increase for the next two Stanley Cup-winning seasons. In 1975-1976, he had 56 goals and 69 assists for 125 points, then 56 goals and 80 assists for 136 points in 1976-1977. Lafleur was also won the Conn Smythe Trophy in 1977 as the most valuable player of the Stanley Cup playoffs. In his last Stanley Cup season with the Canadiens, 1977-1978, he posted 132 points, including 60 goals and 72 assists. Lafleur's impressive statistics continued in the 1978-1979 and 1979-1980 seasons, with 129 and 125 points respectively. For his efforts, Lafleur was named a First Team All-Star from 1975 to 1980.

The reasons for Lafleur's success on the ice were simple. A passionate player, he was speedy and had a powerful, accurate shot that was difficult to stop. Lafleur also was known for his elegant passes, strong instincts, and skating artistry, with the ability to move more quickly than his opponents. Lafleur also used these skills in the service of his country, playing for Team Canada in the 1976 and 1981 Canada Cup tournaments.

Had Serious Car Accident

In the 1980-1981 season, Lafleur only played in 51 games, posting 27 goals and 43 assists. It was the beginning of the end of Lafleur's dominance. He suffered a knee injury that season, then was in a serious car accident after a night of drinking and partying led to him falling asleep while driving late one night. Though he suffered relatively minor injuries, Lafleur considered the event life changing. Lafleur decided to slow down and focus more on his family. Lafleur's numbers improved in 1981-1982, when he played 66 games and had 84 points, including 27 goals.

But Lafleur's skills were in decline, and he soon had less playing time and regularly clashed with coach Jacques Lemaire. From 1982-1983, he played in 68 games and had 76 points. In his final full season with the Canadiens, 1983-1984, Lafleur played in a full 80 games but had only 30 goals and 40 assists. At the beginning of the 1984-1985 season, Lafleur played in 19 games, posting only five points. Essentially forced to quit by his team because the Canadiens would not trade him and having lost confidence in himself, he announced his retirement in November 1984, at the age of 33. The move was unexpected in the hockey world, and the Canadiens retired his number ten jersey in 1985.

Returned After First Retirement

In retirement, Lafleur briefly worked in the Canadiens' front office, but soon realized he was not ready to leave the game. Already one of the all-time leading scorers in the NHL, Lafleur was inducted into the Hockey Hall of Fame in 1988. Soon after, he decided to come out of retirement and return to the NHL.

Lafleur told Robert Fachet of the *Washington Post,* "People laughed and said I was crazy. . . . I didn't want to wake up when I was 50 years and be second-guessing myself, telling myself I should have given it another shot. When I left Montreal, I was fed up with the game, but then I started to enjoy it again and I wanted to try it before I was too old."

Signing with the New York Rangers for the 1988-1989 season, he played in 67 games, netting 18 goals and 27 assists before another knee injury cut it short. Though he had a million dollar offer to play with the Los Angeles Kings, Lafleur signed with the Quebec Nordiques, preferring to play in the Canadian province where his career began. He played for two more seasons, appearing in 39 games with 34 points in 1989-1990 and in 59 games for 28 points.

Retired for a Second and Final Time

When Lafleur finally retired at the end of the 1991 season, his second to last regular season game was played at the Montreal Forum, the home of the Canadiens. He was honored with a six-minute standing ovation. In his final game, played at the home of the Nordiques, he was venerated with an hour-long pregame ceremony.

At the end of his NHL playing days, Lafleur had scored a whopping 560 goals and 835 assists. He also won numerous honors. They included the Art Ross Trophy (for scoring the most points) three times, the Hart Trophy (most valuable player) twice, and the Lester B. Pearson Trophy (most outstanding player in the NHL) once.

After his second and final retirement, Lafleur spent a season working in the Nordiques' front office as the director of corporate affairs. He also focused on his own business ventures. Having done numerous commercial endorsements in the late 1970s for products like Bauer, Yoplait, and Shasta, he returned to such business enterprises beginning in the early 1990s. In 1991, for example, he introduced an energy drink called Flower Power in Ontario. (Lafleur means 'the flower' in French.) In 2001, he became a commercial spokesman for Viagra in Canada.

More businesses followed, including opening a restaurant, a franchise of the Mikes chain in Canada, in late 2002. Called Mikes Signature Guy Lafleur Resto-Bar, it was located in Berthierville, Quebec, and was operated by his sons, Martin and Mark, as well as his wife, Lise. The restaurant was open for about a decade. In December 2012, he sold the restaurant building and closed the business after his sons showed no interest in continuing it.

Arrested and Convicted

Though Lafleur generally avoided any notoriety, both during his playing days and after they ended, this situation changed in 2008 and 2009. His younger son, Mark, was charged with more than 20 counts including sexual assault and forcible confinement. In January 2008, Lafleur was charged with giving contradictory evidence while testifying at two of his son's hearings in the fall of 2007. Lafleur lied about his son respecting a court-ordered curfew while remaining in the custody of Lafleur and his wife. While Mark Lafleur later pled guilty to 14 counts, Lafleur was found guilty in May 2009 and given a suspended sentence, which was thrown out in 2010. Lafleur also filed a $3.5 million lawsuit against the Montreal police and the solicitor general of Quebec because of his very public arrest.

Despite this difficult situation, Lafleur retained his passion for hockey, serving as an ambassador for the Montreal Canadiens and the Legends of Hockey after having been a regular on the Oldtimer's Hockey Challenge tour and other old-time hockey related events. Though he stopped playing even in these events in 2011, he continued to participate as a coach and in other capacities. In 2013, he was involved in Hockey Day in Canada, playing with NHL alumni in a celebration of Canada's national game. Lafleur was still a star, across the United States and Canada but especially in Quebec. As Quebec native and gifted NHL player Luc Robitaille explained to the *USA Today*'s Kevin Allen, "Guy Lafleur is Guy Lafleur. In Quebec, he is bigger than you can imagine. Even when involved in controversy, Guy Lafleur was still Guy Lafleur."

Books

Gale Canada in Context, Gale, 2009.
Great Athletes: Olympic Sports, Volume 2, Salem Press, 2010.

Periodicals

CBC News, June 18, 2009.
Hamilton Spectator (Ontario, Canada), September 5, 2001.
National Post (Canada), July 27, 2002.
Record (Kitchener-Waterloo, Ontario, Canada), January 31, 2008.
States News Service, March 8, 2013; March 10, 2013.
Toronto Star, July 31, 1991; June 18, 2008.
USA Today, February 27, 1991.
Vancouver Sun (British Columbia, Canada), March 22, 2003.
Washington Post, October 19, 1988.□

Ferruccio Lamborghini

The Italian manufacturing executive Ferruccio Lamborghini (1916–1993) founded the sports car company Automobili Ferruccio Lamborghini in 1963 and went on to produce some of the most distinctive high-performance cars of the modern era.

The 1960s were a golden age for sports cars, and Lamborghini had plenty of competition from Porsche in Germany and Britain's Jaguar, as well as from Ferrari at home in Italy. Lamborghini's cars, however, were marked by a fearlessness of design and an insistence on devising engineering solutions that made possible the realization of a vision—a vision that often came from Lamborghini himself. The Lamborghini firm had top-notch engineers, but Lamborghini's most important hires as an executive were automotive designers who asked for and got cars that looked like nothing that had ever been manufactured before. Lamborghinis, especially the Countach model introduced in 1974, created a model for the futuristic automobiles that appeared in films and television programs. Prior to his automotive endeavors, Lamborghini was already a leading Italian industrialist who was successful as a maker of tractors and of heating and air conditioning equipment.

Served in Italian Air Force

Ferruccio Lamborghini was born in Cento, Italy, a small town between the cities of Ferrara and Modena, on April 28, 1916. He grew up on a farm but showed mechanical aptitude from the beginning, tinkering with his father's tractors. He studied at a technical school in Bologna, planning to become a mechanical engineering apprentice and pursue that profession, but the entry of Italy into World War II sidelined his plans. Lamborghini was drafted into the Italian air force and stationed in a repair facility on the Greek island of Rhodes. As the war began to go badly for Italy, Lamborghini and his fellow engineers had to improvise spare parts from whatever vehicles and materials they happened to have at hand.

Lamborghini's wartime apprenticeship continued after he was captured by British troops, held as a prisoner of war, and forced to repair military vehicles under difficult field conditions. By this time Lamborghini was a skilled mechanic, and after the war ended he returned to Cento and opened a small repair shop. His true love was cars, and he was reputed to have built a Fiat himself from scratch. But in the hard times that followed the war in Italy, farmers in his hometown needed tractors, so Lamborghini set about building them, using parts from decommissioned military vehicles—even from German tanks.

Starting with one hand-built tractor a month, the Lamborghini Trattori (Lamborghini Tractors) firm expanded rapidly as Italy recovered. Lamborghini tractors featured air-cooled engines, an innovation in the industry. By 1960, the company was building and selling 400 machines a month, and Lamborghini diversified the company's operations into the manufacture of heating and air conditioning units. By the early 1960s, he was one of Italy's wealthiest individuals, and like many other wealthy Italians he had a passion for fast cars.

Dissatisfied with Ferrari Car

What happened next has become the stuff of legend. Lamborghini is said to have ruined the clutch of his Ferrari while trying to overtake another high-performance car on the *autostrada* superhighway, to have gone personally to Ferrari chief executive Enzo Ferrari to complain, and to have been impolitely received. He then installed a modified version of one of his tractor clutches in the car and had no further problems. Lamborghini himself told the story occasionally, but it exists in several different variants, suggesting that it was at least partly fictional: in one version, Ferrari simply refused to see Lamborghini, while in another he insulted Lamborghini by saying that learning to drive a tractor did not qualify him to drive a Ferrari. Whatever the truth of the story (and it should also be noted that the economic climate in prosperous early 1960s Europe was ready for a new high-end auto firm), Lamborghini decided to open a new factory in Sant'Agata, Italy, not far from Ferrari headquarters, to make his own sports cars, with 12-cylinder engines. Friends warned him against the venture, but he disregarded their advice as he learned more about how his competitors' cars were put together.

Hiring engineer Giampolo Dallara away from Ferrari, Lamborghini develped a new aluminum-and-steel engine with four cams, capable of 350 horsepower. The designer of the first Lamborghini car, the GTV, was ready with the chassis for the 1963 Turin Auto Show, but the engine at that point would not fit under the car's hood. The car was exhibited at the show with bricks under the hood to give it the right ride height. The GTV was replaced by the 350 GT, which went on the market in 1964 with a 280-horsepower engine. The 400 GT followed in 1966, featuring a 12-cylinder engine providing 320 horsepower. The GT name stood for Gran Turismo, or Grand Touring Car in English. Lamborghinis were produced only in dozens or hundreds, and the two GT models are now worth up to $300,000 at auction. Lamborghini's management style was relaxed: he worked closely with employees on new projects, and he continued to maintain a hobbyist's enthusiasm.

The next Lamborghini to reach the market was the Miura, whose name came from that of a breed of bulls used in Spain in bullfights. The car began as a side project on the part of Dallara and several other Lamborghini engineers, but Lamborghini soon realized its marketability and presented a prototype himself at the Turin Auto Show in late 1965. By the time the Geneva Auto Show began in Switzerland in March of 1966, the car was ready for market. With its engine mounted crosswise, toward the rear of the car, it was unlike anything else on the market except for Formula 1 race cars. The car could hit a top speed of 186 miles per hour, faster than any other regular-production car on the market at the time.

Marketed Model with Lifted Doors

The Miura was an instant hit among lovers of high-end sports cars, but even more sensational was the Lamborghini Countach, which went on the market in 1974 after several years of buzzed-about auto show presentations. The car's appearance was absolutely distinctive with its high rear spoiler, its air intakes mounted on the top of the back of the car, and above all its two doors, which did not open sideways but swung upward on front hinges, known as scissor doors. In the words of *Motor Trend,* "The definitive sci-fi fantasy on wheels, it anticipated a radical new era of sharply angular supercars."

As the Countach took hold in the market, the process of Lamborghini's departure from the company he founded had already begun. The company ran into financial trouble when a large order of tractors (which had remained part of Lamborghini operations) was cancelled in South America due to local economic conditions, and labor problems and a slowdown in Italy itself worsened the situation. In 1972, Lamborghini sold 51 percent of the company to the Swiss clockmaker Rosetti; later in the 1970s, he sold off the rest of his stock.

The Lamborghini firm continued to operate despite going into receivership in 1977, and it has always carried Lamborghini's name. Under various owners, including the Chrysler

Corporation and Tommy Suharto, the son of Indonesia's strongman president, the company continued to release new models that reflected Ferruccio Lamborghini's vision. Lamborghini himself took up residence at a 740-acre estate overlooking Italy's Lake Trasimeno, where he supervised a line of wines and opened a Lamborghini Museum. Lamborghini was married three times. His first wife, Clelia Monti, died giving birth to the couple's son, named Antonio and nicknamed Tonino. Lamborghini's second marriage, to Annita Borgatti, ended in divorce; his third marriage, to Maria-Teresa Cane, produced a daughter, Patrizia.

Ferruccio Lamborghini died on February 20, 1993, in Perugia, Italy, after suffering a heart attack. The Lamborghini firm, by then under Volkswagen's ownership, remained in operation as of 2013. In May of that year, the company's 50th anniversary was marked by a cavalcade of old and new Lamborghinis that toured Italy, stopping for celebrations under a 750-mile route.

Books

Cockerham, Paul W., *Lamborghini: Spirit of the Bull,* Smithmark, 1996.

Periodicals

Daily Telegraph (London, England), March 2, 2013.
Motor Trend, June 1993.
New York Times, February 22, 1993; April 21, 2013.
Times (London, England), February 23, 1993.
Toronto Star, August 11, 2012.

Online

"Ferruccio Lamborghini," *LamboWeb,* http://lambo.dk/history/ferruccio.hgm (November 14, 2013).
"Ferruccio Lamborghini, the Man and His Dreams (1916–1993)," *LamboCARS.com,* http://www.lambocars.com/lambonews/ferruccio_lamborghini_a_biography.html (November 14, 2013).□

Mauricio Lasansky

The Argentine-born American artist Mauricio Lasansky (1914–2012) was one of the figures responsible for the elevation of printmaking to its prominent place in the American art world.

Lasansky's influence was built on a three-legged base: he was technically ingenious, inspired equally by classical and contemporary models, and motivated as to subject matter by broad, humanistic concerns. Lasansky's prints used a great variety of printmaking techniques, some of them quite obscure, and he often combined multiple techniques in the same work. He drew on styles as diverse as Surrealism and Renaissance-era Spanish art, applying them to contemporary scenes and issues. Lasansky's most famous work, a set of tinted pencil works called *The Nazi Drawings,* constituted one of the first exhibitions shown at New York's Whitney Museum of American Art. As an educator Lasansky was also highly influential, introducing a new emphasis on printmaking into American art education.

Father Worked for U.S. Mint

Mauricio Leib Lasansky was born in Buenos Aires, Argentina, on October 12, 1914. His father, an immigrant Jew from Poland, had previously lived in the United States, where he worked in the printing department of the U.S. Mint; one of his uncles was also in the printing trade. As a child he hoped to become a musician, but he switched to art after some instruction from his father and began taking art lessons at age 13. The lessons paid off: Lasansky won awards in successive years at the Mutualidad art exhibition in Buenos Aires during his teens, and in 1933 he enrolled at the Superior School of Fine Arts. He was already making notable prints during this period and using an unusual technique involving relief etching on zinc. The so-called *zincográfia* technique had also been used by the Mexican popular printmaker Joś Guadalupe Posada, and popular Latin American printmaking was an important influence on Lasansky's work.

It was far from the only one, however. Lasansky would go on to absorb influences from both previous artists and the places where he lived and worked. In an interview with Jan Muhlert quoted on his website, Lasansky was asked about his influences and responded, "Everyone who came before me. Picasso to say somebody. To me [Andrea] Mantegna is one of the most important artists; through him you can decipher the Renaissance. [Francisco] Goya, of course, and [Matthias] Schöngauer. . . . Mantegna, Schöngauer and Rembrandt." Some of his early works appear to be influenced by the Surrealist style, but Lasansky maintained that Spanish Surrealism was unknown in Argentina at the time, and that he had been inspired instead by Latin American poetry. He was also quoted (in an essay appearing on his website) by Cedar Rapids Museum of Art director Joseph Czestochowski as saying that "my great teacher was the Depression. There were lots of ugly things then."

When he was 22, Lasansky became the director of the Free Fine Arts School in the small city of Villa María. "I was a city boy, like you, like anybody. I did not see a tree in my life. I didn't know what a tree was all about . . . what life is all about," he recalled to Muhlert on his website. Among his duties was to teach elementary school, and his students there also exerted an influence: "A child came into my studio one day and looked at what I was doing and said, 'I never saw a head without a body!' It made me stop and think." Children, he realized, "are so much more related to reality—and reality is an object in space—with all the mechanics of this object, whatever the object is, that conquers space or is conquered by space. You see, that is what you need to decide on—what you are, are you becoming conquered by the space or do you destroy that space and create a new one."

Examined Museum's Entire Print Collection

In 1943, Lasansky won a Guggenheim fellowship that enabled him to study in the U.S. Upon arriving he headed quickly for the Metropolitan Museum of Art in New York, and specifically for its print room. Astonished museum staff reported that he examined each of the museum's some 150,000 prints, an unprecdented feat. He was also a habitué of Atelier 17, a printmaking workshop founded in France by English artist Stanley William Hayter and moved to New York during World War II. There he gained facility in the intaglio technique, whereby a metal surface is etched with an image and covered with ink; the ink is then wiped off from the surface but remains in the cut groove, and a print can be made by compressing paper onto the metal.

After his Guggenheim funding ran out, Lasansky faced difficult times. Disillusioned by the rule of Argentine strongman Juan Perón, he did not want to return to Argentina. But he was married, had started a family that eventually grew to include four sons (William, Leonardo, Phillip, and Tomás) and two daughters (Nina and Jimena), and had few immediate prospects for work in the U.S. His command of English was inadequate, and he was working mostly in media that as yet had little commercial potential. Lasansky's prints from this period have a troubled tone. Things turned around for him, however, when he was invited to become a visiting lecturer in graphic arts at the University of Iowa in the fall of 1945.

Lasansky wasted no time getting to work in Iowa. He liked life in Iowa City immediately, for the move from New York to small-town Iowa reminded him of his earlier move from Buenos Aires to Villa María. Working quickly to improve his English, he proved an effective and energetic teacher, and he brought a selection of new printmaking equipment to Iowa's graphic arts department. After a year, Lasansky was made an assistant professor. He reorganized the department, essentially creating a full-scale printmaking program from scratch, advanced to the rank of associate professor in 1947, and became a tenured full professor the following year—an extremely fast rise through the academic ranks. Under Lasansky's leadership, Iowa would become one of the most prestigious graphic arts programs in the U.S.

Lasansky's own career as a printmaker also flourished at Iowa. His subject matter varied widely and was difficult to characterize; the images in his work ranged from members of his own family to Latin American folkloric material to war and American history. Perhaps the defining characteristic of Lasansky's work in the print medium was its ambition: he was known for large works that could involve as many as 60 individual plates, and, noted Margalit Fox of *The New York Times,* for "his vivid color and the complex layering of multiple techniques—including engraving, etching, drypoint, electric stippling and aquatint—in a single work." Lasansky's printing processes were so complex that he had special paper custom-made for him in France in a heavy-duty style that would stand up to multiple processes.

Drew Holocaust Scenes

In 1966 Lasansky completed his most famous work, *The Nazi Drawings,* consisting not of prints but of 30 individual drawings plus a triptych. They were drawn with lead pencil and also employed elements of collage. Lasansky had already addressed the brutality of Germany's concentration camps during World War II in his large print *Dachau* (1946) and other works. He worked on *The Nazi Drawings* between 1961 and 1966 in a period of intense creative ferment. "[W]hen I made the Nazi drawings, I made them as an angry young man, I wanted to spit it out, my point of view, no rules, no nothing, an instinctive reaction. I was upset, I wanted people to know that the world was upset," Lasansky recalled to Muhlert. One of the drawings shows a Nazi officer whose helmet is adorned with human teeth. *The Nazi Drawings* formed one of the opening exhibitions at New York's Whitney Museum in 1967, and have since been shown in numerous prestigious museums.

Lasansky returned to the theme of the Holocaust in *Kaddish* (1975), a series of eight prints. Another notable Lasansky work of the late 1970s was *Quetzalcoatl,* a giant image of a pre-Columbian Mexican god that used 54 separate plates. Lasansky believed it to be the largest print ever made using the intaglio technique. In 1976, the University of Iowa Museum of Art mounted a retrospective exhibition of his work, producing an exhibition catalogue that served as an overview of his career.

After his retirement from Iowa's faculty, Lasansky remained active as professor emeritus, and the vibrant printmaking workshop he had established continued to turn out recognized artists. Lasansky died at home in Iowa City, Iowa, on April 2, 2012, at the age of 97. University of Iowa professor Anita Jung told Logan Edwards of the *Daily Iowan* that Lasansky "was a passionate artist and had incredible discipline. He made art every day of his life." The National Gallery of Art in Washington, the Art Institute of Chicago, and the Brooklyn Museum are among the hundreds of museums internationally whose permanent collections include his works.

Books

Encyclopedia Judaica, Gale, 2007.

Lasansky, Mauricio, *Lasansky: Printmaker,* University of Iowa, 1975.

Periodicals

New York Times, December 18, 1988; April 8, 2012.

Online

"Mauricio Lasansky," *Cedar Rapids Museum of Art,* http://www.crma.org/collection/lasansky/lasansky.htm (October 12, 2013).

Mauricio Lasansky Official Website, http://www.lasanskyart.com/ (October 12, 2013).

"Renowned Local Artist Mauricio Lasansky Dies at 97," *Daily Iowan,* http://www.dailyiowan.com/2012/04/05/Metro/27781.htm (October 12, 2013).□

Niki Lauda

Austrian race car driver Niki Lauda (born 1949) won the Formula One world championship in 1975 and 1977, but is perhaps best known for surviving a horrific crash during the German Grand Prix in 1976. In addition to being a successful race car driver and team manager, Lauda also founded and owned two airlines and was a pilot himself.

© Heritage Image Parnership Ltd/Alamy

Born Andreas Nikolaus Lauda on February 22, 1949, in Vienna, Austria, his family was privileged and wealthy because of their newspaper and banking interests. By the time he was in his teens, Lauda was interested in driving race cars, and worked hard driving and testing them. He bought his first car when he was too young to drive, a 1949 drophead Volkswagen coupe, for about $100.

As Lauda explained to the *Toronto Star,* "I got it over to my family's place, where there was enough land to drive without a driver's license. When I drove this car, being so young, I suddenly felt what it is to control these cars in extremes. From then on, I got bigger in my passion." The fearless Lauda would take endless risks driving and jumping the car until the car broke down.

Defied Family to Race

An indifferent student who failed two years of the Austrian equivalent of high school, Lauda only gained a diploma by having his name forged on his girlfriend's diploma. Lauda's father wanted him to go to college. The 18-year-old Lauda, however, wanted to focus on racing. Because Lauda's father would not support his son's ambitions, Lauda approached his grandmother, who allowed him to borrow the funds for Lauda to buy a Mini Cooper S for hill-climbing events.

Showing skill as a driver, Lauda began driving competitively at the age of 19. His family was unsupportive, forbidding him from having a racing career. Breaking with them and moving to Salzburg, he made his own way in racing. He soon moved into Formula Three races, then Formula Two. By the early 1970s, Lauda was ready to move into Formula One races. Sponsorship and finding the right cars was always a difficult process, however.

Though Lauda was hired by the March Racing Team and landed sponsorship from an Austrian bank, his family interfered with his burgeoning career. Like Lauda's father, Lauda's grandfather wanted him to join the family business and went as far as to convince the bank to withdraw its sponsorship. Determined to race in Formula One, he borrowed $100,000 to begin his career on this level. It took him only two years to pay back the funds with interest.

Began Competing in Formula One

By 1974, Lauda had signed a contract with Ferrari not only to race its cars but also to test them. Lauda excelled at both, an unusual skill among drivers. While there is a similar skill set, the drivers must understand the cars in different ways. The test driver must be able to explain how to make the car perform better while the race car driver is only focused on driving fast.

Also in 1974, Lauda showed he could compete on the Formula One level, posting his first victories at the Spanish Grand Prix and the Netherlands Grand Prix. He even competed for the Formula One championship, but his loss in the British Grand Prix prevented him from winning that prize.

Lauda returned ready to win in 1975, and was able to pull it off. That year, he won numerous Formula One races, including the Swedish Grand Prix, United States Grand Prix, Belgian Grand Prix, the Monaco Grand Prix, Italian Grand Prix, French Grand Prix, and Dutch Grand Prix. Though he finished eighth in the British Grand Prix—in part because of weather conditions which flooded the track and caused an early end to the race—Lauda was able to hold on to his points lead and overcome criticisms of his skills and courage. At the end of the 1975 season, he won the Formula One championship and was named the World Champion of Drivers.

Nearly Died at German Grand Prix

Lauda also hoped to repeat in 1976, but faced unexpected trials and challenges. Lauda posted victories in the Belgian Grand Prix, Monaco Grand Prix, Brazilian Grand Prix, South African Grand Prix, and the ever elusive British Grand Prix. But it was the events at the German Grand Prix that provided a dark but definitive moment in his career.

The race was held at Nürburgring, the longest, most difficult, and most dangerous of the Grand Prix courses. Numerous drivers lost their lives there over the years. During the race's second lap, a wheel came off Lauda's car. Two other cars slammed into Lauda's wrecked vehicle, and it became engulfed in flames. It took more than a minute for Lauda to free himself from the inferno in his car, breathing in fumes and flames all the while.

After Lauda removed himself from the car, he was transported to the hospital for treatment. Given little chance to survive, Lauda was given last rites by a Roman Catholic priest. Deeply in pain and scarred from the fire, the driver willed himself to survive. He had numerous operations to remove smoke and debris from his lungs, lost half an ear, and his face was scarred and disfigured by burns. Within a week, he began walking, and then went to his country home in Austria to recuperate. For the next ten weeks, he did physical therapy, and returned to the racetrack at the end of the period.

Continuing to compete, Lauda regained the points lead, but only by a slim margin. The Formula One champion was decided at the last race of the season, the Japanese Grand Prix. Held in Fuji, Japan, the weather conditions were poor as rain had been falling at least eight hours before race time. Race officials started the grand prix after a two hour delay. Lauda began the race, but quit after two laps. Because of his decision, James Hunt became the new Formula One champ.

Won Two More Formula One Championships

Because Lauda essentially gave away his championship without a fight, there were questions about his courage. Despite the outcry, Lauda retained his Ferrari contract. Proving his detractors wrong, Lauda won his second Formula One championship easily in 1977. He posted wins in the Netherlands Grand Prix, South African Grand Prix, and German Grand Prix, and placed high in other races on the year.

Lauda only won one race in the 1978 Formula One season, the Italian Grand Prix. In 1979, he decided to take on new challenges by opening his own airline. Announced in April 1979 and beginning operations in May 1979, the airline formally known as Lauda Air Luftfahrtgesellschaft, A.G., was co-owned by Lauda, at 51 percent, and ITAS Austria, at 49 percent. Originally, Lauda Air began by flying two planes. Between 1980 and 1982, Lauda, who was the company's president and chief executive officer (CEO), piloted many of the flights himself after earning his commercial pilot's license.

Citing politics as the reason for being unable to continue to offer scheduled flights in 1982, Lauda leased his two planes to Egyptair and returned to Formula One racing with McLaren that year. He won the British Grand Prix in both 1982 and 1983. In 1984, Lauda won his third Formula One championship, after winning the Italian Grand Prix, French Grand Prix, South African Grand Prix, British Grand Prix, and the Austrian Grand Prix. It was the last time that Lauda would be named the World Champion of Drivers. He raced again in Formula One in 1985, posting his third win at the Netherlands Grand Prix and winning the Dutch Grand Prix. These would be his last Formula One victories as a driver, and he would formally retire in 1985.

Faced Airline Disaster

Returning his focus to his airline, Lauda made it a joint-stock concern and acquired two planes in 1984. In 1985, two more planes were acquired and the company focused on charter and inclusive tour flights to holiday destinations. Lauda's airline continued to expand throughout the late 1980s and early 1990s, adding more planes, personnel, and destinations in Europe, Asia, Australia, the Caribbean, and North America. In 1991, Lauda's airline had its worst disaster to date when one of its jets crashed a few minutes after take-off outside of Bangkok, Thailand. There were no survivors.

After the disaster, the airline continued to grow throughout the 1990s, as passenger boardings increased along with flights offered worldwide. By this time period, Lauda was acting as the airline's chairman as well, and, after 1993, controlled less than 40 percent of the company. The rest was traded on the Austrian stock exchange or was owned by Condor Flugdienst, GmbH. In 1997, after signing an agreement with Austrian Airlines, Lauda gave up 36 percent of his shares and majority control. He remained CEO, however.

By 2000, Lauda was facing a crisis with his airline, despite expansion of service and some growth in the late 1990s. In 2000, the company lost more than 558 million Austrian schillings on the year, and Lauda announced a rescue plan. The airline's partners and management later discovered that the foreign currency dealings within the company lacked internal financial control.

Forced Out of Airline

The board members of Austrian Airlines, which was buying a majority of Lauda Airlines stock, voted Lauda out of the management of the carrier. As this process was taking place, Lauda spoke out against Austrian Airline efforts to take over Lauda Air. In December 2000, Lauda resigned as CEO and took on a pilot's contract. Lauda was fired from this position within a few days by Lauda Air's new CEO, Ferdinand Schmidt, though Lauda became a captain with a company subsidiary a week later. In early 2001, Lauda Air was reduced to a charter operator as Austrian Airlines Group underwent a restructuring.

After being forced out of his airline, Lauda returned to racing. During the 2001 Formula One season, he was named Jaguar Racing's team chief. He also became the head of Ford's Premier Performance division. (Jaguar had been sold to Ford in this time period.) After 15 months, in November 2002, Lauda was fired from both posts, in part because he allegedly lacked the technical depth for those positions.

Two years later, Lauda returned to the airline business. He founded a new, low-cost airline, FlyNiki or just Niki, with five Airbus jets. Based in Austria, Lauda again flew jets regularly for his airline. He sold the company later in the decade. In the early 2000s, Lauda had other businesses as well, including Lauda Motion, which rented Smart cars in Vienna and Munich, Germany, and served as a commentator for Formula One races for German television.

Served as Subject of Film

By 2013, Lauda returned to racing as the non-executive chairman of the Mercedes AMG Petronas Formula One team. He also regained international attention because of a dramatic film by director Ron Howard, *Rush*. Released in the fall of 2013, it focused on the rivalry between Lauda and another Formula One racer, James Hunt, during the 1976 Formula One season, and included a dramatic depiction of Lauda's crash and its aftermath.

Seeing an early screening of *Rush* clarified aspects of Lauda's accident for him. He explained to Chrissy Iley of the London *Sunday Telegraph*, "When after the accident I came out into the world and people looked at me, they were shocked. It upset me. I thought they were impolite not to hide their negative emotions about my look. When I saw the movie it let me see the story from the other side .... It helped me understand why people were shocked." He added later in the interview, "I've been through a lot and I realise the future can't be controlled. I'm not worried. You can always learn to overcome difficulties."

Books

Smith, Myron, Jr. *Airline Encyclopedia: 1909-2000*, Vol. 2., Scarecrow Press, 2002.

Great Athletes: Racing & Individual Sports, Salem Press, 2010.

Periodicals

Birmingham Post, November 27, 2002.

Guardian (London), November 6, 2004.

Sahara Times, October 22, 2011.

Sunday Telegraph (London), August 25, 2013.

Toronto Star, June 8, 2013.□

AP Photo/Seth Perlman

Paul Lauterbur

The American scientist Paul C. Lauterbur (1929–2007) is best known for the invention of magnetic resonance imaging (MRI), now an extremely common medical procedure.

The MRI grew out of an earlier phenomenon, nuclear magnetic resonance (NMR), which was first explored in the late 1940s. Lauterbur was among the handful of scientists who developed the potential of NMR in its early years, even when his ideas faced considerable skepticism. A 1971 Lauterbur paper sketching out the ideas that led directly to the MRI was turned down for publication by the prestigious journal *Nature*, causing Lauterbur to quip later that the history of modern science might be traced by using papers that had been rejected by academic journals. Lauterbur's work was marked throughout his career by an intense, unconventional curiosity—qualities that were recognized when he was awarded the Nobel Prize in Physiology or Medicine in 2003.

Inspired by Aunt

Paul Christian Lauterbur was born in Sidney, Ohio, near Dayton, on May 6, 1929. He was of Luxembourgish and German descent. His father, Edward Joseph Lauterbur, was an engineer and part-owner of a local bakery-machinery firm. Lauterbur did not conform well to the rules of the Catholic school to which he was sent, but he greatly enjoyed the natural environment around the family's home in small-town Sidney. A special influence was an aunt, Anna Lauterbur, who, he recalled in his Nobel Prize autobiography, "was fascinated by natural history, always kept a terrarium in her elementary school classroom, and gave me a subscription to *Natural History* magazine." An incident in which Lauterbur tried to make rocket fuel from strike-anywhere match heads landed the boy in the hospital but confirmed his adventurous spirit; the glass shards from the explosion were never removed from his body.

Another figure who recognized the young Lauterbur's talent was a high school chemistry teacher, John McDermott, who excused him from normal classes and allowed him to pursue experiments, at college level, on his own. The teacher's instincts were vindicated when Lauterbur placed first in Ohio's statewide chemistry exams, and the family decided that he should go to college. Lauterbur attended the Case Institute of Technology in Cleveland (now part of Case Western Reserve University), matriculating in the industrial chemistry program but switching to a chemistry major shortly before graduating in 1951. A professor quoted by Joan Dawson in her biographical sketch *Paul Lauterbur, 1929–2007*, recalled Lauterbur as "a bright Case undergrad who refused to let his coursework get in the way of his education."

For two years after graduating from college, Lauterbur worked for the Dow Corning Corporation at its Mellon Institute research branch in Pittsburgh, Pennsylvania. Through an arrangement the institute had with the University of Pittsburgh, Lauterbur was able to take graduate science courses at the university without having to subject himself to the restrictions of working for a degree. He did original work in the chemical maniupulation of rubber and was exposed to the idea of NMR from visiting lecturers. In the then-new technique of NMR spectroscopy, a substance would be bombarded with electromagnetic radiation. The nuclei of the atoms of the substance would then emit some of the radiation that had struck them, as if in a kind of electronic reflection that showed the internal structure of the object.

Did Research While in Military

Before he had the chance to work much with NMR, Lauterbur was drafted into the United States Army. He was sent at first to a tank battalion at a Kentucky army base, but his superiors soon recognized his scientific accomplishments and transferred him to the Army Chemical Center in Edgewood, Maryland. He worked on chemical weapons for several months and then managed to get another transfer to a research unit that had a new NMR spectrometer—but no personnel who knew how to operate it. Lauterbur presented himself as an expert and was soon doing state-of-the-art research in the field of electronic imaging. He and a group of highly educated fellow draftees published four research papers while still in uniform.

After Lauterbur was discharged, he was ready to hit the ground running. He read widely in the imaging literature, began to investigate the use of NMR to display the structure of organic compounds, and published more than a dozen papers. He returned to Dow Corning in Pittsburgh after the company agreed to buy him his own NMR machine, but he grew increasingly restive as his superiors began to demand to know when they would see a commercial payoff from his work. After being refused permission to deliver a lecture before a scientific society in England, Lauterbur moved over to the University of Pittsburgh and quickly completed a Ph.D. thesis, receiving his degree in 1962. The following year he became an associate professor at the State University of New York at Stony Brook. Lauterbur had, he wrote in his Nobel Prize autobiography, "gotten over my distaste for professors by becoming one myself."

By the late 1960s, Lauterbur was able to take sabbatical leaves and do research at universities where the chemistry department's interests and facilities closely matched his own. One of those was Stanford University, where Lauterbur spent the 1969–1970 school year developing greater sophistication with NMR observations. Taking over a struggling scientific-instrument called Varian for a time (he had been on its board of directors), he became aware of the potential for a medical device that could produce images of internal organs without surgery or the dangerous effects of X-rays. Then, in 1971, he read a paper by Raymond V. Damadian that described how some tumors responded differently to magnetic fields than to normal tissue.

All these factors converged on the evening of September 2, 1971, when Lauterbur went out to a Big Boy restaurant in Pittsburgh. NMR observation by itself produced not an image of the internal structure of an object but instead numerical data that had to be computationally manipulated. Lauterbur realized that by introducing gradations or variations into the magnetic field applied, he could use the re-emitted energy from bodies inside the structure to produce actual images of those internal bodies. This key discovery, which led directly to the development of MRI machines, was first sketched out on a paper napkin.

Made Image of Clam's Interior

Lauterbur's first experiments with the new technology were necessarily rudimentary. He made an MRI image of a clam his daughter had collected at the beach. It "looked pretty much like a clam," Lauterbur's Stony Brook colleague David Hanson told the *New York Times.* "Some people thought it was sort of wacky." *Nature* initially rejected Lauterbur's first paper describing the breakthrough, then accepted it after a key section was deleted. As MRI technology developed, many hospitals refused to use it, holding on to time-honored X-ray imaging despite the hazards involved for both patients and technicians. Lauterbur pressed on, confident of the value of his discovery. He joined the faculty of the University of Illinois in 1985.

At first Lauterbur called his new discovery zeugmatography, using the Greek word "zeugma" ("yoke") because the technique linked, or yoked, chemistry and spatial imaging. The name did not catch on, and neither did versions of the nuclear magnetic resonance name—patients feared the association of the technique with nuclear radiation, even though the word "nuclear" in the term referred only to the nuclei of ordinary atoms. Gradually, however, and partly because of further refinements developed by Lauterbur himself, the MRI became common. By 2013, an estimated 400 million individuals had undergone MRIs. Lauterbur and British physicist Peter Mansfield, who had developed a mathematical technique for analyzing MRI data and independently from Lauterbur devised the gradient-field idea, shared the 2003 Nobel Prize for Physiology or Medicine; Damadian took out full-page newspaper advertisements protesting his exclusion.

In his later years, Lauterbur took up a typically ambitious task: he began to investigate the chemical origins of life, or, as he put it in his Nobel Prize autobiography, "the origin of biology from chemistry." Before his new ideas could be fully evaluated, he died from kidney disease in Urbana, Illinois, on March 27, 2007. Lauterbur was married twice; his first marriage, to Rose Mary Caputo, produced two children, Daniel and Sharon (who renamed herself Sharyn), but ended in divorce. During his second marriage, to Illinois physiology professor Joan Dawson, Lauterbur had a second daughter, Elise.

Books

Notable Scientists from 1900 to the Present, Gale, 2008.

World of Chemistry, Gale, 2006.

Periodicals

American Scientist, May-June 2007.
Economist, April 7, 2007.
New York Times, March 28, 2007.
Times (London, England), April 17, 2007.

Online

"Paul C. Lauterbur—Biographical," *Nobelprize.org,* http://www.nobelprize.org/nobel_prizes/medicine/laureates/2003/lauterbur-bio.html (October 14, 2013).
"Paul C. Lauterbur: Biography," *IEEE Global History Network,* http://www.ieeeghn.org/wiki/index.php/Paul_C._Lauterbur (October 14, 2013).
"Paul Lauterbur, 1929–2007: A Biographical Memoir by Joan Dawson," *National Academy of Sciences,* http://www.nasonline.org/publications/biographical-memoirs/memoir-pdfs/lauterbur-paul.pdf (October 14, 2013).
"Paul Lauterbur, 77; 'The Father of the MRI,' *Los Angeles Times,* http://www.latimes.com/news/science (October 14, 2003). □

Louis Le Brocquy

Louis le Brocquy (1916–2012) is widely considered the most important Irish artist of the 20th century.

WENN/Dardis Mcdonnell

Le Brocquy's work continued to develop over his long career, and he is not classifiable under a single style umbrella. Self-taught, he explored new sources of inspiration constantly, and as he digested them his work took sharp stylistic turns. He began painting in a realistic style inspired by French and Spanish art, turned to an intensive examination of the lives of tinkers (Irish Travellers), began in the 1950s to cultivate an increasingly minimal style marked by the use of gray and increasingly white in his paintings, and finally, late in life, painted a unique series of heads of famous figures in contemporary Irish culture. These finally brought le Brocquy recognition at home; for much of his career, he lived abroad and was better appreciated by critics in France and Britain than in Ireland itself. Even at the height of the influence of abstract art in the 1960s, le Brocquy held to representational styles. Human isolation in the modern world was a common theme in his work.

Planned to Work at Family Refinery

Louis le Brocquy (pronounced le BROCK-ey) was born in Dublin, Ireland, on November 10, 1916. Despite its French name, his family had lived in Ireland for many generations; his grandfather had founded a small oil refinery in Dublin. As a student at Trinity College in Dublin, Le Broczquy majored in chemistry, planning to join the family oil business. As a child, however, he was interested in art, and his creative instincts may have been nurtured by his family's friendship with the Irish poet William Butler Yeats.

As an artist, le Brocquy was completely self-taught. As a university student he became increasingly interested in painting, and the acceptance of two of his first efforts—perhaps the very first two—for an exhibition at the Royal Hibernian Academy only intensified his desire to change careers. (Later, with a considerably larger portfolio of work to his credit, he would suffer rejections from that highly traditionalist institution.) After he graduated in November of 1938, despite the increasingly dire political situation in Europe, le Brocquy embarked on a grand tour of major museums. He and his first wife, Jean Stoney, settled in the south of France and had a daughter, Seyre. They were forced to return to Ireland by the German invasion of France in 1940, and the marriage dissolved soon after that.

Such early works as *Southern Window* (1939) followed the styles of French artists Eduard Manet and Edgar Degas. In the words of le Brocquy's website, they "establish the artist's ongoing preoccupation with the inward isolation of the individual." *The Picnic* (1940) was an unusual depiction of that generally enjoyable recreational event: le Brocquy depicts a group of figures, each lost in his or her own thoughts and not communicating with one another. In 1943, le Brocquy and his sister Melanie, a sculptor, joined with other young artists to launch the Irish Exhibition of Living Art. The theme of isolation continued in his work after the war in a series of increasingly modern paintings of the tinkers, now more often known as Irish Travellers, an indigenous Irish group that lives on the road like the gypsies of Eastern Europe.

Won Prize at Venice Biennale

One of the first le Brocquy paintings to gain international attention was *A Family* (1951). Painted in a style reminiscent of the Cubism of Pablo Picasso and Georges Braque, it depicts in gray and brown colors a nude, partially featureless family on or beside a bed, with a threatening-looking cat emerging from under a bedsheet. The work was rejected for exhibition at the Municipal Gallery in Dublin and was condemned by many in the Irish art world. Undaunted, le Brocquy entered the work at the prestigious biannual Venice Biennale in Italy in 1956. It won a major prize there and was purchased by the Nestlé Foundation for its offices in Milan. The year 1956 was a propitious one for le Brocquy personally as well: he met the painter Anne Madden, and the two married in 1958. The marriage lasted until le Brocquy's death.

The couple settled in the French Alps, where they raised two sons, Alexis and Pierre. Le Brocquy would not make Dublin his permanent home again until 1996. He found a ready market for his work in Paris and London galleries. Although le Brocquy's works in the 1940s had been very colorful, *A Family* marked a move toward gray and finally almost entirely white paintings that were called Presences. In the works of le Brocquy's so-called White Period, lasting from roughly 1956 to 1966, figures appear as ghost-like apparitions, with sparse lines showing details only vaguely.

The minimal quality of le Brocquy's paintings led to comparisons of his style with that of Picasso's later work, but he seems to have arrived at some of his stylistic traits independently. As Michael McNay noted in the London *Guardian,* even le Brocquy's tinker paintings "suggest late-period Picasso before the event." In 1963 le Brocquy experienced a crisis of inspiration and destroyed about 40 of his own paintings. According to the London *Independent,* he told a friend that the destroyed paintings had been executed by "Henry, the monkey which lurks in us all."

Inspired by Polynesian Heads

Le Brocquy began to emerge from this crisis when he visited the Musée de l'Homme anthropology museum in Paris in 1964, and saw there some preserved and decorated skulls from Polynesia, covered with clay to preserve the ancestral spirits inside. Inspired, Le Brocquy began to paint a series he called Ancestral Heads, with a minimal style similar to that of his earlier work, but with definite human personalities. The Ancestral Heads did not depict any particular individuals, but in the 1970s, he began to paint heads of famous cultural figures from Ireland and elsewhere, including Yeats, James Joyce, Picasso, and later U2 frontman Bono. The Bono head was used in an international advertising campaign, "The Irish Mind," intended to showcase Ireland's creative economy.

The Polynesian example led le Brocquy to find similar beliefs in his own culture. "Like the Celts I tend to regard the dead as this magic box containing the spirit," he was quoted as saying by Mark Axelrod in *Irish America.* "Enter that box, enter behind that billowing curtain of the face, and you have the whole landscape of the spirit." Le Brocquy worked from photographs of his subjects, mostly from memory rather than directly. "Where I have worked from them directly," he was quoted as saying by Axelrod, "I have consulted two or more at the same time and—since these photographs bear little consistent resemblance to each other—I have encouraged differing and sometimes contradictory images to emerge spontaneously . . ." Le Brocquy's heads have an uncanny quality of capturing multiple qualities of a subject's personality.

A distinctive feature of le Brocquy's artistic career was his activity in unusual media, including textile design, tapestry, stained glass, mosaics, book illustration, and stage and costume design. In 1969, he provided illustrations for a translation of the ancient Irish epic *The Táin,* by Irish poet Thomas Kinsella. He later turned those prints into a set of tapestries, and in later life he had a successful career as a tapestry designer—a profession rare among modern artists.

Toward the end of his life, le Brocquy finally attained the prestige in his home country that he had already received abroad. In 2002, *A Family* was acquired by the National Gallery of Ireland, making le Brocquy the first living Irish artist to have a work included in the museum's permanent collection. In the United States, his works are owned by the Albright-Knox Museum in Buffalo, New York, the Detroit Institute of Arts, the Guggenheim Museum in New York, and the Hirshhorn Museum in Washington, D.C. A display of the *Táin* tapestries at the Irish Museum of Modern Art in 2004 attracted record crowds for the institution. Le Brocquy's 90th birthday celebration in 2006 was celebrated with a round of retrospective exhibitions at London's Gimpel Fils gallery, the Galerie Jeanne Bucher in Paris, and museums and galleries across Ireland. In 2007, he received the Freedom of the City of Dublin award, the city's highest honor. Le Brocquy died at home in Dublin on April 25, 2012, with Madden at his side.

Books

Contemporary Artists, Gale, 2001.

Walker, Dorothy, *Louis le Brocquy,* Ward River, 1981.

Periodicals

Globe & Mail (Toronto, Ontario, Canada), April 27, 2012.

Guardian (London, England), April 28, 2012.

Independent (London, England), April 26, 2012.

Telegraph (London, England), April 28, 2012.

Online

"Bio," Louis le Brocquy Official Website, http://www.lebrocquy.com/ (October 15, 2013).

"Louis le Brocquy," *Tate Gallery* (London), http://www.tate.org.uk/art/artists/louis-le-brocquy-1480 (October 15, 2013).

"Louis le Brocquy (Irish, 1916–2012): A Family, 1951," *National Gallery of Ireland,* http://www.nationalgallery.ie/en/Collection/Irelands_Favourite_Painting/Final_brocquy.aspx (October 15, 2013).

"Portrait of an Irish Artist: Louis le Brocquy," *Irish America,* http://irishamerica.com/2011/07/portrait-of-an-irish-artist-louis-le-brocquy/ (October 15, 2013).□

Brian Lenihan Jr.

Irish politician Brian Lenihan Jr. (1959–2011) was a popular public figure and a member of a prominent political family. He served Ireland in several positions, including Minister of Finance (from 2008–2011). He assumed that role during a global financial crisis, which compelled him to make some controversial decisions that would have substantial impact on Ireland's economy.

-/AFP/Getty Images

Brian Lenihan Jr. was a member of one of Ireland's most prominent political families. His father, Brian Lenihan Sr. (1930–1995), who died from complications resulting in a liver transplant, served in a number of cabinet positions including Minister for Foreign Affairs and Minister for Justice. The senior Lenihan's grandfather, Patrick Lenihan, served in the conservative, Republican Fianna Fáil party, as did the younger Lenihan's aunt Mary O'Rourke (cabinet) and brother Conor Lenihan (minister).

Brian Lenihan Jr. entered politics in 1996 after a successful early career as a barrister and law lecturer. His first political triumph came in 1996 when he was elected as a Fianna Fáil TD (or Teachtaí Dála) for Dublin West, which is a political constituency in the Irish Parliament. He held that position until his death from pancreatic cancer in 2011. He also served as Irish Minister of State for Children (2002–2007), Irish Minister for Justice, Equality, and Law Reform (2007–2008), and Irish Minister of Finance (2008–2011). O'Rourke described him as a family "torch bearer."

As Ireland's financial minister, Lenihan was appointed during a period of economic turmoil: he assumed the post during the 2008 global recession. His subsequent strategies were designed to help Ireland through this difficult period, but what he developed proved controversial and drew harsh criticism, although he remained a popular figure—a friendly, constantly smiling man—and one of the period's most dedicated public servants. Indeed, he had to help Ireland avoid national bankruptcy during the worst global economic crisis since the Great Depression.

Lenihan was born as Brian Joseph Lenihan Jr. in Dublin, Ireland, on May 21, 1959, into what his aunt Mary O'Rourke described as a political "dynasty." She also used the phrase "Camelot," to describe her family's dynastic nature, which suggested that she thought the Lenihan heritage was the equivalent of the United States' Kennedy family. Brian Lenihan's popularity in part justified this assessment.

Became a Lawyer

Lenihan's father entered politics in 1961, and his grandfather followed in 1965, an unusual set of circumstances: This was the first time a parent followed a child into the Irish Parliament. Meanwhile, the younger Lenihan received education at Belvedere College and Trinity College (both in Dublin) where he studied law and received an honorary degree. The accomplishment led to a scholarship at the University of Cambridge in England. Again, he gained top honors and by 1984, he was admitted to the bar. For the next several years, he worked as a barrister, an activity he combined with part-time lecturing at Trinity College.

However, his education and youthful experience—as well as his family heritage—led to a career in politics. Starting with his teenage years, he had been involved with the local Fianna Fáil party, which was a smaller faction of a political entity that had resulted from Ireland's ongoing fight for independence. The party, whose name translates into "soldiers of destiny," is a conservative, Republican organization that extends as far back as March 1926, when it was founded by Eamon De Valera (1882–1975), a leading force in Irish politics and independence. Lenihan helped canvas for his father during his election campaigns. During his political career, the senior Lenihan held cabinet posts that included Justice, Foreign Affairs, and Tanaiste. He suffered a devastating presidential election defeat in 1990, however. One year after his father died in 1995, Brian Lenihan Jr. ran for office, something that required much persuasion. But his advisors made a good point: there was a political gap that needed to be filled in Dublin West, and only a Lenihan family member could effectively close the fissure.

This would mean a hard, even bitter, political fight. Even Noel Dempsey, Fianna Fáil's director of elections, predicted a loss for his faction. But Lenihan pulled out a narrow win over his opponent, Joe Higgins (born 1949) of the Socialist Party. The margin of victory was a mere 252 votes. The next year, 1997, in the general election, Lenihan kept his seat. That same year, he married Patricia Ryan, who became a circuit court judge. Lenihan would then become a perennial winner, retaining his seat in each subsequent election.

Following the 1997 election, the then-Taoiseach (or prime minister of Ireland) Patrick Bartholomew "Bertie" Ahern (born 1951) positioned Lenihan to lead a new Constitutional Review Committee. Observers had expected Lenihan to gain a junior ministry position. Meanwhile, Lenihan would lead in popularity polls with his constituents. In 2002, instead of gaining a cabinet post, Lenihan became a junior minister at the Department of Health. In this post, he was charged with responsibility for the general welfare of Irish children. Lenihan provided oversight on the reform of Irish adoption laws and the suitability of childcare workers. In 2005, he oversaw publication of the controversial Ferns Report, which investigated child sexual abuse by clerics in the Roman Catholic Diocese of Ferns, located in County Wexford, Ireland. In 2006, he addressed a United Nations committee on child rights.

It had been no secret that Ahern had a great dislike for Lenihan. However, Ahern had to ultimately acquiesce to public opinion. Ahern appointed him to the post of Minister for Justice. Lenihan's position was relatively brief, in political terms. Meanwhile, Ahern resigned amid a 2008 scandal about his personal and professional financial transactions. This led to the placement of a new Fianna Fáil head, Brian Cowen, who had been Minister of Finance. In a move that surprised some, he chose Lenihan as his ministerial replacement.

Faced Potential Financial Collapse

Lenihan's delight about gaining his new appointment did not last long, for he ran head-first into major problems in Ireland: an end of a robust building boom, the 2008 recession, and a projected budget deficit of frightening proportions. There were justified fears that the Irish banking system would itself collapse following the collapse of Lehman Brothers in the United States and the credit crunch on global financial markets. Ireland's banking system was left exposed and vulnerable. Up to this point, the Irish economy had been experiencing robust growth. But the Lehman Brothers collapse and the global credit market freeze revealed something disturbing: years of incautious spending by Irish banks to support an overstated property market. The Irish economy was in danger of going down with its banking system.

The situation led to the introduction of a controversial, government-based banking guarantee in September 2008. Essentially, taxpayer money would help throw a life line to six sinking banking institutions. Lenihan presented his first emergency budget in October 2008, which included a highly criticized proposal that would eliminate the automatic right of citizens over 70 years of age to medical cards. Within fourteen months, three budgets would be proposed, the third being one of the most severe in Ireland's economic history. All the while, Lenihan was up front with the public, trying to provide full disclosure, as he appeared frequently on television and commented extensively on radio about his perceptions of the problems and how the situation could be best handled.

Made Two Controversial Economic Decisions

As Minister of Finance, Lenihan made two of the most significant decisions ever by anyone in his position: introduction of a blanket guarantee on all debt of Ireland's banks, and the signing of an emergency financial assistance deal with the European Union (EU) and the International Monetary Fund (IMF).

The first decision involved guaranteed deposits of a great part of Irish banks' debt. Lenihan felt his decision would avoid a marketplace panic and a potential subsequent banking system collapse. But it proved to be a wrong decision, as the government would have to pay the bill. The country's budget deficit greatly increased. Investors had no interest in buying more of Ireland's debt. As it turned out, the government could not handle the costs. This led to Lenihan's second decision, a rescue deal, negotiated at $93 billion in November 2010, with the EU and the IMF. As quoted in the *New York Times* (via a radio interview with the British Broadcasting Corporation), Lenihan said, "I had fought for two and a half years to avoid this conclusion. I believed I had fought the good fight and taken every measure possible to delay such an eventuality. And now hell was at the gates."

This negotiated bailout exacted a substantial toll. It compelled Ireland to promise to observe a harsh, four-year austerity program. Further, the interest rates were severe. While the terms were humiliating, Lenihan remained a popular figure in Ireland. The fact is a bit mystifying, for as *Vanity Fair* magazine reported in its March 2011 issue in Michael Lewis' feature story, taxpayers were stuck with a big portion of the bill. Lewis wrote, "That had been the strangest consequence of the Irish bubble: to throw a nation which had finally clawed its way out of centuries of indentured servitude back into it."

Diagnosed with Cancer

Lenihan was diagnosed with pancreatic cancer in late 2009. In December of that year, he was suffering from insomnia, and he was hospitalized. At first, it was thought that his sleepless nights resulted from a hernia condition. But on December 26, it was officially announced that he had been diagnosed with pancreatic cancer. In January 2010, Lenihan explained to his country that he would have to undergo intensive treatment, which would include chemotherapy and radiotherapy. Treatment seemed to be going well, and Lenihan remained positive, at least in public statements. He succumbed to his disease on June 10, 2011, at his home in Dublin, however. He was survived by his wife Patricia and their two teenage children, Tom and Claire.

Irish Prime Minister Enda Kenny commented (as recorded in the *New York Times,* "During his illness, which he fought with serenity, he courageously continued to fully perform his ministerial responsibilities in the most challenging and difficult circumstances."

Immediately after his death, a flood of positive official comments were issued, even from those who disagreed with his decisions. His hand may have been moved by misinformation, they conceded. This revisionist perspective indicates the high regard in which Lenihan was held: His integrity was never in doubt, his skills at using media to communicate were deemed honest and effective, and his commitment to public service—even as he was dying—never faltered.

Periodicals

Independent, June 10, 2011.

The Irish Examiner, June 14, 2011.

The Journal, June 10, 2011.

The New York Times, June 10, 2011.

Vanity Fair, March, 2011.

Online

"Michael Lewis on How Merril Lynch and Brian Lenihan Stuck the People of Ireland a Debt of 106 Billion," *Vanity Fair,* http://www.vanityfair.com/online/ (October 31, 2013)

"Brian Lenihan," *NNDB,* http://www.nndb.com/people/587/000274762/ (October 31, 2013.□

Zivia Lubetkin

Polish resistance fighter Zivia Lubetkin (1914–1976) held a military-rank leadership role in the Warsaw Ghetto Uprising of 1943. A holdout in the Warsaw Ghetto as its population was being liquidated in Nazi German death camps, Lubetkin put her life at risk on an almost-daily basis. She was the only woman on the high command of the Jewish Fighting Organization, which in April of 1943 mounted the only open, armed civilian rebellion against German occupation anywhere in Europe during World War II.

Zivia Lubetkin came from a modest family of Polish Jews in present-day Belarus. Born on November 9, 1914, in Byteń, near the larger city of Słonim, she was one of seven children, with a single brother among the six sisters. She studied the Hebrew language in her teens and was drawn to the Zionist youth movement at an early age. Zionism was a political movement that asserted the Jews' right to a safe homeland under their own rule, free of the discrimination and violence that had followed them for centuries through Europe and Eurasia. The Zionist movement itself had two wings: there were right-wing groups like Betar at odds with left-leaning factions like Dror (Freedom), a Socialist-allied youth organization.

Delegate to World Zionist Conference

Lubetkin joined Dror and moved to Warsaw when she finished her schooling. Among Zionism's goals were building up a young self-defense force and also providing training for artisan occupations and even farming for future self-sufficiency in Eretz Israel, the hoped-for Jewish homeland. By the time Lubetkin was in her late teens there were pockets of Zionist settlements in the British Mandate for Palestine, near the original kingdom of the Israelites of ancient times. Lubetkin worked in a bakery and as a farmhand before moving up to positions of increased responsibility as a Dror recruiter and regional organizer.

Lubetkin eventually became a member of Dror's executive council and in the mid-1930s helped Dror merge with another Zionist group, HeHalutz (The Pioneer), to become Dror-HeHalutz. She was elected to a seat on the National Jewish Council of Poland as the group's representative, and traveled to Switzerland in the summer of 1939 as a delegate to the World Zionist Congress in Basel. She came back to Poland just in time for the country's invasion by Nazi Germany on September 1, 1939. The Polish Army attempted to stave off collapse, but after a month Nazi troops marched through Warsaw's streets in triumph. This also marked the start of World War II, as France and Britain went to war against Germany and its increasingly aggressive leader, Adolf Hitler.

Lubetkin spent the first weeks of the war in Kowel, a city in present-day Ukraine that was a center of HeHalutz leadership. She worked to build an underground resistance network to aid Jews both there and in Lviv, a larger Ukrainian city. These were both in disputed border areas near Poland and had large Jewish populations; when the war began these areas were seized by the Soviet Union as part of a Soviet-Nazi non-aggression pact of 1939.

Went Underground in Warsaw

Daringly, Lubetkin opted to re-enter Warsaw in January of 1940, now under strict German military occupation. She was well aware that Nazi Germany's drastic laws restricting rights of its Jewish citizens—indeed, stripping them of any citizenship rights at all—would apply in occupied lands, too. In Poland, Jewish businesses were forced to close and Jewish assets seized. Nazi officials also began issuing relocation orders, forcing cities with large Jewish populations to wall off the old Jewish quarter. The Warsaw Ghetto was sealed off on November 16, 1940, after Jewish laborers were forced to build the high brick walls that kept them from the "Aryan" or German part of the city. The Ghetto, with nearly half a million Jews forced into it, became a place of severe food shortages, disease outbreaks, and abject misery.

The 840-acre Warsaw Ghetto was also the site of a flourishing underground network. Lubetkin worked out of a Dror house at 34 Dzielna Street and did her best to organize teens, who were among the hardest hit by malnutrition. The Nazi occupiers had enlisted the help of cowed, cooperative elders among the Warsaw Jewry, inviting them to set up a *Judenrat,* or Jewish Council, to manage the slave-labor factory assignments, charity relief efforts, and even police themselves with a specially trained (but unarmed) Jewish police force. There was a flourishing black market, and smuggled goods made their way into the Ghetto via ingenious methods, including secret basement passages.

Lubetkin became close to Yitzhak Zuckerman, a native of Vilnius, Lithuania, who came to work for the Zionist underground in Warsaw in the spring of 1940. The fate of their respective families was doomed, and reaffirmed their commitment to the cause: in June of 1941 the Germans mounted an attack on the Soviet Union, and several key regions were seized. Lubetkin's parents plus four of her sisters went into hiding in Belarus, but all were discovered in 1942 and killed; similarly, Zuckerman's family were among the 70,000 Vilnius Jews rounded up by German and Lithuanian soldiers and executed at an abandoned construction-site pit in Ponary in 1941.

Many in Warsaw's Zionist underground warned the Judenrat that mass executions would happen in Poland, too. Yet even Lubetkin later spoke of the cognitive dissonance they all experienced, despite mounting evidence of the Nazi plan to eliminate all of Europe's Jews. "Jews simply refused to believe they would be exterminated," she said at a 1961 war-crimes trial, according to a *New York Times* report. "We could not believe that in the twentieth century a nation would pronounce a sentence of death on a whole people."

Jolted into Action

On July 22, 1942, mass deportations began in Warsaw and went on daily for the next eight weeks. Jews were ordered to report to a collection point known as *Umschagplatz* for "resettlement in the East." In reality, they were taken to a newly built camp called Treblinka, and gassed in specially built bunkers that could kill at a rate of hundreds an hour. Mass crematoriums then burned their remains, saving the Germans the trouble of digging mass graves. Similar camps were set up at Auschwitz-Birkenau, Belżec, and other sites in Poland.

The deportations, which decimated the Warsaw Ghetto, finally propelled the resistance fighters to prominence. The head of the Judenrat, a once-esteemed ex-senator of Poland named Adam Czerniaków, was so traumatized by his inability to halt the deportations that he committed suicide. Five days later, Lubetkin and Zuckerman founded the *Żydowska Organizacja Bojowa,* or Jewish Fighting Organization, with several others. ŻOB, as it was known, began to build secure bunkers inside the Ghetto and collect weapons from the black market and other outside sources. On its high command were Lubetkin, Zuckerman, plus Shmuel Braslav, Josef Kaplan, and Mordechai Tenenbaum. In October, a young activist named Mordechai Anielewicz returned to Warsaw. Once considered too unmanageable to be an effective leader, "Aniolek," as he was called, was a charismatic figure and rallied many younger Jews to the resistance group. It was agreed that Anielewicz would be the ŻOB commander in chief.

Recruited Couriers, Instilled Discipline

Lubetkin's main role in the ŻOB was to recruit, train, and manage female couriers. These young women, some of them Jewish and others affiliated with the AK, moved more easily between the Ghetto and Aryan parts of the city than the men, and even managed to travel to other cities in Poland, Germany, and Russia as links in the underground communication network. Lubetkin was known only as Celina, her *nom de guerre.* Zuckerman also had little trouble passing between borders because of his Slavic looks, and in December of 1942, he went to the Polish city of Krakow in an attempt to breach security at a German military weapons depot to steal guns and ammunition. The scheme was foiled and Zuckerman was chased down, shot, and left for dead. He spent several hours with a grave leg wound and only barely made it onto a train back to Warsaw, even escaping a sudden station round-up for slave labor work.

Lubetkin nursed Zuckerman back to health at a safe house at the intersection of Zamenhof and Low Streets in the Warsaw Ghetto. From their fourth-floor perch on January 18, 1943, they witnessed the start of a new round of deportations, and feared for their lives. German secret police, the SS (*Schutzstaffel*) stormed the building, but Anielewicz had posted an unobtrusive armed guard in the building's lobby, who fired into the backs of the Germans and then fled. Elsewhere, near Umschlagplatz and other parts of the Ghetto, similar actions were taking place, and the Germans quickly retreated and even halted deportations altogether a few days later. This was the start of the Warsaw Ghetto Uprising. The remaining 60,000 or so Ghetto residents were revitalized by the action, and there was a renewal of efforts to supply them with arms. A key moment came when ŻOB agreed to work with another group, the *Żydowski Związek Wojskowy,* or Jewish Military Union. ŻZW actually predated ŻOB and had its roots inside the former army of independent Poland. There were some ideological differences between the groups and Lubetkin played a crucial role in bringing the sides to cooperation.

ŻOB and ŻZW units were prepared for a renewal of hostilities on the night of April 19, 1943, when German forces surrounded the Ghetto to begin a new round of deportations. From secured bunkers and various hideouts Lubetkin and about 500 other members of the Resistance fought back by sniper attack, Molotov cocktails, and homemade pipe bombs. Unfortunately Zuckerman had been sent as an emissary to the Aryan part of Warsaw and was trapped there when the fighting began. Lubetkin worked with Anielewicz, Edelman, and other fellow high-ranking commanders to move supplies and information from one bunker to another throughout the Ghetto. "When ... we threw those hand grenades and bombs and saw German blood flowing on the streets of Warsaw there was rejoicing among us," she recalled at the 1961 trial of Nazi war-crimes fugitive Adolf Eichmann, according to the *New York Times.*

Discovered Tragic Death Scene

Lubetkin moved between several bunkers and lived under extreme duress for the duration of the uprising, and even more so after it. Finally, running low on ammunition and faced with German aerial bombardment and systematic arson, a decision was made to evacuate once they had discovered a sewer route that led them to below-ground Aryan Warsaw. Lubetkin and Edelman waited for word from Anielewicz, who was at the ŻOB command post at 18 Miła Street. When no courier came, they set out after dark and discovered that Anielewicz and about 80 others had taken their own lives rather than surrender to Germans, or die by German bullets, after an ambush. That was on May 8, 1943. Within a week, the Warsaw Ghetto Uprising had concluded and every last known Jew in the Ghetto was rounded up. About 56,000 residents had remained; some 7,000 were killed on site during the uprising and its aftermath, and another 7,000 were sent to Treblinka. The rest were dispersed to other camps, where the final death toll for the Holocaust, when World War II ended exactly two years after the Miła Street tragedy, was six million Jews.

On May 10, 1943, Lubetkin made a 20-hour trek through Warsaw's sewers to safety with other ŻOB and ŻZW fighters. They were then spirited out to the countryside in a truck, where her group hid in a forest. Lubetkin was among a fabled subset of Jews to survive not just the Holocaust, but the Warsaw Ghetto and the revolt: of the estimated 500 resistance fighters, she was one of just 33 who survived to tell the story.

Lubetkin hid in Poland until the AK's Warsaw Uprising of August-September 1944, which was another disastrous event. After that, she spent weeks hiding in a hospital with Zuckerman, whom she eventually married, until Warsaw was liberated by the Soviet Red Army in January of 1945. They then worked to help Holocaust survivors reach Palestine, and emigrated there in 1946. Home became a kibbutz called Lohamei HaGeta'ot, or the Ghetto Fighters, where she died on July 14, 1976. She was survived by Zuckerman, who died in 1981, and their two children.

Books

Brzezinski, Matthew, *Isaac's Army: The Jewish Resistance in Occupied Poland,* Random House, 2012.

Periodicals

New York Times, May 4, 1961; April 18, 2013.□

Ludwig I, King of Bavaria

King Ludwig I of Bavaria (1786–1868) left a lasting mark on Munich and its surrounding environs. Obsessed with classical art and antiquities, he commissioned numerous grandly scaled architectural projects and continued his father's mission to remake the sleepy Bavarian *burg* into a breathtaking, boulevarded royal capital. In 1848 he was ousted from power after a scandalous affair with an Irish-born woman who called herself Lola Montez.

Ludwig was descended from a complex web of German dynastic powers that ruled dozens of small- to medium-sized principalities and duchies across Western Europe. On his father's side he was heir to the House of Palatinate-Zweibrücken-Birkenfeld, a branch of the mighty House of Wittelsbach. The Wittelsbach nobles had reigned in this part of southern Germany since the 1100s. Their power stretched back even further, to the early-medieval German kings Otto and Henry, who were by marriage descendants of Charlemagne, the first Holy Roman Emperor.

Named After Doomed French King

Ludwig was born on August 25, 1786, in Strasbourg, France, as the first son of his father, who was a *graf,* or count. His father's formal title was Count Palatine Maximilian Joseph of Zweibrücken. At the time, his father was a military commander stationed in Strasbourg, a strategically located city on the Rhine River that would pass several times between French and German control over the centuries. Ludwig's mother was Augusta Wilhelmine of Hesse-Darmstadt, daughter of another venerable line of royals, but this one from north-central Germany. The couple had three more children after the birth of Ludwig: the sisters Augusta and Caroline, and a second son, Karl Theodor.

Ludwig's parents Maximilian and Augusta were on friendly terms with the king and queen of France, Louis XVI and his Austrian-born wife, Marie Antoinette. In fact, King Louis XVI was godfather to Ludwig. But Ludwig's childhood was marked by the turmoil of events related to the anti-royalist French Revolution of 1789, which spilled over the borders into German lands. The family had to flee Strasbourg north to Mannheim, another important port on the Rhine River. The enmity between France and Germany resumed and French forces stormed Mannheim, too, in December of 1794. In March of 1796, Ludwig's mother Augusta died at the age of 30 from a lung infection related to the pestilence and unsafe sanitary conditions of wartime. French revolutionary forces, meanwhile, moved eastward to unite with the kingdom of Austria, on Bavaria's southern border.

Ludwig's father concluded a peace treaty with France that forced him to give up some lands of the Palatinate but allowed him sovereignty over an independent Bavaria. In 1799 Maximilian became the Elector of Bavaria; these Elector princely titles referred to certain royals who convened with the bishops of the Roman Catholic Church to choose the next Holy Roman Emperor. While the Protestant faith had its very origins in Germany, in Martin Luther's defiant *95 Theses* nailed to the door of the Wittenberg Cathedral in Saxony in 1517, Bavaria and other parts of southern German had remained staunchly Roman Catholic even after decades of religious war elsewhere in Germany related to the Protestant Reformation. Ludwig's late mother was raised in the Lutheran faith of northern Germany, as was his future wife.

Ludwig was 19 years old when his father became King Maximilian I of Bavaria on January 1, 1806. By that time, Ludwig was immersed in studies, first at Landshut, an old Bavarian city and longtime Wittelsbach stronghold. The University of Ingolstadt, which dated back to the late 1400s, had been moved by his father from Ingolstadt—a city just north of Munich—when Ingolstadt was overrun by French troops. Maximilian decided to permanently establish the school in the heart of Munich once peace was restored, and it was eventually renamed Ludwig-Maximilians-Universität München, or LMU. The "Ludwig" was in honor of Duke Ludwig IX of Bavaria-Landshut, the school's founder, and plus "Maximilian" in honor of the reigning king.

Marriage Celebrated at Oktoberfest

Ludwig also studied in Goöttingen, another center of learning in pre-imperial Germany. On October 12, 1810, he married an 18-year-old princess of the house of Mecklenburg, Therese of Saxe-Hildburghausen. As noted, Bavaria was a relatively new state at the time and its borders had been negotiated, contested, and redrawn several times. Ludwig's father sought to prevent the calamity of the French Revolution of 1789 from occurring in German lands, and initiated a series of reforms to secure the peace, curry public favor, and position Munich as a proper royal capital. The marriage of Ludwig, the crown prince, offered another opportunity to bolster this idea of Bavarian nationalism and unity, and the King ordered that a two-week-long public fair be held in celebration of the marriage. There were to be horse races and games, and later an agricultural fair, but the autumn event became famous as a showcase of German beer-brewing mastery known as Oktoberfest.

All of Munich was invited to attend the first-ever Oktoberfest on the Theresien-*wiese,* or meadow, in honor of the royal wedding of 1810. The field was just outside one of the city's gates at Sendlinger Tor. Billed as the world's largest "people's festival," Oktoberfest became an annual tradition during Ludwig's lifetime and a source of regional pride for Bavarians. The peaceful gathering of thousands of Müncheners, encouraged to consume vast quantities of superior German *bier,* was a pointed rebuke to the unrest and impoverishment that had prompted mass riots in Paris just two decades before and resulted in the public executions of the king and queen of France.

Ludwig had a productive if not entirely harmonious marriage. He and Therese had nine children, eight of whom survived to adulthood, but Ludwig carried on several extramarital affairs, the most notorious of which would lead to his downfall. As a young man, when his father was still king, the crown prince commanded military forces in the ongoing problems with France and other neighbors. He and Therese lived in Würzburg on the Main River from 1816 to 1825, but he traveled often to Italy, clocking more than 50 visits in his lifetime. He even acquired a piece of real estate in Rome, the Villa Malta, but preferred the Tuscan city of Florence, whose rulers and benefactors had revived interest in the cultural and intellectual achievements of ancient Greece and Rome. This period became known as the Italian Renaissance, and even three centuries later in Ludwig's lifetime the neoclassical Revival architecture signified the epitome of European culture and power.

Envisioned Munich as Resplendent Showcase

Ludwig ascended to the throne of Bavaria on October 13, 1825, when his father, known as Old Max, died. The first years of Ludwig's reign were marked by a continuance of his father's reforms, which included an 1818 constitution that gave Bavaria a bicameral legislature and some rights and freedoms, modeled on the French Revolutionary spirit. Nobles made up the *Kammer der Reichsräte* or house of lords, while limited political suffrage—granted to men with financial assets above a certain *thaler* amount—was enacted to elect members of the *Kammer der Abgeordneten,* or House of Commons. The king also had a cabinet of advisors and a fairly competent civil service.

Ludwig continued the massive building projects designed to make Munich a showcase of German pomp and progress. He had actually been working on his vision for the city even as crown prince, meeting with court architect Leo von Klenze to remap the city from its four original medieval gates to a larger, grander urban center. They created Odeonsplatz, just outside of the Altstadt (Old City), and a splendid avenue later named after Ludwig, Ludwigstrasse, and three other "royal" avenues that led to the city center. When Ludwig became king, he continued to lavish funds on monuments, museums, and other projects. These included the Glyptothek, a neoclassical palace designed to house a trove of antiquities Ludwig had been steadily acquiring, and the Alte Pinakothek, which was the world's largest museum when its doors opened in 1836. It housed an immense collection of Old Masters artworks collected by the Wittelsbach rulers over generations.

Ludwig and his family lived at the Residenz in Munich, another complex of buildings designed in part by von Klenze. Walhalla, built near another Bavarian urban center at Regensburg that overlooked the Danube, was Ludwig's commission of an exact replica of the famous Parthenon of Athens, considered one of the masterpieces of classical Greek architecture. Ludwig and von Klenze designed theirs as a shrine to Germanic heroes of history. So enamored was Ludwig of anything Greek that he actually funded the Greeks' war to separate from the Ottoman Empire, and then offered his son Otto as the new "king." Otto and some capable Bavarian junior ministers laid the foundations of a modern Greek state; even the two colors of both the Bavarian and Greek flags, blue and white, serve as reminders of the unusual new alliance created in the 1830s.

Enjoyed Years of Popular Approval

Ludwig also spent his treasury's funds on more practical projects. He built a new Rhine River port at Ludwigshafen to supplant Mannheim's, and revived an ambitious canal-building project designed to link the Rhine and Danube rivers. The Danube-Main Canal, a failed dream of Charlemagne's in the ninth century, went into operation in 1845 and remained in use until World War II. Ludwig also consented to the construction of the first railroad line in Germany, which ran between Fürth and Nuremburg. Munich's beer-centric culture is another enduring legacy of Ludwig's reign. In addition to sanctioning the annual Oktoberfest, in 1828 he declared the Royal Court Brewery, or *Hofbrähaus,* open to the public. It became one of the city's most famous tourist destinations, but its original intent was to showcase Munich as a royal capital where princes and laborers stood at the same bar and drank from the same beer kegs.

Ludwig was brought down by private decisions that became publicly known and spiraled into a political flashpoint. In 1846, he met a renowned beauty and likely courtesan who called herself Lola Montez. Though she claimed to come from Andalusia, Montez was actually a 25-year-old Irish-born semi-burlesque performer named Elizabeth Rosanna Gilbert James who had previously caused havoc in several European cities as she charmed well-known men and provoked scandalous behavior. Predictably, her arrival in Munich caused a stir, and she was initially banned from performing in public.

Montez requested a private meeting with the 61-year-old king of Bavaria, who found her irresistible and soon added her to his Gallery of Beauties, a famous portrait gallery at his Schloss Nymphenburg. The affair continued for more than a year, with Montez ensconced in luxury quarters at 7 Barerstrasse near the resplendent architectural masterpieces of Königsplatz. She was lively and outspoken, and frequented Munich's raucous beer halls and student-drinking haunts, where she regaled fellow drinkers with stories about the king. When Ludwig attempted to grant Montez a title of nobility as the Countess of Landsberg and Baroness of Rosenthal, his ministers refused the request. Her ascension would have included Bavarian citizenship and provided the dancer with an annual income, and Ludwig was so incensed at their refusal that he fired some of them and appointed more amenable ones in their stead.

Forced to Abdicate

There were other issues in Bavarian politics, including a right-wing Roman Catholic movement, and Ludwig's decisions and reversals were said to have been unduly influenced by Montez, who was loathed by the conservatives at Ludwig's court. Even the city's highly regarded university became a source of dissent, and Ludwig's attempt to close it prompted LMU students to riot. Montez was forced to flee, and Ludwig was pressured to abdicate and hand over power to his eldest son, Maximilian, on March 20, 1848. Montez later moved on to a moderately successful career on Broadway. Ludwig spent his final years finessing his monuments in Munich and Bavaria, apparently content to be free from political concerns. He lived in the Leopoldskron castle near Salzburg, and died in Nice, in the south of France, on February 29, 1868. His namesake nephew inherited the throne in 1864 and was called "Mad Ludwig." It was Ludwig II who retreated from public view at his alpine aerie, Neuschwanstein, that was the inspiration for the storybook castle of Sleeping Beauty in the Walt Disney animated film, and replicated at all the Disney theme parks.

Books

Gaab, Jeffrey S., *Munich: Hofbräuhaus & History: Beer, Culture, & Politics,* Peter Lang, 2006.

Periodicals

New York Times, June 19, 1988.

World of Hibernia, Autumn 1998.

Online

"The Royal Wedding and Civil Contributions," Bavarian Library Online/Bayerische Landesbibliothek Online, http://www.bayerische-landesbibliothek-online.de/oktoberfest-1810-english (December 2, 2013).□

M

Donald Maclean

Donald Maclean (1913–1983) furnished the Soviet Union with classified information and state secrets for nearly two decades as a member of the notorious "Cambridge Five" espionage ring. The senior-rank British Foreign Office associate was posted to embassies in Paris, Washington, and Cairo during World War II and the onset of the Cold War. Threat of exposure forced Maclean to make a midnight run to Moscow in 1951, where he spent the remainder of his life.

Donald Duart Maclean was born on May 31, 1913, in Marylebone, London, but his father's family had Scottish roots. His mother Gwendolen Devitt Maclean was the daughter of a local magistrate in Surrey, and Maclean was the second of her five children. By the time of his birth his father, also named Donald, had already risen to prominence in Liberal Party circles and held a seat in the House of Commons; in subsequent years the elder Maclean would serve as Leader of the Opposition in Parliament and was appointed president of the National Board of Education. For his long career in public service, which included his co-founding of the National Society for the Prevention of Cruelty to Children, Maclean's father was knighted by King George V.

Studied Languages at Cambridge

Maclean was sent off to boarding school at an early age. He attended St. Ronan's in Worthing and then Gresham's School in Norfolk. In 1931 he entered Trinity College of Cambridge University, where he studied modern languages and was active in Communist Party circles.

Britain in the 1920s and early '30s was still reeling from the aftershocks of World War I. The country suffered from an underperforming economy exacerbated by the Great Depression, and there were hunger marches and other protest actions that failed to win much sympathy from the government. Young, well-educated Britons of Maclean's generation were drawn to leftist political movements in part because of the transformative success of the Russian Revolution of 1917–18; a mere decade after the overthrow of the Romanov dynasty and the establishment of the world's first Communist regime. Russia seemed a modern, egalitarian nation with a booming economy—and, moreover, one that was seemingly insulated from the global financial crisis that occurred in the aftermath of the Wall Street Crash of 1929.

In Britain, by contrast, there was a lumbering, protocol-obsessed royal dynasty propped up by a snobbish and occasionally dissolute aristocracy; these elites owed their titles and income-producing lands to royal patronage of generations past. Among the upper echelons of British society was a thinly veiled anti-Semitism. Some members of parliament were even supportive of right-wing fascist movements in Germany and Italy, arguing that it took a strong, populist-minded leader like Adolf Hitler to control the working classes and root out so-called "undesirable" elements in society.

Joined Foreign Office

In 1934 Maclean was recruited by Harold Adrian Russell (Kim) Philby, another Trinity College student, into what would become the Cambridge spy ring. Philby had been approached by Arnold Deutsch, an Austrian graduate

© Pictorial Press Ltd/Alamy

student in London who was working clandestinely for the Soviet foreign intelligence services. Deutsch was also the link between Philby and Maclean and three other men with Cambridge connections: history major Guy Burgess, a slightly older art-history graduate student named Anthony Blunt, and a fifth man thought to be John Cairncross. Instead of openly flouting their Communist sympathies, the young graduates were urged to appear as blandly apolitical as possible and even seek out right-wing associates. Maclean graduated from Cambridge in 1934 then spent several months preparing for the Civil Service exam, which he passed in 1935. In his application for a job with the British Foreign Office, he was asked about his Communist Party activities and reported that he become disenchanted with the ideology. In October of 1935, he entered His Majesty's Diplomatic Service at the British Foreign Office, becoming the first of the Cambridge ring to secure a government job with access to classified information.

During this early part of his career Maclean passed on information to another London-based agent named Kitty Harris, who had once been romantically involved with Earl Browder, head of the American Communist Party and a well-known dissident. Maclean and Harris began a relationship that involved trysts at her apartment while she photographed the documents he brought every evening from the Foreign Office. Harris then passed the film on to other Soviet agents in London for processing, encryption, and cabling to Moscow. She even followed Maclean to Paris when he was promoted to the post of third secretary at the British Embassy in Paris in 1938. Their romance cooled after Maclean was introduced to a wealthy, well-connected American woman named Melinda Marling in January of 1940. Marling came from a socially prominent East Coast family and the announcement of her wedding to Maclean in June of 1940 ran in the *New York Times.* Both were forced to flee France as Nazi German troops invaded on France's eastern borders and marched westward. Maclean returned to a desk job at the Foreign Office in London, where he continued to pass on classified information to his Soviet handlers, including details about uranium production and top-secret scientific weapons research related to U.S.-led efforts to build the world's first atomic bomb.

Sent to Washington

Maclean gained even more access to sensitive, war-related plans in 1944 when he was posted to the British Embassy in Washington, D.C. as its first secretary. He spent four years there—and his two sons with Marling were born during this period, conferring upon them automatic U.S. citizenship—and from 1947 to 1948 even served as Secretary of the Combined Policy Committee on Atomic Development, which included British, American, and Canadian scientists and officials. Maclean was not privy to vital technical data, but did know of rollout dates and remote tests. The war in Europe ended with the Allies' victory over Nazi Germany in May of 1945, but the war against Japan—Germany's ally—did not conclude until August of 1945, when U.S. military planes dropped atomic bombs on Hiroshima and Nagasaki, Japan.

The strain of leading secret lives, both during World War II and the even more perilous years that marked the start of the nuclear terror of the Cold War, seemed to have taken a psychological toll on members of the Cambridge Five. Guy Burgess was already an unstable figure, prone to drunken tirades and reckless behavior in pursuit of anonymous same-sex encounters. His utter unsuitability for the role of a spy—a job that required constant and irreproachable conduct—has remained one of the more curious sidenotes in the story of the Cambridge Five.

Maclean's own behavior became increasingly erratic after 1948, when the British Foreign Office posted him to Cairo as chief of the Chancery there. When he drank he was prone to rants against American imperialism and, in one incident in May of 1950, brawled with another man during a boat party on the Nile River. In a second debacle, a drunken Maclean visited an apartment shared by two women who worked for the American Embassy in Cairo and smashed up furniture in an inexplicable rage. Melinda Maclean contacted close friends and urged that her husband be recalled to London immediately. He underwent a psychiatric examination and was deemed fit to return to his Foreign Office post. In October of 1950 he was assigned as chief of the Foreign Office's American desk in Whitehall, where British cabinet ministries are housed.

Eluded Interrogation by Defection

Kim Philby, the so-called "Third Man" of the Cambridge Five, had taken over from Maclean as first secretary at the British Embassy in Washington in 1948. It is thought that Philby became aware of the fact that U.S. intelligence services had finally cracked a code that let them decipher cables sent from the British Embassy in Washington to Moscow during Maclean's tenure as first secretary. The sender code-named "Gomer" or "Homer" was narrowed down to a few key suspects, and Philby arranged a plan to have Burgess recalled to London so that he could warn Maclean personally that he was in danger of being exposed as spy.

Maclean's superiors in Britain's Secret Intelligence Service (SIS) balked when presented with evidence that there had been a Soviet agent, or "mole," inside the British Embassy during the war years. Nevertheless, Maclean was placed under surveillance. His office in Whitehall and his home in the village of Tatsfield on the outskirts of London were "bugged," or implanted with electronic listening devices, as were the telephone lines at both sites. A pair of low-level security personnel was assigned to tail him in London, but they clocked off duty when he boarded the train to Tatsfield at the end of his workday. Fearful and depressed, Maclean once tore a postcard in half and told his wife that should anything happen to him, she should only speak to the person who produced the second half.

Burgess arrived back in England in early May of 1951, and met with Maclean, warning him that U.S. intelligence agents had detected him as Gomer/Homer. On Friday, May 25, 1951, Maclean took the 5:19 p.m. train home for a 38th birthday celebration with his wife, who was pregnant with their third child. Burgess turned up and was introduced to Melinda as "Roger Styles" for the benefit of any eavesdropping devices. Burgess and Maclean left in a car Burgess had rented and drove to the port of Southampton. Just before midnight they boarded a ferry bound for St. Malo, France. So regular were these excursions that French port officials did not bother with passport controls. The next morning Burgess and Maclean made their way to Paris, and then on to Zurich, Switzerland, where Soviet agents aware of their situation made contact and provided them with false passports and tickets for a flight to Prague, the capital of Communist-allied Czechoslovakia. Philby had warned Burgess not to defect, lest he expose the Cambridge ring entirely, but both men vanished behind the Iron Curtain after the plane landed in Prague. Intelligence analysts believe that Burgess had been tricked into defecting with Maclean, and had probably been promised that he would be allowed to return to England.

Part of Cold War Lore

News of Maclean's disappearance was revealed on June 7, 1951, causing a minor international crisis. There was consternation in London, and in Whitehall and Westminster, where the houses of parliament debated the security breach heatedly for months. In September of 1953 Maclean's wife pulled off an even more daring defection, leaving Switzerland with her three children on a night train bound for Vienna, Austria, which was still under post-war Allied control and rife with Soviet agents who likely aided her flight to Moscow.

In February of 1956, Maclean and Burgess reappeared suddenly at a five-minute-long press conference held at a Moscow hotel—another event that made international headlines. They appeared calm and in good health, and admitted that they had harbored Communist sympathies but had never committed acts of espionage. In an official joint statement they said they had grown disillusioned with life in the West and believed their mission to forge peace between nations would be more effective inside the Soviet sphere.

Maclean spent the remainder of his life in Moscow, learning Russian and working for the Soviet Foreign Ministry. His wife and children later returned to England and America. The defection of Burgess had exposed Philby, who denied being a member of the Cambridge Five, but Philby, too, defected to the Soviet Union in 1963—the same year that Burgess died in Moscow at the age of 52. Maclean lived another twenty years in the Soviet Union and, like Burgess, requested that his remains be returned to England. He died of a heart attack on March 6, 1983, at age 69.

Books

Hamrick, S.J., *Deceiving the Deceivers: Kim Philby, Donald Maclean, and Guy Burgess,* Yale University Press, 2004.

Periodicals

Times (London, England), February 13, 1956; March 12, 1983.□

Sir Peter Mansfield

Physicist Sir Peter Mansfield (born 1933) helped develop and refine Magnetic Resonance Imaging (MRI), the computerized scanning system that produces internal images of body structures and is now widely used as a non-surgical medical diagnostic tool. Considered one of the world's greatest living scientists, the much honored college professor was awarded the Nobel Prize in Physiology or Medicine, shared with American Paul Lauterbur who worked separately, in 2003.

Born on October 9, 1933, in Lambeth, London of the United Kingdom, Peter Mansfield is the youngest son of Sidney George Mansfield, a gas fitter for the South Metropolitan Gas Company, and his wife Rose Lilian, a waitress. Along with his brothers Conrad William and Sidney Albert, young Peter was raised in Camberwell near London, a slum area that was evacuated at least three times due to German airplane raids, V1 and V2 bombings during World War II. Peter, who collected and studied an impressive amount of shrapnel when home, spent most of the war years in Seven Oaks and Torquay. Once the

AP Photo Sang Tan

Mansfield family returned to the London area, their youngest child was not fully prepared for the intellectual rigors dictated by his country's 1944 Education Act. Commanded by his school master to take the 11+ examination—something he had never heard of or prepared for—the youngster scored too low to achieve entrance into a local Grammar school. Attending the Peckham Central School—a London area facility much further away—the boy excelled in woodworking and metal works, but did not particularly distinguish himself academically. Further, he considered himself useless at physical sports with his PT master noting aloud during boxing lessons that the young man proved a better dancer than fighter.

Worked as Printer's Assistant

Mansfield attended William Penn School, a secondary school, until he was 15 years old. Prior to dropping out, he was asked by a guidance counselor what career interested him. Inspired by trips to the Science Museum in South Kensington and articles in the local newspapers about young men working in rocket science, the teen proclaimed that he too wanted to be a rocketeer. Unimpressed by Mansfield's scholastic background, the counselor noted his lack of qualifications and suggested he look elsewhere. One of Mansfield's hobbies was printing letterheads and cards along with a small magazine. These interests allowed him to secure a job as a printer's assistant which he held for two years. Still intrigued by rocketry, he taught himself enough about weapons and explosives to land a job as a scientific assistant in the Ministry of Supply at the Rocket Propulsion Department in Westcott, Buckinghamshire, with the understanding that he would study for his A-levels (or high school equivalency diploma).

Eighteen months later, Mansfield was called up for National Service and served two years in the Royal Army. Once discharged, he returned to Westcott and his hard work in night classes resulted in a scholarship to attend the Queen Mary College at London University at age 23. Studying physics under Dr. Jack G. Powles, Mansfield's third undergraduate year was spent studying both experimental physics and mathematical (or theoretical) physics, which was unusual at the time—normally a student chose one or the other. One of Powles' assignments, the building of a transistorized Nuclear Magnetic Resonance (NMR) system for detecting underground objects, earned him top marks and an offer to join his mentor's research group.

Mansfield's work with Powles' group developed an approach that allowed spin echoes of the NMR to occur in solids. They published a groundbreaking paper on the subject although Mansfield was quick to credit scientists whose work paved the way. "The names that were common in the laboratory were [Nicolaas] Bloembergen, [Edward Mills] Purcell and [Robert] Pound—a famous paper which kicked off the whole business of NMR," Mansfield told Richard Thomas of the video archive project *Today's Neuroscience, Tomorrow's History.* "There was [Erwin] Hahn's paper and, of course, we were using Hahn spin echoes in those very early days, and people before me. . .were using Hahn spin echoes to study the properties of liquids. So, there was before us quite a number of important paper and important contributions which really started the whole business and, of course, without them we would have had nothing."

Tested MRI on Himself

Earning both his Bachelor of Science degree and P.h.D. at Queen Mary College, Mansfield married his fiancé Jean Margaret Kibble on September 1, 1962. Appointed a Research Associate at the Physics Department at the University of Illinois in Urbana, he engaged in an NMR study of doped metals, while his wife worked as a secretary at the University Health Center. Working in Charlie Slichter's laboratory, Mansfield's experiments conducted with a double resonance spectrometer did not provide the results he expected, but the experience and knowledge gained would prove valuable in the long run. Towards the end of his stay, he worked with fellow Briton Doug Cutler, also at UI, and ran NMR experiments on aluminum powder. Those results, along with experimental data supplied by colleague Dr. John Strange at Cornell University, inspired Mansfield to issue a strictly theoretical paper extending his theories.

After leaving Urbana, Illinois, Mansfield returned to England where the University of Nottingham offered him a post as the Appointed Lecturer in Physics. This position allowed him to continue studying and experimenting while conferring with other eminent scientists in his field. At

Nottingham, Mansfield was promoted to Senior Lecturer in Physic in 1968, promoted to reader in Physics, 1970, and appointed Professor of Physics in 1979. In 1971, Mansfield, working closely with Dr. Alan Garroway and his student Peter Grannell, used an SRC research grant to make a computer controlled spectrometer that allowed them to more easily study the response of the NMR's echoes to a number of suitable compounds. Reworking calculations and running numerous experiments on single crystals of Calcium Fluoride, the academics evolved a theory that eventually led to the birth of the MRI.

The following year, Mansfield took a sabbatical leave to work in Professor Karl Hausser's group during an appointment as Senior Visitor at the Max Planck-Institute for Medical Research in Heidelberg, Germany. While there, he exchanged letters with Grannell about NMR diffraction based on calculations Mansfield had made before leaving. During a subsequent trip to a conference in Krakow, Poland, the traveling academic first heard about the works of American Professor Paul Lauterbur (1929–2007) Lauterbur's work on his NMR Zeugmatography, as he had titled it, included no structural algorhythm, but the crude images of test tubes he observed were the first positive indication that the type of imaging Mansfield sought was possible.

After years of trial, error, dealing with academic politics concerning grants from the Medical Research Council, and conferring with scientists at home and abroad, Mansfield presented the first working version of the MRI in 1973. The device, used successfully for the first time in 1974, was barely large enough to accommodate the finger of Andrew Maudsley, one of his students. In 1978, with an important conference looming, a larger scale version of the MRI scanner was completed but needed a willing test subject. Mansfield volunteered. Previously, his group had only recorded images of plants and dead animal tissue and Mansfield later admitted that he worried about the risks of experimenting with his own body.

The experience of this first full body scan was retold in a 2009 article for *Eureka Alert.* "There was an audible crack but I felt nothing," Mansfield recalled. "I then signaled to start the scan. The magnet was enclosed in aluminum sheeting forming an RF screen. Due to lack of time there was no light inside. I was therefore clamped in the magnet vertically and in pitch darkness for 50 minutes until the procedure was completed." Mansfield's wife Jean was on hand to help pull the scientist out of the magnet in an emergency, but no help was needed. "[T]he whole experiment went well and images were recorded successfully," the academic/inventor reported.

Won Nobel Prize

Mansfield was not the only scientist working on Magnetic Resonance Imaging, however. His colleagues at Nottingham, Dr. Raymond Andrew and Dr. Paul Morris, as well as many notable figures outside the University, headed up their own research projects and made important contributions to the field. When Andrew and Morris left for greener academic pastures, Mansfield and his group remained despite several lucrative offers from Universities in the United States. He did not need to leave his home country to reap the rewards of his life's work. Once the MRI became commercially available during the 1980s, it revolutionized medicine, allowing physicians to detect cancer, signs of damage in bones, tissues, organs and to study brain injury and disorders. Eventually, the use of MRI spread to medical facilities all over the world and Mansfield, who owns the patents to a great many of the devices associated with the machine, has benefitted financially.

A Professor of Physics since 1979, Mansfield became a Medical Research Council Professorial Research Fellow from 1983 and 1988, when he resumed his professorship. Continually working on ways to make MRI technology faster and safer, the Professor's achievements began attracting a slew of awards and honors throughout the 1980s and 1990s, culminating in a much-prized knighthood in 1993. Now addressed as Sir Peter Mansfield, the scientist's greatest accolade came in 2003 when he was announced as the joint-winner of the Nobel Prize in Physiology or Medicine with Professor Paul Lauterbur. Initially, when his wife told him the news, Mansfield believed she was making a joke. "I didn't expect anything like this at all," he recalled for the Royal Society of New Zealand. "If someone just told you, you had won the Nobel Prize, I think the reaction of 90 percent of the population would be 'Yeah, go on pull the other one'."

In his Nobel Prize website biography, Mansfield, who collected a check for 800,000 pounds from the committee, took a moment to humbly recognize his co-workers and contributors. "None of the work in MRI could have been achieved without the enthusiasm and dedicated support of a highly motivated team of technical and academic staff, research students and post-docs sustained over the period from 1972—to the present day."

Mansfield's scientific contributions were also recognized by his University, where the ever expanding Magnetic Resonance Center, established in 1991, was renamed the Sir Peter Mansfield Magnetic Resonance Center in 2003. Still an Emeritus Professor at Nottingham well past the formal age of retirement, he released *The Long Road to Stockholm, The Story of Magnetic Resonance Imaging—An Autobiography,* published by Oxford University Press in 2013.

A soft spoken family man with two daughters and four grandchildren, he is often surprised that his activities have garnered him any recognition whatsoever. "Most people don't think about where MRI scanners come from" Mansfield mused for the *Daily Mirror*on the occasion of his Best of Britain Award in 2009. "But I feel very pleased and proud when I receive letters from patients, thanking me for saving their lives."

Online

"MRI pioneer awarded Millennium Medal,"*EurekaAlert!,* http://www.eurekaalert.org/ (December 10, 2013).

"Nobel winner did not know he would help millions,"*the Royal Society of New Zealand,* http://www.royalsociety.org.nz/ (November 14, 2013).

"Paul C. Lauterbur," *IEEE Global History Network,* http://www.ieeeghn.org/wiki/index.php/Paul_C._Lauterbur, (December 10, 2013).

"Peter Mansfield," *NNDB,* http://www.nndb.com/people/660/000136252/, (December 10, 2013).

"Peter Mansfield," *Oxford University Press,* http://www.ukcatalogue,oup.com/product/9780199664542, (November 6, 2013).

"Professor Sir Peter Mansfield Interviewed by Richard Thomas," *Today's Neuroscience, Tomorrow's History,* http://www2.history.omul.ac.uk/ (November 14, 2013).

"Sir Peter Mansfield," *Pride of Britain Awards,* http://www.prideof Britain.com/contentpages/winners/2009/sir-peter-mansfield.aspx, (November 14, 2013).

"Sir Peter Mansfield—Biographical," *NobelPrize.Org,* http://www.nobelprize.org/nobel_prizes/medicine/laureated/2003/mansfield-bio.htm,(November 14, 2013).□

Juan Marichal

The Dominican baseball player Juan Marichal (born 1937) won more games in the 1960s than any other pitcher in Major League Baseball's National League. He was part of the first wave of players from Latin America who made a major impact on the game of baseball in that decade.

Focus on Sport/Getty Images

Marichal's distinctive windup was immediately recognizable to anyone who watched his San Francisco Giants play in person or on television. Not a large, naturally athletic man, he generated power and momentum as he planted his right foot, leaned backward, and kicked his left foot high in the air. His right hand might almost hit the ground behind him. It was a graceful, elegant motion, and it made Marichal a remarkably consistent player who averaged 20 wins per year between 1962 and 1971 and turned him into a linchpin of the perennially pennant-contending Giants. (His generally elegant style earned him the nickname the Dominican Dandy.) He was slightly overshadowed at the height of his career by the Los Angeles Dodgers ace Sandy Koufax, but Marichal's career lasted longer. That career was shadowed by a 1965 incident in which Marichal hit Los Angeles Dodgers catcher John Roseboro with a bat, but he was eventually forgiven both by Roseboro and the baseball establishment, which elected him to the Baseball Hall of Fame in 1983. He was the first Dominican player so honored.

Used Homemade Bats, Balls, and Gloves

Juan Antonio Marichal Sánchez was born in the small town of Laguna Verde in the Dominican Republic on October 20, 1937. His surname is pronounced Mahr-ee-CHAHL in Spanish but has often been rendered as Mahr-ee-SHAHL or MARE-uh-shall by Anglophones. Marichal grew up in a poor farming family, and things went from bad to worse after his father died when he was three. Marichal was almost given up for dead at age ten after spending nine days in a coma after falling into a river. His older brother Gonzalo taught him to play baseball, and played against neighborhood boys using a bat made from the branch of a wassama tree, gloves made from truck tarpaulin, and a golf ball wrapped in cloth to increase it to baseball size. Among those other boys were Felipe, Mateo, and Jesús Rojas, who used the surname Alou when they all became American baseball stars themselves.

Quitting high school in eleventh grade, Marichal got a job driving a truck and quickly made several local corporate baseball teams. He was drafted into the Dominican Republic's air force after the son of the country's dictator saw him play and hoped that his talents would augment the air force's own team. The stint in the air force helped Marichal develop his arm and his soon-to-be-famous control, and after he was mustered out he was already a formidable player. He was signed by what was then the New York Giants organization in the spring of 1957, and given a $500 bonus, which helped to soften his mother's resistance to his dream of a baseball career.

Marichal's progression through the minor leagues was rapid. Playing for the Giants-associated Escogido Lions in the 1957–1958 season, he moved to a team in Michigan City, Indiana, in 1958 and scored the first of his many 20-game-winning seasons. In 1959, he won 18 games for the Eastern League's Springfield, Massachusetts, franchise, winning 18 games with a 2.39 earned run average (ERA). He started the 1960 season with the AAA-level Tacoma Giants and was elevated to the new San Francisco Giants squad on July 19. He pitched a shutout with 12 strikeouts in his debut appearance against the Philadelphia Phillies, allowing only one hit, and his major-league career was assured.

Injured in World Series

Marichal's 1961 season was only moderately strong, with a 13–10 won-lost record and a 3.89 ERA. He might have lost a step in spring training when he asked for and was granted permission to return to the Dominican Republic in late March to marry Alma Rosa Carvajal. The couple had six children and, as of this writing, 13 grandchildren and one great-grandchild. Marichal matured fully in 1962, leading the Giants with a 3.36 ERA, winning 18 games, pitching two scoreless innings in the All-Star Game, and helping lead the Giants to the World Series against the New York Yankees. He injured his hand while trying to bunt in the fourth game and had to be taken out of the game. That would be the only World Series appearance for Marichal, although the Giants generally finished high in the National League standings for the rest of the decade.

The 1963 season was one career high point for Marichal, who won 25 games while losing eight, leading the National League with 321 1/3 innings pitched, and scoring a no-hitter against the Houston Astros on June 15. On July 2, he emerged the winner in a titanic 16-inning struggle against the Milwaukee Braves' Warren Spahn, an epic pitchers' duel that later became the subject of an entire book (Jim Kaplan, *The Greatest Game Ever Pitched*). Marichal had another strong season in 1964, with a 21–8 record and a 2.48 ERA, but he was edged out for the coveted annual Cy Young pitching award (then awarded only once per season) by Koufax in 1963 and by Dean Chance in 1964.

By 1965 the Marichal-Koufax rivalry had reached a fever pitch, and tensions were high as the Giants and the Dodgers met on August 22. Both Marichal and Koufax were throwing pitches close to the opposing batters. When Marichal came to the plate, Koufax brushed him back twice, and then Dodgers catcher John Roseboro returned the ball to Koufax with a throw that came very close to Marichal's head. The normally mild-mannered pitcher became enraged and attacked Roseboro with a bat, opening a large cut in his forehead. A bench-clearing brawl ensued, and in its aftermath Marichal was fined $1,750 and suspended for nine games. Roseboro filed a lawsuit against him, but later Marichal apologized for using the bat, and the two players reconciled and even became close friends.

Perhaps Marichal's best season came in 1966, when he notched a 25–6 record, pitched 25 complete games, and led the league in a variety of pitching categories, He was again edged out for the Cy Young Award by Koufax, whose ERA in his final season was 1.73. Despite his dominant performances in the 1960s, Marichal never won the award. Marichal started strong in the 1967 season but was hampered by a hamstring injury and finished with a 14–10 record. In 1968 he led the league with 26 wins against nine losses, and in 1969 he achieved a 21–11 record and a very strong 2.10 ERA.

Suffered Drug Reaction

Marichal's fastball was permanently ruined by an allergic reaction to a penicillin shot during spring training for the 1970 season. From then on he suffered from arthritis and constant back pain. Marichal's control enabled him to bounce back as a smart aging pitcher in 1971, winning 18 games and appearing in the postseason for a second time. He pitched a complete game in the National League Championship Series (NLCS), but lost to the soon-to-be-champions Pittsburgh Pirates. Marichal suffered poor seasons in 1972 and 1973, and was sold to the Boston Red Sox. He managed a 5–1 record with a high ERA in 1974 and was then sold to the Los Angeles Dodgers, where Roseboro appealed to his teammates to give him friendly treatment. Marichal retired in the spring of 1975, after starting two games.

With the Roseboro incident still hanging over his reputation, Marichal was not elected to the Baseball Hall of Fame for several years after he first became eligible in 1981. He fell only seven votes short in 1982, and was finally chosen in 1983 after Roseboro campaigned on his behalf. He has continued to be associated with baseball since his retirement, returning to the Dominican Republic and leading an Oakland Athletics farm program there in the 1980s and 1990s. He has broadcast baseball games on Spanish-language radio and for the Spanish-language service of the ESPN cable network. He served in the Dominican government as Minister of Sports and Physical Education from 1996 to 2000.

Marichal owns a farm in the Dominican Republic, where he tends to farm animals as he did as a child. "I come almost every afternoon," he was quoted as saying by Jan Finke of the Society for American Baseball Research. "I really enjoy spending time with the animals and talking to my workers. It's very relaxing." Marichal has issued two memoirs, *A Pitcher's Story* (1967, with Charles Einstein), and *Juan Marichal: My Journey from the Dominican Republic to Cooperstown* (with Lew Freedman, 2013).

Books

Klein, Dave, *Bob Gibson, Juan Marichal, Vida Blue, Hoyt Wilhelm* (Great Pitchers Series 2), Grosset & Dunlap, 1972.

Marichal, Juan, with Lew Freedman, *Juan Marichal: My Journey from the Dominican Republic to Cooperstown,* MVP, 2011.

Periodicals

National Pastime, Annual 2007.

New York Times, April 28, 1998; July 2, 2008; December 7, 2009.

Washington Times, August 23, 2004.

Online

"Juan Antonio (Sanchez) Marichal," *Latino Legends in Sports,* http://www.latinosportslegends.com/Marichal_Juan-bio.htm

"Juan Marichal," *BaseballLibrary.com,* http://www.baseball library.com/ballplayers/player.php?name=Juan_Marichal_ 1937 (September 28, 2013).

"Juan Marichal," *Society for American Baseball Research,* http:// sabr.org/bioproj/person/5196f44 (September 28, 2013).

"Marichal, Juan," *Baseball Hall of Fame,* http://baseballhall.org/ hof/marichal-juan (September 28, 2013).□

Marie de Médicis, Queen of France

Marie de Médicis (1573–1642) was the queen of France in 1610 and ruled the country as regent for her young son, later King Louis XIII, from 1610 to 1617.

Marie was Italian by birth, and her involvement in French history began with one of the royal marriages that helped to cement so many alliances among the European powers in those days. She became France's ruler during a chaotic period in European history, when tension between Catholics and Protestants was rising to dangerous levels, and she had to negotiate a variety of internal tensions of France as well. Marie's life, during which she was deposed, imprisoned, and banished by her own son, was a dramatic one. She wrangled the most powerful man in 17th-century French politics, Armand Jean du Plessis, known as Cardinal Richelieu. Marie was a vigorous patron of the arts, and her activities in the fields of visual art and architecture have provided rich materials for modern scholars seeking to understand the relationship between art and politics in the court life of the day.

Enjoyed Strong Education

Known in France as Marie de Médicis, Marie was born in Italy into the powerful Medici family of financiers that wielded power equal to that of Europe's monarchical families. She was born in Florence, at the city's Pitti Palace, on April 26, 1573, and in Italian her name was Maria de' Medici—Maria of the Medicis. She received a wide education that was unusual for women at the time; it included mathematics and was particularly strong in the fine arts (she was apparently an artist of modest skills herself), covering such arcane topics as precious stones. The Medici family did not pursue the arts for their own sake but rather deployed them in the service of splendid events such as marriages of members of the family to powerful outsiders.

Thus the young Marie would have witnessed the wedding of Ferdinando de' Medici to the French princess Christine of Lorraine in 1589—a dazzling spectacle that included music, dramatic presentations, ballet jousts, and other elaborate forms of pageantry. In 1600, it was Marie's turn to enter into an arranged marriage, this one even more advantageous to the Medici family: she was betrothed to Henri IV, the king of France. The wedding banquet table was set with nearly life-size sculptures of Marie and her husband (who was not himself present), made from sugar. The following year she took up residence in the Louvre, then the home of the French royal family and now a major museum.

The royal couple wasted no time starting a family. Marie's first child, Louis, was born in 1601 and, as Henri's oldest son, was immediately groomed as the future king. Marie had six children in all, three boys (one of whom died as a small child) and three girls. All of her daughters married into major European ruling families. The most politically important of her children would be the fifth, Gaston, who would emerge as her supporter in her future battles with Louis.

Marie's art and architecture projects began during the 1600–1610 decade: she commissioned an expansion of the château of Montceaux-en-Brie, a castle that had been given to her as a gift by the king on the occasion of Louis's birth. The task would have been emotionally complicated for Marie by the fact that the castle had until recently been owned by one of the king's many mistresses, Gabrielle d'Estrées. Moreover, it had first been built by another Italian bride, Catherine de' Medici, a distant relative of Marie, who had to be sensitive to the fact that she was seen to a degree as a foreign interloper.

Became Regent After Husband's Assassination

The image Marie wanted to present through architecture and art increased in importance after Henri IV was assassinated—stabbed as his carriage was stopped in heavy traffic—in 1610 by a Catholic fundamentalist who had experienced visions telling him to persuade the king to convert the French Protestant Huguenots to Catholicism. Her nine-year-old son Louis, known as the Dauphin, became king, but he was not yet old enough to rule. The Parliament of Paris, somewhere between a legislature and a royal advisory body, installed Marie as regent.

In the words of Katherine Crawford, writing in the *H-France Review,* historians have considered Marie "variously inept, irascible, stupid, politically backward, conniving, greedy, and shrill. She has been accused of complicity in her husband's death, stalling the development of state institutions, and being mindlessly devout." Crawford noted, however, that recent research has challenged this view, and certainly the challenges Marie faced were substantial: her husband had left her on the brink of war with Spain, and at home she had to contend with a host of noble families intent on reducing the monarch's power. Marie directed that large payments be made to certain nobles, but this left the royal treasury in a precarious position. She made peace with the Catholic Habsburg monarchy in Spain and betrothed her son Louis to the Infanta Anna, the daughter of Spain's King Philip II.

Intent on legitimizing her rule, Marie turned again to architecture and art. She planned a new royal residence, the Palais Luxembourg (Luxembourg Palace), which she originally called the Palais Médicis. Modeled on the Pitti Palace where she had grown up, the new residence was begun in 1615 and completed by 1623 as construction continued after Marie's downfall. It included a gallery containing 24 giant paintings by Peter Paul Rubens depicting Marie's life up to that point; the entire series is one of the artistic masterpieces of the period. The palace is now used by France's Senate.

Exiled to Small Town

Marie, however, stirred enmity at court by promoting another Italian, Concino Concini, whom she had brought from Italy with his wife, her childhood friend. In 1617 Louis, then 15, seized power from his mother, ordering her arrest and that of Concini, who was eventually killed. At the advice of the young king's advisor Richelieu, Marie was exiled from Paris and installed under a kind of house arrest in the small town of Blois, more than a hundred miles away. Louis then took the reins of power and installed his own favorite, Albert de Luynes, as Concini's replacement.

The deposed Marie did not accept her defeat. In 1619, she escaped from her Blois house, talked Luynes into making her an administrator in the city of Anjou, and used that as a springboard to attract new backers. She joined with Louis's younger brother Gaston d'Orléns to try to overthrow the teenage king. Their attacking army was defeated in August of 1620, in a battle at the town of Les-Ponts-de-Cé Marie was forgiven once again at the behest of Richelieu, and when Luynes died in 1621, Marie's standing at court reached a new high point.

It was not long, though, before Marie turned against her protector Richelieu. The issue was France's relationship to Spain, which Marie had improved. Richelieu favored confrontation with the Habsburg powers, and he eventually got his way, deepening the continent-wide conflict that would become known as the Thirty Years' War. She tried to have Richelieu fired, once again joining with Gaston to menace the king. But Louis had finally tired of his mother's machinations. On November 12, 1630, known as the Day of the Dupes, he pretended to agree to Marie's terms, and her supporters believed that the influential minister had been defeated. The king, however, had sat out the tumult at the royal hunting lodge in Versailles. Richelieu went there, learned that the king supported him fully, and returned to Paris after Louis had ordered Marie's arrest once again. She was exiled this time to a house in Compiègne.

Once again Marie was able to escape, but her future in France had ended. She fled to the Netherlands, where she was received in royal style and continued to attempt to organize resistance against Louis with little success. She lived in England for a time, but as a Catholic in that increasingly Protestant country she got little political traction. Marie died in Cologne, Germany, on July 3, 1642; Louis outlived her by only a single year.

Books

Europe, 1450 to 1789, Gale, 2004.

Goyau, Georges, *Maria de' Medici: A Short Biography,* Shamrock Eden, 2011.

Lawrence, Cynthia Miller, *Women and Art in Early Modern Europe: Patrons, Collectors, and Connoisseurs,* Pennsylvania State University Press, 1997.

Online

"Jean-François Dubost, Marie de Médicis, La reine dévollé" *H-France Review,* http://www.h-france. net/vol9reviews/vol9no135crawford.pdf (October 28, 2013).□

Ante Marković

The Croatian political leader Ante Marković (1924–2011) was the last prime minister of the nation of Yugoslavia.

Marković attempted to forestall the breakup of Yugoslavia into separate countries, each dominated by a different ethnic group. Had he succeeded, the country might have avoided the years of bloodshed that followed in the 1990s. As prime minister and then president of Croatia, which was then part of the federated Yugoslavia, Marković devised free-market reforms of the kind that have also been attempted in other parts of the Communist world, and as prime minister his

TANJUG/AFP/Getty Images

economic policies met with substantial success. For a short time he was personally popular, and it looked as though his economic model might provide the opportunity for reform of the Communist system. The country soon dissolved under the weight of its internal conflicts, however, and Marković's reign as prime minister came to an end in December of 1991—a date that essentially marked the end of the nation of Yugoslavia.

Fought Against Nazis

Ante Marković (AHN-teh MARK-o-vitch) was born in the small town of Konjic, in what is now Bosnia and Herzegovina, on November 5, 1924. At the time the town was in the Kingdom of Serbs, Croats, and Slovenes, the direct ancestor of the multi-ethnic nation of Yugoslavia that took shape in 1929. Although the area was predominantly Bosnian, and was ruled by Serbs, Marković's family was of Croat background. In the 1930s, he joined the League of Communist Youth, and in 1943, the Communist Party of Yugoslavia. The formative experience of his youth was World War II, during which Yugoslavia was the scene of intense fighting among supporters of the country's prewar monarchy, invading German and Italian forces, and Communists, aided in the later stages of the war by the Soviet Red Army. Marković fought on the Communist side, which prevailed in the maneuvering after the war and declared the new Socialist Federal Republic of Yugoslavia in January of 1946. In the country's new form, all its constituent ethnic groups—Serbs, Bosnians, Macedonians, Kosovars, and Slovenes, as well as a host of smaller groupings, were to have equal rights, and to live in federated states called republics.

Attending schools in the Croatian seaside city of Dubrovnik, Marković moved on to the University of Zagreb, where he received a degree in electrical engineering in 1954. Marković spent most of his career not as a politician but as an industrial manager. He married, and he and his wife raised two children. Marković held regional Communist Party positions in Croatia, but the position in which he exerted the most influence was that of director of the Rade Končar electrical engineering plant in Zagreb, one of Yugoslavia's largest industrial concerns. Marković would serve in that position from 1961 to 1986. Croatian nationalist movements flared up in the late 1960s and early 1970s, only to be put down by the forces of Yugoslav strongman Josip Broz, known as Marshal Tito.

Marković drew mixed conclusions from this experience. He believed in the central Yugoslav government and in the long-term viability of the Communist system. But he had seen firsthand the negative effects of centralized bureaucratic control over state enterprises, and he began to entertain ideas of economic liberalization and the transfer of some economic responsibilities to local control. In this way of thinking he was generally aligned with Tito, who, alone among Eastern European leaders, had steered a course independent of the Soviet Union. Marković hoped to open Yugoslavia to trade with western Europe and to make Yugoslav products more competitive on the world market.

Gained Reformist Reputation

Thus Marković emerged as a strong candidate for advancement within the Yugoslav Communist hierarchy. He also had a clean image: he was perceived as working for the goals of reform rather than trying to increase his own wealth. Marković was named prime minister of Croatia in 1982, serving in that position until he was named the republic's president in 1986. Although he had little real autonomy in these positions, Marković, who spoke several Western languages well and had a personal charisma that led to his being dubbed The Man with the Smile, was able develop a set of policies advocating closer economic ties with the West, increased foreign investment, and various other reform measures.

Like other countries in the Communist East Bloc, Yugoslavia spiraled into economic crisis in the late 1980s. Deteriorating conditions forced Yugoslav prime minister Branko Mikulic to resign on December 30, 1988, and Marković was chosen as the new prime minister by the Communist leadership in a close vote over the country's actual Communist Party chair. He was seen as an economic reformer akin to Soviet head of state Mikhail Gorbachev, who had liberalized both economic and social institutions in the Soviet Union. He took office on March 16, 1989.

At the beginning Marković commanded broad support across Yugoslav society. He was trusted by reform-minded members of the Yugoslav intelligentsia and by politicians in the country's constituent republics, although Serbia's often-demagogic leader, Slobodan Milošević, emerged as a thorn in his side. In his first months in office, Marković took bold steps to restore economic confidence and to slash Yugoslavia's disastrous inflation rate, which was running at more than 300 percent a year when he took over. He pegged the value of Yugoslavia's dinar currency to that of the German deutschmark (used in Germany prior to the introduction of the Euro currency) and loosened foreign trade regulations. These measures slashed the inflation rate to about 50 percent by the end of Marković's first year in office, and by the middle of 1990s, it reached zero.

For a short time, Marković enjoyed considerable popularity, but the seeds of Yugoslavia's eventual dissolution were already in motion. Marković was hampered by the country's loosely federal system, which had aided him as a Croatian manager; Croatia and Yugoslavia's other constituent republics printed currency on their own, undermining Marković's anti-inflation program, and delayed payments to the central government. Most crucially, they objected to funding for Yugoslavia's national army (JNA), which they saw as inimical to their own interests: the JNA had already begun an action against ethnic Albanian separatists in Yugoslavia's Kosovo province.

Formed Political Party

Marković was also pressed from the Serbian-nationalist side: the pro-Serb faction led by Milošević objected to the pro-Western slant of Marković's policies, and Milošević himself clearly had national ambitions. Marković formed a party of his own, the Alliance of Reformist Forces, that attempted to mix economic reform and pro–Yugoslav federalism planks in its platform, but the party had little success in elections in 1990. Marković sought support from the West, visiting the United States in October of 1990. But his reception was chilly at best; he ended having to pay for all of his own meals except for one breakfast at the Council of Foreign Relations. Things came to a head with the official secession of Croatia and Slovenia in June of 1991.

Marković deployed JNA troops to Slovenia, resulting in a ten-day war that claimed dozens of lives. With the help of western European countries, he succeeded in negotiating a three-month moratorium on the implementation of independence measures on the part of the secessionist republics. However, when the moratorium expired, conflict flared anew and almost cost Marković his life: Yugoslav air force jets fired rockets at the Croatian presidential palace in Zagreb while Marković was in the building. "It was by sheer miracle that we stayed alive," Marković told the *New York Times.* Increasingly presiding over a government with no power, and correctly fearing the bloodletting to come as former Yugoslav citizens fell into ethnic conflicts in their new independent countries, Marković resigned the Yugoslav presidency on December 20, 1991.

"If Markovic succeeded as a technocrat, he failed as a politician," observed the London *Times.* Within a few years, the country he loved and to which he had devoted his career was engulfed in horrific violence. Marković stayed out of politics. He did business consulting work in Austria and in various states of the former Yugoslavia before retiring in Zagreb. In 2003, he appeared at the International Criminal Tribunal for the former Yugoslavia in The Hague, in the Netherlands, and testified against Milošević, who was held responsible for much of the violence. Marković died in Zagreb, Croatia, on November 28, 2011.

Books

Current Leaders of Nations, Gale, 1998.

Periodicals

Economist, February 18, 1989.
Guardian (December 16, 2011).
Independent (London, England), November 30, 2011.
New York Times, October 8, 1991; December 13, 2011.
Times (London, England), December 9, 2011.

Online

"What Have I Learnt from Ante Markovic?" *Dalje.com,* http://dalje.com/en-croatia/what-have-i-learnt-from-ante-markovic/39902 (October 15, 2013).□

John McCarthy

The American computer scientist John McCarthy (1927–2011) coined the term "artificial intelligence" (or AI) and was a major pioneer in that field. His influence loomed large in American computer science generally, and his fingerprints appear in many of the technologies taken for granted by ordinary computer users.

McCarthy made one major error in foreseeing the future: he dismissed the personal computer as a toy and as a passing fad. But even that innovation would have been impossible without McCarthy's accomplishments. McCarthy invented the LISP programming language, which underlay the interactivity computers developed as they evolved into something more than high-speed calculators. He devised the system of time-sharing, in which individual users shared the resources of a large mainframe computer; time-sharing was of critical importance in the diffusion of computing into daily life, and it was an important precursor to what is now known as cloud computing. One of his early papers sketched out the idea of what would become online retailing. McCarthy's Stanford Artificial Intelligence Laboratory (SAIL) was a key incubator for new ideas in computing in the last quarter of the 20th century. McCarthy devoted much of his life to the task of building computers with human-like mental processes, and he lived long enough both to recognize the problems in the way of true artificial intelligence and to see it begin to make great new strides.

Father Patented Orange Squeezer

John McCarthy was born on September 4, 1927, in Boston, Massachusetts. His childhood was marked by both leftist politics and a spirit of curiosity and free inquiry: his father, John Patrick McCarthy, was a labor organizer who held a patent on a hydraulic orange squeezer. McCarthy's mother, Ida Glatt, was also an immigrant from Lithuania, and an activist, on behalf of women's suffrage. Both parents were members of the Communist Party in the 1930s. After McCarthy began to suffer from poor health as a child and the family lost its home during the Great Depression, they moved to Los Angeles to make a fresh start.

Attending public schools in Los Angeles and skipping three grades along the way, McCarthy taught himself higher mathematics with books borrowed from the library of the California Institute of Technology (CalTech). He enrolled at CalTech in 1944. After interrupting his studies to serve as a clerk in the United States Army, McCarthy graduated from CalTech in 1948. He went on to Princeton University for a P.h.D., which he earned in 1951, and the faculty there was so impressed that he was added to the university's mathematics faculty immediately. In 1953 McCarthy, who preferred California's mild climate, moved west to take a position at Stanford University, but in 1955 he was drawn back to the Northeast by a position as assistant professor of mathematics at Dartmouth College, which had a pioneering presence in computer science.

Arriving at Dartmouth in 1955, McCarthy organized a two-month conference of ten researchers devoted to what he called artificial intelligence—apparently the first use of the term. McCarthy himself believed that he had heard the term previously, but he never succeeded in locating an earlier source. The conference took place in 1956, and McCarthy stated its goals this way (as quoted from a Stanford news release by *States News Service*): "The study is to proceed on the basis of the conjecture that every aspect of learning or any other feature of intelligence can in principle be so precisely described that a machine can be made to simulate it." This conference is now regarded as a landmark in the history of computer science, which itself barely existed at the time as an academic discipline.

Developed Programming Language

McCarthy took a new faculty position as associate professor at the Massachusetts Institute of Technology (MIT) in 1958, and once again notched a major accomplishment shortly after his arrival: in a paper he sketched out the LISP programming language. The second-oldest high-level computer language still in use, LISP (the name was short for List Processing Language) was a novel advance in several respects upon Fortran, which had dominated the programming field until that time. Its physical text consisted of symbols, not numbers. Most importantly, it was more flexible in its organization than Fortran and was thus more suited to research in artificial intelligence, in machines that would, as the *Economist* put it, "talk back" to humans. McCarthy devised a programming technique known as garbage collection in which code no longer needed in an ongoing operation is discarded from a computer's random access memory; the feature was added to LISP and proved important in the development of later computer languages.

McCarthy organized an artificial intelligence lab at MIT, and then, after moving to Stanford University to accept a full-professor position in 1962, created SAIL there. Both labs have been fertile spawning grounds for new developments in computer technology. In the 1970s McCarthy invited the members of a local group called the Homebrew Computer Club to meet at the Stanford lab; two of its members, Steve Jobs and Steve Wozniak, soon became the founders of the computer maker Apple.

In 1965, McCarthy became the director of SAIL. Among his accomplishments there was the concept of computer timesharing, whereby individual workstations allowed multiple individuals to access a central mainframe computer. The research that led to timesharing was funded by the U.S. Defense Department's Advanced Research Projects Agency (ARPA, later DARPA). The timesharing system allowed ordinary individuals to use computers for, among other things, playing games, and its individual display screen was an important precursor to the personal computer, which quickly supplanted timesharing even though McCarthy dismissed it. McCarthy's Stanford lab was also the site of important early experiments in the development of android-like computer capabilities such as vision, hearing, limb control, and even the self-driving car.

The game of chess, combining creativity with brute computational strength, was often seen as a prime field for artificial intelligence experimentation, and McCarthy, who enjoyed chess himself, began working on computer chess programs at Dartmouth in the 1950s. In 1965 his Stanford team challenged a group of Soviet Russian scientists from the Moscow Institute for Theoretical and Experimental Physics to a computer chess match. The Soviets won the match, which was played by telegraph, but McCarthy developed friendships with several Russian computer scientists, learned to speak Russian, and visited the Soviet Union several times.

Realized AI Problems

McCarthy, however, eventually grew to discount the value of chess and other games in the development of artificial intelligence. He even blamed the game's focus for the slow development of artificial intelligence in the 1980s and 1990s, writing in 1997 (as quoted by the London *Daily Telegraph*) that the situation resembled what would have happened if the early geneticists who had studied fruit flies had tried to breed them for racing: "We would have some science, but mainly we would have very fast fruit flies." More generally, he began to realize that artificial intelligence rested on an understanding of human thinking, and that, as he was quoted as saying in a National Academy of Sciences biography by Nils J. Nilsson, "we understand human mental processes only slightly better than a fish understands swimming."

Even later in his career McCarthy showed an uncanny knack for exploring the issues that would become central to the computer world years or even decades later. As early as the 1960s, he warned of what he saw as a coming tendency for governments to try to exert control over electronic information, and he proposed the extension of the U.S. Constitution's Bill of Rights to electronic data and communications. McCarthy had a strong interest in the growing field of robotics. He lambasted portrayals of artificial intelligence in popular culture, stating (according to the London *Times*) that "[t]here is no more of the science of AI in the [the Steven Spielberg film] *A.I.* than there is in the Pinocchio story of more than 100 years ago. One should also not take seriously any of the ideas of the movie of what robots might really be like."

McCarthy disavowed his earlier left-wing tendencies after witnessing the ideas and techniques of 1960s counterculture groups, and many of his positions in later life—he supported nuclear power, disparaged organic agriculture, and rejected the idea of global warming—might be characterized as conservative, and he had faith in human development through science and technology. McCarthy was an atheist; he noted, according to Nilsson, that "[t]o count oneself as an atheist one need not claim to have a proof that no gods exist. One need merely think that the evidence on the god question is in about the same state as the evidence on the werewolf question."

McCarthy's ideas, expressed in dozens of papers over his long career, continued to influence artificial intelligence and computer science in general, and even the almost forgotten concept of timesharing resurfaced in the development of cloud computing in the 2000s. He received numerous honors in his later years, notably the Turing Award from the Association for Computing Machinery in 1972, the Kyoto Prize in 1988, and the National Medal of Science in 1990. McCarthy was married three times; his second wife, Vera Watson, shared his passion for the outdoors and was the first woman to climb Aconcagua mountain in South America. She later died in a climbing accident. McCarthy had two daughters by his first wife, and one son by his third wife, Carolyn. He died in Stanford, California, on October 24, 2011.

Books

Hilts, Philip J., *Scientific Temperaments: Three Lives in Contemporary Science,* Simon & Schuster, 1982.

Notable Scientists from 1900 to the Present, Gale, 2008.

Periodicals

Daily Telegraph (London, England), October 27, 2011.

Economist, November 5, 2011.

New York Times, October 26, 2011.

States News Service, October 25, 2011.

Times (London, England), November 2, 2011.

Online

"John McCarthy: 1927–2011, a Biographical Sketch by Nils J. Nilsson," *National Academy of Sciences,* http://www.nasonline.org/publications/biographical-memoirs/memoir-pdfs/mccarthy-john.pdf (October 15, 2013).□

Larry McMurtry

A prominent Texas writer, Larry McMurtry (born 1936) has long been known for his realistic fictional depictions of contemporary life in Texas, as well as his myth-breaking portrayals of the Old West in historical novels, including the Pulitzer Prize-winning *Lonesome Dove* (1985). His remarkable output includes more than 30 novels as well as several memoirs, biographies of Crazy Horse and Custer, collections of essays, and scripts, including the Academy Award–winning screenplay for the movie *Brokeback Mountain,* which he co-wrote.

McMurtry has written everything from pure Westerns to stories of contemporary relationships, but many of his tales draw in one way or another on the tension between the mythic cowboy past of Texas and its increasingly urban life over the past century. This disconnect between a glorified past and a bleak present was particularly evident in McMurtry's third novel, *The Last Picture Show* (1966). The novel is set in the dying and desiccated Texas town of Thalia, a once-prosperous ranching community now filled with boarded-up storefronts. Although Thalia is a fictional town, it was based on McMurtry's hometown of Archer City, Texas. *The Last Picture Show* follows several teenagers who, lacking guidance from parents or role models, drift towards adulthood. The lack of jobs in Thalia leads some of them to seek opportunities elsewhere, including the distant and unfamiliar city. Many characters in McMurtry's novels struggle with physical and emotional isolation resulting from the stifling and inhospitable places where they live.

Reinterpreted "Herdsmen Tradition"

On June 3, 1936, Larry Jeff McMurtry was born in Wichita Falls, Texas, to William Jefferson and Hazel Ruth McMurtry. William McMurtry was a cattle rancher, and Larry, the oldest of four children, was raised on the family ranch in Archer County in north central Texas. While working on the ranch, Larry McMurtry learned the stories and myths that defined the American West. This idealized history of brave and honorable men had inspired Larry McMurtry's father and uncles to become ranchers. These stories profoundly shaped Larry, too, but rather than follow in his father's footsteps and become a rancher, Larry would pursue a livelihood in which he dismantled and rebuilt these tales from a critical and more realistic perspective. In interviews as an adult, McMurtry has indicated that he does not consider his choice of a literary career as a break with his family's tradition. "The tradition I was born into was essentially nomadic, a herdsmen tradition, following animals across the earth," he told Mark Horowitz of the *New York Times.* "Writing is a form of herding, too; I herd words into little paragraphlike clusters."

Larry McMurtry attended Archer City High School, where he was an athlete and honor student. He deeply enjoyed reading, but his hometown had few books to offer. Once able to drive, McMurtry traveled the back roads of Texas and visited abandoned Dust Bowl–era farmhouses, where he would occasionally discover old books—and keep them. So began McMurtry's lifelong passion for hunting down and collecting antiquarian books. After graduating from high school in 1954, he left Archer City for Houston to attend Rice University, where he was provided with a wide selection of books to read. ''[W]hen I stepped into a university library, at age eighteen, the whole of the world's literature lay before me unread, a country as vast, as promising, and, so far as I knew, as trackless as the West must have seemed to the first white men who looked upon it,' McMurtry wrote in *In a Narrow Grave: Essays on Texas.* He attended Rice only for one year, and then transferred to the University of North Texas, where he completed his B.A. in English in 1958. He then returned to Rice University to pursue his Master's degree, while also working as a manager of a Houston bookstore.

In 1960, McMurtry was awarded a prestigious Stegner Fellowship at Stanford University, where he studied fiction writing with the renowned writer Wallace Stegner. After that he returned to Texas, where he wrote freelance book reviews for the *Houston Post* and taught writing, first at Texas Christian University from 1961 to 1962, and then at Rice University from 1963 to 1969.

Received Critical Acclaim

McMurtry's first two books, the novels *Horseman, Pass By* (1961) and *Leaving Cheyenne* (1963), are similar in setting and concerns. They are both set on ranches, and explore issues of loneliness and questions of how to live in the shadow of the spectacular frontier days. In *Horseman, Pass By,* the 17-year-old narrator Lonnie Bannon, an orphan, lives and works on his grandfather's cattle ranch. When an epidemic of hoof-and-mouth disease sweeps through the region and threatens the grandfather's herd and livelihood, Lonnie observes the developing conflict between his honest and humble grandfather and his ambitious, materialist half-brother Hud. *Horseman, Pass By* anticipated much of McMurtry's later work in its downbeat portrayal of life on the Great Plains. *Leaving Cheyenne* is about a love triangle between a woman, rancher, and cowboy. While these two novels failed to find a large reading audience, they were critically praised, and *Horseman, Pass By* earned McMurtry a Guggenheim Fellowship in 1964.

McMurtry's third novel, *The Last Picture Show,* catapulted him to public fame and solidified his reputation as a serious writer of Southwestern literature. Not everyone was happy about his portrayal of small-town life in Texas, though. Residents of his hometown, Archer City, were shocked by its graphic depictions of teenage sexuality, and thought that it cast an extremely negative light on their community. With the help of director Peter Bogdanovich, McMurtry adapted the novel into an Academy Award–winning movie screenplay of the same name. He penned four more novels following Duane Moore, the central (and perhaps autobiographical) character in *The Last Picture Show: Texasville* (1987), *Duane's Depressed* (1999), *When the Light Goes* (2007), and *Rhino Ranch* (2009).

While his literary career was taking off, McMurtry was experiencing difficulties in his personal life. In 1959, he had married Josephine Ballard, with whom he had a son, James (later a noted singer and songwriter). In 1966, the couple divorced. In interviews, McMurtry refused to talk about their split, but the subject of divorce surfaced in his next three novels: *Moving On* (1970), *All My Friends Are Going to Be Strangers* (1972), and *Terms of Endearment* (1975). These novels, referred to as his ''urban trilogy,'' share a cast of characters who have relocated to the Houston suburbs. In *Moving On,* a young married couple on the eve of divorce searches for individual fulfillment. In the critically acclaimed *Terms of Endearment,* the protagonist Emma Horton, who was first introduced in *Moving On,* experiences a deterioration of her marriage.

Left Texas and Teaching

McMurtry was living in Washington, D.C. when he wrote his ''urban trilogy.' In 1969, he had left Houston for Fairfax, Virginia, where he taught for a year at George Mason University before settling in Washington, D.C., to teach at American University. He gave up teaching creative writing in 1971, however, following doubts about the necessity of the profession. ''[M]ost of the kids that are really going to write will go ahead and do it anyway,'' he said, as quoted in the *Dictionary of Literary Biography.* Around this time,

McMurtry and some of his friends opened a used and rare bookstore named Booked Up. From this original store in Washington, D.C., McMurtry expanded his book-selling business to include locations in Phoenix, Arizona, and Archer City, Texas. McMurtry opened his Archer City bookstore in 1987, with the help of his sister, Sue Deen. The store was originally named Blue Pig; when it outgrew its original location, McMurtry moved the operation to a larger building and renamed it Booked Up as well.

In the late 1970s and early 1980s, while living in Washington, D.C., McMurtry published three novels set outside the borders of Texas: *Somebody's Darling* (1978), set in Hollywood; *Cadillac Jack* (1982), set across the country; and *The Desert Rose* (1983), set in Las Vegas. In his next novel, the widely beloved *Lonesome Dove,* McMurtry returned readers to his home state. Set in 1876, the story follows two aged Texas Rangers, Woodrow Call and Augustus McCrae, as they lead a cattle drive to Montana. The book was praised for its credible descriptions of the open range, and its sense of humor. *Lonesome Dove* won the 1985 Pulitzer Prize, and in 1989 was adapted into a popular TV miniseries. McMurtry later wrote a sequel to *Lonesome Dove, Streets of Laredo* (1994), as well as two prequels: *Dead Man's Walk* (1995) and *Comanche Moon* (1997).

McMurtry's other novels set in the dying days of the Wild West include a unique retelling of the Billy the Kid myth in *Anything for Billy* (1988), and *Buffalo Girls* (1990), whose wretched pageant of characters includes a never-sober Calamity Jane, Wild Bill Hickok, Buffalo Bill Cody, and Sitting Bull, all well past their glory days. "I'm a critic of the myth of the cowboy," said McMurtry in a *New York Times* interview quoted in *Contemporary Authors Online.* "I don't feel that it's a myth that pertains, and since it's a part of my heritage I feel it's a legitimate task to criticize it."

Battled Health Issues

In 1989, McMurtry was chosen to serve as the head of the PEN American Center, a prestigious New York City–based literary organization; in this capacity he organized American writers' defense of the menaced Pakistani-British novelist Salman Rushdie. At around the same time, he bought a house in Archer City. In 1991, he hit a Holstein cow with his car while driving and shortly after that suffered a major heart attack. During the following period, while recuperating in the Tucson home of his friend and writing partner Diana Ossana, McMurtry battled depression. He eventually recovered, and with Ossana went on to write TV adaptations of *Streets of Laredo* and *Dead Man's Walk.* McMurtry and Ossana also wrote the Academy Award–winning movie screenplay of writer Annie Proulx's short story "Brokeback Mountain," about two cowboys who fall in love.

In the early 2000s, McMurtry was spending most of his time writing and working at Booked Up in Archer City. By then, it was the largest used bookstore in Texas. In 2012, however, McMurtry announced he would be selling more than two-thirds of the store's inventory, or 300,000 books, in an auction he dubbed the "Last Book Sale." In interviews, McMurtry said the reason for the sale was to reduce the burden he would be passing along to his heirs. McMurtry kept about 28,000 books for his personal library. Booked Up remained open in Archer City, with an inventory of around 125,000 books.

In 2011 in Archer City, McMurtry married Faye Kesey, the widow of writer Ken Kesey, with whom McMurtry had studied at Stanford University. His literary productivity has continued unabated into his old age: between 2008 and 2011 he issued three volumes of autobiography (*Books: A Memoir, Literary Life: A Second Memoir,* and *Hollywood: A Third Memoir*) and his biography of General George Armstrong Custer was slated to appear in late 2013. A new Western novel, *The Last Kind Words Saloon,* with Western figures Wyatt Earp and Doc Holliday as characters, was scheduled for publication the following year.

Books

Busby, Mark, *Larry McMurtry and the West: an Ambivalent Relationship,* University of North Texas, 1995.

Dictionary of Literary Biography, Volume 2 (*American Novelists Since World War II: Third Series*), Gale, 1994.

McMurtry, Larry, *Books: A Memoir,* Simon & Schuster, 2008.

McMurtry, Larry, *In a Narrow Grave: Essays on Texas,* Encino, 1968.

Periodicals

New York Times, August 19, 2013.

New York Times Magazine, December 7, 1997; May 29, 2005.

Online

"Larry McMurtry," *The Wittliff Collections* (Texas State University), http://www.thewittliffcollections.txstate.edu/research/a-z/mcmurtry.html (October 15, 2013).

"McMurtry's Booked Up Store in Archer City," *Lubbock Online,* http://lubbockonline.com/filed-online/ (October 15, 2013).□

Graham McNamee

Graham McNamee (1888–1942) was a pioneering radio announcer and one of the first celebrities to emerge in the new medium. Known for his enthusiastic, blow-by-blow coverage of major sporting events for NBC Radio, by 1927 he was famous enough to appear on the cover of *Time.* "Things happen fast in the U. S., and, wherever in the U. S. anything nationally important is happening, Graham McNamee sits there telling the world," the magazine asserted.

Graham McNamee was born on July 10, 1888, in Washington, D.C. At the time, his lawyer-father was serving as legal counsel to Lucius Q. C. Lamar, the U.S. Secretary of the Interior for President Grover Cleveland. The family later moved to the Minneapolis/St. Paul area, where his father served as corporate counsel for the Northern Pacific Railroad. Both his father

AP Photo

and his mother, Anne Liebold McNamee, were originally from Ohio. McNamee inherited a love of music from his mother and trained to become a concert singer.

Moved to New York City

After graduating from the Roman Catholic-affiliated Cretin-Derham Hall High School in St. Paul, McNamee played semiprofessional hockey and went to work as a clerk for the Rock Island Railroad in Minnesota. To further develop his musical ambitions he moved to Chicago, where he continued to train while working as a salesperson for meat-packing giant Armour. McNamee had a pleasing, sturdy baritone and was also a skilled pianist. His father was disappointed that his only child had not chosen a more respectable profession, like the law, but when Anne McNamee was widowed in 1912, she and her son moved to Weehawken, New Jersey, to further his career.

McNamee's years of musical training reached fruition with his professional debut in New York City on November 22, 1920, in a concert recital at Aeolian Hall. He nevertheless struggled to earn a living, and chanced into his radio career by accident: in early 1923, on his way to jury duty, he took a shortcut through the American Telephone and Telegraph Company building, which was running a limited program on its new radio station, WEAF-AM. When he spoke to someone who worked there, they were impressed by his voice and he was offered an audition on the spot.

McNamee started at WEAF as a general announcer and all-around studio go-fer, with a starting salary of $50 a week. Commercial radio was then in its infancy, with only locally available stations broadcasting from major cities, often via large antennas on multistory buildings. Plays, serial dramas, and dramatic readings were developed to fill up airtime, along with news and music. Coverage of live sporting events was another popular feature that helped bring the masses to the new medium. WEAF sent McNamee to a boxing ring set up at the New York Polo Grounds on August 31, 1923, to report from a middleweight title fight between Harry Greb and Johnny Wilson. Six weeks later McNamee took over from sports journalist Grantland Rice in providing coverage of Games Three through Six of baseball's 1923 World Series. This was a "Subway Series," between two New York teams, the Yankees and Giants, and it was only the second time the World Series games were announced over the radio.

Became Baseball-Broadcast Legend

Apart from his brief career in hockey, McNamee had little knowledge of sports. When he began his career, radio coverage of baseball, football, boxing, and other games was the province of newspaper sportswriters, who were not trained in broadcasting nor were they comfortable with extemporaneous speaking. McNamee compensated for his lack of technical knowledge with exciting color commentary, but his blunders were numerous. Ring Lardner, one of America's leading sportswriters of the 1920s, once quipped, "there was a doubleheader yesterday—the game that was played and the one McNamee announced," according to a 1964 *Sports Illustrated* profile of McNamee.

McNamee's stamina for live radio coverage served him well for the 1924 Democratic National Convention, held that year in New York City at Madison Square Garden and the longest in the history of U.S. presidential elections. Deadlocked between two contenders, the delegates went through 103 balloting rounds before reaching a decision. McNamee stayed on the air for 16-hour coverage for 15 days. "He was voluble in extemporaneous description and narration of events that took place before his eyes while a live microphone was before him and he developed a technique for portraying accurately and interestingly, in fluent language, the sights at fast-moving sports contests," the *New York Times* reported about McNamee's appeal to a growing American radio audience. "Unlike most of the voluble, excited broadcasters who imitated his style, he managed to keep his running commentary intelligible and connected."

Wrote Memoir at 38

McNamee began to receive truckloads of mail from radio listeners across the United States, making him one of the first nationally known celebrities created by the new medium. By then AT&T had abandoned its attempt to become a broadcaster, selling off the WEAF station to the Radio Corporation of America (RCA), a manufacturer of radio sets. In 1926, RCA set up the National Broadcasting Corporation (NBC) with WEAF and WJZ, which broadcast from New Jersey, as the flagship stations for a new coast-to-coast network. The 38-year-old McNamee was so well-known by that point that he wrote his autobiography, *You're on the Air,* which was published by Harper in 1926. Drama critic and newspaper columnist Heywood Broun provided the preface, and examined the ardent following that McNamee had garnered over America's airwaves in the space of a few short years. "A thing may be a marvelous invention and still as dull as ditchwater," Broun reflected, according to a *New York Times* review. "It will be that unless it allows the play of personality. Graham McNamee has been able to take a new medium of expression and through it transmit himself—to give out vividly a sense of movement and of feeling. Of such is the kingdom of art."

McNamee co-authored his memoir with Robert G. Anderson and gave some fascinating behind-the-scenes details about what went on in the broadcast booth and how many things might go wrong during a live broadcast. The *New York Times* review of *You're on the Air* found the read a compelling one. "It is the first time the story of this marvelous infant industry, only four years old but already making and losing fortunes and filling the air all around the globe with thousands of voices, has been told from the inside," its book critic wrote.

Witnessed Both Dempsey-Tunney Bouts

McNamee is best remembered for his commentary on two legendary boxing matches of the decade between icons Jack Dempsey and Gene Tunney. The first was on September 23, 1926, in Philadelphia, when the pair fought for the world heavyweight championship title. This was the first bout to be transmitted over the fledgling NBC network, and some 15 million listeners tuned in, according to the *New York Times.* The newspaper also ran the full account of McNamee and White's commentary as transcribed by professional stenographers. "Incidentally, this is probably the first time that the radio story of a big news event has been reported verbatim in a newspaper," the introductory paragraph noted.

Three months later, NBC made history with the first live, coast-to-coast broadcast of a sporting event, with McNamee at the microphone for the 1927 Rose Bowl college football contest in Pasadena, California. Later in 1927, he was stationed at a New York City wharf to greet returning hero Charles Lindbergh, the aviator who had just made the first solo transatlantic flight. On September 22, 1927, McNamee traveled to Chicago to announce the play-by-play in a Tunney-Dempsey rematch. This was the famous "Long Count" fight, with Dempsey ignoring newly implemented rules and inadvertently giving Tunney a few more seconds to recover after being knocked down. This fight had an estimated 50 million listeners and proved so nerve-wracking that it was said ten American listeners died of heart attacks during the broadcast. This event, and McNamee's excitable narration, cemented his contribution to American sports broadcasting. "The Metropolitan Life Insurance Company hastily calculated that in a half-hour of such excitement only 5.4 persons out of the estimated 50 million listeners should have died, which meant either that McNamee had a much larger audience or that his account was almost twice as stimulating as it should have been," wrote Thomas F. Moore in *Sports Illustrated.* "McNamee always regarded this fight as the high point of his sportscasting career."

McNamee's status as a national celebrity was enshrined by his cover appearance on the October 3, 1927, issue of *Time* magazine. "Sports experts grumble that he does not know the sport he is describing," the profile writer said of McNamee. "Radio executives answer that neither do most of the listeners; that colorful, general reports are more satisfying to the masses than accurate technical descriptions."

Became Highest Paid Announcer

In the spring of 1928, McNamee made broadcasting history once again, covering the Indianapolis 500 motor race for NBC before heading on to Kansas City, Missouri, for the Republican National Convention. Again, McNamee's reportage of the nominating process drew millions of listeners, and helped usher American politics into the electronic age.

McNamee had a 19-year run on radio, but NBC executives began to give major sports assignments to a newly trained generation of writer-broadcasters in the early 1930s. One of his final athletic contests was the 1934 Poughkeepsie Regatta of the U.S. Intercollegiate Rowing Association. McNamee attempted to broadcast from a boat on the Hudson River, but his eyewitness account was troubled by poor sight lines and he called the scull of the U.S. Naval Academy as the winner, when actually Navy came in third.

McNamee's first marriage, to professional soprano Josephine Garrett, ended in divorce in 1932. In January of 1934, he wed Anne Lee Simms, a Louisiana native. His NBC contract made him the highest earning announcer in radio by the mid-1930s, and he had some relatively easy years at NBC on a variety program that featured vaudeville comedian Ed Wynn, and another with popular crooner Rudy Vallee. He also earned a reported $700 a week as the narrator for Universal Newsreels, a short rundown of current events and global news stories that ran before the feature film in movie theaters.

Downed by Go-Kart

In August of 1935, McNamee visited Akron, Ohio, for the All-American Soap Box Derby. One entrant crashed into the broadcast booth and McNamee was hospitalized for his injuries, but recovered. "For 13 years, I have taken chances while broadcasting in airplanes, atop skyscrapers, in speeding autos and dozens of other ways—and then I'm knocked for a loop by a 14-year-old kid," he told a newspaper reporter, according to the *Akron Beacon Journal.*

McNamee's final broadcast was on April 24, 1942, for gossip columnist Elsa Maxwell's *Party Line* show. He fell ill at his home on 25 Central Park West, a landmark Art Deco high rise, and was hospitalized for a streptococcus infection. On May 9, 1942, he died of a cerebral embolism at St. Luke's-Roosevelt Hospital Center in New York City at the age of 53.

McNamee's name appears often in scholarly and popular works about baseball's popularity in twentieth-century America. An image of him on the job even appears on the cover of *Baseball Over the Air: The National Pastime on the Radio and in the Imagination,* which recounts McNamee's work with sound engineers in placing microphones around the stadium to capture the excitement. "It is hard for a man at a distance to feel that he is at a ballgame if he hears just a voice talking and talking," the book quoted McNamee as saying. "But that roar makes him believe it—he can see the figure sliding in under the catcher's outstretched hand—even the cloud of dust as the runner reaches his goal."

Books

McNamee, Graham, and Robert G. Anderson, *You're on the Air* with preface by Heywood Broun, Harper & Brothers, 1926.

Silvia, Tony, *Baseball Over the Air: The National Pastime on the Radio and in the Imagination,* McFarland and Company, 2007.

Periodicals

Akron Beacon Journal, September 17, 2012.

New York Times, September 5, 1926; September 24, 1926; June 10, 1928; May 18, 1942.

Sports Illustrated, October 12, 1964.

Time, October 3, 1927.□

valerie Macon/Getty Images

Jiří Menzel

The Czech film and theater director Jiří Menzel (born 1938) was a key figure in the creative flowering of Czech film in the late 1960s, known as the Czech New Wave. Unlike several of his contemporaries in the movement, Menzel remained in Czechoslovakia and continued to work there; after the fall of Communism and the division of Czechoslovakia into the Czech Republic and Slovakia, he has gained new recognition.

Menzel is best known for a single film, known in the United States as *Closely Watched Trains* and in Britain as *Closely Observed Trains.* Released in 1966, the film mixed humor and political content in a way that set the tone for much of his output: many Menzel films featured satire and sexually based comedy that nevertheless had overtones of resistance to totalitarian rule, fascist of Communist. Like his contemporaries, Menzel fell afoul of Communist authorities after the Czechoslovak liberalization movement known as the Prague Spring was crushed by Soviet military forces in 1968. He remained active in Prague as a theater director and actor and gradually returned to making films, many of them based on the works of writers whose work had been banned by the authorities.

Rejected by Theater School

Jiří Menzel was born in Prague, Czechoslovakia, on February 23, 1938. His early childhood spanned the World War II years, but the rapid German occupation of Czechoslovakia may have saved him from trauma. "I was a boy then," he recalled to Clara Rodrigues of the *Times of India.* "There was no war in my city. There were only war airplanes in the sky, and then we had to hide underground. For me it was more like an adventure." He hoped to become a theater director and applied to a theater school but was rejected. Instead he enrolled at FAMU, the Film and TV School of the Academy of the Performing Arts in Prague, graduating in 1962.

At FAMU, Menzel was influenced by several slightly older colleagues who provided the initial spark for the New Wave moment in Czech film. "I was the youngest. I was innocent. I had no ambitions," he recalled to Steve Rose of the London *Guardian.* But along the way Menzel was making a close study of contemporary Czech literature, favoring writers like Josef Škvorecký and Bohumil Hrabal, whose satires and outrageous plots pushed at the boundaries of Socialist Realist orthodoxy. In 1965 Menzel was recruited by one of his mentors, Věra Chytilová, to direct an episode of *Pearls of the Deep,* a collection of short films paying tribute to Hrabal, who has been called the Charles Bukowski of Czech literature. That year he also directed his first feature, the comedy *Crime at a Girls' School,* based on a novel by Škvorecký

In 1966, Menzel released *Closely Watched Trains,* a central document of the Czech New Wave and a film that quickly received international distribution. *Closely Watched Trains* told the story of a young railway employee who loses his virginity during the German occupation of Czechoslovakia during World War II. The film was simple, naturalistic, and often humorous, but it set a coming-of-age story against a background of political repression effectively, and in so doing it exerted an influence on other filmmakers in Czechoslovakia and across Communist Eastern Europe, where creative young people were chafing against the restrictions of Soviet Russian domination. *Closely Watched Trains* won the Academy Award for Best Foreign Film in 1967.

Remained in Czechoslovakia

The film stimulated offers that would have allowed Menzel to emigrate to the West like his contemporary Miloš Forman, who went on to direct such films as *One Flew Over the Cuckoo's Nest, Amadeus,* and *Man in the Moon.* Instead Menzel remained in Czechoslovakia, where he quickly released several more films. These included *Capricious Summer* (1968), in which Menzel himself appeared as a tightrope walker, doing his own stunts; *Crime in a Night Club* (1968); and *Larks on a String* (1969). All these films were based on writings by Czech novelist; the comedy *Crime in a Night Club* was an original story suggested by Škvorecký.

By the time Menzel completed *Larks on a String,* troops from the Soviet Union and other Communist Eastern European countries had invaded Czechoslovakia in August of 1968 and put an end to the Prague Spring. *Larks on a String* went unreleased; Menzel's earlier films were banned; and Menzel found himself blacklisted within the Czech film industry. "Nothing was ever said to me. You would just hear from people that your film had been shelved," he recalled to Rose. Menzel was forced to disown his work up to the end of the Prague Spring, but he refused to return his Academy Awards as the government demanded. His passport was canceled, making it impossible for him to attend film festivals in Western countries.

In 1974 Menzel managed to return to the government's good graces by making *Who Looks for Gold?,* a socialist-realist tale about the construction of a dam. (He has since disowned that film.) Continuing to work in theater (he has appeared as an actor in some 70 productions), he was gradually able to return to making films in which he was personally more interested. In 1980, he returned to form with *Short Cut* (also known as *Shortcuts* or *Cutting It Short*), an adaptation of a novel by Hrabal that mixed erotic and comic elements with subtly disguised political commentary.

During this repressive period, Menzel and other Czech artistic figures managed to keep a spirit of freedom alive by exchanging materials underground. The Russian word for such underground exchanges was *samizdat,* but the same phenomenon occurred in Czechoslovakia. The novels of writers such as Hrabal, Škvorecký, and Milan Kundera were removed from libraries and bookstores, and sent to disposal facilities."But Hrabal's wife worked at the recycling plant," Menzel recalled to Rose, "so she stored these books and distributed them secretly to friends. I have many at home."

Won Golden Bear Award

Meanwhile, Menzel's films continued to circulate abroad and to gain new fans there. His influence was evident in the gentle comedy-drama of such British films as *Local Hero* (1983). As restrictions in the Communist world eased in the late 1980s, Menzel's earlier films were once again permitted to be shown at home, and *Larks on a String* was finally released. The film told the story of a group of officially disapproved characters in the early 1950s—a philosophy professor, a jazz musician, and an honest state's attorney—who are sent to work in a metal scrapyard. *Larks on a String* won the prestigious Golden Bear award at the Berlin Film Festival in 1990.

Ironically, Menzel faced new obstacles to his filmmaking after the fall of Communism: he now had to compete in a free film marketplace, and he found it difficult to obtain funding. In the 1990s, he worked mostly in television and theater. He had worked with Hrabal on an adaptation of the latter's novel *I Served the King of England,* but a producer sold rights to the film to a new television production company behind Menzel's back. Later he met the producer at a film festival and hit him with a stick on stage while condemning him as the audience cheered. "I had to go to the police later and pay a fine, but I was glad I had done it," he explained to Rose. Menzel was finally able to film *I Served the King of England* in the next decade, and the film was released in 2006.

Menzel won Lifetime Achievement Awards at the International Film Festival of India and the Transilvania International Film Festival in Romania in 2013. He kept those, along with the other awards he had received over his long career, in his bathroom. Increasingly active in the international film festival world, Menzel released his 16th film, *The Don Juans,* in 2013; it dealt with rehearsals of the opera *Don Giovanni* at a small regional Czech theater.

Books

Hames, Peter, *The Czechoslovak New Wave,* Berkeley, 1985.

International Dictionary of Films and Filmmakers, Gale, 2000.

Periodicals

Globe & Mail (Toronto, Ontario, Canada), September 19, 2008.

Guardian (London, England), May 9, 2008.

New Republic, March 13, 1991.

New Yorker, September 1, 2008.

Online

"Jiri Menzel," *AllMovie,* http://www.allmovie.com (October 28, 2013).

"Jiri Menzel—Lifetime Achievement Award at TIFF 2013," *Slavorum,* http://www.slavorum.com/ (October 28, 2013).

"Jiri Menzel's Work Is Full of Life," *Montreal Gazette* (August 25, 2013), (October 28, 2013).

"A Man Who Can't Laugh Can Be Sick," *Times of India,* http://articles.timesofindia.indiatimes.com/2013-11-22/theatre/44366664_1_humour-theatre-school-films (October 28, 2013).□

Freddie Mercury

The lead singer and pianist of the pioneering British glam-rock band Queen, Freddie Mercury (1946–1991) was recognized for his flamboyant stage presence and distinctive, powerful vocals, which—in the years following his early death from an AIDS-related illness—have led him to be consistently ranked among the best rock vocalists of all time. Mercury wrote some of Queen's best-known hits, including "Killer Queen," "Somebody to Love," "We Are the Champions," and the chart-topping, seven-minute rock operetta "Bohemian Rhapsody."

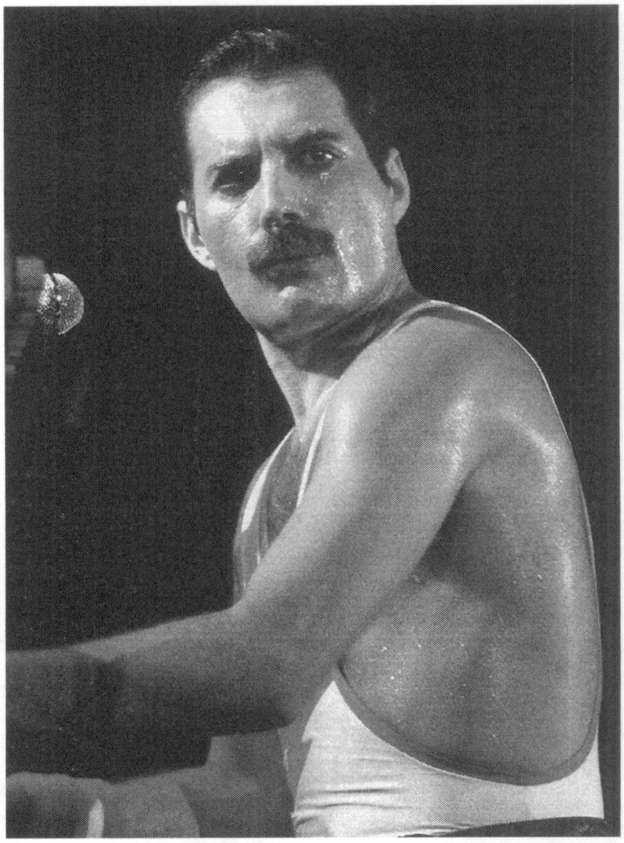

© AF archive/Alamy

During the 1970s and 1980s, Queen achieved tremendous worldwide popularity. Their music was a potent blend of progressive rock and heavy metal, characterized by layered guitars and intricate vocal harmonies. Much of Queen's appeal can also be attributed to Mercury's commanding tenor vocals and onstage personality. Clad in extravagant outfits including ermine capes and leather pants, he would strut and prance across stages before record-breaking live crowds. This majestic persona overshadowed an intensely private and shy individual who divulged few personal details to interviewers and gave coy answers when asked about his sexuality. He publicly acknowledged his struggle with AIDS only one day prior to his death. Mercury also released a solo album, *Mr. Bad Guy* (1985), and engaged in two notable musical collaborations: with the English musician Dave Clark on songs for the West End musical *Time,* and the world-renowned operatic soprano Montserrat Caballé on the album *Barcelona.*

Born into Zoroastrian Family

On September 5, 1946, Freddie Mercury was born Farrokh Bomi Bulsara on Zanzibar, an island off the east coast of Africa that is now part of Tanzania. His father and mother were Bomi and Jer Bulsara. At the time of Farrokh's birth, Zanzibar was under colonial rule by Great Britain, and Farrokh's father, Bomi, was a British civil servant who cashiered at the Zanzibar High Court. Farrokh's parents were Parsis—followers of the religion of Zoroastrianism, whose ancestors had arrived in India from Persia between the seventh and eigth centuries.

In 1955, Farrokh was sent to Panchgani, India, to attend St. Peter's School, an English-style boarding school with an authoritarian environment. During school holidays, he occasionally stayed with relatives in Bombay rather than travel all the way back to Zanzibar. It was during these stays that one aunt taught Farrokh how to draw and play piano. Back at school, he started a band named the Hectics and adopted the nickname "Freddie."

In 1963, Mercury returned to Zanzibar to continue his education at St. Joseph's Convent School. The next year, political unrest in Zanzibar drove Freddie, his parents, and his younger sister, Kashmira, to emigrate to Middlesex, England. Here he expressed a desire to attend art school but found he lacked the proper qualifications to gain admission. He spent two years at Isleworth Polytechnic School before he was able to enter the prestigious Ealing College of Art in 1966 and study graphic design and illustration. At Ealing, Freddie became friends with a fellow student and musician, Tim Staffel. Staffel played bass in a band called Smile and introduced Freddie to Smile's other band members, drummer Roger Taylor and guitarist Brian May.

Co-founded Queen

During his teenage years, Mercury was extremely conscientious about his appearance. "He always used to take hours in front of the mirror, looking after his locks," said his sister in an interview with the *Mail on Sunday* reproduced on the *Queen Archive* website. At one point, he cut apart his mother's tablecloths and refashioned them into a stylish shirt. After graduating from Ealing in 1969, Mercury moved to London, where he and Roger Taylor managed a clothes stall in the Kensington market. Around this time he also put together a short-lived blues band named Wreckage. In order to be a successful rock star, Mercury believed, it was not enough to be a great musician. Artists and bands needed to be interesting, to visually engage and entertain listeners. Sometimes Mercury would attend Smile's concerts and heckle the band's members for their lack of a distinctive stage presence. "Why are you wasting your time doing this?" he would shout, according to *The Times.* "You should be more demonstrative." When Smile broke up in 1970, Mercury asked Roger Taylor and Brian May to join him in starting a new rock band with the campy, attention-grabbing name of Queen. After several months of auditions, Queen invited bassist John Deacon to join in March of 1971.

"In the beginning, I didn't realise how serious he was about a musical career," said Brian May, as quoted by Phil Gould in *The Birmingham Post.* "I thought Freddie was a flamboyant character who was going to be an artist and who saw music as a hobby." The singer, however, was determined to achieve superstardom with Queen. He changed his last name to Mercury—his ruling planet in astrology—with the belief that a rock star needed a great name. In his pursuit of success, Mercury was more interested in creatively marketing Queen through glam imagery than slogging through the traditional live circuit, performing to small crowds in bleak pubs. During its first two years of existence, the band explored the growing realm of sound production in the recording studio. By 1973, Queen had recorded and released its debut self-titled album with the British music recording company EMI. Mercury, May, and Taylor also lent their musical talents to a recording of two singles, "I Can Hear Music" and "Goin' Back," which were released under the pseudonym of Larry Lurex. Neither the album nor the singles garnered mainstream attention.

Mercury and Queen received their big break in 1974 when they were asked to perform as a last-minute substitute for David Bowie on the weekly British television show Top of the Pops. Queen performed the song "Seven Seas of Rhye," which went on to become the band's first top-ten single. In 1974, Queen released two albums: *Queen II* and *Sheer Heart Attack.* The latter album landed on the top ten of music charts in the United States and included the hit single "Killer Queen," which earned Mercury the Ivor Novello songwriting award in 1975. That year brought additional fame and success for Queen, including a headlining tour of the United States and the release of Mercury's most popularly beloved single, "Bohemian Rhapsody." This monumental song, which took three weeks to record and featured the overdubbing of 180 backing voices, was the number one single in the United Kingdom for nine weeks, and earned Mercury another Ivor Novello award. "Bohemian Rhapsody" appeared on Queen's chart-topping fourth album, *A Night at the Opera.*

The crowd-pleasing pomp of Queen's live concerts featured Mercury frolicking with a bottomless microphone stand (a prop he regularly used after breaking his microphone stand during one performance) amid massive set and lighting displays, including a 5,000-pound crown-shaped lighting rig. His unpredictable costumes ranged from sequined leotards and ballet slippers to a baseball cap and shorts. "I like people to go away from a Queen show feeling fully entertained, having had a good time," said Mercury in an interview with *Melody Maker* magazine. "I don't want to change the world with our music. … I like to write songs for fun, for modern consumption. People can discard them like a used tissue afterwards."

In 1970, around the time of Queen's emergence, Freddie had begun dating Mary Austin, a fellow worker at the Kensington market. The two shared much in common and were inseparable early on in their relationship. "Each had a 'tip of the iceberg' personality and tended to reveal little of their true selves," wrote Lesley-Ann Jones in her biography *Mercury: An Intimate Biography of Freddie Mercury.* "Each could give the impression of being shallow, flippant, and frivolous, with materialistic tendencies and a live-for-the-moment style, particularly in their younger days. But most of this boiled down to image and to deliberate concealment of innate shyness." The couple dated for six years, and even after their separation, they continued to remain close friends for the duration of Mercury's life.

Created Grandiose Live Shows

During the late 1970s, Queen's worldwide popularity continued to explode. They released a string of albums—*A Day at the Races* (1976), *News of the World* (1977), *Jazz* (1978), and *Live Killers* (1979)—and embarked on several epic international tours. Their 1980 album *The Game* included the immensely popular singles "Crazy Little Thing Called Love" and "Another One Bites the Dust." Throughout the 1980s, Queen's music was influenced by dance rhythms; this evolving sound reflected Mercury's desire to continuously develop the band's style. "I hate doing the same thing again and again," said Mercury, as quoted on the Rock and Roll Hall of Fame and Museum website. "I like to see what's happening now in music, film and theater and incorporate all of those things." Mercury's desire to be original led to increasingly grandiose live shows before world record-breaking crowds, such as their performance before more than 200,000 people at the 1985 Rock in Rio festival. Queen was widely regarded as a leader in stadium rock, thanks to Mercury's ability to mesmerize hundreds of thousands of concertgoers.

Mercury partied as extravagantly as he rocked. Queen was known for holding lavish and outrageous parties that included entertainment by strippers, dwarfs, and fire-eaters. For his 41st birthday, Mercury flew 80 friends on a DC-9 jet to the Spanish island of Ibiza, where the festivities included flamenco dancing, fireworks that spelled out his name, and a 20-foot-long birthday cake. During these years of partying, Mercury had numerous male partners, and admitted that he "lived for sex" (as quoted in the London *Sunday Times*). He became more reticent with the press, however, after tabloids published cruel articles about his sexual identity. In 1985, Mercury became involved with Jim Hutton, an Irish hairdresser. They were to remain steady partners until Mercury's death.

In 1985, Mercury and Queen delivered a charged and unforgettable performance at the Live Aid concert, which was televised to hundreds of millions of viewers. The following year, Queen set off on its final tour, the Magic Tour, which coincided with the release of the album *A Kind of Magic.* Queen performed its last concert on August 9, 1986, at Knebworth Park in England, before a crowd of 125,000.

Duetted with Opera Star

Mercury's musical recordings outside of Queen included his 1985 solo album, *Mr. Bad Guy,* which wasn't widely embraced but still managed to chart in the U.K. In 1986, Mercury's interest in theater led him to collaborate with Dave Clark on songs for the musical *Time.* And in 1987, Mercury recorded with one of his musical idols, the revered Spanish opera singer Montserrat Caballé. His contributions to their pop-opera album *Barcelona* included the title track, which went on to become the theme song for the 1992 World Olympics.

Mercury spent his last few years outside the public eye. There were rumors of his failing health, and a handful of published photographs showing him to be thin and ailing. Mercury had informed the other members of Queen that he was HIV–positive some years before his death; he informed his sister of his disease on August 18, 1990. Less than a year later, on November 23, 1991, he announced to the world that he had AIDS. The following day, Mercury died of AIDS-related broncho-pneumonia. His death was widely mourned, but the funeral, like his life, was private. The service, conducted in Persian by Parsi priests, was attended by family and close friends, including Dave Clark and Elton John. There were flowers and tributes from around the world. Mercury bequeathed his London mansion and a significant portion of his wealth to his former girlfriend, Mary Austin.

Mercury had continued to make music up to the end. Queen's final studio albums included *The Miracle* (1989); *Innuendo* (1991), released before Mercury's death; and the posthumous *Made in Heaven* (1995). In the decades following his death, Mercury has been regarded as one of rock music's inimitable entertainers. Queen's music—which Mercury has been widely quoted as deeming "disposable pop"—also endures to this day, with songs such as "We Are the Champions" played frequently to large crowds in sporting arenas.

Books

Evans, David and David Minns, *Freddie Mercury: This is the Real Life,* Britannia, 1992.

Jones, Lesley-Ann, *Mercury: An Intimate Biography of Freddie Mercury,* Touchstone, 2011.

Freestone, Peter, *Freddie Mercury,* Omnibus, 2001.

Periodicals

Mail on Sunday, November 26, 2000.

Melody Maker, May 2, 1981.

The Birmingham Post, December 7, 2000.

The Times, November 26, 1991.

Online

"Freddie Mercury," *Queen official Home page,* http://www.queenonline.com/en/the-band/members/freddie-mercury/ (October 19, 2013).

"Queen Biography," *Rock and Roll Hall of Fame and Museum,* http://rockhall.com/inductees/queen/bio/ (October 22, 2013).□

John Molson

Anglo-Canadian entrepreneur John Molson (1763–1836) founded the Molson Brewing Company, one of the most successful brands in the history of Canadian business. Just 22 years old when he launched his venture in 1786 in Montreal, Quebec, Molson became one of British-ruled Canada's richest citizens and opportunely diversified his fortunes as his city and province expanded in the early 1800s. His firm survived into the 21st century as North America's oldest continuously operating brewery.

John Molson was born on December 28, 1763, more than three years after church parish records in Lincolnshire, England, record the marriage of his father, also named John, to a woman named Mary Elsdale. He was their eldest surviving son and the first of five children. His birthplace is cited as Moulton, a village near the larger market town of Spalding, and he spent his early years at Snake Hall, a small manor house that his father had inherited along with some local farmlands. The Molsons were minor landed gentry, but the Elsdales counted among their achievers one Robinson Elsdale, a notorious pirate who made his fortune harrying French ships in the Caribbean. That ancestor's unpublished autobiography was later used as the basis for Frederick Marryat's *Extracts from the Log of a Privateersman One Hundred Years Ago,* a popular novel of the 1840s also published as *The Privateersman.*

Emigrated to Canada

Molson's childhood was not an idyllic one. His father died in 1770, and then his mother followed him to the grave two years later. A paternal uncle and then his late mother's father took over legal guardianship of the child, and the Molson siblings were separated and sent off to other families when the grandfather decided to rent out the Snake Hall home for revenue. As a youngster Molson boarded with a family named Robinson and then the Whiteheads, who sent him to school. Awaiting access to the financial capital he would fully inherit on his 21st birthday, Molson joined the wave of newcomers to British North America at the age of 18, arriving in Quebec City on June 25, 1782. He ventured inland to Montreal and first went into business with two butchers, the Pells, whom he had met on the Atlantic Ocean crossing.

Montreal was a strategically sited former French trade and military garrison on the St. Lawrence River, which connected it to the Atlantic Ocean and Canada's maritime provinces. Montreal's its island geography and connection to two other inland water resources—to Lake Champlain on what is now the state borders of New York and Vermont, and to the Great Lakes region further down the St. Lawrence River that fed into Lake Ontario—had made it a favorable site for human habitation for some four millennia before the French arrived in the early 1600s. They set

CNW Group/MOLSON COORS CANADA

up a fur trading operation, built settlements, and warred with the Mohawk and First Nations; there was also enmity with the British, who had colonized the Atlantic seaboard and were also settling in Quebec province and Montreal. New France ceased to exist after the Seven Years' War between Britain and France was concluded by a peace treaty in 1763, the year Molson was born. After that point, Quebec and the rest of Canada became British-ruled territories.

Montreal had been under English rule for two decades by the time Molson arrived in the growing metropolis. Its French-speaking, largely Roman Catholic population had stayed on after English subjugation, but enjoyed special legal rights granted by the British pertaining to their French language and culture in order to secure Francophone allegiance to the British during the American Revolutionary War. After that war came to a close in favor of American independence, Montreal became one of the primary destinations for British Loyalists, who were forced to flee to Canada. With an influx of some 10,000 Loyalists to British Canada, Molson knew there were untapped consumer-goods markets because of this surge in population. The British liked their ales and porters, the malted quaffs made from barley and other plentiful grains that had been the alcoholic beverage of choice in northern Europe for the past several hundred years. The French, by contrast, preferred wine, made from fermented grapes, and other colonial settlers drank rum, made from West Indian sugarcane.

Imported Advanced Brewing Technology

A man named Thomas Loid became Molson's next business partner. Loid had started up a small brewing operation just outside Montreal's old fort walls in 1782, and Molson joined the operation in 1783. Neither were familiar with the chemistry of brewing and hired a professional named John Wait as their first brewmaster. This set-up became the basis for the Molson Brewing Company, the oldest continuously operating brewery in North America. It was not the first brewery in Canada or the United States, but it was the first to survive and thrive.

Documents reveal that Molson filed a lawsuit against Loid in June of 1784, six months before Molson reached his 21st birthday upon which he would inherit Snake Hall and the other Lincolnshire assets. It seems that he and Loid likely conspired together so that Molson could purchase the property at auction after making a private financial arrangement with Loid. On January 5, 1785, Molson became sole owner of the brewery and its site on the St. Lawrence River. He returned to England to claim his inheritance in the spring of 1785, and stayed for a year. It is thought he may have visited London breweries like Whitbread and gleaned some information about emerging techniques and new scientific instruments that permitted brewers to make much larger batches to satisfy consumer demand. The invention of the thermometer and the hydrometer were two relatively recent advances that enabled factory-type brewing. Molson also read one of the first textbooks on brewing chemistry, *Theoretic Hints on an Improved Practice in Brewing,* a 1777 work by John Richardson, a copy of which he brought back to Montreal when he returned in May of 1786.

Molson had also invested in top-quality barley seed, a cereal grain whose fermentation yields malt, the key ingredient in beer. Another crucial ingredient was fresh water, which Quebec had in abundance. Hops, another plant, was used to give the beverage its distinctive, tangy flavor. In the era before refrigeration, there was actually an annual brewing season in the fall and winter as the barley and hops were processed. With the help of a few hired assistants, Molson barreled his first batches of a traditional English-style ale in late 1786, and sold them at a cheaper price than the heavier porter beers shipped over from England. Over the next few years he invested all of his resources into expanding operations, and the diligence paid off. In 1791, the Molson Brewing Company, after five years in business, was producing 30,000 gallons a year to serve a thirsty Montreal and Quebec province population. Molson arranged deals with farmers to provide him with top-quality barley and even bought a lumber yard so that he could control the cost of barrelmaking.

Entered Quebec Politics

Molson became one of Montreal's leading citizens in the 1790s and early 1800s. He was active in various civic groups and socialized with other middle-class English and Scottish émigrés like himself, who collectively controlled much of the city's commerce and governance. Loaning money to other entrepreneurs was one of his first business ventures, and that eventually became the Molson Bank. He led a drive to build a new wharf for the city and also invested early in new steamship technology, which he recognized would cut his beer-transportation costs. The steamship firm he founded, the St. Lawrence Shipping Company, was known as the Molson Line and was the first to use the newly invented steam-powered engine in Canadian shipping. He also recognized the potential for new rail transportation, and was a major investor in the Champlain and St. Lawrence Railroad, which connected Montreal to New York State. The Molson Bank eventually became part of the Bank of Montreal. Molson's original Brewing Company is often cited as the second oldest company in Canada, after the Hudson's Bay Company, which is usually designated as the oldest commercial corporation in the world.

Molson's rise to become one of Canada's first millionaires might only have happened in a colonial atmosphere, where one's background and family status was of far less importance on the path to economic power and political influence. It is known that after he came back from England in 1786, he hired a housemaid named Sarah Insley Vaughan at a new residence he moved into next to his brewery. She bore him four sons—one of whom died in infancy—but the two were not married until 1801, the year their eldest son, John Jr., turned 14. The delay may have been due to the legal status of her previous marriage, for Vaughan had a curious backstory: she came from a well-born family in Northumberland, England, and had come to North America with a husband named David Tetchley, whom she left after ten years of marriage. She was four years older than Molson and the circumstances that led her to leave her first marriage and take on the lowly occupation of domestic servant are unknown. Two more sons, Thomas and William, were born to the couple in 1791 and 1793, respectively. She suffered from rheumatism and became addicted to laudanum, an opiate, which was said to have hastened her death in 1829.

Molson's list of business investments in and civic contributions to Montreal included an opulent hotel, the Mansion House Hotel, that twice burned, and the Montreal General Hospital. He also opened the city's first sizable performing-arts venue, the Theatre Royal, in 1825. After 1815, he sat in the Legislative Assembly of Lower Canada, the lower house of Lower Canada's colonial government, and in 1829, was appointed to the upper chamber, the Legislative Council.

In 1816, Molson had new articles of incorporation drawn up for the Molson Brewing Company and his assorted holdings. One of the many ironclad clauses in the document, which caused decades of family turmoil, was a stipulation that the brewery would always remain in control of the Molson family and their descendants. This particular item nearly derailed a 2005 merger with the Adolph Coors of Golding, Colorado, to become the Molson Coors Brewing Company.

Left Strong Canadian Brand Identity

Molson was taken ill with a high fever in the winter of 1835–36, and died at age 72 on January 11, 1836, at Boucherville on the Île des Sainte-Marguérite, now a Quebec province park. His descendants continued to prosper from the Molson brewery operations and his other timely investments for generations to come. His son John Jr., was one of the founders of Montreal gaslight utility company, while Thomas was a major shareholder in the company that first lit the streets of New York City. His third son, William, was one of the co-founders of the Grand Trunk Railway, which connected Maine to the Great Lakes states. Molson's great-grandson Harry Molson died on the R.M.S. *Titanic* maritime disaster in April of 1912. The Molson brand name became practically synonymous with Canadian beer and remained so for decades. In the 1950s, Molson's descendants purchased the Montreal Canadiens hockey team of the National Hockey League, and its home ice rink, the Montreal Forum. The family later donated a substantial sum to Concordia University in Montreal, which established the John Molson School of Business in his honor.

Books

Coutts, Ian, *Brew North: How Canadians Made Beer and Beer Made Canada,* Greystone Books, 2010.

Dubuc, Alfred, "Molson, John (1763–1836)," in *Dictionary of Canadian Biography,* vol. 7, University of Toronto/Université Laval, 2003.

Gasbarre, April Dougal, and David E. Salamie, "The Molson Companies Limited," in *International Directory of Company Histories,* edited by Jay P. Pederson, Vol. 26, St. James Press, 1999.□

N

Alla Nazimova

Russian-born stage and screen star Alla Nazimova (1879–1945) captivated audiences with her exotic glamour and expressive performances. One of the highest paid women in the arts in the early decades of the 20th century, Nazimova forged a successful career on Broadway in the years before World War I, then headed to California with the nascent motion-picture industry. She was a legendary fixture on the Hollywood party circuit of the 1920s and '30s, and was said to have seduced a number of high-profile figures.

Alla Nazimova's fabled beauty was in part a genetic gift passed on by her Russian and Ukrainian Jewish origins, though she would reveal years later that she was teased as a plump, clumsy child. Born Mariam Edez Adelaida Leventon on June 3, 1879, she was the second daughter and last of three children born to Sofia Horowitz Leventon and her husband Yakov, a pharmacist. They lived above the pharmacy in Yalta, a port and resort city on the Black Sea, in Ukraine's temperate Crimea region, but the Leventon marriage was a turbulent one, filled with violence and adultery, and eventually the couple left Russia for Switzerland, where they were able to divorce.

Joined Moscow Art Theater

For a time, Nazimova, along with her brother Vladimir and sister Nina, were taken in by a Swiss farm family who needed farmhands. From the foster family she picked up French and German, and also learned to play the violin by age seven. Eventually Yakov Leventon brought her back to Yalta, but he was violent toward her and her new stepmother loathed her. The end of Nazimova's unhappy youth came at a boarding school in Odessa, where she continued her violin studies. When the school was destroyed by fire, some sympathetic local families offered to take in students as boarders, and Nazimova was placed with a household full of amateur actors. She loved the props, the makeup, and the magical atmosphere of the theater, and decided to apply for a place at a Moscow drama school.

In Moscow Nazimova's fellow acting students derided her looks, and she worked diligently to transform herself into a slender, graceful presence both on stage and off. Her compelling stage presence and ability to quickly master a character gained the attention of Vladimir Nemirovich-Danchenko, co-founder of the prestigious Moscow Art Theater. She studied under him and the other founder, Constantin Stanislavski. To spare her family the taint of her career choice—deemed an unsavory one in the waning days of the Russian Empire for a woman of a modest middle-class background—she took the diminutive "Alla" from her middle name plus "Nazimova" after a character in a novel she liked.

Nazimova's career on the stage began with regional theater companies near Minsk and then Vilnius, the Lithuanian capital. In 1899 she married another actor, Sergei Golovin, but managed to keep her status secret from almost everyone she knew; later biographers surmise she did it to spite a man she was seeing, an assistant to Stanislavski. Her professional and possibly romantic partnership with another actor, Pavel Orlenev, proved the most important one of her early career. He secured lead roles for her in St. Petersburg, the imperial Russian capital, and in 1904 Orlenev staged a play called *The Chosen People* that was

© AF archive/Alamy

banned by tsarist censors for its frank depiction of anti-Semitism in Russia. They took it abroad, playing to audiences in Berlin and London, before bringing it to New York City's Herald Square Theater for a Russian-language performance in March of 1905. A *New York Times* reviewer reported that some in the audience wept at scenes of pogroms and other anti-Semitic violence.

Given Warm Welcome in America

Nazimova and Orlenev decided to stay in New York City, where she found almost instant success. One of her most ardent new supporters was the poet and radical activist Emma Goldman, who reportedly developed a crush on Nazimova after seeing her in *The Chosen People.* Goldman introduced the actor to influential figures and encouraged her to perfect her English-language abilities. She landed the title role in a relatively recent import to the New York theater scene, Norwegian playwright Henrik Ibsen's bleak drama *Hedda Gabler.* Nazimova's stirring embodiment of an unhappy, overspending, competitive housewife won favorable notice when she debuted in November of 1906. The *New York Times*' theater critic asserted the lead performance "places her at one bound in the very first rank of English-speaking actresses."

Nazimova also earned strong critical accolades for another lead in another Ibsen masterpiece, *A Doll's House,* in February of 1907. Both plays are considered classics of modern literature, especially for their realistic depictions of human psychology. In a lengthy profile that ran in the *New York Times* in late 1906, Nazimova said that typically the range of dramatic roles for women were emotionally stilted—that a female character is usually shown adoring a man, plotting to best a romantic rival, or pining over a lost love. "That's the sort of thing we women generally have to do," she told the reporter. "We must always be in love. We are the butterflies, the adventuresses, the abandoned girls. We are always made to revolve about the men."

Nazimova's career came under the management of a prominent New York actor and producer, Henry Miller, one of the founders of the Lyceum Theater Company. With Miller as her manager Nazimova worked with the highly successful theater impresarios, the Shubert brothers and even appeared on the stage of a newly built venue that had her name on it, Nazimova's 39th Street Theater. There she premiered a new work from Ibsen, *Little Eyolf,* in the spring of 1910. By then she had sent for her sister Nina to help run her household, which included a delightful farm she called "Who-Torok" in Westchester County, New York. By then Nazimova was "married" to another actor, a British expatriate named Charles E. Bryant, but the marriage that was announced in the newspapers in December of 1912 did not actually take place—a fact that later came to light when Nazimova finally obtained a divorce from Sergei Golovin in 1923. Nevertheless, the cover of a heterosexual marriage allowed both Nazimova and Bryant to pursue same-sex affairs.

Transitioned into Film

Nazimova worked steadily on Broadway until World War I, when a short anti-war play she had done called *War Brides* was adapted for film and earned a small fortune. Again, Nazimova showed herself a versatile performer and readily embraced the new medium of moviemaking. In 1917 Metro Pictures, the forerunner of the Metro-Goldwyn-Mayer (MGM) studio empire, signed her to a contract that provided a stunning salary of $13,000 a week. She made her first Metro Picture, *Revelation,* in 1918.

Nazimova moved to Los Angeles and, flush with her extravagant salary, purchased a recently built Spanish-Mediterranean villa on Sunset Boulevard near Crescent Heights Boulevard in 1920. On its grounds she installed a swimming pool in the shape of the Black Sea, to remind her of her childhood in Yalta. The house soon became the epicenter of riotous parties at which new Russian émigrés, having fled the tumult of the 1917 Bolshevik Revolution, congregated and mixed with Hollywood stars, writers, and entertainment-industry professionals who also loved the year-round sunshine.

Nazimova's feature films from the silent era included *Billions* and *The Heart of a Child.* Her faux-husband Bryant appeared in or was credited as a writer on many of her projects, and he took a ten percent cut of her salary, too. She was so famous that she was billed simply as "Nazimova." She appeared with Rudolph Valentino in 1921's *Camille,* their only film together, which she also produced. She also brought to the screen a silent-era version of *A*

Doll's House in 1922 in which she reprised her role as Nora, and a daring *Salomé* of 1923, based on the salacious Oscar Wilde play of the same name in which she took the title role.

Hosted Fabled Parties

Nazimova was rumored to have had a relationship with Jean Acker, who had married Valentino in 1919 but then separated, and also knew Natacha Rambova, who married the handsome actor before his divorce from Acker was finalized. Rambova's Russian-sounding name was entirely manufactured; she was an American debutante who pursued a career in dance before becoming a set designer. Her avant-garde work for *Salomé* and other projects set a highly stylized, Art Deco look for films of the era. Nazimova also aided the career of an ambitious young Los Angeleno named Dorothy Arzner, a script supervisor who became a film editor and then one of Hollywood's first women directors. Nazimova had a long-term relationship with the poet Mercedes de Acosta, a notorious seducer of both men and women.

Nazimova was said to have coined the term "sewing circle" to describe the all-female get-togethers she held at Who-Torok and her Sunset Boulevard home, which she dubbed "The Garden of Allah." The Hollywood villa was rumored to be the site of much debauchery and wild parties, but the rumors of illicit lovers, plus the revelation of Nazimova's sham marriage to Bryant, damaged her career. Her work in movies came to a standstill after 1925. Desperate for money, she returned to the New York stage, most notably in a revival of the Anton Chekhov play *The Cherry Orchard* in 1928, but there were fewer roles available to her as she approached her 50th birthday. She decided to convert her Sunset Boulevard property into The Garden of Allah Hotel, with private bungalows, a restaurant, and other amenities. The effort bankrupted her and she was forced to sell it, but remained there as a resident of one of its units. The bungalow strategy was copied by the newly erected Chateau Marmont, located almost directly across Sunset Boulevard from Nazimova's fabled home.

Nazimova had a 15-year hiatus from films, until she appeared in *Escape* in 1940, a drama about a man who tries to rescue his mother from one of Nazi Germany's concentration camps. She died of coronary thrombosis at Good Samaritan Hospital in downtown Los Angeles on July 13, 1945. Her former Garden of Allah property fell into disrepair, though during its heyday it had been home to a number of celebrated figures, among them Humphrey Bogart, Lauren Bacall, Errol Flynn, Marlene Dietrich, Dorothy Parker, Ernest Hemingway, and F. Scott Fitzgerald, who wrote his last uncompleted novel, *The Last Tycoon* on the property. Gossip columnist Sheilah Graham later wrote a 1969 book about the landmark, *The Garden of Allah,* ten years after it was demolished.

Nazimova's legacy as an almost openly gay public figure remains her most enduring act. She featured prominently in 2001's *The Girls: Sappho Goes to Hollywood,* a nonfiction work by Diana McLellan, and Brett L. Abrams's 2008 tome *Hollywood Bohemians: Transgressive Sexuality and the Selling of the Movieland Dream.* Among Nazimova's wider circle of platonic friends was a New York actor named Edith Luckett, who in 1921 had a child during her first marriage and asked Nazimova to serve as godmother to little Nancy, as she was called. Luckett's second husband adopted the girl, who went on to a minor career in Hollywood as Nancy Davis in the 1940s then married a future politician, Ronald Reagan. Nazimova's goddaughter is better known as former First Lady Nancy Reagan.

Books

Abrams, Brett L., *Hollywood Bohemians: Transgressive Sexuality and the Selling of the Movieland Dream,* McFarland & Company, 2008.

McLellan, Diana, *The Girls: Sappho Goes to Hollywood,* Macmillan, 2001.

Periodicals

New York Times, November 14, 1906; November 18, 1906.□

LeRoy Neiman

The American artist LeRoy Neiman (1921–2012) was among the most popular painters of the 20th century. Neiman's kinetic paintings of athletes in action remain immediately recognizable to sports fans and to readers of *Playboy* magazine, where he worked as an illustrator for more than 50 years.

Neiman's work was generally not well received by mainstream art critics, who disliked his hedonism, his uncritical embrace of professional sports and celebrities, and his repetition of a small core of themes over his long career. Yet his popular appeal hardly faded as he made drawings for five sets of Olympic games and built a business empire based on the several dozen paintings he produced each year. Neiman deftly combined elements of French Impressionist painting and Abstract Expressionism in his work, reacting enthusiastically when he first encountered the paintings of artists such as Jackson Pollock in the 1950s. Developing a unique style based on the broad, rough application of enamel paint, he applied it to materials of modern consumerist enjoyment: sports, travel, and sex.

Grew Up in St. Paul

LeRoy Neiman was born LeRoy Leslie Runquist. His autobiography, *All Told: My Art and Life Among Athletes, Playboys, Bunnies, and Provocateurs,* gives his birthdate as June 8, 1921, and suggests that he was born in Duluth, Minnesota; birthplaces of Braham, Minnesota, and St. Paul, Minnesota have also been reported, as have various other birthdates. Neiman may well have been uncertain about his origins; his father, Charles Runquist, was a railroadman in his 40s who abandoned the family. "Charlie's only contribution to the marriage," Neiman wrote in *All Told,* "was

© Everett Collection Inc/Alamy

to sire three kids in quick succession." He was closer to his mother, whom he described as "wild and irresponsible ... Feisty, she wouldn't put up with this or that guy's nonsense. She was a big influence on me." Neiman later took the surname of a stepfather. After his mother moved the family to St. Paul, he grew up mostly in the city's tough Frogtown neighborhood.

Attending Catholic schools, Neiman quickly showed talent as an artist and won a national prize for a painting he made of a fish, and in high school he hired himself out as a commercial artist to local grocery stores. "I'd sketch a turkey, a cow, a fish, with the prices," he said in a *Cigar Aficionado* interview quoted in *The New York Times.* "And then I had the good sense to draw the guy who owned the store." Neiman was drafted into the United States Army in 1942, serving in a company that landed in France shortly after D-Day. Neiman was a cook, and he amused his fellow soldiers by painting risqué murals on the walls of army mess halls.

After the war, Neiman studied art in St. Paul and then enrolled at the Art Institute of Chicago, where he continued to teach after graduating. Until coming to Chicago he had painted and drawn in traditional styles, but at the Institute he encountered modern art. "The big shock of my life was Abstract Expressionism—Pollock, de Kooning, those guys," he was quoted as saying by the London *Independent.* "It changed my work. I was an academically trained student, and suddenly you could pour paint, smear it on, broom it on!" Around that time Neiman happened upon some partially used cans of enamel house paint discarded by a custodian. He began to apply the paints as Pollock might have, using them to create broad, vital fields of color that seemed to be in motion. Neiman created a painting of boats that won first prize at the Twin City art show in 1953.

Met Hugh Hefner

Another key event in Neiman's development occurred at downtown Chicago's Carson Pirie Scott department store, to which he contributed artwork as a freelancer in the early 1950s. There he befriended Hugh Hefner, a copywriter in the store's advertising department. Soon after that, Hefner began to publish *Playboy* magazine, and after Hefner saw some of Neiman's paintings of strip clubs, among other things, Neiman was commissioned to illustrate a story about a jazz musician for the magazine. That began an association with *Playboy* that would last for the rest of Neiman's life. His most durable and recognizable contribution there was the Femlin, a small cartoon figure of a woman wearing only stockings, high-heeled shoes, and opera gloves. The Femlin has appeared in every issue of the magazine, sometimes on the cover, since 1955. At Carson Pirie Scott, Neiman also met his wife, copywriter Janet Byrne; the marriage lasted until his death.

In 1958, Neiman devised a *Playboy* feature called "Man at His Leisure." It featured Neiman's depictions of famed scenes around the world, such as the running of the bulls in Pamplona, Spain, or nude beaches in Europe. He also executed large amounts of artwork for the Playboy clubs that were opening rapidly around the world in the 1960s. "Playboy made the good life a reality for me and made it the subject matter of my paintings—not affluence and luxury as such, but joie de vivre itself," Neiman was quoted as saying in *The New York Times.*

Neiman's most recognizable images, though, were associated with professional sports. He seemed not to have a favorite sport, illustrating scenes from perhaps two dozen different sports—including the 1972 world chess championship between the American Bobby Fischer and the Russian Boris Spassky. He made sketches on the spot and was a familiar presence at live sporting events of all kinds. One of Neiman's favorite subjects was the boxer Muhammad Ali, whom he painted for the first time in 1964. Ali later said that he found Neiman and his sketchpad a familiar sight during his workouts. With his distinctive handlebar mustache, Neiman was an immediately identifiable figure.

Perhaps Neiman's most prestigious assignment was the Olympic games, for which he was the official painter five times: in Squaw Valley, California, in 1960; in Munich, Germany, in 1972; in Montreal, Canada, in 1976; in Lake Placid, New York, in 1980; and at the 1984 Winter Olympics in Sarajevo, Yugoslavia, and Summer Olympics in Los Angeles. For representations of the Olympics he began with a sketch and often used a complex mixture of materials, including watercolor, colored pencils, ink, chalk, gouache, marker, graphite, and even charcoal. Neiman also covered football's Super Bowl several times, using an electronic pen to sketch the action live on the air.

Endowed Print Studies Center

All of this activity brought Neiman considerable wealth. His paintings, often large, were produced at the rate of a few dozen a year; one of them, *Le Mans*, brought $107,550 at an auction in 1969. But those paintings spawned an immense industry in Neiman prints, in both limited and mass market editions. According to one 1996 estimate, 150,000 Neiman prints with a market value of about $400 million had been sold up to that time. Neiman also published nine books, two of them autobiographies: *Art and Life Style* (1974) and *All Told* (2012). He gave $6 million to endow the LeRoy Neiman Center for Print Studies at Columbia University.

Despite, or perhaps because of, his popularity, Neiman never enjoyed high esteem among art cognoscenti "whose orbit included *New York Times* critics, *Artforum* and *Art in America* magazines, institutions like the Whitney Museum of American Art and the Museum of Modern Art, and galleries like those lining the streets of Chelsea," wrote Ken Johnson in *The New York Times*. From that exclusive vantage point, Mr. Neiman was the archetypal hack, his immense popularity explicable only by his ambitiously opportunistic personality and his position as Hugh Hefner's court artist, which gave him monthly visibility to millions in the pages of *Playboy*." Often he was simply ignored by critics. Neiman generally appeared untroubled by this critical neglect, but he protested vigorously when *St. Paul Pioneer Press* critic Katherine Lanpher wrote that his work "stinks" and compared it to Precious Moments figurines. Neiman's popularity extended beyond the U.S., and foreign collections holding his work include the Hermitage Museum in St. Petersburg, Russia.

Neiman remained active into old age, creating artwork for the 2008 Ryder Cup golf matches. He continued to paint even after medical problems necessitated the amputation of his right leg in 2010. Neiman died in New York on June 20, 2012, at the age of 91, shortly after his autobiography *All Told* was published.

Books

Neiman, LeRoy, *All Told: My Art and Life Among Athletes, Playboys, Bunnies, and Provocateurs,* Lyons, 2012.

Periodicals

Art Business News, February 2008.

Independent (London, England), June 25, 2012.

New York Times, June 21, 2012; June 23, 2012.

Palm Beach Daily News, July 5, 2012.

Times (London, England), June 22, 2012.

Online

"Artist Biography," LeRoy Neiman Official Website, http://www.leroyneiman.com/leroy-neiman-biography.asp (November 5, 2013).

"St. Paul Played Big Role in Painter Neiman's Colorful Life," *St. Paul Pioneer Press,* http://www.twincities.com/news/ (November 5, 2012). □

Solomon Northup

The African American memoirist Solomon Northup (1808–c.1863) told his story in the book *12 Years a Slave,* made into a widely acclaimed film of the same name in 2013. A freeborn African American, Northup was kidnapped and sold into slavery in Louisiana.

Among the roughly 100 slave narratives published before the Civil War, Northup's story is unusual in several respects. First, it was the first to be made into a theatrical film, and it gave filmgoers around the world, whose previous visual experiences of slavery had come through such sanitized depictions as that in *Gone with the Wind* (1939), a jolting introduction to the brutality of the institution. Another distinctive feature of Northup's *12 Years a Slave* is that, unlike narratives by escaped slaves such as Frederick Douglass and Harriet Tubman, it was the product of a man who had not grown up as a slave. As his narrative abundantly showed, Northup's experiences were not more brutal than those of other slaves, but he described them to some extent as an outsider, with excruciating detail, insight, and even humor. A third unusual feature of Northup's story, as compared with those of the many other free African Americans who were forced into slavery, is that he was eventually freed.

Worked as Raftsman

According to his narrative, Solomon Northup was born in Minerva, in upstate New York north of Albany, in July of 1808. His father, Mintus, had been a slave owned by a family in Rhode Island named Northup; after the family moved to New York state, Mintus's owner died and left directions in his will that Mintus should be freed. Northup married a mixed-race woman, Anne Hampton, in 1829, and the couple had two children, Elizabeth and Margaret. Anne was pregnant with a son, Alonzo, when Northup was kidnapped. Northup owned land, farmed it, and worked on a raft on the Champlain Canal connecting Lake Champlain to the Hudson River. On the side he played the fiddle at local taverns and gatherings.

The family settled in the Saratoga Springs, New York, area. "Though always in comfortable circumstances, we had not prospered," Northup wrote in *12 Years a Slave.* Thus, when two men claiming to be part of a traveling circus approached him and offered wages of a dollar a day plus three dollars for each performance he gave on the fiddle, Northup accepted enthusiastically. The proposed journey was at first purported to extend only to New York, and Northup, thinking that he would be away from home for only a short time, took no steps to inform his wife of what was happening.

Once in New York, however, the men asked Northup to press on to Washington, D.C., where their circus and a lucrative northern tour awaited. Northup agreed, and before they began the carriage trip he registered, at the men's suggestion, as a free black man. "A reference to the entries [at the New York Custom House] during the latter part of March, or first of April, 1841, I have no doubt will satisfy the incredulous, at least so far as this particular transaction is concerned,'' Northup wrote in *12 Years a Slave.*

Awoke in Chains

After arriving in Washington, Northup's companions showed him the city and treated him to food and drink. Soon, however, Northup began to feel unwell; complaining of a headache and nausea, he went to bed. He awoke chained, in complete darkness in, he learned, the Williams Slave Pen near the United States Capitol. Northup was sold to a slave trader, James Burch, and severely whipped when he tried to explain what had happened. Handcuffed to a chain of other slaves, he was put aboard a steamboat to New Orleans under miserable conditions. Northup tried to escape, but his plan was aborted when one of his co-conspirators contracted smallpox; Northup then got the disease himself.

In New Orleans, Northup was given the name of Platt and sold by a slave trader, Theophilus Freeman, to a preacher named William Ford in northwestern Louisiana. At many places in his narrative he recounted the stories of his fellow slaves; a woman named Eliza who was sold at the same time begged that her young daughter be sold along with her, but Freeman refused. Ford, though no abolitionist, did not physically abuse his slaves, and Northup spoke highly of him in his memoir. He suggested that lumber be shipped by river from Ford's plantation, benefiting Ford financially, and he constructed a loom for Ford's household.

More serious problems for Northup began when Ford encountered financial problems and sold him to a carpenter named John Tibeats. After being ordered to strip for a whipping for essentially no reason, Northup recalled in his narrative, ''Master Tibeats, I will *not,''* attacked Tibeats, held him down, and beat him. Tibeats and two friends prepared to hang Northup, but an armed overseer who had witnessed the confrontation demanded that Northup be spared. Tibeats later attacked Northup with a hatchet, resulting in another struggle in which Northup emerged the winner. This time Northup fled into a swamp, to elude pursuing dogs, and made his way back to Ford's plantation.

Ford eventually persuaded Tibeats that it would be easier to sell Northup than to kill him. Northup was sold to cotton planter Edwin Ebbs of Bayou Boeuf, Louisiana, whom Northup described as ''a roystering, blustering, noisy fellow, whose chief delight was in dancing with his 'niggers,' or lashing them about the yard with his long whip, just for the pleasure of hearing them screech and scream, as the great welts were planted on their backs.'' Northup's narrative described in detail Epps's plantation, the house of which still exists, and the sugar plantations on which he sometimes worked. Northup remained with Epps for ten years and was forced during the later part of this period to work as a slave driver for Epps himself.

Entrusted Letter to Carpenter

Finally Northup was put to work building a new house for Epps and was teamed with a Canadian carpenter named Bass, who sympathized with his plight. Northup had already tried once to escape by writing a letter and had been betrayed. But after hearing Bass debate the slavery issue with Epps, Northup decided to trust him. Bass, at considerable risk to his own safety, mailed several letters to friends in New York, including Henry B. Northup, a friend of his father's original owner. After lengthy negotiations based on the fact that the distinction between slave and free man should be upheld, Henry Northup arrived in Louisiana to bring Solomon Northup home. He had no idea that Northup was known as Platt, but through a chance meeting with Bass he managed to locate Northup and take him first to Washington, where Northup unsuccessfully tried to file suit against Burch, and then back to his family. His two daughters did not recognize him.

Several months after Northup's release, *12 Years a Slave* was published in American and British editions. A white lawyer and New York state legislator, David Wilson, was credited as the book's editor. For several years Northup was active as a lecturer on the abolitionist circuit, but he gradually faded from view. No evidence of his activities after 1863 has been uncovered. At the time, rumors circulated that he had been kidnapped again, or killed by Southern sympathizers, or started a new life on the Western frontier, but it is likely that he died that year in an unknown location.

Between 1853 and 1856, *12 Years a Slave* sold 30,000 copies, more than poet Walt Whitman's *Leaves of Grass,* essayist Henry David Thoreau's *Walden,* and philosopher Ralph Waldo Emerson's *English Traits* put together. After that it lay mostly forgotten for decades. In 1936, Louisiana writer Sue Eakin bought a copy in a used bookstore for 25 cents. Although the bookseller and later apologists for slavery have questioned the tale's authenticity, Eakin and later scholars have checked it against other sources from the period and verified many parts of Northup's story. Eakin issued Northup's memoir in book form in 1968.

Shaft director Gordon Parks made a television film about Northup in 1985, telling *The New York Times* that ''[s]o little is said about slavery. This was our holocaust, and it's always hushed, hushed, hushed.'' British director Steve McQueen's film of *12 Years a Slave,* with a screenplay by African American writer John Ridley (who had never heard of Northup prior to the project) and actor Chiwetel Ejiofor in the role of Northup, appeared in 2013 to wide acclaim and multiple awards the following winter and spring. John Podhoretz, writing in *The Weekly Standard,* ''assumed the movie was a more graphic version of the 1853 memoir ... Then I read Northup's book. It offers a portrait of slave life far more brutal and grinding and unimaginably dehumanizing than the movie's. If we were to see on screen what Northup put on the page, the film would be unendurable.''

Books

Fiske, David, *Solomon Northup: The Complete Story of the Author of* 12 Years a Slave, ABC-CLIO, 2013.

Periodicals

Guardian (London, England), January 12, 2014.

New York Times, February 11, 1985.

Star Tribune (Minneapolis, M), October 27, 2013.

Weekly Standard, December 16, 2013.

Online

12 Years a Slave (full text), *Documenting the American South,* http://docsouth.unc.edu/fpn/northup/menu.html (January 8, 2014).

"12 Years a Slave: Who Was Solomon Northup?," *BBC,* http://www.bbc.co.uk/news/entertainment-arts-25589598 (January 8, 2014).

"Solomon Northup," *Documenting the American South,* http://docsouth.unc.edu/fpn/northup/summary.html (January 8, 2014).

"What Really Became of Solomon Northup After His '12 Years a Slave'?," *Wall Street Journal,* http://blogs.wsj.com/speakeasy/2013/10/23/ (January 8, 2014).

Other

All Things Considered (transcript), December 23, 2013.□

O

Ögedei Khan

The Mongol ruler Ögedei (c. 1186–1241), the son of Genghis Khan, ruled the Mongol Empire during the period of its greatest geographical extent. At the peak of his power, the empire covered a wider area than any other in human history, stretching from Europe to the Pacific Ocean.

Under Ögedei's leadership, the Mongols overran huge swaths of territory, relying on their superb cavalry and their unmatched sense of military discipline and planning. The leaders of many small fiefdoms, terrified, simply submitted to their rule without fighting, and other major powers were defeated. Ögedei's troops overran Georgia, Armenia, Persia, Korea, the northern part of China, and much of Russia. They met little resistance during an incursion into eastern Europe, and historians disagree as to why they did not proceed to the Atlantic, as they probably could have. Ögedei transformed the Mongol Empire from a group of marauding tribes into an extensive state, with a central palace, a system of postal communications, and a cadre of specialized governmental advisors that allowed the empire to govern and support its far-flung lands. The Mongol Empire was known for its brutality, and Ögedei's armies were no exception to the rule. But Ögedei himself was said to be a generous ruler, one who enjoyed food and good wine, and preferred to spend time in his newly built palace of Karakorum rather than traveling thousand of miles by horse to the front lines.

Specified as Genghis's Successor

Ögedei (the term "Khan" is a title, meaning leader, and the name Ögedei has been transliterated from Mongolian in many ways) was the third son of Genghis Khan by Borte, the first of his many wives. He was born around 1186. Little is known of his early life, but he apparently impressed his father as level-headed and intelligent: Genghis left instructions at his death in 1227 that Ögedei was to be named his successor. The Mongols were notorious for vicious succession struggles, and it took two years before Ögedei was installed as Khan. His father's recommendation carried a great deal of weight, as did the fact that his older brothers had each received enormous grants of land according to Mongol custom—almost empires in their own right.

"The prime reason for Ögedei's selection" by a council of chiefs called a *kurultai,* in addition to Genghis Khan's endorsement, "was because of his temperament," noted Timothy May in *The Mongol Conquests in World History.* "Wise and calm, Ögedei possessed a talent for finding compromises between his more quarrelsome brothers, Jochi and Chaghatai." Still, Ögedei's younger brother Tolui was restive. But in 1229, Ögedei was named Khan, and according to an old chronicle quoted by Bertold Spuler in *History of the Mongols,* "all the princes, in service and obeisance to [Khan], knelt three times to the sun outside the *ordu* (royal tent); then reentering they held an assembly of mirth and sport and cleared the plains of merriment of the thorns of sorrow."

The force Ögedei inherited was, in the words of James Chambers (writing in *The Devil's Horsemen*) "the best army in the world. Its organization and training, its tactical principles and its structure of command would not have been unfamiliar to a soldier of the 20th century." Ögedei had at his disposal enormous armies, with attacking forces

© INTERFOTO/Alamy

of up to 150,000 men at a time, led by fearsome cavalry with crack horseback-mounted archers. Ögedei conscripted the peoples he conquered into his armies and deployed them intelligently in future conflicts. The Mongols attacked during winter, when their cavalry could cross frozen rivers and lay siege to the capital cities of their adversaries; in the summer, less able to advance, they kept to their traditions and tended to stay in one place.

Renewed Conflict with Persians

Despite his natural inclinations—in the words of J.J. Saunders in *The History of the Mongol Conquests,* he was "devoid of his father's volcanic energy"—Ögedei continued his father's expansionist ways. He began by sending the general Chormaqan to attack the sole empire that had successfully resisted Genghis Khan's depradations, the Persians, who under leader Jalal ad-Din Mingburn had defeated Mongol forces in battles at Parwan and Dameghan, in present-day Iran. In 1230 and 1231, as Jalal was pressed by rival chieftains, Chormaqan mustered an army of 30,000 that quickly overran Jalal's kingdom and forced him into an ignominious flight during which he was killed by a Kurdish peasant. Ögedei's empire now stretched from central Asia to the Persian Gulf.

At the same time, beginning in 1231, Ögedei himself led a force that built upon the successes Genghis Khan had scored against the Jin dynasty that ruled northern China at the time. Ögedei's general Sübedei laid siege to the Jin capital of K'ai-feng, which fell in 1233; the emperor Ai-tsung, like Jalal, fled in disgrace and a year later committed suicide. Now Ögedei turned his attention to the larger Sung dynasty to the south, which was stronger and more firmly rooted in Chinese traditions. The Sung could probably have blocked Ögedei's advance, but, like several others adversaries of the Mongols, they failed to take Ögedei seriously, considering the Mongols a band of uncivilized barbarians. The Sung used the opportunity to consolidate their own power over previously Jin-ruled lands, leaving the door open to a declaration of war and attack by Ögedei in 1235. Forty years of war followed, ending in victory by Kublai Khan, Genghis's grandson, in 1279.

Ögedei's armies also subdued many smaller lands, including Armenia, Georgia, and Korea, then mostly under northern Chinese control. Princes in all these lands paid tribute to the Mongols, and Ögedei, although hardly a benevolent ruler, put in place a modern administrative structure to deal with them. He established what was in essence a postal service that made possible communication across the empire's far-flung lands. Posts were established at regular points (sources differ as to whether they were an hour or a day apart by horseback) where letters and edicts would be officially collected and distributed. Travelers and envoys with an ornate tablet of authority, known as a *paiza,* were able to obtain fresh horses and fodder to continue their journeys. Ögedei imported scribes and scholars from Christian and Islamic lands, making use of their expertise when it was to his advantage to do so.

Built Palace and Capital City

At the beginning of Ögedei's reign, the center of Mongol authority consisted of little more than a complex of tents, but he set Islamic and Chinese craftsmen against each other in building the castle and administrative center of Karakorum, completed in the late 1230s. Karakorum was destroyed by Chinese invaders in the 17th century but has been partially excavated and reconstructed by Mongolian and Russian archaeologists. Ögedei taxed defeated nobles, but stories of his mercy toward poor individuals abounded during his reign. A Muslim, it was said, violated Mongol law, killing a sheep by slitting its throat instead of cutting it open at the breast and pulling out the heart as was the Mongol custom. A tribesman, taking the law into his own hands, tied up the Muslim and brought him to Ögedei, who spared the Muslim's life but had the tribesman executed.

Ögedei had expensive tastes, and, noted May, "much to the consternation of his officials," he "repeatedly paid top dollar for any item that crossed his path." Meeting an arrowsmith who was deep in debt, Ögedei gave him a contract to supply the Mongol army with 10,000 arrows a year. His free-spending ways, May opined, "brought international commerce to Karakorum. What merchant would not risk traveling there when they knew that, regardless of what they brought, they would be paid twice its value after determining the cost of transportation?" The center of trade between East and West Ögedei established would flower during the reign of Kublai Khan several decades later.

Ögedei's last military campaign was his most ambitious. After forces under Jochi's son Batu and the general Sübedei conquered major Russian cities including the capital of Kiev, a massive force of Mongols, backed by Persian and Chinese engineers, moved on Hungary and engaged the forces of King Bela IV and Holy Roman Emperor Frederick II, backed by Italian mercenaries and fighters from Poland and Germany, in 1241. The resulting carnage was one of the grimmest events in the history of medieval Europe, leaving perhaps a third of Hungary's population dead and many of its adult males conscripted into the Mongol army. Fire arrows brought from China were fired into the city of Buda (now Budapest), burning it to the ground. Bela, like so many other leaders who opposed Ögedei, fled the scene, boarding a ship in the Mediterranean Sea.

Hungary's army was one of the largest in Europe at the time, and there were few others capable of fighting the Mongols. Ögedei gave his approval for Mongol troops to press on to the Atlantic Ocean, what the Mongols called the Great Western Sea. "The Mongols," noted Saunders, "had the same effect here as everywhere: they were treated as something more than human, a dreadful visitation from hell; the frantic reports of refugees intensified instead of diminishing the fear and paralysis which gripped every land they approached ..." Back at Karakorum, however, Ögedei was in the late stages of alcoholism. An alarmed adviser begged him to drink only one cup of wine per day, but Ögedei responded by ordering an extra-large cup to be made, and he soon began to disregard even that limit. After what was apparently a drinking binge, he died on December 11, 1241.

That event probably forestalled a full-scale Mongol invasion of Europe, an event that might have substantially altered the course of world history. Correctly foreseeing an epic succession battle to come, Mongol commanders withdrew from Hungary, laying waste to villages and countryside as they went. They headed for centers closer to Mongolia, where they hoped to be able to influence the events to come. The Mongol Empire was ruled for several years by Ögedei's widow, Tšregene, but finally Ögedei's branch of the family was displaced by that of Tolui, whose son Kublai became the next great emperor of the Mongols and founded a Chinese dynasty that lasted for more than a century.

Books

Chambers, James, *The Devil's Horsemen: The Mongol Invasion of Europe,* Weidenfeld and Nicolson, 1979.

May, Timothy, *The Mongol Conquests in World History,* Reaktion Books, 2012.

Morgan, David, *The Mongols,* Basil Blackwell, 1986.

Prawdin, Michael, *The Mongol Empire: Its Rise and Legacy,* translated by Eden and Cedar Paul, George Allen and Unwin, 1940.

Saunders, J.J., *The History of the Mongol Conquests,* Routledge & Kagan, 1971.

Spuler, Bertold, *History of the Mongols: Based on Eastern and Western Accounts of the Thirteenth and Fourteenth Centuries,* translated by Helga and Stuart Drummond, University of California, 1972.□

Willie O'Ree

The Canadian hockey player Willie O'Ree (born 1935) was the first person of African descent to play in the National Hockey League.

O'Ree has been called the Jackie Robinson of the NHL, referring to the athlete who broke baseball's color barrier in 1947. Indeed, he was comparable to Robinson in several ways. Like Robinson, he faced racism as a person of African descent trying to break into a previously all-white sport. As he tried to ascend from hockey's minor leagues to the NHL's Boston Bruins, he was told that blacks were physiologically unsuited to playing hockey, and fans taunted him with racist abuse. Again like Robinson, O'Reel drew on a long tradition of athletics in the black community, in this case the little-known institution of hockey in the African Canadian community in Canada's Maritime provinces. O'Ree played in parts of two seasons with the Bruins, and his overall record was not comparable to Robinson's. However, he enjoyed a long career playing hockey and has remained active as a supporter of the sport and specifically of black hockey players, whose numbers have grown over the course of his life.

Descended from Underground Railroad Refugees

Willie O'Ree was born in Fredericton, New Brunswick, Canada, on October 15, 1935. He was one of 13 children. One set of his grandparents were American slaves who had fled to Canada via the Underground Railroad. His father, Harry O'Ree, was a road maintenance worker for the city of Fredericton. The O'Rees were one of just two African Canadian families in the entire city of Fredericton. Like other young Canadian boys, he loved to play hockey—perhaps even more so, for, as he recalled in *Willie O'Ree: The Story of the First Black Player in the NHL,* "There were four outdoor rinks within 15 minutes of where I lived ... and then there was the river and ponds and lakes and creeks."

Often in the winter, O'Ree could skate to school, where he excelled in many subjects. Racism in Fredericton was more silent than overt, but on one occasion O'Ree was stared down when he walked into a white-owned shop and asked for a haircut. He persisted, and got his haircut, and on the ice he was confident as well. "In retrospect, I think my living around whites made me feel I could play in the pros. I always knew I was as good or better than they were," he was quoted as saying by Mike Walsh of *missionCREEP.*

Many of O'Ree's siblings played one sport or another, and his older brother Richard instructed him in the art of body-checking. O'Ree proved a fast learner, breaking the collarbone of the coach's son during a school team practice, and getting kicked off the team as a result. That was only a minor setback: O'Ree tried out for and won a spot on the Fredericton Junior Capitals team as a teen, after which his coach invited him to come back. But O'Ree was already on his way to bigger things. On the rink, he faced physical abuse from white players. "Players on other teams came after me with high sticks and head shots," he

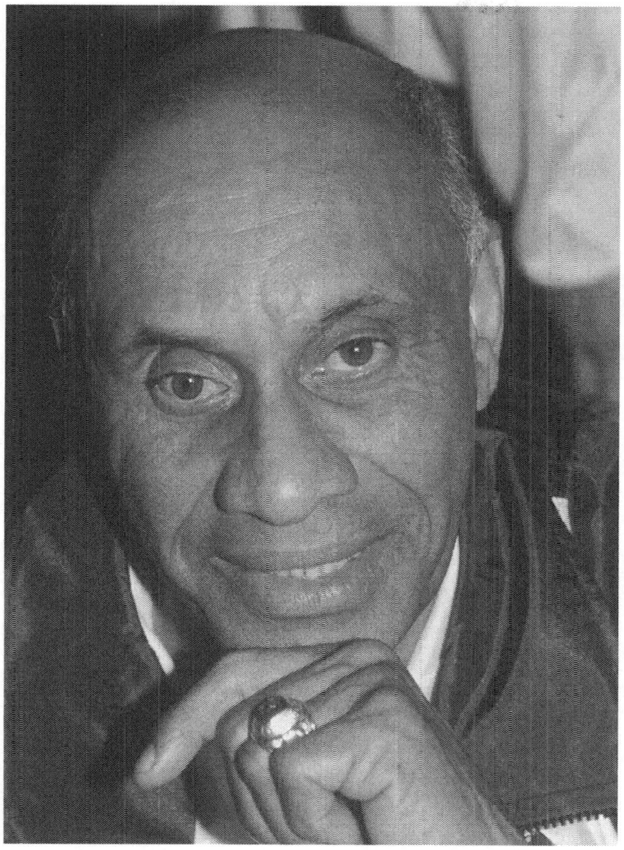

John Giamundo/Bruce Bennett/Getty Images

remembered, "but I was determined not to let anyone run me out of the rink or off the field," O'Ree recalled to Marty Kaminsky of *Boys' Life.*

For a time, however, it looked as though those bigger things might be in the game of baseball rather than on the hockey rink. O'Ree, a gifted athlete, played as many as nine sports in all, and he showed special talent as a baseball player. His team won Fredericton's city championship in 1948, and he was inspired still further when the prize turned out to be a trip to New York to see the Brooklyn Dodgers and the New York Yankees play. Robinson, whose career outside baseball's Negro Leagues had begun with the minor-league Montreal Royals in Canada, had already joined the Dodgers, and O'Ree now had a powerful role model.

Repelled by Southern Racism

In 1956, O'Ree was offered a tryout by major league baseball's Milwaukee Braves at the team's training camp in Atlanta. Experiencing the full force of Southern segregation, he was surprised to find segregrated hotels, restaurants, and restrooms. Discouraged, he gave up on his baseball ambitions. "To be honest," he told Kaminsky, "I don't know if I could have concentrated on baseball with all that prejudice." In hockey he already had another option at hand: he had played a season with the Quebec Frontenacs of the Quebec Provincial Junior Hockey League in 1954 and 1955, and the following year he had begun playing for the Kitchener Canucks of the junior Ontario Hockey Association.

So O'Ree had a growing career to return to when he gave up on baseball. But during the 1955–1956 season disaster struck: wearing no protective gear (like most other hockey players at the time), he was hit in the face by a puck. His nose and part of his jaw were broken, and he lost 95 percent of the vision in his right eye. Doctors and family members counseled O'Ree to give up, but he resolved to carry on and keep his disability a secret. He later said that as far as he knew, the NHL never knew that he was nearly blind in one eye.

In the 1956–1957 and 1957–1958 seasons, O'Ree moved up to the Quebec Hockey League's Quebec Aces, playing in 68 games in the 1956–1957 season and scoring 22 goals with 12 assists. The Aces were a top-level NHL farm team, and after O'Ree got off to another strong start in the 1957–1958 season, he was among the top candidates to be called up to the NHL. On January 18, 1958, he took to the ice for the Boston Bruins in Montreal at the position of winger, becoming the NHL's first black player. He played two games for the Bruins before regular players returned to the Bruins' roster and he returned to Quebec. The move gained little publicity, something that disappointed O'Ree in retrospect: he wished that he would have been given more of a chance to influence other young black players.

After two more years in Quebec, O'Ree was called up to join the Bruins once again early in the 1961 season. This time he played the rest of the year with the team, finishing with four goals and ten assists. Once again, O'Ree had to contend with prejudice from American hockey fans. "Racist remarks from fans were much worse in the U.S. cities than in Toronto and Montreal. I particularly remember a few incidents in Chicago," he recalled to Walsh. "The fans would yell, 'Go back to the south' and 'How come you're not picking cotton.' Things like that. It didn't bother me. Hell, I'd been called names most of my life."

Traded to Montreal

Brawls between O'Ree and white players were common, and one especially ugly incident in Chicago left O'Ree with two missing teeth and a broken nose after he was hit in the face with a stick by Chicago Black Hawks right winger Eric Nesterenko. O'Ree retaliated, and Nesterenko went to the hospital to receive 15 stitches in his head. There were also positive moments, such as a game-winning goal against the Bruins' arch-rival, the Montreal Canadiens, and O'Ree received encouragement from the Bruins coaching staff based on his speed. At the end of the season, however, he was traded to Montreal—a bitter disappointment, for the Canadiens dominated pro hockey at the time, and O'Ree had little chance of making the organization's NHL-level squad. The Bruins gave him no explanation for the trade, but it would be 25 years before another black player would take to the ice in the NHL.

O'Ree played until 1962 for Montreal's Hull-Ottawa farm team and then was traded once again to the Los Angeles Blades of the Western Hockey League. He entertained little hope of reaching the NHL again, and he never made an annual salary of more than $17,500, but he enjoyed the game and continued to perform well in minor league hockey. He won the Western Hockey League scoring title in 1964 with Los Angeles and again in 1969 with the San Diego Gulls, at the age of 34. After the Western Hockey League was dissolved in 1974 O'Ree retired, but he joined a new San Diego team, the Hawks, in 1978 at the age of 43 and played in 64 games of the 70-game season. O'Ree stayed on in San Diego with his wife, Deljeet. The couple had one daughter, Chandra.

In later life O'Ree worked as an auto salesman, fast food restaurant manager, and, as of 1998, security guard at the Hotel del Coronado on San Diego Bay. At that time, when there were still very few minority players in the NHL, the league approached O'Ree to become director of youth development for its diversity task force. In that capacity, O'Ree wrote a biweekly column, "Words O'Reason" for the NHL's website, and in 2000 he issued a memoir for young readers, *The Autobiography of Willie O'Ree.* He remained active with the NHL into his 70s and received several major honors, including the Order of Canada in 2008.

Books

Mortillaro, Nicole, *Willie O'Ree: The Story of the first Black Player in the NHL,* Record, 2012.

O'Ree, Willie, *The Autobiography of Willie O'Ree: Hockey's Black Pioneer,* NHL, 2000.

Periodicals

Boys' Life, November 2001.

Buffalo News, February 19, 2012.

Duluth News-Tribune, April 19, 2012.

Parks & Recreation, January 2005.

Spectator (Hamilton, Ontario, Canada), February 3, 2011.

USA Today, January 15, 2008.

Online

"Soul on Ice: The Willie O'Ree Story," *missionCREEP,* http://www.missioncreep.com/mw/oree.html (October 12, 2013).

"Willie O'Ree," *Internet Hockey Database,* http://www.hockeydb.com/ihdb/stats/pdisplay.php?pid=8354 (October 12, 2013).

"Willie O'Ree," *Sports Illustrated/CNN,* http://sportsillustrated.cnn.com/vault/article/magazine/MAG1141807/index.htm (October 12, 2013).

"Willie O'Ree: Celebration of a Hockey Legend," City of Frederiction, http://www.fredericton.ca/en/recleisure/2007Nov14OreeBio.asp (October 12, 2013).□

Nagisa Oshima

The Japanese filmmaker Nagisa Oshima (1932–2013) was, in the words of the *Criterion Collection* film sales website, "Japanese cinema's preeminent taboo buster." In a series of films in the 1960s and 1970s, Oshima presented a vision of the edges of Japanese society, populated by misfits, criminals, and outcasts.

Several of Oshima's films involved graphic scenes of sex and violence, and one of his most notorious productions, *In the Realm of the Senses* (1976), was banned in Japan and even had to be sent abroad for development and processing due to its explicit sexual nature. Yet Oshima insisted that his intent was not to shock viewers. "A work of art is made without any kind of certainty. It is produced in fear, apprehension and doubt," he observed in a *UNESCO Courier* interview. "It isn't a purposeful, deliberate undertaking that knows exactly where it is going. It doesn't want to 'express' anything. It is always possible that it may, incidentally, offend certain taboos, but that is not the aim." Far from being mannered or grotesque, Oshima's films dealt with important themes in post–World War II Japanese society, and several of his most graphic works were in fact rooted in true stories.

Reportedly Descended from Samurai

Nagisa Oshima was born on March 31, 1932, in Kyoto, Japan. His father, reputed to have been descended from Japan's warrior samurai caste, was a government fisheries researcher; he died when Oshima was six, and Oshima in later interviews referred to his father's early death as a crucial part of his childhood. The devastation wrought in Japan by World War II was another factor that predisposed Oshima to question the traditional norms of Japanese society; only 13 when the war ended, he avoided the actual fighting, but he was vividly impressed by the collapse of Japan's propaganda machinery. When Japan's defeat was announced, he played the game of *go* for the entire day.

Oshima's father had been interested in socialist ideas, and Oshima himself became interested in leftist politics as a young man. Attending law school at Kyoto University, he served as an officer in a left-wing student organization and participated in Japan's first wave of student activism, which preceded similar movements in the West by several years. Fearing a new kind of militarism in Japanese society, Oshima led demonstrations against a Japanese-American security pact. At one point he and his cohorts disrupted a campus visit by the Japanese emperor. Partly as a result of his activist record, Oshima despaired of finding a job after graduating in the mid-1950s. Following a suggestion from a friend, he applied for admission to the highly competitive assistant-director apprenticeship program at Japan's venerable Shochiku film studio. Out of 2,000 applicants, he was one of five candidates chosen.

Joining Shochiku in 1954, Oshima spent several years learning the ropes by working on scripts and assisting better-known directors. On the side he wrote acerbic pieces of film criticism lambasting the state of Japanese cinema. In 1959, Shochiku''s management suffered a series of box-office failures and decided to follow the example of French students who had promoted the young directors of the so-called New Wave in that country and reaped large profits. So Oshima was given the chance to direct his first film, *A Town of Love and Hope*. Realistic in style, the film followed a young man who sold a homing pigeon repeatedly by training it to return to him after it had been sold. The studio urged Oshima to change the film''s downbeat ending, but he refused. Oshima soon became known as the voice of the Japanese New Wave. His second film, *Cruel Story of Youth* (1960), has been compared to the American classic of youth rebellion, *Rebel Without a Cause.*

Formed Own Studio

As his reputation grew, Oshima felt more able to take direct aim at Japanese society. The title of his third film, *The Sun's Burial* (1960), mocked the common description of Japan as the Land of the Rising Sun; the film depicted warring gangs in an Osaka slum. Oshima was dropped from Shochiku's roster after the appearance of the highly political *Night and Fog in Japan* in 1960 happened to coincide with the assassination of a leading Japanese politician. He formed his own studio, Sozosha, meaning "Creation." Two 1968 Oshima films dealt with the question of discrimination against Koreans in Japan: the comedy *Three Resurrected Drunkards* and the stylistically innovative social critique *Death by Hanging.* The latter film, based on a true story, marked Oshima's first breakthrough with international audiences; his films of the 1960s have for the most part not been widely seen in the West.

Oshima's films grew more and more ambitious in the late 1960s and early 1970s. *Boy* (1969) was one of Oshima''s most accessible and successful films; it told the story of a young boy who is forced by his parents to step in front of moving cars so that they can extort money from the drivers. *The Man Who Left His Will on Film* (1970) involved a film-within-a-film and was a highly novel sort of Marxist mystery. Among Oshima's most highly regarded works was *The Ceremony* (1971), which Nelson Kim, writing in *Senses of Cinema,* called "a multigenerational family saga in the mode of *The Godfather 1* and *2* (Francis Coppola, 1972, 74) and *City of Sadness* (Hou Hsiao-hsien, 1989)." The family saga structure was used by Oshima to express his skeptical attitude toward Japanese traditional values.

As far back as 1967's *A Treatise on Japanese Bawdy Song* and *Diary of a Shinjuku Thief* (1968), in which a young couple finds sexual ecstasy in the midst of a street riot, Oshima had begun to push boundaries in terms of sexual material. *In the Realm of the Senses* (1976, also known as *Ai No Corrida*) took that tendency to a whole new level; as Ronald Bergan noted in the London *Guardian,* "it was, for many, in the realms of pornography." Seemingly intended to outdo the internationally successful erotic classic *Last Tango in Paris* (1972), the film told the story of an inn owner and a maid who embark on a sexual odyssey and featured unsimulated scenes involving a variety of sexual practices. *In the Realm of the Senses* was made with a Japanese cast but had to be sent to France to be developed and processed. Even after several decades it has rarely been shown in Japan. Oshima bitterly attacked Japanese censorship laws in his 1992 book *Cinema, Censorship, and the State*.

Won Award at Cannes Festival

In the Realm of the Senses was financed partly with French money, and by the late 1970s Oshima was growing more popular abroad even as he had trouble getting his work shown in Japan. *Empire of Passion* (1978), which Bergan called "a less sexually explicit companion piece to *In the Realm of the Senses*, won the Best Director award for Oshima at the Cannes Film Festival in France. The film told the story of a rickshaw driver who is murdered by his wife and a young man with whom she is having an affair; the rickshaw driver returns as a ghost to torment the lovers with guilt.

Oshima made one fully English-language film, *Merry Christmas, Mr. Lawrence* (1983). Based on a novel by Laurens van der Post, the film depicted life in a Japanese prisoner-of-war camp on the Indonesian island of Java during World War II. The film featured two popular music stars: Japanese vocalist Ryuichi Sakamoto played a Japanese commander, while British glam-rocker David Bowie appeared as a South African–born British officer, Jack Celliers, who realizes that the Japanese officer is sexually attracted to him and begins to undermine his will. Bowie spoke enthusiastically to Ryan Gilbey of the *New Statesman* about Oshima's high-powered, anti-perfectionist approach on the set: "And that really fired us up; I think that got us through the movie more than anything else, this terrific momentum. You'd go through a scene, you'd be done, and then you'd be moving on to the next scene immediately, so you were always your character, with no chance to see the overall thing." The 1986 film *Max, Mon*

Amour, in which Oshima was influenced by the Spanish surrealist director Luis Buñuel, was also filmed partly in English.

Financial problems derailed a film Oshima had planned to set in the United States: *Hollywood Zen* was intended to be a biographical film about the Japanese American actor Sessue Hayakawa. Oshima was sidelined by a stroke in 1996 but recovered enough to direct his last film, *Taboo,* from a wheelchair. The film, released in 1999, was set in feudal Japanese times among a group of samurai serving Japan's shogun, or military governor. It returned to the theme of homosexual desire, once again using that element in the story to challenge imagery of traditional Japan.

Oshima married the actress Akiko Koyama in 1960, and they had two sons. After further strokes he was unable to work, but he lived long enough to see his body of work receive considerable recognition from film buffs. A five-DVD set of Oshima's earlier films, *Oshima's Outlaw Sixties,* appeared in 2010. Oshima died in Fujisawa, Japan, on January 15, 2013. The *Japan Times* eulogized him this way: "His films earned respect around the world and broke restraints on what could be shown and told within cinematic art. Japan could use more iconoclasts like him. Mr. Oshima's films were provocative and bold, two attitudes that are rare in Japanese society."

Books

Turim, Maureen, *The Films of Oshima Nagisa,* University of California, 1998.

Periodicals

Cineaste, Winter 2010.

Daily Telegraph (London, England), January 16, 2013.

Guardian (London, England), January 16, 2013.

Independent (London, England), January 16, 2013.

International Herald Tribune, January 17, 2013.

Japan Times, January 20, 2013.

New Statesman, September 14, 2009.

Times (London, England), January 17, 2013.

UNESCO Courier, July-August 1995.

Online

"Nagisa Oshima," *AllMovie,* http://www.allmovie.com/artist/nagisa-oshima-p105229 (October 15, 2013).

"Nagisa Oshima," *Criterion Collection,* http://www.criterion.com/explore/83-nagisa-oshima (October 15, 2013).

"Nagisa Oshima," *Internet Movie Database,* http://www.imdb.com/name/nm0651915/bio?ref_=nm_ov_bio_s (October 15, 2013).

"Nagisa Oshima," *Senses of Cinema,* http://sensesofcinema.com/2004/great-directors/oshima/ (October 15, 2013).

"Oshima Nagisa," *JapanZone,* http://www.japan-zone.com/modern/oshima_nagisa.shtml (October 15, 2013).□

Wilhelm Ostwald

Chemist, philosopher, and theorist Wilhelm Ostwald (1853–1932) lead the charge in establishing physical chemistry as a legitimate branch of science. Awarded the 1909 Nobel Prize in Chemistry for his work on chemical equilibria, reaction velocities, and catalysis, he also advanced groundbreaking theories on the scientific standardization of shapes and colors.

Russian Born and Educated

Born on September 2, 1853, in Riga, Latvia, in the old Russian Empire, Friedrich Wilhelm Ostwald was the son of German immigrants Gottfried Wilhelm Ostwald, a master cooper smith or barrel maker/repairer, and Elisabeth Leuckel, the daughter of a baker. The second son between brothers Eugen and Gottfried, the youngster attended high school at the Riga State Gymnasium, No. 1, where he studied physics, chemistry, mathematics, natural history and learned to speak French, English, Latin and Russian. Despite his father's wishes that he study engineering, young Wilhelm entered the University of Dorpat, eventually renamed University of Tartu, to study chemistry. Initially, Ostwald was not particularly serious about his avowed discipline and paid more attention to classes in art, music, and philosophy—which remained lifelong interests. However, hard last-minute study earned him a chance to study chemistry under Carl Schmidt and Johann Lemberg and physics with Arthur von Oettingen.

After writing an essay on the mass action of water, Ostwald received his Candidate's degree in 1875, which led to Oettingen bringing him into his laboratory as an assistant, which allowed him time to stage a series of investigative chemistry experiments. After earning his Master's degree in 1876, he began lecturing on physical chemistry while continuing his research on chemical affinity by physical means, while refining methods related to the scientific process. Earning his doctorate in 1878, he became Schmidt's part–time assistant the following year. Married to Helene von Reyher in 1880, Ostwald accepted a Professorship of chemistry at Riga Polytechnicum where he proved a popular and creative instructor.

Working ceaselessly, as he would all his life, he built upon and extended the works of Norwegian scholars Peter Guldberg and Cato Waage when he published his *Lehrbuch der Allgemeinen Chemie* (Textbook of General Chemistry). Later, he worked closely with Svante Arrhenius—who extended the theories of Dutch physical chemist Jacobus van't Hoff—on *Zeitschrift für Physikalische Chemie* (Journal for Physical Chemistry), of which Ostwald personally edited 100 volumes until 1922. During this era, the prolific scientist's contributions came via the clarification, reorganizing and furthering the ideas of other scientists. In the process, he discovered what is now known as Ostwald's Law of Dilution and Conductivity, which defines the relationship between the disassociation constant and the degree of disassociation of weak electrolytes. Ostwald and his associates demonstrated that hundreds of water-soluble acids and bases

obeyed the dilution law while their behavior in solutions conformed to the general ionic theory. This discovery hailed a new era in the field of physical chemistry.

University of Leipzig and Catalysis

In 1887, Ostwald's efforts at Dorpat resulted in an offer to chair the Department of Physical Chemistry at the University of Leipzig in Germany, where he and his wife became naturalized citizens in 1888. Rigorously raising the profile of his subject by republishing over 40 books by other scientists in his *Klassider exakten Wissenschraften* (Classics of Exact Sciences) series during his first four years at the University, he eventually published 250 volumes. Moreover, he wrote or co-wrote texts that became standard issue in the field such as *Grundriss der Allgemeinen Chemie* (Outline of general chemistry) and *Hand- und Hilfsbuch zur Ausführung physiko-chemischer messunge* (Handbook for physiochemical measurements). In these and many other texts, Ostwald not only systemized the subject of general, physical and inorganic chemistry but applied them to other fields. He also organized his school along those lines. Subsequent to this approach, the Leipzig Institute of Physical Chemistry grew dramatically drawing topflight students from all over the globe, a great many of whom became professors of physical chemistry in their respective countries.

Revolutionizing analytical chemistry through solution theory and his theory of indicators, Ostwald and his research students also measured the rates at which reactions proceeded towards the equilibrium state. These kinetic investigations demonstrated that while catalysts could alter the rates of reactions, they did not change the proportion of the final products. A groundbreaking discovery with many implications for industrial use, Ostwald's work on catalysis would be cited as the principal reason for Ostwald's 1909 Nobel award. "Catalysis, which formerly appeared to be a hidden secret," declared the award's presenter, "has thus become accessible to exact scientific study."

Perhaps his most lasting commercial achievement became known as the Ostwald Process, used widely in industry to convert ammonia to nitric acid through oxidation, which results in an economically feasible large scale production of fertilizers and explosives. The basis of the discovery had been patented six decades earlier, but Ostwald's version proved more amenable to mass commercial production. However, commercial successes and his founding of the German Bunsen Society for Applied Physical Chemistry in 1894 notwithstanding, Ostwald's interest in physical chemistry had begun to wane.

Explored Alternate Theories

By the early 1890s, Ostwald was studying the concept of energy and asserting the primacy of energy over matter in opposition to widespread scientific materialism. Energetics as a comprehensive scientific program contained two main features: a new system of absolute measurement and a new interpretation of the second law of thermodynamics. Instead of reducing all other kinds of energy to the mechanical energy, Ostwald saw them in mutually functional relations to each other: "one cannot change the factors of one kind of energy without simultaneously changing the factors of the other kinds of energy," Ostwald was quoted saying in the *Hyle Biography.* His 1896 book *Elektrchemie: Ihre Geschicte und Lehre* (Electrochemistry: Its History and Teaching), was intended to illustrate this functional coordination between different forms of energy and different branches of science. Mathematicians, physicists, and chemists at the 1895 Naturforscherversammlung (Meeting of Natural Scientists), were appalled by Ostwald's interest in monistic and holistic energetics—and killed the concept of energetics as a scientific program.

In 1894, a disappointed Ostwald semi-retired from the University of Leipzig, staying on only as a research professor. Years later, in his Nobel Prize acceptance address, archived at *NobelPrize.org,* Ostwald confessed of exhausting his creative well in physical chemistry and references a study that describes how certain parts of the brain are so worn out by excessive strain that they function less perfectly than before. He specifically explained, "I have repeatedly stressed in the past that this selfsame, extremely heavy strain imposed by research most readily produces this type of partial invalid and in respect of certain functions which I could once perform perfectly I must count myself such an invalid."

Continuing his Nobel committee speech, Ostwald seemed more optimistic as he spoke of the revival of his mind as it relates to fresh interests. "Hence it was only necessary to make my subsidiary work my main work in order first subjectively to eliminate the cheerless feeling of being an invalid, and second objectively to derive from what remained to me as much useful work as possible in the prevailing circumstances." This subsidiary work Ostwald spoke of was his growing love of Natural Science which resulted in the publications of *Moderne Naturphilosophie* (Modern Natural Philosophy) and particularly *Annalen der Naturphilosphie* (Annals of Natural History), which shunned mechanism and materialism while advocating historicism and organicism. Founding the latter journal in 1902, he edited 14 succeeding volumes up until 1921.

Won the 1909 Nobel Prize for Chemistry

Ostwald retired from the University of Leipzig in 1906, devoting more time to energetics with such publications as *Der energetische Imperativ* (The Energetic Imperative). Employing the motto: "Waste no energy, utilize it," he believed that an organized society was similar to a well-functioning body that coordinated individual organs to maximize its energetic efficiency, which he believed was the measure of cultural progress. He further asserted that energetic efficiency should put provide the underlying rationale for the organization of labor.

Ostwald had been honored by universities and various associations throughout his career starting with his tenure at the University of Leipzig. Already well-known among his peers, the awarding of the 1909 Nobel Prize in chemistry for a time placed him in the forefront of the international scene. After donating half of his Nobel Prize award money to the Ido movement—an improved version of the international language Esperanto—he used his new-found position to advance some of his later interests and theories. His public stance on monism—the philosophical view that all things can be explained in terms of a single reality or substance—resulted in his becoming president of the Monistic Alliance in 1911. An avowed atheist, he believed he could decisively fight the Church's claim to power in the field of natural sciences and spread a more modern scientific ideology. Subsequently, Ostwald and Germany's social democrats led an exodus from the church. The famed scientist also used his alliances with international peace organizations and various international organizations to help him promote social Darwinism, eugenics, and euthanasia and he challenged church dogma with his science-based "Sunday sermons." However, his involvement with utopian biologist—philosopher Ernst Haeckel and his Monist League—gained little traction and caused Ostwald considerable financial loss. Further, his pacifist visions of energetics' monistic future were derailed by the outbreak of the First World War, during which he was severely criticized for his pacifistic views.

An avid painter, Ostwald mounted his most successful later study with his systematic analysis of color phenomena and our perception of them, which may have begun as early as 1904 with the publishing of *Malerbriefe* (Letter to a Painter). With help from the Werkbund, an association of painters and architects, he supplemented the subjective and qualitative classification of colors with a quantitative and objective one, establishing principles underlying our awareness of harmony and proportion, which provide the basis for his books *Die Farbenlehre* (Color Theory), *Die Harmonie der Farben* (Harmony of Colors), *Der Farber fibel* (The Color Primer), and his journal *Die Farbe* (Color) first published in 1916. After the war, he continued to establish rules of standardization and laws of color harmony, which he felt would be his most enduring and beneficial contribution to world culture.

Ostwald spent his later years comfortably ensconced at his estate at Grossbothen in Saxony, working on art, music, color theory, energetics, and monism. A family man with five children, two daughters and three sons, his legacy was carried forward by his son Dr. Karl Wilhelm Wolfgang. Known in scientific literature as Wo. Ostwald, Wolfgang was a Lecturer at the University of Leipzig and editor of the *Zeitschrift fur Chemie un Industrie der Kolloide* (Journal for Chemical Industry of the Colloids). After an extremely busy life during which he edited several scientific and philosophical journals, wrote 45 books, and approximately 500 scientific papers, Wilhelm Ostwald, suffering from health problems involving the bladder and prostate, died on April 4, 1932, in a hospital near his country estate, where he was buried.

Ostwald student Wilder Dwight Bancroft paid tribute to his mentor in a quote archived on *Goodreads.com.* "Ostwald was a great protagonist and inspiring teacher, He had the gift of saying the right thing in the right way. When we consider the development of chemistry as a whole, Ostwald's name like Abou Ben Adhems leads all the rest. . .Ostwald was absolutely the right man right place. He was loved and followed by more people than any chemist of our time."

Online

"Quotes about Wilhelm Ostwald," *Goodreads.Com,* http://www.goodreads.com/quotes/tag/wilhelm-ostwald, (December 10, 2013).

"The Father of Physical Chemistry," *Royal Society of Chemistry,* http://www.rsc.org/chemistryworld/issues/2003/may/Physicalchem.asp, (December 10, 2013).

"Wilhelm Ostwald," *Encyclopedia Britannica,* http://www.britannica.com/EBchecked/topic/434499/Wilhelm-Ostwald, (December 10, 2013).

"Wilhelm Ostwald," *Famous Scientists,* http://www.famousscientists.org/wilhelm-ostwald/, (December 10, 2013).

"Wilhelm Ostwald (1853-1932)," *Hyle Biography,* http://www.hyle.org/journal/issues/12-1/bio_kim.htm, (December 10, 2013).

"Wilhelm Ostwald," *NNDB,* http://www.nndb.com/people/883/0000092607/, (December 10, 2013).

"Wilhelm Ostwald," *NobelPrize.org,* http://www.nobelprize.org/nobel_prizes/chemistry/laureates/1909/ostwalkd-bio.html, (December 10, 2013).□

P

Michael Palin

The British actor and writer Michael Palin (born 1943) was one of the major creative forces behind the anarchic Monty Python television and film franchise in the 1960s and 1970s. Since then he has enjoyed a long career as a comic actor, writer, and star in a series of television travelogues.

Palin made numerous contributions to the Monty Python troupe, most of whose members he had met as a university student in the mid-1960s. He, along with cartoonist and animator Terry Gilliam, was responsible for the show's unpredictable surreal edge, and many of his individual characterizations and routines, such as his rendition of Queen Victoria, are among the show's most famous. After the end of the *Monty Python's Flying Circus* television series, Palin went on to co-write the four successful films the show spawned. He has appeared in many comic and serious films, both with and without his former Monty Python cohorts. In 1989, with *Around the World in Eighty Days,* Palin began a second career as host of a series of television travel documentaries, and many Britons who may be only vaguely familiar with his earlier activities have become enthusiastic followers of his work.

Took Comic Roles in School Plays

Michael Edward Palin was born in Sheffield, United Kingdom, on April 5, 1943. His family life, noted Ray Connolly of the *Times* of London, was "a struggle of slightly faded gentility and penny pinching." His father had been well educated at Cambridge University but had fallen on hard times during the Depression years until landing a job as a manager of a toilet paper factory. Palin's mother was the daughter of a former High Sheriff of Oxfordshire. The family scrimped and saved to send Palin to good private schools: the Birkdale preparatory school and then the Shrewsbury School, which spawned the careers of several noted British comedians. At one point a third of Palin's father's salary went to his school tuition. Palin's talent as a comic actor was already showing itself in school plays. As a child he enjoyed the radio comedy program *The Goon Show,* to which various British comics have pointed as an influence.

Palin matriculated at Oxford University's Brasenose College in 1962, majoring in history. Oxford, with its profusion of student dramatic societies and events offering the chance to present comic skits, gave Palin plenty of opportunities to develop his comic gifts, especially after he met future Monty Python cast member Terry Jones. He and Jones, along with fellow student Robert Hewison, penned a show called the *Oxford Revue* that was presented in 1964 at the prestigious Edinburgh Festival in Scotland. In the audience was television presenter David Frost, who promised to keep in contact with Palin and the other young comedy writers.

Soon after graduating from Oxford in 1965, Palin began working as a television host and writer. "I've never had a proper job—not a salary, nor an office, nor a long-term contract," he observed to Sue Gaisford of the London *Independent.* "I just sort of slipped through the net." Palin landed a job as host of a regional television program called *NOW!* and then, urged on by Jones, began to submit scripts to comedy shows airing on the British Broadcasting Company (BBC). Frost kept his promise and recruited the pair as writers for his innovative satirical program *The Frost Report* in 1966. That writing staff brought Palin and Jones together with most of the rest of the Monty Python cast: John Cleese, Eric Idle, and Graham Chapman.

© Presselect/Alamy

Created Legendary Comedy-Sketch Program

Palin and Jones worked on two more BBC comedy series in the late 1960s: *Do Not Adjust Your Set,* which began as a children's show but soon gained a cult adult following, and *The Complete and Utter History of Britain.* Then he and the rest of the British Monty Python cast had the idea for a more experimental program of sketch comedy that Palin at first wanted to call *Gwen Dibley* after a name he had once read in one of his mother's magazines. A BBC producer wanted to call it *Owl Stretching Time,* and several other names with a "Flying Circus" component were considered. The American cartoonist Terry Gilliam, who knew Cleese and was working for an advertising agency in London, joined the cast and creative team, and *Monty Python's Flying Circus* went on the air in October of 1969.

Monty Python's Flying Circus was unlike anything previously shown on television. Palin often worked with Jones and Gilliam as a writing team, contributing a strong surrealist element to such sketches as one involving a cross-dressing lumberjack, or a series of sketches in which a character who complains about an inquisition is suddenly visited by a group of medieval cardinals who point out that "Nobody expects the Spanish Inquisition!" Much of the show's humor was based on the interactions between the comic personalities of its principals, for instance in a routine in which Palin played a pet shop owner who sells a dead parrot but refuses a refund to a distraught Cleese. *Monty Python's Flying Circus* ran until 1974 and then had a new round of success when it was shown on the Public Broadcasting System in the United States.

Monty Python's Flying Circus has had a long life since its initial showings on television. "I always found that twenty minutes into a Python show, I'd think 'This must be the end,' yet there's more and more! So it's like a thick, well-filled comic book. People are always finding new things in Python," Palin observed to Kim Howard Johnson in an interview quoted in *Contemporary Authors.* Sketches from the first two years were collected and adapted into the film *And Now for Something Completely Different* (1971), and the series spawned three more full-length films: *Monty Python and the Holy Grail* (1975), *Monty Python's Life of Brian* (1979), and *Monty Python's The Meaning of Life.* (1983). The troupe also released a live video, *Monty Python Live at the Hollywood Bowl.* In the controversial *Life of Brian,* which brashly depicted a Christ-like figure, Palin played Pontius Pilate, and he co-wrote all the films.

Appeared in *Brazil*

Palin had plenty of energy left over for non–Monty Python projects, including the television series *Ripping Yarns* and a variety of films. He and Gilliam wrote the hit children's film *Time Bandits* in 1981, and the following year he wrote, produced, and starred in the comedy *The Missionary.* He rejoined Gilliam in 1986, playing the serious role of a torturer in Gilliam's dark futuristic fantasy *Brazil,* and Cleese in 1988, playing a hitman in Cleese's comedy *A Fish Called Wanda.* That film stirred controversy due to Palin's use of a stammer for comic effect, but Palin responded that the routine had affectionate roots in his father's persistent stammer.

Even after two decades of high-profile success, Palin was still setting whole new challenges for himself. "I look at everything I have done and think, why wasn't that better?" he explained to John Plunkett of the London *Guardian.* "Part of my motivation is from crippling self-doubt—I have got to prove myself wrong." Palin wrote a novel, *Hemingway's Chair,* four children's books, and a book of limericks; he also collaborated with other Python cast members on *The Pythons: Autobiography* (2005), and released several volumes of his own diaries from different phases of his career. In 1989 his career took an entirely new turn: he starred in a BBC television travel documentary, *Around the World in Eighty Days,* in which he retraced the steps of the journey depicted in the classic Jules Verne adventure novel of the same name, using the same modes of transport boarded by the novel's British main character, Phineas Fogg.

Around the World in Eighty Days was successful enough that it generated four more adventure-packed Palin travelogues: *Pole to Pole with Michael Palin* (1992), *Full Circle: A Pacific Journey* (1997), *Sahara* (2002), and *Himalaya* (2004). Palin declined offers to reunite with his *Monty Python* comrades, believing that the group would inevitably disappoint viewers in comparison with their earlier work. Instead, he became a fellow of Britain's Royal Geographical Society and accepted an offer to become the group's president in 2009. He explained to Olivia

Edward of *Geographical* that he hoped to stimulate interest in the study of geography, which was "seen as a slightly nerdy subject and I can't really begin to think why when you look at what's happening in the world. Whether it's [epidemics], or terrorism, or global warming, knowing the geography is so vitally important." After completing his terms as president, Palin received the society's Patron's Medal.

Palin married Helen Gibbins in 1966 after the pair met on a holiday trip. The pair raised three children. Palin remained active into the 2010s, starring in a new BBC drama, *The Wipers Times,* in 2013. The program dealt with a newspaper produced amidst trench warfare by soldiers in World War I. Palin intended to continue creating new material. As he said to Rosa Silverman of *The Telegraph Online:* "I find as I get older I've learned more about the world, and I want to share with people rather than sit in a chair and shut up." In late 2013, Palin and the four other surviving members of the original Monty Python troupe (Graham Chapman died in 1989) announced plans to reunite for a series of live shows.

Books

Novick, Jeremy, *Life of Michael: An Illustrated Biography of Michael Palin,* Headline, 2001.

Palin, Michael, *Diaries: 1969–1979: The Python Years,* St. Martin's, 2007.

Palin, Michael, *Halfway to Hollywood: Diaries, 1980–1988,* St. Martin's, 2011.

(with Terry Gilliam, et al.) *The Pythons: Autobiography,* St. Martin's, 2005.

Periodicals

Geographical, October 2009; August 2013.

Guardian (London, England), July 5, 2013.

Independent (London, England), October 1, 2004.

New York Times, November 19, 2013.

Telegraph Online, October 8, 2013.

Times (London, England), February 24, 1990; November 4, 2004.

Online

"Michael Palin," *BBC Guide to Comedy,* http://www.bbc.co.uk/comedy/people/michael_palin_person_page.shtml (October 15, 2013).

"Michael Palin," *Contemporary Authors Online,* Gale, 2012.

"Michael Palin," *Cardinal Fang's Python Site,* http://www.cardinalfang.net/biographies/palin_biog.html (October 15, 2013).

"Palin, Michael (1943–)," *British Film Institute,* http://www.screenonline.org.uk/people/id/510300/ (October 15, 2013).□

Spencer Perceval

Spencer Perceval (1762–1812) is one of the forgotten names in British political history. An ally of the Tory (Conservative) members in Parliament, the sober-minded, rather uncharismatic barrister held high-ranking cabinet posts before becoming prime minister in October of 1809. He governed at a time of economic adversity, political turmoil, and widespread public discontent. On May 11, 1812, Perceval became the only British prime minister ever to be assassinated in office.

Spencer Perceval was born on November 1, 1762, at a home on Audley Square in London. His father was John Perceval, the 2nd Earl of Egmont, an Irish peerage. The future prime minister was the seventh son of his father, and the second born from the Earl's second marriage to Catherine Compton. Perceval's father was politically active and an advisor to King George III, who appointed him to a newly created post as Lord of the Admiralty in 1763. The family lived at Charlton House, a manor home in Greenwich, London, and Perceval also spent several formative years at the Harrow School, an elite boys' academy. His father died in 1770, and as one of the younger sons Perceval inherited no property and negligible assets. With an eye toward a potentially profitable career in law, the young Perceval devoted himself to his studies at Trinity College of Cambridge University. He won a prize for oratory before graduating in 1782, then took up the study of law at the Inns of Court in London. After finishing that course of training in 1786, he began working for one of the divisions of the Crown court, the Midlands Circuit.

Eloped with Brother's Sister-in-Law

In the 1780s, Perceval met, through his brother Charles, a woman named Jane Maryon Wilson. Jane's sister Margaretta had married Perceval's older brother, but the Wilsons' father did not believe Perceval could earn a sufficient enough salary as a circuit-court attorney and refused to condone their engagement. For this reason the couple eloped in the summer of 1790, shortly after Jane's 18th birthday.

Some of Perceval's extended family members helped him secure permanent civil-service jobs that brought a steadier income than his law practice. Through his Compton cousins on his mother's side he was appointed Deputy Recorder of Northampton, then became a Commissioner of Bankrupts. In 1791, he was given the titles Surveyor of the Maltings and Clerk of the Irons in the Mint. In 1794 he was appointed counsel to the Board of Admiralty, which put him in the position of arguing the government's case against defendants like Thomas Paine, whose writings had helped spark the American revolution. Paine was tried in absentia for his work *Rights of Man,* which was widely read in England in the early 1790s and prompted calls for political reform in Britain, too.

Became Attorney General

Perceval was called to the bar of Lincoln's Inn in 1796, which qualified him as a barrister with the title King's Counsel, or K.C. In May of that year he also won a seat in the House of Commons as a Member of Parliament (M.P.)

for Northampton, prevailing in a hard-fought contest in the district. It was a time when only a small proportion of the population—men who owned property above a certain value—were permitted to cast votes, and in Northampton Perceval had the backing of a few staunch Tory supporters. He was able to hold on to the seat by running unopposed in the 1802, 1806, and 1807 elections. He rose to prominence in Westminster, the London palace that houses the assembly rooms of the House of Lords and the House of Commons, through his talent for public speaking. When parliament was not in session he continued arguing cases as K.C., or King's Counsel. In 1801 he was appointed Solicitor General and then Attorney General a year later.

Britain was divided by major internal conflict during this era. The American Revolutionary War had been a serious financial drain, and a renewal of hostilities with France in 1792 also sapped the treasury. Outside of parliament, there were calls for electoral reform, to allow more men to participate in the political process by loosening the qualifications, but Perceval's Conservative (Tory) Party allies staunchly opposed this.

Perceval and his wife Jane began a family that would number an astonishing dozen children. A daughter named Jane was born in 1791, followed by another girl, Frances, in 1792 and then Maria in 1794. His first son, also named Spencer, was born in 1795. Before the century closed Perceval and Jane became parents to sons Frederick, Henry, and Dudley. Isabella was born in 1801, a fifth son they named John arrived in 1803, and daughters Louise and Frederica were born, respectively, in 1804 and 1805. Ernest was Perceval's twelfth and last child, born in 1807. The family lived at several places, beginning with rented rooms above a carpet shop on Bedford Row, then a larger place at the address No. 59 Lincoln's Inn Fields. They eventually settled at Belsize House, a sizable property in the hilly Hampstead Heath section of London, and then moved to Ealing, on what was then the outskirts of London.

Led Parson's-Type Life

Perceval and his wife were devout Anglicans who adhered to a Puritan-inspired evangelical branch. They were staunch sabbatarians, believing that Sunday should be a day devoted to churchgoing and reflection. Unlike many of his barrister colleagues and M.P.s., Perceval rarely drank alcohol. He was openly disdainful of other popular pursuits such as gambling, which he deemed a waste of money that might be better spent on charity, and thought hunting and other blood sports were foolish, status-conscious pursuits.

As Attorney General, Perceval was compelled to conduct an inquiry into a supposed illegitimate birth by Princess Caroline, the spurned wife of George, the Prince of Wales and son of an ailing, aging King George III. The prince was a foppish, profligate figure who was openly disdainful of his father and moved to ally himself with M.P.s and members of the House of Lords who wanted to see him rule as Prince Regent in his father's stead. The prince's 1795 marriage to his cousin, Princess Caroline of Brunswick, was brief but produced a daughter, the Princess Charlotte. Prince George then banned his wife from court and returned to his longtime paramour, a twice-divorced Roman Catholic. When Caroline was accused of concealing a second pregnancy, Perceval was forced to undertake the "Delicate Investigation." His inquiries determined that the infant in her household was indeed a foundling whom Caroline had taken in, and in an epic legal brief of 1806 he recommended that the princess be allowed to return to court. Perceval, his wife, and the German-born princess became close, and Caroline served as godmother to the Percevals' youngest child, Ernest. One of the princess's first public appearances in London again was to attend Perceval's maiden speech as Chancellor of the Exchequer from March of 1807.

Perceval had objected to this appointment, rightfully asserting that he had little financial background. But Tory political operatives, including the Duke of Portland, convinced him to join the cabinet at a time when funds were badly needed for the still-ongoing war against France. When the Duke of Portland became prime minister, Perceval became Leader of the House of Commons. Parliament and both Tory and Whig parties were driven by factions and intense partisanship over the war against Napoleon, the issue of Catholic Emancipation—English, Scottish, and Irish adherents to the Church in Rome were subject to various restrictions—and parliamentary reform. Perceval supported the war to vanquish French imperialism, and was against the proposed Catholic Emancipation laws and any type of electoral reform.

Headed New Government

Perceval ascended to the post of prime minister on October 4, 1809, after the resignation of the Duke of Portland due to declining health. King George, then in the 47th year of his rule, was again afflicted with the collection of symptoms that disabled him and gave him the sobriquet "Mad King George," and the Prince of Wales finally became Prince Regent in 1811. During the first year of Perceval's term, in 1810, the Royal Navy conducted a mostly disastrous sea war against French ships, and there were troubles at home, too. Punitive laws and high unemployment caused the infamous Luddite riots, which spread across England in 1811. Luddites were anti-machinery activists and rallied mobs of impoverished, unemployed workers to smash textile looms and other labor-saving new machinery of the Industrial Revolution. One of Perceval's most decisive acts as prime minister was to reclassify frame-breaking as a capital offense, thereby punishable by death. Perceval also supported the abolition of the slave trade in the British Empire, adhering with William Wilberforce's efforts to outlaw the importation or transport of African slaves in British colonies or vessels; slavery itself would not be abolished in Britain's overseas colonies until 1833.

Shot Point-Blank

Perceval's wife and children made Elm House in Ealing their main residence. When in London Perceval lived at No. 10 Downing Street, the prime minister's official residence. Shortly after 5 p.m. on May 11, 1812, Perceval left No. 10 for Westminster after being summoned to hear another inquiry into the Orders in Council, another controversial bill and one that dealt directly with maritime trade and the war against France.

Perceval's assassination as he hurried through the Westminster lobby was carried out by John Bellingham, a disgruntled Liverpool merchant. Bellingham had done business in Russia and was accused of fraud by the Russian authorities in Arkhangelsk, a northern Russian port on the White Sea. Bellingham was eventually cleared of the charges and released, but had lost a substantial sum of money from the debacle and first appealed to the British ambassador in St. Petersburg for help. After returning to Liverpool, Bellingham made several more attempts to receive restitution, with no result, and decided to kill the prime minister as a way of attracting attention to his plight. Arriving in London early in 1812, Bellingham bought a pair of pistols and even had a special pocket constructed by a tailor for his waistcoat to conceal the weapon. He visited sessions of the House of Commons in order to identify Perceval.

Perceval was caught entirely off-guard as he entered Westminster. "As he came through the lobby doors, he was confronted by a looming figure, who put a pistol against his chest and fired," wrote Andrew Holgate in the London *Sunday Times.* "Perceval, shouting 'Murder, oh, murder,' reeled backwards and all hell broke loose, with shouts of 'Close the doors, close the doors' ringing round the chamber." A fatally injured Perceval was carried off to the secretary's room, while a man named Henry Burgess disarmed Bellingham, who simply took a seat on a bench and waited to be arrested.

Perceval's body was removed to No. 10 Downing Street. "After Bellingham struck, there were riots outside parliament, and the cabinet, terrified that Perceval's death heralded the start of a revolution, tried to stop the news spreading by ordering all mail coaches to remain in London," wrote Holgate in the *Sunday Times.* Perceval's family held a quick, private funeral and Bellingham was swiftly tried, found guilty, and hanged on May 18. As prime minister Perceval was succeeded by his Minister of War, Lord Liverpool, who eliminated the Orders in Council and led the country into the disastrous War of 1812 with the United States.

Perceval remains the only prime minister to be assassinated in office, though Irish Republican Army operatives did come perilously close with a 1984 bomb detonated at a hotel in Brighton, England, where Tory leader and Britain's first female prime minister, Margaret Thatcher, was staying. Only one of Perceval's six sons followed him into politics; this was Spencer Perceval the Younger, who served in the House of Commons from 1818 to 1832.

Books

Gray, Denis, *Spencer Perceval: The Evangelical Prime Minister, 1762–1812,* Manchester University Press, 1963.

Periodicals

Guardian (London, England), May 10, 2012; May 12, 2012.
Independent on Sunday (London, England), May 14, 2012.
Sunday Times (London, England), May 6, 2012.□

Charles Ponzi

Charles Ponzi (1882–1949) was an Italian-born schemer whose name is synonymous with an infamous and often-duplicated type of financial fraud. For several months in 1920, Ponzi's sham firm in Boston collected an estimated $10 million from hopeful investors who had been drawn in by his pledge to pay a 50 percent return on the money via the selling of overseas postal reply coupons. The savvy con artist, who targeted Boston's Italian American community and other working-class folk, merely paid his first round of investors with funds deposited by newcomers.

Charles "Carlo" Ponzi never became a naturalized American citizen, and was finally deported back to his homeland by U.S. immigration officials after several years in prison. Born Carlo Pietro Giovanni Guglielmo Tebaldo Ponzi on March 3, 1882, he was the only child of Oreste, a postal worker, and Imelde, whose family connections stretched back into minor Italian

© Everett Collection Inc/Alamy

nobility in the former Duchy of Parma. The Ponzis lived first in Lugo, a town near Bologna where he was born, and eventually settled in Parma. Imelde told her son endless stories about the splendid homes and finery of her distant relatives, and both she and her husband dreamed their son would become a respected professional, pointing him toward a career in law. At the age of ten he was sent away to a private academy, where he proved a gifted student with a facility for languages. When he was in his teens his father died and left him a small inheritance, which was just enough to cover his fees and expenses for a degree at Rome's prestigious La Sapienza University, at which he had been accepted.

Flunked Out of College

In Rome the good-looking, charming Ponzi fell in with a fast crowd of wealthy students from the Roman aristocracy. He drank, gambled, and spent lavishly on clothes and restaurant dinners; after two years his academic record was an embarrassment and he had spent all of his inheritance. An uncle suggested he apply for a position as a business or civil-service clerk, but Ponzi was appalled at the idea of a desk job. His uncle suggested he try to earn his fortune in America, and Ponzi agreed. Family members—hounded by gambling-debt collectors and repeatedly paying fines for Ponzi's recklessness—bought him a steamship ticket and gave him a generous sendoff gift of $200, almost all of which Ponzi had gambled away by the time the *S.S. Vancouver* sailed into Boston Harbor in November of 1903.

Ponzi quickly taught himself English aboard a train to Pittsburgh, where a distant relative had agreed to hire him for his freight company. The owner occasionally falsified invoices and bills of lading in order to earn a little extra money on the side, and it was here that Ponzi first learned the rudiments of U.S. commerce. Loathing Pittsburgh's steel-furnace polluted air, Ponzi moved on, taking a variety of jobs in New Jersey, New York, and Rhode Island. He waited tables, learned sign-painting, and pressed shirts at a laundry—all low-wage, exhausting jobs that only intensified his distaste for a conventional life. The prospect of a quick buck through gambling continued to lure him, but in the rogues' world of early twentieth century life in America, the immigrant was usually outfoxed by shady dealers and fellow poker-table players who knew the skill of counting cards. Finally, in 1907, Ponzi set out for Montreal, Canada.

Convicted of Check Forgery

A bustling river port, Montreal was a center of Francophone Canada and emerging as a major financial capital. Ponzi had heard about a successful bank in Montreal that catered to the city's growing Italian-immigrant population. Hired as a teller at Banco Zarossi, Ponzi was quickly promoted to a management post and realized the bank's founder and president, Luigi Zarossi, was running a fraudulent enterprise. In an era before bank deposits were covered by federal insurance, Zarossi was paying the six-percent interest dividends to his loyal savings-account customers with the funds of new depositors. Once the scheme began to fall apart, Zarossi fled to Mexico to avoid prosecution. Ponzi stayed in Montreal for a time, ostensibly to help auditors and the Zarossi family, but on August 29, 1908, he cashed a check with a forged signature that he had taken from one of the Zarossi Bank's depositors. A teller at the Bank of Hochelaga cashed the $423.58 check drawn on the Canadian Warehousing account, but the nonconsecutive check number aroused suspicion later that day and police began searching for Ponzi, who had spent nearly $200 of it in a few hours on new clothes. He served 20 months in a Quebec province prison, eventually finessing his way into a plum job inside the warden's office.

After his release, Ponzi was roped into a labor-agency scheme to smuggle immigrants across the U.S.-Canadian border. For that he was convicted on federal fraud charges and sent to the U.S. federal penitentiary in Atlanta, Georgia. After his release he tried to win a contract to bring electricity to mining camps in Alabama, which failed, then looked for opportunities in the Florida real-estate market. After a stint working as a college librarian in Mobile, Alabama—a job that gave him ample time to complete his informal education—he hustled up sign-painting jobs in New Orleans after a 1915 hurricane ravaged the city, and then moved on to Wichita Falls, Texas, where a local flat-bed truck manufacturer was selling the durable freight vehicles to overseas markets. The multilingual Ponzi was hired to handle its foreign business, which propelled him back to Boston in search of similar work. He was hired at an import-export firm and began courting a young woman from an Italian-émigré family, Rose Gnecco, whose father ran a wholesale produce business. The two were married in 1918 and Ponzi took over his father-in-law-s business, quickly mismanaging it into bankruptcy.

Devised Arbitrage Scheme

Ponzi disliked the grocery business anyway. He tried to start another business with a publication called the *Traders' Guide,* which would serve as an international business directory. A Boston bank, Hanover Trust Company, refused his application for a loan, and the venture failed. But in August of 1919, a potential customer in Spain replied and asked for a copy of the *Trader's Guide,* enclosing a postal-reply slip. These were called international reply coupons, or IRCs, and were issued by postal services in countries that belonged to the Universal Postal Union (UPU). A letter-writer could buy a coupon at their hometown post office for a reply and enclose it in a letter bound for an overseas address; the post office of the recipient country then exchanged the coupon for reply postage. "Theoretically, someone who bought a postal reply coupon in Spain could redeem it in the United States for about a 10 percent profit," explained *Smithsonian* writer Mary Darby. "Purchasing coupons in countries with weaker economies could increase that margin substantially, he reasoned."

This was the basis for Ponzi's epic fraud. He set up business in December of 1919 at 27 School Street in the heart of Boston, renting out two floors of the Niles Building. He sent out some trial letters to France, Spain, and Italy, and was able to make a profit when he redeemed the IRCs, which had been in use since 1906. What made his idea even more appealing was the fact that unlike banks or the stock market, consumers on both sides of the Atlantic trusted their postal service, and that his scheme appeared to be entirely legal.

Amassed Fortune by "Affinity Fraud"

The first "mark" for Ponzi's scheme was a furniture dealer named Joseph Daniels, who had sold him office furniture on a payment plan. By December of 1919, Ponzi was behind in payments and confronted by Daniels. He offered the businessman an opportunity to invest in his new scheme, convincing him to take a promissory note that pledged a 100 percent return on an initial cash loan of $200 in two months' time. Daniels agreed to give him a short-term loan, and with that Ponzi registered as a sole proprietor of his newly created Securities Exchange Company at Boston City Hall on December 13, 1919. Ponzi had business stationery and promissory notes printed up and began taking deposits. His first investors were those he knew in the North End of Boston, the center of its Italian-émigré community. He promised a 50 percent return on investment (ROI)—in other words, if an investor ponied up $100, he would receive $150 at the end of the first 45 days, and or 100 percent profit in 90 days, for a total of $200. If the funds were continually reinvested, in a single year a depositor could make $2,500, and after two years the ROI would be an astonishing $65,000.

Within weeks Ponzi was taking in hundreds of dollars a day, and then thousands each week. He paid off early investors, and the success of the scheme spread through word-of-mouth. Wisely, Ponzi invested in real estate and bought shares in the Hanover Trust bank. An even cannier move was inviting local newspaper reporters and even Boston police officers to invest, and he bought a palatial house in leafy Lexington, Massachusetts, for his devoted wife. On Saturday, July 24, 1920, the *Boston Post* ran an article about Ponzi under the headline "Doubles the Money within Three Months," and Ponzi's chauffeur-driven luxury car pulled up to the School Street office confronting a mob scene of Bostonians eager to invest in his Securities Exchange Company.

The burst of publicity brought unwelcome attention from state and federal investigators, and Ponzi managed to stave off collapse for a few more weeks. "He claimed to have elaborate networks of agents throughout Europe who were making bulk purchases of postal reply coupons on his behalf," wrote Darby in the *Smithsonian.* "In the United States, Ponzi asserted, he worked his financial wizardry to turn those piles of paper coupons into larger piles of greenbacks. Pressed for details on how this transformation was achieved, he politely explained that he had to keep such information secret for competitive reasons."

Exposed as Scam Artist

At first, Ponzi paid out nervous investors who wanted their funds back and promised to stop taking new investors until government agents and postal inspectors completed their investigation. In the end, a public relations expert he had hired named William McMasters uncovered evidence that Ponzi was, in effect, operating a massive pyramid scheme. Journalists also uncovered details about his prior criminal record, and Ponzi turned himself in to authorities on August 12, 1920.

Ponzi was charged with 86 counts of mail fraud by federal authorities. He struck a plea deal and entered the Plymouth Colony jail on December 12, 1920, almost one year after registering his business. He had had a spectacular run: a *New York Times* report from a few days earlier disclosed the results of an audit, revealing that the Securities Exchange Company had assets of $1.5 million and a debt load of $6.3 million. While serving his sentence, the Commonwealth of Massachusetts attempted to bring additional charges against Ponzi, which he fought on the principal of double jeopardy. His court cases lasted years, and at one point a jury even agreed with him and voted for acquittal. In one instance, free on bail, the infamous fraudster attempted to flee back to Italy disguised as a common sailor, but was flushed out in a manhunt. Finally released from the state prison at Charlestown in 1934, he was promptly deported back to Italy. Later in the 1930s, he worked for an airline run by the Italian government, then under the control of right'wing Fascist Party leader Benito Mussolini, that operated an air route to Brazil, but flights were halted in 1941 during World War II. He was by then divorced from Rose, who had wanted to remain near family in Boston.

Ponzi lived the remaining years of his life in Rio de Janeíro, Brazil, in deep poverty and failing health. He died in a charity hospital in the city on January 18, 1949.

Books

Zuckoff, Mitchell, *Ponzi's Scheme: The True Story of a Financial Legend,* Random House, 2005.

Periodicals

New York Times, December 7, 1920.
New Yorker, March 23, 2009.
Smithsonian, December 1998.□

Andrée Putman

French interior designer Andrée Putman (1925-2013) was a leading creator of the 1980s who set international trends in hotels, commercial spaces, residences, and objects. She also designed the first boutique hotel, helping develop the concept. According to design critic Stephen Bayley, as quoted in the *Daily Mail,* Putman was "the Simone de Beauvoir of interior design."

Bertrand Rindoff Petroff/French Select/Getty Images

Born Andrée Christine Aynard on December 23, 1925, in Paris, France, Putman's family was quite wealthy. Her paternal grandfather was a successful banker, while her father was well-educated at the École Normale Supérieure before becoming a multilingual intellectual. Her mother was a virtuoso piano player who could have had, but did not pursue, a professional playing career. While there were many eccentrics in the family, including her maternal grandmother, some of the family were descendants of the inventors of the hot-air balloon, the Montgolfiers.

Studied Piano at the Paris Conservatoire

Raised on the Left Bank in Paris, her upbringing emphasized music and literary pursuits. Like her mother before, Putman studied piano and composition at the Paris Conservatoire, where she was taught by composer Francis Poulenc. She even won first prize at the conservatory. Poulenc encouraged his promising student to spend a decade focusing on nothing but music.

Putman also had an interest in design as well. As a 15-year-old, foreshadowing her own spare creations, she emptied her room of furniture in the family apartment, leaving it with simply a steel bed, spoons from China and Africa displayed on a bench, and a few other furnishings. The look was influenced by some Art Deco magazines she had found.

When Putman was 19 years old, she suffered a near fatal accident involving her bike. The collision not only compelled her to give up her musical ambitions and leave behind any notion that she might want to focus solely on music for the next ten years, but her injuries also left her with a perpetually erect, stiff posture. After the accident, Putman pursued employment first by becoming a courier at a woman's magazine called *Femina.* At the same time, her burgeoning interest in design led her to decorate and arrange the apartments of friends. As her daughter Olivia explained to the Agence France Presse, "when she went over to a friend's house for dinner, she would offer to haul around sofas, or drape a dishcloth over a lamp to soften the mood."

Launched Career in Magazines

Learning much about fashion in Paris from the experience, Putman soon became a writer. Finding she had a talent for it, she wrote a design column for the fashion magazine *Elle* from 1952 to 1958, then became the interiors editor for the art magazine *L'oeil.* For the latter, she also wrote pieces about art and design. In this period, Putman began to collect artworks as well.

By the late 1950s, Putman increased her connections to the artistic Left Bank culture. Her access and interest deepened when she married Jacques Putman, an art critic and publisher, with whom she would have two children, Olivia and Cyrille. Through her own work and her husband, Putman had daily contact with seminal Left Bank artistic figures like Niki de Saint Phalle, Juliette Gréco, playwright Samuel Beckett, Pierre Alechinsky, and Bram van Velde.

Became Artistic Director of Prisunic

In 1958, Putman became the artistic director of the retail chain, Prisunic, after meeting Denis Fayolle through her Left Bank contacts, then being invited to design a tableware line. Because of Putman's influence, Prisunic began selling reasonably priced (approximately 100 francs) lithographs of contemporary art works. Putman believed that style and art should be accessible, and the selling of these prints supported both Putman and her artist friends. By this point, Putman had a well-defined persona and appearance that would remain strong throughout her life. It included a shock of blonde or auburn hair, chiseled face, high heels, flawless clothing and makeup, a cigarette handled like a move star, and a gravelly smoking-deepened voice.

After about a decade at Prisunic, she moved to Mafia, a Montmare-based company that was a pioneer in discerning fashion trends. Putman was lured away from Mafia by fashion entrepreneur Didier Grumbach to become the artistic director for a new agency, Créateurs & Industriels, in 1971. Créateurs focused on promoting a broad range of young design and fashion talent, including Jean-Paul Gaultier, Emmanuelle Khanh, Issey Miyake, and Thierry Mugler. She designed the interior of the company's new headquarters, which was located in industrial buildings once used by the national rail service in France. This marked the first time she worked specifically in interior design.

Founded Écart International

By 1976, the agency was unable to continue operations; two years later, she was divorced. After these events, Putman founded her own agency, Écart International, which initially focused on furniture sales and design. Through this company, she sold works by and based on undervalued early twentieth century French modernist designers like Jean-Michel Frank, Eileen Gray, Robert Mallet-Stevens, Mariano Fortuny, and Pierre Chareau. A fan of such modernists in her youth, Putman's passion for them was re-ignited when she found many pieces of their furniture in flea markets. At the same time, monochrome was a popular design trend in the 1980s, and the pieces of such modernists complemented the look, increasing their fame and Putman's sales in this time period. For example, Écart sold 30,000 chairs originally designed by Gray and updated by Putman.

As Putman's company grew, she also began designing interiors herself, though she had no formal education in design or architecture. She began working on residential projects for friends, such as fashion designer Karl Lagerfeld, then did bigger spaces after she generated publicity for her work. She used her skills to convert the interior of a Bordeaux-based warehouse into the CACP Museum of Contemporary Art. By the mid-1980s, Putman took a commission to design the interior of Morgans Hotel, in New York City, which became the first boutique hotel in the world. A boutique hotel is one that is small and artistically designed as opposed to a luxury hotel that is very standardized and mass market-oriented.

Offered Unique Design for Morgans

Opened by Ian Schrager and Steve Rubell (former owners of famed nightclub Studio 54) on Madison Avenue in 1984, Putman's interiors at Morgans helped re-define the concept of designer accommodations in what had once been a drab, run-down brick building in Manhattan. As expressed in Morgans and other hotel projects, luxury was modernist and sober, not excessive, clichée, or flowery. She rejected flounces and antiques in favor of a more minimalist, hushed look with uncomplicated lines, painstaking detail, and deceptive simplicity. Putman favored a few interesting pieces in an environment she made essentially hushed and monochromatic. Her bathrooms, for example, often included her signature black and white checkerboard tiling and chrome fixtures. When Morgans opened, it was a hit with critics and the public.

After Morgan's, Putman and Écart landed more commissions for hotels, including the Sheraton-Roissy Hotel at Paris's Charles de Gaulle airport, Peshing Hall and St. James Club in Paris, the Hotel im Wasserturm in Cologne, and the Hotel le Lac in Kawaguchi, Japan. More prestigious contracts followed, such as redesigning the interior of the Concorde supersonic jet, and the Putman, a thirty-one story apartment skyscraper in Hong Kong. Putman also designed many private residences in Europe, Asia, the Middle East, and the United States as well as the elegant but spare offices for Jack Lang, who was the culture minister for France for a time.

In addition, Putman designed retail commercial store interiors including outlets for fashion icons like Lagerfeld, Balenciaga, and Yves Saint-Laurent both in France and overseas. For the French label Guerlain, she designed the interior of the flagship store on the Champs-Élysées. Other projects included serving as set designer for a film by Peter Greenaway, a 1996 adaptation of a Japanese erotic novel *The Pillow Book.* Over the years, her designs became a combination of luxury and austerity, glamour and accessibility. They were inventive, rebellious, and a little unconventional.

As a designer, Putman was influenced by literary and philosophical sensibilities affected by her years of contact with Left Bank intellectuals. According to the *New York Times,* Putman once wrote in a monograph, "Materials are not objects, like letters in a vocabulary. They have connotations, they belong to a code, like shapes or words."

Established Own Company

In 1997, Putman had a falling out with a financial partner at Écart International, and she formed a new company as she continued to be active later in life. Through Andrée Putman Studio, she continued to work with high-end commercial clients like Louis Vuitton, and well-heeled private citizens. In 1997, she founded a line of furniture and home accessories, tableware, carpets, scents, towels, and sheets.

Still working in the late 1990s and early 2000s, Putman designed a house for leading French intellectuals, Bernard-Henri Lèvy, a philosopher, and his wife, Arielle Dombasle, an actress and singer. In 2000, Putman designed a ring for Christofle, a brand of jewelry, that was imperfectly shaped. Five years later, the lavish book *Putman Style* was published, detailing her life and work. It was written by Stephane Gerschel, who explained why she was an icon of design and French good taste.

Continued Designing Late in Life

By 2007, Putman had ceded control of her company to her daughter, Olivia. Though she was no longer in charge, she continued to design pieces like jewelry and a distinctive piano for Pleyel, which made pianos for the likes of Frédéric Chopin and Charles-Camille Saint-Saëns. In 2008, Putman designed a digital photo frame for Parrot, a French cellular telephone company. It was the first object in its planned line of artistic wireless audiovisual products. That same year, a retrospective of her career, "Beyond Style—Andrée Putman," was curated by her son Cyrille and exhibited at New York City's French Cultural Services building.

At 85, Putman remained active, with daily gym workouts, reading, and listening to opera. After her activities became curtailed by the gradual onset of Alzheimer's, Putman died on January 19, 2013, at her home in Paris.

Despite her vast successes and cultural influence, according to the London *Times*, Putman once told *House Beautiful*, "I've had so many occasions to start believing in myself, and I never will. Strange. I am protected by a lot of angels from any self-esteem, from the capacity to feel content with myself. Perhaps that also gives me a certain capacity for wonder at the world, like a child before a Christmas tree. This is very strong in my life, and maybe it's what opens me to other people, and to new ventures and experiences. In French, we have a nice word for that—partant, 'ready to go.' I'm always ready."

Periodicals

Agence France Press—English, November 10, 2010.

Business Day (South Africa), November 1, 2005.

Business Wire, May 6, 2008.

Daily Telegraph (London), April 19, 2013.

New York Sun, September 17, 2008.

New York Times, January 21, 2013.

Times (London), January 26, 2013.□

R

Otis Redding

The African American vocalist Otis Redding (1941–1967) has been considered one of the greatest singers in the soul music genre. His career advanced rapidly between 1962 and 1967, when it was cut short by his death in a plane crash.

Redding was discovered almost accidentally when he was allowed to record a few tracks during some free time at the end of a session at the Stax Records label in Memphis. His gospel-drenched debut single, "These Arms of Mine," sold 800,000 copies and propelled him to popularity in live shows, where his emotion-wracked performances became legendary. Like one of his main influences, Sam Cooke, Redding moved to take control of his career at a time when African American artists were often exploited. He wrote much of his own material, including several songs made popular by other artists; his "Respect," as recorded by Aretha Franklin, became one of the most famous soul songs of all. Just before his death, Redding had made major inroads among white audiences and had written and recorded the classic ballad "Dock of the Bay." Released posthumously, it would become Redding's biggest hit.

Won Consecutive Talent Contests

Born in the small city of Dawson in south Georgia on September 9, 1941, Otis Ray Redding Jr., moved with his family to the musically rich city of Macon when he was five. There he heard the music of rock and roll star Little Richard, who was his hero as a teen, and he would also have been exposed to the music of soul shouter James Brown. Another influence was the gospel music he heard—and played, on guitar and piano—at Vineville Baptist Church. Redding grew up in the rough Tindall Heights housing project and attended Macon's Ballard Hudson High School. He was forced to drop out of school and work as a well-driller when his father fell sick. In his free time, Redding entered talent contests at the Hillview Springs Social Club. After he won for 15 weeks in a row, performing convincingly in the style of Little Richard and taking home a five-dollar prize, he was banned from further competition.

Redding played in Little Richard's band, the Upsetters, and in 1959, he met Zelma Atwood. The relationship took time to deepen, but they married in August of 1961, and raised four children (Dexter, Karla, Otis III, and Demetria) amid what quickly became a very busy career on Redding's part. In 1960, Redding moved to another band, the Pinetoppers, fronted by vocalist Johnny Jenkins. He also gained live performing experience at talent shows hosted by a disc jockey, Hamp Swain, who called himself King Bee.

In 1962 Jenkins, who did not have a driver's license, landed an audition at the new Stax label in Memphis, which was beginning to score major success with a gospel/rhythm-and-blues hybrid that would soon be called soul music. Redding, hoping to be noticed by Stax co-owner Jim Stewart, agreed to serve as Jenkins's driver. Jenkins's performances made little impact, but a visiting Atlantic label executive encouraged Stewart to give Redding a chance. Redding cut a pair of sides, "Hey Hey Baby" was rejected as too derivative of Little Richard, but his impassioned delivery of "These Arms of Mine," impressed Stewart, and Redding was signed to Stax. His recordings would appear variously on Stax, the Stax subsidiary Volt, Atlantic, and Atlantic's subsidiary Atco.

© Pictorial Press Ltd/Alamy

Often working with Stax session guitarist Steve Cropper and with the label's house backing band, the Bar-Kays, Redding quickly became one of Stax's most productive properties. In the words of Peter Guralnick, writing in *Sweet Soul Music,* "With [Redding's] arrival Stax entered a whole new phase, and though he did not return to the studio for another nine months, it was his subsequent success ... that made Stax a byword in soul circles, that would eventualy open up the world of Southern soul to a large-scale white audience." After "These Arms of Mine" hit *Billboard* magazine's rhythm and blues top 20, Redding scored a nearly unbroken string of rhythm and blues top-20 singles between 1963 and 1967. The highest-ranking were "Pain in My Heart" (1963), "Chained and Bound" (1964), "I've Been Loving You Too Long," "Respect," and "I Can't Turn You Loose" (1966), and "Try a Little Tenderness," "Tramp," and "Knock on Wood" (1967). The last two were recorded with Stax's first female vocalist, Carla Thomas.

Redding released several albums, mostly on the Atlantic label, but at this time he was less successful among white audiences. He had close relationships with Stax's legendary studio musicians; Cropper recalled to Craig Rosen of *Billboard* that "[w]hen you were with Otis, he was your brother, he was like your best friend, he was like family. You were bonded. It wasn't like he was sitting over there and you're sitting over here"you were one when you were with Otis." Stax instrumentalist Booker T. Jones, according to Guralnick, said that Redding "was just like [conductor] Leonard Bernstein. He was the same type person. He was a leader. He'd just lead with his arms and his body and his fingers."

Formed Own Label

Redding was a noted performer on the circuit of black-oriented Southern theaters known as the chitlin' circuit, and at a time when African American artists were still routinely exploited by record companies and often ended up in poverty, he accumulated considerable wealth. Like his second idol, Sam Cooke, he formed his own publishing firm and label, Jotis Records. "While it was not Otis's prime motivation," his family website noted, "he was seen as a role model by blacks. He was someone who got paid, and paid well ... without the usual horror stories of being ripped off by promoters, agents, managers, or record company executives."

Although he could hold his own with uptempo Stax soul shouters, Redding was increasingly identified with slower numbers, especially after the release of the 1963 album *The Great Otis Redding Sings Soul Ballads.* His nickname, Mr. Pitiful, came from the title of one of his early singles. Most of Redding's biggest hits while he was still alive, including "I've Been Loving You Too Long," and "Try a Little Tenderness," were ballads. "Tramp," recorded with Thomas on the duet album *King & Queen,* was atypical in its broad humor.

By that time, Redding was looking to gain wider audiences. He headlined the Stax/Volt Revue package tour that appeared in Europe that year, and he edged Elvis Presley as top male singer in an annual poll carried out by Britain's *Melody Maker* magazine. In the United States he appeared at the large Monterey Pop Festival in California; a live album later culled from the festival's program featured his performers along with those of rock guitarist Jimi Hendrix. Aware that the Rolling Stones had covered his "That's How Strong My Love Is" and "Pain in My Heart," Redding covered that British band's standard "Satisfaction," reaching the higher ranks of British charts.

Wrote Song on Houseboat

Also around 1967, Redding began to notice the rise of folk rock in the hands of artists like Bob Dylan and the Byrds. He and Cropper wrote a simple, timelessly melancholy tune called "(Sittin' On) The Dock of the Bay," working on it partly while sitting on a houseboat docked in Sausalito, California. The recording of the song was completed three days before Redding's death and released posthumously on Volt in January of 1968, becoming Redding's first number-one pop hit (it stayed at the top spot for four weeks) and his first million-selling single. The song has remained a timeless soul standard.

On December 10, 1967, Redding chartered a plane from Cleveland, Ohio, to Madison, Wisconsin, where he was scheduled to perform at a club called The Factory. His opening act was to be the band Grim Reaper. On approach to Madison, his twin-engine Beechcraft crashed into Lake Monona, near the University of Wisconsin. Redding and most of the rest of his band were killed; trumpeter Ben Cauley was the sole survivor.

The immediate impact of Redding's death was devastating for Stax, which was about to discover that the deal they had signed with Atlantic had given ownership of all of their music to the larger label. But Redding proved one of those artists whose reputations loom larger in death than they ever had during the artists' lifetimes. Material already recorded provided the basis for four more Redding albums, one of them live, as well as classic Redding singles such as "I've Got Dreams to Remember." Redding was inducted into the Georgia Music Hall of Fame in 1981, and the Rock and Roll Hall of Fame in 1989; for the latter award, Little Richard was the presenter. In 1999, he received a posthumous Grammy award for lifetime achievement. *Rolling Stone* listed Redding as one of the ten greatest singers of all time in 2008.

Books

Contemporary Musicians, volume 5, Gale, 1991.
Guralnick, Peter, *Sweet Soul Music,* Back Bay, 1999.

Periodicals

Billboard, September 15, 2007.
Guardian (London, England), December 5, 1992.
Jet, September 17, 2007.

Online

"Biography," Otis Redding Family Website, http://www.otisredding.com/ (December 3, 2013).
"Otis Redding," *AllMusic,* http://www.allmusic.com (December 3, 2013).
"Otis Redding: Biography," *Rolling Stone,* http://www.rollingstone.com/music/artists/otis-redding/biography (December 3, 2013).
"Otis Redding Biography," *Rock and Roll Hall of Fame,* http://rockhall.com/inductees/otis-redding/bio (December 3, 2013).□

Lou Reed

American musician Lou Reed (1942–2013) co-founded the influential rock band the Velvet Underground with John Cale during the 1960s. After leaving the group, he launched a successful solo career that lasted from the early 1970s right up until his death in 2013. Reed was inducted into the Rock and Roll Hall of Fame as a member of the Velvet Underground in 1996.

For nearly 50 years, Lou Reed—a songwriter, singer, and musician—assumed a position at the avant-garde of American rock and roll music, a genre based on musical minimalism. The majority of song lyrics produced by others in his early era tended to communicate he-loves-you/she-loves you simplicity. Reed extended the boundary. He wrote words that were uncompromising, and he got his inspiration from the harsh existence of New York City streets. He was unrelenting when it came to lyrical depictions of human relationships, in his view far more complex than previously musically depicted. The long playing album would become his recording venue. His lyrics, which have often been described as "brutal" brought a new honesty into the recording world. Reed predated—even created—what would come to be known as "glam-rock" and his music would be embraced by the financially disenfranchised youth that would come to be known as "punk rockers"—a faction that pushed the barriers of societal and sexual norms. Reed was their pioneer. The Associated Press's Hillel Italie wrote in Reed's October 28, 2013 obituary, "Reed's New York was a jaded city of drag queens, drug addicts but it was also as wondrous as any [Woody] Allen comedy, with so many of Reed's songs explorations of right and wrong and quests for transcendence." Reed, Italie said, was as essential a New York artist as [film director] Martin Scorsese or Allen.

Reed demanded attention, and attention is what he got–even if his early recordings with the Velvet Underground did not initially sell well. After Reed's death in October 27, 2013, *The Economist* commented, "He had to get there, wherever it was. Wade through seas of blood if necessary, like Macbeth. Or, in his case, wade through New York streets filled with rain-soaked mattresses, prostitutes, transvestites, exploding Uzis and men selling heroin at $26 a time."

Indeed, Reed lyrics were about sex, drugs and rock and roll–but there was more. His words provided a new dimension to—even a cautious acceptance of—a seemingly squalid, sordid environment and existence. Reed offered listeners a carefully countenanced profile, even if the faces of the better-off chose to look away. For those who were tempted to listen, Reed forced a glance. In Reeds's obituary published in *Rolling Stone* magazine, Jon Dolan wrote, "As a restlessly inventive solo artist, from the seventies into the 2010s, he was chameleonic, thorny and unpredictable, challenging his fans at every turn. Glam, punk and alternative rock are all unthinkable without his revelatory example."

Reed's main mode of expression was rock and roll, with its minimal, but compelling, musical structure. Dolan quoted Reed about his adherence to the simplistic: "One chord is fine. Two chords are pushing it. Three chords and you are into jazz." That attitude made Reed's songs such as "Sweet Jane" enduring rock and roll classics, even if there were actually three basic guitar chords involved, and these were chords that any amateur garage rock band could easily master.

Inspired by Early Rock and Roll

Lou Reed was born Lewis Allan Reed on March 2, 1942, in Brooklyn, New York. His parents were Sidney Joseph Reed, an accountant, and Toby (Futterman) Reed. A member of a conservative Jewish family, Reed grew up in Long Island, New York. Perhaps to the dismay of his parents, in his early years, he became a fan of seminal rock and roll artists such as Dion DiMucci (born 1939), who recorded songs like "Runaround Sue" and "The Wanderers" with his group Dion and the Belmonts. Reed was never without a radio close by, especially when he was doing his school homework.

Reportedly, Reed's early life was somewhat conventional, as he grew up in the New York suburbs. But he was a boy who literally and figuratively liked to climb out of the bedroom window to chase after dreams and experience. The dichotomy of his suburban background and his urban-incited predispositions were perfectly summarized by the lyrics of "I'm Waiting for the Man," his song about a reckless suburbanite—already zombiefied by drugs—hanging out on an inner city street to purchase much-desired illicit substances, hoping and praying he had enough cash to make the deal.

These words rang with the truth of experience. It was a far cry from the romanticized street sale that Bob Dylan sang about in "Mr. Tambourine Man" (1965). Reed described the 1960s street basics of satisfying a pharmacologic obsession (i.e. addiction)—there was nothing romantic about it—and the rest of his lyrics in that particular song sink even deeper into such a dark sidewalk barter.

Reed really wanted to be a novelist, closer to the gritty William Burroughs than to the elegant F. Scott Fitzgerald. It was an elusive quest, but Reed finally found his voice through rock and roll. Driven by his interests in "doo wop" and rhythm and blues music, he learned to play the guitar. He joined several bands when he was in high school.

During this period, he was a horror to his parents. Reportedly, Reed underwent electroshock therapy to cure him of his bisexual urges. As his later life would prove, the strategy was by no means effective, and his subjection to such treatment embittered him.

Influenced by a Famous Poet

After graduating from high school, Reed attended Syracuse University, where he studied film and writing. One of his educators was famed poet Delmore Schwartz (1913–1966). Reed and Schwartz developed a student-mentor relationship, as well as a strong friendship. Schwartz's poetic works would greatly influence the thematic and stylistic direction of Reed's later song lyrics. A troubled, sexually ambivalent man felled early by alcohol addition, Schwartz used simple street language, and it revealed to Reed that a typically unheard voice could speak volumes about the human condition and everyday existence. Reed said that Schwartz inspired him to write and to express himself in hard language. As Jon Dolan wrote in *Rolling Stone*, "With the Velvet Underground in the late Sixties, Reed fused street-level urgency with elements of European avant-garde music, marrying beauty and noise, while bringing a whole new lyrical honesty to rock & roll poetry." But like his hero, Reed had a predilection for addictive substances.

When he graduated from Syracuse, Reed moved to New York City. He secured a job as a staff songwriter for Pickwick Records, a label that specialized in novelty songs. In 1964, Reed had a minor hit single with "The Ostrich," a dance-song parody. But the entire experience at the company dissatisfied him; he found that writing to-order song lyrics was too confining. He did not see himself as a Tin Pan Alley, Brill Building pop songwriting drudge. His aims were far more ambitious. He wanted to compose lyrics the same way that the greatest novelists composed sentences.

Founded the Velvet Underground

Still, at Pickwick, Reed found himself in a situation that would advance his career: At this time, the label hired John Cale, a Welsh musician who was a classically trained violist and pianist. Cale had performed with avant-garde composer La Monte Young (born 1935), who came to be recognized as the first-ever minimalist composer. Cale provided musical backing to Reed's vocals, and the two men became friends and roommates. They formed a band called the Primitives, later known as the Warlocks. With guitarist Sterling Morrison and drummer Maureen Tucker, they formed the Velvet Underground, which would eventually prove to be a very influential rock group.

The band had a very distinctive—even ominous—look. For one thing, at the time it was unusual that a rock group would have a female drummer. Also, the band members liked to dress in black and wear dark sunglasses. Their look, combined with Reed's stark lyrics, attracted the attention of Andy Warhol (1928–1987), the famous pop artist who embraced decadence. Warhol made the Velvet Underground part of his "Exploding Plastic Inevitable," a series of multi-media events that combined music with film. The group proved perfect for Warhol's artistic vision.

Wrote Dolan, "Reed's matter-of-fact descriptions of New York's bohemian demimonde, rife with allusions to drugs and S&M, pushed beyond even the Rolling Stones' darkest moments, while the heavy doses of distortion and noise for its own sake revolutionized rock guitar." In other words, Reed was writing about things that just were not spoken about in pop music, and he was accompanying these with the most appropriate musical score—discordant, dissonant, or even lushly harmonic (but, of course, in minimal fashion).

Found No Commercial Appeal

While Warhol introduced The Velvet Underground to the eccentric but well-moneyed element of New York City's vibrant art scene, the group's albums did not sell very well. Warhol produced the first Velvet Underground album and, as he felt he had ownership of the band, he insisted that the group be fronted by a very attractive European model and singer named Nico. The self-protective group initially balked at the demand, but Nico's inclusion led to a stunning debut album, *The Velvet Underground & Nico,* released in 1967. At the time, it was considered a commercial failure, but it is now regarded as one of the most important and influential albums in a period that saw the release of the Beatles' *Revolver* and *Sgt. Pepper's Lonely Hearts Club Band;* the Beach Boys' *Pet Sounds;* Bob Dylan's *Blonde on Blonde* and *John Wesley Harding;* the Rolling Stones' *Aftermath;* and the Byrds' *The Notorious Byrd Brothers*—all of which are albums regarded as hallmarks of rock music evolution. Later, rock critics would point out that the Velvet's output could hold its own with any of these more popular works. Musician and music producer Brian Eno underscored Reed's influence when he reflected on the mere 30,000 copies the first album sold: "I think everyone who bought one of those 30,000 copies started a band," he wryly noted (as reported in *Rolling Stone*).

Italie placed the group in historical context: "Indie rock essentially began in the 1960s with Reed and the Velvets. Likewise, punk, New Wave, and alternative rock movements of the 1970s, '80s and '90s were indebted to Reed." Like many musical groups in that period, the Velvet Underground had too much talent confined in the restrictive rock band format. Egos clashed and brought about the inevitable breakup. Within the Velvet Underground, peaceful coexistence proved impossible. With the band's next album *White Light/White Heat,* released in 1968, Nico was gone and Warhol had no interest in participating in the trouble-plagued group's career. Cale and Reed frequently argued. Cale either left or was thrown out of the band, depending on whose version is to be believed.

The Velvet Underground would release two more albums, *The Velvet Underground* (1969) and *Loaded* (1970). Again, these did not initially sell very well, but in time they would come to be recognized and purchased by post-1960s generations. Reed would describe *White Light/ White Heat,* as recorded in *Business Wire,* "the Statue of Liberty of Punk, with the light on top." He was disappointed by the album's initial lack of acceptance. But the distortortion and feedback techniques may have been just a few years ahead of late 1960 listeners' ability to grasp. The work never went above the number 199 position on the *Billboard Magazine* charts. But Reed proudly proclaimed in later years, "No one goes near it." Rock critics would agree.

Despite all of the ugly internal conflicts, later honors came: The Velvet Underground was inducted into the Rock and Roll Hall of Fame in 1996, and the *The Velvet Underground & Nico* album was included in the United States' Library of Congress registry in 2006, reported Italie.

Famous Velvet Underground songs include "Heroin," "Sweet Jane," "Rock & Roll," "All Tomorrow's Parties," "White Light/White Heat," "I'm Waiting for the Man," "Venus in Furs," and "The Black Angel's Death Song." These compositions offered a dark counterpoint to the *flower power* optimism of much of the late 1960s music scene. For instance, the song "Sister Ray," which appeared on the *White Light/White Heat* album, provided both a romantic and realistic depiction of the hard-scrabble life of a drag queen plying his/her street trade in New York City's Harlem area. Both Reed and Cale were inspired to compose this song based on the harsh lifestyle of someone they knew.

Left Velvet Underground

In 1970, the inevitable occurred: A frustrated Reed left the Velvets. Curiously enough, he would work for two years as a typist in his father's accountancy business. As David Fricke reports in the *Rolling Stone* magazine tribute to Reed, " Lou had a difficult adolescence. He was prone to mood swings and at war with his parents, who detected what they considered worrying signs of homosexuality in their teenage son." This led to two electroshock therapy treatments at the Creedmore State Psychiatric Hospital in Queens, New York. This, reported Fricke, was recalled with bitterness in the "Kill Your Sons" song that was included on Reed's 1974 *Sally Can't Dance* solo album.

A reported anecdote helps reveal the kind of emotional pain Reed experienced. In Fricke's *Rolling Stone* magazine article, a Reed friend (and a filmmaker) Julian Schnabel related a story Reed recalled from his childhood: "He was standing with his father. He put his hand near his father, and his father kind of smacked him. [Lou] never got over that. He felt the cruelty of that."

During the post-Velvet period, Reed found time to travel to Europe and record his first solo album, with musical backing from the rock band Yes. It was eventually released in 1972. This first solo album included re-structured and re-recorded versions of songs that the troubled Velvet Underground never had a chance to place on vinyl—and like the Velvet albums, it was not a commercial success.

Found Commercial Success

With his next solo album, *Transformer*—began in 1972 and released in America in December—Reed achieved his highest level of commercial and mainstream success. The song, "Walk on the Wild Side," released as a single, became a major radio hit in the late spring/early summer of 1973. It was an unlikely success, as it described the drag queens and drug addicts that populated the Warhol scene in the late 1960s. Radio, at the time, was still conservative when it came to lyric subject matter, and this one slipped through the cracks, mainly because it was so listenable, and Reed's monotone recitation was so charismatic. The album was produced by David Bowie, who was greatly influenced by Reed and scored a major artistic, critical, and commercial triumph with the 1972 release of his *Ziggy Stardust and the Spiders from Mars* album, which celebrated an androgyny that Reed advanced.

Throughout his solo career, the ever-prolific Reed would release more than 20 studio albums and numerous live albums. His major studio works included *Berlin* (1973), *Sally Can't Dance* (1974), *Coney Island Baby* (1975), *Rock and Roll Heart* (1976), and *Street Hassle* (1978). Appropriate to Reed's creative and musically adventurous nature, many of these albums were applauded by some critics and lambasted by others. For instance, when released in 1975, the experimental *Metal Music Machine* was considered a critical and commercial disaster. Reed felt this work was an exercise in artistic noise: there were no songs in the conventional sense—no recognizable structure, no melody, no rhythm, no words, no bridges between choruses. Essentially, it was a sonic catalogue of demonstrated guitar feedback effects. Reed did the production mixing, and he played with the speed of the noise, speeding it up or slowing it down. It was a so-called double-album, as this goes back to the days of vinyl recordings, and even Reed admitted to knowing no one who could listen to the entire work in one sitting.

If Reed seemed intent on career destruction with *Metal Music Machine*, he redeemed himself with a live album titled *Rock 'n' Roll Animal*. The cover art depicted him in what was considered a late 1970s fashion statement: tight black outfit, butch haircut, manacled wrists, and makeup that formed raccoon eyes, and heavily lacquered lips. But what was more important were the songs performed. These were Velvet Underground compositions, both updated and backdated, to form a set that rock and roll was supposed to be all about: ringing guitars playing a minimal number of chords but in the most attractive way.

Married Twice

During his life, Reed's relationships could be as unconventional as his music. In the 1970s, he reportedly had a live-in relationship with a drag queen, a period when he embraced an ambiguous sexuality and also indulged in drugs. However, in 1980, he married British designer Sylvia Morales, which provided an element of stability into this troubled man's life. He reflected on the happiness the relationship brought him in the 1982 album *The Blue Mask*. The couple divorced in the early 1990s.

During that decade, Reed met famed musician and performance artist Laurie Anderson and began a relationship, the couple becoming inseparable. For whatever reason, they waited until 2008 to marry. "For 21 years, we tangled our minds and hearts together," wrote Anderson for *Rolling Stone* magazine, after Reed's death.

Reed experienced failing health in these later years. As Anderson described for *Rolling Stone*: "Lou was sick for the last couple of years, first from treatments of interferon, a vile but sometimes effective series of injections that treats hepatitis C and comes with a lot of nasty side effects. Then he developed liver cancer, topped off with advancing diabetes."

His life, often marked by pain but happy at the end, ended on October 27, 2013, in Amagansett, New York, in a home he shared with his last and most loving, tolerant partner. Anderson continued: "[In April 2013], at the last minute, he received a liver transplant, which seemed to work perfectly, and he almost instantly regained his health and energy. Then that, too, began to fail, and there was no way out." Doctors told the couple that there were no more options.

Anderson described Reed's final moments. "I was holding in my arms the person I loved most in the world, and talking to him as he died," she wrote for *Rolling Stone*. "His heart stopped. He wasn't afraid." Lou Reed was 71 years old when he passed away.

Books

Stokes, Geoffrey; Tucker, Ken; Ward, Ed, *Rock of Ages: The Rolling Stone History of Rock & Roll,* Rolling Stone Press/ Summit Books, 1986.

Periodicals

Associated Press, October, 28 2013.

Business Wire, October, 2013.

Rolling Stone, October 27, 2013; November 21, 2013.

The Economist, October 27, 2013.

Online

"Lou Reed," *American Masters,* http://www.pbs.org/wnet/americanmasters/episodes/lou-reed/about-lou-reed/687/ (October 31, 2013)

"Lou Reed," *bio.True Story,* http://www.biography.com/people/lou-reed-9453959 (October 31, 2013.

"Lou Reed," *Rolling Stone.,* www.rollingstone.com/music/artists/lou-reed/biography (October 31, 2013). □

Grantland Rice

The American journalist Grantland Rice (1880–1954) was one of the most famous sportswriters in history. He did much to establish the cult of celebrity around professional athletes, and much of the literary vein of American sportswriting flowed originally from his pen.

Rice was an avid amateur writer of poetry, and poems might show up in his daily sports columns, describing the action on the field. One of his poems contained a line that became, in modified form, the maxim

Hulton Archive/Getty Images

"It's not whether you win or lose; it's how you play the game." Rice dubbed football halfback Red Grange "The Galloping Ghost." He mythologized athletes, and some of his writing seems overwrought by modern journalistic standards. But, as sportswriter Red Smith was quoted as saying by Mark Inabinett in *Grantland Rice and His Heroes,* "Make no mistake about Granny: he was a giant. Some of his stuff seems like immature gushing today, but he was exactly right for his time, and if he had lived in another time he would have been right for that one."

Farmed Acreage on Family Land

Henry Grantland Rice was born in Murfreesboro, Tennessee, on November 1, 1880, and grew up mostly in Nashville. His father was a Civil War veteran and prosperous farmer who dabbled in banking and was able to buy a house in the upper-middle-class suburb of Edgefield east of the city. The family soon moved even farther out, to a country home on Vaughan Pike, and Rice was told to farm several acres to teach him the value of hard work. He raised a variety of crops, plus, he later wrote (as quoted by William A. Harper in *How You Played the Game: The Life of Grantland Rice*), "practically everything else that grows including all the kissin' kin of the worm and grub family."

Sent to a pair of military schools, the Nashville Military Institute and the Tennessee Military Institute, Rice was exposed to organized sports for the first time. He moved on to a local prep school, Wallace University School, and he would later say that the school's headmaster, who insisted on the importance of the ancient Latin and Greek languages, was the figure who had influenced him most as a writer. Rice played several sports at Vanderbilt University, from which he graduated in 1901 as a classics major. Football left him with several broken bones, and he broke a toe after dropping a weight on it during the hammer throw in track, but he was captain of the basketball team and did well enough on the baseball diamond to attract pro scouts.

Rice's father, however, was not keen on the idea of a sports career, and a football shoulder injury still bothered him. So Rice turned to the second love of his college years: writing. Hired at the *Nashville Daily News* as sports editor for five dollars a week, he made an impression on his bosses by including poetry in his leads and stories. Rice moved briefly to a paper in Washington, D.C., and then to the *Atlanta Journal,* where he interviewed the rising baseball star Ty Cobb. He wrote for the *Cleveland News* for a year and a half and then returned to Nashville to take a position at the city's new paper, the *Tennessean.*

Coined Phrase That Became Proverb

Rice remained at the *Tennessean* for four years, and it was there, in 1908, that he wrote a poem for publication in the paper that included this stanza: "For when the One Great Scorer comes / To write against your name, / He marks not that you won or lost— / But how you played the game." In 1911, he moved to New York to take a job at the *Evening Mail* newspaper and then at the widely syndicated *New York Tribune* (later the *New York Herald Tribune*). He enlisted in the U.S. Army during World War I and was sent to France as an artilleryman, but he was then recruited for the staff of the military newspaper *The Stars and Stripes.*

After Rice returned home from the war, the peak period of his fame began. His daily sports column appeared in more than 100 newspapers with a circulation in the millions. In addition to that, Rice edited *American Golfer* magazine, wrote a column for the weekly magazine *Collier's,* and moved into new media as they appeared with a weekly program on NBC radio and a series of one-reel films dealing with sports that viewers themselves might participate in, such as tennis or fishing.

Among sportswriters active at the time, Rice came closest, in Harper's words, "to becoming a genuine public personality and a national celebrity ... hobnobbing with presidents, radio and movie stars, writers, and larger-than-life sports figures ... as famous and easy to recognize in person or in voice as those rarefied sports figures whose feats he preserved in words." Rice retained his Southern accent after moving north and had a kind of quiet charisma that endeared him to associates and radio listeners. One of his few rivals among sportswriters, the more acerbic and satirical Ring Lardner, was also his close friend.

Idealized Sports Heroes

In Rice's writing, sports figures were larger than life. That seems natural enough at a time when professional athletes are paid millions of dollars each year, but when Rice began his career baseball was something of a ragtag game, played by uneducated men who made very little money at it. Rice not only reported on the rise of sports as they became big-time entertainment; he contributed to that change himself. Rice, wrote Inabinett, "is celebrated as the pioneer and leading practitioner of a writing style employing hyperbole and lyricism to convey vivid images. Even his attitude seems to fit the mold of a legend maker, for he said, 'When a sportswriter stops making heroes out of athletes, it's time to get out of the business.'"

Rice had a knack for imagery that stuck in readers' minds; one of Rice's most famous pieces was written in 1924, when he described the backfield of the Notre Dame University football team as "The Four Horsemen" in a story for the *New York Herald Tribune.* The lead paragraphs of the story became a standard part of sports curricula in journalism schools. They read in full: "Outlined against a blue-gray October sky, the Four Horsemen rode again. In dramatic lore they are known as Famine, Pestilence, Destruction and Death. These are only aliases. Their real names are Stuhldreher, Miller, Crowley and Layden."

During World War II, Rice toured military training camps giving sports lectures. His prolific output slowed somewhat after the war, but he continued to write a daily syndicated column. Much of his energy was devoted to his autobiography, *The Tumult and the Shouting: My Life in Sports,* which appeared after his death. He also wrote six books of poetry and two on golf, which was his favorite game. In 1951, an anonymous donor put up $50,000 to create the Grantland Rice Fellowship in Journalism at Columbia University.

Rice married the former Katherine Hollis of Americus, Georgia, in 1906. The couple raised a daughter, Florence, who became a successful stage and film actress. He died in New York on July 13, 1954. His writing fell out of fashion after his death as a cleaner, more streamlined style came to the fore, but such sportswriters as Red Smith and Jim Murray cited him as an influence, and echoes of his writing may be heard in the entire tradition of literary sportswriting, from George Plimpton to the pages of *Sports Illustrated* in its classic years.

Books

Fountain, Charles, *Sportswriter: The Life and Times of Grantland Rice,* Oxford, 1993.

Harper, William A., *How You Played the Game: The Life of Grantland Rice,* University of Missouri, 1999.

Inabinett, Mark, *Grantland Rice and His Heroes: The Sportswriter as Mythmaker in the 1920s,* University of Tennessee, 1994.

Rice, Grantland, *The Tumult and the Shouting: My Life in Sports,* Barnes, 1954.

Periodicals

American Journalism Review, October-November 2004.

New York Times, July 14, 1954

Online

"Grantland Rice," *American Society for Baseball Research,* http://tennessee.sabr.org/Grantland%20Rice.htm (October 17, 2013).

"Grantland Rice," *Baseball Library,* http://www.baseballlibrary.com/ballplayers/player.php?name=Grantland_Rice (October 17, 2013).□

Bobby Riggs

The American tennis player Bobby Riggs (1918–1995) was one of the best in the game at the peak of his career, from about 1939 to 1948. He is most often remembered, however, for his part in the so-called Battle of the Sexes, a mixed-gender tennis match he played against Billie Jean King in 1973.

Robert Lorimore Riggs was born in Los Angeles on February 25, 1918. The son of a traveling evangelist preacher, he was the youngest of six children: five brothers and one sister. He had a strongly religious upbringing that included evening Bible readings. Growing up with five older brothers, Riggs developed strong competitive instincts. "Sometimes I think I was born in a contest," he was quoted as saying in the *Times* of London. "I grew up believing I was going to become a champion. At something, I didn't know what." A natural gambler, Riggs won a tennis racket from a friend in a marbles contest. He took up tennis because an older brother needed a practice partner, and he was entering tournaments in southern California's tough junior circuit within a month.

Trained by Female Coaches

At about five feet eight and 130 pounds, Riggs did not fit the usual image of a tennis player, and he had an awkward, toes-out stance. But he was both fast and canny, and he often surprised players with greater reach and natural facility. He was a master of such precise techniques as the drop shot and the lob. As a junior player, Riggs had two coaches, both female: university professor and top amateur player Esther Bartosh and Eleanor Tennant. Riggs would later play the role of a male chauvinist in order to hype interest his match against King, but family members reported that it was all an act, and that he regarded women as equals. Riggs won the United States national junior singles championship when he was 16.

In his late teens, against the advice of family and coaches, Riggs decided he was ready for the world of adult tennis. He acquired an old car and took off for the East Coast so that he could enter tournaments there. The trip was eventful—his clothes and wallet were stolen, forcing him to sell his spare tire and a second tennis racket to raise money. By the end of the trip, the car itself was gone. But Riggs's instincts were vindicated as he quickly rose through the national rankings of adult players. En route he won a national clay court championship in Chicago, but his debut at New York's prestigious Forest Hills was marred when he performed poorly after staying up for all of the previous night playing craps.

In 1938, Riggs played on the U.S. Davis Cup team, winning two matches and losing two en route to a 3–2 U.S. win over Australia. The international Davis Cup competition was one of the most prestigious events in tennis at that time, and it was an honor for such a young player to be named to the team. But during the tournament his tendency toward gambling, present since childhood, showed itself: just before a critical match in the finals, in which Riggs was scheduled to play Australia's Adrian Quist, he could not be located. Officials finally found him a basement room at the venue, shooting pool. Called to the court, Riggs went on to win his match.

The highlight of Riggs's amateur career was the Wimbledon tournament in London in 1939, where he won the singles, men's doubles, and mixed doubles competitions—a feat that remains unprecedented. Prior to the match, Riggs noticed that London bookies had listed the odds against his winning the singles tournament at 25-to-1. Confidently, he bet on himself to win not only the singles but the other two competitions as well. The resulting payoff of $108,000 was worth more than $1.7 million in 2013 dollars. "I blew it all back on gambling like any young kid will do," Riggs recalled in a *Tennis Week* interview quoted by Don Van Natta of ESPN. "I liked to go to the casinos and bet on the horse races and play gin. I got overmatched a few times."

Served in Navy

With the outbreak of World War II, Wimbledon was suspended, and Riggs never played in the tournament again. In 1939 and 1941, he won the U.S. singles championship at Forest Hills. Then he was drafted into the U.S. Navy and served, reluctantly, on ships in the Pacific. He played and bet on tennis whenever he could, and on one occasion in Hawaii he won a car, a house, and a large amount of money from a player in Hawaii who did not know who he was. Riggs returned the house and the car but kept $500 as a fee.

Discharged from the Navy in 1942, Riggs turned professional. At the time, major tennis tournaments such as Wimbledon were restricted to amateur players, and pros made money mostly through exhibition match tours. Riggs played well against such top pros as Don Budge, and he won the new U.S. national professional singles championship in 1946, 1947, and 1949. In exhibition matches beginning in late 1947 against a new young competitor, Jack Kramer, Riggs dominated the beginning of the series, winning the first match on December 27, 1947, comfortably despite snowfall; a crowd of 16,000 turned out to see the event. But Riggs then began to lose as the younger player evolved ways to deal with his on-court wiles, and Kramer dominated later matches on their tour.

Riggs issued an autobiography, *Tennis Is My Racket*, in 1950. He retired in 1951 and worked as a promoter of the careers of female players Gussie Moran and Pauline Betz for a time. Riggs was executive vice president with the American Photograph Corporation in New York from 1953 to 1971. He also took up golf and became skilled enough to apply his hustler ways, often devising unusual handicaps to draw wealthy players into matches against him; he used a rake, a hoe, and a baseball bat as clubs playing against singer Bing Crosby. "I love millionaires," he is reported to have said (according to the *Times* of London). "They're the salt of the earth. Wherever I go, they're lining up waiting for me."

Challenged Female Players

By 1973, Riggs's reputation was fading. So, with American society in the midst of a heated debate about women's roles, he decided to challenge leading women player to tennis matches, accompanying the challenges with a barrage of rhetoric stating that domestic roles were proper for women, and claiming that any good male club player would defeat the world's best women. The world's number-one female player, Australia's Margaret Court, accepted the challenge, and a match was set for Mother's Day of 1973 Riggs handed Court a bouquet of roses prior to the match. Although the six-foot, one-inch Court was several inches taller than Riggs, he dominated the match, winning 6-2, 6-1.

Public interest ran even higher when promoter Jerry Perenchio arranged a match between Riggs and the world's number-two player, the American Billie Jean King, and put up a $100,000 winner-take-all prize, billing the event as the Battle of the Sexes. King had been a vocal advocate for the rights of women tennis players, and Riggs applied a fresh layer of male-chauvinist goading, telling a New York news conference (as quoted by Van Natta), "Personally, I would wish that the women would stay in the home and do the kitchen work and take care of the baby and compete in areas where they can compete in because it's a big mistake for them to get mixed up in these mixed-sex matches." Although he had trained hard for the Court match, Riggs was heavily favored in advance of the King contest and did little training. At the Houston Astrodome, on September 20 1973, a crowd of more than 30,000 attended (still the largest crowd to attend a tennis match), and Riggs faced King on national prime-time television. King won the match in straight sets, 6-4, 6-4, 6-3, and Riggs, as quoted vy Van Natta said, "I know I said a lot of things she made me eat tonight. I guess I'm the biggest bum of all time now. But I have to take it."

Van Natta's ESPN article, published in 2013, suggested that Riggs had conspired with organized-crime figures to lose the match intentionally, reaping large profits for those who had bet on King given the strong odds against her. Van Natta relied partly on the recollections of a Florida golf professional, Hal Shaw, who said that he had heard a group of men planning a thrown match; Riggs's motivation was allegedly that he owed large gambling debts to organized criminal enterprises. Rumors about the match had swirled for years, with seasoned tennis observers pointing to aspects of Riggs's play that seemed uncharacteristically lackluster and poorly thought out. However, King herself did not believe that Riggs had intentionally lost the match, and Kramer, a neutral observer who in the past had been critical of Riggs's gambling, also discounted it, as did Riggs biographer Tom LeCompte.

Riggs was married and divorced twice, and had five children. Continuing to play in senior tennis tournaments and achieving top rankings, he was inducted into the International Tennis Hall of Fame in 1967. Diagnosed with prostate cancer in 1988, he formed the Bobby Riggs Tennis Museum Foundation, which also included a prostate cancer awareness component. He and Billie Jean King became close friends during his later years. Bobby Riggs died in Leucadia, California, on October 25, 1995.

Books

LeCompte, Tom, *The Last Sure Thing: The Life and Times of Bobby Riggs,* Black Squirrel, 2003.

Riggs, Bobby, with Robert Larrimore, *Tennis Is My Racket,* S. Paul, 1950.

Periodicals

American Heritage, August-September 2005.

Economist, November 4, 1995.

Globe & Mail (Toronto, Ontario, Canada), October 27, 1995.

New York Times, October 27, 1995.

Times (London, England), October 27, 1995.

Online

"'The Battle of the Sexes': It Isn't What You Think," *WBUR Radio,* http://cognoscenti.wbur.org/2013/09/03/bobby-riggs-billie-jean-king-tom-lecompte (October 18, 2013).

"Bobby Riggs," *International Tennis Hall of Fame,* http://www.tennisfame.com/hall-of-famers/bobby-riggs (October 18, 2013).

"Bobby Riggs, the Mafia and the Battle of the Sexes," *ESPN Outside the Lines,* http://espn.go.com/espn/feature/story/_/id/9589625/ (October 18, 2013).□

Bill Robinson

The African American dancer Bill "Bojangles" Robinson (1878–1949) was the best-known tap dancer of the 20th century, and a pioneer in the world of African American entertainment generally.

As a dancer, Robinson created an entirely new style. While the dances of the minstrel tradition from which he emerged featured shuffling dance steps demeaning to African Americans, Robinson was light on his feet, elegant and agile, rarely moving the top half of his body much but instead relying on the varied rhythms and textures his feet could produce. He often claimed that he could run faster backwards than most people could run forwards. As a choreographer of his own routines, Robinson was highly imaginative, and several sequences from the films and musicals later in his career, when it finally became possible for him to perform for white audiences, have remained classics of cinematic dance. Prior to that period, Robinson was in the forefront of the movement to expand opportunities for African American dancers in a largely segregated theatrical world. He has influenced dancers from Fred Astaire, who specifically acknowledged him as a model, to Gregory Hines in the present day.

Raised by Grandmother

Robinson was a native of Richmond, Virginia. Records of his early life are sparse, but he was probably born there as Luther Robinson on May 25, 1878. He adopted the name Bill as a youth because he disliked his given name. Many stories have been told about the origin of his nickname, Bojangles; a childhood friend of the dancer quoted by Robinson biographers Jim Haskins and N.R. Mitgang, stated that it originated from the mispronunciation by neighborhood children of Boujasson, the name of a local hatmaker the children knew. Robinson himself said that the name came from his early life in Richmond. Both of Robinson's parents died when he was young, and he was raised by a grandmother, Bedilia Robinson, who had grown up as a slave.

A natural performer, Robinson began dancing on the street corners where he shined shoes to earn a few coins. Performing opportunities in those days meant the minstrel shows, and Robinson managed to sign on with the troupe of white vaudevillian Mayme Remington, singing and dancing for several years in a revue called *The South*

Before the War. He made his way to Washington, D.C., probably by riding a freight train, and for a time got a job as a stable boy at a horse track. He continued to give impromptu performances whenever he could, sometimes working with white singers; one of those, according to Haskins and Mitgang, was a Jewish performer who had also run away from home with hopes of making it in show business, Al Jolson.

Robinson had a knack for publicity, and in 1900 he made a splash upon arriving in New York by challenging star tap dancer Harry Swinton to a dance contest, and winning. Early in his career he coined the term "copacetic" (spelled various ways, and meaning, roughly, "cool"), and the term has remained part of the English language. In the first years of the century in New York, African Americans were allowed on the vaudeville stage only in pairs, under what was known as the two-colored rule, and Robinson teamed with dancer George Cooper. They appeared on the Keith and Orpheum vaudeville circuits. At first they were often exploited financially, but after Robinson acquired a manager, Marty Forkins, in 1908, he prospered. The partnership with Cooper lasted until 1914, surviving Robinson's jailing and trial on an unjust armed robbery charge. Unlike other African American performers, they did not wear the blackface makeup of the minstrel show.

Developed Innovative Tap Style

During this first part of his career, Robinson developed his distinctive style as a tap dancer. Constance Vallis Hill, writing on the website of the Tap Dance Hall of Fame, has described his dancing as "delicate and clear." Robinson was the first to assemble tap dancing moves into larger routines. He could perform complex dance sequences, all while bantering with an audience if the situation called for it. Robinson, noted Hill, "danced in split clog shoes, ordinary shoes with a wooden half-sole and raised wooden heel. The wooden sole was attached from the toe to the ball of the foot and left loose, which allowed for greater flexibility and tonality." Filmed examples of Robinson's dancing come from movies he made toward the end of his career; his powers as a younger man must have been impressive indeed.

After splitting with Cooper, Robinson performed as a solo act. Often he was billed as the "Dark Cloud of Joy." Like singer and blackface comedian Bert Williams, Robinson began to appeal to white audiences. He headlined major theaters in New York, and seven different New York newspapers named him the greatest dancer alive. By the mid-1920s, Robinson was earning an estimated $3,500 a week. During World War I, Robinson performed for members of the United States military, and tours took him as far as London, England. His race still kept him from appearing on Broadway—the pinnacle of the American theatrical profession.

One of Robinson's most famous numbers was the Stair Dance, which he introduced in 1918 and refined over the years, fighting off a challenge from a rival troupe that claimed to have invented the idea. Robinson would dance up one side of a free-standing staircase and down the other side, producing a different tone and rhythm on each step as if the steps were keys on a piano. Gregory Hines, who replicated the Stair Dance for a 2001 cable television film about Robinson, found the dance particularly difficult. "It was really very complicated stuff," he told Jennifer Dunning of the *New York Times*. "And he was always dancing up on his toes, so he had this elevation that made him look almost like he was a puppet with somebody above just pulling him up the stairs. I'm telling you, I am only taking escalators from now on."

Appeared in Films

The Stair Dance was incorporated into the all-black revue *Blackbirds of 1928*, which was performed on Broadway and finally brought Robinson, at the age of 50, to a general audience. He appeared in several more stage shows, including *Brown Buddies* (1930) and *Blackbirds of 1933*. The advent of the sound film made it possible for Robinson to exploit that medium as well, and he made his film debut in *Dixiana* (1930) a Technicolor musical about a Southern circus with a mostly white cast. In 1933, he appeared in the all-black film revue *Harlem Is Heaven*.

Robinson had a successful film career in the late 1930s and early 1940s, appearing in such films as *In Old Kentucky* (1935), *One Mile from Heaven* (1937), *By an Old Southern River* (1941), and *Stormy Weather* (1943). The last-named of these also starred Lena Horne, Cab Calloway, and Katherine Dunham, and was one of the most ambitious of Hollywood's all-black film musicals. Robinson also appeared in a series of films with white child start Shirley Temple, including *The Little Colonel* and *The Littlest Rebel* (1935) and *Just Around the Corner* and *Rebecca of Sunnybrook Farm* (1938); in *Rebecca of Sunnybrook Farm* he was shown teaching Temple how to tap dance. On stage he appeared in *The Hot Mikado* (1939), a jazz version of the Gilbert & Sullivan operetta *The Mikado*, playing the Mikado himself.

At the height of his career, Robinson was extraordinarily popular among African Americans, and he became known as the unofficial "mayor" of Manhattan's Harlem neighborhood, where he liked to spend his spare time gambling and playing pool. Some of the younger figures in the Harlem Renaissance movement deplored Robinson's Hollywood film appearances, in which he often played subservient roles such as butlers. Robinson, however, remained active in support of the rights of black performers, co-founding and energetically raising funds for the new Negro Actors Guild of America in the late 1930s. On several occasions he stood up to racist treatment from white police officers.

Robinson married Fannie Clay in 1922. She became his business manager, but the marriage ended in divorce in 1943; Robinson married Elaine Plaines the following year. Robinson suffered financial setbacks in his final years but continued to perform. Suffering from a heart condition, he is said to have danced up the steps to New York's Columbia Presbyterian Medical Center because he found it easier than walking. He died there on November 15, 1949. The memory of Robinson's name was kept alive by the 1968 Jerry Jeff Walker composition "Mr. Bojangles," which ironically was written about a different dancer; Robinson rarely if ever used the Mr. Bojangles designation.

Books

Haskins, Jim, and N.R. Mitgang, *Mr. Bojangles: The Biography of Bill Robinson,* Morrow, 1988.

Stearns, Marshall and Jean Stearns, *Jazz Dance: The History of American Vernacular Dance,* Da Capo, 1994.

Periodicals

Investor's Business Daily, August 18, 2011.

New York Times, February 4, 2001.

Online

"Bill 'Bojangles' Robinson," *Tap Dance Hall of Fame,* http://atdf.org/awards/bojangles.html (January 2, 2014).

"Robinson, Bill 'Bojangles,'" *The Black Past,* http://www.blackpast.org/aah/robinson-bill-bojangles-1878-1949 (January 2, 2014).□

Gene Roddenberry

The American television producer, film producer, and screenwriter Gene Roddenberry (1921–1991) was the creator of the *Star Trek* science fiction television series, which went on the air in 1966.

Ron Sachs/Consolidated News Pictures/Getty Images

Roddenberry made other creative contributions in television and film, several of them highly regarded. But his greatest legacy undoubtedly lies in the three seasons of *Star Trek,* for which he served as executive producer. The future technological world Roddenberry imagined in *Star Trek* was startlingly prescient in many respects, and the show's vision of an essentially peaceful, multicultural future was novel and pioneering. A commercial failure in its original run, *Star Trek* spawned a series of television shows and immensely successful feature films that have continued to the present day.

Joined Civilian Pilot Program

Eugene Wesley Roddenberry was born in El Paso, Texas, on August 19, 1921. While he was a baby, the family was awakened during a house fire by a milkman who probably saved their lives. Roddenberry's father, Eugene Edward Roddenberry, moved the family to Los Angeles when Roddenberry was three, and Roddenberry attended Franklin High School there. He went on for an associate's degree at Los Angeles Community College, studying law enforcement and aeronautical engineering, and graduating in 1941. During his studies there he joined the United States Army Civilian Pilot Program, and in the fall of 1941, he volunteered for the Army Air Corps.

With the entry of the U.S. into World War II, Roddenberry was sent to Kelly Field, Texas, to begin flying cadet training, and after his marriage to Eileen Rexroat in 1942 he was sent to the Pacific theater. He flew about 90 bombing missions, many of them from the Henderson Field airstrip on the island of Guadalcanal. Roddenberry was awarded the Distinguished Flying Cross and the Air Medal. He also began writing during the war, selling stories to flying magazines and also getting a poem published in *The New York Times.* Later in the war he worked as an Air Force crash investigator.

With a growing family (he and Rexroat had two daughters), Roddenberry took a job as a pilot with Pan American Airways. Still interested in writing, he took literature courses at Columbia University in New York. After he had taken off from Calcutta, India, Roddenberry's plane developed engine trouble and crashed in the desert in Syria, but Roddenberry and his crew survived. Later, upon seeing a television for the first time in 1948, Roddenberry immediately decided on a change of career and moved to California with his family, intending to work as a television writer.

Worked as Police Officer

At first, with the dramatic aspect of the new medium slow to develop, Roddenberry had trouble finding work. He decided to follow his father and brother into the Los Angeles Police Department, which turned out to provide some screenwriting experience: the television series *Dragnet* solicited technical advice from Los Angeles police officers and paid them for story ideas. Roddenberry himself submitted several sketches for *Dragnet* episodes. Slowly Roddenberry began to succeed in selling television scripts, first to the series *Mr. District Attorney* (1954). In 1956, he resigned from the police department to work full-time in television, and soon after that he became the head writer on the series *The West Point Story*.

In the late 1950s and early 1960s, Roddenberry was busy as a writer for various series, including *Have Gun, Will Travel, The Jane Wyman Theater, Highway Patrol, Naked City, The Detectives, Bat Masterson, The Kaiser Aluminum Hour,* and *Dr. Kildare*. In 1963, he created a series of his own, *The Lieutenant*. The series ran for only a single season; like *Star Trek* it used a military setting (the Camp Pendleton Marine Corps base in California) to examine sociological issues. The actors Leonard Nimoy, Majel Barrett, and Nichelle Nichols appeared on the show and followed Roddenberry to *Star Trek;* Nichols performed in an unaired episode that dealt with racial prejudice. An episode of *Have Gun, Will Travel* earned Roddenberry an Emmy award in 1957.

For many years before that, Roddenberry had nursed the idea of a series resembling the *Wagon Train* western series, but transferred to a science fiction setting that would allow him to explore social issues. Some of Roddenberry's progressive ideas were motivated by his humanist outlook; although raised in a religious family, he had become an agnostic. In 1964, he developed the idea for *Star Trek* and began to pitch it to television executives. The opening line of each episode, "Space: the final frontier," echoed the language of western films and television shows, and the configuration of a strong leader accompanied by character actors of various kinds resembled the *Wagon Train* cast.

First Roddenberry presented the show to executives from the CBS network, but they declined because they had their own science fiction series, *Lost in Space,* under development. Roddenberry had more luck at NBC, where he received funding for a pilot, "The Cage," that differed substantially from the series as it was eventually aired. That pilot was rejected as too complex, but Roddenberry gained strong support from Desilu Productions, the production company with which he had partnered, and NBC agreed to consider a second pilot, "Where No Man Has Gone Before." According to some reports, comedienne and Desilu principal Lucille Ball championed the show and prevented its demise.

Fought to Retain Spock as Character

NBC accepted the second pilot, which starred William Shatner as Captain James T. Kirk and Leonard Nimoy as his pointy-eared Vulcan first officer on the *U.S.S. Enterprise* spaceship. Mr. Spock, and *Star Trek* went on the air in September of 1966. In one of a series of disagreements with NBC executives, Roddenberry refused to deemphasize the character of Spock, whom the executives feared would be considered satanic. With Roddenberry as executive producer and his cohort on *The Lieutenant* Gene L. Coon often serving as writer, *Star Trek* was unlike any other show on television with its multicultural and multiracial cast. African American actress Nichols, who hoped for a stage career, was persuaded by the Rev. Martin Luther King Jr., to remain with the show.

The technological universe imagined by Roddenberry and his creative team was likewise remarkable. "We had to explain computers," Roddenberry pointed out (according to Robert L. Mcfadden of *The New York Times*), and the computer envisioned on the show, with its individual terminals accessible for crew-member searches, little resembled the mainframe computers of the day but proved strikingly anticipatory of the era of search engines. The crew's communication devices prefigured the appearance of flip-style cellular phones. Despite the show's high-tech sheen, *Star Trek* was a low-budget production; each episode cost just $186,000, and the celestial scenes viewed by the crew through the set's screen consisted of a black cloth with holes and a light to the rear.

Star Trek never performed well in the ratings, but it was twice saved from cancellations by vigorous letter-writing campaigns on the part of its fans. Roddenberry bitterly protested NBC's decision to move the show to an undesirable 10 p.m. time slot in its third season; unsuccessful, he removed himself from the show's day-to-day activities, although he continued to serve as executive producer. Another cast member of *Star Trek* was Barrett, whom Roddenberry married after his divorce from Rexroat. They had one son, Rod Roddenberry, who later made a documentary film, *Trek Nation. Star Trek* finally went off the air in 1969. Its rise to perennial cult-favorite status began almost immediately as television stations began to air it in syndication, gaining young fans known as Trekkies who provided the nucleus of the *Star Trek* franchise's success for decades to come.

Roddenberry remained active in connection with *Star Trek*–related materials. He wrote and produced the first in a series of *Star Trek* films, *Star Trek: The Motion Picture,* in 1979, and he had a consulting role on later films in the series. He was executive producer of the *Star Trek: The Next Generation* television series that premiered in 1987, and spawned its own series of films. In his later years, Roddenberry was associated with several projects unrelated to *Star Trek,* including the film *Pretty Maids All in a Row* (1971). In 1981, the first space shuttle was given the name *Enterprise.* Roddenberry died in Los Angeles on October 24, 1991. In 2014 his ashes, along with Majel's remains and those of *Star Trek* actor James Doohan, were scheduled to be sent into orbit around the sun by a private company, Celestis; Roddenberry had requested at his death that his remains be sent into space when possible.

Books

Alexander, Davis, *Star Trek Creator: The Authorized Biography of Gene Roddenberry,* ROC, 1994.

Engel, Joel, *Gene Roddenberry: The Myth and the Man Behind Star Trek,* Hyperion, 1994.

Periodicals

Guardian (London, England), October 28, 1991.

Humanist, July-August 1995.

New York Times, October 26, 1991; December 20, 2008.

Times (London, England), October 26, 1991.

USA Today, November 29, 2011.

World Entertainment News Network, June 21, 2013.

Online

"Gene Roddenberry," *AllMovie,* http://www.allmovie.com/artist/gene-roddenberry-p108615 (December 3, 2013).

"Gene Roddenberry," Roddenberry Family Official Website, http://www.roddenberry.com/corporate-gene-biography (December 3, 2013).

"Roddenberry, Gene," *Museum of Broadcast Communication,* http://www.museum.tv/eotv/roddenberry.htm (December 3, 2013).

"Roddenberry, Gene," *Star Trek,* http://www.startrek.com/database_article/roddenberry (December 3, 2013).□

Félicien Rops

The Belgian artist Félicien Rops was a popular and often outrageous figure in Paris in the last third of the 19th century.

© INTERFOTO/Alamy

Active as a printmaker as well as a painter, Rops was well-acquainted with many of the leading French writers of the day, and he cultivated a special friendship with the similarly boundary-pushing poet Charles Baudelaire. Rops's art was difficult to categorize. He often depicted female nudes, and some of his work verged on the pornographic. Yet he thought of himself as a serious artist, and he issued many realistic works showing the horrors of war and the depredations of poverty. Perhaps Rops's most characteristic works were those in which he displayed a satirical edge; like another of his friends, writer Guy de Maupassant, he turned an unforgiving lens on the lives of the Parisian well-off. Largely forgotten after his death, Rops's works have been revived by collectors and museums in his native Belgium and elsewhere.

Thrown Out of Catholic School

Félicien Rops (pronounced, roughly, Rawps) was born in Namur, in the French-speaking Belgian region of Wallonia, on July 7, 1833. His father, Nicolas Rops, was an industrialist. An only child, Rops was a promising student and was enrolled in a high-quality Catholic high school, the Collège Notre-Dame de la Paix in Namur. Rops mastered the Latin language and got good grades. However, his rebellious streak also began to show itself, and he was apparently expelled from the school for expressing criticism of the priesthood. Rops finished his high school education at a public school, the Athenée in Namur.

Deciding to become an artist, Rops registered at Namur's Academy of Art but decided to enroll at the University of Brussels. The school proved stimulating for the young artist as he fell in with a group of intellectual students who were satirically minded and critical of the institutions of the time. Rops developed skills as a caricaturist and published two of his drawings each week in a magazine called *Uylenspiegel,* which he founded with the Belgian novelist Charles de Coster. By the late 1850s, Rops was creating major works of his own, mostly lithographs and drawings. His first major work was the almost surreal print *Médeaille de Waterloo* (Waterloo Medal, 1858).

Rops married Charlotte Polet de Faveaux, the daughter of a local lawyer, in 1857. The couple had two children; only a son, Paul, survived. By the early 1860s, Rops had gained attention for such distinctive works as *L'ordre régne Varsovie* (Order Reigns in Warsaw), an allegorical painting showing a fearsome two-headed bird of prey swooping over a landscape showing the word "Liberté" (Freedom). In 1864 he created one of his best-known works, the drawing *L'enterremen en pays Wallon* (Funeral in Walloni). In the words of Roderick Conway Morris of the *International Herald Tribune,* the work "teeters on caricature, but its acute and unforgiving observation rescues this pathetic scene, in which a tiny, motionless orphan gazes down into the grave, from facile sentimentality."

Befriended by Baudelaire

Such unorthodox works drew the attention of, among others, Baudelaire, who said that Rops was the only true artist he had been able to find in Belgium. Finding that they were both fascinated by skeletons, the two men became friends, and Baudelaire urged Rops to begin spending more time in the artistic capital of Paris. Rops took art lessons in Paris, focusing on graphic arts, and soon he was a master of major print techniques such as etching, aquatint, and drypoint. Baudelaire asked Rops to draw a frontispiece (an illustration printed opposite a book's title page) for his book *Epaves* (Scraps), which included several of the poems from his pioneering collection *Les Fleurs du Mal* (The Flowers of Evil) that had been suppressed by censors due to subject matter that included lesbianism.

For several years Rops divided his time between Brussels and Paris. In Brussels he founded an International Society of Engravers and co-founded the Free Society of Fine Arts, serving as its vice-president. For recreation he was also involved with the formation of the Royal Nautical Club of the Sambre and Meuse [rivers]. Meanwhile, Rops's reputation in Paris was beginning to spread, aided partly by a story he devised about a fictional Hungarian ancestor who had gone AWOL from the army of the Habsburg empire. As Rops moved in with a pair of fashion-designer sisters, Leontine and Aurélie Duluc, and fathered a daughter with Lélontine, he began to reap still more publicity. He carried on numerous other short-term relationships on the side. The Italian writer Gabriele D'Annunzio, associated with a growing trend called the Decadent movement, praised Rops as an artist who could capture (as quoted by Morris) "the flowers of evil, flowers that flourish fertilized by the putridness of contemporary life."

In 1874, Rops moved to Paris for good. His works were popular among the city's artistic community, and he was soon in demand for frontispieces and illustrations for books by writers and poets such as Maupassant and the poets Théophile Gautier, Stéphane Mallarmé, and Paul Verlaine. Soon he was the city's highest-paid illustrator. He founded a sort of intellectual dining club that attracted the young pioneers of the Impressionist movement, Claude Monet and Pierre Renoir.

Rops tried to broaden his experiences and to address serious themes in some of his works. He and a friend were on the scene of the disastrous Battle of Sedan in 1870, where French troops under emperor Napoleon III were routed by German forces, and he turned what he saw into a new series of antiwar graphics. Rops traveled extensively. He went to Hungary in 1879, where he claimed to be uniquely inspired by the landscape and by the lifestyle of the region's Gypsy minority, producing a series of drawings he called Hungarian Rhapsodies after the famous compositions of Hungarian composer Franz Liszt.

Depicted Semi-Nude Figures

The primary subject matter of Rops's work, however, was sexuality, and some of his works verged on pornography. He often drew entiredly nude women, showing one kissing her reflection in a mirror under the title "In Love with Herself," but more characteristic were his explorations of the *demi nu* or half-nude, a woman clothed only in what Morris called "fetishistic accessories." One of Rops's most notorious works was *Pornokrates* (1878), showing a woman naked except for shoes, stockings, garters, a belt, silk gloves, earrings, a blindfold, and a hat, with a pig on a leash. Rops was a habitual visitor to Paris bars and cabarets, and his *The Absinthe Drinker* showed a young woman in liquor's deadly grip.

Rops continued to develop innovations in the graphic arts; together with his fellow Belgian artist Armand Rassenfosse he devised a new type of print varnish they dubbed Ropsenfosse. He developed vision problems in his later years but was able to retire comfortably to his estate, the Demi-Lune, in the Paris suburb of Essonnes. He was an enthusiastic gardener in his last years and created several new varieties of roses. He died on August 23, 1898, in Essonnes, attended by the Duluc sisters and his daughter, Léontine.

Although he was a celebrated figure in his own time, Rops was mostly forgotten after his death. Reasons for this neglect include the fact that prints carried less prestige than one-of-a-kind works (Rops did create a number of oil paintings) and the risque subject matter of much of his art. A museum in his hometown of Namun, the Musée Provincial Félicien Rops, has spearheaded a revival of his works, collecting many of them and loaning them out to other museums and galleries. An exhibition of Rops's works at the Palazzo Venezia in Venice, Italy, increased familiarity with his works. Even prints by Rops may now command prices of several thousand dollars or more.

Periodicals

International Herald Tribune, August 3, 1996.

Online

"Biography," *Campbell Fine Art,* http://www.campbell-fine-art.com/artists.php?id=94 (October 15, 2013).

"Biography," *Musée Provincial Félicien Rops,* http://www.museerops.be/biography/bio01.html (October 15, 2013).

"Félicien Rops (Namur, 1833–Essonnes, 1898," *University of Liège,* http://www.wittert.ulg.ac.be/fr/flori/opera/rops/rops_notice.htm (October 15, 2013).

"Félicien Rops, Hungarian Wannabe," *Budapest Times,* http://www.budapesttimes.hu/2010/11/30/felicien-rops-hungarian-wannabe/ (October 15, 2013).

"Rops, Félicien (1833–1898), 'La Dame au Cochon ou Pornokrates,', Etching," *Gerrish Fine Art,* http://www.gerrishfineart.com/(October 15, 2013).□

Arnold Rothstein

The American racketeer Arnold Rothstein (1882–1928) was a central figure in the development of organized crime in the United States.

Rothstein, an elegant man in his personal habits, was not a street thug like many of his associates and predecessors. Instead, wrote his biographer Leo Katcher, he was "'The Brain,' 'The Bankroll,' 'The Man Uptown.' His connections came from the top and went to the top, with Rothstein a central switchboard and one-man nerve center." Rothstein loved to gamble, and in his planning of crime operations, as well as at the horse track or card table, he was willing to risk millions of dollars, usually winning much more than he lost. His genius lay in planning: underworld figure Meyer Lansky, as quoted in the *Jewish Virtual Library,* said that "Rothstein had the most

FPG/Getty Images

remarkable brain. He understood business instinctively and I'm sure that if he had been a legitimate financier he would have been just as rich as he became with his gambling and the other rackets he ran.'' Rothstein profited handsomely during the era of Prohibition, when the manufacture, sale, and transportation of liquor were forbidden in the U.S. He did the same with drugs, largely laying the foundations of the modern narcotics trade, and his tentacles extended into real estate, labor, and sports: he is widely thought to have colluded in the fixing of the 1919 baseball World Series.

Gambled from Early Age

According to family recollections (no birth certificate exists), Arnold Rothstein was born in New York on January 17, 1882. His father, Abraham Rothstein, was a businessman and observant Jew who had a reputation for unusual honesty. Few records exist pertaining to Rothstein's childhood, but he apparently had an ability to carry out complex mathematical calculations in his head and was a consistent winner at dice and card games even in his teens. At 16 he dropped out of Boys High School and took a job as a traveling salesman of caps and hats, but by 1904, he moved back home and was working as a clothing stocker. He frequented gaming places and learned to dress well, although for several years he seemed to have no regular job.

In 1909, Rothstein married Jewish-Catholic showgirl Carolyn Green in the racetrack town of Saratoga Springs, New York. On their wedding night Rothstein (according to Nick Tosches, writing in *Vanity Fair*) told Green, ''Sweet, I had a bad day today, and I'll need your jewelry for a few days.'' The union lasted until 1927 despite Rothstein's several affairs on the side. Later in 1909, Rothstein borrowed $2,000 from his father-in-law to open a gambling parlor on West 46th Street in Manhattan. The operation prospered as it began to attract high rollers, one of whom lost $40,000 in a single session.

In 1910, Rothstein was able to buy out his partner, a local political ward boss named Willie Shea. For the rest of his life, Rothstein would remain close to figures in New York City politics and to the police officers they controlled. These connections helped him avoid being directly connected legally to his growing criminal enterprises and their front companies, whose legal documentation often did not list his name. Rothstein prospered further as one of his main bookmaking rivals, Herman ''Beansy'' Rosenthal, was killed under murky circumstances, and several men, including a police officer, were convicted of his murder and executed.

Alleged to Have Fixed Baseball Series

Part of Rothstein's genius was that he never depended on a single source of income but continually diversified his enterprises. Over the course of the 1910s, he started insurance and real estate operations. One of his favorite ploys was to extend large loans to individuals whose favors he might need to call in later; one of those was Saratoga Springs gambling house operator Harry Tobin. One of Rothstein's most ambitious operations was his alleged fixing of the 1919 World Series. In what became known as the Black Sox scandal, eight Chicago White Sox players were accused of arranging intentional losses to the Cincinnati Reds in return for cash payments from Rothstein and his associates; they in turn profited from bets on the Reds. In another trademark maneuver, Rothstein had apparently arranged payments through associates and could never be tied directly to the events of the series.

By 1914, Rothstein was worth $300,000 (about $7,000,000 in 2014 dollars). By 1921, he might bet that much in a single day or even on a single horserace. On July 4 of that year he won $850,000 betting on Sidereal, a longshot horse he owned, at Queens, New York's Aqueduct Racetrack, and six weeks later he won $500,000 at the Travers Stakes in Saratoga Springs. On the other side of the balance sheet was a $270,000 loss at Aqueduct in the fall. In 1921, Rothstein paid $35.25 in taxes on a declared gross income of $31,544.48 and net income of $7,257.29

The beginning of Prohibition in 1920 proved a bonanza for Rothstein, who was not content to distribute bootleg liquor but instead imported it, making the apparatus of illicit liquor dependent on his activities. Together with underworld figure Dapper Dan Collins he started an operation that brought rum from the Bahamas, and he purchased his own freighter from Norway that could bring as many as 20,000 cases of scotch whiskey to the U.S. at a time. On the rare occasions when ''blind pig'' nightclubs or liquor trucks were raided by police, the chain of distribution was already far from Rothstein's influence.

Rothstein did not smoke or drink; gambling was his only vice, and he was a canny gambler who won more often than not. Betting on boxer Gene Tunney over the celebrated Jack Dempsey in 1926, he took home $500,000. Many aspects of his life were necessarily kept under wraps, but his wagers were famous; for a time in the 1920s, he was known as America's greatest gambler. He once said that he would gamble on anything except the weather, which could not be predicted. Although he speculated that he might have gambled initially as a rebellion against his religious father, the two remained in contact, and in 1926, Rothstein may have helped his father settle a garment workers' strike.

Inspired Fictional Characters

Unlike the street criminals who enforced his orders at times, Rothstein was a man of impeccable personal style. Younger gangsters who entered his organization remembered that he taught them how to dress well, how to hold doors for women. Novelist F. Scott Fitzgerald, who met Rothstein, later based the character of Meyer Wolfsheim in his book *The Great Gatsby* on Rothstein, and the character of Nathan Detroit in the Damon Runyon short stories that became the musical *Guys and Dolls* was modeled on Rothstein as well.

Correctly foreseeing the end of Prohibition, Rothstein looked for new illicit substances to exploit. He quickly realized that he could duplicate his liquor operations with drugs, since the Harrison Narcotics Act of 1914 had ended the legal sale and distribution of heroin, morphine, and cocaine in the U.S. Rothstein arranged for large purchases of drugs in European countries where they were still legal, and in one case he had 225 pounds of heroin imported in boxes marked "bowling balls and pins." The traffickers in that case were arrested and bailed out by Rothstein for $25,000 each. That raised the suspicions of federal investigators, who were preparing indictments connected to Rothstein's narcotics activities when he was killed. The networks Rothstein established, increasingly populated by Italians instead of Jews, remained in place for decades, until the advent of South American cocaine trafficking in the 1970s.

On November 4, 1928, two days before Election Day, Rothstein was confidently awaiting a $500,000 payoff on his bet that Herbert Hoover would win the U.S. presidency over Al Smith. Invited to a card game at the Park Central Hotel by his friend George "Hump" McManus, he sent his driver to bring some cash and went to room 349. At ten minutes before 11:00, a hotel detective spotted Rothstein staggering down a staircase, saying that he had been shot. Rushed to Polyclinic Hospital, he lingered for two days after a .38 slug was removed from his body but, true to the gangster code of silence, refused to say who had shot him, at one point asserting that his mother had done it. Rothstein died on the morning of November 6, 1928. McManus, gangster Dutch Schultz, and others have been proposed as possible killers, but the murder remains unsolved. Rothstein's father outlived him and arranged for an Orthodox Jewish funeral.

Books

Katcher, Leo, *The Big Bankroll: The Life and Times of Arnold Rothstein,* Da Capo, 1994.

McManus, James, *Cowboys Full: the Story of Poker,* Farrar, Straus & Giroux, 2009.

Outlaws, Mobsters & Crooks, Gale, 1998.

Pietrusza, David, *The Life, Times and Murder of the Criminal Genius Who Fixed the 1919 World Series,* Carroll & Graf, 2003.

Tosches, Nick, *King of the Jews,* Ecco, 2005.

Periodicals

American Heritage, February-March 1993.

Vanity Fair, May 2005.

Online

"An Arnold Rothstein Chronology," http://www.davidpietrusza.com/Rothstein-Chronology.html (January 18, 2014).

"Arnold Rothstein," *Jewish Virtual Library,* http://www.jewishvirtuallibrary.org/jsource/biography/Rothstein.html (January 18, 2014).□

Anton Rubinstein

The Russian pianist and composer Anton Rubinstein (1829-1894) was one of the most famous piano virtuosos of the 19th century. He was also a composer who produced a few evergreen works and a large number of other works that were well known in his own time and have been rediscovered after decades in which they were largely forgotten.

Rubinstein's influence as an educator was also immense: he laid the foundation for the splendid conservatory system that still exists and produces classical music stars in Russia today. As a composer he largely rejected Russian musical nationalism and urged his compatriots to open their ears to German music. His compositions influenced a host of younger Russian composers, most notably Tchaikovsky. But it was as a pianist that Rubinstein became a true celebrity, almost his era's equivalent of a rock star. Ticket buyers sometimes formed such long lines that police had to be called. Rubinstein's international tours included a nine-month tour of the United States, during which he often performed two or three concerts in a single day. The tour made him rich, for his reputation had preceded him, and promoters were willing to pay him handsomely.

Toured at a Young Age

Anton Grigor'yevich Rubinstein was born in Vikhvatintsï, Russia, on November 20, 1829. His brother, Nikolay Rubinstein, also became a noted composer. At the age of seven, Anton started piano lessons, and soon it was clear that he had talents far removed from the norm. European

Picture History/Newscom

promoters were keen to discover the next child prodigy, and Rubinstein seemed to fill the bill. His teacher, Alexander Villoing, brought him to Paris, France, in 1839, and for the next four years the youngster toured the capitals of Europe giving concerts. He met Fryderyk Chopin, the Polish composer who had become the taste of France, and he had an audience with Queen Victoria of England. The celebrity who made the greatest impression on him, however, was the foremost piano-composer virtuoso of the day, Franz Liszt, whose works included thunderous cascades of sound new to the world of piano music. Rubinstein emulated Liszt, and by the time he was 13 he was often breaking the strings of his piano during a concert by sheer force.

The teenage Rubinstein decided to further his musical education in Vienna, taking composition lessons from Siegfried Dehn and barely making a living by offering piano lessons. Things quickly improved, however: as a traveling prodigy he had once played for the Russian czar's family, and when he returned to Russia he made contact with the Grand Duchess Yelena Pavlovna, sister-in-law of Czar Nicholas I, who took a liking to the young pianist and installed him in an apartment in her palace, asking him only to play at her evening parties. This gave Rubinstein all the space he needed to develop his skills to the highest level, and in 1853, he launched his formal adult career with a European tour.

For some years, Rubinstein divided his time between concerts and educational activities. Russian musical education lagged far behind that in Western countries, and even in the late 19th century several major composers were essentially brilliant self-taught amateurs. Meeting Yelena Pavlovna in Nice, France, in the winter of 1856–1857, Rubinstein, with the support of his highly placed patron, planned to establish a system of music conservatories and concert series along Western lines. With himself as conductor, Rubinstein opened the Russian Musical Society in 1859, and in 1861 Rubinstein wrote a controversial article in which he lambasted what he considered the amateurish state of Russian music-making. That earned him the enmity of Russian composers and musicians of a more nationalistic vein. The St. Petersburg Conservatory, still one of the most prestigious music schools in the world, opened under Rubinstein's direction in 1862, and by his death his dream of a national system of fine music schools had been fulfilled. The conservatory system he established survived even a century of war, revolution, and Communist bureaucratic control.

Rubinstein stayed on as director in St. Petersburg until 1867, but then he resigned in order to return to his own career. He made another major European tour in the late 1860s, and by that time he was famous well beyond Russia, and for his composing and conducting as well as his mastery of the piano. In 1871 and 1872 he was engaged as the conductor of the Philharmonic Concerts in Vienna, the ancestor of today's Vienna Philharmonic Orchestra and then as now one of the top positions in the world of classical music.

Suffered from Stage Fright

But it was as a pianist that Rubinstein was best known. A Rubinstein concert was a major event, with crowds stretching for blocks along city streets to purchase tickets. In addition to sheer physical virtuosity, he possessed great personal magnetism that seemed to be borne of an overwhelming desire to communicate. He was famous for extreme nervousness before performing, but when he took the stage he would explode in a performance with a compelling mixture of power and spontaneity. A Rubinstein performance often contained missed notes, but no one cared. The Viennese critic Eduard Hanslick, as quoted by Harold C. Schonberg in *The Great Pianists,* wrote, "Yes, he plays like a god, and we do not take it amiss if, from time to time, he changes, like Jupiter, into a bull."

One of Rubinstein's most impressive feats was his tour of the United States between September 10, 1872, and May 24, 1873. In that time, before air travel, he played 215 concerts, sometimes performing two or three times in a single day. He composed a set of variations on "Yankee Doodle," and the tour was popular enough to be mentioned in comic newspaper columns. Rubinstein, as quoted by Schonberg, noted that the tour "laid the foundation of my prosperity," and that "[o]n my return I hastened to invest in real estate," but that "[u]nder these conditions there is no chance for art—one simply grows into an automaton, performing mechanical work; no dignity remains to the artist; he is lost."

Much Russian music of the second half of the 19th century exploited Russian national music materials, but Rubinstein's orientation was toward the West—especially toward Germany and Austria, which were considered the centers of transcendent musical art. His own outlook was cosmopolitan and international, and he realized that that endeared him to few in an ethnically factionalized society. Of Jewish background, Rubinstein had been born to a Russian father and a Jewish mother. Both converted to Christianity. "To the Christians I am a Jew, to the Jews I am a Christian, to the Russians I am a German, to the Germans I am a Russian," he lamented (as quoted by pianist Marius van Paassen on his website).

Composed Popular Opera

During his own day, Rubinstein was a well-known composer who strongly influenced Tchaikovsky (who attended classes organized by the Russian Musical Society) and other younger composers. His opera *The Demon* (1871) was performed at least 100 times between its premiere in 1875 and 1900. He composed not only piano music but operas, choral music, six symphonies, concertos for violin and orchestra and cello and orchestra, songs, and a variety of other works. Among his piano pieces, a small work called the Melody in F has remained a standard of the piano repertory.

Although several other works, most notably the Piano Concerto No. 4 in D minor (1864), have received frequent performances, Rubinstein's compositions fell out of fashion over the years. He wrote a great deal of music, and even during his own lifetime it was criticized as uneven in quality. His rival, the Polish pianist Ignacy Paderewski, said (according to *The New Grove Dictionary of Music and Musicians*) that he "had not the necessary concentration of patience for a composer." Yet there have been signs of a revival in the reputation of Rubinstein's compositions. The British pianist Leslie Howard has championed his works, telling the *Times* of London that Rubinstein in his own time was "significant enough to be imitated. There are bits of his Fourth Concerto in Brahms's Second, and bits of the First Piano Sonata in almost everything Tchaikovsky ever wrote." *The Demon* was revived in a French production in 2003.

Until the end of his life, Rubinstein remained most famous as a pianist. He broke new ground in a Russian and European tour he mounted in 1885 and 1886, playing works by Renaissance- and Baroque-era composers such as William Byrd, and Jean-Jacques Rameau that were almost unknown until the revival of so-called early music in the second half of the 20th century. By the time he died in Peterhof (now Petrodvorets), Russia, on November 20, 1894, he was a legendary figure.

Books

Encyclopedia Judaica, Gale 2007.

Sadie, Stanley, ed., *The New Crove Dictionary of Music and Musicans,* 2nd ed., Macmillan, 2001.

Schonberg, Harold C., *The Great Pianists,* Simon and Schuster, 1963.

Periodicals

New Statesman, February 10, 2003.

Times (London, England), February 2, 1994.

Online

"Anton Rubinstein," *AllMusic,* http://www.allmusic.com (October 17, 2013).

"Anton Rubinstein," *Marius van Paassen Plays on CD I,* http://members.chello.nl/mvpaasse/rubinstein.htm (October 17, 2013). □

S

Peter Safar

American anesthesiologist and professor Dr. Peter Safar (1924-2003) is widely recognized as the father of cardiopulmonary resuscitation, commonly known as CPR or the "kiss of life." He also developed other life-saving techniques, and conducted important research in areas such as emergency medicine and critical care medicine.

Peter Safar was born on April 12, 1924, in Vienna, Austria. His father was an eye surgeon and professor while his mother was a pediatrician. When the Nazis gained power and took over Germany, then Austria, his father was fired from his teaching post for refusing to join the Nazi party, and his mother lost her post because she had a Jewish grandmother. Safar had an early interest in medicine which began after his father let him look through a microscope when Safar was small. Safar himself was drafted into the German army but avoided serving more than briefly as a paramedic because of a skin condition, along with intervention by friends and some luck.

Attended Medical School in Europe

Instead, in 1943, Safar was admitted to the University of Vienna's medical school, despite his Jewish ancestry because an administrator deliberately overlooked it. After the war ended and he had earned his a medical degree, Safar continued his studies from 1948 to 1949 at the University of Vienna, focusing on pathology research, oncology, and surgery. Safar then came to the United States to complete a surgical residency at Yale University from 1949 to 1950. There, he focused on the same subjects, and

realized that the methods used to keep patients alive during surgery could be used when people were near death and lives could be saved.

From 1950 to 1952, Safar was a fellow at the University of Pennsylvania, where he received anesthesiology training. During this period, in 1950, he married Eva Kyzivat, with whom he had three children. After completing his education, Safar began his career in Lima, Peru, in 1952. There, he worked at the National Cancer Institute of Peru and played a key role in founding, developing, and chairing its academic anesthesiology department.

Returning to the United States in 1955, Safar took a position at the Baltimore City Hospital, later known as the Johns Hopkins Bayview Medical Center. While working as an anesthesiologist, he also founded the academic anesthesiology department. Also at the Baltimore City Hospital, he was a pioneer in putting together modern intensive care units. In 1958, he started and developed the first intensive care unit that was medical-surgical and physician staffed. At this time, there were critical care units for specific ailments, but Safar founded the modern intensive care unit commonly found today. Safar also began developing prototypes of the modern ambulance when he concluded that patients were not receiving appropriate treatment on the way to the hospital.

Developed CPR Technique

It was during the 1950s while at Baltimore City Hospital that Safar developed what came to be known as CPR. Through his research, Safar combined mouth to mouth resuscitation with closed-chest cardiac compression to form the CPR technique. (Mouth-to-mouth had been known as early as the 18th century but generally ignored, while external heart massage had been known as early as the 19th century.) Commonly known as the ABC of resuscitation, airway, breathing and circulation, Safar's method involved tilting the head back to open the airway, breathing mouth-to-mouth, then stimulating the circulation of the blood through massaging the heart. Through experiments on human volunteers, Safar documented the effectiveness of his technique.

Safar believed, and subsequent studies proved, that CPR was better than the technique recommended at the time which involved pushing on the victim's back to expel air, then inflating the chest by lifting the arms. Initially, CPR was used to help revive victims of heart attacks, drowning, and choking, saving thousands of people annually. After helping to develop CPR and publishing related findings in 1958, Safar believed in the importance of teaching CPR to the general public, believing it would save more lives as they were often first on the scene. As the director of the Safar Center for Resuscitation Research at the University of Pittsburgh, Dr. Patrick Kochanek, told Allison Schlesinger of the Associated Press, "He was a firm believer that it was something that the masses needed to learn." In addition to CPR techniques, Safar created 'Resusci Annie,' the doll used to teach those enrolled in life-saving classes how to perform CPR and mouth-to-mouth techniques.

Continuing further research into these life-saving techniques, Safar extended CPR into cardiopulmonary-cerebral resuscitation (CPCR) in 1961. Through the nine steps of CPCR, Safar developed a method of basic, advanced, and prolonged life support, used by critical care physicians and other medical personnel. Leaving Baltimore City Hospital for the University of Pittsburgh Medical Center in 1961, Safar again founded, developed, and chaired an academic anesthesiology department there.

Created Multidisciplinary Critical Care Training

Safar and his colleagues turned the department at the University of Pittsburgh into one of the largest of its kind in the United States. In 1962, he created the first multidisciplinary critical care medicine physician training fellowship in the world. It trained more than 500 physicians in critical care medicine between 1962 and 1999. The department also launched ten new programs in critical and emergency medicine, including anesthesiology, pain control, respiratory therapy, intensive care medicine, emergency medical services, resuscitation research, and disaster reanimatology. Safar also developed the first guidelines for community-wide emergency medical services.

While helping to set up this pioneering program for intensive care training, Safar also continued research into life support. Safar developed a number of emergency revival techniques for paramedics and hospital staff, including life supporting first aid. Some of his research was influenced by his own experiences. In 1966, Safar's eleven-year-old daughter Elizabeth died after suffering an asthma attack and falling into a coma. Safar and his wife were away from home when the attack happened, and she suffered from cardiac arrest before he could reach her. Though she was revived and circulation was restored, tragically, she had brain damage and suffered a brain death.

After her death, Safar began researching the potential for cooling patients to help save them and prevent brain damage after being resuscitated in the wake of cardiac arrest or shock. He realized that the essential challenge of resuscitation was not the heart but the brain, because its cells were more delicate; permanent brain damage occurred after five minutes, while a heart can recover twenty minutes after it stops beating. Focusing more intensely on the concept in the 1980s, Safar conducted animal research, then human trials, which showed the value of mild hypothermia.

In 2003, a month before Safar's death, other research was published in *Circulation*, a journal of the American Heart Association (AMA), which demonstrated that Safar was correct in his theory that chilling the bodies of some heart attack victims left unconscious was valuable. The AMA ultimately endorsed cooling comatose patients after their hearts had been restarted so that they could be brought slowly back to life and suffer less brain damage in the process. According to the London *Times,* Safer once explained, "A little bit of cold is good. Cold reduces oxygen demand and, equally important, suppresses chemical reactions which tend to kill cells."

Founded Professional Groups

During the 1960s, Safar also served as a founding member of the CPR Committee for the American Heart Association as well as founding member of the Committee on Emergency Medical Services for the National Research Council. Through his work with these agencies, he established the guidelines needed to set up such agencies, in addition to helping organize emergency units, initiating the first guidelines on CPR, ambulance design and equipment. His work included defining standards for training emergency medical technicians and paramedics. Of the whole of Safar's emergency training development, Frank Poliafico, the executive director of the AED Instructor Foundation, told Schlesinger of the Associated Press, "He wanted [to] prepare the people who show up at an accident scene first— the passer-by—so they can sustain a victim until a paramedic arrives. And then, the paramedic cares for the patient until they reach the emergency room and so on."

During the 1970s, Safar not only co-founded and served as the president of the Society of Critical Care Medicine, his research focus became honed on disaster reanimatology research. He started research programs into cerebral resuscitation after prolonged cardiac arrest. At the end of the decade, Safar instigated and developed the first controlled international multicenter means for clinical studies of sudden death and CPCR. Dubbed the Brain Resuscitation Clinical Trial, it was conducted by twenty teams in seven countries with 15 years of funding from the National Institutes of Health.

In 1979, Safar stepped down as the academic anesthesiology department head at the University of Pittsburgh and founded the International Resuscitation Research Center (IRRC) there. Under his guidance and role in development, the institute focused on research into the secondary injuries which occur after medical events like traumatic brain injury, cardiopulmonary arrest, and severe hemorrhage. Safar also served as mentor to some 60 physicians and 20 medical student research fellows during his time at the helm of the IRRC. In addition, in 1982, he launched the journal *Prehospital and Disaster Medicine.*

Continued Research

When Safar reached the age of 70 in 1994, he stepped down as head of the IRRC. His successor, Dr. Patrick Kochanek, changed the name of the institute to the Safar Center for Resuscitation Research. Though Safar had left his post, he remained an advisor and played a leading role in research programs on cardiac arrest, traumatology, and suspended animation there.

Safar also remained active in peace medicine, human rights, and roots of war issues as he had been for much of his career. In addition to working for a number of non-governmental organizations such as the World Association for Disaster and Emergency Medicine, which he co-founded in 1976, he was a member of the Physicians for Social Responsibility as well as the International Physicians for Prevention of Nuclear War. Safar also advised the casualty care research programs for the U.S. Army and U.S. Navy. Outside of his work, Safar enjoyed classical music, and was an accomplished pianist and ballroom dancer.

In May 2002, a malignant pelvic tumor was discovered, after which he had many surgeries and therapies. Safar did not let illness interfere with his work or his life, continuing to enjoy both until its end. Over the course of his long career, he published more than thirty books and manuals as well as over 1,300 entries in professional publications.

In August 3, 2013, Safar died of the cancer he had fought at the age of 79 in his home in Pittsburgh, Pennsylvania. Upon Safar's death, the chancellor of the University of Pittsburgh, Mark Nordenberg, was quoted by PR Newswire as saying "Throughout this distinguished career, Peter Safar worked tirelessly and effectively to cheat death. He fundamentally re-shaped approaches to medical treatment and helped save hundreds of thousands of lives. His own life was characterized by intellectual power, uncompromising standards and personal grace."

Periodicals

Associated Press, August 4, 2003.
Express, August 20, 2003.
Guardian (London), August 13, 2003.
New York Times, August 6, 2003.
PR Newswire, August 4, 2003.
Times (London), August 6, 2003. □

Coluccio Salutati

The Italian statesman Coluccio Salutati (1331–1406) was the chancellor of the city-state of Florence from 1375 until the end of his life. He was one of the first learned figures in Italy to practice and argue in favor of the revival of knowledge of ancient Greek literature that gave rise to the Renaissance era in European history.

Salutati's name is little known among general students of European history. In the field of literature and scholarship he was overshadowed by his older contemporary Francesco Petrarca, known as Petrarch, who rediscovered the writings of the Roman orator and political theorist Marcus Tullius Cicero. Indeed, comparing himself to Petrarch, Salutati wrote (according to Stephen Greenblatt, writing in *The Swerve: How the World Became Modern*), "I do not like myself." As a political leader Salutati was active at a chaotic time when Italy was torn apart by competing religious factions and by warlords from the Italian peninsula's many small city-states who tried to broaden their own realms. Yet Salutati was a crucial figure who held the citizens of Florence together when they were in mortal danger. And yet more important was that he used the ideas of classical literature to do so. He is one of the forefathers of the splendid city Florence became over the next three centuries.

Family Fled Southern Italy

Coluccio Salutati was born in Stignano, in southern Italy, on February 16, 1331. Salutati's childhood was marked by the conflict between the Pope in Rome and the northern Catholic monarch, the Holy Roman Emperor: his father, a Guelph, or supporter of the Pope, was forced to flee to Bologna after a military victory there by the Ghibellines, or supporters of the Emperor. Salutati was trained in Bologna as a notary, then a literate individual capable of creating and executing legal documents. In 1350, he was able to return to Stignano. He apparently prospered: around 1366 he married, and for his marriage banquet he provided 3,000 oranges, at the time a luxury item. He was active as an assistant to one of the Pope's secretaries from 1368 to 1370. He was married twice, fathering a total of ten children. Generally, little is known of the first several decades of his life.

Salutati became the chancellor (essentially the mayor) of Florence in 1375 and moved into the magnificent Palace of the Signoria that had been built at the end of the last century. Then an independent city-state, Florence was a prosperous banking and merchant city but had been hit hard by the continent-wide outbreak of bubonic plague, known as the Black Death, in 1348. The first stirrings of the Renaissance had become evident in Petrarch's writings, but the thinking of medieval Florence was still mostly shaped by religious leaders. Salutati soon became one of the most learned men of his time. At a time when books existed only in manuscript form and few people possessed even a single one, he accumulated a collection of 800 of them.

Most of these were writings by Catholic Church fathers, but Salutati, although personally devout, became discouraged by the formulaic nature of what he was reading. An active correspondent who left a voluminous record of his impressions, he "found almost nothing to cherish, at least stylistically, in anything written between Cassiodorus in the sixth century and Dante in the thirteenth" (according to Greenblatt). Instead he turned to the writings of the ancients, many of which had only recently been unearthed. Rejecting religious formulas, he sought to develop a writing style of his own, rooted in the classics of ancient Rome but suited to the challenges of his own day.

Argued for Value of Classical Texts

The official Catholic position at the time was that classical literature, which was considered pagan, should essentially be banned. By the late 14th century, educated Florentines were beginning to disregard the ban, but they did so mostly surreptitiously. Salutati went a step further: he directly challenged the Church's reasoning in his own writings. He argued that the Bible had nothing to say about secular learning and that truth came ultimately from God, whatever its source. Moreover, the belief system based on the ancient Greek gods no longer presented any threat to Christianity.

Salutati's most important argument, however, was a practical one: political leaders of his own time needed the lessons writers like Cicero could impart. He believed that, in the words of historian Vincent Cronin (writing in *The Florentine Renaissance*) that "[c]lassical historians could provide lessons in practical politics, statecraft, and political philosophy which simply did not exist in Christian works." Too, in an age when diplomatic correspondence was of paramount importance in the relationship between Florence and places beyond its city walls, the classical authors provided a more forceful and persuasive rhetoric than did exclusively Christian works.

Such ideas were duly attacked by religious leaders of the day. One of them, a fiery preacher named Giovanni Dominici, who claimed that he had been miraculously cured of a speech impediment by St. Catherine of Siena, wrote an entire book called *The Firefly* devoted to first enumerating and then demolishing Salutati's views, arguing that the ultimate goal of human existence was beatitude, and that any form of knowledge not directly connected with that should be discarded. Dominici approvingly referred to Pope Gregory the Great (c. 540–604), who had burned the *History* of the Roman writer Livy because it mentioned the pagan gods. Numerous church leaders of Salutati's time shared Dominici's views, and one church leader knocked down a statue of the Roman writer Virgil and pushed it into the Mincio River in Mantua.

How the dispute might have played out had historical events not intervened is unknown, but Salutati, as Florence's leader, was soon provided with a practical test of his beliefs that the ancient writings provided counsel and rhetorical models for the modern statesman. Beginning around 1390, Florence was menaced by the warlord Giangaleazzo Visconti, who came from the northwestern city of Pavia and had conquered the cities of Verona, Vicenza, and Milan, where his troops began using an emblem (still visible in the city today) of a blue snake with seven coils, holding a struggling human in its mouth. Rome, consumed by inter-religious struggles, and Venice, with its gaze pointed east toward new trading partners, remained neutral as Visconti's troops attacked the city of Bologna. His heralds, bearing the snake emblem, soon arrived in Florence and declared war on the city.

Rallied Florentine Populace

In a series of manifestos, Salutati rallied Florentines to the cause. He wrote that Florence was a city of laws, not of tyranny "obedient to one single man who governs everything according to his caprices" (as translated and quoted by Cronin). Visconti recognized the power of Salutati's writings, reportedly saying that they did more damage to his campaign than a thousand troops mounted in horseback. He even tried to discredit Salutati by issuing a counterfeit pamphlet that made it appear that Salutati planned to commit treason. Salutati denied the pamphlet's authorship in front of a packed Florentine assembly, where he was universally believed.

For several years, the battle seesawed. At one point Florentine mercenaries nearly reached Milan, but in 1399, the port city of Pisa, just over 50 miles from Florence, fell to Visconti, who regarded himself as a modern-day emperor. Salutati, by contrast, cast Florence as a modern equivalent of the ancient Roman republic, where citizens shared in the making of laws and in the defense of the city against invaders. Although Florence was virtually isolated against Visconti's onslaught, and was further weakened by a new outbreak of plague in 1400, the tide turned in Florence's favor when Visconti fell ill and died of an unidentified disease. Soon his heirs and his allies were fighting among themselves, and Florence was saved.

Although Florence had not survived purely through military means, Florentines recognized that it was Salutati and the power of his ideas that had sustained them through 13 years of war, and often famine as the city's trade routes were cut off. Salutati continued to serve as Florence's chancellor and to supervise a new alliance with Pisa after the defeat of an anti-Papal faction there. In his later years he passed on his knowledge of classical lore to Gian Francesco Poggio Bracciolini, a scholar who recovered from monastery libraries many of the classical writings that are known today. Unusually aged by the standards of the day, Salutati died in Florence on May 4, 1406.

Books

Cronin, Vincent, *The Florentine Renaissance,* Dutton, 1967.

Greenblatt, Stephen, *The Swerve: How the World Became Modern,* Norton, 2011.

Martines, Lauro, *The Social World of the Florentine Humanists, 1390–1460,* University of Toronto, 2011.

Witt, Ronald G., *In the Footsteps of the Ancients,* Brill, 2003.

Online

"Coluccio Salutati," *Christian Humanism,* http://aromagosa.easycgi.com/christianhumanism/Biographies/Salutati.htm (October 28, 2013).□

Andrew Sarris

The American film critic Andrew Sarris (1928–2012) introduced the French auteur theory to American journalism. In the words of the *Times* of London, Sarris "was almost single-handedly responsible for introducing to English-speaking readers a then revolutionary idea that quickly became critical orthodoxy: the notion that the primary author of a film is its director."

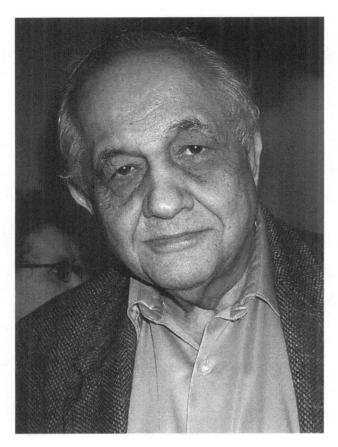

© ZUMA Press, Inc./Alamy

S arris came of age in the 1960s, a time when Americans interested in film were discovering the works of renowned European directors such as France's François Truffaut, Sweden's Ingmar Bergman, and Italy's Federico Fellini. Part of his accomplishment was to define their contributions for American readers. But he also championed the work of such American directors as John Ford and Orson Welles, and he helped to define the Hollywood film as a legitimate object of serious criticism and study. Sarris's writing also helped nurture the talents of the younger American directors who began their careers during his career, including Martin Scorsese, Francis Ford Coppola, and Robert Altman—directors who combined commercial considerations with strong individual styles. Sarris's celebrated clashes with fellow critics Pauline Kael and John Simon were the stuff of controversy in their own time but in retrospect may be seen as having elevated the prestige of American film criticism in general. Over a career lasting more than 50 years, Sarris influenced numerous younger writers on film.

Impressed by Film as Toddler

The son of Greek immigrants George and Themis Sarris, Andrew Sarris was born in Brooklyn, New York, on October 31, 1928, and grew up in the Ozone Park neighborhood in the New York City borough of Queens. There were early indications of his choice of career: when he was about four,

he saw a film based on a short story by French science fiction writer Jules Verne, and, he later recalled (as quoted by Michael Powell in the *New York Times*), "The liquidity of the scene and the film," he recalled, "was truly magical, especially to someone not many years out of the womb himself." At John Adams High School, one of his classmates was the future star columnist Jimmy Breslin. Sarris attended Columbia University, graduating in 1951 after having spent as much time as he could in New York's movie theaters.

After graduation, Sarris served for three years in the United States Army Signal Corps. His writing career began with a film column in a magazine aimed at members of the military. Discharged in 1954, he returned briefly to New York to live with his mother and to take a job with the U.S. Census Bureau. He wrote briefly for a new magazine called *Film Culture.* Then, while his fellow veterans were establishing themselves in careers and houses, he departed for Paris, France, for a year, where he met Truffaut and the even more radical young director Jean-Luc Godard. Fascinated by new French ideas about the role of the director, he managed to land a job as editor of an English-language edition of the influential French film journal *Cahiers du Cinéma* (Film Notebooks) when he returned to the U.S.

In 1960, thanks to a recommendation from one of *Film Culture*'s editors, Sarris achieved his breakthrough: he was hired to write film criticism for the *Village Voice*, the New York publication that pioneered the alternative-weekly format. Sarris showed a gift both for elegant writing and controversy with his very first review for the *Voice*, in which he praised Alfred Hitchcock's horror thriller *Psycho*. The film had been panned as sensationalistic by mainstream critics, but Sarris wrote (as quoted by Powell) that it "is overlaid with a richly symbolic commentary on the modern world as a public swamp in which human feelings and passions are flushed down the drain."

Complaints flooded into the *Voice*'s offices, based mostly on the supposed unacceptability of its critic having praised a product of mainstream Hollywood. But the paper's editors realized that controversy was its lifeblood and let Sarris remain. He would continue to write for the *Voice* for 29 years and to become a major voice in American film criticism. His tastes ran equally to foreign and American films, and as the famous products of the French New Wave, such as Truffaut's *Shoot the Piano Player* (1960) arrived on American shores, it was Sarris who confidently introduced them to audiences.

Popularized Auteur Theory

The term "auteur," or author, had been applied to film by French critics, but it was Sarris who brought it into general circulation in English. The auteur was the film's director, who gave the film a consistent tone and style, and related the look of the film to its story. A good actor, in Sarris's view, might be worth watching in isolation, but what made for great cinematic art was the contribution of the director. Sarris applied his ideas to American films, which French critics had begun to consider in artistic terms but at home had mostly been considered purely commercial products. Witty and erudite, Sarris was an able spokesman for these new critical ideas.

The most extended presentation of Sarris's ideas came in his book *The American Cinema: Directors and Directions, 1929–1968,* which was published in 1968 and reissued by Da Capo Press in 1996. The book remains the central statement of auteur theory in English, and it contained a controversial group of lists that classified directors into various categories. His "Pantheon Directors" included Robert Flaherty, John Ford, Orson Welles, Charles Chaplin, Fritz Lang, F.W. Murnau, Howard Hawks, D.W. Griffith, Buster Keaton, Max Ophuls, Alfred Hitchcock, Ernst Lubitsch, Josef von Sternberg, and Jean Renoir, while the unflattering "Less than Meets the Eye" group included such critical favorites as John Huston.

In 1966, at a film screening, Sarris met Molly Haskell, a young feminist-oriented film critic. He invited her out for a sundae at Howard Johnson's restaurant, and the pair married in 1969. Sarris's chief rival in the world of New York film criticism, *New Yorker* magazine critic Pauline Kael, was invited to the wedding but (according to Powell) declined with the words "That's O.K. I'll go to Molly's next wedding." As it turned out, the marriage lasted until Sarris's death. The pair lived in an apartment on New York's Upper East Side.

Feuded with Other Critics

The exchange between Sarris and Kael was part of a longer critical feud, rooted in contrasting outlooks on film: Kael, who called films "movies," favored a more direct emotional response in contrast to Sarris's more intellectual approach. Film buffs of the time were divided, French-style, into "Sarristes" and "Paulettes," but the rivalry helped draw readers to both critics. Sarris also feuded with John Simon, who wrote reviews for *New York* magazine and other outlets; Simon criticized Sarris's auteur theory, which in his opinion placed insufficient emphasis on storytelling, to which Sarris (as quoted by Powell) responded that "Simon is the greatest film critic of the 19th century."

Sarris wrote for the *Village Voice* until 1989, moving then to the *New York Observer* and remaining there until 2009. In 1998, he published the book *You Ain't Heard Nothing Yet: The American Talking Film, History and Memory 1927–1949.* Sarris's large body of crtiicism influenced both filmmakers and numerous younger critics. Director Scorsese, with whom Sarris once shared an office, was quoted by Hillel Italie of the Toronto *Globe & Mail* as saying that Sarris was "a fundamental teacher" who had helped him "see the genius in American movies."

Sarris earned a master's degree from Columbia in 1998. He was a founding member of the National Society of Film Critics. His other books include several collections of essays and columns, a survey of the work of director John Ford, and a study, *Politics and Cinema.* A finalist for a Pulitzer Prize in 2000, he was laid off from the *Observer* in 2009, but taught film courses at Columbia until 2011. In later years he reversed his negative evaluations of several major directors, including Billy Wilder and Stanley Kubrick, the latter after viewing *2001: A Space Odyssey* under the influence of marijuana at the suggestion of a friend. Sarris died on June 20, 2012, in New York.

Books

Sarris, Andrew, *The American Cinema: Directors and Directions, 1929–1968,* Dutton, 1968.

Periodicals

Globe & Mail (Toronto, Ontario, Canada), June 21, 2012.
Guardian (London, England), June 23, 2012.
Independent (London, England), June 30, 2012.
New York Times, July 9, 2009; June 21, 2012.
Times (London, England), July 2, 2012.□

Terry Sawchuk

Canadian professional hockey player Terry Sawchuk (1929–1970) set records for most shutouts and victories for goalies in the National Hockey League (NHL). Though plagued by alcoholism and personal problems off the ice, Sawchuk is often considered one of, if not the, best goalies in the history of the NHL.

Born December 28, 1929, in Winnipeg, Manitoba, Canada, he was the son of Louis and Anne Maslak Sawchuk. His father had immigrated to Canada from Ukraine as a child, and was a factory worker and tinsmith, while his mother was a factory worker and homemaker. Sawchuk himself was raised in Winnipeg's Ukrainian neighborhood, East Kildonan, with three brothers and a sister. His childhood was marred by tragedy, as his two older brothers passed away in their youth. His oldest brother, Mitch, an aspiring goalie, died unexpectedly of a heart attack at the age of 17, while his second oldest brother, Roger lost his life to scarlet fever, as a small child.

Demonstrated Athletic Skills in Childhood

Sports provided an outlet for Sawchuk from an early age. He learned how to skate at the age of four, and with Mitch, began playing hockey as a small child. The pair were inseparable until Mitch's death. By the age of 12, Sawchuk was also playing football. Dislocating his right elbow while playing, the young Sawchuk hid the injury to avoid punishment. Because it was not treated, the elbow did not heal properly, had limited mobility, and left his right arm a bit shorter then his left arm. The injury, however, did not prevent him playing athletics.

After his eldest brother died, the teenaged Sawchuk was given his brother's goalie equipment and began playing as a goalie instead of forward. He displayed considerable talent while playing in a local league. By the time he was 14 years old, a talent scout for the NHL's Detroit Red Wings arranged for Sawchuk to work out with the team in Detroit. In 1946, Sawchuk then signed an amateur contract with the team and played for the Red Wings' junior team in Galt, Ontario, Canada. While playing for the team, Sawchuk attended eleventh grade,

Bruce Bennett Studios/Getty Images

which was most likely the end of his education because he was playing professionally the next year.

Signed First Professional Contract

In November 1947, Sawchuk's prowess in Galt compelled the Red Wings to sign the goalie to a professional contract. (Sawchuk also played baseball, and turned down an offer to play for the St. Louis Cardinals around this time.) For the next few seasons, Sawchuk moved through Detroit's developmental system, playing in the U.S. Hockey League for Omaha for 1947-1948 and the American Hockey League for Indianapolis in 1948-1949. He was named rookie of the year for both leagues, and won the Calder Cup in Indiana in 1950.

By this time, Sawchuk had developed an atypical playing style. Because of his quick reflexes, impressive lower body strength, and propensity to play with abandon, he eschewed the widely accepted style of bending at the knees and keeping the upper body erect. Instead Sawchuk bent deeply at his waist as he crouched in the goal because he found that he could move more quickly from a crouched position. But, as a result, his face was forward and closer to the ice, allowing him to see the puck better but also putting him at greater risk for injury. At the time, goalies did not wear masks or helmets, so Sawchuk's face was exposed. Despite the risks, Sawchuk's positioning eventually became the norm in the NHL, especially after

goalie masks became more common. Sawchuk himself began wearing a mask in 1962, after acquiring more than 400 stitches on his face.

Joined Detroit Red Wings

Sawchuk was soon given a chance to shine in the NHL. In January 1950, during the Red Wings' successful run for the Stanley Cup in the 1949-50 season, Harry Lumley, Detroit's goalie, injured his ankle. Sawchuk filled in for seven games as Lumley recovered, and played well. Because of Sawchuk's success, the Red Wings traded Lumley to Chicago after the season ended so they could bring up Sawchuk as their primary goalie, even though Lumley backstopped them to the league championship.

The move paid off, as Uke—as Sawchuk was nicknamed—demonstrated his outstanding abilities. In his first season with Detroit, Sawchuk played in every game, had 11 shutouts, and a goals against average of 1.98. He won rookie of the year honors. The Red Wings won the Stanley Cup Sawchuk's second year in goal, one of three over the first five years that he was their goalie. In the 1951-1952 playoffs, Detroit swept both the Blackhawks and the Montreal Canadiens, and Sawchuk did not let in a goal during any home playoff games.

During this period, Sawchuk was selected as an All-Star five times. He also won three Vezina Trophies, given to goalies who allowed the fewest goals on the season. The other two years, Sawchuk missed winning the award by only one goal. He also posted 56 shutouts and had an average goals against average of under 2.00 over these seasons. A Detroit defenseman of this era, Bob Goldham, told John U. Bacon of the *Michigan History Magazine*, "When I look back on those Stanley Cups, what I remember is Ukey making one big save after another. We could always count on him to come up with the big save. Ukey was the greatest goaltender who ever lived."

Though Sawchuk continued to be a dominant goalie, his personality transformed after the 1952 Stanley Cup victory. Always pudgy to this point, Sawchuk was told to lose weight by Jack Adams, the general manager of the Red Wings. Though he dropped 40 pounds from his 219 pounds at the beginning of training camp, Sawchuk became surly and remote, doing few to no interviews nor satisfying fans. His dark temper, which included rages, also emerged in this time period, as did burgeoning alcoholism. By February 1955, Adams temporarily benched Sawchuk because of his drinking and ordered him to receive psychiatric treatment.

Also beginning in this period, Sawchuk's playing style and injuries began catching up to him. Unless he was injured, he had no days off during the season because there were no backup goalies at this time in the NHL. Not only did his long-hurt right elbow undergo three operations, he also had a collapsed lung, severed hand tendons, and a permanent stoop and swayback.

Traded to Boston

Though Sawchuk was still in his playing prime, Adams traded Sawchuk to the Boston Bruins in the summer of 1955. The Red Wings had another young goaltender in

Glenn Hall, and Sawchuk seemed expendable. The trade was hard on the self-critical Sawchuk and he lost confidence in his abilities. Sawchuk played well during his first season with nine shutouts, but during his second, he developed mononucleosis, returned too quickly, and did not play well because he was physically weak. In early 1957, the goalie, who was near a nervous breakdown, announced his retirement. His coach, Boston team executives, and newspaper writers called him a quitter because of the decision.

Finally able to recuperate, Sawchuk temporarily worked as a car dealer, insurance salesman, and bartender. He soon found himself back in Detroit, after Adams traded for him. Sawchuk then played solidly for Detroit for seven more seasons, though he was unable to match the success of his first stint with the Red Wings. His confidence was especially affected when the team converted to the two-goalie system, and Sawchuk had to share the net with Hank Bassen. The team did again make it to the Stanley Cup finals against the Toronto Maple Leafs in the 1963-64 season, despite Sawchuk playing with a pinched nerve. The Wings pushed it to seven games before losing to Toronto.

By 1964, Detroit had another young goalie ready, Roger Crozier, and left Sawchuk eligible in the intraleague waver draft that summer. He was claimed by the Toronto Maple Leafs. In Toronto, Sawchuk played well as part of goaltending tandem with another veteran goalie, Johnny Bower. Together, the pair won the 1965 Vezina Trophy, and the Stanley Cup at the end of the 1966-1967 season, Sawchuk's fourth. This despite having back surgery to fuse two vertebrae and doctors' warnings that he might never play again.

Played Final Seasons as a Backup

Despite this success, Toronto chose to leave Sawchuk unprotected in the 1967 expansion draft. At this time, the NHL expanded from six to 12 teams. The new Los Angeles Kings selected Sawchuk, who played there for one season. In 1968, the goalie was traded back to Detroit for the 1968-69 season. His last season of NHL play was spent with the New York Rangers in 1969-70. For all three times Sawchuk was primarily a backup goalie, though he had the last shutout of his career, number 103, while playing for New York.

By this time, Sawchuk's alcoholism, mental issues, and behavioral problems were widely known. Not only did they affect his relationships with his team and the public, they affected his family life as well. He had married receptionist Patricia Ann Bowman Morey on August 6, 1953, and the couple had seven children. Throughout his marriage, especially as his problems increased on and off the ice, he became verbally and physically abusive. He also repeatedly cheated on his wife. After several attempts to end the marriage ended in reconciliation, Morey finally divorced him in 1969.

Unexpected Early Death

Sawchuk unexpectedly died the following year. After his season with New York ended in 1970, Sawchuk and Ron Stewart, his roommate with the Rangers, had been drinking when they got into an argument about shared chores and expenses for their rented house at the end of April. The incident turned into a physical fight, and Sawchuk suffered internal injuries when he fell either on Stewart's knee or a barbecue grill. The hospitalized Sawchuk told police that he accepted responsibility for the incident. Initially expected to survive, he had multiple operations to remove his gallbladder and address his bleeding liver, and ultimately died of a pulmonary embolism on May 31, 1970. After Sawchuk's death, a grand jury ruled that it was an accident and Stewart was not charged. Sawchuk was buried in Pontiac, Michigan.

When he died, Sawchuk held a number of records, including the most shutouts by a goalie as well as regular season games played by a goaltender, with 971. He also held the record for regular season wins with 447, which was only bested by Patrick Roy in 2000. Hockey honored Sawchuk in a number of ways in the years after his early demise. In 1971, he was posthumously given the Lester Patrick Memorial Trophy for his service to hockey in the United States. That same year, the Hockey Hall of Fame waived the three-year waiting period and inducted him. In 1994, the man many considered the best goaltender ever, had his number retired by the team with whom he had his greatest success, the Detroit Red Wings.

Books

Notable Sports Figures, Volume 3, edited by Dana R. Barnes, Gale, 2004.

Scribner Encyclopedia of American Lives, Thematic Series: The 1960s, edited by William L. O'Neill and Kenneth T. Jackson, Charles Scribner's Sons, 2002.

Periodicals

Gazette (Montreal), March 10, 2008; December 16, 2009.

Globe and Mail (Canada), November 15, 1996.

Michigan History Magazine, November-December 2000.□

Elsa Schiaparelli

Italian-born fashion designer Elsa Schiaparelli lived a life as vivid as the shade of shocking pink long associated with her name. During the 1930s, her Paris atelier was a trendsetting hub frequented by stylish socialites, film stars, and the Surrealists. With almost no formal training in the visual arts or the business of fashion, Schiaparelli managed to create a multimillion-dollar business with collections that set new directions for 20th century women's wear. Knit separates, shoulder pads, and even bright, attention-getting colors are all part of the legacy "Schiap," as she was called by friends and fans, imprinted upon fashion.

Time Life Pictures/Getty Images

Elsa Schiaparelli was born in the heart of Rome, at her family's spectacular Palazzo Corsini, on September 10, 1890. On her mother's side she was descended from an aristocratic lineage that included the Grand Dukes of Tuscany, among the most influential statesmen and religious leaders of Renaissance and Baroque-era Italy. Schiaparelli's father was from a distinguished family of intellectuals; he was a scholar of Arabic and Sansrkit cultures and served as dean at the University of Rome. His brother was Giovanni Schiaparelli, the astronomer who discovered what he called *canali,* or channels, on the surface of the planet Mars, a term incorrectly disseminated in the press of the 1870s as "canals."

Dreamed of Bohemian Life

Schiaparelli and her older sister Beatrice were raised in the rigid traditions of the aristocracy in predominantly Roman Catholic Italy. Unlike Beatrice, however, Elsa was rebellious from an early age and once went on a hunger strike when her parents installed her in a single-sex boarding school run by Roman Catholic nuns. She tried various schemes to elude her parents' control and live independently as an artist, most of which failed. At 21 she managed to have a book of love poetry published, titled *Arethusa,* without her parents' knowledge. Finally, a decision was made to send her to England to work as a governess to a wealthy family, and Schiaparelli made a detour to Paris to see the city for the first time. While working in Kent in southeast England, Schiaparelli spent her free time in London, where she met Count Wilhelm Wendt de Kerlor, a half-Swiss, half-French theosophist. Theosophical societies were a popular trend among forward-thinking Westerners with an interest in Eastern religions. Schiaparelli and de Kerlor fell in love and decided to get married within the space of a few short days. They carried out their plans at a London registry office before Schiaparelli's parents could make a countermove to prevent it.

Schiaparelli's marriage took place just before World War I. In 1916, the couple sailed to America, settling in New York City, where they reveled in Greenwich Village's bohemian spirit. Schiaparelli became pregnant with her first and only child, but the count disappeared and was later found to have run off with the dancer Isadora Duncan. As a single parent Schiaparelli struggled to care for the daughter born Countess Maria Luisa Yvonne Radha de Wendt de Kerlor, whom she dubbed "Gogo." The child was taken in by sympathetic friends in Connecticut for a time, but was stricken with polio. Desperate to obtain treatment and financially imperiled, Schiaparelli joined the flood of expatriates who made Paris their home in the early 1920s. She and Gogo lived on a small monthly amount sent by Schiaparelli's widowed mother, who urged her to return to Italy. In Paris, however, rents were cheap and an influx of creative minds had settled there. Among them were a multinational bunch of avant-garde visual artists Schiaparelli had known from her Greenwich Village days.

Encouraged by Paul Poiret

Schiaparelli had been experimenting with her wardrobe for many years by then. Once, she was asked to a formal dance and had no ball gown with her; she bought a bolt of fabric and pinned it into an evening dress. An aunt had married an Egyptologist who excavated ancient tombs, and often sent her curious fabrics woven from centuries-old traditions. Schiaparelli had no training in fashion, but she liked to sketch designs and had a rampant imagination fueled by her friendships with the Surrealists and Dada artists, including Salvador Dalí, Jean Cocteau, Man Ray, and Marcel Duchamp. Another major influence was the successful French couturier Paul Poiret, who liked both her sketches and sense of personal style. Poiret encouraged her to pursue a career in fashion and provided her with free dresses—a luxury she could never afford on her own limited income.

The business of fashion was a tough one, requiring not just vision but the financial resources to manufacture the goods plus a public-relations knack to drum up interest. Schiaparelli possessed the first and third attributes, and knew a little of the business end from working with Gabrielle Picabia, wife of the artist Francis Picabia, back in New York. Picabia held informal trunk shows of designs imported from Paris. Schiaparelli eventually began working as a freelance fashion illustrator in Paris and was hired in 1925 to design a collection for Maison Lambal, a firm that ran into financial trouble and closed within a year.

Schiaparelli had a keen eye for cutting-edge fashion trends and was fascinated by unusual materials and embellishments. She discovered a small community of Armenian-émigré women in France who knitted fantastic sweaters Schiaparelli knew were unique: the women used an unusual double-layered stitch that meant the garment retained its original shape. Schiaparelli also loved the black-and-white butterfly print on one sweater. She asked one knitter to make a similar version, with a clever trompe-l'oeil bow instead of a butterfly at the neckline, and Schiaparelli's friends found it delightful and demanded their own. Schiaparelli took orders for several sweaters, then paid the Armenian woman to help recruit other knitters who were skilled in that technique. This was the start of her fashion house, in small rented rooms on the Rue de la Paix in early 1927. The sweater made an appearance in the February issue of French *Vogue,* and in December of 1927 was featured in American *Vogue.* Schiaparelli found a financial backer in the form of Charles Kahn, an executive with the Galeries Lafayettes department store in Paris, but was able to buy him out with her share of the profits within two years.

Built Multifaceted Brand

The House of Schiaparelli was an instant success and catapulted its head designer quite suddenly into the upper echelons of Paris fashion. Within a few short years she employed 400 knitters and seamstresses at her atelier. Incessant in her quest to innovate, she was also skilled at courting publicity for her company. When she visited England on a tweed-buying trip in 1930, she appeared in public in one of her own designs, a pair of loose-fitting divided pants that resembled a skirt from a distance. These were culottes, and Schiaparelli convinced a Spanish tennis champion, Lili de Alvarez, to wear them for her 1931 appearance at the famously formal Wimbledon tournament.

Schiaparelli managed to prosper even through the Great Depression. In 1932 she opened the "Schiap Shop" in Paris, making her the first designer to offer ready-to-wear pieces. *Time* magazine put her on its cover in August of 1934 for a feature story about French fashion and how ideas there migrate to U.S. department stores. "There is a handful of houses now at or near the peak of their power as arbiters of the ultra-modern haute couture," the magazine's writer remarked, and counted Schiaparelli along with the houses of Vionnet, Lanvin, Mainbocher, and Molyneux as among the cutting-edge designers. "Madder and more original than most of her contemporaries, Mme'.' Schiaparelli is the one to whom the word 'genius' is applied most often," the *Time* profile asserted.

Schiaparelli's company made swimsuits and she even applied for and received a U.S. patent for a built-in bra for a backless swimsuit. She used this backless bra design on an evening gown, pairing it with a bolero jacket—to reduce the shock of seeing so much of a woman's skin exposed—and the backless gown and a long dress with a matching short jacket both became staples of women's eveningwear for decades. She sought out and embraced new or odd materials, including synthetic fabrics and zippers. When she discovered a new, see-through plastic, she created jewelry for it with metallic insects, so it appeared the wearer was actually sporting a glittering beetle.

Dressed Duchess of Windsor

Schiaparelli introduced her first fragrance, "S," in 1928, but her most memorable was called "Shocking!" at its launch in 1937. Its bottle was shaped like a woman's torso and had been created for the company by the artist Leonor Fini. During these years Schiaparelli's collections had an unusually universal appeal—they were favored by tastemakers and trendsetters of the era on both sides of the Atlantic, but many of her less-extreme ideas were borderline-quirky enough to translate to the mass-retail level. Amusing hats were another signature, along with the bold shade of pink she favored. Once, Salvador Dalí's wife snapped a photograph of him wearing one of Schiaparelli's slippers on his head, which gave Schiaparelli the idea for the famous Shoe hat, a head covering that cleverly resembled an upside-down woman's pump.

Schiaparelli knew Wallis Simpson, the American divorcée who captured the heart of England's King Edward VIII. In 1936, the king abdicated the throne in favor of his younger brother, the Duke of York, in order to marry Simpson. For the official engagement portrait, society photographer Cecil Beaton persuaded Simpson to wear a Schiaparelli dress with a lobster print created by Dalí. Crustacean-themed fashion failed to catch on with the public, but Schiaparelli is credited for adding enormous shoulder pads to women's suit jackets and dresses as a trick to slim the silhouette. Joan Crawford brought some Schiaparelli items back to Hollywood with her from one European jaunt in 1932, and showed them to Adrian, the renowned studio costumer. Soon the extravagantly padded jackets and dresses appeared in boutiques and department stores as women eagerly adopted the trend.

Interrupted by War

In 1935, the House of Schiaparelli moved into palatial quarters on the Place Vendôme in Paris. Like her archrival, Gabrielle "Coco" Chanel, she could be slightly terrifying in person, and the two were said to loathe one another. When Nazi Germany invaded France in 1940, Schiaparelli went to New York City while Chanel stayed in Paris. In New York City Schiaparelli had a few exciting years, working for war-relief charities but refusing to turn out any new work because of wartime shortages, and in solidarity with her French design colleagues who had been unable to flee. Her now-grown, glamorous daughter Gogo married shipping executive Robert B. Berenson—great-nephew of famed art historian and collector Bernard Berenson.

After the war's end in 1945, Schiaparelli returned to Paris, excited about restarting her business. But tastes had changed, and Schiaparelli's zany dictums and quirky shapes failed to catch on with store buyers and fashion-forward clientele. In 1954 she was forced to file for bankruptcy, and lived the next 19 years remembered little more than as an eccentric footnote to interwar fashion. She died in Paris on November 13, 1973, at age 83 after a stroke and several weeks in a coma. By that point her two granddaughters, Berry and Marisa Berenson, were the new trendsetting model/actors of the era. Berry married the actor Anthony Perkins and perished on one of the flights that crashed into New York City's World Trade Center on September 11, 2001.

The rights to the Schiaparelli brand were eventually acquired by Diego della Valle, the Italian luxury-goods executive, who relaunched a limited line in 2013. Schiaparelli's influence on fashion was marked by a lavish show at New York's Costume Institute of the Metropolitan Museum in 2012. Despite her reputation as provocateur, Schiaparelli believed that genuine style was much harder to purchase than fashion. The modern woman, she told Virginia Pope in a 1933 *New York Times* article, "should have a few distinguished clothes.... it is a manifestation of good taste to dress very simply and very well rather than fill one's wardrobe with a lot of makeshift cheap clothes."

Books

Bolton, Andrew, and Harold Koda, *Schiaparelli & Prada: Impossible Conversations,* Metropolitan Museum of Art, 2012.

Periodicals

New York Times, March 5, 1933; November 15, 1973.

New Yorker, October 27, 2003.

Time, Time, August 13, 1934.□

Ayrton Senna

The Brazilian race car driver Ayrton Senna (1960–1994) was, in the words of the *Times* of London, "one of the outstanding talents of the modern racing age."

Senna's domain was the mostly European and Asian Grand Prix races of the Formula One circuit, which has produced the fastest race cars in the world. Within that realm, Senna was dominant over a period of about a decade when his career reached its peak. Senna won three Formula One world championships, given to the driver who wins the highest number of races in a single season. He won 35 individual races and took the pole position, the advantageous starting position given to the racer who has achieved the fastest times in qualifying heats, a record 65 times. A brooding, philosophical man, Senna attracted new fans to the sport of auto racing through what even his detractors conceded was tremendous charisma. His tremendous rivalry with French driver Alain Prost also compelled the attention of race fans. He died as he wished to—in a high-speed crash at the San Marino Grand Prix that took his life instantly.

© Presselect/Alamy

Kart Solved Coordination Problems

Ayrton Senna da Silva was born into a wealthy family in São Paulo, Brazil, on March 21, 1960. He later dropped the surname of his father, Milton da Silva, because it was such a common name in Brazil and decided to use the name of his mother, Neyde Senna. As a small child, Senna showed such problems with coordination that his parents feared that he suffered from a disability. But after they gave him a go-kart when he was four, those fears dissolved: behind the wheel he showed perfect coordination. He loved to watch Grand Prix races on television, and he had a passion for cars nurtured by his father's business (he was an auto parts magnate).

Senna was an indifferent student at school, and it was soon clear to which career he would devote his life. But Brazilian law forbade him to race professionally until he reached the age of 13. When he did enter his first race at a São Paulo kart track, he won, and within a few years he was the dominant go-kart driver on the continent. He won the South American Kart Championship for four consecutive years, between 1977 and 1980, by which time he had realized that only racing in Europe would bring him the new challenges he needed. At his first kart race in Europe, at Le Mans, France, Senna finished sixth. He finished near the top of the field in several other major karting races but never won the Karting World Championship—something he regretted in later life.

Driving in the small-car open-wheel Formula Ford race series, Senna began to give indications of his skills, placing fifth in his first race on his way to a pair of wins. The Formula Ford series involved no compensation for drivers, however, and Senna's marriage to Liliane Vasconcelos was in trouble: she had moved to England to be with him, but she spoke little English and hated London's cold climate. Frustrated, Senna returned to Brazil and took a position in his father's firm.

Overtook Monaco Field in Heavy Rain

The marriage ended in divorce, and Senna's hiatus from racing did not last more than a few months. Soon he was back in Europe. He never married again, although he was linked romantically with Xuxu Menegel, a television news personality, and Adriane Galisteu, a model. In 1982 and 1983, he took several titles as top driver in the Formula Ford 2000 and Formula Three circuits, regarded as primary training grounds for Formula One racing. His Formula One Grand Prix debut came in 1984, at the Brazilian Grand Prix race. In front of a crowd in his home country, he was forced to leave the race due to a blown turbocharger, and he was plagued by mechanical problems for much of his first year. But Senna soon notched the kind of thrilling performance for which he would become famous: in heavy rain at the Monaco Grand Prix he nearly won the race after qualifying in 13th place and steadily advancing through the field over 19 laps. Some race observers felt that the eventual winner, Prost, had been helped by an unfair ruling from race director Jackie Ickx.

Driving for the Toleman and Lotus teams, Senna scored several race wins in the mid-1980s and built a reputation as a daring drive who could prevail under difficult conditions. In 1985, at the Estoril, Portugal Grand Prix he won his first race, taking the wet-course championship that had been denied him the previous year, and he won two championships each in 1986 and 1987. Constantly pushing his teams of mechanics to deliver greater speed, Senna was frustrated by inadequate equipment. Nevertheless, he was one of the top drivers in the world, and was still clearly on the way up. In 1988, Senna jumped to the McLaren team, which made him Prost's teammate.

At first their relationship was cordial, but it soon developed into a fierce rivalry—one that probably honed the skills of both drivers and inaugurated the most successful period of Senna's career. At the Monaco race in 1988 he was denied victory once again by a crash after leading the race by two seconds. "[S]uddenly I realised I was no longer driving the car consciously, I was driving it by a kind of instinct, only I was in a different dimension. ... I was way over the limit but still able to find even more," he was quoted as saying by Jeremy Calkins in the *Daily Telegraph.* But he won six of his next eight races on his way to an eventual eight wins and his first world championship.

In 1989 and 1990, Senna and Prost traded places at the top of the Formula One world, with Prost winning the championship in 1989 after a controversial crash in Suzuka, Japan, in which officials once again played a role in denying Senna the win; in 1990, at the same race, Senna, now a member of the Ferrari team, forced Prost off the track on his way to six victories and a second championship. In 1991, he won seven races and a third world championship.

Motivated by Religious Belief

Prost, among other drivers, complained about Senna's aggressive style; Prost was quoted as saying by the British Broadcasting Company that "Ayrton has a small problem. He thinks he can't kill himself, because he believes in God, and I think that's very dangerous." Senna actually spoke often of his own mortality, but he agreed that religion had been a major motivator in his success. "There is no end to the knowledge you can get or the understanding or the peace by going deeper and deeper. I pray regularly, not because it is a habit but because it has innovated my life. I hardly go to church because the only time I feel really good in a church is when there's nobody there," he was quoted as saying by ESPN.

For the last few years of his life, Senna was hampered by inadequate vehicles but won several races each year and still remained in the top handful of Formula One drivers in the world. His earnings during this period were estimated at $10 milllion a year, large amounts of which he shared with charitable enterprises. In 1993 alone he spent $5 million on the Senninha Brazilian educational project. Senna flew his own plane between races. In 1994, signing with the Williams team, he seemed poised to reach the top spot once again—especially since Prost, now again his teammate at Williams, promptly retired.

But on May 1, 1994, in his third race of the 1994 season, the San Marino Grand Prix at Imola, Italy, his car veered to the right at a corner and hit a concrete wall at a speed of more than 190 miles per hour. He died almost instantly, but the exact cause of death remained a matter of debate, for several other drivers had walked away from crashes at the same corner. His car's designers were tried for manslaughter, based on their inadequate design of the car's steering column; one was eventually convicted but remained free due to the expiration of the statute of limitations. Senna's funeral in São Paulo was attended by a million mourners in person, and many more watched on television. In the words of his teammate Michael Andretti, as quoted by Joseph Siano in *The New York Times,* Senna "might have been the greatest driver of all time."

Books

Contemporary Hispanic Biography, Gale, 2003.

Hilton, Christopher, *Ayrton Senna: The Whole Story,* Haynes, 2004.

Rubython, Tom, *The Life of Senna,* Business F1, 2005.

Periodicals

Daily Telegraph (London, England), May 21, 2011.

New York Times, May 2, 1994.

Sunday Age (Melbourne, Australia), March 10, 1996.

Times (London, England), May 2, 1994.

Online

"Ayrton Senna," *ESPN F1,* http://en.espnf1.com/f1/motorsport/driver/1095.html (October 22, 2013).

"Ayrton Senna," *F1: Formula One, Hall of Fame,* http://www.formula1.com/teams_and_drivers/hall_of_fame/45/ (October 22, 2013).

"Ayrton Senna: In His Own Words," *ESPN UK,* http://www.espn.co.uk/espn/sport/story/13315.html# (October 22, 2013).

"Ayrton Senna: Tragic Hero," *History and Legends of Grand Prix Racing,* http://www.f1-grandprixhistory.net/Senna.html#Introduction (October 22, 2013).

"Formula 1's greatest drivers. Number 1: Ayrton Senna," *BBC Sport Formula 1,* http://www.bbc.co.uk/sport/0/formula1/20324109 (October 22, 2013).□

Jagjit Singh

The Indian vocalist Jagjit Singh (1941–2011) was widely known in India, and throughout the Indian diaspora, as the King of Ghazals. The ghazal is an ancient poetic and musical form, dating back to Arabic and Persian sources more than 1,000 years old.

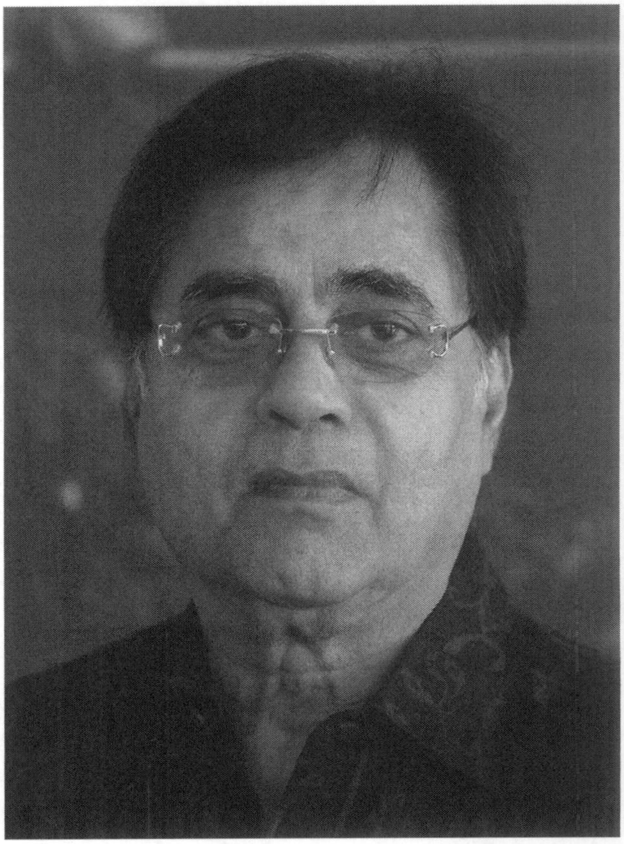

AP Photo/Ajit Solanki

The texts of the ghazal focus on the pain of love, and the sadness of separation and loss. In the music of the Indian subcontinent, the ghazal was allied with Indian classical music; it was an ancient form best appreciated by musical connoisseurs. Singh changed that situation. In the words of the *Times* of London, "Singh had a skill for transforming the traditional, and often elite, ghazal into a form of music that cut across class barriers." He simplified the ghazal, sang ghazals in multiple Indian languages, and enriched the ghazal tradition with the use of Western instruments. Singh spread the ghazal's popularity in Hindu India; before him it had been a predominantly Pakistani and Muslim form, although its texts are not religious. Above all these factors was Singh's remarkable and instantly recognizable voice. "Very few people are blessed with the *kharaj* (bass) he had in his voice," Sufi vocalist Hans Raj Hans was quoted as saying in the New Delhi magazine *Tehelka.* "He had so much depth in his voice, as if the voices of 50 people were in one man."

Name Changed on Guru's Advice

Singh was born Jogmohan Singh on February 8, 1941, in Sri Ganganagar, a city in the Rajasthan region of British-occupied India. His father, a government public works employee, renamed him Jogmohan Jagjit after he was advised to do so by a local holy man in the family's Sikh religion. Singh had four sisters and two brothers. The elder Singh hoped that his son would follow him into government service. But after Singh's unusual talent won notice from his family, his father enrolled him for lessons in Indian classical music with a blind instructor, Pandit Chhaganalal Sharma. He later studied for six years with a renowned teacher Ustad Jamal Khan, and became familiar with major Indian classical genres. He also had the opportunity to hone his vocal skills singing in Sikh religious services, which emphasized a musical component.

In an interview with Sonira Gulhati of *The Hindu,* Singh would stress the importance of classical training. "The strong base in classical music is very essential for success in music," The artistes who get into music without formal classical training may do well for a while, but after that they fade away. To survive in the industry today, it is important to have a good grounding. It gives one a broader base and trains the voice thoroughly." He continued to experiment with music during his college education at a government training school in Sri Ganganagar and then at D.A.V. College in Jalandhar, where he switched his major to arts. As a student he performed in All India Radio and appeared in college stage shows.

"I knew I had to be a singer," he was quoted as saying by Asjad Nazir of the London *Guardian.* "Although my father helped me train in my childhood, he wanted me to be an engineer. I soon realized that I would never understand science." Singh managed to delay his choice of career for a few years by enrolling in graduate school, earning a degree in history from Kurukshetra University. In March of 1965, however, he decided to move alone to Bombay (now Mumbai), hoping to find work in the city's film industry, known as Bollywood. At this time, he cut off the long hair and removed the turban that were required by his Sikh faith.

Lived in Cheap Hostel

Quickly exhausting his minimal savings, Singh checked into a hostel where his room was infested with bedbugs and with rats that chewed on his toes as he tried to sleep. A bright spot came as he met singer Chitra Dutta, who at the time was married to someone else. The pair married in 1969 and had a son, Vivek, in 1971. They later had a daughter, Monica. By that time Singh was making a living singing advertising jingles and performing at weddings and other gatherings. He recorded a four-track EP for the record company HMV, which had noted that several Pakistani ghazal singers had begun to accumulate fans in India despite the fact that the two countries were perpetually close to a state of war.

The stars aligned for Singh in 1976, when he and Chitra, now known as Chitra Singh, recorded a full-length album (Singh's first), called *The Unforgettables.* The album remained a strong seller in India decades later. It included ten ghazals set to music by Singh himself, often simple enough to be suitable for audience singalongs. He and Chitra each took solo selections, and they sang two duets at the end. Although Singh's style took some criticism from performers in the pure ghazal tradition, Singh and his wife became stars almost overnight. One selection, "Baat Niklegi," was an especially big hit.

The Unforgettables exemplified Singh's style, which updated the ghazal for modern Indian audiences. His settings included Western instruments such as guitars and saxophones along with the traditional sarangi, a small bowed stringed instrument, and tabla drum. Singh paid little attention to traditional performers who criticized his style, saying (according to the London *Daily Telegraph*) that "tradition is a fake word, used by people as an excuse to avoid progress. Maybe, 50 years from now, what I've done will be tradition." Indeed, as Singh's style was supplanted by contemporary Indian dance genres, his ghazals would come to be regarded as classics.

Singh and Chitra followed up *The Unforgettables* with a live album, *Come Alive* (1979). Their popularity quickly spread to Indians in Britain, where they recorded two more live albums, *Live in Concert at the Wembley* (1980) and *Live in Royal Albert Hall* (1983), both of them recorded at massive British venues (Wembley Stadium had a capacity of more than 80,000). Both in duets with his wife and solo, Singh was extraordinarily prolific through the 1980s and 1990s, recording dozens of albums, including the hits *Ecstasies, A Sound Affair,* and *Passions.*

Shaken by Son's Death

By 1990, Singh and his wife were among the most popular artists in India. At the height of their fame they were afflicted by tremendous personal tragedy: their son, Vivek, was killed in an auto accident. Chitra gave up singing permanently. Singh, however, continued to perform. The nature of his repertory changed somewhat: he began to perform Sikh religious music and Hindu devotional songs known as bhajans. The ghazals at the core of his performances took on new meaning as their lyrics of loss and melancholy came to reflect Singh's own suffering. His productivity and popularity increased as he poured his emotions into his music, telling *The Hindu* that "I used my music to get over the grief I was going through. During my tour in the U.S., which was immediately after that, it was exceptionally hard to deal with the tragedy. Constantly being at my music helped me deal with the tragedy. Music is very therapeutic."

Although he sometimes had doubts about their lightweight emotional content and demanded veto power over the songs he was asked to sing, films were at the center of Indian popular music, and Singh contributed music to more than 50 of them. His ghazal compositions for the films *Prem Gheet* (1981) and *Arth* (1982) "added a classic touch to the soundtrack," in the words of Shlpa Bharatan Iyer of *Variety.* Singh continued to perform and record frequently in his later years, by which time he was regarded as something of a national treasure. In 2007 he performed before India's parliament, singing a ghazal composed by the Moghul emperor Bahadur Shah Zafar (1775–1862) in commemoration of the 150th anniversary of the unsuccessful Indian Rebellion of 1857 against Britain, known in India as the First War of Independence. In 2011, he performed at Britain's House of Commons.

Singh was awarded the Padma Bhushan, a major civilian award conferred by India's president, in 2003. His daughter, Monica, committed suicide in 2009. In 2011, Singh suffered a stroke and died after more than two weeks in a Mumbai hospital on October 10. Among the many tributes flowing in to Indian publications after his death was one quoted by Kanchan Srivastava in *DNA,* from Indian income tax commissioner Paramjeet Singh: "God, you called Steve Jobs because you wanted an iPod, and now you want ghazals in it!" In 2013 Singh's birthday was marked with a doodle by Google India, showing Singh sitting with a harmonium, a small keyboard instrument.

Periodicals

Daily Telegraph (London, England), October 12, 2011.

DNA (*Daily News & Analysis*), October 11, 2011.

Economic Times (India), October 12, 2011.

Guardian (London, England), October 26, 2011.

Independent (London, England), October 13, 2011.

New York Times, October 11, 2011.

Right Vision News, October 12, 2011.

Tehelka (New Delhi, India), October 22, 2011.

Times (London, England), November 11, 2011.

Times of India, December 19, 2009.

Variety, October 12, 2011.

Online

"Google Celebrates Jagjit Singh's Birthday with a Doodle," *Business Standard* (India), February 8, 2013, http://www.business-standard.com/ (October 27, 2013)

"Music is Therapeutic" [Interview with Jagjit Singh], *The Hindu,* http://www.hindu.com/thehindu/mp/2002/05/20/stories/2002052000720200.htm (October 18, 2013).□

Curt Siodmak

The German-born American screenwriter and novelist Curt Siodmak (1902–2000) set several key patterns in the American film genres of science fiction, fantasy, and horror.

In the words of the *International Directory of Films and Filmmakers,* Siodmak "described himself as an idea man, and he has certainly come up with ideas on which he and others have rung variations, time and time again." The themes of Siodmak's films of the 1940s and 1950s—werewolf lore, the manipulation of the brain by a mad scientist, and fears of radioactivity, to name a few—seem familiar today, and it is easy to forget that many of them originated in Siodmak's prolific and fertile mind, working from a deep foundation of historical German lore. Siodmak was the author of several popular horror novels, which served as inspiration for his own films and those of others. Many of his films, particularly those for which he served as director in the later part of his career, were considered B movies (low-budget genre films with minimal production values) when they were made, but their influence has vastly outrun their prestige.

AP Photo/Jockel Finck

Published Story in Children's Magazine

Kurt Siodmak (he anglicized his first name to Curt upon emigrating to the United States) was born in Dresden, Germany, on August 10, 1902. He was the brother of director Robert Siodmak. "We never had a 'real' family which would supply the love children thrive on," Kurt recalled in an interview with Dennis Fischer reproduced on the website *Notes on Cinematograph.* "My parents' marriage wasn't a happy one, and though we were brought up in our early life with governesses in an affluent surrounding, we were rebels and left the family at a very early age." Siodmak began writing at age eight and had a story published in a children's magazine the following year.

Robert Siodmak began training as an actor early, but Kurt had a more varied early life that included factory work and a stint as a steam engine driver for a German railroad. He attended several schools before earning a doctoral degree in mathematics from the University of Zurich in Switzerland. After that, Siodmak landed a job as a reporter for a Berlin newspaper. One of his assignments in 1926 took him to the set of the pioneering silent German science fiction film *Metropolis.* The day was eventful in several respects: Siodmak landed a part in the film as an extra and became fascinated by the world of cinema. Another extra was Henrietta de Perrot, who became Siodmak's wife and survived him.

Soon Siodmak was working regularly on screenplays in the German filmmaking center of Babelsberg, near Berlin. He contributed to the classic 1929 film *Menschen am Sonntag* (People on Sunday), which, he observed, helped spawn the careers of no fewer than six filmmakers who later became successful beyond Germany: his brother Robert, Billy Wilder (who was born in Austria), Edgar G. Ulmer, Eugene Shuftan, Fred Zinneman, and Siodmak himself. Siodmak worked with his brother on the 1931 film *Der Mann, der seinen Mörder sucht* (The Man Who Searches for His Murderer), but otherwise the two brothers rarely collaborated. In 1932 Siodmak, who was Jewish, heard a speech by Adolf Hitler's associate Joseph Goebbels and correctly estimated the dangers to come. He left Germany for France and then England, where he made a modest living writing screenplays in his second and third languages.

In 1937 Siodmak decided to follow the exodus of creative German Jews who were landing in Hollywood and finding work in the rapidly growing U.S. film industry. He landed a contract for the screenplay to *Her Jungle Love* (1938), a vehicle, in color, for actress Dorothy Lamour, but he endured several slow years during which one of his screenplays was rejected by the messenger boy who had picked it up from his apartment, who had in the meantime become a reader for the MCA studio. In 1940, however, Siodmak was hired to write the screenplay for *The Invisible Man Returns,* the debut film of legendary horror actor Vincent Price. The film was a success, and Siodmak found himself in demand for horror film scripts.

Included Poem in Film

At times he felt stereotyped as a writer, but horror stories came easily to him. "I wrote many horror films," he told

Fischer. "The fantastic and macabre is a German trait. Look at their fairy tales, which are pretty gruesome. We refugees suffer from the past, the Hitler persecution, which we will never be able to absorb completely. We were often so close to death that we are branded for life. No success could wipe out the past which we went through." One of Siodmak's greatest successes came early in his career with *The Wolf Man* (1941), an elegant reworking of German werewolf lore that more than one writer has compared to a Greek tragedy. The film, which starred Lon Chaney Jr., contains a familiar poem: "Even a man who's pure in heart / And says his prayers at night / May become a wolf when the wolfbane blooms / And the autumn moon is bright." Its influence on werewolf films down to the present day has been fundamental.

For Siodmak, *The Wolf Man* also drew on his own experiences. "I am the Wolf Man," he said in a Writers Guild of America interview quoted by Douglas Martin in the *New York Times.* 'I was forced into a fate I didn't want: to be a Jew in Germany. I would not have chosen that as my fate. The swastika represents the moon. When the moon comes up, the man doesn't want to murder, but he knows he cannot escape it, the Wolf Man destiny." The World War II period was a creatively fertile one for Siodmak, who wrote 23 films during the war, including nine in 1943 alone. He also penned the classic horror novel *Donovan's Brain* (1942).

That novel tells the story of a brain researcher whose consciousness is taken over by a brain that he saves after an auto accident. It was filmed three times, as *The Lady and the Monster* (1944), *Donovan's Brain* (1953), and *The Brain* (1963), with the screenplays for the first two being written by Siodmak himself. The tale was also adapted for radio by actor and writer Orson Welles. Siodmak wrote other influential films during the 1940s, including *I Walked with a Zombie* (1943) and *The Beast with Five Fingers* (1946).

Wrote Scripts Rapidly

In the 1950s, Siodmak wrote a number of science fiction films that often treated a fantastic premise in a straightforwardly melodramatic matter. His sheer speed as a writer sometimes worked against the consistency of his films. A producer Siodmak knew, he told Fischer, would say, "'Give it [a film project] to Siodmak; we'll get the script and we can shoot it in a few weeks.' That was my reputation." One of Siodmak's best films in the science fiction genre was *The Magnetic Monster* (1953), which involved a radioactive isotope that increases in size every 11 hours. The film inventively incorporated footage from a lost German film of 1934, *Gold.*

The Magnetic Monster was the second of seven films Siodmak directed, after *Bride of the Gorilla* (1951), an unsuccessful film whose problems Siodmak blamed partly on studio tampering. With the exception of *The Magnetic Monster,* the films Siodmak directed, including *Curucu, Beast of the Amazon* (1956) and *Love Slaves of the Amazon* (1957), have not been well-regarded critically. In the 1960s he returned to Europe to direct the German-language sex comedy *Liebesspiel im Schnee* (Love Play in the Snow).

In later life Siodmak wrote several more novels, including *Hauser's Memory* (1968), a sequel to *Donovan's Brain;* most of them were in a science fiction vein. Though he spoke eloquently about the poor financial treatment given to screenwriters in Hollywood, he was eventually able to afford a ranch in Three Rivers, in California's Central Valley. According to Richard Chatten in the London *Independent,* he said, "Every night I say, 'Heil Hitler,' because, without the son of a bitch, I wouldn't be in Three Rivers, California. I'd still be in Berlin." Siodmak wrote an autobiography, *Even a Man Who Is Pure in Heart. . .,* which appeared in 1997, and at the time of his death at age 98, in Three Rivers on September 2, 2000, he was at work on a sequel to *Metropolis.*

Books

International Dictionary of Films and Filmmakers, Gale, 2000.

McGilligan, Pat, *Backstory 2: Interviews with Screenwriters of the 1940s and 1950s,* University of California, 1997.

Periodicals

Independent (London, England), September 12, 2000.

New York Times, November 19, 2000.

Variety, September 18, 2000.

Online

"Cinema's Exiles: From Hitler to Hollywood," *Public Broadcasting System,* http://www.pbs.org/wnet/cinemasexiles/biographies/the-writers/biography-curt-siodmak/117/ (October 18, 2013).

"I'm a Poor Writer: Curt Siodmak on Siodmaks," *Notes on Cinematograph,* http://notesoncinematograph.blogspot.com/ (October 18, 2013).□

Robert Siodmak

A master of the black-and-white film noir crime thriller, German-born moviemaker Robert Siodmak (1900–1973) made his mark in the United States during the 1940s with dark, suspenseful, atmospheric dramas like *Phantom Lady* (1944), *The Killers* (1946), and *Criss Cross* (1948). Despite his contributions to the industry's film noir opus, Siodmak lacked the enduring name recognition enjoyed by his Hollywood counterparts.

Senses of Cinema writer Chris Justice acknowledged that Siodmak's career "is one of the more underrated and misunderstood in the history of Hollywood." Justice noted that while cinephiles consider Siodmak "the primary architect" of the film noir genre, others dismiss the magnitude of his contributions to the film industry because he never broke through in another genre.

Album/Newscom

Began Film Career in Germany

Robert Siodmak was born August 8, 1900, in Dresden, Germany, to Rosa and Ignatz Siodmak. His parents were Jewish. Siodmak's father grew up in Podgorze, a poor, Jewish settlement in Krakow, Poland. At 16, Ignatz Siodmak stole some money and sailed to the United States, hoping for a better life. Ultimately, he returned to Europe, settled in Germany, married and became a banker. Despite being born in Germany, Siodmak was not given German citizenship because nationality in Europe at that time was determined by the principle of jus sanguinis (right of blood), meaning Siodmak acquired the nationality of his parents. This lack of a definitive citizenship would come to haunt him later.

Siodmak attended the University of Marburg and dabbled with acting, joining local theater productions. Later, he joined his father in the banking profession but was forced to switch careers after rising inflation crippled the banking industry in the run-up to the Great Depression. In the mid-1920s, Siodmak secured a job in Berlin at Universum Film A.G. (UFA), writing the intertitles used to narrate imported silent films. By 1927, he had graduated to film cutter.

In 1929, Siodmak used his industry connections to persuade noted film producer Seymour Nebenzal to finance *Menschen am Sonntag (People on Sunday),* a neo-realistic silent film based on a screenplay co-written by his brother Curt Siodmak and Billy Wilder, an Austrian-born Jew who went on to win a handful of Academy Awards after immigrating to the United States. Robert Siodmak directed the film. Released in 1930, *People on Sunday* followed the lives of five city-dwellers over the course of a single weekend. The movie blurred the lines between fiction and reality. It was part documentary, with the actors loosely "playing" themselves in long, improvisational takes shot outdoors over a series of weekends. According to Bruce Bennett of *Humanities,* film historian Philip Kemp called *People on Sunday* "fresh, light hearted, and remarkably forward looking, deftly anticipating several future revolutions in movie making technique."

After the film's release, Siodmak received a contract with UFA and entered into the first major phase of his film career, coming of age during Germany's expressionist period. During this time German directors experimented with techniques like asymmetrical camera angles and atmospheric lighting to create stark contrasts between the light and the darkness. Siodmak directed several movies while living in Berlin and gained notice for 1931's *Der Mann, der seinen Mörder Sucht* (Looking for his Murderer), a film about a cowardly, suicidal guy who hires a hit man to end his life. After learning his contract has been sold, the man has second thoughts and seeks his would-be killer.

Siodmak hit his stride with 1931's *Voruntersuchung* (The Investigation). In this thriller, Siodmak relied on unusual camera angles, unconventional sounds and atmospheric lighting to convey the emotions. He employed forensics to tell the story, featuring street signs, addresses and name plates prominently in the cinematography to help the viewer unravel the mystery. Siodmak followed with *Stürme der Leidenschaft* (Storms of Passion) in 1932. This thriller followed a gangster wanted by police for murdering the man who seduced his unfaithful girlfriend. As with *People on Sunday,* this film utilized an observational approach, giving it an air of documentary, though the storyline was fictional.

Fled to France

Siodmak fled Germany in 1933 after Adolf Hitler became chancellor. He ended up in Paris and, lacking nationality papers, was marooned there as a stateless refugee because he could not get a passport to leave. The next few years marked one of the roughest periods of Siodmak's life, according to *Exiles Traveling* editor Johannes F. Evelein. "I had no passport, and my wife only had a German one that could be declared invalid at any moment," Siodmak wrote in his autobiography, according to a translation by Evelein. "My stay [in France] was only tolerated. No work permit. I can't even count the number of days that we spent in the courthouse. Hundreds and hundreds of us sat on wooden benches, people of all nations who, like me, didn't know if our residence permits would be extended. If they were denied, there was nowhere for us to go." Frequently behind on rent, he begged producers for work.

Unlike other exiled filmmakers who had taken up residency in Paris, Siodmak had experience with the French film industry. Previously, he had worked on two French-German productions—*Autour d'une enquête* and

Tumultes—which were French adaptations of *Voruntersuchung* and *Stürme der Leidenschaft.* Because of his reputation in Europe, Siodmak was able to secure some work. In 1933, Siodmak directed his first French feature, *Le Sexe Faible* (The Weaker Sex). He made about eight films while in France, his last being 1939's *Pièges* (Personal Column), a brooding, fast-paced thriller about a serial killer.

Moved to Hollywood

In 1939, Siodmak obtained a U.S. passport by lying about his birthplace. Siodmak claimed he had been born in Memphis, Tennessee, while his parents were on a trip, thus making him a U.S. citizen. That is why some biographies on Siodmak list the United States as his birthplace. In August 1939, Siodmak left Paris just as France was mobilizing for war. After arriving in the United States, Siodmak headed for Hollywood. He landed a contract with Paramount in 1941 but had to accept low-budget assignments because he had yet to establish himself in the United States.

Siodmak's first Hollywood film, *West Point Widow,* was released in 1941. Siodmak was less than happy with the final product and struggled during production to get along with the assistant director who chastised Siodmak for his German accent, telling him that if he wanted to work in the United States, he needed to learn proper English. Later in his career, Siodmak was known for showing up on the set in a blue blazer emblazoned with his name spelled phonetically on the back—SEE-ODD-MACK.

In 1943, Siodmak received a break when he reunited with his brother for *Son of Dracula.* Curt Siodmak had immigrated to Hollywood in 1937 and earned a reputation as a horror screenwriter. Curt Siodmak wrote the screenplay for the *Dracula* film and persuaded Universal to hire his brother as director. It was with this film that Siodmak's unique style began to emerge. In *Son of Dracula* Siodmak created a high-contrast world using fog machines and white makeup to offer a visual flair.

Mastered Film Noir Style

Siodmak hit his mark with the 1944 atmospheric thriller *Phantom Lady,* in which Siodmak demonstrated his mastery of the film noir style. *Phantom Lady* told the tale of a husband who fights with his wife on the night of their anniversary. Angry, the man leaves the house, picks up a woman at a bar and takes her to a show. He returns home to find the police there investigating his wife's murder. Unable to find the "phantom lady" who can provide an alibi, he is sentenced to death, but his faithful secretary vows to set him free.

In this creepy whodunit, Siodmak relied heavily on Foley effects to set the mood. "Foley" effects (an innovation of Universal sound engineer Jack Donovan Foley) involve adding ambient sounds post-production—sounds like footsteps, drapes rustling in a breeze, glass breaking, and so forth. In addition, Siodmak enhanced the atmospheric mood by filming the actors in darkness, then placing them in pools of light, thus demonstrating his mastery of low-key lighting. The densely shadowed world Siodmak created in the film was meant to mimic the deeply nightmarish mess the main character finds himself in. One of the film's most memorable scenes involved a crazed drum solo at a jazz club, which served as a metaphor for sexual climax. When the film was screened in Baltimore in 1998, *Sun* film critic Ann Hornaday called it a film noir classic and wrote that *Phantom Lady* "shimmers with velvety black and white photography . . . evocative sexual subtext and glamour that characterizes the best of the genre."

Siodmak followed with the bleak *Christmas Holiday* in 1944, which starred Gene Kelly and Deanna Durbin. In 1945, Siodmak made a film about a serial killer called *The Spiral Staircase.* In *Staircase,* Siodmak relied on crazy visuals to mimic the killer's warped point of view. Two of Siodmak's best-known film noirs were released in 1946—*The Killers* and *The Dark Mirror.* Both were box office hits for Universal and exemplified a moody intensity that recalled its foundations in German expressionism.

The Killers opened with a long, single-take heist scene during which Siodmak relied heavily on tracking and high-angle shots. The scene was filmed by a crane-mounted camera, thus making viewers feel detached from the drama. In making the film, Siodmak fully exploited the possibilities of chiaroscuro lighting, showing a stark contrast between the light and dark. In his film noir treatise *Out of the Shadows,* author Gene D. Phillips raved about the film. "In keeping with the conventions of film noir, the movie is characterized throughout by an air of grim, unvarnished realism, typified by the payroll robbery sequence. Siodmak photographed the scene with a harsh, newsreel-like quality." The story was mostly told through a series of labyrinthine flashbacks. The film marked Burt Lancaster's debut. Siodmak received an Academy Award nomination for best director.

Siodmak earned praise for the craftsmanship of 1949's *Criss Cross,* which starred Lancaster and included lots of shadow-line lighting. In addition, Siodmak created another dramatic action sequence, this one filmed in a haze of smoke bombs. Siodmak's great run of film noir came to a close with 1951's *Deported.* Siodmak ended his Hollywood career with *The Crimson Pirate* in 1952. During the making of the Technicolor film, Siodmak's growing dissatisfaction with Hollywood came to a head. Lancaster starred in the film but also co-produced. Lancaster's antics, as he vied for control, drove Siodmak over the edge.

Returned to Europe

After making 23 films, Siodmak returned to Europe in 1952. During his dozen years in the United States, Siodmak struggled to assimilate his directing style to match the Hollywood studio machine. Siodmak lamented that in Hollywood, producers had too much control over the casting, script and editing. According to *Exiles Traveling,* Siodmak complained about the Hollywood studios in a letter to his brother, Werner, writing, "Here, a good director is someone who makes money for the company. I long for the old days when I could make the kind of films that I wanted to make. . . . I have worked in Germany and France—and successfully—but I have to say that the path to success was never as difficult as it was here in Hollywood."

After leaving Hollywood, Siodmak settled in Ascona, Switzerland, an artists community on Lake Maggiore. He continued to make films through the 1950s and '60s. Noteworthy films from this era included *Die Ratten* (The Rats) (1955) and *Nachts, Wenn der Teufel Kam* (The Devil Strikes Again) (1957). The latter was an anti-Nazi crime film and earned an Academy Award nomination for best foreign language film. Siodmak directed his last film, a two-part sandal-and-sword flick titled *Kampf um Rom* (The Last Roman) in 1968. Siodmak died on March 10, 1973, in Switzerland.

Perhaps Siodmak remains a fringe figure in the collective film consciousness because he, himself, was humble about his accomplishments. As Siodmak noted in Richard Koszarski's book *Hollywood Directors 1941-1976,* "Do I like all my pictures? No, there is only five minutes in each of them that I really like. Lastly, what do I promise the audience that comes to see my films? Well, I never promise them a good picture ... only a better one than they expected."

Books

Brook, Vincent, *Driven to Darkness: Jewish Émigré Directors and the Rise of Film Noir,* Rutgers University Press, 2009.

Evelein, Johannes F., ed., *Exiles Traveling: Exploring Displacement, Crossing Boundaries in German Exile Arts and Writings 1933-1945,* Rodopi, 2009.

Koszarski, Richard, *Hollywood Directors 1941-1976,* Oxford University Press, 1977.

Phillips, Gene D., *Out of the Shadows,* Scarecrow Press, 2012.

Periodicals

Humanities, July/August 2008.

New York Times, July 8, 2012.

Online

"He Made His Home on the Dark Side," *Los Angeles Times,* http://articles.latimes.com/2005/jul/03/entertainment/ca-siodmak3 (November 30, 2013).

"Orpheum Screens 'Phantom Lady,'" *Baltimore Sun,* http://articles.baltimoresun.com/1998-07-10/features/1998191084_1_phantom-lady-trailers-for-movies-lauren-bacall (December 1, 2013).

"Robert Siodmak," *Senses of Cinema,* http://sensesofcinema.com/2003/great-directors/siodmak/ (November 30, 2013).□

Osbert Sitwell

British writer Osbert Sitwell (1892–1969) had a long and prolific career that scythed through the better part of the 20th century. The poet and novelist was known for his acerbic wit and central place inside a trio of siblings with an equally prodigious literary output, his sister Edith and their younger brother, Sacheverell. The three Sitwells were skilled self-promoters and briefly reigned over London's cultural scene in the 1920s. Though Sitwell himself authored more than 60 titles, he is best remembered for a five-volume set of autobiography that proved a surprise bestseller in post-World War II Britain.

Francis Osbert Sacheverell Sitwell was born on December 6, 1892, in London, England, as the first-born son of the fourth baron of Renishaw, Sir George Reresby Sitwell. The family's ancestral home was Renishaw Hall in Derbyshire, which dated back to 1625. The Sitwell fortune originally came from the Sheffield-area ironworks they owned that produced the bulk of the world's nails in the 17th century; coal was later discovered beneath family-held lands and generated a fresh source of steady revenue. Sitwell's mother was born Ida Emily Augusta Denison and came from a deeply eccentric and even wealthier clan, the Earls of Londesborough. Lady Ida's maternal ancestry was quite grand, too: her mother was the daughter of the Duke of Beaufort, and the family claimed to be linked, through an illegitimate birth, to the House of Plantagenet whose kings had ruled England until the 1480s.

Education Concluded at Eton

Sitwell's birth followed that of his sister Edith, born in 1887, and preceded that of Sacheverell, born in 1897. Sir George commissioned the American artist John Singer Sargent to paint a family portrait in 1900, which depicts a lush, privileged household. In reality the Sitwell parents' marriage was an unhappy one, and Sitwell clashed often with his father, a brilliant, Oxford-educated polymath and inventor who occupied his time by researching obscure historical topics and tending to his lands. A classic example of the Victorian-era country squire, Sir George showed off his riding boots in the Sargent portrait and famously told his firstborn son that he would never become a leader of men unless he mastered the game of table tennis.

In addition to Renishaw Hall, which Sitwell would also inherit, the family also owned a manor home called Wood End, in Scarborough, a North Yorkshire resort town on the North Sea. In his boyhood he followed tradition and entered Ludgrove, a boys' boarding school, and then went on to Eton College, where he stayed until 1909. When he left the latter at age 17, his future seemed unclear. He showed little academic promise and even scarcer aptitude for sports, which were an integral part of life at schools like Eton. His father pushed him toward a career in the military, but he failed the examination entrance for the Royal Military Academy Sandhurst twice. Family connections eventually secured him a place in the elite Sherwood Rangers Yeomanry, a mounted guard, though Sitwell loathed horses, too. In 1912, he managed to transfer to the London-based Grenadier Guards, and went overseas with his unit when World War I began in 1914. The experience, which he found as equally pointless as team sports and fox-hunting, turned him into a lifelong pacifist.

Caron/Hulton Archive/Getty Images

Sitwell's literary debut came with a collection of poems he wrote with his sister Edith, *Twentieth Century Harlequinade, and Other Poems,* which appeared in 1916. It marked the start of a career in letters for both that would envelope their youngest brother "Sachie," too, who was still at Eton. With it they also hoped to close the chapter of an embarrassing family scandal related to their mother's unfortunate acquaintance with a con artist. Lady Ida had spent lavishly for years and ran up massive bridge-game gambling debts, which she tried to hide from her husband, who spent long stretches of time in Italy. The trickster's scheme ensnared several friends of Ida's, who then filed lawsuits to recover their money. When her husband refused to help her repay the debts, Lady Sitwell was sent to Holloway Prison after a court convicted her of fraud. The 1915 case made headlines across Britain and Sitwell and his siblings felt themselves ostracized from their elite peers because of it.

Enlivened London's Cultural Scene

The Sitwells remade themselves into patrons of the arts and promoters of modern art, surrealist poetry, and avant-garde theater. They wrote plays together, championed the works of up-and-coming writers, composers, and artists, and produced a voluminous amount of copy that included fiction, essays, and criticism. As *Observer* journalist David Cannadine remarked, "'the Sitwells' promoted themselves as a provocative, revolutionary trio, mocking the philistine middle classes and the Victorian old men, and proclaiming the arrival of a new, irreverent generation of bright and belligerent young things."

Shortly after the war, Sitwell and his brother organized an exhibition of modern French art in London, which included works by Pablo Picasso and Henri Matisse. Sachie had gone on to Oxford University, though he did not complete his Balliol College degree, and established himself as an art historian and architecture specialist. Edith was forging ahead with her own career as a writer, and her elder brother was involved in staging one of the Sitwell trio's most talked-about events of the 1920s: a performance of Edith's *Façade* poems at Aeolian Hall in London in June of 1923. Her nonsensical verse was accompanied by a musical score written explicitly for it by their friend William Walton. The composer-protégé conducted musicians as Edith declaimed verse through a special papier-mâché trumpet called a Sengerphone. The spectacle caused a minor sensation that was widely covered by the newspapers of the day.

Sitwell's solo literary output during this decade includes a 1924 short-story collection, *Triple Fugue,* and his debut novel *Before the Bombardment,* which appeared in 1926. The latter's title refers to the pre-World War I life of a quaint seaside village called Newborough and was drawn from Sitwell's youth in Scarborough. He also published some essays, *Discursions on Travel, Art and Life,* and another volume of poems titled *England Reclaimed.* His 1929 novel, *The Man Who Lost Himself,* won modest acclaim for its time-travel, detective-story set-up.

Collected Numerous Enemies

Like his sister Edith, Osbert led a fairly unconventional life: he remained unmarried, though as a future titleholder he was expected to produce an heir. Edith lived with her longtime governess until the other woman's death in 1938. After living with Walton, Sitwell took up with a young man named David Horner in the mid-1920s, and the two lived together in London in a house Sitwell bought at 2 Carlyle Square, the site of many dinner events and parties recounted by other writers. Among the visitors were the novelist Aldous Huxley and American-born poet T. S. Eliot. Future society chronicler and portrait photographer Cecil Beaton was a protégé of the Sitwells during this period and took a classic, oft-reproduced photograph of the trio in profile. It was Sitwell who underwrote the costs of Beaton's first gallery exhibition in 1927, which launched his career.

The year 1927 also marked the end of the three Sitwell siblings last joint effort together, a play that ran for three nights at the Arts Theatre titled *All at Sea: A Social Tragedy in Three Acts for First-Class Passengers Only.* It earned terrible reviews, and from thereafter Sachie pursued his own career and settled down into a more sedate family life. All three, however, remained notorious for engaging in long-running feuds with other creative professionals. Sitwell was particularly skilled at this and his forte was the deliberately scathing, barely concealed fictional portrayal. Occasionally his efforts were returned in kind, which further enraged him. Novelist D.H. Lawrence based part of the hapless Sir Clifford, the husband of *Lady Chatterley's Lover,* on Osbert, and a trio of siblings turn up in a particularly long and biting chapter of *The Apes of God,* a 1930 novel in which Wyndham Lewis satirized much of literary London of the 1920s. Playwright Noël Coward savagely mocked them in a theater sketch titled "The Swiss Family Whittlebot," in particular Edith and her poetry.

One of Sitwell's most infamous works was never meant for publication, but was widely circulated among his circle and wound up being attributed to him when an excerpt was quoted in a magazine called *Cavalcade.* Titled "National Rat Week," the poem dealt with the scandal gripping Britain in late 1936, as the new king, Edward VIII, announced he would abdicate the throne in favor of his brother, the Duke of York, in order to marry a twice-divorced American woman, Wallis Simpson. Sitwell's "Rat Week" derided the circle of dilettantes and acolytes who had abandoned the former Prince of Wales and his paramour when their situation became intractable. In a curious twist, Sitwell was on friendly terms with the Yorks, especially Elizabeth Bowes-Lyon, the future Queen Mother, and was aghast when his name was attached to the piece.

Retired to Italy

Sitwell had traveled extensively since his childhood. His father first took him to Italy in the early 1900s, and in 1909 Sir George purchased Castello Montegufoni in Tuscany, a rundown castle he spent years restoring. Sitwell roamed for many years, and his accounts of exotic locales appeared in several volumes, including *Escape with Me! An Oriental Sketchbook* in 1939. When World War II erupted that same year, his excursions were sharply curtailed. His father died in Locarno, Switzerland, in 1943, and Sitwell became the fifth Baron of Renishaw. He spent the war years writing his epic autobiography, the first of which was titled *Left Hand! Right Hand!* and appeared in 1944. It was followed by four more volumes—*The Scarlet Tree* in 1946, *Great Morning!* a year later, *Laughter in the Next Room* in 1948, and a fifth and final tome, *Noble Essences,* in 1950. The works were surprise bestsellers in Britain in the late 1940s, a time of austerity and nostalgia for a vanished British Empire of the Victorian and Edwardian era. Sitwell's reminiscences were even appreciated by American readers, and he and Edith were invited to give a series of lectures in 1948, which began with a reading of selections from their works in New York City.

In the late 1940s, Sitwell began to suffer from hand tremors, a warning sign of oncoming Parkinson's disease. He and Horner grew apart, and Sitwell also became estranged from Sachie, who had married and produced two sons. Edith died in 1964, and a year later Sitwell moved permanently to Castello Montegufoni, partly in order to avoid the onerous death-duty taxes that would be imposed on his designated heirs. He left Renishaw Hall to Sachie's son, Reresby Sitwell, and died on May 4, 1969, in Montagnana, Italy, at age 76. The family sold Castello Montegufoni a few years later and it became a hotel.

Sitwell's rapier wit had earned him countless enemies among the British literary establishment, and the poetry and fiction he wrote was generally dismissed as vacuous even in his own lifetime. His travel writing and journalism fared much better over time, as did the exhaustive autobiography, which is considered an excellent chronicle of England's descent from a grand imperial world power to a quirky island nation of eccentrics. Sitwell's *Times* of London obituary asserted the volumes "provide lavish entertainment, a social document of singular interest and value, examples of portraiture done with the nicest mingling of affection and witty ruthlessness, a studied record of the growth of artistic sensibility, and an altogether remarkable essay in deliberate, fine writing."

Books

Pearson, John, *Facades: Edith, Osbert, and Sacheverell Sitwell,* Bloomsbury Publishing, 2011.

The Sitwells and the Arts of the 1920s and 1930s, edited by Sarah Bradford and Honor Clerk, National Portrait Gallery, 1994.

Ziegler, Philip, *Osbert Sitwell,* Chatto & Windus, 1998.

Periodicals

Observer (London, England), May 24, 1998.

Times (London, England), May 6, 1969.□

Howard W. Smith

American politician Howard Worth Smith (1883–1976) used his position as chair of the House Rules Committee to hinder or halt civil rights legislation during the mid 20th century.

American politician Howard Worth Smith (1883–1976)—popularly known as "the Judge" from his tenure on the bench in his home state of Virginia—spent more than three decades in the U.S. House of Representatives. An ardent segregationist and fervent anti-communist, Smith used his position as the chair of the House Rules Committee to shape the federal debate on issues such as civil rights, national security, and organized labor; he also actively opposed what he saw as dangerous foreign and radical influence in the United States through the introduction of the Smith Act. Late in his career, Smith helped support the women's rights movement by seeking to protect employment equality for white women. Yet his efforts to block civil rights legislation made him a controversial figure well after his death.

Born February 2, 1883, on a former plantation in Broad Run, Virginia, Smith was the son of farmers William Worth Smith and his wife, the former Lucinda Lewis. Growing up in the Shenandoah Valley, Smith was indoctrinated with the core values of the former Confederacy; he came to believe in the inherent superiority of the white race over others, in the precedence of states' rights over

Thomas D. Mcevoy/Time Life Pictures/Getty Images

federal jurisdiction, and in the threat of the Republican Party to the Southern way of life. Smith's father was frequently absent to attend to farm business, and his mother instilled a love of politics in the Smith children through renting rooms to regional politicians and through visits to the nation's capital, some 40 miles away, for presidential inaugurations and other events.

After graduating from the Bethel Military Academy and the University of Virginia law school, Smith settled in Alexandria. He married Lillian Proctor in 1913, and the couple had two children before her death during the flu epidemic of 1919; Smith later remarried to Ann Corcoran, his children's nanny, in 1923. Yet his primary focus was on his career as a lawyer and in local politics. At that time, the Democratic Party dominated Virginia's political affairs, and Smith fit well with the party organization. He served as a judge in the Alexandria Corporation Court and on the state Circuit Court during the 1920s, retaining by preference the title "Judge Smith" throughout his life.

Gained Election to Congress

In 1930, Smith won election to the U.S. House of Representatives. After several years of Republican dominance, the federal government underwent a decided shift toward Democratic control as the Great Depression gripped the country. As a firm supporter of small government policies, however, the conservative lawmaker often found himself out of step with the dominant liberal wing of the party during the New Deal era. By the late 1930s, Smith was a leader of the coalition of Southern Democrats and Northern Republicans who managed to grind the expansion of federal programs under the New Deal to a halt.

Became Master Obstructionist

During the late 1930s and 1940s, Smith was at the forefront of conservative efforts to block the power of labor unions and radicals. He believed that communists were the driving force behind what he saw as these overly liberal measures, and in 1940, introduced the Alien Registration Act, commonly known as the Smith Act, to lesson foreign radical influence in the United States. At the time, the world was undergoing significant turmoil; fascist governments had seized power in Italy and Spain, and the Nazi government was aggressively undertaking the conquest of Eastern Europe. With Americans increasingly worried that foreigners could create similar situations in the United States, the Smith Act required non-citizens residing in the United States to register with the federal government. It also criminalized calls for violent resistance to the U.S. government. Roosevelt signed the Smith Act into law in 1940.

After World War II, public concern over the perceived communist threat to U.S. democracy reached a fever pitch. Government officials rounded up and prosecuted members of American communist organizations and radical labor groups under the tenets of the Smith Act. In 1951, the U.S. Supreme Court upheld its provisions, although a 1957 decision limited the act's criminalization of anti-government speech to include only that overtly calling for the violent overthrow of the government. The Smith Act remained in force on the whole, however.

In the 1940s, Smith also continued efforts to limit the influence of organized labor. He led a high-profile investigation into the relatively new National Labor Relations Board that influenced later legislation weakening labor protections. During World War II, he co-sponsored the War Labor Disputes, or Smith-Connally, Act to limit the rights of workers to strike in industries that could affect production or transport of war goods. Smith's contribution to the 1947 Taft-Hartley Act, which amended key portions of the 1935 Wagner Act, outlawed the closed shop, or a workplace that required workers to join a union. This act became law over the veto of a fellow Democrat, President Harry S. Truman.

Smith achieved a new level of political influence when he became the chairman of the House Rules Committee in 1955. The Congressman had served on the committee, a powerful body with the responsibility for determining how a measure is debated within the legislature, since the New Deal era. He therefore had a deep understanding of how to use its myriad powers—the Rules Committee can, with the approval of a majority of House members, do virtually anything to a measure under debate including rewriting it substantially—to further his own conservative political ideals.

During his tenure as chair, Smith became known as a master obstructionist. He succeeded in preventing the passage of legislation that increased federal funding for social welfare programs such as Social Security and public housing through the power of the Rules Committee. With less success but at least equal effort he sought to block measures that expanded civil rights to African Americans, one of the main U.S. political issues of the 1950s and 1960s.

As a leader of the Southern "Dixiecrat" movement, Smith spearheaded efforts within the Southern Democrat coalition to affirm states' legal right to segregate residents based on race, effectively deny African Americans the vote, and generally relegate non-white Americans to second-class citizenship. During committee debate on the Civil Rights Act of 1957, Smith explained his reasoning in a statement that summed up the white supremacist ideology of many civil rights opponents. "The Southern people have never accepted the colored race as a race of people who had equal intelligence and education and social attainments as the whole people of the South," he said, according to Henry Waxman in *The Waxman Report: How Congress Really Works.*

As the more liberal wing of the Democratic Party gained ascendancy, however, other party leaders worked to lesson Smith's control of House proceedings. Progressive pressures led Democratic Speaker of the House Sam Rayburn to push through changes to the Rules Committee that dramatically lessened its ability to block legislation. The changes hamstrung Smith and allowed for a flood of measures expanding federal support for social welfare programs and civil rights during the 1960s.

Yet Smith continued to seek ways to block civil rights. In 1964, Smith was an arguably accidental proponent of the women's rights movement when he added language to the 1964 Civil Rights Act that secured equal employment and workplace rights for women. Although Smith maintained in later years that he truly believed in the importance of gender equality, some historians have maintained that Smith's action was primarily intended to make the legislation less palatable to some members of Congress and so encouraged its overall defeat. The law did pass, however, and Smith's additions have been used as a key to promoting equal rights for women at the federal level ever since.

Lost Seat in a Primary Challenge

Smith's long tenure in the U.S. Congress came to an end after the election of 1966. Despite winning 18 consecutive terms as representative and continuing to wield considerable power in the House, he faced his first serious primary challenge since 1938 in the form of Democrat George C. Rawlings, Jr. A Fredericksburg lawyer and state legislator, Rawlings represented the new, growing liberal wing of the Democratic Party in a stark contrast to Smith's more traditional, Dixiecrat views.

Political watchers widely agreed that the 1966 primary was the toughest political battle that Smith had faced in his long career. Virginia's redistricting after the 1960 census and a U.S. Supreme Court decision outlawing the state's poll tax, which had prevented most African Americans from voting, meant that Smith's Eighth District was home to more progressive voters—including more black voters who opposed his anti-civil rights efforts—than ever before. "It is a more rapidly shifting, more affluent population than I have been used to," Smith admitted in an interview with Ben A. Franklin in the *New York Times.* "These are people who have a lot of contact with Government and are very highly educated. They are rated as more liberal."

Indeed, these liberal voters proved to be Smith's undoing. When the primary vote was held in July, Smith lost by a narrow margin of 645 votes out of more than 53,000 cast. In the general election, however, conservative Democrats who might otherwise have supported Smith put their support behind the Republican candidate, Fairfax lawyer William L. Scott. The seat shifted from Democratic to Republican control, and six years later Scott became the first Republican elected to the U.S. Senate from Virginia since the Reconstruction era just after the Civil War. Smith's primary loss, therefore, stands as a an example of the political shift of the "Solid South" from practical one-party Democratic dominance from the 1870s through the 1960s to the nearly as total dominance of the region by the Republican Party by the end of the 20th century.

Out of office, Smith returned to his home in Alexandria, Virginia. He lived out the remainder of his days there, dying from heart failure on October 3, 1976, at the age of 93. By the time of his death, the role of the federal government in protecting civil rights and other domestic affairs had expanded, showing that Smith's obstructionist tactics could hinder but not halt the changes of the era. Writing in the *New York Times* shortly after Smith's primary loss in 1966, Tom Wicker summed up Smith's position in history thus: "as revolutions—nonviolent but irrestible—broke all around him, Howard Smith remained unchanged. He was a man of another age, of older in not more profound values, of a world that had passed into legend."

Yet even two decades after his death, Smith was able to generate controversy on the House floor. In 1995, Republican leaders took control of the U.S. House of Representatives in an apparent wave of conservatism. As part of this shift, the Rules Committee fell to the chairmanship of Republican Representative Gerald B.H. Solomon of New York. One of Solomon's prerogatives was to choose which portraits were displayed in the Rules Committee's hearing room. Despite being of differing parties, Solomon chose to display the portrait of his Democratic predecessor Smith—much to the dismay of Democrats. By that time, party leaders had disowned Smith and his legacy, with former House Speaker Tip O'Neill once declaring Smith "an ultra-conservative who was no more a Democrat than the man in the moon" according to a *New York Times* report by Katharine Q. Seelye.

Democrats, and, later, members of the Democratic Black Caucus were infuriated by the honor given to a long-time opponent of civil rights, and issued demands that the portrait be removed. At first, Solomon refused, pointing to Smith's long tenure in office and stating the House should not ignore its history. The matter ignited a minor political firestorm before Solomon relented.

Books

Waxman, Harry, with Joshua Green, *The Waxman Report: How Congress Really Works,* Hachette, 2009.

Periodicals

New York Times, June 16, 1966; July 25, 1966; October 4, 1976; January 24, 1995.

Online

"Howard W. Smith (1883–1976)," *Encyclopedia Virginia,* http://www.encyclopediavirginia.org/Smith_Howard_Worth_1883-1976 (December 15, 2013).

"Smith, Howard Worth," *American National Biography Online,* http://www.anb.org/articles/07/07-00278.html (December 15, 2013).□

Mamie Smith

Mamie Smith (1883–1946) became the first African American to make a recording in the blues genre with her "Crazy Blues" of 1920. She was one of the first African American women to make recordings of any kind.

Smith's career set the pattern for all the classic blues singers of the 1920s: African American female performers who dressed sumptuously and drew huge crowds to their flamboyant stage shows. Like those of later performers such as Bessie Smith, Mamie Smith's concert tours and recordings served as a training ground for instrumentalists who would go on to make their marks in the world of jazz. The success of "Crazy Blues" was a milestone in the history of the music industry as well, showing the existence of a large market among African Americans for music made by African American performers, and carving out a market segment for what became known as race records. In spite of the breadth of her influence, Smith and her music have not received sustained attention from historians or blues and jazz reissue labels.

Left Home to Perform with Dance Act

Mamie Smith was in her late 30s when she recorded "Crazy Blues," and in general her life up to that point has been sparsely documented. A native of Cincinnati, Ohio, she was born on May 26, 1883. Her name at birth may have been Mamie Robinson. Smith apparently worked in show business for most of her life, leaving home at age ten in order to perform with a white troupe, the Four Dancing Mitchells. Some time after that she signed on with a traveling vaudeville company, the Smart Set, organized by African American vaudeville pioneer Salem Tutt Whitney. With this group Smith seems to have made her way to the emerging black entertainment mecca of New York, where she married a comedian, Sam Gardner, and then a singer, William "Smitty" Smith. She continued to use Smith's surname as a performer but was romantically linked with other men later on.

Smith's breakthrough as a performer began when she met the African American songwriter and entrepreneur Perry Bradford, who heard Smith perform at a nightclub and cast her in a musical called *Maid of Harlem* (or *Maid in Harlem*). The musical included a Bradford composition called "Harlem Blues," which later evolved into "Crazy Blues." Bradford had trouble promoting his blues-like songs among black performers in New York, who hoped to create stage extravaganzas that would rival those of the white theater and had little use for a form that reminded them of rural Southern origins. But Bradford realized the potential market for African American music that was closer to the roots, and he began to shop Smith around to the record companies of the day.

© Pictorial Press Ltd/Alamy

One of his first stops was at the Victor label, where Smith recorded a Bradford composition called "That Thing Called Love" to her own piano accompaniment. The song was turned down for release by Victor, but reportedly copies leaked out to dealers and enjoyed strong sales. That gave Bradford ammunition to continue his quest, and he became known as "Mule" among recording-industry people of the time. He talked his way into an interview with OKeh label director Fred Hager, giving him sheet music of "That Thing Called Love" and another song, "You Can't Keep a Good Man Down."

Recorded for OKeh

Hager, who had received boycott threats warning him against allowing blacks to record, suggested having white vocalist Sophie Tucker cut the songs, but Bradford persisted, telling Hager (as quoted on the *Jas Obrecht Music Archive* site) that "[t]here are fourteen million Negroes in our great country, and they will buy records if recorded by one of their own, because we are the only folks that can sing and interpret hot jazz songs just off the griddle correctly." Hager agreed to record Smith singing "That Thing Called Love" and "You Can't Keep a Good Man Down" on Valentine's Day of 1920. She was accompanied by an all-white band called the Rega Orchestra.

The 78 rpm record was heavily covered in African American media such as the large *Chicago Defender,* which enthused that "you've heard all the famous stars of the white race chirping their stuff on the different makes of phonograph records ... but we have never—up to now—been able to hear one of our own ladies deliver the cannded goods." Bradford reported strong sales for the record in the South, just as he had predicted, and leading blues arranger W.C. Handy recalled long lines at a Chicago record store in his book *Father of the Blues.* The record's sales performance was good enough to erase any further doubts on OKeh's part, and Bradford was able to persuade Hager to bring Smith into the studio again, in advance of an upcoming tour she had booked. "Crazy Blues" was recorded on August 10, 1920, and credited to Mamie Smith and Her Jazz Hounds. This time the backing musicians were black; they were dubbed her Jazz Hounds.

Strictly speaking, "That Thing Called Love" was a popular song following the structural models of white hits of the day, and even "Crazy Blues" was not a true blues but a hybrid of blues and pop elements. Accordingly, Smith has sometimes been classified as a pop rather than as a blues singer. Yet there was no mistaking the emotional authenticity of Smith's singing as she belted out such lines as "I can't sleep at night, / I can't eat a bite, / 'Cause the man I love, / He don't treat me right." "Crazy Blues" was reported to have sold 75,000 copies in a month in Harlem alone, and music trade magazines began to take notice of its success. Bradford noticed that Pullman porters on trains would buy the record in lots and resell copies in remote locations. Obrecht cited reports that it was not uncommon to hear "Crazy Blues" coming out of windows in African American neighborhoods, and Smith's music began to make inroads among musically progressive whites as well.

After a third OKeh recording, "Fare Thee Honey Blues," Smith was booked for a concert in Norfolk, Virginia, at a fee of $2,000, and by the end of 1920, she and her band were earning $400 and up weekly at running New York theater engagements. Smith responded by adding glamor to her image. "Thousands of people who come to hear me ... expect much, and I do not intend that they shall be disappointed," she told the *Washington Post* (according to Obrecht). "I believe my audiences want to see me becomingly gowned, and I have spared not expense of pains ... for I feel that the best is none too good for the public that pays to hear a singer." By 1922 she was earning up to $1,500 a week.

Attracted Young Jazz Player to Band

Smith's glitzy stage look paved the way for a host of female singers through the 1920s, and beyond, for whom a star image was as important as musical considerations. Soon Smith had competition from younger singers on other labels, but through the early 1920s, she was the preeminent singer of the blues. Player piano rolls were made of some of her recordings, and young jazz players who would later become famous, such as saxophonist Coleman Hawkins and cornetist and trumpeter "Bubber" Miley, jockeyed for places in her band. In 1923 Smith faced more serious competition from singers who had absorbed the blues from Southern roots, such as Bessie Smith and Gertrude "Ma" Rainey. Mamie Smith by then was known as the Queen of the Blues, but Bessie Smith was soon dubbed the Empress. Mamie was dropped from OKeh's roster but made several more recordings for the Ajax and Victor labels.

In 1929, Smith experimented with the new medium of sound film, appearing in a short subject called *Jail House Blues.* In the early 1930s, she toured with a jazz revue called Yelping Hounds under bandleader "Fats" Pichon, and with her own Mamie Smith's Struttin' Revue she is said to have toured Europe. She appeared in several full-length films: *Paradise in Harlem* (1939), *Mystery in Swing* (1940), *Murder on Lenox Avenue* (1941), *Sunday Sinners* (1941), and *Because I Love You* (1943).

Although she had earned a reported $100,000 in royalties during the peak of her career, Smith died in poverty. Even the date of her death is uncertain; it has been reported as August 16, September 16, or October 30, 1946. She was buried in an unmarked grave, but in 1964 a group of German fans sent a headstone by ship for a reinterment at Frederick Douglass Memorial Park on New York's Staten Island. Although Smith recorded some three dozen sides that are crucial in tracing the transition from pop to blues among African American vocalists, she has not been especially well served by blues and jazz reissues. Her complete works have appeared on the small Document label, and some of her films are available as Internet downloads.

Books

Harrison, Daphne Duval, *Black Pearls: Blues Queens of the 1920s,* Rutgers, 1988.

Notable Black American Women, Gale, 1992.

Online

"Cincinnati's Own, Mamie Smith," *African American Registry,* http://www.aaregistry.org/historic_events/view/cincinnatis-own-mamie-smith (October 23, 2013).

"Mamie Smith," *AllMusic,* http://www.allmusic.com (October 23, 2013).

"Mamie Smith," *Red Hot Jazz,* http://www.redhotjazz.com/mamie.html (October 23, 2013).

"Mamie Smith: The First Lady of the Blues," *Jas Obrecht Music Archive,* http://jasobrecht.com/mamie-smith-the-first-lady-of-the-blues/ (October 23, 2013).□

Ronnie Spector

American singer and musician Ronnie Spector (born 1943) led one of the most popular girl groups of the 1960s, the Ronettes.

American singer and musician Ronnie Spector became known as the "original rock'n'roll bad girl" as the lead vocalist of the 1960s girl group the Ronettes. Known for songs such as "Be My Baby" and "Baby I Love You," the Ronettes recorded their hits with producer Phil Spector, to whom the singer was married for several tumultuous years before the pair split in a highly acrimonious divorce. Although the singer launched a post-divorce solo career, her offerings failed to excite at the same level of commercial and critical success as her recordings with the Ronettes. Yet she remained a powerfully talented singer who inspired younger artists and continued to command respect from her peers, with the Ronettes gaining a spot in the Rock and Roll Hall of Fame in 2007.

Began Career in New York

A native of the Spanish Harlem neighborhood of New York, New York, Spector was born Veronica Bennett on August 10, 1943. Her white father, Louis, was a subway laborer who dreamed of being a jazz drummer; her African American and Cherokee mother, Beatrice, worked as a waitress and cared for Spector and her sister Estelle. Spector was drawn to music and performing practically from birth, claiming to have sung "Jingle Bells" on a New York subway train at the age of just 16 months. "Even as a baby, I loved having an audience," she admitted in her autobiography, *Be My Baby: How I Survived Mascara, Miniskirts, and Madness or My Life as a Fabulous Ronette.*

Inspired by the youthful rock singer Frankie Lymon, she continued to sing and dance for friends and family, making her proper debut with a group of family members performing at an amateur night at the borough's Apollo Theatre. "I didn't win Amateur Night, mind you," Spector told Gillian G. Gaar in *Goldmine.* "But when they applauded me, that little applause I got made my future. You know how they say if you make it in New York, you can make it anywhere? I say that about the Apollo Theater." The success of this effort spurred the Bennett family to encourage Spector, sister Estelle, and cousin Nedra to pursue their musical dreams.

Before long, the trio had begun picking up some local work singing and dancing at parties, sockhops, and nightclubs under the names Darling Sisters and Ronnie and the Relatives, in time settling on the Ronettes—a combination of elements of all three girls' names. Before long they had a record deal with Colpix, recording a handful of singles including "What's So Sweet About Sweet Sixteen" and "I Want A Boy" that failed to catch fire. But they made regular appearances on a New York rock and roll radio show and developed a reputation as a popular live act.

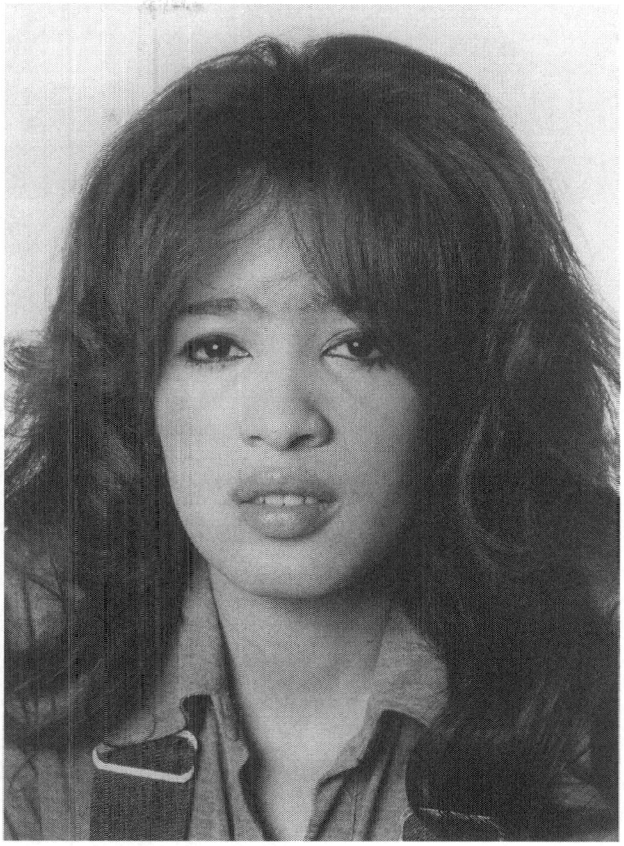

© Pictorial Press Ltd/Alamy

Recorded Popular Singles

By 1963, however, the Ronettes had not had a major breakthrough. Taking a chance, they called producer Phil Spector, already known for hits such as "He's a Rebel" and "Zip-a-Dee-Doo-Dah." The young hit maker agreed to audition the Ronettes, and drawn to Ronnie Spector's distinctive voice, signed them on the spot to his Phillies label. Spector and her group were on their way to major stardom.

The Ronettes' new producer at first put them to work recording backing vocals to provide part of his signature "wall of sound" for other Phillies artists. Soon, however, he recorded what became the Ronettes' breakout hits: "Be My Baby" and "Baby I Love You." After its release in the fall of 1963, "Be My Baby" became a quick radio hit, gaining exposure through Dick Clark's *American Bandstand* television show. The single climbed to number two, achieved platinum-selling status, and made Spector and her backing singers international sensations.

The trio toured England with another new rock act, the Rolling Stones, and befriended members of the Beatles. Known for their signature style of high beehive hairdos, elongated cat-eye eyeliner, and tight skirts, the Ronettes had the appearance of being rock and roll's bad girls even as they traveled with their mothers. Their multiracial heritage—Spector and her sister a mix of white, African American, and Native American, and cousin Nedra a blend of African American and Puerto Rican—made them exotic and unexpected. "Boys wanted to be with them, girls wanted to be like them, and record buyers of both genders devoured their Spector-produced mini-operas," explained a Rock and Roll Hall of Fame online biography of the Ronettes' appeal.

At the same time, Spector developed a romantic relationship with the group's producer. She chose to forego some of the group's scheduled tours—including a domestic slot opening for the Beatles at the height of Beatlemania—allowing another cousin to fill in for her on lead vocals. The producer also seemed to try to distance Spector from her family members, often recording just with the Ronettes' lead vocalist in Los Angeles while the remainder of the trio toured or remained at home in New York. His interest in recording the group also seemed to wane, and by 1965, the Ronettes had lost their command of the charts.

Endured Difficult Marriage

After returning from a tour of U.S. military bases in Germany in 1966, the Ronettes dissolved. "We never made any big plan to split up, but...it just seemed like a natural thing to do," Spector explained in her autobiography. She moved into Phil Spector's Beverly Hills mansion, and in 1968, the couple wed. The marriage proved problematic from its inauguration, however. Spector's husband had been possessive and subject to fits of jealousy throughout their courtship, and marriage did not lesson these tendencies. He was also becoming increasingly reclusive, and made his young wife a virtual prisoner in her own home. Spector later wrote in her autobiography that her husband psychologically, but never physically, abused her, and made her routinely question her worth as a musician, wife, and human being.

In 1968, Spector cut a song written for her by her husband called "You Came, You Saw, You Conquered," but it flopped after its release the following year; another single, the George Harrison-penned "Try Some," suffered the same fate in 1971. The couple adopted a son, Donté, in 1969, and later added a set of adopted twins to the family. But Spector remained depressed, and began drinking to deal with her problems. After beginning to attend Alcoholics Anonymous meetings, she determined that her marriage was no longer tenable. Spector left her husband, and the couple formally divorced in 1974. "I don't think either one of us wanted the divorce, but I had to get a divorce because I would have died there and I knew it, I felt it," she told Ann Kolson of the Philadelphia *Inquirer* years later. "I knew that I loved him, but I loved my career, too."

Freed of her professional and personal relationship with her former producer, Spector tried to capture some of her earlier successes by reforming the Ronettes. Her original backing vocalists declined to participate, however, and Spector performed with two other singers as Ronnie Spector and the Ronettes. But the reformed trio lacked the fire of the 1960s and failed to revive the singer's career. Spector cut backing vocals on tracks for groups such as Bruce Springsteen and the E Street Band and notably with Eddie Money, singing a hook inspired by "Be My Baby" on his 1986 hit "Take Me Home Tonight." Her solo work faltered, however, with albums such as 1980's *Siren* and 1987's *Unfinished Business* barely registering on listeners' consciousnesses.

In 1988, the Ronettes sued Phil Spector for back royalties. The case took nearly 15 years to wend its way through the courts, and eventually ended mostly in the producer's favor. Under the contract that the trio had signed in 1963, the court denied the Ronettes payment for the usage of their performances on screen or in commercials and rejected their claims for industry standard royalties; in total, the three had garnered less than $15,000 total in royalties from their songs over the years. Despite these setbacks, Ronnie Spector actually won a personal victory when the court found that she was entitled to her share of the reduced royalties, a point that her ex-husband contested based on their divorce agreement. Speaking to Robert F. Worth of the *New York Times* upon the court decision in 2002, Spector's lawyer Ira G. Greenberg said, "while we are pleased with the decision on Ronnie's right to royalties, we are obviously disappointed" with the overall outcome.

Continued Performing in Later Years

With these exceptions, Spector spent much of the 1980s and 1990s out of the public eye. In 1983, she remarried to her tour manager, Jonathan Greenfield; the couple had two sons, Austin and Jason. Thrilled with her new and much happier marriage and her role as a mother, Spector dedicated much of her energies to her family.

Yet Spector's own recording history and her longtime ties to legendary producer Phil Spector helped her maintain a certain level of notoriety and influence within the music industry, however. She befriended musician Joey Ramone, and in 1999 released an EP, *She Talks to Rainbows,* that Ramone produced. Never a songwriter, Spector sang tracks penned by others, including the Ramones' "She Talks to Rainbows" and the Beach Boys' "Don't Worry Baby." Although critics embraced the release—Denise Sullivan of AllMusic called it an "extraordinary 'comeback'"—the album, like Spector's earlier solo efforts, was not a commercial success.

In 2006, Spector returned with a new full-length solo album, *The Last of the Rock Stars.* Featuring collaborators including Sune Rose Wager of the Raveonettes, Patti Smith, and garage rockers the Greenhornes. Reviewing the album for the *Guardian,* Betty Clarke compared the singer to a "frayed and muddied Snow White [who] picks up where she left off with the Ronettes... Spector leaves you in no doubt that she is flesh, blood and undiminished spirit."

Spector thrilled at performing well into her 60s, releasing a short Christmas EP, *Ronnie Spector's Best Christmas Ever* in 2010 and recording a tribute version of the Amy Winehouse track "Back to Black" after that artist's death in 2011. The following year, Spector developed a one-woman show called *Behind the Beehive* and appeared on-stage in a special Christmas show, *Ronnie Spector's Best Christmas Party Ever!* "That's the secret," she told Gaar. "You have to have love and passion for what you do.... If you don't have that love and passion for it, you're just going to go out there and not really care. ... I'm still here, and I'm still singing good, and having a ball out there. That's my best fun ever is being on stage. That's the main thing in this business. If you can't have fun with the work you're doing, don't do it."

Books

Spector, Ronnie, with Vince Waldron, *Be My Baby: How I Survived Mascara, Miniskirts, and Madness or My Life as a Fabulous Ronette,* Harmony, 1990.

Periodicals

Goldmine, July 2011.
New York Times, October 18, 2002.
Philadelphia Inquirer, August 1, 1987.

Online

"Ronettes Biography," *Rock & Roll Hall of Fame,* http://rockhall.com/inductees/the-ronettes/bio/ (December 10, 2013).
"She Talks to Rainbows," *AllMusic,* www.allmusic.com/album/she-talks-to-rainbows-uk-mw0000931616 (December 11, 2013).□

Jim Stewart

Charlie Gillett Collection/Redferns/Getty Images

The American music executive and producer Jim Stewart (born 1930) was the co-founder, with his sister Estelle Axton, of the Stax label, the Memphis, Tennessee, recording company that played a key role in popularizing soul music and other African American popular styles.

Stewart's contributions were only rarely musical. He produced some Stax recordings during the label's early days, but his own background was in country music, not in soul, and he left performing and writing to others. Axton, not Stewart, was Stax's primary talent spotter in the label's early years. Yet Stewart's contribution was critical. In the 1960s, a time when Memphis was a hotbed of white resistance to racial integration, Stewart was a bold pioneer, building a fully integrated talent roster and corporate organization. More than one Stax musician recalled the label's heyday as a musical expression of the ideals of the civil rights movement—a connection made explicit in such Stax hits as the Staple Singers' "Respect Yourself" and "I'll Take You There." Stewart's career was a case study in the difficulties faced by small labels as they competed with corporate music giants, but despite this difficulty the label generated 167 hit singles during the years of his leadership from 1958 to 1975. Stewart was inducted into the Rock and Roll Hall of Fame in 2002.

Earned Business Degree

Jim Stewart was born in Middleton, east of Memphis in rural Tennessee, on July 29, 1930. He enjoyed music and was given a guitar by his father when he was ten, later switching to country fiddle and playing in a band called the Canyon Cowboys that imitated the western swing style of Bob Wills & His Texas Playboys. Stewart moved to Memphis after graduating from high school, worked at a Sears store, and continued to play music on the side. He joined the United States Army in the early 1950s and served for two years, then used Servicemen's Readjustment Act (G.I. Bill) money to earn a business degree at Memphis State University. He also took music courses there, and Estelle Axton quipped that he had played the fiddle until he went to college, but then played violin. Stewart graduated from Memphis State in 1956 and took a job in a bank.

Like many other musicians around Memphis, Stewart was fascinated by the success of the homegrown Memphis label Sun Records, which had nurtured the careers of Elvis Presley and several other superstar musicians. After a barber explained the business of music copyrights to Stewart, he began recording music in a garage and soon formed the Satellite label. Turning to Axton for financial help, he set up a studio in the small town of Brunswick, Tennessee, in 1958, after Axton persuaded her husband to remortgage their home. Stewart released a variety of singles, beginning with a country record called "Blue Roses." None had much impact, but a recording by a black vocal group, the Vel-Tones, made a minor splash.

Satellite did not really begin to hit its stride until 1960, when Stewart and Axton, who had joined the label as a partner the previous year, moved its offices to a disused movie theater on East McLemore Avenue on Memphis's south side. They made the move on the suggestion of engineer (and later influential producer and songwriter) Chips Moman, who may have been attracted by the acoustics of the large main theater space. The neighborhood, in the process of changing from predominantly white to predominantly African American, was musically rich, with new arrivals steeped in the church gospel styles of the Mississippi River delta to the south. African American musicians mixed freely with hip young white players such as guitarist Steve Cropper and Axton's saxophonist son Charles, known as Packy. Stewart and Axton opened a record store in the old theater's front vending area, and the shop did double duty as a local talent magnet and music analysis studio: Axton joined with the young musicians who worked there to dissect what worked and what did not in the recordings they sold.

Changed Label Name to Stax

Before long, the scene Stewart and Axton had created began to bear commercial fruit. In 1960, the label had three hits: "Cause I Love You", by the duet of disc jockey Rufus Thomas and his daughter Carla; the rhythm and blues romantic ballad "Gee Whiz," by Carla Thomas alone; and the instrumental "Last Night" by the Mar-Keys, a group that included Cropper and Packy Axton. The company's growing commercial success got attention from a West Coast label also called Satellite, which demanded that Stewart change the name of his own label. Stewart and Axton complied, renaming the label Stax after the first two letters of each of their surnames. More important, the leading rhythm and blues label Atlantic signed a distribution deal with Stewart after hearing the releases by the young Carla Thomas. When Atlantic head Jerry Wexler came to Memphis to meet with Stewart and Stax's multiracial staff, the group had to ride in his hotel's freight elevator to avoid the controversy that would have resulted from their integration of a public facility.

The early and middle 1960s were a period of consistent growth for Stewart's young label. Stewart served as producer for some of the early Stax recordings, but for the most part his contribution was not musical; he oversaw the label's business affairs. Those became increasingly complex as Stax signed such artists as singer Eddie Floyd, the instrumental group Booker T. and the MGs, and most of all vocalist Otis Redding, who came to Stax while working as a driver for another Stax aspirant, Johnny Jenkins. Recording for Stax's new subsidiary Volt, Redding scored such hits as "Pain in My Heart" (1964).

Stewart's most important hire was Washington, D.C., disc jockey Al Bell, who was brought to Stax as national sales director in 1965, and immediately began to influence the label's artistic direction. Bell was African American, but other members of both Stax's roster and its office staff were white, and the racial integration that prevailed at the label's headquarters was rare indeed in rigidly segregated Memphis. The harmonious atmosphere was at least partly the work of Stewart and Axton, who according to both their own testimony and that of black musicians at Stax, were personally unprejudiced.

Stax suffered multiple setbacks in 1967 and 1968 with the deaths of Redding and several other Stax musicians in a plane crash in December of 1967 and the discovery that the distribution deal Stewart had negotiated with Atlantic gave that label ownership of all of Stax's master recordings. When Stax's contract with Atlantic expired, the label was in a poor position to negotiate a new one. Desperate for cash and independence, Stewart sold Stax to the corporate conglomerate Gulf and Western in 1968. The move, along with the assassination of the Rev. Martin Luther King Jr. in the same year, damaged Stax's creative chemistry, and the label's sales declined despite the emergence of new star Isaac Hayes and his *Hot Buttered Soul* album in 1969.

Sold Share in Company

In 1970, Stewart and Bell bought Stax back from Gulf and Western and went on a major talent acquisition spree, signing such artists as the idealistic gospel-tinged family group the Staple Singers, and comedian Richard Pryor, whose early best-seller *That Nigger's Crazy* first appeared on Stax. For several years Stax challenged its Detroit rival Motown at the top of R&B sales charts. Bell signed a new distribution deal with the large Columbia label in 1972 and used his own profits from the deal to buy Stewart out; Stewart stayed on as president. That year, the label organized the Wattstax music festival in Los Angeles, chronicled in a documentary of the same title whose production Stewart assisted.

Once again, Stax's artistic instincts outstripped its business acumen. By 1973, Stax had the fifth-highest revenue among all black-owned American businesses, but much of it was built on borrowed money. The distribution deal with Columbia turned out not to guarantee the agreed-upon payment rates to Stax, and the label faced a variety of other distribution problems at the retail level. Stewart poured much of his personal fortune into trying to keep the label afloat as its financial problems snowballed, but in 1975, the company spiraled toward bankruptcy. A judge ordered Stax dissolved in January of 1976, and the McLemore Street building fell into disrepair. Ownership of the post-Atlantic Stax masters eventually passed into the hands of the San Francisco label Fantasy.

After Stax was shuttered, Stewart remained mostly out of the limelight. He did not emerge even for his induction (with Axton) into the Rock and Roll Hall of Fame in 2002, sending relatives to the induction ceremony. Stewart lived to see the Stax Museum of American Soul Music open in 2003 on the site of the original label headquarters. He has continued to make his home in the Memphis area, and he has given occasional interviews on musical subjects. In the words of the Rock and Roll Hall of Fame website, "The label begun by Jim Stewart back in the late Fifties is finally being recognized as a priceless institution that contributed substantially to America's musical culture."

Books

Bowman, Rob, *Soulsville, U.S.A.: The Story of Stax Records,* Schirmer, 2003.

Gordon, Robert, *Respect Yourself: Stax Records and the Soul Explosion,* Bloomsbury, 2013.

Periodicals

Commercial Appeal (Memphis), March 19, 2002.

Daily Telegraph (London, England), March 4, 2004.

Detroit News, January 4, 2014.

Sunday Age (Melbourne, Australia), December 28, 2008.

Online

"Jim Stewart," *AllMusic,* http://www.allmusic.com (November 12, 2013).

"Jim Stewart & Estelle Axton," *Memphis Music Hall of Fame,* http://memphismusichalloffame.com/inductee/jimstewartestelleaxton/ (November 12, 2013).

"Jim Stewart Biography," *Rock and Roll Hall of Fame,* http://rockhall.com/inductees/jim-stewart/ (November 12, 2013).

"The Stax/Volt Story, by David Edwards and Mike Callahan," *The Stax/Volt Story,* http://www.bsnpubs.com/stax/staxvolt.html (November 12, 2013).□

T

Big Mama Thornton

Willie Mae Thornton (1926–1984) was an American southern blues singer whose enormous size and forceful, shouted vocals earned her the nickname "Big Mama." While she never achieved general commercial success, her musical style and swaggering onstage personality influenced a generation of popular rock and roll musicians, including Elvis Presley and Janis Joplin, who respectively covered her two best-known songs: "Hound Dog" and "Ball and Chain."

In a musical career spanning 40 years, Thornton performed with blues luminaries such as bandleader Johnny Otis and singer Johnny Ace, and she also toured nationally and internationally, performing before adoring crowds at prominent blues festivals. Music critics acclaimed her raw and impassioned singing style, which echoed notable African American blues singers of the 1920s and 1930s such as Bessie Smith, Memphis Minnie, and Ma Rainey. A self-taught drummer and harmonica player who could not read music, Thornton emerged from poverty in the deep South, yet as an African American woman who performed in men's clothing, she was never able to escape the era's broader social constraints and garner mainstream appeal like Elvis or Joplin. After decades of heavy drinking, she died penniless.

Came from Humble Origins

On December 11, 1926, Willie Mae Thornton was born in a rural area outside of Montgomery, Alabama. She was one of seven children born to Mattie and George W. Thornton, a minister. As a child, Willie Mae sang gospel music with her mother in her father's church choir. In 1940, when Willie Mae was 14, her mother died, and Willie Mae was required to help earn money for her family by scrubbing floors in a saloon. Drudgery changed into opportunity when, one night, the saloon's regular blues singer failed to arrive and Willie Mae was asked to sing in her place.

Thornton's musical performing career was set in motion after she won an amateur talent show, where she attracted the attention of Atlanta-based promoter Sammy Green. He invited her to join his Hot Harlem Revue, a vaudeville troupe that toured the South. While performing with the Revue, she honed her singing abilities and also learned how to dance, perform comedy routines, and play harmonica and drums. Her commanding vocals led the revue to bill her as the "new Bessie Smith," and "Bessie Smith's younger sister," referring to the iconic blues singer who also performed as a singer and comedienne in vaudeville tours between 1900 and 1930. While Thornton was undoubtedly influenced by Smith, Thornton preferred to emphasize her own personal efforts to develop her talent. "My singing comes from my experience," she told author Arnold Shaw (as quoted in *Notable Black American Women*). "My own experience. My own thing. I got my feelin's for everything. I never had no one teach me nothin'. I never went to school for music or nothin'. I taught myself to sing and to blow harmonica and even to play drums by watchin' other people. I can't read music but I know what I'm singing. I don't sing like nobody but myself."

Signed Contract in Houston

In 1948, Thornton left the Hot Harlem Revue and settled in Houston. Here she signed a contract to sing exclusively as a nightclub performer for Don Robey, a songwriter, record producer, and founder of the Peacock Records label. Robey

elevated Thornton's musical career to a professional level by helping her to book nightclub performances and record singles. Thornton made her recording debut with a group called The Harlem Stars, and in 1951, she released her first singles, "Partnership Blues" and "I'm All Fed Up." The next year Robey made her a featured singer with Johnny Otis's touring Rhythm & Blues Caravan, which was well known and received among black communities in the U.S.

In addition to earthy, booming vocals that could shake an audience, Thornton possessed a harsh yet charismatic stage presence that included jokes and cross-dressing. One notable performance took place in 1952, at the Apollo Theater in Harlem. Thornton was scheduled as the opening act, but her loud, coarse persona so enthralled the audience that she ended up replacing Little Esther as the headliner the next night. Her appearance at the Apollo not only introduced Thornton to northern crowds, but it earned her the nickname "Big Mama," owing to the magnitude of her voice and size: she was six feet tall and weighed nearly 350 pounds.

In the early 1950s, in addition to touring with the Rhythm and Blues Caravan, Thornton recorded about 30 songs with Robey's Peacock Records. Her most famous single, "Hound Dog," was released in 1953. It found a receptive audience among urban African Americans and went on to reach number one on *Billboard*'s Rhythm and Blues chart and sell over 500,000 copies. Though "Hound Dog" was written by white songwriters Jerry Lieber and Mike Stoller, Thornton made the song her own by adding some of her own lyrics—noted for their overt sexuality—and attitude. Her version of "Hound Dog" is significant because it differed from most of the other popular rhythm and blues songs at the time. These other songs featured prominent saxophone solos and piano flourishes, while the spare instrumentation of "Hound Dog" consisted of backing guitar, bass, and drums. "Hound Dog" was recorded by ten other musicians before Elvis Presley released his 1956 version, which imitated Big Mama's aggressive vocal style. Despite its influence among musicians and popularity among rhythm and blues listeners, "Hound Dog" failed to make Big Mama universally famous or wealthy. She received no royalties for the song, having signed away her rights for $500.

Moved to California

The 1953–1956 period was a busy one for Thornton, who toured with Johnny Ace, Junior Parker, and Clarence "Gatemouth" Brown. Following a 1954 performance at the Apollo Theater, Johnny Ace and Thornton were dubbed the reigning king and queen of blues by one African American–oriented newspaper. The late 1950s and early 1960s, however, saw a decline in blues music's popularity. In 1956, Thornton moved from Houston to the San Francisco Bay area, where she spent the next several years giving infrequent performances at small clubs throughout northern California. Her influence was limited during these years, since she had no recording contract or regular backing band.

With the blues revival of the mid- to late 1960s, Thornton experienced a renewed surge of interest in her music, mostly from young, white followers. In 1965, Thornton was invited to tour Europe with the American Folk Blues Festival, and she signed a recording contract with Arhoolie Records, which released the albums *Big Mama in Europe* (1965) and *Big Mama Thornton with the Chicago Blues Band* (1967). These featured musical appearances by blues legends Muddy Waters and Lightnin' Hopkins. Arhoolie also released Thornton's single "Ball and Chain," which was made popular by the singer-songwriter and Thornton admirer Janis Joplin; she emulated Thornton's gruff vocals and appearance. As with "Hound Dog," Thornton had signed away her rights to the song.

Performed Through Failing Health

Little is known about Thornton's personal life, except that she was a notoriously heavy drinker. Her health began to fail in the 1970s, as decades of drinking whiskey and corn moonshine ravaged her liver. Yet she continued to perform. She had to be helped on stage, where she would sing seated beside a table that held her harmonicas, cigarettes, and alcohol. Cirrhosis chipped away at her weight, shrinking her from a robust 350 pounds to a gaunt 95. In order to hide her skeletal appearance, she wore one of two costumes on the stage: a billowing African robe, or a man's business suit with a straw cowboy hat and boots. Thornton never married or had children.

Throughout the 1970s, she continued to perform at national and international jazz, folk, and blues festivals. Some of her recordings from the decade include *Saved* with Pentagram Records and *The Complete Vanguard Recordings, Sassy Mama, Jail,* and *Big Mama Swings* with the record label Vanguard. She closed out the decade with a passionate performance at the 1979 San Francisco Blues Festival, which gave her an award for her lifetime contributions to the blues.

In 1981 Thornton was seriously injured in a car accident. After recovering, she performed with the veteran blues shouter Big Joe Turner at a cabaret club in Pasadena. During the last few months of her life, she gave no performances, and on July 25, 1984, at age 57, she died of a heart attack in a boarding house in Los Angeles. Her funeral was led by the Reverend Johnny Otis and included spirituals sung by the blues vocalists Jimmy Witherspoon and Margie Evans. Because Thornton died broke, the Southern California Blues Society organized a benefit concert to raise funds to cover her funeral expenses. In 1984, Thornton was inducted into The Blues Foundation's Blues Hall of Fame in recognition of her formidable contributions to American music.

Books

Herzhaft, Gérard, Brigitte Debord, trans., *Encyclopedia of the Blues,* 2nd. ed., The University of Arkansas Press, 1997.

Smith, Jessie C., ed., *Notable Black American Women, Book 2,* Gale, 1996.

Sporke, Michael, *Big Mama Thornton: The Life and Music,* McFarland & Co., 2014.

Periodicals

Living Blues, Summer/Fall 1984.

New York Times, July 28, 1984.

Philadelphia Inquirer, July 28, 1984.

Rolling Stone, September 13, 1984.

Online

"Mama"s Voice: The lasting influence of Willie Mae 'Big Mama' Thornton," *Rock and Roll Hall of Fame and Museum,* http://rockhall.com/(November 26, 2013).

"Thornton, Willie Mae [Big Mama]," *Texas State Historical Association,* http://www.tshaonline.org/handbook/online/articles/fthpg (November 26, 2013). □

István Tisza

The Hungarian political leader Istvn Tisza (1861—1918) served two terms as prime minister of Hungary, before and during World War I. In the words of his biographer Gabor Vermes, he was "one of the Austro-Hungarian Monarchy's most outstanding statesmen."

© DIZ Muenchen GmbH, Sueddeutche Zeitung Photo/Alamy

Tisza was difficult to classify under the large historical categories of liberal and conservative. He saw that power would inevitably pass out of the hands of Hungary's traditional aristocracy, and he was one of the legislative movers behind the country's industrialization. He was a staunch opponent of anti-Semitism. Yet he supported only the gradual expansion of suffrage to all Hungarians, and his basic outlook was religious, and above all nationalistic. That was the key to Tisza's political thinking, which was rooted in the unique position of Hungary within the Austro-Hungarian empire before World War I: Hungary was subordinate to the main center of imperial power in Vienna, Austria, but at the same time was threatened by the variety of Czechs, Slovaks, and south Slavic groups that surrounded it and all had their own national aspirations. A classical economic liberal and a gradual reformer by nature, Tisza prized above all strength and autonomy of the Hungarian nation.

Mastered Complex Card Game as Child

István Tisza (in Hungarian order Tisza István, and in full Count István Tisza de Borosjenö et Szeged, pronounced TEE-sa) was born in Pest, Hungary, soon to become part of the united city of Budapest, on April 22, 1861. He came from an old Hungarian noble family, and his father, Kálmán Tisza, was an important Hungarian politician. So was his uncle, Lajos Tisza, a key supporter of the Austro-Hungarian Compromise of 1867, which established the final form of the Austro-Hungarian state. By the time he was four, Tisza had already mastered the difficult Hungarian card game of taroc. He attended a Calvinist preparatory school in the city of Debrecen, where he fell in love with a cousin, Ilona Tisza. The two married in 1883, and had a son and a daughter; the daughter died from diphtheria in infancy.

Studying at universities in Budapest, Berlin, and Heidelberg, Tisza devoted himself to textbooks in law, economics, public finance, and statistics, taking only occasional breaks for riding and hunting. Tisza traveled to western Europe, a trip that for students then as now could easily have been an opportunity to experiment with the loosening of social restrictions, but he only made note of the orderliness of German society under leader Otto von Bismarck, and of the British parliament, democratic but ruled by the country's educated upper crust. Tisza received a doctorate in political science from the University of Budapest in 1881, and then spent a year in the Hungarian army, serving in a unit that required him to do little more than hone his horseback riding skills.

Tisza seemed to have been groomed for political life, but between 1882 and 1886, he concerned himself primarily with the management of his family's estates in Csegöd and Kocsord, Hungary. During this time a cholera epidemic broke out in Kocsord, where there was no doctor, and Tisza personally attended to some of the sick farmhands on his estate. Later, though, in Vermes's opinion, this episode made Tisza "insensitive to the grave ills plaguing the Hungarian countryside. Because he was able to establish a good personal rapport with his farmhands and because his example as a hard-working, strict but just landlord brought a favorable response, Tisza romanticized the Magyar [Hungarian] peasants as fundamentally virtuous and good, capable of pulling themselves up by their own bootstraps."

Elected to Parliament

In 1886, Tisza, who believed that political service was a moral responsibility of the wealthy, was elected to Hungary's parliament as a member of the Liberal Party, which his father had helped organize and had used as a vehicle to the Hungarian prime ministership. Tisza was a quiet legislator, also working as president of the Hungarian Industrial and Commercial Bank and served on several corporate boards. He also received from his uncle the noble title of Count during this time. As a legislator he absorbed the outlooks that would mark his own years of leadership: in domestic affairs he supported reorganization of Hungary's economy along the lines of new western European models, while outside of Hungary he hoped to restrict the electoral power of the empire's Slavic minorities.

In 1903, a year after the death of his father, the Liberal Party chose Tisza as Hungary's Prime Minister. During his term, Tisza managed to obtain the return of the remains of Hungarian national hero Francis II Rákóczi from his burial place in Turkey. He was combative toward emerging socialist elements in Hungary, ordering that a railway workers' strike be broken up and that its participants be drafted into the army. He did not, however, take large-scale actions against Hungarian unionism, although large demonstrations were dealt with harshly. Tisza also took a confrontational attitude toward the Hungarian parliament's opposition parties, ramming through a series of parliamentary measures designed to increase the majority's power.

This move, in November of 1904, precipitated a crisis that led to the defection of several key members of Tisza's government. A chaotic scene ensued in which fistfights broke out on the parliament floor and Tisza (according to Vermes) yelled at his adversaries, "And you who are transforming this parliament into a farce, you call us the lackeys of Vienna." The scene was abhorrent to Tisza, who prized decorum and order. The vote that followed was disputed, with controversy breaking out over a handkerchief waved by a Liberal Party leader, and Hungary's King Francis Joseph I finally dissolved the parliament and called for new elections in which Tisza's Liberal Party, for the first time since the 1870s, was defeated.

Second Term as Prime Minister

Tisza continued to serve in the parliamentary opposition from 1906 to 1910, when he formed a new National Party of Work to replace the faltering Liberals. This party won the elections held in June of 1910. Tisza demurred when his name was brought up as the next prime minister, partly because he objected to the promotion of universal suffrage by Austria's Archduke Franz Ferdinand, which Tisza feared would dilute the power of Hungarians in the empire as a whole. But in 1912 he was elected speaker of the House of Representatives, becoming the new party's leader, and in June of 1913, he became Hungarian prime minister for a second time.

Resistance to the wholesale implementation of universal suffrage was typical of Tisza's political worldview. He was not anti-democratic, but he was convinced that the right to vote should be extended in gradual stages. Tisza disliked the revolutionary philosophies that were sweeping Europe during his two administrations, and he reserved special disapprobation for the atheistic component of Communism—not so much because he was a strict Calvinist, but because he foresaw the social divisions the new philosophies could bring: "The peace of nations and societies becomes a victim of this horrible bifurcation of the world view," he wrote (according to the *Tisza István Friends Society* website). "Nations are divided into two hostile groups and they no longer understand each other, they fight with each other as enemies. Consequently, there two opposing trends torture the seeking human spirit. The two noblest human instincts become enemies of each other: the one that seeks knowledge and the one that seeks God."

On June 28, 1914, Tisza's worst fears about Slavic unrest came true when Franz Ferdinand was assassinated by Yugoslav nationalist Gavrilo Princip in Sarajevo, Bosnia. Tisza at first feared the consequences of Hungary's entry into World War I, but later he came to believe that the only hope for Austria-Hungary's survival as a world power lay in alliance with Germany against France and England. Tisza resigned as prime minister at the request of the moderate King Charles IV in 1917, but continued to serve in the parliament, and he even led a cavalry regiment to the war's front lines that year.

The war's final year in 1918 was chaotic in Hungary, and Tisza, seen as both a representative of the old monarchy and of the failed war effort, survived several assassination attempts, one of them in front of the parliament building on October 16, 1918. On October 31, a group of soldiers entered Tisza's home in Budapest. His butler advised him to escape through a window, but Tisza refused, reportedly saying (according to Vermes), "I shall not jump anywhere. I wish to die upright, the way I have lived." Carrying a revolver, he met the group of soldiers, one of whom said that Tisza had made him rot in trenches for four years. After he dropped his gun, several shots were fired; he fell to the ground, said the words "it had to happen this way," and died. Tisza was a character in the historical *Transylvanian Trilogy* novels of Miklos Banffy, depicting Hungary's situation during the World War I era.

Books

Kann, Rober A., *A History of the Habsburg Empire, 1526–1918,* University of California, 1974.

Vermes, Gabor, *István Tisza: The Liberal Vision and Conservative Statecraft of a Magyar Nationalist,* Eastern European Monographs, 1985.

Periodicals

Contemporary Review, October 1998.

Online

"The Standpoint of the Tisza István Friends Society Concerning the Historical Figure of Count István Tisza," *Tisza István Friends Society,* http://www.tiszaistvan.hu/index.php/english (January 20, 2014).

"Who's Who—Count István Tisa de Boros-Jeno," *firstworldwar.com,* http://www.firstworldwar.com/bio/tisza.htm (January 20, 2014).□

Aleksey Tolstoy

Russian writer Aleksey Nikolayevich Tolstoy (1883–1945) carried the surname of his more famous ancestor well into the 20th century and into the Soviet cultural era. A descendant of Count Leo Tolstoy, the playwright and novelist who produced such classics as *War and Peace* and *Anna Karenina,* the younger writer gained renown for his science fiction tales, plays, and works of historical fiction that reexamined major figures in Russian history. He was called the "Comrade Count" after returning from abroad in the early 1920s, following Russia's turbulent period of revolution and civil war.

© Heritage Image Partnership Ltd/Alamy

The Tolstoys' titles and lands dated back to the late 1600s and the era of Tsar Peter I, who modernized the hermetic, medieval Russian Empire and forged historic ties with Western European powers. Tolstoy came from a side branch of the same family that produced Leo Tolstoy, who penned much of his lasting output on an estate near Tula. Aleksey Nikolayevich Tolstoy, by contrast, was born on January 10, 1883, in Nikolaevsk, in the Russian oblast of Samara. On his mother's side he was distantly related to another famous name in Russian letters, Ivan Turgenev. His parents were Alexandra Leontievna Turgeneva and Count Nikolai Alexandrovich Tolstoy, a cavalry officer who habitually clashed with his peers, his family, and neighbors. There were three children that preceded Tolstoy's birth—brothers Alexander and Mstislav plus sister Elizabeth—but Tolstoy would have scant contact with them during his lifetime.

Parents Endured Epic Divorce

Count Nikolai's long history of troublemaking finally forced his wife to leave him when she was pregnant with her fourth child. She took up with a left-leaning figure, Alexei Appollonovich Bostrom, and her act, unsurprisingly, further enraged Nikolai, who tried to kill Bostrom. The Tolstoy name and influence produced imbalanced rulings in two court cases related to the dissolution of the marriage: Nikolai suffered no serious repercussion for his attack on Bostrom; then a separate ecclesiastical court, which handled family-law matters like divorce, ruled against Alexandra Leontievna, who was forced to claim that her youngest child had been fathered by Bostrom if she hoped to retain custody. The Russian Orthodox church considered her transgression so serious that she was even forbidden from marrying Bostrom. Because of these circumstances Tolstoy was raised in poverty, with a mother and stepfather considered outcasts by their own family. They instilled in their son a deep distrust of the establishment, including the church and the nobility. Tolstoy did not uncover the details of the divorce until his teens, including the fact that Bostrom was not his biological father.

Tolstoy read both Leo Tolstoy and Ivan Turgenev as a youth, and he was encouraged to write his own stories at a young age. He attended high school in the city of Samara and planned for a practical career in engineering, a goal that was made possible when Nikolai died in 1900 and left part of his estate to him. Tolstoy was able to move to the capital of imperial Russia and enroll at the St. Petersburg Technological Institute. Like other students from modest backgrounds, he was awakened by his education to the principles of democracy and the relative freedoms enjoyed by Europeans in the West. He joined the Russian Social Democrat Party and took part in street protests, and eventually shifted his focus toward literary pursuits full-time. His first poems were published in journals like *Apollon* and *Shipovnik.*

Tolstoy seemed doomed to relive the trauma of his parents' ill-fated match, and repeat the error many times over. He first married a young woman named Julia Rozhansky around 1902, against his parents' wishes, and they had a son, Yuri. His marriage to Rozhansky fell apart after a few short years when he left her for Sophia Dymshits Rosenfeld, the already-married sister of a friend. Again, both parties were rebuked by their extended families, which in turn propelled them to seek a new life in Paris. During this period Tolstoy's son Yuri died of meningitis.

Torn Between East and West

Tolstoy had already spent time in Germany and Italy, but Paris in the decade just before World War I was the center of exciting modernist currents in the arts. He and Sophia fell in with other émigrés of Russian origin whose creative temperaments and progressive ideas had forced them to move abroad, and Tolstoy's career as a writer flourished. Moving from poems to short stories, he found an especially rich trove of inspiration when he considered his maternal ancestors, who were aristocrats with greatly reduced fortunes; each successive generation seemed to be more dissolute and unconventional than the last. He produced a pair of novels, *Chudaki* (The Eccentrics) in 1912 and *Khromoi barin* (The Lame Prince) in 1915, that explored these themes of a nobility rotting from the inside.

Tolstoy was homesick in Paris, however, and he and Sophia returned to Russia and took up residence in St. Petersburg. By that point the couple had a child together, which predictably propelled him into affairs with other women. In 1915 he took up with another married woman, the poet Natalia Vasilievna Volkenstein, who was able to obtain a divorce under less draconian statutes that followed the February Revolution of 1917. This event forced Tsar Nicholas II to abdicate, a major event in the 300-year-old history of the Romanov dynasty. Tolstoy spent World War I working as a newspaper correspondent following the events of the European conflict and then the Russian Civil War, when the new hardline Communist Bolsheviks battled against moderates, monarchists, and militia units supplied by foreign powers. Initially reluctant to support the Bolshevik side, Tolstoy produced a 1919 play, *Smert' Dantona* (The Death of Danton), about the 1794 execution of noted French revolutionary figure Georges Danton, who advocated terrorist methods but then was brought to the guillotine himself.

In 1920, Tolstoy returned to Paris, a city now overrun with an enormous population of refugee Russian aristocrats. Natalia worked as a seamstress to support him and their toddler son Nikita. They moved to Berlin, which was home to a more intellectual community of Russian expatriates, and Tolstoy's reputation as a writer was bolstered when prominent figures back in Moscow and St. Petersburg like Vladimir Mayakovsky and Maxim Gorky championed his work. Soviet diplomats in Berlin reportedly encouraged Tolstoy and his family to think about returning home, promising him artistic freedom and a few perks that would allow the family to maintain a certain standard of living. By then the couple was about to have a second son, Dmitri, and he still had contact with Mariana, his daughter by Sophia. Years later, after two decades of marriage to Volkenstein, he left her for his assistant, Liudmila Ilichna Barsheva.

Wrote Russian Sci-Fi Fable

Tolstoy moved his family to Moscow in 1922, and began an intensely prolific period of his career. His best known works from this era include the first novel in what would become a trilogy published in English translation as *The Road to Calvary.* Volume One is titled *Sestry* (Sisters) and follows the separate paths taken by two sisters, Daria and Katia, in imperial Russia at the onset of World War I. Subsequent novels track their struggles during the tumultuous years of revolution and civil war with partners and other figures. Tolstoy concluded the story in 1942's *Khmuroe utro* (Bleak Morning).

Tolstoy undoubtedly spent years writing *The Road to Calvary,* but a short science fiction tale he titled *Aelita* proved to be one of his most influential works and have a lasting impact in the groundbreaking era of new Soviet art. Published in 1923, *Aelita* features a Soviet scientist named Mstislav Los who invents a rocket that takes him to Mars—known around the world as the *Red Planet* for its curiously rusty pallor in the night sky—along with a veteran soldier of the Red or Bolshevik side, the army that prevailed in the Russian Civil War. Los and Gusev discover an advanced civilization on Mars, but one with a dramatic wealth gap: a minority elite controls almost all capital and resources, while armies of workers are forced to live and toil underground. Los falls in love with Aelita, a princess who reveals that Mars is on the brink of environmental disaster because of its imprudent use of natural resources. Gusev, the soldier, rallies the masses to rebel against their overlords, but the uprising is brutally suppressed and the two Russians are forced to flee back to Earth.

In the end, Los picks up radio signals from Mars hinting that both Aelita and the revolutionary spirit are still alive.

Tolstoy's *Aelita* became the first science fiction film produced by the new state studio called Sovkino. The distinctive, avant-garde Russian Futurist sets and costumes set a high stylistic bar for successive creative professionals conjuring up what interplanetary travel might look like. The 1924 film version was directed by Yakov Protazanov, a pioneer of Soviet film during the silent era, and was shown in New York City later in the 1920s; other works by Tolstoy, such as the play *Rasputin* were staged by left-leaning theater companies in Berlin and other major cities. Tolstoy was permitted to keep the lucrative foreign rights and royalties from his plays and books, a perk that Soviet-era artists only with an elite, state-sanctioned status enjoyed. Nicknamed "Comrade Count," Tolstoy had a spacious Moscow apartment in the same building as Gorky and had managed to retain his longtime personal valet, a relic from his modest aristocrat origins. He rose within the political ranks, too, even during the risky period of Stalinist terror in the 1930s, when many artists or even those who had spent time abroad were targeted as political enemies of the state. He became president of the Writers' Union in 1936, and was elected to the Supreme Soviet in 1937.

Won Stalin Prize

Among Tolstoy's works from the 1930s was an epic historical biography of Peter the Great, also known as Tsar Peter I. He portrayed the legendary ruler as a figure of revolutionary importance whose efforts to modernize feudal Russia foreshadowed the rise of Soviet Communism. *Petr Pervyi* (Peter the First) won the first-ever Stalin Prize in 1941, a new honor created to reward innovators in Soviet arts and sciences. When Germany invaded Poland in September of 1939, launching World War II, Tolstoy criticized the reactionary forces that urged England to declare war on Germany. But less than two years later, when Nazi German troops launched a massive invasion of the Soviet Union, Tolstoy predicted that in the end, the Soviets would prevail and Germany would be vanquished. In newspaper and magazine pieces he laid out his beliefs that the Soviet model had the capacity to both win a war and keep its unique political system intact.

Tolstoy died in Moscow on February 23, 1945, just a few months short of the Soviet victory in World War II that he had predicted. For decades his former apartment at 2 Ulitsa Spiridonovka remained a museum, even after the fall of the Soviet Union. Tolstoy's *Times* of London obituary declared that "Comrade Count" "ranked high as a writer who understood his people and knew the colour and force of their language. But it is as a man who wrote at a time when Russia's aims were, first, to survive the disaster that had overtaken her at German hands, and then to secure victory that he will be chiefly remembered."

Books

Smith, Alexandra, "Alexey Nikolaevich Tolstoy," in *Russian Prose Writers Between the World Wars,* edited by Christine Rydel, in Vol. 272 of *Dictionary of Literary Biography,* Gale, 2003.

Periodicals

New York Times, November 11, 1927.
Times (London, England), February 26, 1945.☐

Tereska Torrès

Tereska Torrès (1920–2012) fled Nazi-occupied France during World War II and joined the Free French Forces in London. Barely out of her teens, the aspiring writer kept a journal that she later turned into a racy novel titled *Women's Barracks* that caused a stir on both sides of the Atlantic when it was published in 1950. "Her frank, moving and funny diaries of life in wartime London," asserted John Lichfield in the *Independent* in 2007 about Torrès's later memoirs, "are among the finest first-hand accounts of Britain in the Blitz. They are also one of the few descriptions of London in wartime to be written from the point of view of a woman soldier of any nationality."

Tereska Torrès was born Tereska Szwarc in Paris on September 3, 1920. She recounted the lives of her Polish-Jewish-émigré parents and their decision to secretly convert to Roman Catholicism in 1919 in *Le Choix: Mémoires à trois voix.* Her father, Marek Szwarc, was a talented sculptor and painter, while her mother Eugenia "Guina" Pinkus Szwarc was a novelist and poet. Torrès was baptized, but it was explained to her at the age of six that her parents wished to keep their Roman Catholic religious practices a secret, for it would have proved too upsetting to their relatives back in Poland, with whom they remained close.

Fled France over Pyrénées

In her teens, Torrès perceived the threat of neighboring Nazi Germany, France's next-door neighbor and a buffer state between her homeland and Poland, where she spent summers with cousins. The Nazi menace emerged fully on September 1, 1939, when German troops launched a full-scale invasion of Poland. This shock came just two days before Torrès's 19th birthday. Germany had already placed severe restrictions on its own Jewish population, stripping them of citizenship rights and eventually establishing slave-labor and extermination camps, and the same fate was to befall Poland's Jews.

In the spring of 1940, France became Germany's next target. Torrès's father had already joined a Polish-émigré unit fighting with the French army, but when the French government capitulated and agreed to a puppet French government under occupation, the joint French and British forces fighting the German invasion were left stranded and had to be evacuated on France's western coastline. German authorities and their French collaborators, meanwhile, began making plans to deport French Jews to labor camps in Eastern Europe.

Louis MONIER/Gama-Rapho/Getty Images

Torrès and her mother were among the hundreds saved by a Portuguese diplomat in France, Aristides de Sousa Mendes, who issued emergency travel visas to French Jews from his office in the city of Bordeaux. Escaping over the border into Spain, Torrès made her way to Lisbon, Portugal, then settled in London in November of 1940. She immediately joined the Volontaires Françaises Corps, a special women's auxiliary group of the military government in exile. A top French army official, Charles de Gaulle, had publicly protested his government's capitulation and urged his fellow French to resist; from London de Gaulle commanded the Free French Forces, which fought with Allied powers against the Nazi occupation. Torrès became personal secretary to de Gaulle and had a high security clearance. Despite the danger of living in London, a city that endured major aerial bombing from German Luftwaffe planes, she recalled with fondness the *esprit de corps* and personal recklessness of the era. "We were young people thrown together," she explained to Lichfield in the *Independent* in 2007. "We became adults very quickly. We had a sense of constant danger but also a sense of constant excitement."

Appealed to Winston Churchill

The impetuous times prompted hasty engagements and weddings. In 1943, Torrès met a young French Jewish soldier, Georges Torrès, the stepson of France's first Jewish prime minister, Léon Blum. Remarkably, the aging Blum was actually arrested and imprisoned by the Nazis and was incarcerated at the Buchenwald concentration camp during this period, where Georges's mother had joined him. Jeanne Blum was divorced from a well-known lawyer and a hero of World War I named Henry Torrès, who was in New York City at the time. Torrès and Georges were shocked to discover they had often lived near one another, first in Paris, then Bayonne, where Torrès had finished her education; he, too, had literary aspirations. "It became clear," as she later wrote in one memoir, quoted in the Israeli newspaper *Ha'aretz,* "that until that point, and during all of our lives, we had moved in the same circles. He had grown up on the Boulevard Montparnasse near our home, he had passed through the towns of Bordeaux, Bayonne and Saint-Jean-de-Luz during the same period as I had and ultimately our paths crossed in London."

Their time in London together was brief, and they decided to wed before Georges was to report for duty with the 2nd Armored Division of the Free French Forces, which would liberate Paris from the Germans in August of 1944. Their marriage certificate required some official documents from his father in New York City, and because of the war normal channels of communication were unavailable. As Torrès recounted in her memoir, the couple took a taxi to No. 10 Downing Street, the official London address of the British prime minister. Clementine Churchill, wife of Winston Churchill, took their request and a telegram was sent to New York and a cable received in time for the ceremony on May 24, 1944, at Our Lady of Victories, a Roman Catholic church in the Kensington district of London. The Churchills even sent a basket of hydrangeas to the bride and groom.

Torrès became a war widow just five months later when Georges was killed in action in the Alsace-Lorraine region. She was also pregnant with the couple's first child, a daughter she named Dominique. Returning to Paris after the war's end in 1945, she completed the novel she had started at age 17, which was published by Gallimard in 1946 as *Le sable et l'écume* (Sand and Spume). She began a relationship with a noted American writer named Meyer Levin, who was 15 years her senior. Born in Chicago, Levin had lived in the British Mandate for Palestine in the 1920s and '30s, written about it, and was an ardent supporter of the Zionist cause, which argued for the establishment of a permanent Jewish homeland. In the years just after the war, Torrès and Levin embarked upon a journalism-documentary project that involved interviewing war refugees and displaced persons (DPs) at camps across Europe. Many Holocaust survivors were determined to settle in Palestine, and Torrès and Levin traveled illegally with one group and filmed the risky Mediterranean journey. Torrès even appeared on screen in the quasi-documentary *Al Tafhidunu* (The Illegals) as a pregnant Jewish refugee. The couple and their film crew were briefly detained by British authorities when the ship arrived in Haifa.

Penned Scandalous, Bestselling Book

Torrès and Levin married in Paris in 1948, and he encouraged her to write a fictional account of her time in London as a member of the women's Volontaires Françaises era. He translated her French text into an English-language manuscript titled *Women's Barracks,* which a New York publisher, Fawcett Books, agreed to issue if a narrator was added to balance out the hedonistic tales of young women living in close quarters in wartime London with relatively few checks on their behavior. Levin appended the disapproving female narrator voice, and Fawcett published it in paperback in 1950 with a lurid cover depicting half-clad young women in uniform eyeing one another. The work became a bestseller but caused a furor in several states, a few of which managed to ban its sale outright. A Canadian high court also prevented its publication in a 1952 decision, but *Women's Barracks* went on to sell five million copies in 14 languages. Feminist scholars later enshrined it as the first lesbian-themed pulp-fiction novel ever published in the United States, but Torrès was aghast and barred its publication in France for many years, feeling she had done a disservice to her fellow Volontaires Françaises service members.

Torrès and Levin had two sons, and worked together on various other projects after moving to Israel in the late 1950s. She drove an ambulance during the Six-Day War in 1967, and the couple traveled to Ethiopia in the early 1970s to promote the cause of a centuries-old population of Jews known as Beta Israelites. She wrote more novels, some of them racy tales of French bourgeois couples that Levin translated for British and American publishers. After he died in 1981, Torrès returned to France.

The success of *Women's Barracks* proved a surprisingly enduring one, and Torrès attempted to block a new reprint in 2005. "Do you know, I now hate to look up Google and type in my own name?" she revealed to Lichfield in the 2007 interview for the *Independent.* "The first thing that always comes up is Women's Barracks.... If you look at Women's Barracks, there are five main characters. Only one and a half of them can be considered lesbian. I don't see why it's considered a lesbian classic. I find it maddening."

"Not So Bad After All"

Torrès finally sat down and revised large sections of it herself for French publication in 2010, issued as *Jeunes Femmes en Uniforme.* She eliminated the scolding narrator Levin had added at the Fawcett editors' request six decades earlier. "You know, finally, I realised that this book was not so bad after all," she admitted to Lichfield in another interview for the *Independent,* this one in 2010. "The second half especially, when you get rid of the stupid narrator, is really quite good."

Torrès's other published works include *Les Années Anglaises: Journal intime de guerre, 1939–1945,* another recounting of her World War II years and later reprinted as *Une Française Libre,* and a memoir of her pre-war childhood titled *The Converts.* Her novels include *The Only Reason, By Cécile, Not Yet..., The Dangerous Games,* and *The Golden Cage.* She also authored an account of her marriage and her second husband's long legal battle with the father of Anne Frank over copyright claims to the stage version of *The Diary of Anne Frank.* Their experiences in the Horn of Africa were recounted in *Mission Secrète: Addis-Abeba-Jérusalem* (Secret Mission: Addis Ababa-Jerusalem).

Torrès spent her final years in the same quarters her family had once occupied before the war, on the Boulevard Arago. She died in Paris on September 20, 2012, at age 92, in the room once used by her father as an art studio, her son Gabriel told *Ha'aretz.* He is a poet and essayist in Israel, his brother Mikael a photographer in New York, and the daughter she had with Georges, Dominique, became a documentary filmmaker in France. One of the few Jewish relatives on either side of her parents' families who survived the Holocaust was Dubi Szwarc. "We kept in touch until her death and we had similar political opinions," the cousin told Gaby Levin in Torrès's *Ha'aretz* obituary. "She was an unusual person who fought for human rights, for social justice, against the occupation. Somehow she was always involved in something, in various places in the world."

Periodicals

Ha'aretz (Jerusalem, Israel), November 16, 2012.

Independent (London, England), June 16, 2007; February 5, 2010; April 4, 2011.

New York Times, September 26, 2012.

Telegraph (London, England), September 25, 2012.

Times (London, England), October 8, 2012.□

V

Stevie Ray Vaughan

American musician Stevie Ray Vaughan (1954-1990) was a guitar virutoso who sparked a blues-rock revival in the 1980s.

American musician Stevie Ray Vaughan (1954-1990) was one of the foremost blues guitarists of his generation, sparking a major popular revival of interest in the genre after the breakthrough of his group, Double Trouble. An exceptional guitar player, Vaughan sold millions of records and won Grammy awards before his career was cut short by a helicopter crash that killed the performer and others in 1990. He built an audience through albums such as 1984's blues hit *Couldn't Stand the Weather* and 1985's *Soul to Soul*, along with live performances at major blues and jazz festivals during the 1980s. The tragic nature of his death at the height of his abilities solidified Vaughan as a music legend, and posthumous releases including *The Sky in Crying* and *In the Beginning* proved equally if not more popular than those of the performer's own lifetime.

Launched Career in Texas

The son of asbestos plant employee Jim and factory secretary Martha, the future blues icon was born on October 3, 1954, in Dallas, Texas. He showed talent with the guitar from a young age, taking inspiration from blues and rock greats such as B.B. King and Jimi Hendrix as well as from his own older brother, Jimmie. Vaughan began playing in Dallas garage bands as a teenager, dropping out of high school at the age of 17 in order to pursue his dreams of making it as a professional musician. He formed his first group, Blackbird, in 1971. With this group he moved to the state capital of Austin, where his brother then lived.

Over the next several years, Vaughan bounced from outfit to outfit, playing around Austin. Writing for *People,* Steve Dougherty, Barbara Sandler, and Beth Austin asserted that Vaughan's "trademark bandito hat, tar-paper voice and potent playing became as familiar as the clubs' watered-down drinks." He formed his own blues group, the Cobras, in 1975. That group enjoyed notable local success, winning the title of Austin's Band of the Year in 1976. Before long the Cobras were offered a record deal but turned it down. Vaughan soon left the group; he began playing with Triple Threat in 1975. Four years later, he formed Double Trouble with some of Triple Threat's members, taking the trio's name from a song by blues artist Otis Rush. At about the same time, Vaughan married an Austin woman he had met while performing at local clubs, Lenora "Lenny" Bailey.

Comprised of Vaughan on guitar and lead vocals, bass player Tommy Shannon, and drummer Chris Layton, Double Trouble developed a local following with its jazz-inflected blues rock sound. They played around Texas, in time catching the ear of the Rolling Stones and of legendary music producer Jerry Wexler. With Wexler's support, Double Trouble landed a slot at the 1982 Montreux Jazz Festival—an unheard-of booking for an unsigned band. Their performance at Montreux raised Double Trouble's profile, and rock singer David Bowie asked Vaughan to play on several tracks on his 1983 *Let's Dance* album. Double Trouble also signed a record deal with Epic, entering the studio in late 1982 to lay down the tracks that would form their debut album. Although Bowie offered Double Trouble a high-profile opening slot on his forthcoming stadium tour, Vaughan's management decided to pass on the opportunity in order to focus on Double Trouble's own burgeoning recording career.

Robert Knight Archive/Redferns/Getty Images

Became Influential Bluesman

With buzz growing about Vaughan in music circles, *Texas Flood* hit shelves in the summer of 1983. The album was an immense, if somewhat unexpected, blues hit, spending several months on the *Billboard* charts, picking up a Grammy nomination, and making Vaughan a star. A blend of blues and rock influences—Vaughan drew near-endless comparisons to guitar great Jimi Hendrix throughout his career—the recording displayed the guitarist's virtuosic musical abilities and his talent at creating sounds that appealed to both genre and mainstream listeners. Vaughan's crossover style, with its rock intensity and radio-friendly flourishes, garnered Vaughan comparisons to fellow Texas rockers Johnny Winter and ZZ Top. In a review of a 1983 live performance, Jon Pareles of the *New York Times* declared that Vaughan's playing "aims for impact instead of subtlety...and, like hard rock, concentrates on texture, not linearity."

In fact, Vaughan's forging of the crossover hit has been noted by critics as one of his key contributions to twentieth-century music. "It's hard to overestimate the impact... *Texas Flood*...had .... At that point, blues was no longer hip, the way it was in the '60s. *Texas Flood* changed all that," argued Stephen Thomas Erlewine in an AllMusic review. Vaughan's live performances exhibited a wild showmanship that served only to further audience interest as the musician played guitar behind his back, while lying on the floor, or in other seemingly impossible stunts.

With Vaughan having sparked a revival of interest in the blues-rock format, listeners were eager for his next release. Double Trouble's follow-up, *Couldn't Stand the Weather,* appeared less than a year after *Texas Flood.* The album, which again showcased Vaughan's guitar chops through a mix of instrumental and vocal tracks, proved even more successful than the outfit's debut. The single "Look at Little Sister" landed in the mainstream rock top 20 even as *Couldn't Stand the Weather* again went gold and earned Double Trouble a second Grammy nomination.

As Double Trouble began work on their next studio album, the outfit added two new members, keyboardist Reese Wymans and saxophonist Joe Sublett, to the mix. With this expanded line-up providing a fuller sound, the group released *Soul to Soul* in 1985—their third album in as many years. Although critics generally agreed that *Soul to Soul* was somewhat less accomplished than its predecessors, the album performed strongly among fans and repeated the chart successes of *Texas Flood* and *Couldn't Stand the Weather.*

Struggled with Substance Abuse

By the mid-1980s, however, Vaughan's abuse of alcohol and drugs had begun to interfere with his ability to play music. On tour, the guitarist battled physical problems resulting from abuse as he struggled to keep up the strenuous demands of traveling and performance. A few weeks of a planned European outing were cancelled after Vaughan's addictions overcame his ability to appear live; he famously collapsed onstage in London in the summer of 1986. In the studio, he and other intimates became increasingly aware that Vaughan's guitar work was sloppy and not up to the standard that he had achieved in the past.

Yet he continued to create recordings that highlighted his lightning-fingered guitar abilities. In a review of the 1986 live album *Live Alive* for the British newspaper *Times,* David Sinclair asserted that "there is no doubting Vaughan's extraordinary technical ability together with the road-hugging security of the Double Trouble backing vehicle."

The death of Vaughan's father from a heart attack in 1986 further spurred the troubled musician to re-evaluate his lifestyle. After completing a North American tour, he quietly entered a rehab center to receive treatment for his addictions. Vaughan and his group spent much of the next year out of the public eye. The guitarist divorced his estranged wife Lenny and worked on songs for Double Trouble's next album. He returned to the stage in 1988, playing at festivals as well as headlining shows with Double Trouble.

What was to be Double Trouble's last studio album, *In Step,* was released in June of the following year. A commercial and critical hit, the recording contained several tracks reflective of Vaughan's battle in overcoming his addictions and announced his artistic revival. Writing for the *Times,* Sinclair observed that *In Step* harkened back to classic blues-rock sounds like those of Eric Clapton but "is at least something different from an artist locked into a genre whose icons tend to ossify at an alarming rate." The album cracked the top 40 on the overall *Billboard* 200, achieved gold-selling status by moving more than 500,000 units, and garnered Double Trouble a Grammy award for Best Contemporary Blues Recording.

Died in Helicopter Crash

During the summer of 1990, Vaughan and Double Trouble hit the road ahead of the planned release of Vaughan's album *Family Style,* recorded with his brother Jimmie, a member of the group the Fabulous Thunderbirds. On August 26, Double Trouble performed a headlining gig before a crowd of some 25,000 at the Alpine Valley Theater near Elkhorn, Wisconsin, where they were joined onstage by legendary guitar player Eric Clapton, blues guitarist Buddy Guy, and another blues musician, Robert Cray. "It was one of the most incredible sets I ever heard Stevie play. I had goose bumps," Guy later told Dougherty, Sandler, and Austin of *People.*

After the show, the performers and some members of their entourage boarded helicopters bound for Chicago, about 75 miles away. Vaughan had planned to drive back to Chicago, where he was staying, with his brother and sister-in-law, but upon learning that a seat was available in the helicopter suite decided to travel that way instead. Despite dense fog, four helicopters departed for Chicago shortly after midnight.

The vehicle carrying Clapton and Cray and the two others landed safely in Chicago soon after; the copter on which Vaughan, Clapton's agent Bobby Brooks, Clapton's bodyguard Nigel Browne, and one of Clapton's tour managers, Colin Smythe, disappeared. A search a few hours later located the chopper's remains near the site of take-off; investigators determined that the helicopter had crashed at a high speed into a ski hill, instantly killing all aboard. "Stevie is the best friend I've ever had, the best guitarist I ever heard and the best person anyone will ever want to know," said Guy in the same *People* article. "He will be missed a lot." Music critics and fans also mourned his loss. Stephen Holden of the *New York Times* hailed Vaughan in his obituary as "a technical virtuoso who played with lightning speed and...a master of...explosive sound effects."

Vaughan's sudden death did not end his musical output, however. Short weeks after the crash, the blues-rock duet album *Family Style* appeared on Epic to a warm reception. Writing for the *New York Times,* Robert Palmer declared that "both brothers play with an effectively taut economy throughout, and their interaction as rhythm players is a special treat." The album made it to the top ten of the *Billboard* 200 and sold more than one million copies in the United States within two months of its initial release. Sales of his older releases also surged, helping *Couldn't Stand the Weather, Texas Flood,* and *In Step* also achieve platinum status. Vaughan also garnered two posthumous Grammy wins, for *Sky is Crying* and the track "Little Wing," both in 1992.

Over the next several years, Vaughan's music lived on in greatest hits collections, live releases, and box sets. Collections including *Blues at Sunrise, Live at Montreux 1982 & 1985,* and *Essential Stevie Ray Vaughan and Double Trouble* all topped the *Billboard* blues albums chart in the 21st century. In 1994, the city of Austin unveiled a memorial statue to the musician near Lady Bird Lake, where Vaughan had performed numerous concerts during his brief but storied career.

Periodicals

New York Times, July 10, 1983; August 28, 1990; October 7, 1990.

People Weekly, September 10, 1990.

Times (London, England), January 10, 1987; July 1, 1989.

Online

"Biography," *AllMusic,* http://www.allmusic.com/artist/stevie-ray-vaughan-mn0000625739/biography (December 14, 2013).

"Biography," Stevie Ray Vaughan Official Website, http://www.srvofficial.com/us/content/biography (December 14, 2013).

"*Texas Flood,*" *AllMusic,* http://www.allmusic.com/album/texas-flood-mw0000090316 (December 14, 2013).□

Shlomo Venezia

Deported to the Auschwitz-Birkenau extermination camp, Greek-born Italian Jew Shlomo Venezia (1923-2012) spent eight months assisting in the massacre of his fellow Jews. Nearly 50 years after his liberation, Venezia came forward to tell his story, offering a rare firsthand account of life in the Sonderkommando—or "special unit"—of Jewish male prisoners given the harrowing task of removing corpses from the gas chamber. First published in France in 2007, Venezia's memoir has been translated into more than 20 languages.

The middle of five children, Shlomo Venezia was born December 29, 1923, in Thessaloniki, Greece. His family had ties to Spain, but like most Jews, they were expelled from the country in 1492. After leaving Spain, Venezia's ancestors fled to Italy and adopted the name Venezia because they settled in Venice. Family members later moved to the Jewish stronghold of Thessaloniki, which was known as the "Jerusalem of the Balkans." Venezia's father was an Italian citizen who fought in World War I. Venezia's mother, Doudoun Angel Venezia, was born in Greece.

Grew Up Poor

When Venezia was 11, his father died. Venezia's father had run a barbershop but none of the children were old enough to manage the business. They let an assistant take over in exchange for a small percentage of each week's profit. It was not enough for the family to live on, so Venezia quit school at 12 and worked in a factory. He also

Victor Sokolowicz/Bloomberg/Getty Images

earned money through odd jobs and took scissors into the poorer sections of the city to give haircuts to those who could not afford a barbershop cut.

At the time of Venezia's childhood, 60,000 Jewish people lived in Thessaloniki. Most of them were of Greek origin, although there were a few hundred Jews like him with an Italian identity. Even as German Chancellor Adolf Hitler came to power and invaded Poland in 1939, the Jews of Thessaloniki did not know much about what was going on because their community was isolated. As Venezia pointed out in his Holocaust memoir *Inside the Gas Chambers,* the Jewish people in his community were so poor and struggling to survive each day, they had no energy to fret about what was happening in the wider world.

Venezia lamented that their state of desperation made them put up little resistance. "This is why ... the Germans had no difficulty at all in deporting the Jews from Greece," Venezia explained. "The Germans easily persuaded them that the occupation forces were going to allocate lodgings to them ... the men would go off to work and the women would stay at home. We were naïve and didn't know what was happening politically.... People believed what they were promised. They didn't have enough to eat, and here people were offering them a place to live in exchange for their labor—it didn't seem such a big deal."

Deported to Auschwitz-Birkenau

Italy invaded Greece in the fall of 1940. Six months later, Germany entered Greece to help its Italian ally. Once the Germans reached Thessaloniki, they sequestered the Jews. Venezia's family fled to Athens but failed to escape. Imprisoned and herded onto a transport train bound for Poland, Venezia arrived at Auschwitz-Birkenau on April 11, 1944, following an 11-day train journey with little food and water. From March 1943 to August 1944, the Germans transferred 55,000 Jews from Greece to Auschwitz. More than 90 percent of Venezia's community would die in the Holocaust.

Most of the Jews who arrived with Venezia were sent directly to the gas chamber, but he was split off to join the labor force. Venezia's brother and two cousins survived the initial "selection" as well. At the concentration camps, after deportees arrived, they went through a "selection" process. The elderly, pregnant women, disabled people and mothers with young children were typically selected for extermination, while those deemed healthy enough to work got to live a little longer.

After making it through the selection process, Venezia was forced to strip and was herded into a room where his head and body were shaved to get rid of lice. Next, he took a group shower and was handed clothing from a previous prisoner. Then, Venezia was tattooed with the number "182727." At this point, the starving Venezia put his ingenuity to work and offered to take the clippers from the worker and shave the other prisoners in exchange for some bread. In his memoir, Venezia said his street skills helped him survive. "This is the sort of thing that makes me often say that people who suffered in their childhood and had to learn to get by on their own had more of a chance of adapting to life in camp and surviving than did people from privileged backgrounds. To survive in the camp, you had to know things that were useful—not philosophy."

Assigned to Crematorium

When asked what jobs he could do, Venezia said hairdresser and was assigned to the Sonderkommando. The Sonderkommandos were the stronger and healthier concentration camp prisoners who serviced the Nazi assembly lines of death. Most prisoners did not last long in the Sonderkommando. Because they were witnesses to the inner workings of the camp, the Sonderkommandos themselves were selected for death every few months. Venezia figured he did not have long to live, yet he never considered suicide. Venezia trudged on, he said in his memoir, remembering the words of his mother, who once told him, "While there's life, there's hope."

Venezia lived in a dorm right inside the crematorium. In this way, the Nazis kept the extermination process going in two shifts—day and night—seven days a week. In his memoir, Venezia detailed the process used at the killing centers. After the convoys arrived, the deportees were lined up and the selection process began. Those selected for death were told to remove their clothing so they could shower. To keep the prisoners calm, the Germans installed numbered hooks in the undressing room for the detainees to hang their clothes and valuables upon. This led the prisoners to think they would be back to collect their things. The gas chamber even had fake shower heads in the ceiling. But once the prisoners were crammed inside, they were gassed. Venezia said that sometimes, he had to lift the heavy cement trapdoor above the gas chamber so the SS officer could toss the Zyklon B pellets through the opening. Then he had to put the door back on.

After the prisoners had died, the ventilation system was switched on to disperse the gas so the bodies could be removed quicker. After about 20 minutes, the Sonderkommandos were sent in. Venezia's job was to remove the hair, which was sold to manufacturers to make rope and mattresses. The bodies were then lifted onto a hoist and pulled up to the next level where the ovens were located. Other times, Venezia carried dead bodies to outdoor ditches, where they were burned. Another job Venezia performed was to grind up the larger bones that failed to burn in the ovens, especially the pelvis because the Germans wanted to dispose of all evidence. Ashes were dumped in the river. "Your only choice was to get used to it," Venezia said in his memoir. "Very quickly, too. On the first days, I wasn't even able to swallow my bread when I thought of all those corpses my hands had touched." Venezia went on to say that after awhile, he just went through the motions. "During the first two or three weeks, I was constantly stunned by the enormity of the crime, but then you stop thinking."

Survived Evacuation

By the fall of 1944, with the Soviet Union's Red Army approaching, German officials halted operations at Auschwitz and began dismantling the crematoria to cover up the crimes. The members of the Sonderkommando were kept alive to take apart the insides of the structure since they were the only ones who had been allowed to see it. The Germans did not want more witnesses who could testify about what had gone on there. Venezia figured that as soon as the work was completed, he would be executed. Other prisoners were allowed to dismantle the outsides of the crematoria structures and at one point, Venezia slipped into the crowd and mingled with other non-Sonderkommando prisoners who were being assembled for an evacuation.

It was in this manner that Venezia escaped death at Auschwitz. Venezia's group of several thousand prisoners began its evacuation in mid-January. Venezia survived by scrounging for food. One night, while the prisoners slept in a barn, he located a secret food cellar. Another time, he caught a loaf of bread thrown by a Polish sympathizer. Many prisoners died along the way. After walking 10 or 12 days, the prisoners were loaded onto trains and later took freight barges across the Danube. Venezia's group ended up at the Mauthausen concentration camp in Austria.

At Mauthausen, Venezia thought the end had come. After arrival, he was told to strip and prepare for a shower. Much to his surprise, he was really given a shower. Later, Venezia was transferred to Melk, a sub-camp of Mauthausen, and onto Ebensee. Ebensee contained a large network of tunnels used for armament storage and Venezia was given the task of digging into the mountainside. After Ebensee was liberated on May 6, 1945, Venezia stayed for two more months because he had nowhere to go. Ill with tuberculosis, Venezia ended up at a sanatorium in Milan, Italy, and spent more than a year there. Venezia lost the use of one lung, but eventually recovered. He lived awhile in a halfway house run by the American Jewish Joint Distribution Committee, which helped former prisoners re-integrate into life.

Haunted by His Story

While living in Grottaferrato, Italy, Venezia met Marika Kaufmann. Venezia was 32; she was 17. They married in 1956 and had three sons—Mario, Alessandro, and Alberto. Venezia spent the rest of his life working in hotels and later owned a souvenir shop in Rome. Many of Venezia's relatives, including his mother, died at Auschwitz. One brother and one sister managed to survive. His brother, who was in a coma at the time of liberation, recovered and moved to the United States. His sister settled in Israel.

Initially, Venezia found that when he tried to talk about his experience, most people thought he was crazy, so he stayed silent. But in 1992—47 years after Venezia was freed—he started talking again. Anti-Semitism was resurfacing in Italy and Venezia felt compelled to speak out. He began lecturing about his experience by speaking at conferences and talking to schoolchildren. In 1997, Venezia served as a historical advisor for the Holocaust film *Life Is Beautiful.* Along the way, he met French journalist Béatrice Prasquier, who conducted an extensive oral interview with Venezia, which was published in France in 2007 as *Inside the Gas Chambers: Eight Months in the Sonderkommando of Auschwitz.* The memoir was published in English in 2009. In the book, Venezia chastised his brother, who never wanted to talk about Auschwitz, pretending instead that it was all a horrible dream. "But I think it's precisely for this reason—because it is so completely unimaginable—that those people who can tell their story must do so."

Venezia died in Rome on October 1, 2012, although as he told it, a part of him died in the concentration camp, never to be revived. In his memoir, Venezia acknowledged he never had a normal life after Auschwitz. "Everything takes me back to the camp. Whatever I do, whatever I see, my mind keeps harking back to the same place. It's as if the 'work' I was forced to do there had never really left my head.... Nobody ever really gets out of the Crematorium."

Books

Venezia, Shlomo, *Inside the Gas Chambers,* Polity Press, 2009.

Periodicals

Pittsburgh Post-Gazette, October 14, 2012.

Times (London), November 8, 2012.

Washington Post, October 12, 2012.□

Michael Ventris

Though professionally an architect, Michael Ventris (1922-1956) is perhaps best known for a linguistic accomplishment, deciphering *Linear B.* This set of cryptic writings from an ancient Greek civilization on Crete had been an archaeological mystery since its discovery in 1900.

Ventris was born on July 12, 1922, the son of a British Army officer. His mother, Dorothea, was the daughter of a Polish immigrant to England. Most of his childhood was spent in privilege, and he spent many of his younger years abroad. Ventris's family life, however, was not particularly happy. His father suffered from tuberculosis, and his mother divorced his father when Ventris was 13 years old. His father died in 1938, and his mother killed herself when her son was 18 years old.

Had Early Interest in Antiquities and Languages

As a small child, Ventris was exposed to archaeology through visits to the British Museum in London with his mother. From the first, Ventris had a fascination with antiquities. Initially educated in Gstaad, Switzerland, Ventris also showed an aptitude for languages. He became a fluent speaker of German and French, after teaching himself Polish at the age of six. Ventris was ultimately fluent in nine languages.

Returning to England to complete his education, he attended the Stowe School in Buckingham, where he focused on the classics before being forced to leave early because his mother could not afford the fees. A friend of his mother's, Marcel Breuer, an acclaimed architect and furniture designer, influenced Ventris's career choice. Deciding to become a professional architect, he began studying at London's Architectural Association school in 1940.

During this period, World War II raged across Europe. Ventris left school temporarily to serve in the Royal Air Force as a navigator, primarily of bombers. After his term of service was complete, he returned to the Architectural Association school and earned his diploma with honors in 1948.

Worked as an Architect

In the late 1940s and early 1950s, Ventris worked as an architect for the Ministry of Education in Great Britain. He focused on designing new and reconstructing old schools in the post-war period. An architect of distinction, he won the first research fellowship given by the *Architects' Journal* in 1956. The subject of his research was called information for the architect.

While Ventris garnered acclaim as an architect, it was his work outside architecture that brought him greater fame. His long-time interest in archaeology was heightened by a lecture given by Sir Arthur Evans in 1936 on the fiftieth anniversary of the founding of the British School of Archaeology at Athens. The then 14-year-old Ventris was part of a school group from Stowe who came to view an exhibit on Greek and Minoan art and who listened to Evans describe his discovery of an ancient Greek civilization on Crete that had its legendary King Minos as its namesake.

Minoan civilization began in about 1850 BCE, and originally wrote in a language called *Linear A* until about 1400 BCE. Mycenaean Greeks, who emerged around that time in the area of the Aegean Sea, modified the script of *Linear A* to fit their own language, resulting in the emergence of *Linear B* in this time period.

In his lecture, Evans noted that *Linear B* had been heretofore undeciphered, and even he, as a great scholar, could not discern them. The language, primarily via inscriptions, was located on Minoan tablets of baked clay which had been discovered by Evans in 1900 in his excavations at Knossos. Evans dubbed these inscriptions *Linear B,* and Ventris was inspired by these lectures to figure out how to decipher the inscriptions and the language. (It was later learned that the tablets and their inscriptions date from 1450 BCE, and represented Europe's oldest readable writings.)

Worked on Deciphering *Linear B*

During his days as an architecture student and later as a young professional architect, Ventris focused on this venture in his spare time. In 1940, he published a piece in the *American Journal of Archaeology* in which he offered his initial theory on the language found on the clay tablets. Because of his war service and the need to complete his education, however, Ventris only worked on deciphering *Linear B* on a limited basis until 1949. But, between 1940 and 1953, Ventris further posited theories and conducted research related to *Linear B.* He even had correspondences with other *Linear B* researchers around the world, including John Chadwick.

Other scholars, such as Emmet Bennett, Jr., and Alice Elizabeth Kober, helped Ventris by laying the groundwork. Bennett showed Ventris that the script on *Linear B* was likely to a syllabary, a phonetic writing system in which symbols stand for syllables, while Kober had conducted some early analysis on inflection patterns in the text. Ventris also had to work through an early, but incorrect, hypothesis that the language on *Linear B* was Etruscan. For his part, Ventris developed a series of working hypotheses and never locked onto one set of assumption about the script as he obsessively focused on solving what he and many others regarded as a puzzle because there was little to no external evidence to help solve it.

Instead, because Ventris was trained as an architect and employed an exacting analytical method, he saw the symbols and language of *Linear B* in unique fashion, using a grid system that involved T-squares and set squares. He also employed the methods used to track U-boats during the Second World War. Ultimately, Ventris created a series of visual grids in which he tested various hypotheses about the symbols' phonetic values and their internal logic. This system ultimately formed the heart of his solution. His elaborate grid system demonstrated the relationship between the symbols and writings found on the tablets. Ventris also employed statistical analysis to confirm his conclusion.

As Sara Paton explained in the *Spectator,* "Largely through internal evidence, without the aid of any bilingual text, Ventris deciphered the ancient script known as Linear B and revealed, to his own and everyone else's astonishment, that the language written in it was an early form of Greek. The result was not just a flood of legible information on the administrative minutiae of the Aegean Bronze Age. A large floating piece of that great fragmentary jigsaw, the history of the ancient world, swung gently round and clicked into place."

Announced His Conclusions

In 1952, Ventris finished deciphering *Linear B,* with the help of Chadwick, and announced his findings on British radio. Ventris and Chadwick then published a related paper in 1953, "Evidence for Greek Dialect in the Mycenaean Archives." He concluded that the language used on the tablets was an archaic dialect of Greek, the earliest known form of Greek. When Ventris announced his solution to the *Linear B* mystery, many scholars reacted with skepticism. Some virulently so, such as a professor of Greek at Edinburgh University named A.J. Beattie, as well as other scholars in Scotland, Germany, and Greece.

However, another tablet was found in 1952, and analysis of it proved that Ventris had been correct. After formulating his solution, Ventris began writing a book with Chadwick. Their *Documents of Mycenaean Greek* offered a detailed explanation of the search for and solution to the linguistic mystery that was *Linear B.*

Describing the impact of Ventris's discovery in its time, the London *Times* claimed in a 1996 articled that "The decipherment of Linear B was an inspirational act. It happened around the same time as the first ascent of Everest and caught the same Coronation spirit. Before Ventris made his discovery the Mycenaeans were a speechless people known for their king, Agamemnon, their glorious golden treasures and a much-disputed place in mythology. After . . . the Mycenaeans became a people with a tongue . . . ."

Once he provided the solution, Ventris announced he had no further interest in *Linear B* or the academic studies of Mycenaean civilization and culture that were spawned. He also claimed no glory for the feat and was relatively unconcerned that other scholars might try to co-opt his discoveries. Ventris even turned down a chance to give the prestigious Waynflete Lectures at Oxford University in 1954.

Honored for His Work

Yet because of his solution, Ventris received several honors in 1955 and 1956 that he did accept. They included an Order of the British Empire, given in honor of his services to Mycenaean paleography (the study of ancient writings). In addition, he was honored with an honorary doctorate from the University of Uppsala in Sweden, and was made an honorary research fellow associated at London's University College.

While Ventris received acclaim for solving *Linear B,* some commentators believe that both the obsession that drove him to solve it as well as the fame that came after negatively impacted both his personal life and his work as an architect. He resigned from his job in this period, disappointed in his own work. It is also known that he had been suffering from severe depression for some time.

On September 6, 1956, Ventris died when his car crashed into a stationary truck while driving late at night on the Great North Road. Friends and observers at the time believed that the accident might have been suicide on Ventris's part as there was no known reason why he would have left his London home and been driving around midnight. He was survived by his wife of more than 30 years, Lois, and their two children.

To honor Ventris, friends established a memorial scholarship in his name in 1957. The annual award is given to students at the Architectura Association and the Institute of Classical Studies at the University of London in alternate years. By offering scholarships to both institutions, his friends believed they could honor both of Ventris's primary interests.

Published Only Book Posthumously

At the time of Ventris's death, *Documents of Mycenaean Greek* was about to be published, and was done so posthumously. It went through at least two more editions, in 1973 and 2009. In 1958, Chadwick wrote another book, *The Decipherment of Linear B,* which outlined the joint effort he and Ventris had made at finding a solution. Ultimately, the work of Ventris and Chadwick proved that the Mycenaens spoke a form of Greek while they lived on the Greek mainland during the period of the events described by Homer in his epics .

Though Ventris and his discovery have been relatively forgotten at the turn of the twenty-first century, a revealing biography was published in 2002, Andrew Robinson's *The Man Who Deciphered Linear B: The Story of Michael Ventris.* Reviewing the book in the London *Evening Standard,* Rowan Moore noted "The fascination of the story lies . . . in a remarkable mind . . . ." Yet, Robinson himself explained the importance of Ventris's feat in the *Times Higher Education Supplement,* "Ventris's achievement was one of a handful of great archaeological decipherments, beginning with Egyptian hieroglyphs in the 1820s and culminating with the Mayan glyphs in the last decades of the 20th century."

Books

Encyclopedia of Language & Linguistics, edited by Keith Brown, Anne H. Anderson, Laurie Bauer, Margie Berns, Graeme Hirst, and Jim Miller, Elsevier, 2005.

Science and Its Times, edited by Neil Schlager and Josh Lauer, Gale, 2000.

Science and Its Times: Volume 7: 1950 to Present, edited by Neil Schlager and Josh Lauer, Gale. 2001.

Periodicals

Building Design, May 10, 2002.

Evening Standard (London), April 15, 2002.

Independent (London), April 24, 2002.

Irish Times, August 24, 2002.
Spectator, May 25, 2002.
Sunday Suteleaph (London), April 21, 2002.
Times (London), September 6, 1996.
Times Higher Education Supplement, May 24, 2002; July 30, 2009.
Weekend Australian, June 29, 2002.□

Pier Paolo Vergerio

Italian cleric Pier Paolo Vergerio (c. 1498–1565) served as a bishop and occasional papal envoy before turning his energies to religious reform. Attacked by colleagues for writings that were critical of the Roman Church and its practices, Vergerio was forced into exile and found shelter in Protestant enclaves in Switzerland and Germany. He holds a minor but noteworthy distinction in the history of Christianity as the first bishop to defect from the Roman Church and adopt Lutheranism.

The rebel bishop is sometimes confused with another Pier Paolo Vergerio the Elder, an ancestor who had an illustrious career in Florence, the birthplace of the Italian Renaissance, and also served as a diplomat for popes and emperors. The elder Vergerio was one of the first scholars of his era to become fluent in both Latin, the language of scholarship and religion in Western Europe, and in ancient Greek. In the first half of the 15th century, Vergerio the Elder authored several works on humanism and education that influenced a generation of philosophers and reformers during the Italian Renaissance.

Earned Law Degree

The younger Pier Paolo Vergerio was born around 1498 and likely named after his esteemed relative, who never married and died in Hungary around 1444. Vergerio the Younger came from Koper, a city on the Istrian coastline of present-day Slovenia. In Vergerio's lifetime, Koper belonged to the Venetian Republic and was called Capodistria, after the Latin term *Caput Histriae,* or Head of Istria. Istria was a providentially sited bulb-shaped peninsula that jutted out into the northeastern waters of the Adriatic Sea. Capodistria rose to influence during the time of the Crusades and was gradually enveloped into the larger Venetian Republic in 1278 as a result of increased economic ties to the powerful city-state. The Venetian Republic came to control much of the Adriatic maritime commerce for the next 500 years and exerted a powerful influence over northern Italy and the Balkan lands to the east.

Vergerio was educated at the University of Padua, from which he was granted a degree in civil law in 1524. During his time there he befriended several figures who would also go on to prominent careers. One was Pietro Bembo, who became a scholar in Florence, leading literary figure in the Italian Renaissance, and high-ranking cardinal in the Church. Another member of Vergerio's student circle in Padua was Reginald Pole, the last Roman Catholic to serve as Archbishop of Canterbury in England.

Moving to the fabled city of Venice, Vergerio married a woman named Diana Contarini in 1526, about whom little is known save for the fact that her surname belongs to one of the oldest aristocratic families of Venice, and that she died within a year or two of their wedding. Until 1532, Vergerio held various civil-service jobs in the Venetian Republic befitting his law degree, but in the early 1530s was motivated to take religious vows, as several of his siblings had done.

Vergerio once said that he traveled on a mission to the Middle East with his brother Aurelio, who was the code secretary to Pope Clement VII. When Aurelio died, Vergerio took over the post, which entailed overseeing sensitive diplomatic documents written in cipher. This was a time of intense turmoil in the Church, roiled by German priest Martin Luther's increasingly successful efforts to reform Christianity. Luther, a respected professor of theology at the University of Wittenberg, challenged the authority of Rome and some of the church's more corrupt practices. For this Luther was excommunicated in 1521 at an official conclave that met in Worms, a German cathedral city. Given protection by a powerful German prince, Luther spent the remainder of his life promoting the Protestant Reformation, which spread across Europe and incited decades of foreign and civil wars.

Enjoyed Diplomatic Intrigues

Pope Clement VII sent Vergerio to serve as his papal nuncio, or ambassador, to the court of Ferdinand, the Archduke of Austria and grandson of Spain's King Ferdinand II. It was during this period that Vergerio first began to travel outside of Italy and was exposed to the ideas and reformist spirit of various Protestant sects who had taken up Luther's daring model.

Pope Clement VII—scion of the rich Medici banking dynasty in the Florentine Republic—died in 1534 and was succeeded by Pope Paul III, who also came from a prominent, wealthy family in Italy, the House of Farnese. Vergerio's career in the church initially appeared to flourish under this new pope, who appointed him Bishop of Modruš in Croatia and then elevated him to Bishop of Capodistria in 1536.

Vergerio first aroused suspicion among his colleagues when visited the French court at Fontainebleau. He befriended Marguerite d'Angoulême, the sister of France's reigning monarch, Francis I. Marguerite was sympathetic to the Protestant cause and corresponded with many prominent theologians and philosophers across Europe. She and Vergerio also exchanged letters for many years. One of Marguerite's most renowned champions was the Dutch humanist cleric and scholar Desiderius Erasmus, who played a decisive role in Martin Luther's evolution into the founder of the Protestant Reformation. Vergerio began to read the works of Erasmus, which discussed certain church doctrines in depth.

Began to Criticize the Church

In Italy, Vergerio became associated with a small movement of Italian evangelicals, who had followed Luther's lead and read the gospels of the New Testament. They called themselves *spirituali.* Back in his Capodistria diocese he began to enact reforms. "Encouraging his flock to embrace a more spiritual religion, he attacked the material aspects of commonplace devotional practices," wrote Robert A. Pierce in *Pier Paolo Vergerio the Propagandist.* These included lit-candle or other "votive offerings to images and statues of saints, veneration of the Virgin, and use of the rosary—which in his view prevented individuals from understanding the spiritual aspects of Christianity," Pierce explained.

There were some elite and influential figures in Capodistria who were aghast by these ideas, and they wrote to church officials to complain. In December of 1544, Vergerio was summoned to a formal inquisition in Rome, but released without charge. Because of that mark against him, however, he was barred from participating in the 1545 Council of Trent, whose decrees marked the onset of the Counter-Reformation. The Counter-Reformation was the Roman Church's concerted effort to check the spread of Luther's teachings across Europe. Under its terms, strict adherence to doctrine was expected, and potential dissenters were rooted out by special ecclesiastical tribunals, summoned to hold formal inquisitions and mete out punishment.

Until that point Vergerio had hoped, along with many influential Catholic reformers and Protestants, that there would be an ecumenical council to resolve these differences and forge a new, united and stronger Christian church. Instead the Roman Church retreated into itself, consolidating control and wielding its enormous financial and political power.

Like Luther and others, Vergerio objected to some practices in Rome and within the Papal Curia, the administrative arm of the Roman Church whose officials controlled revenues and patronage. Pope Paul III, for example, had fathered children with a mistress while he was Cardinal Farnese, and upon becoming pope elevated two of his teenaged grandsons to become cardinals. When Paul died in 1549, he was succeeded by Julius III, a pope who lived with his adopted "nephew," a former street beggar.

Resented Patronage System

Vergerio's ties to Rome began to unravel in earnest over a financial matter in his diocese. A Capodistrian man served as secretary to one of Pope Paul's grandson-cardinals, Alessandro Farnese, and as Bishop of Capodistria, Vergerio was expected to pay this secretary's salary, which was 50 ducats a year. Vergerio's annual stipend as bishop was 200 ducats a year to maintain his entire household. He resented having to submit to this patronage and blatant nepotism, having no family wealth of his own upon which he might draw, and sought in vain to have the 50-ducat obligation reversed. Certainly his background in law gave him a solid intellectual grounding in his written and oral arguments, but in the end the dispute alienated senior officials in Rome. He felt himself increasingly isolated professionally, and came to resent the Curia and its influence. In Capodistria he continued to write treatises on church doctrine, and these circulated among reform-minded northern Italians.

In 1548, Vergerio traveled to Padua to visit a prominent figure among the Italian evangelicals known as *spirituali.* Francesco Spiera was a respected jurist but his experience with the Venetian Inquisition prompted a widely publicized breakdown that hastened his death in December of 1548. Forced to recant his evangelical beliefs or be cast out of the Roman Church, Spiera abjured and returned to his Padua home, where he soon fell ill. For six months he underwent a crisis of conscience while experiencing intense physical distress, openly despairing that he had made the wrong decision and would die a sinner.

Fled Italy Forever

After witnessing Spiera's death and openly criticizing the Bishop of Padua for his conduct in the matter, Vergerio was summoned to present himself for questioning before the Venetian Inquisition on May 1, 1549. He refused to appear and was subsequently convicted in absentia on 34 counts of heresy, formally deposed as Bishop of Capodistria, and stripped of all rights and privileges as a member of good standing of the Roman Church.

By then, Vergerio had fled over the Alps to Basel, Switzerland, a new refuge for Protestant adherents. He spent the remaining 16 years of his life writing polemics against the Roman Church. His outlaw status gave him some minor celebrity in Western Europe as the first bishop to defect from Rome and assert his allegiance to Lutheranism. In 1553 an influential German duke, Christoph of Württemberg, invited him to serve as his advisor. A staunch Protestant and ardent social reformer, Christoph underwrote several notable efforts to establish Lutheranism in southern Germany.

Another patron of Vergerio's was a high-born German noble, Albrecht of Prussia, who inherited vast lands in eastern Germany and Poland. After being appointed Grand Master of the Teutonic Knights—the original Crusader force who had once taken back Jerusalem from Muslim rule—Albrecht converted to Lutheranism and declared a new Duchy of Prussia, considered Europe's first secular state. Vergerio spent the late 1550s at Albrecht's court in Prussia, continuing to write and publish. Duke Albrecht's historic move was not entirely surprising: he was the great-grandson of the Lithuanian prince who finally capitulated to Christianity and ordered his Baltic nation to convert in the 1380s; until then, the Lithuanians had been the last pagan holdouts in Europe.

Vergerio was never able to return to Italy or his birthplace of Capodistria, whose population was decimated by outbreaks of the Black Death in the sixteenth century. The region of Istria eventually passed out of Venetian control and evolved into a larger territory known as Slovenia, which was part of the Austro-Hungarian Empire. The Slovene ethnic identity was partly shaped by a Protestant cleric named Primož Trubar, who developed the first written form of this Slavic tongue elsewhere while serving in Ljubljana, a city with closer ties to German-speaking Austrian lands.

The Istrian part of Slovenia, however, remained staunchly Roman Catholic well into the twentieth century.

Vergerio spent the final months of his life in Tübingen, a leading university in Württemberg that was an important center of Protestant theology in southern Germany. He died there on October 4, 1565, at the age of 66 or 67.

Books

Pierce, Robert A., *Pier Paolo Vergerio the Propagandist,* Edizioni di Storia e Letteratura, 2003.

Schutte, Anne Jacobson, *Pier Paolo Vergerio: The Making of an Italian Reformer,* Librairie Droz, 1977.□

Geza Vermes

British scholar Geza Vermes (1924-2013) was a leading Jewish academic who wrote extensively about Jesus Christ as a Jewish, historical figure and published a popular English translation of the Dead Sea Scrolls.

Geza Vermes was born on June 22, 1924, in Makó, Hungary, the son of Ernó and Terézia Vermes. His father was a journalist and poet, while his mother was a teacher. His parents were of Jewish ancestry, but his family had not practiced since the first half of the 1800s, and he was part of an essentially assimilated Jewish middle class in Hungary. Vermes was raised in an atmosphere which emphasized educational and intellectual pursuits, and one in which Hungarian was the language spoken at home.

Decided to Become a Priest

Vermes' parents converted to Roman Catholicism when Vermes was six years old, in the face of rising anti-Semitism in Europe. Though Vermes was educated at a Roman Catholic gymnasium and was a gifted student, he learned that he could only continue his education if he entered a seminary because anti-Jewish laws prevented him from being admitted to a university as World War II commenced. Vermes decided to become a priest to move his life forward.

In 1942, the 18-year-old Vermes enrolled in a Catholic seminary located in the diocese of Nagyvarad in Budapest, Hungary. He wanted to become a priest but also wanted to protect himself from Nazi Germany, to which Hungary was allied. Beginning in 1941, Germany compelled Hungary to fight on the side of the Axis powers after invading the country.

The decision to become a priest most likely saved his life, as the priests at the seminary kept Vermes in hiding for two years, including the time when Hungarian Jews underwent a mass deportation in 1944. Vermes lost his parents after they were arrested and taken to a Nazi concentration camp in 1944. He never heard from them again.

After being liberated by the Red Army in Budapest in December 1944, Vermes formally became a Roman Catholic priest in 1946. Unable to join the Dominicans because of his Jewish background, he joined the order of the Fathers of Notre-Dame de Sion in Louvain, Belgium. This order had been founded by two French Jewish converts to Roman Catholicism, and focused on praying for the Jewish people. A year later, the order supported Vermes' scholarly ambitions by allowing him to study theology and Asian history and languages at the Catholic University of Louvain.

Donald maclellan/Hulton Archive/Getty Images

Wrote Dissertation on the Dead Sea Scrolls

To complete his Ph.D., Vermes was originally planning to write his thesis on Isaiah. After learning of the discovery of the Dead Sea Scrolls and other writings, his topic changed. The Dead Sea Scrolls were written between 200 BC and 200 AD. They were discovered in caves at Qumran, near Jericho, located near the Dead Sea in Israel, between 1947 and 1956. The first scrolls were accidentally found by an Arab shepherd. Written in ancient Hebrew and Aramaic, the scrolls offer insights into the religious, cultural, and political life of the era in which Jesus Christ and Christianity emerged. They gave particular insight into Jewish practices and thought.

Beginning in 1950, Vermes specialized in Old Testament Studies and began translating and interpreting the Dead Sea Scrolls. He earned his doctorate in theology from Catholic University in 1953. His Dead Sea Scrolls-focused dissertation, *Manuscripts from the Judean Desert,* was one of the first written on that topic. After earning his Ph.D. with highest honors, Vermes moved to Paris where he continued to do research on the Dead Sea Scrolls and became an assistant editor at *Cahiers Sioniens,* a journal which focused on improving the relationship between Catholics and Jews. During this period, Vermes fought the rampant anti-Semitism found in the Roman Catholic church.

Vermes' plans to be a scholar-priest were stymied when he fell in love with a married English woman, Pamela Hobson Curle, in 1955. The English poet and scholar had two children. In 1957, Vermes formally left behind Roman Catholicism and the priesthood, and returned to Judaism. He and Curle married in 1958. It was not only his love affair which compelled the change, however. Vermes later explained that it was his studies of Jesus which convinced him to return to Judaism, as his studies showed that Jesus was a Jewish person, with Jewish ideas who could only be understood within Judaism.

Published English Translation of the Scrolls

The same year he left the priesthood, Vermes moved to England to be with Curle and became a professor of divinity at King's College, which was then part of Durham University, located in Newcastle upon Tyne. (It is now Newcastle University.) During his tenure there, which lasted until 1962, Vermes taught a little but primarily focused on research and writing. He published his translation of the Dead Sea Scrolls, *The Dead Sea Scrolls in English* in 1962. This translation became arguably the most widely read version of the scrolls. Through various updates and new versions he would publish over the years, Vermes achieved his goal of broadly publishing the scrolls.

One of the main translators of the scrolls, Vermes spent years irritated that direct access to the scrolls was limited to a few scholars. In 1977, when he published *The Dead Sea Scrolls: Qumran in Perspective,* he expressed these frustrations by speaking out on the matter. Vermes continued to speak out over the next decade, and the scrolls eventually became more accessible both through photographs and in their original form. Because of his work, Vermes came to be regarded as the foremost authority on the Dead Sea Scrolls.

Became Professor at Oxford

After leaving Newcastle, Vermes became a reader in Jewish studies at Oxford University in 1965, then a fellow of Oxford's Wolfson College in 1966. In 1972, Vermes also was appointed a Governor of the Oxford Centre for Postgraduate Hebrew Studies, later known as the Oxford Centre for Hebrew and Jewish Studies. At Oxford, Vermes did not teach undergraduates, but was among the first members of the humanities faculty to attract graduate students by creating and teaching masters courses in Jewish Studies focused on the Greco-Roman period. He taught by example, used various methodologies in his research and approach to scholarship, and many of his students became academics themselves.

During this period, Vermes came to be seen as a leading Jewish historian, as evidenced by his being named the editor of the *Journal of Jewish Studies* in 1971, a position he would hold until 1996. He would serve as senior editor of the periodical, which focused on the scholarly discussion of Jewish history and literature, from 1996 until his death. Under his leadership, the publication became one of the leaders in its field. Vermes was also part of a greater trend of post-World War II scholars who sought to explore a historical picture of Jesus, beginning with his roots in Nazareth and his place before Christianity. Personally, he became a member of the Liberal Jewish Synagogue but did not take part in a standard, modern Jewish sect.

Vermes published many books on Jesus and Christianity, beginning with the provocatively titled *Jesus the Jew* in 1973. The book caused a furor with the public as Vermes insisted that Jesus should be exclusively understood within the Jewish environment in which he lived. At the time, Jesus's Jewishness was often overlooked by the Christian public and the book had a profound impact. Within a few decades, Jesus's Jewishness and Jewish roots would be more commonly accepted and studied. In 1983, Vermes explored *Jesus and the World of Judaism.* Through these books, Vermes often depicted Jesus as an individualistic holy man who diverged from the religious tenets of the Judaism of his time. Through such studies, Vermes also insisted on independently reading the evidence, and had little concern with the related history of scholarly discussion.

Continued to Publish Challenging Works

By 1989, Vermes was promoted to full professor, and in 1991 he retired and was named a professor emeritus at Oxford. At the same time, he became the director of the Oxford Forum for Qumran Research at the Oxford Centre for Hebrew and Jewish studies. Vermes also continued to write and publish provocative books, many of which challenged basic beliefs of some Christians, including *The Religion of Jesus the Jew,* published in 1993. His first wife died of cancer that year, and he married his second wife, the Polish scientist Margaret Unarska, in 1996. Two years later, Vermes published the scholarly book *The Religion of Jesus the Jew,* and in 1998, produced his autobiography, *Providential Accidents.*

Over the years, other volumes written by Vermes considered various moments in the life of Jesus including his birth, trial, and the resurrection. Such books included *The Changing Faces of Jesus,* a 2000 tome which looked at the various ways Jesus was represented in the New Testament. Another was his 2003 book, *The Authentic Gospel of Jesus.* In this work, Vermes offered a commentary on the sayings of Jesus that appeared in the gospels of Matthew, Mark, and Luke. He also wrote the 2010 book, *Searching for the Real Jesus: Jesus, the Dead Sea Scrolls, and Other Religious Themes,* a collection of 29 of his shorter pieces which reflected on Jesus from a number of angles.

In 2012, Vermes published *Christian Beginnings: From Nazareth to Nicea.* It would be his last book. Well-received, *Christian Beginnings* covered the first 300 years of Christianity, focusing on the development of the Christian doctrine until the formation of the Nicene Creed.

Honored for Life's Work

Widely respected by many religious scholars, Vermes spent much of his career trying to improve relations between Christians and Jews. He also helped build Jewish studies as an academic discipline, and was the first president of both the British Association for Jewish Studies and the European Association for Jewish Studies. Vermes was recognized for his scholarly accomplishments in a number of ways, including being elected a fellow of the British Academy and the European Academy of Arts, Sciences, and Humanities. In 1988, Vermes was given a D.Litt by Oxford, one of the many honorary degrees he received over the years. Near the end of his life, in 2009, the U.S. House of Representatives recognized his contributions through a vote of congratulation.

Vermes died on May 8, 2013, in Oxford, England, at the age of 88. At the time of his death, he had plans to write a new book. In 2004 Donald Harman Akenson wrote of Vermes in the *Globe and Mail* in a review of *The Authentic Gospel of Jesus,* "If Geza Vermes, as a historian of Yeshua of Nazareth, here reveals himself as having feet of clay, we will still have to honour him as a hero for having tried to absorb in his own person, and thus in his scholarship, the terrible, soul-rendering torsion that deep knowledge of ancient Judaism and of Christianity inevitably produces."

Periodicals

Associated Press, May 11, 2013.
Daily Telegraph (London), May 13, 2013.
Globe and Mail (Canada), December 20, 2003.
Guardian (London), May 15, 2013.
New York Times, May 17, 2013.
Sunday Times (London), April 18, 2010.
Times (London), May 10, 2013; May 13, 2013.□

Edward Vernon

British naval officer Edward Vernon (1684–1757) was a British hero during the War of Jenkins' Ear. He also served for several terms in the British Parliament. Vernon's nickname was "Old Grog" and the daily issuing of rum diluted by water—instead of spirits neat—to British sailors became known as Grog.

Born November 12, 1684, in Westminster, England, Edward Vernon was the second son of James and Mary Vernon. His father served as secretary of state to King William III and as the editor of the London *Gazette.* James Vernon was also a member of Parliament for a time. Mary Vernon was the daughter of Sir John Buck. Little is known about Vernon's childhood, upbringing, and family life, save that he was educated at the Westminster School from 1692 to 1700. His education included the classics, mathematics, and French.

Hulton Archive/Getty Images

Joined the Royal Navy

It is not known why Vernon was sent to the navy, other than that his father saw opportunity for his son to stretch his political and diplomatic skills because of the growth of global conflict. On May 10, 1700, Vernon joined the Royal Navy as a volunteer and first served on the HMS *Shrewsbury.* Vernon immediately experienced war at sea as the *Shrewsbury* was sent as a part of an Anglo-Dutch squadron deployed to the Baltic Sea as the relationship between Sweden and Denmark deteriorated. The British had orders to bring about a peaceful resolution to the conflict if possible, but support Sweden if a conflict ensued, as it briefly did.

Vernon served on several ships over the next few years, and gained more exposure to war in Spain. Promoted to third lieutenant in September 1702, he was appointed to the HMS *Lennox,* which was originally part of the Chanel squadron but was later transferred to a Mediterranean deployment. On the *Lennox,* he again saw an amphibious expedition in the Baltic, but primarily was involved in convoy duties.

Throughout his naval career, Vernon witnessed or was part of some of the greatest battles in naval history. In 1704, for example, Vernon served on the HMS *Barfluer* in the Mediterranean when the ship saw the capture of Gibraltar by British forces and the Battle of Málaga. Both occurred as part of the War of the Spanish Succession, and the latter was the largest naval battle of the war. In December 1704, Vernon was transferred to the HMS *Britannnia,* and was present when Barcelona was captured by a multinational army helmed by Lord Peterborough the following year.

Promoted to Captain

Vernon's naval career continued to move forward. In January 1706, Vernon was promoted to captain and was given his first command on the HMS *Dolphin.* Later that year, he was assigned to HMS *Rye* and continued to serve in the Mediterranean through 1707. Returning to England that year, Vernon went back to sea in November 1707 on the HMS *Jersey,* which first was deployed to the French coast. By April 1708, Vernon was given command of the West Indies station in the Caribbean. Seeing battle in the War of the Spanish Succession, he broke a Spanish squadron near Cartagena, a coastal city in present-day Colombia.

The War of the Spanish Succession ended in 1712, and Vernon then returned to Britain. Vernon spent the next three years at home, then served on the HMS *Assistance* in the Baltic Sea for about two years. He faced challenging situations in 1716 and 1717 related to the transport of British ambassadors to and from Constantinople, a ship damaged at sea, and securing the release of British sailors impressed by the Venetians.

After an 18 month period in which he was on half pay (not in active service), Vernon returned to service when he was appointed to the HMS *Mary* and again served in the Baltic and the Caribbean, where he saw some action around Port Royal, Jamaica, and Havana, Cuba. British trade was already being negatively impacted by Spanish privateers and pirates.

Elected to Parliament

Vernon's political career began in the early 1720s. From 1721 to 1726, Vernon was again on half pay. He was elected a member of Parliament (MP) as a Whig representing Penryn. As an MP, Vernon was active in debates regarding the navy and naval actions.

In 1726, Vernon returned to sea when he was appointed to serve on the HMS *Grafton* which served in the Baltic until the winter of 1727. When Spain declared war on Great Britain, the ship became part of the fleet at Gibraltar. After peace was reached with Spain in May 1728 to end the relatively brief Anglo-Spanish War, Vernon requested half pay and went back to Great Britain and his parliamentary seat representing Penryn. In 1729, Vernon married Sarah Best. Their three children died before them. The couple primarily made their home in Nacton.

Britain's peace with Spain was tenuous over the next decade. Part of the agreement with Spain allowed for smuggling and oppression in Spanish colonies, and British merchants in the West Indies were struggling with major losses because Spanish coastguards were preventing foreign trade. Vernon became involved in this situation, championing the case of Robert Jenkins, a British merchant seaman. In 1731, Jenkins claimed the Spanish boarded his ship and cut off his ear. Jenkins' story reached Parliament several years later as the Spanish continued to act against foreign trade in the region. When the British government declared war against Spain in 1739, the conflict became known as the War of Jenkins' Ear.

Became Vice Admiral

With the start of this conflict, Vernon was promoted to Vice Admiral in July 1739. He had been an outspoken proponent of the war and the Royal Navy, and was given command of a five-ship squadron in the West Indies. Vernon was set up to fail, however, as his squadron was charged with destroying as much of the Spanish shipping and settlements as they could, by any means necessary. Vernon's detractors hoped that he and his ships could not achieve any of these goals and that Vernon would be held responsible.

Vernon defied their expectations. His small group was able to capture the Spanish fort in the stronghold of Porto Bello—located in present-day Panama—as well as the city itself. In the process, Vernon and his sailors also destroyed all the war stores located there. To support Vernon and his accomplishments, the British had to send reinforcements to attack other Spanish possessions. Vernon became a war hero, honored by the city of London.

Ordered Grog Rations

For nonheroic reasons, it was during this period that Vernon's historical legacy was cemented. With an order issued on August 21, 1740, Vernon changed the composition of the daily ration of rum given to sailors of the British fleet to combat drunkenness and disciplinary issues. Beginning in 1655, sailors were given a daily half-pint ration of rum neat. Vernon ordered that the rum ration be watered down to three parts water to one part rum.

This ration became known as Grog after Vernon. Vernon was fond of wearing a cloak made of grogram—composed of silk, mohair, and wool fibers that were stiffened with gum—and his nickname was "Old Grog." The Grog ration was given daily to British sailors until 1970. Today, grog is the name given to a number of alcoholic beverages, with the definition changing from country to country.

By April 1741, Vernon had a larger fleet, land support from General Thomas Wentworth, and focused his attention on Cartegna. Vernon had failed to subdue this settlement with his smaller squadron, and did not succeed a second time. In addition to the British suffering from an outbreak of yellow fever, Wentworth's lack of ability as a commander led to delays in attacking and being repelled by the Spanish.

Struggled in Jamaica

After returning to Port Royal, located in present-day Jamaica, at the end of May 1741, Vernon and Wentworth were charged with attacking Cuba. The outcome was similar, as Wentworth's inability to lead his men into battle effectively and another outbreak of illness forced the attack to be abandoned by the end of the year. Vernon was incensed with Wentworth, causing an outburst of ill will between them. Both parties were recalled to Britain in December 1742.

At home, Vernon returned to Parliament, having been elected in his absence to represent Ipswich. In Parliament, Vernon continued to speak out on naval affairs. He also was the alleged author of perhaps some of the many anonymous pamphlets that appeared deriding the government on naval issues and criticizing the Admiralty. Though Vernon denied he was the author, many scholars believe he penned at least a few of them.

In 1745, Vernon was promoted to admiral and given the command of the North Sea Fleet. There, the British faced a threat from French forces that were supporting Charles Edward Stuart, commonly known as Bonnie Prince Charlie, a Jacobite pretender to the British throne. Vernon, however, was unhappy because he was not given the position of commander in chief by the Admiralty and asked to be relieved of his duties on December 1, 1745. Vernon's request was granted. In 1746, Vernon was removed from the list of flag officers (senior commissioned officer).

Served in Parliament until Death

Until his death over a decade later, Vernon remained a member of parliament and was interested in naval affairs. He might have authored more pamphlets as well. Vernon died on October 30, 1757, in Nacton, England, and was buried next to his wife, who died in 1756, in Nacton. After his death, he was remembered as an effective naval commander who worked to improve naval procedures, the Admiralty, maneuvers, and gun drills.

Vernon's nephew Francis, Lord Orwell, had a flattering monument—created by sculptor Michael Rysbrack—erected to his uncle at Westminster Abbey in 1763. According to the Westminster Abbey website, Francis's inscription on the monument lauded "The testimony of a good conscience was his reward, the love and esteem of all good men, his glory. In battle; through calm, he was active, & through intrepid, prudent: successful yet not ostentatious, ascribing the glory to God. In the Senate, he was disinterested, vigilant and stead. On the XXXth day of October MDCCLVII he died as he lived, the friend of Man, the lover of his Country, the father of the poor, aged LXXIII."

Though Vernon's reputation as a naval officer fluctuated from the mid-eighteenth to the early twentieth century, his contributions and complexities were realized later in the 1900s. In *Precursors of Nelson: British Admirals of the Eighteenth Century,* contributor Richard Harding explained "He never fought the great sea battles that would have placed him in the first rank of naval heroes. Nor did he hold high office in naval administration. Yet his pamphlets, his parliamentary speeches and his correspondence while commander in the Channel do give him an important place in the development of the navy." Harding added, "For a short but significant time, Vernon was the most prominent public face of maritime war, arguing for its utility and the means by which it could be waged."

Books

Hart, Francis Russell, *Admirals of the Caribbean,* Houghton Mifflin Company, 1922.

Palmer, Michael A., *Command at Sea: Naval Command and Control Since the Sixteenth Century,* Harvard University Press, 2005.

Precursors of Nelson: British Admirals of the Eighteenth Century, edited by Peter Le Fevre and Richard Hardin, Stackpoole Books, 2000.

Periodicals

Daily Telegraph (Australia), February 16, 2012.

Roanoke Times (VA), November 25, 2009.

Townsville Bulletin (Australia), March 7, 2009.

Online

"Biography: Edward Vernon," *National Museum of the Royal Navy,* http://www.royalnavalmuseum.org/info_sheets_edward_vernon.htm (December 12, 2013).

"Edward Vernon," *Westminster Abbey,* http://www.westminster-abbey.org/our-history/people/edward-vernon (December 12, 2013).☐

W

Edgar Wallace

Wildly popular and extraordinarily prolific, British crime writer Edgar Wallace (1875–1932) gained notoriety for his quick output and ability to dictate an entire novel in a two- to three-day period. Over the course of his literary career, Wallace wrote 175 novels, 30 plays, and 957 short stories. Among 20th century authors, Wallace holds the distinction of having the most movies made from his work—some 160 films have been produced from his writing, with his most enduring contribution being the towering feature creature King Kong.

Richard Horatio Edgar Wallace was born April 1, 1875, in London. His mother, Polly Richards, was a widow who lost her sea captain husband while pregnant with his older sister, Josephine. As a single mother, Polly Richards struggled to support her daughter but found work with a London theater company run by a woman known as Miss Marriott. Miss Marriott took Polly Richards and her daughter under her wing, casting them both in plays. At some point, Polly Richards fell for Richard Edgar, the dashing son of Miss Marriott. After becoming pregnant with his child, Polly Richards hid the pregnancy and gave birth in secret.

Eager to re-join her acting troupe, Polly Richards left her newborn in the hands of George Freeman. Freeman worked as a porter at the Billingsgate fish market. He and his wife had ten children and agreed to take the child for five shillings a week. The Freemans were not highly educated; George Freeman could read a bit but he could not write. Nonetheless, they sent Wallace to school.

Entered Workforce Early

When Wallace was 12, the Freemans pulled him from school and sent him to work. Over the next several years, Wallace worked numerous jobs. He worked at a printing press, sold newspapers, and labored in a shoe shop and rubber factory. Wallace, however, grew tired of the monotony of manual labor and ran away to sea in 1890, signing on as a cook for a fish trawler. The rough seas made him so sick he jumped ship one day when the trawler was docked.

Next, Wallace worked on a dairy farm and as a plasterer and road maker. Poor, tired, and starving, the 18-year-old Wallace joined the Royal West Kent Regiment in 1893. Eventually, Wallace worked his way into the medical staff corps and was sent to Aldershot, a major garrison for the British army. After training, Wallace became an orderly in a military hospital. This job offered a lot of down time, during which Wallace wrote poems and stories about his fellow soldiers, often reciting them in the canteen.

Launched Writing Career in Africa

In 1896, Wallace sailed for South Africa to his new post at the Royal Navy base in Simon's Town. The base hospital held few patients, leaving Wallace free time to pursue his newfound passion for writing. Soon after his arrival in South Africa, Wallace got a poem published in the *Cape Times* and began writing poems for the *Owl,* a Cape Town weekly. Wallace also wrote election jingles for South African papers and contributed poems to London papers back home.

Seeing his name in print bolstered Wallace's confidence. He yearned to write full-time, so he bought his way out of the army. Discharged in May 1899, Wallace began his freelance career reporting on the Boer Wars for several South African papers, including the *Cape Times.*

© DIZ Muenchen GmbH, Sueddeutsche Zeitung Photo/Alamy

The Boer Wars were fought between British and Dutch settlers in South Africa. Wallace also signed on with the international news agency Reuters. Filled with lively descriptions, Wallace's war narratives from South Africa were picked up by papers around the globe.

In 1900, Wallace published his first collection. Titled *Writ in Barracks,* the book included poems about British patriotism, war, army doctors, and commanders. Though many of the poems had been previously published, the book was not well-received. London publisher Methuen printed 2,000 copies but sold only 977. According to Margaret Lane's book *Edgar Wallace: The Biography of a Phenomenon,* the London *Daily Mail* offered a lukewarm review: "Though Mr. Wallace's rhymes, being essentially journalism, deserved the places they have held in our newspapers, we do not think that they were ever worth collecting between two covers."

In 1902, Wallace became editor of the *Rand Daily Mail,* a Johannesburg newspaper owned by a wealthy South African businessman named Harry Freeman Cohen. Given a sizable salary for the first time in his life, Wallace lived the high life. He moved into a lavish bungalow in Johannesburg, hired servants and bought himself expensive suits, hats, and gloves. He also spent money betting on horses and entertaining his peers. Wallace went into debt living beyond his means and frustrated Cohen by buying and printing sensational material at exorbitant prices. Wallace's tenure with the *Rand Daily Mail* lasted less than two years. He was fired for adopting an editorial stance that ran in contrast to the owner's wishes.

Returned to London

Wallace returned to London and set up house with his wife. Wallace had married after leaving the army. For years he had courted Ivy Caldecott, the daughter of a Methodist missionary he met after first arriving in South Africa. In London, Wallace found work as a reporter for the *Daily Mail.* In April 1904, Ivy gave birth to a son, Bryan Edgar Wallace. Their first child, a daughter, had died of meningitis while they still lived in South Africa. From 1904-05, Wallace traveled overseas, covering the Russo-Japanese War for the *Daily Mail.*

After returning to London, Wallace hit upon an idea for a novel and began work on the manuscript that would become *The Four Just Men,* his first best-seller. The murder mystery centered on four vigilantes who commit murder in the name of justice. In this particular tale, a British foreign secretary dies. Prior to the book's release, Wallace created hype through an extensive—and expensive—advertising campaign. He encouraged sales by offering a cash reward to readers who could predict how the book would end and ran the contest through the *Daily Mail.*

After the book's release in 1905, thousands of solutions poured in, yet months passed without any rewards being presented. Wallace found himself in a bind—he failed to include a clause that limited the number of winners and found himself obligated to pay for every correct answer. The public grew angry and denounced the contest as a scam. Though sales were brisk, Wallace ended up in debt over his huge advertising campaign and could not afford to pay the rewards. Eventually, *Daily Mail* owner Alfred Harmsworth paid the reward money to alleviate the bad press his newspaper was receiving through its affiliation with the contest. Wallace further irritated Harmsworth when the *Daily Mail* had to pay damages for two libel suits involving Wallace. He was soon fired.

Turned to Fiction

In 1908, Wallace desperately needed money. His wife had given birth to another child, Patricia Marion Caldecott Wallace, in late 1907. At this point, Wallace gave up journalism and decided to write fiction instead of seeking a job at another newspaper. Wallace began publishing stories in the *Weekly Tale-Teller* and earned a reputation for his fictionalized accounts of his time spent in the Congo. Prior to being let go by the *Daily Mail,* Wallace had traveled to the Congo to report on alleged abuse by the Belgians who controlled the area.

Wallace used his South African experiences to create a magazine serial called *Sanders of the River* about a British district commissioner named Sanders who ruled over South Africans during Africa's colonial days. The series, launched around 1909, proved highly popular, prompting Wallace to create *The People of the River* series, which also featured Sanders. The stories appealed to readers interested in Wallace's vivid descriptions of South Africa and its people. Sanders became a movie in 1935.

Other recurring characters included Bosambo, chief of the Ochori, and Bones, another British official. These books would be considered politically incorrect in the 21st century for their callous portrayal of African natives but at the time echoed popular European sentiment toward Africa's indigenous population. Another popular character developed from Wallace's personal experiences was Private Selby, who offered British citizens a look at army life.

While Wallace's writing life was proving successful, his marriage was not. His third child, Michael Blair Wallace, was born in 1916, but within two years, Wallace and his wife separated. In 1921, he married Violet King. King had become Wallace's secretary some years earlier—when she was still a teenager. There was a 23-year age difference between Wallace and King. They had one daughter, Penelope, born in 1923.

Wrote Books, Plays, Movie Scripts

During the early 1920s, Wallace signed a book deal with Hodder and Stoughton, which offered him royalties for the first time in his career. In addition, Hodder and Stoughton said it would publish his books as fast as he could write them. During the first decade of the agreement, Wallace published 46 books. Wallace also made money by slipping "ads" into his stories. He would mention a specific product by name—and often have it relate directly to the plot—and receive payment from the manufacturer.

Along the way, Wallace got involved with theater. In 1919, *The Whirligig* hit London's Palace Theater. Wallace wrote the revue in conjunction with British director Albert de Courville. It was a moderate success. Wallace followed with *M'Lady* in 1922. Wallace—ever confident in his abilities—decided to produce the play himself to keep expenses down and profits up. Critics scorched the play. A colossal failure, Wallace pulled it from the stage within two weeks of opening night. Wallace kept at it, though, and in 1926 staged *The Ringer,* a play about an assassin. Wallace consulted British actor Gerald Du Maurier during production. This play was so successful it ran for over a year and was made into a silent film, as well as a talkie. Prolific as usual, Wallace wrote some 16 plays in a six-year period and became the first playwright to have three plays running simultaneously in London.

In the late 1920s, Wallace became affiliated with the British Lion Film Corp., which put him under contract so as to have the first option of turning his works into film. Later, Wallace directed his own movies. In late 1931, Wallace traveled to Hollywood to work on movie scripts for RKO Pictures. He had just finished the scenario for King Kong—relying heavily on the beauty and beast theme—when he became ill and died of pneumonia on February 10, 1932. Released in 1933, *King Kong* remains one of Hollywood's most memorable characters. The script was finished without Wallace but his touches remained. It was Wallace's idea to capture the beast and bring him to the United States for a finale on the Empire State Building.

Known for Quantity Over Quality

Wallace was popular with readers but serious literary critics dismissed his work, saying his books lacked the enduring quality of real classics. Wallace was known to work quickly. He cranked out his material from a home office, reporting to his desk by 6 a.m. Working from notes, Wallace dictated entire novels and stories into a Dictaphone while drinking sweet tea and smoking incessantly. His secretary typed the dictation into a manuscript and Wallace and his wife edited it for grammar and errors. At this point, Wallace considered the work done—he balked at rewrites.

The press even joked about the pace of Wallace's output. There was a popular cartoon that referred to the "midday Wallace," as if he rolled out several editions a day. According to *Edgar Wallace,* the *Daily Telegraph,* in May 1931, offered this take: "How Edgar Wallace accomplishes and executes all the work that passes under his name he only can tell.... If only Edgar Wallace would give himself sufficient time to write a really first-class play he could take a very much higher place in the esteem of the general public than he now occupies. People have come to expect nothing from him but thrills and excitement, relieved by a low order of comicality."

Wallace lived a lavish lifestyle beyond his means. He gambled, owned mediocre racehorses, employed servants, threw frequent house parties, and drove a yellow Rolls-Royce. Wallace was often in debt and this necessitated his writing pace. Wallace reportedly began 1931's *The Devil Man* on a Friday night and 60 hours later had 80,000 words. Despite the minor errors that slipped into his work (a character's name might change during the course of a novel), Wallace remained incredibly popular with the masses, who enjoyed his fun reads that took them away from their lives for a while. Enormously popular, books like *The Crimson Circle* (1922) and *The Green Archer* (1923) sold hundreds of thousands of copies. During the 1920s, Wallace's publisher claimed that in England, one-quarter of all books read were written by Wallace.

Books

Lane, Margaret, *Edgar Wallace: The Biography of a Phenomenon,* Doubleday, Doran & Co., 1938.

Periodicals

Age (Melbourne, Australia), October 23, 2012.

Journal of Popular Culture, Summer 1998.

Lantern, February 1992.□

Mike Wallace

The American broadcast journalist Mike Wallace (1918–2012) was one of the best-known and most controversial figures in 20th-century American television. He was famed for his aggressive interview style, displayed most prominently on the CBS television news magazine *60 Minutes.*

© Everett CollectionInc/Alamy

At the peak of his fame as a *60 Minutes* correspondent, Wallace was an instantly recognizable face. An advertisement (quoted in the *New York Post*) had only to state "The four most feared words in the English language: Mike Wallace is here," and viewers would know the reference: Wallace with a camera trained on an uncomfortable wrongdoer was a formidable adversary, using timing and silence to frame and prolong the contradictions in which the victim had been caught. Wallace came from a tradition of crusading journalism that defended the underdog and exposed the misdeeds of the powerful, and he was a perennial award-winner whose interviews were regarded as classics. Equally, he used techniques that were widely regarded as unfair, and he was hit hard professionally and personally by several well-publicized missteps. Wallace's career was unusually long, beginning in Michigan in the early 1940s, and continuing until 2008, his 90th year.

Gained Broadcasting Experience on Campus

Wallace was born Myron Leon Wallace on May 9, 1918. He parents, Friedan (Frank) and Zina, were Russian Jewish immigrants whose surname has been variously given as Wallik and Wallechinsky. Wallace's father was a grocer and later an insurance salesman. At Brookline High School, Wallace was a solid but unspectacular student. He attended the University of Michigan, majoring in English and getting involved with an early example of campus broadcasting there. The latter experience inspired Wallace to pursue a media career. He remained involved with his alma mater in later life, helping to establish the Livingston Awards and the Knight-Wallace Fellowships, a pair of prestigious journalism fellowships.

After graduating, Wallace landed a $20-a-week writing job at a station in Grand Rapids, Michigan. He moved on to Detroit, where he served as an announcer and actor on such hit radio series as *The Lone Ranger* and *The Green Hornet.* After narrating a radio program used by the United States Navy in its recruiting, he was inspired to join the Navy himself, serving as a communications officer in the Pacific. In the late 1940s, Wallace worked at various jobs including radio game show host, cigarette advertising pitchman (Wallace himself was a smoker for years), and professional wrestling announcer. In 1949, Wallace and his second wife, Buff Cobb, co-hosted a talk show called *Mike and Buff* that began on the radio and then moved to the new medium of television. The controversy and bickering built into the show's format eventually had a negative impact on their marriage, and they divorced in 1954.

In 1951, Wallace had moved to New York, and as the television industry grew there he quickly found his place within it and his life's work. The characteristic Wallace personality that later became famous was largely invented during the run of a talk show called *Night Beat* that ran on the DuMont television network from 1956 to 1958. Here Wallace found production values that matched his own ability to manipulate a situation through his own acting skills. "We had lighting that was warts-and-all close-ups," he recalled (according to Tim Weiner of *The New York Times*). "I was asking tough questions. And I had found my bliss." *Night Beat* was picked up and renamed *The Mike Wallace Interview* by the ABC network, achieving national distribution before it was canceled by skittish network executives; the confrontational tone of the program had led critics to dub the host Mike Malice.

Shaken by Son's Death

In 1962, Wallace's oldest son, Peter, was reported missing during a hiking trip in Greece. Arriving by plane in Athens, Wallace went to look for his son and suffered the trauma of finding his dead body at the bottom of a cliff. The experience fixed Wallace's commitment to serious journalism; he resolved in the future to do only work of which his son would have been proud. But the experience also left Wallace with a propensity toward serious depression. In 1963, *The CBS Morning News with Mike Wallace* went on the air; he remained the program's host for three years and then continued at CBS as a full-time reporter.

In 1968, Wallace was offered the position of press secretary in the ultimately successful presidential campaign of Richard M. Nixon but turned it down, keeping true to his vow to pursue only serious journalistic work. Instead, he joined the cast of the new CBS newsmagazine program *60 Minutes,* which featured a rotating series of hosts and correspondents who would research and conduct their own stories and interviews. Wallace remained one of the program's hosts until 2006 and continued to appear until

2008. Wallace, who once remarked (according to the London *Independent*) that "[t]here's no such thing as an indiscreet question," defined the program's tone with his take-no-prisoners interviews. "Without him and his iconic style, there probably wouldn't be a '60 Minutes,'" CBS News chairman Jeff Fager told Ashley Hayes of the news channel CNN.

Wallace had the combination of tenacity and contacts necessary to land interviews with most of the world's top newsmakers, and he treated them all, from presidents Nixon and Ronald Reagan to the mercurial Libyan strongman Moammar Gaddafi to Russian president Vladimir Putin, absolutely fearlessly. He asked Iran's theocratic leader Ayatollah Ruhollah Khomeini what he thought of being called a lunatic by Egyptian president Anwar Sadat (Khomeini laughed and responded that Sadat was a heretic). The Mike Malice side of his personality could surface, as in an interview in which he badgered singer Barbra Streisand about her long course of psychotherapy treatment, but Wallace was never dull, and he helped turn *60 Minutes* into a top-ten ratings powerhouse for many years—something very rare for a news program in American television.

Program Provoked Lawsuit

More serious than Wallace's disagreeable moods was the controversy that followed the airing of a 1982 CBS documentary, hosted by Wallace, called *The Uncounted Enemy: A Vietnam Deception.* The program alleged that U.S. commander General William C. Westmoreland had deliberately falsified estimates of North Vietnamese and Viet Cong troop strength. Westmoreland launched a $120 million libel suit against CBS in 1984. When the case went to trial, many of Wallace's charges were corroborated, but unethical procedures in assembling the story, including a $25,000 payment to one of the show's interviewees, were also uncovered. The bad publicity propelled Wallace into a deep depression, during which, on December 30, 1984, he attempted to commit suicide by taking an overdose of sleeping pills.

Wallace continued to suffer from depression for the rest of his life. He maintained a home on the island of Martha's Vineyard in Massachusetts, where he became friends with the novelist William Styron and the political humorist Art Buchwald, also depression sufferers. "We walked around in the rain together on Martha's Vineyard and consoled each other," Wallace said in an interview quoted by Weiner. "We named ourselves the Blues Brothers." He credited his fourth wife, Mary Yates, as a stabilizing influence, but a biography of Wallace by Peter Rader was one of several sources alleging that he harassed female CBS staffers into his old age.

Despite personal problems, Wallace's skills as an interviewer remained undimmed. His 2005 *60 Minutes* interview with outfielder José Canseco was a key step in exposing the use of performance-enhancing drugs in professional baseball. Wallace slowed his pace in his late 80s but appeared as late as 2008 with an interview of baseball pitcher Roger Clemens. By that time, *60 Minutes* and Wallace's contributions to it had spawned a host of imitations. Wallace won 20 Emmy awards, including a Lifetime Achievement Emmy in 2003, and he was inducted into the Television Academy Hall of Fame in 1991.

Wallace was married four times in all; Chris Wallace, a host on the Fox News cable channel, was his son by his first wife. He underwent triple bypass surgery in 2008 and recovered, but after that he finally retired from television. Wallace died at an assisted care facility in New Canaan, Connecticut, on April 7, 2012.

Books

Encyclopedia Judaica, Gale, 2007.

Rader, Peter, *Mike Wallace: A Life,* Dunne, 2012.

Periodicals

CNN Wire, April 9, 2012.

Independent (London, England), April 11, 2012.

National Review, April 30, 2012.

New York Post, March 4, 2012.

New York Times, April 9, 2012.

Times (London, England), April 10, 2012.

Variety, April 9, 2012.

Online

"Wallace, Mike," *Museum of Broadcast Communications,* http://www.museum.tv/eotv/eotv.htm (October 23, 2013).□

John Wheelwright

The colonial American minister John Wheelwright (c. 1592–1679) was a key player in the Antinomian controversy, one of the most serious theological disputes to trouble the young Massachusetts Bay Colony in its first decades. Forced to leave Massachusetts, Wheelwright founded the town of Exeter, New Hampshire.

The Antinomian controversy flared over an issue central to Protestant faith: does the Christian reward of eternal life flow from faith (the covenant of grace) or from good works (the covenant of works)? Wheelwright arrived in the midst of the dispute and immediately became a strong backer of the covenant-of-faith position and of its chief proponent, Anne Hutchinson. Expressing his views strongly and showing himself unwilling to compromise, he was exiled from the colony in a stormy court proceeding. By means unknown he made his way to what is now Exeter, where he and his followers purchased land from local Native Americans and proceeded to carve a small colony out of the wilderness. When Massachusetts asserted its control over southeastern New Hampshire, Wheelwright was forced to move again. He spent the rest of his long life in Maine, Massachusetts, and back in England among adherents of the radical Puritan movement that had shaped his outlook.

Attended Cambridge University

Records of Wheelwright's life are incomplete. He was probably born in Saleby, in eastern England's Lincolnshire region, in 1592. Wheelwright's family seems to have consisted of small landowners; he inherited substantial real estate holdings and passed them along to his own children when he died. He was admitted to Cambridge University sizar—with a scholarship—in 1611, receiving a bachelor's degree in 1614 or 1615 and a master's degree in 1618. One of his classmates at Cambridge was Oliver Cromwell, who went on to overthrow the English monarchy temporarily and become England's Lord Protector and leader.

Wheelwright was apparently a physically vigorous man: Cromwell said, according to Wheelwright's early biographer Charles H. Bell, that "I remember the time when I was more afraid of meeting Wheelwright at football, than I have been since of meeting an army in the field, for I was infallibly sure of being tripped up by him." In 1619, Wheelwright was ordained as a minister, and two years later he married Marie Storre, the daughter of the vicar of Bilsby in Lincolnshire. When his father-in-law died, Wheelwright became vicar himself. He and Marie had three children. Marie died in 1629, and the following year he married Mary Hutchinson. Mary's brother William and his wife, Anne, would soon depart for Massachusetts with their 11 children.

Both Wheelwright and Cromwell became attached to the dissident Puritan sect within the Church of England, which wanted to purge all aspects of Catholic ritual from Anglican worship, some years after they completed their educations. It was apparently in the early 1630s that Wheelwright began to run seriously afoul of church authorities. In 1633, he lost his post as vicar of Bilsby, perhaps because he had tried to sell his position (a misdeed known as simony), perhaps because church authorities were already trying to silence him. For several years, Wheelwright seems to have traveled around Lincolnshire, trying to find a church that would have him. In 1636, he, his wife, and their five children set sail for Boston; they arrived on May 26 and were given a hearty welcome in the growing town, but soon the divisions within Puritanism itself began to assert themselves.

Pastored Small-Town Church

Wheelwright hoped to become a teacher at Boston's new church, but the colony leader and soon-to-be governor John Winthrop realized that Wheelwright was part of the Antinomian camp of John Cotton (who was from Lincolnshire), who already held a position at the church, and maneuvered to block his selection. He became minister of a newly built church in Mount Wollaston (now Quincy, Massachusetts) about ten miles to the south. Winthrop hoped to keep in balance the forces of the growing Antinomian controversy, stoked by the at first all-female meetings at the home of Anne Hutchinson, who had helped arrange Wheelwright's appointment in Mount Wollaston.

The peace did not last long. The colony set a Fast Day, a day of general fasting and prayer, for January 19, 1637, with the intention of promoting peaceful reflection on the issues that divided the colonists. But Wheelwright, invited to preach at the Boston church, gave a fiery sermon that attacked the ministers on Winthrop's side, who made up the majority of the Massachusetts clergy. And Winthrop himself, who was running against Henry Vane for the post of colonial governor in 1637, was suspicious of Wheelwright's philosophy, which seemed to threaten civil law and community cohesion, making its adherents answerable only to God.

Wheelwright was summoned to court after this sermon, charged with sedition and contempt for civil authority, and found guilty. But his backers, who included Governor Henry Vane, protested the decision, and no action was taken. The situation began to turn against Wheelwright when Winthrop was elected governor in May of 1637 and Vane departed for England. At a synod in September Wheelwright lost another key supporter when Cotton joined the larger group of ministers opposing him. Wheelwright refused, however, to retract any of the offending passages in his sermon.

Banished from Massachusetts

When the Massachusetts Bay General Court met in November, therefore, Wheelwright's fate was sealed, and he was banished from the colony. He was given 14 days to leave. Still refusing to recant, he requested a chance to appeal to England's king, but the court ruled that it had final authority. Wheelwright was offered a place with other dissenters in Roger Williams's new colony of Rhode Island, but he wanted to be free to follow his own conscience. So, during the notably severe winter of 1637–1638, he headed north, spending the winter in a tiny settlement called Squamscot, New Hampshire. He left no record of how he made the 55-mile trip in what was probably dismal weather, nor of how he financed the next stage of his career or obtained the materials and livestock necessary to establish a new settlement. In a later pamphlet called the *Mercurius Americanus,* quoted on the website of the Exeter Historical Society, he wrote (describing himself in the third person), "I confess it was marvelous he got thither [to New Hampshire] at that time, when they expelled him, by reason of the deep snow in which he might have perished."

At the time, what is now southeastern New Hampshire was under no real government authority; it was part of a disputed English land grant that became ensnared in the deepening political crisis in England. For Wheelwright, therefore, it was perfect. In April of 1638, he made two land purchases from local Native Americans. About 35 families soon joined him from Boston, and the new settlement of Exeter quickly established its own government, courts, and church, with Wheelwright as minister. The group included a pair of carpenters who built some reliable houses, and the settlement flourished, raising livestock and feeding them with plants from salt marshes, farming upland plots, and fishing in the Exeter and Merrimac rivers.

After five years, however, Wheelwright was back where he had started: the Massachusetts Bay Colony succeeded in extending its jurisdiction over an area that included Exeter, and Wheelwright, still under sentence of banishment, had to leave once again. In 1643, he moved to Wells, Maine, but apparently tired of life on the run; the following year he sent letters to Winthrop and the General Court, finally apologizing for his conduct in 1637. The Antinomian controversy was still a live issue in Boston; Anne Hutchinson had been banished to Rhode Island and had been killed by Native Americans in 1643. Winthrop and Thomas Weld issued an anti-Wheelwright pamphlet, *A Short Story of the Rise, Reign and Ruine of the Antinomians,* to which *Mercurius Americanus* was a response. In May of 1644, the court reversed Wheelwright's banishment sentence.

Wheelwright did not immediately leave Wells, where he had become pastor of a church. He stayed on for two years, then preached in Hampton, New Hampshire from 1647 to 1656. He returned to England and supported Cromwell's Commonwealth government, but when the monarchy was restored in 1660, his position there again became difficult. The 70-year-old Wheelwright returned to America in 1662, and accepted a position as pastor at a church in Salisbury, New Hampshire. He continued to preach there until his death on November 15, 1679.

Books

Bell, Charles H., *John Wheelwright,* Prince Society, 1876.

Elliott, Emory, ed., *American Colonial Writers, 1606–1734* (*Dictionary of Literary Biography,* Vol. 24), Gale, 1984.

Heard, John, Jr., *John Wheelwright 1592–1679,* Houghton Mifflin ,1939.

Online

"Early Exeter History, 1638–1887," *Exeter Historical Society,* http://www.exeterhistory.org/ (November 20, 2013).

"Joseph Dow's History of Hampton: Rev. John Wheelwright," *Lane Memorial Library* (Hampton, NH), http://www.hampton.lib.nh.us/hampton/history/dow/chap19/dow19_3.htm (November 20, 2013).□

Lenny Wilkens

American professional basketball player and coach Lenny Wilkens (born 1937) was only the second African American coach in the National Basketball Association (NBA) and all-time leader in coaching victories. Wilkens is also one of only two men inducted into the Basketball Hall of Fame as both a player and a coach.

Born Leonard Randolph Wilkens Jr., on October 28, 1937, he was the son of Leonard Sr., a chauffeur, and his wife, Henrietta, a candy factory worker. Because Wilkens' father was African American and his mother was white, he and his three siblings faced taunting and other acts of discrimination throughout their childhood. Leonard Wilkens Sr., died unexpectedly when his son was five years old, and the family lived in poverty in a tenement in the tough Bedford-Stuyvesant, Brooklyn neighborhood after his death. Wilkens later remembered that no one helped his mother and her family after her husband's death and he saw people looking down at them.

Despite his age, Wilkens took on responsibilities and helped take care of his younger siblings. He took his first job at the age of seven, delivering groceries. He also focused on doing well at school and avoiding trouble. Wilkens was educated at Catholic schools in the neighborhood.

Found Release in Basketball

One release was basketball, a game Wilkens often played in his spare time. After learning to play street ball, he soon played in youth leagues around Brooklyn, where he learned the mechanics of the game. Wilkens attended Boys High School, a basketball powerhouse. Though he made the basketball team as a freshman, he quit the team in part because he believed he did not have the skills to start, but also because he lacked playing time. Instead, he was a starter for a CYO (Catholic Youth Organization) league, where his coach was Father Tom Mannion.

Because of Mannion's influence, Wilkens landed an athletic scholarship to a Catholic university in Rhode Island, Providence College, after he graduated from high school in 1956. Here, Wilkens also experienced racism as he was one of only six African Americans among the 1,200 member student body. Yet, he also grew as a basketball player, learning skills that made him a strong point guard and defender for the Friars. During his junior year,

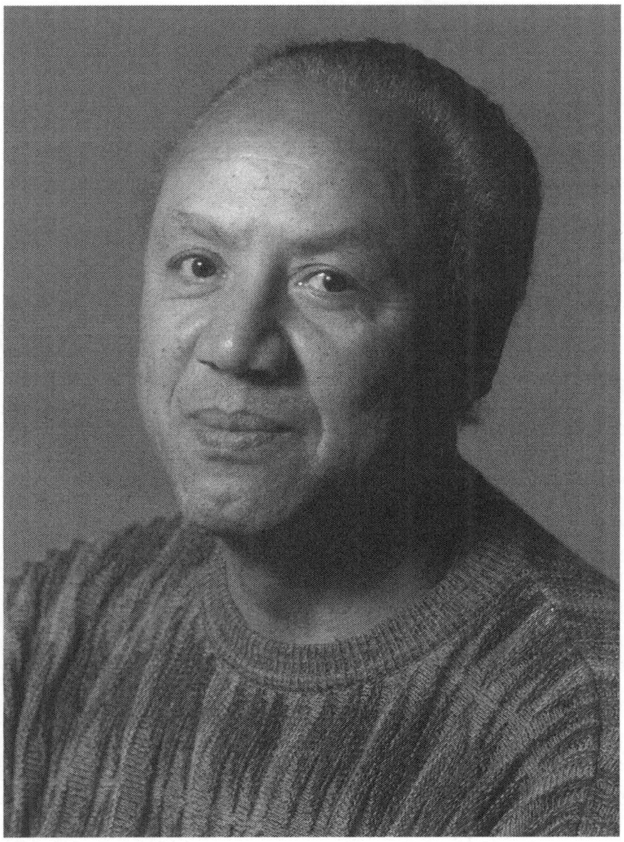

Steve Russell/Toronto Star/Getty Images

Providence reached the semifinals of the National Invitational Tournament (NIT). When Wilkens was a senior, the Friars reached the NIT finals and Wilkens won the tournament's Most Valuable Player award. Over the course of his three-year varsity career with the Friars, Wilkens averaged 14.9 points per game.

Wilkens graduated from Providence in 1960 with a degree in economics, and had a number of offers to play professional basketball. In the 1960 NBA (National Basketball Association) draft, Wilkens was selected by the St. Louis Hawks with the sixth pick in the first round. Though the Hawks offered him a paltry salary of $8000 with a $1500 signing bonus, Wilkens chose the NBA and to play for St. Louis.

Played in the NBA

As a rookie, Wilkens was a starter and soon was a star, albeit one known as a team player instead of for his individual skills, in the NBA. During his second year, he only played in 20 games because he served in the U.S. Army from 1961 to 1962, reaching the rank of second lieutenant. After his return to the NBA full time, he was regularly chosen as an All-Star, selected to nine All-Star teams between 1963 and 1973. Wilkens had his best season as a player in 1967-68 when he averaged 20 points per game. At season's end, he finished second in voting for the NBA's most valuable player award to superstar Wilt Chamberlain.

Also in 1968, the Hawks moved from St. Louis to Atlanta, and had a new team owner. Because the new owner and star player could not reach a deal in contract negotiations, Wilkens was traded to the Seattle SuperSonics for Walt Hazzard. Though initially it seemed that Seattle was basketball purgatory for Wilkens—the SuperSonics were a second-year expansion team with minimal chance to make the playoffs—the basketball player ended up finding a new career path.

Became Player/Coach

At the beginning of the 1969-70 NBA season, Wilkens was asked by the Sonics' general manager Dick Vertlieb to become a player-coach for Seattle. Though he had no coaching background, Wilkens agreed. In doing so, he became only the second African-American head coach in the NBA, after Bill Russell.

Wilkens drew on his own deep understanding of the fundamentals of basketball while learning the basics of coaching on the job. He taught and drilled his teammates/players especially on defense, passing, and the correct assignments. Because of Wilkens, the SuperSonics had their first ever winning season in 1971-72 at 47–35.

At the beginning of the 1972-73 season, the SuperSonics asked Wilkens to choose between coaching and playing. Wilkens was not ready to stop playing, however, so he gave up his coaching duties. The new coach, Tom Nissalke, immediately traded Wilkens to the Cleveland Cavaliers, an expansion club. Though Wilkens initially refused to report, he eventually played and remained for two seasons.

In 1974, Wilkens joined the Portland Trail Blazers, where he was again a player-coach. Ending his playing days in 1975, he served solely as a coach for Portland until he was fired in 1976. Though he considered moving out of basketball entirely at this time, Wilkens received an offer to become a head coach early in the 1977-78 season.

Returned to Seattle as Coach

Returning to Seattle, Wilkens turned around the failing team. When he arrived in 1977, the SuperSonics had a record of 5–17. By season's end, however, their record was 47–35 and the team reached the NBA finals. Though Seattle lost the finals in seven games to the Washington Bullets, Wilkens had demonstrated his skills as a coach.

The following year, the SuperSonics again made the playoffs, this time winning the NBA championship. Wilkens was denied coach of the year honors both years, despite his success. This snub was considered racist by some observers, since he was only the second black head coach in the NBA.

Wilkens remained in Seattle for a total of eight years, then served as the SuperSonics' general manager for an additional season. In the 1986 off-season, Wilkens took a job with the Cleveland Cavaliers. He served as Cleveland's head coach for seven seasons, and again turned the team around.

In the 1985-86 season, the Cavaliers won only 29 games. In five of the next six seasons, Cleveland posted more than 50 victories and went deep into the playoffs. Their success was limited, however, because this was also the era in which Michael Jordan was a dominant player with the Chicago Bulls.

Helped Coach the Dream Team

During his time in Cleveland, Wilkens enjoyed some recognition for his accomplishments as a player and coach. In 1989, he was inducted into the Basketball Hall of Fame as a player. Three years later, Wilkens was an assistant coach for the "Dream Team," the U.S. Olympic basketball team that won a gold medal in the Summer Olympics at Barcelona, Spain. While in Spain, Wilkens suffered a life-threatening injury after he tore an Achilles tendon, then suffered blood clots that moved from his legs to his lungs.

Though Wilkens had a year remaining on his contract with the Cavaliers, he walked away from Cleveland in 1993. A still in-demand coach, Wilkens soon signed a lucrative contact to helm the Atlanta Hawks. The five-year deal was worth $6.5 million.

In Atlanta, as in his other stops, Wilkens transformed a losing team. The first year he coached the Hawks, he took a team—of which little was expected—and turned it into a Central Division champion with a record of 57–25. At the end of the 1993-94 season, Wilkens finally won his first coach of the year award.

More milestones came in the 1994-95 season. In early 1995, Wilkens had his 939th career victory, pulling him past the legendary Red Auerbach for more victories than anyone in professional basketball. Wilkens also held the record for having taken part in more NBA games as a player or head coach than anyone else.

Posted 1,000th Career Victory

During the next season, Wilkens' Hawks had a record of 46–36 and he reached his 1,000th career victory. Atlanta also reached the Eastern Conference semi-finals that year. After the season ended, Wilkens coached the 1996 U.S. Olympic basketball team, which included such players as Shaquille O'Neal and Charles Barkley. The Americans again won gold.

Wilkens remained with Atlanta through the end of the 1999-2000 season. The coach led the Hawks to another playoff berth in 1996-97 season, then signed a four-year contract extension worth $20 million. Another bright spot was his 1998 induction into the Basketball Hall of Fame as a coach, making him the only person besides the celebrated John Wooden to be inducted as both a player and a coach.

The last season Wilkens spent with the Hawks was the worst of his coaching career. Atlanta's record on the year was 28–54, with 25 losses in the last 31 games. After the season ended, Wilkens quit.

Though there was speculation on Wilkens' future in coaching, he signed a new, four-year coaching deal in June 2000. Becoming the head coach of the Toronto Raptors, Wilkens' team included high profile veterans and young players, and did well in its first season. In 2000-01, Toronto had a record of 47–35, and reached the second round of the Eastern Conference playoffs. During 2001, Wilkens also published his autobiography, *Unguarded: My Forty Years Surviving in the NBA.*

Coached in Toronto, New York

However, Wilkens' touch as a coach seemed to be in decline as the next two seasons he spent with Toronto saw the team lose more and more games. In the 2002-03 season, the Raptors posted a lowly record of 24–58. Wilkens was blamed for the team's demise, and even set a record for the most career loses by an NBA coach with 1107. Wilkens resigned at season's end.

Though Wilkens pursued other opportunities for several months, he returned to the NBA and coaching in January 2004 when he was hired to become the head coach of the struggling New York Knicks. He replaced Don Chaney, who had been unceremoniously fired by team president (and former NBA star) Isaiah Thomas. Wilkens led the Knicks to the playoffs at season's end. But New York started poorly at the beginning of the 2004-05 season, and Wilkens resigned in January 2005.

At the end of his coaching career, Wilkens had a record 1332 regular season victories. This record would stand until the 2009-10 season when Don Nelson, the head coach of the Golden State Warriors, passed Wilkens. Though Wilkens left coaching behind, he remained involved in basketball.

Focused on His Charity

In 2006, Wilkens returned to Seattle to become the vice chairman of the SuperSonics. Though Seattle remained his home, he left the post in 2007 after feeling that his role in the organization had declined. That year, he founded and helmed the Lenny Wilkens Foundation, which focused on providing access to healthcare and education for underprivileged youth and their families. Charity and humanitarian work took most of his attention at this time in his life.

Wilkens still had some basketball-related commitments, however. He became a consultant to the Korean national basketball team in 2010, and the team won a silver medal in the Asian Games. Also in 2010, Wilkens became part of the movement to bring the NBA back to Seattle. Much to the disappointment of fans in Seattle, ownership moved the SuperSonics to Oklahoma in 2008 and the team became the Oklahoma City Thunder.

Throughout his career, Wilkens displayed a low-key demeanor and was known for his work ethic and perseverance. Upon Wilkens' induction into the Hall of Fame in 1998, Marty Blake, the general manager of the St. Louis Hawks and the man responsible for drafting Wilkens, told Jeffrey Denberg of the *Atlanta Journal and Constitution,* "You knew he was going to be a great player. You knew he was a coach on the floor at Providence. I mean, he ran the show. There was no question who was in charge. You had a sense watching him that Lenny could someday become a coach, but all this? That was impossible to forecast."

Books

African Americans, Volume 5, edited by Carl L. Bankston III, Salem Press, 2011.

Contemporary Black Biography, Volume 88, Gale, 2011.

Scribner Encyclopedia of American Lives, Thematic Series: The 1960s, edited by William L. O'Neill and Kenneth T. Jackson, Charles Scribner's Sons, 2002.

Periodicals

Associated Press, July 7, 2007.

Atlanta Journal and Constitution, October 2, 1998; April 25, 2000.

New York Times, January 15, 2004; January 28, 2005.

State News Service, July 18, 2012.

St. Louis Post-Dispatch, December 25, 1994.

USA Today, August 1, 1996; May 14, 2001.□

Amy Winehouse

British singer-songwriter Amy Winehouse (1983–2011) became famed as one of the finest updaters of the soul sound for a new century before personal troubles and her sudden death nearly overshadowed her talents.

© Geoffrey Robinson/Alamy

British singer-songwriter Amy Winehouse was recognized as the possessor of one of the most powerful voices of her generation during her critically-acclaimed but tragically short career. Her Grammy-award-winning recordings channeled classic soul and jazz sounds into a contemporary pop blend enhanced by the singer's throaty contralto singing voice. Yet Winehouse's celebrated musical career was troubled by ongoing personal struggles with drug and alcohol abuse. By the time of her death at the age of 27, Winehouse had released a 2003 debut *Frank* and a 2006 international breakthrough, *Back to Black.* A posthumous collection, *Lioness: Hidden Treasures,* followed a few months after her demise from alcohol poisoning.

Early Career as Jazz Singer

Born on September 14, 1983, in the northern suburb of Southgate, London, England, Winehouse was the younger child of cab driver Mitchell Winehouse and his wife, pharmacist Janis Winehouse. The Winehouse family was a musical one; her paternal grandmother had once dated famed British jazz musician Ronnie Scott, and her maternal uncles were professional jazz musicians. Winehouse's own parents enjoyed listening to performers such as Frank Sinatra and Ella Fitzgerald, and even as a child Winehouse showed an interest in performing. "It's always been her dream to be a singer," Janis Winehouse told the *Daily Mirror* in 2007. "That was all she ever wanted. She was always singing around the house." The young WInehouse expanded on her parents' tastes by listening to contemporary female artists such as En Vogue and Salt-N-Pepa—she and a friend formed a childhood hip-hop duo—as well as classic 1960s girl groups including the Shangri-Las. Inspired by older brother Alex, she also learned to play the guitar.

In her early teens, Winehouse enrolled in the Sylvia Young Theatre School and the BRIT School for Performing Arts and Technology, a London training ground for many popular entertainers. She was a bright and obviously talented student, but also rebellious and headstrong. Before long, however, Winehouse's behavior and her decision to pierce her nose led to her expulsion from school. The experience was not fruitless, however. A school friend, Tyler James, passed a teenaged Winehouse's demo recording on to an A&R representative at Island. In time, that record label sied Winehouse to a recording contract.

Winehouse's 2003 debut album, *Frank,* made her a quick success in the United Kingdom. Although Winehouse was just 20 years old, elements of the style that would make her a worldwide star were already apparent. Produced by Salaam Remi—a collaborator whose hip-hop sensibilities helped inform Winehouse's hybridized sound—*Frank* blended soul, jazz, pop, hip-hop, and rhythm and blues into a distinctive and eminently listenable style. Critics widely praised the album, with Beccy Lindon of the *Guardian* hailing Winehouse's "colossal vocal talent" and *Entertainment Weekly* reviewer Chris Willman favorably assessing *Frank*'s "[fierce] intelligence" upon its U.S. reissue in 2007. British music critics nominated *Frank* for some of the nation's top accolades, including the Mercury Music Prize—an award given to that year's best British album—and Winehouse herself was nominated as for the Brit Award for best British female solo artist. Album track "Stronger Than Me" received a 2004 Ivor Novello Award, a British songwriting prize, for best contemporary song.

Even as Winehouse's fledgling career flourished, however, her personal life began to deteriorate. The singer entered into an on-again, off-again romantic relationship with Blake Fielder-Civil, a London-based music video production assistant. The relationship was a tumultuous one fueled by partying and alcohol, and the couple made the gossip pages for their public outbursts and occasionally violent arguments. Winehouse's substance abuse began to interfere with her ability to perform, and her managers suggested that she enter an alcohol abuse treatment program. Winehouse not only refused, but also fired her managers.

Back to Black Garnered Worldwide Acclaim

The conflict between the singer and her management company served as fodder for what became Winehouse's international breakthrough hit, "Rehab." "They tried to make me go to rehab and I said no, no, no," sang Winehouse bluntly of the experience in the song's main hook. Led by that number, Winehouse's sophomore effort, *Back to Black,* channeled what she claimed were autobiographical tales of substance abuse and romantic infidelity through a retro filter of 1960s girl groups and classic soul singers. Winehouse also combined the two eras in her own distinctive personal appearance, mixing tattoos and low-rise jeans with cat-eye black eyeliner and a towering beehive hairstyle. This blend of vintage and modern influences in Winehouse's persona added greatly to her critical appeal. "If Ms. Winehouse were a purely old-fashioned soul singer, she'd just be a nostalgia act, though one with some telling songs," asserted Jon Pareles of the *New York Times.* "Her self-consciousness, and the bluntness she has learned from hip-hop, could help lead soul into 21st-century territory," he continued.

Thoroughly contemporary lyrical twists made the classic sounds produced by Remi and Mark Ronson a fit with the modern listener and helped *Back to Black* debut in the highest *Billboard* chart position achieved by a British female singer in the United States to date. The album peaked at number two on the *Billboard* 200, and eventually sold enough copies to achieve platinum status. "Rehab" and, to a lesser extent, follow-up single "You Know I'm No Good" both made waves on the singles chart, and Winehouse seemed to be well on her way to a high-flying musical career.

By the spring of 2007, Winehouse and Fielder-Civil had resumed their relationship amidst a period of growing personal turmoil for the singer. Fielder-Civil later admitted that during this period he introduced Winehouse to heroin, and over time she became a regular user of the drug. That spring, the couple married in Miami, Florida, but this did not lessen the poisonous aspects of their relationship. Together the two delved deeper into drug and alcohol abuse, frequently fighting and becoming regular tabloid fixtures for their actions. Around the end of 2007, footage rumored to be of Winehouse smoking crack cocaine circulated through the British media, and under pressure from her record label and family she entered a rehab center. The scandal prevented Winehouse from attending the Grammy Award ceremony soon after, and she accepted her five awards—including Best New Artist, Record of the Year, and Song of the Year—via satellite. At the time, her victories tied her with Beyoncé Knowles as the most decorated female artist at any one Grammy ceremony.

Personal Problems Steal the Limelight

Despite these critical accolades, Winehouse remained largely in the public eye due to her ongoing personal struggles. Tabloids tracked her every move, and less sensational publications began discussing the singer as an exemplar of excess and a global celebrity-obsessed pop culture. "What made 'Rehab' amusing when it appeared was that Ms. Winehouse was mocking what had become such a standard celebrity way station," commented Pareles in a separate *New York Times* story. Nevertheless, he added, in light of her somewhat notorious status in the time since its release, "she would do well to disappear for a while, into rehab or private recovery, and then to hole up in a recording studio and work up some new songs.... In the era of total exposure Ms. Winehouse would serve herself and her listeners best by working behind closed doors."

As time went, on the singer continued to lash out violently and faced deteriorating health as drug abuse took its toll on her lungs and heart. Although Winehouse reportedly managed to kick her drug habit, she still drank heavily, occasionally engaging in intense bouts of binge drinking. A court required Fielder-Civil to serve jail time and enter drug rehab after he was separately arrested and convicted on assault charges, and by the end of 2008, the couple's marriage had irrevocably failed amidst allegations of adultery. They filed for divorce in January of 2009. Speaking to British television presenter Jeremy Kyle in a 2013 interview quoted by Sarah Bull of the *Daily Mail,* Fielder-Civil expressed his regrets at introducing Winehouse to hard drugs and setting her on a downward path. "The fact is that of course I regret it; not only just because of the damage it's caused Amy, and the loss of her life and the damage to her family, but also to my family and also to me. We've all gone through this addiction," he added.

Substance Abuse Led to Early Death

Winehouse's substance abuse problems seemed to grow worse after her split with Fielder-Civil, however. Her live performances had long been inconsistent at best, with the singer sometimes unable to perform as well as expected and even, on occasion, forgetting the lyrics to the numbers she was attempting to sing. Nevertheless Winehouse hoped to make a professional comeback, working on new songs in the studio and planning a brief European tour for the summer of 2011. However, these efforts ended in disaster after a highly intoxicated performance resulted in Winehouse being booed off stage at the tour's opening night show in Belgrade, Serbia, that June. Summarizing the show in the *Daily Mail,* one journalist commented that the singer "arrived an hour late, dropped her microphone, threw away one of her shoes and forgot her lyrics [in]. . .a vintage Winehouse performance." Shortly after the highly publicized incident, the singer cancelled the remainder of the tour.

The ill-fated show proved to be her swan song. About a month later, Winehouse appeared briefly onstage to support a performance by her goddaughter, singer Dionne Bromfield; within short days she was dead. On July 23, 2011, a member of Winehouse's security staff found her dead in her bed at her home in the north London borough of Camden. Struggling with both substance abuse and bulimia, Winehouse had spent the evening before her death at home surfing the Internet, watching television, and drinking vodka. A later inquest determined that the amount of alcohol in her bloodstream had been well above the levels considered fatal and sufficient to interfere with her ability to breathe, and her death was determined to be the result of an accidental overdose.

Rumors that Winehouse had intended to end her life circulated, but family and friends were adamant that the artist was not suicidal. "The last 18 months of her life were possibly the best 18 months of her life," Winehouse's father said in a later interview with Washington, D.C. radio station 106.7 The Fan. "She had a new boyfriend. They were very happy. There were times when she was drinking heavily, and there were large periods when she wasn't drinking at all." Nevertheless, he acknowledged, when Winehouse did drink she often consumed huge amounts of liquor, and this time the effects of that consumption had killed her.

Music fans around the world reacted intensely to news of the singer's death. Mourners created makeshift memorials, especially near Winehouse's Camden home, and fellow artists issued statements expressing their grief at the loss of such a respected if troubled talent. Shortly after Winehouse's death, her parents established the Amy Winehouse Foundation, primarily to support young people struggling with substance abuse. In December of 2011, a collection of Winehouse singing covers and unreleased material entitled *Lioness: Hidden Treasures* was released with profits supporting the singer's memorial foundation. A documentary about Winehouse's life and death helmed by British director Asif Kapadia was slated for released in 2014. Commenting about the documentary in a statement reprinted in a story by the *New York Times*'s Dave Itzkoff, the Winehouse family said that they believed the documentary would "look at Amy's story sensitively, honestly and without sensationalizing her."

Periodicals

Daily Mail (London, England), June 25, 2011.

Entertainment Weekly, November 16, 2007.

Guardian (London, England), October 16, 2003.

New York Times, May 10, 2007; January 24, 2008; July 23, 2011; April 25, 2013.

Online

"'Amy trying heroin for the first time was MY doing': Blake Fielder-Civil takes responsibility for Winehouse's addiction as he opens up to Jeremy Kyle," *Daily Mail,* http://www.dailymail.co.uk/tvshowbiz/article-2285258/Blake-Fielder-Civil-takes-responsibility-Amy-Winehouses-heroin-addiction.html (November 2, 2013).

"Tiny Winehouse," *Daily Mirror,* http://www.mirror.co.uk/news/uk-news/tiny-winehouse-452855 (November 2, 2013).

"Two Years Later: What Really Caused the Death of Amy Winehouse," CBS DC, washington.cbslocal.com/2013/07/16/two-years-later-what-really-caused-the-death-of-amy-winehouse-2/ (November 2, 2013).□

P. G. Wodehouse

British-American author and humorist P.G. Wodehouse (1881–1975) became internationally known as a prolific writer of light fiction.

British-American author and humorist P.G. Wodehouse is best remembered as the writer of the popular books and short stories featuring the characters Bertie Wooster and his valet, Jeeves, who have outlived their creator not only in print but also in stage and screen adaptations. Himself a member of the British upper classes, Wodehouse presented antics of the nation's aristocracy through light-hearted tales featuring an array of domineering aunts, foppish young men, eccentric elders, and mischievous school boys. Wodehouse's humorous pieces made him widely popular in his own day, but his radio broadcasts on Nazi airwaves from World War II-era Germany turned his name from famous to notorious for a time in his native country. By the end of his life, however, his reputation had been restored, Wodehouse had been knighted, and he had penned hundreds of stories, poems, lyrics, and other written works.

Created Famous Characters

Born Pelham Granville Wodehouse on October 15, 1881, in Guildford, England, Wodehouse was the third son of Ernest Wodehouse and his wife, Eleanor. Wodehouse's father was a judge in British-controlled Hong Kong, and the Wodehouse family had a long and respectable lineage that included numerous knights and minor peers, although Wodehouse himself had no inherited title. With his parents typically stationed in Asia, Wodehouse—who went by the nickname of "Plum" throughout his life—grew up in a series English boarding schools including Dulwich College and in the homes of aunts who remained in the British Isles. This collection of influences was apparent throughout his literary canon in later years. From an early age, Wodehouse was a dedicated reader and writer, and he determined to pursue a career as an author as a youth.

After completing his education, Wodehouse was groomed for a job with the Hong Kong and Shanghai Bank through a position at the institution's London office. The

Edward Gooch/Hulton Archive/Getty Images

work was not to his liking, however, and he began writing a column for the London *Globe.* At the same time, he began composing short, comic stories drawing on his own boarding school experiences. In 1902, *Public School Magazine* serialized his first major school story, *The Pothunters.* Before long, Wodehouse had left the bank to attempt to build a full-time writing career and was met with near-immediate, if moderate, success. He wrote numerous stories, poems, and lyrics that appeared in British publications such as *Punch* and the *Daily Express.* In 1904, he traveled to New York City, and he spent much of the next few decades crossing back and forth between Britain and the United States, where he wrote songs and collaborated on stage productions. From 1915, he had a long and fruitful working relationship with librettist Guy Bolton.

During this same period, the author continued to write short stories and novels. Wodehouse first found widespread popular acclaim with his stories featuring the protagonist Psmith, who made his debut in the 1909 novel *Mike.* One of Wodehouse's recurring characters, Psmith is a youthful dandy and, when the reader first meets him, recently expelled Etonian who goes on to engage in a series of misadventures that drew in part on Wodehouse's own experiences working in London. Psmith in time crossed over into another successful Wodehouse series set at Blandings Castle that was inaugurated with the serialized publication of *Something Fresh* in 1914. The home of British aristocrat Lord Emsworth and a menagerie of supporting characters including a pig known as the Empress of Blandings, Blandings Castle served as the backdrop for a typically light-hearted array of absurd happenings. At about the same time, Wodehouse married an English widow he met in New York, Ethel Newton Rowley, and adopted her daughter by her earlier marriage.

Wodehouse introduced the duo that became his best-known and most popular characters in the 1917 story "Extricating Young Gussie." Young British gadabout Bertie Wooster and his valet, Jeeves, epitomized Wodehouse's writing: Wooster is wealthy, thoroughly disinclined to anything resembling work, and given to finding himself in trouble caused by foolishly but enthusiastically concocted schemes executed by himself and his cadre of like-minded friends. Jeeves, by contrast, is a clever and sometimes sardonic personality who devises ingenious and hilarious solutions to Wooster's dilemmas—often at the price of forcing his employer to abandon an article of clothing offensive to the valet's discerning tastes. Together, the pair faces situations ranging from helping Wooster dodge the requests of his somewhat domineering Aunt Agatha to arranging romantic matches for Wooster's friends with mixed success. The humorous relationship and quirky situations of the story made them enduring favorites that helped Wodehouse establish himself as a high-earning and in-demand popular author of fiction.

During the Great Depression of the 1930s, Wodehouse enjoyed two year-long stints as a Hollywood screenwriter that he deemed required him to be underworked and overpaid. Screenwriting—despite its low requirements that left him with ample time to pursue a lifelong love, golf—failed to thrill the author, however, and he rededicated himself to other efforts after his contracts were completed. Later that decade, Wodehouse's characters Wooster and Jeeves came to the silver screen for the first time in the films *Thank You, Jeeves,* and *Step Lively, Jeeves!*

Made Questionable Broadcasts

World War II presented a series of unexpected personal and professional challenges for Wodehouse. Living in Le Touquet in northern France at the time of the Nazi invasion, Wodehouse remained at his home, believing that the conflict was unlikely to affect him directly far from the front lines. As the front lines came closer and closer in the spring of 1940, however, Wodehouse and his wife belatedly and unsuccessfully attempted to travel south; by this time German forces controlled enough French territory to prevent this effort. That summer, Wodehouse and some other British nationals living at Le Touquet were interned by the Germans. He was imprisoned at a series of German prison camps, places that were uncomfortable and frightening but far from the horrifying fates experienced by those detained at the infamous Nazi concentration camps. Wodehouse spent much of late 1940 and early 1941 at an internment camp in Tost, Poland.

Wodehouse made the best of his situation, continuing to write light comedies essentially free of wartime references or influence. His imprisonment was international news, and supporters in Britain worked to achieve Wodehouse's release. But the author by all accounts found the experience to be a bit of a lark. In June of 1941, he was transferred to Berlin and released from internment. There, he recorded five radio broadcasts on non-political subjects that were broadcast toward British and U.S. audiences, telling of his thoughts and experiences on camp life. A *New York Times* article quoted some of the author's thoughts on the experience: "I have been living rather in camp lately.... Here [in Berlin] the food is very good. But there are only three meals a day. In camp my tea and could nibble chocolate in between."

Wodehouse's broadcasts, which he rather naïvely believed to be harmless, infuriated the British public and generated a great deal of suspicion about the author's character and intentions among national authorities. Documents declassified in 1999 suggested that British intelligence believed Wodehouse to be in the pay of the Nazi regime for creating propaganda and that officials there planned to arrest and prosecute the author for treason if he returned to the country. Wodehouse himself claimed that the broadcasts were simply a terrible mistake, and his true culpability remains a question of debate among fans and historians. "It is as likely that Wodehouse performed treacherous acts as it is for the sun not to rise tomorrow," asserted P.G. Wodehouse Society head Norman Murphy in the *New York Times.* The French police, however, did arrest Wodehouse in Paris in 1944 on charges of treason that were eventually dropped. Writing in Wodehouse's *New York Times* obituary, Alden Whitman noted that contemporary assessments "agreed that at best [Wodehouse] was singularly thick-skulled in failing to realize the implications of his broadcasts."

Later Life in the United States

With his reputation in tatters in Great Britain, Wodehouse decided to emigrate to the United States after the close of World War II. He and his wife settled in New York City, where the author sold a trickle of stories to U.S. magazines and dedicated much of his energies to theatrical productions, frequently alongside longtime collaborator Guy Bolton. By the early 1950s, Wodehouse had begun to restore his creative energies even as the public had begun to forgive his wartime misjudgments. He created new novels and plays featuring Wooster and Jeeves, and returned to Blandings Castle with *Pig Have Wings.* In 1953, Wodehouse published *Performing Flea,* a collection of letters to a lifelong school friend that essentially stood as the author's autobiography.

Although the British public was again buying Wodehouse's writing, he remained worried that his reputation would prevent him from ever returning to his native country for good. Believing his future to lie in the United States, Wodehouse became a U.S. citizen in 1955. "I had always been a sort of honorary American," the author explained wryly in *America, I Like You,* "but it seemed to me that the time had come when I ought to start running things." By now in his seventies, Wodehouse moved to Long Island but refused to fully retire. He continued to produce new stories featuring his signature characters and scenarios throughout the 1960s and into the 1970s. Wodehouse's consistency was in itself remarkable. "The comparative lack of development in his writing is one of its unique features: no other 20th century English writer of consequence evolves in his mature work as little as Wodehouse," argued Robert McCrum in *Wodehouse: A Life.* "He had created a world that was complete, self-sufficient and almost faultless."

While Wodehouse continued to produce new works, his older ones found new audiences through television adaptations of Jeeves and Wooster stories on the BBC entitled *The World of Wooster.* In 1974, London museum Madame Tussaud's flattered the writer by commissioning a wax figure of him for its famed galleries. The following year, Wodehouse received an even greater honor: Queen Elizabeth II made him a knight. Wodehouse's reputation was fully restored.

Just weeks after his investiture, Wodehouse—still at work on a new Blandings Castle novel—fell ill. He checked into a local hospital for tests and, despite seeming reasonably well, died there of a heart attack on the evening of February 14, 1975. Newspapers around the world reported Wodehouse's death, with Whitman of the *New York Times* eulogizing him as "one of this century's most prolific, popular and durable writers of light fiction."

Indeed, Wodehouse's works endured well beyond his own lifetime. Andrew Lloyd Webber scored a musical based on Wodehouse's characters entitled *Jeeves* that flopped in London shortly after the author's death. A 1990s television revival of Jeeves and Wooster starring British actors Hugh Laurie and Stephen Fry fared better, as did a long-running BBC radio series of Wodehouse's Jeeves and Wooster stories. In the twenty-first century, these characters were revived in a pastiche by British author Sebastian Faulks entitled *Jeeves and the Wedding Bells* that was officially sanctioned by Wodehouse's estate. At the same time, Wodehouse's own century-old stories continued to delight readers with visits to a madcap fictional world.

Books

McCrum, Robert, *Wodehouse: A Life,* W.W. Norton and Co., 2004.

Wodehouse, P.G, *America, I Like You,* Simon and Schuster, 1956.

Periodicals

New York Times, June 29, 1941; February 15, 1975; September 18, 1999.

Online

"Wodehouse, P.G." *American National Biography Online,* http://www.anb.org/articles/16/16-02803.html (December 5, 2013).□

Ed Wood Jr.

The American film director and screenwriter Ed Wood Jr. (1924–1978), whose films were ridiculed as the worst ever made, became a cult figure after his death.

The biographical film *Ed Wood* (1994), by acclaimed director Tim Burton, aided in the revival of Wood's films. The film, although not historically accurate in all respects, captured the qualities that have endeared Wood to younger viewers: his unquenchable optimism, his originality, and his honesty about the themes that mattered to him. Yet Wood's rise to popularity had begun before the release of Burton's film. Film buffs had started to watch them, and they had started to appear in video stores and on the programs of college film societies, after Wood was named the worst director of all time by a prominent film critic. What viewers found was a director who was incompetent, to be sure, but whose films—most prominently the transvestite-themed drama *Glen or Glenda* (1953)—resembled nothing else being made at the time, and they never lacked for energy. "Wood's films are certainly inept in most departments," noted Geoff Brown of the London *Times.* "But they are never unwatchable. *Plan 9 [from Outer Space]* especially has a lunatic, dishevelled charm, while no film on earth can match Glen or Glenda for its quirky yet earnest exploration of the pleasures and pains of cross-dressing."

Served in Marines in World War II

Edward Davis Wood Jr. was born in Poughkeepsie, New York, on October 10, 1924. His father was a maintenance worker at a local post office. Wood enjoyed comic books and science fiction stories as a child. Although Burton's *Ed Wood* depicted scenes in which his mother dressed him in girls' clothing as a child, it is not clear whether this actually occurred. In his late teens Wood got a job as an usher and then, in 1942, enlisted in the United States Marine Corps. By that time his own transvestite tendencies had developed: he wore a bra and panties underneath his uniform. Wood saw action in heavy fighting in the Pacific theater, and, perhaps fearful of exposure, he apparently became an exceptional solder and was given several military medals.

Exactly what Wood did after his discharge is not known for certain, but he later told his wife Kathy that he had studied at Northwestern University in suburban Chicago and lived in an abandoned theater. The following year he headed for Hollywood and its rapidly growing film industry. He landed bit parts in stage productions, worked at the scheduling department at Universal Studios, and made a 30-minute short subject, *Crossroads of Laredo* (also known as *Streets of Laredo*), which was never released or even given a soundtrack. Wood appeared in the film as a bad guy on horseback, even though he had never ridden a horse previously.

In 1952, Wood wrote the script under a pseudonym for a reasonably successful Western, *The Lawless Rider,* and the following year that film's producer, who had paid Wood a flat fee for his contribution, offered him the chance to direct a film about a famous transsexual woman of the day, Christine Jorgenson. After Jorgenson's name was removed from the story due to legal issues, Wood was apparently given control over the direction of the film, and he injected elements of his own life as a transvestite into the story. The result was *Glen or Glenda,* which remains one of Wood's two most notorious films.

Film Endorsed Tolerance of Transsexuals

Glen or Glenda featured Wood's trademark low-budget style, complete with extremely rudimentary set design and overly melodramatic narrative style. It included a performance by the aging horror film actor Bela Lugosi as a semi-godlike scientist narrator whose presence is never explained; Lugosi apparently took on the role out of financial need. The film flopped financially, but later viewers noticed that it differed substantially from the low-budget, so-called B-movie fare with which it competed at theaters and drive-ins: its earnest plea for tolerance of transsexuals, for example, was unusual for its time.

That film starred actress Dolores Fuller as the fianceé of its title character. Fuller (later a songwriter who contributed heavily to Elvis Presley's catalogue) was also Wood's girlfriend at the time, and the pair, unusually for the time, lived together without marrying. Wood, like many other transvestites, was not homosexual. Sometimes he used the pen name Ann Gora, derived from his fondness for women's angora sweaters. Fuller appeared in a second Wood film, the crime drama *Jail Bait* (1954), probably the closest to the mainstream stylistically among Wood's films. Wood and Fuller later split up, and Wood married Kathy O'Hara in 1959. That marriage endured until Wood's death.

Wood's next film, *Bride of the Monster,* appeared in 1955, and once again featured Lugosi (who had also been slated to appear as a plastic surgeon in *Jail Bait* but had been forced to withdraw for health reasons). That year Wood began work on his next film, the science fiction drama *Plan 9 from Outer Space.* It was again intended for Lugosi, but the Hungarian actor died shortly after shooting began. Wood rather haphazardly worked his brief footage of Lugosi into the story, which dealt with an invasion of alien beings who transform deceased humans into murderous zombies. By this time Hollywood financiers had soured on Wood, who persuaded the members of the First Baptist Church of Beverly Hills, California, to finance the film. The result was a classically laughable set of special effects, including flying saucers made from pie pans attached to wires visible in the finished film. *Plan 9 from Outer Space* was not released until 1959.

Made Pornographic Films

Wood made several more low-budget mainstream releases before turning to pornography later in his career. He managed to cobble together financing for several films despite his bad reputation, probably because his earlier films had been made on a shoestring and had, if not made money, at least not lost a great deal. His later films included juvenile-delinquency drama *The Violent Years* (1956), *Night of the Ghouls* (1959, released posthumously in 1987), and the crime drama *The Sinister Urge* (1961). Wood also wrote the pilot for a television series, *Final Curtain* (1957), and screenplays for several other films

By the mid-1960s B-movies had declined in popularity, and Wood turned to the growing pornographic film industry to support himself and his wife. He wrote the screenplay for the surreal erotic film *Orgy of the Dead* (1965) and then directed three full-length pornographic features: *Take It Out in Trade* (1970), and *Necromania* and *The Young Marrieds* (both 1971). Wood also acted in and wrote screenplays for other erotic-themed releases, sometimes using the pseudonym Akdov Telmig (the words "vodka gimlet" spelled backward). In the 1970s, Wood suffered from alcoholism and depression, and he and his wife lived in a rundown apartment on Yucca Street in Hollywood. They were evicted and moved into the apartment of a friend, where Wood died while watching football on television on December 10, 1978.

For some years, Wood's films were mostly forgotten. But the adage that there is no such thing as bad publicity was demonstrated anew when Wood was listed as cinema's worst director in the book *The Golden Turkey Awards* (1980), by film critics Michael and Harry Medved, which also named *Plan 9 from Outer Space* history's worst film. Curious film buffs began to seek out Wood's films, which were still available at low cost for rental and quickly began to circulate among B-movie devotees with the advent of the videocassette recorder.

The defining event in the enshrinement of Wood in the history of popular culture was the release of the film *Ed Wood* in 1994. Accompanied by a Wood biography, *Ed Wood: Nightmare of Ecstasy (The Life and Art of Edward D. Wood, Jr),* the film and its star, Johnny Depp, treated Wood sympathetically and explored the imaginative elements of his films. Since then Wood has been a full-fledged cult favorite, regarded in some quarters as an ingenious outsider artist. His work has been explored in detail by critic Rob Craig in *Ed Wood, Mad Genius: A Critical Study of the Films* (2009). In 2013, a resident of Poughkeepsie was reported to be raising funds to erect a statue of Wood in his native city.

Books

Craig, Rob, *Ed Wood, Mad Genius: A Critical Study of the Films,* McFarland, 2009.

Grey, Rudolph, *Ed Wood: Nightmare of Ecstasy (The Life and Art of Edward D. Wood, Jr.),* Feral House, 1994.

St. James Encyclopedia of Popular Culture, St. James, 2000.

Periodicals

Artforum International, December 1994.

Billboard, October 15, 1994.

Spectator (Hamilton, Ontario, Canada), May 30, 2013.

Online

"Edward D. Wood Jr.," *Internet Movie Database,* http://www.imdb.com/name/nm0000248/bio?ref_=nm_ov_bio_sm (December 3, 2013).

"The Life of Edward D. Wood Jr.," *The Church of Ed Wood,* http://www.edwood.org/bio.html (December 3, 2013).□

John Wooden

Known as the Wizard of Westwood, American basketball coach John Wooden (1910–2010) helmed the men's basketball team at the University of California Los Angeles (UCLA) for 27 years, winning ten national championships.

John Wooden was born October 14, 1910, the son of Joshua and Roxie Anna Wooden, on a primitive farm located near Martinsville, Indiana. His father grew wheat, corn, and alfalfa. As a child, the young Wooden focused his life around sports after his father built a baseball diamond on the family's land. Wooden and his brother Maurice not only played baseball but also basketball on a hoop nailed on the hayloft. Wooden's childhood had its struggles, however, as his family lost their farm during his youth.

Won High School Basketball Championships

Though Wooden initially preferred baseball to basketball, the latter proved to be his best sport and he led his Martinsville High School team to the Indiana state basketball championship in 1927. He also lost another state championship by one point. After high school, Wooden entered Purdue University, where he continued to play elite basketball as a guard. Playing hard on both offense and defense, he was an All-America in 1930, 1931, and 1932, and the Boilermakers won the national championship when he was a senior. That year, Wooden was the college basketball player of the year and earned the nickname "the Indiana Rubber Man" because of his habit of diving on the basketball court.

After completing his degree, Wooden worked as a high school teacher. He began teaching and serving as the basketball coach at Dayton High School in Kentucky. His first season as a high school basketball coach, he had a losing record, the only one of his whole career. After two years, Wooden returned to Indiana were he spent nine years at South Bend Central High School. In addition to teaching English, he coached basketball, baseball, and tennis.

During World War II, Wooden served in the U.S. Navy as a physical education instructor. After his service ended, he became the basketball coach at the Indiana State Teachers College. He landed the job because his predecessor at the college, Glenn Curtis, had been Wooden's coach at Martinsville High School when the team won the 1927 state championship. Curtis left coaching to take a position

© ZUMA Press, Inc./Alamy

in private business, and recommended Wooden to the college's president.

Hired as College Basketball Coach

At Indiana State Teachers College, Wooden set a trend by recruiting a number veterans of World War II who were attending college on the GI Bill. A number were former players for South Bend High School. This decision proved initially unpopular because many returning, locally recruited players were forced into reserve roles to make room for the veterans on the seventeen-man roster. Despite criticism, Wooden believed in his decision because it helped the team win.

Over two seasons, Wooden's teams posted a total record of 47–17, a school record. In this first year, his team won the Indiana Collegiate Conference title. Though the team was invited to the NAIB (National Association of Intercollegiate Athletics) tournament, he refused the invitation because he had an African-American player, Clarence Walker, on the team and African Americans were banned from the tournament. The rule was changed for the next season. Wooden's team played after winning another conference title, and Walker became the first African-American to play in a post-season college basketball tournament. Also while coaching at Indiana State, Wooden developed and displayed characteristics that would become the blueprint for his later coaching success.

It was at this point that Wooden's career path took an unexpected trajectory. In 1948, he headed west to the University of California at Los Angeles (UCLA). Wooden took the job at UCLA almost by accident. He was waiting for a call from the University of Minnesota about its head coaching job that year, and assumed he did not get the job because the call had not come. While he was waiting, UCLA called and offered Wooden its head coaching position. Wooden accepted the job on the spot. Minnesota called later that night, giving Wooden the job and explaining the call had not come earlier because of a snowstorm. Wooden actually wanted the post in Minnesota more than the one in Los Angeles, but headed west because he had already given the word to UCLA.

Built Bruins Dynasty

When Wooden took over the Bruins, the UCLA team began winning, though it would be sixteen seasons before a championship would be won. As the head men's basketball coach at UCLA, his teams won ten NCAA (National Collegiate Athletic Association) championships over his twenty-seven years as head coach. The first came in 1964 with a team led by Walt Hazzard that went 30–0, while his tenth came in the 1974-75 season. Seven championships in a row came between 1967 and 1973. During this time, the Bruins were 330–19 and had four 30–0 seasons. This period marked perhaps his greatest years as a coach.

Over the course of his career, Wooden's teams at UCLA had a record of 620–147, including 88 straight wins from January 1971 to January 1974. Because of his continued success, Wooden attracted and coached some of the greatest players in college basketball, including Bill Walton, Kareem Abdul-Jabbar (then known as Lew Alcindor), Jamaal Wilkes, Lucius Allen, and Gail Goodrich. Overall, Wooden coached 24 All Americans and his record as a college coach was 664–162.

There were many reasons for Wooden's success. Not only did he take psychology classes and seek out players and coaches who would challenge him to better relate to players, he broke ground and set trends as coach through his stress on discipline and hard work. His UCLA teams played an up-tempo, running style, and he insisted his players stay in peak condition and understand the value of fundamentals to meet the demands of the style. Wooden also emphasized a team game that used all the players on the court instead of putting the whole game on the shooters. In addition, he conducted team drills which underscored the importance of hitting the open man on offense and playing aggressive, sustained defense from game to game. Though Wooden's teams varied in quality, talent, size, and ability, he worked to get the best out of them. As a player on his first two championship teams, high-scoring guard Gail Goodrich, told Michael Mink of the *Investor's Business Daily,* "Coach Wooden focused on the process and what it took to become a winning team. What gave him joy was the challenge; he was an incredible competitor."

Yet Wooden also emphasized leadership and life instruction, often in small ways. Wooden had only three firm team rules: no use of profanity, no tardiness, and no criticizing of teammates. Unofficially, Wooden taught and expected his players to put on socks and sneakers properly, keep hair short, and faces clean shaven. He also emphasized his so-called pyramid of success, a chart that summarized his life code to an essence including values such as industriousness, enthusiasm, faith, patience, loyalty, self-control, and competitive greatness. Ultimately, he stressed being a good, well-rounded person with a strong character, more than a good basketball player. Personally, Wooden always remained humble, gracious, and true to himself. He eschewed the nickname "Wizard of Westwood" because the name implied that he somehow was successful for a reason other than hard work.

Perhaps the greatest professional basketball coach of all time, Red Auerbach, explained to the *Washington Post*'s John Feinstein, "He was genuinely a humble guy, never pointed out how well he'd coached or how he had outsmarted the other guy. He just did it, smiled and moved on to the next thing. The thing he did best, though, was he could coach anybody: Some of those guys he had, especially Abdul-Jabbar and Walton, weren't exactly easy to deal with. But they never questioned him. People didn't give him credit for how much he got out of those guys and all the guys who played for him."

Remained Active in Retirement

Wooden retired in 1975 at the age of 64 after UCLA defeated Kentucky to win the coach's tenth national championship. Through 2013, no college coach had come close to Wooden's record, nor his effect on the game. University of Connecticut basketball coach Jim Calhoun told Beth Harris of the Associated Press, "There has been no greater influence on college basketball not just about the game but about the team. He gave so much to basketball and education. In my opinion if he's not as important as Dr. Naismith, he's right next to him."

In retirement, Wooden was a sought-after public speaker and wrote numerous books including *Pyramid of Success.* This book explained the values by which he lived his life and the values that were the basics of a competitive team. *Pyramid of Success* proved influential not only for other coaches but also for business leaders. Wooden also penned an insightful autobiography, *Wooden: A Lifetime of Observations and Reflections On and Off the Court,* and a book on strategies for competitive greatness, *Wooden on Leadership: How to Create a Winning Organization.*

Wooden continued to attend UCLA games until he was about 97 years old. Working late in life, he published a book he co-wrote on his 99th birthday, *The Wisdom of Wooden: A Century of Family, Faith, and Friends.* Among the topics explored was how to live life and raise children. Wooden and his late wife and high school sweetheart Nell Reilly, who died in 1985, had a son, James, and a daughter, Nancy, as well as numerous grandchildren and great-grandchildren. He also completed his last book only a short time before his death, 2010's *John Wooden: My Century On and Off the Court.*

Inducted into Basketball Hall of Fame Twice

The recipient of numerous honors, Wooden was twice inducted into the Basketball Hall of Fame, both as a player and a coach. At the time, he was the only person to be so inducted. He also turned down at least two chances to be a head coach in the National Basketball Association (NBA)—including one reportedly with the Los Angeles Lakers—primarily because his family believed it was best to stay at UCLA. Yet, during his first four years at UCLA he worked an early shift as a dairy dispatcher because his coaching income was then quite small.

In ill health for several weeks before his demise, Wooden died of natural causes on June 4, 2010, at the Ronald Reagan UCLA Medical Center in Los Angeles, California. In October 2012, an eight-foot-tall statue of the coach was unveiled outside of UCLA's Pauley Pavilion. After Wooden's death, Abdul-Jabbar explained to Harris of the Associated Press, "It's kind of hard to talk about Coach Wooden simply, because he was a complex man. But he taught in a very simple way. He just used sports as a means to teach us how to apply ourselves to any situation. He set quite an example. He was more like a parent than a coach. He really was a very selfless and giving human being, but he was a disciplinarian. We learned all about those aspects of life that most kids want to skip over. He wouldn't let us do that."

Periodicals

Associated Press, June 5, 2010; October 14, 2010; October 27, 2012.

Christian Science Monitor, June 5, 2010.

Daily News of Los Angeles, June 6, 2010.

Investor's Business Daily, April 8, 2013.

New York Times, June 7, 2010.

Times (London), June 7, 2010.

Tribune-Star (Terre Haute, IN), June 19, 2010.

Washington Post, June 5, 2010.□

Y

Nikolai Yezhov

Nikolai Yezhov (1895–1940) rose to a position of terrifying political power in the Soviet Union as the head of Josef Stalin's secret police. During a period known as the Great Terror in the mid-1930s, Yezhov conducted a ruthless purge of Russian Communist Party ranks, and his dragnet grew to include ordinary citizens, many of whom vanished into the prison-camp system or mass graves. Predictably he, too, fell victim to the state domestic-surveillance apparatus. "My great guilt lies in the fact that I purged so few," he infamously said at his trial, according to the 2010 work *Road to Terror: Stalin and the Self-Destruction of the Bolsheviks, 1932–1939.*

Nikolai Ivanonich Yezhov was born on May 1, 1895, in St. Petersburg, the capital city of imperial Russia. In the tsarist era, his was one of the millions of struggling families in the cities and countryside; just 30 years earlier, the peasant class known as serfs had been freed from the complex network of bondage-statutes dating back to the feudal era that tied them to the land and the local landowners, known as boyars. Yezhov was fortunate to have been born in a major city and received some rudimentary schooling. He began work at a young age as an assistant at a tailor, then found a place at the massive Putilov ironworks in St. Petersburg. Putilov built Russia's railroad cars and networks and then its ships, and its massive workforce was one of the first to form a legal union after Tsar Nicholas II was forced to make some concessions after a near-revolution in 1905.

Joined Bolsheviks as Factory Worker

Yezhov was drafted into the Imperial Russian Army after the outbreak of World War I in 1914, but his short stature made him unfit for combat duty, and he spent much of the war working at an artillery plant in Vitebsk. He joined the Bolshevik Party in 1917 and quickly proved himself a capable organizer, party propagandist, and savvy political operator. After participating in the October Revolution of 1917, Yezhov became a leader of Vitebsk's newly formed Red Guard unit, the armed militias tasked with ensuring Bolshevik control of the local area, its lands and businesses, and its citizens. Russian revolutionaries, led by Vladimir I. Lenin and other prominent leftists, had turned the former imperial empire into the world's first socialist state.

In 1919, Yezhov was drafted into military service once again, this time in the Red Army during Russia's civil war in 1919-1922. He married a university student named Antonina Alekseevna Titova, who went on to work for the newly Sovietized chemical workers' union. After leaving military service, Yezhov had a remarkable rise within the ranks of the Communist Party, and then the Soviet government, that occurred in the span of a little over a decade. Some of it was thanks to the patronage of Lazar Kaganovich, who was close to Josef Stalin, the leader who succeeded Lenin after the latter's death in 1924. Yezhov was just 26 when he was appointed a regional party boss for the Mari province. He was transferred to Semipalatinsk in 1923, taking over a much larger party organization there. After that he served in Kirgiz in Central Asia, then Kazakh, before landing a plum post in Moscow at the offices of the party's governing body, the Central Committee, as a bureaucrat within the Secretariat's Assignments and Records Department.

Appointed to Internal-Affairs Investigation

In 1929, Yezhov was made a deputy people's commissar for agriculture, which coincided with Stalin's concerted effort at the collectivization of farmlands, which prompted massive unrest at the local level. Resisters were dealt with punitively, and entire regions starved for noncompliance, as was the case with the fertile "breadbasket" region of Ukraine. In late 1930, Yezhov accepted a series of simultaneous promotions as chief of department of special affairs, department of personnel, and department of industry inside the Central Committee Secretariat. He also divorced Titova to marry Yevgenia Feigenberg, who had a reputation as somewhat of a minx inside Soviet cultural circles. An editor in Moscow, she preferred literary men, had been twice married before Yezhov, and lived in London and then Berlin with one of her spouses. Both Yevgenia and Yezhov were reported to have conducted numerous extramarital affairs during their marriage, and at one point they adopted a two-year-old girl whose parents had been condemned to one of Stalin's emerging prison camps known by their Russian-language shorthand term gulag.

In early 1934, Yezhov was elevated to critical insider-level status within the Soviet state when he was elected to become a member of the Central Committee of Communist Party at the 17th Party Congress. Later that year, Sergei Kirov, head of the Communist Party in Leningrad—the renamed St. Petersburg—was assassinated at his office, which initially prompted panic and fear at the highest levels of the party leadership. Kirov was a respected member of the party's founding cadre, known as the Old Bolsheviks, and his death was first believed to be the work of foreign agents, possibly working on behalf of new right-wing Fascist powers in Western Europe. Yezhov was appointed to head up the investigation into Kirov's death, but modern historians believe that Stalin himself was likely behind the death and that the incident was an excuse for a massive purge of Communist Party members who had resisted Stalin's rise to power after the death of Lenin.

Kirov's death in December of 1934 and Yezhov's own execution are considered the bookends of Stalin's Great Terror, as the purge became known. After having successfully expelled and exiled Leon Trotsky, who with Lenin had been the most venerated of Bolshevik revolutionary leaders, Stalin targeted other potential rivals for elimination. To do this he needed a flawless state security apparatus, and that had been created by Lenin in 1917 as the Vserossiyskaya Chrezvychaynaya Komissiya, known in shortened acronym form as the VcheKA, or simply Cheka. That police agency was reorganized in 1922 as the People's Commissariat of Internal Affairs, known in Russian as the Narodnyy Komissariat Vnutrennikh Del, or NKVD.

Oversaw Mass Executions

The NKVD was headed by a famously corrupt and brutal Old Bolshevik named Genrikh Grigoryevich Yagoda. Yezhov initially worked with Yagoda to purge high-ranking party members. The first high-profile attacks were against Lev Kamenev and Grigory Zinoviev, both of whom had played crucial roles in the 1917 revolution and went on to high-ranking government posts under Lenin. In a shocking move, Kamenev and Zinoviev were arrested and charged with treason. Their court proceedings were among the infamous Moscow Show Trials of the 1930s, in which the accused confessed a range of crimes, from wrecking (a catchall term used to accuse others of hampering the party's socialist agenda) to espionage on behalf of the West. A significant number of Old Bolsheviks were arrested, tortured into signing false confessions, then sentenced to death with the help of falsified evidence and the spurious confessions of others. Even Yagoda was arrested and put on trial, and Stalin replaced him with Yezhov as the new People's Commissar for Internal Affairs on September 26, 1936.

Yezhov's headquarters at the NKVD was the most feared address in Moscow, the Lubyanka building and attached prison. He oversaw the arrest, detention, and torture operations against some of the Soviet Union's highest-ranking officials, including war hero Mikhail N. Tukhachevsky and Nikolai Bukharin, editor of *Pravda.* After his NKVD directive known as Order No. 447 in July of 1937, party officials were instructed to fulfill quota numbers and turn in ordinary non-party citizens suspected of wrecking or anti-Communist sentiments. In a memo he sent to Stalin in 1937, Yezhov discussed plans to eliminate political opposition and create a more perfect Soviet state. It would be swift, he assured Stalin, and done in two stages. "The first category, to shoot," he wrote, according to J. Arch

Getty and Oleg V. Naumov, authors of *Yezhov: The Rise of Stalin's "Iron Fist."* "The second category, ten years in prison plus ten years in exile.... We should shoot a pretty large number. Personally I think it must be done in order to finally finish with this filth. It is understood that no trials are necessary. Everything can be done in a simplified process."

Yezhov supervised mass executions in a special basement section of Lubyanka that featured a sloped concrete floor that could be hosed down more easily once the bodies were trucked away to a mass grave. He signed orders for thousands of Soviet citizens to be sent to prison camps in Siberia and other remote corners of Russia where conditions were so harsh and rations so meager that many died of cold, malnutrition, and disease.

His family and Stalin's were close, and spent warm-weather breaks at neighboring dachas outside Moscow. On December 20, 1937, Yezhov was feted at a 20th anniversary celebration for the NKVD at the Bolshoi Theater in Moscow, but Stalin seemed unmoved by spoken tributes to Yezhov's leadership—nearly everyone in the inner circle knew what power the NKVD chief possessed—and some saw this as a sign that the end of Yezhov's career was about to come to a swift and bureaucratically efficient end.

Vanished into Penal System

The first sign of trouble for Yezhov came when he was given added duties in April of 1938 as People's Commissar for Water Transport. In August, one of Yezhov's own enemies, Lavrenty Beria, was made his NKVD deputy. Sensing an ignominious end, Yezhov began drinking heavily and informed Yevgenia that he wanted a divorce. There were rumors that he had engaged in homosexual conduct, and her affairs with high-ranking officials were a barely concealed secret inside Moscow's intelligentsia. The last time Yezhov appeared with Stalin at a public event was in late October of 1938, at the 40th anniversary of the Moscow Art Theater. A terrified Yevgenia, well aware of the horrors of Lubyanka's basement rooms and the gulag camps, committed suicide on November 19, 1938. Yezhov resigned from his post as NKVD Commissar four days later. Beria succeeded him and ordered an immediate review of all arrests and detentions carried out during Yezhov's era.

At a Central Committee meeting in February of 1939, Stalin rebuked Yezhov and accused him of plotting to have him killed. Shortly afterward, Yezhov was removed from all posts except the Water Transport, which he then lost a few weeks later when it was divided into two new sections, each with their own department head. Finally, the dreaded NKVD agents came for Yezhov, arresting him on April 10, 1939. His secret trial was conducted on February 2. 1940, after months of torture. He had signed a confession admitting to a long list of crimes, including plotting to kill Stalin, the ubiquitous wrecking, and even sodomy. In a written statement he delivered at trial, however, Yezhov claimed he was innocent of the charges of conspiracy and espionage, and said that he had been a committed party member for 25 years. "I personally exposed ... enemies of the people, who had infiltrated the organs of the NKVD and who had occupied important positions in it," he asserted, according to another book by Getty and Naumov, *Road to Terror: Stalin and the Self-Destruction of the Bolsheviks, 1932–1939.* "Tell Stalin that I shall die with his name on my lips." He was executed by firing squad on February 4, 1940, and his remains cremated and interred in a mass grave. After the fall of the Soviet Union in 1991, his daughter Natasha, who had spent the remainder of her childhood in an orphanage, attempted to have his name officially cleared and his Communist Party reputation rehabilitated, but the Russian Federation's Supreme Court ruled against it in 1998.

Books

Getty, J. Arch, and Oleg V. Naumov, *Yezhov: The Rise of Stalin's "Iron Fist,"* Yale University Press, 2008.

Getty, J. Arch, and Oleg V. Naumov, *Road to Terror: Stalin and the Self-Destruction of the Bolsheviks, 1932–1939,* Yale University Press, 2010.

Periodicals

New York Times, December 25, 1937.

Sunday Times (London, England), January 31, 1999.□

Buson Yosa

Though Japanese poet and artist Yosa Buson (1716-1784) is remembered as a haiku master, he is also known one of the best painters of his era, especially with haiga. He lived during Japan's Edo Period, which lasted from 1603 to 1867, and is considered perhaps the greatest haiku writers of the 18th century and one of the greatest haiku writers in Japanese history.

Buson, sometimes known as Yosa no Buson, was most likely born Yosa Saicho in Kema, Japan, in 1716. Kema was a small village of Settsu (later Osaka). Buson revealed little of his family life, though there was speculation that he was the son of a wealthy farmer and a household maid. What is more certain is that he lost both of his parents at a young age. Buson also apparently enjoyed painting in his youth. He lived in Settsu until he was about 20 years old.

Studied under Hajin

About that time, Buson, an impoverished young man, left Settsu to move to Edo (now Tokyo). His intent was to study both painting and haiku. Within a year, Buson became an apprentice of the well-known haiku master Hayano Hajin, who had founded the Yahantei haiku school. During his apprenticeship, he not only learned haiku and haikai (comic verse), but also haiga, a form of painting and drawing that incorporates haiku.

Hajin died in 1742, and after his death, Buson spent much of the next decade traveling. He traveled in the Chiba area, the nearby countryside, Yuki, and the northern part of Oku. He visited these and other areas to meet with other disciples of Haijin. Some of his travels followed the path of Matsuo Basho, who had made haiku writing an art in the late 17th century and is credited with elevating the form to perfection. Basho outlined this path in his poetic diary, *Oku No Hosomichi* (1694, *The Narrow Road to the Deep North*). Buson was greatly influenced by Basho, and Hajin had been a disciple of two of Basho's disciples, Kikaku and Ransetsu. Indeed, some called Buson the heir apparent to Basho.

Became Buson

Buson made one significant change. In about 1743, he changed his name from Saicho to Buson. Buson is a compound of two words which mean "ceases to be" and "village." Buson also continued to evolve as a poet and artist. While living in Yuki, he wrote his first poem that anticipated modern free verse entitled "Hokuju Rosen wo itamu" (Elegy to the old poet Hokuju). (He would write several other such poems over his life.) In 1747, Buson also edited an anthology of women haikai poets, *Tamamo Shu.*

By the winter of 1751, Buson settled in Kyoto. It is believed that he made the move to study art, though he also might have moved there to be closer to his birth city. While Kyoto was his primary home, he lived at the Kenshoji temple in the coastal city of Miyazu from 1754 to 1757. At a later date, he traveled and spent much time on the island of Shikoku to paint screens at a temple.

During this period, Buson spent much of his time painting. Mostly self-taught, he became a skilled painting master over the years and focused much of his energy on his visual art. He experimented with a number of Japanese and Chinese painting styles while developing his own style amidst many hardships and learning the art of self-discipline. It was tradition in this time period for artists and writers to live in social exile, as wandering priests or other type of itinerant. Buson was, for a period in the 1740s, an unordained Buddhist priest of the Jodo sect.

Became Established Artist and Writer

By the age of 45, Buson was established with a wide reputation as an artist and he married a woman named Tomo in this period. Together they had a daughter named Kuno. By 1770, Buson had acquired a number of haiku followers as well, and he succeeded Haijin as the head of the Yahantei haiku school. Buson took on the poet name of Yahantei at this time. As the head of the school, Buson was relatively indifferent about haiku, perhaps because of what he regarded as the vulgarity in much contemporary haiku. Yet he was friendly with many fellow haiku poets, including Katyo Kyotai and Tan Taigi.

Instead, Buson focused primarily on his visual art, and used the school as a source of new clients for his paintings. It was in this period, from about 1770 until his death, that Buson created perhaps his finest works as an artist in such mediums as hand scrolls, hanging scrolls, albums, and six-fold screens. In addition to perfecting haiga, sketches which include haiku, he also became a distinguished Bunjinga, or literary style, painter. Bunjinga was inspired by Chinese literati. Well-read in the classics and a student of numerous other Japanese and Chinese artistic styles, Buson worked in a variety of styles, though he did his best work in the nanga style after the age of 62.

Much is known about this period of Buson's professional life because many of his letters have survived. He wrote a little about haikai theory but the letters reveal much about being a working poet and painter in Kyoto in this period. Some letters were to patrons about works, others to the important haikai poets of the day. Still other letters were written to members of the Yahantei haikai group, and the most were to his key followers, including perhaps his most loyal disciple, Matsumura Gekkei, better known as Kito.

Matured as a Painter and Poet

In this era, Buson's paintings were done both alone and with other artists. In 1770, Buson created a work entitled *Meishi genkou,* a six-fold screen. The six panels depict the friendship between a master and his pupils and is based on a historical event in China. The piece also features phrases from kanbun classic Chinese texts, and demonstrates Buson's strong admiration for China. In 1771, Buson and literati star Ike no Taiga painted a set of ten screens together.

Buson still published haiku. He was included in a 1772 anthology *Sono Yuki Kage* (*Light from the Snow*). He also wrote linked verse with other leading haiku writers of the era, including Kyotai from Nagoya and Chora from Ise. One such poem was 1774's "Yukaze ya" (Evening Breeze), a kasen that had 36 total verses. It was written by Buson along with Saiba, Tairo, and others, and offers beautiful descriptions of the length of a heron, cattails, and bamboo cane.

Though Buson suffered ill health in early 1775 and suffered from anxiety about the unhappy marriage of his daughter to a Kyoto-based merchant in 1776, he continued to write, publish, and paint. More of his haiku were included in *Zoku-Ake Garasu* (Another Crow at Dawn), also published around this time.

Recognized as Haiku Master

By this time, Buson was considered a master of haiku, as well as his specializations of haikai and haiga forms that emerged from haiku. Like Basho, Buson was especially identified with haiga, perhaps more than haiku and other forms of poetry. In terms of haiku, however, it is believed that 2,850 haiku can be attributed to Buson, and most of these, 2,650, can be dated. More than half were written in the last eight years of his life. Much of his poems emphasized quality haiku, and his verse often focused on Japanese society's lower section. Another preferred topic was common creatures, many of whom were often overlooked.

In late 1776 or early 1777, Buson published his next book of poems, *Yahan-Raku.* This volume included longer poems such as "Shunpu Batei Kyoku" (Spring Wind at the River Bank of Kema) and "Denga-ka" (Slow-River Song). Early in 1777, he started a notebook, *Shin Hanatsumi* (New Flower Picking), which was originally intended to include the ten haiku he would write for 100 days. Illness around day 17 prevented him from reaching this goal, though the notebook included essays about his past.

Expanded His Art Forms

In 1780, Buson wrote a collection of linked verse haikai, "Momosumomo," with his primary disciple, Kito. There were two sequences written when the pair exchanged letters over several months, though Japanese linked verse was usually written in one session. Buson's letters of the period show that he realized he was a great painter and his works were valuable, and that he lived relatively simply. Throughout these years, a significant amount of Buson's time was spent on paintings as well as haiku. As Yvonne Tan wrote on *Asian Art,* "He had a rare understanding of form and exploited its boundaries to create anew."

For example, Buson established the concept of bunjin-ga paintings. These were the Japanese version of the literati paintings, also known as China's Southern School. Bunjin-ga were paintings by nonprofessional artists, and Buson's textured version included poetry and Japanese nature themes. Both his painting and his poetry were influenced by his travels. In 1782, Buson viewed the cherry blossoms by making the trip to the Yoshino Mountains near Nara, and in 1783, he visited one of his haiku disciples in Uji and collected mushrooms.

Remained Important After Death

Buson became ill during the latter trip and returned home. By the end of 1783, he was reportedly suffering from chest pains, and dictated his last three haiku to Kito shortly before his death on December 24, 1783. He was buried in a small cemetery above the temple of Konpukuji in Kyoto. His widow became a Buddhist nun, and was buried next to him after her death. After Buson's death, he was succeeded as the head of the Yahantei school by Kito, who was the school's third and last leader. Unlike Buson, Kito took charge of the editorial work of Yahantei anthologies.

In the years after his death, Buson was primarily known for his paintings, not his poetry. Interest was revived in Buson as a poet because of nineteenth century haiku poet Masaoka Shiki, who wrote an essay in which he praised Buson, and compared Buson and Basho, in 1897. This essay renewed interest in Buson, which continued into the 20th and 21st centuries. Buson's paintings are also the subject of scholarly interest, and they are publicly exhibited from time to time. In 2012, for example, a major retrospective of his works was held at the Miho Museum in Shaigaraki, Japan. Both his art and his poetry were represented.

Describing Buson and his impact, Makoto Ueda wrote in his book *The Path of the Flowering Thorn: The Life and Poetry of Yosa Buson,* "he took delight in the natural beauty of colors and forms as well as in the artistic beauty of composition. A seeker of ideals that were more aesthetic than religious or moral, he would freely let himself wander into a land of exotic beauty far removed from contemporary society and indulge in otherworldly dreams to his heart's content."

Books

Sawa, Yuki, and Edith Marcomeb Shiffert, *Haiku Master Buson: Translations from the Writings of Yosa Buson—Poet and Artist—With Related Materials,* Heian International Publishing Company, 1978.

Ueda, Makota, *The Path of the Flowering Thorn: The Life and Poetry of Yosa Buson,* Stanford University Press, 1998.

Periodicals

Christian Science Monitor, September 4, 2012.

Daily Yomiuri, July 15, 1997.

Europe Intelligence Wire, November 2, 2005.

Japan Economic Newswire, March 26, 2009.

Japan Times, February 9, 1999.

Record (Bergan County, NJ), March 26, 2004.

Southeast Review of Asian Studies, 2008.

Online

McFadden, Edward, "Yosa Buson—Haiku Master," *Kyoto Journal,* http://www.cerisepress.com/01/03/a-selection-of-haiku-by-buson, December 12, 2013.

"A Selection of Haiku by Buson, " *Cerise Press,* http://www.cerisepress.com/01/03/a-selection-of-haiku-by-buson/view-all, December 12, 2013.

Tan, Yvonne, "Yosa Buson," *Asian Art,* http://www.asianartnewspaper.com/article/yosa-buson, December 12, 2013.

"Yosa Buson (1716-1784/Osaka/Japan)," *PoetHunter.com,* http://www.poemhunter.com/yosa-buson/biography/, December 12, 2013.□

Z

Meles Zenawi

The Ethiopian political leader Meles Zenawi (1955–2010) was the president of Ethiopia from 1991 until his death in 2012.

Zenawi was in many ways Ethiopia's first modern head of state, succeeding the Marxist ruler Mengistu Haile Mariam and before him the traditional emperor Haile Selassie (Ras Tafari Markonnen). His rule was controversial both at home and abroad, for it was marked by widespread human rights abuses, violent represssion of Ethiopian dissidents, and military conflict. In spite of these problems, Zenawi ultimately won the favor of both international aid organizations and the Ethiopian people themselves, for he was relatively efficient in the administration of aid and of economic policies that began to improve conditions in one of the world's poorest nations. Zenawi's ideas about Africa's economic future exerted an influence on other African leaders, and he became a staunch ally of Western attempts to contain radical Islamic terrorist movements in the continent's northeastern part.

Studied Medicine

Zenawi was born Legesse Zenawi in Adwa, in northern Ethiopia, on May 8, 1955. His father, Zenawi Asresu, was a member of the area's Tigray ethnic group; his mother, Alemash Gebreleul, was from what is now the nation of Eritrea. Zenawi attended an elementary school in Adwa and then, showing promise in his studies, was sent to the capital of Addis Ababa to study at the prestigious General Wingate High School. He moved on the University of Addis Ababa, where he majored in medicine. During these studies Zenawi acquired a fluent command of English and of southern Ethiopia's Amharic language in addition to his native tongue, Tigrayan.

In the chaos surrounding the overthrow of Haile Selassie in 1974, Zenawi dropped out of the university to join a rebel group fighting for the rights of Ethiopia's Tigray people. He took the name of a Tigrayan fighter, Meles Tekle, who had been killed by the Marxist Derg regime. In the late 1970s Zenawi served as a fighter himself in the Tigrayan People's Liberation Front (TPLF). In 1979 he became part of the group's central committee, and from 1983 to 1989 he served on its executive committee, and in 1989 he became its chairman.

During this period Zenawi dutifully adopted the regime's Marxist principles, but behind the scenes he worked to forge alliances with other small groups to form a broader Ethiopian People's Revolutionary Democratic Front (EPRDF). This group succeeded in overthrowing Mengistu in 1991 and establishing a transitional government. Meles, with his long rebel record, ability to speak articulately in several languages, and membership in one of Ethiopia's smaller ethnic groups, seemed an ideal compromise candidate to rule the country, and the EPRDF appointed him as president in 1991 and then as post-Communist Ethiopia's first prime minister in 1995. As prime minister, he began to embrace free-market economic principles.

Allowed Eritrean Secession

Zenawi promoted national reconciliation with a policy he called ethnic federalism that allowed the country's patchwork of provinces to make some decisions on their own. The national language would remain Amharic, but individual provinces were free to set their own working languages.

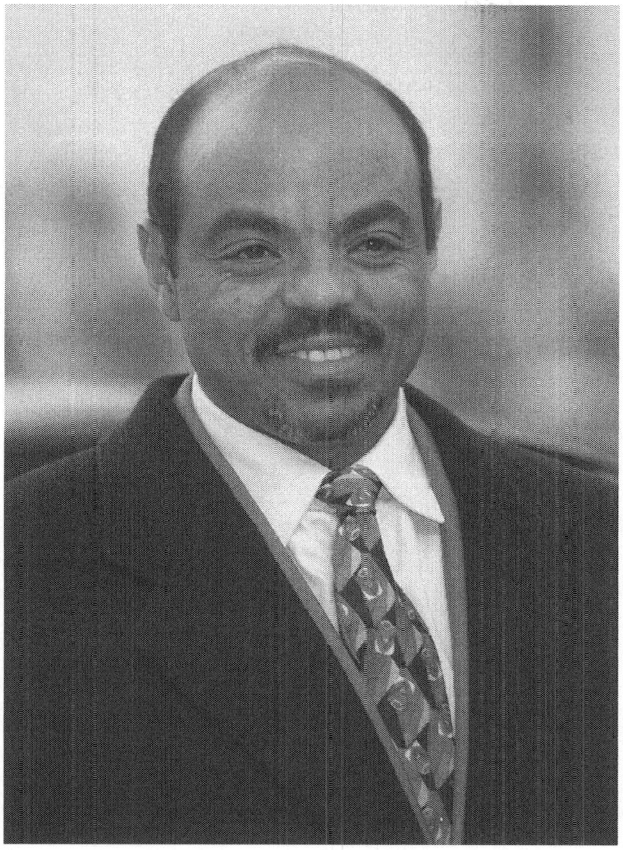

© vario images GmbH & Co.KG/Alamy

Zenawi's most dramatic step to end conflict in the region was to forge an agreement with Eritrea, which when he took office was part of Ethiopia but had waged a long and bloody rebellion against Ethiopian control. Aided by the fact that he was distantly related to Eritrean leader Isaias Afewerki, Zenawi worked out an agreement leading to the independence of Eritrea in 1993.

At home, Zenawi's programs were equally ambitious. Cooperating with both the West and with the increasingly important African investment strategy launched by China, he launched large infrastructure projects including the Great Ethiopian Renaissance Dam (formerly known as the Millennium Dam) on the Nile River. Education funding helped increase Ethiopia's literacy rate by nearly a third in just five years, from 1997 to 2002, and food production, aided by government investments in agriculture, doubled over the years of Zenawi's reign. Economic growth averaged about nine percent a year in the 2000s decade and hit double digits in some years. "While life remains a struggle for many Ethiopians, millions of others have been lifted out of abject misery in just a generation. Anyone who has visited the country more than once notes the transformation taking place constantly as infrastructure is built out, and will remark on the dynamism of the people," said an African observer quoted in the London *Independent*.

Relations with Eritrea, never good, deteriorated over the first years of Zenawi's rule as the two countries wrangled over the rights of landlocked Ethiopia to parts of Massawa and Assab, rights that had been promised in the 1992 peace agreement. In 1998, a trade dispute centered on the border town of Badme flared into war, and the resulting two-year conflict is estimated to have caused 100,000 deaths before a United Nations buffer zone was established. A 2002 ruling by an independent commission awarded Badme, which has a population of only about 1,500, to Eritrea, but Zenawi refused to accept the ruling, and tensions between the two countries have remained high.

Clamped Down on Election Opposition

Ethiopia's council of representatives reappointed Zenawi as prime minister for a new five-year term in 2000. With both domestic and international successes under his belt, Zenawi decided to contest the 2005 presidential race in open elections. The plan ran aground after opposition parties began to show strength, and the night before the election was to take place, Zenawi declared a state of emergency that outlawed all public gatherings. His election win was widely regarded as illegitimate, and as government security forces clamped down on the demonstrations that soon broke out, an estimated 200 demonstrators were killed and 800 injured, with the number imprisoned running into the thousands.

One of the reasons Western countries continued to support Zenawi in spite of his poor human rights record was his cooperation in the international war on terror. Drones operated by the United States Central Intelligence Agency that patrolled the terrorist hot spot of Somalia were based in Ethiopia, and Zenawi, with U.S. support, invaded Somalia in 2006, aiming to displace the fundamentalist Islamic Courts Union that had seized control of the Somali capital of Mogadishu. Ethiopian troops prevailed, but after they withdrew, a power vacuum resulted in the ascent of the al-Qaida-affiliated al-Shabaab militia, and the invasion was widely regarded as a failure.

Nevertheless, Zenawi continued to enjoy support from the West. His economic record remained impressive, and his accomplishments did not rely on environmental destruction; in 2005, he received Norway's Green Revolution Prize. Zenawi pursued policies that favored gender equality and consequently enjoyed support among women. Ethiopia's health ministry under Zenawi was held up as a model of evidence-based planning, and infant mortality under his rule plunged. Zenawi won respect among other African leaders for trying to restrict Western corporate influence in favor of a process he called the democratic developmental state, favoring a free but state-guided economy. Such policies might well have led Zenawi to victory in his quest for a new five-year term in elections held in 2010, but the actual 99 percent share of the vote he eventually obtained was widely regarded as fraudulent.

Zenawi married fellow TPLF militant Azeb Mesfin in the mid-1980s, and the couple had three children, Semhal, Senay, and Marda. Azeb earned the negative nickname Queen Mega due to her high position in several Ethiopian corporations, but Zenawi himself was generally not regarded as personally corrupt. He landed the impressive new African Union headquarters for Addis Ababa, and the building opened in 2012. But concern over his health surfaced when he skipped a summit held at the new headquarters in July of that year, and grew when he disappeared from public view. News of Zenawi's condition and location was shielded from the Ethiopian public, but he was reported to be receiving treatment for liver cancer in a hospital in Brussels, Belgium. He died there on August 20, 2012.

Books

Worldmark Encyclopedia of Nations, Gale, 2003.

Periodicals

African Business, December 2011; August-September 2013.

Daily Telegraph (London, England), August 23, 2012.

Economist, August 25, 2012.

Guardian (London, England), August 23, 2012.

Independent (London, England), August 22, 2012.

International Herald Tribune, August 22, 2012.

Maclean's, September 17, 2012.

Times (London, England), August 23, 2012.

Online

"Ethiopian PM Zenawi Dies After Illness," *BBC News,* http://www.bbc.co.uk/news/world-africa-19328356 (October 22, 2013).

"Meles Zenawi's Biography," *Durame,* http://www.durame.com/2011/09/meles-zenawis-biography.htmlDurame (October 22, 2013).□

HOW TO USE THE *SUPPLEMENT* INDEX

The *Encyclopedia of World Biography Supplement (EWB)* Index is designed to serve several purposes. First, it is a cumulative listing of biographies included in the entire second edition of *EWB* and its supplements (volumes 1-33). Second, it locates information on specific topics mentioned in volume 34 of the encyclopedia—persons, places, events, organizations, institutions, ideas, titles of works, inventions, as well as artistic schools, styles, and movements. Third, it classifies the subjects of *Supplement* articles according to shared characteristics. Vocational categories are the most numerous—for example, artists, authors, military leaders, philosophers, scientists, statesmen. Other groupings bring together disparate people who share a common characteristic.

The structure of the *Supplement* Index is quite simple. The biographical entries are cumulative and often provide enough information to meet immediate reference needs. Thus, people mentioned in the *Supplement* Index are identified and their life dates, when known, are given. Because this is an index to a *biographical* encyclopedia, every reference includes the *name* of the article to which the reader is directed as well as the volume and page numbers. Below are a few points that will make the *Supplement* Index easy to use.

Typography. All main entries are set in boldface type. Entries that are also the titles of articles in *EWB* are set entirely in capitals; other main entries are set in initial capitals and lowercase letters. Where a main entry is followed by a great many references, these are organized by subentries in alphabetical sequence. In certain cases—for example, the names of countries for which there are many references—a special class of subentries, set in small capitals and preceded by boldface dots, is used to mark significant divisions.

Alphabetization. The Index is alphabetized word by word. For example, all entries beginning with *New* as a separate word *(New Jersey, New York)* come before *Newark.* Commas in inverted entries are treated as full stops *(Berlin; Berlin, Congress of; Berlin, University of; Berlin Academy of Sciences).* Other commas are ignored in filing. When words are identical, persons come first and subsequent entries are alphabetized by their parenthetical qualifiers (such as *book, city, painting*).

Titled persons may be alphabetized by family name or by title. The more familiar form is used—for example, *Disraeli, Benjamin* rather than *Beaconsfield, Earl of.* Cross-references are provided from alternative forms and spellings of names. Identical names of the same nationality are filed chronologically.

Titles of books, plays, poems, paintings, and other works of art beginning with an article are filed on the following word *(Bard, The).* Titles beginning with a preposition are filed on the preposition *(In Autumn).* In subentries, however, prepositions are ignored; thus *influenced by* would precede the subentry *in* literature.

Literary characters are filed on the last name. Acronyms, such as UNESCO, are treated as single words. Abbreviations, such as *Mr., Mrs.,* and *St.,* are alphabetized as though they were spelled out.

Occupational categories are alphabetical by national qualifier. Thus, *Authors, Scottish* comes before *Authors, Spanish,* and the reader interested in Spanish poets will find the subentry *poets* under *Authors, Spanish.*

Cross-references. The term *see* is used in references throughout the *Supplement* Index. The *see* references appear both as main entries and as subentries. They most often direct the reader from an alternative name spelling or form to the main entry listing.

This introduction to the *Supplement* Index is necessarily brief. The reader will soon find, however, that the *Supplement* Index provides ready reference to both highly specific subjects and broad areas of information contained in volume 34 and a cumulative listing of those included in the entire set.

INDEX

A

"A"
see Arnold, Matthew

"A.B."
see Pinto, Isaac

AALTO, HUGO ALVAR HENRIK (1898-1976), Finnish architect, designer, and town planner **1** 1-2

AARON, HENRY LOUIS (Hank; born 1934), American baseball player **1** 2-3

ABAKANOWICZ, MAGDALENA (Marta Abakanowicz-Kosmowski; born 1930), Polish sculptor **25** 1-3

Abarbanel
see Abravanel

ABBA ARIKA (c. 175-c. 247), Babylonian rabbi **1** 3-4

ABBAS I (1571-1629), Safavid shah of Persia 1588-1629 **1** 4-6

ABBAS, FERHAT (1899-1985), Algerian statesman **1** 6-7

ABBAS, MAHMOUD (Abu Masen; born 1935), Palestinian statesman **27** 1-3

Abbas the Great
see Abbas I

Abbé Sieyès
see Sieyès, Comte Emmanuel Joseph

ABBEY, EDWARD (Edward Paul Abbey; 1927-1989), American author and environmental activist **27** 3-5

ABBOTT, BERENICE (1898-1991), American artist and photographer **1** 7-9

Abbott, Bud
see Abbott and Costello

ABBOTT, DIANE JULIE (born 1953), British politician and journalist **26** 1-3

ABBOTT, EDITH (1876-1957), American social reformer, educator, and author **26** 3-5

ABBOTT, GRACE (1878-1939), American social worker and agency administrator **1** 9-10

ABBOTT, LYMAN (1835-1922), American Congregationalist clergyman, author, and editor **1** 10-11

ABBOTT AND COSTELLO (Bud Abbott; 1895-1974, and Lou Costello; 1908-1959), American comedic acting team **32** 1-4

ABBOUD, EL FERIK IBRAHIM (1900-1983), Sudanese general, prime minister, 1958-1964 **1** 11-12

ABD AL-MALIK (646-705), Umayyad caliph 685-705 **1** 12-13

ABD AL-MUMIN (c. 1094-1163), Almohad caliph 1133-63 **1** 13

ABD AL-RAHMAN I (731-788), Umayyad emir in Spain 756-88 **1** 13-14

ABD AL-RAHMAN III (891-961), Umayyad caliph of Spain **1** 14

Abd al-Rahman ibn Khaldun
see Ibn Khaldun, Abd al-Rahman ibn Muhammad

ABD AL-WAHHAB, MUHAMMAD IBN (Muhammad Ibn Abd al-Wahab; 1702-1703-1791-1792), Saudi religious leader **27** 5-7

ABD EL-KADIR (1807-1883), Algerian political and religious leader **1** 15

ABD EL-KRIM EL-KHATABI, MOHAMED BEN (c. 1882-1963), Moroccan Berber leader **1** 15-16

Abdallah ben Yassin
see Abdullah ibn Yasin

ABDELLAH, FAYE GLENN (born 1919), American nurse **24** 1-3

Abdu-l-Malik
see Abd al-Malik

ABDUH IBN HASAN KHAYR ALLAH, MUHAMMAD (1849-1905), Egyptian nationalist and theologian **1** 16-17

ABDUL-BAHA (Abbas Effendi; 1844-1921), Persian leader of the Baha'i Muslim sect **22** 3-5

ABDUL-HAMID II (1842-1918), Ottoman sultan 1876-1909 **1** 17-18

ABDUL RAHMAN, TUNKU (1903-1990), prime minister of Malaysia **18** 340-341

Abdul the Damned
see Abdul-Hamid II

ABDULLAH II (Abdullah bin al Hussein II; born 1962), king of Jordan **22** 5-7

ABDULLAH, MOHAMMAD (Lion of Kashmir; 1905-1982), Indian political leader who worked for an independent Kashmir **22** 7-9

'ABDULLAH AL-SALIM AL-SABAH, SHAYKH (1895-1965), Amir of Kuwait (1950-1965) **1** 18-19

ABDULLAH IBN HUSEIN (1882-1951), king of Jordan 1949-1951, of Transjordan 1946-49 **1** 19-20

ABDULLAH IBN YASIN (died 1059), North African founder of the Almoravid movement **1** 20

ABE, KOBO (born Kimifusa Abe; also transliterated as Abe Kobo; 1924-1993), Japanese writer, theater director, photographer **1** 20-22

ABE, SHINZO (born 1954), Japanese prime minister **28** 1-3

ABEL, IORWITH WILBER (1908-1987), United States labor organizer **1** 22-23

ABEL, NIELS (1802-1829), Norwegian mathematician **20** 1-2

ABELARD, PETER (1079-1142), French philosopher and theologian **1** 23-25

ABERCROMBY, RALPH (1734-1801), British military leader **20** 2-4

ABERDEEN, 4TH EARL OF (George Hamilton Gordon; 1784-1860), British statesman, prime minister 1852-55 **1** 25-26

ABERHART, WILLIAM (1878-1943), Canadian statesman and educator **1** 26-27

ABERNATHY, RALPH DAVID (born 1926), United States minister and civil rights leader **1** 27-28

ABIOLA, MOSHOOD (1937-1998), Nigerian politician, philanthropist, and businessman **19** 1-3

Abolitionists, English
Perceval, Spencer **34** 289-291

Aborigines, Australian
policy
Hancock, Lang **34** 153-155

ABRAHAM (Abraham of the Chaldrrs; Father Abraham; c. 1996 BCE - c. 1821 BCE), considered the "father of the world's three largest monotheistic religions" **23** 1-3

ABRAHAMS, ISRAEL (1858-1925), British scholar **1** 29

ABRAMOVIĆ, MARINA (born 1946), Serbian artist **33** 1-3

ABRAMOVITZ, MAX (1908-2004), American architect **18** 1-3

ABRAMS, CREIGHTON W. (1914-1974), United States Army commander in World War II and Vietnam **1** 29-31

ABRAVANEL, ISAAC BEN JUDAH (1437-1508), Jewish philosopher and statesman **1** 31

Abreha
see Ezana

Abstract expressionism (art)
Neiman, LeRoy **34** 273-275

ABU BAKR (c. 573-634), Moslem leader, first caliph of Islam **1** 31-32

ABU-L-ALA AL-MAARRI (973-1058), Arab poet and philosopher **1** 32

ABU MUSA (born Said Musa Maragha; c. 1930-2013), a leader of the Palestinian Liberation Organization **1** 32-33

ABU NUWAS (al-Hasan ibn-Hani; c. 756-813), Arab poet **1** 33-34

Abubacer
see Ibn Tufayl, Abu Bakr Muhammad

Abyssinia
see Ethiopia

ABZUG, BELLA STAVISKY (1920-1998), lawyer, politician, and congresswoman **1** 34-35

ACEVEDO DIAZ, EDUARDO (1851-1924), Uruguayan author and activist **24** 3-4

Achad Haam
see Ahad Haam

ACHEBE, CHINUA (1930-2013), Nigerian novelist **1** 35-37

ACHESON, DEAN GOODERHAM (1893-1971), American statesman **1** 37-38

ACKERMAN, FORREST J (1916-2008), American editor and archivist **32** 4-6
Harryhausen, Ray **34** 157-163

Acquired immune deficiency syndrome (AIDS)
Barré-Sinoussi, Françoise **34** 18-20

Action painting
see Abstract expressionism (art)

Activists
Chinese
Fang Lizhi **34** 113-115

Activists, American
gay rights
Kameny, Franklin **34** 196-198

ACTON, JOHN EMERICH EDWARD DALBERG (1834-1902), English historian and philosopher **1** 38

Actors and entertainers, American
dancers
Robinson, Bill "Bojangles" **34** 306-308
directors/filmmakers
Wood, Ed, Jr. **34** 383-384
film actors
Darin, Bobby **34** 77-79
Fontaine, Joan **34** 121-124
singers
Darin, Bobby **34** 77-79
vaudeville
Robinson, Bill "Bojangles" **34** 306-308

Actors and entertainers, European
GREAT BRITAIN
comedians
Palin, Michael **34** 287-289
stage performers
Cibber, Colley **34** 56-58
television performers
Palin, Michael **34** 287-289
THE CONTINENT
actors
Darrieux, Danielle **34** 79-81
Deneuve, Catherine **34** 88-90
filmmakers/directors
Ciulei, Liviu **34** 58-61
Menzel, Jiří **34** 264-265
Sarris, Andrew **34** 319-321
Siodmak, Curt **34** 330-331
Siodmak, Robert **34** 331-334
opera singers
Della Casa, Lisa **34** 86-88
stage directors
Ciulei, Liviu **34** 58-61
Menzel, Jiří **34** 264-265

Actors and entertainers, Japanese
Oshima, Nagisa **34** 282-284

Actors and entertainers, Russian
actors
Nazimova, Alla **34** 271-273

Actors Studio (New York City)
Adler, Stella **34** 1-3

ADAM, JAMES (1730-1794), Scottish architect **1** 38-40

ADAM, ROBERT (1728-1792), Scottish architect **1** 38-40

ADAMS, ABIGAIL (Abigail Smith; 1744-1818), American first lady **18** 3-7

ADAMS, ANSEL (1902-1984), landscape photographer and conservationist **1** 40-41

Adams, Brooks
see Adams, Peter Chardon Brooks

ADAMS, CHARLES FRANCIS (1807-1886), American diplomat and politician **1** 41-42

ADAMS, EDDIE (Edward Thomas Adams; 1933-2004), American photojournalist **25** 3-5
Faas, Horst **34** 109-111

ADAMS, GERALD (born 1948), president of the Sinn Fein Irish political party **1** 42-44

ADAMS, HANK (born 1944), Native American activist **1** 45

ADAMS, HENRY BROOKS (1838-1918), American historian and author **1** 45-47

ADAMS, HERBERT BAXTER (1850-1901), American historian and teacher **1** 47

ADAMS, JAMES LUTHER (1901-1994), American social ethicist, theologian, and defender of religious and political liberalism **1** 47-48

ADAMS, JOHN (1735-1826), American statesman and diplomat, president 1797-1801 **1** 48-51

ADAMS, JOHN COUCH (1819-1892), English mathematical astronomer **1** 51-52

ADAMS, JOHN QUINCY (1767-1848), American statesman and diplomat, president 1825-29 **1** 52-54

ADAMS, LOUISA (born Louisa Catherine Johnson; 1775-1852), American first lady **32** 6-8

ADAMS, PETER CHARDON BROOKS (1848-1927), American historian **1** 54

ADAMS, SAMUEL (1722-1803), American colonial leader and propagandist **1** 55-56

ADAMSON, JOY (Friederike Victoria Gessner; 1910-1980), Austrian naturalist and painter **18** 7-9

ADDAMS, JANE (1860-1935), American social worker, reformer, and pacifist **1** 56-57

Addis Ababa, Duke of
see Badoglio, Pietro

ADDISON, JOSEPH (1672-1719), English essayist and politician **1** 57-58

ADDISON, THOMAS (1793-1860), English physician **1** 58-59

ADENAUER, KONRAD (1876-1967), German statesman, chancellor of the Federal Republic 1949-63 **1** 59-61

ADLER, ALFRED (1870-1937), Austrian psychiatrist **1** 61-63

ADLER, FELIX (1851-1933), American educator and Ethical Culture leader **1** 63-64

ADLER, LARRY (Lawrence Cecil Adler; 1914-2001), American harmonica player **26** 5-7

ADLER, MORTIMER JEROME (1902-2001), American philosopher and educator **22** 9-11

ADLER, RENATA (born 1938), American author **26** 8-9

ADLER, STELLA (1901-1992), American acting teacher **34** 1-3

Adolphe I
see Thiers, Adolphe

ADONIS ('Ali Ahmad Said; born 1930), Lebanese poet **1** 64-65

ADORNO, THEODOR W. (1903-1969), German philosopher and leader of the Frankfurt School **1** 65-67

ADRIAN, EDGAR DOUGLAS (1st Baron Adrian of Cambridge; 1889-1977), English neurophysiologist **1** 67-69

Advanced Research Projects Agency (ARPA)
McCarthy, John **34** 257-259

ADZHUBEI, ALEKSEI IVANOVICH (1924-1993), Russian journalist and editor **18** 9-11

AELFRIC (955-c. 1012), Anglo-Saxon monk, scholar, and writer **1** 69-70

Aelita (short story)
Tolstoy, Aleksey Nikolayevich **34** 350-352

AEROSMITH (began 1969), American rock band **24** 4-7

AESCHYLUS (524-456 BCE), Greek playwright **1** 70-72

AESOP (c. 620 BCE-c. 560 BCE), Greek fabulist **24** 7-8

AFFONSO I (c. 1460-1545), king of Kongo **1** 72

Afghanistan (nation, Central Asia)
British and
Khan, Abdur Rahman **34** 200-202
centralization of power
Khan, Abdur Rahman **34** 200-202

AFINOGENOV, ALEKSANDR NIKOLAEVICH (1904-1941), Russian dramatist **1** 72-73

'AFLAQ, MICHEL (1910-1989), Syrian founder and spiritual leader of the Ba'th party **1** 73-74

African American art
see African American history

African American history
"SEPARATE BUT EQUAL" (1896-1954)
segregation supporters
Smith, Howard Worth **34** 336-339
SOCIETY AND CULTURE
music
Axton, Estelle **34** 13-15
Cooke, Sam **34** 63-64
Redding, Otis **34** 297-299
Smith, Mamie **34** 339-340
sports
Wilkens, Lenny **34** 375-378

African Americans
see African American history (United States)

AGA KHAN (title), chief commander of Moslem Nizari Ismailis **1** 74-76

AGAOGLU, ADALET (Adalet Agoglu; born 1929), Turkish playwright, author, and human rights activist **22** 11-13

AGASSIZ, JEAN LOUIS RODOLPHE (1807-1873), Swiss-American naturalist and anatomist **1** 76-78

AGEE, JAMES (1909-1955), American poet, journalist, novelist, and screenwriter **1** 78-79

AGESILAUS II (c. 444-360 BCE), king of Sparta circa 399-360 B.C. **1** 79-80

AGHA MOHAMMAD KHAN (c. 1742-1797), shah of Persia **1** 80-81

AGIS IV (c. 262-241 BCE), king of Sparta **1** 81-82

AGNELLI, GIOVANNI (1920-2003), Italian industrialist **1** 82-83

AGNES (c. 292-c. 304), Italian Christian martyr **24** 8-10

AGNESI, MARIA (1718-1799), Italian mathematician, physicist, and philosopher **20** 4-5

AGNEW, DAVID HAYES (1818-1892), American physician **28** 3-5

AGNEW, HAROLD MELVIN (born 1921), American physicist **32** 8-10

AGNEW, SPIRO THEODORE (1918-1996), Republican United States vice president under Richard Nixon **1** 83-85

AGNODICE (born c. 300 BCE), Greek physician **20** 5-5

AGNON, SHMUEL YOSEPH (1888-1970), author **1** 85-86

AGOSTINO DI DUCCIO (1418-c. 1481), Italian sculptor **1** 86

Agricola
see Crèvecoeur, St. J.

AGRICOLA, GEORGIUS (1494-1555), German mineralogist and writer **1** 86-87

AGRIPPINA THE YOUNGER (Julia Agrippina; 15-59), wife of Claudius I, Emperor of Rome, and mother of Nero **20** 5-8

AGUINALDO, EMILIO (1869-1964), Philippine revolutionary leader **1** 88

Agustin I
see Iturbide, Augustin de

AHAD HAAM (pseudonym of Asher T. Ginsberg, 1856-1927), Russian-born author **1** 88-89

AHERN, BERTIE (Bartholomew Ahern; born 1951), Irish Prime Minister **18** 11-13
Lenihan, Brian, Jr. **34** 240-242

AHIDJO, AHMADOU (1924-1989), first president of the Federal Republic of Cameroon **1** 89-90

AHMADINEJAD, MAHMOUD (Mahmoud Ahmadi Nejad; born 1956), Iranian politician **27** 7-10

AI QING (1910-1996), Chinese poet **34** 3-4

AI WEIWEI (born 1957), Chinese artist and activist **33** 3-5
Ai Qing **34** 3-4

AICHER, OTL (1922-1991), German graphic designer **34** 4-6

AIDOO, AMA ATA (Christina Ama Aidoo; born 1942), Ghanaian writer and educator **20** 8-10

AIDS
see Acquired immune deficiency syndrome (AIDS)

AIKEN, CONRAD (1889-1973), American poet, essayist, novelist, and critic **1** 90-91

AIKEN, HOWARD (1900-1973), American physicist, computer scientist, and inventor **20** 10-12

AILEY, ALVIN (1931-1989), African American dancer and choreographer **1** 91-94

AILLY, PIERRE D' (1350-1420), French scholar and cardinal **1** 94

Air pioneers
see Aviators

AITKEN, WILLIAM MAXWELL (Lord Beaverbrook; 1879-1964), Canadian businessman and politician **1** 94-96

AKBAR, JALAL-UD-DIN MOHAMMED (1542-1605), Mogul emperor of India 1556-1605 **1** 96

AKHENATEN (Amenhotep IV; c. 1385-c. 1350 BCE), Egyptian pharaoh and religious leader **25** 5-7

AKHMATOVA, ANNA (pseudonym of Anna A. Gorenko, 1889-1966), Russian poet **1** 96-97

AKIBA BEN JOSEPH (c. 50-c. 135), Palestinian founder of rabbinic Judaism **1** 97-98

AKIHITO (born 1933), 125th emperor of Japan **1** 98-99

AKIYOSHI, TOSHIKO (born 1929), Japanese musician **24** 10-12

AKUTAGAWA, RYUNOSUKE (Ryunosuke Niihara; 1892-1927), Japanese author **22** 13-14

AL-ABDULLAH, RANIA (Rania al-Yasin; born 1970), Queen Rania of Jordan **25** 8-10

AL AQQAD, ABBAS MAHMOUD (Abbas Mahmud al Aqqad; 1889-1964), Egyptian author **24** 25-27

AL-BANNA, HASSAN (1906-1949), Egyptian religious leader and founder of the Muslim Brotherhood **1** 104-106

AL-BATTANI (Abu abdallah Muhammad ibn Jabir ibn Sinan al-Raqqi al Harrani al-Sabi al-Battani; c. 858-929), Arab astronomer and mathematician **25** 10-12

AL-KASHI (Ghiyath al-Din Jamshid Mas'ud Al-Kashi; 1380-1429), Iranian mathematician and astronomer **26** 12-13

AL-SHUKAIRY, AHMAD (1908-1980), Lebanese diplomat and Arab nationalist **25** 20-21

ALA-UD-DIN (died 1316), Khalji sultan of Delhi **1** 102-103

ALAMÁN, LUCAS (1792-1853), Mexican statesman **1** 99-100

Alamein, 1st Viscount Montgomery of
see Montgomery, Bernard Law

ALARCÓN, PEDRO ANTONIO DE (1833-1891), Spanish writer and politician **1** 100-101

ALARCÓN Y MENDOZA, JUAN RUIZ DE (c. 1581-1639), Spanish playwright **1** 101

ALARIC (c. 370-410), Visigothic leader **1** 101-102

Alau
see Hulagu Khan

ALAUNGPAYA (1715-1760), king of Burma 1752-1760 **1** 103

ALBA, DUKE OF (Fernando Álvarez de Toledo; 1507-1582), Spanish general and statesman **1** 103-104

Albategnius
see Battani, al-

ALBEE, EDWARD FRANKLIN, III (born 1928), American playwright **1** 106-108

Albemarle, Duke of
see Monck, George

ALBÉNIZ, ISAAC (1860-1909), Spanish composer and pianist **1** 108-109

ALBERDI, JUAN BAUTISTA (1810-1884), Argentine political theorist **1** 109-110

ALBERS, JOSEF (1888-1976), American artist and art and design teacher **1** 110

ALBERT (1819-1861), Prince Consort of Great Britain **1** 110-112

ALBERT I (1875-1934), king of the Belgians 1909-1934 **1** 112

ALBERT II (born 1934), sixth king of the Belgians **1** 112-113

Albert of Prussia, (1490-1568), German noble
Vergerio, Pier Paolo **34** 362-364

Albert the Great
see Albertus Magnus, St.

ALBERTI, LEON BATTISTA (1404-1472), Italian writer, humanist, and architect **1** 113-115

ALBERTI, RAFAEL (1902-1999), Spanish poet and painter **18** 13-15

ALBERTUS MAGNUS, ST. (c. 1193-1280), German philosopher and theologian **1** 115-116

ALBRIGHT, MADELEINE KORBEL (born 1937), United States secretary of state **1** 116-118

ALBRIGHT, TENLEY EMMA (born 1935), American figure skater **23** 3-6

ALBRIGHT, WILLIAM (1891-1971), American archaeologist **21** 1-3

ALBUQUERQUE, AFONSO DE (c. 1460-1515), Portuguese viceroy to India **1** 118-119

Alcántara, Pedro de
see Pedro II

ALCIBIADES (c. 450-404 BCE), Athenian general and politician **1** 119-120

ALCORN, JAMES LUSK (1816-1894), American lawyer and politician **1** 120-121

ALCOTT, AMOS BRONSON (1799-1888), American educator **1** 121

ALCOTT, LOUISA MAY (1832-1888), American author and reformer **1** 122

ALCUIN OF YORK (c. 730-804), English educator, statesman, and liturgist **1** 122-123

ALDRICH, NELSON WILMARTH (1841-1915), American statesman and financier **1** 123-124

Aldrin, Buzz
see Aldrin, Edwin Eugene, Jr.

ALDRIN, EDWIN EUGENE, JR. (Buzz Aldrin; born 1930), American astronaut **18** 15-17

ALDUS MANUTIUS (Teobaldo Manuzio; c. 1450-1515), Italian scholar and printer **21** 3-5

ALEICHEM, SHOLOM (Sholom Rabinowitz; 1859-1916), writer of literature relating to Russian Jews **1** 124-125

ALEIJADINHO, O (Antônio Francisco Lisbôa; 1738-1814), Brazilian architect and sculptor **1** 125-126

ALEMÁN, MATEO (1547-c. 1615), Spanish novelist **1** 126

ALEMÁN VALDÉS, MIGUEL (1902-1983), Mexican statesman, president 1946-1952 **1** 126-127

ALEMBERT, JEAN LE ROND D' (1717-1783), French mathematician and physicist **1** 127-128

ALESSANDRI PALMA, ARTURO (1868-1950), Chilean statesman, president 1920-1925 and 1932-1938 **1** 128-129

ALESSANDRI RODRIGUEZ, JORGE (1896-1986), Chilean statesman, president 1958-1964 **1** 129-130

ALEXANDER I (1777-1825), czar of Russia 1801-1825 **1** 130-132

Alexander I, king of Yugoslavia
see Alexander of Yugoslavia

ALEXANDER II (1818-1881), czar of Russia 1855-1881 **1** 132-133

ALEXANDER III (Orlando Bandinelli; c. 1100-1181), Italian pope 1159-1181 **24** 12-14

ALEXANDER III (1845-1894), emperor of Russia 1881-1894 **1** 133-134

Alexander III, king of Macedon
see Alexander the Great

ALEXANDER VI (Rodrigo Borgia; 1431-1503), pope 1492-1503 **1** 134-135
opponents
Innocent VIII **34** 183-185

ALEXANDER VII (Fabio Chigi; 1599-1667), Roman Catholic pope **25** 12-13

ALEXANDER, JANE (nee Jane Quigley; born 1939), American actress **26** 9-12

ALEXANDER, SADIE TANNER MOSSELL (1898-1989), African American lawyer **25** 13-15

ALEXANDER, SAMUEL (1859-1938), British philosopher **1** 141

Alexander Karageorgevich (1888-1934)
see Alexander of Yugoslavia

Alexander Nevsky
see Nevsky, Alexander

ALEXANDER OF TUNIS, 1ST EARL (Harold Rupert Leofric George Alexander; born 1891), British field marshal **1** 135-136

ALEXANDER OF YUGOSLAVIA (1888-1934), king of the Serbs, Croats, and Slovenes 1921-1929 and of Yugoslavia, 1929-1934 **1** 136-137

ALEXANDER THE GREAT (356-323 BCE), king of Macedon **1** 137-141

Alexeyev, Constantin Sergeyevich
see Stanislavsky, Constantin

ALEXIE, SHERMAN (born 1966), Native American writer, poet, and translator **1** 141-142

ALEXIS MIKHAILOVICH ROMANOV (1629-1676), czar of Russia 1645-1676 **1** 142-143

Alexis Nikolaevich, (1904-1918), czarevitch of Russia
Feodorovna, Alexandra **34** 7-9

ALEXIUS I (c. 1048-1118), Byzantine emperor 1081-1118 **1** 143-144

Alfa Romeo
Ferrari, Enzo **34** 117-119

ALFARO, JOSÉ ELOY (1842-1912), Ecuadorian revolutionary, president 1895-1901 and 1906-1911 **1** 144-145

ALFIERI, CONTE VITTORIA (1749-1803), Italian playwright **1** 145-146

ALFONSÍN, RAÚL RICARDO (1927-2009), politician and president of Argentina (1983-89) **1** 146-148

ALFONSO I (Henriques; c. 1109-1185), king of Portugal 1139-1185 **1** 148

Alfonso I, king of Castile
see Alfonso VI, king of León

ALFONSO III (1210-1279), king of Portugal 1248-1279 **1** 148-149

ALFONSO VI (1040-1109), king of León, 1065-1109, and of Castile, 1072-1109 **1** 149

ALFONSO X (1221-1284), king of Castile and León 1252-1284 **1** 150-151

ALFONSO XIII (1886-1941), king of Spain 1886-1931 **1** 151

Alfonso the Wise
see Alfonso X, king of Castile and León

ALFRED (849-899), Anglo-Saxon king of Wessex 871-899 **1** 151-153

Alfred the Great
see Alfred, king of Wessex

Algazel
see Ghazali, Abu Hamid Muhammad al-

ALGER, HORATIO (1832-1899), American author **1** 153-154

Algeria, Democratic and Popular Republic of (nation, North Africa)
international role
Bendjedid, Chadli **34** 27-30

ALGREN, NELSON (Abraham; 1909-1981), American author **1** 154-155

Alhazen
see Hassan ibn al-Haytham

ALI (c. 600-661), fourth caliph of the Islamic Empire **1** 155-156

ALI, AHMED (1908-1998), Pakistani scholar, poet, author, and diplomat **22** 16-18

Ali, Haidar
see Haidar Ali

ALI, MUHAMMAD (Cassius Clay; born 1942), American boxer **1** 156-158

ALI, MUSTAFA (1541-1600), Turkish historian and politician **31** 1-2

ALI, SUNNI (died 1492), king of Gao, founder of the Songhay empire **1** 158-159

Ali Ber
see Ali, Sunni

Ali Shah (died 1885)
see Aga Khan II

Ali the Great
see Ali, Sunni

ALIA, RAMIZ (1925-2011), president of Albania (1985-) **1** 159

Alien Registration Act (1940)
Smith, Howard Worth **34** 336-339

ALINSKY, SAUL DAVID (1909-1972), U.S. organizer of neighborhood citizen reform groups **1** 161-162

All-American Girls Professional Baseball League
Foxx, Jimmie **34** 124-128

All Russian Extraordinary Commission
see Cheka (secret police, Russia)

ALLAL AL-FASSI, MOHAMED (1910-1974), Moroccan nationalist leader **1** 162

ALLAWI, IYAD (born 1945), Iraqi prime minister **25** 15-17

Allegri, Antonio
see Correggio

ALLEN, ELSIE (Elsie Comanche Allen; 1899-1990), Native American weaver and educator **27** 10-11

ALLEN, ETHAN (1738-1789), American Revolutionary War soldier **1** 163-164

ALLEN, FLORENCE ELLINWOOD (1884-1966), American lawyer, judge, and women's rights activist **1** 164-165

ALLEN, GRACIE (1906-1964), American actress and comedian **22** 18-20

ALLEN, MEL (1913-1996), American broadcaster **32** 10-12

ALLEN, PAUL (Paul Gardner Allen; born 1953), American entrepreneur and philanthropist **25** 17-19

ALLEN, PAULA GUNN (1939-2008), Native American writer, poet, literary critic; women's rights, environmental, and antiwar activist **1** 165-167

ALLEN, RICHARD (1760-1831), African American bishop **1** 168

ALLEN, SARAH (Sarah Bass Allen; 1764-1849), African American missionary **27** 12-13

ALLEN, STEVE (1921-2000), American comedian, author, and composer **22** 20-22

ALLEN, WOODY (born Allen Stewart Konigsberg; b. 1935), American actor, director, filmmaker, author, comedian **1** 169-171

ALLENBY, EDMUND HENRY HYNMAN (1861-1936), English field marshal **1** 171-172

ALLENDE, ISABEL (born 1942), Chilean novelist, journalist, dramatist **1** 172-174

ALLENDE GOSSENS, SALVADOR (1908-1973), socialist president of Chile (1970-1973) **1** 174-176

Alleyne, Ellen
see Rossetti, Christina Georgina

ALLSTON, WASHINGTON (1779-1843), American painter **1** 176-177

ALMAGRO, DIEGO DE (c. 1474-1538), Spanish conquistador and explorer **1** 177-178

ALMENDROS, NÉSTOR (Nestor Almendrod Cuyas; 1930-1992), Hispanic American cinematographer **27** 13-15

ALMODOVAR, PEDRO (Calmodovar, Caballero, Pedro; born 1949), Spanish film director and screenwriter **23** 6-9

ALN
see Armée Nationale de Libération (ALN; Algeria)

Alompra
see Alaungpaya

Alonso (Araucanian chief)
see Lautaro

ALONSO, ALICIA (Alicia Ernestina de la Caridad dei Cobre Martinez Hoya; born 1921), Cuban ballerina **24** 14-17

ALP ARSLAN (1026/32-1072), Seljuk sultan of Persia and Iraq **1** 178-179

Alpetragius
see Bitruji, Nur al-Din Abu Ishaq al-

ALPHONSA OF THE IMMACULATE CONCEPTION, ST. (1910-1946), Indian nun and Roman Catholic saint **30** 1-3

Alphonse the Wise
see Alfonso X, king of Castile

ALTAMIRA Y CREVEA, RAFAEL (1866-1951), Spanish critic, historian, and jurist **1** 179

ALTDORFER, ALBRECHT (c. 1480-1538), German painter, printmaker, and architect **1** 179-180

ALTERMAN, NATAN (1910-1970), Israeli poet and journalist **24** 17-18

ALTGELD, JOHN PETER (1847-1902), American jurist and politician **1** 180-182

ALTHUSSER, LOUIS (1918-1990), French Communist philosopher **1** 182-183

ALTIZER, THOMAS J. J. (born 1927), American theologian **1** 183-184

ALTMAN, ROBERT (1925-2006), American filmmaker **20** 12-14

ALTMAN, SIDNEY (born 1939), Canadian American molecular biologist **23** 9-11

ALUPI, CALIN (Calinic Alupi; 1906-1988), Romanian artist **24** 18-19

Alva, Duke of
see Alba, Duke of

ALVARADO, LINDA (Linda Martinez; born 1951), American businesswoman **25** 21-23

Alvarez, Jorge Guillén y
see Guillén y Alvarez, Jorge

ÁLVAREZ, JUAN (1780-1867), Mexican soldier and statesman, president 1855 **1** 184-185

ALVAREZ, JULIA (born 1950), Hispanic American novelist, poet **1** 185-187

ALVAREZ, LUIS W. (1911-1988), American physicist **1** 187-189

ÁLVAREZ BRAVO, MANUEL (1902-2002), Mexican photographer **31** 2-6

ALVARIÑO, ANGELES (Angeles Alvariño Leira; 1916-2005), Spanish American marine scientist **27** 15-17

AMADO, JORGE (1912-2001), Brazilian novelist **1** 189-190

AMBEDKAR, BHIMRAO RAMJI (1891-1956), Indian social reformer and politician **1** 190-191

AMBLER, ERIC (1909-1998), English novelist **1** 191-192

Ambrogini, Angelo
see Poliziano, Angelo

AMBROSE, ST. (339-397), Italian bishop **1** 192-193

AMBROSE, STEPHEN E. (1936-2002), American historian **32** 12-14

Ambulances
Safar, Peter **34** 316-318

AMENEMHET I (ruled 1991-1962 BCE), pharaoh of Egypt **1** 193-194

AMENHOTEP III (ruled 1417-1379 BCE), pharaoh of Egypt **1** 194-195

Amenhotep IV
see Ikhnaton

Amenophis IV
see Ikhnaton

American Football League (AFL)
Davis, Al **34** 81-84

American Heart Association
Safar, Peter **34** 316-318

AMERICAN HORSE (aka Iron Shield; c. 1840-1876), Sioux leader **1** 195-198

American literature
poetry
Bly, Robert **34** 38-40

American Michelangelo
see Rimmer, William

American music
20th century
Americana
Helm, Levon **34** 165-167
country and western
Dickens, Hazel **34** 93-94
Jackson, Wanda **34** 191-193
folk and national themes
Dickens, Hazel **34** 93-94
recording industry
Axton, Estelle **34** 13-15
rock and roll
Jackson, Wanda **34** 191-193
soul and funk
Cooke, Sam **34** 63-64

American Rembrandt
see Johnson, Jonathan Eastman

American Woodsman
see Audubon, John James

AMES, ADELBERT (1835-1933), American politician **1** 198

AMES, EZRA (1768-1836), American painter **29** 1-3

AMES, FISHER (1758-1808), American statesman **1** 199-200

AMHERST, JEFFERY (1717-1797), English general and statesman **1** 200-201

AMICHAI, YEHUDA (Yehuda Pfeuffer; Yehudah Amichai; 1924-2000), German-Israeli poet **24** 19-21

AMIET, CUNO (1868-1961), Swiss Postimpressionist painter **1** 201-202

AMIN DADA, IDI (c. 1926-2003), president of Uganda (1971-1979) **1** 202-204

AMINA OF ZARIA (Amina Sarauniya Zazzau; c. 1533-c. 1610), Nigerian monarch and warrior **21** 5-7

AMIS, KINGSLEY (Kingsley William Amis; 1922-1995), English author **28** 5-8

Amitabha Buddha
see Buddha (play)

AMMA (Amritanandamayi, Mata; Ammachi; Sudhamani; born 1953), Indian spiritual leader **28** 8-10

AMMANATI, BARTOLOMEO (1511-1592), Italian sculptor and architect **30** 3-5

AMONTONS, GUILLAUME (1663-1705), French physicist **29** 3-5

AMORSOLO, FERNANDO (1892-1972), Philippine painter **1** 204

AMORY, CLEVELAND (1917-1998), American author and animal rights activist **26** 14-16

AMOS (flourished 8th century BCE), Biblical prophet **1** 205

AMPÈRE, ANDRÉ MARIE (1775-1836), French physicist **1** 205-206

AMPÈRE, JEAN-JACQUES (1800-1864), French essayist **29** 5-7

AMUNDSEN, ROALD (1872-1928), Norwegian explorer **1** 206-207

AN LU-SHAN (703-757), Chinese rebel leader **1** 239-240

ANACLETUS II (c. 1090-1138), antipope 1130-1138 **29** 7-9

ANACREON (c. 570-c. 490 BCE), Greek lyric poet **29** 9-11

ANAN BEN DAVID (flourished 8th century), Jewish Karaite leader in Babylonia **1** 207-208

ANAND, DEV (1923-2011), Indian actor **33** 5-7

ANANDA MAHIDOL (1925-1946), king of Thailand 1935-1946 **31** 7

Anatomy (science)
educators
Bartholin, Thomas **34** 21-23

ANAXAGORAS (c. 500-c. 428 BCE), Greek philosopher **1** 208-209

ANAXIMANDER (c. 610-c. 546 BCE), Greek philosopher and astronomer **1** 209-210

ANAXIMENES (flourished 546 BCE), Greek philosopher **1** 210

ANAYA, RUDOLFO ALFONSO (born 1937), Chicano American author **27** 17-19

ARCHIPENKO, ALEXANDER (1887-1964), Russian-American sculptor and teacher **1** 280-281

Architecture
Aicher, Otl **34** 4-6
Ito, Toyo **34** 186-188
Koolhaas, Rem **34** 214-217

ARCINIEGAS, GERMAN (1900-1999), Colombian historian, educator, and journalist **24** 27-29

ARDEN, ELIZABETH (Florence Nightingale Graham; c. 1878-1966), American businesswoman **1** 281-282

ARDEN, JOHN (1930-2012), British playwright **33** 11-13

Ardler, Stella
see Adler, Stella

ARENDT, HANNAH (1906-1975), Jewish philosopher **1** 282-284

ARENS, MOSHE (born 1925), aeronautical engineer who became a leading Israeli statesman **1** 284-285

ARETE OF CYRENE (c. 400 BCE-c. 340 BCE), Grecian philosopher **26** 18-20

ARETINO, PIETRO (1492-1556), Italian satirist **29** 16-18

ARÉVALO, JUAN JOSÉ (1904-1951), Guatemalan statesman, president 1944-1951 **1** 285-286

ARGALL, SAMUEL (1580-1626), English mariner **29** 18-20

Argentina (Argentine Republic; nation, South America)
economics
Kirchner, Néstor **34** 206-208
21st century
Kirchner, Néstor **34** 206-208

ARGÜELLES, JOSÉ (1933-2011), American philospher and art historian **32** 14-16

Ari Ha-qodesh
see Luria, Isaac ben Solomon

ARIAS, ARNULFO (1901-1988), thrice elected president of Panama **1** 286-287

ARIAS SANCHEZ, OSCAR (born 1941), Costa Rican politician, social activist, president, and Nobel Peace Laureate (1987) **1** 287-289

ARINZE, FRANCIS (born 1932), Nigerian Roman Catholic cardinal **26** 20-22

ARIOSTO, LUDOVICO (1474-1533), Italian poet and playwright **1** 289-290

ARISTARCHUS OF SAMOS (c. 310-230 BCE), Greek astronomer **1** 290-291

ARISTIDE, JEAN-BERTRAND (born 1953), president of Haiti (1990-91 and 1994-95); deposed by a military coup in 1991; restored to power in 1994 **1** 291-293

Aristio
see Unánue, José Hipólito

ARISTOPHANES (450/445-after 385 BCE), Greek playwright **1** 293-294

ARISTOTLE (384-322 BCE), Greek philosopher and scientist **1** 295-296

ARIUS (died c. 336), Libyan theologian and heresiarch **1** 297-298

ARKWRIGHT, SIR RICHARD (1732-1792), English inventor and industrialist **1** 298

ARLEDGE, ROONE (1931-2002), American television broadcaster **32** 16-18

ARLEN, HAROLD (born Hyman Arluck; 1905-1986), American jazz pianist, composer, and arranger **19** 7-9

ARLT, ROBERTO (Roberto Godofredo Christophersen Arlt; 1900-1942), Argentine author and journalist **23** 11-13

ARMANI, GIORGIO (1935-1997), Italian fashion designer **1** 299-301

Armée Nationale de Libération (Algeria)
Bendjedid, Chadli **34** 27-30

ARMINIUS, JACOBUS (1560-1609), Dutch theologian **1** 301-302

ARMOUR, PHILIP DANFORTH (1832-1901), American industrialist **1** 302

ARMSTRONG, EDWIN HOWARD (1890-1954), American electrical engineer and radio inventor **1** 302-303

ARMSTRONG, HENRY (Henry Jackson, Jr.; 1912-1988), American boxer and minister **21** 9-11

ARMSTRONG, JOHN (1758-1843), American diplomat **31** 13-14

ARMSTRONG, LANCE (born 1971), American cyclist **23** 13-15

ARMSTRONG, LILLIAN HARDIN (1898-1971), African American musician **23** 15-17

ARMSTRONG, LOUIS DANIEL (1900-1971), African American jazz musician **1** 303-304

ARMSTRONG, NEIL ALDEN (1930-2012), American astronaut **1** 304-306

ARMSTRONG, SAMUEL CHAPMAN (1839-1893), American educator **1** 306-307

Army, United States
see U.S. Army
McCarthy, Joseph Raymond **10** 388-389

ARNAZ, DESI (Desiderio Alberto Arnaz y De Acha; 1917-1986), American musician and actor **21** 12-14

ARNE, THOMAS AUGUSTINE (1710-1778), English composer **1** 307-308

ARNIM, ACHIM VON (Ludwig Joachim von Achim; 1781-1831), German writer **1** 308-309

ARNOLD, BENEDICT (1741-1801), American general and traitor **1** 309-310

Arnold, Franz
see Lieber, Francis

ARNOLD, HENRY HARLEY (Hap; 1886-1950), American general **1** 310-311

ARNOLD, MATTHEW (1822-1888), English poet and critic **1** 311-313

ARNOLD, THOMAS (1795-1842), English educator **1** 313-314

ARNOLD, THURMAN WESLEY (1891-1969), American statesman **1** 314

ARNOLD, VLADIMIR IGOREVICH (1937-2010), Russian mathematician **31** 15-17

ARNOLD OF BRESCIA (c. 1100-1155), Italian religious reformer **1** 314-315

ARNOLFO DI CAMBIO (c. 1245-1302), Italian sculptor and architect **1** 315-316

ARON, RAYMOND (1905-1983), academic scholar, teacher, and journalist **1** 316-317

Arouet, François Marie
see Voltaire

Around the World in Eighty Days (novel)
Palin, Michael **34** 287-289

ARP, JEAN (Hans Arp; 1887-1966), French sculptor and painter **1** 317-318

ARRAU, CLAUDIO (1903-1991), Chilean American pianist **23** 17-18

ARRHENIUS, SVANTE AUGUST (1859-1927), Swedish chemist and physicist **1** 318-320
Ostwald, Wilhelm **34** 284-286

ARROYO, MARTINA (born c. 1936), African American opera singer **27** 23-25

Ars, Curé of
see Vianney, St. Jean Baptiste

ARTAUD, ANTONIN (1896-1948), developed the theory of the Theater of Cruelty **1** 320-321

ARTHUR, CHESTER ALAN (1830-1886), American statesman, president 1881-1885 **1** 321-323

Artificial intelligence
McCarthy, John **34** 257-259

ARTIGAS, JOSÉ GERVASIO (1764-1850), Uruguayan patriot **1** 323

Artists, American
fashion designers
Schiaparelli, Elsa **34** 323-326
painters (20th century)
Neiman, LeRoy **34** 273-275
printmakers
Lasansky, Mauricio **34** 232-233

B

Babur, Zahir-ud-din Muhammed
see Babar the Conqueror

BACA-BARRAGÁN, POLLY (born 1943), Hispanic American politician **1** 412-414

BACALL, LAUREN (born 1924), American actress **29** 29-31

BACH, CARL PHILIPP EMANUEL (1714-1788), German composer **1** 414-415

BACH, JOHANN CHRISTIAN (1735-1782), German composer **1** 415-416

BACH, JOHANN SEBASTIAN (1685-1750), German composer and organist **1** 416-419

BACHARACH, BURT (born 1928), American composer **22** 38-39

BACHE, ALEXANDER DALLAS (1806-1867), American educator and scientist **1** 420

Baciccio
see Gaulli, Giovanni Battista

BACKUS, ISAAC (1724-1806), American Baptist leader **1** 420-421

BACON, SIR FRANCIS (1561-1626), English philosopher, statesman, and author **1** 422-424

BACON, FRANCIS (1909-1992), English artist **1** 421-422

BACON, NATHANIEL (1647-1676), American colonial leader **1** 424-425

BACON, PEGGY (Margaret Francis Bacon; 1895-1987), American artist and author **25** 29-31

BACON, ROGER (c. 1214-1294), English philosopher **1** 425-427

Bad Hand
see Fitzpatrick, Thomas

BAD HEART BULL, AMOS (1869-1913), Oglala Lakota Sioux tribal historian and artist **1** 427-428

BADEN-POWELL, ROBERT (1857-1941), English military officer and founder of the Boy Scout Association **21** 16-18

BADINGS, HENK (Hendrik Herman Badings; 1907-1987), Dutch composer **23** 26-28

BADOGLIO, PIETRO (1871-1956), Italian general and statesman **1** 428-429

BAECK, LEO (1873-1956), rabbi, teacher, hero of the concentration camps, and Jewish leader **1** 429-430

BAEKELAND, LEO HENDRIK (1863-1944), American chemist **1** 430-431

BAER, GEORGE FREDERICK (1842-1914), American businessman **22** 39-41

BAER, KARL ERNST VON (1792-1876), Estonian anatomist and embryologist **1** 431-432

BAEZ, BUENAVENTURA (1812-1884), Dominican statesman, five time president **1** 432-433

BAEZ, JOAN (born 1941), American folk singer and human rights activist **1** 433-435

BAFFIN, WILLIAM (c. 1584-1622), English navigator and explorer **1** 435-436

BAGEHOT, WALTER (1826-1877), English economist **1** 436-437

BAGLEY, WILLIAM CHANDLER (1874-1946), educator and theorist of educational "essentialism" **1** 437-438

BAHÁ'U'LLÁH (Husayn-'Ali', Bahá'u'lláh Mírzá; 1817-1982), Iranian religious leader **28** 21-23

BAHR, EGON (born 1922), West German politician **1** 438-440

BAIKIE, WILLIAM BALFOUR (1825-1864), Scottish explorer and scientist **1** 440

BAILEY, F. LEE (born 1933), American defense attorney and author **1** 441-443

BAILEY, FLORENCE MERRIAM (1863-1948), American ornithologist and author **1** 443-444

BAILEY, GAMALIEL (1807-1859), American editor and politician **1** 444-445

BAILEY, JAMES A. (1847-1906), American circus owner **30** 26-28

BAILEY, MILDRED (Mildred Rinker, 1907-1951), American jazz singer **23** 28-30

BAILLIE, D(ONALD) M(ACPHERSON) (1887-1954), Scottish theologian **1** 445

BAILLIE, ISOBEL (Isabella Baillie; 1895-1983), British singer **26** 27-29

BAILLIE, JOANNA (1762-1851), Scottish playwright and poet **28** 23-25

BAILLIE, JOHN (1886-1960), Scottish theologian and ecumenical churchman **1** 445-447

BAIN, ALEXANDER (1818-1903), Scottish psychologist, philosopher, and educator **32** 28-30

BAIUS, MICHAEL (1513-1589), Belgian theologian **29** 31-33

BAKER, ELLA JOSEPHINE (1903-1986), African American human and civil rights activist **18** 26-28

BAKER, GEORGE PIERCE (1866-1935), American educator **29** 33-35

BAKER, HOBEY (1892-1918), American athlete **34** 16-18

BAKER, HOWARD HENRY, JR. (born 1925), U.S. senator and White House chief of staff **18** 28-30

BAKER, JAMES ADDISON III (born 1930), Republican party campaign leader **1** 447-448

BAKER, JOSEPHINE (1906-1975), Parisian dancer and singer from America **1** 448-451

BAKER, NEWTON DIEHL (1871-1937), American statesman **1** 451

BAKER, RAY STANNARD (1870-1946), American author **1** 451-452

BAKER, RUSSELL (born 1925), American writer of personal-political essays **1** 452-454

BAKER, SIR SAMUEL WHITE (1821-1893), English explorer and administrator **1** 454-455

BAKER, SARA JOSEPHINE (1873-1945), American physician **1** 455-456

BAKHTIN, MIKHAIL MIKHAILOVICH (1895-1975), Russian philosopher and literary critic **1** 456-458

BAKSHI, RALPH (born 1938), American director **32** 30-32

BAKST, LEON (1866-1924), Russian painter **29** 35-37

Bakufu (shogun military government)
see Japan–1185-1867

BAKUNIN, MIKHAIL ALEKSANDROVICH (1814-1876), Russian anarchist **1** 458-460

BALAGUER Y RICARDO, JOAQUÍN (1907-2002), Dominican statesman **1** 460-461

BALANCHINE, GEORGE (1904-1983), Russian-born American choreographer **1** 461-462

Balanchivadze, Georgi Melitonovitch
see Balanchine, George

BALBO, ITALO (1896-1940), Italian air marshal **29** 37-39

BALBOA, VASCO NÚÑEZ DE (c. 1475-1519), Spanish explorer **1** 462-463

Balbulus, Notker
see Notker Balbulus

BALCH, EMILY GREENE (1867-1961), American pacifist and social reformer **1** 463-464

BALDOMIR, ALFREDO (884-1948), Uruguayan president 1938-1943 **29** 39-41

BALDWIN I (1058-1118), Norman king of Jerusalem 1100-1118 **1** 464-465

BALDWIN, JAMES ARTHUR (1924-1987), African American author, poet, and dramatist **1** 465-466

BALDWIN, ROBERT (1804-1858), Canadian politician **1** 466-468

BALDWIN, ROGER NASH (1884-1981), American civil libertarian and social worker **25** 31-33

BALDWIN, STANLEY (1st Earl Baldwin of Bewdley; 1867-1947), English statesman, three times prime minister **1** 468-469

Baldwin of Bewdley, 1st Earl
see Baldwin, Stanley

Baldwin of Boulogne
see Baldwin I, king

BALENCIAGA, CRISTÓBAL (1895-1972), Spanish fashion designer **30** 28-30

BALFOUR, ARTHUR JAMES (1st Earl of Balfour; 1848-1930), British statesman and philosopher **1** 469-470

Bali (island)
see Indonesia

Baline, Israel
see Berlin, Irving

BALL, GEORGE (1909-1994), American politician and supporter of an economically united Europe **1** 470-471

BALL, LUCILLE (Lucille Desiree Hunt; 1911-1989), American comedienne **1** 472-473

Ball and Chain (song)
Thornton, Willie Mae **34** 346-348

BALLA, GIACOMO (1871-1958), Italian painter **1** 473-474

BALLADUR, EDOUARD (born 1929), premier of the French Government **1** 474-475

BALLANCE, JOHN (1839-1893), New Zealand journalist and statesman **29** 42-44

BALLARD, J. G. (1930-2009), British author **30** 30-32

BALLARD, LOUIS WAYNE (1913-2007), Native American musician **26** 29-31

BALLARD, ROBERT (born 1942), American oceanographer **19** 10-12

BALLIVIÁN, JOSÉ (1805-1852), Bolivian president 1841-1847 **1** 475

BALMACEDA FERNÁNDEZ, JOSÉ MANUEL (1840-1891), Chilean president 1886-1891 **1** 475-476

BALTHUS (Balthasar Klossowski; 1908-2001), European painter and stage designer **1** 476-477

BALTIMORE, DAVID (born 1938), American virologist **1** 477-478

BALZAC, HONORÉ DE (1799-1850), French novelist **1** 478-480

BAMBA, AMADOU (1850-1927), Senegalese religious leader **1** 481-482

BAMBARA, TONI CADE (1939-1995), African American writer and editor **1** 482-483

Bamewawagezhikaquay
see Schoolcraft, Jane Johnston

BAN KI-MOON (born 1944), South Korean diplomat **27** 29-31

BAN ZHAO (Pan Chao, Ban Hui-ji, Cao Dagu; c. 45-51-c. 114-120), Chinese author and historian **24** 38-40

BANCROFT, ANN (born 1955), American explorer **30** 32-34

BANCROFT, ANNE (nee Anna Maria Louisa Italino; 1931-2005), American actress **26** 31-33

BANCROFT, GEORGE (1800-1891), American historian and statesman **1** 483-484

BANCROFT, HUBERT HOWE (1832-1918), American historian **1** 484-485

BANCROFT, MARY (Mary Bancroft Badger; 1903-1997), American author and intelligence analyst **27** 31-33

Band, The (music group)
Helm, Levon **34** 165-167

BANDA, HASTINGS KAMUZU (1905-1997), Malawi statesman **1** 485-486

BANDARANAIKE, SIRIMAVO RATWATTE DIAS (1916-2000), first woman prime minister in the world as head of the Sri Lankan Freedom party government (1960-1965, 1970-1976) **1** 486-488

Bandera de Provincias (Mexican artists group)
Anguiano, Raul **34** 9-11

Bandinelli, Orlando
see Alexander III, pope

BANERJEE, SURENDRANATH (1848-1925), Indian nationalist **1** 488

BANGS, LESTER (1948-1982), American journalist **32** 32-34

BANKS, DENNIS J. (born 1932), Native American leader, teacher, activist, and author **1** 488-489

BANKS, SIR JOSEPH (1743-1820), English naturalist **1** 489-490

BANNEKER, BENJAMIN (1731-1806), African American mathematician **1** 490-491

BANNISTER, EDWARD MITCHELL (1828-1901), African American landscape painter **1** 491-493

BANNISTER, ROGER (born 1929), English runner **21** 18-20

BANTING, FREDERICK GRANT (1891-1941), Canadian physiolgist **1** 493-494

BAÑUELOS, ROMANA ACOSTA (born 1925), Mexican businesswoman and American government official **24** 40-42

BANZER SUÁREZ, HUGO (1926-2002), Bolivian president (1971-1979) **1** 494-496

BAO DAI (1913-1997), emperor of Vietnam 1932-1945 and 1949-1955 **1** 496-497

BAR KOCHBA, SIMEON (died 135), Jewish commander of revolt against Romans **2** 5

BARAGA, FREDERIC (Irenej Frederic Baraga; 1797-1868), Austrian missionary and linguist **27** 33-35

BARAK, EHUD (born 1942), Israeli prime minister **1** 497-498

BARAKA, IMAMU AMIRI (Everett LeRoi Jones; born 1934), African American poet and playwright **1** 498-499

Barakzai dynasty (Afghanistan)
Khan, Abdur Rahman **34** 200-202

BARANOV, ALEKSANDR ANDREIEVICH (1747-1819), Russian explorer **1** 499-500

BARBARA, AGATHA (1923-2002), Maltese politician **27** 36-38

BARBARO, FRANCESCO (1390-1454), Italian diplomat and author **31** 18-19

Barbarossa, Frederick
see Frederick I, (1657-1713)

BARBAULD, ANNA (MRS.) (nee Anna Laetitia Aiken; 1743-1825), British author **27** 38-40

BARBEAU, MARIUS (1883-1969), Canadian ethnographer, anthropologist, and author **24** 42-44

BARBER, RED (Walter Lanier Barber; 1908-1992), American broadcaster **31** 20-21

BARBER, SAMUEL (1910-1981), American composer **1** 500-501

Barbera, Joseph
see Hanna and Barbera

Barberini, Maffeo
see Urban VIII

Barbie (doll)
Handler, Elliot **34** 155-157

BARBIE, KLAUS (Klaus Altmann; 1913-1991), Nazi leader in Vichy France **1** 501-503

Barbieri, Giovanni Francesco
see Guercino

BARBIROLLI, JOHN (Giovanni Battista Barbirolli; 1899-1970), British conductor **24** 44-46

Barbo, Pietro
see Paul II, pope

BARBONCITO (1820-1871), Native American leader of the Navajos **20** 25-27

BARBOSA, RUY (1849-1923), Brazilian journalist and politician **1** 503-504

BARCLAY, EDWIN (1882-1955), Liberian statesman, twice president **29** 44-45

BARCLAY, MCCLELLAND (1891-1943), American artist **33** 17-19

BARDEEN, JOHN (1908-1991), American Nobel physicist **2** 1-3

Bardi, Donato di Niccolò
see Donatello

BARENBOIM, DANIEL (born 1942), Israeli pianist and conductor **2** 3-4

BARENTS, WILLEM (died 1597), Dutch navigator and explorer **2** 4-5

Baring, Evelyn
see Cromer, 1st Earl of

BARING, FRANCIS (1740-1810), English banker **21** 20-22

BARKLA, CHARLES GLOVER (1877-1944), English physicist **29** 46-48

BARLACH, ERNST (1870-1938), German sculptor **2** 5-6

BARLOW, JOEL (1754-1812), American poet **2** 6-7

BARNARD, CHRISTIAAN N. (1922-2001), South African heart transplant surgeon **2** 7-8

BARNARD, EDWARD EMERSON (1857-1923), American astronomer **2** 8-9

BARNARD, FREDERICK AUGUSTUS PORTER (1809-1889), American educator and mathematician **2** 9-10

BARNARD, HENRY (1811-1900), American educator **2** 10

BARNES, DJUNA (Lydia Steptoe; 1892-1982), American author **2** 11-13

BARNETT, ETTA MOTEN (1901-2004), African American actress and singer **25** 34-36

BARNETT, MARGUERITE ROSS (1942-1992), American educator **21** 22-24

BARNEY, NATALIE CLIFFORD (1876-1972), American writer **33** 19-21

BARNUM, PHINEAS TAYLOR (1810-1891), American showman **2** 13-15

Barocchio, Giacomo
see Vignola, Giacomo da

BAROJA Y NESSI, PÍO (1872-1956), Spanish novelist **2** 15-16

BARON, SALO WITTMAYER (1895-1989), Austrian-American educator and Jewish historian **2** 16-17

BARONESS ORCZY (Emma Magdalena Rosalia Maria Josefa Orczy; 1865-1947), Hungarian-British author **28** 25-27

Barozzi, Giacomo
see Vignola, Giacomo da

BARRAGÁN, LUIS (1902-1988), Mexican architect and landscape architect **2** 17-19

BARRAS, VICOMTE DE (Paul François Jean Nicolas; 1755-1829), French statesman and revolutionist **2** 19

BARRE, RAYMOND (1924-1981), prime minister of France (1976-1981) **2** 19-20

BARRÉ-SINOUSSI, FRANÇOISE (born 1947), French scientist **34** 18-20

BARRÈS, AUGUSTE MAURICE (1862-1923), French writer and politician **2** 20-21

Barrett, Elizabeth
see Browning, Elizabeth Barrett

BARRIE, SIR JAMES MATTHEW (1860-1937), British dramatist and novelist **2** 21-22

BARRIENTOS ORTUÑO, RENÉ (1919-1969), populist Bolivian president (1966-1969) **2** 22-23

BARRIOS, AGUSTIN PÌO (1885-1944), Paraguayan musician and composer **28** 27-29

BARRIOS, JUSTO RUFINO (1835-1885), Guatemalan general, president 1873-1885 **2** 23-24

Barrow, Joe Louis
see Louis, Joe

BARROWS, ISABEL CHAPIN (1845-1913), American missionary, stenographer, and physician **30** 34-36

BARRY, ELIZABETH (1658-1713), English actress **30** 36-38

BARRY, JAMES (Miranda Stuart Barry; 1795-1865), First British female physician **27** 40-41

BARRY, JOHN (1745-1803), American naval officer **2** 24-25

BARRY, JOHN (1933-2011), British film music composer **33** 21-23

BARRY, MARION SHEPILOV, JR. (born 1936), African American mayor and civil rights activist **2** 25-28

BARRY, PHILIP (Philip James Quinn Barry; 1896-1949), American playwright **31** 22-23

BARRYMORES, American Theatrical Dynasty **2** 28-30

BARTH, HEINRICH (1821-1865), German explorer **2** 30-31

BARTH, KARL (1886-1968), Swiss Protestant theologian **2** 31-32

BARTHÉ, RICHMOND (1901-1989), African American sculptor **2** 33-34

BARTHOLDI, FRÉDÉRIC-AUGUSTE (1834-1904), French sculptor **28** 29-31

BARTHOLIN, THOMAS (1616-1680), Danish scientist **34** 21-23

BARTHOLOMAEUS ANGLICUS (Bartholomew the Englishman; Bartholomew de Glanville; flourished 1220-1240), English theologian and encyclopedist **21** 24-25

BARTIK, JEAN (1924-2011), American computer programmer **32** 34-36

BARTLETT, SIR FREDERIC CHARLES (1886-1969), British psychologist **2** 34-35

BARTÓK, BÉLA (1881-1945), Hungarian composer and pianist **2** 35-36

BARTON, BRUCE (1886-1967), American advertising business executive and congressman **2** 36-37

BARTON, CLARA (1821-1912), American humanitarian **2** 37-39

BARTON, SIR EDMUND (1849-1920), Australian statesman and jurist **2** 39-40

BARTRAM, JOHN (1699-1777), American botanist **2** 40-41

BARTRAM, WILLIAM (1739-1823), American naturalist **2** 41-42

BARUCH, BERNARD MANNES (1870-1965), American statesman and financier **2** 42-43

BARYSHNIKOV, MIKHAIL (born 1948), ballet dancer **2** 43-44

BARZIZZA, GASPARINO (1360-c. 1430), Italian humanist **30** 38-40

BARZUN, JACQUES (1907-2012), American writer **30** 40-42

BASCOM, FLORENCE (1862-1945), American geologist **22** 42-43

Baseball Hall of Fame (Cooperstown, New York)
Cepeda, Orlando **34** 52-53
Foxx, Jimmie **34** 124-128
Frick, Ford **34** 132-135
Marichal, Juan **34** 252-254

Baseball players
see Athletes

BASEDOW, JOHANN BERNHARD (1724-1790), German educator and reformer **2** 44-45

BASHO, MATSUO (1644-1694), Japanese poet **2** 45-48
Buson, Yosa **34** 389-391

BECHET, SIDNEY (1897-1959), American jazz musician **22** 50-52

BECHTEL, STEPHEN DAVISON (1900-1989), American construction engineer and business executive **2** 98-99

BECK, JÓZEF (1894-1944), Polish statesman **29** 48-50

BECK, LUDWIG AUGUST THEODER (1880-1944), German general **2** 99-100

Beckenbauer, Franz, (born 1945), German soccer player and coach
Chinaglia, Giorgio **34** 53-56

BECKER, CARL LOTUS (1873-1945), American historian **2** 100-101

BECKET, ST. THOMAS (c. 1128-1170), English prelate **2** 101-102

BECKETT, SAMUEL (1906-1989), Irish novelist, playwright, and poet **2** 102-104

BECKHAM, DAVID (David Robert Joseph Beckham; born 1975), British soccer player **26** 36-38

BECKMANN, MAX (1884-1950), German painter **2** 104-105

BECKNELL, WILLIAM (c. 1797-1865), American soldier and politician **2** 105-106

BECKWOURTH, JIM (James P. Beckwourth; c. 1800-1866), African American fur trapper and explorer **2** 106-107

BÉCQUER, GUSTAVO ADOLFO DOMINGUEZ (1836-1870), Spanish lyric poet **2** 107-108

BECQUEREL, ANTOINE HENRI (1852-1908), French physicist **2** 108-109

BEDE, ST. (672/673-735), English theologian **2** 109-110

BEDELL SMITH, WALTER (1895-1961), U.S. Army general, ambassador, and CIA director **18** 30-33

BEEBE, WILLIAM (1877-1962), American naturalist, oceanographer, and ornithologist **22** 52-54

BEECHAM, THOMAS (1879-1961), English conductor **24** 46-48

BEECHER, CATHARINE (1800-1878), American author and educator **2** 110-112

BEECHER, HENRY WARD (1813-1887), American Congregationalist clergyman **2** 112-113

BEECHER, LYMAN (1775-1863), Presbyterian clergyman **2** 113

Beer, Jakob Liebmann
see Meyerbeer, Giacomo

BEERBOHM, MAX (Henry Maximilian Beerbohm; 1872-1956), English author and critic **19** 16-18

BEETHOVEN, LUDWIG VAN (1770-1827), German composer **2** 114-117
influence of
Czerny, Carl **34** 68-70
interpretations
Damrosch, Walter **34** 73-75

Beethoven of America
see Heinrich, Anthony Philip

BEETON, ISABELLA MARY (Isabella Mary Mayson; Mrs. Beeton; 1836-1865), English author **28** 34-36

BEGAY, HARRISON (1917-2012), Native American artist **2** 117-118

BEGIN, MENACHEM (1913-1992), Israel's first non-Socialist prime minister (1977-1983) **2** 118-120

BEHAIM, MARTIN (Martinus de Bohemia; c. 1459-1507), German cartographer **21** 30-32

Behmen, Jacob
see Boehme, Jacob

BEHN, APHRA (c. 1640-1689), English author **18** 33-34

BEHRENS, HILDEGARD (1937-2009), German soprano **2** 120-121

BEHRENS, PETER (1868-1940), German architect, painter, and designer **2** 121-122

BEHRING, EMIL ADOLPH VON (1854-1917), German hygienist and physician **2** 122-123

BEHZAD (died c. 1530), Persian painter **2** 123

BEISSEL, JOHANN CONRAD (1690-1768), German-American pietist **2** 123-124

BELAFONTE, HARRY (Harold George Belafonte, Jr.; born 1927), African American singer and actor **20** 31-32

BELASCO, DAVID (1853-1931), American playwright and director-producer **2** 124-125

BELAÚNDE TERRY, FERNANDO (1912-2002), president of Peru (1963-1968, 1980-1985) **2** 125-126

Belgian art
Rops, Félicien **34** 310-311

BELGIOJOSO, CRISTINA TRIVULZIO (1808-1871), Italian aristocrat and writer **34** 25-27

BELGRANO, MANUEL (1770-1820), Argentine general and politician **2** 126-127

BELINSKY, GRIGORIEVICH (1811-1848), Russian literary critic **2** 128

BELISARIUS (c. 506-565), Byzantine general **2** 128-129

Bell, Acton
see Brontë, Anne

Bell, Al, American disc jockey and record label executive
Stewart, Jim **34** 343-345

BELL, ALEXANDER GRAHAM (1847-1922), Scottish-born American inventor **2** 129-131

BELL, ANDREW (1753-1832), Scottish educator **2** 131-132

Bell, Currer
see Brontë, Charlotte

BELL, DANIEL (born Daniel Bolotsky; 1919-2011), American sociologist **2** 132-133

Bell, Ellis
see Brontë, Emily

BELL, GERTRUDE (1868-1926), British archaeologist, traveler, and advisor on the Middle East **22** 54-55

BELL, GLEN (1923-2010), American restaurateur **31** 24-25

BELL, VANESSA (Vanessa Stephen; 1879-1961), British painter **25** 36-38

BELL BURNELL, SUSAN JOCELYN (born 1943), English radio astronomer **2** 133-134

BELLAMY, CAROL (born 1942), American activist and political servant **25** 38-40

BELLAMY, EDWARD (1850-1898), American novelist, propagandist, and reformer **2** 134-135

BELLÁN, ESTEBAN (1849-1932), Cuban baseball player **32** 38-40

BELLARMINE, ST. ROBERT (1542-1621), Italian theologian and cardinal **2** 135-136

Bellay, Joachim du
see Du Bellay, Joachim

Belle du jour (film)
Deneuve, Catherine **34** 88-90

BELLECOURT, CLYDE (born 1939), Native American activist **2** 136-137

BELLI, GIACONDA (born 1948), Nicaraguan author and activist **24** 48-50

Bellingham, John, (c. 1769-1812), British assassin
Perceval, Spencer **34** 289-291

BELLINI, GIOVANNI (c. 1435-1516), Itlaian painter **2** 137-138

BELLINI, VINCENZO (1801-1835), Italian composer **2** 138-139

BELLMAN, CARL MICHAEL (1740-1794), Swedish poet and musician **25** 40-42

BELLO, ALHAJI SIR AHMADU (1909-1966), Nigerian politician **2** 139-140

BELLO Y LÓPEZ, ANDRÉS (1781-1865), Venezuelan humanist **2** 140-141

BELLOC, JOSEPH HILAIRE PIERRE (1870-1953), French-born English author and historian **2** 141

BELLOC LOWNDES, MARIE ADELAIDE (1868-1947), English novelist **30** 49-51

BELLOW, SAUL (1915-2005), American novelist and Nobel Prize winner **2** 141-143

BELLOWS, GEORGE WESLEY (1882-1925), American painter **2** 143

BELLOWS, HENRY WHITNEY (1814-1882), American Unitarian minister **2** 143-144

BELMONT, AUGUST (1816-1890), German-American banker, diplomat, and horse racer **22** 56-57

BELO, CARLOS FELIPE XIMENES (born 1948), East Timorese activist **25** 42-44

Beltov
see Plekhanov, Georgi Valentinovich

BEMBERG, MARIA LUISA (1922-1995), Argentine filmmaker **25** 44-46

BEMBO, PIETRO (1470-1547), Italian humanist, poet, and historian **2** 144-145
Vergerio, Pier Paolo **34** 362-364

BEMIS, POLLY (Lalu Nathoy; 1853-1933), Chinese American pioneer and businesswoman **25** 46-47

BEN AND JERRY, Ice Cream Company Founders **18** 35-37

BEN BADIS, ABD AL-HAMID (1889-1940), leader of the Islamic Reform Movement in Algeria between the two world wars **2** 147-148

BEN BELLA, AHMED (1918-2012), first president of the Algerian Republic **2** 148-149
Bendjedid, Chadli **34** 27-30

BEN-GURION, DAVID (1886-1973), Russian-born Israeli statesman **2** 160-161

BEN-HAIM, PAUL (Frankenburger; 1897-1984), Israeli composer **2** 161-162

BEN YEHUDA, ELIEZER (1858-1922), Hebrew lexicographer and editor **2** 181-182

BENACERRAF, BARUJ (1920-2011), American medical researcher **27** 42-44

BENALCÁZAR, SEBASTIÁN DE (died 1551), Spanish conquistador **2** 145-146

BENAVENTE Y MARTINEZ, JACINTO (1866-1954), Spanish dramatist **2** 146-147

BENCHLEY, ROBERT (1889-1945), American humorist **2** 150-151

BENDA, JULIEN (1867-1956), French cultural critic and novelist **2** 151-152

BENDIX, VINCENT (1881-1945), American inventor, engineer, and industrialist **19** 18-20

BENDJEDID, CHADLI (1929-2012), president of the Algerian Republic (1979-92) **34** 27-30

BENEDICT XIV (Prospero Lorenzo Lambertini; 1675-1758), pope, 1740-1758 **23** 32-35

BENEDICT XV (Giacomo della Chiesa; 1854-1922), pope, 1914-1922 **2** 153-154

BENEDICT XVI (Joseph Alois Ratzinger; born 1927), Roman Catholic pope (2005-2013) **26** 295-297

BENEDICT, RUTH FULTON (1887-1948), American cultural anthropologist **2** 154-155

BENEDICT, ST. (c. 480-547), Italian founder of the Benedictines **2** 154-155

Benedict of Nursia, St.
see Benedict, St.

BENEŠ, EDWARD (1884-1948), Czechoslovak president 1935-1938 and 1940-1948 **2** 155-157

BENÉT, STEPHEN VINCENT (1898-1943), American poet and novelist **2** 157-158

BENETTON, Italian family (Luciano, Giuliana, Gilberto, Carlo and Mauro) who organized a world-wide chain of colorful knitwear stores **2** 158-159

BENEZET, ANTHONY (1713-1784), American philanthropist and educator **2** 159-160

Bengan Korei
see Muhammad II, Askia

BENJAMIN, ASHER (1773-1845), American architect **2** 162-163

BENJAMIN, JUDAH PHILIP (1811-1884), American statesman **2** 163-164

BENJAMIN, WALTER (1892-1940), German philosopher and literary critic **20** 32-34

BENN, GOTTFRIED (1886-1956), German author **2** 164

BENN, TONY (Anthony Neil Wedgewood Benn; 1925-2014), British Labour party politician **2** 164-166

BENNETT, ALAN (born 1934), British playwright **2** 166-167

BENNETT, ARNOLD (1867-1931), English novelist and dramatist **2** 167-168

BENNETT, JAMES GORDON (1795-1872), Scottish-born American journalist and publisher **2** 168-169

BENNETT, JAMES GORDON, JR. (1841-1918), American newspaper owner and editor **2** 169-170

BENNETT, JOHN COLEMAN (1902-1995), American theologian **2** 170-171

BENNETT, RICHARD BEDFORD (1870-1947), Canadian statesman, prime minister 1930-1935 **2** 171-172

BENNETT, RICHARD RODNEY (1936-2012), English composer **2** 172

BENNETT, ROBERT RUSSELL (1894-1981), American arranger, composer, and conductor **21** 32-34

BENNETT, WILLIAM JOHN (born 1943), American teacher and scholar and secretary of the Department of Education (1985-1988) **2** 172-174

Bennett of Mickleham, Calgary, and Hopewell, Viscount
see Bennett, Richard Bedford

BENNY, JACK (Benjamin Kubelsky; 1894-1974), American comedian and a star of radio, television, and stage **2** 174-176

Benso, Camillo
see Cavour, Conte di

BENTHAM, JEREMY (1748-1832), English philosopher, political theorist, and jurist **2** 176-178

BENTLEY, ARTHUR F. (1870-1957), American philosopher and political scientist **2** 178

BENTON, SEN. THOMAS HART (1782-1858), American statesman **2** 178-179

BENTON, THOMAS HART (1889-1975), American regionalist painter **2** 178-179

BENTSEN, LLOYD MILLARD (1921-2006), senior United States senator from Texas and Democratic vice-presidential candidate in 1988 **2** 180-181

BENZ, CARL (1844-1929), German inventor **2** 182-183

BERCHTOLD, COUNT LEOPOLD VON (1863-1942), Austro-Hungarian statesman **2** 183-184

BERDYAEV, NICHOLAS ALEXANDROVICH (1874-1948), Russian philosopher **2** 184-185

BERELSON, BERNARD (1912-1979), American behavioral scientist **2** 185-186

BERENSON, BERNARD (1865-1959), American art critic and historian **20** 34-35

BERENSON ABBOTT, SENDA (1868-1954), American athletic director **31** 26-27

BERENSTAIN, STAN AND JAN (Stan Berenstain; 1923-2005, and Jan Berenstain; 1923-2012), American author-illustrator duo **33** 25-27

BERG, ALBAN (1885-1935), Austrian composer **2** 186-187

BERG, MOE (1902-1972), American baseball player and spy **29** 50-52

BERG, PAUL (born 1926), American chemist **2** 187-189

BERGER, VICTOR LOUIS (1860-1929), American politician **2** 189-190

BERGIUS, FRIEDRICH KARL RUDOLPH (1884-1949), German chemist **30** 51-53

BERGMAN, (ERNST) INGMAR (1918-2007), Swedish film and stage director **2** 190-191

BERGMAN, INGRID (1917-1982), Swedish actress **20** 35-37

BERGSON, HENRI (1859-1941), French philosopher **2** 191-192

BERIA, LAVRENTY PAVLOVICH (1899-1953), Soviet secret-police chief and politician **2** 192-193
Yezhov, Nikolai **34** 387-389

BERING, VITUS (1681-1741), Danish navigator in Russian employ **2** 193-194

BERIO, LUCIANO (1925-2003), Italian composer **2** 194-195

BERISHA, SALI (born 1944), president of the Republic of Albania (1992-) **2** 195-197

BERKELEY, BUSBY (William Berkeley Enos; 1895-1976), American filmmaker **20** 38-39

BERKELEY, GEORGE (1685-1753), Anglo-Irish philosopher and Anglican bishop **2** 197-198

BERKELEY, SIR WILLIAM (1606-1677), English royal governor of Virginia **2** 198-199

BERLAGE, HENDRICK PETRUS (1856-1934), Dutch architect **30** 53-55

BERLE, ADOLF AUGUSTUS, JR. (1895-1971), American educator **2** 199-200

BERLE, MILTON (1908-2002), American entertainer and actor **18** 37-39

Berlin (city, Germany)
sectors
Blake, George **34** 34-36

BERLIN, IRVING (1888-1989), American composer **2** 200-201

BERLIN, ISAIAH (1909-1997), British philosopher **2** 201-203

BERLINER, ÉMILE (1851-1929), American inventor **20** 39-41

BERLIOZ, LOUIS HECTOR (1803-1869), French composer, conductor, and critic **2** 203-205

BERLUSCONI, SILVIO (born 1936), Italian businessman and politician **25** 48-50

BERMEJO, BARTOLOMÉ (Bartolomé de Cárdenas; flourished 1474-1498), Spanish painter **2** 205

BERNADETTE OF LOURDES, ST. (Marie Bernarde Soubirous; 1844-1879), French nun and Roman Catholic saint **21** 34-36

BERNADOTTE, JEAN BAPTISTE (1763-1844), king of Sweden 1818-1844 **2** 205-206

BERNANOS, GEORGES (1888-1948), French novelist and essayist **2** 206-207

BERNARD, CLAUDE (1813-1878), French physiologist **2** 208-210

BERNARD OF CLAIRVAUX, ST. (1090-1153), French theologian, Doctor of the Church **2** 207-208

Bernardi, Francesco
see Senesino

BERNARDIN, CARDINAL JOSEPH (1928-1996), Roman Catholic Cardinal and American activist **2** 210-211

Bernardone, Giovanni di
see Francis of Assisi, St.

BERNAYS, EDWARD L. (1891-1995), American public relations consultant **2** 211-212

BERNBACH, WILLIAM (1911-1982), American advertising executive **19** 20-22

BERNERS-LEE, TIM (born 1955), English computer scientist and creator of the World Wide Web **20** 41-43

BERNHARDT, SARAH (Henriette-Rosine Bernard; 1844-1923), French actress **2** 212-214

BERNHEIM, HIPPOLYTE (1837-1919), French physician **30** 55-57

BERNIER, JOSEPH E. (Joseph-Elzéar Bernier; 1852-1934), Canadian explorer **23** 35-37

BERNINI, GIAN LORENZO (1598-1680), Italian artist **2** 214-216

BERNOULLI, DANIEL (1700-1782), Swiss mathematician and physicist **2** 216

BERNOULLI, JAKOB (Jacques or James Bernoulli; 1654-1705), Swiss mathematician **23** 37-39

BERNSTEIN, CARL (born 1944), investigative reporter **29** 52-54

BERNSTEIN, DOROTHY LEWIS (1914-1988), American mathematician **2** 217

BERNSTEIN, EDUARD (1850-1932), German socialist **2** 218

BERNSTEIN, ELMER (1922-2004), American composer **27** 44-46

BERNSTEIN, LEONARD (1918-1990), American composer, conductor, and pianist **2** 218-219

Bernstein, Ludvik
see Namier, Sir Lewis Bernstein

BERRA, YOGI (born 1925), American baseball player, coach, and manager **29** 54-57

Berrettini, Pietro
see Cortona, Pietro da

BERRI, NABIH (born 1939), leader of the Shi'ite Muslims in Lebanon **2** 220-222

BERRIGAN, DANIEL J. (born 1921), activist American Catholic priest **2** 222-223

BERRUGUETE, ALONSO (1486/90-1561), Spanish sculptor **2** 223-224

BERRY, CHUCK (born 1926), African American musician **2** 224-226

BERRY, MARY FRANCES (born 1938), African American human/civil rights activist and official **2** 226-229

BERRY, RAYMOND (born 1933), American football player and coach **29** 57-59

BERRYMAN, JOHN (John Allyn Smith, Jr.; 1914-1972), American poet and biographer **19** 22-25

BERTHIER, LOUIS ALEXANDRE (1753-1815), French soldier and cartographer **20** 43-44

BERTHOLLET, CLAUDE LOUIS (1748-1822), French chemist **2** 229-230

BERTILLON, ALPHONSE (1853-1914), French criminologist **2** 230-231

BERTOLUCCI, BERNARDO (born 1940), Italian film director **18** 39-41

BERZELIUS, JÖNS JACOB (1779-1848), Swedish chemist **2** 231-233

BESANT, ANNIE WOOD (1847-1933), British social reformer and theosophist **2** 233-234

Besht
see Baal Shem Tov

BESSEL, FRIEDRICH WILHELM (1784-1846), German astronomer **2** 234-235

BESSEMER, SIR HENRY (1813-1898), English inventor **2** 235-236

BEST, CHARLES HERBERT (1899-1978), Canadian physiologist **2** 236-237

Beta
see Eratosthenes of Cyrene

BETANCOURT, RÓMULO (1908-1990), Venezuelan statesman **2** 237-238

BETHE, HANS ALBRECHT (1906-2005), Alsatian-American physicist **2** 238-239

BETHMANN HOLLWEG, THEOBALD VON (1856-1921), German statesman **2** 239-240

BETHUNE, HENRY NORMAN (1890-1939), Canadian humanitarian physician **2** 240-241

BETHUNE, MARY MCLEOD (1875-1955), African American educator **2** 241-242

BETI, MONGO (Alexandre Biyidi; born 1932), Cameroonian novelist **2** 242-243

BETJEMAN, JOHN (1906-1984), Poet Laureate of Britain 1972-1984 **2** 243-245

BETTELHEIM, BRUNO (1903-1990), Austrian-born American psychoanalyst and educational psychologist **2** 245-246

BETTERTON, THOMAS (1635-1710), English actor **33** 27-29
Cibber, Colley **34** 56-58

BETTI, UGO (1892-1953), Italian playwright **2** 246

BEUYS, JOSEPH (1921-1986), German artist and sculptor **2** 246-248

BEVAN, ANEURIN (1897-1960), Labour minister responsible for the creation of the British National Health Service **2** 248-249

BEVEL, JAMES LUTHER (1936-2008), American civil rights activist of the 1960s **2** 250-251

BEVERIDGE, ALBERT JEREMIAH (1862-1927), American statesman **23** 39-41

BEVERIDGE, WILLIAM HENRY (1st Baron Beveridge of Tuccal; 1879-1963), English economist and social reformer **2** 251-252

BEVERLEY, ROBERT (c. 1673-1722), colonial American historian **2** 252

BEVIN, ERNEST (1881-1951), English trade union leader and politician **2** 252-253

Beyle, Marie Henri
see Stendhal

BHABHA, HOMI JEHANGIR (1909-1966), Indian atomic physicist **2** 253-254

BHAKTIVEDANTA PRABHUPADA (Abhay Charan De; 1896-1977), Hindu religious teacher who founded the International Society for Krishna Consciousness **2** 254-255

BHASHANI, MAULANA ABDUL HAMID KHAN (1880-1976), Muslim leader who promoted nationalism in Assam, Bengal, and Bangladesh **2** 255-257

BHAVE, VINOBA (1895-1982), Indian nationalist and social reformer **2** 257-258

BHUMIBOL ADULYADEJ (born 1927), king of Thailand (1946-) representing the Chakri Dynasty **2** 258-259

BHUTTO, BENAZIR (1953-2007), prime minister of Pakistan (1988-1990) **2** 259-261

BHUTTO, ZULFIKAR ALI (1928-1979), Pakistan's president and later prime minister (1971-1979) **2** 261-262

BIALIK, HAYYIM NAHMAN (1873-1934), Russian-born Hebrew poet **2** 262-263

BIBER, HEINRICH VON (Heinrich Ignaz Franz von Biber; 1644-1704), Austrian composer and violinist **26** 38-40

BICHAT, MARIE FRANÇOIS XAVIER (1771-1802), French anatomist, pathologist, and physiologist **2** 263-264

BIDDLE, NICHOLAS (1786-1844), American financier **2** 264-265

BIDEN, JOE (born 1942), American statesman **33** 29-32

BIDWELL, JOHN (1819-1900), American pioneer and agriculturist **2** 265

BIEBER, OWEN (born 1929), American union executive **2** 266-268

BIENVILLE, SIEUR DE (Jean Baptiste Le Moyne; 1680-1768), French colonizer and administrator **2** 268-269

BIERCE, AMBROSE GWINETT (1842-c. 1914), American journalist and author **2** 269-270

BIERSTADT, ALBERT (1830-1902), American painter **2** 270-271

BIFFEN, SIR ROWLAND HARRY (1874-1949), English geneticist **29** 59-61

BIGELOW, JOHN (1817-1911), American journalist, editor, and diplomat **2** 271-272

BIGELOW, KATHRYN (born 1951), American director **32** 40-42

BIGGE, JOHN THOMAS (1780-1843), English judge and royal commissioner **2** 272

BIGGS, HERMANN MICHAEL (1859-1923), American physician **2** 272-273

Bigordi, Domenico di Tommaso
see Ghirlandaio, Domenico

Bihzad
see Behzad

BIKILA, ABEBE (1932-1973), Ethiopian marathon runner **20** 44-46

BIKO, STEVE (Stephen Bantu Biko; 1946-1977), political activist and writer and father of the Black Consciousness movement in the Union of South Africa **2** 273-274

Bill, Max, Swiss architect
Aicher, Otl **34** 4-6

BILLINGS, JOHN SHAW (1838-1913), American physician and librarian **22** 57-60

BILLINGS, WILLIAM (1746-1800), American composer **2** 274-275

BILLINGTON, JAMES HADLEY (born 1929), American scholar and author **2** 275-276

BILLY THE KID (W.H. Bonney; 1859-1881), American frontiersman and outlaw **2** 277

BIN LADEN, OSAMA (1957-2011), Saudi terrorist **22** 60-62

BINCHY, MAEVE (1939-2012), Irish author **34** 30-31

BINET, ALFRED (1857-1911), French psychologist **2** 277-278

BINGHAM, GEORGE CALEB (1811-1879), American painter **2** 278-279

BINGHAM, HIRAM (1875-1956), American explorer **20** 46-48

BINNIG, GERD KARL (born 1947), German physicist **24** 50-52

BIOY CASARES, ADOLFO (1914-1999), Argentine writer **33** 32-34

Bird
see Parker, Charles

BIRD, ISABELLA (Isabella Bird Bishop; 1831-1904), English explorer and author **23** 41-42

BIRD, LARRY (born 1956), American basketball player **2** 279-281

BIRD, ROBERT MONTGOMERY (1806-1854), American dramatist and novelist **2** 281-282

BIRDSEYE, CLARENCE (1886-1956), American naturalist, inventor, and businessman **19** 25-27

BIRENDRA (Bir Bikram Shah Dev; 1945-2001), King of Nepal (1972-2001) **2** 282-283

BIRGER, ZEV (1926-2011), Israeli official **33** 34-36

BIRINGUCCIO, VANNOCCIO (1480-1539), Italian mining engineer and metallurgist **2** 283

BIRNEY, JAMES GILLESPIE (1792-1857), American lawyer and abolitionist **2** 283-284

Birth control (medicine)
oral contraceptive
Djerassi, Carl **34** 95-97

BIRUNI, ABU RAYHAN AL- (973-c. 1050), Arabian scientist and historian **2** 284-285

BIRYUKOVA, ALEKSANDRA PAVLOVNA (1929-1990), a secretary of the Central Committee of the Communist party of the Soviet Union and a deputy prime minister (1986-1990) **2** 285-287

BISHARA, ABDULLAH YACCOUB (born 1936), Kuwaiti statesman and first secretary-general of the Gulf Cooperative Council **2** 287-288

Blixen-Finecke, Baroness
see Dinesen Blixen-Finecke, Karen

BLOCH, ERNEST (1880-1959), Swiss-born American composer and teacher **2** 326-327

BLOCH, ERNST (1885-1977), German humanistic interpreter of Marxist thought **2** 327-328

BLOCH, FELIX (1905-1983), Swiss/American physicist **2** 328-330

BLOCH, KONRAD (1912-2000), American biochemist **2** 330-332

BLOCH, MARC (1886-1944), French historian **2** 332-333

BLOCK, HERBERT (Herblock; 1909-2001), American newspaper cartoonist **2** 333-334

BLODGETT, KATHARINE BURR (1898-1979), American physicist **24** 54-56

BLOK, ALEKSANDR ALEKSANDROVICH (1880-1921), Russian poet **2** 335

BLONDIN, JEAN FRANCOIS GRAVELET (Charles Blondin; 1824-1897), French tightrope walker and acrobat **27** 48-50

Bloody Mary
see Mary I

BLOOM, ALLAN DAVID (1930-1992), American political philosopher, professor, and author **2** 335-337

BLOOM, HAROLD (born 1930), American literary critic and educator **28** 38-40

BLOOMBERG, MICHAEL (Michael Rubens Bloomberg; born 1942), American businessman and politician **28** 40-42

BLOOMER, AMELIA JENKS (1818-1894), American reformer and suffrage advocate **2** 337

BLOOMFIELD, LEONARD (1887-1949), American linguist **2** 338

BLOOR, ELLA REEVE ("Mother Bloor"; 1862-1951), American labor organizer and social activist **2** 338-340

BLÜCHER, GEBHARD LEBERECHT VON (Prince of Wahlstatt; 1742-1819), Prussian field marshal **2** 340-341

BLÜCHER, VASILY KONSTANTINOVICH (1889-1938), Soviet military leader **30** 59-61

Bluegrass (music)
Dickens, Hazel **34** 93-94

Blues (music)
Smith, Mamie **34** 339-340
Thornton, Willie Mae **34** 346-348
Vaughan, Stevie Ray **34** 355-357

BLUFORD, GUION STEWART, JR. (born 1942), African American aerospace engineer, pilot, and astronaut **2** 341-343

BLUM, ARLENE (born 1940), American mountaineer **30** 61-63

BLUM, LÉON (1872-1950), French statesman **2** 343-344
Torrès, Tereska **34** 352-354

BLUMBERG, BARUCH (1925-2011), American medical researcher **32** 44-46
Gajdusek, Carleton **34** 138-140

BLUME, JUDY (born Judy Sussman, 1938), American fiction author **2** 344-345

BLUMENTHAL, WERNER MICHAEL (born 1926), American businessman and treasury secretary **2** 345-346

BLUNT, ANTHONY (1907-1983), British art historian and spy **34** 36-38
Burgess, Guy **34** 44-47

BLY, NELLIE (born Elizabeth Cochrane Seaman; 1864-1922), American journalist and reformer **2** 346-348

BLY, ROBERT (born 1926), American poet **34** 38-40

BLYDEN, EDWARD WILMOT (1832-1912), Liberian statesman **2** 348-349

Blythe, Vernon William
see Castle, I. and V.

Boadicia
see Boudicca

BOAL, AUGUSTO (1931-2009), Brazilian director and author **30** 63-65

Boanerges
see John, St.

Boardwalk Empire (television program)
Johnson, Enoch "Nucky" **34** 193-195

BOAS, FRANZ (1858-1942), German-born American anthropologist **2** 349-351

BOCCACCIO, GIOVANNI (1313-1375), Italian author **2** 351-353

BOCCIONI, UMBERTO (1882-1916), Italian artist **2** 353-354

BÖCKLIN, ARNOLD (1827-1901), Swiss painter **2** 354-355

BODE, BOYD HENRY (1873-1953), American philosopher and educator **2** 355-356

Bodenstein, Andreas
see Karlstadt

BODENSTEIN, MAX ERNST (1871-1942), German chemist **32** 46-48

Bodhisattva Emperor
see Liang Wu-ti

BODIN, JEAN (1529/30-1596), French political philosopher **2** 356-357

BOECKH, AUGUST (1785-1867), German classical scholar **30** 63-67

BOEHME, JACOB (1575-1624), German mystic **2** 357

BOEING, WILLIAM EDWARD (1881-1956), American businessman **2** 357-358

BOERHAAVE, HERMANN (1668-1738), Dutch physician and chemist **2** 358-359

BOESAK, ALLAN AUBREY (born 1945), opponent of apartheid in South Africa and founder of the United Democratic Front **2** 359-360

BOETHIUS, ANICIUS MANLIUS SEVERINUS (c. 480-524/525), Roman logician and theologian **2** 360-361

BOFF, LEONARDO (Leonardo Genezio Darci Boff; born 1938), Brazilian priest **22** 69-71

BOFFRAND, GABRIEL GERMAIN (1667-1754), French architect and decorator **2** 361

BOFILL, RICARDO (born 1939), post-modern Spanish architect **2** 362-363

BOGART, HUMPHREY (1899-1957), American stage and screen actor **2** 363-364

Bogdanovich, Peter, American film director
McMurtry, Larry **34** 259-261

BOHEMUND I (of Tarantò; c. 1055-1111), Norman Crusader **2** 364

BOHLEN, CHARLES (CHIP) EUSTIS (1904-1973), United States ambassador to the Soviet Union, interpreter, and presidential adviser **2** 364-366

BÖHM, GEORG (1661-1733), German organist **31** 28-29

BÖHM-BAWERK, EUGEN VON (1851-1914), Austrian economist **2** 366

Böhme, Jakob
see Boehme, Jacob

BOHR, AAGE NIELS (1922-2009), Danish physicist **25** 53-55

BOHR, NIELS HENRIK DAVID (1885-1962), Danish physicist **2** 366-368
theory acceptance/rejection
Fang Lizhi **34** 113-115

BOIARDO, MATTEO MARIA (Conte di Scandiano; 1440/41-1494), Italian poet **2** 369

BOILEAU-DESPRÉAUX, NICHOLAS (c. 1636-1711), French critic and writer **2** 369-371

Boisy, Francis
see Francis of Sales, St.

BOITO, ARRIGO (1842-1918), Italian composer, librettist, and poet **30** 67-69

BOIVIN, MARIE GILLAIN (née Marie Anne Victorine Gillain; 1773-1841), French midwife and author **25** 55-56

BOK, DEREK CURTIS (born 1930), dean of the Harvard Law School and president of Harvard University **2** 371-372

BOK, EDWARD WILLIAM (1863-1930), American editor and publisher **22** 71-73

BOK, SISSELA ANN (born 1934), American moral philosopher **2** 372-374

BOLAÑO, ROBERTO (1953-2003), Chilean author **28** 42-45

BOLEYN, ANNE (c. 1504-1536), second wife of Henry VIII **18** 47-49

Bolingbroke, Henry
see Henry IV (king of England)

BOLINGBROKE, VISCOUNT (Henry St. John; 1678-1751), English statesman **2** 374-375

BOLÍVAR, SIMÓN (1783-1830), South American general and statesman **2** 375-377

BOLKIAH, HASSANAL (Muda Hassanal Bolkiah Mu'izzaddin Waddaulah; born 1946), Sultan of Brunei **18** 49-51

BÖLL, HEINRICH (1917-1985), German writer and translator **2** 377-378

Bolshevik Revolution
see Russian Revolution (1917; October)

Bolsheviks (Russian politics)
supporters
Yezhov, Nikolai **34** 387-389

BOLT, ROBERT (1924-1995), British screenwriter and playwright **30** 69-71

BOLTWOOD, BERTRAM BORDEN (1870-1927), American radiochemist **2** 378-379

BOLTZMANN, LUDWIG (1844-1906), Austrian physicist **2** 379-380

BOLZANO, BERNHARD (1781-1848), Bohemian mathematician and philosopher **33** 38-40

BOMANI, PAUL (1925-2005), Tanzanian politician **29** 63-65

BOMBAL, MARÍA LUISA (1910-1980), Chilean novelist and story writer **2** 380-381

Bonaparte, Charles Louis Napoleon
see Napoleon III

BONAPARTE, JOSEPH (1768-1844), French statesman, king of Naples 1806-1808 and of Spain 1808-1813 **2** 381-382

BONAPARTE, LOUIS (1778-1846), French statesman, king of Holland 1806-1810 **2** 382-383

Bonaparte, Napoleon
see Napoleon I

BONAVENTURE, ST. (1217-1274), Italian theologian and philosopher **2** 383-384

Boncompagni, Ugo
see Gregory XIII

BOND, HORACE MANN (1904-1972), African American educator **2** 384-386

BOND, JULIAN (born 1940), civil rights leader elected to the Georgia House of Representatives **2** 386-387

BONDEVIK, KJELL MAGNE (born 1947), Norwegian politician **27** 51-53

BONDFIELD, MARGARET GRACE (1873-1953), British union official and political leader **2** 388-389

BONDI, HERMANN (1919-2005), English mathematician and cosmologist **18** 51-52

Bonesana, Cesare
see Becarria, Marchese di

BONHAM CARTER, HELEN VIOLET (nee Helen Violet Asquith; 1887-1969), English author and orator **26** 42-44

BONHEUR, ROSA (Marie Rosalie Bonheur; 1822-1899), French artist **19** 29-31

BONHOEFFER, DIETRICH (1906-1945), German theologian **2** 389-391

BONIFACE, ST. (c. 672-754), English monk **2** 391

BONIFACE VIII (Benedetto Caetani; c. 1235-1303), pope 1294-1303 **2** 392-393

BONIFACIO, ANDRES (1863-1897), Filipino revolutionary hero **2** 393-394

BONINGTON, RICHARD PARKES (1802-1828), English painter **2** 394-395

BONNARD, PIERRE (1867-1947), French painter **2** 395-396

Bonnie Prince Charlie
see Charles Edward Louis Philip Casimir Stuart

BONNIN, GERTRUDE SIMMONS (Zitkala-Sa; Red Bird; 1876-1938), Native American author and activist **18** 52-54

BONNY, ANNE (Anne Bonn; Anne Burleigh; 1700-1782), Irish American pirate **25** 56-58

BONO (Paul Hewson; born 1960), Irish musician and activist **24** 56-59

BONO, SONNY (Salvatore Bono; 1935-1998), American entertainer and U.S. Congressman **18** 54-56

BONTEMPS, ARNA (Arnaud Wendell Bontemps| 1902-1973), American author and educator **21** 47-50

BONVALOT, PIERRE GABRIEL ÉDOUARD (1853-1933), French explorer and author **2** 396

Bookmaking (gambling)
Rothstein, Arnold **34** 311-313

BOOLE, GEORGE (1815-1864), English mathematician **2** 396-397

BOONE, DANIEL (1734-1820), American frontiersman and explorer **2** 397-398

BOORSTIN, DANIEL J. (1914-2004), American historian **2** 398-400

BOOTH, BRAMWELL (1856-1929), English Salvation Army leader **29** 65-67

BOOTH, CATHERINE MUMFORD (1829-1890), English reformer **29** 67-69

BOOTH, CHARLES (1840-1916), English social scientist **2** 400-401

BOOTH, EDWIN (1833-1893), American actor **2** 401-402

BOOTH, EVANGELINE CORY (1865-1950), British/American humanist **2** 402-403

BOOTH, HUBERT CECIL (1871-1955), English inventor of the vacuum cleaner **21** 50-52

BOOTH, JOHN WILKES (1838-1865), American actor **2** 404

BOOTH, JOSEPH (1851-1932), English missionary in Africa **2** 404-405

BOOTH, WILLIAM (1829-1912), English evangelist, Salvation Army founder **2** 405-406

Boothe, Clare
see Luce, Clare Boothe

BOOTHROYD, BETTY (born 1929), first woman speaker in Great Britain's House of Commons **2** 406-407

Bootleggers (United States)
Johnson, Enoch "Nucky" **34** 193-195
Rothstein, Arnold **34** 311-313

BORA, KATHARINA VON (1499-1552), German nun **29** 256-258

BORAH, WILLIAM EDGAR (1865-1940), American statesman **2** 408

BORDABERRY, JUAN MARÍA (1928-2011), Uruguayan statesman **33** 40-42

BORDEN, GAIL (1801-1874), American pioneer and inventor of food-processing techniques **2** 409

BORDEN, LIZZIE (Lizzie Andrew Borden; 1860-1927), American murderer **28** 45-47

BORDEN, SIR ROBERT LAIRD (1854-1937), Canadian prime minister, 1911-1920 **2** 409-411

BORDONI, FAUSTINA (1697-1781), Italian opera singer **31** 30-31

BORELLI, GIOVANNI ALFONSO (1608-1679), Italian physicist **29** 69-72

BORGES, JORGE LUIS (1899-1986), Argentine author and critic **2** 411-412

Borghese, Camillo
see Paul V, pope

BORGIA, CESARE (1475-1507), Italian cardinal, general, and administrator **2** 412-413

BORGIA, FRANCIS (1510-1572), Spanish noble and priest **33** 42-44

BORGIA, LUCREZIA (1480-1519), Italian duchess of Ferrara **2** 413-416

Borgia, Rodrigo
see Alexander VI

BORGLUM, JOHN GUTZON DE LA MOTHE (1867-1941), American sculptor and engineer **2** 416-417

BORI, LUCREZIA (Lucrezia Gonzá de Riancho; 1887-1960), Spanish American opera singer **23** 44-45

BORJA CEVALLOS, RODRIGO (born 1935), a founder of Ecuador's Democratic Left (Izquierda Democratica) party and president of Ecuador (1988-1992) **2** 417-418

BORLAUG, NORMAN ERNEST (1914-2009), American biochemist who developed high yield cereal grains **2** 418-420

BORN, MAX (1882-1970), German physicist **2** 420-421

Borneo (island)
see Indonesia

BOROCHOV, DOV BER (1881-1917), early Zionist thinker who reconciled Judaism and Marxism **2** 421-422

BORODIN, ALEKSANDR PROFIREVICH (1833-1887), Russian composer **2** 422-423

BORODIN, MIKHAIL MARKOVICH (1884-1951), Russian diplomat **29** 72-74

BOROUGH, STEPHEN (1525-1584), English navigator **29** 74-76

BORROMEO, ST. CHARLES (1538-1584), Italian cardinal and reformer **2** 423-424

BORROMINI, FRANCESCO (1599-1667), Italian architect **2** 424-425

BOSANQUET, BERNARD (1848-1923), English philosopher **2** 425-426

BOSCAWEN, EDWARD (1711-1761), British admiral **31** 32-33

BOSCH, CARL (1874-1940), German industrial chemist **29** 76-78

BOSCH, HIERONYMUS (1453-1516), Netherlandish painter **2** 426-428

BOSCH, JUAN (1909-2001), Dominican writer, president, 1963 **2** 428-429

BOSE, SIR JAGADIS CHANDRA (1858-1937), Indian physicist and plant physiologist **2** 430-431

Bose, Satyendra Nath
see Bose, S.N.

BOSE, S.N. (1894-1974), Indian physicist **29** 78-80

BOSE, SUBHAS CHANDRA (1897-1945), Indian nationalist **2** 430-431

BOSOMWORTH, MARY MUSGROVE (Cousaponokeesa;1700-1765), Native American/American interpreter, diplomat, and businessperson **20** 54-56

BOSSUET, JACQUES BÉNIGNE (1627-1704), French bishop and author **2** 431-432

Boston Bruins (hockey team)
O'Ree, Willie **34** 280-282
Sawchuk, Terry **34** 321-323

Boston Red Sox (baseball team)
Foxx, Jimmie **34** 124-128
Marichal, Juan **34** 252-254

Boston Strong Boy
see Sullivan, John Lawrence

BOSWELL, JAMES (1740-1795), Scottish biographer and diarist **2** 432-434

BOTERO, FERNANDO (born 1932), Colombian artist **24** 59-61

BOTHA, LOUIS (1862-1919), South African soldier and statesman **2** 434-436

BOTHA, PIETER WILLEM (1916-2006), prime minister (1978-1984) and first executive state president of the Republic of South Africa **2** 436-438

BOTHE, WALTHER (1891-1957), German physicist **2** 438-439

Boto, Eza
see Beti, Mongo

BOTTICELLI, SANDRO (1444-1510), Italian painter **2** 439-440

Bou Kharouba, Mohammed Ben Brahim
see Boumediene, Houari

BOUCHER, FRANÇOIS (1703-1770), French painter **2** 440-442

BOUCICAULT, DION (1820-1890), Irish-American playwright and actor **2** 442-443

Boudiaf, Mohammed, (1919-1992), Algerian statesman
Bendjedid, Chadli **34** 27-30

BOUDICCA (Boadicea; died 61 A.D.), Iceni queen **18** 56-58

BOUDINOT, ELIAS (Buck Watie; Galagina; 1803-1839), Cherokee leader and author **21** 52-54

BOUGAINVILLE, LOUIS ANTOINE DE (1729-1811), French soldier and explorer **2** 443-444

Boulanger, N. A.
see Holbach, Baron d'

BOULANGER, NADIA (1887-1979), French pianist and music teacher **20** 56-58

BOULEZ, PIERRE (born 1925), French composer, conductor, and teacher **2** 444-445

BOULT, ADRIAN CEDRIC (1889-1983), English conductor **24** 61-64

BOUMEDIENE, HOUARI (1932-1978), Algerian revolutionary, military leader, and president **2** 445-446

BOURASSA, JOSEPH-HENRI-NAPOLEON (1868-1952), French-Canadian nationalist and editor **2** 446-447

BOURASSA, ROBERT (1933-1996), premier of the province of Quebec (1970-1976 and 1985-94) **2** 447-449

Bourcicault, Dion
see Boucicault, Dion

BOURDELLE, EMILE-ANTOINE (1861-1929), French sculptor **2** 449-450

BOURGEOIS, LÉON (1851-1925), French premier 1895-1896 **2** 450-451

BOURGEOIS, LOUISE (1911-2010), American sculptor **2** 451-452

BOURGEOIS, LOUYSE (Louise Bourgeois; c. 1563-1636), French midwife **25** 58-60

BOURGEOYS, BLESSED MARGUERITE (1620-1700), French educator and religious founder **2** 452-453

Bourgogne, Jean de
see Mandeville, Sir John

BOURGUIBA, HABIB (1903-2000), Tunisian statesman **2** 453-455

BOURIGNON, ANTOINETTE (1616-1680), Flemish mystic **29** 80-83

BOURKE-WHITE, MARGARET (1904-1971), American photographer and photojournalist **2** 455-456

BOURNE, RANDOLPH SILLIMAN (1886-1918), American pacifist and cultural critic **2** 456-457

Boursiquot, Dionysius Lardner
see Boucicault, Dion

BOUTMY, ÉMILE (1835-1906), French educator **29** 83-84

BOUTON, JIM (James Alan Bouton; b. 1939), American baseball player **31** 34-36

BOUTROS-GHALI, BOUTROS (born 1922), Egyptian diplomat and sixth secretary-general of the United Nations (1991-) **2** 457-458

BOUTS, DIRK (c. 1415-1475), Dutch painter **2** 458-459

Bouvier, Jacqueline Lee
see Kennedy, Jacqueline

BOVERI, THEODOR HEINRICH (1862-1915), German biologist **25** 60-62

Bovine spongiform encephalopathy
see Mad cow disease

BOW, CLARA (1905-1965), American actress **31** 37-38

BOWDITCH, HENRY INGERSOLL (1808-1892), American physician **2** 459-460

BOWDITCH, NATHANIEL (1773-1838), American navigator and mathematician **2** 460-461

BOWDOIN, JAMES (1726-1790), American merchant and politician **2** 461-462

BOWEN, EDWARD GEORGE (1911-1991), Welsh physicist **29** 84-86

BOWEN, ELIZABETH (1899-1973), British novelist **2** 462-463

BOWERS, CLAUDE GERNADE (1878-1958), American journalist, historian, and diplomat **2** 463

BOWIE, DAVID (David Robert Jones; born 1947), English singer, songwriter, and actor **18** 58-60
Deneuve, Catherine **34** 88-90
Oshima, Nagisa **34** 282-284
Reed, Lou **34** 299-302

BOWIE, JAMES (1796-1836), American soldier **30** 71-73

BOWLES, PAUL (1910-1999), American author, musical composer, and translator **19** 31-34

BOWLES, SAMUEL (1826-1878), American newspaper publisher **2** 464

BOWMAN, ISAIAH (1878-1950), American geographer **2** 464-465

BOXER, BARBARA (born 1940), U.S. Senator from California **2** 465-468

Boxers
see Athletes–boxers

Boy bachelor
see Wolsey, Thomas

Boycott
see Civil rights movement (United States); Labor unions (United States)

BOYD, LOUISE ARNER (1887-1972), American explorer **22** 73-74

Boyd, Nancy
see Millay, Edna St. Vincent

Boyd Orr, John
see Orr, John Boyd

BOYER, JEAN PIERRE (1776-1850), Haitian president 1818-1845 **2** 468-469

BOYER, PAUL DELOS (born 1918), American biochemist **25** 62-65

BOYLE, ROBERT (1627-1691), British chemist and physicist **2** 469-471

BOYLSTON, ZABDIEL (1679-1766), American physician **2** 471

Boz
see Dickens, Charles

BOZEMAN, JOHN M. (1837-1867), American pioneer **2** 471-472

Bozzie
see Boswell, James

BRACCIOLINI, POGGIO (1380-1459), Italian humanist **32** 48-50

BRACEGIRDLE, ANNE (c. 1663-1748), English actress **30** 73-75

BRACKENRIDGE, HUGH HENRY (1749-1816), American lawyer and writer **2** 472-473

BRACTON, HENRY (Henry of Bratton; c. 1210-1268), English jurist **21** 54-55

BRADBURY, RAY (1920-2012), American fantasy and science fiction writer **2** 473-474
Harryhausen, Ray **34** 157-163

Bradby, Lucy Barbara
see Hammond, John and Lucy

BRADDOCK, EDWARD (1695-1755), British commander in North America **2** 474-475

BRADFORD, WILLIAM (1590-1657), leader of Plymouth Colony **2** 475-476

BRADFORD, WILLIAM (1663-1752), American printer **2** 476-477

BRADFORD, WILLIAM (1722-1791), American journalist **2** 477

BRADLAUGH, CHARLES (1833-1891), English freethinker and political agitator **2** 478

BRADLEY, ED (1941-2006), African American broadcast journalist **2** 478-481

BRADLEY, FRANCIS HERBERT (1846-1924), English philosopher **2** 481-482

BRADLEY, JAMES (1693-1762), English astronomer **2** 482-483

BRADLEY, JOSEPH P. (1813-1892), American Supreme Court justice **22** 74-77

BRADLEY, LYDIA MOSS (1816-1908), American businesswoman and philanthropist **30** 75-77

BRADLEY, MARION ZIMMER (1930-1999), American author **18** 60-62

BRADLEY, OMAR NELSON (1893-1981), American general **2** 483-484

BRADLEY, TOM (1917-1998), first African American mayor of Los Angeles **2** 484-485

BRADMAN, SIR DONALD GEORGE (1908-2001), Australian cricketer **2** 485-486

BRADSTREET, ANNE DUDLEY (c. 1612-1672), English-born American poet **2** 486-487

BRADWELL, MYRA (Myra Colby; 1831-1894), American lawyer and publisher **24** 64-66

BRADY, MATHEW B. (c. 1823-1896), American photographer **2** 487-488

BRAGG, BRAXTON (1817-1876), American general **31** 39-41

BRAGG, SIR WILLIAM HENRY (1862-1942), English physicist **2** 488-489

BRAHE, TYCHO (1546-1601), Danish astronomer **2** 489-490

BRAHMAGUPTA (c. 598-c. 670), Indian mathematician and astronomer **26** 44-46

BRAHMS, JOHANNES (1833-1897), German composer **2** 490-492

BRAID, JAMES (1795-1860), British surgeon **31** 42-43

BRAILLE, LOUIS (1809-1852), French teacher and creator of braille system **2** 492-493

BRAINARD, BERTHA (Bertha Brainard Peterson; died 1946), American radio executive **28** 47-48

BRAMAH, JOSEPH (Joe Bremmer; 1749-1814), English engineer and inventor **20** 58-59

BRAMANTE, DONATO (1444-1514), Italian architect and painter **2** 493-494

BRANCUSI, CONSTANTIN (1876-1957), Romanian sculptor in France **2** 494-496

BRANDEIS, LOUIS DEMBITZ (1856-1941), American jurist **2** 496-497

BRANDES, GEORG (Georg Morris Cohen Brandes; 1842-1927), Danish literary critic **23** 45-47

Branding (marketing design)
Aicher, Otl **34** 4-6

BRANDO, MARLON (1924-2004), American actor **2** 497-499
Adler, Stella **34** 1-3

BRANDT, KARL (1904-1948), German physician **33** 44-46

BRANDT, WILLY (Herbert Frahm Brandt; 1913-1992), German statesman, chancellor of West Germany **2** 499-500

BRANSON, RICHARD (born 1950), British entrepreneur **19** 34-36

BRANT, JOSEPH (1742-1807), Mohawk Indian chief **2** 500-501

BRANT, MARY (MOLLY) (1736-1796), Native American who guided the Iroquois to a British alliance **2** 501-503

BRANT, SEBASTIAN (1457-1521), German author **2** 503-504

BRAQUE, GEORGES (1882-1967), French painter **2** 504-505

Braschi, Gianangelo
see Pius VI

BRATTAIN, WALTER H. (1902-1987), American physicist and co-inventor of the transistor **2** 505-507

Bratton, Henry de
see Bracton, Henry de

BRAUDEL, FERNAND (1902-1985), leading exponent of the *Annales* school of history **2** 507-508

BRAUN, FERDINAND (1850-1918), German recipient of the Nobel Prize in Physics for work on wireless telegraphy **2** 508-509

BRAVO, CLAUDIO (1936-2011), Chilean artist **33** 46-48

BRAY, JOHN RANDOLPH (1879-1978), American animator and cartoonist **21** 55-57

Brazil, Federative Republic of (nation, South America)
1990s
Franco, Itamar **34** 130-132

Brazil (film)
Palin, Michael **34** 287-289

BRAZILE, DONNA (born 1959), American political strategist **32** 51-53

BRAZZA, PIERRE PAUL FRANÇOIS CAMILLE SAVORGNAN DE (1852-1905), Italian-born French explorer **2** 509-510

BREASTED, JAMES HENRY (1865-1935), American Egyptologist and archeologist **2** 510-511

BRÉBEUF, JEAN DE (1593-1649), French Jesuit missionary **2** 511-512

BRECHT, BERTOLT (1898-1956), German playwright **2** 512-514

BRECKINRIDGE, JOHN CABELL (1821-1875), American statesman and military leader **22** 77-79

BRECKINRIDGE, MARY (1881-1965), American nurse **31** 44-45

Brède, Baron de la
see Montesquieu, Baron de

BREER, ROBERT (1926-2011), American artist **33** 48-50

BREGUET, ABRAHAM-LOUIS (1747-1823), French instrument maker **29** 86-88

BREMER, FREDRIKA (1801-1865), Swedish author **26** 46-48

BRENDAN, ST. (Brenainn; Brandon; Brendan of Clonfert; c. 486- c. 578), Irish Abbott and explorer **22** 79-80

BRENNAN, WILLIAM J., JR. (1906-1997), United States Supreme Court justice **2** 514-515

Brent of Bin Bin
see Franklin, Miles

BRENTANO, CLEMENS (1778-1842), German poet and novelist **2** 515-516

BRENTANO, FRANZ CLEMENS (1838-1917), German philosopher **2** 516-517

BRESHKOVSKY, CATHERINE (1844-1934), Russian revolutionary **2** 517-519

BRESLIN, JIMMY (born c. 1930), American journalist **33** 50-51

BRESSON, ROBERT (1901-1999), French filmmaker **25** 65-67

BRETON, ANDRÉ (1896-1966), French author **2** 519-520

Bretton, Henry de
see Bracton, Henry de

BREUER, JOSEF (1842-1925), Austrian physician **30** 77-79

BREUER, MARCEL (1902-1981), Hungarian-born American architect **2** 520-521

BREUIL, HENRI EDOUARD PROSPER (1877-1961), French archeologist **2** 521-522

Breweries
Labatt, John Kinder **34** 226-228
Molson, John **34** 268-270

BREWSTER, KINGMAN, JR. (1919-1988), president of Yale University (1963-1977) **2** 522-523

BREWSTER, WILLIAM (c. 1566-1644), English-born Pilgrim leader **2** 523-524

BREYER, STEPHEN (born 1938), U.S. Supreme Court justice **2** 524-527

BREYTENBACH, BREYTEN (Jan Blom; born 1939), South African author and activist **24** 66-68

BREZHNEV, LEONID ILICH (1906-1982), general secretary of the Communist party of the Union of Soviet Socialist Republics (1964-1982) and president of the Union of Soviet Socialist Republics (1977-1982) **2** 527-528

BRIAN BORU (c. 940-1014), Irish king **18** 62-64

BRIAND, ARISTIDE (1862-1932), French statesman **2** 528-529

BRICE, FANNY (1891-1951), vaudeville, Broadway, film, and radio singer and comedienne **3** 1-2

BRIDGER, JAMES (1804-1881), American fur trader and scout **3** 2-3

BRIDGES, HARRY A.R. (1901-1990), radical American labor leader **3** 3-5

BRIDGET OF SWEDEN (Saint Birgitta of Sweden; Birgitta Birgersdotter; 1303-1373), Swedish Catholic Saint **27** 53-55

BRIDGMAN, LAURA DEWEY (1829-1889), sight and hearing impaired American **29** 88-91

BRIDGMAN, PERCY WILLIAMS (1882-1961), American physicist **3** 5-6

BRIGHT, CHARLES TILSTON (1832-1888), English telegraph engineer **29** 91-93

BRIGHT, JOHN (1811-1889), English politician **3** 6-7

BRIGHT, RICHARD (1789-1858), English physician **3** 7-8

BRIGHTMAN, EDGAR SHEFFIELD (1884-1953), philosopher of religion and exponent of American Personalism **3** 8-9

BRINK, ANDRE PHILIPPUS (born 1935), South African author **22** 80-83

Brinkley, David
see Huntley and Brinkley

BRISBANE, ALBERT (1809-1890), American social theorist **3** 9

BRISBANE, ARTHUR (1864-1936), American newspaper editor **29** 93-95

BRISBANE, THOMAS MAKDOUGALL (1773-1860), Scottish military leader, colonial governor, and astronomer **30** 79-81

BRISTOW, BENJAMIN HELM (1832-1896), American lawyer and Federal official **3** 9-10

British Broadcasting Corporation (BBC)
Burgess, Guy **34** 44-47

British East India Company
see East India Company (British)

British Royal Society
see Royal Society (Britain)

BRITTEN, BENJAMIN (1913-1976), English composer **3** 10-11

BROAD, CHARLIE DUNBAR (1887-1971), English philosopher **3** 12

Broadcasting
Corwin, Norman **34** 65-67
King, Larry **34** 204-206
McNamee, Graham **34** 261-264
Wallace, Mike **34** 371-373

BROCA, PIERRE PAUL (1824-1880), French surgeon and anthropologist **32** 53-55

BROCK, SIR ISAAC (1769-1812), British general **3** 12-13

BROD, MAX (1884-1968), German writer **29** 95-97

BRODSKY, JOSEPH (Iosif Alexandrovich Brodsky, 1940-1996), Russian-born Nobel Prize winner and fifth United States poet laureate **3** 13-15

Broglie, Louis de
see de Broglie, Louis Victor Pierre Raymond

Brokaw, Clare Boothe
see Luce, Clare Boothe

BROKAW, TOM (Thomas John Brokaw; born 1940), American television journalist and author **25** 67-69

Brokeback Mountain (short story and film)
McMurtry, Larry **34** 259-261

Broken Hand
see Fitzpatrick, Thomas

BRONN, HEINRICH GEORG (1800-1862), German zoologist and paleontologist **29** 97-99

Bronstein, Lev Davidovich
see Trotsky, Leon

BRONTË, ANNE (1820-1849), English novelist **29** 99-101

BRONTË, CHARLOTTE (1816-1855), English novelist **3** 17-18

Bronte, Duke of
see Nelson, Viscount

BRONTË, EMILY (1818-1848), English novelist **3** 18-19

BRONZINO (1503-1572), Italian painter **3** 19

BROOK, PETER (born 1925), world-renowned theater director **3** 19-21

BROOKE, ALAN FRANCIS (Viscount Alanbrooke; 1883-1963), Irish military leader **20** 59-61

BROOKE, SIR JAMES (1803-1868), British governor in Borneo **3** 21-22

BROOKE, RUPERT (1887-1915), English poet **3** 22-23

BROOKNER, ANITA (born 1928), British art historian and novelist **3** 23-24

BROOKS, GWENDOLYN (1917-2000), first African American author to receive the Pulitzer Prize for Literature **3** 24-26

BROOKS, HERB (1937-2003), American hockey coach **30** 81-83

BROOKS, MEL (Melvin Kaminsky; born 1926), American actor, playwright, and film and theatre producer/director **23** 48-50

BROOKS, PHILLIPS (1835-1893), American Episcopalian bishop **3** 26

BROOKS, ROMAINE (1874-1970), American painter **32** 55-57

BROTHERS, JOYCE (Joyce Diane Bauer; 1927-2013), American psychologist who pioneered radio phone-in questions for professional psychological advice **3** 26-28

BROUDY, HARRY SAMUEL (1905-1998), American philosopher, teacher, and author **3** 28-29

BROUGHAM, HENRY PETER (Baron Brougham and Vaux; 1778-1868), Scottish jurist **22** 83-85

BROUN, HEYWOOD (1888-1939), American journalist **29** 97-99

BROUN, HEYWOOD, JR. (Heywood Hale Broun; 1918-2001), American broadcast journalist **31** 46

BROUWER, ADRIAEN (c. 1605-1638), Flemish painter **3** 29-30

BROWDER, EARL RUSSELL (1891-1973), American Communist leader **3** 30-31

BROWN, ALEXANDER (1764-1834), American merchant and banker **3** 31-32

BROWN, BENJAMIN GRATZ (1826-1885), American politician **3** 32-33

BROWN, CHARLES BROCKDEN (1771-1810), American novelist **3** 33

BROWN, CHARLOTTE EUGENIA HAWKINS (Lottie Hawkins; 1882-1961), African American educator and humanitarian **3** 34

BROWN, GEORGE (1818-1880), Canadian politician **3** 35-36

BROWN, GORDON (James Gordon Brown; born 1951), British politician **28** 48-50

BROWN, HALLIE QUINN (c. 1849-1949), American educator and reformer **30** 83-85

BROWN, HELEN GURLEY (1922-2012), American author and editor **3** 36-37

BROWN, JAMES (1928-2006), African American singer **3** 37-39

BROWN, JOHN (1800-1859), American abolitionist **3** 39-41

BROWN, JOSEPH EMERSON (1821-1894), American lawyer and politician **3** 41-42

BROWN, LES (Leslie Calvin Brown; born 1945), American motivational speaker, author, and television host **19** 36-39

BROWN, MOSES (1738-1836), American manufacturer and merchant **3** 42-43

BROWN, RACHEL FULLER (1898-1980), American biochemist **3** 43-44
Hazen, Elizabeth Lee **34** 163-165

BROWN, ROBERT (1773-1858), Scottish botanist **20** 61-63

BROWN, RONALD H. (1941-1996), African American politician, cabinet official **3** 44-47

BROWN, RUTH (1928-2006), American singer **34** 41-42

BROWN, STERLING (Sterling Allen Brown; 1901-1989), American literary critic **28** 51-54

BROWN, TINA (Christina Hambly Brown; born 1953), British editor who transformed the English magazine *Tatler*, then the United States magazines *Vanity Fair* and the *New Yorker* **3** 47-48

BROWN, TONY (William Anthony Brown; born 1933), African American radio personality **24** 68-70

BROWN, WILLIAM WELLS (1815/16-1884), African American author and abolitionist **3** 48-49

Browne, Charles Farrar
see Ward, Artemus

BROWNE, SIR THOMAS (1605-1682), English author **3** 49-50

BROWNE, THOMAS ALEXANDER (Rolf Boldrewood; 1826-1915), Australian author **22** 85-87

BROWNER, CAROL M. (born 1955), U.S. Environmental Protection Agency administrator **3** 50-52

BROWNING, ELIZABETH BARRETT (1806-1861), English poet **3** 52-53

BROWNING, JOHN (1855-1926), American firearms designer **30** 85-87

BROWNING, ROBERT (1812-1889), English poet **3** 53-55

BROWNLOW, WILLIAM GANNAWAY (1805-1877), American journalist and politician **3** 55-56

BROWNMILLER, SUSAN (born 1935), American activist, journalist, and novelist **3** 56-57

BROWNSON, ORESTES AUGUSTUS (1803-1876), American clergyman and transcendentalist **3** 57-58

Broz, Josip
see Tito, Marshal

BRUBACHER, JOHN SEILER (1898-1988), American historian and educator **3** 58-59

BRUBECK, DAVE (1920-2012), American pianist, composer, and bandleader **3** 59-61

BRUCE, BLANCHE KELSO (1841-1898), African American politician **3** 62-63

BRUCE, DAVID (1855-1931), Australian parasitologist **3** 63

BRUCE, JAMES (1730-1794), Scottish explorer **3** 63-64

Bruce, James (1811-1863)
see Elgin, 8th Earl of

BRUCE, LENNY (Leonard Alfred Schneider; 1925-1966), American comedian **19** 39-41

Bruce, Robert
see Robert I (king of Scotland)

BRUCE OF MELBOURNE, 1ST VISCOUNT (Stanley Melbourne Bruce; 1883-1967), Australian statesman **3** 61-62

BRUCKNER, JOSEPH ANTON (1824-1896), Austrian composer **3** 64-65

BRUEGEL, PIETER, THE ELDER (1525/30-1569), Netherlandish painter **3** 65-67

BRÛLÉ, ÉTIENNE (c. 1592-1633), French explorer in North America **3** 67-68

BRUNDTLAND, GRO HARLEM (1939-1989), Norwegian prime minister and chair of the United Nations World Commission for Environment and Development **3** 68-69

Brunei, Sultan of
see Bolkiah, Hassanal

BRUNEL, ISAMBARD KINGDOM (1806-1859), English civil engineer **3** 69-70

BRUNELLESCHI, FILIPPO (1377-1446), Italian architect and sculptor **3** 70-72

BRUNER, JEROME SEYMOUR (born 1915), American psychologist **3** 72-73

BRUNHOFF, JEAN DE (1899-1937), French author and illustrator **19** 41-42

BRUNI, LEONARDO (1370-1444), Italian writer and historian **33** 52-54

BRUNNER, ALOIS (1912-1996), Nazi German officer who helped engineer the destruction of European Jews **3** 73-74

BRUNNER, EMIL (1889-1966), Swiss Reformed theologian **3** 74-75

BRUNO, GIORDANO (1548-1600), Italian philosopher and poet **3** 75-76

Bruno of Toul (Egisheim)
see Leo IX, St.

BRUTON, JOHN GERARD (born 1947), prime minister of Ireland **3** 76-77

BRUTUS, DENNIS (1924-2009), exiled South African poet and political activist opposed to apartheid **3** 77-78

BRUTUS, MARCUS JUNIUS (c. 85-42 BCE), Roman statesman **3** 79-80

Brutus, Quintus Caepio
see Brutus, Marcus Junius

BRYAN, WILLIAM JENNINGS (1860-1925), American lawyer and politician **3** 80-82

BRYANT, PAUL ("Bear;" 1919-1983), American college football coach **3** 82-83

BRYANT, WILLIAM CULLEN (1794-1878), American poet and editor **3** 83-85

BRYCE, JAMES (1838-1922), British historian, jurist, and statesman **3** 85

BRZEZINSKI, ZBIGNIEW (1928-1980), assistant to President Carter for national security affairs (1977-1980) **3** 85-87

BUBER, MARTIN (1878-1965), Austrian-born Jewish theologian and philosopher **3** 87-89

Buccleugh
see Monmouth and Buccleugh Duke of

BUCHALTER, LEPKE (Louis Bachalter; 1897-1944), American gangster **19** 42-44

BUCHANAN, JAMES (1791-1868), American statesman, president 1857-1861 **3** 89-90

BUCHANAN, PATRICK JOSEPH (born 1938), commentator, journalist, and presidential candidate **3** 90-91

BUCHWALD, ART (Arthur Buchwald; 1925-2007), American journalist **27** 55-57

BUCK, JACK (John Francis Buck; 1924-2002), American sportscaster **27** 57-59

BUCK, PEARL SYDENSTRICKER (1892-1973), American novelist **3** 91-93

BUCKINGHAM, 1ST DUKE OF (George Villiers; 1592-1628), English courtier and military leader **3** 93-94

BUCKINGHAM, 2D DUKE OF (George Villiers; 1628-1687), English statesman **3** 94-95

BUCKLE, HENRY THOMAS (1821-1862), English historian **3** 95-96

BUCKLEY, WILLIAM F., JR. (1925-2008), conservative American author, editor, and political activist **3** 96-97

BUDDHA (c. 560-480 BCE), Indian founder of Buddhism **3** 97-101

BUDDHADĀSA BHIKKHU (Nguam Phanich; 1906-1993), founder of Wat Suan Mokkhabalārama in southern Thailand and interpreter of Theravāda Buddhism **3** 101-102

BUDÉ, GUILLAUME (1467-1540), French humanist **3** 102-103

BUDGE, DON (J. Donald Budge; 1915-2000), American tennis player **21** 57-59

BUECHNER, FREDERICK (born 1926), American novelist and theologian **3** 103-105

BUEL, JESSE (1778-1839), American agriculturalist and journalist **3** 105

Buell, Sarah Josepha
see Hale, Sarah Josepha

BUFFALO BILL (William Frederick Cody; 1846-1917), American scout and publicist **3** 105-106

BUFFETT, WARREN (born 1930), American investment salesman **3** 106-109

BUFFON, COMTE DE (Georges Louis Leclerc; 1707-1788), French naturalist **3** 109-111

BUGEAUD DE LA PICONNERIE, THOMAS ROBERT (1784-1849), Duke of Isly and marshal of France **3** 111

BUICK, DAVID (1854-1929), American inventor and businessman **19** 44-45

BUKHARI, MUHAMMAD IBN ISMAIL AL- (810-870), Arab scholar and Moslem saint **3** 111-112

BUKHARIN, NIKOLAI IVANOVICH (1858-1938), Russian politician **3** 112-113
Yezhov, Nikolai **34** 387-389

BUKOWSKI, CHARLES (1920-1994), American writer and poet **3** 113-115

BULATOVIC, MOMIR (born 1956), president of Montenegro (1990-1992) and of the new Federal Republic of Yugoslavia (1992-) **3** 115-116

BULFINCH, CHARLES (1763-1844), American colonial architect **3** 116-117

BULGAKOV, MIKHAIL AFANASIEVICH (1891-1940), Russian novelist and playwright **3** 117

BULGANIN, NIKOLAI (1885-1975), chairman of the Soviet Council of Ministers (1955-1958) **3** 118-119

Bulgaroctonus (Bulgar-Slayer)
see Basil II, (1415-1462)

BULL, OLE (Ole Bornemann Bull; 1810-1880), Norwegian violinist and composer **28** 54-56

BULLER, CHARLES (1806-1848), British politician **34** 42-44

Bullock, Anna Mae
see Turner, Tina

BULOSAN, CARLOS (1911-1956), American author and poet **21** 59-61

BULTMANN, RUDOLF KARL (1884-1976), German theologian **3** 119-120

BULWER-LYTTON, EDWARD (1st Baron Lytton of Knebworth; 1803-1873), English novelist **22** 87-88

BUNAU-VARILLA, PHILIPPE JEAN (1859-1940), French engineer and soldier **3** 120-121

BUNCH, CHARLOTTE (born 1944), American activist **31** 47-49

BUNCHE, RALPH JOHNSON (1904-1971), African American diplomat **3** 121-122

BUNDY, MCGEORGE (1919-1996), national security adviser to two presidents **3** 122-124

BUNIN, IVAN ALEKSEEVICH (1870-1953), Russian poet and novelist **3** 124

Bunjin-ga painting (Japanese art)
Buson, Yosa **34** 389-391

BUNSEN, ROBERT WILHELM (1811-1899), German chemist and physicist **3** 124-125

BUNSHAFT, GORDON (1909-1990), American architect **3** 125-127

BUNTING-SMITH, MARY INGRAHAM (Polly Bunting; 1910-1998), American educator **27** 59-61

BUNTLINE, NED (c. 1821-1886), American writer and publisher **30** 88-90

BUÑUEL, LUIS (1900-1983), Spanish film director **3** 127-128
Deneuve, Catherine **34** 88-90

BUNYAN, JOHN (1628-1688), English author and Baptist preacher **3** 128-129

BURBAGE, RICHARD (c. 1567-1619), British actor **24** 70-72

BURBANK, LUTHER (1849-1926), American plant breeder **3** 129-131

BURBIDGE, E. MARGARET (Eleanor Margaret Burbidge; born 1919), British-American astronomer and physicist **26** 48-50

BURCHFIELD, CHARLES (1893-1967), American painter **3** 131-132

BURCKHARDT, JACOB CHRISTOPH (1818-1897), Swiss historian **3** 132-133

BURCKHARDT, JOHANN LUDWIG (1784-1817), Swiss-born explorer **3** 133

Bureau of Investigation
see Federal Bureau of Investigation (FBI)

BURGER, WARREN E. (1907-1986), Chief Justice of the United States Supreme Court (1969-1986) **3** 133-136

BURGESS, ANTHONY (John Anthony Burgess Wilson; 1917-1993), English author **3** 136-137

BURGESS, GUY (1911-1963), British intelligence officer and spy **34** 44-47
Blunt, Anthony **34** 36-38
Maclean, Donald **34** 247-249

BURGOYNE, JOHN (1723-1792), British general and statesman **3** 137-138

BURKE, EDMUND (1729-1797), British statesman, political theorist, and philosopher **3** 138-141

BURKE, JOHN BERNARD (1814-1892), British genealogist and publisher **30** 90-91

BURKE, KENNETH (1897-1993), American literary theorist and critic **3** 141-142

BURKE, ROBERT O'HARA (1820-1861), Irish-born Australian policeman and explorer **3** 142-143

BURKE, SELMA (1900-1995), African American sculptor **3** 143-144

BURLIN, NATALIE CURTIS (Natalie Curtis; 1875-1921), American ethnomusicologist **23** 50-52

BURLINGAME, ANSON (1820-1870), American diplomat **3** 144-145

BURMAN, RAHUL DEV (R. D. Burman; 1939-1994), Indian musician **26** 50-52

BURNE-JONES, SIR EDWARD COLEY (1833-1898), English painter and designer **3** 145-146

BURNET, SIR FRANK MACFARLANE (1899-1985), Australian virologist **3** 146-147

BURNET, GILBERT (1643-1715), British bishop and historian **3** 147

BURNETT, CAROL (born 1933), American television entertainer **23** 52-55

BURNETT, FRANCES HODGSON (Frances Eliza Hodgson Burnett; 1849-1924), English-born American author **18** 64-67

BURNETT, LEO (1891-1971), American advertising executive **19** 45-47

BURNEY, FANNY (Frances Burney; 1752-1840), English novelist and diarist **3** 147-148

BURNHAM, DANIEL HUDSON (1846-1912), American architect and city planner **3** 148-149

BURNHAM, FORBES (1923-1985), leader of the independence movement in British Guiana and Guyana's first prime minister **3** 149-151

BURNS, ANTHONY (1834-1862), African American slave **3** 151

BURNS, ARTHUR (1904-1987), American economic statesman **3** 151-153

BURNS, GEORGE (born Nathan Birnbaum; 1896-1996), American comedian and actor **3** 153-155

BURNS, KEN (Kenneth Lauren Burns; born 1953), American documentary filmmaker **20** 63-65

BURNS, ROBERT (1759-1796), Scottish poet **3** 155-156

BURR, AARON (1756-1836), American politician, vice president 1801-1805 **3** 156-159

BURRI, ALBERTO (1915-1995), Italian painter **3** 159-160

BURRITT, ELIHU (1810-1879), American pacifist, author, and linguist **3** 160

BURROUGHS, EDGAR RICE (1875-1950), American author **18** 67-68

BURROUGHS, JOHN (1837-1921), American naturalist and essayist **3** 160-161

BURROUGHS, WILLIAM S. (1914-1997), American writer **3** 162-163

BURROUGHS, WILLIAM S. (William Seward Burroughs; 1855-1898), American inventor **28** 56-57

BURTON, RICHARD (Richard Jenkins; 1925-1984), Welsh actor **3** 163-164

BURTON, SIR RICHARD FRANCIS (1821-1890), English explorer, author, and diplomat **3** 164-166

BURTON, ROBERT (1577-1640), English author and clergyman **3** 166-167

Burton, Tim, (born 1958), American film director and producer
Wood, Ed, Jr. **34** 383-384

BUSCH, ADOLPHUS (1839-1913), American brewer and businessman **19** 47-49

BUSH, GEORGE (George Herbert Walker Bush; born 1924), United States vice president (1981-1989) and president (1989-1993) **3** 167-169

BUSH, GEORGE WALKER (born 1946), United States president (2001-2009) **21** 61-64

BUSH, LAURA WELCH (born 1946), American first lady **25** 69-72

BUSH, VANNEVAR (1890-1974), American scientist and engineer **3** 169-171

BUSH-BANKS, OLIVIA WARD (1869-1944), American author **27** 61-63

BUSHNELL, DAVID (1742-1824), American inventor **21** 64-65

BUSHNELL, HORACE (1802-1876), American Congregational clergyman **3** 171-172

BUSIA, KOFI ABREFA (1914-1978), Ghanaian premier and sociologist **3** 172-173

Business and industrial leaders
Australian
Hancock, Lang **34** 153-155
Austrian
Lauda, Niki **34** 233-236
Canadian
Labatt, John Kinder **34** 226-228
Molson, John **34** 268-270
English
Ecclestone, Bernie **34** 100-102
Italian
Ferrari, Enzo **34** 117-119
Lamborghini, Ferruccio **34** 230-232

Business and industrial leaders, American
beer, wine, and spirits industry
Daniel, Jack **34** 75-77
entertainment industry
Axton, Estelle **34** 13-15
musical instrument industry
Fender, Leo **34** 115-117
sports industry
Frick, Ford **34** 132-135
toy industry
Handler, Elliot **34** 155-157

BUSON, YOSA (1716-1784), Japanese poet and artist **34** 389-391

BUSONI, FERRUCCIO BENVENUTO (1866-1924), Italian musician **3** 173-174

BUSSOTTI, SYLVANO (born 1931), Italian composer **3** 174-175

BUSTAMANTE, WILLIAM ALEXANDER (1884-1977), Jamaican labor leader and first prime minister (1962-1967) **3** 175-177

BUTCHER, SUSAN (1954-2006), American dog sled racer **30** 91-93

BUTE, 3D EARL OF (John Stuart; 1713-1792), British statesman, prime minister 1762-1763 **3** 177-178

BUTENANDT, ADOLF FRIEDRICH JOHANN (1903-1995), German chemist **25** 72-74

BUTHELEZI, MANGOSUTHU GATSHA (born 1928), chief of the Zulu "homeland" and an important figure in the struggle to end apartheid in South Africa **3** 178-179

BUTLER, BENJAMIN FRANKLIN (1818-1893), American politician and military leader **21** 65-67

BUTLER, JOHN (1728-1796), British Indian agent and Loyalist leader **3** 180

BUTLER, JOSEPH (1692-1752), English philosopher and theologian **3** 180-181

BUTLER, NICHOLAS MURRAY (1862-1947), American educator **3** 181

BUTLER, OCTAVIA E. (1947-2006), African American novelist and essayist **3** 182-183

BUTLER, SAMUEL (1613-1680), English poet **3** 183-184

BUTLER, SAMUEL (1835-1902), English novelist and essayist **3** 183

BUTTERFIELD, JOHN (1801-1869), American financier and politician **3** 184-185

BUTTON, DICK (Richard Totten Button; born 1929), American figure skater and sports commentator **23** 55-57

BUXTEHUDE, DIETRICH (1637-1707), Danish composer and organist **3** 185-186

BYRD, RICHARD EVELYN (1888-1957), American admiral and polar explorer **3** 186-187

BYRD, WILLIAM (c. 1543-1623), English composer **3** 187-188

BYRD, WILLIAM (1652-1704), English colonial planter and merchant **3** 188-189

BYRD, WILLIAM II (1674-1744), American diarist and government official **3** 189-190

BYRNE, JANE (born 1934), first woman mayor of Chicago **3** 190-191

BYRNES, JAMES FRANCIS (1879-1972), American public official **3** 191-192

BYRON, GEORGE GORDON NOEL (6th Baron Byron; 1788-1824), English poet **3** 193-194

Byzantine Church
see Orthodox Eastern Church

Byzantine Empire (395-1453; Eastern Roman Empire 395-474)
decline and fall
Kydones, Demetrius **34** 67-68

Byzantium
see Byzantine Empire (395-1453; Eastern Roman Empire 395-474)

C

CABALLÉ, MONTSERRAT (born 1933), Spanish opera singer **33** 55-57

CABELL, JAMES BRANCH (1879-1958), American essayist and novelist **3** 195-196

CABET, ÉTIENNE (1788-1856), French political radical **3** 196

CABEZA DE VACA, ÁLVAR NÚÑEZ (c. 1490-c. 1557), Spanish explorer **3** 197

CABEZÓN, ANTONIO (1510-1566), Spanish composer **3** 197-198

CABLE, GEORGE WASHINGTON (1844-1925), American novelist **3** 198-199

Cable News Network (CNN)
King, Larry **34** 204-206

CABOT, JOHN (flourished 1471-1498), Italian explorer in English service **3** 199-200

CABOT, RICHARD CLARKE (1868-1939), American physician **3** 200

CABOT, SEBASTIAN (c. 1482-1557), Italian-born explorer for England and Spain **3** 200-201

Caboto, Giovanni
see Cabot, John

CABRAL, AMÍLCAR LOPES (1924-1973), father of modern African nationalism in Guinea-Bissau and the Cape Verde Islands **3** 202-203

CABRAL, PEDRO ÁLVARES (c. 1467-1520), Portuguese navigator **3** 203-204

Cabrera, Manuel Estrada
see Estrada Cabrera, Manuel

CABRERA INFANTE, GUILLERMO (1929-2005), Cuban-British writer **33** 57-58

CABRILLO, JUAN RODRÍGUEZ (died 1543), Portuguese explorer for Spain **3** 204-205

CABRINI, ST. FRANCES XAVIER (1850-1917), Italian-born founder of the Missionary Sisters of the Sacred Heart **3** 205

CACCINI, GIULIO (c. 1545-1618), Italian singer and composer **3** 205-206

CACHAO (1918-2008), Cuban musician **29** 104-106

CADAMOSTO, ALVISE DA (c. 1428-1483), Italian explorer **3** 206-207

CADILLAC, ANTOINE DE LAMOTHE (1658-1730), French explorer and colonial administrator **18** 69-71

CADMUS, PAUL (1904-1999), American painter **27** 64-66

CAEDMON (650-c.680), English Christian poet **20** 66-67

CAESAR, (GAIUS) JULIUS (100-44 BCE), Roman general and statesman **3** 207-210

CAESAR, SHIRLEY (born 1938), African American singer **3** 210-211

Caetani, Benedetto
see Boniface VIII

CAGE, JOHN (1912-1992), American composer **3** 211-214
influence of
Cale, John **34** 48-51

CAGNEY, JAMES (1899-1986), American actor **21** 68-71

CAHAN, ABRAHAM (1860-1951), Lithuanian-American Jewish author **3** 214

Cahiers du cinéma (periodical)
Sarris, Andrew **34** 319-321

CAILLIÉ, AUGUSTE RENÉ (1799-1838), French explorer **3** 214-215

CAIN, JAMES (1892-1977), American journalist and author **19** 50-52

Cairncross, John, (1913-1995), British spy
Blunt, Anthony **34** 36-38
Burgess, Guy **34** 44-47
Maclean, Donald **34** 247-249

CAIUS, JOHN (1510-1573), English physician **31** 50-51

CAJETAN, ST. (1480-1547), Italian reformer; cofounder of the Theatines **3** 215-216

CHÉNIER, ANDRÉ MARIE (1762-1794), French poet **3** 500-501

CHENNAULT, CLAIRE LEE (1893-1958), American military aviator **29** 114-116

Cheops
see Khufu

CHERENKOV, PAVEL ALEKSEEVICH (1904-1990), Russian physicist **3** 502-503

CHERNENKO, KONSTANTIN USTINOVICH (1911-1985), the Soviet Union general secretary from February 1984 to March 1985 **3** 503-504

CHERNYSHEVSKY, NIKOLAI GAVRILOVICH (1828-1889), Russian journalist, critic, and social theorist **3** 504-505

CHERUBINI, LUIGI CARLO ZANOBI SALVATORE MARIA (1760-1842), Italian-born French composer **3** 505-506

CHESNUT, MARY BOYKIN (1823-1886), Civil War diarist **3** 506-508

CHESNUTT, CHARLES WADDELL (1858-1932), African American author and lawyer **20** 78-82

Chess (game)
McCarthy, John **34** 257-259

CHESS, LEONARD (1917-1969), Polish-American record executive **30** 110-112

CHESTERTON, GILBERT KEITH (1874-1936), English author and artist **3** 508-509

CHEUNG, KATHERINE (Katherine Sui Fun Cheung; 1904-2003), Chinese American aviator **25** 88-90

CHEVALIER, MAURICE (1888-1972), French singer and actor **26** 66-68

Chevalier de Saint-Goerge, Joseph Boulogne
see Saint-George, Joseph Boulogne, Chevalier de

CHEVROLET, LOUIS (1878-1941), auto racer and entrepreneur **20** 82-84

CHEYNE, GEORGE (1671-1743), Scottish physician and author **28** 74-76

Chi Fa
see Wu wang

Ch'i Heng
see Ch'i Pai-shih

CH'I PAI-SHIH (1863-1957), Chinese painter and poet **3** 526-527

Chi Tan
see Chou kung

Ch'i Wei-ch'ing
see Ch'i Pai-shih

CH'I-YING (c. 1786-1858), Chinese statesman and diplomat **4** 12

Chia
see Hui-yüan

CHIA SSU-TAO (1213-1275), Chinese statesman **3** 514-515

Chiang Ch'ing
see Jiang Qing

CHIANG CHING-KUO (1910-1988), chairman of the Nationalist party and president of the Republic of China in Taiwan (1978-1988) **3** 509-510

CHIANG KAI-SHEK (1887-1975), Chinese nationalist leader and president **3** 510-513

Chiaramonti, Luigi Barnabà
see Pius VII

CHIARI, ROBERTO (1905-1981), president of Panama (1960-1964) **3** 513-514

CHICAGO, JUDY (Judith Cohen; born 1939), American artist and activist **3** 515-516

Chicago Defender (newspaper)
Smith, Mamie **34** 339-340

CHICHERIN, GEORGI VASILYEVICH (1872-1936), Russian statesman **3** 516-517

CHICHESTER, FRANCIS (1901-1972), British yachter **24** 83-85

CHIEN-LUNG (Hung-li; Qianlong; 1711-1799), Chinese emperor (1735-1799) **21** 78-79

CHIEPE, GAOSITWE KEAGAKWA TIBE (born 1926), intellectual, educator, diplomat, politician, and cabinet minister of external affairs of Botswana **3** 517

Chiesa, Giacomo della
see Benedict XV

CHIFLEY, JOSEPH BENEDICT (1885-1951), Australian statesman **3** 518

CHIH-I (Chih-k'ai, 538-597), Chinese Buddhist monk **3** 518-519

CHIKAMATSU, MONZAEMON (1653-1725), Japanese playwright **23** 70-72

CHILD, JULIA MCWILLIAMS (1912-2004), chef, author, and television personality **3** 519-520

CHILD, LYDIA MARIA FRANCIS (1802-1880), American author and abolitionist **3** 520-521

CHILDE, VERE GORDON (1892-1957), Australian prehistorian and archeologist **3** 521-522

Children's literature
see Literature for children

CHILDRESS, ALICE (1920-1994), African American dramatist, author, and poet **3** 522-524

CH'IN KUEI (1090-1155), Chinese official **3** 524-525

Ch'in-shan
see Yüan, Ma

China, People's Republic of (Communist)
Tiananmen Square, 1989
Fang Lizhi **34** 113-115

China, Republic of (Nationalist)
Chinese opposition
Ai Qing **34** 3-4

CHINAGLIA, GIORGIO (1947-2012), Italian soccer player **34** 53-56

Chinese Communist party
see Communist party (China)

Chingiz-Khan
see Genghis Khan

CHINMAYANANDA, SWAMI (1916-1993), Indian spiritual leader **30** 112-114

CHINN, MAY EDWARD (1896-1980), African American physician **3** 525-526

CHINO, WENDELL (1923-1998), Native American tribal leader and activist **27** 86-88

Chino-Japanese War
see Sino-Japanese War (1937-1945)

CHIPPENDALE, THOMAS (1718-1779), English cabinetmaker **4** 1-2

CHIRAC, JACQUES (born 1932), French prime minister **4** 2-3

CHIRICO, GIORGIO DE (1888-1978), Italian painter **4** 4

CHISHOLM, CAROLINE (1808-1877), British author and philantropist **4** 4-7

CHISHOLM, SHIRLEY ANITA ST. HILL (1924-2005), first African American woman to serve in the United States Congress **4** 7-9

CHISSANO, JOAQUIM ALBERTO (born 1939), a leader of Mozambique's war for independence and later president of Mozambique (1986-) **4** 9-11

CHISUM, JOHN SIMPSON (1824-1884), American rancher **4** 11

CHMIELNICKI, BOGDAN (1595-1657), Cossack leader of Ukrainian revolt **4** 12-13

CHOATE, JOSEPH HODGES (1832-1917), American lawyer and diplomat **22** 103-106

CHOATE, RUFUS (1799-1859), American lawyer and statesman **22** 106-107

CH'OE CH'UNG-HN (1149-1219), Korean general **4** 13

Chomedey, Paul de
see Maisoneuve, Sieur de

CHOMSKY, NOAM AVRAM (born 1928), American linguist and philosopher **4** 13-15

CHONG CHUNG-BU (1106-1179), Korean general **4** 15

CHONGJO (1752-1800), king of Korea **4** 15-16

CHOPIN, FRÉDÉRIC FRANÇOIS (1810-1849), Polish-French composer and pianist **4** 16-18
friends
Czerny, Carl **34** 68-70

CHOPIN, KATHERINE ("Kate"; born Katherine O'Flaherty; 1851-1904), American writer, poet, and essayist **4** 18-20

Chopinel, Jean
see Jean de Meun

CHOPRA, DEEPAK (born 1946), Indian physician, author, and educator **20** 84-86

Chorus Line, A (musical)
Hamlisch, Marvin **34** 151-153

Chou, Duke of
see Chou kung

CHOU EN-LAI (1898-1976), Chinese Communist premier **4** 20-22

CHOU KUNG (flourished c. 1116 BCE), Chinese statesman **4** 22-23

Chou Shu-jen
see Lu Hsün

CHRESTIEN DE TROYES (flourished 12th century), French poet **4** 23-24

CHRÉTIEN, JOSEPH-JACQUES-JEAN ("Jean"; born 1934), French Canadian politician and Canada's 20th prime minister **4** 24-25

Christ, Jesus
see Jesus of Nazareth

CHRISTIAN IV (1577-1648), king of Denmark and Norway 1588-1648 **20** 86-89

CHRISTIAN V, (1646-1699), King of Denmark
Bartholin, Thomas **34** 21-23

CHRISTIAN, CHARLIE (1916-1942), American jazz musician **32** 71-72

CHRISTIANSEN, OLE KIRK (1891-1958), Danish inventor and entrepreneur **28** 76-78

CHRISTIE, AGATHA (Agatha Mary Clarissa Miller; 1890-1976), best selling mystery author **4** 25-26

CHRISTINA OF SWEDEN (1626-1689), queen of Sweden 1632-1654 **4** 26-29

CHRISTINE DE PISAN (1364/65-c. 1430), French author **4** 29-30

CHRISTO (Christo Vladimiroff Javacheff; born 1935), Bulgarian-born sculptor noted for large-scale environmental artworks **4** 30-31

CHRISTOPHE, HENRI (1767-1820), Haitian patriot and king **4** 32

CHRISTOPHER, WARREN MINOR (1925-2011), United States secretary of state **4** 32-33

CHRISTUS, PETRUS (c. 1410-1472/73), Flemish painter **4** 33-34

CHRISTY, EDWIN P. (1815-1862), American minstrel **4** 34-35

CHRYSIPPUS (c. 280-c. 206 BCE), Greek Stoic philosopher **4** 35-36

CHRYSLER, WALTER PERCY (1875-1940), American manufacturer **4** 36-37

CHRYSOLORAS, MANUEL (c. 1355-1415), Byzantine scholar and diplomat **32** 72-74

Chrysostom
see John Chrysostom, St.

CHU, PAUL CHING-WU (born 1941), Chinese-American experimentalist in solid-state physics **4** 37-39

CHU, STEVEN (born 1948), American physicist **32** 75-76

CHU HSI (Chu Fu-tzu; 1130-1200), Chinese scholar and philosopher **4** 40-43

CHU TEH (1886-1976), Chinese Communist military leader **4** 54-55

Chu Ti
see Yung-lo

CHU YUAN-CHANG (Hongwu; Hung-Wu; T'ai Tsu; Kao-ti; 1328-1398), Chinese Ming emperor (1368-1398) **21** 79-81

Chub
see Ward, Artemus

CHULALONGKORN (Rama V; 1853-1910), king of Thailand 1868-1910 **4** 43-45

CHUN DOO HWAN (born 1931), army general turned politician and president of the Republic of Korea (South Korea); 1981-1988 **4** 45-47

CHUNG, CONNIE (born 1946), American correspondent and resporter **4** 47-48

CHUNG, JU YUNG (1915-2001), Korean businessman **23** 72-74

CHUNG, KYUNG WHA (born 1948), Korean violinist **23** 74-76

Ch'ung Ch'eng
see Shih Ko-fa

Chung-shan
see Sun Yat-sen

CHUNG-SHU, TUNG (c. 179-104 BCE), Chinese man of letters **4** 48-49

Ch'ungnyong, Prince
see Sejong

CHURCH, FRANK FORRESTER, III (1924-1984), American politician **28** 78-80

CHURCH, FREDERICK EDWIN (1826-1900), American painter **4** 49-50

Church of England
see England, Church of

Church of Rome
see Roman Catholic Church

Churchill, John
see Marlborough, 1st Duke of

CHURCHILL, WINSTON (1871-1947), American novelist **4** 50-51

CHURCHILL, SIR WINSTON LEONARD SPENCER (1874-1965), English statesman **4** 51-53

CHURRIGUERA, JOSÉ BENITO DE (1665-1725), Spanish architect and sculptor **4** 53-54

CHYTILOVÁ, VERA (1929-2014), Czech filmmaker **24** 85-87

CIA
see Central Intelligence Agency (United States)

CIBBER, COLLEY (1671-1757), English actor and dramatist **34** 56-58

Cibo, Giovanni Battista
see Innocent VIII

CICERO, MARCUS TULLIUS (106-43 BCE), Roman orator and writer **4** 55-58

CID, THE (Cid Campeador; 1043-1099), Spanish medieval warrior **4** 58-59

ÇILLER, TANSU (born 1946), prime minister of Turkey (1993-96) **4** 59-60

CIMABUE (flourished late 13th century), Italian painter **4** 60-61

CIMAROSA, DOMENICO (1749-1801), Italian opera composer **4** 61-62

CINQUE, JOSEPH (c. 1813-c. 1879), West African slave leader **4** 62

CINTRÓN, CONCHITA (1922-2009), American-Peruvian bullfighter **30** 114-115

Cione, Andrea di
see Orcagna

Cisneros, Francisco Jiménez de
see Jiménez de Cisneros, Francisco

CISNEROS, HENRY G. (born 1947), first Hispanic mayor in Texas **4** 62-64

CISNEROS, SANDRA (born 1954), Hispanic American short story writer and poet **4** 64-65

CISSÉ, SOULEYMANE (born 1940), Malian filmmaker **4** 65-66

CLEVELAND, STEPHEN GROVER (1837-1908), American statesman, twice president **4** 108-110

CLIFF, JIMMY (born 1948), Jamaican singer **34** 61-62

CLIFFORD, ANNE (1590-1676), English author and philanthropist **27** 88-90

CLINE, PATSY (born Virginia Patterson Hensley; 1932-1963), American singer **4** 110-112

CLINTON, DEWITT (1769-1828), American lawyer and statesman **4** 112-113

CLINTON, GEORGE (1739-1812), American patriot and statesman **4** 113-114

CLINTON, SIR HENRY (c. 1738-1795), British commander in chief during the American Revolution **4** 114-115

CLINTON, HILLARY RODHAM (born 1947), American politician and first lady **4** 115-117

CLINTON, WILLIAM JEFFERSON ("Bill"; born 1946), 42nd president of the United States **4** 117-119

CLIVE, ROBERT (Baron Clive of Plassey; 1725-1774), English soldier and statesman **4** 119-120

CLODION (1738-1814), French sculptor **4** 121

CLODIUS PULCHER, PUBLIUS (died 52 BCE), Roman politician **4** 121-122

CLOONEY, ROSEMARY (1928-2002), American singer and actress **27** 90-93

Clopinel, Jean
see Jean de Meun

Clostridium botulinum
Hazen, Elizabeth Lee **34** 163-165

Cloud computing
McCarthy, John **34** 257-259

CLOUET, FRANÇOIS (c. 1516-c. 1572), French portrait painter **4** 122-123

CLOUET, JEAN (c. 1485-c. 1541), French portrait painter **4** 122-123

CLOUGH, ARTHUR HUGH (1819-1861), English poet **4** 123-124

CLOVIS I (465-511), Frankish king **4** 124

Clurman, Harold, American theater founder
Adler, Stella **34** 1-3

Clyens, Mary Elizabeth
see Lease, Mary Elizabeth Clyens

CNN
see Cable News Network (CNN)

Cnut
see Canute I

COACHMAN, ALICE (Alice Coachman Davis; born 1923), African American athlete **26** 71-73

COANDĂ, HENRI (1886-1972), Romanian engineer **31** 54-55

COBB, JEWEL PLUMMER (born 1924), African American scientist and activist **22** 112-114

COBB, TYRUS RAYMOND (1886-1961), baseball player **4** 124-126

COBBETT, WILLIAM (1763-1835), English journalist and politician **4** 126-127

COBDEN, RICHARD (1804-1865), English politician **4** 127-128

COCHISE (c. 1825-1874), American Chiricahua Apache Indian chief **4** 128

COCHRAN, JACQUELINE (Jackie Cochran; 1910-1980), American aviator and businesswoman **18** 94-96

COCHRAN, JOHNNIE (1937-2005), African American lawyer **4** 128-131

COCHRANE, THOMAS (Earl of Dundonald; 1775-1860), British naval officer **20** 91-93

COCKCROFT, JOHN DOUGLAS (1897-1967), English physicist **4** 131-132

COCTEAU, JEAN (1889-1963), French writer **4** 132-133
Darrieux, Danielle **34** 79-81

Cody, William Frederick
see Buffalo Bill

COE, SEBASTIAN (born 1956), English track athlete **20** 93-95

COEN, JAN PIETERSZOON (c. 1586-1629), Dutch governor general of Batavia **4** 133

COETZEE, J(OHN) M. (born 1940), South African novelist **4** 133-135

COFFIN, LEVI (1789-1877), American antislavery reformer **4** 135

Coffin, Lucretia
see Mott, Lucretia Coffin

COFFIN, WILLIAM SLOANE, JR. (1924-2006), Yale University chaplain and activist **4** 135-137

COHAN, GEORGE MICHAEL (1878-1942), American actor and playwright **4** 137-138

Cohen, Bennett, (Ben Cohen; born 1951)
see Ben & Jerry

Cohen, George Morris
see Brandes, Georg Morris

COHEN, HERMANN (1842-1918), Jewish-German philosopher **4** 138-139

COHEN, LEONARD (born 1934), Canadian musician and writer **32** 79-81

COHEN, MORRIS RAPHAEL (1880-1947), American philosopher and teacher **4** 139-140

COHEN, WILLIAM S. (born 1940), American secretary of defense **18** 96-98

COHN, FERDINAND (1829-1898), German botanist **20** 95-97

COHN, HARRY (1891-1958), American movie industry executive **31** 56-59

COHN, MILDRED (1913-2009), American biochemist **32** 81-84

COHN, ROY MARCUS (1927-1986), American lawyer and businessman **29** 116-118

COHN-BENDIT, DANIEL (born 1946), led "new left" student protests in France in 1968 **4** 140-141

COKE, SIR EDWARD (1552-1634), English jurist and parliamentarian **4** 141-142

Colbath, Jeremiah Jones
see Wilson, Henry

COLBERT, CLAUDETTE (1903-1996), French actress **33** 77-80

COLBERT, JEAN BAPTISTE (1619-1683), French statesman **4** 142-143

COLBY, WILLIAM E. (1920-1996), American director of the Central Intelligence Agency (CIA) **4** 143-145

COLDEN, CADWALLADER (1688-1776), American botanist and politician **4** 145-146

COLDEN, JANE (1724-1766), American botanist **29** 118-119

COLE, GEORGE DOUGLAS HOWARD (1889-1959), English historian and economist **4** 146-147

COLE, JOHNNETTA (born 1936), African American scholar and educator **4** 147-149

COLE, NAT (a.k.a. Nat "King" Cole, born Nathaniel Adams Coles; 1919-1965), American jazz musician **4** 149-151

COLE, THOMAS (1801-1848), American painter **4** 151-152

COLEMAN, BESSIE (1892-1926), first African American to earn an international pilot's license **4** 152-154

COLERIDGE, SAMUEL TAYLOR (1772-1834), English poet and critic **4** 154-156

COLERIDGE-TAYLOR, SAMUEL (1875-1912), English composer and conductor **28** 80-83

COLES, ROBERT MARTIN (born 1929), American social psychiatrist, social critic, and humanist **4** 156-157

CURIE, ÈVE (Eve Curie Labouisse; 1904-2007), French musician, author and diplomat **18** 109-111

Curie, Irène
see Joliot-Curie, Irène

CURIE, MARIE SKLODOWSKA (1867-1934), Polish-born French physicist **4** 339-341

CURIE, PIERRE (1859-1906), French physicist **4** 341-344

CURLEY, JAMES MICHAEL (1874-1958), American politician **4** 344-345

CURRIE, SIR ARTHUR WILLIAM (1875-1933), Canadian general **4** 345

CURRIER AND IVES (1857-1907), American lithographic firm **4** 345-346

CURRY, JABEZ LAMAR MONROE (1815-1903), American politician **4** 346-347

CURTIN, ANDREW GREGG (1815-1894), American politician **4** 347-348

CURTIN, JOHN JOSEPH (1885-1945), Australian statesman, prime minister **4** 348-349

CURTIS, BENJAMIN ROBBINS (1809-1874), American jurist, United States Supreme Court justice **4** 349

CURTIS, CHARLES BRENT (1860-1936), American vice president (1929-1932) and legislator **21** 99-100

CURTIS, GEORGE WILLIAM (1824-1892), American writer and reformer **4** 349-350

CURTISS, GLENN HAMMOND (1878-1930), American aviation pioneer **4** 350-351

CURTIZ, MICHAEL (1888-1962), Hungarian-born film director **29** 130-132

CURZON, GEORGE NATHANIEL (1st Marquess Curzon of Kedleston; 1859-1925), English statesman **4** 351-352

CUSA, NICHOLAS OF (1401-1464), German prelate and humanist **4** 352-353

CUSHING, HARVEY WILLIAMS (1869-1939), American neurosurgeon **4** 353-354

CUSHMAN, CHARLOTTE (1816-1876), American actress **4** 354-355

CUSTER, GEORGE ARMSTRONG (1839-1876), American general **4** 355-356

CUTLER, MANASSEH (1742-1823), American clergyman, scientist, and politician **4** 356-357

CUVIER, BARON GEORGES LÉOPOLD (1769-1832), French zoologist and biologist **4** 357-359

CUVILLIÉS, FRANÇOIS (1695-1768), Flemish architect and designer **4** 359-360

CUYP, AELBERT (1620-1691), Dutch painter **4** 360-361

CUZZONI, FRANCESCA (1696-1778), Italian singer **29** 132-134

CYNEWULF (8th or 9th century), Anglo-Saxon poet **20** 103-104

CYPRIANUS, THASCIUS CAECILIANUS (died 258), Roman bishop of Carthage **4** 361-362

CYRIL (OF ALEXANDRIA), ST. (died 444), Egyptian bishop, Doctor of the Church **4** 362

CYRIL, ST. (827-869), Apostle to the Slavs **4** 362

CYRUS THE GREAT (ruled 550-530 BCE), founder of the Persian Empire **4** 363-364

Czaczkes, Shmuel Yoseph
see Agnon, Shmuel Yoseph

Czech film
Menzel, Jiří **34** 264-265

Czech literature
Hrabal, Bohumil **34** 173-176

CZERNY, CARL (1791-1857), Austrian pianist and composer **34** 68-70

D

Da Gama, Vasco
see Gama, Vasco da

DA PONTE, LORENZO (Emanuele Conegliano; 1749-1838), Italian librettist and poet **20** 105-106

DAGUERRE, LOUIS JACQUES MANDÉ (1787-1851), French painter and stage designer **4** 365-366

DAHL, ROALD (1916-1990), Welsh-born English author **4** 366-367

DAIGO II (1288-1339), Japanese emperor **4** 367-368

DAIMLER, GOTTLIEB (1834-1900), German mechanical engineer **4** 368

DALADIER, ÉDOUARD (1884-1970), French statesman **4** 369

DALAI LAMA (Lhamo Thondup; born 1935), 14th in a line of Buddhist spiritual and temporal leaders of Tibet **4** 369-371

DALE, SIR HENRY HALLETT (1875-1968), English pharmacologist and neurophysiologist **4** 371-373

D'Alembert, Jean
see Alembert, Jean le Rond d'

DALEN, NILS GUSTAF (1869-1937), Swedish engineer and inventor **25** 99-101

DALEY, RICHARD J. (1902-1976), Democratic mayor of Chicago (1955-1976) **4** 373-375

DALEY, RICHARD M. (born 1942), mayor of Chicago **24** 102-104

DALHOUSIE, 1ST MARQUESS OF (James Andrew Broun Ramsay; 1812-1860), British statesman **4** 375-376

DALI, SALVADOR (1904-1989), Spanish painter **4** 376-377
Schiaparelli, Elsa **34** 323-326

DALL, CAROLINE HEALEY (1822-1912), American reformer **31** 71-72

DALLAPICCOLA, LUIGI (1904-1975), Italian composer **4** 377-378

DALRYMPLE, ALEXANDER (1737-1808), Scottish hydrographer **34** 71-73

DALTON, JOHN (1766-1844), English chemist **4** 378-379

DALY, MARCUS (1841-1900), American miner and politician **4** 379-380

DALY, MARY (1928-2010), American feminist theoretician and philosopher **4** 380-381

DALZEL, ARCHIBALD (or Dalziel; 1740-1811), Scottish slave trader **4** 381-382

DAM, CARL PETER HENRIK (1895-1976), Danish biochemist **4** 382-383

Damadian, Raymond V., American scientist
Lauterbur, Paul C. **34** 236-238

DAMIEN, FATHER (1840-1889), Belgian missionary **4** 383

DAMPIER, WILLIAM (1652-1715), English privateer, author, and explorer **4** 384

DAMROSCH, WALTER (1862-1950), American musical director **34** 73-75

DANA, CHARLES ANDERSON (1819-1897), American journalist **4** 384-385

DANA, RICHARD HENRY, JR. (1815-1882), American author and lawyer **4** 385-386

DANDOLO, ENRICO (c. 1107-1205), Venetian doge 1192-1205 **4** 386-387

DANDRIDGE, DOROTHY (1922-1965), African American actress and singer **18** 112-114

DANIEL, JACK (c. 1849-1911), American distiller **34** 75-77

DANIELS, JOSEPHUS (1862-1948), American journalist and statesman **4** 387

Daniels, W.
see Wallace-Johnson, Isaac

D'ANNUNZIO, GABRIELE (1863-1938), Italian poet and patriot **4** 388

DE FOREST, MARIAN (1864-1935), American dramatist and journalist **30** 138-139

DE GASPERI, ALCIDE (1881-1954), Italian statesman, premier 1945-1953 **4** 462-463

DE GAULLE, CHARLES ANDRÉ JOSEPH MARIE (1890-1970), French general, president 1958-1969 **4** 463-465
supporters
Torrès, Tereska **34** 352-354

DE GOUGES, MARIE OLYMPE (born Marie Gouzes; 1748-1793), French author **23** 85-88

DE GOURNAY, MARIE LE JARS (1565-1645), French author **23** 88-90

DE HAVILLAND, SIR GEOFFREY (1882-1965), British aviator and aeronautical engineer **25** 101-103

DE HAVILLAND, OLIVIA (born 1916), British-American actress **33** 92-94
Fontaine, Joan **34** 121-124

DE HIRSCH, MAURICE (Baron de Hirsch; 1831-1896), Austro-Hungarian financier and philanthropist **24** 104-106

DE KLERK, FREDRIK WILLEM (born 1936), state president of South Africa (1989-1994) **4** 466-468

DE KOONING, WILLEM (1904-1997), Dutch-born American painter **4** 468-469

DE LA BARRA, FRANCISCO LEÓN (1863-1939), Mexican statesman **29** 245-247

DE LA MADRID HURTADO, MIGUEL (1934-2012), president of Mexico (1982-1988) **4** 471-472

DE LA ROCHE, MAZO LOUISE (1879-1961), Canadian author **4** 474-475

DE LA WARR, THOMAS (1577-1618), English colonial governor of Virginia **30** 140-142

DE LEMPICKA, TAMARA (Maria Gorska; Tamara Kuffner; 1898-1980), Polish American artist **24** 106-109

DE LEON, DANIEL (1852-1914), American Socialist theoretician and politician **4** 479-480

DE L'ORME, PHILIBERT (1510-1570), French architect **9** 519

DE MILLE, AGNES (1905-1993), American dancer, choreographer, and author **4** 486-488

DE NIRO, ROBERT (born 1943), American actor and film producer **21** 103-106

DE PISAN, CHRISTINE (1363-1431), French poet and philosopher **24** 109-111

DE PRIEST, OSCAR (1871-1951), American politician **30** 142-144

DE QUINCEY, THOMAS (Thomas Quincey; 1785-1859), British author **27** 98-100

De Revoire, Paul
see Revere, Paul

DE SANCTIS, FRANCESCO (1817-1883), Italian critic, educator, and legislator **4** 505

DE SAUSSURE, FERDINAND (1857-1913), Swiss linguist and author **24** 111-113

DE SICA, VITTORIO (c. 1901-1974), Italian filmmaker **29** 138-139

DE SMET, PIERRE JEAN (1801-1873), Belgian Jesuit missionary **4** 509-510

DE SOTO, HERNANDO (1500-1542), Spanish conqueror and explorer **4** 510-511

DE VALERA, EAMON (1882-1975), American-born Irish revolutionary leader and statesman **4** 514-515

DE VALOIS, NINETTE (Edris Stannus; 1898-2001), English choreographer and ballet dancer **25** 103-105

DE VARONA, DONNA (born 1947), American swimmer **30** 144-146

DE VERE, EDWARD (Earl of Oxford; 1550-1604), English author **25** 105-107

DE VRIES, HUGO (1848-1935), Belgian botanist in the fields of heredity and the origin of species **4** 516-518

DE WOLFE, ELSIE (1865-1950), American interior decorator **20** 107-108

Dead Sea Scrolls (ancient manuscripts)
Vermes, Geza **34** 364-366

Deadwood Dick
see Love, Nat

DEÁK, FRANCIS (1803-1876), Hungarian statesman **4** 431-432

DEAKIN, ALFRED (1856-1919), Australian statesman **4** 432-433

DEAN, DIZZY (Jay Hanna "Dizzy" Dean; c. 1910-1974), American baseball player **33** 90-92

DEAN, JAMES (James Byron Dean; 1931-1955), American actor and cult figure **4** 433-434

DEANE, SILAS (1737-1789), American merchant lawyer and diplomat **4** 435-437

DEARBORN, HENRY (1751-1829), American military officer and politician **31** 76-77

DEB, RADHAKANT (1783-1867), Bengali reformer and cultural nationalist **4** 437

DEBAKEY, MICHAEL ELLIS (1908-2008), American surgeon **4** 437-438

DEBARTOLO, EDWARD JOHN, SR. AND JR., real estate developers who specialized in large regional malls **4** 438-440

DEBS, EUGENE VICTOR (1855-1926), American union organizer **4** 444-445

Debt (economics)
Kirchner, Néstor **34** 206-208

DEBUSSY, (ACHILLE) CLAUDE (1862-1918), French composer **4** 445-447

DEBYE, PETER JOSEPH WILLIAM (1884-1966), Dutch-born American physical chemist **4** 447-448

DECATUR, STEPHEN (1779-1820), American naval officer **4** 448-449

Decimus Junius Juvenalis
see Juvenal

Decoin, Henri, French director
Darrieux, Danielle **34** 79-81

DECROW, KAREN (born 1937), American journalist and activist **31** 78-80

DEE, JOHN (1527-1608), British mathematician and astronomer **25** 107-110

DEE, RUBY (born Ruby Ann Wallace; born 1924), African American actor **4** 449-452

Dee, Sandra, American actress
Darin, Bobby **34** 77-79

DEER, ADA E. (born 1935), Native American social worker, activist, and director of Bureau of Indian Affairs **4** 452-454

DEERE, JOHN (1804-1886), American inventor and manufacturer **4** 455

DEERING, WILLIAM (1826-1913), American manufacturer **4** 455-456

DEES, MORRIS S., JR. (born 1936), American civil rights attorney **4** 456-457

Defense Advanced Research Projects Agency (DARPA)
McCarthy, John **34** 257-259

DEFOE, DANIEL (1660-1731), English novelist, journalist, and poet **4** 457-459

DEGANAWIDA (also DeKanahwidah; c. 1550-c. 1600), Native American prophet, leader, and statesman **4** 460-461

DEGAS, (HILAIRE GERMAIN) EDGAR (1834-1917), French painter and sculptor **4** 461-462

DEHLAVI, SHAH WALIULLAH (Qutb-ud-Din; 1703-1762), Indian religious leader **28** 92-94

DEISENHOFER, JOHANN (born 1943), German biochemist and biophysicist **23** 90-93

Deutsch, Arnold, Austrian spy
Blunt, Anthony **34** 36-38
Burgess, Guy **34** 44-47
Maclean, Donald **34** 247-249

DEUTSCH, KARL WOLFGANG (1912-1992), American political scientist **4** 512-514

DEVERS, GAIL (Yolanda Gail Devers; born 1966), American athlete **25** 113-115

DEVLIN, BERNADETTE (McAliskey; born 1947), youngest woman ever elected to the British Parliament **4** 515-516

DEVOE, EMMA SMITH (1848-1927), American voting rights activist **31** 83-84

DEVOL, GEORGE (1912-2011), American inventor **34** 90-93

DEVRIES, WILLIAM CASTLE (born 1943), American heart surgeon **4** 518-519

DEW, THOMAS RODERICK (1802-1846), American political economist **4** 519

DEWEY, GEORGE (1837-1917), American naval officer **4** 520

DEWEY, JOHN (1859-1952), American philosopher and educator **4** 520-523

DEWEY, MELVIL (1851-1931), American librarian and reformer **4** 523-524

DEWEY, THOMAS EDMUND (1902-1971), American lawyer and politician **4** 524

DEWSON, MARY WILLIAMS (Molly; 1874-1962), American reformer, government official, and organizer of women for the Democratic party **4** 525

D'HÉRELLE, FÉLIX HUBERT (1873-1949), Canadian bacteriologist **29** 140-142

DHLOMO, R.R.R. (1901-1971), Zulu writer **29** 142-144

Dhu'l-Aktaf
see Shahpur II

Diachronic historical linguistics
see Linguistics (science)

DIAGHILEV, SERGEI (1872-1929), Russian who inspired artists, musicians, and dancers to take ballet to new heights of public enjoyment **4** 525-527

DIAGNE, BLAISE (1872-1934), Senegalese political leader **4** 527

DIAMOND, DAVID (1915-2005), American composer and teacher **4** 527-529

DIAMOND, NEIL (born 1941), American singer and songwriter **33** 98-100

DIANA, PRINCESS OF WALES (born Diana Frances Spencer; 1961-1997), member of British royal family **4** 529-533

DIAS DE NOVAIS, BARTOLOMEU (died 1500), Portuguese explorer **4** 533-534

DIAZ, ABBY MORTON (nee Abigail Morton; 1821-1904), American author and activist **26** 87-89

Díaz, Manuel Azaña
see Azaña Díaz, Manuel

DÍAZ, PORFIRIO (José de la Cruz Porfirio Díaz; 1830-1915), Mexican general and politician **4** 534-536

Diaz, Rodrigo
see Cid, The

DÍAZ DEL CASTILLO, BERNAL (c. 1496-c. 1584), Spanish soldier and historian **4** 536-537

DÍAZ ORDAZ, GUSTAVO (1911-1979), president of Mexico (1964-1970) **4** 537-538

DIBANGO, MANU (born 1933), Cameroonian musician **31** 85-86

DICK, PHILIP K. (Philip Kindred Dick; 1928-1982), American science fiction writer **28** 96-98

DICKENS, CHARLES JOHN HUFFAM (1812-1870), English author **4** 538-541

DICKENS, HAZEL (1935-2011), American singer and songwriter **34** 93-94

DICKEY, JAMES (1923-1997), American poet **19** 87-89

DICKINSON, EMILY (1830-1886), American poet **4** 541-543

DICKINSON, JOHN (1732-1808), American lawyer, pamphleteer, and politician **4** 543-544

DICKSON, LAURIE (William Kennedy Laurie Dickson; 1860-1935), British inventor and filmmaker **20** 112-113

DIDDLEY, BO (1928-2008), American musician **29** 144-146

DIDEROT, DENIS (1713-1784), French philosopher, playwright, and encyclopedist **5** 1-2

DIDION, JOAN (born 1934), American author **20** 113-116

DIEBENKORN, RICHARD (1922-1993), American abstract expressionist painter **5** 2-4

DIEFENBAKER, JOHN GEORGE (1895-1979), Canadian statesman **5** 4-5

DIELS, (OTTO PAUL) HERMANN (1876-1954), German organic chemist **5** 5-6

DIEM, NGO DINH (1901-1963), South Vietnamese president 1955-1963 **5** 6-7

DIESEL, RUDOLF (1858-1913), German mechanical engineer **5** 7

DIETERLE, WILLIAM (1893-1972), German-American film director **32** 94-97

DIETRICH, MARLENE (née Marie Magdalene Dietrich; 1901-1992), German actor **25** 115-117

Digestion (anatomy)
Bartholin, Thomas **34** 21-23

DIKE, KENNETH (Kenneth Onwuka Dike; 1917-1983), African historian who set up the Nigerian National Archives **5** 7-8

DILLINGER, JOHN (1903-1934), American criminal **5** 9
Floyd, Charles **34** 119-121

DILTHEY, WILHELM CHRISTIAN LUDWIG (1833-1911), German historian and philosopher **5** 10

Dilution
Ostwald, Wilhelm **34** 284-286

DIMAGGIO, JOE (born Giuseppe Paolo DiMaggio, Jr.; 1914-1999), American baseball player **5** 10-11

DIMITROV, GEORGI (1882-1949), head of the Communist International (1935-1943) and prime minister of Bulgaria (1944-1949) **5** 11-13

Din, Muslih-al-
see Sadi

DINESEN BLIXEN-FINECKE, KAREN (a.k.a. Isak Dinesen; 1885-1962), Danish author **5** 13-14

DINGANE (c. 1795-1840), Zulu king **5** 14-15

DINKINS, DAVID (born 1927), African American politician and mayor of New York City **5** 15-18

DINWIDDIE, ROBERT (1693-1770), Scottish merchant and colonial governor **5** 18-19

DIOCLETIAN (Gaius Aurelius Valerius Diocletianus; 245-c. 313), Roman emperor 284-305 **5** 19-20

DIOGENES (c. 400-325 BCE), Greek philosopher **5** 20-21

DIONYSIUS EXIGUUS (c. 465-c. 530), Roman theologian and mathematician **28** 99-100

DIOP, CHEIKH ANTA (1923-1986), African historian **5** 21-22

DIOP, DAVID MANDESSI (1927-1960), French Guinean poet **24** 117-118

DIOR, CHRISTIAN (1905-1957), French fashion designer **5** 22

Diplomats
Algerian
Bendjedid, Chadli **34** 27-30

Diplomats, Italian
Faliero, Marino **34** 111-113

DORSEY, THOMAS ANDREW (1900-1993), African American gospel singer and composer **22** 149-151

DOS PASSOS, RODERIGO (1896-1970), American novelist **5** 69-71

DOS SANTOS, JOSÉ EDUARDO (born 1942), leader of the Popular Movement for the Liberation of Angola and president of Angola **5** 71-72

DOS SANTOS, MARCELINO (born 1929), Mozambican nationalist insurgent, statesman, and intellectual **5** 72-74

DOSTOEVSKY, FYODOR (1821-1881), Russian novelist **5** 74-77

DOUBLEDAY, FRANK NELSON (1862-1934), American publisher **29** 146-148

DOUGLAS, LORD ALFRED BRUCE (1870-1945), English author **33** 106-109

DOUGLAS, DONALD WILLS (1892-1981), American aeronautical engineer **5** 77

DOUGLAS, GAVIN (c. 1475-1522), Scottish poet, prelate, and courtier **5** 77-78

DOUGLAS, SIR JAMES (c. 1286-1330), Scottish patriot **5** 80-82

DOUGLAS, SIR JOHN SHOLTO (1844-1900), English boxing patron **29** 148-150

DOUGLAS, MARJORY STONEMAN (1890-1998), American conservationist **31** 89-91

DOUGLAS, MARY TEW (1921-2007), British anthropologist and social thinker **5** 79-80

DOUGLAS, STEPHEN ARNOLD (1813-1861), American politician **5** 80-82

Douglas, Thomas
see Selkirk, 5th Earl of

DOUGLAS, THOMAS CLEMENT (1904-1986), Canadian clergyman and politician, premier of Saskatchewan (1944-1961), and member of Parliament (1962-1979) **5** 82-83

DOUGLAS, WILLIAM ORVILLE (1898-1980), American jurist **5** 83-85

DOUGLAS-HOME, ALEC (Alexander Frederick Home; 1903-1995), Scottish politician **20** 117-119

DOUGLASS, FREDERICK (c. 1817-1895), African American leader and abolitionist **5** 85-86

DOUHET, GIULIO (1869-1930), Italian military leader **22** 151-152

DOVE, ARTHUR GARFIELD (1880-1946), American painter **5** 86-87

DOVE, RITA FRANCES (born 1952), United States poet laureate **5** 87-89

"Doves" (United States politics)
see Vietnam war (1956-1976)–opponents (United States)

DOVZHENKO, ALEXANDER (Oleksandr Dovzhenko; 1894-1956), Ukrainian film director and screenwriter **25** 120-122

DOW, CHARLES (1851-1902), American journalist **19** 95-97

DOW, HERBERT H. (Herbert Henry Dow; 1866-1930), American chemist and businessman **28** 100-102

DOW, NEAL (1804-1897), American temperance reformer **5** 89-90

DOWLAND, JOHN (1562-1626), British composer and lutenist **5** 90

DOWNING, ANDREW JACKSON (1815-1852), American horticulturist and landscape architect **5** 90-91

DOYLE, SIR ARTHUR CONAN (1859-1930), British author **5** 91-92

D'Oyly Carte
see Carte, Richard D'Oyly

Dracula (novel and film)
Siodmak, Robert **34** 331-334

DRAGO, LUIS MARÍA (1859-1921), Argentine international jurist and diplomat **5** 92-93

DRAKE, DANIEL (1785-1852), American physician **5** 93-94

DRAKE, EDWIN (1819-1880), American oil well driller and speculator **21** 108-110

DRAKE, SIR FRANCIS (c. 1541-1596), English navigator **5** 94-96
Grenville, Sir Richard **34** 148-150

DRAPER, JOHN WILLIAM (1811-1882), Anglo-American scientist and historian **5** 96-97

Drapier, M.B.
see Swift, Jonathan

DRAWBAUGH, DANIEL (1827-1911), American inventor **31** 92-93

DRAYTON, MICHAEL (1563-1631), English poet **5** 97-98

Dream Lover (song)
Darin, Bobby **34** 77-79

DREBBEL, CORNELIUS (Jacobszoon Drebbel; Cornelius Van Drebbel; 1572-1633), Dutch inventor and engineer **28** 102-104

DREISER, (HERMAN) THEODORE (1871-1945), American novelist **5** 98-100

DREW, CHARLES RICHARD (1904-1950), African American surgeon **5** 100-101

DREW, DANIEL (1797-1879), American stock manipulator **5** 101-102

DREXEL, KATHERINE (1858-1955), founded a Catholic order, the Sisters of the Blessed Sacrament **5** 102-103

DREXLER, KIM ERIC (born 1955), American scientist and author **20** 119-121

DREYER, CARL THEODOR (1889-1968), Danish film director **22** 152-155

DREYFUS, ALFRED (1859-1935), French army officer **5** 103-105

DRIESCH, HANS ADOLF EDUARD (1867-1941), German biologist and philosopher **5** 105

Dror-HeHalutz (Zionist youth organization)
Lubetkin, Zivia **34** 242-244

DRUCKER, PETER (1909-2005), American author and business consultant **21** 110-112

Drummond, James Eric
see Perth, 16th Earl of

DRUON, MAURICE (1918-2009), French author **31** 94-96

Drury Lane Theatre (London)
Cibber, Colley **34** 56-58

DRUSUS, MARCUS LIVIUS (c. 124-91 BCE), Roman statesman **5** 105-106

DRYDEN, JOHN (1631-1700), English poet, critic, and dramatist **5** 106-107

DRYDEN, KEN (born 1947), Canadian hockey player **33** 109-111

DRYSDALE, SIR GEORGE RUSSELL (1912-1981), Australian painter **5** 107-109

DU BELLAY, JOACHIM (c. 1522-1560), French poet **5** 113-114

DU BOIS, WILLIAM EDWARD BURGHARDT (1868-1963), African American educator, pan-Africanist, and protest leader **5** 116-118

DU BOIS-REYMOND, EMIL (1818-1896), German physiologist **5** 118-119

DU MAURIER, DAPHNE (Lady Browning; 1907-1989), English author **18** 125-127

DU PONT, PIERRE SAMUEL (1870-1954), American industrialist **5** 154-155

DU PONT, ÉLEUTHÈRE IRÉNÉE (1771-1834), French-born American manufacturer **5** 154

DU PONT DE NEMOURS, PIERRE SAMUEL (1739-1817), French political economist **5** 155-156

DU SABLE, JEAN BAPTISTE POINTE (Jean Baptiste Point Desable; c. 1745-1818), African-American explorer and founder of Chicago, IL **28** 104-106

EDMISTON, ALTHEA MARIA (Althea Maria Brown; 1874-1937), African American missionary **27** 108-111

EDMONDS, EMMA (1841-1889), Canadian soldier, nurse, and spy **32** 107-109

Education (Europe)
Austria
Czerny, Carl **34** 68-70

EDWARD I (1239-1307), king of England 1272-1307 **5** 208-210

EDWARD II (Edward of Carnarvon; 1284-1327), king of England 1307-27 **5** 210

EDWARD III (1312-1377), king of England 1327-77 **5** 211-212

Edward IV (1330-1376)
see Edward the Black Prince

EDWARD IV (1442-1483), king of England 1461-70 **5** 212-213

EDWARD VI (1537-1553), king of England and Ireland 1547-53 **5** 213-214

EDWARD VII (1841-1910), king of Great Britian and Ireland 1901-10 **5** 214-215

EDWARD VIII (1894-1972), King of England (1936) and Duke of Windsor after abdicating his throne **5** 215-217

Edward of Carnarvon
see Edward II

EDWARD THE BLACK PRINCE (1330-1376), English soldier-statesman **5** 217-218

EDWARD THE CONFESSOR (reigned 1042-1066, died 1066), last king of the house of Wessex **5** 218-219

EDWARD THE ELDER (died 924), king of England 899-924 **5** 219-220

Edwards, Eli
see McKay, Claude

EDWARDS, JONATHAN (1703-1758), American Puritan theologian **5** 220-222

EDWARDS, MELVIN (born 1937), African-American sculptor **5** 222-223

EDWARDS, SIAN (born 1959), British conductor **26** 96-98

EGGLESTON, EDWARD (1837-1902), American Methodist minister and historian **5** 223-224

EHRENBURG, ILYA GRIGORIEVICH (1891-1967), Russian author **5** 224-225

EHRLICH, JAKE W. (1900-1971), American lawyer and author **30** 160-162

EHRLICH, PAUL (1854-1915), German bacteriologist **5** 225-226

EICHMANN, ADOLF (1906-1962), German Nazi war criminal **5** 226-227

EIFFEL, ALEXANDRE GUSTAVE (1832-1923), French engineer **5** 227-228

EIJKMAN, CHRISTIAN (1858-1930), Dutch physician and biologist **5** 228

EIMER, THEODOR (1843-1898), German zoologist **32** 109-110

EINHORN, DAVID RUBIN (1809-1879), German theolgian **22** 164-166

EINSTEIN, ALBERT (1879-1955), German-born American physicist **5** 228-231

EISAI (1141-1215), Japanese Buddhist monk **5** 231-232

EISELEY, LOREN COREY (1907-1977), American interpreter of science for the layman **5** 232-233

EISENHOWER, DWIGHT DAVID (1890-1969), American general and statesman, president 1953-61 **5** 233-236

EISENHOWER, MAMIE DOUD (1896-1979), American first lady **5** 236-237

EISENHOWER, MILTON (Milton Stover Esisenhower; 1899-1985), American adviser to U.S. presidents and college president **5** 237-238

EISENMAN, PETER D. (born 1932), American architect **5** 239-240

EISENSTAEDT, ALFRED (1898-1995), American photographer and photo-journalist **19** 100-102

EISENSTEIN, SERGEI MIKHAILOVICH (1898-1948), Russian film director and cinema theoretician **5** 240-242

EISNER, MICHAEL (born 1942), American businessman **19** 102-104

EITOKU, KANO (1543-1590), Japanese painter of the Momoyama period **5** 242

Ejiofor, Chiwetel, (born 1977), English actor
Northup, Solomon **34** 275-277

EKWENSI, CYPRIAN (1921-2007), Nigerian writer **5** 242-243

El-Hajj Malik El-Shabazz
see Malcolm X (film)

ELBARADEI, MOHAMED (born 1942), Egyptian diplomat **26** 98-100

Elchingen, Duke of
see Ney, Michel

ELDERS, JOYCELYN (born 1933), first African American and second woman U.S. surgeon general **5** 243-246

ELEANOR OF AQUITAINE (c. 1122-1204), queen of France 1137-52, and of England 1154-1204 **5** 246-247

Electrolyte (chemistry)
Ostwald, Wilhelm **34** 284-286

ELGAR, SIR EDWARD (1857-1934), English composer **5** 247-248

ELGIN, 8TH EARL OF (James Bruce; 1811-63), English governor general of Canada **5** 248-249

Elia
see Lamb, Charles

ELIADE, MIRCEA (1907-1986), Rumanian-born historian of religions and novelist **5** 249-250

ELIAS, TASLIM OLAWALE (1914-1991), Nigerian academic and jurist and president of the International Court of Justice **5** 250-251

Eliezer, Israel ben
see Baal Shem Tov

ELIJAH BEN SOLOMON (1720-1797), Jewish scholar **5** 251-252

ELION, GERTRUDE B. (1918-1999), American biochemist and Nobel Prize winner **5** 252-254

ELIOT, CHARLES WILLIAM (1834-1926), American educator **5** 254

ELIOT, GEORGE (pen name of Mary Ann Evans; 1819-80), English novelist **5** 254-256

ELIOT, JOHN (1604-1690), English-born missionary to the Massachusetts Indians **5** 256-258

ELIOT, THOMAS STEARNS (1888-1965), American-English poet, critic, and playwright **5** 258-261

ELISABETH, EMPRESS OF AUSTRIA (1837-1898), German empress of Austria **28** 111-113

Elisabeth, Princess of Bohemia, (1618-1680)
Labadie, Jean de **34** 224-226

ELIZABETH (Elizabeth Petrovna; 1709-61), empress of Russia 1741-61 **5** 261-263

ELIZABETH I (1533-1603), queen of England and Ireland 1558-1603 **5** 263-266
court
Grenville, Sir Richard **34** 148-150
in Ireland
Grenville, Sir Richard **34** 148-150

ELIZABETH II (born 1926), queen of Great Britain and Ireland **5** 266-269
Blunt, Anthony **34** 36-38

ELIZABETH BAGAAYA NYABONGO OF TORO (born 1940), Ugandan ambassador **5** 269-271

ELIZABETH BOWES-LYON (Elizabeth Angela Marguerite Bowes-Lyon; 1900-2002), queen of Great Britain and Ireland (1936-1952) and Queen Mother after 1952 **5** 261-263

ELIZABETH OF HUNGARY (1207-1231), saint and humanitarian **5** 271-272

Elizabethan literature
see English literature–Elizabethan

ELLINGTON, "DUKE" EDWARD KENNEDY (1899-1974), American jazz composer **5** 273-274

ELLIS, HAVELOCK (Henry Havelock Ellis; 1959-1939), British psychologist and author **20** 126-128

ELLISON, RALPH WALDO (1914-1994), African American author and spokesperson for racial identity **5** 274-275

ELLSBERG, DANIEL (born 1931), U.S. government official and Vietnam peace activist **5** 275-277

ELLSWORTH, LINCOLN (1880-1951), American adventurer and polar explorer **5** 277

ELLSWORTH, OLIVER (1745-1807), American senator and Supreme Court Chief Justice **21** 115-117

ELON, AMOS (1926-2009), Israeli writer **32** 111-112

ELSASSER, WALTER MAURICE (1904-1991), American physicist **5** 277-278

ELSSLER, FANNY (1810-1884), Austrian ballet dancer **31** 107-108

ELUARD, PAUL (1895-1952), French poet **34** 108-109

ELWAY, JOHN (born 1960), American football player **23** 98-100

ELY, RICHARD (1854-1943), American economist and social reformer **21** 117-120

Emergency medicine
Safar, Peter **34** 316-318

EMERSON, RALPH WALDO (1803-1882), American poet, essayist, and philosopher **5** 278-280

EMINESCU, MIHAIL (1850-1889), Romanian poet **5** 280-281

EMMET, ROBERT (1778-1803), Irish nationalist and revolutionary **5** 281-282

EMPEDOCLES (c. 493-c. 444 BCE), Greek philosopher, poet, and scientist **5** 282

ENCHI, FUMIKO UEDA (1905-1986), Japanese author **23** 100-102

ENCINA, JUAN DEL (1468-c. 1529), Spanish author and composer **5** 283

ENDARA, GUILLERMO (1936-2009), installed as president of Panama by the U.S. Government in 1989 **5** 283-284

ENDECOTT, JOHN (1588-1655), English colonial governor of Massachusetts **5** 284-285

ENDERS, JOHN FRANKLIN (1897-1985), American virologist **5** 285-286

Energetics (science)
Ostwald, Wilhelm **34** 284-286

ENGELBART, DOUGLAS (born 1925), American inventor **31** 109-111

ENGELS, FRIEDRICH (1820-1895), German revolutionist and social theorist **5** 286-288

Engineering
mechanical
Devol, George **34** 90-93

ENGLAND, JOHN (1786-1842), Irish Catholic bishop in America **5** 288

England, Church of
separation from Rome
Godfrey, Edmund Berry **34** 141-143

English literature
Victorian (prose)
Sitwell, Osbert **34** 334-336

ENNIN (794-864), Japanese Buddhist monk **5** 288-289

ENNIUS, QUINTUS (239-169 BCE), Roman poet **5** 289

ENRICO, ROGER (born 1944), American businessman **27** 111-112

ENSOR, JAMES (1860-1949), Belgian painter and graphic artist **5** 289-290

EPAMINONDAS (c. 425-362 BCE), Theban general and statesman **5** 291-292

EPÉE, CHARLES-MICHEL DE L' (1712-1789), French sign language developer **21** 120-122

EPHRON, NORA (1941-2012), American author, screenwriter and film director **18** 130-132

EPICTETUS (c. 50-c. 135), Greek philosopher **5** 292

EPICURUS (c. 342-270 BCE), Greek philosopher, founder of Epicureanism **5** 292-294

Epimanes
see Antiochus IV (king of Syria)

Epsom Derby (race)
Davison, Emily Wilding **34** 84-86

EPSTEIN, ABRAHAM (1892-1945), Russian-born American economist **5** 294-295

EPSTEIN, SIR JACOB (1880-1959), American-born English sculptor **5** 295-296

EQUIANO, OLAUDAH (1745-c. 1801), African author and former slave **5** 296-297

ERASISTRATUS (c. 304 BCE- c. 250 BCE), Greek physician and anantomist **5** 297-298

ERASMUS, DESIDERIUS (1466-1536), Dutch author, scholar, and humanist **5** 298-300

ERASMUS, GEORGES HENRY (born 1948), Canadian Indian leader **5** 300-301

ERATOSTHENES OF CYRENE (c. 284-c. 205 BCE), Greek mathematician, geographer, and astronomer **5** 301-302

ERCILLA Y ZÚÑIGA, ALONSO DE (1533-1594), Spanish poet, soldier, and diplomat **5** 302

ERDOS, PAUL (1913-1996), Hungarian mathematician **22** 166-168

ERDRICH, LOUISE (Karen Louise Erdrich; born 1954), Native American author **23** 102-105

ERHARD, LUDWIG (1897-1977), German statesman, West German chancellor 1963-66 **5** 302-304

ERIC THE RED (Eric Thorvaldsson; flourished late 10th century), Norwegian explorer **5** 304

ERICKSON, ARTHUR CHARLES (1924-2009), Canadian architect and landscape architect **5** 304-306

ERICSON, LEIF (971-c. 1015), Norse mariner and adventurer **5** 306-307

ERICSSON, JOHN (1803-1889), Swedish-born American engineer and inventor **5** 307-308

ERIGENA, JOHN SCOTUS (c. 810-c. 877), Irish scholastic philosopher **5** 308-309

ERIKSON, ERIK HOMBURGER (1902-1994), German-born American psychoanalyst and educator **5** 309-310

Eritrea (former Italian colony, East Africa)
Zenawi, Meles **34** 392-394

ERLANGER, JOSEPH (1874-1965), American physiologist **5** 310-311

ERMAN, ADOLF (1854-1937), German Egyptologist and lexicographer **29** 154-156

ERNST, MAX (1891-1976), German painter **5** 311-312

ERNST, RICHARD (Richard Robert Ernst; born 1933), Swiss chemist **27** 112-114

ERSHAD, HUSSAIN MOHAMMAD (born 1930), Bengali military leader and president of Bangladesh (1982-1990) **5** 312-314

ERSKINE, THOMAS (1750-1823), British lawyer **22** 168-170

ERTÉ (Romain de Tirtoff; 1892-1990), Russian fashion illustrator and stage set designer **5** 314-316

ERTEGUN, AHMET (1923-2006), Turkish-American record company executive **30** 162-164
Brown, Ruth **34** 41-42

ERVIN, SAM J., JR. (1896-1985), lawyer, judge, U.S. senator, and chairman of the Senate Watergate Committee **5** 316-317

ERVING, JULIUS WINFIELD (a.k.a. Dr. J.; born 1950), African American basketball player **5** 317-319

ERZBERGER, MATTHIAS (1875-1921), German statesman **5** 319-320

ESAKI, LEO (Reiona Esaki; born 1925), Japanese physicist **24** 127-130

ESCALANTE, JAIME (1930-2010), Hispanic American educator **5** 320-321

ESCHER, MAURITS CORNELIS (M.C. Escher; 1898-1972), Dutch graphic artist **18** 132-134

ESCOFFIER, AUGUSTE (Georges Auguste Escoffier; 1846-1935), French chef **21** 122-124

ESENIN, SERGEI ALEKSANDROVICH (1895-1925), Russian poet **5** 321

ESQUIVEL, LAURA (born 1950), Mexican writer **31** 112-113

Essex, Earl of (circa 1485-1540)
see Cromwell, Thomas

ESSEX, 2D EARL OF (Robert Devereux; 1567-1601), English courtier **5** 321-322

Estabanico
see Estevan

Estenssoro, Victor Paz
see Paz Estenssoro, Victor

ESTES, RICHARD (born 1932), American realist painter **5** 322-323

ESTEVAN (a.k.a. Estabanico, Estevanico the Black; c. 1500-1539), Moroccan explorer **5** 324-325

ESTHER (Hadasseh; 522-c. 460 BCE), queen of Persia **25** 126-128

ESTRADA CABRERA, MANUEL (1857-1924), Guatemalan president 1898-1920 **5** 325-326

ESTRADA PALMA, TOMÁS (1835-1908), Cuban president 1902-1906 **5** 326-327

ETHELRED THE UNREADY (c. 968-1016), Anglo-Saxon king of England 978-1016 **5** 327

Ethiopia, Empire of (nation, East Africa)
rulers (21st century)
Zenawi, Meles **34** 392-394

Ethiopian People's Revolutionary Democratic Front (EPRDF)
Zenawi, Meles **34** 392-394

Ethiopian War (1935)
see Ethiopia–Italy and

Ethnomethodology
Garfinkel, Harold **34** 140-141

EUCKEN, RUDOLF (Rudolf Christof Eucken; 1846-1926), German philosopher **25** 128-130

EUCLID (flourished 300 BCE), Greek mathematician **5** 327-329

EUDOXUS OF CNIDUS (c. 408-c. 355 BCE), Greek astronomer, mathematician, and physician **5** 329-330

EUGENE OF SAVOY (1663-1736), French-born Austrian general and diplomat **5** 330-331

EULER, LEONARD (1707-1783), Swiss mathematician **5** 331-332

EURIPIDES (480-406 BCE), Greek playwright **5** 332-334

EUSTACHI, BARTOLOMEO (c. 1500-1574), Italian anatomist **30** 164-166

EUSTIS, DOROTHY HARRISON (1886-1946), American philanthropist and executive **32** 112-114

EUTROPIUS (flourished 4th century), Roman historian and official **20** 128-130

EUTYCHES (c. 380-455), Byzantine monk **5** 335

EVANS, ALICE (1881-1975), American bacteriologist **19** 104-106

EVANS, SIR ARTHUR JOHN (1851-1941), English archeologist **5** 335-336
Kober, Alice **34** 213-214
Ventris, Michael **34** 360-362

EVANS, EDITH (1888-1976), English actress who portrayed comic characters **5** 336-337

EVANS, GEORGE HENRY (1805-1856), American labor and agrarian reformer **5** 337-338

Evans, Mary Ann
see Eliot, George

EVANS, OLIVER (1755-1819), American inventor **5** 338

EVANS, WALKER (1903-1975), American photographer of American life between the world wars **5** 339

EVANS-PRITCHARD, SIR EDWARD EVAN (1902-1973), English social anthropologist **5** 340

EVARTS, WILLIAM MAXWELL (1818-1901), American lawyer and statesman **5** 340-341

EVATT, HERBERT VERE (1894-1965), Australian statesman and jurist **5** 341-343

EVELYN, JOHN (1620-1706), English author **5** 343-344

EVERETT, EDWARD (1794-1865), American statesman and orator **5** 344

EVERGOOD, PHILIP (1901-1973), American painter **5** 345

EVERS, MEDGAR (1925-1963), African American civil rights leader **5** 345-348

EVERS-WILLIAMS, MYRLIE (born Myrlie Louise Beasley; 1933), civil rights leader, lecturer, and writer **5** 348-350

EVERT, CHRIS (Christine Marie "Chris" Evert, born 1954), American tennis player **33** 112-114

EWING, WILLIAM MAURICE (1906-1974), American oceanographer **5** 350-351

EWONWU, BENEDICT CHUKA (1921-1994), Nigerian sculptor and painter **5** 351-352

Executions
Soviet Union
Yezhov, Nikolai **34** 387-389

Exiles (literary)
from China
Ai Qing **34** 3-4

Exiles (religious)
from Italy
Vergerio, Pier Paolo **34** 362-364
from U.S.
Wheelwright, John **34** 373-375

Explorers, English
of North America
Grenville, Sir Richard **34** 148-150

Explorers, Scottish
Dalrymple, Alexander **34** 71-73

Expressionism (film)
Siodmak, Robert **34** 331-334

EYCK, HUBERT VAN (died 1426), Flemish painter **5** 352-354

EYCK, JAN VAN (c. 1390-1441), Flemish painter **5** 352-354

EYRE, EDWARD JOHN (1815-1901), English explorer of Australia **5** 354

EZANA (flourished 4th century), Ethiopian king **5** 354-355

EZEKIEL (flourished 6th century BCE), Hebrew priest and prophet **5** 355-356

EZRA (flourished 5th century BCE), Hebrew priest, scribe, and reformer **5** 356-357

F

FAAS, HORST (1933-2012), German photographer **34** 109-111

FABERGÉ, CARL (Peter Carl Fabergé; Karl Gustavovich Fabergé; 1846-1920), Russian jeweler and goldsmith **21** 125-127

FABIUS, LAURENT (born 1946), prime minister of France in the 1980s **5** 358-359

FABRICI, GIROLAMO (1537-1619), Italian anatomist and surgeon **30** 167-169

Fabricius ab Aquapendente, Hieronymus
see Fabrici, Girolamo

FACKENHEIM, EMIL LUDWIG (1916-2003), post-World War II Jewish theologian **5** 359-361

Fackel, Die (journal)
Kraus, Karl **34** 219-221

Facundo, Juan
see Quiroga, Juan Facundo

FADIL AL-JAMALI, MUHAMMAD (1903-1997), Iraqi educator, writer, diplomat, and politician **5** 361-362

FADLALLAH, SAYYID MUHAMMAD HUSAYN (1935-2010), Shi'i Muslim cleric and Lebanese political leader **5** 362-364

FAHD IBN ABDUL AZIZ AL-SAUD (1920-2005), son of the founder of modern Saudi Arabia and king **5** 364-366

FAHRENHEIT, GABRIEL DANIEL (1686-1736), German physicist **5** 366

FAIDHERBE, LOUIS LÉON CÉSAR (1818-1889), French colonial governor **5** 366-367

Fair, A. A.
see Gardner, Erle Stanley

FAIR, JAMES RUTHERFORD, JR. (1920-2010), American chemical engineer and educator **20** 131-131

FAIRBANKS, DOUGLAS (Douglas Elton Ulman; 1883-1939), American actor and producer **19** 107-108

FAIRCLOUGH, ELLEN LOUKS (1905-2004), Canadian Cabinet minister **5** 367-368

FAIRUZ (née Nuhad Haddad; born 1933), Arabic singer **5** 368-369

Fairy tale (literary form)
Bly, Robert **34** 38-40

FAISAL I (1883-1933), king of Iraq 1921-33 **5** 370-371

FAISAL II (1935-1958), king of Iraq, 1953-1958 **20** 132-132

FAISAL IBN ABD AL AZIZ IBN SAUD (1904-1975), Saudi Arabian king and prominent Arab leader **5** 371-372

Faith (religion)
Wheelwright, John **34** 373-375

FALCONET, ÉTIENNE MAURICE (1716-1791), French sculptor **5** 372

FALIERO, MARINO (1285-1355), Venetian doge, 1354 **34** 111-113

Falkland Islands (Southern Atlantic Ocean)
Kirchner, Néstor **34** 206-208

FALLA, MANUEL DE (1876-1946), Spanish composer **5** 372-373

FALLACI, ORIANA (1929-2006), Italian journalist **27** 115-117

FALLETTA, JOANN (born 1954), American conductor **5** 373-375

FALLOPPIO, GABRIELE (1523-1562), Italian anatomist **29** 157-159

FALWELL, JERRY (1933-2007), fundamentalist religious leader who also promoted right-wing political causes **5** 375-376

Family, A (painting)
Le Brocquy, Louis **34** 238-239

FAN CHUNG-YEN (989-1052), Chinese statesman **5** 376-377

FANEUIL, PETER (1700-1743), American colonial merchant and philanthropist **5** 377

FANFANI, AMINTORE (1908-1999), Italian prime minister **5** 378-379

FANG LIZHI (1936-2012), Chinese scientist and dissident **34** 113-115

FANGIO, JUAN MANUEL (1911-1995), Argentine race car driver **33** 115-117

FANON, FRANTZ (1925-1961), Algerian political theorist and psychiatrist **5** 379-380

FARABI, AL- (Abou Nasr Mohammed ibn Tarkaw; 870-950), Turkish scholar and philosopher **22** 14-16

FARADAY, MICHAEL (1791-1867), English physicist and chemist **5** 380

FARAH, NURUDDIN (born 1945), Somali author **28** 114-116

FARGO, WILLIAM GEORGE (1818-1881), American businessman **5** 380-381

FARINA, MIMI (Margarita Mimi Baez Farina; 1945-2001), American singer and activist **27** 117-119

FARLEY, JAMES A. (1888-1976), Democratic Party organizer and political strategist **5** 381-383

FARMER, FANNIE MERRITT (1857-1915), American authority on cookery **5** 383

FARMER, JAMES (1920-1999), American civil rights activist who helped organize the 1960s "freedom rides" **5** 383-385

FARMER, MOSES GERRISH (1820-1893), American inventor and manufacturer **5** 385

Farnese, Alessandro (1468-1549)
see Paul III

Farnese, Alessandro, (1520-1589), Italian cardinal
Vergerio, Pier Paolo **34** 362-364

FARNESE, ALESSANDRO (Duke of Parma; 1545-1592), Italian general and diplomat **20** 132-135

FARNSWORTH, PHILO T. (1906-1971), American inventor of the television **5** 386-387

FAROUK I (1920-1965), king of Egypt 1937-1952 **5** 387-388

FARRAGUT, DAVID GLASGOW (1801-1870), American naval officer **5** 388-389

FARRAKHAN, LOUIS (Louis Eugene Walcott, born 1933), a leader of one branch of the Nation of Islam popularly known as Black Muslims and militant spokesman for Black Nationalism **5** 389-390

FARRAR, GERALDINE (1882-1967), American opera singer **23** 106-108

FARRELL, EILEEN (1920-2002), American singer **27** 119-121

FARRELL, JAMES THOMAS (1904-1979), American novelist and social and literary critic **5** 390-391

FARRELL, SUZANNE (née Roberta Sue Ficker; born 1945), American classical ballerina **5** 391-393

FARRENC, LOUISE (Jeanne Louise Dumont; 1804-1875), French pianist **27** 121-122

FASSBINDER, RAINER WERNER (1946-1982), German filmmaker **26** 101-103

Fathers of the Church
see Religious leaders, Christian–Fathers

Fatih
see Mehmed the Conqueror

FAUCHARD, PIERRE (1678-1761), French dentist **26** 103-105

FAULKNER, BRIAN (1921-1977), prime minister of Northern Ireland (1971-1972) **5** 393-395

FAULKNER, WILLIAM (1897-1962), American novelist **5** 395-397

FAURÉ, GABRIEL URBAIN (1845-1924), French composer **5** 397-398

FAUSET, JESSIE REDMON (1882-1961), African American writer and editor **20** 135-138

FAUST, DREW GILPIN (Catherine Drew Gilpin; born 1947), American historian and university president **28** 116-118

FAVALORO, RENE GERONIMO (1923-2000), Argentine physician **24** 131-133

FAWCETT, MILLICENT GARRETT (1847-1929), British feminist **5** 398-400

FAWKES, GUY (Guido Fawkes; 1570-1606), English soldier and conspirator **27** 123-125

FAYE, SAFI (born 1943), Senegalese filmmaker and ethnologist **5** 400-401

FBI
see Federal Bureau of Investigation (United States)

FECHNER, GUSTAV THEODOR (1801-1887), German experimental psychologist **5** 401-402

Federal Bureau of Investigation (United States)
Greene, Danny **34** 146-148

FEE, JOHN GREGG (1816-1901), American abolitionist and clergyman **5** 402-403

FEIFFER, JULES RALPH (born 1929), American satirical cartoonist and playwright and novelist **5** 403-404

FEIGENBAUM, MITCHELL JAY (born 1944), American physicist **5** 404-405

FEIGL, HERBERT (1902-1988), American philosopher **18** 135-137

FEIJÓ, DIOGO ANTÔNIO (1784-1843), Brazilian priest and statesman **5** 405-406

FEININGER, LYONEL (1871-1956), American painter **5** 406-407

FEINSTEIN, DIANNE (Goldman; born 1933), politician, public official, and San Francisco's first female mayor **5** 407-408

FELA (Fela Anikulapo Kuti; 1938-1997), Nigerian musician and activist **21** 127-129

FELICIANO, JOSÉ (born 1945), Hispanic American singer and guitarist **19** 109-110

Feliks
see Litvinov, Maxim Maximovich

Felious, Odetta Holmes
see Odetta

FELLER, BOB (Robert William Andrew Feller; 1918-2010), American baseball player **21** 129-131

FELLINI, FEDERICO (1920-1993), Italian film director **5** 408-409

FELT, W. MARK (1913-2008), FBI Associate Director and "Deep Throat" **30** 169-171

FELTRE, VITTORINO DA (1378-1446), Italian humanist and teacher **5** 409-410

Feminist movement
see Women's rights

Feminists
American
Dickens, Hazel **34** 93-94

FENDER, LEO (1909-1991), American musical instrument manufacturer **34** 115-117

FÉNELON, FRANÇOIS DE SALIGNAC DE LA MOTHE (1651-1715), French archbishop and theologian **5** 410-411

FENG KUEI-FEN (1809-1874), Chinese scholar and official **5** 411-412

FENG YÜ-HSIANG (1882-1948), Chinese warlord **5** 412-413

Feodorovich, Pëtr
see Peter III, (Peter Feodorovich; 1728-62)

FEODOROVNA, ALEXANDRA (1872-1918), empress of Russia **34** 7-9

FERBER, EDNA (1887-1968), American author **5** 413

FERDINAND (1865-1927), king of Romania 1914-1927 **5** 413-414

FERDINAND I (1503-1564), Holy Roman emperor 1555-1564, king of Hungary and Bohemia 1526-64 and of Germany 1531-1564 **5** 414-415

FERDINAND II (1578-1637), Holy Roman emperor 1619-1637, king of Bohemia 1617-1637 and of Hungary 1618-1637 **5** 415

FERDINAND II (1810-1859), king of the Two Sicilies 1830-1859 **5** 415-416

Ferdinand II (king of Aragon)
see Ferdinand V (king of Castile)

FERDINAND III (1608-1657), Holy Roman emperor 1637-1657, king of Hungary 1626-1657 and of Bohemia 1627-1657 **5** 416-417

Ferdinand III (king of Naples)
see Ferdinand V (king of Castile)

FERDINAND V (1452-1516), king of Castile 1474-1504, of Sicily 1468-1516, and of Aragon 1479-1516 **5** 417-418

Ferdinand V (king of Spain)
see Ferdinand V (king of Castile)

FERDINAND VII (1784-1833), king of Spain 1808 and 1814-1833 **5** 418-420

Ferdinand von Hohenzollern-Sigmaringen
see Ferdinand (king of Romania)

FERGUSON, ADAM (1723-1816), Scottish philosopher, moralist, and historian **5** 420-421

FERGUSON, HOWARD (1908-1999), Irish musician and composer **18** 137-138

FERLINGHETTI, LAWRENCE (Lawrence Monsato Ferling; born 1919), American poet, publisher and bookstore owner **27** 125-127

FERMAT, PIERRE DE (1601-1665), French mathematician **5** 421-422

FERMI, ENRICO (1901-1954), Italian-American physicist **5** 422-424

Fermoselle
see Encina, Juan del

FERNÁNDEZ, CRISTINA (born 1953), Argentine president **33** 117-119
Kirchner, Néstor **34** 206-208

FERNÁNDEZ, EMILIO (1904-1986), Mexican film director and actor **31** 114-115

Fernández, José Manuel Balmaceda
see Balmaceda Fernández, José Manuel

FERNÁNDEZ DE LIZARDI, JOSÉ JOAQUIN (1776-1827), Mexican journalist and novelist **5** 424-425

Fernando
see Ferdinand

FERNEL, JEAN FRANÇOIS (c. 1497-1558), French physician **5** 425-426

Ferrante
see Ferdinand

FERRARI, ENZO (1898-1988), Italian automaker **34** 117-119
Lamborghini, Ferruccio **34** 230-232

Ferrari S.p.A.
Ferrari, Enzo **34** 117-119
Lauda, Niki **34** 233-236

FERRARO, GERALDINE (1935-2011), first woman candidate for the vice presidency of a major U.S. political party **5** 426-428

FERRER, GABRIEL MIRÓ (1879-1930), Spanish author **5** 428

FERRER, IBRAHIM (1927-2005), Cuban musician **26** 105-107

FERRER, JOSÉ FIGUÉRES (1906-1990), Costa Rican politician **5** 428-429

FERRERO, GUGLIELMO (1871-1942), Italian journalist and historian **5** 429-430

FERRI, ENRICO (1856-1929), Italian criminologist **29** 159-162

FERRIER, SIR DAVID (1843-1928), Scottish anatomist **31** 116-117

FERRY, JULES FRANÇOIS CAMILLE (1832-1893), French statesman **5** 430

FEUCHTWANGER, LION (1884-1958), post-World War I German literary figure **5** 430-432

FEUERBACH, LUDWIG ANDREAS (1804-1872), German philosopher **5** 432

Fever (song)
Blackwell, Otis **34** 32-33

FEYNMAN, RICHARD PHILLIPS (1918-1988), American physicist **5** 432-434

Fianna Fail (Irish political party)
Lenihan, Brian, Jr. **34** 240-242

Fiat (Fabrica Italiana Automobili Torino)
Ferrari, Enzo **34** 117-119

FIBIGER, JOHANNES (Johannes Andreas Grib Fibiger; 1867-1928), Danish bacteriologist and pathologist **21** 131-133

FIBONACCI, LEONARDO (c. 1180-c. 1250), Italian mathematician **5** 434-435

FICHTE, JOHANN GOTTLIEB (1762-1814), German philosopher **5** 435-436

FICINO, MARSILIO (1433-1499), Italian philosopher and humanist **5** 436-437

FIEDLER, ARTHUR (1894-1979), American conductor of the Boston Pops **5** 437-438
Kenton, Stan **34** 198-200

FIELD, CYRUS WEST (1819-1892), American merchant **5** 438-439

FIELD, DAVID DUDLEY (1805-1894), American jurist **5** 439-440

FIELD, MARSHALL (1834-1906), American merchant **5** 440-441

FIELD, SALLY (Field, Sally Margaret; born 1946), American actress and director **24** 133-135

FIELD, STEPHEN JOHNSON (1816-1899), American jurist **5** 441-442

Fielder-Civil, Blake
Winehouse, Amy **34** 378-380

FIELDING, HENRY (1707-1754), English novelist **5** 442-444
enemies
Cibber, Colley **34** 56-58

FIELDS, DOROTHY (1905-1974), American lyricist **26** 107-109

FIELDS, W. C. (stage name of William Claude Dukenfield; 1879-1946), American comedian **5** 444

FIENNES, CELIA (Cecelia Fiennes; 1662-1741), British travel writer and diarist **28** 118-121

Fieschi, Sinibaldo de'
see Innocent IV

FIGUEIREDO, JOÃO BATISTA DE OLIVEIRA (1918-1999), Brazilian army general and president (1979-1985) **5** 445-446

Figuéres Ferrer, José
see Ferrer, José Figuéres

FIGUEROA, GABRIEL (1907-1997), Mexican cinematographer **31** 118-119

Filioque doctrine (Roman Catholic theology)
Kydones, Demetrius **34** 67-68

FILLMORE, MILLARD (1800-1874), American statesman, president 1850-1853 **5** 447-448

FILMER, SIR ROBERT (died 1653), English political theorist **5** 448

FILONOV, PAVEL (1883-1941), Russian artist **33** 119-121

FINCH, ANNE (Anne Kingsmill Finch; 1661-1720), English poet **27** 127-129

FINK, ALBERT (1827-1897), American railroad engineer and economist **21** 133-135

FINKELSTEIN, RABBI LOUIS (1895-1991), American scholar and leader of Conservative Judaism **5** 448-450

FINLAY, CARLOS JUAN (1833-1915), Cuban biologist and physician **5** 450

FINNEY, CHARLES GRANDISON (1792-1875), American theologian and educator **5** 450-451

FIORINA, CARLY (Cara Carleton Sneed; born 1954), American businesswoman **25** 131-133

FIRDAUSI (934-1020), Persian poet **5** 451-452

FIRESTONE, HARVEY SAMUEL (1868-1938), American industrialist **5** 452-453

FIRESTONE, SHULAMITH (1945-2012), Canadian feminist **27** 129-131

FIRST, RUTH (1925-1982), South African socialist, anti-apartheid activist, and scholar **5** 453-454

FISCHER, BOBBY (1943-2008), American chess player **5** 454-456

FISCHER, EMIL (1852-1919), German organic chemist **5** 456-457

FISCHER, HANS (1881-1945), German organic chemist **5** 457-459

FISCHER VON ERLACH, JOHANN BERNHARD (1656-1723), Austrian architect **5** 459-461

FISH, HAMILTON (1808-1893), American statesman **5** 461-462

Fish Called Wanda, A (film)
Palin, Michael **34** 287-289

FISHER, ANDREW (1862-1928), Australian statesman and labor leader **5** 462

FISHER, IRVING (1867-1947), American economist **5** 462-463

FISHER, JOHN ARBUTHNOT (Baron Fisher of Kilverstone; 1841-1920), British admiral **22** 171-173

FISHER, SIR RONALD AYLMER (1890-1962), English statistician **5** 463-464

FISHER, RUDOLPH (Rudolph John Chauncey Fisher; 1897-1934), African American author **28** 121-123

FISK, JAMES (1834-1872), American financial speculator **5** 464-465

Fiske, Helen Marie
see Jackson, Helen Hunt

FISKE, JOHN (1842-1901), American philosopher and historian **5** 465-466

FISKE, MINNIE MADDERN (Mary Augusta Davey; 1865-1932), American "realistic" actress who portrayed Ibsen heroines **5** 466-467

FITCH, JOHN (1743-1798), American mechanic and inventor **5** 467-468

FITCH, VAL LOGSDON (born 1923), American physicist **24** 135-138

Fitz-Boodle, George Savage
see Thackeray, William Makepeace

FITZGERALD, ELLA (1918-1996), American jazz singer **5** 468-469

FITZGERALD, FRANCES (born 1940), American author **5** 469-470

FITZGERALD, FRANCIS SCOTT KEY (1896-1940), American author **5** 470-472
Baker, Hobey **34** 16-18
Rothstein, Arnold **34** 311-313

FITZGERALD, GARRET (1926-2011), Irish prime minister (1981-1987) **5** 472-474

FITZHUGH, GEORGE (1806-1881), American polemicist and sociologist **5** 474

FITZPATRICK, THOMAS (1799-1854), American trapper, guide, and Indian agent **5** 474-475

FIZEAU, HIPPOLYTE ARMAND LOUIS (1819-1896), French physicist **5** 475

FLAGLER, HENRY (1830-1913), American industrialist **21** 135-137

FLAGSTAD, KIRSTEN MALFRID (1895-1962), Norwegian opera singer **25** 133-135

FLAHERTY, ROBERT (1884-1951), American documentary filmmaker **5** 476-477

FLAMININUS, TITUS QUINCTIUS (c. 228-174 BCE), Roman general and diplomat **5** 477

FLAMSTEED, JOHN (1646-1719), English astronomer **5** 477-478

FLANAGAN, HALLIE (1890-1969), American director, playwright, and educator **5** 478-479

FLANNAGAN, JOHN BERNARD (1895-1942), American sculptor **5** 480

FLAUBERT, GUSTAVE (1821-1880), French novelist **5** 480-482

Flavius Claudius Julianus
see Julian the Apostate

FLEISCHER, MAX (1883-1972), American animator, cartoonist, and inventor **22** 173-175

GARCIA, JERRY (Jerome John Garcia; 1942-1995), American musician **21** 150-152

GARCÍA MÁRQUEZ, GABRIEL (1928-2014), Colombian author **6** 208-209

GARCÍA MORENO, GABRIEL (1821-1875), Ecuadorian politician, president 1861-1865 and 1869-1875 **6** 209-210

GARCÍA ROBLES, ALFONSO (1911-1991), Mexican diplomat **23** 117-119

Garcia y Sarmiento, Félix Rubén
see Dario, Rubén

GARCILASO DE LA VEGA, INCA (1539-1616), Peruvian chronicler **6** 210-211

GARDEN, ALEXANDER (c. 1730-1791), Scottish-born American naturalist and physician **30** 176-178

GARDINER, SAMUEL RAWSON (1829-1902), English historian **6** 211

GARDNER, AVA (Ava Lavinia Gardner; 1922-1990), American actress **25** 151-154

GARDNER, ERLE STANLEY (1889-1970), American mystery writer **22** 193-195

GARDNER, GERALD (1884-1964), British witch and writer **30** 178-180

GARDNER, ISABELLA STEWART (1840-1924), American art patron and socialite **21** 152-155

GARDNER, JOHN W. (1912-2002), American educator, public official, and political reformer **6** 211-213

GARFIELD, JAMES ABRAM (1831-1881), American general, president 1881 **6** 213-214

GARFIELD, LUCRETIA RUDOLPH (1832-1918), American first lady **32** 124-126

GARFINKEL, HAROLD (1917-2011), American educator **34** 140-141

GARIBALDI, GIUSEPPE (1807-1882), Italian patriot **6** 215-217

GARLAND, HANNIBAL HAMLIN (1860-1940), American author **6** 217-218

GARLAND, JUDY (1922-1969), American actress and singer **6** 218-219
Hamlisch, Marvin **34** 151-153

GARNEAU, FRANÇOIS-XAVIER (1809-1866), French-Canadian historian **6** 219-220

GARNER, JOHN NANCE ("Cactus Jack" Garner; 1868-1967), American vice president (1933-1941) **21** 155-157

GARNET, HENRY HIGHLAND (1815-1882), African American clergyman, abolitionist, and diplomat **24** 155-158

GARNIER, FRANCIS (Marie Joseph François Garnier; 1839-1873), French naval officer **6** 220-221

GARNIER, JEAN LOUIS CHARLES (1825-1898), French architect **6** 221-222

GARRETT, JOHN WORK (1820-1884), American railroad magnate **6** 225

GARRETT, PATRICK FLOYD (1850-1908), American sheriff **30** 180-182

GARRETT, THOMAS (1789-1871), American abolitionist **6** 225-226

GARRETT (ANDERSON), ELIZABETH (1836-1917), English physician and women's rights advocate **6** 222-225

GARRISON, WILLIAM LLOYD (1805-1879), American editor and abolitionist **6** 226-228

GARROS, ROLAND (1888-1918), French aviator **32** 126-128

GARVEY, MARCUS MOSIAH (1887-1940), Jamaican leader and African nationalist **6** 228-229

GARY, ELBERT HENRY (1846-1927), American lawyer and industrialist **6** 229-230

GASCA, PEDRO DE LA (c. 1496-1567), Spanish priest and statesman **6** 230-231

Gascoyne-Cecil, Robert Arthur Talbot
see Salisbury, 3rd Marquess of

GASKELL, ELIZABETH (1810-1865), English novelist **6** 231-232

Gaspé, Philippe Aubert de
see Aubert de Gaspé, Philippe

GATES, HORATIO (c. 1728-1806), Revolutionary War general **29** 169-172

GATES, THOMAS SOVEREIGN (1873-1948), American educator and businessperson **32** 128-130

GATES, WILLIAM HENRY, III ("Bill"; born 1955), computer software company co-founder and executive **6** 232-234

GATLING, RICHARD JORDAN (1818-1903), American inventor of multiple-firing guns **6** 234-235

GAUDÍ I CORNET, ANTONI (1852-1926), Catalan architect and designer **6** 235-236

GAUGUIN, PAUL (1848-1903), French painter and sculptor **6** 236-238

GAULLI, GIOVANNI BATTISTA (1639-1709), Italian painter **6** 238-239

GAULTIER, JEAN PAUL (born 1952), French avant-garde designer **6** 239-240

GAUSS, KARL FRIEDRICH (1777-1855), German mathematician and astronomer **6** 240-242

GAUSTAD, EDWIN (1923-2011), American historian **32** 130-131

Gautama, Prince
see Buddha (play)

GAUTIER, THÉOPHILE (1811-1872), French writer **31** 133-134

GAVIRIA TRUJILLO, CESAR AUGUSTO (born 1947), president of Colombia **6** 242-243

GAY, JOHN (1685-1732), English playwright and poet **6** 243-244

GAY-LUSSAC, JOSEPH LOUIS (1778-1850), French chemist and physicist **6** 245-246

GAYE, MARVIN (Marvin Pentz Gay; 1939-1984), American musician **26** 119-123

GAYLE, HELENE DORIS (born 1955), African American epidemiologist and pediatrician **6** 244-245

Geber
see Jabir ibn Hayyan

GEDDES, SIR PATRICK (1854-1932), Scottish sociologist and biologist **6** 246-247

GEERTGEN TOT SINT JANS (Geertgen van Haarlem; c. 1460/65-1490/95), Netherlandish painter **6** 248

GEERTZ, CLIFFORD (1926-2006), American cultural anthropologist **6** 248-249

GEFFEN, DAVID LAWRENCE (born 1943), American record and film producer **23** 119-122

GEHRIG, LOU (Henry Louis Gehrig; 1903-1941), American baseball player **19** 119-121

GEHRY, FRANK O. (née Goldberg; born 1929), American architect **6** 250-251

GEIGER, HANS (born Johannes Wilhelm Geiger; 1882-1945), German physicist **6** 251-253

GEISEL, ERNESTO (1908-1996), Brazilian army general, president of Brazil's national oil company (Petrobras), and president of the republic (1974-1979) **6** 253-255

GEISEL, THEODOR (a.k.a. Dr. Seuss; 1904-1991), American author of children's books **6** 255-256

Geiseric
see Gaiseric

GELERNTER, DAVID (born 1955), American computer scientist **32** 131-133

GELL-MANN, MURRAY (born 1929), American physicist **6** 257-258

Gellée, Claude
see Claude Lorrain

GELLER, MARGARET JOAN (born 1947), American astronomer **6** 256-257

GLASS, PHILIP (born 1937), American composer of minimalist music **6** 362-364

GLASSE, HANNAH (Hannah Allgood; 1708-1770), English cookbook author **21** 166-167

GLEASON, JACKIE (Herbert Walton Gleason Jr.; 1915-1987), American actor **31** 139-140

GLEDITSCH, ELLEN (1879-1968), Norwegian chemist **23** 124-126

Glen or Glenda (film)
Wood, Ed, Jr. **34** 383-384

GLENDOWER, OWEN (c. 1359-c. 1415), Welsh national leader **6** 364-365

GLENN, JOHN HERSCHEL, JR. (born 1921), military test pilot, astronaut, businessman, and United States senator from Ohio **6** 365-367

GLIDDEN, JOSEPH (1813-1906), American businessman and inventor **21** 167-170

GLIGOROV, KIRO (1917-2012), first president of the Republic of Macedonia **6** 367-369

GLINKA, MIKHAIL IVANOVICH (1804-1857), Russian composer **6** 369-370

GLISSANT, ÉDOUARD (born 1928), Martiniquais writer **31** 141-142

Global Economic Recession (2008-2012)
Lenihan, Brian, Jr. **34** 240-242

GLOUCESTER, DUKE OF (1391-1447), English statesman **6** 370-371

Gloucester, Richard, Duke of
see Richard III (play; Shakespeare)

GLUBB, SIR JOHN BAGOT (1897-1986), British commander of the Arab Legion 1939-56 **6** 371-372

GLUCK, CHRISTOPH WILLIBALD (1714-1787), Austrian composer and opera reformer **6** 372-374

GLUCKMAN, MAX (1911-1975), British anthropologist **6** 374-375

GLYN, ELINOR (born Elinor Sutherland; 1864-1943), British author and filmmaker **23** 126-128

Glyndyfrdwy, Lord of Giyndwr and Sycharth
see Glendower, Owen

GOBINEAU, COMTE DE (Joseph Arthur Gobineau; 1816-1882), French diplomat **6** 375-376

GODARD, JEAN-LUC (born 1930), French actor, film director, and screenwriter **19** 126-128

GODDARD, ROBERT HUTCHINGS (1882-1945), American pioneer in rocketry **6** 376-377

GÖDEL, KURT (1906-1978), Austrian-American mathematician **6** 377-379

GODFREY, EDMUND BERRY (1621-1678), English magistrate **34** 141-143

GODKIN, EDWIN LAWRENCE (1831-1902), British-born American journalist **6** 380

GODOLPHIN, SIDNEY (1st Earl of Godolphin; 1645-1712), English statesman **6** 380-381

GODOY Y ÁLVAREZ DE FARIA, MANUEL DE (1767-1851), Spanish statesman **6** 381-382

GODUNOV, BORIS FEODOROVICH (c. 1551-1605), czar of Russia 1598-1605 **6** 382-383

GODWIN, WILLIAM (1756-1836), English political theorist and writer **6** 383-384

GOEBBELS, JOSEPH PAUL (1897-1945), German politician and Nazi propagandist **6** 384-385

GOEPPERT-MAYER, MARIA (1906-1972), American physicist **6** 385-387

GOETHALS, GEORGE WASHINGTON (1858-1928), American Army officer and engineer **6** 387-388

GOETHE, JOHANN WOLFGANG VON (1749-1832), German poet **6** 388-391

GOGOL, NIKOLAI (1809-1852), Russian author **6** 391-393

GOH CHOK TONG (born 1941), leader of the People's Action Party and Singapore's prime minister **6** 393-395

GOIZUETA, ROBERTO (1931-1997), Cuban American businessman and philanthropist **18** 160-162

GÖKALP, MEHMET ZIYA (1875/76-1924), Turkish publicist and sociologist **6** 395-396

GÖKÇEN, SABIHA (Sabiha Geuckchen; 1913-2001), Turkish aviator **27** 147-149

GOKHALE, GOPAL KRISHNA (1866-1915), Indian nationalist leader **6** 396

GOLD, THOMAS (1920-2004), American astronomer and physicist **18** 162-164

GOLDBERG, ARTHUR JOSEPH (1908-1990), U.S. secretary of labor, ambassador to the United Nations, and activist justice of the U.S. Supreme Court **6** 397-398

GOLDBERG, WHOOPI (born Caryn E. Johnson; born 1949), African American actress **6** 398-402

GOLDEN, HARRY (1902-1981), Jewish-American humorist, writer, and publisher **6** 402-403

Goldfish, Samuel
see Goldwyn, Samuel

GOLDIE, SIR GEORGE DASHWOOD TAUBMAN (1846-1925), British trader and empire builder **6** 404

GOLDING, WILLIAM (1911-1993), English novelist and essayist **6** 404-406

GOLDMAN, EMMA (1869-1940), Lithuanian-born American anarchist **6** 406-407

Goldmann, Max
see Reinhardt, Max

GOLDMARK, JOSEPHINE (1877-1950), advocate of government assistance in improving the lot of women and children **6** 407-408

GOLDMARK, PETER CARL (1906-1977), American engineer and inventor **21** 170-172

GOLDONI, CARLO (1707-1793), Italian dramatist, poet, and librettist **6** 408-409

GOLDSMITH, JAMES MICHAEL (1933-1997), British-French industrialist and financier **6** 409-411

GOLDSMITH, OLIVER (1730-1774), British poet, dramatist, and novelist **6** 411-413

GOLDSMITH, OLIVER (1794-1861), Canadian poet **6** 411

GOLDWATER, BARRY (1909-1998), conservative Republican U.S. senator from Arizona (1952-1987) **6** 413-415

GOLDWYN, SAMUEL (1882-1974), Polish-born American film producer **6** 416

Golitsyn, Anatoliy, (born 1926), Soviet KGB defector
Blunt, Anthony **34** 36-38

GOMBERT, NICOLAS (c. 1500-1556/57), Franco-Flemish composer **6** 416-417

GOMBRICH, ERNST HANS JOSEF (1909-2001), British author and educator **27** 149-151

GÓMEZ, JUAN VICENTE (1857-1935), Venezuelan dictator **6** 417-418

GÓMEZ, MÁXIMO (1836-1905), Dominican-born Cuban general and independence hero **6** 418-419

GÓMEZ CASTRO, LAUREANO ELEUTERIO (1889-1965), Colombian statesman, president **6** 419-420

GOMPERS, SAMUEL (1850-1924), American labor leader **6** 420-422

GOMULKA, WLADISLAW (1905-1982), Polish politician **6** 422-424

GONCHAROV, IVAN ALEKSANDROVICH (1812-1891), Russian novelist **6** 424

GONCHAROVA, NATALIA (1881-1962), Russian painter and theatrical scenery designer **6** 424-426

GONCOURT BROTHERS (19th century), French writers **6** 426-427

Gondola, Andrea di Pietro dalla *see* Palladio, Andrea

Gongon Musa *see* Musa Mansa

GÓNGORA Y ARGOTE, LUIS DE (1561-1627), Spanish poet **6** 427-428

GONNE, MAUD (c. 1866-1953), Irish nationalist **20** 158-160

Gonzalez, José Victoriano *see* Gris, Juan

GONZÁLEZ, JULIO (1876-1942), Spanish sculptor **6** 428-429

GONZÁLEZ MARQUEZ, FELIPE (born 1942), Socialist leader of Spain **6** 429-431

GONZÁLEZ PRADA, MANUEL (1848-1918), Peruvian essayist and poet **6** 431

GONZALO DE BERCEO (c. 1195-c. 1252), Spanish author **6** 431-432

GOOCH, GEORGE PEABODY (1873-1968), British historian and political journalist **6** 432-433

GOODALL, JANE (born 1934), British scientist who studied primates **6** 433-434

GOODE, MAL (Malvin Russell Goode, 1908-1995), African American journalist **27** 151-153

GOODLAD, JOHN INKSTER (born 1917), American education researcher and prophet **6** 434-436

GOODMAN, BENNY (Benjamin David Goodman; 1909-1986), jazz clarinetist and big band leader (1935-1945) **6** 436-438

GOODMAN, ELLEN HOLTZ (born 1941), American journalist **6** 438-439

GOODNIGHT, CHARLES (1836-1926), American cattleman **6** 439

GOODPASTER, ANDREW JACKSON (1915-2005), American Army officer active in organizing NATO forces in Europe and adviser to three presidents **6** 439-441

GOODYEAR, CHARLES (1800-1860), American inventor **6** 441

GOOLAGONG, EVONNE (born 1951), Australian tennis player **33** 126-128

Goon on Earth *see* Antiochus IV (king of Syria)

GORBACHEV, MIKHAIL SERGEEVICH (born 1931), former president of the Union of Soviet Socialist Republics. **6** 441-444

GORBACHEV, RAISA MAXIMOVNA (née Titorenko; 1932-1999), first lady of the Soviet Union **6** 444-446

GORDEEVA, EKATERINA (born 1971), Russian ice skater and author **18** 164-166

GORDIMER, NADINE (born 1923), South African author of short stories and novels **6** 446-447

GORDIN, JACOB (1853-1909), Russian playwright **33** 128-130

GORDON, AARON DAVID (1856-1922), Russian-born Palestinian Zionist **6** 447-448

GORDON, BEATE SIROTA (1923-2012), Austrian-American cultural expert **34** 143-145

GORDON, CHARLES GEORGE (1833-1885), English soldier and adventurer **6** 448-449

Gordon, George Hamilton *see* Aberdeen, 4th Earl of

GORDON, JOHN BROWN (1832-1904), American businessman and politician **6** 449-450

GORDON, PAMELA (born 1955), Bermudan politician **18** 166-167

GORDY, BERRY, JR. (born 1929), founder of the Motown Sound **6** 450-451

GORE, ALBERT, JR. (born 1948), Democratic U.S. representative, senator, and 45th vice president of the United States **6** 452-453

Gorenko, Anna Andreyevna *see* Akhmatova, Anna

GORGAS, JOSIAH (1818-1883), American soldier and educator **6** 453-454

GORGAS, WILLIAM CRAWFORD (1854-1920), American general and sanitarian **6** 454-455

GORGES, SIR FERDINANDO (1568-1647), English colonizer and soldier **6** 455-456

GORGIAS (c. 480-c. 376 BCE), Greek sophist philosopher and rhetorician **6** 456

GÖRING, HERMANN WILHELM (1893-1946), German politician and air force commander **6** 457-458

GORKY, ARSHILE (1905-1948), American painter **6** 458

GORKY, MAXIM (1868-1936), Russian author **6** 458-460

GORMAN, R.C. (Rudolph Carl Gorman; 1931-2005), Native American artist **23** 128-130

GORRIE, JOHN (1803-1855), American physician and inventor **21** 172-174

GORTON, SAMUELL (c. 1592-1677), English colonizer **6** 460

GOSHIRAKAWA (1127-1192), Japanese emperor **6** 460-461

GOSHO, HEINOSUKE (1902-1981), Japanese filmmaker **22** 199-200

Gospel music
Cooke, Sam **34** 63-64

Gösta *see* Gustavus II

Got, Bertrand de *see* Clement V

Gothart, Mathis Neithart *see* Grünewald, Matthias

GOTTFRIED VON STRASSBURG (c. 1165-c. 1215), German poet and romancer **6** 461-462

GOTTLIEB, ADOLPH (1903-1974), American Abstract Expressionist painter **6** 462-463

Gottrecht, Friedman *see* Beissel, Johann Conrad

GOTTSCHALK, LOUIS MOREAU (1829-1869), American composer and pianist **6** 463-464

GOTTWALD, KLEMENT (1896-1953), first Communist president of Czechoslovakia (1948-1953) **6** 464-466

GOUDIMEL, CLAUDE (c. 1514-1572), French composer **6** 466

GOUJON, JEAN (c. 1510-1568), French sculptor **6** 466-467

GOULART, JOÃO (1918-1976), Brazilian statesman **6** 467-469

GOULD, GLENN (1932-1982), Canadian musician **6** 469-470

GOULD, JAY (1836-1892), American financier and railroad builder **6** 470-472

GOULD, STEPHEN JAY (1941-2002), American paleontologist **6** 472-473

Goulden, Emmeline *see* Pankhurst, Emmeline

GOUNOD, CHARLES FRANÇOIS (1818-1893), French composer **6** 473-474

GOURLAY, ROBERT (1778-1863), British reformer in Canada **6** 474

GOURMONT, REMY DE (1858-1915), French author, critic, and essayist **6** 475

GOWER, JOHN (c. 1330-1408), English poet **6** 475-476

GOYA Y LUCIENTES, FRANCISCO DE PAULA JOSÉ DE (1746-1828), Spanish painter and printmaker **6** 476-478

Goyakla *see* Geronimo

GOYEN, JAN VAN (1596-1656), Dutch painter **6** 478-479

GOYTISOLO, JUAN (born 1931), Spanish writer **31** 143-144

GRACCHUS, GAIUS SEMPRONIUS (c. 154-121 BCE), member of a Roman plebeian family referred to as the Gracchi **6** 479-480

GRACCHUS, TIBERIUS SEMPRONIUS (c. 163-133 BCE), member of a Roman plebeian family referred to as the Gracchi **6** 479-480

GRACE, WILLIAM RUSSELL (1832-1904), Irish-born American entrepreneur and politician **6** 480-481

GRACIÁN Y MORALES, BALTASAR JERÓNIMO (1601-1658), Spanish writer **6** 481-482

GRADY, HENRY WOODFIN (1850-1889), American editor and orator **6** 482-483

GRAETZ, HEINRICH HIRSCH (1817-1891), German historian and biblical exegete **6** 483

GRAF, STEFFI (born 1969), German tennis player **30** 184-186

Graft
see Corruption, political (government)

Graham, John
see Phillips, David Graham

GRAHAM, KATHARINE MEYER (1917-2001), publisher who managed *The Washington Post* **6** 483-485

GRAHAM, MARTHA (1894-1991), American dancer and choreographer **6** 485-486

GRAHAM, OTTO (1921-2003), American football player and coach **21** 174-176

GRAHAM, SHEILAH (1904-1988), English-born American columnist **29** 174-176

GRAHAM, SYLVESTER (1794-1851), American reformer and temperance minister **6** 486-487

GRAHAM, WILLIAM FRANKLIN, JR. ("Billy"; born 1918), American evangelist **6** 487-488

GRAHAME, KENNETH (1859-1932), British author **28** 138-140

GRAINGER, PERCY (Percy Aldridge Grainger; George Percy Grainger; 1882-1961), Australian American musician **25** 160-161

GRAMSCI, ANTONIO (1891-1937), Italian writer and Communist leader **6** 488-489

GRANADOS, ENRIQUE (1867-1916), Spanish composer and pianist **6** 489-490

GRANATO, CAMMI (born 1971), American hockey player **32** 138-140

GRAND DUCHESS OLGA NIKOLAEVNA (Grand Duchess Olga Nikolaevna; 1895-1918), Russian grand duchess **28** 141-143

GRANDA, CHABUCA (Isabel Granda Larco; 1920-1983), Peruvian singer and songwriter **28** 143-144

GRANDVILLE, J.J. (Jean-Ignace-Isidore Gérard; 1803-1847), French artist and cartoonist **28** 144-146

GRANGE, RED (Harold Edward Grange; 1903-1991), American football player **19** 128-130
Rice, Grantland **34** 302-304

GRANT, CARY (born Archibald Alexander Leach; 1904-1986), English actor **6** 490-492
Fontaine, Joan **34** 121-124

GRANT, MADISON (1865-1937), American conservationist and eugenics supporter **31** 145-146

GRANT, ULYSSES SIMPSON (1822-1885), American general, president 1869-1877 **6** 492-494

GRANVILLE, CHRISTINE (Krystyna Skarbek; c. 1915-1952), Polish secret agent **27** 153-154

GRANVILLE, EVELYN BOYD (born 1924), African American mathematician **6** 494-496

GRASS, GÜNTER (born 1927), German novelist, playwright, and poet **6** 496-497

GRASSELLI, CAESAR AUGUSTIN (1850-1927), third generation to head the Grasselli Chemical Company **6** 497-498

GRASSO, ELLA T. (1919-1981), American politician **32** 140-142

GRATIAN (died c. 1155), Italian scholar, father of canon law **6** 498-499

GRATTAN, HENRY (1746-1820), Irish statesman and orator **6** 499

GRAU SAN MARTIN, RAMÓN (1887-1969), Cuban statesman and physician **6** 499-500

GRAUNT, JOHN (1620-1674), English merchant and civil servant **21** 176-178

GRAVES, EARL GILBERT, JR. (born 1935), African American publisher **23** 130-132

GRAVES, MICHAEL (born 1934), American Post-Modernist architect **6** 500-502

GRAVES, NANCY STEVENSON (1940-1995), American sculptor **6** 502-504

GRAVES, ROBERT RANKE (1895-1985), English author **6** 504-506

GRAY, ASA (1810-1888), American botanist **6** 506-507

GRAY, ELISHA (1835-1901), American inventor **29** 176-178

GRAY, HANNAH HOLBORN (born 1930), university administrator **6** 507-508

GRAY, ROBERT (1755-1806), American explorer **6** 508-509

GRAY, THOMAS (1716-1771), English poet **6** 509-510

GRAY, WILLIAM H., III (born 1941), first African American to be elected House Whip for the U.S. House of Representatives **6** 510-511

Grayson, David
see Baker, Ray Stannard

Great Balls of Fire (song)
Blackwell, Otis **34** 32-33

Great Britain (United Kingdom of Great Britain and Northern Ireland; island kingdom; northwestern Europe)
1603-1714 (STUART AND COMMONWEALTH)
1660-1685 (Charles II)
Godfrey, Edmund Berry **34** 141-143

Great Proletarian Cultural Revolution
see Cultural Revolution (China)

Great Purge (1936-38; Union of Soviet Socialist Republics)
perpetrators
Kirov, Sergei **34** 208-211
Yezhov, Nikolai **34** 387-389
victims
Kun, Béla **34** 221-223

Great Reform Act
see Reform Bill of 1832 (England)

GRECO, EL (1541-1614), Greek-born Spanish painter **6** 511-514

Greek art and architecture (classical)
influence of
Ludwig I of Bavaria **34** 244-246

Greek (language)
Kober, Alice **34** 213-214
Ventris, Michael **34** 360-362

Greek literature (classical)
influence of
Salutati, Coluccio **34** 318-319

GREELEY, ANDREW M. (born 1928), American Catholic priest, sociologist, and author **6** 514-515

GREELEY, HORACE (1811-1872), American editor and reformer **6** 515-517

GREELY, ADOLPHUS WASHINGTON (1844-1935), American soldier, explorer, and writer **6** 517-518

GREEN, CONSTANCE MCLAUGHLIN (1897-1975), American author and historian **6** 518-519

GREEN, EDITH STARRETT (1910-1987), United States congresswoman from Oregon (1954-1974) **6** 519-520

H

HAMLISCH, MARVIN (1944-2012), American composer and pianist **34** 151-153

HAMM, MIA (born 1972), American soccer player **30** 197-199

HAMM-BRÜCHER, HILDEGARD (born 1921), Free Democratic Party's candidate for the German presidency in 1994 **7** 101-103

HAMMARSKJÖLD, DAG (1905-1961), Swedish diplomat **7** 100-101

HAMMER, ARMAND (1898-1990), American entrepreneur and art collector **7** 103-104

HAMMERSTEIN, OSCAR CLENDENNING II (1895-1960), lyricist and librettist of the American theater **7** 104-106

HAMMETT, (SAMUEL) DASHIELL (1894-1961), American author **7** 106-108

HAMMOND, JAMES HENRY (1807-1864), American statesman **7** 108-109

HAMMOND, JOHN (1910-1987), American music producer **31** 155-156

HAMMOND, JOHN LAWRENCE LE BRETON (1872-1952), English historian **7** 108-109

HAMMOND, LUCY BARBARA (1873-1961), English historian **7** 109

HAMMURABI (1792-1750 BCE), king of Babylonia **7** 109-110

HAMPDEN, JOHN (1594-1643), English statesman **7** 110-111

HAMPTON, LIONEL (1908-2002), African American jazz musician **22** 211-213

HAMPTON, WADE (c. 1751-1835), American planter **7** 111-112

HAMPTON, WADE III (1818-1902), American statesman and Confederate general **7** 112

HAMSUN, KNUT (1859-1952), Norwegian novelist **7** 113-114

HAN FEI TZU (c. 280-233 BCE), Chinese statesman and philosopher **7** 124-125

Han Kao-tsu
see Liu Pang

HAN WU-TI (157-87 BCE), Chinese emperor **7** 136

HAN YÜ (768-824), Chinese author **7** 136-137

HANAFI, HASSAN (born 1935), Egyptian philosopher **7** 114

HANCOCK, JOHN (1737-1793), American statesman **7** 114-116

HANCOCK, LANG (Langley George Hancock; 1909-1992), Australian industrialist **34** 153-155

HAND, BILLINGS LEARNED (1872-1961), American jurist **7** 116

Händel, Georg Friedrich
see Handel, George Frederick

HANDEL, GEORGE FREDERICK (1685-1759), German-born English composer and organist **7** 116-119

HANDKE, PETER (born 1942), Austrian playwright, novelist, screenwriter, essayist, and poet **7** 119-121

HANDLER, ELLIOT (1916-2011), American toy manufacturer **34** 155-157

HANDLER, RUTH (Ruth Mosko; 1916-2002), American businesswoman **25** 183-185

HANDLIN, OSCAR (1915-2011), American historian **7** 121-122

Handschuchsheim, Ritter von
see Meinong, Alexius

HANDSOME LAKE (a.k.a. Hadawa' Ko; c. 1735-1815), Seneca spiritual leader **7** 122-123

HANDY, WILLIAM CHRISTOPHER (1873-1958), African American songwriter **7** 123-124
  Smith, Mamie **34** 339-340

HANEKE, MICHAEL (born 1942), Austrian filmmaker **33** 135-137

HANKS, NANCY (1927-1983), called the "mother of a million artists" for her work in building federal financial support for the arts and artists **7** 126-127

HANKS, TOM (Thomas Jeffrey Hanks; born 1956), American actor **23** 135-137

HANNA AND BARBERA (William Hanna, 1910-2001; Joseph Barbera, 1911-2006), American producers and directors of animated cartoons **28** 156-159

HANNA, MARCUS ALONZO (1837-1904), American businessman and politician **7** 127-128

Hanna, William
see Hanna and Barbera

HANNIBAL BARCA (247-183 BCE), Carthaginian general **7** 128-130

Hanover dynasty (Great Britain)
see Great Britain–1714-1901 (Hanover)

HANSBERRY, LORRAINE VIVIAN (1930-1965), American writer and a major figure on Broadway **7** 130-131

HANSEN, ALVIN (1887-1975), American economist **7** 131-132

Hansen, Emil
see Nolde, Emil

HANSEN, JULIA BUTLER (1907-1988), American politician **7** 132-133

HANSON, DUANE (1925-1990), American super-realist sculptor **7** 133-135

HANSON, HOWARD (1896-1981), American composer and educator **7** 135-136

HAPGOOD, NORMAN (1868-1937), American author and editor **7** 137-138

Hapsburg (European dynasty; ruled 1273-1918)
  Spain (ruled 1516-1700)
    Médicis, Marie de' **34** 254-255

HARA, KEI (1856-1921), Japanese statesman and prime minister 1918-1921 **7** 138

HARAND, IRENE (born Irene Wedl; 1900-1975), Austrian political and human rights activist **7** 139-145

HARAWI, ILYAS AL- (Elias Harawi; 1930-2006), president of Lebanon **7** 145-146

HARBURG, EDGAR YIPSEL (Irwin Hochberg; E.Y. Harburg; 1896-1981), American lyricist **26** 140-142

Hardenberg, Baron Friedrich Leopold von
see Novalis

HARDENBERG, PRINCE KARL AUGUST VON (1750-1822), Prussian statesman **7** 146-147

Harder They Come, The (film)
  Cliff, Jimmy **34** 61-62

HARDIE, JAMES KEIR (1856-1915), Scottish politician **7** 147-148

HARDING, FLORENCE KLING (Florence Kling DeWolfe Harding; 1860-1924), American first lady **28** 159-161

Harding, Stephen, Saint
see Stephen Harding, Saint

HARDING, WARREN GAMALIEL (1865-1923), American statesman, president 1921-1923 **7** 148-149

Hardouin, Jules
see Mansart, Jules Hardouin

HARDY, HARRIET (1905-1993), American pathologist **7** 150

HARDY, THOMAS (1840-1928), English novelist, poet, and dramatist **7** 150-152

HARE, ROBERT (1781-1858), American chemist **7** 152-153

HARGRAVES, EDWARD HAMMOND (1816-1891), Australian publicist **7** 153-154

HARGREAVES, ALISON (1962-1995), British mountain climber **26** 142-144

HARING, KEITH (1958-1990), American artist tied to New York graffiti art of the 1980s **7** 154-155

HARINGTON, JOHN (1560-1612), English author and courtier **21** 193-195

HARIRI, RAFIC (1944-2005), politician and businessman **28** 161-163

HARJO, JOY (Born 1951), Native American author, musician, and artist **25** 185-187

HARJO, SUZAN SHOWN (born 1945), Native American activist **18** 183-185

HARKNESS, GEORGIA (1891-1974), American Methodist and ecumenical theologian **7** 155-156

HARLAN, JOHN MARSHALL (1833-1911), American jurist **7** 156-157

HARLAN, JOHN MARSHALL (1899-1971), U.S. Supreme Court justice **7** 157-159

Harlem (New York City)
Robinson, Bill "Bojangles" **34** 306-308

HARLEY, ROBERT (1st Earl of Oxford and Earl Mortimer; 1661-1724), English statesman **7** 159-160

HARLOW, JEAN (1911-1937), American film actress **29** 182-184

Harmonica (musical instrument)
Thornton, Willie Mae **34** 346-348

HARNACK, ADOLF VON (1851-1930), German theologian **7** 160

HARNETT, WILLIAM MICHAEL (1848-1892), American painter **7** 160-161

Harold "Fairhair"
see Harold I

Harold Haardraade
see Harold III

HAROLD I (c. 840-933), king of Norway 860-930 **7** 161-162

HAROLD II (Harold Godwinson; died 1066), Anglo-Saxon king of England of 1066 **7** 162

HAROLD III (1015-1066), king of Norway 1047-1066 **7** 163

Harold the Ruthless
see Harold III

HARPER, FRANCES (Frances Ellen Watkins Harper; 1825-1911), African American author, abolitionist and women's rights activist **18** 185-187

HARPER, JAMES (1795-1869), American publisher **22** 213-216

HARPER, MARTHA MATILDA (1857-1950), American entrepreneur **31** 157-158

HARPER, STEPHEN (born 1959), Canadian prime minister **27** 159-161

HARPER, WILLIAM RAINEY (1856-1906), American educator and biblical scholar **7** 163-164

HARPUR, CHARLES (1813-1866), Australian poet and author **22** 216-218

HARRIMAN, EDWARD HENRY (1848-1909), American railroad executive **7** 164-165

HARRIMAN, PAMELA (1920-1997), American ambassador and patrician **18** 187-189

HARRIMAN, W. AVERELL (1891-1986), American industrialist, financier, and diplomat **7** 165-166

HARRINGTON, JAMES (1611-1677), English political theorist **7** 166-167

HARRINGTON, MICHAEL (1928-1989), American political activist and educator **7** 167-169

HARRIOT, THOMAS (1560-1621), English scientist and mathematician **23** 137-139

HARRIS, ABRAM LINCOLN, JR. (1899-1963), African American economist **7** 169-171

HARRIS, BARBARA CLEMENTINE (born 1930), African American activist and Anglican bishop **7** 171-172

HARRIS, FRANK (1856-1931), Irish-American author and editor **7** 172-173

HARRIS, JOEL CHANDLER (1848-1908), American writer **7** 173-174

HARRIS, LADONNA (born 1931), Native American activist **18** 189-191

HARRIS, PATRICIA ROBERTS (1924-1985), first African American woman in the U.S. Cabinet **7** 174-175

HARRIS, ROY (1898-1979), American composer **7** 175-176

HARRIS, TOWNSEND (1804-1878), American merchant and diplomat **7** 176-177

HARRIS, WILLIAM TORREY (1835-1909), American educator and philosopher **7** 177-178

HARRISON, BENJAMIN (1833-1901), American statesman, president 1889-1893 **7** 178-179

HARRISON, CAROLINE LAVINIA SCOTT (1832-1892), American first lady **30** 199-202

HARRISON, GEORGE (1943-2005), English musician **25** 187-191

HARRISON, JAMES (born c. 1936), Australian blood donor **32** 149-150

HARRISON, PETER (1716-1775), American architect and merchant **7** 179-180

HARRISON, WILLIAM HENRY (1773-1841), American statesman, president 1841 **7** 180-181

HARRYHAUSEN, RAY (1920-2013), American animator **34** 157-163

HARSHA (Harshavardhana; c. 590-647), king of Northern India 606-612 **7** 181-182

Hart, Emma
see Hamilton, Lady; Willard, Emma Hart

HART, GARY W. (born 1936), American political campaign organizer, U.S. senator, and presidential candidate **7** 182-184

HART, HERBERT LIONEL ADOLPHUS (1907-1992), British legal philosopher **22** 218-219

HART, LORENZ (1895-1943), American lyricist **29** 184-186

HARTE, FRANCIS BRET (1837-1902), American poet and fiction writer **7** 184-185

HARTLEY, DAVID (1705-1757), British physician and philosopher **7** 185

HARTLEY, MARSDEN (1877-1943), American painter **7** 186

HARTSHORNE, CHARLES (1897-2000), American theologian **7** 186-187

HARUN AL-RASHID (766-809), Abbasid caliph of Baghdad 786-809 **7** 188

HARUNOBU, SUZUKI (c. 1725-1770), Japanese painter and printmaker **7** 188-189

HARVARD, JOHN (1607-1638), English philanthropist **21** 195-197

Harvard University (Cambridge, Massachusetts)
architecture
Koolhaas, Rem **34** 214-217

HARVEY, CYRUS (1925-2011), American entrepreneur **32** 150-152

HARVEY, WILLIAM (1578-1657), English physician **7** 189-190

HARWELL, ERNIE (William Earnest Harwell; 1918-2010), American sports broadcaster **30** 202-204

HARWOOD, GWEN (nee Gwendoline Nessie Foster; 1920-1995), Australian poet **26** 144-146

HASAN, IBN AL-HAYTHAM (c. 966-1039), Arab physicist, astronomer, and mathematician **7** 190-191

Hasan, Mansur ben
see Firdausi

Hasan Ali Shah
see Aga Khan

Hasan ibn-Hani, al-
see Abu Nuwas

HAŠEK, JAROSLAV (1883-1923), Czech writer **31** 159-160

Hashomer Hatzair (Zionist youth group)
Anielewicz, Mordechai **34** 11-13

HASKINS, CHARLES HOMER (1870-1937), American historian **7** 191-192

Hasong, Prince
see Sonjo

HASSAM, FREDERICK CHILDE (1859-1935), American impressionist painter **7** 192

HASSAN, MOULEY (King Hassan II; 1929-1999), inherited the throne of Morocco in 1961 **7** 194-195

HASSAN, MUHAMMAD ABDILLE (1864-1920), Somali politico-religious leader and poet **7** 194-195

HASTINGS, PATRICK GARDINER (1880-1952), British lawyer and politician **22** 219-221

HASTINGS, WARREN (1732-1818), English statesman **7** 195-196

HATCH, WILLIAM HENRY (1833-1896), American reformer and politician **7** 196

HATFIELD, MARK (1922-2001), American politician and educator **33** 137-139

Hathorne, Nathaniel
see Hawthorne, Nathaniel

HATSHEPSUT (ruled 1503-1482 BCE), Egyptian queen **7** 196-197

HATTA, MOHAMMAD (1902-1980), a leader of the Indonesian nationalist movement (1920s-1945) and a champion of non-alignment and of socialism grounded in Islam **7** 197-199

HAUPTMAN, HERBERT AARON (1917-2011), American mathematician **24** 165-167

HAUPTMANN, GERHART JOHANN ROBERT (1862-1946), German dramatist and novelist **7** 199-201

HAUSHOFER, KARL (1869-1946), German general and geopolitician **7** 201

HAUSSMANN, BARON GEORGES EUGÈNE (1809-1891), French prefect of the Seine **7** 201-202

Hauteclocque, Philippe Marie de
see Leclerc, Jacques Philippe

HAVEL, VACLAV (1936-2011), playwright and human rights activist who became the president of Czechoslovakia **7** 202-205

HAVEMEYER, HENRY OSBORNE (1847-1907), American businessman **22** 222-224

HAVILAND, LAURA SMITH (1808-1898), American anti-slavery activist **27** 161-163

HAWES, HARRIET ANN BOYD (1871-1945), American archeologist **22** 224-225

HAWKE, ROBERT JAMES LEE (born 1929), Australian Labor prime minister **7** 205-206

Hawkesbury, Baron
see Liverpool, 2nd Earl of

HAWKING, STEPHEN WILLIAM (born 1942), British physicist and mathematician **7** 206-208

HAWKINS, COLEMAN (1904-1969), American jazz musician **7** 208-210

HAWKINS, SIR JOHN (1532-1595), English naval commander **7** 210-211

HAWKS, HOWARD WINCHESTER (1896-1977), American film director **22** 225-226

HAWKSMOOR, NICHOLAS (1661-1736), English architect **7** 211-212

HAWTHORNE, NATHANIEL (1804-1864), American novelist **7** 212-215

HAY, JOHN (1838-1905), American statesman **7** 215-216

HAYA DE LA TORRE, VICTOR RAUL (1895-1979), Peruvian political leader and theorist **7** 216-217

HAYDEN, FERDINAND VANDIVEER (1829-1887), American geologist and explorer **22** 227-229

HAYDEN, ROBERT EARL (1913-1980), African American poet **22** 229-231

HAYDEN, THOMAS EMMET (born 1939), American writer and political activist **7** 217-219

HAYDN, FRANZ JOSEPH (1732-1809), Austrian composer **7** 219-221

HAYEK, FRIEDRICH A. VON (1899-1992), Austrian-born British free market economist, social philosopher, and Nobel Laureate **7** 221-223

HAYES, HELEN (1900-1993), American actress **7** 223-224

HAYES, LUCY WEBB (Lucy Ware Webb Hayes; 1831-1889), American Fist Lady **28** 163-166

HAYES, CARDINAL PATRICK JOSEPH (1867-1938), American cardinal **7** 224-225

HAYES, ROLAND (1887-1977), African American classical singer **7** 225-227

HAYES, RUTHERFORD BIRCHARD (1822-1893), American statesman, president 1877-1881 **7** 227-228

HAYES, WOODY (Wayne Woodrow "Woody"; 1913-1987), American football coach **33** 139-141

HAYEZ, FRANCISCO (1791-1882), Italian painter and printmaker **32** 152-154

HAYFORD, J. E. CASELY (1866-1903), Gold Coast politician, journalist, and educator **7** 228-230

HAYKAL, MUHAMMAD HUSAIN (born 1923), Egyptian journalist and editor of *al-Ahram* (1957-1974) **7** 230-231

HAYNE, ROBERT YOUNG (1791-1839), American politician **7** 231-232

HAYNES, ELWOOD (1857-1925), American inventor and businessman **22** 231-234

HAYS, WILL (William Harrison Hays; 1879-1954), American film censor **21** 197-199

HAYWOOD, ELIZA (Eliza Fowler Haywood; 1693-1756), English author **27** 163-165

HAYWOOD, WILLIAM DUDLEY (1869-1928), American labor leader **7** 232-233

HAYWORTH, RITA (born Margarita Carmen Cansino; 1918-1987), American actress **7** 233-235

HAZA, OFRA (1959-2000), Israeli singer **24** 167-169

Hazaken (Elder)
see Shammai

HAZEN, ELIZABETH LEE (1885-1975), American scientist **34** 163-165

HAZLITT, WILLIAM (1778-1830), English literary and social critic **7** 235-236

HEAD, EDITH (1898-1981), American costume designer **18** 191-193

HEADE, MARTIN JOHNSON (1819-1904), American painter **7** 236

HEALY, BERNADINE (1944-2011), American physician and administrator **7** 237-238

HEANEY, SEAMUS JUSTIN (1939-2013), Irish poet, author, and editor **7** 238-240

HEARN, LAFCADIO (1850-1904), European-born American author **7** 240

HEARNE, SAMUEL (1745-1792), English explorer **7** 241-242

HEARST, GEORGE (1820-1891), American publisher and politician **7** 242

HEARST, PATRICIA (born 1954), kidnapped heiress who became a bank robber **7** 242-243

HEARST, PHOEBE APPERSON (1842-1919), American philanthropist **27** 165-167

HEARST, WILLIAM RANDOLPH (1863-1951), American publisher and politician **7** 243-244

HEARTFIELD, JOHN (1891-1968), German artist **32** 154-157

HEATH, EDWARD RICHARD GEORGE (1916-2005), prime minister of Great Britain (1970-1974) **7** 244-246

Herzfelde, Helmut
see Heartfield, John

HERZL, THEODOR (1860-1904), Hungarian-born Austrian Zionist author **33** 141-143

HERZOG, CHAIM (1918-1997), president of the State of Israel **7** 354-355

HERZOG, ROMAN (born 1934), president of the German Federal Constitutional Court (1987-1994) and president of Germany **7** 355-357

HERZOG, WERNER (Werner Stipetic; born 1942), German film director and producer **25** 194-197

HESBURGH, THEODORE MARTIN (born 1917), activist American Catholic priest who was president of Notre Dame (1952-1987) **7** 357-358

HESCHEL, ABRAHAM JOSHUA (1907-1972), Polish-American Jewish theologian **7** 358-359

HESELTINE, MICHAEL (born 1933), British Conservative politician **7** 359-361

HESIOD (flourished c. 700 BCE), Greek poet **7** 361-362

HESS, MYRA (1890-1965), British pianist **27** 169-171

HESS, VICTOR FRANCIS (1883-1964), Austrian-American physicist **7** 362-363

HESS, WALTER RICHARD RUDOLF (1894-1987), deputy reichsführer for Adolf Hitler (1933-1941) **7** 363-365

HESS, WALTER RUDOLF (1881-1973), Swiss neurophysiologist **7** 365

HESSE, EVA (1936-1970), American sculptor **7** 365-367

HESSE, HERMANN (1877-1962), German novelist **7** 367-369

HESSE, MARY B. (born 1924), British philosopher **7** 369-371

HEVESY, GEORGE CHARLES DE (1885-1966), Hungarian chemist **7** 371

HEWITT, ABRAM STEVENS (1822-1903), American politician and manufacturer **7** 371-372

HEYDLER, JOHN (1869-1956), American sports executive **32** 161-163

HEYDRICH, REINHARD (1904-1942), German architect of the Holocaust **20** 176-178

HEYERDAHL, THOR (1914-2002), Norwegian explorer, anthropologist and author **18** 194-196

HEYSE, PAUL JOHANN LUDWIG (1830-1914), German author **7** 372-373

HEYWOOD, THOMAS (1573/1574-1641), English playwright **7** 373-374

HIAWATHA (c. 1450), Native American Leader **23** 143-145

HICKOK, JAMES BUTLER ("Wild Bill"; 1837-1876), American gunfighter, scout, and spy **7** 374-375

HICKS, BEATRICE (1919-1979), American engineer **31** 163-164

HICKS, EDWARD (1780-1849), American folk painter **7** 375

HIDALGO Y COSTILLA, MIGUEL (1753-1811), Mexican revolutionary priest **7** 375-377

HIDAYAT, SADIQ (1903-1951), Persian author **7** 377-378

Hideyoshi
see Toyotomi Hideyoshi

Higgins, Margaret
see Sanger, Margaret

HIGGINS, MARGUERITE (1920-1966), American journalist **7** 378-380

HIGGINSON, THOMAS WENTWORTH (1823-1911), American reformer and editor **7** 380

HIGHTOWER, ROSELLA (1920-2008), Native American dancer **26** 154-156

HILBERT, DAVID (1862-1943), German mathematician **33** 143-146

Hildebrand
see Gregory VII, Pope

HILDEBRANDT, JOHANN LUCAS VON (1663-1745), Austrian architect **7** 380-381

HILDRETH, RICHARD (1807-1865), American historian and political theorist **7** 382

HILFIGER, TOMMY (born 1952), American fashion designer **19** 144-146

HILL, ANITA (born 1956), African American lawyer and professor **7** 382-385

HILL, ARCHIBALD VIVIAN (1886-1977), English physiologist **7** 385-386

HILL, BENJAMIN HARVEY (1823-1882), American politician **7** 386-387

HILL, BENNY (Alfred Hawthorn Hill; 1924-1992), English comedian **28** 170-172

HILL, HERBERT (1924-2004), American scholar and civil rights activist **7** 387-388

HILL, JAMES JEROME (1838-1916), American railroad builder **7** 388-389

HILL, ROWLAND (1795-1879), British educator, postal reformer, and administrator **21** 202-204

HILLARY, EDMUND (1919-2008), New Zealander explorer and mountaineer **7** 389-390

Hillel Hazaken
see Hillel I

HILLEL I (c. 60 BCE -c. 10 A.D.), Jewish scholar and teacher **7** 390-391

HILLEMAN, MAURICE RALPH (1919-2005), American microbiologist **26** 156-158

HILLIARD, NICHOLAS (c. 1547-1619), English painter **7** 391-392

HILLMAN, SIDNEY (1887-1946), Lithuanian-born American labor leader **7** 392-393

HILLQUIT, MORRIS (1869-1933), Russian-born American lawyer and author **7** 393-394

HILLS, CARLA ANDERSON (born 1934), Republican who served three presidents as lawyer, cabinet member, and U.S. trade representative **7** 394-396

HILTON, BARRON (William Barron Hilton; born 1927), American businessman **19** 146-148

HILTON, CONRAD (1887-1979), American hotelier **20** 178-180

HIMES, CHESTER BOMAR (1909-1984), American author **22** 242-244

HIMMELFARB, GERTRUDE (born 1922), American professor, writer, and scholar **7** 396-398

HIMMLER, HEINRICH (1900-1945), German Nazi leader **7** 398-399

HINDEMITH, PAUL (1895-1963), German composer **7** 399-400

HINDENBURG, PAUL LUDWIG HANS VON BENECKENDORFF UND VON (1847-1934), German field marshal, president 1925-1934 **7** 400-401

HINE, LEWIS WICKES (1874-1940), American photographer **28** 172-174

Hiner, Cincinnatus
see Miller, Joaquin

HINES, GREGORY OLIVER (1946-2003), American dancer and actor **7** 401-403
Robinson, Bill "Bojangles" **34** 306-308

HINKLER, BERT (1892-1933), Australian aviator **34** 169-171

HINOJOSA, ROLANDO (born 1929), Hispanic-American author **7** 403-405

HINSHELWOOD, SIR CYRIL NORMAN (1897-1967), English chemist **7** 405-406

HINTON, SUSAN ELOISE (born 1950), American novelist and screenwriter **7** 406-407

HYDE, IDA HENRIETTA (1857-1945), American physiologist and educator **22** 252-254

HYMAN, FLO (Flora Jean Hyman; 1954-1986), American volleyball player **26** 165-167

HYMAN, LIBBIE HENRIETTA (1888-1969), American zoologist **8** 83-84

HYNDE, CHRISSIE (born 1951), American musician **34** 180-182

HYPATIA OF ALEXANDRIA (370-415), Greek mathematician and philosopher **8** 85

Hypochondriack, The
see Boswell, James

I

IACOCCA, LIDO (LEE) ANTHONY (born 1924), American automobile magnate **8** 86-88

IBÁÑEZ DEL CAMPO, CARLOS (1877-1960), Chilean general and president **8** 88

IBÁRRURI GÓMEZ, DOLORES (1895-1989), voice of the Republican cause in the Spanish Civil War **8** 88-90

IBERVILLE, SIEUR D' (Pierre le Moyne; 1661-1706), Canadian soldier, naval captain, and adventurer **8** 90-91

IBN AL-ARABI, MUHYI AL-DIN (1165-1240), Spanish-born Moslem poet, philosopher, and mystic **8** 91

IBN BAJJA, ABU BAKR MUHHAMAD (c. 1085-1139), Arab philosopher and scientist **29** 207-209

IBN BATTUTA, MUHAMMAD (1304-1368/69), Moslem traveler and author **8** 91-92

IBN GABIROL, SOLOMON BEN JUDAH (c. 1021-c. 1058), Spanish Hebrew poet and philosopher **8** 92

IBN HAZM, ABU MUHAMMAD ALI (994-1064), Spanish-born Arab theologian and jurist **8** 93

IBN KHALDUN, ABD AL-RAHMAN IBN MUHAMMAD (1332-1406), Arab historian, philosopher, and statesman **8** 93-94

Ibn Rushd
see Averroës

IBN SAUD, ABD AL-AZIZ (1880-1953), Arab politician, founder of Saudi Arabia **8** 94-95

Ibn Sina
see Avicenna

IBN TASHUFIN, YUSUF (died 1106), North African Almoravid ruler **8** 95-96

IBN TUFAYL, ABU BAKR MUHAMMAD (c. 1110-1185), Spanish Moslem philosopher and physician **8** 96

IBN TUMART, MUHAMMAD (c. 1080-1130), North African Islamic theologian **8** 96-97

IBRAHIM PASHA (1789-1848), Turkish military and administrative leader **8** 97-98

IBSEN, HENRIK (1828-1906), Norwegian playwright **8** 98-100

IBUKA, MASARU (1908-1997), Japanese inventor and businessman **28** 184-186

ICHIKAWA, KON (1915-2008), Japanese filmmaker **29** 209-211

ICKES, HAROLD LECLAIRE (1874-1952), American statesman **8** 100-101

ICTINUS (flourished 2nd half of 5th century BCE), Greek architect **8** 101

Idle, Eric, (born 1943), British comedian, actor, and singer
Palin, Michael **34** 287-289

IDRIS I (1889-1983), king of Libya 1950-69 **8** 102

IDRISI, MUHAMMAD IBN MUHAMMAD AL- (1100-c. 1165), Arab geographer **8** 102-103

IGLESIAS, ENRIQUE V. (born 1930), Uruguayan economist, banker, and public official **8** 106-107

IGNATIUS OF ANTIOCH, ST. (died c. 115), Early Christian bishop and theologian **8** 107-108

IGNATIUS OF LOYOLA, ST. (1491-1556), Spanish soldier, founder of Jesuits **8** 108-109

IKEDA, DAISAKU (born 1928), Japanese Buddhist writer and religious leader **8** 109-110

IKEDA, HAYATO (1899-1965), Japanese prime minister **29** 211-213

IKHNATON (ruled 1379-1362 BCE), pharaoh of Egypt **8** 110-111

ILIESCU, ION (born 1930), president of Romania (1990-96, 2000-04) **8** 111-112

ILITCH, MIKE (born 1929), American businessman **19** 163-165

ILLICH, IVAN (1926-2002), theologian, educator, and social critic **8** 112-114

IMAI, TADASHI (1912-1991), Japanese film director **22** 255-257

IMAM, ALHADJI ABUBAKAR (1911-1981), Nigerian writer and teacher **8** 114-115

IMAMURA, SHOHEI (1926-2006), Japanese film director and producer **25** 207-210

IMAOKA, SHINICHIRO (1881-1988), progressive and liberal religious leader in Japan **8** 115

IMF
see International Monetary Fund (established 1945)

IMHOTEP (c. 3000 BCE-c. 2950 BCE), Egyptian vizier, architect, priest, astronomer, and magician-physician **8** 116-117

Imouthes
see Imhotep

In the Realm of the Senses (film)
Oshima, Nagisa **34** 282-284

INCE, THOMAS (1882-1924), American film producer and director **21** 213-215

INCHBALD, ELIZABETH (Elizabeth Simpson; 1753-1821), British novelist and playwright **27** 174-176

Indian music (Asia)
Singh, Jagjit **34** 328-329

Indonesia, Republic of (nation, southeast Asia)
independence (1945)
Koolhaas, Rem **34** 214-217

Indulgences (Roman Catholic Church)
Innocent VIII **34** 183-185

Inflation (economics)
Brazil
Franco, Itamar **34** 130-132

INGE, WILLIAM RALPH (1860-1954), Church of England clergyman, scholar, social critic, and writer **8** 118-119

INGENHOUSZ, JAN (1730-1799), Dutch physician, chemist, and engineer **8** 119-120

INGERSOLL, ROBERT GREEN (1833-1899), American lawyer and lecturer **8** 120-121

INGLIS, ELSIE MAUD (1824-1917), British physician and suffragist **26** 168-170

Ingolstadt, University of (West Germany)
Ludwig I of Bavaria **34** 244-246

INGRES, JEAN AUGUSTE DOMINIQUE (1780-1867), French painter **8** 121-123

INNESS, GEORGE (1825-1894), American painter **8** 123-124

INNIS, HAROLD ADAMS (1894-1952), Canadian political economist **8** 124-125

INNOCENT III (Lothar of Segni; 1160/1161-1216), pope 1198-1216 **8** 125-127

INNOCENT IV (Sinibaldo de' Fieschi; died 1254), pope 1243-1254 **23** 165-167
Faliero, Marino **34** 111-113

INNOCENT VIII (Giovanni Battista Cibo; 1432-1492), pope 1484-1492 **34** 183-185

Ives, James Merritt, (1824-1895)
see Currier and Ives

IVORY, JAMES (born 1928), American film director and producer **20** 186-188

IWAKURA, TOMOMI (1825-1883), Japanese statesman **8** 160-161

IWERKS, UB (1901-1971), American animator **31** 178-179

IYENGAR, B.K.S. (Bellur Krishnamachar Sundararaja Iyengar; born 1918), Indian yoga educator and author **27** 178-180

IZETBEGOVIC, ALIJA (1926-2003), president of the eight-member presidency of the Republic of Bosnia-Herzegovina **8** 161-163

Izvekov, Sergei Mikhailovich
see Pimen I, Patriarch of Moscow

J

JA JA OF OPOBO (c. 1820-1891), Nigerian politician **8** 201-204

JABBAR, KAREEM ABDUL (Ferdinand Lewis Alcinor, Junior ; born 1947), American basketball player **8** 164-165
Wooden, John **34** 384-386

JABER AL-SABAH, JABER AL-AHMAD AL- (1926-2006), emir of Kuwait **8** 166-167

JABIR IBN HAYYAN (flourished latter 8th century), Arab scholar and alchemist **8** 167

JABOTINSKY, VLADIMIR EVGENEVICH (1880-1940), Russian Zionist **8** 167-168

JACKSON, ANDREW (1767-1845), American president 1829-1837 **8** 168-172

JACKSON, HELEN HUNT (1830-1885), American novelist **8** 172

JACKSON, HENRY MARTIN (Scoop; 1912-1983), United States senator and proponent of anti-Soviet foreign policy **8** 172-174

JACKSON, JESSE LOUIS (born 1941), U.S. civil rights leader and presidential candidate **8** 174-176

JACKSON, JOE (David Ian "Joe" Jackson; born 1954), British songwriter and musician **34** 189-190

JACKSON, JOHN HUGHLINGS (1835-1911), British neurologist **30** 214-216

JACKSON, MAHALIA (1911-1972), American singer **19** 166-168
Blackwell, Otis **34** 32-33

JACKSON, MAYNARD HOLBROOK, JR. (1938-2003), first African American mayor of Atlanta, Georgia (1973-81 and 1989-1993) **8** 176-178

JACKSON, MICHAEL JOE (1958-2009), American singer **8** 178-180

JACKSON, NELL (1929-1988), American track and field athlete and coach **30** 216-218

JACKSON, PETER (born 1961), New Zealander actor and filmmaker **25** 211-213

JACKSON, RACHEL (Rachel Donelson Jackson; 1767-1828), American first lady **31** 180-181

JACKSON, REGINALD "REGGIE" MARTINEZ (born 1946), African American baseball player **8** 180-182

JACKSON, ROBERT HOUGHWOUT (1892-1954), American jurist **8** 182-183

JACKSON, SHIRLEY ANN (born 1946), African American physicist **8** 183-184

JACKSON, THOMAS JONATHAN ("Stonewall"; 1824-1863), American Confederate general **8** 184-185

JACKSON, WANDA (born 1937), American singer **34** 191-193

JACOB, JOHN EDWARD (born 1934), African American activist and president of the National Urban League **8** 185-188

JACOBI, ABRAHAM (1830-1919), American physician **8** 188-189

JACOBI, DEREK (born 1938), British actor **19** 168-170

JACOBI, FRIEDRICH HEINRICH (1743-1819), German philosopher **8** 189-190

JACOBI, MARY PUTNAM (1834-1906), American physician **8** 188-189

JACOBS, ALETTA HENRIETTE (1854-1929), Dutch physician and social reformer **26** 171-173

JACOBS, FRANCES (1843-1892), American activist **31** 182-184

JACOBS, HARRIET A. (1813-1897), runaway slave and abolitionist **8** 190-193

JACOBS, JANE (Jane Butzner; 1916-2006), Canadian author and urban planning activist **27** 181-183

JACOBSEN, JENS PETER (1847-1885), Danish author **8** 193-194

JACOBSON, DAN (born 1929), South African author **22** 266-268

Jacopo, Giovanni Battista di
see Rosso, Il

JACOPONE DA TODI (c. 1236-1306), Italian poet and mystic **8** 194

JACQUARD, JOSEPH MARIE (1752-1834), French inventor **21** 216-218

JAELL, MARIE TRAUTMANN (1846-1925), French pianist and composer **24** 189-191

Jafar, Abu
see Mansur, al-

JAGGER, MICHAEL PHILIP ("Mick"; born 1944), lead singer for the Rolling Stones **8** 194-196

JAHAN, NUR (Mihrunnissa; Nur Mahal; 1577-1646), Indian queen **24** 191-193

JAHANGIR (1569-1627), fourth Mughal emperor of India **8** 196-199

JAHN, HELMUT (born 1940), German-American architect **8** 199-201

Jalal al-Din, (died 1231), shah of Khwarizm
Ögedei Khan **34** 278-280

Jalal-ed-Din Rumi
see Rumi, Jalal ed-Din

JAMERSON, JAMES (1936-1983), American bassist **30** 218-220

JAMES I (1394-1437), king of Scotland 1406-1437 **8** 206-207

JAMES I (James VI of Scotland; 1566-1625), king of England 1603-1625 **8** 204-206

JAMES II (1633-1701), king of England, Scotland, and Ireland 1685-1688 **8** 207-208
relatives
Henrietta Maria of France **34** 167-169

JAMES III (1451-1488), king of Scotland 1460-1488 **8** 208-209

James VI, king of Scotland
see James I (king of England)

James VII, king of Scotland
see James II (king of England)

JAMES, DANIEL, JR. ("Chappie"; 1920-1978), first African American man in the U.S. to become a four star general **8** 209-211

JAMES, ETTA (Jamesetta Hawkins; 1938-2012), African American singer **25** 213-215

JAMES, HENRY (1843-1916), American novelist **8** 211-212

JAMES, JESSE WOODSON (1847-1882), American outlaw **8** 212-213

JAMES, P. D. (born 1920), British crime novelist **8** 213-215

JAMES, WILLIAM (1842-1910), American philosopher and psychologist **8** 215-217

JAMESON, SIR LEANDER STARR (1853-1917), British colonial administrator **8** 218

JAMI (Maulana Nur al-Din Abd al-Rahman; 1414-1492), Persian poet **8** 218-219

K

KACZYNSKI, TED (born 1942), American terrorist **33** 165-167

KADALIE, CLEMENTS (c. 1896-1951), South Africa's first Black national trade union leader **8** 401-402

KADÁR, JÁN (1918-1979), Czech filmmaker and screenwriter **25** 227-229

KÁDÁR, JÁNOS (1912-1989), Hungarian statesman **8** 402-403

Kael, Pauline, American film critic
Sarris, Andrew **34** 319-321

KAFKA, FRANZ (1883-1924), Czech-born German novelist and short-story writer **8** 403-406

KAHANAMOKU, DUKE (1890-1968), Hawaiian swimmer **20** 197-199

KAHLO, FRIDA (1907-1954), Mexican painter **8** 406-407

KAHN, ALBERT (1869-1942), American architect **8** 407-408

KAHN, LOUIS I. (1901-1974), American architect **8** 408-410

KAIFU TOSHIKI (born 1931), Japanese prime minister (1989-1991) **8** 410-411

KAISER, GEORG (1878-1945), German playwright **8** 411-412

KAISER, HENRY JOHN (1882-1967). American industrialist **8** 412-413

Kakuyu
see Toba Sojo

KALAKAUA, DAVID (1836-1891), king of Hawaiian Islands 1874-1891 **8** 413-414

KALASHNIKOV, MIKHAIL (Mikhail Timofeyevich Kalashnikov; (1919-2013)), Russian inventor **28** 190-192

KALIDASA (flourished 4th-5th century), Indian poet and dramatist **8** 414-415

KALINE, AL (born 1934), American baseball player **33** 167-170

Kalish, Sonya
see Tucker, Sophie

KALMAN, RUDOLF EMIL (born 1930), Hungarian scientist **24** 199-201

KALMUS, NATALIE (Natalie Mabelle Dunfee; c. 1883-1965), American inventor and cinematographer **21** 233-235

Kamako
see Fujiwara Kamatari

Kamakura Period
see Japan–1185-1338

KAMARAJ, KUMARASWAMI (1903-1975), Indian political leader **8** 415

KAMBONA, OSCAR (1928-1997), Tanzanian statesman **32** 175-177

KAMEHAMEHA I (c. 1758-1819), king of the Hawaiian Islands 1795-1819 **8** 416

KAMEHAMEHA III (c. 1814-1854), king of the Hawaiian Islands 1825-1854 **8** 416-417

KAMENEV, LEV BORISOVICH (1883-1936), Russian politician **8** 417-418
Kirov, Sergei **34** 208-211
Yezhov, Nikolai **34** 387-389

KAMENY, FRANKLIN (1925-2011), American activist **34** 196-198

KAMERLINGH ONNES, HEIKE (1853-1926), Dutch physicist **8** 418-420

Kamisori
see Tojo, Hideki

Kamitsumiya no Miko
see Shotoku Taishi

KAMMU (737-806), Japanese emperor 781-806 **8** 420

KAMROWSKI, GEROME (1914-2004), American artist **27** 197-199

KANDER, JOHN (born 1927), American composer and lyricist **21** 235-237

KANDINSKY, WASSILY (1866-1944), Russian painter **8** 420-422

KANE, JOHN (1860-1934), Scottish-born American primitive painter **8** 422

KANE, PAUL (1810-1871), Canadian painter and writer **8** 422-423

K'ANG-HSI (1654-1722), Chinese emperor 1661-1722 **8** 423-426

K'ANG YU-WEI (1858-1927), Chinese scholar and philosopher **8** 426-428

Kanis, Saint Peter
see Peter Canisius, Saint

KANISHKA (c. 78-c. 103), Kashan ruler **8** 428-429

Kankan Musa
see Musa Mansa

Kano school
see Japanese art–Kano school

KANT, IMMANUEL (1724-1804), German philosopher **8** 430-432

KAO-TSUNG (1107-1187), Chinese emperor **8** 433

KAPIOLANI, JULIA ESTHER (1834-1899), Hawaiian dignitary **31** 185-186

KAPITSA, PYOTR LEONIDOVICH (1894-1934), Soviet physicist **8** 433-435

KAPLAN, MORDECAI MENAHEM (1881-1933), American Jewish theologian and educator **8** 435-436

KAPP, WOLFGANG (1858-1922), German nationalist politician **8** 436

KAPTEYN, JACOBUS CORNELIS (1851-1922), Dutch astronomer **8** 436-437

KARADZIC, RADOVAN (born 1945), leader of the Serbian Republic **8** 437-440

KARAJAN, HERBERT VON (1908-1989), Austrian conductor **26** 190-192

KARAMANLIS, CONSTANTINE (1907-1998), Greek member of parliament, prime minister (1955-1963; 1974-1980), and president (1980-1985) **8** 440-441

KARAMZIN, NIKOLAI MIKHAILOVICH (1766-1826), Russian historian and author **8** 441-442

KARAN, DONNA (born 1948), American fashion designer and businesswoman **8** 442-444

KARENGA, MAULANA (born Ronald McKinley Everett; born 1941), African American author, educator, and proponent of black culturalism **8** 444-447

Karim, Prince
see Aga Khan IV

KARIM KHAN ZAND (died 1779), Iranian ruler, founder of Zand dynasty **8** 447

KARLE, ISABELLA (born 1921), American chemist and physicist **8** 447-449

KARLOFF, BORIS (William Henry Pratt; 1887-1969), English actor **26** 192-194

KARLOWICZ, MIECZYSLAW (1876-1909), Polish composer **33** 170-172

KARLSTADT, ANDREAS BODENHEIM VON (c. 1480-1541), German Protestant reformer **8** 449

KARMAL, BABRAK (1929-1996), Afghan Marxist and Soviet puppet ruler of the Democratic Republic of Afghanistan (1979-1986) **8** 449-451

KÁRMÁN, THEODORE VON (1881-1963), Hungarian-born American physicist **8** 451-452

KÁROLYI, MIHÁLY (1875-1955), Hungarian count **33** 172-174
Kun, Béla **34** 221-223

KARP, NATALIA (1911-2007), Jewish Polish pianist **28** 192-194

KARSAVINA, TAMARA (1885-1978), Russian ballet dancer **32** 177-180

KARSH, YOUSUF (1908-2002), Canadian photographer **23** 184-187

Karski, Jan, (1914-2000), Polish resistance fighter
Edelman, Marek **34** 102-104

KARTINI, RADEN AJENG (1879-1904), Indonesian activist **24** 201-203

KARUME, SHEIKH ABEID AMANI (1905-1972), Tanzanian political leader **8** 452-453

KASAVUBU, JOSEPH (c. 1913-1969), Congolese statesman **8** 453-455

Kasimir, Karl Theodore
see Meyerhold, Vsevolod Emilievich

KASPAROV, GARRY (Garri Kimovich Weinstein; born 1963), Russian chess player and politician **28** 194-196

KASSEBAUM, NANCY (born 1932), Republican senator from Kansas **8** 455-457

KASTRIOTI-SKANDERBEG, GJERGJ (1405-1468), Albanian military leader **23** 187-189

KATAYAMA, SEN (1860-1933), Japanese labor and Socialist leader **8** 457

KAUFFMAN, ANGELICA (Maria Anna Angelica Catherina Kauffman; 1741-1807), Swedish artist **25** 229-231

KAUFMAN, GEORGE S. (1889-1961), American playwright **8** 457-458

KAUFMAN, GERALD BERNARD (born 1930), foreign policy spokesman of the British Labour Party **8** 458-460

KAUFMANN, EZEKIEL (1889-1963), Jewish philosopher and scholar **8** 460

KAUNDA, KENNETH DAVID (born 1924), Zambian statesman **8** 460-461

KAUTILYA (4th century BCE), Indian statesman and author **8** 462

KAUTSKY, KARL JOHANN (1854-1938), German Austrian Socialist **8** 462-463

KAWABATA, YASUNARI (1899-1972), Japanese novelist **8** 463-464

KAWAWA, RASHIDI MFAUME (1929-2009), Tanzanian political leader **8** 464-465

KAYE, DANNY (David Daniel Kaminsky; 1913-1987), American film and stage actor **25** 231-234

KAZAN, ELIA (1909-2003), American film and stage director **8** 465-466

KAZANTZAKIS, NIKOS (1883-1957), Greek author, journalist, and statesman **8** 466-468

KEAN, EDMUND (1789-1833), English actor **21** 237-239

KEARNEY, DENIS (1847-1907), Irish-born American labor agitator **8** 468

KEARNY, STEPHEN WATTS (1794-1848), American general **8** 468-469

KEATING, PAUL JOHN (born 1944), federal treasurer of Australia (1983-1991) **8** 469-470

KEATON, BUSTER (Joseph Frank Keaton; 1895-1966), American comedian **20** 199-201

KEATS, JOHN (1795-1821), English poet **8** 470-472

KECKLEY, ELIZABETH HOBBS (Elizabeth Hobbs Keckly; 1818-1907), African American seamstress and author **28** 196-199

KEENAN, BRIAN (1940-2008), Irish peace activist **29** 223-225

KEFAUVER, CAREY ESTES (1903-1963), U.S. senator and influential Tennessee Democrat **8** 472-474
Gaines, William M. **34** 136-138

KEILLOR, GARRISON (Gary Edward Keillor, born 1942), American humorist, radio host, and author **22** 271-273

KEITA, MODIBO (1915-1977), Malian statesman **8** 474-475

KEITEL, WILHELM (1882-1946), German general **18** 224-226

KEITH, SIR ARTHUR (1866-1955), British anatomist and physical anthropologist **8** 475-476

KEITH, MINOR COOPER (1848-1929), American entrepreneur **8** 476-477

KEKKONEN, URHO KALEVA (1900-1986), Finnish athlete and politician **23** 189-191

KEKULÉ, FRIEDRICH AUGUST (1829-1896), German chemist **8** 477-478

KELLER, ELIZABETH BEACH (Elizabeth Waterbury Beach; 1918-1997), American biochemist **25** 234-235

KELLER, GOTTFRIED (1819-1890), Swiss short-story writer, novelist, and poet **8** 478-479

KELLER, HELEN ADAMS (1880-1968), American lecturer and author **8** 479-480

KELLEY, FLORENCE (1859-1932), American social worker and reformer **8** 483-484

KELLEY, HALL JACKSON (1790-1874), American promoter **8** 480

KELLEY, OLIVER HUDSON (1826-1913), American agriculturalist **8** 480-481

KELLOGG, FRANK BILLINGS (1856-1937), American statesman **8** 481

KELLOGG, JOHN HARVEY (1852-1943), American health propagandist and cereal manufacturer **21** 239-242

KELLOGG, W. K. (Will Keith Kellogg; 1860-1951), American cereal manufacturer and philanthropist **28** 199-201

KELLOR, FRANCES (1873-1952), American activist and politician **8** 481-482

KELLY, ELLSWORTH (born 1923), American artist **8** 482-483

KELLY, GENE (born Eugene Curran Kelly; 1912-1996), American actor, dancer, and choreographer **8** 484-486

KELLY, GRACE (Grace, Princess; 1929-1982), princess of Monaco **19** 174-176

KELLY, LEONTINE (1920-2012), American bishop **31** 187-188

KELLY, NED (1854-1880), Australian horse thief, bank robber, and murderer **29** 226-228

KELLY, PATRICK (1954-1990), African American fashion designer **22** 273-275

KELLY, PETRA (1947-1992), West German pacifist and politician **8** 486-487

KELLY, WALT (Walter Crawford Kelly; 1913-1973), American cartoonist **22** 275-278

KELLY, WILLIAM (1811-1888), American iron manufacturer **8** 487-488

KELSEY, FRANCES OLDHAM (born 1914), Canadian American scientist **31** 189-190

KELSEY, HENRY (c. 1667-1724), English-born Canadian explorer **8** 488

KELVIN OF LARGS, BARON (William Thomson; 1824-1907), Scottish physicist **8** 488-489

Kemal, Mustapha (Kemal Atatürk)
see Atatürk, Ghazi Mustapha Kemal

KEMAL, YASHAR (born 1922), Turkish novelist **8** 489-491

KEMBLE, FRANCES ANNE (Fanny Kemble; 1809-1893), English actress **8** 491

KEMP, JACK FRENCH, JR. (1935-2009), Republican congressman from New York and secretary of housing and urban development **8** 491-493

KEMPE, MARGERY (1373-1440), English religious writer **29** 228-230

KEMPIS, THOMAS À (c. 1380-1471), German monk and spiritual writer **8** 493-494

KENDALL, AMOS (1789-1869), American journalist **8** 494

KENDALL, EDWARD CALVIN (1886-1972), American biochemist **8** 495

KENDALL, THOMAS HENRY (Henry Clarence Kendall; 1839-1882), Australian poet **23** 191-194

Kendrake, Carleton
see Gardner, Erle Stanley

KENDREW, JOHN C. (1917-1997), English chemist and Nobel Prize winner **8** 495-496

KENEALLY, THOMAS MICHAEL (born 1935), Australian author **18** 226-228

KOUFAX, SANDY (Sanford Braun; born 1945), American baseball player **20** 208-210
Marichal, Juan **34** 252-254

KOUSSEVITZKY, SERGE (Sergey Aleksandrovich Kusevitsky;1874-1951), Russian-born American conductor **24** 213-215

KOVACS, ERNIE (1919-1962), American comedian **19** 186-188

KOVALEVSKY, SOPHIA VASILEVNA (Sonya Kovalevsky; 1850-1891), Russian mathematician **22** 280-282

KOZYREV, ANDREI VLADIMIROVICH (born 1951), Russian minister of foreign affairs and a liberal, pro-Western figure in Boris Yeltsin's cabinet **9** 92-93

KPD
see Communist party, German

KRAMER, LARRY (born 1935), American AIDS activist and author **20** 210-212

KRAMER, STANLEY (1913-2001), American filmmaker **32** 186-189

KRASNER, LEE (Lenore; 1908-1984), American painter and collage artist **9** 93-94

KRAUS, KARL (1874-1936), Austrian writer **34** 219-221

KRAVCHUK, LEONID MAKAROVYCH (born 1934), president of the Ukraine (1991-1994) **9** 94-95

KREBS, SIR HANS ADOLF (1900-1981), German British biochemist **9** 95-97

KREISKY, BRUNO (1911-1983), chancellor of Austria (1970-1983) **9** 97-98

KREISLER, FRITZ (Friedrich Kreisler; 1875-1962), Austrian violinist **26** 201-203

Kremer, Gerhard
see Mercator, Gerhardus

KRENEK, ERNST (1900-1991), Austrian composer **9** 98-99

KREPS, JUANITA MORRIS (1921-2010), economist, university professor, United States secretary of commerce (1977-1979), and author **9** 99-101

KRIEGHOFF, CORNELIUS (1815-1872), Dutch-born Canadian painter **9** 101

KRISHNAMURTI, JIDDU (1895-1986), Indian mystic and philosopher **9** 101-103

KRISHNAMURTI, UPPALURI GOPALA (1918-2007), Indian philosopher and author **28** 201-203

KRLEZA, MIROSLAV (1893-1981), Croatian author and poet **24** 215-217

KROC, RAYMOND ALBERT (1902-1984), creator of the McDonald's chain **9** 103-104

KROCHMAL, NACHMAN KOHEN (1785-1840), Austrian Jewish historian **9** 104-105

KROEBER, ALFRED LOUIS (1876-1960), American anthropologist **9** 105-106

KROGH, SCHACK AUGUST STEENBERG (1874-1949), Danish physiologist **9** 106

KRONE, JULIE (Julieanne Louise Krone; born 1963), American jockey **24** 217-220

KROPOTKIN, PETER ALEKSEEVICH (1842-1921), Russian prince, scientist, and anarchist **9** 107-108

KROTO, HAROLD WALTER (Harold Walter Krotoschiner; born 1939), British Chemist **27** 216-218

KRUGER, STEPHANUS JOHANNES PAULUS ("Paul"; 1825-1904), South African statesman **9** 108-109

KRUPP FAMILY (19th-20th century), German industrialists **9** 109-111

KU CHIEH-KANG (1893-1980), Chinese historian **9** 120-121

KU K'AI-CHIH (c. 345-c. 406), Chinese painter **9** 125-126

KUANG-HSÜ (1871-1908), emperor of China 1875-1908 **9** 111-112

KUANG-WU-TI (6 BCE - 57 A.D.), Chinese emperor ca. 25-57 **9** 112-113

KUBITSCHEK DE OLIVEIRA, JUSCELINO (1902-1976), president of Brazil 1956-1961 **9** 113-115

KUBLAI KHAN (1215-1294), Mongol emperor **9** 115-118

KÜBLER-ROSS, ELISABETH (1926-2004), Swiss-born American psychiatrist **9** 118-120

KUBRICK, STANLEY (1928-1999), American filmmaker **18** 237-239

KUCAN, MILAN (born 1941), President of the Republic of Slovenia **18** 239-242

Kuerti, Anton, (born 1938), Austrian-Canadian pianist
Czerny, Carl **34** 68-70

KUFUOR, JOHN AGYEKUM (born 1938), president of Ghana **27** 218-220

KUHN, BOWIE (1926-2007), American baseball commissioner **33** 183-185

KUHN, MAGGIE (1905-1995), American activist and founder of the Gray Panthers **19** 188-190

KUHN, THOMAS SAMUEL (1922-1996), American historian and philosopher of science **9** 121-123

Kuehnle, Louis "Commodore", (1857-1934), American entrepreneur
Johnson, Enoch "Nucky" **34** 193-195

KUK, ABRAHAM ISAAC (1865-1935), Russian-born Jewish scholar **9** 123-124

KUKAI (774-835), Japanese Buddhist monk **9** 124-125

KUKRIT PRAMOJ, MOMRAJAWONG (M.R.; 1911-1995), literary figure and prime minister of Thailand (1975-1976) **9** 126-127

KULTHUM, UMM (Ibrahim Umm Kalthum; 1904-1975), Egyptian musician **24** 220-222

Kumara Siladitya
see Harsha

KUMARAJIVA (c. 344-c. 409), Indian Buddhist monk **9** 127

KUMARATUNGA, CHANDRIKA (Chandrika Bandaranaike; born 1945), Sri Lankan politician **25** 252-254

KUMIN, MAXINE WINOKUR (1925-2014), American poet and author **26** 203-206

KUN, BÉLA (1885-1937), Hungarian revolutionary **34** 221-223

Kunani
see Suleiman I

KUNDERA, MILAN (born 1929), Czech-born author **9** 128-129

KÜNG, HANS (born 1928), Swiss-born Roman Catholic theologian **9** 129-130

Kung-sun Yang
see Shang Yang

KUNIN, MADELEINE MAY (born 1933), first woman governor of Vermont **9** 130-131

KUNITZ, STANLEY JASSPON (1905-2006), American poet laureate **22** 282-284

KUNSTLER, WILLIAM M. (1919-1995), American civil rights attorney and author **9** 131-133

KUO MO-JO (1892-1978), Chinese author **9** 133-134

KUPKA, FRANTISEK (Frank; 1871-1957), Czech painter and illustrator **9** 134-135

Kupper, C.E.M.
see Doesburg, Theo van

Kuprili, Ahmed
see Köprülü, Ahmed

KURAS, ELLEN (born 1959), American cinematographer and director **32** 189-191

KURON, JACEK (Jacek Jan Kuron; 1934-2004), Polish trade union advisor and politician **28** 203-206

L

LE CARRE, JOHN (born David Cornwell, 1931), British spy novelist **9** 270-271

LE CORBUSIER (Charles Édouard Jeanneret-Gris; 1887-1965), Swiss architect, city planner, and painter **9** 274-275

LE DUAN (1908-1986), North Vietnamese leader and later head of the government of all Vietnam **29** 150-153

LE FANU, JOSEPH SHERIDAN (1814-1873), Irish author **23** 206-208

LE GUIN, URSULA KROEBER (born 1929), American author **18** 249-251

LE JEUNE, CLAUDE (c. 1530-1600), Flemish composer **9** 314-315

Le Moyne, Pierre
see Iberville, Sieur d'

LE NAIN BROTHERS, 17th-century French painters **9** 321-322

LE NÔTRE, ANDRÉ (or Le Nostre; 1613-1700), French landscape architect **9** 328-329

LE PEN, JEAN MARIE (born 1928), French political activist of the radical right **9** 348-350

LE PLAY, GUILLAUME FRÉDÉRIC (1806-1882), French sociologist and economist **9** 350-351

Le Prestre, Sébastien
see Vauban, Marquis de

LE VAU, LOUIS (1612-1670), French architect **9** 360-361

LEA, HENRY CHARLES (1825-1909), American historian **9** 261-262

LEA, TOM (1907-2001), American artist and author **32** 201-202

LEACOCK, RICHARD (1921-2011), British filmmaker **32** 202-205

LEADBELLY (Huddie William Leadbetter; 1885-1949), African American folk singer **23** 208-211

LEAKEY, LOUIS SEYMOUR BAZETT (1903-1972), British anthropologist **9** 262

LEAKEY, MARY DOUGLAS (1913-1996), English archaeologist **9** 263-264

LEAKEY, RICHARD ERSKINE FRERE (born 1944), Kenyan researcher in human prehistory and wildlife conservationist **9** 264-265

LEAN, DAVID (1908-1991), English film director and producer **29** 239-241

LEAR, EDWARD (1812-1888), English writer and artist **9** 265-266

LEAR, NORMAN (born 1922), American author and television director and producer **19** 193-195

LEARY, TIMOTHY (1920-1996), American psychologist, author, lecturer, and cult figure **9** 266-267

LEASE, MARY ELIZABETH CLYENS (1853-1933), American writer and politician **9** 268

LEAVITT, HENRIETTA SWAN (1868-1921), American astronomer **23** 211-213

LEBED, ALEXANDER IVANOVICH (1950-2002), Russian general and politician **18** 245-247

LEBLANC, NICOLAS (1742-1806), French industrial chemist **21** 256-258

LECKY, WILLIAM EDWARD HARTPOLE (1838-1903), AngloIrish historian and essayist **9** 271-272

Leclerc, Georges Louis
see Buffon, Comte de

LECLERC, JACQUES PHILIPPE (1902-1947), French general **9** 272-273

LECLERCQ, TANAQUIL (Tanny; 1929-2000), French American dancer **27** 234-235

LECONTE DE LISLE, CHARLES MARIE RENÉ (1818-1894), French poet **9** 273-274

LECUONA, ERNESTO (Ernesto Sixto de la Asuncion Lecuona y Casado; 1896-1963), Cuban musician **23** 213-216

LED ZEPPELIN (1968-1980), British "Heavy Metal" band **23** 216-218

LEDBETTER, LILLY (born 1938), American women's equality advocate **32** 205-207

LEDERBERG, JOSHUA (1925-2008), Nobel Prize winning geneticist **9** 275-277

LEDERER, ESTHER PAULINE (Ann Landers; 1918-2002), American Columnist **25** 255-257

LEDOUX, CLAUDE NICOLAS (1736-1806), French architect **9** 277-278

LEE, MOTHER ANN (1736-1784), religious and social reformer and founder of the Shakers **9** 289-290

LEE, ARTHUR (1740-1792), American statesman and diplomat **9** 288-289

LEE, BRUCE (1940-1973), Asian American actor and martial arts master **18** 247-249

LEE, CHARLES (1731-1782), American general **22** 294-297

LEE, HARPER (Nelle Harper Lee; born 1926), American author **20** 220-222

LEE, MING CHO (born 1930), American scene designer for theater and opera **9** 289-290

LEE, PEGGY (1920-2002), American singer **32** 207-209
Blackwell, Otis **34** 32-33

LEE, RICHARD HENRY (1732-1794), American patriot and statesman **9** 291-292

LEE, ROBERT EDWARD (1807-1870), American army officer and Confederate general in chief **9** 292-294

LEE, ROSE (Rose Hum; 1904-1964), American sociologist **21** 258-260

LEE, SPIKE (born Sheldon Jackson Lee; born 1957), African American actor, author, and filmmaker **9** 295-299

LEE, STAN (born 1922), American comics artist **30** 253-255

LEE, TSUNG-DAO (born 1926), Chinese-born American physicist **9** 299-300

LEE, YUAN TSEH (born 1936), Taiwanese American scientist and educator **23** 218-220

LEE HSIEN LOONG (born 1952), Singaporean soldier and deputy prime minister **9** 280-281

LEE JONG-WOOK (1945-2006), Korean physician and head of the World Health Organization **27** 235-238

LEE KUAN YEW (born 1923), prime minister of Singapore (1959-1988) **9** 281-283

LEE TENG-HUI (born 1923), president of the Republic of China (1988-) **9** 283-285

LEEKPAI, CHUAN (born 1938), Thai prime minister **24** 225-228

LEEUWENHOEK, ANTON VAN (1632-1723), Dutch naturalist and microscopist **9** 300-301

LEFEBVRE, GEORGES (1874-1959), French historian **9** 301-302

Léger, Alexis Saint-Léger
see Perse, Saint-John

LÉGER, FERNAND (1881-1955), French painter **9** 302-303

LEGHARI, SARDAR FAROOQ AHMED KHAN (1940-2010), president of the Islamic Republic of Pakistan **9** 303-305

LEGINSKA, ETHEL (Ethel Liggins; 1886-1970), English American musician **23** 220-222

LEGUÍA Y SALCEDO, AUGUSTO BERNARDINO (1863-1932), Peruvian president 1908-12 and 1919-30 **9** 305-306

LEHMAN, ERNEST (1915-2005), American screenwriter **26** 226-229

LEHMAN, HERBERT HENRY (1878-1963), American banker and statesman **9** 306-307

LEHMANN, LOTTE (1888-1976), German-American soprano **31** 204-206

Lehmann, Walter
see Harwood, Gwen

LEHMBRUCK, WILHELM (1881-1919), German sculptor **9** 307

Leiber, Jerry
see Leiber and Stoller

LEIBER AND STOLLER (Jerry Leiber; 1933-2011, and Mike Stoller; born 1933), American songwriters and producers **32** 209-212
Thornton, Willie Mae **34** 346-348

LEIBNIZ, GOTTFRIED WILHELM VON (1646-1716), German mathematician and philosopher **9** 307-310

LEIBOVITZ, ANNIE (born 1949), Ameircan photographer **9** 310-312

LEICESTER, EARL OF (Robert Dudley; c. 1532-1588), English politician **9** 312-313

Leicester, 6th Earl of
see Montfort, Simon de

LEIGH, MIKE (born 1943), British director and screenwriter **23** 222-225

LEIGH, VIVIEN (Vivian Mary Hartley; 1913-1967), British actress **18** 251-253

Leipzig, University of (Germany)
scientists
Ostwald, Wilhelm **34** 284-286

LEISLER, JACOB (1640-1691), American colonial leader **9** 313-314

LEITZEL, LILLIAN (born Leopoldina Altitza Pelikan; 1892-1931), German aerialist **23** 225-227

LELY, SIR PETER (1618-1680), German-born painter active in England **9** 315

LEM, STANISLAW (1921-2006), Polish author **27** 238-240

LEMAÎTRE, ABBÈ GEORGES ÉDOUARD (1894-1966), Belgian astronomer **9** 315-316

LEMAY, CURTIS E. (1906-1990), United States combat leader (World War II) and Air Force chief of staff **9** 316-318

LEMBEDE, ANTON (1913-1947), leader of black resistance to white supremacy in South Africa **9** 318-319

LEMIEUX, MARIO (born 1965), Canadian hockey player and team owner **20** 222-224

LEMMON, JACK (John Uhler Lemmon; 1925-2001), American actor **22** 297-299

LEMNITZER, LYMAN LOUIS (Lem; 1899-1988), American soldier-statesman and strategist and NATO architect **9** 319-320

LENARD, PHILIPP (Philipp Eduard Anton von Lenard; 1862-1947), Hungarian-born German physicist **25** 259-261

L'ENFANT, PIERRE CHARLES (1754-1825), French-born American architect **9** 322-323

L'ENGLE, MADELEINE (1918-2007), American author **18** 253-255

LENGLEN, SUZANNE (1899-1938), French tennis player **19** 195-197

LENIHAN, BRIAN, JR. (1959-2011), Irish politician **34** 240-242

Lenihan, Brian, Sr., (1930-1995), Irish politician
Lenihan, Brian, Jr. **34** 240-242

Lenihan, Patrick, (1902-1970), Irish politician
Lenihan, Brian, Jr. **34** 240-242

LENIN, VLADIMIR ILICH (1870-1924), Russian statesman **9** 323-326
influence of
Kirov, Sergei **34** 208-211

LENNON, JOHN (1940-1980), English songwriter and musician **9** 326-328

LENYA, LOTTE (1900-1981), Austrian-American singer **29** 241-242

LENZ, WILHELM VON (1809-1883), Russian musicologist **29** 243-245

LEO I (c. 400-461), saint and pope 440-461 **9** 329-330

LEO III (the Isaurian; c. 680-741), Byzantine emperor 717-741 **9** 330-332

LEO IX, ST. (Bruno of Egisheim; 1002-1054), pope 1049-1054 **9** 332

LEO X (Giovanni de' Medici; 1475-1521), pope 1513-1521 **9** 332-334

LEO XII (Annibale Sermattai della Genga; 1760-1829), Italian Roman Catholic pope (1823-1829) **26** 297-299

LEO XIII (Vincenzo Gioacchino Pecci; 1810-1903), pope 1878-1903 **9** 334-336

Leo Hebraeus
see Levi ben Gershon

LEON, MOSES DE (c. 1250-1305), Jewish mystic **9** 336

LEONARD, BUCK (1907-1997), American baseball player **33** 192-194

LEONARD, DANIEL (1740-1829), American loyalist lawyer and essayist **9** 336-337

LEONARD, ELMORE (1925-2013), American writer **32** 212-214

LEONARD, SUGAR RAY (Ray Charles Leonard; born 1956), American boxer **24** 228-231

LEONARDO DA VINCI (1452-1519), Italian painter, sculptor, architect, and scientist **9** 337-340

Leonardo of Pisa
see Fibonacci, Leonardo

LEONIDAS I (c. 530 BCE - 480 BCE), Spartan king **9** 340-343

LÉONIN (Leoninus; flourished c. 1165-1185), French composer **9** 343-344

LEOPARDI, CONTE GIACOMO (1798-1837), Italian poet **9** 344-345

LEOPOLD I (1790-1865), king of Belgium 1831-1865 **9** 345-346

Leopold I (Duke of Tuscany)
see Leopold II (Holy Roman emperor)

LEOPOLD II (1747-1792), Holy Roman emperor 1790-1792 **9** 346

LEOPOLD II (1835-1909), king of Belgium 1865-1909 **9** 346-347

LEOPOLD III (1901-1983), king of Belgium 1934-1951 **9** 347-348

LEOPOLD, ALDO (1887-1948), American author and conservationist **28** 211-213

Leopold, Duke of Brabant
see Leopold III (king of Belgium)

Lepoqo
see Moshweshwe

LEPSIUS, KARL RICHARD (1810-1884), German Egyptologist and linguist **30** 256-258

LERDO DE TEJADA, MIGUEL (1812-1861), Mexican liberal politician **9** 351-352

LERMONTOV, MIKHAIL YURIEVICH (1814-1841), Russian poet and prose writer **9** 352-353

LERNER, ALAN JAY (1918-1986), American lyricist/librettist **20** 224-226

LESAGE, ALAIN RENÉ (1668-1747), French novelist and playwright **9** 353-354

LESCHETIZKY, THEODOR (1830-1915), Polish composer and pianist **31** 207-208

LESCOT, PIERRE (1500/1515-1578), French architect **9** 354

LESPINASSE, JULIE DE (1732-1776), French writer **32** 214-216

LESSEPS, VICOMTE DE (Ferdinand Marie; 1805-1894), French diplomat **9** 354-355

LESSING, DORIS (Doris May Taylor; 1919-2013), South African expatriate writer **9** 355-357

LESSING, GOTTHOLD EPHRAIM (1729-1781), German philosopher, dramatist, and critic **9** 357-359

LETCHER, JOHN (1813-1884), American politician **9** 359-360

LETTERMAN, DAVID (born 1947), American comedian **26** 229-231

LEVANT, OSCAR (1906-1972), American composer and pianist **19** 197-199

LEVERRIER, URBAIN JEAN JOSEPH (1811-1877), French mathematical astronomer **9** 361-362

LÉVESQUE, RENÉ (1922-1987), premier of the province of Quebec, Canada (1976-1985) **9** 362-363

Levi
see Matthew, Saint

LEVI, CARLO (1902-1975), Italian writer and painter **9** 364

LEVI, PRIMO (1919-1987), Italian author and chemist **9** 365-366

LÉVI, SYLVAIN (1863-1935), French scholar and Asian cultures expert **30** 258-260

LEVI BEN GERSHON (1288-c. 1344), French Jewish scientist, philosopher, and theologian **9** 363-364

LEVI-MONTALCINI, RITA (1909-2012), Italian-American biologist who discovered the nerve growth factor **9** 366-368

LÉVI-STRAUSS, CLAUDE GUSTAVE (1908-2009), French social anthropologist **9** 371-372

LEVINAS, EMMANUEL (1906-1995), Jewish philosopher **9** 368-369

LEVINE, JAMES (born 1943), American conductor and pianist **9** 369-371

LEVITT, HELEN (1913-2009), American photographer **30** 260-261

LEVITT, WILLIAM (1907-1994), American real estate developer **19** 199-201

LÉVY, BERNARD-HENRI (BHL; born 1948), French philosopher and author **28** 213-215

LEVY, DAVID (born 1937), Israeli minister of foreign affairs and deputy prime minister **9** 373-374

LÉVY-BRUHL, LUCIEN (1857-1939), French philosopher and anthropologist **9** 374-375

LEWIN, KURT (1890-1947), German-American social psychologist **9** 375-376

LEWIS, ANDREW (c. 1720-1781), American general in the Revolution **9** 376-377

LEWIS, CARL (born Frederick Carlton Lewis; born 1961), African American track and field athlete **9** 377-380

LEWIS, CECIL DAY (1904-1972), British poet and essayist **9** 380

LEWIS, CLARENCE IRVING (1883-1964), American philosopher **9** 381

LEWIS, CLIVE STAPLES (C.S.; 1898-1963), British novelist and essayist **9** 381-382

LEWIS, EDMONIA (Mary Edmomia Lewis; Wildfire; c. 1840-c. 1909), American sculptor **28** 215-217

LEWIS, ESSINGTON (1881-1961), Australian industrial leader **9** 382-384

LEWIS, GILBERT NEWTON (1875-1946), American physical chemist **9** 384-385

LEWIS, HARRY SINCLAIR (1885-1951), American novelist **9** 385-387

LEWIS, JERRY (born 1926), American comedian **30** 261-264

Lewis, Jerry Lee, (born 1935), American musician
Blackwell, Otis **34** 32-33

LEWIS, JOHN LLEWELLYN (1880-1969), American labor leader **9** 387-388

LEWIS, JOHN ROBERT (born 1940), United States civil rights activist and representative from Georgia **9** 388-390

LEWIS, MATTHEW GREGORY (1775-1818), English novelist and playwright **9** 390-391

LEWIS, MERIWETHER (1774-1809), American explorer and army officer **9** 391-392

LEWIS, OSCAR (1914-1970), American anthropologist **9** 392-393

LEWIS, REGINALD FRANCIS (1942-1993), African American businessman, attorney, and philanthropist **25** 261-263

Lewis, Sinclair
see Lewis, Harry Sinclair

LEWIS, WILLIAM ARTHUR (1915-1991), St. Lucian economist **27** 240-242

LEWIS, WYNDHAM (Percy Wyndham Lewis; 1882-1957), Canadian-born British author and artist **28** 217-219

LEWITT, SOL (1928-2007), American Minimalist and Conceptualist artist **9** 393-395

LEYSTER, JUDITH (1609-1660), Dutch artist **30** 264-266

Li Erh
see Lao Tzu

Li Fei-kan
see Pa Chin

LI HUNG-CHANG (1823-1901), Chinese soldier, statesman, and industrialist **9** 407-409

Li Ma-t'ou
see Ricci, Matteo

LI PENG (born 1928), premier of the People's Republic of China **9** 433-435

LI PO (701-762), Chinese poet **9** 437-439

Li Shih-min
see Tai-tsung, T'ang

LI QINGZHAO (1084-1150), Chinese poet **25** 263-265

LI SSU (c. 280-208 BCE), Chinese statesman **9** 442-443

LI TA-CHAO (1889-1927), Chinese Communist revolutionist **9** 447

LI TZU-CH'ENG (c. 1606-1645), Chinese bandit and rebel leader **9** 452

LIANG CH'I-CH'AO (1873-1929), Chinese intellectual and political reformer **9** 395-396

LIANG WU-TI (464-549), Chinese emperor of Southern dynasties **9** 396-397

LIAQUAT ALI KHAN (1896-1951), Pakistani statesman **9** 397

LIBBY, LEONA MARSHALL (1919-1986), American nuclear scientist **26** 231-233

LIBBY, WILLARD FRANK (1908-1980), American chemist **9** 397-398

Liberal party
Brazil
Franco, Itamar **34** 130-132
Hungary
Tisza, Istvan **34** 348-350

LICHTENSTEIN, ROY (1923-1997), American painter, sculptor, and printmaker **9** 398-399

LIE, TRYGVE HALVDAN (1896-1968), Norwegian statesman and UN secretary general **9** 400-401

LIEBER, FRANCIS (c. 1798-1872), German American political scientist **9** 401-402

Lieber, Stanley Martin
see Lee, Stan

LIEBERMANN, MAX (1847-1935), German painter **9** 402-403

LIEBIG, BARON JUSTUS VON (1803-1873), German chemist **9** 403-404

LIGACHEV, YEGOR KUZ'MICH (born 1920), member of the Central Committee of the Communist Party of the Soviet Union (1966-1990) **9** 404-406

LIGETI, GYÖRGY (1923-2006), Austrian composer **9** 406-407

LIGHTNER, CANDY (born 1946), American activist and founder of Mothers Against Drunk Driving **19** 201-203

LILBURNE, JOHN (1615-1657), English political activist and pamphleteer **9** 409-410

LILIENTHAL, DAVID ELI (1899-1981), American public administrator **9** 410-411

LILIENTHAL, OTTO (1848-1896), Prussian design engineer **21** 260-262

LLOYD, HAROLD (1893-1971), American actor **20** 226-229

LLOYD GEORGE, DAVID, (1st Earl of Dwyfor; 1863-1945), English statesman, prime minister 1916-1922 **9** 469-471

LLOYD-JONES, ESTHER MCDONALD (1901-1991), school personnel specialist who focused on development of the whole person **9** 471-472

LOBACHEVSKII, NIKOLAI IVANOVICH (1792-1856), Russian mathematician **9** 472-474

LOBENGULA (died c. 1894), South African Ndebele king **9** 474-475

LOBO, REBECCA ROSE (born 1973), American basketball player **31** 209-210

LOCHNER, STEPHAN (c. 1410-1451), German painter **9** 475

LOCKE, ALAIN (1886-1954), African American educator, editor, and author **9** 475-478

LOCKE, JOHN (1632-1704), English philosopher and political theorist **9** 478-480

LOCKE, PATRICIA (1928-2001), American educator **31** 211

LOCKWOOD, BELVA (1830-1917), American lawyer, suffragist, and reformer **19** 205-207

LODGE, DAVID (born 1935), English novelist **9** 480-482

LODGE, HENRY CABOT (1850-1924), American political leader **9** 482-483

LODGE, HENRY CABOT, JR. (1902-1985), American congressman, senator, ambassador, and presidential adviser **9** 483-485

Lodovico il Moro
see Sforza, Lodovico

LOEB, JACQUES (Isaak Loeb; 1859-1924), German-American biophysiologist **22** 299-301

LOESSER, FRANK (Francis Henry Loesser; 1910-1969), American lyricist **18** 257-259

LOEW, MARCUS (1870-1927), founder of a theater chain and Metro-Goldwyn-Mayer **9** 485-486

LOEWI, OTTO (1873-1961), German-American pharmacologist and physiologist **9** 486-487

LOFTING, HUGH (1886-1947), British author of children's books **19** 207-209

LOGAN, GEORGE (1753-1821), American politician and diplomat **23** 231-234

LOGAN, JAMES (1674-1751), American colonial statesman and jurist **9** 487-488

LOGAN, MYRA ADELE (1908-1977), American physician and surgeon **30** 266-268

LOGAN, SIR WILLIAM EDMOND (1798-1875), Canadian geologist **9** 488-489

Loges, François des
see Villon, François

LOISY, ALFRED FIRMIN (1857-1940), French theologian and biblical historian **9** 489-490

LOMAX, ALAN (1915-2002), American folklorist, author and musician **27** 242-244

LOMAX, ALMENA (1915-2011), American journalist and activist **32** 216-218

LOMAX, JOHN AVERY (1867-1948), American musicologist **28** 224-225

LOMBARD, CAROLE (1909-1942), American actress **29** 249-251

LOMBARD, PETER (c. 1095-1160), Italian bishop and theologian **9** 490-491

LOMBARDI, VINCE (1913-1970), American football coach **9** 491-492

LOMBARDO, GUY (Gaetano Alberto Lombardo; 1902-1977), Canadian band leader **23** 234-236

Lombardy (province; Italy)
Belgiojoso, Cristina Trivulzio **34** 25-27

LOMBROSO, CESARE (1835-1909), Italian criminologist **9** 493

LOMONOSOV, MIKHAIL VASILEVICH (1711-1765), Russian chemist and physicist **9** 494

LON NOL (1913-1985), Cambodian general and politician **29** 251-253

LONDON, JACK (1876-1916), American author **9** 494-495

LONDONDERRY, ANNIE (1870-1947), American cyclist **29** 253-256

Londonderry, 2nd Marquess of
see Castlereagh, Viscount

Lonesome Dove (novel)
McMurtry, Larry **34** 259-261

LONG, CRAWFORD WILLIAMSON (1815-1878), American physician **9** 495-496

LONG, HUEY PIERCE (1893-1935), American politician **9** 496-497

LONG, IRENE D. (born 1951), African American aerospace medicine physician **9** 497-498

Long Parliament (England; 1640-48)
Henrietta Maria of France **34** 167-169

LONGFELLOW, HENRY WADSWORTH (1807-1882), American poet **9** 499-500

LONGINUS (flourished 1st or 3rd century), Latin author and rhetorician **9** 500-501

LONGSTREET, JAMES (1821-1904), American army officer **22** 301-305

LONGUS (flourished 3rd century), Greek author **20** 229-230

LONNROT, ELIAS (1802-1884), Finnish author and physician **25** 271-273

LONSDALE, KATHLEEN (born Kathleen Yardley; 1903-1971), Irish crystallographer **9** 501-502

LOOS, ADOLF (1870-1933), Viennese architect **9** 502-503

LOOS, ANITA (1893-1981), American actress and writer **21** 262-265

LOPE FÉLIX DE VEGA CARPIO (1562-1635), Spanish dramatist **9** 503-506

LÓPEZ, CARLOS ANTONIO (1792-1862), Paraguayan president-dictator 1844-1862 **9** 506-507

LÓPEZ, FRANCISCO SOLANO (1826-1870), Paraguayan president-dictator **9** 507-508

López, Israel
see Cachao

LOPEZ, NANCY (born 1957), American golfer **30** 268-270

LÓPEZ, NARCISO (1798-1851), Venezuelan military leader **9** 508

LOPEZ ARELLANO, OSWALDO (1921-2010), Honduran military officer and president **20** 230-231

LÓPEZ DE AYALA, PEDRO (1332-1407), Spanish statesman, historian, and poet **9** 508-509

LÓPEZ MATEOS, ADOLFO (1910-1970), president of Mexico (1958-1964) **9** 509-510

LÓPEZ PORTILLO, JOSÉ (1920-2004), president of Mexico (1976-1982) **9** 510-511

LOPOKOVA, LYDIA (1891-1981), Russian ballerina **31** 212-214

LORCA, FEDERICO GARCÍA (1898-1936), Spanish poet and playwright **9** 511-513

LORD, BETTE BAO (born 1938), Chinese American writer and activist **32** 218-220

Lord Haw Haw
see Joyce, William

LORDE, AUDRE (1934-1992), African American poet **9** 513-515

LOREN, SOPHIA (Sofia Villani Scicolene; born 1936), Italian actress and author **18** 259-261

LORENTZ, HENDRIK ANTOON (1853-1928), Dutch physicist **9** 515-516

LUDENDORFF, ERICH FRIEDRICH WILHELM (1865-1937), German general **10** 27-28

LUDLUM, ROBERT (a.k.a. Jonathan Ryder and Michael Shepherd; 1927-2001), American suspense novelist **10** 28-29

LUDWIG I OF BAVARIA (1786-1868), king of Bavaria 1825-1848 **34** 244-246

Ludwig II
see Louis II (king of Bavaria)

LUDWIG, DANIEL KEITH (1897-1992), American shipping magnate **10** 29-31

LUDWIG, KARL FRIEDRICH WILHELM (1816-1895), German physiologist **10** 31

LUGARD, FREDERICK JOHN DEALTRY (1st Baron Lugard; 1858-1945), British soldier and colonial administrator in Africa **10** 31-32

Lugosi, Bela, (1882-1956), Hungarian-American actor
Wood, Ed, Jr. **34** 383-384

LUHAN, MABEL DODGE (1879-1962), American writer, salon hostess, and patron of artists, writers, and political radicals **10** 32-34

LUHMANN, NIKLAS (1927-1998), German sociologist who developed a general sociological systems theory **10** 34-35

LUKÁCS, GYORGY (1885-1971), Hungarian literary critic and philosopher **10** 37-38

Lukar, Cyril
see Lucaris, Cyril

LUKASIEWICZ, IGNACY (1822-1882), Polish pharmacist and inventor of the kerosene lamp **28** 225-227

LUKE, ST. (flourished A.D. 50), Evangelist and biblical author **10** 38

LUKENS, REBECCA (née Rebecca Webb Pennock; 1794-1854), American industrialist **25** 275-277

LUKS, GEORGE BENJAMIN (1867-1933), American painter **10** 38-39

LULA DA SILVA, LUIZ INÁCIO (Lula; born 1945), president of Brazil **27** 244-247
Franco, Itamar **34** 130-132

LULL, RAYMOND (1232/35-1316), Spanish theologian, poet, and missionary **10** 39-40

LULLY, JEAN BAPTISTE (1632-1687), Italian-born French composer **10** 40-41

Lully, Raymond
see Lull, Raymond

LUMET, SIDNEY (1924-2011), American filmmaker and television director **22** 305-307

LUMIÈRE BROTHERS (Auguste Marie Louis, 1862-1954, and Louis Jean, 1864-1948), French inventors **10** 41-43

LUMMIS, CHARLES FLETCHER (1859-1928), American adventurer and journalist **33** 199-201

LUMUMBA, PATRICE EMERY (1925-1961), Congolese statesman **10** 43-45

LUNDY, BENJAMIN (1789-1839), American journalist **10** 45-46

LUNS, JOSEPH (1911-2002), West European political leader **10** 46-47

LUPER, CLARA (1923-2011), American equal rights activist **33** 201-203

LURIA, ISAAC BEN SOLOMON ASHKENAZI (1534-1572), Jewish mystic **10** 47-48

LUTHER, MARTIN (1483-1546), German religious reformer **10** 48-51
excommunicated
Vergerio, Pier Paolo **34** 362-364

Lutheranism (religion)
in Europe
Vergerio, Pier Paolo **34** 362-364

LUTHULI, ALBERT JOHN (1898-1967), South African statesman **10** 51-52

LUTOSLAWSKI, WITOLD (1913-1994), Polish composer **10** 52-53

LUTYENS, EDWIN LANDSEER (1869-1944), English architect **10** 54-55

LUXEMBURG, ROSA (1870-1919), Polish revolutionary **10** 55-56

LUZ, ARTURO ROGERIO (born 1926), Philippine painter and sculptor **10** 56-57

LUZHKOV, YURI MIKHAYLOVICH (born 1936), mayor of Moscow **18** 266-268

LUZZATO, MOSES HAYYIM (1707-1747), Jewish mystic and poet **10** 57-58

LUZZI, MONDINO DE' (c. 1265-1326), Italian anatomist **10** 58

LWOFF, ANDRÉ (1902-1994), French microbiologist and geneticist **10** 58-59

LY, ABDOULAYE (born 1919), Senegalese politician and historian **10** 60

LYAUTEY, LOUIS HUBERT GONZALVE (1854-1934), French marshal and colonial administrator **10** 60-61

LYDGATE, JOHN (c. 1370-1449/50), English poet **10** 61-62

LYELL, SIR CHARLES (1797-1875), Scottish geologist **10** 62-63

Lymphatic system (anatomy)
Bartholin, Thomas **34** 21-23

LYND, HELEN MERRELL (1896-1982), American sociologist and educator **10** 63-64

LYND, ROBERT STAUGHTON (1892-1970), American sociologist **10** 64-65

LYND, STAUGHTON (born 1929), historian and peace militant **10** 65-66

LYNDSAY, SIR DAVID (c. 1485-1555), Scottish poet and courtier **10** 66-67

LYON, MARY (1797-1849), American educator, religious leader, and women's rights advocate **10** 67-69

LYONS, ENID MURIEL (1897-1981), Australian politician **29** 258-260

LYONS, JOSEPH ALOYSIUS (1879-1939), Australian statesman, prime minister 1932-39 **10** 69-70

LYSANDER (died 395 BCE), Spartan military commander and statesman **10** 70

LYSENKO, TROFIM DENISOVICH (1898-1976), Soviet agronomist and geneticist **10** 71

Lytton, 1st Earl of, (Edward Robert Bulwer Lytton; 1831-1891), English statesman
Khan, Abdur Rahman **34** 200-202

Lytton of Knebworth, 1st Baron
see Bulwer-Lytton, Edward

M

MA, YO-YO (born 1955), American cellist **20** 232-234

MAAS, PETER (1929-2001), American author **27** 248-251

MAATHAI, WANGARI MUTA (1940-2011), Kenyan environmental activist **18** 269-271

MABILLON, JEAN (1632-1707), French monk and historian **10** 72

MABINI, APOLINARIO (1864-1903), Filipino political philosopher **10** 72-73

Mabovitch, Golda
see Meir, Golda

MABUCHI, KAMO (1697-1769), Japanese writer and scholar **10** 73-74

MACAPAGAL, DIOSDADO P. (1910-1997), Filipino statesman **10** 74-76

MACAPAGAL-ARROYO, GLORIA (Gloria Arroyo; born 1947), president of the Philippine islands **25** 278-280

MACARTHUR, DOUGLAS (1880-1964), American general **10** 76-78
Japan occupied (1949-1952)
Gordon, Beate Sirota **34** 143-145

MACARTHUR, ELLEN (born 1976), English yachtswoman **33** 204-206

MACARTHUR, JOHN (c. 1767-1834), Australian merchant, sheep breeder, and politician **10** 78

MARTINEZ, MARIANNE (Marianne von Martinez; Anna Katherina Martinez; 1744- 1812), Austrian musician **27** 256-258

MARTINEZ, MARIA MONTOYA (Maria Antonia Montoya; Marie Poveka; Pond Lily; c. 1881-1980), Pueblo potter **24** 241-243

MARTÍNEZ, MAXIMILIANO HERNÁNDEZ (1882-1966), president of El Salvador (1931-1944) **10** 297-298

MARTINEZ, VILMA SOCORRO (born 1943), Hispanic American attorney and activist **18** 276-279

Martinez Ruíz, José
see Ruíz, José Martinez

MARTINI, SIMONE (flourished 1315-1344), Italian painter **10** 298-299

MARTINU, BOHUSLAV (1890-1959), Czech composer **10** 299-300

MARTY, MARTIN E. (born 1928), Lutheran pastor, historian of American religion, and commentator **10** 300-301

MARVELL, ANDREW (1621-1678), English poet and politician **10** 301-303

MARX, KARL (1818-1883), German political philosopher **10** 304-308

MARX BROTHERS, 20th-century American stage and film comedians **10** 303-304

Marxism (philosophy)
England
Hobsbawm, Eric **34** 171-173

MARY I (1516-1558), queen of England 1553-1558 **10** 308-309

MARY II (1662-1694), queen of England, Scotland, and Ireland 1689-1694 **10** 309-310

MARY, QUEEN OF SCOTS (1542-1587), queen of France and Scotland **10** 308-309

MARY, ST. (Blessed Virgin Mary; late 1st century BCE-1st century A.D.), New Testament figure, mother of Jesus **10** 308-309

MARY MAGDALENE (Mary of Magdala), Catholic saint and biblical figure **24** 243-246

MASACCIO (1401-1428), Italian painter **10** 312-313

Masafuji
see Mabuchi, Kamo

Masahito
see Goshirakawa

Masanobu
see Mabuchi, Kamo

MASARYK, JAN (1886-1948), Czech foreign minister **20** 243-246

MASARYK, TOMÁŠ GARRIGUE (1850-1937), Czech philosopher and statesman, president 1919-1935 **10** 314-315

Mascots
Aicher, Otl **34** 4-6

MASINA, GIULIETTA (1921-1994), Italian actress **29** 268-270

MASINISSA, KING OF NUMIDIA (240 BCE - 148 BCE), prince of the Massylians who consolidated the Numidian tribes to form a North African kingdom **10** 315-317

MASIRE, QUETT KETUMILE (born 1925), a leader of the fight for independence and president of Botswana **10** 318-319

MASON, BRIDGET (Biddy Mason; 1818-1891), African American nurse, midwife, and entrepreneur **22** 312-314

MASON, GEORGE (1725-1792), American statesman **10** 319-320

MASON, JAMES MURRAY (1796-1871), American politician and Confederate diplomat **10** 320-321

MASON, LOWELL (1792-1872), American composer and music educator **10** 321-322

Mass production (industry)
development
Devol, George **34** 90-93

Massachusetts (state, United States)
religion (colonial era)
Wheelwright, John **34** 373-375

Massachusetts Bay Company (1628-1684)
Wheelwright, John **34** 373-375

Massachusetts Institute of Technology (Cambridge)
computing
McCarthy, John **34** 257-259

MASSAQUOI, HANS J. (1926-2013), American journalist and author **29** 270-272

MASSASOIT (1580-1661), Native American tribal chief **10** 322-324

MASSEY, VINCENT (Charles Vincent Massey, 1887-1967), Canadian governor-general **24** 246-248

MASSEY, WILLIAM FERGUSON (1856-1925), New Zealand prime minister 1912-1925 **10** 324

MASSINGER, PHILIP (1583-1640), English playwright **10** 324-325

MASSYS, QUENTIN (1465/66-1530), Flemish painter **10** 325-326

Mastai-Ferretti, Giovanni Maria
see Pius IX

Master Meng
see Mencius

Master of Flémalle
see Campin, Robert

MASTERS, EDGAR LEE (1869-1950), American author and lawyer **10** 326-327

MASTERS, WILLIAM HOWELL (1915-2001), American psychologist and sex therapist **10** 327-328

MASTERSON, BAT (William Barclay Masterson; 1853-1921), American sheriff and sportswriter **29** 272-274

MASTROIANNI, MARCELLO (1924-1996), Italian actor **33** 208-210
Deneuve, Catherine **34** 88-90

MASUDI, ALI IBN AL- HUSAYN AL- (died 956), Arab historian **10** 328-329

MASUR, KURT (born 1927), German conductor and humanist **20** 246-248

MATA HARI (Margaretha Geertruida Zelle; 1876-1917), Dutch spy **21** 279-282

MATAMOROS, MARINO (1770-1814), Mexican priest and independence hero **10** 329-330

MATHER, COTTON (1663-1728), American Puritan clergyman and historian **10** 330-332

MATHER, INCREASE (1639-1723), American Puritan clergymen, educator, and author **10** 332-333

MATHEWSON, CHRISTY (Christopher Mathewson; 1880-1925), American baseball player **21** 282-284

MATHIAS, BOB (Robert Bruce Mathias; 1930-2006), American track and field star **21** 284-286

MATHIEZ, ALBERT (1874-1932), French historian **10** 333-334

MATILDA OF TUSCANY (c. 1046-1115), Italian countess **10** 334-336

MATISSE, HENRI (1869-1954), French painter and sculptor **10** 336-337

MATLIN, MARLEE (born 1965), American actress **19** 228-230

MATLOVICH, LEONARD (1943-1988), American gay rights activist **20** 248-250

Matoaka
see Pocahontas (ballet)

Matsumura Goshun, (1752-1811), Japanese painter
Buson, Yosa **34** 389-391

MATSUNAGA, SPARK MASAYUKI (1916-1990), Asian American U.S. senator **18** 279-281

MATSUSHITA, KONOSUKE (1918-1989), Japanese inventor and businessman **19** 230-232

Matsys, Quentin
see Massys, Quentin

MATTA ECHAURREN, ROBERTO SEBASTIAN ANTONIO (Matta, 1911-2002), Chilean artist **24** 248-250

MATTEI, ENRICO (1906-1962), Italian entrepreneur **10** 337-339

Mattel (toy company)
Handler, Elliot **34** 155-157

MATTEOTTI, GIACOMO (1885-1924), Italian political leader **10** 339-340

MATTHAU, WALTER (Walter Matthow; Walter Matuschanskayasky; 1920-2000), American Actor **22** 314-316

MATTHEW, ST. (flourished Ist century), Apostle and Evangelist **10** 340-341

MATTHEW PARIS (c. 1200-1259), English Benedictine chronicler **10** 341-342

MATTHEWS, MARJORIE SWANK (1916-1986), American bishop **32** 240-242

MATTHEWS, VICTORIA EARLE (1861-1907), American journalist and social reformer **32** 242-245

MATTINGLY, GARRETT (1900-1962), American historian, professor, and author of novel-like histories **10** 342-344

MATZELIGER, JAN (1852-1889), American inventor and shoemaker **19** 232-234

MAUCHLY, JOHN (1907-1980), American computer entrepreneur **20** 250-252

MAUDSLAY, HENRY (1771-1831), British engineer and inventor **21** 286-288

MAUGHAM, WILLIAM SOMERSET (1874-1965), English author **10** 344-345

MAULBERTSCH, FRANZ ANTON (1724-1796), Austrian painter **10** 345

MAULDIN, BILL (1921-2003), cartoon biographer of the ordinary GI in World War II **10** 345-346

MAUPASSANT, HENRI RENÉ ALBERT GUY DE (1850-1893), French author **10** 347

MAURIAC, FRANÇOIS (1885-1970), French author **10** 347-348

MAURICE, JOHN FREDERICK DENISON (1805-1872), English theologian and Anglican clergyman **10** 349-350

MAURICE OF NASSAU, PRINCE OF ORANGE (1567-1625), Dutch general and statesman **10** 348-349

MAURRAS, CHARLES MARIE PHOTIUS (1868-1952), French political writer and reactionary **10** 350-351

MAURY, ANTONIA (1866-1952), American astronomer and conservationist **20** 252-254

MAURY, MATTHEW FONTAINE (1806-1873), American naval officer and oceanographer **10** 351-352

MAUSS, MARCEL (1872-1950), French sociologist and anthropologist **10** 352-353

MAWDUDI, ABU-I A'LA (1903-1979), Muslim writer and religious and political leader in the Indian sub-continent **10** 353-354

MAWSON, SIR DOUGLAS (1882-1958), Australian scientist and Antarctic explorer **10** 354-355

MAXIM, SIR HIRAM STEVENS (1840-1916), American-born British inventor **10** 355-356

Maximianus, Gaius Galerius Valerius
see Galerius

Maximilian (emperor of Mexico)
see Maximilian of Hapsburg

MAXIMILIAN I (1459-1519), Holy Roman emperor 1493-1519 **10** 356-357

Maximilian I Joseph of Bavaria, (1756-1825), elector and king of Bavaria
Ludwig I of Bavaria **34** 244-246

MAXIMILIAN II (1527-1576), Holy Roman emperor 1564-1576 **10** 357-358

MAXIMILIAN OF HAPSBURG (1832-1867), archduke of Austria and emperor of Mexico **10** 358-360

MAXWELL, IAN ROBERT (née Ludvik Hock; 1923-1991), British publishing magnate **10** 360-361

MAXWELL, JAMES CLERK (1831-1879), Scottish physicist **10** 361-364

May, Brian, (born 1947), English musician
Mercury, Freddie **34** 266-268

MAY, KARL (1842-1912), German author **26** 248-250

Maya Indians (North America)
artistic portrayals
Anguiano, Raul **34** 9-11

MAYAKOVSKY, VLADIMIR VLADIMIROVICH (1893-1930), Russian poet **10** 364-365

MAYBACH, WILHELM (1846-1929), German automobile builder **29** 274-277

MAYER, JEAN (1920-1993), nutritionist, researcher, consultant to government and international organizations, and president of Tufts University **10** 365-366

MAYER, LOUIS BURT (Eliezer Mayer; 1885-1957), American motion picture producer **19** 234-235

Mayerling (film)
Darrieux, Danielle **34** 79-81

MAYFIELD, CURTIS (1942-1999), American musician **30** 273-275

MAYNARD, ROBERT CLYVE (1937-1993), African American journalist and publisher **10** 366-367

MAYO, WILLIAM J. AND CHARLES H. (1861-1939; 1865-1939), American physicians **10** 367-369

MAYO-SMITH, RICHMOND (1854-1901), American statistician and sociologist **10** 371-372

MAYOR ZARAGOSA, FEDERICO (born 1934), Spanish biochemist who was director-general of UNESCO (United Nations Educational, Scientific, and Cultural Organization) **10** 369-371

MAYR, ERNST (1904-2005), American evolutionary biologist **10** 372-374

MAYS, BENJAMIN E. (1894-1984), African American educator and civil rights activist **10** 374-376

MAYS, WILLIE (William Howard Mays, Jr.; born 1931), African American baseball player **10** 376-379
Cepeda, Orlando **34** 52-53

Mayson, Isabella Mary
see Beeton, Isabella Mary

MAZARIN, JULES (1602-1661), French cardinal and statesman **10** 379-380

MAZEPA, IVAN STEPANOVICH (c. 1644-1709), Ukrainian Cossack leader **10** 381

Mazzarini, Giulio
see Mazarin, Jules

MAZZINI, GIUSEPPE (1805-1872), Italian patriot **31** 224-225

Mazzola, Francesco
see Parmigianino

M'BOW, AMADOU-MAHTAR (born 1921), director general of UNESCO (United Nations Educational, Scientific, and Cultural Organization) **10** 383-384

MBOYA, THOMAS JOSEPH (1930-1969), Kenyan political leader **10** 384-385

MCADOO, WILLIAM GIBBS (1863-1941), American statesman **10** 385-386

MCAULIFFE, ANTHONY (1898-1975), American army officer **19** 236-239

MCAULIFFE, CHRISTA (nee Sharon Christa Corrigan; 1948-1986), American teacher **20** 254-257

MCCAIN, JOHN SIDNEY, III (born 1936), American politician **25** 285-287

MCCANDLESS, BRUCE (born 1937), American astronaut **23** 243-246

MCCARTHY, EUGENE JOSEPH (1916-2005), American statesman **10** 386-388

MCCARTHY, JOHN (1927-2011), American computer scientist **34** 257-259

MCCARTHY, JOSEPH RAYMOND (1908-1957), American politician **10** 388-389

Meng-tzu
see Mencius

MENGELE, JOSEF (1911-1979), German physician and war criminal **10** 502-503

MENGISTU HAILE MARIAM (born 1937), head of state of Ethiopia **10** 503-505

MENGS, ANTON RAPHAEL (1728-1779), German painter **10** 505

MENKEN, ALAN (born 1949), American composer **20** 263-266

MENNO SIMONS (c. 1496-1561), Dutch reformer **10** 505-506

MENOCAL, MARIO GARCIA (1866-1941), Cuban statesman, president 1913-1921 **10** 506-507

Menon, Balakrishnan
see Chinmayananda, Swami

MENON, VENGALIL KRISHNAN KRISHNA (1897-1974), Indian statesman **10** 507-509

MENOTTI, GIAN CARLO (1911-2007), Italian-born American composer **10** 509-510

Men's movements
Bly, Robert **34** 38-40

Mensheviks (Russian Social Democratic movement)
Kirov, Sergei **34** 208-211

MENTEN, MAUD L. (1879-1960), Canadian biochemist **24** 259-260

MENUHIN, YEHUDI (1916-1999), American and British violinist and conductor **20** 266-268

MENZEL, JIŘÍ (born 1938), Czech theater and film director **34** 264-265

MENZIES, SIR ROBERT GORDON (1894-1978), Australian statesman **10** 510-511

MENZIES, WILLIAM CAMERON (1896-1957), American film director, producer, and set designer **21** 291-293

Meor Ha-Golah
see Gershom ben Judah

MERCATOR, GERHARDUS (1512-1594), Flemish cartographer **10** 511-512

MERCHANT, ISMAIL (Ismail Noor Mohammed Abdul Rehman; 1936-2005), Indian filmmaker **26** 252-254

MERCK, GEORGE WILHELM (1894-1957), American chemist and executive **29** 279-281

MERCKX, EDDY (Edouard Louis Joseph Merckx; born 1945), Belgian cyclist **28** 241-243

MERCURY, FREDDIE (1946-1991), British singer **34** 266-268

MEREDITH, GEORGE (1828-1909), English novelist and poet **10** 512-513

MEREDITH, JAMES H. (born 1933), African American civil rights activist and politician **10** 514-515

MEREZHKOVSKY, DMITRY SERGEYEVICH (1865-1941), Russian writer and literary critic **10** 515-516

Merezhkovsky, Zinaida
see Gippius, Zinaida

MERGENTHALER, OTTMAR (1854-1899), German-American inventor of the Linotype **10** 516-517

MERIAN, MARIA SIBYLLA (1647-1717), German artist and entomologist **20** 268-269

MERICI, ANGELA (St. Angela; 1474-1530), Italian nun and educator **21** 293-295

MÉRIMÉE, PROSPER (1803-1870), French author **10** 517

Merisi, Michelangelo
see Caravaggio

MERKEL, ANGELA (Angela Dorothea Kasner; born 1954), German politician **28** 243-245

MERLEAU-PONTY, MAURICE (1908-1961), French philosopher **10** 518

Merlotti, Claudio
see Merulo, Claudio

MERMAN, ETHEL (Ethel Agnes Zimmermann; 1909-1984), American singer and actress **21** 295-297

Merovingian dynasty
see France–481-751

MERRIAM, CHARLES EDWARD (1874-1953), American political scientist **10** 518-519

MERRILL, CHARLES E. (1885-1956), founder of the world's largest brokerage firm **10** 519-520

MERRILL, JAMES (1926-1995), American novelist, poet, and playwright **10** 521-522

Merry Christmas, Mr. Lawrence (film)
Oshima, Nagisa **34** 282-284

MERTON, ROBERT K. (1910-2003), American sociologist and educator **10** 522-523

MERTON, THOMAS (1915-1968), Roman Catholic writer, social critic, and spiritual guide **10** 523-525

MERULO, CLAUDIO (1533-1604), Italian composer, organist, and teacher **10** 525-526

MESMER, FRANZ ANTON (1734-1815), German physician **10** 526-527

MESSALI HADJ (1898-1974), founder of the Algerian nationalist movement **10** 527-528

MESSERSCHMIDT, FRANZ XAVER (1736-1783), German sculptor **33** 217-219

MESSERSCHMITT, WILLY (Wilhelm Emil Messerschmitt; 1898-1978), German aircraft designer and manufacturer **25** 291-293

MESSIAEN, OLIVIER (1908-1992), French composer and teacher **10** 528-529

MESSNER, REINHOLD (born 1944), Austrian mountain climber and author **22** 316-318

METACOM (a.k.a. King Philip; 1640-1676), Wampanoag cheiftain **10** 529-531

METCALFE, CHARLES THEOPHILUS (1st Baron Metcalfe; 1785-1846), British colonial administrator **10** 531-532

METCHNIKOFF, ÉLIE (1845-1916), Russian physiologist and bacteriologist **10** 532-533

Method acting (theater)
Adler, Stella **34** 1-3

METHODIUS, SAINT (825-885), Greek missionary and bishop **4** 362-363

Metropolitan Museum of Art (New York City)
Lasansky, Mauricio **34** 232-233

Metsys, Quentin
see Massys, Quentin

METTERNICH, KLEMENS VON (1773-1859), Austrian politician and diplomat **10** 533-536

Meun, Jean de
see Jean de Meun

Mexican art
Anguiano, Raul **34** 9-11

MEYERBEER, GIACOMO (1791-1864), German composer **10** 536-537

MEYERHOF, OTTO FRITZ (1884-1951), German biochemist **10** 537-539

MEYERHOLD, VSEVOLOD EMILIEVICH (1874-c. 1942), Russian director **10** 539

MEYNELL, ALICE (1847-1922), British poet **32** 255-257

MFUME, KWEISI (born Frizzell Gray; born 1948), African American civil rights activist and congressman **10** 539-542

MI FEI (1051-1107), Chinese painter, calligrapher, and critic **11** 12-13

MI5 (British security service)
Blunt, Anthony **34** 36-38

MI6 (British intelligence service)
Blake, George **34** 34-36
Burgess, Guy **34** 44-47
Maclean, Donald **34** 247-249

MUSTE, ABRAHAM JOHANNES (1885-1967), American pacifist and labor leader **11** 276-277

MUTESA I (c. 1838-1884), African monarch of Buganda **11** 277

MUTESA II (1924-1969), Monarch of Buganda **11** 277-278

MUTIS, JOSÉ CELESTINO (1732-1808), Spanish-Colombian naturalist **11** 278-279

MUTSUHITO (a.k.a. Meiji; 1852-1912), Japanese emperor **11** 279-282

Muttathupandatu, Anna
see Alphonsa of the Immaculate Conception, Saint

MUYBRIDGE, EADWEARD (1830-1904), English photographer **21** 305-308

MWANGA (c. 1866-1901), Monarch of Buganda **11** 282-283

Mycenaean civilization (Greece)
Kober, Alice **34** 213-214
Ventris, Michael **34** 360-362

MYDANS, CARL (1907-2004), American photojournalist **11** 283-284

Myerson, Golda
see Meir, Golda

Myongsong Hwanghu
see Min

MYRDAL, ALVA (1902-1986), Swedish social reformer and diplomat **24** 274-276

MYRDAL, KARL GUNNAR (1898-1987), Swedish economist and sociologist **11** 284

MYRON (flourished c. 470-450 BCE), Greek sculptor **11** 285

Mystery fiction (literary genre)
Wallace, Edgar **34** 369-371

MZILIKAZI (c. 1795-1868), South African warrior leader **11** 285-286

N

NABOKOV, VLADIMIR (1899-1977), Russian-born American writer, critic, and lepidopterist **11** 287-288

NABUCO DE ARAUJO, JOAQUIM AURELIO (1849-1910), Brazilian abolitionist, statesman, and author **11** 288-289

NADELMAN, ELIE (1882-1946), Polish-American sculptor and graphic artist **11** 289-290

NADER, RALPH (born 1934), American lawyer and social crusader **11** 290-291

NADIR SHAH (born Nadir Kouli; 1685-1747), Emperor of Persia **20** 278-281

NAGEL, ERNEST (1901-1985), American philosopher of science **11** 291-292

NAGUMO, CHUICHI (1887-1944), Japanese admiral **19** 263-266

NAGURSKI, BRONKO (Bronislaw Nagurski; 1908-1990), Canadian football player **21** 309-311

NAGY, IMRE (1896-1958), prime minister of Hungary (1953-55, 1956) **11** 292-293

NAHMANIDES (1194-1270), Spanish Talmudist **11** 293-294

NAIDU, LEELA (1940-2009), Indian actress **31** 247-248

NAIDU, SAROJINI (1879-1949), Indian poet and nationalist **11** 294-295

NAIPAUL, V. S. (born 1932), Trinidadian author of English-language prose **11** 295-296

NAISMITH, JAMES (1861-1939), Canadian inventor of basketball **21** 311-313

NAJIBULLAH, MOHAMMAD (1947-1996), Soviet-selected ruler of the Republic of Afghanistan **11** 296-298

NAKASONE, YASUHIRO (born 1918), prime minister of Japan (1982-1987) **11** 298-300

Nakayama
see Sun Yat-sen

NAMATJIRA, ALBERT (1902-1959), Australian Aboriginal artist **11** 300-301

NAMIER, SIR LEWIS BERNSTEIN (1888-1960), English historian **11** 301-303

NAMPEYO (Numpayu; Tsumana; c. 1859-1942), Hopi-Tewa potter **25** 303-306

NANAK (1469-1538), Indian reformer, founder of Sikhism **11** 303

NANSEN, FRIDTJOF (1861-1930), Norwegian polar explorer, scientist, and statesman **11** 304-305

NAOROJI, DADABHAI (1825-1917), Indian nationalist leader **11** 305

NAPIER, JOHN (1550-1617), Scottish mathematician **11** 306

NAPOLEON I (1769-1821), emperor of the French 1804-1815 **11** 306-310

NAPOLEON III (Louis Napoleon; 1808-1873), emperor of the French 1852-1870 **11** 310-312

Napoleon Bonaparte
see Napoleon I

NARAYAN, JAYAPRAKASH (1902-1979), Indian nationalist and social reformer **11** 312-313

NARAYAN, R. K. (Narayanswami; 1906-2001), Indian author **11** 313-314

Narcotics (drugs)
trade
Rothstein, Arnold **34** 311-313

NARIÑO, ANTONIO (1765-1823), Colombian patriot **11** 314-315

NARVÁEZ, PÁNFILO DE (c. 1478-1528), Spanish soldier and explorer **11** 315

Naseby, Battle of (1645)
Henrietta Maria of France **34** 167-169

NASH, JOHN (1752-1835), English architect and town planner **11** 316

NASH, JOHN FORBES, JR. (born 1928), American mathematician **22** 336-338

NASH, OGDEN (Frediric Ogden Nash; 1902-1971), American poet **18** 304-306

Nasier, Alcofribas
see Rabelais, François

NASMYTH, JAMES (1808-1890), Scottish engineer and inventor **11** 316-317

Naso, Publius Ovidius
see Ovid

NASSER, GAMAL ABDEL (1918-1970), Egyptian statesman, president 1956-1970 **11** 317-318

NAST, CONDÉ (1873-1942), American publisher **19** 266-268

NAST, THOMAS (1840-1902), American caricaturist and painter **11** 318-319

NATHAN, GEORGE JEAN (1882-1958), American author, editor, and critic **11** 319-321

NATION, CARRY AMELIA MOORE (1846-1911), American temperance reformer **11** 321-322

National Basketball Association (United States)
Wilkens, Lenny **34** 375-378

National Broadcasting Company (NBC)
McNamee, Graham **34** 261-264
Roddenberry, Gene **34** 308-310

National Football League (United States)
Davis, Al **34** 81-84

National Hockey League (North America)
Lafleur, Guy **34** 228-230
O'Ree, Willie **34** 280-282
Sawchuk, Terry **34** 321-323

National Inventors Hall of Fame
Devol, George **34** 90-93
Hazen, Elizabeth Lee **34** 163-165

National Labor Relations Act (United States; 1935)
Smith, Howard Worth **34** 336-339

National Labor Relations Board (United States)
Smith, Howard Worth **34** 336-339

NURSÎ, SAID (Bediüzzaman Said Nursî; 1876-1960), Turkish theologian **28** 259-261

NUSSLEIN-VOLHARD, CHRISTIANE (born 1942), German biologist **25** 314-316

Nuvolara, Count of
see Castiglione, Baldassare

NYE, GERALD (1892-1971), American senator **21** 320-323

NYERERE, JULIUS KAMBERAGE (1922-1999), Tanzanian statesman **11** 447-449

NYGREN, ANDERS (1890-1978), Lutheran bishop of Lund and representative of the so-called Lundensian school of theology **11** 449-451

NYKVIST, SVEN (Sven Vilhelm Nykvist; 1922-2006), Swedish cinematographer **28** 261-263

NYRO, LAURA (1947-1997), American singer-songwriter **31** 254-256

Nystatin
Hazen, Elizabeth Lee **34** 163-165

NZINGA, ANNA (Pande Dona Ana Souza; 1582-1663), queen of Angola **23** 270-271

Nzinga Mvemba
see Affonso I

NZINGA NKUWU (died 1506), king of Kongo **11** 451-452

O

Oakland Raiders (football team)
Davis, Al **34** 81-84

OAKLEY, ANNIE (1860-1926), American markswoman and Wild West star **11** 453-454

OATES, JOYCE CAROL (born 1938), American author **11** 454-456

OATES, TITUS (1649-1705), English leader of the Popish Plot **11** 456
Godfrey, Edmund Berry **34** 141-143

OBAMA, BARACK (born 1961), American president 2009- **32** 280-282

OBAMA, MICHELLE (born 1964), American first lady **33** 229-232

OBERTH, HERMANN JULIUS (1894-1989), Romanian physicist **29** 296-298

OBOTE, APOLO MILTON (1925-2005), Ugandan politician **11** 457

OBRADOVIĆ, DOSITEJ (Dimitrije Dositej Obradović c. 1740-1811), Serbian author and educator **24** 282-284

OBRECHT, JACOB (1450-1505), Dutch composer **11** 457-458

OBREGÓN, ÀLVARO (1880-1928), Mexican revolutionary general and president **11** 458-459

O'BRIEN, WILLIS (1886-1962), American film special effects pioneer **21** 324-326
Harryhausen, Ray **34** 157-163

Obscure, the
see Heraclitus

O'CASEY, SEAN (1880-1964), Irish dramatist **11** 459-460

Occam, William of
see William of Ockham

OCHOA, ELLEN (born 1958), Hispanic American electrical engineer and astronaut **11** 460-461

OCHOA, SEVERO (1905-1993), Spanish biochemist **11** 461-464

OCHS, ADOLPH SIMON (1858-1935), American publisher and philanthropist **11** 464

OCKEGHEM, JOHANNES (c. 1425-1495), Netherlandish composer **11** 464-465

O'CONNELL, DANIEL (1775-1847), Irish statesman **11** 465-467

O'CONNOR, CARROLL (1924-2001), American actor **22** 343-345

O'CONNOR, JOHN JOSEPH (1920-2000), American Roman Catholic cardinal and archbishop **22** 345-347

O'CONNOR, (MARY) FLANNERY (1925-1964), American author of short stories and novels **11** 467-468

O'CONNOR, SANDRA DAY (born 1930), United States Supreme Court justice **11** 468-470

Octavian (Octavianus, Octavius)
see Augustus

ODETS, CLIFFORD (1906-1963), American playwright and film director **11** 470-471
Adler, Stella **34** 1-3

ODETTA (1930-2008), American singer **31** 257-258

ODINGA, AJUMA JARAMOGI OGINGA (1912-1994), Kenyan politician **11** 471-473

ODOACER (433-493), Germanic chieftain **11** 473

O'DONNELL, RED HUGH (1572-1602), Irish chieftan **32** 282-284

Odría, Manuel Arturo
see Odriá Amoretti, Manuel Apolinario

ODRIÁ AMORETTI, MANUEL APOLINARIO (1897-1974), Peruvian army officer, dictator-president (1948-1957), and politician **11** 473-474

ODUM, HOWARD WASHINGTON (1884-1954), American sociologist, educator, and academic administrator **11** 474-476

ODUMEGWU OJUKWU, CHUKWUEMEKA (born 1933), Nigerian army general and rebel **18** 311-313

OE, KENZABURO (born 1935), Japanese author **24** 284-286

OERSTED, HANS CHRISTIAN (1777-1851), Danish physicist **11** 476-478

OERTER, AL (Alfred Adolph Oerter Jr.; 1936-2007), American discus thrower **21** 326-328

O'FAOLAIN, NUALA (1940-2008), Irish author **29** 294-296

OFFENBACH, JACQUES (1819-1880), German-French composer **11** 478-479

Ogadai
see Ögedei

OGATA, SADAKO (born 1927), United Nations High Commissioner for Refugees **11** 479-480

OGBURN, WILLIAM FIELDING (1886-1959), American sociologist **11** 480

OGDEN, PETER SKENE (1794-1854), Canadian fur trader and explorer **11** 480-481

OGILBY, JOHN (1600-1676), Scottish cartographer **30** 291-293

OGILVY, DAVID MACKENZIE (1911-1999), British-American advertising executive **11** 481-482

OGLETHORPE, JAMES EDWARD (1696-1785), English general and colonizer **11** 482-483

ÖGEDEI KHAN (c. 1186-1241), Mongol khan 1227-41 **34** 278-280

OGOT, GRACE EMILY AKINYI (born 1930), Kenyan author and politician **11** 483-484

OH, SADAHARU (born 1940), Japanese baseball player **31** 259-260

O'HAIR, MADALYN MURRAY (1919-1995), American atheist author and radio commentator **11** 484-485

O'HARA, JOHN (1905-1970), American novelist **11** 485

O'HARA, MAUREEN (born 1920), Irish-American actress **33** 232-233

O'HIGGINS, BERNARDO (1778-1842), Chilean soldier and statesman **11** 486

OHM, GEORG SIMON (1789-1854), German physicist **11** 486-487

OJUKWU, CHUKWUEMEKA ODUMEGWU (1933-2011), Nigerian colonel, Biafran leader **29** 298-301

Oxford, 1st Earl of
see Harley, Robert

Oxford and Asquith, 1st Earl of
see Asquith, Herbert Henry

Oxford University (England)
Jewish studies
Vermes, Geza **34** 364-366

OYONO, FERDINAND LEOPOLD (1929-2010), Cameroonian author and diplomat **24** 290-292

OZ, AMOS (born 1939), Israeli author **12** 45-47

OZAL, TURGUT (1927-1993), Turkish prime minister and president **12** 47-49

OZAWA, SEIJI (born 1935), Japanese musician and conductor **12** 49-51

OZU, YASUJIRO (1903-1963), Japanese film director **23** 279-281

P

PA CHIN (pen name of Li Fei-kan; 1904-2005), Chinese novelist **12** 53-54

PAAR, JACK HAROLD (1918-2004), American comedian and radio personality **26** 284-286

PABST, G. W. (Georg Wilhelm Pabst; 1885-1967), Austrian film director **23** 282-284

Pacelli, Eugenio Maria Giuseppe
see Pius XII

Pacheco, Máximo, (1907-1992), Mexican artist
Anguiano, Raul **34** 9-11

Pacheco y Padilla, Juan Vicente Güemes
see Revillagigedo, Conde de

PACHELBEL, JOHANN (1653-1706), German composer and organist **12** 52

PACHER, MICHAEL (c. 1435-1498), Austro-German painter and wood carver **12** 53

Pacific Ocean
Dalrymple, Alexander **34** 71-73

PACINO, AL (Alfredo James Pacino; born 1940), American actor and film director **23** 284-286

PACKARD, DAVID (1912-1996), cofounder of Hewlett-Packard Company and deputy secretary of defense under President Nixon **12** 54-56

PADEREWSKI, IGNACE JAN (1860-1941), Polish pianist, composer, and statesman **12** 56-57
Rubinstein, Anton **34** 313-315

PADMORE, GEORGE (1902/03-1959), Trinidadian leftist political activist **12** 57-58

PÁEZ, JOSÉ ANTONIO (1790-1873), Venezuelan general and president 1831-46 **12** 58

Päffgen, Christa
see Nico

PAGANINI, NICCOLO (1782-1840), Italian violinist and composer **12** 58-59

PAGE, THOMAS NELSON (1853-1922), American author and diplomat **12** 59-60

PAGE, WALTER HINES (1855-1918), American journalist and diplomat **12** 60-61

PAGELS, ELAINE HIESEY (born 1943), historian of religion **12** 61-62

PAGLIA, CAMILLE (born 1947), American author and social critic **23** 286-288

PAIGE, SATCHEL (Leroy Robert Paige; 1906-1982), African American baseball player **12** 62-65

PAINE, JOHN KNOWLES (1839-1905), American composer **12** 65

PAINE, THOMAS (1737-1809), English-born American journalist and Revolutionary propagandist **12** 66-67

PAISLEY, IAN K. (born 1926), political leader and minister of religion in Northern Ireland **12** 67-69

Pak Chong-hŭi
see Park, Chung Hee

PALACKÝ, FRANTIŠEK (1798-1876), Czech historian and statesman **12** 69-70

PALAMAS, KOSTES (1859-1943), Greek poet **12** 70

Palamism (Eastern Orthodox doctrine)
Kydones, Demetrius **34** 67-68

PALESTRINA, GIOVANNI PIERLUIGI DA (c. 1525-1594), Italian composer **12** 70-72

PALEY, GRACE (1922-2007), American author and activist **22** 348-350

PALEY, WILLIAM (1743-1805), English theologian and moral philosopher **12** 72

PALEY, WILLIAM S. (1901-1990), founder and chairman of the Columbia Broadcasting System **12** 72-75

PALIN, MICHAEL (born 1943), British comedian and writer **34** 287-289

PALLADIO, ANDREA (1508-1580), Italian architect **12** 75-77

PALMA, RICARDO (1833-1919), Peruvian poet, essayist, and short-story writer **12** 77

PALME, OLOF (Sven Olof Joachim Palme; 1927-1986), Swedish prime minister (1969-1973; 1982-1986) **28** 267-269

PALMER, ALEXANDER MITCHELL (1872-1936), American politician and jurist **12** 77-78

PALMER, ARNOLD DANIEL (born 1929), American golfer **12** 78-80

PALMER, NATHANIEL BROWN (1799-1877), American sea captain **12** 80-81

PALMER, PHOEBE WORRALL (1807-1847), American evangelist **23** 288-290

PALMERSTON, 3D VISCOUNT (Henry John Temple; 1784-1865), English prime minister 1855-65 **12** 81-83

Pamfili, Giovanni Batista
see Innocent X

PAMUK, ORHAN (born 1952), Turkish novelist and Nobel Prize Winner **28** 269-272

PAN KU (32-92), Chinese historian and man of letters **12** 86-87

Pan-Slavism
see Nationalism, Slavic

Pancreas (anatomy)
Bartholin, Thomas **34** 21-23

PANDIT, VIJAYA LAKSHMI (1900-1990), Indian diplomat and politician **12** 83-84

PANETTA, LEON E. (born 1938), Democratic congressman from California and chief of staff to President Clinton **12** 84-85

PANINI (flourished c. 5th century BCE), Indian grammarian **24** 293-295

PANKHURST, CHRISTABEL HARRIETTE (1880-1948), English reformer and suffragette **22** 350-352

PANKHURST, EMMELINE (1858-1928), English reformer **12** 85-86
Davison, Emily Wilding **34** 84-86

PANKHURST, SYLVIA (1882-1960), English reformer **29** 309-311

PANNENBERG, WOLFHART (born 1928), German Protestant theologian **12** 87-88

PANUFNIK, ANDRZEJ (1914-1991), Polish/British composer and conductor **24** 295-298

PAPANDREOU, ANDREAS (1919-1996), Greek scholar and statesman and prime minister **12** 88-91

PAPERT, SEYMOUR (born 1928), South African-born computer scientist and educator **32** 290-292

PAPINEAU, LOUIS-JOSEPH (1786-1871), French-Canadian radical political leader **12** 91

Papua New Guinea, Republic of (nation, southeast Asia)
Gajdusek, Carleton **34** 138-140

PIAGET, JEAN (1896-1980), Swiss psychologist and educator **12** 287-288

PIANKHI (ruled c. 741-c. 712 BCE), Nubian king **12** 288-289

Piano (musical instrument)
Czerny, Carl **34** 68-70

PIANO, RENZO (born 1937), Italian architect, lecturer, and designer **12** 289-291

PIATETSKI-SHAPIRO, ILYA (1929-2009), Russian-Israeli mathematician **30** 303-304

PIAZZOLLA, ASTOR (Astor Pantaleón Piazzolla; 1921-1992), Argentine musician **26** 291-293

Pibul Songgram, Luang
see Songgram, Luang Pibul

PICABIA, FRANCIS (1879-1953), French artist, writer, and bon vivant **12** 291-292

PICASSO, PABLO (1881-1973), Spanish painter, sculptor, and graphic artist **12** 292-295

PICASSO, PALOMA (born 1949), Spanish fashion designer **12** 295-297

PICCARD, AUGUSTE (1884-1962), Swiss scientist **12** 297-298

PICCARD, JACQUES ERNEST JEAN (1922-2008), Swiss explorer, scientist, oceanographer, and engineer **18** 320-322

Piccolomini, Aeneas Sylvius de'
see Pius II

PICKENS, THOMAS BOONE, JR. (T. Boone Pickens; born 1928), American businessman **19** 284-286

PICKERING, EDWARD CHARLES (1846-1919), American astronomer **12** 298

PICKERING, TIMOTHY (1745-1829), American Revolutionary soldier and statesman **12** 298-299

PICKETT, BILL (1870-1932), American rodeo cowboy **19** 286-288

PICKFORD, MARY (Gladys Louise Smith; 1893-1979), Canadian-American actress, screenwriter, and film producer **19** 288-290

PICO DELLA MIRANDOLA, CONTE GIOVANNI (1463-1494), Italian philosopher and humanist **12** 299-300
Innocent VIII **34** 183-185

PICON, MOLLY (1898-1992), American actress **27** 290-292

Pictographs (art)
Aicher, Otl **34** 4-6

PIERCE, FRANKLIN (1804-1869), American statesman, president 1853-57 **12** 300-301

PIERCE, JOHN ROBINSON (1910-2002), American electronics engineer and author **21** 349-351

Pierluigi, Giovanni
see Palestrina, Giovanni Pierluigi da

PIERO DELLA FRANCESCA (c. 1415-1492), Italian painter **12** 301-302

Pierre de Maricourt
see Peregrinus, Petrus

Pietro Pierleoni
see Anacletus II

PIGOU, ARTHUR CECIL (1877-1959), English economist **12** 302

PIKE, ZEBULON (1779-1813), American soldier and explorer **12** 302-304

Pilar, Marcelo H. del
see Del Pilar, Marcelo H.

PILLSBURY, CHARLES ALFRED (1842-1899), American businessman **12** 304

PILON, GERMAIN (c. 1535-1590), French sculptor **12** 305

PILSUDSKI, JOSEPH (1867-1935), Polish general, president 1918-21 **12** 305-306

PIMEN I, PATRIARCH OF MOSCOW (1910-1990), Russian church leader **30** 304-306

PIN-CHIN CHIANG (Wei-Chih Chiang; Ling Ding; 1904-1986), Chinese author and feminist **24** 310-312

PINCHBACK, PINCKNEY BENTON STEWART (1837-1921), African American politician **12** 306-308

Pincherle, Alberto
see Moravia, Alberto

PINCHOT, GIFFORD (1865-1946), American conservationist and public official **12** 308-309

PINCKNEY, CHARLES (1757-1824), American politician and diplomat **12** 309-310

PINCKNEY, CHARLES COTESWORTH (1745-1825), American statesman **12** 310

PINCKNEY, ELIZA (Elizabeth Lucas; 1722-1793), American business woman **25** 334-336

PINCUS, GREGORY GOODWIN (1903-1967), American biologist **12** 310-312
Djerassi, Carl **34** 95-97

PINDAR (c. 518-c. 438 BCE), Greek lyric poet **12** 312-313

PINEL, PHILIPPE (1745-1826), French physician **12** 313-314

PINERO, ARTHUR WING (1855-1934), English playwright **18** 322-324

Pingwoldang
see Sol Ch'ong

Pinilla, Gustavo Rojas
see Rojas Pinilla, Gustavo

PINKERTON, ALLEN (1819-1884), American detective **12** 314-315

PINKHAM, LYDIA ESTES (1819-1883), American patent medicine manufacturer **21** 351-353

PINKNEY, WILLIAM (1764-1822), American attorney, diplomat, and statesman **22** 355-357

PINOCHET UGARTE, AUGUSTO (1915-2006), Chilean military leader and dictator **12** 315-317

PINTER, HAROLD (1930-2008), English playwright **12** 317-318

PINTO, ISAAC (1720-1791), Jewish merchant and scholar **12** 318

PINZÓN, MARTIN ALONSO (c. 1440-1493), Spanish navigator **22** 358-360

PINZÓN, VICENTE YÁÑEZ (c. 1460-c. 1524), Spanish navigator **22** 360-361

PIO, PADRE (Francesco Forgione; 1887-1968), Italian priest **20** 297-299

PIPPIN, HORACE (1888-1946), African American painter **12** 318-319

PIRANDELLO, LUIGI (1867-1936), Italian playwright novelist, and critic **12** 319-321

PIRANESI, GIOVANNI BATTISTA (1720-1778), Italian engraver and architect **12** 321-322

PIRENNE, JEAN HENRI (Jean Henri Otto Lucien Marie Pirenne; 1862-1935), Belgian historian **12** 322-323

PIRI REIS (c. 1465-1554), Turkish navigator and mapmaker **31** 280-281

Pisan, Christine de
see Christine de Pisan

PISANELLO (Antonio Pisano; before 1395-1455), Italian painter and medalist **12** 323-324

Pisano
see Pisanello

PISANO, GIOVANNI (c. 1250-c. 1314), Italian sculptor **12** 324-325

PISANO, NICOLA (Nicola d'Apulia; c. 1220-c. 1278), Italian sculptor **12** 325

PISCATOR, ERWIN (1893-1966), German theatrical producer **29** 315-317

PISCOPIA, ELENA LUCREZIA CORNARO (1646-1684), Italian philosopher **26** 293-295

PISSARO, CAMILLE (1830-1903), French painter **12** 326-327

PISTON, WALTER (1894-1976), American composer **12** 327-328

Q

R

REVEL, BERNARD (1885-1940), Talmudic scholar and educator **13** 108-109

REVELS, HIRAM RHOADES (1822-1901), African American clergyman, statesman, and educator **13** 109-110

REVERE, PAUL (1735-1818), American patriot, silversmith, and engraver **13** 110-111

REVILLAGIGEDO, CONDE DE (Juan Vicente Güemes Pacheco y Padilla; 1740-1799), Spanish colonial administrator, viceroy of New Spain **13** 111-112

REYES, ALFONSO (1889-1959), Mexican author and diplomat **13** 112-113

REYES, RAFAEL (1850-1920), Colombian military leader, president 1904-09 **13** 113

REYMONT, WLADYSLAW STANISLAW (Wladyslaw Rejment; 1868-1925), Polish author **25** 352-353

REYNOLDS, ALBERT (born 1932), prime minister of Ireland **13** 113-115

REYNOLDS, SIR JOSHUA (1723-1792), English portrait painter **13** 115-116

REYNOLDS, RICHARD JOSHUA, JR. (R.J. Reynolds; 1906-1964), American businessman and philanthropist **19** 308-310

REZA SHAH PAHLAVI (Reza Khan; 1878-1944), Shah of Iran 1925-41 **13** 116-117

RHEE, SYNGMAN (1875-1965), Korean independence leader, South Korean president 1948-60 **13** 117-120

RHETT, ROBERT BARNWELL (1800-1876), American statesman **13** 120

RHODES, CECIL JOHN (1853-1902), English imperialist and financier **13** 120-122

RHODES, JAMES FORD (1848-1927), American historian **13** 122

RHYS, JEAN (Ella Gwendolen Rees Williams; 1890-1979), English author **19** 310-312

Rhythm and Blues Foundation
Brown, Ruth **34** 41-42

RIBERA, JUSEPE DE (1591-1652), Spanish painter **13** 122-123

RICARDO, DAVID (1772-1823), English economist **13** 123-124

RICCI, MATTEO (1552-1610), Italian Jesuit missionary **13** 124-125

Quebec Nordiques (hockey team)
Lafleur, Guy **34** 228-230

RICE, ANNE (born 1941), American author **13** 125-126

RICE, CONDOLEEZZA (born 1954), African American national security advisor **23** 335-338

RICE, ELMER (1892-1967), American playwright and novelist **13** 126-127

RICE, GRANTLAND (1880-1954), American journalist **34** 302-304

RICE, JOSEPH MAYER (1857-1934), American education reformer **13** 127-128

RICH, ADRIENNE (1929-2012), American poet **13** 128-130

RICHARD I (1157-1199), king of England 1189-99 **13** 130

RICHARD II (1367-1400), king of England 1377-99 **13** 130-131

RICHARD III (1452-1485), king of England 1483-85 **13** 132-133

Richard III (play; Shakespeare)
Cibber, Colley **34** 56-58

Richard, Duke of Gloucester
see Richard III (play; Shakespeare)

RICHARD, MAURICE ("Rocket" Richard; 1921-2000), Canadian hockey player **19** 312-313

Richard the Lion-Hearted
see Richard I

RICHARDS, ANN WILLIS (1933-2006), Democratic governor of Texas **13** 133-134

RICHARDS, ELLEN H. (born Ellen Henrietta Swallow; 1842-1911), American chemist and educator **13** 134-136

RICHARDS, IVOR ARMSTRONG (1893-1979), English-born American semanticist and literary critic **13** 137

RICHARDS, THEODORE WILLIAM (1868-1928), American chemist **13** 137-138

RICHARDSON, HENRY HANDEL (pen name of Ethel Florence Lindesay Richardson; 1870-1946), expatriate Australian novelist **13** 139

RICHARDSON, HENRY HOBSON (1838-1886), American architect **13** 139-141

RICHARDSON, RALPH DAVID (1902-1983), British actor **24** 332-334

RICHARDSON, SAMUEL (1689-1761), English novelist **13** 141-142

RICHELIEU, ARMAND JEAN DU PLESSIS DE (1585-1642), French statesman and cardinal **13** 142-144
Médicis, Marie de' **34** 254-255

RICHET, CHARLES ROBERT (1850-1935), French physiologist **13** 144-145

RICHIER, GERMAINE (1904-1959), French sculptor **13** 145-146

RICHLER, MORDECAI (1931-2001), Canadian author **22** 371-373

RICHTER, BURTON (born 1931), American physicist **25** 354-356

RICHTER, CHARLES F. (1900-1985), American seismologist **13** 146-148

RICHTER, CONRAD MICHAEL (1890-1968), American novelist and short-story writer **13** 148-149

RICHTER, GERHARD (born 1932), German artist **23** 338-340

RICHTER, HANS (Johann Siegried Richter; 1888-1976), German-born film director **13** 149-150

RICHTER, JOHANN PAUL FRIEDRICH (1763-1825), German humorist and prose writer **13** 150-151

RICHTHOFEN, BARON MANFRED VON (1892-1918), German aviator **29** 322-324

RICIMER, FLAVIUS (died 472), Germanic Roman political chief **13** 151-152

RICKENBACKER, EDWARD VERNON (1890-1973), World War I fighter pilot and airline president **13** 152-153

RICKEY, WESLEY BRANCH (1881-1965), innovative baseball executive **13** 153-155

RICKOVER, HYMAN GEORGE (1900-1986), U.S. Navy officer **13** 155-157

RICOEUR, PAUL (1913-2005), French exponent of hermeneutical philosophy **13** 157-158

RIDE, SALLY (1951-2012), American astronaut and physicist **13** 158-160

RIDGE, JOHN ROLLIN (Yellow Bird; 1827-1867), Native American author **22** 373-375

RIDGE, THOMAS JOSEPH (born 1946), American governor of Pennsylvania and first secretary of the Department of Homeland Security **24** 334-337

RIDGWAY, MATTHEW BUNKER (1895-1993), American general **13** 160-161

RIDGWAY, ROZANNE LEJEANNE (born 1935), American diplomat **24** 337-338

RIEFENSTAHL, LENI (1902-2003), German film director **13** 161-163

RIEL, LOUIS (1844-1885), Canadian rebel **13** 163-164

RIEMANN, GEORG FRIEDRICH BERNARD (1826-1866), German mathematician **13** 164-165

RIEMENSCHNEIDER, TILMAN (1468-1531), German sculptor **13** 166

RIENZI, COLA DI (or Rienzo; c. 1313-1354), Italian patriot, tribune of Rome **13** 166-167

RIESMAN, DAVID (1909-2002), American sociologist, writer, and social critic **13** 167-168

S

SADI, SHAIKH MUSLIH-AL-DIN
see Sa'di

SADR, MUSA AL- (Imam Musa; 1928-c. 1978), Lebanese Shi'ite Moslem religious and political leader **13** 420-422

SAFAR, PETER (born 1924), Austrian-American anesthesiologist **34** 316-318

SAFIRE, WILLIAM (1929-2009), American journalist **13** 422-424

SAGAN, CARL E. (1934-1996), American astronomer and popularizer of science **13** 424-425

SAGER, RUTH (1918-1997), American biologist and geneticist **13** 425-426

Sagoyewatha
see Red Jacket

SAHA, MEGHNAD N. (1893-1956), Indian astrophysicist **30** 312-314

SAICHO (767-822), Japanese Buddhist monk **13** 426-428

SAID, EDWARD WADIE (1935-2003), American author and activist **27** 312-314

SAID, SEYYID (1790-1856), Omani sultan **13** 428-429

SAIGO, TAKAMORI (1827-1877), Japanese rebel and statesman **13** 429

St. Albans, Viscount
see Bacon, Sir Francis

ST. CLAIR, ARTHUR (1736-1818), Scottish-born American soldier and politician **13** 429-430

ST. DENIS, RUTH (c. 1878-1968), American dancer and choreographer **13** 430-431

SAINT-EXUPÉRY, ANTOINE DE (1900-1944), French novelist, essayist, and pilot **13** 431-432

SAINT-GAUDENS, AUGUSTUS (1848-1907), American sculptor **13** 432

SAINT-GEORGE, JOSEPH BOULOGNE, CHEVALIER DE (1745-1799), French musician, athlete and soldier **27** 314-316

St. John, Henry
see Bolingbroke, Viscount

SAINT-JUST, LOUIS ANTOINE LÉON DE (1767-1794), French radical political leader **13** 433

ST. LAURENT, LOUIS STEPHEN (1882-1973), Canadian statesman **13** 434

ST. LAURENT, YVES (1936-2008), French fashion designer **20** 327-329
Deneuve, Catherine **34** 88-90

Saint-Léger Léger, Alexis
see Perse, Saint-John

St. Louis Cardinals (baseball team)
Cepeda, Orlando **34** 52-53

St. Louis Hawks (basketball team)
Wilkens, Lenny **34** 375-378

SAINT-PIERRE, ABBÉ DE (Charles Irénée Castel; 1658-1743), French political and economic theorist **13** 434-435

SAINT-SAËNS, CHARLES CAMILLE (1835-1921), French composer **13** 435-436

SAINT-SIMON, COMTE DE (Claude Henri de Rouvroy; 1760-1825), French social philosopher and reformer **13** 436-437

SAINT-SIMON, DUC DE (Louis de Rouvroy; 1675-1755), French writer **13** 436

SAINTE-BEUVE, CHARLES AUGUSTIN (1804-1869), French literary critic **13** 438

SAINTE-MARIE, BUFFY (Beverly Sainte-Marie; born 1941), Native American singer and songwriter **26** 334-336

SAIONJI, KIMMOCHI (1849-1940), Japanese elder statesman **13** 438-439

SAKHAROV, ANDREI (1921-1989), Russian theoretical physicist and "father of the Soviet atomic bomb" **13** 439-441

SALADIN (Salah-ad-Din Yusuf ibn Aiyub; 1138-93), Kurdish ruler of Egypt and Syria **13** 441-442

SALAM, ABDUS (1926-1996), Pakistani physicist **24** 344-346

SALAZAR, ANTÓNIO DE OLIVEIRA (1889-1970), Portuguese statesman **13** 442-443

Salcedo, Augusto Bernardino Leguía y
see Leguía y Salcedo, Augusto Bernardino

SALCEDO, DORIS (born 1958), Colombian artist **33** 276-278

SALIERI, ANTONIO (1750-1825), Italian composer **29** 333-335

SALIH, ALI'ABDALLAH (born 1942), president of the Yemeni Arab Republic (North Yemen) and first president of the United Republic of Yemen **13** 443-445

SALIH, TAYEB (1929-2009), Sudanese author **31** 317-318

SALINAS DE GORTARI, CARLOS (born 1948), president of Mexico 1988-1994 **13** 445-447

SALINGER, J. D. (1919-2010), American author **13** 447-448

SALISBURY, HARRISON EVANS (1908-1993), American journalist **13** 449-451

SALISBURY, 3D MARQUESS OF (Robert Arthur Talbot Gascoyne-Cecil; 1830-1903), English statesman and diplomat **13** 448-449

SALK, JONAS EDWARD (1914-1995), American physician, virologist, and immunologist **13** 451-452

SALLE, DAVID (born 1952), American artist **13** 452-453

SALLINEN, AULIS (born 1935), Finnish composer **25** 368-370

SALLUST (Gaius Sallustius Crispus; 86-c. 35 BCE), Roman statesman and historian **13** 454

SALOMON, CHARLOTTE (1917-1943), German artist **13** 454-455

SALOMON, HAYM (c. 1740-1785), American financier **20** 329-331

SALUTATI, COLUCCIO (1331-1406), Italian humanist and chancellor **34** 318-319

SALVEMINI, GAETANO (1873-1957), Italian historian **13** 455-456

SAMAR, SIMA (born 1957), Afghan physician and human rights activist **25** 370-372

SAMOSET (1590-1653), Native American chief and interpreter **27** 316-319

SAMPSON, EDITH (nee Edith Spurlock; 1901-1979), African American social worker, judge, and promoter of the United States **23** 356-358

SAMUEL (c. 1056-1004 BCE), Hebrew prophet, last judge of Israel **13** 457-458

SAMUELSON, PAUL ANTHONY (1915-2009), American economist **13** 458-459

San Francisco Giants (baseball team)
Cepeda, Orlando **34** 52-53
Marichal, Juan **34** 252-254

SAN MARTÍN, JOSÉ DE (1778-1850), Argentine soldier and statesman **13** 468-469

San Martín, Ramón Grau
see Grau San Martín, Ramón

SANA'I, HAKIM (Adam al-Ghaznawi; Abu al-Majd Majdud ibn Adam; c. 1050-c. 1131), Persian mystic poet **24** 346-347

SANAPIA (Mary Poafpybitty; 1895-1979), Comanche medicine woman **23** 358-360

SANCHEZ, SONIA (Wilsonia Benita Driver; born 1934), African American author and educator **24** 347-350

SANCTORIUS (1561-1636), Italian physician and physiologist **13** 459

SAND, GEORGE (1804-1876), French novelist **13** 459-461

SANDAGE, ALLAN REX (1926-2010), American astronomer **21** 383-384

SANDBURG, CARL (1878-1967), American poet, anthologist, and biographer **13** 461-462

SANDERS, BARRY (born 1968), African American football player **25** 372-374

SANDERS, COLONEL (Harland David Sanders; 1890-1980), American businessman **19** 323-325

SANDINO, AUGUSTO C. (1894-1934), Nicaraguan guerrilla leader **13** 462-463

Sandracottus
see Chandragupta Maurya

SANDYS, SIR EDWIN (1561-1629), English statesman and colonizer in America **13** 463-464

SANGALLO FAMILY (flourished late 15th-mid-16th century), Italian artists and architects **13** 464-466

SANGER, FREDERICK (1918-2013), English biochemist **13** 466-467

SANGER, MARGARET HIGGINS (1884-1966), American leader of birth control movement **13** 467-468

SANMICHELI, MICHELE (c. 1484-1559), Italian architect and military engineer **13** 469-470

SANSOVINO, JACOPO (1486-1570), Italian sculptor and architect **13** 470-471

SANTA ANA, ANTONIO LÓPEZ DE (1794-1876), Mexican general and statesman, six times president **13** 471-472

SANTA CRUZ, ANDRÉS DE (1792-1865), Bolivian general and statesman, president 1829-39 **13** 472-473

SANTAMARIA, BARTHOLOMEW AUGUSTINE (1915-1998), Australian Roman Catholic publicist and organizer **13** 473-474

SANTANA, CARLOS (born 1947), American guitarist **33** 278-280

SANTANA, PEDRO (1801-1864), Dominican military leader, three times president **13** 474-475

SANTANDER, FRANCISCO DE PAULA (1792-1840), Colombian general and statesman **13** 475

SANTAYANA, GEORGE (Jorge Agustin de Santayana; 1863-1952), Spanish-American philosopher **13** 475-477

Santorio, Santorio
see Sanctorius

SANTOS-DUMONT, ALBERTO (1873-1932), Brazilian inventor **13** 477-478

Sanzio, Raffaello
see Raphael

SAPIR, EDWARD (1884-1939), American anthropologist **13** 478-479

SAPPHO (c. 625-570 BCE), Greek lyric poet **13** 479-480

SAPRU, SIR TEJ BAHADUR (1875-1949), Indian lawyer and statesman **13** 480-481

SARAMAGO, JOSE (1922-2010), Portuguese author **25** 374-376

SARANDON, SUSAN (Susan Abigail Tomalin; born 1946), American actress and activist **18** 358-360

SARASATE, PABLO DE (Martín Melitón Sarasate y Navascuéz 1844-1908), Spanish violinist and composer **26** 336-338

Saraswati, Swami Dayananda
see Dayananda Saraswati, Swami

SARGENT, JOHN SINGER (1856-1925), American portrait painter **13** 481-482

SARGON II (ruled 722-705 BCE), king of Assyria **13** 482

SARGON OF AGADE (c. 2340-2284 BCE), first Semitic king of Mesopotamia **13** 483

SARIT THANARAT (1908-1963), Thai army officer, prime minister 1957-63 **13** 483-484

SARKOZY, NICOLAS (born 1955), French president, 2007-2012 **33** 280-282

SARMIENTO, DOMINGO FAUSTINO (1811-1888), Argentine statesman, president 1868-74 **13** 484-485

SARNOFF, DAVID (1891-1971), American television and radio broadcasting executive **13** 485-486

SAROYAN, WILLIAM (1908-1981), American short-story writer, dramatist, and novelist **13** 486-487

SARPI, PAOLO (1552-1623), Italian prelate and statesman **13** 487-488

SARRAUTE, NATHALIE TCHERNIAK (1900-1999), French author of novels, essays, and plays **13** 488-490

SARRIS, ANDREW (1928-2012), American film critic **34** 319-321

Sarto, Andrea del
see Andrea del Sarto

Sarto, Giuseppe Melchiorre
see Pius X

SARTON, GEORGE (1884-1956), Belgian-born American historian of science **13** 490-491

SARTRE, JEAN PAUL (1905-1980), French philosopher and author **13** 491-492

SASSETTA (c. 1400-50), Italian painter **13** 492

SASSOON, SIEGFRIED (1886-1967), English poet **13** 492-493

SASSOON, VIDAL (1928-2012), British beautician and executive **33** 282-284

SATANTA (White Bear; 1830-1878), Native American orator and leader of the Kiowa tribe **13** 493-494

Satellite Records
Axton, Estelle **34** 13-15
Stewart, Jim **34** 343-345

SATIE, ERIK (1866-1925), French composer **13** 494-495
Cale, John **34** 48-51

Satire (literature)
Austrian
Kraus, Karl **34** 219-221

SATO, EISAKU (1901-1975), Japanese statesman, prime minister 1964-72 **13** 495-496

Sato, Nobusuke
see Kishi, Nobusuke

SAUER, CARL ORTWIN (1889-1975), American geographer and anthropologist **13** 496-497

SAUGUET, HENRI (1901-1986), French composer, writer, and thinker on art and music **13** 497-498

SAUL (c. 1020-1000 BCE), first King of Israel **13** 498

SAUND, DALIP SINGH (1899-1973), Indian-American U.S. congressman **28** 310-312

Saunders, Sir Alexander Morris Carr
see Carr-Saunders, Sir Alexander Morris

SAUNDERS, SIR CHARLES EDWARD (1867-1937), Canadian cerealist **13** 498-499

SAUNDERS, CICELY (Cicely Mary Strode Saunders; 1918-2005), English doctor and social worker **25** 376-378

SAVAGE, AUGUSTA CHRISTINE (born Augusta Christine Fells; 1892-1962), African American sculptor and teacher **13** 499-501

SAVAGE, MICHAEL JOSEPH (1872-1940), New Zealand labor leader, prime minister 1935-40 **13** 501-502

SAVARKAR, VINAYAK DAMODAR (Veer Savarkar; 1883-1966), Indian political leader **28** 312-314

SAVIGNY, FRIEDRICH KARL VON (1779-1861), German jurist **13** 502-503

SAVIMBI, JONAS MALHEIROS (1934-2002), founder and leader of UNITA (National Union for the Total Independence of Angola) **13** 503-505

SAVONAROLA, GIROLAMO (1452-1498), Italian religious reformer and dictator of Florence **13** 505-506

SAW MAUNG (1928-1997), leader of armed forces that took power in Burma (now Myanmar) in a 1988 military coup **13** 506-507

SAWALLISCH, WOLFGANG (1923-2013), German orchestra conductor **28** 314-316

SAWCHUK, TERRY (1929-1970), Canadian hockey player **34** 321-323

SAX, ADOLPHE (Antoine-Joseph Sax; 1814-1894), Belgian musician and inventor of musical instruments **28** 316-318

SAXE, COMTE DE (1696-1750), marshal of France **13** 507-508

Saxe-Coburg-Gotha dynasty (Great Britain)
see Great Britain-since 1901 (Windsor)

SAY, JEAN BAPTISTE (1767-1832), French economist **13** 508-509

SAYERS, DOROTHY L. (1893-1957), English author and translator **29** 335-337

SAYERS, GALE (born 1943), American football player **21** 377-379

SAYRE, FRANCIS BOWES (1885-1972), American lawyer and administrator **13** 509

SAYYID QUTB (1906-1966), Egyptian writer, educator, and religious leader **13** 509-511

SCALFARO, OSCAR LUIGI (1918-2012), Christian Democratic leader and president of the Italian Republic **13** 511-512

SCALIA, ANTONIN (born 1936), U.S. Supreme Court justice **13** 513-514

Scams
Ponzi, Charles **34** 291-294

Scandal, political
see Corruption, political (government)

Scandiano, Conte di
see Boiardo, Matteo Maria

SCARGILL, ARTHUR (born 1938), president of the British National Union of Mineworkers **13** 514-515

SCARLATTI, DOMENICO (1685-1757), Italian harpsichordist and composer **13** 515-517

SCARLATTI, PIETRO ALESSANDRO GASPARE (1660-1725), Italian composer **13** 517-518

SCARRY, RICHARD (1919-1994), American author and illustrator **33** 284-286

SCHACHT, HJALMAR HORACE GREELEY (1877-1970), German economist and banker **13** 518-519

SCHAFF, PHILIP (1819-1893), Swiss-born American religious scholar **13** 519-520

SCHAPIRO, MIRIAM (born 1923), Artist **13** 520-521

SCHARNHORST, GERHARD JOHANN DAVID VON (1755-1813), Prussian general **13** 521-522

SCHARPING, RUDOLF (born 1947), minister-president of Rhineland-Palatinate and chairman of the German Social Democratic Party **13** 522-524

SCHECHTER, SOLOMON (1849-1915), Romanian-American Jewish scholar and religious leader **13** 524

SCHEELE, KARL WILHELM (1742-1786), Swedish pharmacist and chemist **13** 525-526

SCHELLING, FRIEDRICH WILHELM JOSEPH VON (1775-1854), German philosopher **13** 526-527

SCHEMBECHLER, BO (1929-2006), Glenn Edward Schembechler, Jr.; American football coach **31** 319-320

Scherer, Jean-Marie Maurice
see Rohmer, Éric

SCHIAPARELLI, ELSA (1890-1973), Italian-American fashion designer **34** 323-326

SCHIELE, EGON (1890-1918), Austrian Expressionist painter and draftsman **14** 1-2

SCHIESS, BETTY BONE (born 1923), American Episcopalian priest **18** 360-362

SCHIFF, JACOB HENRY (1847-1920), German-American banker **14** 2-3

SCHIFRIN, LALO (born 1932), Argentine composer and pianist **33** 286-288

SCHILLEBEECKX, EDWARD (1914-2010), Belgian Roman Catholic theologian **14** 3-4

SCHILLER, JOHANN CHRISTOPH FRIEDRICH VON (1759-1805), German dramatist, poet, and historian **14** 4-7

SCHINDLER, ALEXANDER MOSHE (1925-2000), American Jewish leader **23** 360-362

SCHINDLER, OSKAR (1908-1974), German businessman and humanitarian **18** 362-365

SCHINDLER, SOLOMON (1842-1915), German-American rabbi and social theorist **14** 7-8

SCHINKEL, KARL FRIEDRICH (1781-1841), German architect, painter and designer **14** 8

SCHLAFLY, PHYLLIS (born 1924), American political activist and author **14** 9-10

SCHLEGEL, FRIEDRICH VON (1772-1829), German critic and author **14** 10-11

SCHLEIERMACHER, FRIEDRICH ERNST DANIEL (1768-1834), German theologian and philosopher **14** 11-12

SCHLEMMER, OSKAR (1888-1943), German painter, sculptor, and stage designer **14** 12-13

SCHLESINGER, ARTHUR MEIER (1888-1965), American historian **14** 13

SCHLESINGER, ARTHUR MEIER, JR. (1917-2007), American historian and Democratic party activist **14** 13-15

SCHLESINGER, JAMES RODNEY (born 1929), American government official **14** 15-16

SCHLICK, FRIEDRICH ALBERT MORITZ (1882-1936), German physicist and philosopher **14** 16-17

SCHLIEMANN, HEINRICH (1822-1890), German merchant and archeologist **14** 17-18

SCHLÜTER, ANDREAS (c. 1660-1714), German sculptor and architect **14** 18-19

SCHMELING, MAX (1905-2005), German boxer **29** 337-339

SCHMIDT, HELMUT (born 1918), Social Democrat and chancellor of the Federal Republic of Germany (the former West Germany), 1974-82 **14** 19-21

Schmidt, Johann Caspar
see Stirner, Max

SCHMITT, JACK (Harrison Hagan Schmitt; borm 1935), American astronaut and geologist **22** 385-386

Schmitz, Ettore
see Svevo, Italo

SCHMOLLER, GUSTAV FRIEDRICH VON (1838-1917), German economist **14** 21

SCHNABEL, ARTUR (1882-1951), Austrian American pianist **27** 319-321

SCHNEERSON, MENACHEM MENDEL (The Rebbe; 1902-1994), Russian-American Hassidic Jewish leader **22** 386-388

SCHNEIDER, ROMY (Rosemarie Magdalena Albach-Retty; 1938-1982), Austrian actress **24** 350-352

SCHNEIDERMAN, ROSE (1882-1972), labor organizer and activist for the improvement of working conditions for women **14** 22-23

SCHNITZLER, ARTHUR (1862-1931), Austrian dramatist and novelist **14** 23-24

SCHOENBERG, ARNOLD (1874-1951), Austrian composer **14** 24-26

SCHOLASTICA, ST. (c. 480-547), Italian abbess **30** 314-316

SCHOLEM, GERSHOM (1897-1982), Jewish scholar **14** 26

Scholl, Sophie, (1921-1943)
Aicher, Otl **34** 4-6

SCHONGAUER, MARTIN (c. 1435-91), German engraver and painter **14** 26-28

SHAW, ARTIE (Arthur Jacob Arshawsky; 1910-2004), American clarinetist and composer **26** 340-342

SHAW, GEORGE BERNARD (1856-1950), British playwright, critic, and pamphleteer **14** 163-164

Shaw, Josephine
see Lowell, Josephine Shaw

SHAW, LEMUEL (1781-1861), American jurist **14** 164-165

SHAW, MARY (born 1943), American computer science professor **14** 165-167

SHAW, RICHARD NORMAN (1831-1912), British architect **14** 167-168

Shaw, T. E.
see Lawrence, Thomas Edward

SHAW BROTHERS (Runme, 1901-1985, and Run Run, 1907-2014), Chinese cinema executives **30** 326-328

SHAWN, WILLIAM (1907-1992), American editor **19** 333-335

SHAYS, DANIEL (c. 1747-1825), American Revolutionary War Captain **14** 168

SHCHARANSKY, ANATOLY BORISOVICH (born 1948), prominent figure of the Helsinki Watch Group **14** 168-170

SHEARER, NORMA (1902-1982), Canadian actress **29** 343-345

SHEBA (Makeda; Bilqis; c. 1075 BCE-c. 955 BCE), queen of Sheba **24** 365-367

SHEELER, CHARLES (1883-1965), American painter **14** 170-171

SHEEN, FULTON J. (1895-1979), American Roman Catholic bishop and television host **14** 171-172

Shehu
see Uthman don Fodio

Sheikh Ibrahim
see Burkhardt, Johann Ludwig

SHELBY, CARROLL (1923-2012), American racecar driver **33** 295-297

SHELDON, CHARLES M. (1857-1946), American social reformer who also wrote *In His Steps* **14** 172-174

Sheldon, May French
see French-Sheldon, May

SHELDON, SIDNEY (1917-2007), American author **28** 323-325

SHELLEY, MARY WOLLSTONECRAFT (1797-1851), English author **14** 174-176

SHELLEY, PERCY BYSSHE (1792-1822), English romantic poet **14** 176-178

Shelomoh Yitzhaki
see Rashi

SHEPARD, ALAN (1923-1998), American astronaut **14** 178-180

SHEPARD, SAM (Samuel Shepard Rogers VII; born 1943), American playwright, rock performer, and film actor **14** 180-181

SHEPPARD, WILLIAM HENRY (1865-1927), African American missionary to Africa **27** 325-327

SHERATON, THOMAS (1751-1806), English furniture designer **14** 181-182

SHERIDAN, PHILIP HENRY (1831-1888), American general **14** 182-183

SHERIDAN, RICHARD BRINSLEY (1751-1816), British playwright and orator **14** 183-184

SHERMAN, CINDY (Cynthia Morris Sherman; born 1954), American photographer **19** 335-337

SHERMAN, JOHN (1823-1900), American politician **14** 184-185

SHERMAN, ROGER (1721-1793), American patriot **14** 185-186

SHERMAN, WILLIAM TECUMSEH (1820-1891), American general **14** 186-187

SHERRINGTON, SIR CHARLES SCOTT (1857-1952), English physiologist **14** 187-189

SHERWOOD, ROBERT EMMET (1896-1955), American playwright **14** 189-190

SHESTOV, LEV (Lev Isaakovich Schwarzmann; 1866-1938), Russian Jewish thinker and literary critic **14** 190-191

SHEVARDNADZE, EDUARD AMVROSEVICH (born 1928), foreign minister of the U.S.S.R. (1985-1990) **14** 191-193

SHEVCHENKO, TARAS GRIGORYEVICH (1814-1861), Ukrainian poet **24** 367-369

SHIBA, RYOTARO (1923-1996), Japanese novelist, historian, and journalist **30** 328-330

Shih-heng
see Lu Chi

SHIH KO-FA (died 1644), Chinese scholar-soldier **14** 194-195

SHIH LE (274-333), Chinese emperor 330-333 **14** 195

SHIHAB, FU'AD (1903-1973), Father of the Lebanese Army and president of Lebanon (1958-1964) **14** 193-194

SHILS, EDWARD ALBERT (1911-1995), American sociologist **14** 195-197

SHIMADA, SHIGETARO (1883-1976), Japanese naval admiral **30** 330-332

SHINRAN (1173-1262), Japanese Buddhist monk **14** 197

SHIPPEN, EDWARD (1728-1806), American jurist **14** 197-198

SHIRER, WILLIAM L. (1904-1993), American journalist and historian who wrote on the history of Nazi Germany **14** 198-199

SHIVAJI
see Śivaji

SHKLOVSKY, VIKTOR (1893-1984), Russian critic **30** 332-334

Shochiku Motion Picture Company
Oshima, Nagisa **34** 282-284

SHOCKLEY, WILLIAM (1910-1989), American physicist **14** 200-202

SHOEMAKER, GENE (Eugene Merle Shoemaker; 1928-1997), American geologist and planetary scientist **20** 335-338

SHOEMAKER, WILLIE (Billy Lee Shoemaker; 1931-2003), American jockey and horse trainer **21** 381-383

Shogunate (Japan)
see Japan–1185-1867

SHOLEM ALEICHEM (Sholem Rabinowitz; 1859-1916), Russian-born American author **14** 202-203

SHOLES, CHRISTOPHER LATHAM (1819-1890), American publisher, inventor, and social reformer **21** 383-385

SHOLOKHOV, MIKHAIL ALEKSANDROVICH (1905-1984), Russian novelist **14** 203-204

SHORE, DINAH (1916-1994), American actress and singer **31** 333-334

SHORT, WALTER (1880-1949), American army officer **19** 337-339

SHOSTAKOVICH, DMITRI DMITRIEVICH (1906-1975), Russian composer **14** 204-205
Ciulei, Liviu **34** 58-61

SHOTOKU TAISHI (573-621), Japanese regent, statesman, and scholar **14** 205-207

SHOUSE, CATHERINE FILENE (1896-1994), American public servant **32** 317-320

Showa Tenno
see Hirohito

SHREVE, HENRY MILLER (1785-1851), American steamboat designer and builder **14** 207

SHRIVER, EUNICE KENNEDY (1921-2009), American activist **19** 339-341

Shu Ch'ing-ch'un
see Lao Shê

Shu Maung
see Ne Win

SHUB, ESTHER (Esfir Ilyanichna Shub; 1894-1959), Ukrainian filmmaker **24** 369-371

SHUBERT BROTHERS (1883-1963), theatrical managers **14** 207-209

SHULTZ, GEORGE PRATT (born 1920), labor and economics specialist, educator, businessman, and international negotiator **14** 209-211

Shunro
see Hokusai, Katsushika

Shuta
see Liang Wu-ti

SIBELIUS, JEAN JULIUS CHRISTIAN (1865-1957), Finnish composer **14** 211-212

Sicily, Duke of
see Guiscard Robert

SICKERT, WALTER RICHARD (1860-1942), English painter **14** 212-213

SICKLES, DANIEL EDGAR (1819-1914), American politician and diplomat **21** 385-388

SIDGWICK, HENRY (1838-1900), English philosopher and moralist **14** 213

SIDNEY, SIR PHILIP (1554-1586), English poet, courtier, diplomat, and soldier **14** 214-215

SIEBERT, MURIEL (1932-2013), American businesswoman **18** 368-370

SIEGEL, BENJAMIN ("Bugsy"; 1906-1947), American gangster **14** 215-216

SIENKIEWICZ, HENRYK (1846-1916), Polish novelist and short-story writer **14** 216-217

SIERRA, JUSTO (1848-1912), Mexican educator, writer, and historian **14** 217

SIEYÈS, COMTE EMMANUEL JOSEPH (1748-1836), French statesman and political writer **14** 217-218

SIFTON, SIR CLIFFORD (1861-1929), politician who helped turn the Canadian West into a premier agricultural area **14** 219-220

SIGISMUND (1368-1437), Holy Roman emperor 1411-37, king of Bohemia 1420-37, and king of Hungary 1385-1437 **14** 220-221

SIGNAC, PAUL (1863-1935), French painter **23** 369-372

SIGNORELLI, LUCA (c. 1445/50-1523), Italian painter **14** 221-222

Sigüenza
see Ferrer, Gabriel Miró

SIHANOUK, PRINCE NORODOM (1922-2012), Cambodian nationalist and political leader **14** 222-223

SIKORSKI, WLADYSLAW (1881-1943), Polish military leader and prime minister **20** 338-340

SIKORSKY, IGOR (1889-1972), Russian-American aeronautical engineer, aircraft manufacturer, and inventor **14** 223-224

SILBER, JOHN (1926-2012), American philosopher and educator **14** 224-226

SILES ZUAZO, HERNAN (1914-1996), Bolivian politician **18** 370-373

SILKO, LESLIE (Leslie Marmon Silko; born 1948), Native American author and poet **14** 226-227

SILKWOOD, KAREN (1946-1974), American antinuclear activist **14** 227-229

SILLIMAN, BENJAMIN (1779-1864), American chemist, naturalist, and editor **14** 229-230

SILLS, BEVERLY (Belle Miriam Silverman; 1929-2007), American child performer, coloratura soprano, and operatic superstar **14** 230-231

SILONE, IGNAZIO (1900-1978), Italian novelist and essayist **14** 231-232

Silva, José Bonifácio de Andrada e
see Andrada e Silva, José Bonifácio de

Silva Paranhos, José Maria da
see Rio Branco, Barão do

Silva Xavier, José Joaquim da
see Tiradentes

SILVER, ABBA HILLEL (1893-1963), American rabbi and Zionist leader **14** 232-233

SILVERSTEIN, SHEL (1932-1999), American author and poet **19** 341-343

Sim, Georges
see Simenon, Georges

SIMENON, GEORGES (1903-1989), Belgian novelist **14** 233-234

SIMEON, KING OF BULGARIA (c. 864-927), Emperor of Bulgaria 893-927 **28** 325-327

Simeon ben Jeshua ben Elazar ben Sira
see Jesus ben Sira

SIMMEL, GEORG (1858-1918), German sociologist and philosopher **14** 234-235

SIMMS, WILLIAM GILMORE (1806-1870), American author **14** 235-236

Simon
see Peter, St.

SIMON, CLAUDE (1913-1984), French novelist **25** 386-388

SIMON, CLAUDE HENRI EUGENE (1913-2005), French author **25** 386-388

SIMON, HERBERT ALEXANDER (1916-2001), American Nobelist in economics **14** 236-237

Simon, John, American film critic
Sarris, Andrew **34** 319-321

SIMON, JULES FRANÇOIS (1814-1896), French philosopher, writer, and statesman **14** 237-238

SIMON, NEIL (Marvin Neil Simon; born 1927), American playwright **18** 373-374

SIMON, PAUL (born 1928), newspaper publisher, Illinois state legislator, lieutenant governor, and U.S. representative and senator **14** 238-239

Simon, Paul, (born 1941), American musician
Cliff, Jimmy **34** 61-62

SIMONE, NINA (Eunice Kathleen Waymon; 1933-2003), African American musician **24** 371-374

SIMONOV, KONSTANTIN MIKHAILOVICH (1915-1979), Soviet poet and novelist **14** 239-240

Simons, Menno
see Menno Simons

SIMPSON, GEORGE GAYLORD (1902-1984), American paleontologist **14** 240-242

SIMPSON, LOUIS ASTON MARANTZ (1923-2012), American poet, critic, and educator **14** 243-244

SIMPSON, WALLIS (Bessie Wallis Warfield Simpson, Duchess of Windsor; 1896-1986), American socialite and wife of Edward VIII, King of England **19** 343-345
Schiaparelli, Elsa **34** 323-326
Sitwell, Osbert **34** 334-336

SIMS, WILLIAM SOWDEN (1858-1936), American admiral **14** 244

SIN, JAIME L. (1928-2005), Filipino cardinal of the Roman Catholic Church **14** 244-245

SINAN, KODJA MIMAR (1489-1578), Ottoman architect **14** 245-246

SINATRA, FRANCIS ALBERT (Frank Sinatra; 1915-1998), American singer **14** 246-248

SINCLAIR, UPTON BEALE, JR. (1878-1968), American novelist and political writer **14** 248-249

SINGER, ISAAC BASHEVIS (1904-1991), Polish-American author **14** 249-250

SINGER, ISAAC M. (1811-1875), American inventor of the sewing machine **14** 250

SINGER, MAXINE (born Maxine Frank, 1931), American biochemist and geneticist **14** 251-252

T

TAFT, LORADO (1860-1936), American sculptor **15** 75-76

TAFT, ROBERT ALPHONSO (1889-1953), American senator **15** 76-78

TAFT, WILLIAM HOWARD (1857-1930), American statesman, president 1909-1913 **15** 78-81

Taft-Hartley Act (United States; 1947)
Smith, Howard Worth **34** 336-339

TAGLIONI, MARIE (Maria Taglioni; 1804-1884), French ballet dancer **28** 345-347

TAGORE, RABINDRANATH (1861-1941), Bengali poet, philosopher, social reformer, and dramatist **12** 529-531

TAHARQA (reigned c. 688-c. 663 BCE), Nubian pharaoh of Egypt **15** 81-82

Tahiti (island, South Southern Pacific Ocean)
Dalrymple, Alexander **34** 71-73

T'AI-TSUNG, T'ANG (600-649), Chinese emperor **15** 83-84

TAINE, HIPPOLYTE ADOLPHE (1828-1893), French critic and historian **15** 82-83

Taiwan
see China, Republic of; Formosa

Taizong
see T'ai-tsung, T'ang

TAKAHASHI, KOREKIYO (1854-1936), Japanese statesman **15** 84-85

Takauji, Ashikaga
see Ashikaga Takauji

TAKEMITSU, TORU (1930-1996), Japanese composer **26** 355-357

TAL, JOSEF (Josef Gruenthal; 1910-2008), Israeli composer, pianist, and professor of music **15** 85-86

TALBERT, MARY MORRIS BURNETT (1866-1923), American educator, feminist, civil rights activist, and lecturer **15** 86-88

Tales from the Crypt (comic book series)
Gaines, William M. **34** 136-138

Taliaferro, Booker
see Washington, Booker Taliaferro

TALLCHIEF, MARIA (born 1925), Native American prima ballerina **15** 88-89

TALLEYRAND, CHARLES MAURICE DE (Duc de Tallyrand-Périgord; 1754-1838), French statesman **15** 89-90

TALLIS, THOMAS (c. 1505-85), English composer and organist **15** 91

TALMA, LOUISE JULIETTE (1906-1996), American composer and educator **27** 336-338

TALON, JEAN (1626-1694), French intendant of New France **15** 91-92

TAM, VIVIENNE (Yin Yok Tam; born 1957), Chinese American designer **24** 400-402

TAMARA (Tamar; 1159-1212), Queen of Georgia (1184-1212) **23** 388-390

TAMBO, OLIVER REGINALD (1917-1993), serves as acting president of the African National Congress **15** 92-94

TAMERLANE (1336-1405), Turko-Mongol conqueror **15** 94-95

TAMIRIS, HELEN (Helen Becker; 1905-1966), American dancer and choreographer **23** 390-392

Tan (historian)
see Lao Tzu

TAN, AMY (born 1952), American author **15** 95-96

TANAKA, KAKUEI (1918-1993), prime minister of Japan (1972-1974) **15** 96-98

TANEY, ROGER BROOKE (1777-1864), American political leader, chief justice of U.S. Supreme Court **15** 98-99

TANGE, KENZO (1913-2005), Japanese architect and city planner **15** 99-101

TANGUAY, EVA (c. 1878-1947), Canadian-American singer and dancer **31** 361-362

TANGUY, YVES (1900-1955), French painter **15** 101

TANIZAKI, JUNICHIRO (1886-1965), Japanese novelist, essayist, and playwright **15** 101-102

TANNAHILL, ROBERT (1774-1810), Scottish poet and songwriter **33** 316-318

TANNER, HENRY OSSAWA (1859-1937), African American painter **15** 102-103

TANNING, DOROTHEA (1925-2012), American artist **33** 318-320

TAO-AN (312-385), Chinese Buddhist monk **15** 103-104

T'AO CH'IEN (365-427), Chinese poet **15** 104-105

TAO-HSÜAN (596-667), Chinese Buddhist monk **15** 105

Tao-lin
see Shih Ko-fa

T'ao Yüan-ming
see T'ao Ch'ien

Tap dancing
Robinson, Bill "Bojangles" **34** 306-308

TAPPAN BROTHERS (19th century), American merchants and reformers **15** 105-106

TAQI KHAN AMIR-E KABIR, MIRZA (c. 1806-52), Iranian statesman **15** 106-107

TARBELL, IDA MINERVA (1857-1944), American journalist **15** 107-108

TARDE, JEAN GABRIEL (1843-1904), French philosopher and sociologist **15** 108-109

TARKINGTON, NEWTON BOOTH (1869-1946), American author **15** 109

TARKOVSKY, ANDREI ARSENYEVICH (1932-1986), Russian film director **23** 392-395

TARLETON, SIR BANASTRE (1754-1833), English soldier; fought in American Revolution **15** 110

TARSKI, ALFRED (1902-1983), Polish-American mathematician and logician **15** 110-111

TARTAGLIA, NICCOLO (1500-1557), Italian mathematician **15** 111-112

TARTINI, GIUSEPPE (1692-1770), Italian violinist, composer, and theorist **15** 112-113

TARZI, MAHMUD (1865-1933), Afghani writer and publisher **33** 320-322

Tashufin, Yusuf ibn
see Ibn Tashufin, Yusuf

TASMAN, ABEL JANSZOON (c. 1603-59), Dutch navigator **15** 113-114

TASSO, TORQUATO (1544-1595), Italian poet **15** 114-116

TATA, JAMSETJI NUSSERWANJI (Jamshedji Nasarwanji Tata; 1839-1904), Indian businessman **24** 402-404

TATE, ALLEN (1899-1979), American poet, critic and editor **15** 116

TATI, JACQUES (Jacques Tatischeff; 1908-1982), French actor and director **22** 410-412

TATLIN, VLADIMIR EVGRAFOVICH (1885-1953), Russian avant garde artist **15** 117-118

Tatti, Jacopo
see Sansovino, Jacopo

TATUM, EDWARD LAWRIE (1909-1975), American geneticist **29** 356-358

Taubman, George Dashwood
see Goldie, Sir George Dashwood Taubman

TAUSIG, CARL (1841-1871), Polish pianist and composer **30** 356-357

TAUSSIG, HELEN BROOKE (1898-1986), American physician **15** 118-120

Tawfiq Pasha
see Pasha, Tewfik

TAWNEY, RICHARD HENRY (1880-1962), British economic historian and social philosopher **15** 120-121

THORNDIKE, SYBIL (Dame Agnes Sybil Thorndike; 1882-1976), English actress and manager **24** 415-417

THORNTON, WILLIE MAE ("Big Mama" Thornton: 1926-1984), American blues singer **34** 346-348

THORPE, JIM (James Francis Thorpe; 1888-1953), American track star and professional football and baseball player **15** 209-211

THORVALDSEN, BERTEL (Albert Bertel Thorvaldsen; 1770-1848), Danish sculptor **23** 403-406

Thorvaldsson, Eric
see Eric the Red

THUCYDIDES (c. 460-c. 401 BCE), Greek historian **15** 211-212

THUKU, HARRY (1895-1970), Kenyan politician **15** 212-213

Thünström, Louis Leon
see Thurstone, Louis Leon

THURBER, JAMES GROVE (1894-1961), American writer and artist **15** 213-214

THURMAN, HOWARD (c. 1899-1981), American author, educator, and minister **32** 334-335

THURMAN, WALLACE HENRY (Patrick Casey; Ethel Belle Mandrake; 1902-1934), African American author and journalist **28** 352-354

THURMOND, JAMES STROM (1902-2003), American lawyer and statesman **15** 214-215

Thurstein, Domine de
see Zinzendorf, Count Nikolaus Ludwig von

THURSTONE, LOUIS LEON (1887-1955), American psychologist **15** 215-216

THUTMOSE III (1504-1450 BCE), Egyptian king **15** 216-217

Tiananmen Square massacre (China; 1989)
Fang Lizhi **34** 113-115

TIBERIUS JULIUS CAESAR AUGUSTUS (42 BCE -A.D. 37), emperor of Rome 14-37 **15** 217-218

TIECK, LUDWIG (1773-1853), German author **15** 218-219

T'ien-wang
see Hung Hsiu-ch'üan

TIEPOLO, GIOVANNI BATTISTA (1696-1770), Italian painter **15** 219-220

TIFFANY, LOUIS COMFORT (1848-1933), American painter and designer **15** 220-221

TIGLATH-PILESER III (ruled 745-727 BCE), king of Assyria **15** 221-222

Tigray people
Zenawi, Meles **34** 392-394

TILBERIS, ELIZABETH (Elizabeth Jane Kelly; Liz Tilberis; 1947-1999), British journalist **27** 340-342

TILDEN, BILL (William Tatem Tilden II; 1893-1953), American tennis player **20** 370-372

TILDEN, SAMUEL JONES (1814-1886), American politician **15** 222-223

TILLEY, SIR SAMUEL LEONARD (1818-1896), Canadian statesman **15** 223-224

TILLEY, VESTA (Matilda Alice Victoria Powles; 1864-1852), British entertainer **26** 359-361

TILLICH, PAUL JOHANNES (1886-1965), German-American Protestant theologian and philosopher **15** 224-225

TILLION, GERMAINE (1907-2008), French anthropologist and author **29** 358-360

TILLMAN, BENJAMIN RYAN (1847-1918), American statesman and demagogue **15** 225-226

TILLY, GRAF VON (Johann Tserclaes; 1559-1632), Flemish general **20** 372-374

TIMERMAN, JACOBO (1923-1999), Argentine journalist and human rights advocate **15** 226-228

Timur
see Tamerlane

TINBERGEN, JAN (1903-1994), Dutch economist **15** 228-229

TINBERGEN, NIKOLAAS (1907-1988), English ethologist and zoologist **15** 229-230

TING, SAMUEL CHAO CHUNG (born 1936), American nuclear physicist **23** 406-408

TINGUELY, JEAN (1925-1991), Swiss sculptor **15** 230-232

TINTORETTO (1518-1594), Italian painter **15** 232-234

TIPPETT, MICHAEL KEMP, SIR (1905-1998), English composer and conductor **15** 234-235

TIPPU TIP (Hamed bin Mohammed bin Juma bin Rajab el Murjebi; c. 1840-1905), Zanzibari trader **15** 235-236

TIPU SULTAN (1750-1799), Moslem ruler of Mysore **15** 236

TIRADENTES (José Joaquim da Silva Xavier; 1748-92), Brazilian national hero **15** 237

TIRPITZ, ALFRED VON (1849-1930), German admiral and politician **20** 374-376

TIRSO DE MOLINA (1584-1648), Spanish dramatist **15** 237-238

TISCH BROTHERS (1923-), real estate developers **15** 238-240

TISELIUS, ARNE WILHELM KAURIN (1902-1971), Swedish biochemist **15** 240-241

TISSOT, JAMES (1836-1902), French-born artist **33** 330-332

TISZA, ISTVAN (1861-1918), Hungarian prime minister 1903-1905 **34** 348-350

Tisza, Kálmán, (1830-1902), Hungarian statesman
Tisza, Istvan **34** 348-350

TITCHENER, EDWARD BRADFORD (1867-1927), English-American psychologist **15** 241-242

TITIAN (c. 1488-1576), Italian painter **15** 242-244

TITO, MARSHAL (1892-1980), Yugoslav president **15** 244-246
Marković, Ante **34** 255-257

TITULESCU, NICOLAE (1882-1941), Romanian statesman **15** 246-247

Titus Flavius Domitianus Augustus
see Domitian

TITUS FLAVIUS VESPASIANUS (39-81), Roman general, emperor 79-81 **15** 247-248

Titus Petronius Niger
see Petronius Arbiter

T'o-pa Hung
see Wei Hs ao-wen-ti

TOBA SOJO (1053-1140), Japanese painter-priest **15** 248-249

TOBEY, MARK (1890-1976), American painter **15** 249-250

TOBIAS, PHILLIP (1925-2012), South African paleoanthropologist **33** 332-334

TOCQUEVILLE, ALEXIS CHARLES HENRI MAURICE CLÉREL DE (1805-1859), French statesman and historian **15** 250-251

TODD, ALEXANDER (1907-1997), English chemist **15** 251-253

TODD, MABEL LOOMIS (1856-1932), American author **29** 360-362

TODD, MIKE (Avron Hirsch Goldenbogen; 1907-1958), American theater and film producer **21** 402-404

TODD, REGINALD STEPHEN GARFIELD (1908-2002), prime minister of Southern Rhodesia and supporter of Zimbabwean independence **18** 391-393

TOER, PRAMOEDYA ANANTA (1925-2006), Indonesian author **27** 342-345

TOGLIATTI, PALMIRO (1893-1964), Italian statesman and a founder of the Italian Communist Party **15** 253-254

TOGO, HEIHACHIRO (1847-1934), Japanese admiral **20** 376-379

Togu Gakushi
see Makibi, Kibi-Ho

TOJO, HIDEKI (1884-1948), Japanese general, premier 1941-44 **15** 254-256

TOKLAS, ALICE B. (1877-1967), American literary figure and editor **29** 362-364

TOKUGAWA IEYASU (1542-1616), founder of Tokugawa shogunate **8** 103-106

Tokugawa shogunate
see Japan–1603-1867

TOKUGAWA YOSHINOBU (1837-1913), last Japanese shogun **29** 382-384

TOKYO ROSE (Ikuko Toguri; Iva Toguri d' Aquino; Iva Toguri; 1916-2006), Japanese American broadcaster and businesswoman **27** 345-348

TOLAND, GREGG (1904-1948), American cinematographer **21** 405-407

TOLAND, JOHN (1670-1722), British scholar **15** 256

TOLEDANO, VICENTE LOMBARDO (1894-1968), Mexican intellectual and politician **15** 256-257

TOLEDO, FRANCISCO DE (1515-1584), Spanish viceroy of Peru **15** 257-259

TOLKIEN, J. R. R. (1892-1973), English author **15** 259-261

TOLLE, ECKHART (born 1948), German-born author **33** 334-336

TOLLER, ERNST (1893-1939), German playwright **15** 261

TOLMAN, EDWARD CHACE (1886-1959), American psychologist **15** 261-262

TOLSTOY, ALEKSEY NIKOLAYEVICH (1883-1945), Russian novelist and dramatist **34** 350-352

TOLSTOY, LEO (1828-1910), Russian novelist and moral philosopher **15** 262-265
relatives
Tolstoy, Aleksey Nikolayevich **34** 350-352

TOLTON, AUGUSTINE (1854-1897), African-American Roman Catholic priest **28** 354-356

Tolui Khan, (reigned 1192-1232), Mongol khan
Ögedei Khan **34** 278-280

TOMLINSON, RAYMOND (born 1941), American computer programmer **31** 363-364

TOMONAGA, SIN-ITIRO (1906-1979), Japanese physicist **15** 265-266

TONEGAWA, SUSUMU (born 1939), Japanese biologist **24** 417-420

TÖNNIES, FERDINAND (1855-1936), German sociologist **15** 266-267

TOOMBS, ROBERT AUGUSTUS (1810-1885), American statesman **15** 267-268

TOOMER, JEAN (Nathan Eugene Pinchback Toomer; 1894-1967), American author **23** 408-410

Toronto Maple Leafs (hockey team)
Sawchuk, Terry **34** 321-323

Toronto Raptors (basketball team)
Wilkens, Lenny **34** 375-378

TORQUEMADA, TOMAS DE (1420-1498), leader of the Spanish Inquisition **21** 407-409

TORRE, JOE (born 1940), American baseball player and manager **33** 336-338

Torre, V. R. Haya de la
see Haya de la Torre, Victor Raúl

TORRENCE, JACKIE (1944-2004), American storyteller **19** 384-386

Torres, Manuel Montt
see Montt Torres, Manuel

TORRÈS, TERESKA (1920-2012), French freedom fighter **34** 352-354

TORRICELLI, EVANGELISTA (1608-1647), Italian mathematician and physicist **15** 268-269

TORRIJOS, OMAR (1929-1981), Panamanian strongman **15** 269-270

TORSTENSSON, LENNART (1603-1651), Swedish military leader **20** 379-381

TOSCANINI, ARTURO (1867-1957), Italian conductor **15** 270-271

Tosei
see Basho, Matsuo

TOSOVSKY, JOSEF (born 1950), banker and prime minister of the Czech Republic **18** 393-395

TOULMIN, STEPHEN EDELSTON (1922-2009), British-American ethical philosopher **15** 271-273

TOULOUSE-LAUTREC, HENRI DE (1864-1901), French painter **15** 273-274

TOURAINE, ALAIN (born 1925), French sociologist **15** 274-275

TOURÉ, SAMORY (1830-1900), Sudanese ruler and state builder **15** 275-277

TOURÉ, SÉKOU (1922-1984), African statesman, president of Guinea **15** 275-277

TOURGÉE, ALBION WINEGAR (1838-1905), American jurist and writer **15** 277-278

TOUSSAINT L'OUVERTURE, FRANÇOIS DOMINIQUE (1743-1803), Haitian military leader **15** 278-279

TOWER, JOAN (born 1938), American composer **15** 279-281

Town planning
Koolhaas, Rem **34** 214-217

TOWNES, CHARLES HARD (born 1915), American physicist **15** 281-282

TOWNSEND, FRANCIS EVERITT (1867-1960), American physician **15** 282-283

TOYNBEE, ARNOLD JOSEPH (1889-1975), English historian and philosopher of history **15** 283-284

Toyo-mike Kashiki-ya-hime
see Suiko

TOYODA, EIJI (1913-2013), Japanese automobile manufacturing executive **15** 284-286

TOYOTOMI HIDEYOSHI (1536-1598), Japanese warrior commander **15** 286-289

TRACY, SPENCER BONAVENTURE (1900-1967), American film actor **15** 289-290

Trade unions
see Labor movement; Labor unions

TRAILL, CATHARINE PARR (1802-1899), Canadian naturalist and author **15** 291

TRAIN, RUSSELL (1920-2012), American conservationist **33** 338-340

TRAJAN (Marcus Ulpius Trajanus; c. 53-117), Roman emperor 98-117 **15** 291-292

Tranquilli, Secondino
see Silone, Ignazio

Translators
Bly, Robert **34** 38-40
Gordon, Beate Sirota **34** 143-145
Kydones, Demetrius **34** 67-68
Vermes, Geza **34** 364-366

TRANSTRÖMER, TOMAS (born 1931), Swedish poet **33** 340-342

Transvestism
Wood, Ed, Jr. **34** 383-384

TRAPP, MARIA VON (1905-1987), Austrian nun and inspiration for The Sound of Music **33** 342-344

TRAVERS, P.L. (Pamela Lyndon Travers; Helen Lyndon Geoff; 1988-1996), British author **27** 348-350

TRAVIS, WILLIAM BARRET (1809-1836), American cavalry commander **15** 292-293

TÚPAC AMARU, JOSÉ GABRIEL (1742-1781), Peruvian revolutionist, last of the Incas **15** 341

TUPOLEV, ANDREI NIKOLAEVICH (1888-1972), Soviet aeronautical engineer and army officer **15** 341-342

TUPPER, SIR CHARLES (1821-1915), Canadian statesman, prime minister 1896 **15** 342-343

TURA, COSIMO (1430-1495), Italian painter **15** 343-344

TURABI, HASSAN ABDULLAH AL- (born 1932), major leader of the Sudan's Islamic fundamentalist movement **15** 344-345

TURENNE, VICOMTE DE (Henri de la Tour d'Auvergne; 1611-1675), French military commander **20** 381-383

TURGENEV, IVAN SERGEYEVICH (1818-1883), Russian novelist, dramatist, and short-story writer **15** 345-348

TURGOT, ANNE ROBERT JACQUES (Baron de l'Aulne; 1721-81), French economist **15** 348-349

TURING, ALAN MATHISON (1912-1954), British mathematician **15** 349-350

TURNER, FREDERICK JACKSON (1861-1932), American historian **15** 350-351

TURNER, HENRY MCNEAL (1834-1915), African American racial leader **15** 351-352

TURNER, JOSEPH MALLORD WILLIAM (1775-1851), English painter **15** 352-354

TURNER, LANA (Julia Jean Mildred Frances Turner; 1920-1995), American actress **19** 388-390

TURNER, NATHANIEL (1800-1831), African American slave leader **15** 354

TURNER, TED (Robert Edward Turner; born 1938), American television entrepreneur **15** 355-357

TURNER, TINA (Anna Mae Bullock; born 1939), African American singer, dancer, and actress **15** 357-359

TUSSAUD, MARIE (Madame Tussaud; Anna Marie Gresholtz Tussaud; Anna Mari Grosholtz; 1761-1850), German wax modeler and museum founder **28** 356-358

TUTANKHAMEN (reigned 1361-1352 BCE), twelfth king of the Eighteenth Egyptian Dynasty **15** 359-360

TUTU, ARCHBISHOP DESMOND (born 1931), South African Anglican archbishop and opponent of apartheid **15** 360-361

TUTUOLA, AMOS (1920-1997), Nigerian writer **15** 361-362

TWACHTMAN, JOHN HENRY (1853-1902), American painter **15** 362-363

TWAIN, MARK (Samuel Langhorne Clemens; 1835-1910), American humorist and novelist **15** 363-366

TWAIN, SHANIA (Eileen Regina Edwards; born 1965), Canadian singer-songwriter **26** 361-363

TWEED, WILLIAM MARCY (1823-1878), American politician and leader of Tammany Hall **15** 366-367

12 Years A Slave (memoir and film)
Northup, Solomon **34** 275-277

TYLER, ANNE (born 1941), American author **15** 367-368

TYLER, JOHN (1790-1862), American statesman, president 1841-45 **15** 368-369

TYLER, MOSES COIT (1835-1900), American historian **15** 369-370

TYLER, RALPH W. (1902-1994), American educator/scholar **15** 370-371

TYLER, ROYALL (1757-1826), American playwright, novelist, and jurist **15** 371-372

TYLOR, SIR EDWARD BURNETT (1832-1917), English anthropologist **15** 372-373

TYNDALE, WILLIAM (c. 1495-1536), English biblical scholar **15** 373-374

TYNDALL, JOHN (1820-1893), Irish physicist **15** 374

Typhoid Mary
see Mallon, Mary

Tyrone, second Earl of
see O'Neill, Hugh

Tyrone's rebellion (Ireland)
see Ireland–Tyrone's rebellion

TYRRELL, GEORGE (1861-1909), Irish-English Jesuit priest and theologian **15** 374-375

TYRRELL, JOSEPH BURR (J.B. Tyrrell; 1858-1957), Canadian geologist and explorer **23** 410-412

TZ'U-HSI (1835-1908), empress dowager of China 1860-1908 **15** 375-376

U

UBICO Y CASTAÑEDA, GENERAL JORGE (1878-1946), president of Guatemala (1931-1944) **15** 377-378

UCCELLO, PAOLO (1397-1475), Italian painter **15** 378-379

UCHIDA, MITSUKO (born 1948), Japanese pianist **23** 413-415

UEBERROTH, PETER VICTOR (born 1937), Former baseball commissioner **15** 379-381

UECKER, BOB (born 1935), American baseball announcer and actor **32** 343-345

UELSMANN, JERRY (born 1934), American photographer **20** 384-385

Ugedey Khan
see Ögödei

UHLENBECK, KAREN (born 1942), American mathematician **15** 381-382

UIJLENBURGH, SASKIA VAN (1612-1642), Dutch model **32** 345-347

Ukiyo-e school
see Japanese art

ULANOVA, GALINA (1910-1998), Russian ballerina **15** 382-383

ULBRICHT, WALTER (1893-1973), East German political leader **15** 383-384

ULFILAS (c. 311-c. 382), Arian bishop of the Visigoths **15** 384

Ulm School of Design
Aicher, Otl **34** 4-6

ULPIAN, DOMITIUS (died 228), Roman jurist **15** 385-386

Umayado no Miko
see Shotoku Taishi

Umdabuli we Sizwe
see Mzilikazi

UNAMUNO Y JUGO, MIGUEL DE (1864-1936), Spanish philosopher and writer **15** 386-387

UNÁNUE, JOSÉ HIPÓLITO (1755-1833), Peruvian intellectual, educator, and scientist **15** 387-388

Underground Railroad
see African American history–Slavery and abolition (Underground Railroad)

UNDERHILL, JOHN (c. 1597-1672), American military leader and magistrate **15** 388

UNDSET, SIGRID (1882-1949), Norwegian novelist **15** 388-389

UNGARETTI, GIUSEPPE (1888-1970), Italian poet **15** 389-390

Unimate (robot)
Devol, George **34** 90-93

Union of Soviet Socialist Republics (former nation, Northern Eurasia)
SOVIET UNION (SINCE 1917)
espionage
Blake, George **34** 34-36
Blunt, Anthony **34** 36-38
Burgess, Guy **34** 44-47
Maclean, Donald **34** 247-249

V

WAUGH, EVELYN ARTHUR ST. JOHN (1903-1966), English author **16** 145-147

WAUNEKA, ANNIE DODGE (1910-1997), Navajo nation leader and Native American activist **18** 409-410

WAVELL, ARCHIBALD PERCIVAL (1st Earl Wavell; 1883-1950), English general, statesman, and writer **16** 147-148

Way We Were, The (film and song) Hamlisch, Marvin **34** 151-153

WAYLAND, FRANCIS (1796-1865), American educator and clergyman **16** 148-149

WAYNE, ANTHONY (1745-1796), American soldier **16** 149-150

WAYNE, JOHN (Marion Mitchell Morrison; 1907-79), American actor **16** 150-151

We Hold These Truths (radio drama) Corwin, Norman **34** 65-67

WEAVER, JAMES BAIRD (1833-1912), American political leader **16** 151-152

WEAVER, PAT (Sylvester Laflin Weaver, Jr.; 1908-2002), American television executive **19** 410-413

WEAVER, ROBERT C. (1907-1997), first African American U.S. cabinet officer **16** 152-153

WEBB, BEATRICE POTTER (1858-1943), English social reformer **16** 153-154

WEBB, JACK (1920-1982), American actor, producer, and screenwriter **29** 375-376

WEBB, SIDNEY JAMES (Baron Passfield; 1859-1947), English social reformer, historian, and statesman **16** 154-155

WEBBER, ANDREW LLOYD (born 1948), British composer **16** 155-156

WEBER, CARL MARIA FRIEDRICH ERNST VON (1786-1826), German composer and conductor **16** 156-157

WEBER, LOIS (1881-1939), American film director **26** 375-378

WEBER, MAX (1864-1920), German social scientist **16** 157-160

WEBER, MAX (1881-1961), American painter **16** 160

WEBERN, ANTON (1883-1945), Austrian composer **16** 160-162

WEBSTER, DANIEL (1782-1852), American lawyer, orator, and statesman **16** 162-164

WEBSTER, JOHN (c. 1580-c. 1634), English dramatist **16** 164

WEBSTER, NOAH (1758-1843), American lexicographer **16** 164-166

WEDEKIND, FRANK (Benjamin Franklin Wedekind; 1864-1918), German dramatist, cosmopolite, and libertarian **16** 166-167

WEDGWOOD, CICELY VERONICA (1910-1997), British writer and historian **16** 167-168

WEDGWOOD, JOSIAH (1730-1795), English potter **16** 168-169

WEED, THURLOW (1797-1882), American politician **16** 169-170

WEEMS, MASON LOCKE (1759-1825), American Episcopal minister and popular writer **16** 170

WEGENER, ALFRED LOTHAR (1880-1930), German meteorologist, Arctic explorer, and geophysicist **16** 170-171

Wei, Prince of *see* Ts'ao Ts'ao

WEI HSIAO-WEN-TI (467-499), Chinese emperor **8** 5

WEI JINGSHENG (born 1950), Chinese human rights activist **18** 410-412

Wei-mo-ch'i *see* Wang Wei

Wei Yang *see* Shang Yang

WEI YÜAN (1794-1856), Chinese historian and geographer **16** 180-181

WEIDENREICH, FRANZ (1873-1948), German anatomist and physical anthropologist **16** 171-172

WEIL, SIMONE (1909-1943), French thinker, political activist, and religious mystic **16** 172-174

WEILL, KURT (1900-1950), German-American composer **16** 174-175

Weimar Republic *see* Germany–Republic

WEIN, GEORGE (born 1925), American concert promoter **33** 362-364

WEINBERG, STEVEN (born 1933), Nobel Prize-winning physicist **16** 175-177

WEINBERGER, CASPER WILLARD (1917-2006), U.S. public official under three presidents **16** 177-178

Weinstein, Nathan *see* West, Nathanael

WEISMANN, AUGUST (1834-1914), German biologist **33** 364-366

WEISSMULLER, JOHNNY (Peter John Weissmuller; 1904-1984), American swimmer and actor **21** 425-427

WEIZMAN, EZER (1924-2005), Israeli air force commander and president of Israel (1993-) **16** 181-182

WEIZMANN, CHAIM (1874-1952), Israeli statesman, president 1949-52 **16** 183-184

WELCH, JACK (John Francis Welch, Jr.; born 1935), American businessman **19** 413-415

WELCH, ROBERT (1899-1985), founder of the John Birch Society **16** 184-185

WELCH, WILLIAM HENRY (1850-1934), American pathologist, bacteriologist, and medical educator **16** 185-186

Weld, Mrs. Theodore *see* Grimké, Angelina Emily

WELD, THEODORE DWIGHT (1803-1895), American reformer, preacher, and editor **16** 186

WELDON, FAY BIRKINSHAW (born 1931 or 1933), British novelist, dramatist, essayist, and feminist **16** 186-188

WELENSKY, SIR ROY (1907-1991), Rhodesian statesman **16** 188

WELK, LAWRENCE (1903-1992), American bandleader and television host **22** 420-422

WELLCOME, HENRY (1854-1936), American chemical manufacturer and explorer **33** 366-368

WELLES, GIDEON (1802-1878), American statesman **16** 188-190

WELLES, ORSON (1915-1985), Broadway and Hollywood actor, radio actor, and film director **16** 190-191

WELLES, SUMNER (1892-1961), American diplomat **16** 191-192

Wellesley, Arthur *see* Wellington, 1st Duke of

WELLESLEY, RICHARD COLLEY (1st Marquess Wellesley; 1760-1842), British colonial administrator **16** 192-193

WELLHAUSEN, JULIUS (1844-1918), German historian **20** 397-400

WELLINGTON, 1ST DUKE OF (Arthur Wellesley; 1769-1852), British soldier and statesman **16** 193-195

WELLS, HERBERT GEORGE (1866-1946), English author **16** 195-196

WELLS, HORACE (1815-1848), American dentist **16** 196

WELLS, MARY GEORGENE BERG (born 1928), American businesswoman **16** 197-198

WELLS-BARNETT, IDA B. (1862-1931), American journalist and activist **30** 376–378

WELTY, EUDORA (1909-2001), American author and essayist **16** 199-201

X

Y

Yatsumimi no Miko
see Shotoku Taishi

YEAGER, CHUCK (born 1923), American pilot **16** 444-445

YEAGER, JEANA (born 1952), American pilot **23** 449-451

YEATS, WILLIAM BUTLER (1865-1939), Irish poet and dramatist **16** 445-447

YEH-LÜ CH'U-TS'AI (1189-1243), Mongol administrator **16** 447-449

YEKUNO AMLAK (ruled c. 1268-1283), Ethiopian king **16** 449

YELTSIN, BORIS NIKOLAEVICH (1931-2007), president of the Russian Republic (1990-) **16** 449-452

YEN FU (1853-1921), Chinese translator and scholar **16** 452

YEN HSI-SHAN (1883-1960), Chinese warlord **16** 452-453

YEN LI-PEN (died 673), Chinese painter **16** 453-454

YERBY, FRANK (Frank Garvin Yerby; 1916-1991), American Author **25** 448-450

YERKES, ROBERT MEARNS (1876-1956), American psychologist **16** 454-455

Yeshayhu
see Isaiah

YEVTUSHENKO, YEVGENY ALEXANDROVICH (born 1933), Soviet poet **16** 455-456

YEZHOV, NIKOLAI (1895-1989), Russian politician **34** 387-389

Yi Ha-ŭng
see Taewon'gun, Hŭngson

YI HWANG (1501-1570), Korean philosopher, poet, scholar, and educator **16** 457

Yi Kong
see Sonjo

Yi Kŭm
see Yongjo

YI SNG-GYE (1335-1408), Korean military leader, founder of the Yi dynasty **16** 458-459

Yi Song
see Chongjo

Yi Song-gye
see Yi Sng-gye

Yi Sung-man
see Rhee, Syngman

YI SUNSIN (1545-1598), Korean military strategist and naval hero **16** 459-461

Yi T'aewang
see Kojong

Yi To
see Sejong

Yi Yu
see Sejo

YO FEI (Yo P'eng-chü; 1103-41), Chinese general **16** 462

YOGANANDA (Mukunda Lal Ghose; 1893-1952), Indian yogi **16** 462-463

YÔNGJO (1694-1776), king of Korea 1724-76 **16** 461-462

YORITOMO, MINAMOTO (1147-1199), Japanese warrior chieftain **16** 463-464

York, Edward, Duke of
see Edward IV

YOSHIDA, SHIGERU (1878-1967), Japanese diplomat and prime minister **16** 464-465

Yoshimichi Mao
see Kukai

YOSHIMUNE, TOKUGAWA (1684-1751), Japanese shogun **16** 465-466

Yoshinobu, Tokugawa
see Tokugawa Yoshinobu

You Send Me (song)
Cooke, Sam **34** 63-64

YOULOU, FULBERT (1917-1972), Congolese president **16** 466-467

YOUNG, ANDREW JACKSON, JR. (born 1932), African American preacher, civil rights activist, and politician **16** 467-469

YOUNG, BRIGHAM (1801-1877), American Mormon leader and colonizer **16** 469-470

YOUNG, COLEMAN ALEXANDER (1918-1997), first African American mayor of Detroit **16** 470-471

YOUNG, CY (Denton True Young; 1867-1955), American baseball player **24** 447-449

YOUNG, FREDDIE (1902-1998), British cinematographer **32** 370-372

Young, La Monte, (born 1935), American musician
Cale, John **34** 48-51

YOUNG, LESTER WILLIS ("Prez";1909-59), American jazz musician **16** 471-473

YOUNG, LORETTA (Gretchen Michaela Young; 1913-2000), American Actress **22** 427-430

YOUNG, OWEN D. (1874-1962), American industrialist and monetary authority **16** 473-474

YOUNG, STARK (1881-1963), drama critic, editor, translator, painter, playwright, and novelist **16** 474-475

YOUNG, THOMAS (1773-1829), English physicist **16** 475-476

YOUNG, WHITNEY MOORE, JR. (1921-1971), African American civil rights leader and social work administrator **16** 476-477

Young Pretender
see Charles Edward Louis Philip Casimir Stuart

YOUNGER, MAUD (1870-1936), American suffragist and trade unionist **26** 392-395

YOUNGHUSBAND, SIR FRANCIS EDWARD (1863-1942), English soldier and explorer **16** 477

YOURCENAR, MARGUERITE (Marguerite Antoinette Ghislaine; 1903-87), French novelist, poet, essayist, dramatist, world traveller, and translator **16** 477-479

YRIGOYEN, HIPÓLITO (1852-1933), Argentine statesman, president 1916-1922 and 1928-1930 **31** 389-391

YÜAN, MA (flourished c. 1190-c. 1229), Chinese painter **10** 379

YÜAN MEI (1716-1798), Chinese author **16** 479-480

YÜAN SHIH-K'AI (1859-1916), Chinese military leader **16** 480-481

Yü-yü
see Hsia Kuei

YUDHOYONO, SUSILO BAMBANG (born 1949), president of Indonesia **27** 375-377

Yugoslav People's Army (JNA)
Marković, Ante **34** 255-257

Yugoslavia, Socialist Federal Republic of (former nation, South Eastern Europe) unified state
Marković, Ante **34** 255-257

YUKAWA, HIDEKI (1907-1981), Japanese physicist **16** 431-482

YUN SONDO (1587-1671), Korean sijo poet **16** 483

YUNG-LO (1360-1424), Chinese emperor **16** 482-483

YUNUS, MUHAMMAD (Mohammad Yunus; born 1940), Bangladeshi economist and developer of microlending **28** 386-388

YUPANQUI, ATAHUALPA (1908-1992), Argentine singer and songwriter **32** 372-373

YZAGUIRRE, RAUL (Raul Humberto Yzaguirre; born 1939), Hispanic American civil rights leader **24** 449-452

YZERMAN, STEVE (born 1965), Canadian hockey player **23** 451-453

Z